MW00714248

FIFTH ANNUAL EDITION

The Antique Trader

ANTIQUES & COLLECTIBLES PRICE GUIDE

Edited by

Kyle Husfloen

A comprehensive price guide to the entire field of antiques and collectibles for the 1989 market.

Illustrated

The Babka Publishing Co.
P.O. Box 1050
Dubuque, Iowa 52001

STAFF

Assistant Editor	Marilyn Dragowick
Assistants	Connie Wagner
	Diane Neumeister
	Carolyn Clark
Subscription Manager	Bonnie Rojemann
Business Manager	Ted Jones
Publisher	Edward A. Babka

Copyright © 1988 by The Babka Publishing Co. All rights reserved. No part of this publication may be reproduced, stored in a retrieval system, or transmitted in any form or by any means, electronic, mechanical, photocopying, recording or otherwise, without prior permission in writing from the publisher.

ISBN: 0-930625-04-8

Library of Congress Catalog Card No. 85-648650

Additional copies of this book may be ordered from:

THE BABKA PUBLISHING CO.
P.O. Box 1050
Dubuque, Iowa 52001

$12.95 plus $1.00 postage and handling.

A WORD TO THE READER

The Antique Trader has been publishing a Price Guide for eighteen years. *The Antique Trader Price Guide to Antiques and Collectors' Items* has been available by subscription and on newsstands across the country, first as a semi-annual and then as a quarterly publication, and since 1984 it has been published on a bi-monthly basis.

In 1985, in response to numerous requests to combine the material of the bi-monthly issues and provide a large, complete price guide, the first edition of *The Antique Trader Antiques & Collectibles Price Guide* was issued. The book you now hold in your hands is the 1989 guide, our Fifth Annual Edition.

This book is the most current price listing available. We think it is also the most reliable book for dealers and collectors to turn to for realistic values of antiques and collectibles. Prices listed in this guide have not been unrealistically set at the whim of an editor who has no material at hand to substantiate the listed values. The Antique Trader Price Guide staff has always used a very methodical compilation system that is supported by experts from across the country as we select listings for the various categories. Prices are derived from antiques shops, advertisements, auctions, and antique shows, and on-going records are maintained. Items are fully described and listings are carefully examined by experts who discard unreasonable exceptions to bring you the most reliable, well-illustrated and authoritative Price Guide available.

Our format enables us to maintain a wide range of both antique and collectible items in a running tabulation to which we are continually adding information and prices. Items are diligently researched and clearly described. As new avenues of collecting interest are aroused, new categories are added and if a definite market is established, this material becomes a part of the Price Guide. New categories included in this edition are: Architectural Items, Barberiana, Books - State & Local Histories, Circus Collectibles, Drugstore & Pharmacy Items, Egg Replicas, Heintz Art Wares, Household Appliances, Olympic Games Memorabilia, Scientific Instruments and Stoves. In the Jewelry section we are now including Rhinestone and Costume Jewelry. Shelley China has been added to our Ceramics section and products of the Consolidated Lamp & Glass Company are now included in our Glass section.

Six popular areas of collecting are highlighted in well-illustrated "Special Focus" features which provide background material and tips on collecting. Our 1989 edition includes focuses on American Belleek China, Bottle Collecting, Greentown Glass, Rocking Chairs, Souvenir Plates and Stereographs & Stereoscopes.

This book should be used only as a *guide* to prices and is not intended to set prices. Prices do vary from one section of the country to another and auction prices, which are incorporated into this guide, often have an even wider variation. Though prices have been double-checked and every effort has been made to assure accuracy, neither the compilers, editor nor publisher can assume responsibility for any losses that might be incurred as a result of consulting this guide, or of errors, typographical or otherwise.

This guide follows an alphabetical format. All categories are listed in alphabetical order. Under the category of Ceramics, you will find all types of pottery, porcelain, earthenware, parian and stoneware listed in alphabetical order. All types of glass, including Art, Carnival, Custard, Depression, Pattern and so on, will be found listed alphabetically under the category of Glass. A complete Index and cross-references in the text have also been provided.

We wish to express sincere appreciation to the following authorities who help in selecting material to be used in this guide: Sandra Andacht, Little Neck, New York; Robert T. Matthews, West Friendship, Maryland; Connie Morningstar, Salt Lake City, Utah; Cecil Munsey, Poway, California; J. Michael and Dorothy T. Pearson, Miami Beach, Florida; Bob Rau, Portland, Oregon and Ruth Schinestuhl, Absecon, New Jersey.

The authors of our "Special Focus" segments deserve special recognition: "American Belleek" by Mary Frank Gaston, Bryan, Texas; "Bottle Collecting" by Cecil Munsey, Poway, California; "Greentown Glass" by James S. Measell, Berkley, Michigan; "Rocking Chairs" by Connie Morningstar, Salt Lake City, Utah; "Souvenir Plates" by Arene Burgess, Bethalto, Illinois and "Stereographs & Stereoscopes" by Laurance Wolfe, North Sutton, New Hampshire.

Photographers who have contributed to this issue include: E.A. Babka, Dubuque, Iowa; Al Bagdade, Northbrook, Illinois; Stanley L. Baker, Minneapolis, Minnesota; Dorothy Beckwith, Platteville, Wisconsin; Louise Boggess, San Mateo, California; Donna Bruun, Galena, Illinois; Marie Bush, Amsterdam, New York; David Carter, Stillwater, Oklahoma; Herman C. Carter, Tulsa, Oklahoma;

J.D. Dalessandro, Cincinnati, Ohio; Don Dipboye, Warren, Michigan; Bill Freeman, Smyrna, Georgia; Vicki Gross, Hillsboro, Oregon; Jeff Grunewald, Chicago, Illinois; Frances Johnson, Gray, Maine; James Measell, Berkley, Michigan; Donald Moore, Alameda, California; Gale Morningstar, Salt Lake City, Utah; Ruth Schinestuhl, Absecon, New Jersey and Bruce Whitehill, Palos Verdes Estates, California.

For other photographs, artwork, data or permission to photograph in their shops, we sincerely express appreciation to the following auctioneers, galleries, museums, individuals and shops: Neal Alford Company, New Orleans, Louisiana; Americana Shop, Chicago, Illinois; Antiques by Doris, Rockford, Illinois; Antiques by the Gross, Hillsboro, Oregon; The Antique Gallery, Phoenix, Arizona; Jim Babcock, Madison, Wisconsin; Susan and Al Bagdade, Northbrook, Illinois; Bell Tower Antique Mall, Covington, Kentucky; Bireley's Antiques, Ft. Wayne, Indiana; Bill Bodell, Auctioneer, Hazel Green, Wisconsin; Boheme Antiques, Romeoville, Illinois; Booknook Parnassus, Evanston, Illinois; Frank H. Boos Gallery, Bloomfield Hills, Michigan; Richard A. Bourne Co., Hyannis, Massachusetts; Brandybow Antiques, Maumee, Ohio; Brass Key, Salt Lake City, Utah; Brown House II Antiques, Scottsdale, Arizona; Bruhn's Auction Gallery, Denver, Colorado; Butterfield & Butterfield, San Francisco, California; Carriage Shed Antiques, Chillicothe, Illinois; Norm and Diana Charles, Hagerstown, Indiana; Christie's, New York, New York; Cobb's Doll Auctions, Columbus, Ohio; Conner-Rosenkranz, New York, New York; Cottonwood Antiques Mall, Salt Lake City, Utah; Mrs. James Craig, Washington, Pennsylvania; Cyr Auctions, Bryant Pond, Maine; S. Davis, Williamsburg, Ohio; Gail DePasquale, Leavenworth, Kansas; Doyle Auctioneers, Fishkill, New York; Edith Dragowick, Dubuque, Iowa; DuMouchelle Art Galleries, Detroit, Michigan; Dunning's Auction Service, Elgin, Illinois; Early Auction Company, Milford, Ohio; Caroline Elizabeth Antiques, Kirkwood, Missouri; T. Ermert, Cincinnati, Ohio; Frasher's Doll Auction Service, Kansas City, Missouri; Garth's Auctions, Inc., Delaware, Ohio; Glick's Antiques, Galena, Illinois and Morton Goldberg Auction Gallery, New Orleans, Louisiana.

Also to Grunewald Antiques, Hillsborough, North Carolina; Hanzel Galleries, Chicago, Illinois; Gene Harris Antique Auction Center, Marshalltown, Iowa; Kenneth S. Hays & Associates, Louisville, Kentucky; House of the Seven Fables, Somonauk, Illinois; Hypoint Farm, Barrington, Illinois; International Carnival Glass Association, Mentone, Indiana; Alice Jacobs Antiques, Illinois; Jane's Antiques, Galva, Illinois; Jeanne & Keith Antiques, Cassville, Wisconsin; James D. Julia Auction Company, Fairfield, Maine; Gary Kirsner, Coral Springs, Florida; Sherry Klabo, Seattle, Washington; Beverly Kubesheski, Dubuque, Iowa; Lionstone International, Ltd., Chicago, Illinois; Marilu Antiques, Livonia, Michigan; J. Martin, Mt. Orab, Ohio; Sybill McFadden, Lakewood, New York; Hanna Mebane Enterprises, Dunwoody, Georgia; Rosemary Meyer, Dubuque, Iowa; Trudy Miller Antiques, Dallas, Texas; Virginia Miller, Raleigh, North Carolina; William Miller, Rockford, Illinois; Virginia Mills, Peabody, Massachusetts; Monroe House Antiques, Anamosa, Iowa; Stephen Morse, Hudson, Ohio; The Nippon Room, Rexford, New York; Richard Oliver Auctions, Kennebunk, Maine; Howard Parzow, Auctioneer, Silver Spring, Maryland; Pettigrew Auction Company, Colorado Springs, Colorado; Phillips, New York, New York; Pioneer Antiques, Muskego, Wisconsin; Radle's Reliques, Tulsa, Oklahoma; Dave Rago, Trenton, New Jersey; Lloyd Ralston, Fairfield, Connecticut; Raven & Dove, Wilmette, Illinois; RC Antiques, Cleveland, Ohio; Jack and Berta Reynolds, Jackson, Michigan; John T. Roth Antiques, Norwalk, Ohio; Tammy Roth, East Dubuque, Illinois; Scheikel Antiques, Milwaukee, Wisconsin; Seventh Street Galleria, Phoenix, Arizona; Dolores Simon, Farmington, Michigan; Robert W. Skinner, Inc., Bolton, Massachusetts; Sotheby's, New York, New York; Doris Spahn, East Dubuque, Illinois; Stein Collectors International, Kingston, New Jersey; Stratford Auction Center, Delaware, Ohio; Sybill's Museum of Antique Dolls & Toys, Lakewood, New York; Robert B. Taylor, Richmond, Virginia; Rose Mary Taylor, Pecatonica, Illinois; Theriault's, Annapolis, Maryland; Time Was Museum, Mendota, Illinois; Town & Country Antiques, Northbrook, Illinois; Trader Lukes, Wilmington, California; Travis Auction Galleries, Milwaukee, Wisconsin; Don Treadway Auction Service, Cincinnati, Ohio; Treasure Hut, Ft. Wayne, Indiana; Trunzo Auctioneers, Inc., Salt Lake City, Utah; Lee Vines, Hewlett, New York; Doris Virtue, Galena, Illinois; Chris Walker Auctions, Potosi, Wisconsin; Whalen Antiques Auction, Neapolis, Ohio; Williams Auctions, Harrisonville, Missouri; Wilson House Antiques, Mineral Point, Wisconsin; Witherell Enterprises, Healdsburg, California and Woody Auction Service, Douglass, Kansas.

The staff of *The Antique Trader Antiques and Collectibles Price Guide* welcomes all letters from readers, especially those of constructive critique, and we make every effort to respond personally.

Kyle Husfloen, Editor

ABC PLATES

A Religious Theme ABC Plate

These children's plates were popular in the late 19th and early 20th centuries. An alphabet border was incorporated with nursery rhymes, maxims, scenes or figures in an apparent attempt to "spoon feed" a bit of knowledge at mealtime. They were made of ceramics, glass and metal. A boon to collectors is the fine book, "A Collectors Guide to ABC Plates, Mugs and Things" by Mildred L. and Joseph P. Chalala.

CERAMIC

5 7/8" d., children's activities & games, polychrome transfer scene of young girl standing in front of piano keyboard, "The Pretty Child on Tiptoe Stands...," embossed alphabet border & narrow beaded edge, Elsmore & Forster, Staffordshire, England, 19th c. $115.00

6" d., occupations, "The Village Blacksmith," black transfer center, embossed alphabet borders, unmarked Staffordshire 75.00

6" d., Poor Richard's Maxims series, "Handle Your Tools With Mittens...," transfer scene of men chopping down large tree, lustre edge, embossed alphabet border, unmarked Staffordshire, 19th c. .. 95.00

6 1/8" d., birds, "Magpie," transfer of bird in center, embossed alphabet border, unmarked Staffordshire 85.00

6 1/8" d., Franklin Maxim, "Now I have a Sheep...," black transfer scene of stocky gentleman standing beside cow & sheep w/rider in distance, embossed alphabet border, unmarked Staffordshire, 19th c. 95.00

6¼" d., farm scene, "Harvest Home," black transfer scene of hay wagon bringing home hay highlighted w/red, blue, green & yellow enameling, embossed alphabet border, Meakin, England, 19th c. 100.00

6¾" d., birds, "Canary, Bullfinch & Goldfinch," black transfer of birds highlighted w/red, white , yellow & green enameling, embossed alphabet border, unmarked Staffordshire 60.00

6¾" d., Indian series, "Chinonca Watching The Departure of the Cavalcade," brown transfer of standing Indian watching distant troops, embossed alphabet border, Charles Allerton & Sons, England, ca. 1890 .... 75.00

7" d., religious, "How Glorious Is' Our Heavenly King," color-trimmed transfer scene of young child kneeling in prayer before open Bible on table w/harp-playing angel nearby, embossed alphabet border, Meakin, England, 19th c. (ILLUS.) 55.00

7 1/8" d., occupations, "London Dog Seller," colored transfer scene of rough-looking man in top hat w/two small dogs, embossed alphabet border, unmarked Staffordshire, 19th c. 125.00

7¼" d., Robinson Crusoe series, "Crusoe At Work," colored transfer scene of Crusoe seated on floor of cabin weaving a basket, printed alphabet border, Brownhills Pottery Co., England, 1880's 75.00

7 5/16" d., wild animals, "The Lion," square transfer scene in center of lion in brown & green, scattered, printed alphabet around edges, Brownhills Pottery Co., England, registration date of Sept. 29, 1882 .... 95.00

Cricket Players ABC Plate

7 3/8" d., sports, colored transfer scene of men playing cricket w/British flag flying in distance, embossed alphabet border, unmarked Staffordshire (ILLUS.) 105.00

8¼" d., Aesop's Fables, "The Dog in the Manger," blue transfer scene center, printed alphabet border, B.P. Co., ca. 1875 .... 90.00

8¼" d., so-called "Deaf & Dumb" sign language type, transfer scene of two kittens skipping rope within circle of sign language alphabet highlighted w/polychrome enameling 140.00

8¾" d., occupations, organ grinder, transfer scene of organ grinder highlighted w/multicolored enameling, embossed alphabet border, Edge Malkin & Co., England, 1871 .... 116.00

GLASS

Ducks Alphabet Plate

2¾" d., dish of ice cream center scene, alphabet border, Federal Glass (Wabash Toy Series) 50.00

6" d., dog standing on grass beside tree center scene, alphabet border, clear 65.00

6" d., ducks & ducklings center scene, alphabet border (ILLUS.) ... 35.00

6" d., elephant w/howdah on back & three tiny figures in howdah waving flag center scene, alphabet border, clear, signed "R&C" on howdah 150.00

6" d., rabbit in meadow center scene, alphabet border 40.00

6" d., Rover (bust of Bulldog) center scene, alphabet border, clear (ILLUS.) 45.00

Rover ABC Plate

6" d., Sancho Panza riding mule, Dapple, center scene, alphabet border, frosted & clear 58.00

7" d., American eagle & "Centennial Exhibition 1776-1876" center, alphabet border 47.50

Carnival Glass ABC Plate

7½" d., flying stork center scene, alphabet & numbers border, marigold Carnival glass (ILLUS.) 65.00

TIN

"Cock Robin" ABC Plate

3½" d., Girl on Swing lithographed center scene, printed alphabet border 45.00

6" d., embossed bust profile of George Washington w/stars around head & "Washington" below, embossed alphabet border .. 85.00

8" d., "Who Killed Cock Robin?," Cock Robin bird & verse embossed center scene, embossed alphabet border (ILLUS.) 65.00

8½" d., Girl on Swing lithographed scene center, printed alphabet border 45.00

ADVERTISING CARDS

"Buckingham's Dye" Card

The Victorian trade card evolved from informal calling cards and hand decorated notes. From the 1850's through the 1890's, the American home was saturated with these black-and-white and chromolithographed advertising cards given away with various products.

Ammunition, "U.S. Cartridge Co.," 1876, commemorating 100 years in business $95.00

Automobiles, "Oakland Car," Model 35 pictured, No. 1075 .... 7.00

Baking soda, "Arm & Hammer," Bird series, set of 15 .... 10.00

Bread, "Homogenized Bond Bread," Movie Star series, 1947, complete set of 52 .... 25.00

Cigarettes, "Fatima," Actress series, portrait of Billie Burke 5.00

Cigarettes, "Helmar Turkish Trophies," chromolithographs of ladies by Hamilton King, set of 10 .... 120.00

Cologne, "Hoyt's German Cologne," chromolithograph of girl holding fan & goldenrod, 1893 calendar reverse 5.00

Cream separator, "Sharples Bros., Philadelphia," chromolithograph of girl & bunny 12.00

Dye, "Buckingham's Dye for the Whiskers," metamorphic, folded shows man w/white beard, extended shows man w/dark beard, 3 3/8" folded, 5½" extended (ILLUS.) 15.00

"Geneva Hand Fluter"

Fluting iron, "Geneva Hand Fluter," young lady w/flowing tresses fluting her petticoat while 2 kittens play under table, 3¾" (ILLUS.).... 5.00

Food product, "Hecker's Buckwheat," hold-to-light 18.00

Graniteware, "Granite Iron Ware," colorful scene of girl on ice, "Won't break the pitcher if she falls" 20.00

Insurance, "Metropolitan Life," die-cut chromolithograph of 3 little girls having tea party w/little boy wearing baker's hat & apron standing & watching, ca. 1900 .... 24.00
Paint, "Granite Floor Paint," black women in kitchens 10.00

Mechanical Advertising Card

Patent medicine, "Dr. Miles' Laxative Tablets," mechanical, "25 doses 25c," patented Nov. 22, 1910, 4½ x 3½" (ILLUS.) 12.00
Patent medicine, "Hood's Sarsaparilla," chromolithograph scene of children looking at projection on wall, reverse w/"Forepoughs Great Show, w/James Donahue, Clog & Jig Dancer," 1888 copyright 15.00
Patent medicine, "Scotts Emuslion," chromolithograph of girl, cats & dogs 12.00
Razors, "Gilette Safety Razor," chromolithograph of baby shaving 8.00
Sewing machines, "Singer," American Song Birds series, 1927, set of 16 .... 25.00
Shoes, "Beals, Torrey & Co. Boots & Shoes," Brownies pictured 6.00
Sled, "Flexible Flyer," die-cut folding model of sled 10.00
Stoves, "Noble Cook Stove," chromolithograph of happy chef at stove 10.00
Thread, "Clark's O.N.T.," chromolithograph of lady & birds 12.00
Thread, "Willimantic Linen Co.," hand-colored scene of boy riding spool of thread, Hatch Lith. Co., New York, 1881 .... 35.00
Tobacco, "Allen & Ginter," Fish series, booklet of 50 .... 75.00
Tobacco, "Seal of North Carolina," black couple holding oversized tobacco pouch, matted & framed 30.00

ADVERTISING ITEMS

"Reddy Kilowatt" Ashtray

Thousands of objects made in various materials, some intended as gifts with purchases, others used for display or given away for publicity, are now being collected. They range from ash and drink trays to toys. Also see ADVERTISING CARDS, BANKS, BASEBALL MEMORABILIA, BOTTLE OPENERS, BOTTLES & FLASKS, BUSTER BROWN COLLECTIBLES, CALENDAR PLATES, CANS & CONTAINERS, CARNIVAL GLASS, CHARACTER COLLECTIBLES, COCA-COLA ITEMS, COOKBOOKS, COOKIE CUTTERS, JEWEL TEA AUTUMN LEAF WARES, SALESMAN'S SAMPLES, STICKPINS, TRADE CATALOGS, WATCH FOBS and WORLD'S FAIR COLLECTIBLES.

Apron & chef's hat, "Borden's Dairy," cotton w/Elsie & Elmer ... $45.00
Ashtray, "Chicago Motor Club," brass, enameled logo center 18.00
Ashtray, "Dr. Hiller's Pfefferminz," bone china 65.00
Ashtray, electric company, clear glass w/silk-screened "Reddy Kilowatt" figure center, 4" sq. (ILLUS.)......................... 10.00
Ashtray, "Mission Orange Soda," clear glass, 3" h. bottle center ... 130.00
Ashtray, "Provident Life & Accident Insurance," brass, 8 x 4"......... 12.00
Baby's rattle, "Heinz 57," metal..... 12.50
Banner, "Doggets Chocolates," canvas, 54 x 22" 40.00
Banner, "Oldsmobile," canvas, 1952, 30' x 3' 250.00
Banner, "Pittsburgh Fences," canvas, elephant center, 48" l. 65.00
Barrel, "Heinz Pickles," counter-type, wooden w/red paint 90.00
Beater jar, "Wesson Oil for Good Things to Eat," utilitarian crockery, blue & white 65.00

Billfold, "John Deere," leather, w/logo & bulldozer 12.00
Billfold, "The Michigan Stove Co.," leather 7.00
Bill hook, "South Bend Malleable Steel Range" 20.00
Biscuit cutter, "American Beauty Flour," aluminum 6.00
Blotter, "Holland Furnace Co.," 8 horses pulling wagon 14.00
Blotter, "Kemble & Mills, Mercantile, Pittsburgh, Pa.," Heroine series, Indian maiden, 8¾ x 4" 12.00
Book, "Old Dutch Cleanser," entitled "Bachelor's Children" 15.00
Book, "Peters Shoes," entitled "The Weatherbird Bag of Tricks" 9.00
Book, "Procter & Gamble," entitled "Guiding Light," 1938 .... 20.00
Booklet, "Alka-Seltzer," entitled "Our Presidents" (through Franklin Roosevelt's 1st term) 10.00
Booklet, "Seal Brand Coffee," entitled "History of Flag," World War I era 6.50
Booklet, "Western Union," entitled "Vogue of the Social Telegram" .. 8.00
Booklet, "Williams Shaving Soap," entitled "A Story for Shavers," dated 1900 .... 15.00
Bowl, "Chicken of the Sea Tuna," chalkware, raised golden-haired mermaid, dark green, red & white 20.00
Bowl, "Coon Chicken Inn," 3½" d. .. 40.00
Bowl, "Diamond Salt," clear glass, 7½" d. 15.00
Bread platter, "Pioneer White Wings Flour," china, 90th anniversary ... 65.00
Bridge score pad, "Singer Sewing Machines," portrait of beautiful woman by Rolf Armstrong 10.00
Broom rack, "Merkles Blue Jay Store," collapsible-type 95.00
Butter dish, cov., "Breakstones Fine Dairy Foods," milk white glass, round 30.00
Cake pan, "Swans Down," tin, round 20.00
Calendar, 1881, "Pierce Paints & Varnishes," chromolithograph of black man painting houses 55.00
Calendar, 1895, "Morison Machine Co.," black boy removing thorn from pal's foot 60.00
Calendar, 1897, "Grand Union Tea Co.," chromolithograph of children 25.00
Calendar, 1899, "Ludwig Pianos," window-type, multicolored scene on cellophane, woman feeding children in old-fashioned kitchen 12.00
Calendar, 1904, "Sleepy Eye Milling Co." 200.00
Calendar, 1906, "Larkin," Art Nouveau style 35.00
Calendar, 1906, "Millar's Coffees," chromolithograph depicting Dutch children chasing rabbit 25.00
Calendar, 1907, "Cardui Medicines," product pictured 20.00
Calendar, 1907, "Hood's Sarsaparilla" 55.00
Calendar, 1909, "Metropolitan Life Insurance" 50.00
Calendar, 1919, "Hercules Gun Powder" 125.00
Calendar, 1925, "McCormick-Deering" 40.00
Calendar, 1927, "Sinclair Oil," entitled "Dream Girl" by Rolf Armstrong, 8 x 21¾" 40.00
Calendar, 1928, "Central Dairy Co., Rockford, Illinois," pretty girl 25.00
Calendar, 1929, "Frigidaire" 35.00
Calendar, 1931, "DeLaval Cream Separators," Norman Price illustration 15.00
Calendar, 1931, "Peters Cartridge Co." 150.00
Calendar, 1933, "Doe-Wah-Jack (Dowagiac, Michigan) Round Oak Stoves," entitled "Fills His Creel" 100.00
Calendar, 1933, "Fairbank's Gold Dust Washing Powder," Gold Dust Twins pictured, 7½ x 10½" 45.00
Calendar, 1933, "Winchester Western Ammunition" 195.00
Calendar, 1936, "Travelers Insurance Co.," Currier & Ives print 9.00
Calendar, 1937, "John Deere," Centennial issue, 26 x 18" 75.00
Calendar, 1939, "Becher's Bar," illustration of nurse by Elvgren 20.00
Calendar, 1944, "International Harvester," woman on tractor, 13 x 20" 17.00
Calender, 1946, "Morrell Meats," Tom Sawyer & Huck Finn illustration by Norman Rockwell 30.00
Calendar, 1948, "Greiner's Bakery," little boy in baker's clothes 28.00
Calendar, 1953, "Royal Crown Cola," Rhonda Fleming pictured, 11 x 24" 65.00
Can opener, "Pet Milk," metal 12.50
Charm, "Bull Durham," 14k gold-plated 12.50
Checkerboard, "Canadian Club Whiskey," wooden fold-up type, dated 1910, 4 x 8" 88.00
Cigarette case w/striker, "Ekers Indian Pale Ale" (Montreal), nickel-plated 32.50

Cigarette set, "Camel Cigarettes," metal recumbent camel, howdah on back holds package of cigarettes & 2 tin ashtrays, embossed camel center & "Camels Are Mild" on rim, 3 pcs. 30.00
Cigar store figure, cast zinc, painted, full figure of an Indian brave w/elaborate headdress & costume carrying a war club in his left hand, on square base w/plaque inscribed "W. Demuth & Co., Manufrs., 501 Broadway, New York," ca. 1870, 63" h. (paint restored) 6,600.00
Clock, "Bachelor Cigars-5 Cents," embossed tin, 2-sided, Baird Clock Co. 1,950.00
Clock, "Buster Brown Shoes," electric wall model, Buster & Tige pictured, Pam Clock Co. 85.00
Clock, "Garfield Tea," wall regulator, "Fig Syrup for Infants, Children & Adults" in gold letters, wooden case w/brass trim, ca. 1900 ....1,150.00
Clock, "Nunn Bush Shoes," electric, brass, man's pocket watch & fob shape, lighted 125.00
Clothespin apron, "Sleepy Eye Milling Co." 650.00

"Summit Stove Co." Comb

Comb, "Summit Stove Co., La Crosse, Wis.," aluminum, w/case, 5" l. (ILLUS.) 12.00
Compact, "Kremola Skin Cream," celluloid w/mirror, girl pictured, dated 1915 .... 15.00
Compass, "Northfield Iron," celluloid, 1¾" 32.00
Counter display, "Dr. West's Germ Fighter Toothbrush," over-sized toothbrush, red Bakelite handle .. 65.00
Counter display, "Red Goose Shoes," plastic goose on straw nest dispenses egg, ca. 1950, 33" h. 135.00
Counter display, "Robeson Suredge Knives," die-cut cardboard figure of Santa, 12" h. 15.00
Counter display, "Rudolph Valentino Cigars," figure of Valentino, "The Sheik of all Five Cent Cigars" 45.00
Counter display cabinet, "DeLaval," embossed tin front w/cream separator pictured 450.00
Counter display case, "Bluejay Corn Plasters," lithographed tin front, 3 drawers in back 125.00
Counter display case, "Sheaffer's Lead," wooden w/glass front, 9¾" w., 9" h. 110.00
Counter display case, "Slidewell Collars," 3 rows of collars, 1913 ..... 400.00
Counter display figure, "Dentyne Gum," die-cut tin Dentyne girl in feathered hat 30.00
Counter display figure, "Mazda Light Bulb," die-cut tin Knaves of Hearts, Maxfield Parrish artwork 750.00

"Nipper" Counter Display Figure

Counter display figure, "RCA," plaster model of mascot dog Nipper, 18" h. (ILLUS.) 135.00
Counter display rack, "Dr. Scholl's Foot Remedies," tin, 2 drawers & shelves 215.00
Counter display rack, "Hohner Harmonicas," hand-crank turn-table stand, "Grand Prix Philadelphia," 1926, 36" h. 125.00
Creamer, "Fairmont Dairy," milk white glass 25.00
Crock, "Weidmann's Since 1870, Meridan, Miss., Have Some Peanut Butter," stoneware w/sgraffito inscription on Albany slip, 4¼" h. 185.00
Cup, "Lion Coffee," china, little pink roses decor, 1¼" h. 12.00
Cup, "Nash Garage, Greybull, Wyoming," tin w/wire handle 15.00

Cup, "Pratt's Food For Horses & Cattle," tin, 2½ x 3" 20.00
Cup & saucer, "Baker's Chocolate," La Belle Chocolatiere pictured, made by Shelley Potteries, Ltd., England for Baker & Co., Boston . . 50.00
Display stand, "Bissel Carpet Sweepers," oak, ca. 1910, 3' 6" h. 115.00

"Crescent Flour" Door Push Plate

Door push plate, "Crescent Flour," lithographed tin (ILLUS.) 55.00
Door push plate, "Ex-Lax," porcelain 50.00
Door push plate, "Keen Kutter," tin 100.00
Dose spoon, "Duffy's Malt," glass . . . 20.00
Dose spoon, "Rexall Drugs," sterling silver 16.00
Egg separator, "South Bend Ranges," tin 8.00
Fan, "Borden's Condensed Milk," cardboard 20.00
Fan, "RCA Victor," record-shaped . . . 19.00
File card box, "Moore's Stoves," oak, Moore Brothers, Joliet, Illinois, 6" l., 4" h. 85.00
First aid kit, "Kellogg's," plane, train & boat pictured 20.00
Flatware, "Planters Peanuts," knife, fork & spoon, silver plate, Mr. Peanut handles, 3 pcs. 60.00
Flour barrel, "Sleepy Eye Milling Co.," w/brass banding, store dipper style, 18" d., 24" h. 1,800.00
Flour sifter, "Calumet Baking Powder," tin, 1-cup 18.00
Fountain pen, "Pepsi Cola" 40.00
Funnel, "Pratt's Animal Regulator," tin, 2½" h. 15.00
Game, "Eagleine Oils," Dominoes, black & white wooden pieces in dovetailed box w/sliding lid 57.00
Game, "Standard Oil," checkerboard & checkers, different product named on checkers & spaces on board 47.50
Gasoline pump top globe, "Champlin," plastic 90.00
Gasoline pump top globe, "Imperial Premier," 1-piece glass 500.00
Gasoline pump top globe, "Indian Gas," etched glass in frame 400.00

Gasoline Pump Top Globes

Gasoline pump top globe, "Richfield Hi-Octane," milk white glass w/eagle pictured (ILLUS. left) . . . . 200.00 to 275.00
Gasoline pump top globe, "Shell," milk white glass shell shape (ILLUS. right) 500.00
Gasoline pump top globe, "Sinclair H-C," 3-piece glass, narrow body 175.00
Gasoline pump top globe, "Standard Blue Crown" (aviation fuel) 285.00
Gasoline pump top globe, "Texaco," leaded stained glass 2,500.00
Grater, "Dining Car Butter, Luxus Ice Cream," tin 15.00
Gravy ladle, "Banner Buggies," silver plate, etched buggy in bowl . . 45.00
Hat, "John Deere," woven straw w/wide brim & cotton band 22.00
Horseshoe, "Simmons Liver Regulator," brass 28.00
Iced tea dispenser, "Maxwell House," ceramic, brown barrel shape, 2-part, 16" h. 65.00
Iced tea dispenser, "Tetley's Iced Tea," ceramic, embossed, brass spigot 95.00
Jigsaw puzzle, "Cocomalt," boy & dog, 1932 . . . . 20.00
Jigsaw puzzle, "Quaker Oats," Dick Daring, 1930's 35.00
Juice reamer, "Sunkist," chocolate slag glass 200.00
Key case, "RCA," leather w/gold embossing, Nipper & phonograph w/"New York Talking Machine" below 65.00
Key chain, "Hood Tires," metal fob, reverse w/policeman, 1½" oval . . 35.00
Knife, "City Ice & Fuel Co., Clinton, Ia.," wooden handle, early 1900's 8.50
Knife, pocket-type, "Robin Hood Shoes" 55.00

Lapel pin, "Archer Tires" 15.00
Lapel pin, "Ceresota Flour," ornate frame 30.00
Letter holder, "Davis, Bradford & Corson Insurance & Bonding, Nashville," brass, 18th Anniversary, Andrew Jackson home engraved on front 35.00
Letter opener, "Dupont Dynamite" .. 45.00
Letter opener, "Gateway Casket Co., Kansas City, Missouri," bronze 10.00
Letter opener, "Planters Peanuts," celluloid 25.00
Mask, "Kleenex," paper, Tubby 15.00
Matchbook, "Nu-Grape Soda" 7.00
Match box holder, "Nu-Grape Soda," copper-plated tin 25.00
Match holder, wall-type, "Edgeworth Tobacco," tin 75.00
Match holder, wall-type, "Old Judson Whiskey," tin, scene of mother helping dad w/coat & daughter, w/striker 110.00
Match holder, wall-type, "Universal Stove & Ranges," tin 35.00
Measuring cup, "Swansdown Cake Flour," tin, 1-cup 8.00
Mechanical pencil, "Armstrong Tires," rhinoceros butting at tire inside clear oil-filled top 20.00
Mechanical pencil, "Bell Telephone," floating bell inside clear oil-filled top 25.00
Mechanical pencil, "Hudson Automobile," floating Hudson auto inside clear oil-filled top 48.00
Menu, "Coon Chicken Inn," 12" 65.00
Menu board, "Camel Cigarettes," glass 75.00
Merry-go-round, "Buster Brown Shoes," pedal-type, 4 silhouette horse shapes w/painted details, on wheels, 6' d., 30" h. to top of horse's heads 2,750.00
Mirror, floor standing type (to view shoes), "Red Goose Shoes," 20½ x 14½" 125.00
Mirror, hand-type, "Emerson-Brantingham," beveled glass, brass frame 75.00
Mirror, pocket-type, "Applegarth's Oysters," 3½" d. 30.00
Mirror, pocket-type, "Baby Ruth" ... 40.00
Mirror, pocket-type, "Brer Rabbit Syrup," Brer Rabbit holding product 150.00
Mirror, pocket-type, "Buffalo Overalls," standing buffalo 50.00
Mirror, pocket-type, "Crescent Macaroni & Cracker, Davenport, Iowa," pretty lady 65.00

"Duffy's Pure Malt Whiskey"

Mirror, pocket-type, "Duffy's Pure Malt Whiskey," inventor at work, 1¾" d. (ILLUS.) 65.00
Mirror, pocket-type, "C.D. Kenny Co.," Dutch family drinking Kenny's Coffee," oval 250.00
Mirror, pocket-type, "Lucky Tiger Cures Dandruff," girl hugging tiger 75.00
Mirror, pocket-type, "Mother's Bread," boy in sailor suit 235.00
Mirror, pocket-type, "Planters Peanuts," "The Nickel Lunch" 32.50
Mirror, pocket-type, "Travelers Insurance Co., Hartford, Conn.," train 65.00
Mirror, pocket-type, "Worcester Elastic Stocking Co." 35.00
Mirror, pocket-type, "Yellow Cab," 1920's 85.00
Mirror, wall-type, "Wm. J. Florence Cigars," framed 225.00
Money clip, "Champion Sparkplug" 16.00
Mug, "Dad's Root Beer," glass, barrel-shaped, embossed 25.00
Mug, "Hires Root Beer," frosted glass, colorful logo, 3" h. 30.00
Mug, "Moxie," clear glass 30.00
Mug, "Wild Cherry, Thompson Phosphate Co., Chicago," glass, embossed, miniature 34.00
Needle book, "Luzianne Coffee," cardboard, die-cut coffee can 8.00
Night light, "Planters Peanuts," plastic, figural Mr. Peanut 75.00
Notebook, "Hamilton Watch Co.," celluloid, railroad engine, factory & flags on cover 20.00
Note pad, "Dr. Siegert's Angostura Bitters," celluloid, 1908 .... 20.00
Nut chopper, "Planters Peanuts," tin, 1938 .... 23.50
Ocarina, "Cracker Jack" 12.00
Paperweight, "Bausch & Lomb Optical," brass 30.00

Paperweight, "Bell System, New York Telephone Co.," blue glass, bell-shaped 75.00
Paperweight, "Crow-Burlingame Parts & Equipment," model of a sad iron, Niloak pottery 37.50
Paperweight, "The Flexible Clipper," cast alumunim, model of a bus, Flexible Co., Londonville, Ohio, 1940's, 7 x 2¼" 65.00

"Imperial Glass Company"

Paperweight, "Imperial Glass Company," glass, bulbous top, white lettering on blue, 3" d. (ILLUS.) ... 40.00
Paperweight, "Independent Stove Co.," cast iron, model of an elephant 50.00
Paperweight, "Keen Kutter," metal, model of an axe head 135.00
Paperweight, "La Belle Creole Cigars, New Orleans," reverse painting on glass 75.00
Paperweight, "National Cash Register," cast iron, model of a cash register 45.00
Paperweight, "Portland Cement Co.," small cement chunks encased in glass 20.00
Paperweight, "Swigart Insurance Associates," cast iron, model of a fireman's helmet 35.00
Pencil box, "Red Goose Shoes," heavy cardboard cylinder w/tin lid 46.00
Pencil sharpener, "Baker's Chocolate," metal, figural La Belle Chocolatiere," 2" h. 35.00
Pickle crock w/bail handle, "National Pickle & Canning Co.," 1 gal. (no cover) 48.00
Pie pan, "Cottolene Shortening," tin 12.00
Pinback button, "Associated Gas Engine," engine 28.00
Pinback button, "Dutch Cleanser," Dutch woman w/stick 12.00
Pinback button, "Imperial Plow" 40.00
Pinback button, "Rickenbacker Motor Co., Detroit," w/hat in the ring logo 18.00
Pinback button, "Stephenson Union Suits," man looking into mirror ... 35.00
Pinback button, "Studebaker," celluloid, spoke wheel, early 1900's 20.00
Radio, "Pepsi-Cola," bottle-shaped, 1930's, 24" h. .... 300.00 to 400.00
Radio, "Pepsi-Cola," model of a cooler, R.C.A. 275.00
Radio, pocket-type, "Sunoco," model of a gas pump 12.00
Razor holder, "Listerine," china, model of donkey 18.00
Recipe file box, "Gold Medal Flour," oak 18.00
Record cleaning brush, "R.C.A.," celluloid handle, black & gold w/red lettering & picture of "Nipper" dog, "His Master's Voice" 25.00
Ring, "Indian Motorcycle," sterling silver 38.00
Rolling pin, "Golden Grain Homemade Bread," utilitarian crockery, brown on gold 60.00
Rolling pin, "Snow White Grocery, W. Langsdale," utilitarian crockery w/original handles 175.00
Rolling pin, "W.P. Stevens Lumber Co.," wooden 14.00
Ruler, "Baby Bear Bread," 12" 8.00
Ruler, "Fireman's Fund Insurance," 12" 6.00
Sad iron, "Grand Union Tea Co.," 1897 .... 95.00
Salt & pepper shakers, "General Electric," milk white glass, model of refrigerator, pr. 26.00
Salt & pepper shakers, "Kool Cigarettes," figural Willie & Millie Kool, pr. 14.00
Salt & pepper shakers, hanging-type, "Ottumwa, Iowa," tin w/match container 65.00
Salt & pepper shakers, "Pepsi Cola," miniature bottles, pr. 40.00
Salt & pepper shakers, "Phillips 66," plastic, model of gas pump, pr. ... 25.00
Salt & pepper shakers, "Planters Peanuts," ceramic, rhinestone monocles, 4½" w., pr. .....60.00 to 80.00
Salt & pepper shakers, "Texaco Fire Chief," figural gas pumps, pr. 20.00
Satchel, "Sunshine Bisquit Co.," black leather, w/company logo ... 75.00
Scales, "Wrigley Gum," brass pan & face, original decals 185.00
School crossing sign, "Pepsi Cola," tin, figural safety kid, "Drive Slow Please!" 75.00
Scoop, "Nabisco," china 65.00
Scoop, "Planters Peanuts," plastic .. 10.00

Scoop, "Swans Down," Beetleware . . 7.00
Screwdriver, "Dayton Scale Co." 6.00
Sewing kit, "Lydia Pinkham Medicines," metal 10.50
Shaving mug, "Vick's Vapo-Rub," scalloped handle, "Serving Modern Health Needs" 52.00
Shaving mug, double cup, Buffalo Pottery, "Wildroot" 125.00
Sheet music, "Moxie," entitled "Moxie Fox Trot Song," 1930 . . . . 22.00

Arbuckles Coffee Crate

Shipping crate, "Arbuckles Roasted Coffees," wooden, nailed construction, 19½ x 29", 16¼" h. (ILLUS.) 135.00
Shipping crate, "Baker's Chocolate," wooden, w/LaBelle Chocolatiere, 6-lb. size 22.00
Shipping crate, "Snow Flake Table Salt," wooden, dovetailed, two mammies in kitchen pouring salt in frying pans 50.00
Shoe brush, "Gregg Lumber, Grand Rapids, Mich.," ebony & leather, long brush w/shoe horn handle, 15" l. 20.00
Shoe horn, "Shinola Shoe Polish," metal, 1907 . . . . 30.00
Soap, "Bendix," washing machine shape, "Now you can wash behind your ears w/a Bendix" on box, 1940's 45.00
Soap dish, "Wright's Coal Tar Dragonfly Soap," stoneware pottery marked "Doulton" 72.00
Soap grater, "Fels Naphtha Soap," tin, 4 x 10" 6.50
Soda fountain syrup dispenser, "Bardwell's Root Beer," stoneware, keg-shaped w/bail handle 575.00
Soda fountain syrup dispenser, "Ward's Orange Crush," ceramic floral base 475.00
Song book, "Sharples Cream Separator," 50 pp. 13.50
Spatula, "Rumford Baking Powder," tin, pierced heart design in blade 13.00
Spoon, "Kellogg's," wooden, long handle 6.50
Spoon, serving, "Planters Peanuts," slotted plastic 15.00
Stickpin, "Cracker Jack," elephant . . 14.00
Stickpin, "Portland Cement" 18.00
Stickpin, "Round Oak Stoves," brass, bust portrait of Indian in relief, 5/8" d. top 22.50
String holder, hanging-type, "Use Handy Box French Shoe Blacking," patd. 1881 . . . . 335.00
Sugar sack, "Quaker," girl, logo & "Sample" 15.00
Table crumb set, "Fuller Brush," celluloid, 2 pcs. 12.00
Tape measure, "Boot & Shoe Workers Union," celluloid & metal, 60" l. 25.00

John Deere Tape Measure

Tape measure, "John Deere," celluloid, 1¾" d. (ILLUS.) 35.00
Tatting shuttle, "Lydia Pinkham Medicines," celluloid 40.00
Tea dispenser, "Maxwell House Iced Tea," stoneware, blue on white, w/push spigot 175.00
Teapot, "James Vandyke Tea/Coffee," pottery, miniature 65.00
Teapot, "Lipton Tea," blue-glazed ceramic, 4-cup size 16.00
Teaspoon, demitasse, "Old Sleepy Eye," silver plate, rose design 115.00
Teaspoon, demitasse, figural "Towle's Log Cabin Syrup," silver plate 15.00
Telephone index, "Moxie," tin 45.00
Thermometer, "Camel Cigarettes," embossed tin, 5½" w., 13" h. 30.00
Thermometer, "Chesterfield Cigarettes," tin 28.00
Thermometer, "Edwards Dependable Coffee," wooden can & woman w/long flowing hair, 9 x 21" 140.00
Thermometer, "Lash's Bitters," wooden, 6 x 20" 250.00
Thimble, "Budweiser," salesman's giveaway, celluloid 14.00

Thimble, "Marshall Wells Stores," celluloid ... 3.50
Tire patch kit, "Camel Cigarettes" ... 12.00
Toy doll, "Aunt Jemima Pancake Flour," uncut cloth, 1924, 16" ... 87.50
Toy doll, "Burger King," cloth, stuffed ... 12.00
Toy duck on wheels, "Triangle Brand Shoes" ... 35.00
Toy whistle, "Endicott Johnson Shoes," tin, yellow ... 10.00
Tumbler, "Moxie," embossed clear glass ... 25.00
Whetstone, "Blanke Coffee," celluloid back ... 7.00
Whiskey jug, "Hecht's Hotel, Isaac Hecht Proprietor, Havre De Grace, Md.," stoneware pottery, brown & cream, w/bail handle, ½ pt. ... 119.00

ALMANACS

Warner's Safe Cure Almanac

Almanacs have been published for decades. Commonplace ones are available at $4 to $12; those representing early printings or scarce ones are higher.

American Telephone & Telegraph Almanac, 1939 ... $7.00
Bucklen's Almanac, 1903 ... 7.00
Brethren Almanac, 1914 ... 7.00
Christian Family Almanac, 1862 ... 7.00
Cumberland Almanac, 1889 ... 8.00
Dr. Jayne's Medical Almanac, 1904 ... 7.00
Dr. J.H. McLean's Almanac, 1894 ... 7.00
Ford Home Almanac, 1939 ... 2.50
Green's Diary Almanac, 1882 & 1883 ... 8.50
Hagerstown Almanac, 1886-1945, 59 issues ... 60.00
Home Almanac (The), Home Insurance Company of New York, 1893, World's Columbian Exposition featured ... 4.00
Hostetter's Bitters Almanac, 1892, 1896, 1899 or 1901, each ... 7.00
Hostetter's Medical Almanac, 1904 or 1905, each ... 5.00
Lum & Abner's Family Almanac, 1937, Horlick's Malted Milk radio premium ... 15.00
Lum & Abner's "Adventures in Hollywood" Family Almanac, 1938 ... 15.00
Mobil Flying Red Horse Almanac, 1939 ... 5.00
National State Almanac, 1866 ... 7.00
New York Tribune Almanac, 1871 ... 9.00
Old Farmer's Almanac (The), 1869 ... 5.00
Pittsburgh Steel Company Almanac, 1913 ... 7.00
Rawleigh's Almanac, 1910, 1912, 1913 or 1916, each ... 5.00
Rawleigh's Cookbook Almanac, 1921 ... 10.00
Schloss's English Bijou Almanac, 1841, illustrated, 9/16 x 13/16" (miniature), 62 pp. ... 350.00
Simmon's Liver Regulator Almanac, 1903 ... 5.00
Watkins Almanac, 1908 ... 5.00
Warner's Safe Cure Almanac, 1890 (ILLUS.) ... 10.00

ARCHITECTURAL ITEMS

In recent years the growing interest in and support for historic preservation has spawned a greater appreciation of the fine architectural elements which were an integral part of early buildings, both public and private. Where, in decades past, fine structures might be razed and doors, fireplace mantels, windows, etc., hauled to the dump, today all interior and exterior details from unrestorable buildings are salvaged to be offered to home restorers, museums and even builders who want to include a bit of history in a new construction project.

Columns, turned wood, carved ionic capitals, painted in shades of green w/gold & black striping & red detail, 81¾" h., pr. ... $225.00

Door, painted & decorated pine, three raised panels & molded edge stiles & rails, original red w/brown "vinegar painted" panels, 21½ x 52" (minor edge damage) 250.00

Doors, entry, molded panels w/ornate wrought-iron grills in top openings, weathered old paint, 27" w., 87½" h., pr. (hardware replaced or missing, some edge damage) 150.00

Door sidelight, Federal-style, glass set w/molded cames in a circle & curved diamond motif accented w/molded rosettes, all within a mortised & tenoned frame, retains some paint & gilding, New England, early 19th c., 13" w., 36" h. 137.50

Federal Doorway

Doorway, Federal-style, painted pine, exterior doorway w/a pitched projecting cornice carved w/dentil molding above a mullioned & glazed fan light, sides w/fluted pilasters headed by rosettes (door not included), Maryland, ca. 1800, 6' 10" w., 10' 8" h. (ILLUS.) 12,100.00

Elevator lintel, cast iron, rectangular w/one L-form end, cast w/two slightly overlapping rows of starbursts w/beaded circles at center below a wavy band enclosing crosses within ovals, designed by Louis Sullivan for the Chicago Stock Exchange Building, 1893, 7' 9 3/8" l., 15" h. 5,500.00

Mantel, cherry, rectangular shelf above molded rectangular supports carved w/stylized flowerhead roundels, America, ca. 1900, 5' l., 4' h. 522.50

Federal Carved Mantel

Mantel, Federal-style, carved & painted wood, long rectangular mantel shelf above carved dentil molding, bands of herringbone-carved reeding & incised floral devices, original black paint, America, early 19th c., 70" w., 64" h. (ILLUS.) 770.00

Mantel, Federal-style, painted pine, molded rectangular top above frieze decorated w/central allegorical figures flanked by garlands & urns, supported by pilasters decorated w/twisted ribbons, w/inset marbleized wooden panels, paint of a later date, Boston, Massachusetts, ca. 1800, 78½" w., 55" h. 4,290.00

Mantel, Federal-style, poplar, top shelf w/molded edge above raised central panel section flanked by simple pilasters w/molded circles at corners, old white paint over earlier colors, 68¼" w., 57¾" h. 325.00

Mantel, George III-style, gesso & pine, overhanging cornice w/beading & leaf tips above a frieze of blossoming rosebuds & a deeper frieze w/five registers incorporating a sea maiden amidst coral & seashells interspersed w/fluting, fluted sides headed by sea horses surmounting urns, England, early 19th c., 5' 4½" w., 4' 7" h. 12,100.00

Mantel, Louis XV, red brocatelle, serpentine shelf w/molded edge above foliate scroll-carved lintel, jambs carved w/shells & leafy pendants, mid-18th c., France, 5' 10" l., 39" h. opening, overall 7' ½" l., 46" h. 3,300.00

Mantel, pine, serpentine shelf w/molded edge over a rectangular panel decorated w/concentric diamonds in pale brown on a grained darker brown ground, raised on rectangular supports on block feet, grain-painted overall in shades of brown, America, 19th c., 4' 4" l., 4' 3" h. (some flaking to paint) 247.50

Mantel, Victorian-style, white veined marble, serpentine-fronted shelf above carved florals & shells, ornate arched opening, ca. 1855 .... 2,700.00

Pediment, four-part, carved & painted wood, three triangular segments surround rectangular center section, light yellow paint w/center section applied w/letters "Shadow Farm" above a floral swag w/ribbons all in dark green, carved random rosettes, carved sun rays in top & side triangular sections, from a dairy farm in Warwick, Rhode Island, 19th c., 7' l., 31" h. 522.50

Roof ornament, molded copper & gilded, full-bodied stylized bird standing on one leg, gold polychrome, in a plexiglass base, America, late 19th-early 20th c., 13½" l., overall 15½" h. 990.00

Screen door frame, carved wood, stiles & rails w/relief-carved leaf, flower & geometric designs on one side, 32 x 81½" 50.00

Staircase balustrade, cast iron, of tapering quadrangular form set w/narrow square upright supports w/three rows of molded rectangular elements between woven rectangular borders, designed by Louis Sullivan for the Chicago Stock Exchange Building, 1893, 7' 2¾" l., 46 5/8" h. 2,200.00

Staircase riser, cast iron, rectangular panel cast on both sides w/frieze of Celtic-inspired decoration including concentric circles & starburst elements, one side also cast w/narrow band of similar geometric patterns, designed by Louis Sullivan for the Chicago Stock Exchange Building, 1893, 42¾" l., 7 5/8" h. 3,300.00

ART DECO

Interest in Art Deco, a name given an art movement stemming from the Paris International Exhibition of 1925, is at an all-time high and continues to grow. This style flowered in the 1930's and actually continued into the 1940's. A mood of flippancy is found in its varied characteristics-zigzag lines resembling the lightning bolt, sometimes steppes, often the use of sharply contrasting colors such as black and white and others. Look for Art Deco prices to continue to rise.

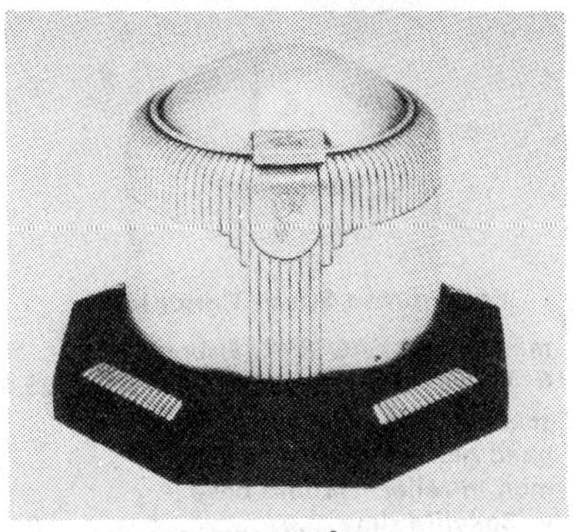

Art Deco Ashtray

Ashtray, metal, figural standing nude w/dark bronze-wash finish, holds original NuArt ceramic ashtray $175.00

Ashtray, silver, cylindrical form w/domed shoulders, partly engraved w/vertical flutes, sliding domed cover, engraved w/the crest of a lily below a crown, octagonal composition base applied w/four silver fluted bands, maker's mark & numbers & engraved "Cartier," Paris, France, ca. 1930, 4 3/8" h. (ILLUS.) 2,860.00

Book ends, metal, figural nudes kneeling, gold satin finish, 3½" base, 5" h., pr. 65.00

Book ends, metal, figural nude w/arched back & long flowing hair, bronze wash finish, 7", pr. ... 79.00

Bottle stopper, china, model of a lady's head w/cloche hat 27.50

Bracelet, faux amber & cream Bakelite 25.00

Bracelet & ring, green onyx, pyramid mark, ca. 1930, set 250.00

Brooch, 14k white gold, bow-shaped, openwork, 3/8 x 1" 45.00

Cake plate, glass, etched crystal w/black handle 15.00

Candy dish, cov., glass, exotic birds on yellow & black ground 49.00

Cigarette box, bronze, rectangular, classical figure carrying grapes w/goats leaping in background, designed by Rockwell Kent, ca. 1920, 5¼ x 6½" 500.00

Candelabrum, 3-light, silver, continuous round hollow tubing forming 3 circular loops, each w/attached cylindrical sconce w/wide flat wax pan, Portuguese,

Portuguese Silver Candelabra

marked "Liet AO & IR, Lisbon," 6" h., pr. (ILLUS. of one) 825.00

Cigarette dispenser, pottery w/applied golfer, fisherman & horseman in relief, chrome base w/Bakelite rim 70.00

Cigarette holder, chrome & Bakelite, 12" l. 10.00

Cigarette lighter, chrome, model of airplane 45.00

Cocktail pitcher, sterling silver, tapered cylindrical body, bracket handle, incised geometric decor, w/monogram "G," Gorham Mfg. Co., ca. 1927, 12" h. 1,210.00

Cocktail set: cocktail shaker & 8 matching glasses; sterling overlay on cobalt blue ground, 9 pcs. 250.00

Coffee urn, electric, chrome w/teak accents, Manning-Bowman, 15" ... 125.00

Compact, black enameled gold-finish metal 8.00

Compact, pretty lady on silver-dust ground 12.00

Dresser set: hand mirror, hair brush, nail file, buffer, shoe horn, clothes brush, bonnet brush & comb holder; sterling silver, Webster, 8 pcs. 275.00

Evening purse, Bakelite, 6-sided black frame, yellow ochre ball, black & red circles w/tiny green glass beads, silk strap, closure w/slide, apricot silk lining, black silk tassel on bottom, signed "Perreta Paris" 300.00

Figure of an Egyptian topless lady, porcelain, Germany, 6½" h. 55.00

Fire screen, wrought iron, rectangular w/serpentine top & truncated fan crest, wrought w/leafy branches & a central fountain, raised on trestle supports, designed by Edgar Brandt, ca. 1925, 49½" l. 7,975.00

Hat box, wooden, pull-out drawer type, w/pedestal inside for hat, original blue paint, 1920's, 12½ x 12¾" 45.00

Lamp, alabaster figure of standing lady, wearing a tiara, armored halter top & robe over legs, one hand holds large urn, other holds hem of robe, brass fittings rise from pedestal in background, 27" h. figure 1,850.00

Lamp, bright bronze-wash nude seated on dark bronze-wash base, silver iridized glass globe marked "NuArt" 225.00

Model of a Polar bear snarling, blue & white china, unmarked (possibly Austrian) 350.00

Necklace, green onyx & marcasite, one large & two small stones, ca. 1930, 20" l. 125.00

Night light, metal & marble base w/millefiori glass sphere shade .. 308.00

Powder jar, cov., pale pink camphor glass, figural nudes form base ... 75.00

Tea & coffee service: coffeepot, teapot, creamer & two-handled cov. sugar bowl; silver & glass, navette form on rectangular base, glass curved strap handles & arched finials, Jean E. Puiforcat, Paris, 20th c., 4 pcs. 16,500.00

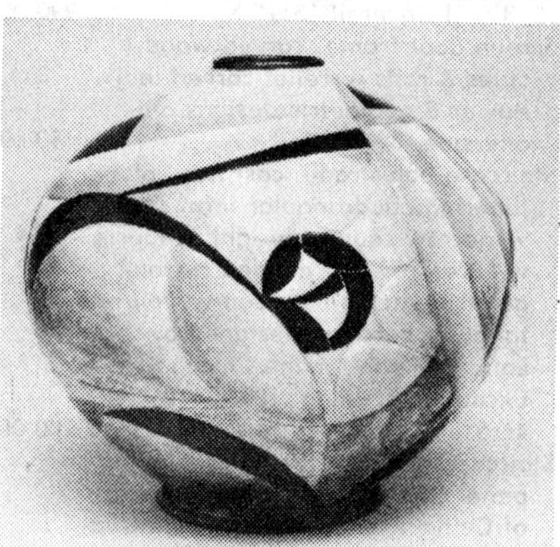

Art Deco Enameled Copper Vase

Vase, enameled copper, spherical, black, white & aquamarine curvilinear pattern, signed "Faure Limoges France," 11½" h. (ILLUS.) 3,520.00

Vase, pottery, cylindrical, enameled bell-shaped flowers on matte yellow ground, signed "Swultmont Belgium," 13" h. 210.00

ART NOUVEAU

Art Nouveau's primary thrust was between 1890 and 1905 but commercial Art Nouveau productions continued until about World War

I. This style was a rebellion against historic tradition in art. Using natural forms as inspiration, it is primarily characterized by undulating or wave-like lines. Many objects were made in materials ranging from glass to metals. Interest in Art Nouveau still remains high, especially for jewelry in the Nouveau taste.

Art Nouveau Metal Frame

Bowl, pewter, tulips, Kayserzinn, Germany, 11" d. $60.00

Bust of maiden, earthenware, lady dressed in blue & green w/delicate rose in her hair, Ernst Wahliss, Austria, 10" h. 700.00

Button hook, sterling silver, woman's head w/flowing hair handle, Simons Bros., 6½" l. 65.00

Button hook, sterling silver, hollow handle, repousse bare bosomed lady w/flowing hair & calla lilies each side, 7 5/8" l. 68.00

Candlesticks, silvered pewter, figural Art Nouveau lady w/partially upswept hair wrapped around two outward-curving stalks, each ending in a single candle socket, probably Germany, ca. 1900, 13½" h., pr. 1,760.00

Card tray, pewter-type metal, woman at top w/flowing hair, 4½ x 7" 78.00

Cup, sterling silver, campana-form, three-handled, wavy rim, repousse & chased w/undulating flowers, three wavy handles capped w/foliage, flowers & shellwork, Reed & Barton, Taunton, Mass., ca. 1900, 9½" h. 2,750.00

Dresser set: hand mirror & brush; quadruple silver plate, heavily embossed Lily pattern, set 65.00

Figure of woman throwing ball, bronze, long flowing gown, chignon hairdo, signed "Burger," 5¼" h. 300.00

Frame, gilt pot metal, ornately scrolling tendrils form sides & meet at top center w/pond lily blossom, young woman's face w/flowing hair at center base, cast artist's signature, ca. 1900, 8¾" w., 12½" h. (ILLUS.) 250.00

Frame, sterling silver, shaped rectangle, repousse iris blossoms & sinuous stems on pebbled ground, blue velvet backing, English, 1904, 8" h. 550.00

Frame, sterling silver, softened architectural form, repousse stylized flowers & twin banded ovals, oak backing, English, 1906, 9" h. 770.00

Lamp, gilt-bronze, figure of Loie Fuller, her dress swirling about her body, tossing her veils up overhead to conceal the light bulbs, signed "Raoul Larche," late 19th-early 20th c., 12¾" h. (wired for electricity) 6,600.00

Mirror, table-type, silver-painted cast iron, figure of a lady w/flowing dress holding 7" oval mirror over her head, 16" h. 125.00

Mirror, table-type, w/easel back, pewter, lady in flowing robes playing pipes, original beveled mirror, marked "W.F.M.," 9½" d., 16½" h. 495.00

Napkin holder, bronze, lady's head w/flowing hair 40.00

Pin, brass, openwork vines w/green Peking glass center, 2½" wide ... 35.00

Pin, lady's, sterling silver, figural lady w/butterfly wings, marcasite borders, 2¾" 110.00

Pitcher, cov., vermeil Martele silver, raised naturalistic form decorated w/chased poppy & wild flower & central monogram, ivory heat stops on handle, Gorham Mfg., Providence, Rhode Island, sold by Shreve, Crump & Low Company, ca. 1900, 8¾" h. 6,160.00

Plate, vermeil Martele silver, raised shaped edge, chased anemone border design, Gorham Mfg. Co., Providence, Rhode Island, sold by Spaulding Company, Chicago, ca. 1900, 11 x 8¾" oval 1,320.00

Tea & coffee service: cov. coffeepot, cov. teapot, creamer, two-handled cov. sugar bowl & silver-mounted wooden tray; silver, embossed & chased w/swirling waves & bubbles, mounted wooden handles, loop finials, Orivit, Germany, early 20th c., 5 pcs. 3,300.00

Tea & coffee service: cov. coffee pot, cov. teapot, cov. hot water kettle on stand w/burner, creamer, two-handled cov. sugar bowl, two-handled waste bowl & two-handled tray; silver, pear-shaped, repousse & chased w/undulating flowers & foliage, domed covers w/carved ivory finials, w/ivory insulators, Martele by Gorham Mfg. Co., Providence, Rhode Island, ca. 1910, 7 pcs. 23,100.00

Thermometer, desk-type, spelter w/gilt finish, easel feet, embossed florals on top & sides & free-standing buffalo at base, 8½" h. 75.00

Art Nouveau Vase

Vase, glass & silver plate, cylindrical green shading to clear glass vase w/engraved floral decoration around base, set in silver plate frame w/sinuous Art Nouveau lady & leaves & scrolls forming sides & handles (ILLUS.). 600.00

AUDUBON PRINTS

John James Audubon, American ornithologist and artist, is considered the finest nature artist in history. About 1820 he conceived the idea of having a full color book published portraying every known species of American bird in its natural habitat. He spent years in the wilderness capturing their beauty in vivid color only to have great difficulty finding a publisher. In 1826 he visited England, received immediate acclaim, and selected Robert Havell as his engraver. "Birds of America," when completed, consisted of four volumes of 435 individual plates, double-elephant folio size, which are a combination of aquatint, etching and line engraving. W.H. Lizars of Edinburgh engraved the first ten plates of this four volume series. These were later retouched by Havell who produced the complete set between 1827 and early 1839. In the early 1840's, another definitive work, "Viviparous Quadrupeds of North America," containing 150 plates, was published in America. Prices for Audubon's original double-elephant folio size prints are very high and beyond the means of the average collector. Subsequent editions of "Birds of America," especially the chromolithographs done by Julius Bien in New York (1859-60) and the smaller octavo (7 x 10½") edition of prints done by J.T. Bowen of Philadelphia in the 1840's are less expensive.

American Widgeon

American Magpie - Plate CCCLVII (357), hand-colored engraving & aquatint plate from "The Birds of America," engraved, printed & colored by Robert Havell, Jr., London, 1827-38, 33 5/8 x 25½" $990.00

American Robin - Plate CXXXI (131), hand-colored engraving & aquatint plate from "The Birds of America," engraved, printed & colored by Robert Havell, Jr., London, 1827-38, 38 x 25 5/8" 4,675.00

American Widgeon - Plate CCCXLV (345), hand-colored engraving & aquatint plate from "The Birds of America," engraved, printed & colored by Robert Havell, Jr., London, 1827-38, 15 x 19 7/8" (ILLUS.) 4,675.00

Baltimore Oriole - Plate XII (12), hand-colored engraving & aquatint plate from "The Birds of America," engraved, printed & colored by Robert Havell, Jr., London, 1827-38, 25¾ x 20 5/8" 4,125.00

Belted Kingfisher - Plate LXXVII (77), hand-colored engraving & aquatint plate from "The Birds of America," engraved, printed & colored by Robert Havell, Jr., London, 1827-38, 26 3/8 x 20½" ......3,000.00 to 4,5000.00

Bemaculated Duck

Bemaculated Duck - Plate CCCXXXVIII (338), hand-colored engraving & aquatint plate from "The Birds of America," engraved, printed & colored by Robert Havell, Jr., London, 1827-39, 18½ x 23¾" (ILLUS.) 5,500.00

Brown Pelican - Plate CCLI (251), hand-colored engraving & aquatint plate from "The Birds of America," engraved, printed & colored by Robert Havell, Jr., London, 1827-38, 37¾ x 24 7/8" 8,250.00

Carbonated Warbler - Plate LX (60), hand-colored engraving & aquatint plate from "The Birds of America," engraved, printed & colored by Robert Havell, Jr., London, 1827-38, 19 3/8 x 12¼" 990.00

Chestnut-Sided Warbler - Plate LIX (59), hand-colored engraving & aquatint plate from "The Birds of America," engraved, printed & colored by Robert Havell, Jr., London, 1827-38, 19½ x 12 3/8" 1,320.00

Cinnamon Bear, hand-colored plate from the "Viviparous Quadrupeds of North America," printed & colored by J.T. Bowen, Philadelphia, ca. 1845, 17¾ x 25 3/8" 880.00

Common Buzzard - Plate CCCLXXII (372), hand-colored engraving & aquatint plate from "The Birds of America," engraved, printed & colored by Robert Havell, Jr., London, 1827-38, 27 1/8 x 23 5/8" 2,750.00

Hawk Owl - Plate CCCLXXVIII (378), hand-colored engraving & aquatint plate from "The Birds of America," engraved, printed & colored by Robert Havell, Jr., London, 1827-38, 26¼ x 22 1/8" 1,870.00

Ivory-Billed Woodpecker - Plate LXVI (66), hand-colored engraving & aquatint plate from "The Birds of America," engraved, printed & colored by Robert Havell, Jr., London, 1827-38, 38¾ x 26" 9,900.00

Loggerhead Shrike - Plate LVII (57), hand-colored engraving & aquatint plate from "The Birds of America," engraved, printed & colored by Robert Havell, Jr., London, 1827-39, 20¾ x 26" 770.00

Long-Tailed Duck - Plate CCCXII (312), hand-colored engraving & aquatint plate from "The Birds of America," engraved, printed & colored by Robert Havell, Jr., London, 1827-39, 21 1/8 x 30 1/8" 3,850.00

Prairie Starling - Plate CCCCXX (420), hand-colored engraving & aquatint plate from "The Birds of America," engraved, printed & colored by Robert Havell, Jr., London, 1827-39, 12¼ x 19½" 825.00

Red-Cockaded Woodpecker - Plate CCCLXXXIX (389), hand-colored engraving & aquatint plate from "The Birds of America," engraved, printed & colored by Robert Havell, Jr., London, 1827-39, 12¼ x 19½" 990.00

Red-Shouldered Hawk - Plate LVI (56), hand-colored engraving & aquatint plate from "The Birds of America," engraved, printed & colored by Robert Havell, Jr., London, 1827-39, 25½ x 38" 3,300.00

Red Texan Wolf, hand-colored plate from the "Viviparous Quadrupeds of North America," printed & colored by J.T. Bowen, Philadelphia, ca. 1845, 13 3/8 x 25¼" 715.00

Rocky Mountain Sheep, hand-colored plate from the "Viviparous Quadrupeds of North America," printed & colored by J.T. Bowen, Philadelphia, ca. 1845, 17¾ x 24 1/8" 660.00

Roseate Spoonbill

Roseate Spoonbill - Plate CCCXXI (321), hand-colored engraving & aquatint plate from "The Birds of America," engraved, printed & colored by Robert Havell, Jr., London, 1827-39, 25 x 37¼" (ILLUS.) 7,150.00

Rough-Legged Falcon - Plate CLXVI (166), hand-colored engraving & aquatint plate from "The Birds of America," engraved, printed & colored by Robert Havell, Jr., London, 1827-39, 25¼ x 37¾" . . . 1,870.00

Rusty Grackle - Plate CLVII (157), hand-colored engraving & aquatint plate from "The Birds of America," engraved, printed & colored by Robert Havell, Jr., London, 1827-38, 25¾ x 20¾" 990.00

Sandwich Tern - Plate CCLXXIX (279), hand-colored engraving & aquatint plate from "The Birds of America," engraved, printed & colored by Robert Havell, Jr., London, 1827-39, 12 1/8 x 19 1/8" 1,650.00

Traill's Flycatcher - Plate XLV (45), hand-colored engraving & aquatint plate from "The Birds of America," engraved, printed & colored by Robert Havell, Jr., London, 1827-39, 12¼ x 19½" 1,210.00

White-Crowned Sparrow - Plate CXIV (114), hand-colored engraving & aquatint plate from "The Birds of America," engraved, printed & colored by Robert Havell, Jr., London, 1827-39, 12¼ x 19½" 990.00

White-Eyed Flycatcher - Plate LXIII (63), hand-colored engraving & aquatint plate from "The Birds of America," engraved, printed & colored by Robert Havell, Jr., London, 1827-38, 19½ x 12¼" . . . 1,430.00

White Heron - Plate CCCLXXXVI (386), hand-colored engraving & aquatint plate from "The Birds of America," engraved, printed & colored by Robert Havell, Jr., London, 1827-39, 25 x 36 3/8" 3,575.00

Whooping Crane - Plate CCLXI (261), hand-colored engraving & aquatint plate from "The Birds of America," engraved, printed & colored by Robert Havell, Jr., London, 1827-39, 22 7/8 x 36" 9,350.00

Wild Turkey...Male - Plate I (1), hand-colored etching & engraved plate from "The Birds of America," engraved by W. H. Lizars, colored by Robert Havell, Sr., London, on paper w/watermark "J. Whatman Turkey Mill, 1827," 25 5/8 x 38¼" 24,200.00

Zenaida Dove - Plate CLXII (162), hand-colored engraving & aquatint plate from "The Birds of America," engraved, printed & colored by Robert Havell, Jr., London, 1827-39, 20¾ x 25 7/8" 2,640.00

AUTOGRAPHS

Values of autographs and autograph letters depend on such factors as content, scarcity and the fame of the writer. Values of good autograph material continue to rise. A.L.S. stands for "autographed letter signed;" L.S. for "letter signed;" D.S. for "document signed" and S.P. for "signed photograph."

Adams, John, (1767-1848) 2nd President of the United States, document signed as President, March 19, 1799, commissioning Nathan Tisdale a surgeon's mate in the U.S. Navy, 1 p. $2,250.00

Barkley, Alben W., (1877-1956) Vice President of the United States under Harry S. Truman, typed L.S., Vice President's Office, to Emil K. Ellis, 1 p. 30.00

Caruso, Enrico, (1873-1921) Italian opera star, photograph signed, dated 1916, New York City 550.00

Catherine the Great, (1729-1796) German princess who became Empress of Russia, document signed, December 30, 1777 . . . . 990.00

Crosby, Bing, (1904-1978) entertainer, letter to fan on studio letterhead w/envelope & autographed card 65.00

Davies, Marion, (1897-1961) actress, photograph signed, 8 x 10" 100.00

Dean, (Jay Hanna or Jerome Herman) Dizzy, (1911-1974) baseball player, autographed picture, 5½ x 3¼" 150.00

Eisenhower, Mamie Doud, (1896-1980) wife of President Eisenhower, inscribed & signed photograph, 1953, 5 x 7" photograph mounted on a board 75.00

Fremont, John C., (1813-1890) American explorer, A.L.S., 1 p. . . . 100.00

Harding, Florence Kling, (1860-1924) wife of President Harding, typed L.S. as First Lady, Augusta, Georgia (but on White House letterhead), April 4, 1923, to Dayton C. Belknap 120.00

Herbert, Victor, (1859-1924) Irish-American composer & conductor, autographed musical manuscript of an unidentified instrumental part of "Anitra's Dance" from his band arrangement of Edvard Grieg's "Peer Gynt Suite," 1 p. . . . 135.00

Hoover, Herbert, (1884-1872) 33rd President of the United States, autograph note signed as President, April 14, 1932 .... 500.00
Jackson, Andrew, (1767-1845) 7th President of the United States, A.L.S. as President, Washington, Oct. 7, 1835, to his adopted son, 1 p. 3,000.00
James, Frank, (1866-1882) outlaw, signature framed 450.00
Jefferson, Thomas, (1743-1826) author of the Declaration of Independence & 3rd President of the United States, A.L.S. as Governor of Virginia, April 13, 1781, to William Davies at the War Office, 1 p. 4,500.00
Jones, Charles "Buck," (1889-1942) movie cowboy, photograph signed, black & white, 1926 ...... 425.00
Kennedy, Robert F. (1925-1968) Attorney General & U.S. Senator, self-typed L.S. 500.00
Lahr, Bert, (1895-1967) comedian, S.P., signed "Best Wishes Bert Lahr," Maurice Seymour photograph, tiny crease in margin, 8 x 10" 85.00
Lee, Henry, "Light-Horse Harry" (1756-1818), American soldier & statesman of the Revolutionary period, D.S., Virginia land grant, 1792 .... 195.00
Lennon, John, (1940-1980) recording star, record album cover signed, "Please Please Me," signed "To Stan and Jan Love John" 385.00
Lombard, Carole, (1909-1942) movie star & wife of Clark Gable, D.S., July 23, 1938, "Change of Beneficiary," 3 pp. 275.00
Marshall, Thomas Riley, (1854-1925) Vice President of the United States under Woodrow Wilson 1913 to 1921, S.P., w/message, dated 1921 .... 175.00
Napoleon I, (1769-1821) French Emperor, L.S., January 7, 1798, to General Berthier, 2 pp. 1,430.00
Nutting, Wallace, (1861-1941) photographer, author, furniture maker, A.L.S., signed & dated letter on authentic stationery w/original postmarked envelope 90.00
O'Neill, Eugene, (1888-1953) American dramatist, A.L.S., Provincetown, Mass., 23 June 1921, to St. John Ervine, the drama critic 2,400.00
Pickford, Mary, (1893-1979) actress, S.P., 8 x 10" 65.00
Smith, Joseph, (1805-1844) founder of the Mormon Church, $5 bank note signed, made out to O.P. Good, Feb. 10, 1837 .... 700.00
Taft, William Howard, (1857-1930) 27th President of the United States, S.P., w/message & dated 1928, mounted & framed 425.00
Van Buren, Martin, (1782-1862) 8th President of the United States, A.L.S., March 5, 1829 (the day he was appointed Secretary of State), to Col. Stebbins of the Senate, 2 pp. 750.00
"We Are The World," poster signed, USA for Africa, United Support of Artists for Africa, printed in black on white ground, signed in vivid colored markers by 22 of the performers: Harry Belafonte, Lindsey Buckingham, Kim Carnes, Sheila E., Daryl Hall, Marlon Jackson, Michael Jackson, Billy Joel, Quincy Jones, Cyndi Lauper, Huey Lewis, Kenny Loggins, Bette Midler, John Oates, Jeffrey Osborne, Steve Perry, Lionel Richie, Smokey Robinson, Kenny Rogers, Paul Simon, Dionne Warwick & Stevie Wonder, 20 x 24" 1,760.00

AUTOMOBILE ACCESSORIES

Early Illinois Chauffeur Badges

Air pump, "Ford" $45.00
Badge, "Chrysler," enameled metal w/three tabs, colorful, 2" d. 10.00
Chauffeur's badge, 1920, New York 10.00
Chauffeur's badge, 1923, Minnesota 15.00
Chauffeur's badges, 1926 & 1927, Illinois, pr. 20.00
Chauffeur's badge, 1930, California 13.00
Chauffeur's badge, 1938, Indiana ... 6.00
Clock, Phinney-Walker, rim wind, w/bracket 30.00
Clock, Waltham, 8 day, w/bracket .. 50.00
Coil, "Model T" 7.00
Display cabinet, "Schrader's Tire Gauge," tin, figural 110.00

Gear shift knob, clambroth glass w/blue & gold swirls 55.00
Gear shift knob, Delftware, 1¼" d. 20.00
Head lamp, "Castle Model 104a," brass 65.00
Head lamps, "Ford Model A," pr. ... 50.00
Headlight, "Cadillac," brass, electric w/bracket, 1914 (some dents in lens door) 50.00
Hood ornament, "Chevrolet," 1932 .. 25.00
Hood ornament, "Dodge," ram 30.00
Hood ornament, "Lincoln," lion 12.00
Hood ornament, chrome nude w/blue wings 95.00
Horn, brass, circular tubing w/rubber bulb, marked "14," 8" d. 98.00
Hubcaps, "Buick," 4½", pr. 15.00
Hubcaps, "Chevrolet," 3½", pr. 15.00
Hubcaps, "Ford Model T" 8.00
Jack, "Ford Model T" 22.00
License plate, 1908, Pennsylvania, porcelain 220.00
License plate, 1910, Massachusetts .. 50.00
License plate, 1913, Pennsylvania, porcelain 22.00
License plate, 1914, Wisconsin 40.00
License plate, 1915, Maine, porcelain (some fading in numbers) .. 45.00
License plate, 1937, Nebraska 12.00
License plate, 1942, Wyoming 12.00
License plate holder, advertising "State Farm Insurance," 1930's ... 14.00
Luggage rack, "Model T Ford" 35.00
Mirror, clamp-on type, unused in original box 20.00
Motometer, "Buick," Boyce 40.00
Motometer, "Hudson Super Six," wreath-type 45.00
Motor heater, kerosene-type, metal 95.00
Oil can, Big Chief, 2-gal. 85.00
Oil can, squirt-type, "Ford" 12.00
Pliers, "Ford" in script lettering 15.00
Pressure gauge, cylinder shape, 3½ w/12" rigid tube & threaded adapter for old cars 75.00
Radiator, "Rolls Royce," 1920's 1,750.00
Radiator cover, ceramic, Roseville Pottery 450.00
Running lights, "Model T," oil-type, 9" h., pr. 125.00
Side lights, "Cadillac," brass, 1914, pr. 100.00
Spare tire cover, "Pontiac," chrome, 2 pcs. 125.00
Spark plug tester w/coil, "Champion" 35.00
Speedometer, "Cadillac," brass, 1900-19 .... 450.00
Spotlight, on arm, "Buick," 1929 .... 25.00
Tire pressure gauge, "Schrader," ca. 1916 .... 12.50
Tire pump, brass, double barrel, "Holstein" 20.00
Tire tester, "Motometer" 10.00
Tune-up kit, "Chevrolet," in the shape of a brass key, 1931 .... 130.00
Wheel cover spinners, "Rambler," Classic & Ambassador, original box, never used, set 42.00
Wrench, "Ford T" in script, adjustable 4.00
Wrenches, "Maxwell," No. 2, 3 & 4, set of 3 .... 16.00

AUTOMOBILE LITERATURE

Automobile Blue Book, 1912, 750 pp. $35.00
Auto Trade Journal, December 1915, new cars illustrated, 356 pp. 26.50
Book, "Fifty Years of Ford," 1903-1953, hardbound 25.00
Books, "Practical Treatise On Automobiles," by Oscar C. Schmidt, 1912, Vols. 1 & 2, 935 pp. 40.00
Buick promotional booklet, 1914, illustrated 50.00
Cadillac "Fleetwood Custom Coachwork," 1931, text & eight chromolithograph plates, 11 x 15" 75.00
Chandler sales brochure, 1919, 12 pp. 25.00
Chevrolet repair manual, 1929 ...... 19.50
Chevrolet showroom catalog, 1937, color illustrations 15.00
Chevrolet showroom catalogs, 1947, one w/colored cellophane slip sheets of car body interior & exterior, other w/automobile motor 75.00
Columbia "Six" Touring Car sales brochure, 1923, fold-out illustration of Deluxe model, 9 x 12" 6.00
Dart, "Centamile" sales brochure, 1925 .... 27.00
DeSoto sales brochure, 1952 .... 8.50
Dodge passenger car maintenance manual, 1935 .... 35.00
Dyke's Auto & Gas Engine Encyclopedia, 1923, 1,226 pp. 50.00
Edsel sales brochure, 1959, color illustrations, 15 x 20", 14 pp., in original envelope 35.00
Edsel maintenance manual, 1959 ... 25.00
Flint "Deluxe" sales brochure, 1925, 7 x 10", 16 pp. 35.00
Ford Model A instruction book, 1929 .... 25.00
Ford Model A sales brochure, 1927-28, "The Story of the Ford Car" 50.00

Hudson owner's manual, 1941 ...... 25.00
Lincoln showroom booklet, 1942 .... 125.00
Nash sales brochure, 1924, all models pictured, 3½ x 6", 12 pp. 15.00
Oakland "Model 34C" owner's manual, 1920, w/price list, 150 pp. ... 30.00
Overland "Model 79" owner's manual, 1913, 118 pp. 30.00
Plymouth "DeLuxe" sales brochure, 1940, color illustrations, 18 pp. ... 25.00
Pontiac "Chieftain" sales brochure, 1934, w/models, specs & prices, Chicago World's Fair edition, 6 pp. 10.00
Program, "Chicago Auto Show," 1935, 9 x 12", 48 pp. 25.00
Reo "Speed Wagons" sales brochure, 1922, trucks, fire trucks & "Auto Bungalows" (early motor homes) illustrated, 8½ x 11", 24 pp. 35.00
Stanley Steam Cars sales brochure, 1912, 32 pp. 65.00
Studebaker owner's manual, 1916, 34 pp. 25.00
Stutz sales brochure, 1920, 32 pp. .. 75.00
Willys sales brochure, 1921, 3½ x 5½", 8 pp. 15.00

AUTOMOBILES

1932 Lincoln Sedan

Bentley, 1935 roadster, open-wheeled $38,000.00
Bentley, 1949, right hand drive, needs new paint & interior repair, runs & drives well 8,000.00
Buick, 1921, five-passenger touring car, new upholstery, side curtains & top 17,500.00
Cadillac, 1931 Coupe, V-16 engine, restored 33,000.00
Cadillac, 1941 series 62 convertible, restorable condition ...10,175.00
Chrysler, 1964 Crown Imperial, four-door hardtop, last push-button transmission, 40,000 miles 3,375.00
Crosley, 1946 pickup truck 4,000.00
Ford, 1906 Model N Runabout, nice older restoration 5,800.00
Ford, 1917 touring car.............7,500.00
Ford, 1921 Model T touring car 6,000.00
Ford, 1926 Model T, original 3,800.00
Ford, 1928 Model A touring car, restored 13,000.00
Ford, 1929 Model A pickup truck ...4,000.00
Ford, 1930 Model A, two-door, needs upholstering 5,500.00
Ford, 1930 Sedan, dual side mounts, trunk, balanced engine, showroom condition, original throughout...10,500.00
Ford, 1953 Crestline Country Squire station wagon 3,500.00
Hupmobile, 1930 Model S, 28,000 original miles, new paint, new tires, new mohair interior 9,000.00
Kaiser, 1953 four-door sedan, running condition 2,100.00
Lincoln, 1932 four-door sedan, outstanding condition (ILLUS.)......34,000.00
Mercedes Benz 280 SE, 1973 ......11,000.00
Mercury, 1958 Monterey four-door, push-button shift, beige & bronze, 56,000 original miles, w/owner's manual, running condition 3,500.00
Oldsmobile, 1960 Super Rocket 88 Holiday, four-door hardtop, ruby red w/white top, factory air conditioning, runs well 950.00
Rolls Royce, 1961 Silver Cloud II convertible, four-door cabriolet, V-8 engine, automatic transmission, power operated leather hood, air conditioning, green leather upholstery interior, green carpet, walnut trim 181,500.00

AVIATION COLLECTIBLES

Recently much interest has been shown in collecting items associated with the early days of the "flying machine." In addition to relics, flying adjuncts and literature relating to the early days of flight, collectors also seek out items that picture the more renowned early pilots, some of whom became folk-heroes in their own lifetimes, as well as the early planes themselves.

Advertisement, "Wright Aeronotical," 1927, w/Lindbergh, black & white, 8½ x 12" $7.00
Badge, wing-shaped, metal, "American Boy Junior Pilot - Future Pilot" 18.00
Book, "Airplane Commander Training Manual," B-29, 1945.......... 100.00

Book, "Boy's Story of Lindbergh, The Lone Eagle," 1928 . . . . . 10.00
Book ends, cast iron, Lindbergh, "The Aviator," 1927, pr. 25.00
Cream soup dish, handled, china, "Trans-World Airlines," made by Rosenthal for the Royal Ambassador Flights, white w/red banner across, center w/gold star w/RA in middle 15.00
First aid kit, "Sentinel Junior Ace First Aid Kit," tin box, 1940's motif 10.00
Jigsaw puzzle, advertising, Thompson Products, "Know Your Planes," full-color, 1940's, set of three different, 10½ x 18" 36.00
Magazine, "Aviation," 1927, March 14 . . . . . 6.00
Model of an airplane, "British Airways," 52" fuselage, 53" wingspan 350.00
Model of an airplane, paper, advertising, "Lindy Brand Bread" 10.00
Model of a jet, "Eastern Airlines 720," on stand, 28½" body, 30" wing 350.00
Perfume bottle, clear glass, "Lucky Lindy Perfume," Nipoli Company, 1927 . . . . . 10.00
Pinback, "National Air Races, 1929, Cleveland," tin 11.00
Plate, 8½" d., china, "Trans-World Airlines," made by Rosenthal for the Royal Ambassador Flights, white w/red banner across, center w/gold star w/RA in middle 15.00
Pocket knife, "The Spirit of St. Louis," Keen Kutter, limited edition, mint in box 165.00
Propeller, oak, 10' l. 550.00
Sheet music, "Hello Lindy," picturesque cover, 1927 . . . . . 17.00
Watch fob, Lindbergh w/compass & braided tassel 135.00

BABY MEMENTOES

Everyone dotes on the new baby and through many generations some exquisite and unique gifts have been carefully selected with a special infant in mind. Collectors now seek items from a varied assortment of baby mementoes, once tokens of affection to the newborn babe. Also see CHILDREN'S BOOKS and CHILDREN'S MUGS.

Baby's record book, illustrations by Charlotte Becker, ca. 1955, original box $15.00
Bowl, cereal, white earthenware china, boy on rocking horse & dog center, gilt design rim, D. E. McNicol Pottery, East Liverpool, Ohio, 1892-1920, 7" d. (ILLUS.) 35.00

Baby's Cereal Bowl

Cup, coin silver, repousse leaf sprays, ca. 1850 . . . . . 145.00
Cup, silver plate, "Little Tommy Tucker" 45.00
Cup, silver, continuous scene of house, lake & trees, Russian, mk. 84, dated 1891 . . . . . 135.00
Cup, sterling silver, engraved lily-of-the-valley spray & monogram, Wave Edge patt. base, Tiffany & Co., New York, ca. 1873 . . . . . 295.00
Cup & napkin ring, sterling silver, engraved "Meinemlieben Patchen," in presentation box from Bremerhaven, Germany, 1890's, 2 pcs. 95.00
Cup & plate, sterling silver, deeply embossed dragonflies, water lilies & clouds against at hammered ground, Dominick & Haff, 2 pcs. . . 950.00
Feeding dish, earthenware china, "Baby Bunting" verse & decal, rolled rim 45.00
Feeding dish, divided, earthenware china, "See Saw Margery Daw," verse & decal, green 35.00
Feeding spoon w/curved handle, sterling silver, Narcissus patt., Fessenden & Company, Providence, Rhode Island 34.00
Feeding spoon w/curved handle, sterling silver, Zodiac sign & "October" on handle, engraved "T.A.G., Jr." in bowl 35.00
Food pusher, sterling silver, Olympian patt., Tiffany & Co., New York 145.00
Fork, sterling silver, alphabet in blocks on handle . . . . . 35.00 to 45.00
Fork & spoon, sterling silver, Forget-Me-Not patt., Stieff Company, Baltimore, Maryland, pr. 75.00
Fork & spoon, sterling silver, cut-out pie-eyed Minnie Mouse on han-

dles, marked International Sterling, S.H. & Miller, pr. 87.50
Fork & spoon, sterling silver, mother-of-pearl handles, pr. 45.00
Hair comb, wooden, fine & coarse teeth 65.00
Mush set: 6½" d., plate, porringer & mug; china, multi-paneled bodies w/various nursery rhymes on each panel, William B. Kerr Co., Newark, New Jersey, 1855-1906, 3 pcs. 400.00
Mush set: plate, porringer & mug; china, "This Is the Maid All Forlorn," 3 pcs. 55.00
Plate, sterling silver, six named birds & animals around border, marked Wallace, 6 1/8" d. 60.00
Rattle, brass, disc hung w/bells, bone & pewter handle, 6" l. 230.00
Rattle, celluloid, doll w/blue dress & pink hat, 1920-30 .... 15.00
Rattle, silver plate, lollipop-style, embossed dog & girl one side, deer & girl reverse, bone handle w/jade sphere on end 165.00
Rattle, sterling silver, acorn shape, Birmingham hallmark, ca. 1903 ... 45.00

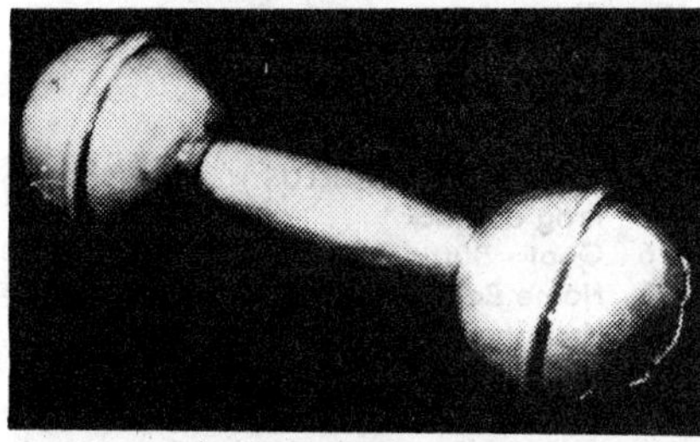

Sterling Silver Rattle

Rattle, sterling silver, dumbbell form (ILLUS.) 45.00
Rattle, sterling silver, ring hung w/bells, coral handle, hallmarked 425.00
Rattle-whistle, silver plate, sphere w/star-like cut-outs, twisted handle ending in small whistle....... 145.00
Rattle-whistle, sterling silver & mother-of-pearl, w/whistle & two bells at sides, engraved, Whiting, 3¼" l. 60.00
Teething ring, celluloid, girl holding lamb & basket of flowers, pink & blue on white, embossed VCO USA monogram on back, 5½" h. 16.00
Teething ring, blue & amber glass bead ring, slender turned ivory handle, 4" l. 150.00

BAKELITE

Bakelite is the trade-mark for a group of thermoplastics invented by Leo Hendrik Baekeland, an American chemist who invented this early form of plastic in 1909, only twenty years after immigrating to New York City from his native Belgium where he had taught at the University of Ghent. Bakelite opened the door to modern plastics and was widely used as an electrical insulating material replacing the flammable celluloid. Jewelry designers of the 1920's considered Bakelite the perfect medium to create pieces in the Art Deco style and today Bakelite bracelets, earrings and pins of this period are finding favor with another generation of modish women.

Backgammon chips, 13 each red & gold, 26 pcs. $28.00
Book rack, carved World War II military scenes on front & ends 35.00
Box, white, in brass frame w/coiled brass trim, 7¾ x 5" 25.00
Bracelet, bangle-type, yellow, ½" w. 12.00
Bracelet, bangle-type, cherry amber marbleized, 1" w. 25.00
Bracelet, cuff-type, black set w/three rhinestones 35.00
Bracelet, hinged, emerald green, ornate carving 45.00
Clip, model of a grape cluster w/leaves, 1930's 12.00
Clock, mantel-type, circular dial in black diamond-shaped frame held in flared rectangular mottled tortoise shell brown mount, silver feet, Bond Electric, 7" h. 45.00
Compact, obverse molded as a tennis-racket head w/an elegantly dressed woman tennis player, beige, unsigned, probably French, ca. 1925, 5½" d. 242.00
Earrings, amber, Accessocraft, ¾", pr. 10.00
Earrings, red w/white polka dots, pr. 30.00
Evening bag, oval, mottled grey set w/two rows of rhinestones, 8" l. 23.50
Napkin ring, model of a chicken 12.50
Napkin ring, model of a Scottie dog 5.00
Necklace, pendant-type, amber, deeply carved & set w/multicolored "jewels," large 40.00
Necklace, gold & black geometric design, Monet 8.00
Pin, model of a horse w/inlaid eyes & brass harness, butterscotch 40.00
Pin, pair of crossed riding boots w/horsehead, brass reins & spurs, 2 x 2½" 25.00

Pin, hinged bracelet & earrings, red, carved, set 100.00
Poker chip holder, two-tone blue marbleized, holds 150 chips 165.00
Ring, green, carved, large 30.00
Salt & pepper shakers, Art Deco style, green w/yellow tops, pr.... 10.00
Toy, crib-type, teddy bear.......... 45.00

BANKS

Original early mechanical and cast-iron still banks are in great demand with collectors and their scarcity has caused numerous reproductions of both types and the novice collector is urged to exercise caution. The early mechanical banks are especially scarce and some versions are seldom offered for sale but, rather, are traded with fellow collectors attempting to upgrade an existing collection. Numbers before mechanical banks refer to those in John Meyer's "Handbook of Old Mechanical Banks." In past years, our standard reference for cast-iron still banks was Hubert B. Whiting's book Old Iron Still Banks, *but because this work is out of print and a beautiful new book,* The Penny Book - Collecting Still Banks *by Andy and Susan Moore pictures and describes numerous additional banks, we will use the Moore numbers as a reference preceding each listing and indicate the Whiting reference in parenthesis at the end. The still banks listed are old and in good original condition with good paint and no repair unless otherwise noted. An asterisk (*) indicates this bank has been reproduced at some time.*

MECHANICAL

Chief Big Moon

42 Chief Big Moon (ILLUS.) $1,150.00
58 Dinah (ILLUS.)............... 375.00
65 Dog - Bulldog - Standing 500.00
67 Dog on Turntable 335.00
69 Dog - Speaking 795.00

Dinah

71 Dog - Trick 400.00

Eagle & Eaglets

75 Eagle & Eaglets (ILLUS.)...... 400.00
101 Frog on Rock ....250.00 to 275.00
116 Goat - Butting 625.00
125 Home Bank 400.00
127 Humpty Dumpty............. 480.00
132 Jolly Nigger - Shepherd Hardware Co., Buffalo, N.Y., March 14, 1882........... 285.00
138 Jonah and the Whale ....950.00 to 1,150.00
143 Leap Frog...................1,100.00
146 Lilliput - Hall's 388.00
147 Lion and Monkeys...450.00 to 550.00
148 Lion Hunter 3,375.00
150 Little Joe 345.00
165 Monkey & Parrot 275.00
169 Mule Entering Barn.......... 625.00
174 New Bank - Building & Guard...................... 500.00
178 Organ Bank - with Monkey, Boy & Girl 376.00
182 Owl - Turns Head 275.00
186 Panorama Bank ..4,000.00 to 4,500.00
194 Pig in High Chair........... 406.00
196 Pony - Trick, worn paint (ILLUS.)................. 280.00
199 Presto - Building 300.00
201 Professor Pugfrog 5,000.00
203 Punch & Judy 790.00
212 Rooster 375.00
214 Santa Claus at Chimney...... 750.00
220 Squirrel & Tree Stump 550.00

Trick Pony

224 Tammany 255.00

226 Teddy and the Bear in Tree .. 920.00

231 Uncle Sam with Satchel & Umbrella 900.00

237 William Tell................ 458.00

240 Wireless Bank 250.00

STILL

Billiken Bank

195 Amish Boy with Pig on Bale of Straw, white metal, key locked trap, 4¾ x 3½" 65.00

219 "Andy Gump Savings Bank," lead, General Thrift Products, 1920's, 5¾ x 5¾" 300.00

1489 Automobile - Yellow Cab, cast iron, rubber tires, Arcade, 1921, 4¼ x 7 7/8" ... 618.00

907 Barrel - White City Puzzle Barrel, No. 1, on 2-wheeled cart, cast iron, Nicol, patd. 1894, 5" l. cart (W. 286)..........300.00 to 350.00

908 Barrel - White City Puzzle Barrel, No. 1, cast iron, Nicol, patd. 1894 (W. 285).. 104.00

917 Basket Bank - woven, cast iron, 2 7/8 x 3¾" 40.00

1439 Battleship "Maine," cast iron, J. & E. Stevens, 1901, 10¼" l., 6" h. (W. 143) 658.00

951 Bean Pot - w/nickel register & bail handle, cast iron, 3 7/8" d., 3" h. 175.00

693 Bear Stealing Pig, cast iron, 5½" h. (W. 246) * 988.00

698 Bear - "Teddy Bear," cast iron, Arcade, 1910-25, 4" l., 2½" h. (W. 331) * 136.00

714 Bear - Bear Seated on Log, cast iron, 7" h. (W. 328) ... 530.00

683 Beehive, cast iron, Kyser & Rex, 1882, 2½" h. * 75.00

74 "Billiken" on base, cast iron, A.C. Williams Co., 1909-12, 2¼" w., 4¼" h., W. 50 (ILLUS.).................. 52.00

79 "Billy Can" on bottom of feet & base of Funny Man, cast iron, ca. 1910, 5 1/8" h. (W. 51) 770.00

664 Bird - Songbird on Stump (Bird Toy Bank), cast iron, A.C. Williams, 1912-20's, 4¾" h. (W. 209)........... 360.00

83 Black Boy - Two-Faced Black Boy, cast iron, A.C. Williams, 1901-19, 4 1/8" h. (W. 43).................... 140.00

84 Black Boy - Two-Faced Black Boy, cast iron, A.C. Williams, 1901-19, 3 1/8" h. (W. 44) 75.00

170 Black Boy - Young Negro Bust, cast iron, England, 4½" h. (W. 42)........... 200.00

166 Black Man - "Give Me A Penny," cast iron, Hubley, 1902-26, 5½" h. (W. 19).... 188.00

176 Black Woman - Mammy with Hands on Hips, cast iron, Hubley, 1914-46, 5¼" h. (W. 20) * 95.00

46 Boy Scout - "Made in Canada" on backpack, cast iron, 5 11/16" h. 365.00

556 Buffalo - "Amherst Stoves" on side, cast iron, 1930's, 8" l. (W. 207) 270.00

954 Building - Castle Bank, cast iron, Kyser & Rex, 1882, 2 13/16" w., 3" h. (W. 354)................... 169.00

968 Building (Church) - Litchfield Cathedral, cast iron, England, 1908, 6¾" h...... 325.00

960 Building (Church) - Little Brown Church, white metal, Hout, 5¼" h. 45.00

974 Building (Church) - Westminster Abbey, cast iron, possibly Sydenham &

McOustra, England, 3¼" w., 6¼" h. (W. 170) .. 125.00

958 Building (Church) - West Side Presbyterian Church, cast iron, ca. 1916, 3½" w., 3¾" h. (W. 282) 400.00

Columbia Bank

1070 Building - Columbia Bank, replica of Columbian Exposition building, cast iron, Kenton, 1893-1913, 4½" sq., 5¾" h., W. 430 (ILLUS.) 223.00

1226 Building - Crown Bank Building, "Bank" over front door, cast iron, J. & E. Stevens, 1873-1907, Grey Iron Casting Co., 1903-28, 3 5/8" h. (W. 373) 105.00

1146 Building - Cupola Bank, cast iron, J. & E. Stevens, 1872, 3½" w., 4¼" h. (W. 306) .. 86.00

1081 Building - "Deposit Bank," large print, cast iron, Columbia Grey Casting Co., 1897, 3" w., 4¼" h. 62.00

1180 Building - Domed "Bank" Building, cast iron, A.C. Williams, 1899-1934, 2" w., 3" h. (W. 424) 30.00

1182 Building - Domed "Bank" Building, cast iron, A.C. Williams, 1899-1934, 3¼" w., 4½" h. (W. 422) .. 38.00

1125 Building - Double Door "Bank" Building, cast iron, A.C. Williams, 1905-20's, 4" w., 5½" h. (W. 368) 145.00

1011 Building - "1876 Bank," cast iron, Judd, 1895, 3" w., 3½" h. (W. 388) * 55.00

1161 Building - Flat Iron Building, cast iron, Kenton, 1912-26, 3" w., 5½" h. (W. 409) 76.50

1121 Building - Four Tower "Bank" Building, cast iron, J. & E. Stevens, 1895-1906, 4¼" w., 5¾" h. (W. 370) * 105.00

1126 Building - Home Savings Bank, cast iron, Shimer Toy Co., 1899, J. & E. Stevens, 1896, 4½" w., 5 7/8" h. (W. 369) 81.00

1122 Building - Roof "Bank" Building, cast iron, J. & E. Stevens, 1887, 5¼" h. (W. 366) 86.00

1007 Building - Six-sided Building, cast iron, 2½" h. (W. 332) 212.00

1238 Building - Skyscraper, cast iron, A.C. Williams, 1900-31, 1¾" sq. base, 3½" h. (W. 414) 39.00

1239 Building - Skyscraper, cast iron, A.C. Williams, 1900-31, 2 1/8" sq. base, 4½" h. (W. 413) 36.00

1080 Building - "State Bank," cast iron, Kenton, ca. 1900, 4½" w., 6" h. (W. 445) 90.00

1633 Building - "State Bank," cast iron, Columbia Grey Iron Casting Co., 1897, Kyser & Rex, 4" w., 5½" h. (W. 444) 90.00

1198 Building - "Tower Bank - 1890," cast iron, Kyser & Rex, 1890, 6 7/8" w., 6 7/8" h. (W. 437) 422.00

1208 Building - Tower bank, cast iron, John Harper, Ltd., 1902-11, 3 7/8" w., 9¼" h. 164.00

998 Building - "Town Hall Bank," clock face in cupola, cast iron, Kyser & Rex, 1882, 3¼" w., 4¾" h. (W. 401) .. 114.00

1008 Building - Two-Story Building, 6-sided, cast iron, 2½" w., 3¼" h. (W. 358) 85.00

1040 Building - "Woolworth Building," cast iron, Kenton, 1915, 8 1/8" h. (W. 386) ... 90.00

1072 Building - "World Fair Administration Building," replica of Columbian Exposition building, cast iron, 1893, 6" h. (W. 399) 675.00

555 Bull - "Aberdeen Angus" embossed inside, aluminum, 7½" l. (W. 190) * 140.00

38 Captain Kidd - with shovel beside tree, cast iron, ca. 1910, 5½" h. (W. 38) ... 283.00

930 Cash Register - "Junior" Cash Register, cast iron, J. & E. Stevens, ca. 1920, 3½" w., 4¼" h. 100.00

931 Cash Register - "Junior" Cash Register, cast iron, J. & E.

Stevens, ca. 1920, 4 5/8" w., 5¼" h. 154.00

358 Cat on Tub, cast iron, A.C. Williams, 1920-34, 4 1/8" h. (W. 53) 122.00

370 Cat with Blue Bow - seated, lead, Germany, 4 1/8" h. .. 42.50

366 Cat with Soft Hair - seated, cast iron, Arcade, 1910-29, 4¼" h. (W. 248) 77.00

298 Chaplin (Charlie) beside Ash Barrel, cast iron & glass (candy container conversion), Borgfeldt & Co., 1920's, 3" w., 3¾" h. (W. 393) 120.00

928 Chest - Treasure Chest, cast iron, 2" w., 2" h. (W. 303) 100.00

1535 Clock - Ornate Hall Clock, cast iron w/paper face, Hubley, 1914-20's, 2 15/16" w., 5 7/8" h. 286.00

1548 Clock - Street Clock, cast iron, A.C Williams, 1920's-31, 6" h. (W. 219) ... 300.00

1539 Clock - Time Around the World - printed cards inside visible windows indicate times at 24 world capitols, cast iron & paper, Arcade, 1910-20, 4" h. (W. 172) 282.00

1317 Coronation (Elizabeth II) Crown, cast iron, England, 1953, 3" d., 3 3/16" h. 48.00

1628 Cross, cast iron, 9¼ x 4 5/8" 1,150.00

31 Devil - Two-Faced Devil, cast iron, A.C. Williams, 1904-12, 4¼" h. (W. 41) * .. 503.00

380 Dog - Basset Hound, cast iron, 4¼" l., 3 1/8" h. (W. 261) 960.00

412 Dog - Labrador Retriever, cast iron, 4½" l. (W. 104) 225.00

407 Dog - "Lost Dog," cast iron, possibly by Judd Mfg. Co., 1890's, 5½" h. (W. 115) 575.00

405 Dog - Pugdog seated, cast iron, Kyser & Rex, 1880, 3" l., 3½" h. (W. 111) 84.00

416 Dog - Puppo (Puppy Dog with Bee), cast iron, Hubley, 1920-30's, 4 7/8" h. (W. 338) 95.00

442 Dog - Puppo on Pillow (Dog on Cushion), cast iron, Hubley, 1920's, little paint, 5 5/8 x 6" (W. 336) * 168.00

437 Dog - St. Bernard with Pack, large, A.C. Williams, 1901-30's, 7¾" l. (W. 113) * 65.00

359 Dog on Tub, cast iron, A.C. Williams Co., 1920-34 4" h. (W. 54) 130.00

944 Dollar Sign - 2 tiny slots in side, tin, key locked trap, 2 5/8" w., 4" h. 40.00

499 Donkey - with saddle, small, cast iron, Arcade & A.C. Williams, 1910-30's, 4½" l., 4½" h. (W. 198) 60.00

616 Duck on Tub - "Save for a Rainy Day" on tub, cast iron, Hubley, 1930-36, 5¼" h. (W. 323) 145.00

181 Dutch Girl holding Flowers, cast iron, Hubley, 1930's, 5¼" h. (W. 35) 76.00

1074 Eiffel Tower, cast iron, Sydenham & McOustra, England, 1908, 8¾" h. 600.00

480 Elephant (no chariot holes), cast iron, Hubley, 1906, 7¾" l., 4¾" h. (W. 62) 145.00

486 Elephant on Bench on Tub, cast iron, A.C. Williams, 1920's-30, 4" h. (W. 55) 165.00

Elephant on Wheels

446 Elephant on Wheels, cast iron, A.C. Williams, 1920's, 4 3/8" l., 4 1/8" h., W. 75 (ILLUS.) 150.00

467 Elephant with Chariot, cast iron, Hubley, 1906, 8" l., 3½" h. (W. 74) 1,080.00

459 Elephant with Howdah, cast iron, A.C. Williams, 1912-34, 4" l., 3" h. (W. 68) * 38.00

474 Elephant with Howdah, cast iron, A.C. Williams, 1910-30's, 6 3/8" l., 4 7/8" h. (W. 63) 66.00

1630 Elephant with Howdah (short trunk), cast iron, Hubley, 1910, 4¾" l., 3¾" h. (W. 64) 45.00

11 Football Player, cast iron, A.C. Williams, 1910-31,

gold repaint, 5¾" h. (W. 12) 310.00

1658 Fox Head, cast iron, Unicast US 1973, 4½ x 2 3/8" 35.00

594 Goats - Two Kids - two goats lock horns over stump, cast iron, possibly Harper, 4" w., 4½" h. (W. 262) .... 1,100.00 to 1,300.00

85 Golliwog, cast iron, John Harper Ltd., England, 1910-25, 6¼" h. (W. 3) * ... 325.00

86 Golliwog, aluminum, John Harper Ltd., England, 6" h. (W. 52) * 108.00

610 Goose - "Red Goose Shoes," cast iron, Arcade, 1920's, 3¾" h. 130.00

628 Goose - "Red Goose School Shoes," cast iron, Arcade, 1920's, 3¾" h. (W. 215) 135.00

1399 Hat - World War I "Buddy" Hat, metal, Stronghart Co., ca. WWI, 3 11/16" w., 1 7/8" h. (W. 167) 196.00

510 Horse - Horse on Tub, cast iron, undecorated, A.C. Williams, 1920's, 5 5/16" h. 157.00

512 Horse - Horse on Wheels, cast iron, A.C. Williams, ca. 1920, 4¼" w., 5" h. (W. 87) 223.00

523 Horse - Saddle Horse, cast iron, Williams, 1934, 3 3/16" l., 2¾" h. (W. 86) .. 158.00

527 Horse - Work Horse with Flynet, cast iron, possibly Arcade, ca. 1910, 4 5/8" l., 4" h. (W. 80) ..... 400.00 to 450.00

786 Liberty Bell - Washington Bell with Yoke - "1732 - 1932" & Washington bust in relief, cast iron, Grey Iron Casting Co., 1932, 2¾" d., 2¾" h. (W. 275) 76.00

742 Lion, small, cast iron, A.C. Williams, 1934, 3½" l., 2½" h. (W. 94) 90.00

754 Lion - tail right, cast iron, A.C. Williams, 1905-31, 6¼" l., 5¼" h. (W. 89) 58.00

759 Lion - tail right, cast iron, A.C. Williams, 1920's, 4½" l., 3½" h. (W. 91) * ... 32.00

107 Man in Top Hat - Transvaal Money Box, cast iron, John Harper Ltd., England, ca. 1885, 4¼" w., 5 3/16" h. * .... 750.00 to 850.00

740 Monkey w/removable hat, bronze, worn polychrome paint, 3 3/8" h. (no hat) 425.00

743 Monkeys - Three Wise Monkeys, cast iron, "See, Hear & Speak No Evil" on base, A.C. Williams, U.S.A., 1910-12, 3½" w., 3¼" h. (W. 236) 225.00

289 Mouse - Sniffles at Tree Trunk, white metal, Metal Moss Mfg. Co., U.S.A., late 1930's, 5¾" l., 5 1/8" h. 40.00

177 Mulligan the Cop, cast iron, A.C. Williams Co., U.S.A., 1905-32, 5½" h. * (W. 8) 145.00

Mutt & Jeff Bank

157 Mutt & Jeff, cast iron, colorful old paint, A.C. Williams, U.S.A., 1912-31, 4¼" h., W. 13 (ILLUS.) 125.00

216 Organ Grinder (conversion), cast iron, Hubley, U.S.A., 6¼" h. 150.00

1320 "Our Empire Bank," cast iron, bust of King George V & Queen Mary in relief, possibly Sydenham & McOustra, England, ca. 1911, 6½" h. * 155.00

597 Owl, cast iron, Vindex, U.S.A., ca. 1930, 2½ x 4¼" 135.00

911 Pail - White City Pail, cast iron, Nicol & Co., U.S.A., ca. 1893, 2 5/8 x 2 5/8" 75.00

620 Pig - The Biggest Pig of All, cast iron, model of seated pig, 7¼" l. 100.00

602 Pig - "Bismark Bank," cast iron, U.S.A., ca. 1883, 7 3/8" l., 3 3/8" h. (W. 174) 132.50

629 Pig - "I Made Chicago Famous" (small), cast iron, J.M. Harper, U.S.A., 1902, 4 1/8" l., 2¼" h. (W. 177) 176.00

631 Pig - "I Made Chicago Famous" (large), cast iron, J.M. Harper, U.S.A., 1902, 5 5/16" l.,

2 5/8" h. 385.00

640 Pig - Laughing Pig, cast iron, no trap, possibly Hubley, U.S.A., 5¼" l., 2½" h........95.00

623 Pig - Pig (small), cast iron, Arcade, U.S.A., 1910-32, 4" l., 2" h. (W. 184)...............85.00

264 Pig - Porky Pig, cast iron, "Porky" on base, Hubley, U.S.A., ca. 1930, 5¾" w. (W. 27) 250.00

Pistol Packing Pirate Bank

341 Pistol Packing Pirate, white metal, pirate holding pistols & sitting on treasure chest, key-locked trap, American-made, ca. 1940, 6¼" h. (ILLUS.).....................45.00

561 Possum, cast iron, Arcade, U.S.A., 1910-13, 4½" l., 2 3/8" h. (W. 205) 350.00

568 Rabbit - seated, small, cast iron, Arcade, U.S.A., 1910-20, 3½" h. (W. 96) * 80.00

569 Rabbit on Base - "Bank" one side, "1884" other, cast iron, American-made, 2¼" h. (W. 97) 765.00

574 Rabbit - Rabbit standing, cast iron, A.C. Williams, U.S.A., ca. 1908 to mid-1920's, 5 5/8" l., 6¼" h. (W. 99) * ..125.00

1335 Refrigerator - "Electrolux," white metal, American-made, 2" l., 4" h. 35.00

737 Reindeer - Large Reindeer (Elk), cast iron, standing animal w/antlers, A.C. Williams, U.S.A., 1910-35, 5¼" l., 9½" h. ....100.00 to 125.00

736 Reindeer - Small Reindeer (Elk), cast iron, standing animal w/antlers, A.C. Williams, U.S.A., 1910-35 & Arcade, U.S.A., 1913-32, 4 7/8" l., 6¼" h. (W. 195)....55.00

120 Roosevelt, Theodore - "Teddy," cast iron, bust of Theodore Roosevelt, A.C. Williams, U.S.A., ca. 1919, 3½" l., 5" h. (W. 309).....155.00 to 175.00

Rooster Bank

547 Rooster, cast iron, Arcade, U.S.A., 1910-25, 4 5/8" h., W. 187 (ILLUS.)..............80.00

882 Safe - "Arabian Safe," cast iron, wording on front & desert scenes on sides, w/key, Kyser & Rex, U.S.A., ca. 1882, 4" sq., 4½" h. (W. 346).............75.00

906 Safe - "Bank of Columbia," cast iron, Arcade, U.S.A., 1891-1913, 3 3/8 x 3¾", 4 7/8" h. 155.00

866 Safe - "Pet Safe" - cast iron, American-made, 1¾ x 2¾", 4½" h. 95.00

"Safe Deposit" Bank

Safe - "Safe Deposit," cast iron, combination-type, "Henry C. Hart Mfg. Co., Detroit, Mich." on door (ILLUS.)......................87.50

891 Safe - "Security Safe Deposit," cast iron, possibly Kyser & Rex, U.S.A., 2 3/8 x 2 13/16", 3 7/8" h. 74.00

886 Safe - "Sport Safe," cast iron, w/keylock, Kyser & Rex, U.S.A., 2¼" sq., 3" h. (W. 374) 58.00

895 Safe - "Time Safe," cast iron, "What Time Does It Open" on clock face, door opens at correct time setting, E.M. Roche Co., U.S.A., 3¾" l., 7 1/16" h. (W. 397) 325.00

913 Safe - White City Puzzle Safe, No. 10, cast iron, Nicol & Co., U.S.A., 2¾" sq., 4½" h. (W. 287) 74.00

881 Safe - "Young America" Safe, cast iron, early American scenes on sides, w/key, Kyser & Rex, U.S.A., ca. 1882, 3 1/8" sq., 4 3/8" h., (W. 350) ....125.00 to 150.00

59 Santa Claus, cast iron, standing figure in old-fashioned red suit, Wing, U.S.A., ca. 1900, 5 7/8" h. (W. 30) * ....250.00 to 300.00

61 Santa Claus - Santa with Tree, cast iron, worn old polychrome paint, Hubley, U.S.A., 1914-30, 5 7/8" h. (connecting bolt an old replacement) 295.00

102 Santa Claus - Sleeping Santa, white metal, figure seated in large chair, original paint, Banthrico, U.S.A., 1950's, 6½" h. 65.00

103 Santa Claus - Sleeping Santa, white metal, figure seated in chair, Banthrico, U.S.A., 1950's, 5 7/8" h. 75.00

732 Sea Lion (Seal on Rock), cast iron, Arcade, U.S.A., 1910-13, 4¼" l., 3½" h. (W. 199) 290.00

596 Sheep - "Feed My Sheep," lead, American-made, 4 1/8" l., 2¾" h. 92.00

1420 Shell - 1½ inch Shell Bank, World War I deactivated artillery shell, Ferrosteel Mfg. Co., U.S.A., ca. 1919, 8 1/16" h. (W. 385) 48.00

1622 Shell - "Shell Out," cast iron, seashell on a base, J. & E. Stevens, U.S.A., ca. 1882, 4¾" w., 2½" h. (W. 293) ...325.00

1459 Ship - Steamboat, cast iron, sidewheeler w/two smokestacks, A.C. Williams, U.S.A., 1912-1920's, 8" l., 2 7/16" h. (W. 148) * 175.00

1461 Ship - Steamboat (6 holes), cast iron, sidewheeler w/sidewheel pierced w/six holes, American-made, 8 1/8" l., 2 11/16" h. (W. 150) 265.00

44 Soldier (Minute Man), cast iron, Hubley, U.S.A., 1905-06, 6" h. (W. 15) * 332.00

1087 Space Heater (Bird), cast iron, six-sided upright heater w/openwork design of Bird of Paradise, Chamberlain & Hill, England, ca. 1892, 4" sq., 6½" h. (W. 320) 65.00

660 Squirrel with Nut, cast iron, American-made, 3" w., 4 1/8" h. (W. 250) ....600.00 to 700.00

1164 Statue of Liberty, cast iron, A.C. Williams, U.S.A., ca. 1910 - early 1930's, 2¼" sq., 6 1/16" h. (W. 269) 65.00

Statue of Liberty Bank

1166 Statue of Liberty, cast iron, Wing, U.S.A., ca. 1900 & Kenton, U.S.A., 1911-32, 3 3/8" x 3 7/16", 9 5/8" h., W. 268 (ILLUS.) 150.00

1479 Stop Sign (small), cast iron, embossed "Stop" & "Save," Dent, U.S.A., ca. 1920, 2" sq., 4½" h. (W. 234) 195.00

1481 Stop Sign (large), cast iron, embossed "Stop" & "Save," Dent, U.S.A., ca. 1920, 2½" sq., 5 5/8" h. (W. 233) 255.00

1350 Stove - "Eureka" Gase Stove, tin, John Wright & Co., England, 5¼" h. 65.00

1364 Stove - Gem Stove, cast iron,

"Gem" on door, Abendroth Bros., New York, 3" d., 4¾" h. (W. 131) 105.00

1363 Stove - Mellow Stove, cast iron, "Mellow" on door, Liberty Toy Co., U.S.A., 3 1/8" d., 3 9/16" h. (W. 129) 85.00

1354 Stove - New Heatrola Bank, cast iron, model of coal-burning stove on four legs, Kenton, U.S.A., 1927-32, 2 5/8" sq., 4½" h. (W. 130) ..72.00

1357 Stove - Parlor Stove, cast iron, American-made, 2¾" sq., 6 7/8" h. (W. 138) 210.00

1341 Stove - Roper Stove (burner covers lift up), cast iron & sheet metal, Arcade, U.S.A., 2¼ x 3¾", 3¾" h. (W. 139) 165.00

1351 Stove - "York Stove," cast iron, model of parlor-type stove, Abendroth Bros., New York, 2¾ x 4", 4" h. (W. 133) 225.00

1549 "Sun Dial," cast iron, hours & compass points on top, Arcade, U.S.A., 1910-16, 2 1/8" sq., 4 5/16" h. (W. 153) 1,250.00

World War I Tank Bank

1435 Tank - "Tank Bank U.S.A., 1918," cast iron, model of a World War I tank, A.C. Williams, U.S.A., 1920's, 3 11/16" l., 3" h., W. 161 (ILLUS.) 135.00

1417 Tank - "Tank Savings Bank," cast iron, model of a World War I tank, Ferrosteel, U.S.A., ca. 1919, 9½" l., 4" h. 550.00

1437 Tank - "U.S. Tank Bank 1918," cast iron, model of a World War I tank, A.C. Williams, U.S.A., 1920's, 4¼" l., 2 3/8" h. (W. 162) 72.00

1438 Tank - U.S. Tank Bank, cast iron, model of a World War I tank, Nelson T. Hasenplug designer, American-made, ca. 1919, 3 7/8" l., 1¾" h. (W. 163) 75.00

1163 Temple Bar (Gateway to City of London), cast iron, England, 2½ x 4 1/8", 4" h. 305.00

1471 Trolley Car - Main Street Trolley (with people), cast iron, A.C. Williams, U.S.A., 1920's, 1¾ x 6½", 3" h. (W. 164) 305.00

1469 Trolley Car - Main Street Trolley (no people), cast iron, A.C. Williams, U.S.A., 1920's, 1¾ x 6½", 3" h. (W. 166) 245.00

1472 Trolley Car - Trolley, cast iron, American-made, ca. 1889, 4 5/8" l., 3 15/16" h. 275.00

1474 Trolley Car, cast iron, Kenton, U.S.A., 1904-22, 5¼" l., 2 11/16" h. 285.00

946 Trunk - Trunk on Dolly, cast iron, Piaget, U.S.A., ca. 1890, 3 9/16" w., 2 5/8" h. (W. 232 without dolly) 40.00

585 Turkey - Large Turkey, cast iron, A.C. Williams, U.S.A., 1905-12, 4" w., 4¼" h. (W. 194) 415.00

587 Turkey - Small Turkey, cast iron, A.C. Williams, U.S.A., 1905-35, 3 3/8" w., 3½" h. (W. 193) * 70.00

842 U.S. Mailbox - Standing Mailbox, small, cast iron, "U.S. Mail" & "Letters" on slot, Hubley, U.S.A., ca. 1928, 1½ x 1 7/8", 3¾" h. (W. 126) 38.00

853 U.S. Mailbox - "U.S. Mail," cast iron, A.C. Williams, U.S.A., 1912-31, 1¼ x 2½", 3 5/8" h. (W. 122) 30.00

856 U.S. Mailbox - "U.S. Mail" (hanging), cast iron, A.C. Williams, U.S.A., 1921-34, 3" w., 5 1/8" h. (W. 382) 82.00

136 Washington, George - Washington (hollow base), cast iron, standing figure of Washington, American-made, ca. 1970, 6 3/8" h. 25.00

153 Washington, George - Washington, Tall Bust, cast iron, Grey Iron Casting Co., U.S.A., late 1920's, 3 7/8" w., 8" h. 750.00

1048 "Washington" Monument, cast iron, A.C. Williams, U.S.A., 1910-12, 2 1/8" sq., 6 1/8" h. (W. 360) 100.00

1049 "Washington" Monument, cast iron, A.C. Williams, U.S.A., 1910-12, 2½" sq., 7½" h. (W. 364) 190.00

1606 Water Wheel, cast iron, American-made, 4" w., 4½" h. (W. 152) 1,600.00

GLASS

Cat, clear figure w/metal cap, container for "Grapette" drink 21.00

Clock, container for "Nash's Mustard," clear, 4" h. 12.50

Clown, clear figure, container for "Grapette" drink . . . . .12.00 to 15.00

"Coin Saver," square, clear 12.00

Donald Duck, clear figure, container for "Nash's Mustard" . . 12.00

Fat man, clear figure, container for "Nash's Mustard" . . 15.00

1561 Fruit jar, advertising "Atlas Strong Shoulder Mason," clear replica w/embossed lettering .17.00

Glass block, advertising "Pittsburgh Paint," clear 26.50

302 Happifats on Drum, clear, Borgfeldt & Co., U.S.A., 1913-21, 4½" h. 167.50

Liberty Bell, container for "Nash's Mustard," clear 16.50

Log cabin, clear 19.00

Owl, "Wise Old Owl" on base, 7" h. 14.00

"Snoopy" dog, clear glass . . . . .7.00 to 10.00

POTTERY

Chalkware Hen Bank

Advertising, "Van Dyke Teas," model of a log cabin, glazed earthenware pottery, marked "Austria," ca. 1930, 2½ x 3½ x 2½" 35.00

Advertising, "Van Dyke Tea & Coffee, Our Own Stores" on bottom, model of a turkey on a pedestal, glazed earthenware pottery, marked "Austria," ca. 1909, 4" h. 22.50

Apple, redware pottery, 2½" h. 105.00

Cylindrical w/sloping sides, stoneware, applied leaves & stars, incised design around coin slot, brushed cobalt blue polka dots, horizontal bands, diagonal slashes & "E.D." on grey, 3¼" h. (made for Edward Dunaway, Greensboro, Pennsylvania druggist) 2,950.00

Cylindrical w/turnip-shaped top, tooled lines at shoulder, brushed dark reddish brown florals on reddish clay pottery, New Geneva, 6 7/8" h. (chips around coin slot & sides) 275.00

Frog seated, buff clay pottery w/speckled green glaze, 3 7/8" h. .30.00

Hen, chalkware, hollow figure painted in tones of red & yellow on white ground, coin slot on back, Pennsylvania, mid-19th c., 6½" h. (ILLUS.) .715.00

Jug, redware pottery, brown & green running glaze, Shenandoah Valley, 4" h. 450.00

Man seated & holding pitcher impressed "Money Taken In Here," mottled brown Rockingham-glazed pottery (minor small flakes) . . . . .60.00 to 75.00

Ovoid, redware pottery, tooled lines at shoulders & knob finial, slightly amber glaze w/brown flecks, 5¼" h. (minor wear) 125.00

Pig, earthenware pottery, brown, salmon, blue & cream marbleized, 4" l. 85.00

Pig standing, yellowware pottery w/mottled brown Rockingham glaze, 3¾" l. (chips) 20.00

Pig standing, yellowware pottery w/green & brown splotches, 4 7/8" l. 105.00

Pig, white clay pottery w/brown sponge-daubed spots 65.00

Turnip, redware pottery, old worn red paint, 4¾" h. 165.00

Turnip, white clay pottery, clear glaze w/blue sponge-daubed bands & "Cora" within sponged wreath, 5" h. 200.00

TIN

Chein Barrel Bank

Advertising, "Amoco Oil," oil can shape 11.50
Advertising, "Atlas Battery," replica of 6-volt car battery . . 16.00
Advertising, "Bokar (A & P) Coffee," coffee can replica, black ground 12.00
Advertising, "Gerber's Orange Juice" 7.00
Advertising, "Harness Soap," black man, round 60.00
Advertising, "John Hancock Insurance," blue & gold leatherette one side, slip-in photo pocket other, w/key, Ell Products, New York, 1940-50, 2 x 4½" 22.00
Advertising, "Lifesavers," replica of Lifesavers package, 10" h. 69.00
Advertising, "Peacock Dried Beef," lithographed 35.00
Advertising, "Pep Boys," w/reminder to buy U.S. Savings Bonds, 1942 . . . . 50.00
Advertising, "Pure Premium Oil," round 12.00
Advertising, "Sinclair Gasoline," gas pump replica 19.00
Advertising, "Standard Permalube," round 15.00
Barrel, "Happy Days," J. Chein & Co. (ILLUS.) . . . . 12.00 to 15.00
1577 Declaration of Independence scene, cylinder, American Can Co., 3½" h. 15.00
Donald Duck, semi-mechanical, "Second National Bank," J. Chein & Co. 45.00
Drum, Civil War type, J. Chein & Co. 9.00
1350 "Eureka" Gas Stove, John Wright & Co., England, 5¼" h. 55.00
1297 George VI Coronation, red & gold, 1937, 3 x 2 9/16" 20.00
Kiddie clock dime bank, tin w/glassine closure, various times of the world printed around edge, side printed "Mfg. J.C. Crossette Co., Jeannette, Pa.," 1 7/8" d. (originally a candy container) 110.00
Liberty Bell, w/key, 1919 . . . . 15.00
"Mr. Zip," Ohio Art Co. 5.00
Safe, 5 x 5" 15.00
Westward Ho, book shape, w/key 30.00

BARBERIANA

A wide variety of antiques related to the tonsorial arts have been highly collectible for many years, especially 19th and early 20th century shaving mugs and barber bottles and, more recently, razors. We are now combining these closely related categories under one heading here for easier reference. A selection of other varied pieces relating to barbering will also be found below.

BARBER BOTTLES

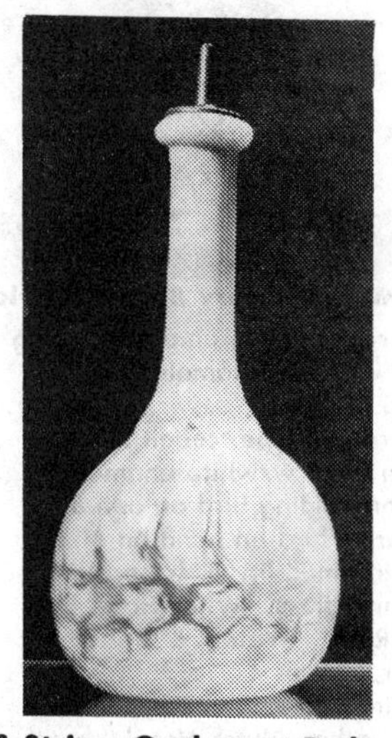

Stars & Stripes Opalescent Barber Bottle

Amber glass, Bay Rum, "Colgate & Co., N.Y." $19.00
Amber glass, pressed Hobnail patt. 35.00
Amethyst glass, blown, enameled floral decoration, open pontil, 8" h. 250.00
Blue opalescent glass, Daisy & Fern patt., rolled lip, ground pontil, 7½" h. 125.00

Blue opalescent glass, Stars & Stripes patt., ground pontil, 7" h. (ILLUS.) 200.00

Clambroth glass, pressed, tapering cone-shape, both embossed in red, "Water," 8" h. w/porcelain stoppers, pr. 36.00

Cranberry craquelle glass, applied clear rim, polished pontil 195.00

Cranberry opalescent glass, vertical stripes, rolled lip, ground pontil, 7½" h. 100.00

Frosted clear glass w/burgundy lip, blown, raised base of neck, ribbed base, decorated w/flowers & leaves, some gold highlighting, pontil, 8" h. w/stopper 90.00

Iridescent blown glass w/"crackled" green iridescence over cobalt blue, similar to Loetz glass, ground pontil, ca. 1900, 7½" h. .. 206.00

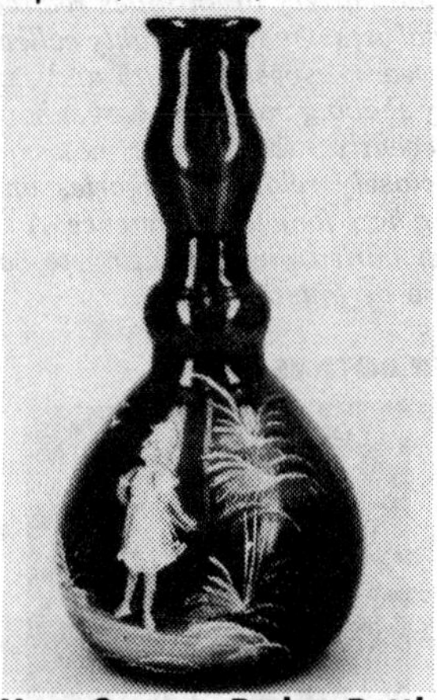

Mary Gregory Barber Bottle

Mary Gregory-type, amethyst blown glass w/white enameled figure (ILLUS.) 250.00

Mary Gregory-type, cobalt blue blown glass w/white enameled woman holding bird on one & hunter w/bird on hand on other, gold trimmed lip, 8" h., pr. 300.00

Milk white glass, "Witch Hazel," "Bay Rum," "Water" & "Toilet Water," set of 4 .... 200.00

Porcelain, one embossed "Tonic" in black, other "Witch Hazel," both w/three sides w/floral decoration, 9" h., pr. 220.00

MUGS *(Porcelain unless otherwise noted)*

Occupational

Artist, h.p. color pallet & brushes below name in gold, "P. Kutner," base marked "J & C Bavaria" 355.00

Automobile dealer, early h.p. touring car in green above name in gold, "C.F. Johns," base marked "Germany" 600.00

Bicyclist, h.p. color scene of man in blue outfit riding safety bike on dirt road, house in background w/fence & trees above name in gold, "Jno. K. Marsh" (tiny repaired chip on underside) 525.00

Cab driver, h.p. scene of man driving black horse cab, name faded 325.00

Delivery man, h.p. delivery wagon full of watermelons being pulled by two horses, driver w/whip in hand, gold scroll either side, w/name "C. Forrino" 275.00

Doctor, h.p. ornate gold & floral decoration, name "A.D. Bradsher M.D." in gold, signed on base "A. Kern B.S. Co. St. Louis" 150.00

Fireman, h.p. w/two horses pulling fire fighting equipment, name in gold 150.00

Jockey, h.p. horse head, jockey, whip & horseshoe decoration, name in gold 355.00

Musician, h.p. brown violin w/light blue & tan background, name above in gold, "Isial F. Jervais," marked on base, "T & V France" .. 250.00

Printer, h.p. w/hand holding printer's composing stick, w/name, "W. ST. T. Havy," T & V Limoges 125.00

Restaurateur, excellent h.p. color interior scene of a restaurant w/waiter w/tray, customer paying tab & woman in red dress serving seated customers, owner's name across top in gold, "F.H. Slouecker" 814.00

Telegraph operator, h.p. color scene of man seated at work at counter below worn name in gold, "Roy West" 326.00

Miscellaneous

Fraternal, B.P.O.E. (Benevolent & Protective Order of Elks), w/name "W.R. Finley," marked on base, "V & D Austria" 54.00

Fraternal, Ancient Order of United Workmen, w/name in gold 95.00

China, "A Close Shave," two black men fighting w/switch blades, marked on base, "K.P.M. Germany" 250.00

China, h.p. Buster Brown scene, w/name in gold, Limoges blank .. 275.00

China, h.p. eagle medallion w/two flags & gold band trim, name "Leon Henry Berry" & roses in lattice scroll, Limoges blank 150.00

China, h.p. floral decoration & "Think of Me," ornate gold trim .. 25.00

China, embossed shape w/light moss & beige florals, R.S. Germany mark 75.00

China, full-color portrait of Victorian woman framed in black oval, light blue ground behind lower portion of portrait, purple ribbon w/faded gold name, "Geo. B. Mc C. Riden," faded gold rim & highlighting 270.00

Ironstone china, Tea Leaf patt., panel mold, Anthony Shaw 175.00

Silver plate w/milk glass insert, waisted shape w/raised flowers on front, ornate handle w/brush rest, marked on bottom, "S & L Co., NY." 26.00

RAZORS

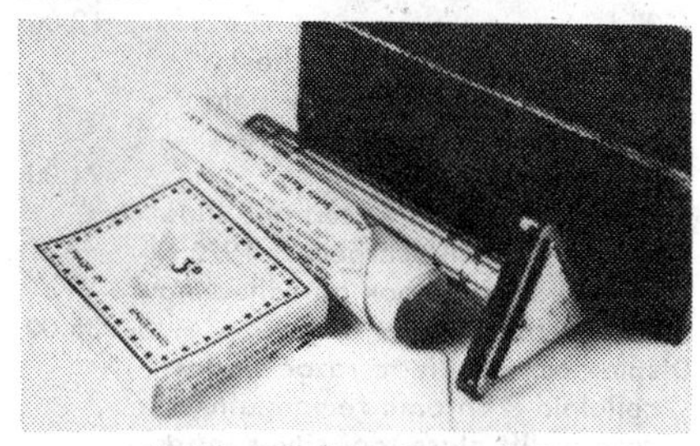

Maktor Safety Razor Set

Corn razor, "Hamilton Corn Razor," etched blade, chased aluminum handle decorated both sides 76.00

Safety razor, "Griffon Safety Razor," in tin 150.00

Safety razor, "Kriss Kross Safety Razor," stropper in box 12.00

Safety razor, "The Laurel," tin container, purple w/light green & gold lettering 40.00

Safety razor, "Maktor," triangular-head model, w/package of blades, instructions & original box, the group (ILLUS.) 80.00

The Mohican Safety Razor Tin

Safety razor, "The Mohican Safety Razor," w/instructions & original Indian-decorated tin (ILLUS. of tin) 551.00

Safety razor, "Torrey No. B," tin container in green & yellow w/gold & black lettering, ca. 1905 .... 182.00

Safety razor, "Winchester," w/red, blue & grey box w/advertising (box end missing) 42.00

Safety razor set: two-part chrome-plated razor & blade holder fitted in leather-covered wood case w/purple lining; Gem Safety, the set 18.00

Safety razor set: impressed ivory handled razor w/wafer blade & blade guard, gold & metal tag w/days of week embossed & places for six additional blades, three extra blades in lower part w/spaces for three more, all fitted in leather-bound wood case lined w/green velvet; Sextoblade Razor Style B, made by E. Weck & Son, Inc., New York, the set 55.00

Safety razor set: silver plated razor, seven blades etched w/days of the week, leather strop, all fitted in oak case; Wilkinson Sword Co., the set 80.00

Straight razor, Allen (Joseph), England, blade etched, "Non XLL," yellow celluloid handle, w/florals 25.00

Straight razor, Almer, celluloid marbleized brown & yellow handle 12.50

Straight razor, Boker (H.) & Co., Germany, impressed ivory handle w/raised beaded pattern w/raised scroll around each end, blade w/"B" in center, ivory tang, w/presentation case 25.00

Straight razor, Case Brothers, Little Valley, N.Y., blade stamped "Tested XX," yellow wrapped rope pattern handle 30.00

Straight razor, Clark Bros. Co., Germany, brown to yellow w/leaves & florals decoration on handle 20.00

Straight razor, Elliott (Joseph) Fine India Steel, black horn handle is pressed across center w/"Boston" surrounded by flowers, blade etched, "Celebrated Razor," ca. 1860's 20.00

Straight razor, "George Washington" lettering on handle & etched bust of Washington on blade 183.00

Straight razor, Golden Rule Cutlery Co., Chicago, USA, photo handle w/four beautiful women, two on each side 65.00

Straight razor, Hitchcock Hill Co., Chicago, Illinois, impressed ivory handle w/leaf & scrolls patterns at ends 56.00

Straight razor, Johnson (Chris.), Sheffield, England, plated-brass handle, wide hollow ground blade 56.00

Straight razor, Keen Kutter, etched black ivory handle 50.00

Straight razor, Keen Kutter, No. K-15, w/box 21.00

Straight razor, Roberts Warranted, straight crude real bone handle, wedge blade w/no distinct tang, iron pin covers, rare & early, ca. 1780 .... 138.00

Straight razor, Shurago model, celluloid handle made of two different colored halves, front orange, back green, blade etched w/gold area showing an open straight razor w/a gentleman's head & "Shumate Registered Trade Mark" 65.00

Straight razor, Wade & Burcher, picked bone handle, blade etched, "Ask For Wade & Burcher's Hollow Ground Razor," excellent condition 100.00

Straight razor, tortoiseshell handle inlaid w/escutcheon plate, tang stamped, "I & S Waranted (sic)," ca. 1815 .... 120.00

Straight razor, Wiss (J.), Newark, New Jersey, picked bone handle resembles stag horn 46.00

GENERAL ITEMS

Pearlware Barber Bowl

Barber bowl, Pearlware, footed bowl h.p. in colored enamels w/stylized foliate garland border at rim & ochre & underglaze-blue floral sprigs in interior, underside h.p. in brown w/trellis diaper band, rims edged in blue, Staffordshire, England, 1810-1820 (hairline crack, restoration), 10 3/8" d. (ILLUS.) 605.00

Barber chair, child's, Koken, w/horse's head 1,200.00

Barber chair, walnut w/velvet upholstery, pat. 1880, "Kochs Eureka" (restored) 550.00

Barber pole, floor-style, Koken, white pedestal base supporting paneled sides made up of red & white striped glass panels, large round white ball at top (restored) 4,900.00

Barber pole, wall-type, Koken, white tapering crest w/acorn finial above panels of red & white striped art glass, white base 1,000.00

Barber pole, turned & painted wood, tall, free-standing pole w/two flat sections divided by ring-turned center section & turned base & top capped w/round ball, worn & weathered red & white stripes & blue trim, added round disk base, 77" h. (age cracks) 470.00

Blade bank, porcelain, model of a donkey, advertising "Listerine," 3" l. 12.00

Blade bank, tin, treasure chest shape, orange & black w/gold highlighting & lettering "Ever-Ready," 1 x 1½ x 2" 24.00

Book, "1000 Razors Priced and Illustrated," by Bill Schroeder, 1970, illustrated, first book on collecting razors, out of print, 71 pp. 35.00

Display case, Gillette razor blades, celluloid & chrome rectangular case w/lift glass top, silver lettering on black background across front edge, 14 x 17", 2" h. 43.00

Razor blade sharpener, "Edge-Bak" 7.50

Razor blade sharpener, Everkeen Magnetic, brown bakelite sharpener marked "Ritz," made by Yates & Grant Inc., Detroit, Michigan, fitted in cardboard box 30.00

Razor hone, "The Apart Hones," Austria, in box 10.00

Razor hone, Hibbard, Spencer, Bartlett & Co., fitted in green, blue & white tin case (case worn) 44.00

Razor strop, ivory handle, w/pressed sheath, 1½" w., 12" l. 21.00

Razor strop, "Never-Fail" stropper, boxed w/instruction sheet 24.00

Shaving brush, Art Nouveau style, embossed sterling silver handle w/floral decoration overall, marked "Stieff Sterling 450," good bristles 26.00

Shaving mirror, table-type, base of red & white porcelain bands in shape of a barber pole, gold trim, round two-sided mirror swivels, bottom marked "C.T.P. 01961" (worn finish) 54.00

Shaving mug rack, golden oak, 28-compartment, w/applied carving, 41" l., 39" h. 625.00

Shaving stand, table-type, gold-plated metal in ornate Art Nouveau style on four feet, tapering up to round opening for milk white glass insert for soap, wooden-handled shaving brush in holder just above insert, back of stand continues up to form rounded opening for mirror, base marked "JB" 54.00

Shaving stand, floor-type, mahogany veneer on pine, Hepplewhite, rectangular mirror plate within inlaid reeded frame w/corner blocks, tilting between reeded posts above base w/dovetailed drawer, ball feet, 14¾" w., 17¼" h. 175.00

Sign, "Associated Master Barbers of America," metal & cardboard, dark blue w/gold & red lettering, green banner, yellow centers, made by Bastian Bros. Co., Rochester, N.Y., w/chain for hanging, 6 x 15" 101.00

Tintype, two barbers standing behind table, one w/open straight razor in hand, table w/two barber bottles, ointment jar, strop & more, 2¼ x 3½" 42.00

Trade catalog, "Buerger Bros. Barber Supply," fully illustrated, mugs, razors, bottles, backbars, chairs, etc., ca. 1905, 152 pp. 138.00

Trade catalog, "J.R. Torrey Razor Co.," ca. 1890's, fully illustrated, 23 pp. 31.00

BASEBALL MEMORABILIA

Baseball was named by Abner Doubleday as he laid out a diamond-shaped field with four bases at Cooperstown, New York, in 1839. A popular game from its inception, by 1869 it was able to support its first all-professional team, the Cincinnati Red Stockings. The National League was organized in 1876 and though the American League was first formed in 1900, it was not officially recognized until 1903. Today, the "national pastime" has millions of fans and collecting baseball memorabilia has become a major hobby with enthusiastic collectors seeking out items associated with players such as Babe Ruth, Lou Gehrig, and others, who became legends in their own lifetimes. Though baseball cards, issued as advertising premiums for bubble gum and other products, seem to dominate the field there are numerous other items available.

Almanac, "Mutual Baseball Almanac," Doubleday, 1954, hard cover $10.00

Baseball, autographed by Don Larson, w/box 42.50

Baseball, "New York Yankees World Champions," autographed by all 25 players, 1950 (some smearing) ....195.00 to 285.00

Baseball card, 1880's, Old Judge Cigarettes, Hatfield of New York 45.00

Baseball card, 1880's, Old Judge Cigarettes, P. Keepe of New York (Hall of Famer) 95.00

Baseball card, 1880's, Old Judge Cigarettes, L.F. O'Neil of St. Louis 45.00

Baseball card, 1953, Bowman Gum, Stan Musial (No. 32) 112.00

Baseball card, 1953, Topps Gum, Yogi Berra (No. 104) 25.00

Baseball card, 1956, Topps Gum, Mickey Mantle (No. 135) 177.00

Baseball card, 1957, Topps Gum, Hank Aaron (No. 20) 31.00

Baseball card, 1957, Topps Gum, Johnny Bench Rookie (No. 247) ... 51.00

Baseball card, 1957, Topps Gum, Willie Mays (No. 10) 26.00

Baseball card, 1959, Fleers Gum, Ted Williams 15.00

Baseball card, 1973, Topps Gum, Ty Cobb 4.00

Baseball card, 1973, Topps Gum, Lou Gehrig 4.50

Baseball card, 1973, Topps Gum, Walter Johnson 4.00

Baseball card, 1973, Topps Gum, Babe Ruth 5.00

Baseball card, 1974, Topps Gum, Mike Schmidt 2.50

Baseball card, 1974, Topps Gum, Dave Winfield 7.00

Baseball cards, 1956, Topps Gum, assorted set of 40 .... 20.00

Bat, oak, miniature, souvenir of 1931 World Series, Cardinals vs. Athletics, w/Cardinal pennant attached 100.00

Book, "Babe Ruth Story," w/photographs, 1948, 1st edition 55.00

Book, "The Baseball Encyclopedia," 1969, 2,336 pp. 35.00

Book, "Dizzy Dean Dictionary," photographs & anecdotes, advertising Falstaff Beer 25.00

Book, "Spalding's 1923 Official Baseball Guide" 60.00

Book, "Strike Out: Story of Bob Feller," by Barnes, 1947 .... 10.00

Cigarette flannel, Walter Johnson .. 39.00

Cigarette flannel, Ty Cobb 79.00

Pen, wooden, model of Louisville Slugger baseball bat, "Mickey Mantle," 8" 5.00
Pen & pencil set, celluloid baseball bat shapes, "Jimmy Foxx," 1930-40, original box, pr. 35.00
Pennant, "Baltimore Orioles," 1955, 12" 15.00
Photograph, Mickey Mantle, autographed, 1950, 8 x 10"....... 35.00
Pinback button, Ted Williams....... 15.00
Program, 1954 World Series, Cleveland Indians vs. San Francisco Giants 15.00
Program, 1958 All-Star Game 50.00
Program & scorecard, 1965, New York Mets, World's Fair edition ... 12.00
Score card, 1935 World Series - Chicago Cubs vs. Detroit Tigers, 6 pp. of photographs of players, 6 x 9" 15.00
Score card, 1943, New York Yankees vs. Philadelphia Phillies 12.00
Sheet music, "Babe Ruth! Babe Ruth! We Know What He Can Do," Babe Ruth on cover, 1928 ... 25.00
Toy, celluloid windup, New York Yankees catcher, made in Occupied Japan, original box 85.00
World Series booster pin, 1926, red cardinal on bat 30.00
Wrist watch, Babe Ruth, 1933-35 ....175.00 to 250.00
Yearbook, 1953 Philadelphia Phillies 10.00
Yearbook, 1953 Washington Nationals 7.50
Yearbook, 1955 New York Giants ... 30.00
Yearbook, 1957 St. Louis Cardinals .. 20.00

BASKETS

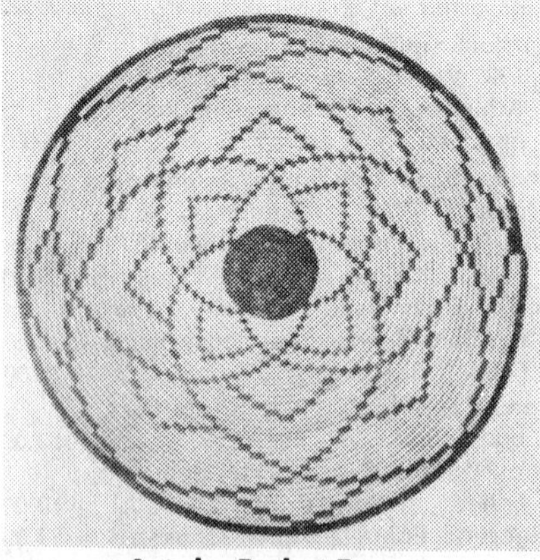

Apache Basket-Tray

The American Indians were the first basket weavers on this continent and, of necessity, the early Colonial settlers and their descendents pursued this artistic handicraft to provide essential containers for berries, eggs and endless other items to be carried or stored. Rye straw, split willow and reeds are but a few of the wide variety of materials used. The Nantucket baskets, plainly and sturdily constructed, along with the baskets woven by American Indians and at the Shaker settlements, would seem to draw the greatest attention in an area of collecting where interest has stabilized because of the wide availability of fine baskets by contemporary basketweavers for art and craft shows across the country.

American Indian cov. basket, Makah, wrap-twined cedar bark & bear grass construction, geometric design, 2½" d., 1½" h. $75.00
American Indian cov. basket, Nootka, wrap-twined construction, whaling scene against light ground, 7" d., 3" h. 70.00
American Indian cov. basket, Woodland, woven splint construction, faded red & blue design on natural, 16 x 13" oblong, 10¾" h. 270.00
American Indian basket, Hupa, twined construction, linear geometric design, 1900's, 5" d. 125.00
American Indian basket, Pima, woven coilwork construction, black Coyote Track patt. on natural, 6¾" d., 4" h. 95.00
American Indian basket, Klamath, twined construction, stylized wild geese design, ca. 1910, 8" d., 4½" h. 160.00
American Indian basket, Pima-Papago, coilwork construction, flaring circular form, woven w/standing figures around sides, 1890-1910, 9" widest d., 3½" h. .. 250.00
American Indian basket-bowl, Apache, woven devil's claw, checkered rectangles & encompassing banded decor near rim & meandering stylized arrow motifs radiating towards central tondo, 14½" d. 770.00
American Indian basket-tray, Apache, broad flat base & flaring sides, woven devil's claw & willow coilwork construction, black & natural radiating terraced snowflake design, 22½" d. (ILLUS.) 1,210.00
Apple basket, woven oak splint, 19" d. 50.00
"Buttocks" basket, miniature, 6-rib construction, woven natural splint, 1¾" l. 130.00

"Buttocks" basket, 20-rib construction, woven oak splint, 7½ x 7", 4½" h. plus bentwood handle 300.00

"Buttocks" basket w/double-hinged cover, 24-rib construction, woven splint, 10½ x 5½", 5½" h. plus twisted splint handle 250.00

"Buttocks" basket, 18-rib construction, woven splint, old red & black paint, eye of God design at base of handle, 12¾ x 12", 5¾" h. plus bentwood handle................ 200.00

Cheese Basket

Cheese basket, woven splint, 23½" d., 6½" h. (ILLUS.)......... 425.00

Egg gathering basket, tightly woven splint, melon-ribbed, 9½ x 8¼" oval, 5" h. plus bentwood handle 115.00

Egg gathering basket, tightly woven splint, melon-ribbed, colorful old painted design, woven eye of God design at base of handle, 10 x 9½", 4½" h. plus bentwood handle 475.00

Field (or gathering) basket, woven willow, dark patina, w/bentwood handle, ca. 1880, 19 x 18", overall 20" h......................... 260.00

Field (or gathering) basket, woven splint, w/bentwood rim & handles, 20½" d., 9¾" h. 55.00

Market (or utility), oval, woven splint w/red, green & black painted decoration, 6 x 8", 4" h. plus well-shaped bentwood handle 305.00

Market (or utility) basket, woven faded brown, yellow & natural splint, radiating splint staves, 13 x 15", 6" h. plus bentwood handle .. 125.00

Market (or utility) basket, woven splint, oval rim tapering to a rectangular base (losses to corners), painted dark green, Eastern Illinois, 19th c., 15" l., 6" h. plus bentwood handle (ILLUS.) 275.00

Woven Splint Market Basket

Market (or utility) basket, woven splint w/kick-up, carved swivel handle, American, 19th c., 14½" d., 6½" h. 440.00

Market (or utility) basket, woven splint, worn orangish tan paint, 14¼" d., 9" h. plus bentwood handle 215.00

Market (or utility) basket, woven reed & splint, round base, oval rim, w/bentwood swivel handle, 14 x 16", 9¼" h. 75.00

Market (or utility) basket, woven splint, 15½ x 28", 14" h. plus bentwood handle................ 195.00

Melon basket, miniature, 12-rib construction, woven splint, eye of God design at base of handle, 6¼" d., 3½" h. plus bentwood handle 195.00

Melon basket, 12-rib construction, woven splint, 11½ x 12½" oval, 6" h. plus bentwood handle 130.00

Melon basket, 14-rib construction, woven splint, eye of God design at handle, 12" d., 5¾" h. 95.00

Melon basket, 20-rib construction, woven splint, old worn finish, bentwood handle, 14 x 17"....... 165.00

Nantucket lightship basket, tightly woven rattan sides, wooden base, pair bentwood swing handles, base signed "Made in Nantucket, Jose Formoso Reyes," 14 x 16½" oval, 7" h. plus handles 2,550.00

Nantucket lightship basket, wooden base, rivet & washer, swing handle, signed on base "Jason Wills, Nantucket, Mass.," 13" d., 9" h. .. 275.00

Nantucket lightship baskets, finely woven ash & willow splint sides, circular pine board base, bentwood swivel handle w/chamfered ears, all marked, R. Folger, Nantucket, Massachusetts, 19th c., 14½" d., 9½" h.; 11" d., 7½" h. (some

Nantucket Lightship Baskets

breaks) & 6" d., 4¼" h., set of 3 (ILLUS.) 3,575.00

Picnic (or storage) hamper w/double-hinged cover, 22-rib construction, woven natural & colored splint, 10¼ x 16", 7¼" h. plus bentwood handle 175.00

Rye straw (bread) basket, coilwork construction, round w/open handles each side, Pennsylvania, 15" d. 60.00

Sewing basket, open, openwork w/a multi-pointed star pattern, woven rye straw interwoven w/pieces of blue, green & red felt & other fabric tied w/tufts on the rim, Pennsylvania, 19th c., 11¼" d., 3" h. 220.00

Storage basket, open, woven splint w/wrapped rim, bentwood rim handles, square base, round top, 10" top d., 3¼" h. 225.00

Storage basket w/hinged lid, woven willow & vine, colorful old paint in stripes of red, blue, yellow, white & green, 13 x 19", 10" h. plus bentwood handle................ 75.00

Storage basket, cov., woven wide splint w/yellow, red & natural w/black potato print designs, 18 x 24", 13½" h. 350.00

Weaver's basket, woven splint, low rectangle w/rounded corners, divided interior, orange & blue watercolor designs, 10½ x 18", 5" h. (minor damage)............ 175.00

BEADED & MESH BAGS

Beaded and mesh bags, popular earlier in this century, are now in great demand. Ladies have found them to be the perfect accessory to the casual long gowns now so fashionable. Sterling silver bags and those set with precious stones bring high prices, but the average glass beaded bag is much lower.

Beaded, amber beading forming an undulating design on bag & handle, envelope clutch-type w/gilt bronze overflap applied w/three oval enameled portraits of beautiful women, each oval within ormolu fishscale frame set w/pearls, gold satin lining, signed Marabito, Paris, 8 x 7" $200.00

Beaded, colorful beading forming scene of a peacock on tree branch, elaborate frame & chain handle, 10 x 7" 75.00

Beaded, iridescent light blue beading, Flapper-style 30.00

Beaded, ivory beading forming roses design, Victorian 35.00

Carnival Glass Beaded Bag

Beaded, marigold Carnival glass beading on mesh fabric, drawstring type (ILLUS.) 35.00

Beaded, midnight blue beading forming looped panels, silver filigree frame, 6½ x 5½" 30.00

Beaded, multicolored florals & geometric designs, jeweled frame w/chain handle, beaded fringe, 7" w., 11" l. 125.00

Beaded, pink & blue beading forming rose buds & forget-me-nots on black fabric, silver plate frame & chain handle.................... 35.00

Beaded, purple Carnival glass beading, ornate frame, 7" l. 85.00

Beaded, red, blue & yellow beading, overall roses design 65.00

Beaded "miser's purse," cut steel beading on tubular burgundy crocheted fabric, w/steel slide rings 45.00

Enameled mesh, black & silver design, Whiting-Davis 35.00

Enameled mesh, multicolored Art Deco style design on silver finish mesh, chain handle, Whiting-Davis 40.00

Enameled mesh, multicolored floral design, chain handle, Whiting-Davis 60.00

Enameled mesh, orange, yellow, blue & white design, gold finish metal frame, Whiting-Davis, ca. 1920, 6 x 4" 45.00

Enameled mesh, red, green & lavender splashes on robin's egg blue shaded to dark blue, Whiting-Davis, ca. 1920.................. 85.00

German Silver Mesh Bag

German silver mesh, Art Nouveau style frame, chain handle, 5 drops at base (ILLUS.) 47.00

Gold finish mesh, child's, taffeta lined, Whiting-Davis, 2¾ x 2¼" .. 38.00

Gold finish mesh, Whiting-Davis, 8 x 5" 125.00

Gold mesh, 14k, 2 long narrow engraved panels either side, ornate engraved frame w/deep blue sapphire clasp & mesh loop handle, chain & seed pearl fringed base, marked Phelps & Perry, Maiden Lane, New York, in original lined leather case 1,600.00

Silver finish mesh, Whiting-Davis ... 28.00

Silver mesh, engraved grapevine decor on frame, German, 7½" l. ... 85.00

Sterling silver mesh, bearded man's face & 2 cupids on each side of frame, pat. Dec. 24, 1901, 7¼" l. 300.00

BELLS

Animal bell, cow, sheet iron w/iron clapper $20.00

Animal bell, sheep, brass w/wooden clapper & leather neck strap .. 24.00

Animal bell, sheep, tin 10.00

Animal bell, turkey, brass, w/buckle & silencer 68.00

Commemorative bell, World War II "Victory" bell, cast from metal of German aircraft shot down over Britain, "V" on handle & embossed bust portraits of Churchill, Stalin & Roosevelt on sides, 5½" h. 62.50

Dinner gong, brass, bell suspended in large frame, marked "China" .. 95.00

Figural bell, brass, bust of Neville Chamberlain, 2¾" d., 5¼" h. 60.00

Figural bell, brass, Sairey Gamp 165.00

Figural bell, brass, Tony Weller..... 65.00

Figural bell, brass, witch from "Hansel & Gretel" 145.00

Figural bell, bronze, Dutch girl w/jug, 4½" h. 125.00

Glass bell, Amberina w/applied clear handle 125.00

Glass bell, Bohemian, ruby w/etched Vintage patt. 55.00

Glass bell, Boston & Sandwich Glass Co., h.p. scene of stork standing near cattails in a marsh, w/original clapper, 5½" h. 195.00

Glass bell, opaque white cut to cranberry, applied clear handle w/cranberry tip, overall gold tracery, 3½" d., 7" h. 385.00

Glass bell, cranberry, Diamond Quilted patt., applied cream opaque handle, clear clapper, 6½" d., 10½" h. 200.00

Glass bell, cranberry w/applied clear handle, green glass clapper, 5½" d., 11 7/8" h. 165.00

Hand bell, brass, either side w/embossed bust of a man and a woman in Teutonic armored headgear, ornate studwork around busts, 2 7/8" d., 4" h. 183.00

Hand bell, brass, figural lion's mask handle, 3 1/8" d., 6" h. 44.00

Hand bell, silver, figural cherub handle, London, 1892, 1 1/8" d., 1 7/8" h. 130.00

Hand bell, silver, Louis XV, molded ribs around bow & removable baluster form handle, w/clapper, Pierre Andre Brun, Uzes, mid-18th c., 6" h. 2,200.00

Locomotive bell, bronze, 1883, 15½" d. 1,100.00

Schoolhouse tower bell, bell metal, embossed "John Gallagher, Pittsburgh," w/wrought iron yoke & ringing arm, 15¼" d., 16" h. (no clapper) 200.00

Schoolhouse tower bell, cast iron, w/yoke, ringing arm & clapper, marked "No. 4 Upright, 1886," 18" d. (pitted).................... 85.00

Schoolhouse tower bell, cast iron, No. 5 size, w/wheel 300.00

School Teacher's Hand Bell

School teacher's hand bell, brass w/turned wood handle, 6½" h. (ILLUS.) 42.50
School teacher's hand bell, brass w/turned fruitwood handle, 13" h. 55.00
Shop entrance bell, brass, w/coiled iron spring & wrought iron mounting, "Abe's Patent," 8" d. 35.00
Sleigh bells, 20 graduated brass crotal-type bells on leather strap 300.00
Sleigh bells, 23 graduated brass bells on original leather strap 450.00
Sleigh bells, 32 graduated cast brass crotal-type bells on leather strap 235.00
Table bell, nickel-plated brass, twist-type, dated 1887 .... 40.00

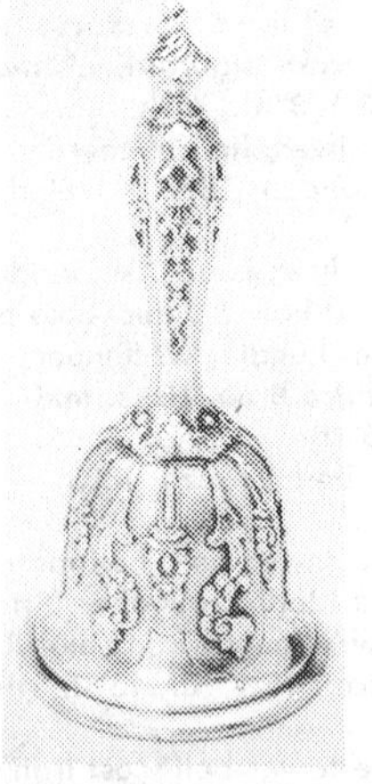

Sterling Silver Table Bell

Table bell, sterling silver, George IV, 2-part w/hexagonal baluster form handle screwed to bow, chased flowers, shells & scrolling foliage, engraved w/contemporary crest, Robert Garrard, London, 1829, 5¼" h. (ILLUS.) 3,575.00
Tap bell, brass dome w/lever to depress, engraved brass base w/beaded trim, last patent date of 1863 on base, 3½" d. 35.00
Tap bell, ornate brass filigree 85.00
Troika bells, two brass bells on metal shaft flanking central orb w/two-headed Imperial eagle finial, Russian, 9" w., 12" h. 285.00

BICYCLES

The early rotary-pedal bicycles of the 19th century were known as "velocipedes" to the French but the English dubbed them "boneshakers" because of their affect on the riders who rode them on the rough unpaved roads of the day. Gradually the front wheels of these early bicycles were enlarged to increase the distance gained by each revolution of the pedal. To offset the weight added to the front wheel, the rear wheel was made smaller and the term "high-wheeler" came into use. All bicycles made before 1900 are desirable but the early high-wheelers are scarce because their popularity was so short-lived for they were difficult to mount, to dismount and quite dangerous to ride.

Bicycle, "Crescent," wood wheel rims & chain guard, 1893 (never used) $1,000.00
Bicycle, "Endurance Flyer," Western Tire Company, 1940 .... 150.00
Bicycle, "Hawthorne," 1947 (good condition) 110.00
Bicycle, "Iroquois" lady's model, wood wheel rims, fender & grips, original pinstriping 375.00
Bicycle, "Remington Arms Co." tandem model, chain-drive steering.. 700.00
Bicycle, "Rouse Hazard Overland," wooden wheel rims & rear fender, original paint, made in Peoria, Illinois, 26" h. (front fender missing) 225.00
Bicycle, "Schwinn" boy's B-6 model, spring shock absorber, tank, ca. 1948, 26" h. 500.00
Tricycle, early adult-size model, "Columbia," two high wheels w/anti-tip pole fastened to rear seat (needs restoration) 985.00

Tricycle, early adult-size model, wooden w/metal rimmed spoked wheels & metal fittings, leatherized seat w/worn fringe, worn original red paint w/black & yellow striping, 52" l., 35" h. (one metal fitting & several bolts replaced) 900.00

BIG LITTLE BOOKS

Buck Rogers Big Little Books

The original "Big Little Books" series of small format was originated in the mid-30's by Whitman Publishing Co., Racine, Wisconsin, and covered a variety of subjects from adventure stories to tales based on comic strip characters and movie and radio stars. The publisher originally assigned each book a serial number. Most prices are now in the $8.00-$20.00 range with scarce ones bringing more.

Ace Drummond, No. 1177, 1935 .... $33.00
Air Fighters of America, "movie flip" page corners, No. 1448, 1941 .... 8.00
Alice in Wonderland, No. 759, 1934 (oversized) 25.00
Apple Mary and Dennie's Lucky Apples, No. 1403, 1939 .... 8.50
Bambi's Children, "movie flip" page corners, No. 1497, 1943 .... 15.00
Blondie, Papa Knows Best, No. 1490, 1945 .... 15.00
Buck Jones and the Rock Creek Cattle War, No. 1461, 1938 .... 33.00
Buck Rogers and the Depth Men of Jupiter, No. 1169, 1935 .... 37.00
Buck Rogers in the City Below the Sea, No. 765, 1934 (ILLUS. left) ... 37.50
Buck Rogers in the War with the Planet Venus, No. 1437, 1938 (ILLUS. center) 40.00
Buck Rogers, 25th Century A.D. vs. the Fiend of Space, No. 1409, 1940 (ILLUS. right) 20.00
Bugs Bunny and His Pals, No. 1496, 1945 .... 15.00
Chester Gump at Silver Creek Ranch, No. 473, 1933 .... 15.00
Chuck Malloy Railroad Detective on the Streamliner, No. 1453, 1938 .. 11.00
Cowboy Lingo, No. 1457, 1938 ...... 18.00
Dan Dunn Secret Operative 48 and the Crime Master, No. 1171, 1937 .... 11.00
Danger Trails in Africa, No. 1151, 1935 .... 10.00
Dick Tracy and the Boris Arson Gang, No. 1163, 1935 .... 25.00
Dick Tracy and the Mad Killer, No. 1435, 1947 .... 15.00
Dick Tracy and the Phantom Ship, No. 1434, 1940 .... 24.00
Dick Tracy and the Racketeer Gang, No. 1112, 1936 .... 45.00
Doctor Doom and the Ghost Submarine, Foreign Spies, No. 1460, 1939 .... 14.00
Flash Gordon and the Witch Queen of Mongo, No. 1190, 1936 .... 40.00
Flash Gordon on the Planet Mongo, No. 1110, 1934 .... 73.00
Gene Autry and Raiders of the Range, No. 1409, 1946 .... 11.00
Gene Autry and the Red Bandit's Ghost, No. 1461, 1949 .... 12.00
Gene Autry Cowboy Detective, No. 1494, 1940 .... 30.00
Guns in the Roaring West, No. 1426, 1937 .... 9.50
Harold Teen Swinging at the Sugar Bowl, No. 1418, 1939 .... 10.00
Houdini's Big Little Book of Magic, No. 715, 1933 .... 22.50
Invisible Scarlet O'Neil Versus the King of the Slums, No. 1406, 1946 .... 8.00
Jane Withers in This Is the Life, No. 1179, 1937 .... 26.50
Jim Craig State Trooper and the Kidnapped Governor, No. 1466, 1938 .... 7.00
Jimmie Allen in the Air Mail Robbery, No. 1143, 1936 .... 11.00
Jim Starr of the Border Patrol, No. 1428, 1937 .... 8.00
John Carter of Mars, No. 1402, 1940 .... 88.00
Junior G-Men, No. 1442, 1937 ...... 20.00
Last Days of Pompeii, No. 1132, 1935 (oversized) 12.00
Laughing Dragon of Oz, No. 1125, 1934 .... 95.00
Li'l Abner Among the Millionaires, No. 1401, 1939 .... 21.00
Little Orphan Annie in the Movies, No. 1416, 1937 .... 25.00
Lone Ranger and His Horse Silver, No. 1181, 1935 .... 15.00

Lone Ranger and the Menace of Murder Valley, No. 1465, 1937 .... 22.50
Lone Ranger and the Secret Killer, No. 1431, 1937 .... 18.00
Mary Lee & The Mystery of the Indian Beads, No. 1438, 1937 .... 10.00
Mickey Mouse, The Detective, No. 1139, 1934 .... 18.00
Mickey Mouse & The Lazy Daisy Mystery, No. 1433, 1947 .... 30.00
Mickey Mouse, The Mail Pilot, No. 731, 1933 .... 25.00
Mickey Mouse Runs His Own Newspaper, No. 1409, 1937 .... 16.00
Pluto the Pup, No. 1467, 1938 .... 35.00
Skippy (Story of), No. 761, 1934 .... 12.00
Snow White & the Seven Dwarfs, No. 1460, 1938 .... 18.00
Tarzan of the Screen, No. 778, 1934 .... 22.00
Terry & the Pirates, No. 1156, 1934 .... 30.00
Tiny Tim (The Adventures of), No. 767, 1935 .... 25.00
Tom Mix and His Circus on the Barbary Coast, No. 1482, 1940 .... 19.95
Tom Mix in the Fighting Cowboy, no number, 1935 .... 30.00
Wash Tubbs & Captain Easy Hunting for Whales, No. 1455, 1943 .... 10.00

RELATED BOOKS

Abbie an' Slats & Becky, Saalfield, Jumbo Books, No. 1182, 1940 .... 10.00
Andy Burnett on Trial (Walt Disney's) Whitman, Big Little Book TV Series, No. 1645, 1958 .... 10.00
Border Eagle (The), Saalfield, Little Big Books, No. 1139, 1938 .... 12.50
Buck Rogers in the City of Floating Globes, Whitman, Big Little Books Cocomalt premium, no number, 1935 .... 75.00
Bugs Bunny and the Giant Brothers, Whitman, New Better Little Books, No. 706-10, 1949 .... 30.00
Danger Trail North, Saalfield, Jumbo Books, No. 1177, 1940 .... 16.50
Dick Tracy Encounters Facey, Whitman, A Big Little Book, No. 2001, 1967 .... 10.00
Gulliver's Travels, Saalfield, Jumbo Books, No. 1172, 1939 .... 7.00
Houdini's Big Little Book of Magic, Whitman, Big Little Books Amoco premium, no number, 1933 (dated 1927) 25.00
Joe Palooka's Great Adventure, Saalfield, Jumbo Books, No. 1168, 1939 .... 16.50
Joyce of the Secret Squadron, A Captain Midnight Adventure, Whitman, Adventure & Mystery Series, No. 2376, 1942 .... 27.00
Little Colonel (The), Saalfield, Little Big Books, No. 1095, 1935 .... 50.00

BOOK ENDS

Alabaster, model of a parrot, green, orange & white, pr. $45.00
Brass, advertising, "Hartford Fire Ins. Co.," stag, dated 1935, pr. ... 35.00
Brass, Art Nouveau, figure of a female w/flowing hair, pr. 75.00
Brass, model of Dachshunds w/five books, 3½ x 4½ x 5", pr. 40.00
Brass-plated, model of an owl, expandable-type, pr. 45.00
Bronze, Art Deco, model of frogs in running position, wearing top hats, green patina, 7½" h., pr. ... 120.00
Bronze, bust of Indian, profile in high relief, pr. 125.00
Bronze, columns & a vignette of a woman reading at a desk, one w/Bradley & Hubbard paper label, 5 x 5 x 2", pr. 50.00
Bronze, figure of a nude girl kneeling on rock, signed "Armor Bronze Co.," pr. 150.00
Bronze, modeled as trumpeting elephant fleeing an alligator emerging from foaming waves, applied ivory tusks, Japanese, 6½" h., pr. 385.00
Bronze-finish pot metal, model of "The Gleaners," pr. 27.00
Cast iron, Amish man & woman on bench, worn original polychrome paint, 4¾" h., pr. 30.00
Cast iron, Art Deco angular design in relief, black, silver & gold repaint, 5½" h., pr. 25.00
Cast iron, model of Airedale dog, painted black, 4¾" h., pr. 40.00
Cast iron, drunken dogs (3) singing, 5", pr. 34.00
Cast iron, 2 Terrier dogs in profile, 1900-20, 2 x 5 x 5½", pr. 45.00
Cast iron, model of "The Thinker," 4" h., pr. 20.00
Cast iron, model of Connestoga wagon, original polychrome paint, marked "Hubley," 6 5/8" h., pr. .. 20.00
Cast iron, model of an open fire w/kettle, original polychrome paint, 5 7/8" h., pr. 12.50
Chalkware, model of well-read books, pr. 295.00
China, figural Colonial lady & gentleman, white decor w/gold trim, marked "Morimura," pr. 35.00

Glass, dimensional triangular shape, cobalt blue, heavy, pr. 55.00
Porcelain, model of Royal Doulton "Little Bridesmaid" (single) 175.00
Pressed glass, figure of horse heads, clear, 3 x 5", 5" h., pr. ... 45.00
Pressed glass, model of lyre, Fostoria, pr. 90.00
Wrought iron, model of Scottie dog, marked "Vernols," pr. 17.00

BOOKMARKS

Advertising Bookmark

Advertising, "Carnation Milk," celluloid $26.50
Advertising, "Columbus Buggy Co.," celluloid 8.00
Advertising, "Cracker Jack," tin, lithographed Scottie 23.00
Advertising, "Cracker Jack," tin, lithographed Terrier 20.00
Advertising, "1st Love Chocolates," celluloid 8.50
Advertising, "W. H. Foote & Co., Clothing, Westfield, Mass.," paper (ILLUS.) 3.00
Advertising, "Pacific Biscuit," celluloid 9.50
Advertising, "Poole Pianos," celluloid 12.50
Celluloid, beehive design, 5" l. 2.50
Celluloid, souvenir, "Pan American Exposition, 1901" 25.00
Leather, cat shape, 1863 .... 13.00
Sterling silver, applied full figure owl, 3" l. 45.00
Sterling silver, Medallion patt., George W. Shiebler & Co., New York 185.00

BOOKS

ANTIQUES RELATED

American Heritage "History of American Antiques," 3 vols., 1968 .... $75.00
Barber, Edwin Atlee, "Artificial Soft Paste Porcelain," 1907, soft cover 30.00
Barret, Richard C., "Bennington Pottery & Porcelain," hardbound, out of print 40.00
Bishop, Robert, "Centuries and Styles of The American Chair, 1640-1970," 1972 .... 30.00
Burgess, Fred W., "Antique Jewelry & Precious Stones," 1937 .... 45.00
Carrick, Alice Van Leer, "A History of American Silhouettes," 1968 ... 30.00
Cox, Warren, "The Book of Pottery & Porcelain," 1946, 2 vols. 60.00
Kauffman, Henry J., "Early American Andirons," 1974 .... 15.00
Kettell, Russell H., "The Pine Furniture of Early New England," 1956 .... 30.00
Lichten, Frances, "Folk Art of Rural Pennsylvania," 1946 .... 110.00
Lockwood, Luke V., "Colonial Furniture in America," Vols. I & II in one volume 35.00
McGregor, Jack, "Early Texas Furniture and Decorative Arts," 1973, paperback 50.00
McKearin, George & Helen, "200 Years of American Blown Glass," 1958, 11¼ x 8½" 38.00
Montgomery, Charles, "American Furniture: The Federal Period In The Henry Francis du Pont Winterthur Museum," 1966 .... 37.50
Nutting, Wallace, "Furniture Treasury," Vol. III, 1933 .... 35.00
Safford, Carleton L. & Bishop, Robert, "America's Quilts and Coverlets," 1974 .... 40.00
Toulouse, Julian Harrison, "Fruit Jars," 1969, 9¼ x 6¼" 25.00

CIVIL WAR RELATED

More books have been written about the Civil War era (1861-65) than any other period in the history of our country. The following listing includes books by and about those directly involved in the fighting, the overall history of the conflict and the years following.

"A History of the Civil War," by Benson J. Lossing, 1912, Brady photographs & Ogden prints, 16 vols. ... 200.00
"The American Soldier & Sailor at War," by Stanley, 1889 .... 150.00
"Civil War in Song & Story," by Frank Moore, 1899, Collier's 50.00

"Confederate Veteran's Association of Kentucky," 1891, constitution & membership w/name, rank, command & other information, Rebel flag in color, hardbound 35.00

"Deeds of Daring by the American Soldier, North and South," by D. M. Kelsey, 1886, over 100 drawings, one color lithograph, 670 pp. (spine loose) 36.00

"General Sherman - His Life and Battles - In Words of One Syllable," 1886, 96 etchings by Forbes, McLoughlin Bros. 75.00

"Grant's Vicksburg Campaign," illustrated by J. Korn 11.00

"The Great Conspiracy, Civil War," by Logan, 1886 .... 12.00

"Harper's Pictorial History of The Great Rebellion," 1866 & 1868, 2 vols. 150.00

"History of the Civil War," by John S. C. Abbott, 1866, 2 vols. 30.00

"Mr. Lincoln's Army," by Bruce Catton, 1951 .... 8.00

"The Photographic History of the Civil War," by F.T. Miller, copyright 1912, 10 vols., 1st edition ... 200.00

"Record of Officers & Men of New Jersey in the Civil War, 1861-1865," published by Authority of the Legislature, William S. Stryker, Adjutant General, Trenton, New Jersey, 2 vols. 175.00

"Reminiscences of the Civil War," by Genl. John B. Gordon, 1903, 474 pp. 29.00

"The Southern Rebellion History," 1862, Vols. 1 & 2 .... 145.00

"Under Both Flags: A Panorama of the Great Civil War," by representatives of each side, 1896, half-leather bound, gilt edges, 591 pp. (spine partially taped) 35.00

PRESIDENTS & HISTORICAL FIGURES

The following listing includes a wide cross-section of books by and about former Presidents of the United States and other persons of note.

"Abraham Lincoln - The Prairie Years," by Carl Sandburg, 1926 ... 10.00

"Eleanor Roosevelt Story," by Eaton, 1956, w/dust jacket 3.75

"Girlhood of Queen Victoria," 1912, 2 vols. 20.00

"Italy Under Mussolini," New York, 1926 .... 8.50

"Last of the Great Scouts - Buffalo Bill Cody," by his sister, Helen Cody, 1899 .... 35.00

"Life of Adolph Hitler," 1932, in German, with 200 photographs 475.00

"Life of Hon. Phineas T. Barnum," by Joe Benton, 1891, 621 pp. 20.00

"Mussolini: My Diary," 1925, illustrated, w/dust jacket 10.00

"Pioneer Life In the West, Autobiography of Rev. James B. Finley," 1853 .... 22.50

"The Romance of Leonardo da Vinci," by Bernard G. Gerney, 1928 .. 25.00

"Story of T.R. (Teddy)," biography of Theodore Roosevelt, by Bill Sewall, 1919, New York, illustrated 12.50

"Struggles & Triumphs," P.T. Barnum autobiography, 1871 .... 35.00

"The Thrilling Lives of Buffalo Bill & Pawnee Bill," 1911, 3rd edition ... 20.00

"Trial of Mrs. Abraham Lincoln," by Homer Croy, 1st edition, w/dust jacket 12.50

"The Winning of the West," by Theodore Roosevelt, 1900, Vol. 1 .... 2.75

"Yarns & Stories by Abraham Lincoln," by Alex K. McClure, 1901 .. 35.00

STATE & LOCAL HISTORIES

CALIFORNIA

"Historical Souvenir of San Francisco, California," 1888, by Heiniger 95.00

"La Reina, Photo History of Los Angeles," 1929 .... 10.00

"U.S. Coast Survey, 1852," 1853, 36 maps plus large map of the City of San Francisco 125.00

CONNECTICUT

"History of Fairfield County, Connecticut," 1881, biographical sketches of prominent citizens by D. Hurd, 878 pp. 60.00

"Memorial History Hartford County, Connecticut, Town Histories, 1633-1884," 1886, by Trumball, 570 pp. 30.00

MASSACHUSETTS

"Atlas of Berkshire, Massachusetts," 1875, maps & pictures 95.00

"History and Traditions of Marblehead," 1897, by Roads 60.00

"History of the Great Fire in Boston," 1873, by Col. R.H. Conwell, illustrated, 312 pp. 65.00

MINNESOTA

"Historical Norwegian People in America," 1925, illustrated, 602 pp. 15.00

"History of the Swedish Americans of Minnesota," 1910, by Strand, 3 vol. 350.00

MISSOURI

"Centennial History of Missouri," 1921, Clarke Publishing Co., Chicago, deluxe edition, 4 vol. ... 100.00

"The State of Missouri," 1904, Walter Williams editor, illustrated, 572 pp. ... 35.00

NEW YORK

"Atlas of Rochester, New York," 1888 ... 90.00

"History of Westchester County," 1925, 4 vol. ... 85.00

"New York City Manual," 1868 ... 115.00

PENNSYLVANIA

"History of Mercer County," 1888, biographical references & sketches of early residents, illustrated, 9 x 7", 1,210 pp. (rebound) ... 115.00

"Pennsylvania: A History," 1926, by George Dunbar, 5 vol. ... 150.00

"Philadelphia Blue Book," 1906, prominent householders, clubs, shopping guide & theater, diagrams, 1,026 pp. ... 50.00

VERMONT

"Atlas of Washington County, Vermont," 1873, F.W. Beers & Co. ... 200.00

"History of Newbury," 1902 ... 50.00

BOTTLE OPENERS

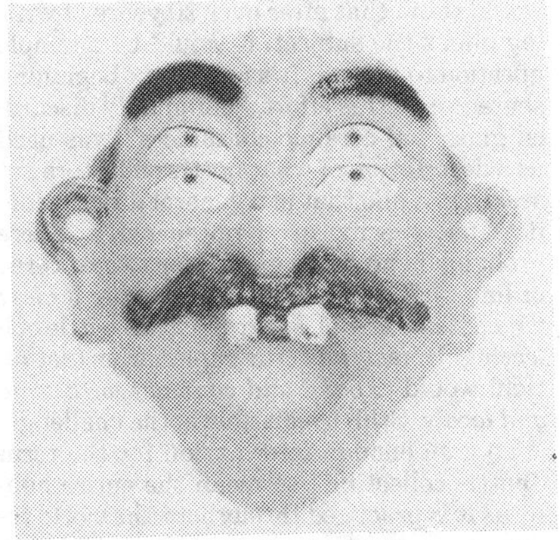

Four-Eyed Man Bottle Opener

Corkscrews were actually the first bottle openers and these may date back to the mid-18th century, but bottle openers, as we know them today, are strictly a 20th century item and came into use only after Michael J. Owens invented the automatic bottle machine in 1903. Avid collectors have spurred this relatively new area of collector interest that requires only a modest investment. Our listing, by type of metal, encompasses the four basic types sought by collectors: advertising openers; full figure openers which stand alone or hang on the wall; flat figural openers such as the lady's leg shape; and openers with embossed, engraved or chased handles.

Advertising, "Calvert Gin," bottle-shaped ... $6.00

Advertising, "Duquesne Brewing Co., Pittsburgh, Pennsylvania," metal ... 5.00

Advertising, "Jack Sprat," metal, spear end, 1926 ... 10.00

Advertising, "Jack Tar Hotel," w/corkscrew ... 25.00

Advertising, "Pabst Blue Ribbon Beer," tin, bottle-shaped ... 12.00

Advertising, "White Rock Water & Ginger Ale" ... 9.00

Aluminum, full figure DoDo bird ... 10.00

Aluminum, full figure squirrel ... 10.00

Brass, full figure pelican ... 40.00

Cast iron, bust of cock pheasant, 4" h. ... 35.00

Cast iron, full figure alligator, original paint, 6 1/8" l. (minor rust) ... 50.00

Cast iron, full figure black boy w/alligator biting boy's seat ... 125.00

Cast iron, full figure bulldog standing ... 60.00

Cast iron, full figure clown, 1936 ... 41.00

Cast iron, full figure donkey w/wide ears ... 42.00

Cast iron, full figure drunk in straw hat at sign post, original paint, 3 7/8" h. ... 50.00

Cast iron, full figure elephant in seated position, original polychrome paint, marked "John Wright Inc.," 3" h. ... 50.00

Cast iron, full figure lobster, original red paint, marked "Maine," 3½" l. ... 35.00

Cast iron, full figure parrot on perch, red, yellow & blue paint, 5½" h. ... 20.00

Cast iron, full figure seahorse, original polychrome paint, marked "John Wright Inc.," 4¼" h. ... 85.00

Cast iron, full figure turtle, worn black paint, marked "Golding, Franklin, Mass.," 3" l. ... 30.00

Cast iron, model of automobile jack ... 15.00

Cast iron, wall-type, four-eyed bald-headed man w/mustache, original paint, Wilton Products, 3½ x 3¼" (ILLUS.) ... 40.00

Stag's horn handle w/sterling silver ferrule, marked "Pat. 1908" ... 32.00

Sterling silver, Bloch patt., Jensen ... 65.00

Sterling silver, Repousse patt., Kirk ... 35.00

Bottle Collecting

by Cecil Munsey

Former President Jimmy Carter does it; television star Bill Cosby does it; people from all walks of life do it; in fact, several hundred thousand individuals from most major countries in the world do it. What is *"it"* that all of these people are doing? They are collecting commonly discarded glass and ceramic containers — they are participating in a hobby generically called...

bottle collecting.

While collecting bottles is indeed a worldwide activity, the majority of collectors are in the United States. For the last two decades of the 1800's and the entire twentieth century thus far, people have gathered both unusual and common bottles and displayed them as collections. Early bottle collectors were considered a bit eccentric, peculiar, or at least quaint. All of that changed in the mid-twentieth century — in 1959 to be exact.

It was in that year when less than two dozen treasure hunters in Sacramento, California made their common interest of digging for old bottles in the urban renewal area an official activity by forming the first bottle collectors' club. In just three years the original 17 members of the *Antique Bottle Collectors Association of California* became 217 members. Since membership was by then national, the "of California" was dropped.

By 1969, just a decade after the hobby's beginning, thousands of collectors of old bottles belonged to over 100 clubs internationally. The hobby had several national/international periodicals furthering the blossoming hobby. There were over 100 club newsletters being shared across the land and a more permanent literature of almost 100 books. The big event of 1969, however, was the formation of the *Federation of Historical Bottle Clubs* (FOHBC). This organization replaced the loosely knit *Antique Bottle Collectors Association* and more firmly established bottle collecting by sponsoring national conventions, educational programs, and an official publication.

A short ten years later, in 1979, bottle collecting found a permanent home. The *National Bottle Museum* was established in Ballston Spa, New York, a few miles from the famous playground of the rich — Saratoga Springs. A 90-year-old Victorian-Gothic mansion was donated to the FOHBC to be its national headquarters and museum. Each year, during the last week in May, bottle collectors gather at the hobby's "Mecca" for the annual re-opening of their museum and an accompanying celebration which includes an important bottle auction and one of the largest shows/sales of the year. The show/sale is held in nearby Saratoga Springs.

That's the short version of bottle collecting's story from a historic and organizational aspect. But what about the reason behind the hobby — the bottles themselves? One would think that after over 20 years of writing about the subject, it would be a simple question to answer. It's not. In the beginning sentences of this effort, "commonly discarded glass and ceramic containers" was used as a description of what bottle collectors are seeking. While that is a general description, it is not specific or comprehensive. There probably is no concise word (or two or three or four...) that does the job of making it clear which items are an integral part of bottle collecting. In fact, any true explanation (definition) would *expand and contract with time and locale.* Still, irresistible is the challenge.

To gain enough information for the term "bottle collecting" to mean the entire hobby as it is practiced throughout the world today, two questions should be asked and answered. One is, *why* are certain bottles valued and collected? The other is, *which* bottles are valued and collected? To add confusion, in some instances it's a combination of answers to both questions which provides the reason or motivation behind the desire to collect some bottles and not others.

WHY ARE BOTTLES COLLECTED?

- SCARCITY — As with many of the collecting hobbies, scarcity is a big factor in determining a bottle's desirability. Limited numbers of a type of common-use container greatly enhance value.

• AGE — Some of the oldest still obtainable bottles range in age from 200 - 400 years. For the most part, the older a bottle the more it is desired.

• MANUFACTURE — How a bottle was constructed is of importance. That is so because it may, for example, indicate age, geographical origin, or a renowned manufacturer. Glass bottles could be free-blown, mold-blown, or machine-blown — and each technique has a direct affect on a bottle's value and collectibility.

• GLASS or CERAMIC — This factor is a bit tricky to deal with because common-use glass and ceramic bottles were almost always made of inexpensive ingredients, *but* in some bottles a more expensive glass or clay was used. Generally, the more expensive glass or stoneware would indicate the higher value, but most often it's more than that one factor which determines collectibility.

• GLASS COLOR — The color of a bottle can radically affect value. An uncommon color would relate to scarcity and increase value. For example, purple induced by exposure to ultra-violet sun rays would boost value. An expensive color such as "ruby red," created by the addition of gold oxide to the original glass mixture, would enhance value. "Puce" (French for "color of the flea"), another rare color, also greatly increases value.

• GLASS CONDITION — Glass deteriorates when exposed to the elements, to harsh use, and to misuse. If a bottle is in a deteriorated condition, its value is lessened proportionally to the deterioration *except* in rare cases where a desired effect is achieved by the disability. Badly worn and/or damaged bottles are predictably worth less than those which are perfect.

• EMBOSSMENTS — Raised lettering and designs (embossments) have more lasting durability than accompanying paper labels so, as such, embossments have come to be one of the desirable traits bottles can have. Coupled with the other factors being discussed, they can be a great asset to value.

• LABELS — Paper labels do not greatly enhance bottle value as a general rule. (In some unusual cases they do.) This has been changing in recent times. *Applied Color Labeling* (ACL) was developed around 1920. Some collectors refer to it as "painted labeling" because it looks like painting on a bottle. ACL is rapidly becoming more interesting to bottle collectors as the hobby necessarily moves toward collecting bottles of the mid-1900's. ACL, therefore, is an indicator of value.

• SIZE — Size of bottles can determine collectibility. Unusual sizes, large or small, are generally of great interest, thus of more value.

• SHAPE — Bottle shape is a prime factor in bottle value. While geometric shapes are interesting, collectors find it hard to resist figurally-shaped bottles, many of which have high values.

• COMPOSITION — The materials from which bottles are made are value indicators. Glass is generally of more value than ceramic, and plastic is of almost no value now. Plastic probably will be of more value in the future as such bottles become historically significant and/or technologically obsolete.

• DECORATION — While decoration on common-use bottles is not consistent, it is on other types of containers. Depending on decoration and other factors the following decorating methods are indicators of value: *cutting, overlaying, engraving, etching, gilding, flashing, staining, enameling,* and the already mentioned *ACL.*

WHICH BOTTLES ARE COLLECTED?

The foregoing factors offer a partial answer to *why* certain bottles are collected. Now to deal with *which* bottles are collected. Basically a list will suffice but before listing the major bottle categories several things should be noted. CONTENTS are important — not what a bottle contains now but what it was made to contain originally. USE is another important consideration. This leads to a distinction between common bottles and bottles made artistically with expensive raw materials for repeated use*. These can be seen in the following listing of bottle collecting categories which provide a means by which collectors "choose up sides:"

-- Historical Flasks
-- Mineral Water Bottles
-- Pictorial Flasks
-- Wine Bottles
-- Perfume Bottles
-- Snuff Bottles *
-- Case Bottles
-- Figural Bottles
-- Soda Pop Bottles
-- Beer Bottles
-- Ink Bottles
-- Whiskey Bottles
-- Ceramic Bottles
-- Fruit Jars
-- Food Bottles
-- Patent Medicine Bottles
-- Poison Bottles
-- Decanters *

- -- Back Bar Bottles *
- -- Barber Bottles *
- -- Bitters Bottles
- -- Drugstore Bottles
- -- Nursing Bottles
- -- Milk Bottles

DETERMINING BOTTLE VALUES

As stated originally, bottle value is determined by a number of factors including bottle type. It is important to remember that *seldom does one factor or type exclusively determine a bottle's desirability. Most often it is a combination of two or more characteristics which make certain bottles of greater interest than others.* To make this specifically evident, the bottles pictured with this special feature are identified by all applicable factors, type, and which factor or type is most important to the value. Then a monetary value is judged.

Primary "value factor" = SCARCITY

Type: Canada Dry soda pop bottle produced in very limited quantity for the "Honorable Lyndon B. Johnson, Vice President of the United States." **Date:** ca. 1962; **height:** 8"; **value factors:** scarcity and labeling; **current value:** $75.

Type: Coca-Cola soda pop bottle made of amber glass. **Date:** ca. 1943; **height:** 7¾"; **value factors:** scarcity (only three known to exist) and color; **current value:** $375.

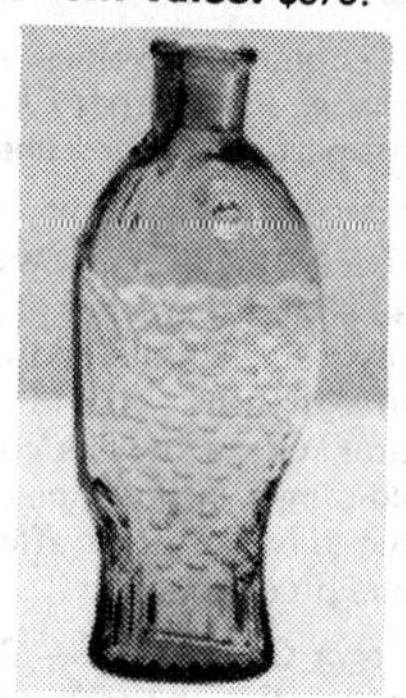

Type: Eli Lilly cod liver oil bottle. **Date:** ca. 1925; **height:** 3"; **value factors:** scarcity (only five known to exist), size (miniature salesman's sample) and shape; **current value:** $375.

Primary "value factor" = AGE

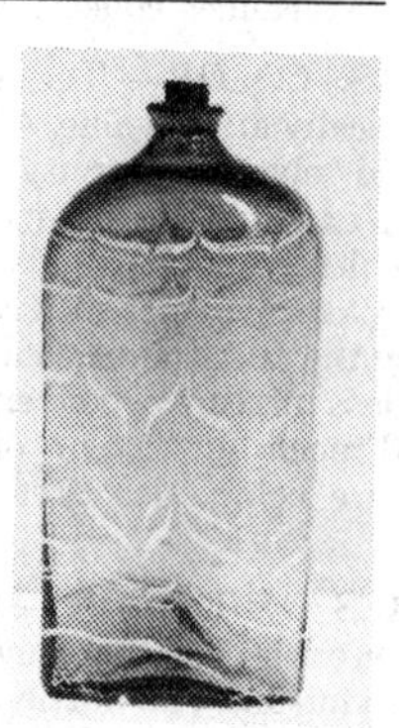

Type: Drug bottle possibly made in America by Henry William "Baron" Stiegel. **Date:** ca. 1770-1775; **height:** 7 3/8"; **value factors:** age, manufacture (free-blown and paddle developed), decoration (white enameling) and color (amber); **current value:** $480.

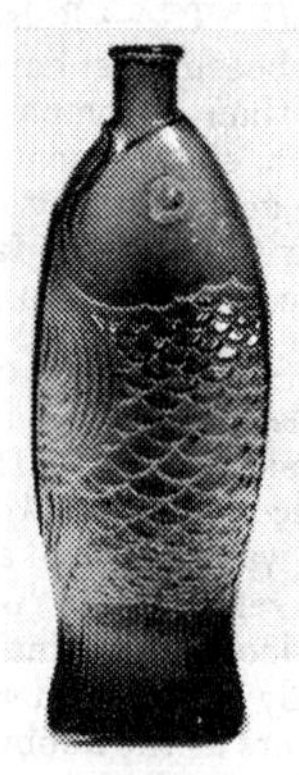

Type: Bitters bottle (patent medicine). **Date:** ca. 1865; **height:** 11½"; **value factors:** age, scarcity, shape and glass condition; **current value:** $260.

Primary "value factor" = MANUFACTURE

Type: Amber Midwestern flask in twisted-swirl design. **Date:** ca. 1830-1850; **height:** 6 5/8"; **value factors:** manufacture (free-blown from dip mold), age and color; **current value:** $250.

Type: Historical flask. **Date:** ca. 1850; **height:** 7¾"; **value factors:** manufacture, geographical origin (Willington Glass Co., West Willington, Connecticut), embossment (American eagle), color (emerald green) and age; **current value:** $210.

Primary "value factor" = GLASS or CERAMIC

Type: Tan and brown pottery beer or ale bottle. **Date:** ca. 1840-1860; **height:** 8¾"; **value factors:** ceramic, age and condition; **current value:** $65. (Next column top left)

Type: Pocket flask. **Date:** ca. 1870-1890; **height:** 7¼"; **value factors:** glass (ribbed design), color (medium to dark amber), age and condition; **current value:** $75. (Next column top right)

Primary "value factor" = COLOR

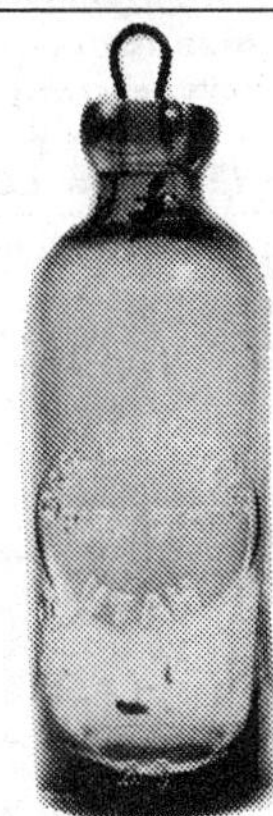

Type: Hutchinson-stoppered "Dan McPolin" soda pop bottle. **Date:** ca. 1890; **height:** 7"; **value factors:** color (medium to dark sun-colored purple), condition, age and embossment; **current value:** $85.

Type: Figural bitters bottle (barrel shape). **Date:** ca. 1870; **height:** 9½"; **value factors:** color (puce), shape, age and condition; **current value:** $325.

Type: Beer bottle ("No Deposit No Return") made to contain Schlitz Beer. **Date:** 1949; **height:** 8 1/8"; **value factors:** color (copper ruby red) and scarcity; **current value:** $400.

Primary "value factor" = CONDITION

Type: Historical flask (Union hands clasped). **Date:** ca. 1860-1880; **height:** 6¼"; **value factors:** condition (clear), age and manufacture (historical flask); **current value:** $90.

Type: Historical flask (Union hands clasped). **Date:** ca. 1860-1880; **height:** 6½"; **value factors:** condition (cloudy), age and manufacture (historical flask); **current value:** $35.

Primary "value factor" = EMBOSSMENT

Type: Mineral water bottle ("Priest Natural Mineral Water"). **Date:** ca. 1875-1895; **height:** 7"; **value factors:** embossment (man wearing a stocking cap and scarf), color (lime green), condition and age; **current value:** $110.

Type: Amber pocket whiskey or wine flask with ground-off neck and screw cap. **Date:** ca. 1890; **height:** 7½"; **value factors:** manufacture, age, condition and color; **current value:** $10.

Type: Amber pocket wine flask with ground-off neck and screw cap. **Date:** ca. 1890; **height:** 6"; **value factors:** embossment (grapes on hanging vine), manufacture, age, condition and color; **current value:** $60.

Primary "value factor" = LABELS

Type: Soda pop bottle. **Date:** ca. 1915; **height:** 8¼"; **value factors:** paper label (Orange Crush), scarcity and condition (near perfect); **current value:** $40.

Type: Soda pop bottle. **Date:** 1934; **height:** 7¾"; **value factors:** paper label (7-UP), scarcity and condition (near perfect); **current value:** $50.

Type: Soda pop bottle. **Date:** 1935; **value factors:** Applied Color Label (7-UP), scarcity, color (amber), shape and condition (no scratches); **current value:** $80. (Top next column)

Primary "value factor" = SIZE

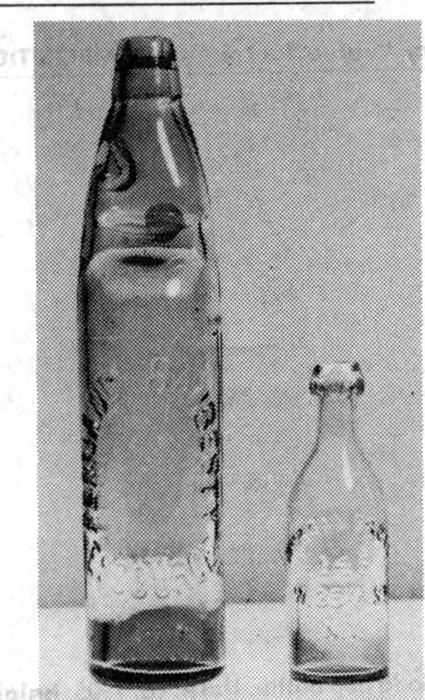

Type: Soda water bottle. **Date:** ca. 1875; **height:** 12"; **value factors:** size (unusually tall), scarcity, manufacture (Codd Marble-stoppered), embossment, condition and age; **current value:** $45. (Left)

Type: Soda water bottle. **Date:** ca. 1850-1870; **height:** 6"; **value factors:** size (unusually short), scarcity, embossment, condition and age; **current value:** $125. (Right)

Primary "value factor" = SHAPE

Type: Bitters bottle. **Date:** 1867; **height:** 12¼"; **value factors:** shape ("Indian Queen"), age and condition; **current value:** $250. (Next page top left)

Type: Mineral water bottle. **Date:** ca. 1900; **height:** 11¾" (with stopper); **value factors:** shape (Moses), age and condition; **current value:** $150. (Next page top right)

Primary "value factor" = COMPOSITION

Type: Soda pop bottle. **Date:** ca. 1905; **height:** 9¾"; **value factors:** composition, paper label (Cliquot Club), scarcity, age and condition; **current value:** $40.

Type: Ginger beer bottle. **Date:** ca. 1910-1920; **height:** 7"; **value factor:** composition (ceramic); **current value:** $5.

Primary "value factor" = DECORATION

Type: Back Bar bottle. **Date:** ca. 1890; **height:** 11½"; **value factors:** decoration (enameling), age and condition; **current value:** $60.

Type: Wine decanter. **Date:** ca. 1915; **height:** 8¾"; **value factors:** decoration (etching), scarcity, age and condition; **current value:** $100.

(End of Special Focus)

BOTTLES & FLASKS

BARBER *(See Barberiana)*

BITTERS

Amazon Bitters, Peter McQuade, New York, square, amber, 9" h. . . $75.00

American Celebrated Stomach Bitters, square, amber, 9½" h. . . . . 135.00 to 175.00

Atwood's Quinine Tonic Bitters, rectangular, aqua, 8 7/16" h. 80.00

Baker's Orange Grove Bitters, square w/roped corners, orange-amber, 9½" h. 145.00

Baker's (E.) Premium Bitters, Richmond, Va., oval, aqua, 6¾" h. . . . 85.00

Ball's (Dr.) Vegetable Stomachic Bitters, Northboro, Mass., rectangular, aqua, 6 7/8" h. 145.00
Beck's Herb Bitters, York, Pa., square, amber, 9½" h. (light haze) 150.00
Bennett's Celebrated Stomach Bitters, Jos. N. Souther & Co. Sole Proprietors, San Francisco, square, amber, 9" h. (light stain) 155.00
Blakes (Dr.) Aromatic Bitters, New York, rectangular, pontil, aqua, 7" h. 145.00
Blue Mountain Bitters, rectangular, aqua, 7 7/8" h. 55.00
Bourbon Whiskey Bitters, barrel-shaped, amber, 9¼" h. 275.00
Boyer's Stomach Bitters, Cincinnati, round, clear, 11" h. 65.00
Brady's Family Bitters, square, amber, 10" h. 110.00
Brophy's Bitters motif encased in crescent, 5-pointed star within crescent, Trade Mark, Nokomis, Illinois, square, aqua, 7½" h. ....150.00 to 185.00

Bitters Bottles

Brown's Celebrated Indian Herb Bitters, Patented 1867, figural Indian Queen, amber, 12¼" h. (ILLUS. right) 250.00
Bryant's Stomach Bitters, 8-sided lady's leg shape, green, pontil, 12 5/8" h. 2,000.00
Bull's (Dr.) Superior Stomach Bitters, W.H. Bull & Co., St. Louis, square, amber, 9" h. 110.00
Bull (The) Wild Cherry Bitters (label), rectangular, clear, 8½" h. .. 120.00
California Herb Bitters, Pittsburgh, Pa., G.W. Frazier, square, amber, 9½" h. 100.00
Capitol (J.F.L.) Bitters, pineapple-shaped, pontil, deep amber 375.00
Carey's (Dr.) Original Mandrake Bitters, Elmira, N.Y., 12-sided, aqua, 6½" h. 50.00
Carter's Liver Bitters, C.M. Co., New York, WT & Co., oval, amber, 8½" h. 125.00
Chandler's (Dr.) Jamaica Ginger Root Bitters, Chas. Nichols, Jr. & Co. Props., Lowell, Mass., oval barrel shape, amber, 10" h. 1,700.00
Dandelion (XXX) Bitters, rectangular strap flask, clear, 7¼" h. . .45.00 to 60.00
Demuth's Stomach Bitters, Philada, square, amber, 9 3/8" h. ....135.00 to 150.00
Drakes Plantation Bitters, square w/five embossed logs above label panels, honey amber, 10" h. 165.00
Drakes Plantation Bitters, square w/six embossed logs above label panels, amber, 10" h. (ILLUS. left) 145.00
Drakes Plantation Bitters, square w/six embossed logs above label panels, green, 10" h. 490.00
Eagle Angostura Bark Bitters, globe-shaped, amber, 4" h. 65.00
"Electric" Brand Bitters, H.E. Bucklen & Co., Chicago, Ill., square, amber, 10" h. ....30.00 to 45.00
Flint's (Dr.) Quaker Bitters, Providence, R.I., rectangular, aqua, 9½" h. 25.00
German Balsam Bitters, W.M. Watson & Co. Sole Agents for U.S., square, milk white, 9" h. 550.00
German Hop Bitters, Dr. C.D. Warner, Reading, Mich, square, amber, 10" h. ....60.00 to 75.00
Globe (The) Tonic Bitters, square, amber, 9 5/8" h. 78.00
Golden Bitters, Geo. C. Hubbel & Co., rectangular w/roofed shoulders, aqua, 10 3/8" h. ...150.00 to 200.00
Great Western Tonic Bitters, Patented Jany 21, 1868, O.P. Bissel & Co., Peoria, Ill., square, amber, 9¼" h. 225.00
Greeley's Bourbon Bitters, barrel-shaped w/ten hoops above & below center band, amber, 9 3/8" h. 265.00
Hardy (Dr. Manly) Genuine Jaundice Bitters, Bangor, Me., rectangular, aqua, 6¼" h. ....125.00 to 150.00
Herb (H.P.) Wild Cherry Bitters, Reading, Pa., square w/cherry tree motif & roped corners, light golden amber, 10" h. 225.00
Hi-Hi Bitters, Hi-Hi Bitters Co., Rock Island, Ill., triangular, amber, 9 3/8" h. ....210.00 to 250.00
Hops & Malt, T (sheaf of wheat motif) M, Bitters, square, amber, 3 5/8" h. 310.00

Hostetter's (Dr. J.) Stomach Bitters, square, citron, 9½" h. 45.00
Hutchings Dyspepsia Bitters, New York, rectangular, pontil, aqua, 8½" h. 150.00
Isham's Stomach Bitters, square, amber, 9 3/8" h. ....150.00 to 175.00
Jewett's (Dr. Stephen) Celebrated Health Restoring Bitters, Rindge, N.H., rectangular, pontil, green, 7½" h. 175.00
Kaiser Wilhelm Bitters Co., San- dusky, Ohio, round, amber, 10 1/8" h. ....95.00 to 125.00
Kauffman's (Dr.) Sulphur Bitters (label), oval, aqua, 8½" h. 30.00
King Solomon's Bitters, Seattle, Wash., rectangular, amber, 8 3/8"h ....85.00 to 100.00
Lawrence's (Dr.) Wild Cherry Family Bitters, square, amber, 5½" h. ... 200.00
Leak's Kidney and Liver Bitters, The Best Blood Purifier and Cathartic, square, amber, 9¾" h. 100.00
Lediard's Morning Call Stomach Bit-ters, square, emerald green, 9½" h. 600.00
Loew's (Dr.) Celebrated Stomach Bit-ters & Nerve Tonic, The Loew & Sons Co., Cleveland, O., square, green, 9¼" h. 150.00
Lovegood's XX (Dr.) Family Bitters, square cabin shape, amber, 10½" h. 1,250.00
Lutz's German Stomach Bitters (label), embossed D. Lutz, Reading, Pa., rectangular, amber, 7¾" h... 85.00
Lyford's (Dr.) Bitters, C.P. Herrick, Tilton, N.H., oval, aqua, 8½" h... 125.00
McKeever's Army Bitters, drum-shaped, shoulders covered w/cannonballs, amber, ¾ qt. 1,725.00
Moulton's Olorso Bitters, embossed pineapple & vertical ribs, aqua ... 205.00
New York Hop Bitters Company, embossed flag, aqua 187.50
Nibol Kidney and Liver Bitters, The Best Tonic Laxative & Blood Purifier, square, amber, 9½" h. 42.50
O'Leary's 20th Century Bitters, square, amber, 8½" h. 170.00
Owen's (Dr.) European Life Bitters, Detroit, aqua, 7" h. .....175.00 to 200.00
Panknin's Hepatic Bitters, New York, dark amber, 8 5/8" h. 210.00
Pepsin Bitters, R.W. Davis Drug Co., Chicago, U.S.A., rectangular, apple green, 8 1/8" h. 92.00
Peychaud's American Aromatic Bit-ter Cordial, L.E. Jung Sole Proprietor, New Orleans, round, amber, 6" h. ....40.00 to 50.00
Pineapple Bitters, W & C NY, green, 8 7/8" h. (ILLUS.) 1,000.00

Pineapple Bitters Bottle

Planett's (Dr.) Bitters, square, aqua, 9¾" h. 600.00
Polo Club Trade F & M (monogram) Mark Stomach Bitters, square, amber, 9 1/8" h. 180.00
Prune Stomach and Liver Bitters, The Best Cathartic and Blood Purifier, square, amber, 9¼" h. ....65.00 to 75.00
Quinine Tonic Bitters Manf. By Q.T.B. Chemical Co., Lexington, Ky., U.S.A., rectangular, clear, 8" h. 40.00
Rainbow Tonic Bitters, rectangular, cobalt blue, w/label, 8 7/8" h. ... 20.00
Red Jacket Bitters, Bennett Pieters & Co., square, amber, 9½" h. 85.00
Red Jacket Bitters, Monheimer & Co., square, amber, 9½" h. 55.00
Red Jacket Bitters, Schwab. Mc.Quaid & Co., square, amber, 9¾" h. 115.00
Rocky Mountain Tonic Bitters, 1840 Try Me 1870, square, amber, 9 7/8" h. ....150.00 to 175.00
Rohrer's Wild Cherry Bitters, Lan-caster, Pa., square, amber, 10½" h. (some haze) 140.00
Rose's (E.J.) Magador Bitters For Stomach, Kidney & Liver, square, amber, 8 5/8" h. 68.00
Rothery's Bitters, The Great English Tonic, Chicago, U.S.A., rectangular, amber, 8" h. (lip nick) 145.00
Royce's Sherry Wine Bitters, rectangular, smooth base, aqua ....100.00 to 125.00
Russ' St. Domingo Bitters, New York, square, amber, 9 7/8" h. ... 75.00
Saint Jacob's Bitters, square, dark blackish amber, 8¾" h. 75.00
Salmon's Perfect Stomach Bitters, square, amber, 9½" h. 125.00
Samson's (Dr. J.) Strengthening Bit-ters, square, amber, 9" h. 200.00

Sarasina Stomach Bitters, square, amber, 9 1/8" h. . . . . .85.00 to 100.00

Smiths (Dr. A.H.) Old Style Bitters, square, amber, 8¾" h. 50.00

Smyrna Stomach Bitters, Prolongs Life, Dayton, Ohio, short lady's leg, amber, 9" h. . . . . . . .175.00 to 200.00

Solomon's Strengthening & Invigorating Bitters, Savannah, Georgia, square, cobalt blue, 9 5/8" h. (dug) 425.00

Stanley's (Dr.) South American Indian Bitters, square, smooth base, yellow amber, 9" h. 130.00

Star Kidney and Liver Bitters, square, amber, 8 7/8" h. 50.00

Stewart's (Dr.) Tonic Bitters, Columbus, O., rectangular, amber, 7¾" h. 115.00

Stockton's Port Wine (monogram motif) SW Trade Mark Bitters, rectangular, amber, 9 1/8" h. 75.00

Stoever's (Dr.) Bitters Established 1837, Kryder & Co., Philadelphia, square, yellow-amber, 9½" h. 105.00

Suffolk Bitters, Philbrook & Tucker, Boston, model of a pig, amber, 10 1/8" l. . . . . .385.00 to 410.00

Sun Kidney and Liver Bitters, Vegetable Laxative, Bowel Regulator and Blood Purifier, square, amber, 9½" h. 110.00

Theilmann's (H.) Bitters, rectangular, aqua, 6¾" h. (small lip chip) 65.00

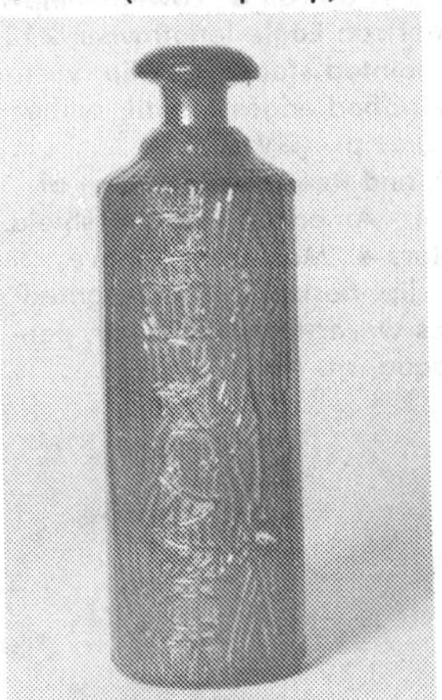

Tippecanoe Bitters Bottle

Tippecanoe (birch bark & canoe motif), H.H. Warner & Co., round, amber, 9" h. (ILLUS.) 97.00

Tip Top, H R & Co Bitters, round, yellow-green, 8½" h. (dug) 150.00

Tonic Bitters, J.T. Higby, Milford, Ct., square, amber, 9½" h. 95.00

Wahoo & Calisaya Bitters, Jacob Pinkerton, square, amber, 9 5/8" h. 175.00

Wakefield's Strengthening Bitters, rectangular w/beveled corners, aqua, 8" h. 42.50

Warren's (Old Dr.) Quaker Bitters, Flint & Co., rectangular, aqua, 9¾" h. . . . . .45.00 to 55.00

Webb's Improved Stomach Bitters, C.W. Webb & Bro., Jackson, Mich., square, amber, 9" h. . . . . .150.00 to 170.00

West India Stomach Bitters, St. Louis, Mo., square, amber, 8½" h. . . . . .35.00 to 50.00

Wheeler's (Dr.) Sherry Wine Bitters, oval, aqua, 7¾" h. 88.00

White's Stomach Bitters, square, amber, 9½" h. 75.00

Whitwell's Temperance Bitters, Boston, rectangular, aqua, pontil, 7¾" h. .75.00 to 90.00

Wild Cherry Bitters, C.C. Richards & Co., Yarmouth, N.S., rectangular, aqua, 6¼" h. . . . . .85.00 to 100.00

Willard's Golden Seal Bitters, oval, aqua, 7¾" h. 95.00

Woodcock Pepsin Bitters, Schroeder's Med. Co., rectangular, amber, 8" h. 120.00

Youngs (Dr.) Wild Cherry Bitters, Brooklyn, N.Y., rectangular, amber, 8½" h. (light stain) 75.00

FLASKS

(Numbers used below refer to those used in the McKearin's "American Glass.")

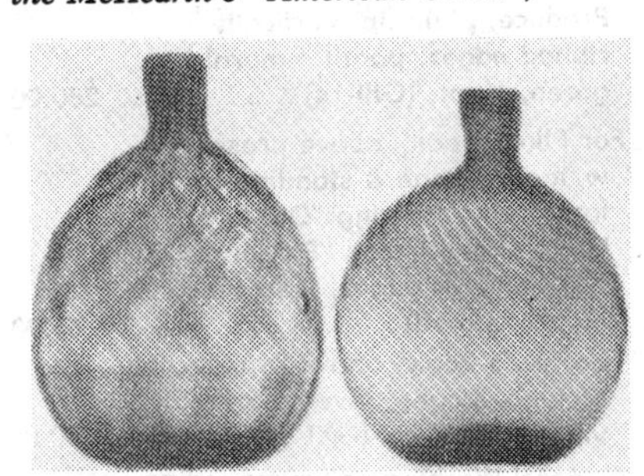

Chestnut Flasks

All-Seeing Eye of God w/lashes on upper lid on 6-pointed star (Star of David) w/"AD" below - 6-pointed star enclosing arm bent at elbow, forearm raised vertically, compass in hand, unidentified emblem on bottom point of star w/"GRJA" below, plain lip, heavy vertical medial rib, deep forest green, pt. (GIV-43) 75.00

American Eagle - American flag w/twenty stars, furled & "For Our Country," plain lip, vertically ribbed edges, pontil, aqua, pt. (GII-54) 55.00

American Eagle - Lyre, plain lip, horizontally corrugated edges w/vertical medial rib, pontil, aqua, pt. (GII-22) 220.00

American Eagle above oval & "Pittsburgh" - American Eagle on plain oval, narrow vertical rib, deep olive yellow, pt. (GII-106) 120.00

Anchor & fork-ended pennants w/"Baltimore" on one & "Glass Works" on other - Phoenix rising from flames & "RESURGAM" in rectangular panel below, round collar, smooth edges, aqua, pt. (GXIII-54) 60.00

"Baltimore" above Monument - "Liberty & Union," plain lip, smooth edges, pontil, olive green, pt. (GVI-3) 625.00

"Baltimore" below Monument - "Corn For The World" above ear of corn, plain lip, smooth edges, pontil, clear green, ½ pt. (GVI-7) 750.00

Chestnut, 24 swirled ribs, golden amber, Zanesville, Ohio, 4¾" h. (ILLUS. right) 375.00

Chestnut, 10 diamond, yellow-amber, Zanesville, Ohio, 5 3/8" h. (ILLUS. left) .1,550.00

Cornucopia with Produce - Urn with Produce, plain lip, vertically ribbed edges, pontil, light green, ½ pt. (GIII-13) 105.00

Cornucopia with Produce - Urn with Produce, plain lip, vertically ribbed edges, pontil, emerald green, ½ pt. (GIII-14) 280.00

"For Pike's Peak" above prospector w/tools & cane & standing on oblong frame reading "Old Rye" - Eagle above frame "Pittsburgh, PA," smooth edges, light blue, ½ pt. (GXI-10) 65.00

"For Pike's Peak" above prospector w/tools & cane obverse & reverse, aqua, qt. (GXI-54) 700.00

"General Washington" surrounding bust - American eagle w/shield on oval frame w/"T.W.D.," plain lip, vertically ribbed edges, pontil, aqua, pt. (GI-16) 150.00

Horseman - Hound, w/pour spout & applied handle, amber, pt. (GXIII-17 variant) 1,150.00

"Jenny Lind" above bust encircled by wreath - "Glass Work's" above house & "S. Huffsey" below, calabash, broad sloping collar, smooth edges, pontil, aqua, qt. (GI-99) . . . 155.00

"Kossuth" above bust - Tall tree in foliage calabash, sloping collar w/beveled ring, smooth edges, pontil, olive yellow, qt. (GI-113) 145.00

"Kossuth" above bust - Tall tree in foliage calabash, sloping collar w/beveled ring, smooth edges, pontil, olive yellow, qt. (GI-113) 500.00

"LaFayette" (sic) above bust, "Coventry C-T" below - French Liberty Cap on pole in oval frame w/semicircle of nine stars above & "S & S" below, plain lip, vertically ribbed edges, pontil, olive green, ½ pt. (GI-86) 650.00

Masonic Emblems - American Eagle on oval frame w/"J.K.B.," tooled neck, vertically ribbed edges, pontil, yellow-green, pt. (GIV-3) . . 350.00

Masonic Emblems - American Eagle on oval frame w/"Ohio," "Zanesville" above & "J. Shepard & Co." (reversed S) below, plain lip, vertically ribbed edges, pontil, bright red amber, pt. (GIV-32) 400.00

Pitkin, 36 ribs in broken swirl, blown, dark olive amber, 5¾" h. 225.00

Pitkin, 36 ribs broken swirl to the left, sheared mouth, pontil, amber, 6 7/8" h. 225.00

Pitkin, 36 ribs in broken swirl, blown, green, 7 1/8" h. 190.00

"Railroad" above horse drawing long cart on rail & "Lowell" below - American Eagle lengthwise & 13 five-pointed stars, plain lip, vertically ribbed edges, pontil, amber olive, ½ pt. (GV-10) 127.50

"Rough and Ready" above bust of Taylor - American Eagle w/shield, 13 stars & "Masterson" above, plain lip, horizontally corrugated edges w/vertical medial rib, pontil, aqua, qt. (GI-77) 750.00

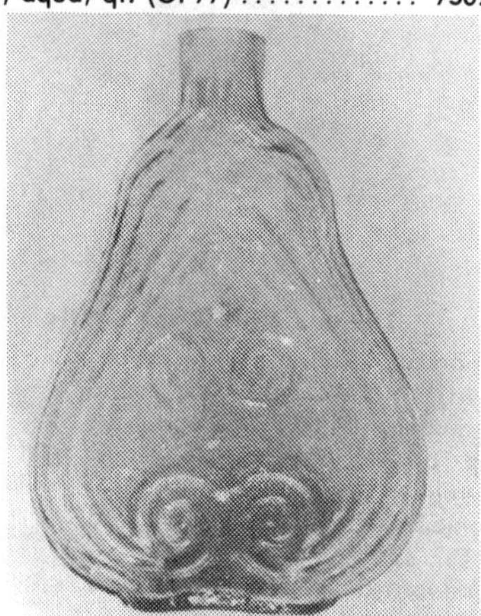

Scroll Flask

Scroll w/"Louisville" obverse & "Glassworks" reverse, plain lip, vertical medial rib, aqua, pt. (GIX-8) 220.00

Scroll, obverse & reverse, plain lip, vertical medial rib, pontil, deep green, pt. (GIX-10) 237.50

Scroll, obverse & reverse, plain lip, vertical medial rib, pontil, sapphire blue, pt., GIX-10 (ILLUS.) ... 700.00

Scroll, obverse & reverse, plain lip, vertical medial rib, pontil, deep yellow-green, qt. (GIX-2) 750.00

Sheaf of Grain - "Westford Glass Co., Westford, Conn.," plain lip, smooth edges, olive amber, pt. (GXIII-35) 75.00

Sloop w/pennant flying to the left & no waves - eight-pointed star without ornaments between rays, plain lip, smooth edges, pontil, sapphire blue, ½ pt. (GX-8a) 3,600.00

Stag w/"Good" below & "Game" at right - Weeping Willow tree, plain lip, vertically ribbed sloping edges sloping to heavy medial rib, pontil, yellow-amber, ½ pt. (GX-2) 10,000.00

Strap flask, "Warranted full pint, M. J. Doran, West Main Street, Rochester, N.Y.," light amethyst 25.00

"Success to the Railroad," obverse & reverse, wording above horse drawing cart on rail, plain lip, vertically ribbed edges, pontil, golden amber, pt. (GV-1)........1,550.00

"Success to the Railroad," obverse & reverse, wording above horse drawing cart on rail, plain lip, vertically ribbed edges, pontil, yellow-amber, pt. (GV-1) 1,400.00

"Summer" Tree - "Winter" Tree, plain lip, smooth edges, pontil, yellow-green, pt. (GX-15) 500.00

Summer Tree - Winter Tree, plain lip, smooth edges, pontil, smokey olive yellow, qt. (GX-19) 825.00

Sunburst, Elliptical, plain lip, horizontally corrugated edges, pontil, dark olive amber, pt. (GVIII-1) 2,550.00

Sunburst w/twenty-four rays, obverse & reverse, plain lip, horizontally corrugated edges, pontil, light clear green, pt. (GVIII-2) 390.00

Sunburst w/twenty-nine rays & "KEEN" reading from top to bottom of oval - Sunburst w/twenty-nine rays & "P & W" in oval, plain lip, horizontal corrugations do not extend around top & bottom, pontil, olive amber, ½ pt. (GVIII-9) .. 200.00

"Union" above clasped hands - American Eagle w/pennants inscribed "A & CO.," yellow-amber, pt. (GXII-22) 300.00

"Union" above clasped hands, oval frame inscribed "FA & Co." - Cannon facing right, American flag w/thirteen stars & stripes flying left, deep bluish aqua, pt. (GXII-40) 60.00

U.S. Army Officer - Daisy w/eleven slender double petals, calabash, vertically fluted edges, pontil, aqua, qt. (GXIII-15).............. 150.00

Washington - American Eagle w/shield & stars, plain lip, heavy vertical medial rib w/narrow rib each side, pontil, clear w/amethyst tint, qt. (GI-26) 100.00

"Washington" above bust - "Jackson" above bust, plain lip, vertically ribbed edges, pontil, amber, pt. (GI-33) 165.00

"Washington" above bust - "Gen. Z. Taylor" above bust, plain lip, smooth edges, aqua, pt. (GI-49) .. 55.00

Washington, "The Father of His Country" - Taylor, "Gen. Taylor Never Surrenders, Dyottville Glass Works, Philad.a," plain lip, smooth edges, pontil, apricot (or topaz), qt. (GI-37) 800.00

INKS

"Sanford's Inks and Library Paste"

Cylindrical, deep cobalt blue mold-blown glass, embossed "Harrison's Columbian Ink," open pontil, 1 7/8" d., 4" h. (lip chip)......... 225.00

Master size, automatic bottle machine-made clear glass, embossed "Sanford's Inks and Library Paste," qt. (ILLUS.) 6.50

Master size, stoneware pottery cylinder w/pouring spout,"Wm. Allen & Co., N.Y. Inks," qt............. 18.00

Master size, stoneware pottery, "Sanford's Ink," Western Stoneware Co., gal. 125.00

Pitkin, olive green glass, 36-rib

mold, ribs swirl to right, open pontil, 2 3/8" d., 1½" h. 550.00
Square, automatic bottle machine-made cobalt blue glass, "Davids Electro Chemical Writing Fluid" 15.00
Square, aqua mold-blown glass, vertical ribbing on three sides, two pen ledges, England, 1¾" sq., 2" h. 15.00
Teakettle-type fountain inkwell w/neck extending up at angle from base, cobalt blue mold-blown glass, 2 3/16" d., 2" h. 350.00
Teakettle-type fountain inkwell w/neck extending up at angle from base, fiery opalescent mold-blown glass, five-lobed body w/embossed floral design, 2 1/16" d., 2" h. 375.00
Teakettle-type fountain inkwell w/neck extending up at angle from base, opaque robin's egg blue mold-blown glass, six-lobed body, 2¾" widest d., 2¾" h. 700.00
Teakettle-type fountain inkwell w/neck extending up at angle from base, white porcelain, eight-panel body, 2 3/16" w., 2¼" h. .. 140.00
Twelve-sided, aqua mold-blown glass, embossed "Harrison's Columbian Ink" on sides & "Patent" on shoulder, open pontil, gal. 875.00
Umbrella-type (eight-panel cone shape), orange amber mold-blown glass, pontil, 2 3/16" w., 2¼" h. 85.00
Umbrella-type (paneled cone shape), deep olive yellow mold-blown glass, tooled lip, smooth base, original label "Unoco Fast Black Writing Ink," 2¾" h. 65.00
Umbrella-type (paneled cone shape), light blue-green mold-blown glass, rolled lip, open pontil, original label "The Granite State Writing Fluid, Julius A. Mahurin, Concord, N.H.," 2 3/16" h. 75.00
Umbrella-type (paneled cone shape), sapphire blue mold-blown glass, rolled lip, open pontil, 2½" h. 500.00

MEDICINES

Alexander (Dr. W.H.) Healing Oil, Columbus, Virginia, clear, cork closure, w/contents, 6" h. 4.50
Allen's (Mrs.) World Hair Balsam, paneled, open pontil, aqua, 7" h. 35.00
Allen's (Mrs.) World Hair Balsam, paneled, open pontil, yellow, 7" h. 155.00
Allen's (Mrs.) World Hair Restorer, amethyst 160.00
Allen's (Mrs.) World Hair Restorer, black amethyst 90.00
Allen's (Mrs.) World Hair Restorer, dark red violet 95.00
Arabian Tonic Blood Purifier, Stuart Howell, New York, aqua 22.00
Ayer's Hair Vigor, cobalt blue, 6½" h. 22.00
Baker's (Dr.) Pain Panacea, rectangular, pontil, aqua, 5" h. 34.00
Baker's (Dr.) Tonic Laxative, Keokuk, Iowa, indented panels, golden amber 14.00
Blodgett's Persian Balm, The Great Home Luxury, aqua, 5" h. 155.00
Blood Wine, embossed, sample 15.00
Bogle's Hyperian Fluid, aqua 15.00
Bonpland's Fever & Ague Remedy, rectangular, pontil, aqua, 5 1/8" h. 48.00
Bosanko's (Dr.) Pile Remedy, aqua, 2½" h. 6.00
Braddock's Pulmonary Cough Mixture, Hartford, Connecticut, aqua 100.00
Brant's Indian Pulmonary Balsam, 8-sided, aqua, 7" h. 60.00
Brant's Indian Purifying Extract, rectangular, aqua, 10" h. 130.00
Browder's (Dr.) Compound Syrup of Indian Turnip, rectangular, aqua, 7" h. ....75.00 to 85.00
Brown's (N.K.) Aromatic Essence Jamaica Ginger, oval, aqua, 5¾" h. 16.00
Bull's King of Pain, oval, deep aqua blue, 5" h. 78.50
Caldwell's Syrup Pepsin, Mf'd by Pepsin Syrup Company, Monticello, Illinois, rectangular, aqua, 7" h. 10.00
Chadwick's Compound Vegetable Liniment, rectangular, applied lip, open pontil, aqua, 5 3/16" h. (open bubble on inside of lip) 60.00
Christie's (Dr.) Ague Balsam 125.00
Cod Liver Oil, square, embossed fish & scales, machine-made w/threaded lip for cap, amber, 9" h. (ILLUS.) 15.00
Corbin's German Drops, pontil, aqua 180.00
Covert's Balm of Life, rectangular w/beveled corners, pontil, olive green, 5 7/8" h. 595.00
Cummings' (Dr.) Vegetine, oval, aqua, 9 5/8" h. 12.00
Curtis & Perkins' Cramp and Pain Killer, round, aqua, 4 7/8" h. 40.00
Daniels (Dr.) Puppy Vermifuge Capsules, w/contents, original box ... 10.00

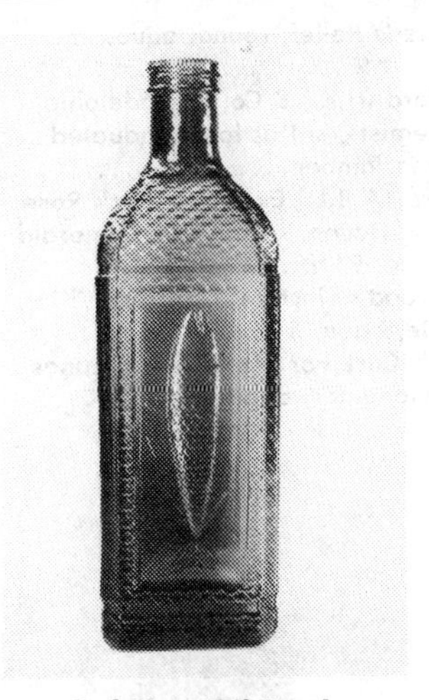

Cod Liver Oil Bottle

Davis (G.W.) Inflammatory Extirpator & Cleanser, aqua 39.00
Davis' (Perry) Pain Killer, rectangular, pontil, aqua, 4 5/8" h 13.50
Davis' (Perry) Pain Killer, rectangular, pontil, aqua, 6" h........... 7.00
Dean's (Prof.) King Cactus Oil, The Great Barbed Wire Remedy, round, embossed house, amber, 9½" h......................... 65.00
Dodge Brothers Melanine Hair Tonic, puce 275.00
Dyer's Healing Embrocation, Providence, Rhode Island, ponti, aqua, 6¼" h......................... 80.00
Elmore's (Dr.) Rheumatine-Goutaline, amber, 7 7/16" h...... 45.00
Empire Company's Nervine Balsam & Indian Remedy 7.50
Fahrney's (Dr.) Celebrated Blood Cleanser or Panacea, ice blue 10.00
Farrell's (H.G.) Arabian Liniment, round, aqua, 5" h. 125.00
Fenning's Fever Cure, rectangular, aqua, 6½" h. 9.50
Fitch (Dr. S.S.), 714 Broadway, N.Y., oval, aqua, 6 3/8" h. (dug) 17.50
Fitler's (Dr.) Rheumatic Remedy, rectangular, aqua, 6 5/8" h. 20.00
Foord's (Dr. A.) Pectoral Syrup, rectangular, aqua, 5½" h. ....80.00 to 95.00
Ganter's (L.F.) Magic Chicken Cholera Cure, L.F. Ganter Med. Co., Glasgo, Ky., amber, 6¼" h....... 20.00
Gardner's (Mrs. M.N.) Indian Balsam of Liverwort, round, pontil, aqua, 5 1/8" h. ....52.00 to 65.00
Gibb's Bone Liniment, 8-sided, open pontil, olive green, 6½" h....... 610.00
Glover's Imperial Distemper Cure, H. Clay Glover, New York, amber, 5 1/8" h. 10.00
Glover's Imperial Distemper Cure, H. Clay Glover, New York, green, 5 1/8" h. 15.00
Goff's (S.B.) Indian Vegetable Cough Syrup & Blood Purifier, rectangular, aqua, 5¾" h. 12.50
Gombault's Caustic Balsam, rectangular, aqua, 6½" h. 11.00
Grove's Tasteless Chill Tonic, aqua, 6" h.......................... 12.50
Hagan's Cleanser For Childrens Hair, aqua 18.00
Hair's (Dr. B.W.) Asthma Cure, square, aqua, 8" h. 36.00
Hall's Balsam for the Lungs, John F. Henry & Co., New York, rectangular, aqua, 7¾" h. 90.00
Hamlin's Wizard Oil, rectangular, aqua, 5¾" h. 4.00
Hart's Swedish Asthma Cure, rectangular, amber, 5" h.............. 18.00
Hay's Hair Health, amber, 7½" 5.00
Healy & Bigelow's Kickapoo Cough Syrup, round, aqua, 6½" h. 6.50
Helmbold (H.T.) Genuine Fluid Extracts, Philadelphia, open pontil, aqua, 7¼" h. (hazed)........... 20.00
Hobensack's Medicated Worm Syrup, Philada., rectangular w/indented panels, aqua, 4½" h.......40.00 to 60.00
Hopkins' Chalybeate, Baltimore, deep green, 7¾" h. 110.00
Hoyt's Poisoned Blood Cure, Indiainapolis (sic), clear, 8¼" h. 80.00
Hunnewell's (John L.) Tolu Anodyne, open pontil, aqua 35.00
Hunter's Pulmonary Balsam or Cough Syrup, J. Curtis Prop., Bangor, Me., rectangular, aqua, 6" h.............................. 82.50
Hunt's Liniment, Sing Sing, N.Y., rectangular, aqua, 4¾" h. 22.50
Jacobs' Cholera & Dysentery Cordial, open pontil, aqua (light inside haze) 65.00
Jayne's (Dr. D.) Carminative Balsam, round, aqua, 5¼" h. 13.50
Jayne's (Dr. D.) Expectorant, rectangular, open pontil, aqua, 5" h. ... 33.00
Jayne's (Dr. D.) Tonic Vermifuge, Philada., square, aqua, 4 7/8" h. 27.50
Johnston's (Dr.) Indian Compound Herbaline, aqua, 10" h. 135.00
Josephus' (Dr.) Great Shoshone Indian Remedy, rectangular, aqua, 8¾" h......................... 65.00
Kennedy's (Donald) Salt Rheum Ointment, 2" h...................... 77.50
Kerr's (Dr. James C.) Great System Renovator, amber 20.00
Kilmer's (Dr.) Ocean Weed Heart Remedy, The Blood Specific, rec-

tangular, embossed heart, aqua, 8½" h. 34.50

Lake's Indian Specific

Lake's Indian Specific, rectangular w/deeply beveled corners & raised frame around embossing, aqua, 8¼" h. (ILLUS.) ...295.00 to 325.00

Liquid Peptonoids, square, amber, 7 5/8" h. 6.00

Long's (Dr.) Vegetable Prairie Flower, aqua, 9" h. 22.00

Liquid Opodeldoc, thin flared lip, pontiled, aqua 20.00

Loudin & Co.'s Indian Expectorant, aqua, 7½" h. (minor inside stain) 75.00

Magnetic Ather, H. Halstead & Co., Rochester, N.Y., nine-sided, open pontil, aqua 135.00

Mathewson's Infallable Remedy, Price 50 Cts., applied lip, open pontil, aqua, 6¾" h. 122.50

McLane's (Dr.) American Worm Specific, round, open pontil, aqua, 3 7/8" h. 35.00

McLean's Volcanic Liniment, rectangular, greenish aqua, 6½" h. 90.00

Merchant's (G.W.) Gargling Oil, rectangular, open pontil, green, 7 1/8" h. 52.50

Mexican Hair Renewer, cobalt blue 28.00

Mexican Mustang Liniment, round, pontil, aqua, 4" h. 12.00

Miles' (Dr.) New Heart Cure, rectangular, aqua, 8 3/8" h. 17.00

Miles' (Dr.) Restorative Blood Purifier, aqua (99% paper label) 25.00

Montgomery's Hair Restorer, light amber 18.00

Morse's Celebrated Syrup, Prov., R.I., large, oval-shaped, huge iron pontil, deep aqua 45.00

Mother's Relief, round, aqua, 8½" h. 225.00

Mulford (H.K.) & Co., Philadelphia, chemists, set of four graduated sizes, amber 24.00

Myers' (A.B.L.) Extract of Rock Rose, New Haven, rectangular, emerald green, 9" h. 900.00

Norwood's Tincture Veratrum Viside, aqua, 5½" h. 25.00

Otto's Cure For The Throat & Lungs, rectangular, aqua, 6" h. 7.00

Parker's Hair Balsam Bottle

Parker's Hair Balsam, New York, amber, 7" h. (ILLUS.) 6.00

Park's Sure Cure for the Liver & Kidneys, rectangular, amber, 9¾" h. (collar repaired)................ 85.00

Peckham's Croup Remedy, The Children's Cough Cure, aqua......... 12.00

Peptenzyme, Reed & Carnick, New York, cobalt blue, 4½" h. 12.00

Pepto-Mangan Gude, six-sided, aqua, 7¼" h. 12.00

Phalon & Sons Chemical Hair Invigorator, aqua, 5½" h. 38.00

Phelp's Arcanum, Worcester, Mass., round w/eight sunken panels, pontil, olive amber, 9" h.........1,000.00

Pierce's (Dr. R.V.) Favorite Prescription, Buffalo, N.Y., rectangular, aqua, 8¼" h. 20.00

Pinkham's (Lydia) Blood Purifier, oval, aqua, 8½" h. 6.00

Pinkham's (Lydia) Emmenagogue, whittled, pontil, aqua............ 84.00

Pinkham's (Lydia) Vegetable Compound, oval, aqua, 8½" h. 12.00

Piso's Cure, Hazeltine & Co., rectangular, amber, 5½" h............. 8.00

Piso's Cure, Hazeltine & Co., rectangular, green, 5¼" h. 6.00

Pitcher's (Dr. S.) Castoria, rectangular, aqua, 6" h. 6.00

Pond's Extract, oval, aqua, 5½" h. 28.00

Radway's Renovating Resolvent (R.R.R. No. 2), 7¼" h. 35.00
Riker's American Hair Restorer, amber 35.00
Roberts's (M.B.) Vegetable Embrocation, round, open pontil, emerald green, 5" h. 130.00
Rubifoam for the Teeth, Put up by E.W. Hoyt & Co., Lowell, Mass., oval, amethyst, 4" h. 6.00
Russian Rheumatic Cure, aqua, rare 30.00
Sandford's (Dr.) Extract of Witch Hazel, rectangular, cobalt blue, 7¼" h. 45.00
Sanital De Midy, Paris, ten-sided, clear, 4¼" h. 6.00
Schrage's Rheumatic Cure, aqua 15.00
Scovell Blood & Liver Syrup, Cincinnati, aqua 18.00
Sharp & Dohme, Baltimore, MD, cobalt blue, 3½" h. 8.00
Silkodono For Hair & Scalp, milk white 30.00
Simmons Liver Regulator, rectangular, aqua, 9¼" h. 9.00
Sims Tonic, Antwerp, N.Y., amber, large 2 x 3¼ x 7¼" 9.00
Sines (Charles) Celebrated Compound Syrup of Tar, Wild Cherry & Hoarhound, Phila., Pa., clear 45.00
Smith's Bile Beans, disc-shaped, clear, 1 5/8" h. 4.00
Smith's (H.K.) Cure All, rectangular, aqua, 5" h. 7.50
Spanish Lustral, Prepared by J.C. Wadleigh, open pontil, aqua 40.00
Sun Flower Cholera Cure, clear, 8¾" h. 80.00
Thompson's Dandelion & Celery Tonic 30.00
Thompson's (Dr.) Eye Water, New London, Conn., round, aqua, 3¾" h. (neck hazy) 22.00
Tobias (Dr.) New York, Venetian Liniment, oval, open pontil, aqua, 5¾" h. 42.00
Tobias' Venetian Liniment, aqua, 8 1/8" h. 165.00
Trask's (A.) Magnetic Ointment, square w/chamfered corners, pontil, aqua, 3 1/8" h. 35.00
University of Free Medicines, Philada., six-sided, aqua 130.00
Vaseline, Cheesebrough Mfg. Co., clear, 3" h. 6.00
Wair Asthma Cure, deep amber 30.00
Warner's Safe Cure, London, emerald green, ½ pt. 52.50
Warner's Safe Cure, London, amber, pt. 32.00
Warner's Safe Cure, w/three cities .. 45.00
Warner's Safe Cure, w/four cities, amber, pt. 55.00
Warner's Safe Nervine, H.H. Warner & Company, Rochester, New York, amber, ½ pt. 36.00
Warner's Safe Rheumatic Cure, London, amber 165.00
Warren's (Dr.) Tonic Cordial, Cincinnati & N.Y., square, aqua, 9½" h. 60.00
Wayne's Diurectic & Alterative Elixir of Buchu, Juniper & Acetate Potash, Cincinnati, Ohio, applied top, cobalt blue 120.00
Welling's (G. S.) Compound Arnica Liniment, open pontil, aqua 90.00
Whitcomb's (C.) Rheumatic Indian Liniment, Apothery, N.H., oval, clear, 5" h. 22.00
Winer's Canadian Vermifuge, round, light green, 4" h. 25.00
Woods (Professor) Hair Restorative, aqua 38.00
Wyeth (John) & Bro., Philadelphia, w/dose cup, pat. May 16, 1899, cobalt blue, 6½" h. 23.00

MILK

Amber, embossed "Rieck's Pure Milk & Cream Registered," qt. 45.00
Amber, embossed "V.M. & I.C.," qt. 75.00
Amber, white pyroglaze "Anchorage Dairy," qt. 40.00
Amber, white pyroglaze "Driftwood Dairy" & cow, square, ½ gal. 20.00
Clear, "baby face" top, embossed "Dunmyer Dairy," qt. 20.00
Clear, "baby face" top, embossed "Sunshine Dairy," square, qt. 35.00
Clear, cream-top, embossed "Brookfield Dairy, Hellertown, Pa., Premium Quality, Mothers Who Care," ½ pt. 18.00
Clear, cream-top, embossed "Otto Milk Co.," ½ pt. 14.00
Clear, cream-top, embossed "Neisen & Schwan," qt. 15.00
Clear, cream-top, embossed "Willow Farms," qt. 20.00
Clear, double, "baby face" top, embossed "Brookfield Dairy," square, qt. 28.00
Clear, double, "baby face" top, orange & red pyroglaze "Dairylea," qt. 30.00
Clear, embossed "Golden Cream," ½ pt. 4.50
Clear, embossed "Maytag Dairy Farm," ½ pt. 15.00
Clear, embossed "Pevely Dairy," ½ pt. 7.00
Clear, embossed "10c Klamath Falls," pt. 7.50
Clear, ribbed, embossed "Union Dairy Co., St. Louis," pt. 7.00
Clear, embossed "Carnation," qt. 10.00

Clear, embossed "Charmed Land Dairies," qt. 8.00
Clear, embossed "City Creamery, Duluth," round, qt. 4.50
Clear, embossed "Mack Farm Dairy, Batesville, Ark.," round, qt. 15.00
Clear, embossed "Miner's Dairy, Butte, Mt.," qt. 6.00
Clear, embossed "Morgan's Dairy" & crying milk bottle "I wanna go home - please return!," qt. 25.00
Clear, embossed "Red Oak Grove, Austin, Minn.," square, qt. 6.00
Clear, embossed "Producer's Dairy," w/war slogan, ½ gal. 25.00
Green, "Big Elm Dairy," qt. 350.00

MINERAL WATERS

G. Klauder Mineral Water Bottle

Artesian Spring Lithia Mineral Water, emerald green, pt. 45.00
Chase & Co. Mineral Water, San Francisco, Cal., blob top, graphite pontil, green 35.00
Clark & White, olive green, qt. 25.00
Felix's (Geo. W.) Mineral Water, Harrisburg, Pa., iron pontil, deep green 250.00
Guilford Mineral Spring Water, Guilford, Vt., w/monogram, emerald green, qt. 44.00
Guilford Mineral Spring Water, Guilford, Vt., w/monogram, light green, qt. 30.00
Hathorn Spring, Saratoga, New York, deep black amber, pt. 24.00
Hathorn Spring, Saratoga, N.Y., amber, qt. 24.00
Klauder (G.), Union Glass Works, Phila., Superior Mineral Water, round w/"mug" base, applied top, iron pontil, deep cobalt blue, small bruise on base (ILLUS.) 275.00
Missisquoi Spring, w/papoose, yellow-green 340.00
Oak Orchard, Acid Springs, C.W. Merchant, Lockport, N.Y., Saratoga-type, emerald green, qt. 52.00
Pacific Congress Water, soda-type crown cap, aqua, 8¼" h. 12.00
Pluto Spring Water, devil & factory pictured, tin cap, embossed "Pluto Corp, French Lick, Indiana" 20.00
Poland (Moses) Water, cylinder, aqua, w/label 65.00
Ryan (John) Excelsior Mineral Water 1859, Savannah, Ga., cobalt blue 55.00
Superior Mineral Water, eight-sided, iron pontil, aqua (dug) 28.00
White Rock Mineral Water, 1910, unopened, paper labels, amber 35.00
Witter Spring Water, W.M.S. Co., San Francisco, cylinder, amber 30.00

PEPPERSAUCES

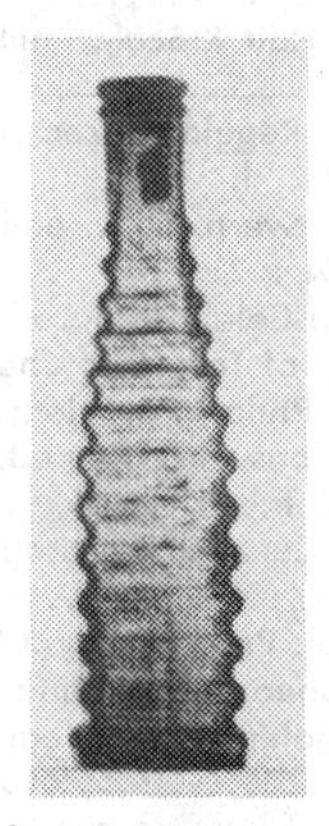

E.R. Durkee Peppersauce Bottle

Cathedral arches, square, applied round collar, came from mold tilted, aqua, 8¾" h. 85.00
Cathedral arches, square, Gothic arches & windows, applied round collar, iron pontil, aqua 85.00
Ridge-sided tapering square, embossed "E.R. Durkee & Co., New York," base embossed "S.Sp.B.," blue-green, pt. (ILLUS.) 35.00
Swirl, jade green, 8" h. 25.00

POISONS

Amber, corner bumps, "Poison," 3½" h. 12.00
Amber, square w/embossed skull & crossbones, paper label, "Tincture Iodine" 12.00
Aqua, flat hobnail pattern, cross on front, scarred base, crude 150.00
Cobalt blue, "The Owl Drug Co." on shoulder, "Poison" down side, 5" h. 55.00

Cobalt blue, triangular, "The Owl Drug Co." on one side, "Poison" on another side, 7¾" h. 375.00
Cobalt blue, square w/ridges, "Poison," 3" h. 15.00
Cobalt blue, triangular w/bumps, "Poison," 3" h. 15.00
Cobalt blue, triangular w/bumps, "Triloids" on one side, "Poison" on another side, 3" h. 24.00
Cobalt blue, diamond-quilted body, "W.T. & Co.," 5 3/8" h. 40.00

SNUFF BOTTLES

Amber glass, square w/chamfered corners, sheared lip, rough pontil, 4½" h. 40.00
Amber glass, square cylinder, flanged lip, 5¾" h. 10.00
Green-amber glass, eight-panel, open pontil, 5¾" h. 90.00
Olive amber glass, embossed "J.J. Mapes, No. 61 Front St., New York," open pontil 375.00
Stoneware pottery, labeled "American Made," w/1902 tax stamps ... 60.00
Stoneware pottery, ovoid w/wide flared neck, marked on base "Weyman's Snuff," grey, 6" h. 20.00
Stoneware pottery, ovoid w/wide flared neck, marked on base "Weyman's Snuff," cream w/brown interior, 9" h. 35.00

SODAS & SARSAPARILLAS

Duensing Soda Bottle

Alameda Soda Water Co., Oakland, Cal., soda, clasped hands, Hutchinson stopper 28.00
American Flag Soda Works, San Francisco, soda, aqua 65.00
Baker (D.H.), Davenport, Iowa, soda, crown top 12.50
Beard (Luke), Howard St., Boston, soda, "This Bottle is Never Sold," squat, emerald green, 6½" h. 50.00
Brandt (G.W.), Carlisle, soda, squat, iron pontil, green 80.00
Caldwell Bottling Works, Caldwell, Idaho, "CWB" monogram (cloudy) 150.00
California Pop, stoneware, cream-colored glaze, soda, signed & dated "Pat. Oct. 29, 1872," 11" h..... 29.00
California Soda Works, embossed eagle, Hutchinson stopper, aqua .. 25.00
Campbell (T.), Philadelphia, soda, squat, iron pontil, green 65.00
Canterbury (P.), Galveston, Texas, soda, blob top, aqua 50.00
Carpenter & Cobb Knickerbocker Soda Water, Saratoga Springs, ten-sided, applied lip, iron pontil, light green (small surface bubble burst on shoulder)............... 325.00
City Bottling, Spokane, Washington, soda, Hutchinson stopper 10.00
Classen & Co., San Francisco, soda, crossed anchors, satin finish 50.00
Coca-Cola, Columbus, Ohio, amber 40.00
Coca-Cola, Huntington, W. Va., amber 45.00
Coca-Cola, Jonesboro, Ark., amber 250.00
Coca-Cola, Knoxville, Tenn., w/arrows, amber 35.00
Coca-Cola, Memphis, Tenn., amber 22.50
Coca-Cola, New York, New York, straight sides, amber 35.00
Coca-Cola, Pittsburgh, Pennsylvania, straight sided, amber........... 30.00
Coca-Cola, Savannah, Ga., straight sides 25.00
Coca-Cola, Biedenhorn, Vicksburg, Miss., straight-sided, aqua 20.00
Coca-Cola, "75th Anniversary Commemorative Bottle," Chattanooga Coca-Cola Bottling Co., 1974 ..... 5.00
Coggeshall (G.D.), No. 421 Pearl St., New York, Soda Water, small tenpin shape, narrow rounded applied lip, scarred base, deep olive amber, 6¾" h. (slight wear spots) 2,900.00
Concord Bottling Co., Concord, N.H., soda, Hutchinson stopper 15.00
Cottle Post & Co., Portland, Oregon, soda, eagle center, blob top, bluish green, 7¼" h. 40.00
Crown Bottling Works, Muskogee, I.T. (Indian Territory), soda, Hutchinson stopper, clear 175.00
Crystal Bottling Co., Nampa, Idaho, soda (dug)......................... 75.00
Crystal Palace Premium Soda Water, W.E. Eagle, Union Glass Works, Phila., embossed Crystal Palace building, round, applied top, iron

pontil, deep teal blue (small base chip) 675.00

Cudworth (A.W.) & Co., San Francisco, soda, blob top, green, 7¼" h. 35.00

Dana's Sarsaparilla, complete back label, aqua, 9" h. 20.00

Duensing (H.), Sr., Chicago Hts., Ill., aqua, interior stains (ILLUS.) 3.50

Eagle Superior Soda Water, New York, applied collar, iron pontil, olive amber 825.00

Eagle Works, Philadelphia, soda, squat, iron pontil, green 55.00

Empire Soda Works, Vallejo, Cal., blob top, aqua 80.00

Ghiradelli's Branch, Oakland, Cal., soda, blob top, cobalt blue, 7¾" h. 100.00

Grant's Sarsaparilla, Fremont, Neb., aqua 15.00

Haight & O'Brien, St. Louis, Mo., soda, blob top, aqua (dug) 15.00

Hires Carbonated Beverages, soda, aqua 9.00

Holland & Rink, Butte, Mont., soda, crown top 10.00

Hood's Sarsaparilla, aqua, ca. 1890, 8¾" h. 12.00

Indian Rock Ginger Ale, ten-pin shape, deep amethyst, 8½" h. 30.00

Leon's Sarsaparilla, Belfast, Maine, aqua, 7¾" h. 50.00

Moxie, soda, pale green, 6¾" h. 12.00

Orange Crush, soda, amber, 7 oz. .. 7.00

Pacific & Puget Sound Soda Works, Seattle, Wash., soda, Hutchinson stopper, aqua, 7" h. 12.00

Pepsi Cola, Escambia Bottling Co., Pensacola, Fla., soda, Hutchinson stopper 395.00

Pepsi Cola, New Bern, N.C., soda, ca. 1906 .... 55.00

Sand's Sarsaparilla, New York, open pontil, aqua, 6" h. 48.50

Seitz Bros., Easton, Pa., Premium Mineral Waters, soda, eight-sided, blob top, cobalt blue 48.00

Seven-Up, Houston, Texas, soda, amber 25.00

Sherwood, (F.), Bridgeport, New Haven, Conn., soda, iron pontil, teal green 125.00

Taylor Soda Water Mfg. Co., Boise, Idaho, soda, panel base, clear, 6¾" h. 30.00

Von Harten (Albert), Savannah, Ga., soda, squatty, teal green 25.00

Wintle (A.J.) & Sons, Bill Mills Nr Ross, soda, ten-pin shape, aqua, 9¼" h. 25.00

WHISKEY & OTHER SPIRITS

Beer, "Buffalo Brewing Company, San Francisco," amber, pt. 15.00

Beer, "Fredericksburg Bottling Co., San Francisco," golden amber, 5½" h. 86.00

Beer, "Fredericksburg Brewery, San Jose," blob top, red-amber, qt. ... 65.00

Beer, "Godensburg Ginger Beer Works/Century Brand/H.N. Daniels, Proprietor," stoneware .. 29.00

Beer, "Honolulu Brewing Co., Honolulu, T.H.," blob top, aqua, qt. ....30.00 to 38.00

Beer, "Phoenix Bottling Co., New York," blob top, 9 1/8" 12.50

Beer, "R. Powley & Co., Dunedin N.Z.," crown cap, yellow-amber, ostrich trade mark, 1920's 12.00

Beer, "Red Wing Brewing Co., Red Wing, Minn." embossed in circle, blob top, light amber, picnic size (½ gal.)................85.00 to 100.00

Beer, "Schlitz," royal ruby, 7 oz. 22.50

Beer, "Schlitz," royal ruby, 32 oz. 38.00

Beer, "Milwaukee Beer, John H. Seiling, Boone, Iowa," aqua, qt. .. 12.00

Beer, Walker & Sons Products Co., amber 5.00

Case gin, "Beste Schiedammer Genever Fabrick van Levert & Co. Amsterdam" label, olive green, 11¾" h. 40.00

Case gin, "Blankenheym & Nolet," sloping collar, olive green, qt..... 25.00

Case gin, "E. Kiderlen," tapered, dark olive green, whittled, 9¼" h. ....30.00 to 45.00

Case gin, "P. Loopuyt & Co., Distillers, Schiedam," dark olive green, 9" h. 25.00

Case gin, "A.C.A. Nolet," green, qt. ....26.00 to 35.00

Case gin, "Rye Malt Gin, Henry H. Shute Ltd. Co.," embossed crown, honey amber 79.00

Case gin, "Daniel Visser & Zonen, Schiedam," olive green, 9¼" h. .. 30.00

Case gin, "Daniel Visser & Zonen, Schiedam, De Graauwehengst, Anno 1714," embossed w/prancing horse, emerald green 150.00

Gin, "Bininger Old London Dock Gin," yellow-amber, qt. 80.00

Gin, "Bininger Old London Dock Gin," olive green ....65.00 to 79.00

Gin, "Bowlin King Cole Dry Gin," embossed on two sides, aqua 6.00

Gin, "London Royal Imperial," dark cornflower blue, qt. 220.00

Gin, "Messenger's London Cordial," iron pontil 110.00

Wildflower Gin Bottle

Gin, "Wildflower," olive green, paper label, ⅓ gal. (ILLUS.) 22.50

Liqueur, "Dunbar & Co. Wormwood Cordial," square, olive green, smooth base, qt. 95.00

Schnapps, "F. J. Dunbar Cordial," emerald green 55.00

Schnapps, "Nolet's (J.A.J.) Aromatic," light olive green, qt. 20.00

Whiskey, "Bininger Old Kentucky Bourbon," square, amber ..65.00 to 75.00

Whiskey, "Bouillon Maggi," seal whiskey, red amber 100.00

Casper's Whiskey Bottle

Whiskey, "Casper's Whiskey - Made by Honest North Carolina People," cobalt blue, qt. (ILLUS.) 365.00

Whiskey, "The Champus Gassler Bros. Prop NW cor 104 St. Columbus Av., N.Y.," jug w/applied red-amber handle 125.00

Whiskey, "Chapin & Gore Sour Mash, 1867," barrel-shaped, amber 75.00

Whiskey, "Chestnut Grove," ewer form w/applied handle, amber ... 165.00

Whiskey, "Class of 1846" on seal, "Dyottville Glassworks Phila." on base, sloping collared mouth w/ring, olive green, 11¼" h...... 200.00

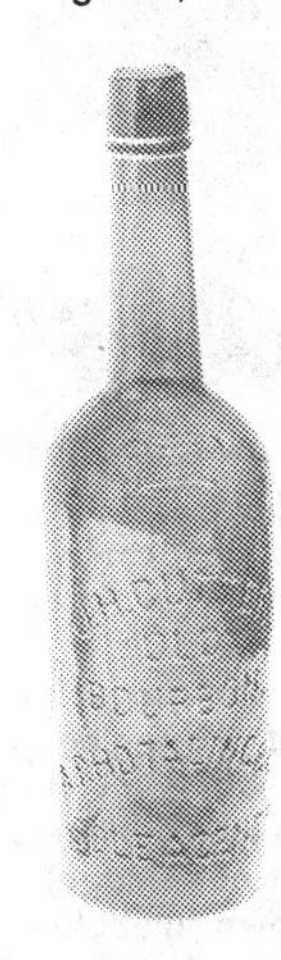

J.H. Cutter Old Bourbon Bottle

Whiskey, "J.H. Cutter Old Bourbon," blob top, light amber (ILLUS.) 60.00

Whiskey, "Diamond Club Whiskey," whittled, pontiled, emerald green, qt. 360.00

Whiskey, "L. Franc & Co's. Brunswick Club Handmade Sour Mash," stoneware pottery, qt. 75.00

Whiskey, "The Hayner Distilling Co., Dayton, St. Louis, Atlanta, St. Paul Distillers," clear, qt. 9.00

Whiskey, "Hildebrant & Posner, San Francisco, California," cylinder, amber, fifth 15.00

Whiskey, "Jorum Roderick Dhue Old Highland Whiskey, Wright & Greiglr Glasgow," miniature, handled, stenciled vines, berries & flowers, 4" h...................... 45.00

Whiskey, "Macy & Jenkins," handled jug, amber 15.00

Whiskey, "Middleton Wheat Whiskey 1825," squat, large applied seal, rare improved pontil, green, qt. .. 365.00

Whiskey, "Mohawk Rock & Rye," miniature stoneware flask, glazed white & brown spatter pattern, colorful orange label, Mohawk Liqueur Corp., Detroit, Michigan, 1/16th pt. 35.00

Whiskey, mold-blown, globular-form, 20-ribs swirled to the right, turned over collar on lip, pontil, light citron, Kent, Ohio, early 19th c., ½ pt., 5 1/8" h. 600.00

Early Zanesville Bottle

Whiskey, mold-blown, globular-form, 24 swirled ribs, citron, Zanesville, Ohio, 7 5/8" h. (ILLUS.) 1,500.00

Whiskey, mold-blown, globular-form, 24 swirled ribs, golden amber, Zanesville, Ohio, 7¾" h. (minor sickness & surface blisters w/small amount of damage) 300.00

Whiskey, mold-blown, globular-form, 24-ribs swirled to the left, turned over collar on lip, pontil, red-amber, Zanesville, Ohio, 8" h. 400.00

Whiskey, "G.H. Moore Old Bourbon & Rye," amber (whittled) 30.00

Whiskey, "Old Continental," acorn-shaped jug, yellow-amber, 3½" h. 1,050.00

Whiskey, "Old Wheat, S.M. & Co.," bulbous, embossed shoulder medallion, amber, 1840-60, 11¼" h. 225.00

Whiskey, "Patent Whiskey," Dyottville Glass Works, Phila. on base, iron pontil, dark olive yellow 28.00

Whiskey, "Patent Whiskey," W. McCully & Co. on base, dark olive green 22.00

Whiskey, "Potts & Thompson Liquors," debossed jug 75.00

Whiskey, "Quaker Maid Whiskey," mold-blown, applied collar, 8" h. 15.00

Whiskey, "Quinn's Quality Quantity-Rye Whiskey, Kansas City, Largest Mail Order Grocer & Liquor Merchant In the West," stoneware pottery jug, 10" d. 295.00

Whiskey, "Red Top Rye," Ferdinand Westleimer & Sons, Cincinnati, St. Joseph, amber, qt. 22.00

Whiskey, "Red Top Rye," Ferdinand Westleimer & Sons, Cincinnati, St. Joseph, Louisville, embossed tip, amber, pt. 10.00

Whiskey, "Star Whiskey New York, W. B. Crowell Jr.," mold-blown, vertical ribs & oval embossed label, well-shaped applied handle & lip, golden amber, 8" h. 400.00

Whiskey, "Upper Blue Lick Water, Stanton & Pierle, Proprietors, Maysville, Ky.," oval, cornflower blue, qt. 550.00

Whiskey, "N. VanBeil New York," seal whiskey, citron 125.00

Whiskey, "Vidvard & Sheehan," handled jug, applied mouth w/pour spout, olive yellow, 10" h. 750.00

Wine demijohn, egg-shaped, open pontil, blue-aqua, 5 gal. 89.00

Wine demijohn, open pontil, blue-green, 2 gal. (small lip chip) 40.00

(End of Bottle Section)

BOXES

Painted Bentwood Bride's Box

The category of Boxes, formerly included in the Furniture section, has been expanded to include not only wooden boxes but those made of glass, ceramic and various metals.

Band box, cylindrical, top & sides covered overall w/floral print wallpaper in blue & white on black ground, New England, early 19th c., 6¼" d., 4" h. (wear to edges) $220.00

Band box, oval, stitched top & conforming body covered overall w/wallpaper stenciled w/stylized floral & foliate bands decorated in green, black & white, the interior & base fixed w/contemporary newspaper, probably New Hampshire, ca. 1840, 12½" l., 6 1/8" h. (some wear) 165.00

Bible box, painted pine, molded lid & base, original brass bat's wing end handles, old worn green paint, 18¼" l. 325.00

Bible box, carved pine, pintel-hinged lid w/thumbnail beading on front & back edges, conforming nailed box w/beveled bottom board, front panel w/interlocking bands of arches above incised line decoration, heart within a heart in center flanked by foliate & heart panels divided by pillars of impressed crosses, Chippendale brass escutcheon, thin wash of light grey paint, possibly New Hampshire, early 18th c., 16½ x 25", 9¼" h. (missing lock) 6,050.00

Bride's box, bentwood oval, lid decorated w/a large floral sprig in yellow, green, blue, black & white, the sides decorated w/continuous tulip sprig frieze in corresponding colors, America, first half 19th c., 12½" l., 5" h. 550.00

Bride's box, bentwood oval, lid painted w/figures of a man & woman walking in a landscape setting w/two trees, sides decorated w/a continuous floral sprig border in red, green & blue on a red ground, some paint flaking, New England, second quarter 19th c., 15 5/8" l., 6¾" h. (ILLUS.) 1,045.00

Bride's box, bentwood oval, lid painted w/a scene depicting man & woman in 18th century dress, he in a dark blue three-quarter length coat, pants & black shoes, holding a walking stick, she in an off-white dress tied at the waist & wearing a string of pearls & hat, buildings in distance, sides painted w/a continous floral sprig frieze in tones of blue, red, green, white & black, 19th c., 19" l., 7½" h. 1,320.00

Bride's box, oval lid w/bentwood loop handle & locking device incised w/various cross-hatched motifs & wrigglework border, the body w/meandering wrigglework, Scandinavia, 19th c., 13½" l., 7¼" h. 165.00

"Bucher" (book) box w/hinged lid, painted pine, top & sides painted w/red, yellow & white tulips, centering on the top the initials "M.A." on black-painted ground, interior inscribed in pencil "Annie Marmott" & initials "SEA," tin hasp, Berks or Lancaster County, Pennsylvania, 8¼ x 9¾", 3" h.... 990.00

"Bucher" box w/fitted lid, bentwood oval, painted w/free-flowing floral sprays in red, white, yellow & green on a black ground, portions of lid & base missing, Berks or Lancaster County, Pennsylvania, ca. 1800, 11¾" l., 2½" h. (ILLUS.) 1,320.00

Bentwood Oval "Bucher" Box

Candle box, curly maple, dovetailed & pegged construction, carved rooster pull on lid 340.00

Candle box, painted & decorated, shaped rim centering a heart, single drawer, painted red, 5¼ x 17" 825.00

Candle box, hanging-type, poplar, dovetail construction, scalloped crest pierced to hang, lift lid opening to divided interior, old red paint, 12½" h. 500.00

Carved birch box, hewn from single piece of wood, two sliding lids opening to round compartment, lids & sides w/Friesian (wheel-form scratch-carved) carving, further carved w/initials "R.H.," good patina, w/hand written note "Box - Ruth Harris Brewster...at least back to 1722," 5" l. (minor damage) 800.00

Curly walnut box, tambour lid w/brass knob, reeded sides, revarnished old natural finish, 5¾ x 10 3/8", 3½" h. 450.00

Document box, painted & decorated, hinged rectangular lid w/applied handles opening to a rectangular storage area, the front blind-fret-carved w/a central hex motif flanked by scrolls, half hexes & geometric strapwork, single drawer below, painted overall in green within black borders, the sides w/free-form yellow, black & green scrollwork, Pennsylvania, early 19th c., 11½" l., 6½" h. ...1,320.00

Document box, inlaid tiger maple, hinged rectangular lid, conforming dovetailed case inlaid w/stringing & a heart-shaped escutcheon over molded base w/bracket feet, New England, late 19th - early 20th c., 6¼ x 10½", 6½" h. 880.00

Dough box w/lid, rectangular top lifting to a plain tapering interior, painted overall in brown, New England, first half 19th c., 28" l., 9½" h. 192.50

Dresser box, bird's-eye maple, rectangular lid academy painted w/polychrome compote of fruit flanked by flower-filled cornucopias, sides & front w/groupings of fruit, interior w/mirror & divided lift-out compartment, each section w/brush line sketches in black, four bun feet, America, ca. 1820, 8¼ x 12¼", 6¼" h. (minor damage) 3,960.00

Game box, bone, sliding lid pierced as cribbage board, two-part interior w/33 small bone dominos & five cribbage pins, tooled design highlighted in worn red & black, single dovetailed corners w/pin fasteners, inscribed "John Esmond 1810" on base, 4 5/8" l. (short edge crack at lid) 450.00

Game box, painted & decorated wood, landscape reserve on lid enclosing four similar boxes containing incised square, circular, rectangular & fish-form mother-of-pearl counters, Continental, 19th c., 7¾" l., 6" h. 165.00

Glass box w/lift-off lid, cobalt blue w/gold bands, pink roses & small blue flowers, center decorated w/yellow flowers & leaves, 2½" d., 2½" h. 75.00

Hat box, wallpaper covered, lid covered in chalky white & brown on blue ground & block-printed w/a scene of the paddlewheel steamer "British Queen," base covered in chalky white, brown & black on a blue ground w/"Merchants Exchange, N.Y.," label inside cover "From, S.M. Hurlbert's Pasteboard, Bandbox & Paper Hangings., No. 25 Court Street, Boston," ca. 1842, overall 14¼ x 18½", 12¼" h. (stains & paint wear on lid) 1,045.00

Knife boxes, inlaid mahogany, serpentine slanted crossbanded hinged lid w/bookend inlaid front above conforming case inlaid w/contrasting dark & light pilasters, interior of lid w/inlaid stellate device, inlaid interior pierced for cutlery, possibly American, ca. 1790, 9¼" w., 14½" h., pr. (one w/repair to lid) 4,950.00

Knife boxes, George III, cross-banded mahogany, hinged serpentine-fronted lid opening to fitted interior, mounted w/silver shield-shaped escutcheons, raised on bracket feet, ca. 1790, 14¾" h., pr. 3,300.00

Marquetry box, fruitwood, square hinged lid w/ribbed sloping borders, top inlaid w/various woods forming a design of blossoms, thorny branches, leaves & a butterfly, above straight sides w/a matching border, signed Galle', ca. 1900, w/key, 8¾" sq. 990.00

Painted & decorated box, rectangular w/sliding lid & molded edge opening to compartmented interior, top & sides w/incised compass-drawn & free-hand drawn flowers & stellate devices in tones of red & white on slate blue ground, 8" l., 2½" h. 2,860.00

Painted & decorated box, free-hand decorated lid w/scene of two rabbits eating greens, painted in shades of brown, green & red, top of sides w/gilt flowers & leafage highlighted w/red & green above deep ochre grain-painted base, lined w/exotic paper depicting various quadrupeds, interior w/two paper labels "Rufus Cole, Mayfield, Fulton County," New York, ca. 1830, 9 x 13½", 5¾" h. 8,250.00

Painted & decorated box, poplar, dovetail construction w/original brown sponging & daubs of red in fanciful designs over a light-colored ground, original lock & hasp, 17¾" l. 775.00

Pill box, sterling silver, hinged lid w/repousse & chased florals, attached ring 80.00

Late 18th Century Pipe Box

Pipe box, hanging-type, pine, rounded backboard pierced to hang, over a deep well, base fitted w/a single drawer, New England, late 18th c., 7¾" w., 22" h. (ILLUS.) . . . 385.00

Porcelain box, lid w/white & gold dotted design on medium blue ground centering scene of a young woman seated in a chair, gilt brass fittings, crossed arrow mark, 3" l. 195.00

Salt box, pine, sloping side & incised fitted cover w/turned peg pull, shaped & pierced bracket, painted red w/highlights & floral motifs in red & black, attributed to John Weber, Lancaster County, Pennsylvania, early 19th c., 8" l., 6½" h. 770.00

Salt box, hanging-type, painted & decorated wood, tulip-form backboard over square base, overhanging lid, overall painted leafy sprigs in black & vermilion on deep yellow ochre ground, ca. 1830, 4¾ x 5¼", 7" h. 385.00

Storage box w/fitted lid, painted & decorated bentwood oval, top painted w/two peaches & yellow & red leafage within a yellow dotted grain-painted border, bottom portion w/meandering vine, feathery leaves & yellow berries within red-painted borders, top & sides w/tapered fingers, probably Pennsylvania, ca. 1840, 11" l., 4½" h. 2,200.00

Storage box, pine, wrought-iron hinges & banding, interior of lid & till lid w/original floral rosemaling, traces of old paint exterior, 23½" l. 425.00

Storage box, tin-covered pine, oblong top w/hinged lid opening to well, sides & top covered overall w/punched tin in designs of florals & trees w/birds, each end w/dog & tree design, 18½ x 28¼", 16¾" h. 300.00

Storage box on feet, curly maple & pine, rectangular top w/breadboard ends above conforming dovetailed case on turned bun feet, 14½" l. (age crack, top end damage) 375.00

Trinket box, painted & decorated, rectangular top painted w/a fruit cluster & floral sprigs in green & red within stylized floral spandrels, the front & sides decorated w/an oval sunburst in orange & green, Pennsylvania, second quarter 19th c., 5¼" l., 2½" h. (wear to paint) 220.00

BREWERIANA

Beer is still popular in this country but the number of breweries has greatly diminished. More than 1,900 breweries were in operation in the 1870's but we find fewer than 40 supplying the demands of the country a century later. The small local brewery has either been absorbed by a larger company or forced to close, unable to meet the competition. Advertising items used to promote the various breweries, especially those issued prior to Prohibition, now attract an ever growing number of collectors. The breweriana items listed are a sampling of the many items available. Also see BOTTLES.

Pabst Foam Scraper

Ale can, cone-top, "Fort Schuyler Ale," 12 oz. $50.00

Ale can, flat-top, "Genesee Ale," 12 oz. 6.00

Ale can, cone-top, "Red Top Ale" ... 45.00

Ale can, cone-top, "Utica Club Pale Cream Ale" 55.00

Ashtray, "Lemp Brewery," ceramic, castle decor, round 325.00

Ashtray, "P & H Special, Lebanon Beer," cast iron, Pennsylvania, steelworker pictured 55.00

Banner, "Anheuser-Busch Beer," cloth, 1899, framed, 13 x 15" 185.00

Beaker, "Crystal Springs," stoneware 150.00

Beaker, "Haberle Lager," stoneware 150.00

Beer can, cone-top, "Ballantine Beer," 32 oz. 52.00

Beer cans, flat-top, "Billy Beer," case of 24 unopened 35.00

Beer can, cone-top, "Bohemian Club" 12.00

Beer can, cone-top, "Duquesne" 20.00

Beer can, cone-top, "Goetz" 40.00

Beer can, flat-top, "Horlacher," 12 oz. 8.00

Beer can, flat-top, "Iron City Beer," pictures 1980 Pittsburgh Steelers, unopened 4.50

Beer can, cone-top, "Kopper Kettle" 125.00

Beer can, cone-top, "Pilsner's Brewing Company," 32 oz. 50.00

Beer can, cone-top, "Schlitz," World War II gold can 250.00

Beer glass, "A.B.C. Beer, St. Louis," embossed 90.00

Beer glass, "Albany Brewing Co.," 1905, Lewis-Clark Centennial pictured 55.00

Beer glass, "Anheuser-Busch," embossed 75.00

Beer glass, "Crystal Rock," frosted .. 35.00

Beer glass, "Excelsior," embossed .. 135.00

Beer glass, "Fred Miller Brewing Co., Milwaukee, Wisconsin," etched, bird emblem 95.00

Beer glass, "Foss Schneider," embossed 55.00

Beer glass, "Anton Mayer," embossed 275.00

Beer glass, "Mt. Hood," etched 70.00

Beer glass, "Pacific Beer, Tacoma, Wash.," etched 29.00

Beer glass, "E. Porter, Joliet,," etched 42.00

Blotter, celluloid, "Bergdoll Brewing Co.," 1909 .... 17.50

Book, "Pabst Brewing Co.," souvenir, 1891 .... 30.00

Book, "Recipes of Quality," Indianapolis Brewing Co., 1912 .... 22.50

Bottle opener, "Favorite Beer, Montana," metal, nude woman-shaped 25.00

Bottle opener, "Fehr's," wooden bottle-shaped handle 12.00

Bottle opener, "Grand Prize Beer," wall-type 5.00

Bottle opener, "White Rock," flat-type, kneeling nymph logo 12.00

Bottle opener, model of wooden shoe w/brass knife-type opener 55.00

Calendar, 1905, "Pabst Malt Extract," Oriental scene, yard-long 145.00

Calendar, 1910, "Stegmaier," pictures brewery, depots & Mr. Stegmaier 895.00

Calendar, 1913, "Crockery City Beer," 14 x 20" 345.00

Calendar, 1945, "Rhinelander Beer" 17.50

Ceiling fixture, "Budweiser," carousel-type, lighted, revolving World Champion Clydesdale Team, 1940's 900.00

Clock, electric, "Ballantine," w/pendulum, lights up 35.00

Coaster, "Dinckel Acker Beer," cardboard, Germany 3.50

Coasters, "Griesedieck Bros.," cardboard, set of 12 .... 4.00

Coaster, "Linden Brewery, Long Island, New York," cardboard, factory scene 35.00

Coaster, "Richbrau Beer" 25.00

Corkscrew, "Anheuser-Busch," bottle-shaped, nickel-plated brass w/brass label, 1898, 3" 17.50

Counter display, "Drewry's, South Bend, Ind.," chalkware figure of Canadian Mountie straddling Drewry's beer bottle 25.00

Counter display, "Fox Brewing Co., Grand Rapids, Michigan," chalkware figure of a fox holding a bottle of "Alpine Beer" 50.00

Cue stick, "Budweiser," wood, 2-piece 30.00

Fly swatter, "Schell's Beer," wood & screen 27.00

Foam scraper, "Anheuser-Busch" 35.00

Foam scraper, "Ballentine," white 10.00

Foam scraper, "Pabst Blue Ribbon," celluloid, 1890's (ILLUS.) 22.00

Goblet, "Moerlein's Cincinnati National Lager Beer, Good Luck," glass, 6¼" 45.00

Goblet, "Pfeiffer Weiss Beer," etched glass 125.00

Knife, pocket-type, "Gilt Top Beer, Spokane" 75.00

Lithograph, "Anheuser-Busch," battle scene of "Custer's Last Stand" on canvas, original wood frame 350.00

Lithograph, "East Buffalo," tavern scene, framed, 14 x 23" 365.00

Lithograph, "Kam Schellinger," lion on world, framed, 22 x 34" 495.00

Loving cup, "Lemp Beer," silver plate, donated by Wm. Lemp for Best Bird in St. Louis County Poultry Show, Lemp logo, dated 1916, 9" h. 325.00

Match holder, "American Brewing Co.," salt glazed stoneware, striker on bottom 65.00

Match holder, "Beverwyck Beer," tin, hanging-type 68.00

Anheuser-Busch Match Safe

Match safe, "Anheuser-Busch," silver plate, large "A" w/eagle, ca. 1900, 2¾" l. (ILLUS.) 40.00

Match safe, "Pabst, Milwaukee," brass 34.00

Medallion, "Anheuser-Busch," bronze, eagle on big letter "A", says "Compliments of Budweiser" 15.00

Mug, "Bezirks Turnfest," Dolgeville, New York, stoneware, 1894 .... 135.00

Mug, "Kuntz Bohemian," china w/lithophane bottom 140.00

Mug, "Oertels Real Lager," pottery 10.00
Pilsner glass, "Excelsior Brewing Co., St. Louis, Mo.," embossed 55.00
Pilsner glass, "Piels Bros." 30.00
Plate, "Compliments Drug Brewing Co.," china, brewery & portrait of Fred Drug, 1909, 9½" d. 95.00
Postcard, "Dick's Beer," factory scene 25.00
Puzzle, jigsaw-type, "Pabst Brewery," 1940, "33-1," cardboard 12.00
Salt & pepper shakers, "Fleck's Beer, Faribault, Minnesota," glass, 4" h., pr. 30.00
Shirt, "Primo Beer," Hawaiian-style 8.00
Sign, "Anheuser-Busch," metal, pictures doctor & stork shadow, ca. 1915 .... 85.00
Sign, "Berghoff Beer," self-framed tin, hunting dogs scene, 13 x 21" 85.00
Sign, "Brazil Beer, Indiana," porcelain corner sign, red, white & blue depicting bull fighter in red 565.00
Sign, "Budweiser," lighted, World Champion Clydesdales pictured, needs switch, 24" d. 275.00
Sign, "Eldredge Portsmouth Ale," cardboard stand-up, 11 x 14" 15.00
Sign, "Hoosier Beer," self-framed tin over cardboard, fisherman in boat drinking beer w/dog watching the one that got away 275.00

Fred. Krug Advertising Sign

Sign, "Fred. Krug Brewing Co., Omaha," tin, colored scene of classically draped young woman standing beside shield & pulling back drapery to show distant scene of brewery, marked at bottom, "Nebraska Unveiling Her Finest Brands of Beer," in ornate gilt-plaster Victorian frame (ILLUS.) 925.00
Sign, "Salzburger Beer," metal, lobster, beer & flowers shown, 1900, 24" d. 550.00
Stein, "Globe Brewing Co. - Baltimore, MD," display size, Arrow Beer 95.00
Tap knob, "Dick's Beer" 28.00
Tap knob, "Hamm's," porcelain 20.00
Tap knob, "Michelob," double faced, brass & enamel insert in plastic frame 15.00
Thermometer, "Gibbons Mellor-Pure Beer & Ale," metal, "If It's Gibbons It's Got To Be Good," 12" l. 19.50
Toddy stick, wooden, double ended, turned tapered shaft, ca. 1840, 12" l. 29.00
Trade card, "Rock Island Brewery - Country Time" 25.00
Watch fob, "Anheuser-Busch," red enameling, "A" w/eagle center .. 165.00
Watch fob, "E. Buffalo Brewery Lager Beer" 38.00

BROWNIE COLLECTIBLES

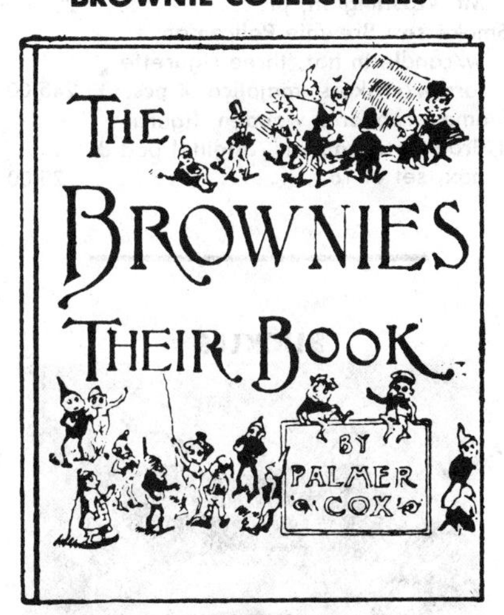

The First Brownies Book

The Brownies were creatures of fantasy created by Palmer Cox, artist-author, in 1887. Early in this century, numerous articles with depictions of or in the shape of Brownies appeared.

Book, "Bomba, The Merry Old King," by Palmer Cox $30.00

Book, "The Brownies Abroad," by Palmer Cox, 1941, 18th printing, w/dust jacket 30.00
Book, "The Brownies & Other Stories," illustrated, published by Donohue Publishing Co. 40.00
Book, "The Brownies - Their Book," by Palmer Cox, first edition, 1887 (ILLUS.) .... 75.00 to 100.00
Book, "The Brownies Through The Union," by Palmer Cox, 1895 .... 62.50
Creamer, china, verse on back, four pipe smoking Brownies on front, 2½" h. 55.00
Game, "Horseshoe" 40.00
Humidor, majolica, head of Brownie Sailor, hat forms cover, French 150.00
Ice cream mold, pewter, figural Brownie 185.00
Plate, china, group of colorful Brownies (7) sitting on log smoking, white ground, late 19th c., 8" oval 85.00
Puzzles, jigsawed Brownies: Uncle Sam, Chinaman, Canadian, Irishman, Indian, Soldier, Highlander, Sailor & Policeman; lithographed paper on wood, copyright 1892 by Palmer Cox, one stand, 12" h., set of 9 (Highlander damaged at base) 440.00
Salt & pepper shakers w/original tops, glass, w/Brownie Sailor on one & Brownie Indian on other, Mt. Washington, pr. 235.00
Smoke set: Brownie Policeman w/candle in hat, three cigarette jars w/strikers; majolica, 4 pcs. 245.00
Stamps, rubber & wooden, figural Brownie & animals, original pad & box, set of 16 .... 25.00

BUCKLES

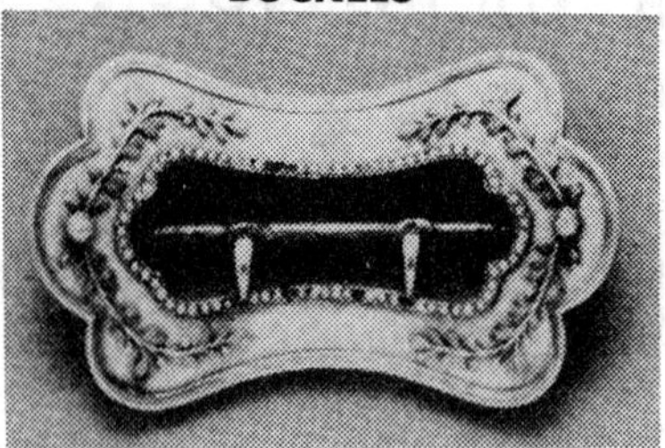

Faberge Belt Buckle

When it was the height of popularity between 1650 and 1800, the lowly buckle was considered a fashionable status symbol denoting the wearer's wealth by the material from which it was made. Gold, silver, pewter, iron and tin buckles were made in a variety of forms. Though buckle collectors strive to acquire at least a few 18th century examples, they also seek out later buckles in desirable forms that are more affordable. Listed by type as well as material, the following buckles sold within recent months.

Belt buckle, lady's, two-part, heart-shaped, champleve, light blue w/dainty flowers $95.00
Belt buckle, lady's, two-part, cloisonne, silver to lavender ground w/pale pink irises, green leaves & blue clouds, 1½ x 1¾" 114.00
Belt buckle, lady's, 14k gold surrounded w/tiny seed pearls, ¾" h. 65.00
Belt buckles, lady's, gold, enamel & diamond, Art Nouveau style, each in the form of a flowering plant & set w/diamonds, one w/tendrils enameled translucent pink over a "guilloche" ground & mounted w/faceted green beryl center, the other w/tendrils enameled translucent apple green over a "guilloche" ground & mounted w/faceted pink quartz center, maker's mark "S.S.," St. Petersburg, Russia, ca. 1900, 3" h., pr. 5,225.00
Belt buckle, lady's, nephrite, Phoenix head terminal, shaft carved in low relief w/an animal design, light brown mottling, 4" l. 330.00
Belt buckle, lady's, nephrite, oblong w/circular hollow at center flanked by pierced dragons, 19th c., 4½" l. 192.50
Belt buckle, lady's, pewter, Art Nouveau butterfly design, ca. 1890 .... 20.00
Belt buckle, lady's, Satsuma, intricate design of butterflies, silver back 50.00
Belt buckle, lady's, silver, gold, enamel & jewels, shaped rectangular form enameled translucent sky blue over a "guilloche" ground & applied w/sprays of berried foliage, each spray set w/a brilliant, inner opening w/a border of seed pearls, workmaster's initials & "Faberge" in Cyrillac, St. Petersburg, Russia, ca. 1900, 2 5/8" l. (ILLUS.) 3,080.00
Belt buckle, man's, sterling silver, horseshoe & cowboy design 35.00
Shoe buckle, butterfly in center set w/rhinestones, marked "Reyco" 15.00
Shoe buckles, cut-steel, rhinestone-studded, in original (worn) leatherized cardboard case, pr. 30.00

BUSTER BROWN

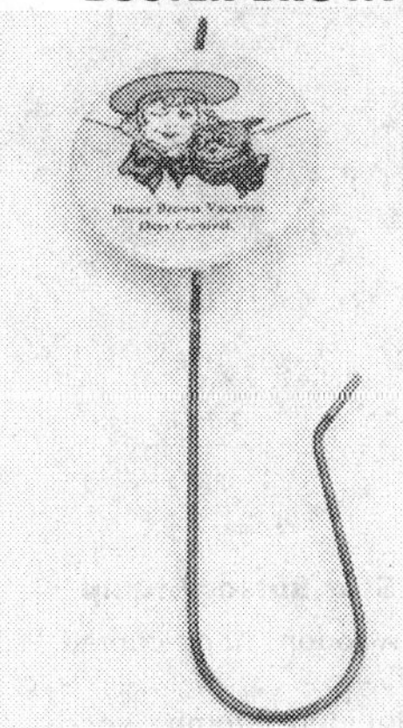

Buster Brown Billhook

Buster Brown was a comic strip created by Richard Outcault in the New York Herald in 1902. It was subsequently syndicated and numerous objects depicting Buster (and often his dog, Tige) were produced.

Billhook, multicolor button w/wire hook, copyright 1946, 2¼" d. button, 6½" l. hook (ILLUS.) $25.00
Blotter 15.00
Book, "Buster Brown Dictionary," Buster & Tige on cover, copyright 1923 .... 15.00
Book, "Buster Brown on His Travels," Cupples & Leon, 1909 .... 50.00
Book, "My Resolutions," 1901, hardbound, small 30.00
Breakfast set: 4½" d. bowl & 6½" d. plate; china, Buster Brown & Tige, pr. 60.00
Camera, No. 3, 1919, w/original instructions 75.00
Cartoon book, "Buster Brown & Company," by Richard Outcault, 1905 .... 250.00
Cereal dish, aluminum, w/advertising 39.00
Clock, wall-type, lighted face, colorful picture of Buster & Tige, "Buster Brown America's Favorite Children's Shoes," 1950's, 15" d. .. 585.00
Coloring book, "Buster & Tige Circus," ca. 1940 .... 8.00
Fan, Buster Brown & Tige pictured, framed 75.00
Figure, cast iron, Buster Brown in cart pulled by dog, 1900 .... 363.00
Game, "Buster Brown & Tige Beebe" 9.00
Knife-bottle opener combination, advertising "Buster Brown Shoes," w/Buster Brown & Tige 125.00
Magazine page, "Saturday Evening Post," advertising featuring Buster Brown & Tige, ca. 1920, framed .. 20.00
Photograph, Buster Brown & Tige standing before crowd in front of drug store, "The Only Original Buster Brown!" lettering, 1910, 16 x 10" framed 100.00
Pinback button, advertising "Buster Brown Walking Club," 1½" oval .. 20.00
Pinback button, tin, advertising "Buster Brown Shoes" 12.50
Postcard, Buster & Tige, Mason City, Ill., 1908 .... 10.00
Puzzle, wooden, 1910 .... 20.00
Shoe tree, figural Buster Brown, 1950's 15.00
String holder, counter top model, cast iron base w/die-cut figure of Buster Brown & 2 of Tige, w/tin windmill at top, 15" h. 550.00
Valentine, Raphael Tuck, 1903 ...... 18.00

BUTTER MOLDS & STAMPS

Flowers & Leaves Butter Mold

While they are sometimes found made of other materials, it is primarily the two-piece wooden butter mold and one-piece butter stamp that attracts collectors. The molds are found in two basic styles, rounded cup form and rectangular box form. Butter stamps are usually round with a protruding knob handle on the back. Many are factory made items with the print design made by forcing a metal die into the wood under great pressure, while others have the design chiseled out by hand.

Acorn mold w/two leaves, wooden, hand-carved, 1½" d. $55.00
Cow mold, wooden, hand-carved, 4¼" d. 75.00
Cow stamp, cherry, hand-carved, 1-piece w/knob handle, 18th c., 4½" d. 385.00
Cow & tree stamp, wooden, hand-carved, 1-piece w/turned wood handle, 4 3/8" d. 155.00

Daisy & leaf mold, wooden, hand-carved, 3-ribbed border, 3½" d. . . 65.00

Eagle & shield "lollipop" double-sided stamp, wooden, relief-carved eagle & shield on one side, star flower on reverse, 4¾" d., 9" l. 575.00

Eagle & star stamp, wooden, hand-carved, w/turned wood handle, 2¾" d. 140.00

Fern leaf stamp, wooden, hand-carved, knob handle, 19th c., round 39.00

Fleur de lis mold, glass, wood handle 45.00

Flower stamp, wooden, deeply hand-carved stylized blossom & foliage, chip-carved edge, 4¼" d. 185.00

Flower & foliage stamp, unglazed redware, reverse w/clear glaze w/brown splotches, handle & tooled lines, 4" d. 800.00

Flowers & leaves mold, wooden, 4-section hand-carved face in square frame w/brass hooks, 5½" sq., 2½" h. (ILLUS.) 78.00

Heart & florals stamp, wooden, hand-carved, almond-shaped, chip-carved edge, back branded "1822," 9 x 3¾" 435.00

Leaf stamp, wooden, hand-carved overall stylized leaf design, 4 7/8" d. (handle missing) 75.00

Musk melon mold, wooden, hand-carved, round, ca. 1830, ½ lb. . . . 65.00

Pineapple mold, wooden, ca. 1866, 1 lb. 70.00

Pineapple stamp, wooden, hand-carved diamond-hatched leaves & fruit, rope-carved edge, 1-piece w/turned wood handle, 4" d. 180.00

Pinwheel "lollipop" stamp, wooden, hand-carved, 7¼" l. 550.00

Pomegranate stamp, wooden, hand-carved, chip-carved edge, w/turned wood handle, 4" d. 165.00

Rose mold, wooden, hand-carved rose blossom, bud & leaves, 4" d. 95.00

Sheaf of wheat stamp, w/"J.C. & J.P. Sharpless" around lower edge, wooden, hand-carved, 1-piece w/turned wood handle, 3 3/8" d. 195.00

Sheaf of wheat half-circle stamp (made to stamp half the top of butter crock), wooden, hand-carved, 3¼ x 6¼" (worn) 130.00

Sheaf of wheat "lollipop" stamp w/starflower design reverse, wooden, hand-carved, 7½" l. (edge wear) 525.00

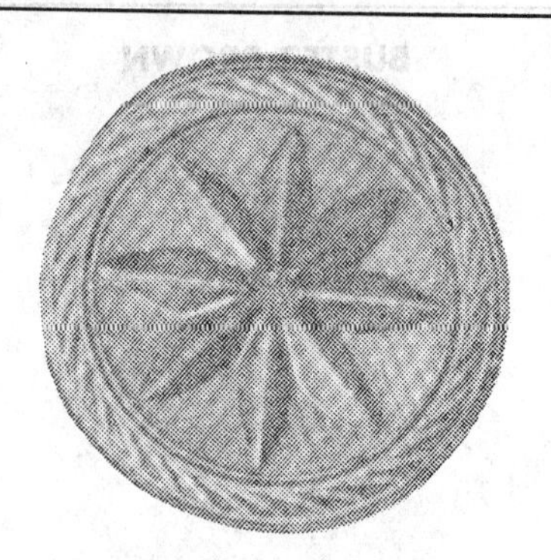

Star Butter Stamp

Star stamp, wooden, hand-carved, 4" d. (ILLUS.) 125.00

Starflower "lollipop" stamp, wooden, hand-carved design on both sides, 9" l. 375.00

Starflower stamp, wooden, deeply carved six-petal starflower w/small stars between each petal, 1-piece w/large turned handle, worn, scrubbed finish, 5" d. 325.00

Sunflower & leaves stamp, birch, hand-carved w/hand hewn handle, 18th c., 3½" d. 120.00

Tulip stamp, wooden, deeply carved tulip & two stars, 1-piece, large turned handle, 4¼" d. 300.00

CALENDAR PLATES

1912 Owl on Book Calendar Plate

Calendar plates have been produced in this country since the turn of the century, primarily of porcelain and earthenwares but also of glass and tin. They were made earlier in England. The majority were issued after 1909, largely intended as advertising items.

1904, holly & berries decoration $22.00
1908, "Santa Monica," w/advertising 35.00
1909, bird holding ribbon in beak w/"1909," calendar months border, Connecticut advertising 55.00
1909, bunches of violets center, w/advertising, 6¼" d. 55.00
1909, Gibson Girl center, Peterson, Iowa advertising 16.00
1909, "Nowlin Drug Co., R. Tester, Prop., Nowlin, South Dakota" advertising 24.00
1909, woman driving car center, calendar months border 35.00
1910, bust of Gibson-type girl center, calendar months, fruit & floral border 20.00
1910, cupids ringing bell center, calendar months border, souvenir of Wausau, Wisconsin 28.00
1910, holly design, "C.A. Joy & Co., Midland, South Dakota" advertising 24.00
1910, roses center, calendar months border 15.00
1910, "Use Mother's Pride Products" advertising 35.00
1911, "Bosco's Cash Grocery & Market - Jacksonville, Fla." advertising 45.00
1911, cupids & roses border, Stamford, Nebraska advertising, 9" d. 22.00
1912, girl sailor & American flag center 24.00
1912, owl perched atop book center, calendar months border w/gold trim, 7½" d. (ILLUS.) 25.00
1912, sunset scene center, "H.C. Ruden Gen. Merchandise, Nowlin, South Dakota" advertising 20.00
1914, woman on horse center, Kansas advertising 18.00
1915, Panama Pacific Exposition souvenir 20.00
1917, battleship scene center, w/advertising 37.50
1918, clock decor center 22.00
1919, "Victory of Allies," World War I, Michigan advertising, 8" d. 17.00

CANDLESTICKS & CANDLEHOLDERS

Candelabrum, clear glass, Cambridge "Caprice" patt., two arms, three sockets $150.00

Candelabrum, gilt-bronze, 7-light, central raised holder flanked by six matching holders w/detachable bobeches, Tiffany Studios, New York, 14" h. 1,430.00

Candleholder, brass, chamberstick-type, saucer base w/ring handle w/thumbrest, 4 x 6" 130.00

Candleholder, wrought iron, miner's "sticking Tommy" type, 10½" l. 70.00

Candlestick, blown glass, hollow socket w/flared rim atop ring & column base w/applied foot, 19th c., 8¾" h. 260.00

Candlestick, brass, "capstan," bell-form base, mid-stem drip pan, plain candle socket, burnished, 5" h. 390.00

Candlestick, brass, simple Neoclassical design, rounded, tapered base w/columnar body & flared lip, w/push-up, 6¾" h. 85.00

Candlestick, bronze, disc foot, slender stem, onion-shaped socket, flat bobeche, Jarvie, Chicago, Illinois, ca. 1910, 12½" h. 1,210.00

Candlestick, bronze, floral form w/green patina, 7¾" h. 412.00

Candlestick, iron, "hogscraper" w/pushup, lip hanger, brass "wedding band," 6¼" h. (base w/rust damage & edge cracks) 155.00

Candlestick, iron, "hogscraper" w/iron ring, pushup & hanging lip, pushup marked "Shaw," 6 5/8" h. 275.00

Candlestick, iron, spiral, in turned wood base, w/hanging tab & lift 230.00

Candlestick, oak, adjustable, of triangular section, three sides pierced & carved, top & triangular reflector w/copper sheathing, by Charles Rohlfs, 1901, 25½" h. 3,520.00

Alabaster Candlesticks

Candlesticks, alabaster, round stepped base, columnar stem supporting baluster-turned socket above graduated drip pan, possibly Russian, 19th c., 18" h., pr. (ILLUS.) 880.00

Candlesticks, brass, domed circular foot, ball baluster, circular drip pan, cylindrical candlecup above ball-turned baluster, Dutch, late 17th c., 7" h., pr. (now fitted for electricity) 825.00

Candlesticks, brass, scalloped base, baluster stem, lobed bobeche, George III, 3rd quarter 18th c., 7½" h., pr. (solder repair to stem) 880.00

Regency Candlesticks

Candlesticks, brass, round domed base, turned columnar stem w/flared socket, Regency period, England, ca. 1820, 8¼" h., pr. (ILLUS.) 225.00

Candlesticks, brass, domed & stepped base, baluster- and ring-turned stem, removable bobeche, 19th c., 9" h., pr. 240.00

Candlesticks, brass, lobed circular base, trumpet turned stem, cylindrical candlecup, lobed bobeche, George III, 3rd quarter 18th c., 9½" h., pr. 1,320.00

Candlesticks, brass, beehive & diamond quilted stem, w/pushups, impressed "England" w/registry mark & "S.A. & Co. Jeruselem," Victorian, 10¾" h., pr. 170.00

Candlesticks, brass, domed & stepped base, beehive & diamond quilted stem, w/push-up, marked "England" w/registry mark, Victorian, 11¾" h., pr. 250.00

Candlesticks, coin silver, circular bobeche & tapered fluted body on square flared plate w/beaded decoration, Cabot monogram, Boston, Mass., by H.B. Stanwood, ca. 1850, 10¼" h., pr. 1,430.00

Candlesticks, French faience, modeled as a playful lion w/large eyes & a long curly mane, resting on his haunches & grasping w/one paw a spiral-molded columnar standard terminating in a pierced candle cup, on molded oval base, mustard & blue, 9 3/8" h., pr. (one base restored, chips to glaze) 3,025.00

Candlesticks, clear glass, pressed hexagonal base, wafer-connected to blown stem & hollow socket, pewter insert, 8¼" h., pr. 800.00

Candlesticks, flint glass, canary, square, stepped base, columnar ribbed stem w/petal socket, 9 3/8" h., pr. 400.00

CANDY CONTAINERS (Glass)

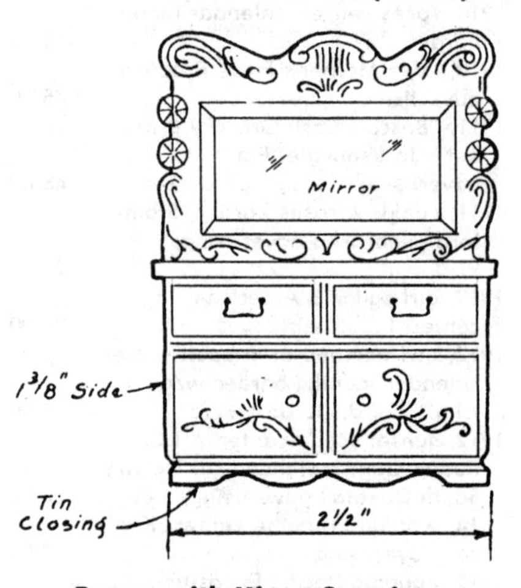

Bureau with Mirror Container

**Indicates the container might not have held candy originally. +Indicates this container might also be found as a reproduction. ‡Indicates this container was also made as a bank. All containers are clear glass unless otherwise indicated. Any candy container that retains the original paint is very desirable and readers should follow descriptions carefully realizing that an identical candy container that lacks the original paint will be less valuable.*

Airplane - "Army Bomber 15-P-7," J.H. Millstein, 1940's, 4 1/8" l. (no closure) $22.00

Airplane - "Spirit of Goodwill," "Victory" under wing, no paint & no closure 77.00

Automobile - streamlined touring car, w/screw-on cap closure, 3 7/8" l. 25.00
Automobile - "Westmoreland Specialty Co. Limousine," w/tin wheel, w/tin closure on top, 4" l. 150.00
Automobile - limousine w/rear trunk & tire, marked "V.G. Co., etc.," original paint, w/tin closure on top, ca. 1930, 4 13/16" l. 120.00
+Automobile - "Station Wagon," w/cardboard closure, 4 7/8" l. 45.00
Baby Chick - standing, painted yellow, w/tin closure, no markings, ca. 1930, 3 3/8"h. 90.00
‡Barney Google beside bank, painted figure, 3 1/16" h. 375.00
Barney Google & Ball - painted, 3¾" h. 195.00
*Bell - "1776 Liberty," blue, 4" base, 4 1/8" h. 75.00
Boat - model cruiser, no cardboard closure, 4½" l. 22.00
Boat - battleship on waves, w/tin closure, Cambridge Glass Co., ca. 1916, 5¼" l. 95.00
*Boat - "Remember the Maine," 2-piece dish container, 7¼" l. 40.00
Boot - Santa Claus, original label, 3¼" h. 22.00
Bureau - w/real mirror above, original paint, w/tin closure, ca. 1913, 3 7/8" h. (ILLUS.) 150.00
Bus - marked "Jitney Bus" on tin top unit on glass body, marked "West Bros. Co., etc." on glass body, ca. 1912, 4¼" l. 275.00
Charlie Chaplin beside barrel - figure beside barrel marked "Geo. Borgfeldt & Co." on base & w/tin closure on barrel slotted for use as bank, ca. 1915, 3 7/8" h. figure w/some paint 120.00
Chicken in "Shell" Auto - some paint on chick & shell, marked "V.G." & "U.S.A.," w/tin closure, 1920's, 4¼" l. 200.00
Chicken on Oblong Basket - painted, w/closure, 3" h. 65.00
"Chicken on the Nest" - marked on cardboard closure, J.H. Millstein, 4 5/8" h. 33.00
Clock - round-top shelf model, milk white glass, no paint, 2½ x 1¾" base, 3¼" h. 108.00
Clock - mantel-type, painted decor, paper dial inside, tin closure on top, 2 7/8" w., 3¾" h. 108.00
Clock - shelf model w/octagon-top case, original paper dial inside face, some painted decoration, tin cap closure behind clock face, slotted for use as bank, early 1900's, 3 7/8" h. 150.00
Dirigible - "Los Angeles" embossed each side, "V.G. Co.," aluminum screw cap closure, 1¾" h., 5¾" l. 150.00
Dog - "Scotty Dog," cardboard closure, head up, 3¼" h. 28.00
Dog - Bulldog on round base, no paint, w/closure, 4¼" h. 44.00
+Fire engine - miniature w/solid glass boiler & hose roll on back, 5" l. 20.00
Gun - "Stough, 1939, Pat. Pending," muzzle end closure (red tin cap), 4 1/8" l., 2 1/8" h. 21.00
*Gun - small revolver, No. 1, 4¾" l. 25.00
Gun - plastic automatic pistol w/glass insert in grip, marked J.H. Millstein Co., 5 5/8" l. 25.00
Nursing Bottle - marked "Baby Dear," w/nipple, ca. 1930, 2¼" h. 29.50
Opera Glasses - plain panels, milk white, painted decoration, w/screw-on cap closures on large ends, ca. 1908, 2 7/8" h. 135.00
Owl - traces of paint, unmarked, w/tin cap closure, 1920's 70.00
Phonograph - w/tin horn & tin record, w/inkwell-type depression, tin closure on base, 2 7/8" w., 4 5/8" to top of tin horn 220.00
Pipe - with ornate bowl, swirl stem at base, 4¼" h. 50.00
Powder Horn - w/hanger & metal closure, 8¾" l. 46.00
Rabbit - w/basket on arm, painted w/closure, Victory Glass Co., 4½" h. 98.00
Rabbit in Egg Shell - gilt-painted rabbit, marked "V.G., etc.," w/metal screw-on cap closure, 1920's, 5 1/8" h. 95.00
Rabbit Eating Carrot, ca. 1947, 4 3/8" h. (no closure) 35.00
Rabbit on Base - sitting w/laid-back ears, heavy glass, w/tin closure, no paint, early 1900's, 4½" h. 75.00
Rabbit - "Peter Rabbit," by Millstein, 6¼" h. 32.00
Rolling pin - glass center, metal cap ends w/turned wood handles, marked "V.G. Co. Jnet Pa ¾ oz," 7" l. 175.00
Santa Claus - with double cuffs, some paint, w/closure, ca. 1927, 4 3/8" h. 95.00
Santa Claus with Plastic Head - marked "J.H. Millstein Co.," etc. inside plastic head, parts of Santa

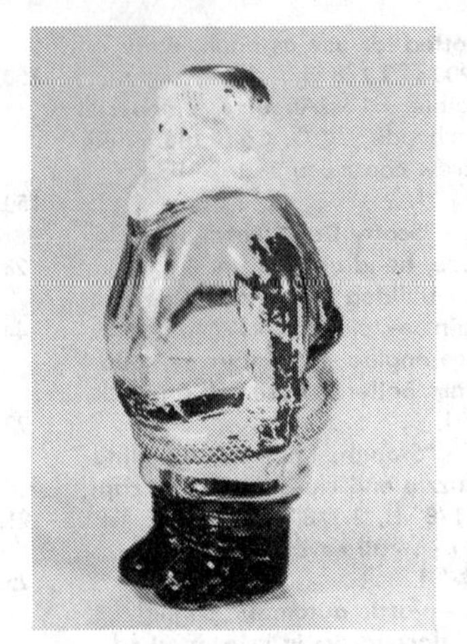

Santa Claus Candy Container
airbrush-painted, 1940's, 5 5/8" h. (ILLUS.) 78.00

Spark Plug Container

"Spark Plug" - marked on side of horse wrapped in blanket, painted, marked "King Features Syndicate, Inc." on base, w/tin closure, 1923, 3" h. (ILLUS.) 136.00

Suitcase - clear, 3 5/8" l., 2½" h. (no closure) 30.00

Suitcase - milk white glass, decal-type "Roosevelt Bears," w/tin slide closure, ca. 1908, 2½" h. . . . 150.00

Tank - World War I, some paint, w/closure, 4 5/16" l. 110.00

Tank - w/man in turret, 1942, 4¼" l. 32.00

Tank with Two Cannons - some parts painted, marked "Victory Glass Inc." on cardboard closure, 1940's, 4¼" l. 30.00

Tank (miniature) - marked "U.S. Army," T.H. Stough Co., 3 1/8" l. 24.00

Telephone - candlestick-type, tall musical toy, w/wooden receiver, ca. 1950, 4¼" h. 25.00

Telephone - "West Bro's Co., 1907," pewter mouthpiece & wooden receiver, 4¼" h. 85.00

Telephone - candlestick-type w/flat-topped hinge, wooden receiver & attached cord, marked "V.G. Co.," w/tin closure, all original, 1920's, 4 3/8" h. 52.00

Telephone - "Victory Glass Co., Dial Type," wire hanger & wooden receiver, ca. 1944, 4 7/8" h. 35.00

Wheelbarrow - w/tin closure over top, 6" l. 62.00

Windmill - Dutch-type, heavy six-sided tower w/tin arms, cardboard closure marked "Pla-Toy Co.," 1940's, 4 7/8" h. 60.00

CANES & WALKING STICKS

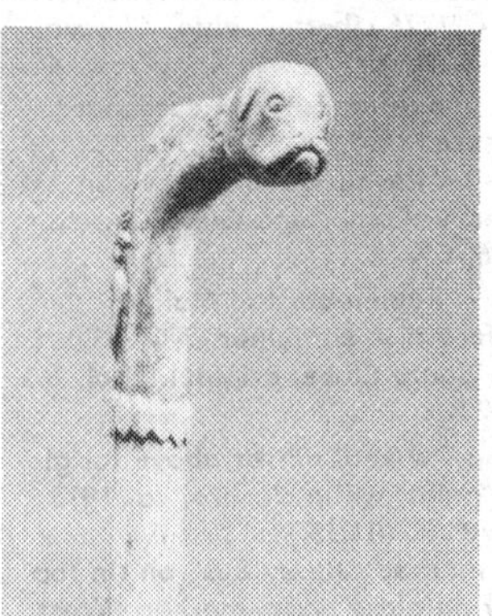

Wooden Dog Head Walking Stick

Canes have been used for thousands of years and probably collected for hundreds of years. Seventeenth and eighteenth century court "dandies" often owned numerous canes, coordinating their use to various costumes and occasions. Today's collector looks for canes made of unique materials in a unique form. Gadget canes, such as those that convert into a weapon or conceal a whiskey flask in the handle, are probably the most elusive type for the collector to acquire.

Antler-handled walking stick, sterling silver trim, dated 1900 . . . . . . $25.00

Bamboo walking stick, pewter knob handle w/hunting dog wearing cap decor 75.00

Glass cane, aqua, 36" l. 45.00

Glass cane, clear w/interior red & white swirled ribbons, 36" l. 175.00

Glass walking stick, bulb head, spatter design in dark red, white & yellow in "barber-pole" swirl, Corning, New York, 1908, 57" l. . . . 225.00

Gold-handled walking stick, gold-filled 1½" d. knob w/ferrule tapering to fit ebony shaft, knob engraved, "17th May, 1879, Albert Lea, Erik L. Peterson," silver tip, 34" l. 160.00

Ivory-handled cane, carved Greyhound dog head handle w/glass eyes & silver band collar 485.00

Pewter-handled walking stick w/2" pewter bee in relief & 1½" pewter band w/raised honey bee, hawthorne wood shaft, 36" l. 65.00

Sword cane w/snap lock, wooden w/brass & ivory decor, 20" l. blade, overall 36" l. 45.00

Sword walking stick, bone handle carved as lion head, sword blade marked "India," 35¾" l. 65.00

Telescope cane, ivory knob surrounding brass telescope forms handle, wood shaft 850.00

Wooden cane, pipe-form handle carved w/alligator decor, plain shaft, 31" l. 50.00

Wooden cane, relief-carved design w/snakes, Indians, eagle & other devices, worn polychrome paint, 35" l. (age cracks) 40.00

Wooden cane, carved snake handle 125.00

Wooden walking stick, shaft w/natural growth carved as black boy w/hatchet & alligator, 14" l. (shaft broken) 50.00

Wooden walking stick, turned ball-shaped knob, shaft carved w/two entwining snakes, worn old brown & green paint, 30½" l. 25.00

Wooden walking stick, curly maple, bone handle w/engraved steel medallion inscribed "S.P. 1835," 34½" l. 65.00

Wooden walking stick, curved carved handle w/figure of strutting rooster, handle terminus carved in form of dog's head w/floppy ears & sawtooth collar, Simmons', probably Pennsylvania, 19th c., 37½" l. (ILLUS.) 1,320.00

CANS & CONTAINERS

The collecting of tin containers has become quite popular within the past several years. Air-tight tins were at first produced by hand to keep foods fresh, and after the invention of the tin-printing machine in the 1870's, containers were manufactured in a wide variety of shapes and sizes with colorful designs.

Anti-Freeze, Quaker Brand 5-gal. can, dated 1935 .... $35.00

Axle grease, Monarch pail, eagles 20.00

Axle grease, Sambo 5-lb. tin, Negro boy 40.00

Baking powder, Calumet 6-oz. can, Indian 10.00

Baking powder, Clabber Girl 2-lb. can, family scene 8.00

Baking powder, Rumford 1-lb. 8-oz. can 13.50

Biscuit, Huntley & Palmers Chinese teak jewelry case w/relief dragon on lid 70.00

Biscuit, Huntley & Palmers Christmas "Literature" books, bound in leather strap, 1901 .... 450.00

Biscuit, Huntley & Palmers "Library" books ("History of Reading, etc."), 1900, 4¾" l., 6¼" h. 135.00

Biscuit, Huntley & Palmers "Paris Exposition," golf scene on lid, various sports on box 75.00

Biscuit, Huntley & Palmers, Queen Elizabeth II & Prince Phillip 25.00

Biscuit, Huntley & Palmers "Toby Jug," 1911, 6½" h. 165.00

Biscuit, Iten Biscuit Co., Omaha, lunch pail, animal cookie decor 88.50

Biscuit, Krispy Crackers Sunshine lift top tin, blue lettering on yellow ground, 9 x 8½", 7" h. 32.50

Biscuit, Laurel Biscuit Co. can, blue & yellow, 11" 32.00

"Hiawatha's Wedding Journey" Box

Biscuit, Loose-Wiles "Hiawatha's Wedding Journey" 2-lb. 8-oz. box **w/bail handle, Hiawatha & Indian maiden by waterfall, w/poem (ILLUS.)** 160.00

Biscuit, Sunshine tin, "America Beautiful," octagonal 18.00

Biscuit, Sunshine tin, colorful picture of U.S. Capitol building, 12½ x 10¾" 20.00

Biscuit, United Biscuit Co. container, "Ye Christmas Feast," 10" d. 30.00

Bluing, Zanzibar 275.00

Candy, Artstyle 2-lb. tin, butterflies on yellow 15.00

Candy, Dilling 15-lb. round tin, yellow 28.00

Candy, Jackie Coogan pail, red 175.00

Candy, King Kup Candies sand pail w/tin shovel, multicolored frog & duck cartoon decor 25.00

Candy, King Leo Stick Candy 2-lb. can, lion standing on striped candy sticks 12.75

Candy, Little Red Riding Hood pail, Lovell & Covel 100.00

Candy, Peter Rabbit pail, Lovell & Covel 125.00

Candy, Plantation 10-lb. tin 15.00

Candy, Reed's Butterscotch Patties 5-lb. can, orange, red & gold lettering, round 28.00

Candy, Smiling Boy Toffee tin 20.00

Candy, Teenie Weenie Toffee tin ... 65.00

Candy, Three Bears can 40.00

Candy, Whitman "Salamagundi" 1-lb. box 16.00

Candy, Y & S Licorice Wafers tin w/hinged lid, "Enjoyed by Smokers" 10.00

Chocolate, Koko tin, Uncle Sam pictured 125.00

Chocolates, Mrs. Stevens 2-lb. box, floral 7.00

Cigarettes, Blue Navy Cut tin 15.50

Cigarettes, Cavalier one hundreds, oval, 4 x 3" 9.00

Cigarettes, Chesterfield flat fifties .. 8.50

Cigarettes, Lord Salisbury Turkish flat one hundreds 19.00

Cigarettes, Lucky Strike round one hundreds, green 27.00

Cigarettes, Player's Navy Cut flat fifties 13.00

Cigarettes, Sweet Corporal flat fifties 13.00

Alles & Fisher's Cigar Box

Cigars, Alles & Fisher's box, 5½" l., 2¾" h. (ILLUS.) 30.00

Cigars, Between the Acts box, 3¼ x 3" 8.00

Cigars, Bold container 40.00

Cigars, Bridgman's Hand Made 5c canister, red & gold, 4¼" sq., 5" h. (ILLUS.) 32.00

Cigars, Buckeye container, beaver & roses 32.00

Cigars, Camel canister, oval 125.00

Bridgman's Cigar Canister

Cigars, Court Royal container 50.00

Cigars, Cuban Daisy container, beautiful girl, 1898 .... 85.00

Cigars, R.G. Dun container 15.00

Cigars, Hauptmann's Panetela flat box 20.00

Cigars, Havanna Cadet container 65.00

Cigars, In-B-Tween box, black & gold 25.00

Cigars, John Ruskin container 85.00

Cigars, Kilbow's Panatela 3 for 5c container, w/lithograph 24.00

Cigars, La Costa container 75.00

Cigars, La Nora container 125.00

Cigars, McBlue "Sunset Trail" container 235.00

Cigars, Our Business Reputation container, oval 75.00

Cigars, Outlook container 40.00

Cigars, Popper's Ace Cigars canister, oval, biplane pictured, 5 x 3" 225.00

Cigars, Portage container 35.00

Cigars, Round Trip horizontal box ... 80.00

Cigars, Simon's Roosevelt Cigars horizontal box, Teddy Roosevelt decor, 4 x 3 x 1" 30.00

Cigars, Tennyson container 50.00

Cigars, T & B container, red & black 18.00

Cigars, Two Orphans canister, Victorian girls, 1909 .... 125.00

Cleanser, Bon Ami sample tin, chick & lady washing windows decoration, unopened, 2½" 18.00

Cleanser, Watch Dog 14-oz. can 6.50

Cocoa, Apex ½-lb. tin 10.00

Cocoa, Armour's Veribest 5-lb. tin .. 20.00

Cocoa, Baker's sample size, round ....75.00 to 95.00

Cocoa, Baker's ½-lb. tin 15.00

Cocoa, Droste's square 8-oz. container, Dutch boy & girl ....15.00 to 18.00

Cocoa, Droste's 1-lb. square tin, Dutch girl & boy decoration (ILLUS.) 20.00

Cocoa, Hasty Lunch tin, cup of cocoa decoration in blue & gold, dated 1923 .... 20.00

Droste's Cocoa Tin

Cocoa, Justice tin, William Baker, Syracuse, N.Y., Miss Liberty on tin, 4" 24.00
Cocoa, McNess sample size 25.00

Monarch Cocoa Tin

Cocoa, Monarch square tin, blue ground, round medallion in center w/lion's head, 6" h. (ILLUS.) 20.00
Cocoa, Montclair Breakfast Brand 5-lb. tin, Sears, Roebuck & Co. 30.00
Cocoa, National container, capitol dome pictured, ca. 1925 .... 85.00
Cocoa, Rawleigh's Good Health 1-lb. can, lithographed scene 15.00
Cocoa, Runkles sample size can 55.00
Coconut, Snowdrift tin, 12" d., 15" h. 10.00
Coffee, Acme 1-lb. canister, good colors 33.00
Coffee, After Glow 5-lb. pail w/bail handle, Marshalltown, Iowa 35.00
Coffee, American Ace tin, pilot decoration 75.00
Coffee, Aristocrat 3-lb. tin 45.00
Coffee, Astor House 1-lb. tin, blue printing on cream ground, "Astor House, Abbott Groc. Co., Keene, N.H. & Athol, Mass." 33.00
Coffee, Beech-Nut trial size container 25.00
Coffee, Beverly Club Steel Cut 1-lb. can 10.00
Coffee, Big Horn 1-lb. can 25.00
Coffee, Blackhawk 5-lb. pail 110.00
Coffee, Blanke's Mojav 2-lb. square container w/round lid, lady riding sidesaddle, salmon & brown 165.00
Coffee, Bluehill 5-lb. pail w/bail handle, blue & white decoration 40.00
Coffee, Bluehill 10-lb. tin 52.00
Coffee, Bokar ½-lb. can 7.00
Coffee, Boston Roasted 1-lb. tin, rectangular 35.00
Coffee, Bouquet 1-lb. can 29.00
Coffee, Breakfast Call 1-lb. can 40.00
Coffee, Breakfast Call 3-lb. tin, woman ringing bell lithographed decoration 50.00
Coffee, Brownie Blended Coffee tin 51.00
Coffee, Butter Nut 1-lb. can, key lid 22.00
Coffee, Butter Nut 2-lb. can 18.00
Coffee, Campbell 4-lb. container, camels pictured, yellow & red 45.00
Coffee, Campbell 5-lb. pail 70.00
Coffee, Caswells tin 32.00
Coffee, Chase & Sanborn 1-lb. can, paper label 50.00
Coffee, Chase & Sanborn 5-lb. pail w/bail handle, blue & white decoration 57.50
Coffee, Chase & Sanborn Butterfly brand 5-lb. pail 150.00
Coffee, Cherry Blossom 1-lb. can 45.00
Coffee, Chocolate Cream 3-lb. container 52.50
Coffee, Chocolate Cream 6-lb. pail 90.00
Coffee, Clark & Host 3-lb. tin, pry-up lid, good lithograph 36.00
Coffee, Conrad's Eagle container 12.00
Coffee, Country Club 1-lb. container, 4 x 6" 48.00
Coffee, Dainty bin 35.00
Coffee, Del Monte 1-lb. tin 13.00
Coffee, Eagle 1-lb. tin 75.00
Coffee, Edward's Dependable 2-lb. can, 1931 .... 12.00
Coffee, El Capitan 1-lb. container 55.00
Coffee, Eureka 1-lb. container 29.00
Coffee, Fararo 1-lb. container 50.00
Coffee, Farrington Castle Brand 3-lb. tin w/handle, paper label, full, 6¼ x 8" 70.00
Coffee, Flaroma 1-lb. tin, screw-on lid 20.00
Coffee, Folger's Steel Cut 1-lb. can 25.00

Coffee, Folger's 5-lb. container, ship decoration . . . 75.00
Coffee, Ft. Bedford Instant Coffee 6 oz. tin . . . 8.00
Coffee, Franco-American 1-lb. tin . . . 85.00
Coffee, French Opera pail . . . 55.00
Coffee, Freshpak 1-lb. can . . . 30.00
Coffee, G. Washington's Instant Coffee 2-oz. tin . . . 11.00
Coffee, Giant 5-lb. tin . . . 95.00
Coffee, Gillies square canister, yellow & gold, 6 x 6", 10" h. . . . 45.00
Coffee, Gillies store bin, mustard yellow, 1880's . . . 135.00
Coffee, Golden West 1-lb. can, cowgirl decoration . . . 15.00
Coffee, Hatchet Brand 1-lb. tin . . . 45.00
Coffee, Hills Bros. Blue Grand container . . . 65.00
Coffee, Hills Bros. 10-lb. tin, man pictured . . . 60.00
Coffee, Holland House 1-lb. tin . . . 38.00
Coffee, Holland House 3-lb. container . . . 17.00
Coffee, Hoosier Boy 1-lb. canister, 4¼" d., 6" h. . . . 155.00
Coffee, J.S.B. 5-lb. pail . . . 120.00
Coffee, Jack Sprat 4-lb. container . . . 188.00
Coffee, Kaffee Hag 1-lb. container . . . 25.00
Coffee, Kar-A-Van 1-lb. tin, camel pictured w/white printing on dark blue ground, "Kar-A-Van Coffee Co., Toledo, Ohio" . . . 30.00
Coffee, King Cole ½-lb. can, king being served pot of coffee decoration, 4½" d., 5" h. . . . 70.00
Coffee, Krink Sum canister w/paper label . . . 18.00
Coffee, Kybo ½-lb. tin, screw-on lithographed lid . . . 21.00
Coffee, Lady Hellen 1-lb. can, ca. 1923 . . . 25.00
Coffee, Lipton 1-lb. container, screw-on lid, yellow label . . . 69.00
Coffee, Louis Sherry 5-lb. square can, 7 x 7", 7¼" h. . . . 51.00
Coffee, Luzianne 1-lb. container . . . 28.00
Coffee, Luzianne 2-lb. container, mammy pictured on label . . . 18.00
Coffee, Luzianne 3-lb. pail w/pry-up lid, mammy on red-orange ground . . . 75.00
Coffee, Mammy's Favorite 4-lb. pail, black mammy on orange . . . 188.00
Coffee, Mammy's Favorite 4-lb. tin . . . 110.00
Coffee, Maunakea Kona 3-lb. can, pry-up lid, paper label w/Hawaiian scene . . . 40.00
Coffee, Mazon 1-lb. tin . . . 20.00
Coffee, McLaughlin "Our Motto" 1-lb. container . . . 20.00
Coffee, Meyer's Bros. Ja-San-Mo 2-lb. container, owl decoration . . . 100.00
Coffee, Milk Maid 5-lb. pail, milk maid carrying pail pictured . . . 125.00
Coffee, Millac's May-Day 1-lb. can . . . 22.00
Coffee, Miss Carolina tin, plantation scene w/blacks . . . 15.00
Coffee, Mocha & Java tin, Harper Brass Co., 10" . . . 26.00
Coffee, Mohican Coffee tin . . . 23.00
Coffee, Monadnock 1-lb. tin . . . 50.00
Coffee, Morning Glory 1-lb. can . . . 10.00
Coffee, Mother's Joy 1-lb. container . . . 18.00
Coffee, Mount Cross 3-lb. tin . . . 44.00
Coffee, Mt. Cross 5-lb. pail . . . 95.00
Coffee, Mt. Cross 10-lb. tin, recessed lid w/bail, nice lithographed decoration, "Product of Denver, Colorado," 13" . . . 85.00
Coffee, Nash Jubilee pail . . . 33.00

Navarre Golden Sun Coffee Canister

Coffee, Navarre Golden Sun canister, paper label, 4" d., 5½" h. (ILLUS.) . . . 18.00
Coffee, Niagara Falls box . . . 10.00
Coffee, Oak Hill 1-lb. container . . . 55.00
Coffee, Old Jewel Coffee container, little girl decoration . . . 275.00
Coffee, Old Judge 3-lb. jar . . . 19.00
Coffee, Old Master 1-lb. can, old gentleman portrait in oval . . . 35.00
Coffee, Old Master 3-lb. can . . . 50.00
Coffee, Old Southern canister, lady in chair decoration, 4¼" d., 6¼" h. . . . 65.00
Coffee, Peak 1-lb. can . . . 35.00
Coffee, Pickwick 1-lb. tin . . . 25.00
Coffee, S.S. Pierce 1-lb. tin . . . 20.00
Coffee, Pilot Knob 5-lb. pail . . . 85.00
Coffee, Plantation 4-lb. pail . . . 125.00
Coffee, Queen's Taste canister . . . 18.00
Coffee, Red Ball 3-lb. can . . . 25.00
Coffee, Red Wolf 6-lb. pail . . . 150.00
Coffee, Royal Dutch 1-lb. container . . . 36.00
Coffee, Sears Special Combination 10-lb. pail . . . 45.00

Coffee, Sears Roasted 25-lb. bin w/lift lid, 1910 .... 200.00
Coffee, Silver Sea container, key lid 16.00
Coffee, Solitaire 5-lb. tin 18.00
Coffee, Strong Heart 1-lb. can, Indians decoration 75.00
Coffee, Thesco container, paper label 50.00
Coffee, Timur 1-lb. tin 160.00
Coffee, Turkey canister, large turkey illustrated, 4¼" d., 5¾" h.... 500.00
Coffee, Union Club 1-lb. can 35.00
Coffee, Universal Blend 1-lb. can, Uncle Sam illustrated 150.00
Coffee, Van Dyke 1-lb. tin, screw-on lid 29.00
Coffee, Veteran Brand canister, portrait of Civil War vet, 4¼ x 5¾".. 70.00
Coffee, Wallen's 5-lb. can, pry-up lid 80.00
Coffee, Wag 1-lb. tin, Syracuse, N.Y. 19.00
Coffee, Ward 1-lb. container, rectangular 29.00
Coffee, Wedding Breakfast 3-lb. can 18.00
Coffee, White House 1-lb. can 35.00
Coffee, White House 2-lb. tin, paper lithographed label in blue & white 35.00
Cookies, Lenz Co. container, decorated w/multicolored pull-toy animals, clowns, giraffes, geese, etc., tin, 5 x 4", 20 oz............ 40.00
Cookies, Murray's container, red, white & blue, 12" 24.00
Cough drops, Bone Eagle Cough Drops 5-lb. tin, colorful graphics .. 90.00
Cough drops, Licorice Lozenges 5-lb. tin, glass front 55.00
Cough drops, Luden's store bin 25.00
Cough drops, Petits & Smiths store bin, Sommers Bros............... 48.00
Cough drops, P.C.W. box 37.50
Cough drops, Stop That Cough tin, glass front....................... 45.00
Crackers, Fairy Soda Crackers box w/lift lid, blue 30.00
Crackers, Johnson's Baby Educator tin 70.00
Crackers, Natl. Biscuit Co. Premium Soda Crackers 2-lb. tin 32.00
Crackers, Sunshine Cheese Wafers container 28.00
Crackers, Uneeda Bakers Graham Crackers sample box, Nabisco in red, wheat design............... 15.00
Crayons, Crayola Dustless box 18.00
Cream, Half & Half sample tin 40.00
Dental floss, Johnson & Johnson "Brunswick" tin, holds 12 yards ... 15.00
Dog food, Nutrena 10-lb. tin, bail handle, dog pictured on orange ground 45.00
Dust absorber, Freeman Dust Absorber tin 4.00
Explosives, Fort Pitt Blasting Caps tin 9.00
Face powder, California Perfume tin, 3" d. 18.00
Face powder, Rosebud tin, Rosebud Perfume Co., young girl w/roses pictured, 1914................. 15.00
Floor polish, Kress container, mop pictured 18.00
Food coloring, Peacock Food tin, large dome top, peacock pictured 20.00
Fruitcake, Hostess tin, gold, red & blue lady decoration............. 18.00
Gelatine, Enzo Gelatine box, early glider plane pictured, 1926, mint, w/contents 10.00
Gum, Huyler's Sweetheart box, heart-shaped, red, small 55.00
Gun powder, Dead Shot drum, falling duck shown 110.00
Gun powder, Dupont, flask-type tin, Indian on label, dated 1908 ...... 55.00
Gun powder, King Semi-Smokless drum........................... 85.00
Gun powder, Oriental can, ca. 1880 .... 225.00
Gun powder, Robin Hood Powder Co. 1-lb. can.................... 120.00
Hair product, Firestone's Pomade container 5.00
Hair product, Koakota Pomade container 5.00
Hair product, Murray's Pomade container, blacks pictured 10.00
Hair product, Queen sample tin, blacks pictured.................. 8.00
Hair product, Royal Crown sample tin, blacks pictured 8.00
Hair product, Susie Q sample tin, blacks pictured................. 8.00
Hair product, Tuskegee Belle container, blacks pictured 25.00
Honey, Manitoba Pure Honey 1-gal. pail w/wire bail handle, dark blue background w/green & yellow lettering, "Western Clover Apiaries, Dufrost, Man.," scene w/boxes for keeping bees, 6¼" d., 7¼" h. 15.00
Honey, Manitoba Pure Honey 1-gal. pail w/wire bail handle, red & black plaid background w/bright yellow lettering, scene of bee on hive in center w/pink flowers & green leaves, "Brandon McGregor's Apiaries" in banner above hive, full-color farm scene

on back showing "Glencarnock Stock Farms - Angus Cattle" 26.00
Ice cream, Abbotts round tin, Amish girl shown, 5" d., 6" h. 18.00
Ice cream cones, Bully Boy can 75.00
Ice cream topping, Planters Chopped Nut tin, Mr. Peanut w/sundae 75.00
Insect powder, Bee Brand, bee 5.50
Knitting needles, Eureka tin, delicate lithography of girl, 9" needles included, 9" l., Germany 25.00
Lard, Armour's 4-lb. pail 16.00
Lard, Farmer Peets 50-lb. container, pigs hunting, fishing, swimming & skating, red, white & blue 35.00
Lard, Hardy's Pure 4-lb. tin, pig dressed up & carrying umbrella... 26.00
Lard, Morrell 50-lb. pail 22.00
Lard, Partridge 8-lb. container 25.00
Lard, Shamokin pail, Indian chief & swastikas shown 125.00
Lard, White Seal pail, seal on iceberg scene 20.00
Malted milk, Borden's 10-lb. tin..... 26.50
Marshmallows, Angelus 5-lb. container 25.00
Marshmallows, Brach's 3-lb. tin 37.50
Marshmallows, Bunte 4-oz. tin, multicolor pink w/Bunte kid, 1914 .... 118.00
Marshmallows, Campfire 5-lb. container 18.00
Marshmallows, Woodwards 5-lb. tin, blue 37.50
Matches, Diamond Match Co. tin, blacks pictured 75.00
Mop, O-Cedar container, scene of lady w/mop, 1929 .... 22.00
Motor oil, Around the World 2-gal. can, orange & yellow 85.00
Motor oil, Bull's Head 2-gal. can, large bull shown, 1920's 45.00
Motor oil, Capitan 2-gal. tin, early car shown, ca. 1930 .... 35.00
Motor oil, D-X H.D. Oil 1-qt. can, old logo, full 9.00
Motor oil, High Grade Oil 1-gal. can, eagle, black & yellow 65.00
Motor oil, Monarch Oil 1-gal. can, eagle, red & black 75.00
Motor oil, Oil Creek Petroleum Products 5-qt. can, green & orange 50.00
Motor oil, Sturdy 2-gal. can 15.00
Motor oil, Wright Aerolube 10-lb. pail 10.00
Motor oil, Zerolene Standard Oil Co. (Calif.) ½-gal. can 65.00
Mustard, Barrus canister, square, yellow & black w/eagle front & back, lithographed standing child each side, 10" h. 33.00
Mustard, McCormick's tin, pictures bees & lists medical uses 15.00
Needles, Verona tin 35.00
Nuts, Festino Almonds, National Biscuit Co. container, square 10.00
Nuts, Kemp Salted Nuts tin 20.00
Nuts, Kemp Golden Glow Mixed Nuts tin, 4 x 6" 50.00
Oil, Grizzly Neats Foot Oil tin, pictures grizzly bear 25.00
Oysters, McNaney's 10-lb. container 15.00
Oysters, Pride of the Chesapeake 1-gal. pail 18.00
Oysters, Wentworth 1-gal. pail 12.50
Paint, Dutch Boy 25-lb. pail, white lead paint 40.00
Patent medicine, Blackstone's Tasty-Lax tin 10.00
Patent medicine, Capsolin Rubefacient mustard plaster container ... 12.00
Patent medicine, Chi-Ches-Ters Diamond Brand Pills tin 4.00
Patent medicine, Dr. Hobson's Arnica Salve tin 9.00
Patent medicine, Dr. Hunter's Sure Relief tin, dated 1906 .... 10.00
Patent medicine, Dr. Sauer's Aspirin tin, pictures doctor, 1920's 10.00
Patent medicine, Ramon's Liver Ailment tin, 3" 4.00
Patent medicine, Rawleigh Medicated Ointment container 3.00
Patent medicine, Victor Ointment tin, rooster standing on slain loser after cock fight 12.00
Patent medicine, Wiley's Dandruff Remover Scalp Treatment 1-gal. container 33.00
Peanut butter, A & P Sultana 1-lb. pail 55.00
Peanut butter, Armour's Veribest 1-lb. pail, Mother Goose scenes .. 62.00
Peanut butter, Big Sister pail 95.00
Peanut butter, Buffalo 1-lb. pail 55.00

Dixie Peanut Butter Container

Peanut butter, Dixie 15-lb. container, blue background w/lithographed lettering (ILLUS.) 37.50
Peanut butter, Forester pail 75.00
Peanut butter, Frontenac 12-oz. pail 45.00

Peanut butter, Lighthouse pail 100.00
Peanut butter, Lovell & Coval pail, Peter Rabbit decoration 125.00
Peanut butter, Peter Pan 25-lb. pail, four Peter Pans shown 95.00
Peanut butter, Peter Rabbit 1-lb. pail 350.00
Peanut butter, Spindlers 10-lb. pail w/bail handle 28.00
Peanut butter, Swift's "Wizard of Oz" 2-lb. pail 30.00
Peanut butter, Teenie Weenie 2-lb. pail, colorful cartoon decoration .. 150.00
Peanut butter, Uncle Wiggly 1-lb. pail 400.00
Peanut butter, Yacht Club 1-lb. pail 250.00
Peanuts, Brundage 10-lb. can 40.00
Peanuts, Bunnies 10-lb. canister 320.00
Peanuts, Harvard Jumbo 5-lb. container 50.00
Peanuts, Planters 1-lb. can w/bail handle, lithographed comics 425.00
Peanuts, Planters Pennant Salted Peanuts 10-lb. canister, blue & red lettering on black background, pennant w/Mr. Peanut across center, w/original lid, 8½" d., 10" h. 150.00
Peanuts, Squirrel Brand Salted Peanuts 10-lb. can w/wire bail handle, orange background w/white & black lettering & gold trim, 8¼" d., 9½" h. (no lid, minor damage) 130.00
Phonograph needles, Best Talking Machine box, phonograph w/horn shown 10.00

Victor Phonograph Needle Tin

Phonograph needles, RCA Victor box, dog & phonograph (ILLUS.) .. 22.00
Popcorn, Jessop's box, old lady on front 7.00
Potato chips, Blue Ribbon Potato Chips container, large 25.00
Potato chips, New Era 1-lb. can 20.00
Potato chips, Old King Cole canister, multicolored Old King Cole, musicians, cat & dog, 7½" d., 11" h. .. 42.50
Radio crystals, Philmore tin, red, pictures crystal, electric beams, crystal inside, round 20.00
Rouge, Princess Pat tin, concave, Art Deco girl decoration 10.00
Scouring powder, Bon Ami sample tin 15.00
Shaving powder, Colgate's Rapid Shave Powder tin, 1920's 20.00
Shoe polish, Gilt Edge Oil Shoe Dressing tin w/screw-in jar 25.00
Shoe polish, Kelly's Slide tin, baseball player decoration 20.00
Shoe polish, Yankee container, boy shining Uncle Sam's shoes, dated 1930 .... 35.00
Shortening, Swift's Jewel Pure 8-lb. pail 18.00
Skin whitener, Queen sample tin, blacks pictured 8.00
Spark plug, Ford Tungsten tin 6.00
Spice, Buster Brown Allspice tin 16.50
Spice, Cody, Ball, Barnhart Co. tin, Grand Rapids, Michigan, lady on front, 12" h. 50.00
Spice, Golden Key Cinnamon can, blue & orange 14.00
Spice, Jack Sprat Allspice tin 12.50

McCormick Behnke Spice Bin

Spice, McCormick Behnke & Co. store bin, rounded top front w/sliding door in black w/gold & red lettering, front decorated w/lithographed color scene of two horses in a field, 6½ x 9 x 11" (ILLUS.) 210.00
Spice, Zanzibar 6-lb. canister, nude blacks depicted 125.00
Stove polish, Quickshine, little girl w/stove shown 19.00
Syringe, Dr. F. Wilhoft's Original & Only Genuine Lady's Syringe rectangular tin, two-tone green exterior illustrating product, instructions inside lid, early, rare, 3 x 4 x 7" 301.00
Syrup, Pepsi Cola 5-gal. can 35.00
Syrup, Towle's Log Cabin 12-oz. tin, cabin-shaped, red 35.00

Syrup, Towle's Log Cabin tin, cabin-shaped, "Dr. R.U. Well" cartoon decoration 120.00

Syrup, Towle's Log Cabin tin, cabin-shaped, girl & mother in doorway, w/cartoon ends 69.00

Talcum powder, Air Float container 32.00

Talcum powder, Bonnie B tin, dated 1923, Art Nouveau style decoration w/storks 45.00

Talcum powder, La Femme tin, 1920's Art Deco decoration 15.00

Talcum powder, Palmer's Talc For Men tin 20.00

Talcum powder, Sweetheart can, lady in evening gown standing between columns 22.50

Talcum powder, Tally-Ho tin, man w/cane & wearing top hat 38.00

Talcum powder, Velta Rose Bouquet tin 15.00

Talcum powder, Vi-Jon Apple Blossom tin 17.00

Talcum powder, Wembdon Lavender tin 12.00

Talcum powder, Yardley tin, maiden w/children 24.00

Tea, Banquet tin w/embossed lid, deep green & red, 3 x 1½ x 1½" 16.00

Tea, Grandmother's A&P 1-lb. tin 15.00

Tea, E.C. Harley 2-lb. tin, red stenciled, 7" 45.00

Monarch Light of Asia Tea Box

Tea, Monarch Light of Asia 8-oz. box (ILLUS.) 32.00

Tea, Montgomery Ward's Oriental 5-lb. canister, lady pictured on four sides 125.00

Tea, Nabob Pure Indian & Ceylon square can, gold-trimmed green background w/red, white & black lettering, 6" w., 7½" h. 20.00

Tea, Norton Bros. Chicago Family can, green w/black, three scenes around outside & reserves printed, "Teas, Coffee, Spices," embossed lid dated 1880, 7½" h. (some flaking) 35.00

Tea, Ocean Blend Indian & Ceylon square can, red background w/gold, black & red lettering above & below center scene of ocean liner, 6½ x 8", 8½" h. (paint loss on back) 75.00

Tea, Red Hill box, hinged lid, Hillman, Waterloo, 18 x 11" 40.00

Tea, Richelieu box, Oriental design 14.50

Tea, Sears & Roebuck 5-lb. pail w/bail handle, shaded red ground 45.00

Tea, Swee-Touch Nee trunk-shaped container, red & gold decoration 25.00

Tea, Tetley's ¼-lb. tin, rectangular, sunflower decoration 13.00

Tire patches, John Bull tin, early "John" embossed, full kit, two smaller tins inside, both embossed "John Bull Tyres" 25.00

Tobacco, Allen & Ginter pocket tin 10.00

Tobacco, Bagdad pocket tin, Turk in fez 70.00

Tobacco, Bagley's Burley Boy pocket tin, little boxer boy, "The White Man's Hope" 600.00

Tobacco, Bagley's Old Colony Mixture pocket tin 75.00

Tobacco, Belfast vertical box, lift top, 7 x 6 x 3" 20.00

Tobacco, Benton square corner container 35.00

Tobacco, Big Ben pocket tin, shows horse 25.00

Tobacco, Bird's Eye tin, hinged lid, 4½ x 3½" 40.00

Tobacco, B-L red label pocket tin 35.00

Tobacco, Blue Jay lunch pail 110.00

Tobacco, Blue Sunset Trail lunch pail 125.00

Tobacco, Boar's Head rectangular counter tin, yellow background w/blue lettering, illustration of boar's head on ends, 5½ x 9", 5½" h. (minor dents) 75.00

Tobacco, Bohemian Perique pocket tin 35.00

Tobacco, Bond Street 1-lb. canister 12.00

Tobacco, Bowl of Roses pocket tin, man before fireplace, bowl of roses on table 165.00

Tobacco, Brotherhood lunch pail 45.00

Tobacco, Buckingham Cut Plug pocket tin 52.00

Tobacco, Bugler canister 18.00

Tobacco, Bunte store bin, tall w/picture of factory 125.00

Tobacco, Carlton Club pocket tin 65.00

Tobacco, Catcher Rough Cut Pipe round canister 45.00
Tobacco, Central Union pocket tin .. 185.00
Tobacco, Checkers pocket tin, white (scarce) 375.00
Tobacco, City Club round canister, man seated in wicker armchair reading paper 110.00
Tobacco, City Club pocket tin, man seated in wicker armchair reading paper 100.00
Tobacco, Cross Swords square corner horizontal box, large swords frame two bust portraits of young ladies 53.00
Tobacco, Culture pocket tin 100.00

Dan Patch Cut Plug Box

Tobacco, Dan Patch Cut Plug box, 6 x 4" (ILLUS.) 40.00
Tobacco, Dereszke pocket tin, oval, pictures Dracula look-a-like 35.00
Tobacco, Dial pocket tin 18.00
Tobacco, Diamond F Mixture tin, Felgner & Son Mfg., Baltimore, Maryland, black, red on yellow printing, 4½ x 3½", 2¼" h....... 30.00
Tobacco, Dixie Kid Cut Plug lunch pail, black baby boy 360.00
Tobacco, Dixie Queen canister, blue knob top 325.00
Tobacco, Edgeworth sample tin 32.00
Tobacco, Edgeworth square container w/concave sides 22.00
Tobacco, Epicure square box, hinged top, embossed flowers on sides .. 35.00
Tobacco, Gold Bond (Old Reliable) pocket tin 25.00
Tobacco, Granulated 54 sample size pocket tin 106.00
Tobacco, Guide pocket tin 125.00
Tobacco, Half & Half sample size pocket tin 93.00
Tobacco, Hiawatha round box, 8½" d., 2" h. 70.00
Tobacco, Hi-Plane pocket tin, single-engine plane 50.00
Tobacco, Idle Hour pocket tin, hour-glass on front 45.00
Tobacco, Just Suits lunch box....... 40.00

Tobacco, Lorillard's Redicut lunch box 68.00
Tobacco, Mayo's lunch box, telescoping-type 130.00
Tobacco, Mayo's Roly Poly Dutchman 550.00
Tobacco, North Pole canister 120.00
Tobacco, Old English Cut Curve store bin 350.00
Tobacco, Omega canister 50.00
Tobacco, Pat Hand pocket tin....... 80.00
Tobacco, Paul Jones pocket tin.....1,100.00

Peachey Pocket Tin

Tobacco, Peachey pocket tin, shows peach (ILLUS.)................. 62.00
Tobacco, Star pocket tin 32.00
Tobacco, Sterling Light round canister, 8 x 14" 80.00
Tobacco, Sweet Burley Light store bin 120.00
Tobacco, Tiger lunch box, red, 9 x 6¾ x 6¼" 38.00
Tobacco, Tuxedo canister, green & gold 32.00
Tobacco, Union Leader Cut Plug lunch box 20.00
Tobacco, Winner Cut Plug canister w/"Starch" in scrolled cartouche on back 125.00

Winner Lunch Box

Tobacco, Winner Cut Plug lunch box, racing car scene on side (ILLUS.) .. 125.00

CARD CASES

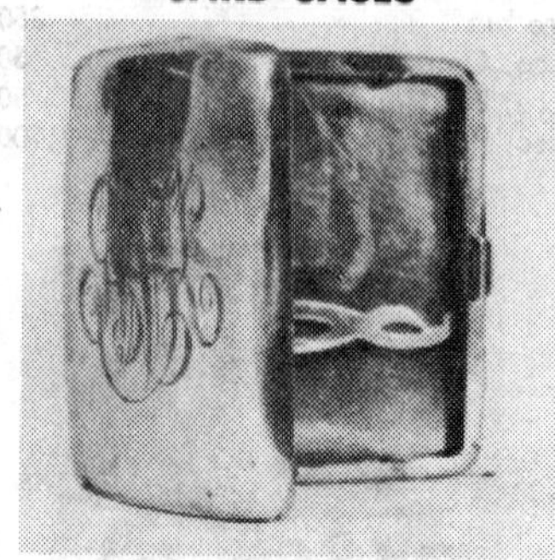

Gentleman's Card Case

In a more leisurely and sociable era, ladies made a ritual of "calling" on new neighbors and friends. Calling card cases held the small cards engraved or lettered with the owner's name and sometimes additionally decorated. The cases were turned out in a wide variety of styles and material which included gold, silver, ivory, tortoise shell and leather. A sampling of collectible calling card cases is listed below.

Mother-of-pearl shell, diamond pattern, ivory trim, 2¾ x 3¾" $40.00
Sterling silver, ornate, late 19th century, 2 x 2½" 37.50
Sterling silver, gentleman's, curved to fit breast pocket, monogrammed, 3½ x 3½" (ILLUS.) 75.00
Sterling silver, delicate filigree border, applied flowers & hovering butterfly within a frame of beading, possibly Chinese, 2½ x 3¾" 110.00
Sterling silver, engraved foliate scrolls & scene of "Witley Court....," Birmingham hallmarks for 1843-44, 4" l. 145.00
Sterling silver, bright-cut design on overall engine-turned ground, marked "Gorham" 195.00
Sterling silver, ornate, Victorian, Birmingham, ca. 1876 .... 350.00

CAROUSEL FIGURES

The ever-popular amusement park merry-go-round or carousel has ancient antecedents but evolved into its most colorful and complex form in the decades from 1880 to 1930. In America a number of pioneering firms, begun by men such as Gustav Dentzel, Charles Looff and Allan Herschell, produced these wonderful rides with beautifully hand-carved animals, the horse being the most popular. Some of the noted carvers included M.C. Illions, Charles Carmel, Solomon Stein and Harry Goldstein.

Today many of the grand old carousels are gone and remaining ones are often broken up and the animals sold separately as collectors search for choice examples. A fine reference to this field is Painted Ponies, American Carousel Art, *by William Manns, Peggy Shank and Marianne Stevens (Zon International Publishing Company, Millwood, New York, 1986.)*

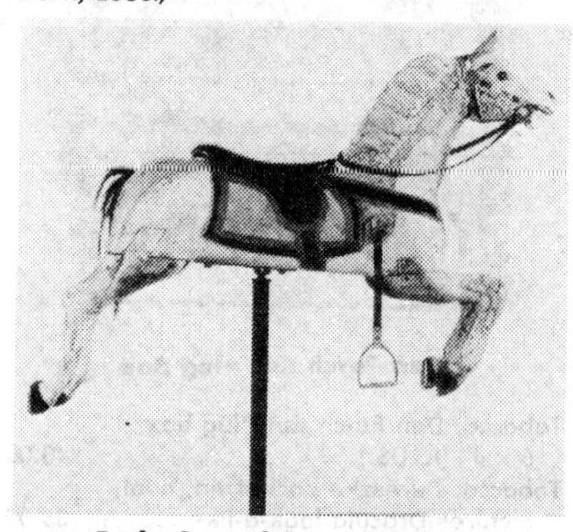

Early Carved Carousel Horse

Bear, glass eyes, carved to simulate bear fur, carved saddle & bow tie, stripped & finished, J.R. Anderson, Bristol, England, ca. 1875, 34" l. $1,430.00
Carousel chariot, girl w/dog at side (restored) 3,000.00
Carousel chariot, three figures, armored, Coney Island style, (Bogota), Charles Carmel 5,000.00
Deer, outside row closed mouth prancer, eagle behind saddle, professionally restored, Gustav Dentzel, ca. 1885 ....17,500.00
Donkey, carved saddle, blanket & nodding head w/brass handle-grip, grey, red, brown, yellow & blue, Bayol of Angers, France, ca. 1880, 43" l. 1,430.00
Goat, stripped, Charles Looff, Jr., small 9,000.00
Horse, child's size trotter w/carved mane, saddle trappings & tail, stripped & finished in a walnut stain, w/stand, Henri Devos of Angers, France, ca. 1900 ....1,100.00
Horse, outside row Indian pony stander, bear skin saddle blanket,

full-faced three-dimensional Indian head carved behind saddle on both sides, jewels, stripped, Charles Carmel 17,000.00

Horse, outside row jumper, heavily jewelled, Illions, ca. 1895 (completely restored) 9,700.00

Horse, outside row stander, carved jewels & peekaboo mane, Charles Looff, ca. 1880 (restored) 7,500.00

Horse, outside row star-gazer jumper, flying horse w/U.S. shield w/stars on chest, eagle behind saddle, jewels & beveled mirrors, stripped, Charles Carmel 13,500.00

Horse, middle row prancer, hand-scraped to original factory paint & pin striping blanket decoration, E.J. Morris .10,500.00

Horse, middle row, carved snake & dove motifs & large tassel at front of mane, reins inscribed "Trevor," green, yellow, blue, red & silver showpaint, J.R. Anderson, Bristol, England, ca. 1880, 68" l. 3,850.00

Horse, inner row jumper w/carved top-knot, stripped, Daniel Muller-Gustav Dentzel 7,500.00

Horse, inner row jumper w/roached mane, stripped, Gustav Dentzel . .7,500.00

Horse, jumper, carved wavy mane & wooden pricked ears, grey & black saddle blanket, white body w/horsehair tail, Hindsley, 19th c., 4' 9" l., 4' 10¾" h. (ILLUS.) 2,090.00

Horse, jumper, hand-carved body by Daniel Muller, head, tail & legs are cast aluminum, original paint, original brass pole, ca. 1920 . . . . .3,000.00

Horse, stander, carved, tassel trim, tongue out & two owls behind the cantle, Philadelphia Toboggan Co. 12,750.00

Lion, fierce but friendly heraldic lion from children's carousel, probably Carl Muller, Germany, pre-1880, stripped 9,500.00

Ostrich Carousel Figure

Ostrich, running bird w/carved feathers & saddle, long neck hinged on body, stripped & finished, Savages of King's Lynn, England, ca. 1875, 58" l., 56" h. (ILLUS.) 3,300.00

Pig, carved oak leaves & acorns on sides, Gustav Dentzel (restored) 9,500.00

Rabbit, Bayol of Angers, France, ca. 1899 (restored) 6,500.00

Rooster, white bird w/red comb, red saddle w/blue trim, Herschell-Spillman 4,700.00

Tiger, walking animal w/raised head, wearing carved saddle, Gustav Dentzel-Daniel Muller, ca. 1895 (restored) 23,000.00

Zebra, outside row, realistic animal in proud pose, fancy straps, parrot peeking beneath saddle cantle, Gustav Dentzel, ca. 1895 (restored) 23,000.00

CASH REGISTERS

National Cash Register

James Ritty of Dayton, Ohio, is credited with inventing the first cash register. In 1882, he sold the business to a Cincinnati salesman, Jacob H. Eckert, who subsequently invited others into the business by selling stock. One of the purchasers of an early cash register, John J. Patterson, was so impressed with the savings his model brought to his company, he bought 25 shares of stock and became a director of the company in 1884, eventually buying a controlling interest in the National Manufacturing Company. Patterson thoroughly organized the company, conducted sales classes, prepared sales manuals and established salesman's territories. The success of the National Cash Register Company is due as much to these well organized origins as to the efficiency of its machines. Early "National" cash registers, as well as other models, are deemed highly collectible today.

Brass, "American," marble shelf (fully restored) $1,595.00
Brass, "Michigan," embossed designs 315.00
Brass, "National" Model 7............ 450.00
Brass, "National" Model 8 (ILLUS.) .. 485.00
Brass, "National" Autographic Register Model 30 (restored).....1,200.00
Brass, "National" Model Pt46 ......1,600.00
Brass, "National" Model 47¼-2-2, double drawer w/original sign ... 675.00
Brass, "National" Model 52¼, extended base 1,200.00
Brass, "National" Model 58, keys up to $20.99, 16½" h. 990.00
Brass, "National" Model 130........ 550.00
Brass, "National" Model 143........ 595.00
Brass, "National" Model 324........ 750.00
Brass, "National" Model 327........ 950.00
Brass, "National" Model 332........ 595.00
Brass, "National" Model 337 (restored) 750.00
Brass, "National" Model 348-2-2, two drawers, bar model 475.00
Brass, "National" Model 420, single drawer 260.00
Brass, "National" Model 597-E 550.00
Brass, "National" Model 1040, ca. 1913 .... 375.00
Cast iron & grained oak, stenciled drawer w/lettering "Amount of Sale" & "Monitor" on small front window 275.00
Mahogany, "National" Model 717, marble top 175.00
Oak, "National" Model 855......... 400.00
Oak, "Standard," ca. 1890 .... 350.00

CASTORS & CASTOR SETS

Castor bottles were made to hold condiments for table use. Some were produced in sets of several bottles housed in silver plated frames. The word also is sometimes spelled "Caster."

Castor set, 3-bottle, clear cut glass bottles in thumbprint pattern & cut tall stoppers, trefoil-form pierced latticework silver stand on three foliate feet & center handle, one side w/cartouche reserve engraved "Regatta, 1849, 1st Class Yachts, 1st Prize," stand by William F. Ladd, New York, stand 16½" h. (ILLUS.) $2,420.00

Ornate Castor Set

Castor set, 3-bottle, clear cut glass bottles w/open salt dip w/spoon, silver plate stand 98.00
Castor set, 4-bottle, etched clear bottles & two amethyst open salts, silver plate stand 120.00
Castor set, 4-bottle, cranberry glass bottles w/original stoppers, handled glass stand 295.00
Castor set, 5-bottle, clear glass bottles, ornate revolving silver plate stand w/ornate center handle, marked Meriden 145.00
Castor set, 5-bottle, clear glass etched bottles, silver plate stand w/figural squirrel on handle 175.00
Castor set, 5-bottle, clear glass Gothic patt. bottles w/original stoppers, pewter stand 105.00
Castor set, 5-bottle, clear glass bottles w/hand-cut finger flutes & florals & cut teardrop stoppers, silver plate stand w/embossed skirt & elaborate bail handle, marked Pairpoint.................. 155.00
Pickle castor, amber glass Cane patt. insert, silver plate frame, cover & tongs, shell edging around base, leaves & twist bail handle 165.00
Pickle castor, amber glass Melon Rib Swirl patt. insert, ornate silver plate frame, marked Derby 135.00
Pickle castor, blue glass Cane patt. insert, silver plate frame & tongs, 11" h. 130.00
Pickle castor, blue glass Inverted Thumbprint patt. insert, silver plate frame w/fork, marked J. Rogers, 11" h. 250.00
Pickle castor, blue glass Netted Swirl mold insert w/pink apple blossoms in relief, cover engraved

"Christmas 1890," resilvered silver plate frame 350.00

Pickle castor, canary glass Daisy & Button patt. insert, ornate silver plate frame, cover & tongs 210.00

Block Pattern Pickle Castor

Pickle castor, clear glass Block patt. insert, silver plate frame & fork (ILLUS.) 110.00

Pickle castor, clear glass Cosmos patt. insert, silver plate frame, cover & tongs 145.00

Pickle castor, clear glass Daisy & Button patt. insert, silver plate frame 85.00

Pickle castor, cranberry glass insert, silver plate frame & tongs, marked Pairpoint 225.00

Pickle castor, cranberry glass insert, w/raised enamel decoration, silver plate frame & tongs, 10½" h 180.00

Pickle castor, cranberry glass Diamond Quilted patt. insert, silver plate frame w/applied bug one side, 4½" d., 10½" h. 195.00

Pickle castor, cranberry glass, egg-shaped, Inverted Thumbprint patt. insert, silver plate frame & cover, marked Tufts 235.00

Pickle castor, cranberry glass insert w/enameled decoration, silver plate footed frame w/full figural bird perched on looped handle ... 385.00

Pickle castor, cranberry glass Inverted Baby Thumbprint patt. insert, silver plate frame & cover 165.00

Pickle castor, Fostoria glass Carmen patt. insert, silver plate frame & tongs 95.00

Pickle castor, Peach Blow glass insert w/enameled flowers, ornate silver plate frame, marked Tufts .. 400.00

Pickle castor, Rubina Crystal glass insert decorated w/coralene florals, silver plate frame 585.00

Pickle castor, Rubina Verde glass Inverted Thumbprint patt. insert w/enameled decoration, silver plate frame 125.00

Pickle castor, sapphire blue glass insert, ornate footed silver plate frame 175.00

Pickle castor, sapphire blue Daisy & Button w/V Ornament patt. insert, silver plate frame, cover & tongs, marked Rogers 170.00

Pickle castor, sapphire blue glass insert w/enameled floral decoration, silver plate frame w/attached hinged lid & tongs, marked Tufts 325.00

Pickle castor, shaded pink glass egg-shaped insert, enameled gold florals & leaves outlined w/white, white interior, original ornate silver plate frame & tongs, marked Meriden 395.00

Pickle castor, white satin glass Coreopsis patt. insert w/decoration, silver plate frame 325.00

CAT COLLECTIBLES

PRINTS

"Five Senses"

"All in a Line," by L. Eugene Lambert, published by J.F. Hill & Co., Augusta, Maine, 1895, framed (slight tear at far left side), overall 25 x 20" $95.00

"Chessie as We Found Her" and "Chessie and Her First Family," old C&O logo at bottom right corner, light wood frames, overall 16 x 16", each 50.00

"Five Senses," by Henry Grant Plumb, 1906, unframed (reproduced item) ....25.00 to 35.00

"Five Senses," by Henry Grant Plumb, 1906, framed (ILLUS.)..................50.00 to 60.00

"Kittens with Spilled Vase of Pansies," published by P.O. Vickery, 1883, unframed, 23½ x 15½" 45.00

Portfolio of 8 - 12 x 16" full-color signed prints by Gladys Emerson Cook, the set 225.00

Portfolio of 16 black on cream prints w/identification chart & booklet about the artists' drawing of cats, Harper & Row, 1956, each 10¼ x 13½", the set.................. 90.00

"Queen of Sheba" and "King of Siam," by Margaret M. Phillips, New York Graphic Society, Fine Art Publishers, w/border, overall 16 x 16", pr. 50.00

"Yard of Kittens," by Guy Bedford .. 100.00

"Yard of Kittens," by C.S. Vredenburgh 125.00

ORIGINAL WORKS OF ART

"Royal Maiden & Her Kitten"

"Adolescence," John Henry Dolph (American, 1835-1903), signed oil on canvas, 12 x 9" 4,500.00

"At It Again," Jules LeRoy (French, 19th c.), signed oil, 14 x 12" 4,500.00

"Girl With Kittens," folk art oil on canvas, 17" w., 30" h. 300.00

Gray cats in wicker basket, B.C. Seymour, signed water-color, overall 5¾" square.............. 18.00

"Kitties with Spilled Vase of Pansies," oil on academy board, copy of 1883 P.O. Vickery print, simple wood frame, 18 x 23½" 125.00

"Seated Royal Maiden and Her Kitten," European School pastel, 18th c., 23" w., 30¾" h. (ILLUS.)......2,100.00

"The Tea Party," Johann Caspar Herterich (German, 1834-1905), signed oil on panel, 31 x 21" ...17,500.00

"Three Kittens in Sewing Basket"

"Three Kittens into the Sewing Basket," Louis-Eugene Lambert, signed oil painting, dated "76" (1876), 15 x 19" (ILLUS.) 3,850.00

MISCELLANEOUS

Terra Cotta Cats

Animal covered dish, cat on lid, lacy base, vaseline, "Westmoreland" .. 95.00

Ashtray, ceramic, black cat w/open mouth, paper label, "#109 Shafford Pottery" 15.00

Candlestick, porcelain, model of a black cat w/green & orange trim on side of stick, 6" h. 62.00

Cologne bottle, w/black cat, "Max Factor," under plastic dome cover 10.00

Compote on metal base, Bristol glass, fluted, h.p. scene of cat in grass 65.00

Creamer w/cat handle, ceramic, souvenir of "Irish Hills, Michigan," marked "Made in Czechoslovakia," 4½" h. 25.00

Cup & saucer, child's, ceramic, two kittens on cup, brilliant pink trim, cup 2" h., saucer 4" d. 30.00

Feeding dish, ceramic, three-section, cat, dog & rooster pictured, marked "Roma," 7¼" d. . . . 40.00

Figure group, "Solitude," lady on seat w/small cat, HN 2810, Royal Doulton 170.00

Group of two cats, terra cotta, marble base, signed "Fiene Yaddo 32," Paul Fiene, United States, 1932, 18 x 18 x 18" (ILLUS.) 8,500.00

Letter opener, brass, cat on handle, marked "England," 9" l. 35.00

Model of a cat, "Lucky," black, K-12, Royal Doulton, 2½" h. 95.00

Model of a cat in reclining position, bisque, white coat, marked "Heubach," 4" l. 125.00

Model of a cat, porcelain, in the Oriental style, white coat w/gold & black spots & grey tail, attributed to Samson, France, red Chinese character mark, ca. 1890, 5" h. 195.00

Night light, bisque, model of a kitten's head, grey coat, blue collar, green glass eyes 485.00

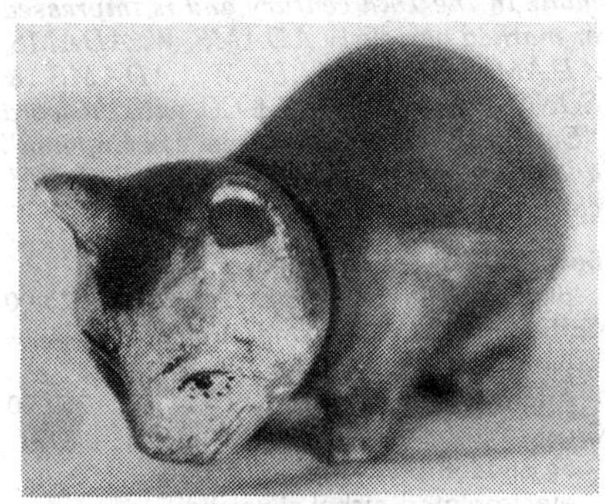

Chalkware Nodder

Nodder, chalkware, model of a cat, original painted features, rich brown patina, ca. 1800, 9" l. (ILLUS.) 450.00

Pipsqueak, papier-mache, model of a black cat wearing cloth suit, marked "Japan," 3¾" h. 55.00

Powder jar, ceramic, girl in lavender dress holding white kitten on cover, marked "Coventry Made in USA #5537A," ca. 1930, 6½" h . . . 30.00

Salt & pepper shakers, ceramic, figural black cats, paper label, "Shafford Pottery," 4" h., pr. 15.00

Silhouette, free-cut figure of a cat, signed "T.G. Brooks," ca. 1840, 6½ x 8" 225.00

Toy, black cloth cat w/black & green eyes, orange felt shirt & green pants, Schuco, 10" h. 125.00

Toy, pull toy, black mohair cat meows when pulled, Germany . . . 185.00

Toy, wind-up tin, Figaro the Cat, Line Mar 60.00

Wall pocket, ceramic, cat face, brown w/blue eyes, pink ears & mouth, yellow bow, unmarked, 5" h. 25.00

CELLULOID

Celluloid Tatting Shuttle

Celluloid was our first commercial plastic and early examples are now "antique" in their own right, having been produced as early as 1868 after the perfection of celluloid by John Wesley Hyatt. Earlier in this century other related "plastics" were also introduced and some examples of these items are also included here.

Bookmark, heart-shaped, creamy ivory, w/advertising $22.00

Box, cov., girl & dog playing piano decor, pretty lady w/large hat on cover, creamy ivory 25.00

Box w/hinged lid, fan-shaped, creamy ivory, 8" w. 46.00

Collar box, pretty girl decor, creamy ivory 25.00

Collar & cuff box, cov., embossed cylinder shape, creamy ivory 16.00

Dresser set: brush, mirror & tray; amber pyralin, signed "LaBelle," 3 pcs. 40.00

Dresser set, mottled brown & amber "tortoise shell," 7 pcs. 28.50

Dresser set, marbleized green, 10 pcs. 50.00

Dresser set, green w/gold Art Nouveau design, w/green moire-lined locking leather case, 11 pcs. 145.00

Dresser set, creamy ivory, 12 pcs. . . 62.50

Dresser set, pink & black marbleized, 21 pcs. 48.00

Glove stretcher, creamy ivory, 7" l. 20.00
Hair comb, butterfly-shaped, brown 20.00
Letter opener, sterling silver figural dog handle 47.50
Mustache scissors, creamy ivory handles 15.00
Napkin ring, model of yellow duck w/glass eyes 22.50
Napkin ring, model of green elephant 18.50
Napkin ring, model of green rabbit w/glass eyes 22.50
Tape measure, model of a pig, creamy ivory 22.00
Tatting shuttle, portrait of Victorian lady, creamy ivory (ILLUS.) 18.00

CERAMICS

ABINGDON

From about 1934 until 1950, Abingdon Pottery Company, Abingdon, Illinois, manufactured decorative pottery, mainly cookie jars, flower pots and vases. Decorated with various glazes, these items are becoming popular with collectors who are especially attracted to Abingdon's novelty cookie jars.

Book end, model of dolphin, No. 444, white glaze (single) $45.00
Book ends, model of horse head, black & white glaze, pr. 42.00
Book ends, model of horse, pr. 85.00
Cookie jar, "Choo Choo," No. 651 .... 50.00
Cookie jar, "Cookie Time," green, white & red glaze 58.00
Cookie jar, "Daisy," h.p. decor 25.00
Cookie jar, "Humpty Dumpty," original sticker 82.50
Cookie jar, "Jack-in-the-Box" 120.00
Cookie jar, "Jack-O-Lantern" .... 60.00 to 90.00
Cookie jar, "Little Bo Peep" 88.00
Cookie jar, model of a pineapple 65.00
Cookie jar, "Money Bag" 40.00
Cookie jar, "Mother Goose" 200.00
Cookie jar, relief-molded Three Bears decor 50.00
Cookie jar, "Yogi Bear" 58.00
Vase, 9" h., double handles, colonial figures, ornate gold decor 46.00
Wall pocket, Daisy patt., brown & yellow glaze 55.00
Wall pocket, Ionic patt., No. 457, matte raspberry glaze 60.00

ADAMS

Columbia Coffeepot

The Adams family has been potters in England since 1650. Three William Adamses made pottery, all of it collectible. Most Adams pottery easily accessible today was made in the 19th century and is impressed or marked variously ADAMS, W. ADAMS, ADAMS TUNSTALL, W. ADAMS & SONS, and W. ADAMS & CO. with the word "England" or the phrase "made in England" added after 1891. Wm. Adams & Son, Ltd. continues in operation today.

Bowl, 6½" d., Winter Season patt., pink transfer $75.00
Coffeepot, cov., octagonal, Columbia patt., blue transfer, W. Adams, ca. 1850 (ILLUS.) 250.00
Cracker jar, enameled medallions on shaded pale orange ground, electroplated nickel-silver lid & bail handle 75.00
Creamer, Cries of London series, milkmaids 27.00
Plate, 8" d., Andalusia patt., gentleman & lady on horses, pink transfer 30.00
Plate, 8" d., transfer decor of two women washing clothes by lake w/viaduct bridge & important looking home in background, ca. 1840 .... 60.00
Plate, 8½" d., Seasons patt., "February," pink transfer 55.00
Plate, 9" d., Caledonia patt., elk & hunter, black transfer 35.00
Plate, 9½" d., Landing of Columbus series - Indians hunting scene, purple transfer 75.00
Plate, 10" d., Dr. Syntax series - "Dr. Syntax Bound To A Tree by Highwaymen," blue transfer 85.00
Plate, 10½" d., Shakespeare series - "Merchant" 42.00

Plate, 10½" d., Shakespeare series - "Richard III" 42.00
Platter, 17½" l., Regent Quadrant patt., dark blue transfer 375.00
Soup plate, fishing scene w/cottage, dark blue transfer, impressed "Adams," 10¼" d. 75.00
Soup plate w/flange rim, Palestine patt., red transfer, 10 5/8" d. 25.00
Soup plate w/flange rim, Spanish Convent patt., sepia transfer, 10¾" d. 35.00

AUSTRIAN

Moose Head Creamer

Numerous potteries in Austria produced good-quality ceramic wares over many years. Some factories were established by American entrepeneurs, particularly in the Carlsbad area, and other factories made china under special brand names for American importers. Marks on various pieces are indicated in many listings. Also see KAUFFMANN (Angelica) CHINA.

Bowl, 10" d., Thistle patt. $20.00
Bowl, 12" diagonal by 2" h., square shape, shades from pale peach to pale blue, large center transfer of five classical maidens, gold foliage around edge (Victoria-Carlsbad) 65.00
Compote, 8½" d., 2¾" h., Alhambra patt. 95.00
Condiment set: cov. mustard pot w/original spoon, salt & pepper shakers, toothpick holder, cruet w/original stopper & 8" d. tray; ornate gold florals w/gold trim decor on mint green ground, 7 pcs. (Royal Austria) 135.00
Creamer, figural moose head, shaded brown to pastel blue at base, 4½" h. (ILLUS.) 50.00
Creamer & cov. sugar bowl, Alhambra patt., pr. 110.00

Cup & saucer, footed cup, Angelica Kauffmann decor on teal green ground, ornate gold trim (Victoria, Carlsbad) 48.00
Dessert set, Bluebird patt., w/bluebird tea cloth, 28 pcs. (Victoria, Carlsbad) 255.00
Dresser set: tray, pin tray & ring tree; yellow roses decor, 3 pcs. . . 75.00
Fish set: 15 x 11½" platter & eight matching 8½" d. plates; fish center w/gold border on scalloped rim, 9 pcs. (M.Z. Austria) 300.00
Fish set: 25" platter, 11 plates & gravy boat w/attached underplate; h.p. speckled trout decor, 13 pcs. (Carlsbad) 350.00
Hatpin holder, h.p. roses decor, gold top 55.00
Muffineer, Blue Bird patt. (Victoria-Carlsbad) 40.00
Pitcher, 13½" h., applied gold lizard handle, floral painting on cream ground, signed "Stellmacher, No. 228" 165.00
Pitcher, tankard, 15" h., h.p. grapes & leaves decoration (Vienna) 198.00
Plaque, pierced to hang, blue windmill scene, 11½ x 11½" 95.00
Plate, 7" d., h.p. Falstaff & Mrs. Ford scene, dark green border w/1" gold rim 60.00
Plates, 8" d., life-like red raspberries & green foliage on soft shaded pastel ground, gold trim, set of 8 . . . . 120.00
Plate, 8½" d., pierced 1¼" blue edge w/dainty flowers in center . . 12.50
Plate, 8½" d., portrait medallions of Josephine, Maria de Medici & Duchess de Bourgogne; floral medallions between portraits, scalloped gilt edge 65.00
Plate, 9½" d., portrait of brunette lady w/name "Amicitia," gold trim, blue underglaze beehive mark on back 175.00
Plate, 12" d., portrait of three women & child in center, burgundy ground w/gold trim (Imperial China Austria) 125.00

Austrian Salt Dip

Plate, 17" d., lovely lady portait center, jade green border w/gold trim (Victoria Austria) 145.00
Salt dip, h.p. open roses & green leaves, gold feet, set of 4 (ILLUS. of one) 60.00
Vase, 7" h., bulbous, 4-handled, glossy enameled Art Deco-type poppies decor on matte ground (Austrian Amphora) 79.00
Vase, 10¾" h., 2 young girls walking in flower garden scene, 2 relief panels, "JS" in shield & "JS" w/numbers 150.00
Vase, 14½" h., h.p. fuchsia decor, cobalt blue on handles extends down sides & around base 355.00
Vase, 16" h., 4 feet, metal handles, portrait front decor, scenic reverse, ornate top, artist-signed 210.00

BAUER POTTERY

The Bauer Pottery was moved to Los Angeles, California from Paducah, Kentucky, in 1909, in the hope that the climate would prove beneficial to the principal organizer, John Andrew Bauer, who suffered from severe asthma. Flower pots, made of California adobe clay, were the first production at the new location, but soon they were able to resume production of stoneware crocks and jugs, the mainstay of the Kentucky operation. In the early 1930's, Bauer's colorfully glazed earthen dinnerwares, especially the popular Ring-Ware pattern, became an immediate success. Sometimes confused with its imitator, Fiesta Ware (first registered by Homer Laughlin in 1937), Bauer Pottery is collectible in its own right and is especially popular with West coast collectors. Bauer Pottery ceased operation in 1962.

Bowl, 8½" d., Plain-Ware patt., yellow $12.00
Bowl, ½-gal., Glossy Pastel Kitchenware patt., No. 12, green 15.00
Bowl, batter, Ring-Ware patt., cobalt blue 28.00
Bowl, cereal, Plain-Ware patt., green 4.00
Butter dish, cov., Ring-Ware patt., red 85.00
Casserole, cov., individual size, Ring-Ware patt., red 55.00
Creamer, Monterey patt., turquoise 5.00
Creamer, individual size, Ring-Ware patt., ivory 14.00
Creamer, Ring-Ware patt., red 12.00
Cup & saucer, Ring-Ware patt., blue 35.00
Custard cups, Ring-Ware patt., green, cobalt blue, red & yellow, set of 4 .... 23.00
Hanging pot, yellow, 9" 90.00
Flower pot, Ring-Ware patt., No. 3, green 4.00
Mixing bowl, Ring-Ware patt., No. 6, orange 65.00
Mixing bowl, Ring-Ware patt., blue, 9½" d. 22.00
Mixing bowl, Ring-Ware patt., No. 12, black 39.00
Mixing bowl, Ring-Ware patt., yellow 18.00
Pitcher, Monterey Modern patt., No. 207, green 15.00
Pitcher, Ring-Ware patt., turquoise 25.00
Refrigerator jar, cov., Monterey patt., burnt orange 65.00
Refrigerator jar w/lid, in metal frame, Ring-Ware patt., green 25.00
Refrigerator jar w/lid, in metal frame, Ring-Ware patt., red 37.00
Salt & pepper shakers, Monterey patt., brown, pr. 7.50
Salt shaker, Ring-Ware patt., No. 88, blue (single) 9.00
Serving bowl, Plain-Ware patt., brown 7.00
Spice jar, carnation decor on turquoise glaze, 8 x 6" 20.00
Teapot, cov., Ring-Ware patt., orange 48.00
Tidbit, 2-tier, Contempo patt., maroon 10.00
Tray, square, Plain-Ware patt., pink 7.00
Tumbler, Plain-Ware patt., yellow 3.00
Tumbler w/wooden handle, Ring-Ware patt., cobalt blue 16.00
Tumbler w/wooden handle, Ring-Ware patt., red 16.00
Vase, 7 x 9½", Indian decor on black ground 100.00

BAVARIAN

Ceramics have been produced by various potteries in Bavaria for many years. Those appearing for sale in greatest frequency today were produced in the 19th and early 20th centuries.

Cake plate, pierced handles, green, tan & white floral decor, 10" d. (H. & Co., Bavaria) $25.00
Cake plate, pierced handles, h.p. roses decor on rainbow shaded

ground, gold border, 10" d. (R.C. Malmaison) 40.00

Centerpiece bowl, 4 ornate gold feet, h.p. florals & blackberries overall decor, gold top rim, mother-of-pearl finish interior, ruffled & scalloped rim, 12 x 6"... 85.00

Charger, beaded & molded rim, h.p. game bird center, roses decor, marked "Bavaria" w/M in circle under crown, 12½" d. 85.00

Chocolate pot, cov., green, blue & brown windmill, houses & people on front, castle reverse decor, 9½" h. (J.P.S.V.) 100.00

Chocolate set: cov. chocolate pot & 6 c/s; bulbous, flower decor, 13 pcs. 125.00

Creamer, shell-shaped, coral handle 30.00

Creamer & cov. sugar bowl, birds & foliage w/silver overlay on copper ground, artist-signed, pr. 250.00

Creamer & cov. sugar bowl, decorated w/violets, gold handles, signed "Hirt," ca. 1870 (Zeh, Scherzer & Co.) 45.00

Dessert set: 8½" and 6½" d. footed scalloped bowls, 7½" d. serving plate, 6 sauce dishes & 1 oval serving dish; h.p. lavender iris w/gold trim decor, 10 pcs. 275.00

Dinner service, h.p. birds on blue, grey & yellow ground, 66 pcs. including 7 serving pcs. (Paul Mueller, Selb).................. 250.00

Dinner service: 3 large platters, cov. tureen w/stand, 12 dinner plates, 12 salad plates, 12 consomme bowls & saucers, 12 tea cups & saucers & 12 demitasse; each w/transfer print foliate band in tones of yellow, blue & red on white, 88 pcs.................... 660.00

Game plate, straight-billed game bird facing right on shaded cream to green to brown ground, 8½" d., Z.S. & Co. (Zeh, Scherzer & Co.)......................... 15.00

Plate, 6½" d., center portrait of beautiful young lady, lacy gold border, marked on back "R.S. Malmaison" (Rosenthal) 30.00

Plate, 9½" d., deep green outer rim w/six medallion portraits of Madame Recamier (ZS Bavaria) 60.00

Plate, 9½" d., gold foliage & peonies in center on cobalt blue ground 45.00

Plate, 10" d., "Melon Eaters" design center, gold & blue floral border, gold beading, artist-signed, 1873 (Jaeger & Co.) 175.00

Powder box, cov., pink & white, 3" female jester in sitting position on lid, hands at back corners, feet center front, 3 x 2½" 72.00

Powder box, figural lady holding rose bouquet, marked "Bavaria 3153" 78.00

Tea set: cov. teapot & cup & saucer, ribbed body w/pink roses & gold trim, 3 pcs. (Z.S. & Co.).......... 65.00

Toothpick holder, h.p overall landscape, dated, marked "R.C. Bavaria" (Rosenthal) 45.00

BELLEEK

Belleek Bust of Clytie

Belleek china has been made in Ireland's County Fermanagh for many years. It is exceedingly thin porcelain. Several marks were used, including a hound and harp (1865-1880), and a hound, harp and castle (1863-1891). A printed hound, harp and castle with the words "Co. Fermanagh Ireland" constitutes the mark from 1891. Belleek-type china was also made in the United States last century by several firms, including Ceramic Art Company, Columbian Art Pottery, Lenox, Inc., Ott & Brewer and Willets Manufacturing Co.

IRISH

Basket, cov., Basket Ware, round, applied tinted florals on cover, small size $2,200.00

Basket, cov., Basket Ware, 3-strand, oval, applied tinted florals on cover 3,500.00

Basket, cov., Basket Ware, 3-strand, no tint, 1865-90, 11" oval 4,500.00

Basket, cov., Basket Ware, 4-strand, applied tinted florals on cover, after 1921, 11" d. 3,000.00

Basket, Basket Ware, 4-strand, Boston shape, applied tinted florals on rim, after 1955 ....1,500.00

Basket, Basket Ware, 4-strand, Erne shape, applied tinted florals on rim, after 1955 .... 695.00

Basket, Basket Ware, 4-strand, Forget-Me-Not shape, applied tinted florals on rim 350.00

Basket, Basket Ware, 4-strand, Heart shape, no flowers, after 1921, 4½ x 4" 325.00

Basket, Basket Ware, 4-strand, center handle, Henshall shape, no tint, 11 x 9" 1,695.00

Beaker, Fan patt., cobalt blue trim, 3rd black mark, 4" h. 95.00

Bowl, 5" w., 6¼" to tab handle, 1¼" deep, Shell patt., pink trim, 1st black mark 145.00

Bowl, Quilted Diamond patt., 1st green mark 65.00

Bread plate, Limpet patt., 3rd black mark 145.00

Bread plate, Tridacna patt., 11½" point to point, 1st black mark 164.00

Bread plate, Shamrock-Basketweave patt., two-handled, 10½" d., 2nd black mark 130.00

Brush tray, Hawthorne patt., 1st black mark 350.00

Bust of Clytie, 11¾" h., 1st black mark (ILLUS.) 1,995.00

Butter plate, Shell patt., 2nd green mark 70.00

Butter tub, Aberdeen patt., 3rd green mark 22.00

Candlestick, Allingham patt., 1st black mark (single) 975.00

Cheese dish, model of cottage, twig handles, yellow lustre ground, 1st green mark, 6½ x 5¼ x 4½" h., 2 pcs. 145.00

Coffeepot, cov., Limpet patt., 3rd black mark 375.00

Coffeepot, cov., Shamrock-Basketweave patt., 3rd black mark 275.00

Coffee set, Limpet patt., 11 pcs., 3rd black mark 550.00

Compote, 9¼" w., 5¼" h., Basket Dessert Ware, 1st black mark 750.00

Compote, 9¾" d., 4¾" h., Greek patt., aqua trim, 2nd black mark 650.00

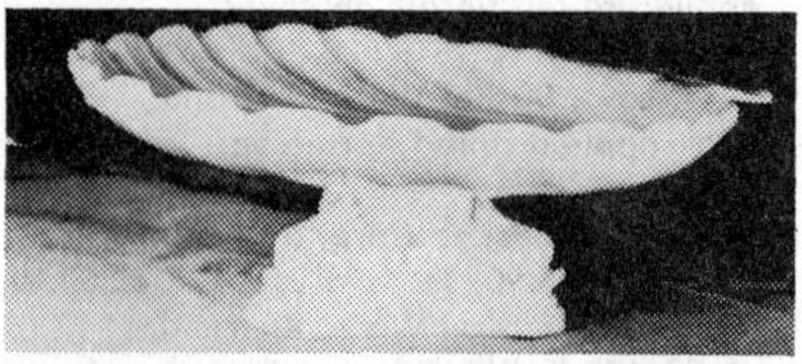

Belleek Shell Compote

Compote, open, 10" d., 4 7/8" h., Shell patt., three-dolphin pedestal, 1st black mark (ILLUS.) 650.00

Condiment set, in ornate holder: open salt, cov. mustard & pepper shaker; Harp Shamrock patt., green trim, 6½" d., 4½" h., 2nd black mark, 4 pcs. 450.00

Cracker jar, cov., Bamboo & Ribbon patt., pink ribbon center & double finial, 1st black mark 414.00

Creamer, Echinus patt., gold trim, rose "E" monogram, 4¼" d., 3 5/8" h., 1st black mark 171.00

Creamer, Lifford patt., 4th green mark 85.00

Creamer, Lily patt., 1st black mark 80.00

Creamer, Lily patt., 1st green mark 33.00

Creamer, Nautilus patt., large, 1st black mark 200.00

Creamer, Ribbon patt., 4th green mark 39.00

Creamer, Scale patt., 1st black mark 70.00

Creamer, Seashell patt., 3 x 5½", 4 5/8" h., 1st black mark 325.00

Creamer, Shamrock-Basketweave patt., yellow trim, 2nd black mark 65.00

Creamer, Shamrock-Basketweave patt., 1st green mark 40.00

Creamer, Toy Shell patt., blue trim, 2nd black mark 80.00

Creamer, Undine patt., 5th green mark 38.00

Creamer & cov. sugar bowl, Cleary patt., 3rd black mark, pr. 95.00

Creamer & open sugar bowl, Ivy patt., 3rd black mark, large, pr. ... 185.00

Creamer & sugar bowl, Limpet patt., gold trim, 3rd black mark, pr. 125.00

Cup & saucer, breakfast size, Tridacna patt., pink trim, 1st black mark 65.00

Cup & saucer, demitasse, h.p. tiny blue flowers, 3rd black mark 225.00

Cup & saucer, demitasse, Limpet patt., 3rd black mark 82.00

Cup & saucer, demitasse, Ring Handle patt., pink trim w/gold bands, 2nd black mark 175.00

Cup & saucer, plain shape w/Belfast Coat of Arms decoration, 1st black mark 125.00

Cup & saucer, Cone patt. w/pink trim, 2nd black mark 188.00

Cup & saucer, Grass patt., 1st black mark 150.00

Cup & saucer, Hawthorne patt., gold trim, 1st black mark 175.00

Cup & saucer, Neptune patt., 1st black mark 65.00

Cup & saucer, Thorn patt., 1st black mark 100.00

Cup marmalade, cov., Shamrock-

Basketweave patt., 4th green mark 55.00
Dish, Echinus patt., gold trim, 7", 1st black mark 90.00
Dish, Shell patt., green trim, 5 x 4", 2nd black mark 79.00
Dish, Sycamore Leaf shape, 4½", 3rd black mark 45.00

Belleek Aberdeen Ewer-Vase

Ewer-vase, Aberdeen patt., applied flowers & leaves decor, 3½" d., 6" h., 2nd black mark (ILLUS.) 410.00
Figurine, Boy Basket Bearer, 8½" h., green mark 250.00
Figurine, Praying Madonna, 12" h., 1st green mark 588.00
Figurine, Leprechaun w/"Good Luck" in English & Irish, gold trim, 2nd black mark 325.00
Flower holder, Imperial Shell patt., coral feet, 6" widest, 5" h., 2nd black mark 475.00
Flower holder, model of a seahorse on base, 3rd black mark 235.00
Flower pot, Finner patt., coral detailed handles, 11 x 6", 2nd black mark 2,495.00
Flower pot, Octagon patt., 2nd black mark 225.00
Honey pot, cov., Grass patt., 1st black mark 435.00
Honey pot, cov., Shamrock-Basketweave patt., 3rd black mark 145.00
Jug spill, Typha patt., 3rd black mark 125.00
Luncheon set: 7" d. plate & cup & saucer; Tridacna patt., yellow trim, 2nd black mark, 3 pcs. 75.00
Marmalade jar, cov., barrel-shaped, Shamrock patt., 3rd black mark 85.00
Menu holder, applied small florals & large daisy, 2nd black mark (some petal damage) 375.00
Milk jug, Shamrock patt., 4½", 5th green mark 85.00
Model of a cauldron, three-footed, 2nd black mark 95.00
Model of a dog, seated Greyhound on base, 3rd black mark 615.00
Model of a harp, shamrock trim, 8½" h., 5th green mark 125.00
Model of a swan, 4½ x 3½", 2nd black mark 175.00
Muffin dish, cov., Artichoke Tea Ware, green trim, 8½" d., 4½" h., 1st black mark 433.00
Plate, 6" d., Tridacna w/coral rim, 1st black mark 80.00
Plate, 8½ x 8", Shell patt., scalloped edge, 1st black mark 90.00
Powder bowl, cov., Mask Ware, 6½" d., 3rd black mark 295.00
Salt dip, master size, Shell patt., 1st black mark 80.00
Sandwich tray, oval, handled, Mask Tea Ware, cobalt blue trim, 3rd black mark 275.00
Spillholder, fish-shaped, 7" h., 1st black mark 475.00
Spillholder, Rock patt., 5¼" h., 3rd black mark 195.00
Sugar bowl, cov., Ivy patt., 3rd black mark 32.00
Sugar bowl, open, Ribbon patt., 3rd green mark 12.50
Teapot, cov., Bamboo patt., 1st black mark 450.00
Teapot, cov., Echinus patt., medium size, 1st black mark 300.00

Belleek Hexagon Teapot

Teapot, cov., Hexagon patt., green trim, 2nd black mark (ILLUS.) 350.00
Teapot, cov., New Shell patt., large, 3rd black mark 450.00
Teapot, cov., Tridacna patt., small, 2nd black mark 250.00
Tea set: cov. teapot, creamer, sugar bowl, tray & two cups & saucers; Neptune patt., green trim, 2nd black mark, 8 pcs. 1,795.00
Tea set: cov. teapot, creamer, sugar bowl, cake plate, four cups & saucers & four individual cake plates; Limpet patt., 3rd black mark, 16 pcs. 750.00
Vase, 7½" h., Celtic Tara patt., gold trim, 3rd black mark 250.00
Vase, 9" h., 4½" d., Princess patt., various flowers in yellow, pink, blue & white, 2nd black mark 795.00

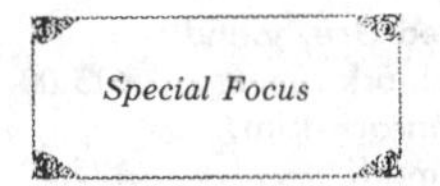

The Irish-Inspired Elegance of American Belleek

by Mary Frank Gaston

Americans have always had a reputation for their "can do" spirit in seeking to accomplish their goals. One interesting example of such zeal can be found in the origin of the American Belleek china industry. Although the word "Belleek" is almost synonymous with Ireland because it is the name of the fine translucent china made by the Irish Belleek Pottery, Limited, a "Belleek" china was also produced at one time in America. "American Belleek" refers to china manufactured between 1883 and 1930 by several potteries in Trenton, New Jersey and a few locations in Ohio.

American Belleek traces its roots back to the Irish firm which perfected this special type of ware in the early 1860's. The Irish porcelain was distinguished by a very thin body and special pearly glaze. The china became famous not only for those characteristics but also because of its creative shapes and decorations. Naturalistic forms with an emphasis on marine life and intricate woven work helped to attract a large market for this particular line of the factory's products.

"Belleek" was used in the marks of the pottery's production to designate the location of the factory, the village of Belleek, Ireland. As interest increased in the uniquely glazed ware, however, "Belleek" became the name used to identify that particular type of china. It is pertinent to note that the name "Belleek" became associated with the china early on and did not slowly evolve. (For complete history of Irish Belleek, see Richard Degenhardt's *Belleek, The Collector's Guide and Illustrated Reference,* 1978).

The popularity of the Irish Belleek was not limited to Europe but spread to America as well. Ott and Brewer, a Trenton, New Jersey pottery, was quite fascinated with the china, and the company strived to duplicate it. They were so determined in their efforts that they hired the son of the Irish plant's production manager to teach them the proper manufacturing techniques. When that ploy was not entirely successful, Ott and Brewer, refusing to give up, simply hired the father, William Bromley, Sr. With Bromley's instruction, Ott and Brewer's goal was soon accomplished.

Ott and Brewer is acknowledged as the first American pottery to make a Belleek china. Their first production of this ware dates from circa 1883. The company incorporated the name "Belleek" in marks on the pieces. By including the name "Belleek," the firm apparently was not trying to fool Americans into thinking that the china was made by the Irish pottery. Rather, the word indicated that the American china was the same type as the Irish.

Ott and Brewer's persistence proved that fine quality china could be made in the United States. Before that time, American ceramics were considered inferior to those manufactured abroad. Porcelain, especially, was imported. The Belleek china made in Trenton, New Jersey, however, was considered by the experts of the day to rival that of its namesake, the Irish Belleek Pottery. American Belleek, like the Irish product, had a thin, translucent body, was very light in weight, and the pieces were superbly crafted.

Shortly after Ott and Brewer's Belleek production was underway, another Trenton pottery, Willets Manufacturing Company, also began making Belleek. They were able to do this because William Bromley, Sr. left Ott and Brewer to work for the Willets factory. The Irishman seemed to have no qualms about teaching others how to make the exquisite Irish china. In fact, Bromley was not the only employee of the Irish factory who left that company and his homeland to work for American pottery manufacturers. Other workers followed this example. Consequently, knowledge of making Belleek spread from one pottery to another in Trenton and even into Ohio during the late 1800's. Like Ott and Brewer, the other American companies also added "Belleek" to their factory marks.

During the late Victorian and Art Nouveau years, a wide assortment of decorative pieces was made by the American potteries. The American Belleek, like its Irish mother, was designed for display even if the items had a utilitarian purpose, such as tea sets. Objects were often elaborately shaped with applied work on the body as well as hand-painted decoration. Gold was used in a variety of ways either to form or accent the decor. Such examples are truly works of art.

European artists worked for some of the companies. Their individual styles of decoration enhance many examples of American Belleek. Signed pieces by noted factory artists command premium prices among collectors today. A large amount of "blank" china was sold by several of the factories during the early 1900's when china painting was a serious hobby. Collectors are quick to differentiate between factory and non-factory decorated items. Rare pieces, unusual shapes, and quality decoration, however, must also be considered before dismissing articles decorated outside the factory.

Some of the American china closely resembles Irish Belleek in shape, pattern, or decoration. But a very large amount of the several companies' production is strikingly different from the Irish, especially in decoration. Often, except for the word "Belleek" in the mark, there is no other visible similarity between American and Irish Belleek. The composition of the china is not easily discernible to the naked eye.

American Belleek production spans a period of less than fifty years. In all, about fourteen companies are known to have made this type of china during that time. Most of the factories were not in business for too many years. Considering so few companies operated over a relatively short time, a large volume of Belleek was made. The most prolific factories in Trenton were Ott and Brewer, Willets, and the Ceramic Art Company which subsequently became Lenox, Inc. Examples from some of the other Trenton firms, such as the American Art China Company and the Columbian Art Pottery, range from rare to very rare!

In East Liverpool, Ohio, the Knowles, Taylor, Knowles Company also endeavored to make Belleek china a few years after Ott and Brewer initiated this type of ware in Trenton. It has been established that Knowles, Taylor, Knowles did make some Belleek between 1887 and 1889. Like the New Jersey companies, they also benefited from the expertise of an Irishman's knowledge. The company's Belleek production was short-lived, however, because the factory was destroyed by fire about 1889. When operations resumed in 1891, Knowles, Taylor, Knowles made a bone china, rather than a true Belleek body, for just a few years. "Lotus Ware" was the name assigned to this particular segment of the factory's production. Lotus Ware resembles American Belleek because of its delicate nature, translucent body, and artistic shapes and decorations as well as the period when it was made. These similarities cause many collectors to include Lotus Ware as part of the American Belleek era.

Quite a few years after Knowles, Taylor, Knowles ceased making Lotus Ware, two other Ohio potteries tried their hand at making Belleek china. The first was the Morgan China Company established in Canton, Ohio in 1924. The second was the Coxon Belleek factory founded in Wooster, Ohio in 1926. Both of these factories' Belleek operations were implemented by people connected with Trenton potteries. The Morgan and Coxon companies were quite successful in making a fine quality translucent ware. Instead of artistic or decorative objects, though, dinnerware services were the chief products. The sets were beautifully decorated and quite costly, designed for the affluent. Both companies were in business for only a few years, and thus examples are scarce and bring top prices today.

The end of the American Belleek era can be attributed to two causes. The first was economic. The manufacturing process was very expensive, and consequently, the finished products were also expensive. While most of the companies had either gone out of business entirely or ceased making Belleek china by the 1920's, the Depression years forced the others out of the market, with the exception of Lenox, Inc.

The second reason for the demise of the American Belleek industry, however, is perhaps more vital than the first. Coinciding with the year the Stock Market crashed, 1929, the courts ruled that only the Irish Belleek Pottery could use the name "Belleek" to identify its china. Evidently the Irish factory decided it was time to claim sole right to the name "Belleek." American manufacturers could no longer designate china by that name, and thus, by 1930, the American Belleek era ended. Lenox, Inc. remained in business, but the word "Belleek" had been omitted from its marks some years prior to the court decision.

American Belleek is held in high esteem by collectors. While numerous American potteries have made many forms of earthenwares, American translucent china is comparatively rare. Prices reflect the quality of the china, but in most cases prices are still competitive with, or sometimes even lower than, European china made during the same period. American Belleek is not really well known or easily found outside its areas of production. Keen interest in the china continues to center around the locations where it was made, Trenton, New Jersey and Ohio. Collectors in those areas have been quick to realize the historical significance of American Belleek as well as to appreciate its beauty and scarceness. As awareness grows, respect and admiration for American Belleek's contribution to our American heritage is more appreciated.

The author expresses appreciation to the following: Marje and Harry Hunsaker for contributing photographs from their American Belleek collection; to Nancy and Denver Wetzel, Quentin W. Welty, and Elizabeth Fowler for permitting pieces to be photographed from their respective collections of Lotus Ware, Coxon Belleek, and Willets Belleek; and to *Collector Books* for allowing us to use several examples from her book *American Belleek,* including items from the collections of Erma and Harry Brown, Mr. and Mrs. Don H. Stinchcomb, and Mr. Horace Mann.

For a complete history of the American Belleek era, including marks, examples, and prices, see Mary Frank Gaston's book, in color, American Belleek, *available from the publisher, Collector Books, P.O. Box 3009, Paducah, KY 42002, $20.95 ppd.*

Bouillon cup & saucer, gold twig handles, molded decor on creamy lustre ground, gold trim, Willets Manufacturing Company, Trenton, New Jersey $85.00

Bouillon cup & saucer, lotus handles, ruffled rim, gold paste decor on blue enameled ground, Willets 100.00

Bowl, 4¼" d., 2½" h., ruffled rim, coral-shaped handles, gold paste buds & leaves w/pink enamel decor, Willets 175.00

Lotus Ware Bowl

Bowl, 13½" d., 6½" h., Lotus Ware, twig-shaped handles, ruffled border, side indentations, pink interior, heavy gold trim on white body, Knowles, Taylor, Knowles, East Liverpool, Ohio, Wetzel Collection (ILLUS.) 3,000.00

Bowl, 7½" d., 4½" h., pink flowers & fleur de lis decor, gold handles, crimped edge, Willets 155.00

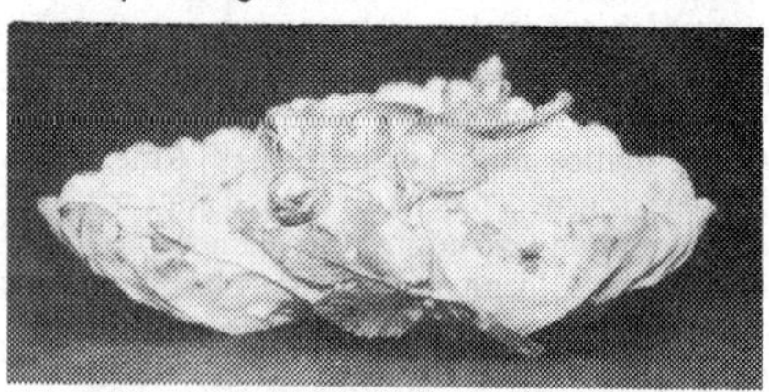

Ceramic Art Company Bowl

Bowl, 12½" l., 7½" w., applied floral & leaf designs decorated in different shades of gold on cream colored body, Ceramic Art Company, Trenton, New Jersey, Hunsaker Collection (ILLUS.).........1,300.00

Lenox Candleholders

Candleholders, undecorated, scalloped bases, Lenox, Inc., Trenton, New Jersey, pr. (ILLUS.) 125.00

Lotus Ware Candleholder Centerpiece

Candleholder centerpiece, Lotus Ware, applied leaves on base, scalloped border & overlapping scallops on bowl, center portrait decor, Knowles, Taylor, Knowles, Wetzel Collection, 8½" d., 5½" h. (ILLUS.) 1,400.00

Candlesticks, cream w/gold trim, Lenox, 8½" h., pr. 85.00

Lotus Ware Chocolate Pot

Chocolate pot, Lotus Ware, raised floral decoration on body & lattice work on base, Knowles, Taylor, Knowles, Wetzel Collection, 8" h. (ILLUS.) 750.00

Cider set: 14½" h. tankard pitcher & six 5½" h. mugs; each piece decorated w/different groups of fruits, berries & foliage, ornate handles & heavily tooled gold trim, Willets, 7 pcs. 750.00

Compote, pedestal base, two-handled, Art Nouveau style w/bright red tulips & heavy gold decor, Lenox 195.00

Willets Creamer

Creamer, gold enamel trim, h.p. rose medallion, Willets, 4" h. (ILLUS.) 150.00

Creamer w/gold dragon handle, "Princeton" on side, Willets, 4½" h. 75.00

Cup & saucer, demitasse, w/dolphin handle, swirl mold, overall florals w/gold decor, Willets 65.00

Cup & saucer, demitasse, embossed veining traced in gold, Willets 85.00

Coxon Cup & Saucer

Cup & saucer, bold multicolored florals w/gold trim, Coxon Belleek Pottery, Wooster, Ohio, Welty Collection (ILLUS.) 200.00

Cup & saucer, blue & pink enameled florals w/green leaves decor, Ott & Brewer, Trenton, New Jersey . . . 125.00

Cup & saucer, Cactus patt., Ott & Brewer 150.00

Cup & saucer, Palmer Cox Brownies decor, Ceramic Art Company 150.00

Pitcher, cider, cherry decor, Willets 105.00

Lenox Cider Pitcher

Pitcher, cider, h.p. grapes on black ground, Lenox blank w/Pickard Studio decoration (ILLUS.) 300.00

Ceramic Art Company Pitcher

Pitcher, 4" h., Art Nouveau curved handle, pink flowers, Ceramic Art Company (ILLUS.) 150.00

Willets Pitcher

Pitcher, 7¾" h., 8½" w., rose & burnished gold decor, coral-shaped handle, Willets, Hunsaker Collection (ILLUS.) 995.00

Ott & Brewer Pitcher

Pitcher, 8" h., applied flowers, h.p. pink water lily, heavy gold paste work, Ott & Brewer, Hunsaker Collection (ILLUS.) 1,400.00

Pitcher, tankard, 10¾" h., dark green handle extends to 6½" d. base, h.p. lemon foliage & blossoms decor on cream shaded to bluish green ground, Ceramic Art Company 245.00

Ceramic Art Company Tankard

Pitcher, tankard, 11" h., "Lady with Doves" decoration, brown tones at neck & base, Ceramic Art Company, Wetzel Collection (ILLUS.) .. 450.00

Pitcher, tankard, 14" h., h.p. grapes, Lenox 230.00

Pitcher, tankard, 14½" h., h.p. purple raspberries, white florals & green leaves overall decor, gold trim w/yellow base, Willets 375.00

Pitcher, tankard, 15" h., serpent handle, portrait of St. Bernard, artist-signed, Willets............. 750.00

Plate, 10" d., scene of mallard duck among rushes, artist-signed, Lenox 140.00

Morgan China "Azure" Plate

Plate, 10½" d., "Azure" patt., Morgan China Co., Canton, Ohio (ILLUS.) 200.00

Coxon Belleek Plate

Plate, 10½" d., blue border w/orange & yellow florals, Coxon, Welty Collection (ILLUS.) 200.00

Plate, 10½" d., "Bouquet" patt., wide inner red border, Coxon, Welty Collection 200.00

Plate, 10½" d., Dresden-type floral decor on cream ground, Coxon 250.00

Plate, 10½" d., sterling silver overlay floral decor, Lenox 65.00

Plate, 11" d., handled, Art Nouveau gold rim, h.p. decoration, 1912, Lenox 70.00

Lotus Ware Covered Rose Bowl

Rose bowl, cov., Lotus Ware, heavy filigree work on sides & lid, Knowles, Taylor, Knowles, Wetzel Collection, 7½" h. (ILLUS.) 1,800.00

Lotus Ware Open Rose Bowl

Rose bowl, open, Lotus Ware, gold tapestry work, apple blossoms decor, artist-signed, Knowles, Taylor, Knowles, Wetzel Collection, 4½" h. (ILLUS.) 600.00

Rose bowl-vase, h.p. roses w/gold tracery 125.00

Salt dip, individual size, h.p. floral decor w/gold scalloped rim, Willets 16.50

Salt dip, Ten Forget-Me-Nots patt., footed, Willets 20.00

Salt dip, ruffled, blue enamel flowers w/gold tracery, Willets 36.00

Stein, cantaloupe colored ground, narrow band of flowers & wide band of hanging cherries decoration, gold trim, 7" h., Lenox 150.00

Sugar bowl, cov., gold dragon-shaped handles, heavy gold sprays around blue enameled flowers, Willets 95.00

Sugar bowl, cov., silver overlay Art Deco design around inverted heart, Lenox 60.00

Sugar & Creamer with Dragon Handles

Sugar & creamer, dragon-shaped handles, mask spout on creamer, Hunsaker Collection, creamer 4½" h., pr. (ILLUS.) 175.00

Coxon Tea Cup, Demitasse Cup & Plate

Tea cup, demitasse cup & plate, scattered floral patt., Coxon, Welty Collection, each (ILLUS.) ... 200.00

Lenox "Hawthorn" Tea Set

Tea set, "Hawthorn" patt., Lenox, 3 pcs. (ILLUS.) 200.00

Tea Set with Silver Overlay

Tea set, sterling silver overlay w/figures in silhouette, decor by Rockwell Silver Co. on Ceramic Art Company china, Hunsaker Collection, 3 pcs. (ILLUS.) 325.00

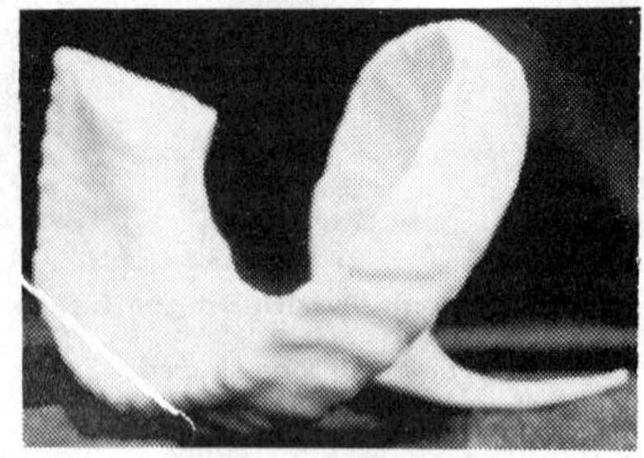

Ram's Horn Vase

Vase, 3½" h., 4¾" w., ram's horn shape, white lustre finish, Ott & Brewer, Hunsaker Collection (ILLUS.) 1,600.00

Lenox Vase with Silver

Vase, 8" h., sterling silver decoration w/pink floral cameo, Lenox (ILLUS.) 550.00

Vase, 9 3/8" h., turquoise blue enamel dots w/gold decor, Lenox 175.00

Vase, 10" h., Art deco pink & blue floral decor w/gold trim, Lenox 65.00

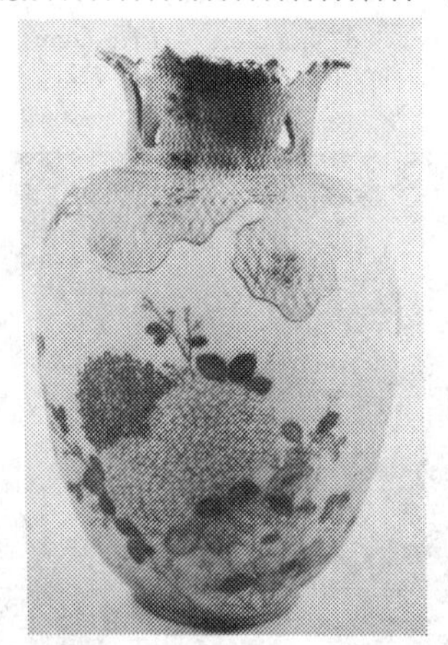

Ceramic Art Company Vase

Vase, 10¼" h., pink & white flowers, gold paste leaves, cream colored body, matte finish covers two-thirds of body while green flowers on diamond patterned ground decorate neck & upper part of vase, Ceramic Art Company (ILLUS.) 450.00

Lotus Ware Vase with Lilacs

Vase, 10½" h., Lotus Ware, lilac flowers, matte finish, gold trim, Knowles, Taylor, Knowles, Wetzel Collection (ILLUS.) 1,200.00

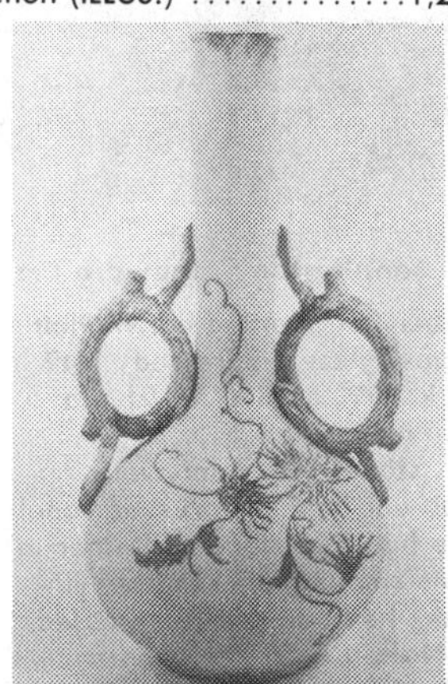

Ceramic Art Company Handled Vase

Vase, 11" h., fancy round handles, gold paste floral decor on cream colored body, Ceramic Art Company (ILLUS.) 350.00

Vase, 11" h., pedestal base, 6-sided narrows into 3" neck, rust colored ground w/gold stylized Art Deco florals, Lenox 60.00

Vase, 11" h., pink roses framed in gold beaded border & gold paste flowers & ribbons, Willets 300.00

Vase, 12" h., h.p. full figure of lady on glossy blue ground, Ceramic Art Company - Lenox 275.00

Vase, 14" h., gold-lined wide mouth, cabbage roses on dark brown ground, artist-signed, Lenox 425.00

Vase, 15" h., Art Nouveau maiden wrapped in diaphanous veil, artist-signed, 1910, Willets 850.00

Vase, 15½" h., ovoid, tiger lilies on brick red ground, artist-signed, Willets 475.00

Vase, 16" h., pansies decor on chocolate brown ground, artist-signed, Ceramic Art Company - Lenox 495.00

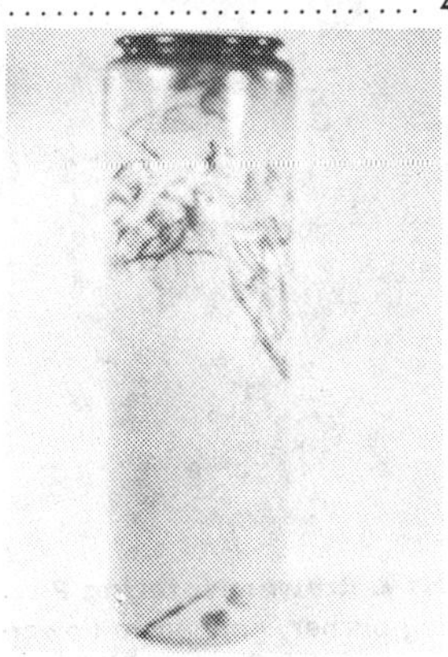

Willets Vase

Vase, 17" h., birds on branch decor, pale blue background, high glaze, Willets (ILLUS.) 500.00

Floral Decorated Ceramic Art Vase

Vase, 18" h., lavender & white flowers, gold trim, Ceramic Art Company (ILLUS.) 500.00

Coxon Vegetable Dish

Vegetable dish, cov., multicolored florals, gold trim, Coxon, Welty Collection (ILLUS.) 350.00

Ott & Brewer Watering Pitcher

Watering pitcher, gold paste flowers & leaves, Ott & Brewer, 8¾" h. (ILLUS.) 700.00

Lotus Ware Rose Bowl

Witches' pot rose bowl, Lotus Ware, pink flowers, green leaves, Knowles, Taylor, Knowles, Wetzel Collection, 7" h. (ILLUS.) 350.00

(End of Special Focus)

BENNINGTON

Bennington wares, which ranged from stoneware to parian and porcelain, were made in Bennington, Vt., primarily in two potteries, one in which Captain John Norton and his descendants were principals, and the other in which Christopher Webber Fenton (also once associated with the Nortons) was a principal. Various marks are found on the wares made in the two major potteries, including J. & E. Norton, E. & L. P. Norton, L. Norton & Co., Norton & Fenton, Edward Norton, Lyman Fenton & Co., Fenton's Works, United States Pottery Co., U.S.P. and others.

The popular pottery with the mottled brown on yellowware glaze was also produced in Bennington, but such wares should be referred to as "Rockingham" or "Bennington-type" unless they can be specifically attributed to a Bennington, Vermont factory.

Bennington Stoneware Crock

Chamber pot, mottled brown Flint Enamel glaze, impressed "1849" mark, 8¾" d., 5½" h. (chip at base of handle) $250.00

Crock, stoneware, semi-ovoid, applied ear handles, brushed cobalt blue figure of standing farmer in boots smoking pipe but w/reindeer's head on grey, impressed "J. Norton & Co., Bennington, Vt.2," ca. 1865, 2 gal., 10 7/8" h. (ILLUS.) 15,400.00

Cuspidor w/side vent, Shell patt., mottled Flint Enamel glaze, 7 3/8" d., 3½" h. 92.00

Cuspidor, octagonal w/paneled sides, mottled brown Rockingham glaze, impressed "1849" mark, 8" d. 110.00

Figure, parian, standing young woman holding large basket of grapes & leaves, personification of Autumn, 13" h. (minor damage) 95.00

Fist, three-dimensional clenched fist, mottled brown Flint Enamel glaze w/blue spots, very rare, 3 7/8" h. (hairline, flake & base chips) 760.00

Jug, stoneware, semi-ovoid, strap handle, brushed cobalt blue leaf sprig on grey, impressed "E. Norton & Co., Bennington, Vt.," 1 gal. (ILLUS.) 235.00

Bennington Stoneware Jug

Lamp, clear pattern glass font joined by brass connector to tapering round pottery base w/Flint Enamel glaze, 9¾" h. 452.50

Mug, slightly waisted, strap handle, mottled Flint Enamel glaze, 3" h. 130.00

Mug, mottled brown Rockingham glaze, impressed "Bennington, Vt.," 3½ x 2½" 45.00

Paperweight, model of a reclining dog, rectangular domed base, mottled brown Rockingham glaze, faintly impressed "1849" mark, 4½" l., 3" h. (tiny muzzle flake, small flakes on base) 650.00

Pitcher, 6½" h., bulbous base, scalloped rim, Sweetheart patt., mottled brown Rockingham glaze 500.00

Pitcher, parian, 18¾" h., tall ovoid shape w/low wide spout & strap handle, Sheaf of Wheat patt., ca. 1850 .... 75.00

Plate, 9½" d., mottled Flint Enamel glaze 135.00

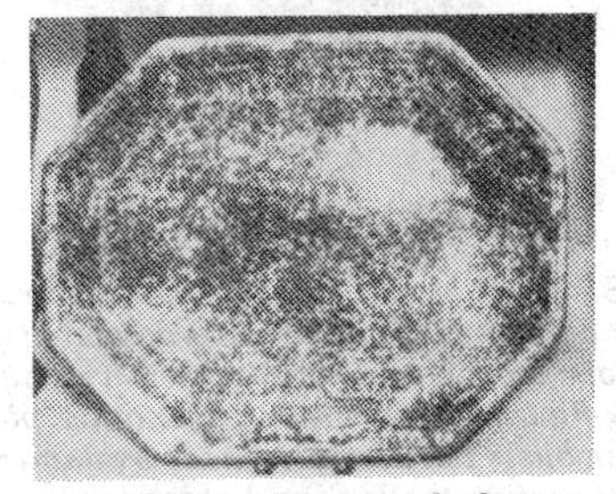

Bennington Octagonal Platter

Platter, octagonal, embossed scalloping at rim, mottled brown glaze, 15" l. (ILLUS.) 350.00

Soap dish, oval, mottled brown Rockingham glaze, "1849" mark, 5 3/8" l. (insert & lid missing, hairline) 35.00

Syrup pitcher w/pewter lid, parian, slightly tapering cylinder w/low, wide spout & strap handle, climbing ivy pattern, 7¾" h. (minor stains) 85.00

Tobacco jar, cov., Gothic Arch patt., mottled brown glaze, 9" h. (small edge chips) 225.00

Bennington Zachary Taylor Pitcher

Toby pitcher, bust portrait of Zachary Taylor w/tricorn hat w/ribbon reading "Rough" on one side, "Ready" on opposite side, green streaked Flint Enamel glaze, ca. 1850, three glaze chips, 13½" w., 13 1/8" h. (ILLUS.) 4,620.00

Vase, 9½" h., parian, applied grape clusters 70.00

BERLIN (KPM)

Painting of "Queen Louise"

The mark, KPM, was used at Meissen from 1723 to 1725, and was later adopted by the

Royal Factory, Konigliche Porzellan Manufaktur, in Berlin. At various periods it has been incorporated with the Brandenburg sceptre, the Prussia eagle or the crowned globe. The same letters were also adopted by other factories in Germany in the late 19th and 20th centuries. With the end of the German monarchy in 1918, the name of the firm was changed to Staatliche Porzellan Manufaktur and though production was halted during World War II, the factory was rebuilt and is still in business. The exquisite paintings on porcelain were produced at the close of the 19th century and are eagerly sought by collectors today.

Bowl, 13" l., 11" w., 3¼" h., leaf-shaped, molded petal edge, applied gold branch handle, interior scene of bird hovering over nest w/eggs amid array of colorful flowers, ferns & leaves, blended pink & light blue background, gold trim $650.00

Cup & saucer, footed, pink floral medallions w/gold enameling on cobalt blue ground 650.00

Cup, cover & stand, 2-handled cup, reserved & painted w/portrait of Alexander I, name in gilt on reverse, within square gilt cartouche, w/gilt floral within trellis band borders beneath gilt rims, iron-red ground, cup w/richly gilt interior & w/gilt artichoke finial, ca. 1830 .... 1,515.00

Flask w/gilt-metal stopper, scroll-molded, painted one side w/chinoiserie figures, reverse w/a flower spray, 19th c., 5" h. ... 110.00

Painting on porcelain, portrait of La Belle Chocolatiere after Jean Etienne Liotard, late 1870's, 6 x 4" 350.00

Paintings on porcelain, portraits of a German couple, signed H. Fritz, w/matching 6" frames, 8 x 10", pr. 10,000.00

Painting on porcelain, gypsy maiden playing a mandolin, artist-signed, ca. 1900, 11½ x 7 7/8" 4,125.00

Painting on porcelain, "The Sisters," fashionably dressed maiden seated in a chair & holding the hand of her sister clad in a black habit & standing near an open window w/a somber downcast gaze, artist- signed, late 19th c. 12 5/8 x 10¼" 2,200.00

Painting on porcelain, Cardinal tasting wine from a goblet, holding a prayer book in his left hand, standing beside a table draped w/a turkoman in an interior, ca. 1860, giltwood frame, overall 10¼ x 12¾" 3,850.00

Painting on porcelain, Queen Louise descending staircase wearing a a flowing white gown w/pink sash & ermine-lined deep blue velvet robe, signed A. Schinzel (after Richter), ca. 1900, 16 x 10¼" (ILLUS.) 5,500.00

Plaque, pierced to hang, jasper ware, 9 white relief portrait busts of Prussian Royal family on light green, simple white relief-molded border, paper on back w/hand written German script identifying each bust, 7¾ x 6½" 495.00

Vase, 6" h., portrait of Young Napoleon, signed Wagner 625.00

Vases, cov., 13½" h., fluted shouldered ovoid, h.p. floral posies & vignettes within raised gilded laurel wreaths, covers surmounted by an eagle, late 19th c., pr. 935.00

BISQUE

Bisque Dutch Girl Figure

Bisque is biscuit china, fired a single time but not glazed. Some bisque is decorated with colors. Most abundant from the Victorian era are figurines and groups, but other pieces from busts to vases were made by numerous potteries in the U.S. and abroad.

Ashtray, figure of pretty girl reclining on pink floral-decorated chaise longue, scantily clothed, fan protruding from one breast, elevated legs which both move, ashtray w/two rests at end, 5½" l. $110.00

Bust of sailor, intaglio eyes, w/earring, excellent coloring, 13" h. ... 695.00

Figure of a baby w/blonde hair sitting in tan bathtub, 2 2/3" l., 3¾" h. 89.00

Figure, "Fat Boy," Dicken's Pickwick Papers, dressed in grey coat w/yellow trim, black hat & boots, Heubach, 2" d., 4½" h. 60.00

Figure of a girl seated on swing wearing blue & tan skirt & blue hat w/gold trim & holding dog, 3" d., 4 5/8" h. 88.00

Figure of young black boy wearing white britches & reclining w/one arm up, 5" h. 58.00

Figure of a Scotsman in kilt, "Mind your own business" on base, lift kilt "Of course I've pants ye fool!," probably Schafer and Vater, 5¼" h. 130.00

Figure of baby sitting in old shoe, w/right arm lifted, toes sticking out the end, unmarked, 6½" l., 7" h. 280.00

Figure of a boy w/cigar, seated on stool & wearing fez & glasses, shades of pastel green & blue, Heubach, 2¾" d., 7" h. 85.00

Figure of a lady standing behind ship's wheel, decorated, Heubach, 11¼" h. 170.00

Figure of a girl in pleated skirt dancing, pastel pink pleated dress w/yellow lace collar, pink florals & gold branches, pink bow on shoulder, pink ballet shoes, standing by pink roses, green leaves, tambourine w/pink streamers on ground, Heubach, 5¾ x 9¾", 16" h. 595.00

Figure of a maiden standing by fountain, frilly cap over blonde locks, camisole neckline falling to reveal a hint of one breast, lovely pastels, soft gold, lavender, lovely face, 19" h. 375.00

Figure group, standing boy in Colonial costume tipping hat w/one hand, holding cane in other, beside standing girl in frilly bonnet & knee-length gown carrying a cylindrical basket, natural coloring on figures, tan base, 7" w., 11" h. 250.00

Figures, Dutch boy & girl, sitting, green, orange & white, Heubach, 3½ x 5", 7¼" h., pr. (ILLUS. of girl) 245.00

Figures, chubby cheeked boy in pastel blue outfit, straw hat w/pink band & chubby cheeked girl in ruffled pink dress trimmed in blue, straw hat w/green plume, 4" d., 11¼" h., pr. 373.00

Match holder, model of dog dressed like man, smoking pipe, resting on stump, molded striker, 4 x 3" 85.00

Model of a dog, tan & white, blue ribbon around neck, brown glass eyes, 6" h. 110.00

Model of a rabbit, wearing vest & top coat, carrying cane & open top egg, 7" h. 95.00

Nodding figure, seated Oriental man, bald head w/queue & moustache, holding pipe, pastel blue & pink, 2" d., 3" h. 65.00

Nodding figure, Mama Katzenjammer, seated, Germany, 4¾" 225.00

Nodding figure, pig, standing upright, Oriental garb w/huge exposed belly & breast, laughing face, overall honey beige variegated glaze, 3½" w., 5¼" h. 115.00

Nodding figures, Oriental man & woman w/arms upraised to hold fan behind his head, lavender pink, powder blue, peach w/ornate gold trim & beading on pearlized ground, Germany, 6¼" w. base, 6½" h., pr. 595.00

Piano baby, seated, white gown w/blue ribbon trim, Heubach, 1 3/8 x 2 1/8", 2½" h. 79.00

Piano baby, crawling, gown frilled around shoulders, blue bow in back, marked "Heubach," 5" 200.00

Piano baby, crawling, clutching a white cat, pale green gown w/gold beading at collar, 7¼" l. (one bead missing) 75.00

Rare Bisque Piano Baby

Piano baby, rare standing baby in long gown leaning on round chair w/pink & white striped painted upholstery, gold tassels & brown painted chair frame, spindles & legs, 12¾" h. (ILLUS.) 775.00

Piano baby, seated, dressed in blue

trimmed gown & bonnet, Scheider mark 65.00

Pin dish, model of ocean waves w/miniature nude on rim, ca. 1920's 125.00

Pin tray-soap dish combination, muzzled Pug puppy sits in dish, intaglio eyes, unmarked, 4" 125.00

Pitcher, 2 7/8" h., 2¼" d., figural colored boy's head, black hair & gold collar 69.00

Snow baby playing tuba, marked Germany, 1½" h. 45.00

Snow Baby, girl on a sled, 2" l. 55.00

Snow baby seated on champagne bottle sliding down hill, 3" h. 125.00

Snow baby night light, back of large head is open cut to accommodate small candle, figure is seated on ground, legs extended wearing ice skates, huge intaglio eyes, surprised mouth, known as "Cliquot Club" baby, 3½" h., marked "Heubach," 7" 450.00

Trinket box, figural, seated Dutch boy in blue, feet turned in, knees out, hands tucked under derriere, head turned right, intaglio eyes, large ears, smiling face, glazed hat, clogs & trousers, white scarf, figure separates at waist revealing container, 5" 450.00

Vase, 6½" h., 3¼" d., bust of Indian chief, black hair w/braids, tan & black feathers, brown shirt w/yellow & green beads 175.00

BOCH FRERES

Boch Freres Vases

The Belgian firm, founded in 1841 and still in production, first produced stoneware art pottery of mediocre quality, attempting to upgrade their wares through the years. In 1907, Charles Catteau became the art director of the pottery and slowly the influence of his work was absorbed by the artisans surrounding him. All through the 1920's wares were decorated in a distinctive Art Deco motif that is now eagerly sought along with the hand-thrown gourd form vessels coated with earth-tone glazes that were produced during the same time. Almost all Boch Freres pottery is marked, but the finest wares also carry the signature of Charles Catteau in addition to the pottery mark.

Vase, 8¾" h., 7¼" d., two gold handles, top & bottom rims, overall decoration of yellow berries & flowers in shades of blue w/gold & green trim, glossy finish $225.00

Vase, 11" d., footed, brown, black & yellow semi-circles separated by black-spotted brown columns on pale yellow crackled ground 770.00

Vases, 12¼" h., ovoid w/everted, rim, vertical waving bands between panels of stylized florals in shades of blue, tan, yellow & cream on crackled ground, pr. (ILLUS. of one right) 825.00

Boch Freres Vase

Vase, 12¼" h., ovoid, turquoise columns & upper navy, caramel & yellow foliage band on white crackled ground, signed (ILLUS.) .. 242.00

Vases, 12½" h., ovoid, irregular alternating sky blue & black panels w/tan scrollwork, pr. 1,100.00

Vase, 13½" h., ovoid, continuous frieze of stylized birds in flight between cloud form decorated neck w/inverted rim & lower portion, yellow, vibrant blue & light blue, crackled ground (ILLUS. left) 770.00

Vase, 17" h., 7½" d., flared rim, Oriental Imari influence w/designs of mums, peonies, flying insects, etc., blue & white Delft-style ground 235.00

BOEHM PORCELAINS

Although not antique, Boehm porcelain sculptures have attracted much interest as Edward Marshall Boehm excelled in hard porcelain sculptures. His finest creations, inspired by the beauties of nature, are in the forms of birds and flowers. Since his death in 1969, his work has been carried on by his wife at the Boehm Studios in Trenton, New Jersey. In 1971, an additional studio was opened in Malvern, England, where bone porcelain sculptures are produced. We list both limited and non-limited editions of Boehm.

ANIMALS

Bunny (Female), glazed, decorated, 1954, 3 x 2" $375.00
Chick, yellow, 1954, 3½" h. 175.00
Chipmunk, preening, 1959-61, 3" h. 170.00
Cocker Spaniel (American), black, 1980, 6½ x 5" 175.00
Cocker Spaniel, white, large, 8½ x 10½" 750.00
Lamb, 3½ x 5" 100.00
Lion cub, ca. 1954-59, 5 x 4½" 300.00
Whippets, standing, undecorated bisque, 1954-61, 7¾ x 5½" 715.00

BIRDS

Black-Capped Chickadee

Baby Cedar Waxwing, 1957-73, 3" h. 165.00
Baby Crested Flycatcher, 1962-72, 7" 320.00
Baby Goldfinch, 1959-72, 4½" h. 165.00
Baby Mockingbird 175.00
Baby Robin, 1957, 3½" h. 200.00
Blackburnian Warbler w/Mountain Laurel, 1958-66, 10½ x 5" 160.00
Black-Capped Chickadee standing on a holly branch, white bisque base, 1957-73, 9" h. (ILLUS.) 575.00
Fledgling Canada Warbler with Monarch Butterfly, 1967, 8½" h. 2,000.00
Fledgling Great Horned Owl, 1965-70, 7 x 5" 1,475.00
Fledgling Magpie, 1964-72, 5½ x 4" 310.00
Fledgling Red Poll, 1968, 4" h. 220.00
Fledgling Western Bluebirds, 1968-73, 5½" h. 288.00
Lesser Prairie Chickens, 1962-74, 10" h., pr. 1,450.00
Macaws, perched on a tree trunk w/shaped base, 1955-60, 9" h., pr. 220.00
Mute Swans (Bird of Peace), Boehm Studios, 1971, 17 x 17" 7,250.00
Nuthatch w/Holly & Moneywort, 1963, 11" h. 825.00
Owl, perched on books, white w/colored eyes & face, 1960-70, 9" h. 395.00
Prothonotary Warbler, 1958, 5½" h. 550.00
White-Throated Sparrow on Cherokee Rose, undecorated bisque, 1957, 9½" h. 1,100.00

MISCELLANEOUS FIGURALS

Ballerina, Swan Lake, 1954-61, 7¼" h. 120.00
Cupid w/horn, white bisque, 1954-59 .... 350.00
Madonna Bust, white bisque, 6" h... 185.00
Madonna La Pieta, white bisque, 1958-70, small 300.00
Neptune with Seahorse, decorated bisque, 1953-59, 7½" h. 800.00
Pigtail Angel, 1953-57, 3½" h. 400.00
Venus, decorated bisque, 1953-59, 7½" h. 800.00

BUFFALO POTTERY

Buffalo Pottery was established in 1902 in Buffalo, N.Y., to supply pottery for the Larkin Company. Most desirable today is Deldare Ware, introduced in 1908 in two patterns, "The Fallowfield Hunt" and "Ye Olden Times," which featured central English scenes and a continuous border. Emerald Deldare, introduced in 1911, was banded with stylized flowers and geometric designs and had varied central scenes, the most popular being from "The Tours of Dr. Syntax." Reorganized in 1940, the company now specializes in hotel china.

DELDARE

Bowl, fruit, 9" d., The Fallowfield Hunt - Breaking Cover $425.00

Deldare Ye Village Tavern Bowl

Bowl, fruit, 9" d., 3¾" h., Ye Village Tavern (ILLUS.) 400.00
Cake plate w/pierced handles, Ye Village Gossips, 10" d. 158.00
Candlestick, shield-back, Village Scenes 650.00
Creamer, Scenes of Village Life in Ye Olden Days 185.00
Creamer, The Fallowfield Hunt - Breaking Cover 150.00
Cup & saucer, Ye Olden Days 185.00
Humidor, cov., octagonal, Ye Lion Inn, 7" h. 700.00
Mug, Breakfast at the Three Pigeons, 4½" h. 242.00
Mug, Ye Lion Inn, 4¼" h. 280.00
Nut bowl, Ye Lion Inn, 1909, 8" d., 3¼" h. 400.00
Pitcher, 7" h., The Fallowfield Hunt - Breaking Cover 500.00
Pitcher, tankard, 12½" h., "All You Have To Do Is Teach the Dutchman English - The Great Controversy" 725.00
Pitcher, tankard, 12½" h., The Hunt Supper 900.00
Plaque, pierced to hang, The Fallowfield Hunt - Breakfast at the Three Pigeons, 12" d. 475.00
Plate, 6" d., Ye Village Street 185.00
Plate, 8½" d., Ye Town Crier (ILLUS.) 150.00
Plate, 9½" d., The Fallowfield Hunt - The Start, artist-signed, 1908 .... 176.00
Plate, 9½" d., Ye Olden Times, artist-signed, 1909 .... 175.00

Ye Town Crier Plate

Plate, 10" d., The Fallowfield Hunt - Breaking Cover, artist-signed 188.00

Fallowfield Hunt Chop Plate

Plate, chop, 14" d., The Fallowfield Hunt - The Start (ILLUS.) 516.00
Relish tray, The Fallowfield Hunt - The Dash, artist-signed, 1909, 12 x 6½" ....300.00 to 325.00
Relish tray, Ye Olden Times, artist-signed, 1908, 12 x 6½" 395.00
Saucer, Ye Olden Days, 1908 .... 82.00
Soup plate w/flange rim, Ye Village Street, 9" d. 250.00

EMERALD DELDARE

Candlesticks, abstract bayberry motif, artist-signed, 9" h., pr. 350.00
Pitcher, 8" h., octagonal, Dr. Syntax Bound to a Tree by Highwaymen 675.00
Plate, 8¼" d., Art Nouveau floral & geometric designs 350.00
Plate, 8½" d., Misfortune at Tulip Hall 450.00

MISCELLANEOUS

Butter tub, Apple Blossom patt. 35.00
Chamber set, Tea Rose patt., pink & yellow roses on white ground, 9 pcs. 335.00
Christmas plate, 1955 . . . . . 34.00
Christmas plate, 1959 . . . . . 42.00
Christmas plate, 1962 . . . . . 143.00
Feeding dish, "Baby Bunting" decoration 40.00

Campbell Kids Feeding Dish

Feeding dish, Campbell Kids decoration, 7¾" d. (ILLUS.) 48.00
Fish plate, Pike, signed "R.K. Beck," 9" d. 30.00
Game platter, buck & doe standing in water w/forest scene background, signed "R.K. Beck," 15 x 11" oval 65.00
Game set: pitcher, oval & rectangular platters & six game plates; Buffalo Hunt design, 9 pcs. 650.00
Gravy boat, Blue Willow patt., 1909 . . . . . 50.00
Jug, Cinderella, 1906, 6" h. 350.00
Jug, Geranium, blue & white, 3¼" h. 125.00
Jug, Geranium, blue & white, 4½" h. 175.00
Jug, George Washington, blue decoration, gold trim, 1905, 7½" h. 400.00
Mug, commemorative, "Souvenir of Calumet Club, Buffalo, N.Y., April 24, 1911" 80.00
Mug, George Washington 225.00
Mug, Roosevelt Bears 165.00
Pitcher, 9" h., Pilgrim, 1908 . . . . . 425.00 to 500.00
Pitcher, 9¼" h., John Paul Jones, 1907 . . . . . 375.00
Pitcher, tankard, 14" h., monk decoration, ca. 1905-08 . . . . . 135.00
Pitcher, Gaudy Willow patt., 1907 . . . 300.00
Pitcher, water, Blue Willow patt., cobalt blue spout & gold trim 150.00
Plate, 7" d., commemorative, Niagara Falls, blue-green border 35.00
Plate, 9¼" d., Blue Willow patt. 16.50
Plate, 10" d., historical series, Niagara Falls, blue & white 65.00
Plate, Temperance, blue & white, 1912 . . . . . 115.00

CANTON

Canton Bowl with Lobed Corners

This ware has been decorated for nearly two centuries in factories near Canton, China. Intended for export sale, much of it was originally inexpensive blue-and-white hand decorated ware. Late 18th and early 19th century pieces are superior to later ones and fetch higher prices.

Bowl, 8 7/8" w., square w/lobed corners, underglaze-blue river landscape within a trellis & cloud border, 19th c. (ILLUS.) $385.00
Dish & domed cover w/bud finial, blue-and-white, bridge scene on cover & dish interior, raincloud border, 19th c., 9¼ x 8" squared form 247.50
Pitcher, water, 15" h., pear-shaped, cane-shaped handle styled as a branch of bamboo, blue-and-white, Willow patt. variant below a trellis-diaper border flanked by a dash-and-scallop edge, 19th c. . . 715.00
Plates, 10" d., blue-and-white, bridge scene center, raincloud border, 19th c., set of 8 . . . . . 990.00
Platter, 10½" sq., squared corners, blue-and-white, mountains & pagoda decor 150.00
Platter, 18¼" oblong w/cut corners, blue-and-white, bridge scene center, raincloud border, 19th c. (one rim chip) 275.00
Serving dish & cover w/pod finial, rectangular w/notched corners, underglaze-blue Chinese river landscapes within cloud & trellis-diaper border on cover & interior, exterior w/floral sprays, 19th c., 9 3/8" l. (top not original, repaired) 330.00

Tea jar, cov., hexagonal w/domed cover, blue-and-white, orchids, prunus, foliage & rocks, shoulders w/fruit & plants, 19th c., 12 5/8" 1,100.00
Teapot, cov., blue-and-white, bamboo wrapped handles, 7" d....... 175.00
Vegetable bowl, cov., blue-and-white, 9 3/8 x 8 5/8" oblong 195.00

CAPO DI MONTE

Capo di Monte Figures

Production of porcelain and faience began in 1736 at the Capo-di-Monte factory in Naples. In 1743 King Charles of Naples established a factory there that made wares with relief decoration. In 1759 the factory was moved to Buen Retiro near Madrid, operating until 1808. Another Naples pottery was opened in 1771 and operated until 1806 when its molds were acquired by the Doccia factory of Florence, which has since made reproductions of original Capo-di-Monte pieces with the "N" mark beneath a crown. Some very early pieces are valued in the thousands of dollars but the subsequent productions are considerably lower.

Bowl-plaque, relief-molded Bachanallian scene w/leopards, ca. 1860, 14" d. $175.00
Chocolate cup & saucer, cov., figural cupid finial on cover, relief-molded figures, ca. 1870 .... 140.00
Chocolate cup & saucer, cov., relief-molded figures, ca. 1860 .... 100.00
Figure of a clown playing a violin & standing next to a drum, 12" h. . . 450.00
Figures, allegorical figures of young maidens representing "The Four Seasons," set of 4 (ILLUS.) 2,400.00
Model of African crowned crane, w/one foot in water, other held up in air, w/water plants, artist-signed, 14" h.................... 160.00
Mug, relief-molded satyr decoration, large, ca. 1900 .... 85.00
Pastille box, cov., relief-molded nudes & putti on cover, interior & exterior decoration 285.00
Pitcher, 8" h., relief-molded satyrs & cherubs w/polychrome enameling & gilt trim 65.00
Platter, 19", relief-molded scene of beautiful draped ladies 85.00
Stein, twisted handle, brass mounts, inlaid lid, 5 liter 1,785.00
Tile, paneled, relief-molded scene of nude maidens at Roman bath 165.00
Urn, two-handled, relief-molded white classical women & cherubs, w/gold trim & handles, 7" h...... 165.00

CARLTON WARE

The Staffordshire firm of Wiltshaw & Robinson, Stoke-on-Trent, operated the Carlton Works from about 1890 until 1958, producing both earthenwares and porcelain. Specializing in decorative items like vases and teapots, they became well known for their lustre-finished wares, often decorated in the oriental taste. The trademark Carlton Ware *was incorporated into their printed mark. Since 1958, a new company,* Carlton Ware Ltd., *has operated the Carlton Works at Stoke.*

Bookends, multicolored Art Deco design, pr......................... $65.00
Bowl, 11" d., twig handles, glossy blue w/relief-molded tree, ribbed 75.00
Box, cov., enameled wisteria tree & bird of paradise on cobalt blue ground 135.00
Centerpiece bowl, handled, four-footed, enameled multicolored florals & birds on cobalt blue ground, gilt trim, 12½" l., 6¼" h.......................... 170.00
Cheese dish, stylized florals on soft beige ground 45.00
Cup & saucer, demitasse, enameled & gilt chinoiserie scene on blue lustre ground, gold interior 55.00
Dish, oval, single molded stepped handle, scalloped rim, enameled blue, yellow & pink spray of daisies w/green & gilt lustre leaves on mottled blue, yellow & pale claret lustre ground, gilt trim, 10 3/8" l................... 66.00
Marmalade jar, cov., mottled orange 65.00
Potpourri jar, footed, enameled wisteria tree w/raised enamel & gilt trim, 6" h. 110.00
Strawberry dish w/underplate, pierced, pink & brown design on

glossy light green ground, 8½" d. 85.00
Vase, 6" h., enameled multicolored florals & birds w/ornate gold trim on cobalt blue ground 80.00
Vase, 6" h., "Vert Royale" (green) 45.00
Vase, 9½" h., 6½" d., scroll footed, chrysanthemums on beige ground, gold trim, 1893 registry mark 98.00
Violet vase, "Noire Royale" (black) 45.00

CAULDON LTD.

Cauldon Flow Blue Plate

The Staffordshire pottery at Cauldon Place, Shelton, was a direct descendant of the famed Ridgway potteries. After John Ridgway dissolved his partnership with his brother, William, in 1830, he operated the Cauldon Place works independently, selling out to T.C. Brown-Westhead, Moore & Co. in 1855. He remained active in the firm several years. Brown-Westhead, Moore & Co. became Cauldon, Ltd. in 1905 and continued in operation until acquired by Pountney & Co. Ltd. of Bristol in 1962.

Plate, 10¾" d., white center, 2" black border w/heavily enameled variegated green leaves & shaggy lavender flowers, made for Tiffany & Co., New York, New York $58.00
Plate, 12¼" d., Peking Star patt., flow blue, 1891-98, set of 4 (ILLUS. of one) 120.00
Tea set: cov. teapot, cov. sugar bowl & creamer; ornate molding of intricate rococo scalloping & swirls, pure white porcelain richly endowed w/heavy enameled gold in a floral & foliage pattern, some gold matte trim, glossy, gold handles, 3 pcs. 125.00
Tea set: cov. teapot, cov. sugar & creamer; wide vertical ribs & handles, white ground, gold trim, made for Davis Collamore, New York, New York, 3 pcs. 135.00
Tureens, cov., ornate rococo molding with gold trim, gold decoration in a spidery network w/tiny hand-enameled pink roses alternating w/yellow pansies every 2", round, pr. 135.00

CELADON

Carved Celadon Jar

Celadon is the name given a highly-fired Oriental porcelain featuring a glaze that ranges from olive through tones of green, blue-green and grey. These wares have been made for centuries in China, Korea and Japan. Fine early Celadon wares are costly, later pieces are far less expensive.

Bowl, 10½" d., shallow, everted rim, cylindrical foot, exterior w/white raised enamel precious emblems & scholar's implements, 19th c. $247.50
Dish, everted lipped rim, shallow sides, incised central peony blossom, crackled deep green glaze, Ming Dynasty, 10½" d. 247.50
Fishbowl, compressed globular body, well-carved w/numerous carp amidst lotus pads & waterweeds beneath scattered prunus blossoms floating on the surface, all w/delicately incised detailing, bubble-suffused glaze of pale green pooling around the ridged rim & above the knife-pared foot, Qing Dynasty, Kangxi period (1662-1722), 20" d., 13" h. 6,600.00

Garden seat, hexagonal, four panels pierced w/trelliswork & two w/lion masks & cash medallions, row of molded bosses between each panel, 17" h. (some glaze flaking) 1,540.00
Jar, boldly carved w/four panels enclosing flowers of the four seasons on a combed ground above lotus leaves, all beneath an even pale green glaze, Yuan Dynasty, 1280-1367, 11¼" h. (ILLUS.) 4,125.00
Rose petal jar w/inner lid, relief-molded blue, pink & red flowers w/green leaves, gold trim, 4½" d. at bulbous shoulders, 5½" h. 95.00
Teapot & oval lid w/knob finial, ovoid, dragon spout, handle emerging from cresting waves on body, olive green glaze, 6" h. 275.00
Vase, 7" h., relief-molded dragon around sides, bluish green glaze 65.00
Vase, 7¼" h., stick-type, flared rim, high rolled foot, incised w/dragon amid *lingzhi* & scrolling clouds, 19th c. 357.50
Vases, cov., 18½" h., tapering bulbous form, prunus branch handles, brown-glazed band of lappets, blue & white lady w/Buddhistic lion, circular gadrooned cover w/stylized flower finial, on circular ormolu base cast w/leaves & berries, late 19th c. (the mounts later), pr. 4,620.00

CERAMIC ARTS STUDIO OF MADISON

Founded in Madison, Wisconsin in 1941 by two young men, Lawrence Rabbitt and Reuben Sand, this company began as a "studio" pottery. In early 1942 they met an amateur clay sculptor, Betty Harrington and, recognizing her talent for modeling in clay, they eventually hired her as their chief designer. Over the next few years Betty designed over 460 different pieces for their production. Charming figurines of children and animals were a main focus of their output in addition to models of adults in varied costumes and poses, wall plaques, vases and figural salt and pepper shakers.

Business boomed during the years of World War II when foreign imports were cut off and, at its peak, the company employed some 100 people to produce the carefully hand-decorated pieces.

After World War II many poor-quality copies of Ceramic Arts Studio figurines appeared and when, in the early 1950's, foreign imported figurines began flooding the market, the company found they could no longer compete. They finally closed their doors in 1955.

Since not all Ceramic Arts Studio pieces are marked, it takes careful study to determine which items are from their production.

Bell, figural, "Winter Belle" $32.50
Figurine, Aphrodite, green & brown 45.00
Figurine, Balinese Dancer, semi-bisque glaze, 9½" h. 28.00
Figurine, Bo-Peep, 5¼" h. 32.00
Figurine, Drummer Girl 34.00
Figurine, modern dancer, "Beth" 22.00
Figurine, Pioneer Susie, standing lady w/broom 29.00
Figurine, Water Sprite, female, green 20.00
Figurine, Winter Willie, kneeling boy w/snowball 28.00
Figurines, "Comedy" & "Tragedy," 10" h., pr. . . . . . 75.00 to 125.00
Figurines, elephants, seated, one wearing pink polka dots, other blue polka dots, 3½" h., pr. 38.00
Figurines, Oriental boy & girl wearing green jackets, 6" h., pr. 40.00
Figurines, Peter Pan & Wendy, on bases w/tall leafy plants, pr. 48.00
Figurines, Shadow Dancers, pr. 64.00
Figurines, Swedish man & woman, large, pr. 85.00
Figurines, Victorian gentleman & lady, pr. 65.00
Model of cat & kitten, shelf-sitter . . . 25.00
Models of horse heads, 3½" h., pr. 35.00
Models of Peter & Polly parrots in cage, pr. 48.00
Models of skunk family, 4 pcs. 75.00
Planter, model of a girl's head, "Barbie" 45.00
Planter, model of a girl's head, "Becky" 39.00
Planter, model of a girl's head, "Bonnie" 46.00
Planter, model of a girl's head, "Mei-Ling" 38.00
Salt shaker, figural East Indian boy sitting w/yellow polka dot turban 12.50
Salt & pepper shakers, figural dog & doghouse, pr. 20.00
Salt & pepper shakers, figural elf w/toadstool, pr. 20.00
Salt & pepper shakers, figural foxes, pr. 40.00
Salt & pepper shakers, figural mother Polar Bear holding cub, pr. 25.00

Salt & pepper shakers, figural mouse w/cheese, pr. 20.00
Salt & pepper shakers, figural roosters, pr. 27.00
Salt & pepper shakers, figural skunks, pr. 25.00
Vase, 4½" h., cylindrical, embossed stylized flying ducks on ivory ground 15.00
Vase, bud, 7" h., three flower holders modeled as bamboo stalks w/standing Oriental girl w/musical instrument beside them on base 35.00
Wall plaques, pierced to hang, figural, Harlequin & Columbine, pr. 85.00
Wall plaques, pierced to hang, figural, Zor & Zorina, pr. 64.00

CHINESE EXPORT

Tobacco Leaf Pattern Cup & Saucer

Large quantities of porcelain have been made in China for export to America from the 1780's, much of it shipped from the ports of Canton and Nanking. A major source of this porcelain was Ching-te-Chen in the Kiangsi province but the wares were also made elsewhere. The largest quantities were blue and white. Prices fluctuate considerably depending on age, condition, decoration, etc.

Basin & water bottle, "famille-rose" palette, circular base w/underglaze-blue diaper border, interior w/gilt scrolling band encompassing panels of flowers, center decorated in enamel depicting a sage surrounded by figures & a side table; matching bottle w/continuous scene of figures, 18th c., 11 3/8" d. basin, 10" h. bottle, 2 pcs. $1,100.00
Bowl, 9¾" sq., painted on interior & exterior rim w/border of gold & maroon foliate whorls flanking at the corners oval wreaths of pink roses & green leaves centering gilt foliate sprays & in center of the sides iron-red & gold leaf motifs above blue & gold circlets substituted on front & reverse of exterior rim by either seated cat crest of Gillespie or gilt initials "TG," all between gilt band borders, ca. 1810 . . . . 1,430.00
Charger, "Skating Lesson," center painted in shades of purple, pink, blue, white & black w/a Dutchman holding a long pick w/which his student companion steadies herself while five smaller figures glide or tumble on the brown ice beyond, cavetto w/four worn gilt floral sprays, rim (hair crack) w/border of flowers & fruit in a full palette of "famille-rose" enamels heightened in worn gilding, ca. 1740, 14" d. 7,700.00
Cups & saucers, Tobacco Leaf patt., minor abrasions, 1770-85, cup 2 1/8" h., saucer 4¾" d., pr. (ILLUS. of one set) 3,850.00
Dishes, oblong w/shaped sides & cut corners, Pseudo Tobacco Leaf patt., decorated w/stylized leaves, cut pomegranates & brocade rings in pink, deep blue, iron-red & chartreuse w/gilt highlights, late 18th c., 11 5/8" l., pr. 4,675.00
Fish bowls, "famille-noire" palette, prunus blossoms, peonies, chrysanthemums & bamboo, symbolizing the four seasons, w/numerous birds, butterflies & rocks, all reserved on a black ground, interior w/goldfish swimming among aquatic plants, 20¼" d., 17½" h., pr. 4,400.00

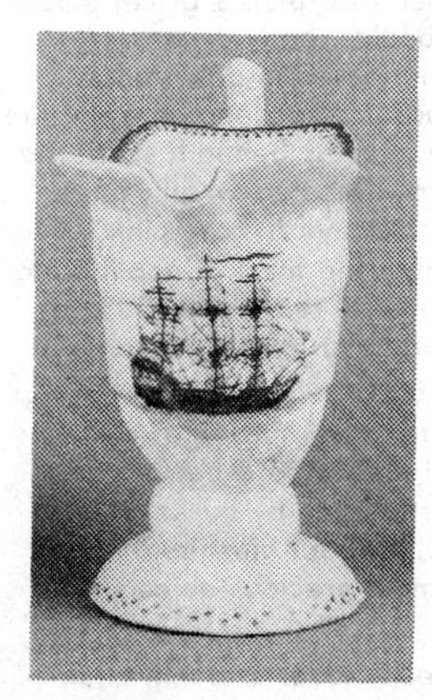

Chinese Export Milk Jug

Milk jug, helmet-shaped, branch handle, brown, black & iron-red fully-rigged ship w/gilt highlights flying an American flag, foot w/brown vintage border, rim w/gilt-dotted band & gilt & brown husk border, ca. 1795, 5 3/8" h. (ILLUS.) 2,200.00

Mug, bell-shaped, "famille-rose" palette, boy w/a couple hand-in-hand & holding fans, watching pair of amorous spotted dogs, S-scroll handle flanked by flowering plants, grey rockwork & plantain trees, rim w/iron-red & gold floral scroll border, ca. 1745, 6 5/16" h. 770.00

Pitchers, cov., 15¾" h., "famille-rose" palette, pear-shaped, continuous winter scene of robed figures strolling & at leisurely pursuits, one vignette showing a gathering around four lambs, neck, spout, covers & base enameled enclosing birds, flowers & landscape in grisaille, gilt, black & iron-red, Qianlong, pr. 9,900.00

Platter, 16¾" l., oval, painted w/scattered pink flowers within a gilt spearhead band at cavetto below slightly flaring rim decorated w/pink & pale turquoise brocade design & ribbon-tied cash emblems, 19th c. 1,760.00

Punch bowl, interior rim w/genre scenes & small floral panels, sides w/butterflies & floral sprays, battle scene or charade depicted on the floor, exterior w/continuous scene of people in a garden engaged in various types of painting, early 19th c., 14¾" rim d., 6" h. 2,310.00

Sauce tureen, cov., diamond-shaped, scalloped rim, blue & green glazed loop handles, body decorated w/broad leaves in pale yellow, pale turquoise & deep blue w/blue outline in veins beneath scattered blossoms accented w/gilt, large central blossom in rose-pink, cover w/finial in the form of applied blossoms in coral-red & yellow, late 18th-early 19th c., 12" l. (some wear) 3,025.00

Soup plate, blue "Fitzhugh" patt., central pine cone & beast medallion surrounded by husks & dumbbells within four clusters of blossoms & precious objects, late 19th c., 9 5/8" d. (ILLUS.) 550.00

Soup tureen, cover & stand, chamfered rectangular shape, tureen & stand w/figures & sampans near pagodas in a river landscape within a ruyi-head band & on stand rim a wide border of scalework, blossoms, ruyi heads & leaves repeated on the cover rim, center of cover w/river view interrupted by scroll knop (reglued), ends of tureen w/pierced kylin-mask handles, blue & white, 19th c., 14 7/8" l., 12" h. overall 1,430.00

Blue Fitzhugh Soup Plate

Tile, fan-shaped, "famille-rose" palette, elaborate diapered border enclosing reserve of court vignettes & flocking birds against foliate tentril ground, in metal frame, 19th c., 9½" l. 467.50

Nanking Tray

Tray, leaf-shaped, blue "Nanking", 8 x 6" (ILLUS.) 175.00

Vase, 34¼" h., "famille-rose" palette, tapered baluster form w/wide flared mouth, applied gilt fu-lion handles, butterflies & flowers surrounded by shaped panels featuring figures in interiors at various pursuits on gilt ground, applied gilt dragons climbing on the shoulder, 19th c. 3,300.00

Vases, cov., 20" h., "famille-jaune" palette, shoulder applied w/two Fu lion masks, painted w/peony blossoms & foliage on yellow ground, matching cover w/Fu lion finial, late 19th c., now mounted as lamps, pr. 3,300.00

Waste bowl, spread-winged American eagle & shield w/monogram, delicate blue & gilt rim decor 400.00

CLARICE CLIFF DESIGNS

"Tonquin" Pattern Bone Dish

Clarice Cliff was a designer for A.J. Wilkinson, Ltd., Royal Staffordshire Pottery, Burslem, England when they acquired the adjoining Newport Pottery Company whose warehouses were filled with undecorated bowls and vases. About 1925, her flair with the Art Deco style was incorporated into designs appropriately named "Bizarre" and "Fantasque" and the warehouse stockpile was decorated in vivid colors. These hand-painted earthenwares, all bearing the signature of designer Clarice Cliff, were produced until World War II and are now finding enormous favor with collectors.

Bone dish, Tonquin patt., blue (ILLUS.)........................ $11.00

Bowl, 3" d., "Bizarre," drip over glaze 50.00

Bowl, 8" d., "Bizarre," Crocus patt.......................... 40.00

Bowl, soup, Tonquin patt., brown ... 6.00

Cache pot, "Fantasque," 3" 48.00

Candleholder, "Bizarre," 2" elevated holder, 3½" d., 2¼" h. 85.00

Cheese dish, cov., "Fantasque" 143.00

Coffee pot, cov., "Bizarre," Gay Day patt., orange, blue, purple & green florals on yellow, tan & brown ground, 3½" d., 7½" h. ... 175.00

Coffee set, "Bizarre," Chintz patt., 15 pcs. 122.00

Cookie jar, cov., "Bizarre," My Garden patt., Art Deco style green w/deep green mottling, finial & handles are flowers & leaves in green, blue & rose, 6½" widest d., 7¼" h. 156.00

Creamer, Tonquin patt., blue 15.00

Cup & saucer, "Bizarre," Geometric patt. 40.00

Cup & saucer, Rural Scene patt. 15.00

Egg set, cov. hen dish w/three egg cups in dish, 6", 4 pcs. 138.00

Flower frog, "Bizarre," Art Deco style, model of pile of rocks w/mottling of brown & green on grey ground, 3½" d., 3¾" h...... 69.00

Gravy boat & platter, Tonquin patt., brown, 2 pcs. 22.50

Honey pot, cov., model of a beehive w/applied bee, Newport Pottery Co., England, 2¾" h. 95.00

Marmalade jar, cov., "Fantasque" .. 60.00

Match holder, "Bizarre," Nasturtium patt., Art Deco orange & yellow flowers w/spattered brown, place for burnt matches & striker, 4¾" d., 6 1/8" h. 140.00

Pitcher, 6 5/8" h., 3½" w., octagonal, "Bizarre," Gay Day patt., orange, & purple Art Deco florals on blue, brown & green ground .. 135.00

Pitcher, 6¾" h., 4¾" d., jug-type, "Bizarre," blue, rose & gold Art Deco florals w/green leaves on cream ground w/blue bands 198.00

Plaque, pierced to hang, Cottage Garden, 18" d. 1,815.00

Plate, 9" d., "Fantasque," Canterbury Bells patt. 22.00

Plate, 9" d., "Bizarre," Islands Moderne patt. 13.00

Platter, 15½" l., Tonquin patt., brown 35.00

Sauce dish, Tonquin patt., brown ... 4.00

Tray, "Bizarre," Crocus patt., Faux handles, dated 1929, 11 x 9½" ... 90.00

Vase, 5 3/8" h., 4¼" d., "Bizarre," blue & green florals w/tan 165.00

Vase, 6¾" h., 5¾" d., "Bizarre," Art Deco pagoda, lavender shrubs, orange tree w/green & orange leaves, green grass, gold sky on cream ground 302.00

COALPORT

Coalport Porcelain Works operated at Coalport, Shropshire, England, from about 1795 to 1926 and has operated at Stoke-on-Trent as Coalport China, Ltd., making bone china since then.

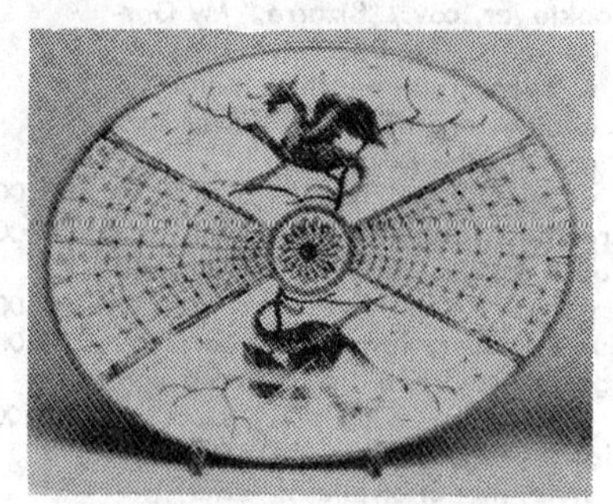

Coalport Oval Dish

Basket, Indian Tree patt., ca. 1891, 3½ x 3" $38.00
Cache pot & stand, tapered cylinder, gilt dolphin head handles, scene of a harbor landscape w/shepherds in the foreground, within gilt border against a gilt scrolled white ground, ca. 1810, 5 5/8" h., 2 pcs. 275.00
Cup & saucer, demitasse, Pembroke patt. 35.00
Dessert service: four oval two-handled cov. sugar bowls w/two stands, four oval dishes, four shell-shaped dishes, three square dishes & 32 plates; specimen flowers named at the reverse in blue within a gilt chain patt. border, rim w/band of foliage on a peach ground, ca. 1800, 49 pcs. (minor chips, hairline & repairs) 48,400.00
Dishes, oval, h.p. w/a flowerhead at the center within gilt-line borders surrounded by fan-shaped panels of turquoise & gilt diaper pattern alternating w/panels of a griffin entwined in branches on a gilt-twigged ground, ca. 1810, 10½" w., pr. (ILLUS. of one).....2,420.00
Dishes, oval, w/gilt foliage border & the Church Gresley pattern in yellow, the center w/a crest below a crown, ca. 1805, 11" w., pr. (some wear) 1,100.00
Dishes, oval, w/shaped gilt-line rim & decorated w/the Church Gresley pattern in yellow, ca. 1810, 15" w., pr. (some wear) 2,420.00
Plates, 9" d., h.p. buildings & ruins in wooded landscape center within gilt circular cartouches, border w/apricot & gilt key pattern, ca. 1810, pr. 550.00
Tureen, cov. & stand, oval, w/gilt scroll finial & handles & decorated w/the Church Gresley pattern in yellow between gilt lines, ca. 1800, the stand 15¼" w. (tureen & cover cracked, some wear), 3 pcs. 1,760.00
Vase, 9" h., baluster shape, blue scale ground, painted w/an urn, strawberries & flowers, the reverse w/fruit & flowers within oval gilt foliate panels, the neck & foot w/a band of stylized pink flowerheads alternating w/green leaves, enriched w/gilt, ca. 1805 (one handle restored) 264.00

COPELAND & SPODE

Copeland Center Bowl

W.T. Copeland & Sons, Ltd., have operated the Spode Works at Stoke, England, from 1847 to the present. The name Spode was used on some of its productions. Its predecessor, Spode, was founded by Josiah Spode about 1784 and became Copeland & Garrett in 1843, continuing under that name until 1847. Listings dated prior to 1843 should be attributed to Spode.

Basket, square-shaped, the center painted w/Spode's "The Rookery near Dorking Surrey," named on the reverse, within a border of gilt trailing foliage, the interlaced strap handle & edge molded w/leaf-tips & vines, ca. 1815, 9¾" w. (handle repaired, gilding rubbed) $308.00
Bowl, 9½" d., Spode's Tower patt., blue transfer.................... 60.00
Bowl, fruit, Spode's Cowslip patt. ... 18.00
Bowl, salad, Spode's Cowslip patt. .. 12.00
Butter pat, Spode's Sorrento patt. ... 8.00
Cake stand, pedestal base, India Tree patt., deep rust w/copper lustre, 12½" d., 5½" h........... 50.00

Center bowl, parian, oval foliate-molded dish tinted pale green w/pale pink interior, supported on the backs of two classical maidens w/long flowing tresses, further supported by glazed coral branches in the center, base molded w/four large scallop shells tinted pale pink, the whole w/gilt details, ca. 1870, 18" w. (ILLUS.) 715.00

Compote, 18½" l., 13¾" h., in the form of an infant Pan w/grape wreath in his hair & pipes in his lap, seated on the tails of two intertwined dolphins supporting two scallop shells w/jets of water, raised on lobed circular base w/gilt highlights, ca. 1880 (one shell restored) 495.00

Cookie plate, Spode's Cowslip patt. 18.00

Creamer & cov. sugar bowl, Spode's Cowslip patt., large, pr. 45.00

Cup, demitasse, Spode's Sorrento patt. 12.00

Cup & saucer, handleless, Oriental scene, blue transfer, gold scalloped rim, marked "Spode" 45.00

Dessert set: two 2-handled 10¾" oval dishes, two 2-handled 9½" oval dishes, 2-handled oblong dish, 2-handled compote, two 2-handled cov. sugar bowls w/stands & 18 plates; painted bouquets of flowers, pale green borders molded w/flowering foliage & enriched in gilding, shaped rims, Spode, ca. 1830, 26 pcs. 770.00

Spode Dessert Set

Dessert set, partial: pr. cov. sugar bowls (one cracked), four shell-shaped dishes, 18 plates, pr. of coolers w/covers & liners (one repaired handle, one cracked liner) & a similar compote; painted in colors w/flower sprays, the pink ground enriched w/gilding of flowering foliage, shaped rims, Spode, patt. no. 3912, ca. 1840, 27 pcs. (ILLUS.) 6,050.00

Foot rest, pair of arched legs supporting curved rectangular rest, blue transfer scene, marked "Spode's Tower, Copeland, England," 13½ x 10", 6¼" h. 295.00

Garden seats, ironstone, octagonal, decorated in the Chinese taste w/polychrome blossoms & borders, 18¾" h., pr. 1,540.00

Pitcher, 5½" h., Spode's Tower patt., blue transfer 65.00

Pitcher, 8" h., Spode's Tower patt., blue transfer 47.00

Pitcher, 8½" h., 7½" w., pioneers, Indian & Chicago fire within creamy cameos on blue ground, F. Burley 180.00

Pitcher, milk, Spode's Tower patt., red transfer 45.00

Plate, 8" d., underglaze-blue Oriental scene w/overglaze polychrome enameling, gilt trim, impressed "Spodes New Stone" 50.00

Plate, 10½" d., Spode's Tower patt., blue transfer 25.00

Plates, 10½" d., scalloped, gadrooned gilt rim & paneled border centering stylized garden motif, iron-red, cobalt blue & green w/gilt highlights, "New Stone, Spode 8330," early 20th c., set of 12 .... 660.00

Plate, bread & butter, Spode's Cowslip patt. 8.00

Plate, dinner, Spode's Cowslip patt. 18.00

Plate, dinner, Spode's Wickerlane patt. 15.00

Plate, salad, Spode's Wickerlane patt. 8.00

Platter, 12", Camilla patt., blue transfer 65.00

Platter, 20¾ x 16" oblong w/cut corners, exotic stylized floral design in brilliant blues & greens, impressed "Spode New Stone," ca. 1815 .... 330.00

Platter, Spode's India patt., ca. 1805 .... 650.00

Punch bowl, Spode's Tower patt., blue transfer, 15½" d. 265.00

Soup tureen, Spode's Bird & Grasshopper patt., 1805-15 ....1,500.00

Vase, 13 3/8" h., 14" l., in the form of two putti, one astride & one attempting to push a large blue nautilus shell w/gilt highlights, base molded as the shore w/blue & gilt waves crashing on the shell, ca. 1877 (restoration to shell rim) 440.00

CORDEY

Founded by Boleslaw Cybis in Trenton,

New Jersey, the Cordey China Company was the forerunner of the Cybis Studio, renowned for its fine porcelain sculptures. A native of Poland, Boleslaw Cybis was commissioned by his government to paint "el fresco" murals for the 1939 New York World's Fair. Already a renowned sculptor and painter, he elected to remain and become a citizen of this country. In 1942, under his guidance, Cordey China Company began producing appealing busts and figurines, some decorated by applying real lace dipped in liquid clay prior to firing in the kiln. Cordey figures were assigned numbers that were printed or pressed on the base. The Cordey line was eventually phased out of production during the 1950's as the porcelain sculptures of the Cybis Studios became widely acclaimed.

Ashtray, rococo form, scrolls, flower, two leaves & gold trim, No. 6034-177, 5½" $12.00
Box, cov., roses in relief on top, No. 6038, 5½" sq. 65.00
Bust of girl w/veil, No. 5026, 7" h. 85.00
Bust of lady, No. 4015 .... 75.00
Bust of lady, No. 5003, blue 52.00
Bust of lady, No. 5004 .... 45.00
Bust of lady, No. 5005 .... 48.00
Bust of lady wearing bonnet, No. 5013-47 .... 60.00
Bust of lady wearing green costume, No. 5024 .... 42.50
Bust of thoughtful lady w/head tilted, eyes closed, "tapestry" bonnet, arms out w/delicate hands, much lace, 14" h. 145.00
Busts: man w/blue tricorn lace hat, No.4013B & lady w/big hat w/pink lace trim, No. 4014P, pr. 115.00
Dresser set: 16" tray, w/rococo scroll & roses, two long neck cologne bottles w/rose festooned stoppers & pedestal covered ring jar w/floral decoration, Nos. 7022, 7024, 3 pcs. 205.00
Figure of an "Old Colony" lady, pink flowers in hair, No. 5054, 9¼" h. 60.00
Figure of a lady w/ringlets in her hair, "Marcelle," wearing a huge flat lace shawl w/flowers & leaves, seated on rococo scroll floral base, No. 5069, 10" h. 155.00
Figure of young girl holding bouquet, No. 4049P, 10½" h. 235.00
Figure of a Can Can dancer w/head tilted forward, roses in red hair, black edge lacy "bateau" neckline over yellow striped top, voluminous skirt w/ruffled lace petticoats, No. 4064, 11" h. 300.00
Figure of Colonial Lady, No. 5084, 11½" h. 95.00
Figure of woman w/hair in ringlets, hat w/leaves, bustle dress, lace & roses in blues & aqua, No. 4073, 13½" h. 120.00
Figure of lady, No. 305, 14" h. 85.00
Figure of lady, mature appearance w/voluminous skirt, shawl & ruffles, No. 482, 15½" h. 105.00
Figure of a man, plum-mauve long jacket, light pink vest over beige shirt, white stockings, plum shoes, left hand at side, right hand holds plum hat w/colorful trim, No. 305, 16½" h. 75.00
Figures: Colonial Man (No. 8710) 12" h., & Colonial Lady (No. 8711), 11½" h., pr. 75.00
Lamp, bust of Victorian lady 115.00
Lamp, floor-type, center metal shaft through white enameled tube w/gold metal details, decorated w/roses, 4' h. 100.00
Model of a bluebird on tree stump, w/roses, petals & leaves, No. 6004, 10" h. 75.00
Model of a lamb, "Bambi," flowers & leaves intact, No. 6025 .... 115.00
Trinket box, cov., footed, rococo style, cream w/lush gold roses, blue flowers & leaves, No. 7038, 5 x 3¾", 3½" h. 33.00
Wall pocket, Victorian lady's face in full relief, ringlets in hair, roses & lace wrap at throat, No. 902, 10¼" h. 150.00

COWAN

Pueblo Mother & Child Group

R. Guy Cowan first opened a studio pottery in 1913 in Cleveland, Ohio. The pottery con-

tinued to operate almost continuously, at various locations in the Cleveland area, until it was forced to close in 1931 due to financial problems. This fine art pottery, which was gradually expanded into a full line of commercial productions, is now sought out by collectors.

Ashtray, shell shaped, gunmetal glaze $13.00
Book ends, model of polar bears eating fish, ivory glaze, Art Deco style, pr. 215.00
Candleholder, double, figural nude woman, ivory glaze, 9½" h. 125.00
Candlesticks, octagonal base, ivory lustre glaze, 3¼" h., pr. 20.00
Candlesticks, figural nude woman, ivory glaze, 12" h., pr. ..200.00 to 300.00
Candlesticks, blue lustre glaze, 13½" h., pr. 60.00
Candlesticks, four-sided, green glaze, pr. 20.00
Cigar tray, model of a duck 28.00
Figure group, Pueblo Mother & Child, mother dressed in brown w/turquoise jewelry & w/blanket around her waist holds child in white blanket, both seated astride a white pony, rounded rectangular base growing w/thicket of brightly glazed blue, green & yellow plants, designed by Francis Luis Mora, molded "F. Luis Mora" & impressed "Cowan," 14½" h. (ILLUS.) 1,100.00
Flower frog, figural nude w/scarf, white, 6¼" 110.00
Flower frog, figures of two dancing nudes 250.00
Flower holder, model of a mushroom, 5" h. 80.00
Model of a flamingo, ivory glaze, 11" h. 195.00
Model of a peacock, turquoise glaze, 12" h. 75.00

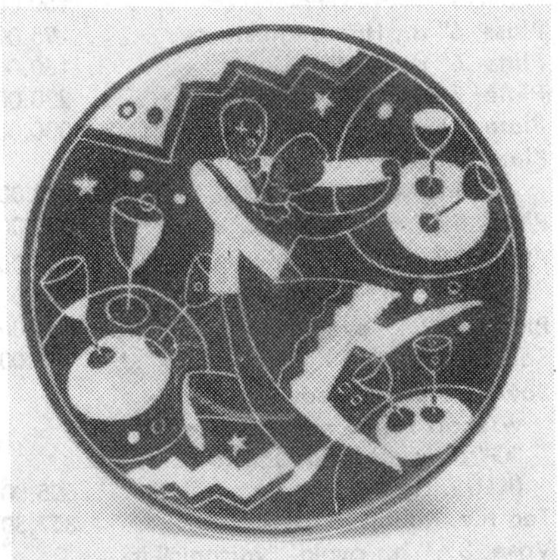

Jazz-age Design Plate

Plate, 11¼" d., Jazz-age stylized scene of couple dancing among martini glasses, turquoise & navy, designed by Viktor Schreckengost, impressed "Cowan" (ILLUS.) 1,100.00
Plate, 11½" d., h.p. rabbit in blue & black glaze 500.00
Trivet, hexagonal, relief-molded florals, multicolor high gloss glaze 325.00
Vase, 5½" h., fat shape, matte apple green blending to rose glaze 55.00
Vase, 7½" h., Chinese Red glaze ... 75.00
Vase, 10" h., handled, deep blue-green glaze 55.00
Vase, 11¼" h., 7¾" d., flared rim vase resting atop a stylized Chinese bird, crackled medium to dark green high gloss glaze 242.00
Vase, 12", flat form, mythical figures at base, glossy royal blue crackle glaze 250.00

CUP PLATES (Staffordshire)

Like their glass counterparts, these small plates were designed to hold a cup while the tea or coffee was allowed to cool in a saucer before it was sipped from the saucer, a practice that would now be considered in poor taste. The forerunner of the glass cup plates, those listed below were produced in various Staffordshire potteries in England. Their popularity waned after the introduction of the glass cup plate in the 1820's. Also see CUP PLATES under Glass.

Staffordshire (unmarked), Garden Scenery patt., blue transfer $38.00
Staffordshire (unmarked), Leeds-type w/blue feather edge, ca. 1790, 4½" d. 55.00
Staffordshire (unmarked), Massacre of the Innocents patt., brown transfer, ca. 1840 .... 32.00
Staffordshire (unmarked), multicolored floral transfer 35.00
Wood, child w/bird center, red transfer 155.00
Wood, country scene, black transfer 55.00

CYBIS

Though not antique, fine Cybis porcelain figures are included here because of the great collector interest. They are produced in both limited edition and non-numbered series and thus there can be a wide price range available to the collector.

Pollyanna

American Wild Turkey, 10½" $400.00
Ariel, 5" 310.00
Ballerina, "Little Princess," 10" 450.00
Blue Headed Vireo Building Nest, 8½" 450.00
Buffalo, 5" 95.00
Burro, "Fitzgerald," 7" 150.00
Calla Lily, 16½" 1,125.00
Child Clown Head, "Funny Face," w/holly, 10½" 375.00
Cinderella, 7½" 450.00
Columbia, 1776 Through 1976, 13" h. plus wooden base 400.00
Deermouse, "In Clover," 3½" 150.00
Elephant, "Alexander," 7½ x 6½" .. 275.00
First Flight, 4½" 150.00
Good Queen Anne, 13¼" 350.00
Great White Heron, 16½" 375.00
Guinevere, 12" 500.00
Indian Girl Head, "Running Deer," 10" 400.00
Jester, 15" 500.00
Juliet, 12" 1,200.00
Little Blue Heron, 9¼" h. plus wooden base 325.00
Little Red Riding Hood, 6½" 225.00
Peter Pan, 7½" 285.00
Pandora, 5" 165.00
Pansies, "China Maid," w/butterfly 275.00
Pollyanna, 7" (ILLUS.) 300.00
Psyche, Eros' True Love, 9¼" 240.00
Raccoon, "Raffles," 7½ x 9" 225.00
Robin Hood, 10" 625.00
Queen Esther, 13½" 1,000.00
Sharmaine, The Sea Nymph, 12½" 325.00
Snail, "Sir Henri Escargot," 3" 225.00
Tiffin, 7 x 5½" 225.00
Wendy, 6½" 135.00

DEDHAM

Dedham Carp Plate

This pottery was organized in 1866 by Alexander W. Robertson in Chelsea, Mass., and became A. W. & H. Robertson in 1868. In 1872, the name was changed to Chelsea Keramic Art Works and in 1891 to Chelsea Pottery, U.S.A. About 1895, the pottery was moved to Dedham, Mass., and was renamed Dedham Pottery. Production ceased in 1943. High-fired colored wares and crackle ware were specialities. The rabbit is said to have been the most popular decoration on crackle ware in blue.

Ashtray, Elephant, 4" d. $300.00
Bacon tray, Grape, 9¾ x 6" 440.00
Bonbon, cov., Rabbit, 4¼" d., 3½" h. 330.00
Bouillon cup & saucer, Rabbit 250.00
Bowl, 5¼" d., Pond Lily 412.50
Bowl, serving, 8" sq., Rabbit 385.00
Chocolate pot, cov., Grape, 9 x 7" .. 632.50
Creamer, cylindrical, Rabbit, 5" h. .. 247.50
Cup & saucer, Azalea 302.50
Cup & saucer, Magnolia 220.00
Humidor, cov., Elephant, ca. 1927 ..2,970.00
Marmalade jar, cov., spherical, Azalea, 4¼" h. 302.50
Pitcher, 5" h., owl & chickens decor 150.00
Plate, 6" d., Horse Chestnuts 95.00
Plate, 6" d., Moths 150.00
Plate, 7½" d., Azalea 220.00
Plate, 7½" d., Swan 330.00
Plate, 8½" d., Carp jumping out of swirling wave (ILLUS.) 1,100.00
Plate, 8½" d., Duck 300.00
Plate, 8½" d., Lobster (ILLUS. left) .. 880.00
Plate, 8½" d., Rabbit ....85.00 to 115.00
Platter, 12½" oval, Dolphin 1,430.00
Salt shaker, tall, Rabbit (single) 195.00
Sauce bottle, tall square form w/short round neck, blue script "G" on crackle ground, 8¼" h. (ILLUS. right) 605.00
Tea tile, Rabbit, 5½" 357.50
Vase, 8½" h., ovoid, "volcanic" irregular red, brick red, navy blue, light blue, green & beige glaze

Lobster Plate & Sauce Bottle

w/light gold iridescence, artist-signed "Hugh Robertson" 6,600.00
Whipped cream bowl, Elephant, 5½" d. 385.00

DELFT

Bristol Delft Plate

Delft, a tin-glazed pottery, is of a type that originated in Belgium and Italy centuries ago. Because Dutch traders made the city of Delft the center of their world-wide trade on these items, the term "delft" became synonymous with "tin-glazed pottery." The use of delft to indicate only blue and white is in error since all potters worked in polychrome as well. Delft, faience, and majolica are all tin-glazed pottery.

Bowl, 10¼" d., iron red, green, blue & yellow w/stylized landscape w/houses, rockwork & foliage, Holland, mid- to late 18th c. (cracked, rim chips) $330.00

Charger, cobalt blue stylized floral design, yellow trim at rim, Holland, late 18th c., 14" d. (repaired chip on underside of rim, small glaze chips) 330.00

Charger, flaring rim, blue, yellow, iron-red & manganese flower-filled urn flanked by flowerheads, probably English, 18th c., 14" d. . . 825.00

Charger, painted wide border band divided into six reserves of intricate blue on white floral decoration, center decorated with intricate blue florals, blue & white, 14" d. (minor edge chips) . . 400.00

Dish, blue & white octagonal harbor scene reserved on the powdered manganese ground, the edge w/shaped reserves containing stylized flowerheads, blue "G" mark, possibly Wincanton or Bristol, England, ca. 1740, 8 7/8" d. 352.00

Dish, painted in iron red, blue, green & yellow w/a parrot perched on a branch issuing from rockwork, within a border of trailing flowers & pinecones, Lambeth, England, ca. 1760, 9" d. (rim chips) 198.00

Dish, painted in blue, manganese, iron red, yellow & green, w/a shaped panel of a vase of flowers, a bird perched in the branches in a landscape bordered by panels of flowers on the manganese ground, Holland, ca. 1740, 12½" d. (chips, rim restored) 220.00

Dish, painted in yellow, green, blue, iron red & brown w/a bird perched on flowering plants issuing from a vase on a blue rockwork ledge within a border of stylized flower sprays reserved on the brown ground, Holland, early 18th c., 13¼" d. (rim chips) 550.00

Dish, painted in blue, iron red, green & yellow w/flowering plants issuing from a terrace within a border of flower sprays divided by trellis-pattern panels, bearing blue mark of Jacobus Halder, Holland, 19th c., 13½" d. (rim chips) 385.00

Dish, painted in yellow, manganese, iron red, blue & green w/a Chinaman in a landscape within borders of stylized scrolling foliage & flowerheads, Holland, ca. 1740, 14" d. (rim & glaze chips) 352.00

Jar w/brass domed lid, ovoid shape w/polychrome floral decoration & "Meryland," Holland, 8" h. (edge chips) 875.00

Plate, 8 7/8" d., blue & white, the center w/fishermen in a landscape within a stenciled border of flowers & pine cones in "white on white," Bristol, England, ca. 1760 (minor glaze chips) 143.00

Plate, 9" d., blue & white w/wavy edge, w/a hunter, blowing a horn, his hound tracking a hare, in a landscape w/sponged trees, Holland, ca. 1750 (rim chips) 330.00

Plate, 9" d., center w/fisherman in a landscape, border w/flowering plants & cone-pattern in "white on white," blue & white center, Bristol, England, ca. 1760, minor glaze chips (ILLUS.) 220.00

Plate, 9¼" d., blue & white, decorated w/The Peacock patt. within a yellow edge, blue mark for "The Three Bells" factory, and "2," Holland, mid-18th c. (rim chips)...... 242.00

Plate, 12¼" d., blue & white, painted in the center w/an exotic bird beneath flying insects, flanked by shrubbery & large blossoms, within narrow & wide borders of stylized flowers & foliage, the barbed rim decorated w/a narrow band of shells & diapering, the reverse w/two blue border lines, De Porceleyne Bijl, Holland, mid-18th c. 467.50

Punch bowl, in blue, green & red w/a hilly landscape w/houses, figures in the foreground, the reverse w/a shepherd & shepherdess, the interior w/a man walking, Holland, mid-18th c., 15½" d. (rim chips, restored) 3,520.00

Shoe, high-heeled, painted in manganese & blue w/stylized overlapping leaves, center w/an oval clasp, arch w/initials "M & B" & date "1769," English, 5" l. (minor chips) 2,200.00

Shoes, high-heeled, pointed toes, h.p. scrolling flowering plants, blue & white, English, dated 1758, 5¼" l., pr. (one w/repairs, minor chips) 1,870.00

Shoe, high-heeled, w/clasp, painted blue & white marbleized bands, heel in blue, English, ca. 1770, 7" l. 2,090.00

Tile picture, rectangular, depicting an urn of spring flowers & a butterfly in manganese, Holland, late 18th c., 15¼ x 10¼" (restoration) 385.00

Tile picture, rectangular, depicting a yellow canary in a manganese cage w/blue feeder & yellow finials, Holland, 18th c., some restoration, cracks, framed, 19¾ x 14¾" (ILLUS.) 462.00

Delft Tile Picture

Tile pictures, rectangular, depicting a seated cat w/a mouse in its mouth, & a seated dog, manganese, Holland, late 18th c., in black painted wooden frames, 15 1/8 x 10 1/8", pr. (both w/cracks & restorations) 1,540.00

Tobacco jars, ovoid, oval panel embellished w/blue foliate garlands emanating from a central floral spray enclosing inscribed numerals "N3" or "N12," blue & white, plain brass cap, Dutch, 12" h., pr. 1,210.00

Tobacco jar, oviform, floral & foliate-scroll cartouche centered at the top w/an urn & stylized flowerheads & leafage, inscribed "RAPPE," blue & white, simple brass cover (damaged), Dutch, 13" h. 935.00

Wall plaque, cartouche-shaped, blue & white w/Abel kneeling beside animals feeding from a trough in a barnyard, Holland, early 18th c., 6 3/8 x 4¼" (rim chips).......... 242.00

DERBY & ROYAL CROWN DERBY

William Duesbury, in partnership with John and Christopher Heath, established the Derby Porcelain Works in Derby, England, about 1750. Duesbury soon bought out his partners and in 1770 purchased the Chelsea factory and six years later, the Bow works. Duesbury was succeeded by his son and grandson. Robert Bloor purchased the business about 1814 and managed successfully until illness in 1828 left him unable to exer-

cise control. The "Bloor" Period, however, extends from 1814 until 1848, when the factory closed. Former Derby workmen then resumed porcelain manufacture in another factory and this nucleus eventually united with a new and distinct venture, Derby Crown Porcelain, Ltd., 1890.

Derby Sweetmeat Figures

Cake stand, Imari patt., 19th c., 5" h. $75.00

Cup & saucer, demitasse, Imari patt., red, cobalt blue & gold on white ground, dated 1889 .... 60.00

Cups & saucers, demitasse, Imari patt., set of 9 .... 350.00

Figure, Andromache weeping over the ashes of Hector, leaning on an urn raised on a pedestal & looking downward, floral wreath held in her left hand, dressed in a purple-flowered white gown highlighted w/small purple dots & gilt leafage & a pale puce mantle, standing on a chamfered rectangular base w/Greek key molded border, ca. 1790, 10¼" h. (firing cracks) 715.00

Figures, bird catchers, he in mint green jacket & breeches enriched in gilding & holding a bird w/dog at his side, she in white bodice, white skirt w/floral clusters & plum shawl holding an empty cage w/a lamb at her side, 9½" h., pr. (losses) 495.00

Fish plates, each painted w/large gilt scallop-shell framing a fish in naturalistic colors on a tranquil sea & flanked by sprays of seaweed & coral, each reserved on a pastel pink, blue, yellow, apricot or beige ground within gilt dentil edge, ca. 1890, 9¼" d., assembled set of 12 .... 880.00

Jardinieres, cov., demi-lune shaped, cover encrusted w/naturalistically molded & painted flower bouquets above conforming bodies w/white ground central panel applied w/flower bunch, reserved against gilt embellished cobalt blue ground, Bloor period, ca. 1830, 7 5/8" l., pr. (chips & restorations) 2,860.00

Pitcher, 8" h., octagonal, Imari patt., ca. 1881 .... 135.00

Plate, 8½" d., footed, hand-enameled floral reserves & floral circular center, separated by gold wheat design on cobalt blue ground, painted red mark, 1825-40 .... 230.00

Rose bowl, cov., bright yellow ground w/h.p. gold flowers decoration, 4" 135.00

Sweetmeat figures, model of shepherd & shepherdess in flowered clothes enriched w/gilding, each seated on rockwork base holding two-handled basket, on tall scroll-molded base w/applied sheep & a dog & flowering foliage trimmed in green & puce, some repairs, each 9½" h., pr. (ILLUS.) .... 1,500.00 to 2,000.00

Teapot, cov., Imari patt., 18th c., 6" h. 195.00

Vase, 10¼" h., shouldered ovoid, salmon pink ground, enameled colors in gilt cartouches below a fluted narrow neck w/floriform rim, retailed by Bailey, Banks & Biddle, Philadelphia 192.00

Royal Crown Derby Vase

Vase, 16" h., baluster-shaped, gilt & enameled sprawling sunflowers & iris buds w/gilt banding around the base & rim, scrolling openwork gilt handles (ILLUS.) 357.00

DOULTON & ROYAL DOULTON

Doulton & Co., Ltd., was founded in Lambeth, London, about 1858. It was operated there till 1956 and often incorporated the words "Doulton" and "Lambeth" in its marks. Pinder Bourne & Co., Burslem was purchased by the Doultons in 1878 and in 1882 became Doulton & Co., Ltd. It added porcelain to its earthenware production in 1884. The "Royal Doulton" mark has been used since 1902 by this factory, which is still in production. Character jugs and figurines are commanding great attention from collectors at the present time.

DICKENSWARE

Cap'n Cuttle Tray

Ash pot, Sairey Gamp, "A" mark ... $85.00
Bowl, 7½" d., shallow, Tony Weller, signed Noke 75.00
Bowl, 8½" sq., shallow, Little Nell 90.00
Bowl, 8¾" sq., 2" h., Mr. Pickwick 92.00
Bowl, 11 x 8", Sairey Gamp 85.00
Bust of Mr. Pickwick, small 82.00
Bust of Tony Weller, miniature 85.00
Cake plate w/silver stand, Bill Sykes 95.00
Candlesticks, Fagin & Sam Weller figures, 6¾" h., pr. 320.00
Charger, Dick Swiveller & the Marchioness, 13" d. 95.00
Charger, Mr. Micawber, 13" d. 95.00
Cheese dish w/dome lid, Dickens' characters ....225.00 to 250.00
Creamer, Fat Boy 60.00
Creamer, Old Peggoty 95.00
Condiment set: mustard pot, salt dip & pepper shaker; Bill Sykes & Mr. Pickwick, 3 pcs. 168.00
Cup, Mr. Micawber, signed Noke ... 40.00
Cup & saucer, demitasse, Poor Jo .. 60.00
Cup & saucer, Mr. Micawber, large breakfast size................. 72.00
Dish, handled, Bill Sykes, 6¾" d. ... 45.00
Dresser set: 11½ x 7" tray & 3 cov. boxes; Bill Sykes & Fat Boy, 4 pcs. 350.00
Figurine, Bill Sykes, 4" h. 50.00
Figurine, Mr. Pickwick, 4" h. 50.00
Jug, Trotty Veck, 7" h................ 92.50
Jug, square, Alfred Jingle, 3 5/8" sq., 7 3/8" h.................. 130.00
Pitcher, 2½" h., Bill Sykes 80.00
Pitcher, 2½" h., 1½" d., Sam Weller 84.00
Pitcher, milk, 7" h., Cap'n Cuttle ... 75.00
Pitcher, cov., 7" h., jug-type, Fagin, signed Noke 158.00
Pitcher, 7" h., square, "Oliver Asks For More" in relief 184.00
Pitcher, 7" h., square jug-type, Pickwick Papers 155.00
Pitcher, 7¼" h., Artful Dodger 95.00
Pitcher, 7¼" h., square jug-type, Mr. Pickwick.................... 155.00
Pitcher, 8" h., Old Peggoty ....250.00 to 275.00
Pitcher, 8¾" h., 3 5/8" h., Barnaby Rudge.......................... 141.00
Pitcher, 9" h., 5½" d., Alfred Jingle 175.00
Plate, 6" sq., Bill Sykes, signed Noke 40.00
Plate, 7½" d., Barkis 60.00
Plate, 7½" d., Mark Tapley 52.50
Plate, 7½" d., Mr. Pickwick 55.00
Plate, 7½" d., Old Peggoty 55.00
Plate, 8½" d., Bill Sykes, signed Noke 68.00
Plate, 9½" d., Fagin.................. 50.00
Plate, 10" d., Barkis 70.00
Plate, 10" d., Bill Sykes or Fat Boy, each 55.00
Plate, 10" d., Fagin.................. 75.00
Plate, 10" d., Sam Weller 60.00
Plate, 10¼" d., Sergeant Buz Fuz ... 90.00
Plate, 10½" d., Alfred Jingle 65.00
Teapot, Artful Dodger 220.00
Tray, Fagin, 8½ x 7¼" 85.00
Tray, Cap'n Cuttle, 10½ x 5" (ILLUS.)......................... 85.00
Vase, 3" h., Fagin.................. 72.00
Vase, 3 7/8" h., 2" sq., Bill Sykes... 65.00
Vase, 5¼" h., 4 1/8" d., 2-handled, Alfred Jingle.................. 93.00
Vase, 7" h., 4½" w., 2-handled, square flattened shape, Mark Tapley 137.50
Vase, 7½" h., 3½" d., 2-handled, Sergeant Buz Fuz................ 144.00
Vase, 10" h., 2-handled, Bill Sykes .. 135.00

MISCELLANEOUS

Ale cooler, dark brown bands (6) decor on light brown ground, Doulton & Co. Lambeth Ltd. (impressed in circle), 5 gal., 13" d., 16" h.......................... 395.00
Ashtray, blue & white razors & blades, Gillette advertising, 6" d. 115.00
Ashtray, Dutch series, 3 5/8" d. 38.00
Ashtray, Welsh Ladies series, dated 1934, 3 5/8" d...................... 48.00

Ashtray, Witch series, witch & cauldron on caramel ground, 3 5/8" d. 33.00
Ashtray, country scene, "flambe" glaze, signed Noke, 4½" 35.00
Bottle, Sandeman Port black transfer 95.00

Shakespeare Series Bowl

Bowl, 5¾" d., 2½" h., Shakespeare series, "Orlando" (ILLUS.) 120.00
Bowl, 8" d., Old Moreton Hall series 125.00
Bowl, 11" oval, gnarled gnomes (6) under shadowy tree roots, gold stars in cobalt blue sky, metallic spiderwebs & tracery overall, signed Noke 357.00
Butter pat, Old English Inns series, "Inn of the Four Seasons," black on white 15.00
Candlestick, Dutch series, 6½" h. (single) 55.00
Candlestick, Woodland series, Pelican shaped, 6½" h. (single) 80.00
Character jug, Apothecary, miniature, 2¼" h. 35.00
Character jug, Apothecary, large 72.50
Character jug, Aramis, large 53.00
Character jug, 'Ard of 'Earing, small, 3½" h. 695.00
Character jug, 'Ard of 'Earing, large, 6" h. 1,033.00
Character jug, 'Arriet, "A" mark, miniature, 2¼" h. 82.00
Character jug, 'Arriet, large 175.00
Character jug, 'Arry, "A" mark, miniature, 2¼" h. 85.00
Character jug, 'Arry, small, 3½" h. 80.00
Character jug, 'Arry, "A" mark, small, 3½" h. 75.00
Character jug, Athos, large 52.00
Character jug, Auld Mac, miniature, 2¼" h. 25.00
Character jug, Auld Mac, "A" mark, miniature, 2¼" h. 52.00
Character jug, Auld Mac, small, 3½" h. 35.00
Character jug, Auld Mac, "A" mark, large, 6¾" h. (ILLUS.) 60.00

Auld Mac Jug

Character jug, Auld Mac, white, "A" mark, large 350.00
Character jug, Beefeater, miniature, 2¼" h. 60.00
Character jug, Beefeater, "A" mark, miniature, 2¼" h. 37.50
Character jug, Beefeater, small, 3½" h. 47.00
Character jug, (Sergeant) Buz Fuz, miniature, 2¼" h. 95.00
Character jug, (Sergeant) Buz Fuz, "A" mark, small, 3½" h. 72.00
Character jug, (Sergeant) Buz Fuz, large 150.00
Character jug, Capt. Ahab, miniature, 2¼" h. 27.50
Character jug, Capt. Ahab, small, 3½" h. 32.50
Character jug, Capt. Ahab, large 65.00
Character jug, Cap'n Cuttle, small, 3½" h. 85.00
Character jug, Cap'n Cuttle, large, 6" h. 145.00
Character jug, Cap'n Cuttle, "A" mark, odd size 200.00
Character jug, Captain Henry Morgan, small, 3½" h. 40.00
Character jug, Captain Henry Morgan, large 70.00
Character jug, Cardinal, "A" mark, miniature, 2¼" h. 48.00
Character jug, Cardinal, small, 3½" h. 65.00
Character jug, Cardinal, "A" mark, small, 3½" h. 62.00
Character jug, Clark Gable 3,250.00
Character jug, Gardener, miniature, 2¼" h. 30.00
Character jug, Gardener, small, 3½" h. 50.00
Character jug, Gardener, large, 6" h. 80.00
Character jug, Guardsman, miniature, 2¼" h. 32.50
Character jug, Guardsman, small, 3½" h. 55.00
Character jug, Guardsman, large 75.00
Character jug, John Peel, miniature, 2¼" h. 45.00
Character jug, John Peel, small, 3½" h. 65.00

Character jug, Mr. Micawber, "A" mark, large 150.00
Character jug, Night Watchman, miniature, 2¼" h. 30.00
Character jug, Old Charley, miniature, 2¼" h. 32.00
Character jug, Old Charley, large ... 67.00
Character jug, Paddy, tiny, 1¼" h. ... 95.00
Character jug, Paddy, miniature, 2¼" h. 45.00
Character jug, Paddy, "A" mark, miniature, 2¼" h. 48.00
Character jug, Paddy, small, 3½" h. 62.00
Character jug, Paddy, large 125.00
Character jug, Parson Brown, small, 3½" h. 60.00
Character jug, Parson Brown, large, 6" h. 135.00
Character jug, Pied Piper, miniature, 2¼" h. 26.00
Character jug, Regency Beau, small, 3½" h. 498.00
Character jug, Regency Beau, large, 6" h. 930.00
Character jug, Robin Hood, "A" mark, miniature, 2¼" h. 55.00
Character jug, Robin Hood, small, 3½" h. 58.00
Character jug, Robin Hood, large ... 135.00

Sairey Gamp Jug

Character jug, Sairey Gamp, miniature, 2¼" h. (ILLUS.) 25.00
Character jug, Sairey Gamp, "A" mark, large 70.00
Character jug, Sam Johnson, small, 3½" h. 163.00
Character jug, Santa Claus, doll & drum handle, large 74.00
Character jug, Toby Philpots, miniature, 2¼" h. 44.00
Character jug, Toby Philpots, large, 6" h. 115.00
Character jug, Uncle Tom Cobbleigh, large 355.00
Charger, Castles & Churches series, Pembroke Castle, blue & white, 13¼" d. 95.00
Coffeepot, cov., Moorish Gateway series, unusual form, 3¾" d., 7" h. 150.00
Coffeepot, cov., Shakespeare series, "Orlando" in brown, tan & purple attire, yellow ground, 3 7/8" d., 7½" h. 165.00
Cracker jar, cov., Dutch series, Dutch man w/cane & Dutch woman on yellow, tan & green ground, silver plate rim, cover & handle, 4 7/8" d., 6¼" h. 225.00
Cracker jar, cov., Sir Roger De Coverley series, cavalier on white horse talking to boy by gate on cream ground, silver plate rim, cover & handle, 4 7/8" d., 6½" h. 225.00
Creamer, Old Moreton Hall series .. 35.00
Creamer, Gallant Fishers series, Isaac Walton 35.00
Creamer, pinched spout, Welsh Ladies series, 2½" h. .....95.00 to 125.00
Creamer, stoneware, hunting scene, Doulton-Lambeth 55.00
Creamer & cov. sugar bowl, Sayings Ware, old lady drinking tea 75.00
Cup & saucer, demitasse, deep teal blue w/lighter blue chrysanthemums, heavy gold trim, gold lined cup, 1896 .... 100.00
Cup & saucer, demitasse, h.p. florals w/brushed gold trim, Doulton-Burslem 110.00
Cup & saucer, demitasse, red & brown w/Art Nouveau sterling silver overlay 130.00
Cup & saucer, Robin Hood series, Robin, Little John & Friar Tuck 65.00
Cup & saucer, Welsh Ladies series .. 80.00
Dish, handled, octagonal, Country Side series 40.00
Dish, Welsh Ladies series, Welsh ladies (3) in colorful dress on green & beige ground, 4¼ x 3¾" rectangle 63.00
Ewer, flow blue, iris blossoms w/gold trim, Doulton-Burslem, 6¾" h. 145.00
Ewer, stoneware, metal banded rim, incised goats within 3 medallions center, ca. 1880, Doulton-Lambeth, signed Hannah Barlow, 9" h. 580.00
Ferner, Dutch series, 5 x 5½" 100.00
Figure of Ellen Terry as Queen Catherine in traditional Elizabethan dress, w/her voluminous train flowing forward, her head slightly tilted, lightly tinted in green & rose, 12½" h. 412.00
Figure of Sir Henry Irving as Cardinal Wolsey, w/his weighty robe draped diagonally across his shoulder & supported by his arm, 13" h. 220.00

Figurine, "Adrienne," HN 2304, blue dress, 1964- 135.00
Figurine, "Affection," HN 2236, brown-purple dress, 1962- 72.00
Figurine, "A La Mode," HN 2544, 1974-79 .... 165.00
Figurine, "All-A-Blooming," HN 1466, 1931-38 ....1,400.00
Figurine, "Angela," HN 1204, red & purple costume, 1926-38 .... 925.00
Figurine, "Annabella," HN 1875, red dress, 1938-49 .... 600.00
Figurine, "Annette," HN1550, red blouse, green underskirt, 1933-49 .... 300.00
Figurine, "Anthea," HN 1526, green dress, 1932-38 .... 650.00
Figurine, "Anthea," HN 1527, purple dress, red umbrella, 1932-49 ..... 620.00
Figurine, "Antoinette," HN 1850, red & white dress, 1938-49 .... 875.00
Figurine, "Apple Maid" (The), HN 2160, 1957-62 .... 345.00
Figurine, "Bridget," HN 2070, 1951-73 ....185.00 to 225.00
Figurine, "Bridesmaid" (The Little), M 12, multicolor gown, 1932-45 ... 253.00
Figurine, "Bridesmaid" (The Little), HN 1433, pale yellow dress, 1930-51 ....135.00
Figurine, "Bridesmaid" (The Little), HN 2196, white dress, pink trim, 1960-76 .... 110.00
Figurine, "Bunny," HN 2214, 1960-75 ....125.00 to 150.00
Figurine, "Calumet," HN 1689, green costume, blue pot, 1935-49 .... 625.00
Figurine, "Camille," HN 1586, red bodice & overskirt, 1933-49 .... 500.00

"Carolyn"

Figurine, "Carolyn," HN 2112, 1953-59 (ILLUS.) 265.00

Figurine, "Charmian," HN 1568, red & white dress, 1933-38 .... 695.00
Figurine, "Charmian," HN 1569, light green-blue skirt, 1933-38 .... 775.00
Figurine, "Chelsea Pair" (female), HN 577, white flowered dress, 1923-38 .... 620.00
Figurine, "Chitarrone," HN 2700, Lady Musicians series, blue overdress, 1974 .... 575.00
Figurine, "Choice" (The), HN 1959, red dress, 1941-49 .... 900.00
Figurine, "Cookie," HN 2218, 1958-75 .... 135.00
Figurine, "Covent Garden," HN 1339, green dress, lavender apron, 1929-38 ....1,010.00
Figurine, "Cynthia," HN 1685, pink & green dress, 1935-49 .... 750.00
Figurine, "Dainty May," M 67, pink skirt, blue overdress, 1935-49 .... 300.00
Figurine, "Dainty May," HN 1639, red dress, green underskirt, 1934-49 .... 285.00
Figurine, "Dancing Years," HN 2235, 1965-71 .... 285.00
Figurine, "Daphne," HN 2268, 1963-75 .... 150.00
Figurine, "Daydreams," HN 1731, pink bodice, light skirt, 1935-..... 105.00
Figurine, "Debbie," HN 2385, 1969-82 .... 75.00
Figurine, "Debutante," HN 2210, 1963-67 .... 300.00
Figurine, "Detective" (The), HN 2359, brown coat, 1977-83 .... 130.00
Figurine, "Diana," HN 1986, red dress, purple hat ties, 1946-75 .... 120.00
Figurine, "Dick Swiveller," M 90, black coat & top hat, tan pants, 1949-83 .... 32.00
Figurine, "Dorcas," HN 1491, light green-blue dress, 1932-38 ....425.00 to 495.00
Figurine, "Dorcas," HN 1558, red dress, 1933-52 .... 275.00
Figurine, "Eleanore," HN 1754, orange dress, white bodice w/flowers, 1936-49 ....1,050.00
Figurine, "Elfreda," HN 2078, 1951-55 ....550.00 to 595.00
Figurine, "Eugene," HN 1520, green & pink dress, 1932-38 .... 715.00
Figurine, "Evelyn," HN 1622, red bodice & hat, 1934-49 .... 840.00
Figurine, "Fat Boy" (The), HN 1893, 1938-52 .... 305.00
Figurine, "Fiona," HN 2694, red & white dress, 1974-80 .... 148.00
Figurine, "First Waltz," HN 2862, 1979-83 ....150.00 to 185.00
Figurine, "Forty Winks," HN 1974, 1945-73 (ILLUS.) 205.00

"Forty Winks"

Figurine, "Fragrance," HN 2334, 1966- 122.00
Figurine, "Gaffer" (The), HN 2053, 1950-59 ....330.00 to 375.00
Figurine, "Giselle," HN 2139, blue dress, 1954-69 .... 305.00
Figurine, "Gloria," HN 1488, grey-blue cape & dress, 1932-38 ....1,450.00
Figurine, "Gossips," HN 1429, red dress, white dress, 1930-49 .... 430.00
Figurine, "Granny's Heritage," HN 2031, green skirt, light multicolored shawl, 1949-69 .... 380.00
Figurine, "Granny's Shawl," HN 1647, red cape, 1934-49 .... 345.00
Figurine, "Greta," HN 1485, off-white dress, red shawl, 1931-53 .. 225.00
Figurine, "Gwendolen," HN 1503, orange-yellow dress, 1932-49 ....1,300.00
Figurine, "Harmony," HN 2824, grey dress, 1978-84 .... 138.00
Figurine, "Harp," HN 2482, Lady Musicians series, brown dress, 1973-78 ....1,200.00 to 1,500.00
Figurine, "He Loves Me," HN 2046, 1949-62 .... 180.00
Figurine, "Henrietta Maria," HN 2005, 1948-53 .... 460.00
Figurine, "Hilary," HN 2335, 1967-80 .... 145.00
Figurine, "Hinged Parasol" (The), HN 1579, red dress, purple ruffles, 1933-49 .... 375.00
Figurine, "In the Stocks," HN 2163, rust jacket, 1955-59 .... 552.00
Figurine, "Invitation," HN 2170, 1956-75 .... 122.00
Figurine, "Irene," HN 1621, pale yellow dress, 1934-51 .... 316.00
Figurine, "Ivy," HN 1768, pink hat, lavender dress, 1936-79 .... 65.00
Figurine, "Jack," HN 2060, 1950-71 .. 124.00
Figurines, "Jack" & "Jill," HN 2060 & HN 2061, 1950-71, pr. 252.00
Figurine, "Janet," M 75, white skirt, shaded rose overdress, 1936-49 ... 300.00
Figurine, "Janet," HN 1538, blue-red dress, 1932-49 .... 200.00
Figurine, "Janet," HN 1916, blue bodice, pink skirt, 1939-49 .... 215.00
Figurine, "Janice," HN 2022, green dress, 1949-55 .... 390.00
Figurine, "Janice," HN 2165, dark overdress, 1955-65 .... 440.00
Figurine, "Karen," HN 1994, red dress, 1947-55 .... 385.00
Figurine, "Katrina," HN 2327, 1965-69 .... 230.00
Figurine, "Kurdish Dancer," HN 2867, Dancers of the World series, blue & purple costume 800.00
Figurine, "Lady Anne Nevill" (The), HN 2006, purple dress, ermine trim, 1948-53 .... 688.00
Figurine, "Lady April," HN 1965, green dress, 1941-49 .... 300.00
Figurine, "Lady Charmian," HN 1948, green dress, red shawl, 1940-73 .. 205.00
Figurine, "Lisa," HN 2310, violet & white dress, 1969-82 .... 140.00
Figurine, "Little Boy Blue," HN 2062, 1950-73 .... 112.00

"Long John Silver"

Figurine, "Long John Silver," HN 2204, dark uniform, 1957-65 (ILLUS.) 445.00
Figurine, "Loretta," HN 2337, rose-red dress, yellow shawl, 1966-80 .... 115.00
Figurine, "Love Letter," HN 2149, pink & white dress, blue dress, 1958-76 .... 285.00
Figurine, "Lucy Lockett," HN 524, yellow dress, 1921-49 .... 504.00
Figurine, "Lunchtime," HN 2485, 1973-80 .... 156.00
Figurine, "Madonna of the Square,"

HN 2034, light green-blue costume, 1949-51 .... 650.00

Figurine, "Maisie," HN 1619, pink dress, 1934-49 .... 357.00

Figurine, "Mandarin" (A), HN 641, onyx style coloring, 1924-38 .....3,500.00

Figurine, "Margaret," HN 1989, 1947-59 .... 250.00

Figurine, "Margaret of Anjou," HN 2012 .... 465.00

Figurine, "Margot," HN 1628, blue bodice, 1934-38 .... 660.00

Figurine, "Marigold," HN 1447, white & purple dress, 1931-49 .... 495.00

"Market Day"

Figurine, "Market Day," HN 1991, 1947-55 (ILLUS.) 240.00

Figurine, "Mary Jane," HN 1990, 1947-59 .... 368.00

Figurine, "Mary Mary," HN 2044, 1949-73 .... 134.00

Figurine, "Masque," HN 2554, 1973-82 .... 142.00

Figurine, "Masquerade" (man), HN 599, red jacket, 1924-49 ...... 650.00

Figurine, "Masquerade," HN 2259, red dress, 1960-65 .... 255.00

Figurine, "Mephistopheles & Marguerite," HN 755, two-sided, lady w/orange dress & purple cloak one side, man w/red outfit & red cloak other side, 1925-49 ....1,900.00

Figurine, "Midinette," HN 2090, blue dress, 1952-65 .... 250.00

Figurine, "Milkmaid" (The), HN 2057, 1975-81 .... 120.00

Figurine, "Minuet," HN 2019, white dress, floral print, 1949-71 .... 238.00

Figurine, "Mirabel," HN 1744, pink dress, 1935-49 ....700.00 to 800.00

Figurine, "Miss Demure," HN 1402, pale pink dress, 1930-75 .... 170.00

Figurine, "Miss Muffet," HN 1936, red coat, 1940-67 .... 150.00

Figurine, "Nadine," HN 1886, orange dress, blue trim, purple ribbon, 1938-49 .... 650.00

Figurine, "Negligee," HN 1454, pink negligee, red base, 1931-38 ...... 999.00

Figurine, "New Bonnet" (The), HN 1728, pink dress, green hat, 1935-49 .... 675.00

Figurine, "Newsboy," HN 2244, dark jacket, plaid hat, 1959-65 .... 470.00

Figurine, "Nina," HN 2347, 1969-76.. 140.00

Figurine, "Old King Cole," HN 2217, ermine-lined robe, 1963-67 .... 480.00

Figurine, "Old Meg," HN 2494, blue dress, purple shawl, 1974-76 ..... 220.00

Figurine, "Old Mother Hubbard," HN 2314, green dress, polka dot apron, 1964-75 .... 270.00

Figurine, "Olivia," HN 1995, 1947-51 .... 435.00

Figurine, "Once Upon a Time," HN 2047, pink dotted dress, 1949-55 .... 276.00

Figurine, "One That Got Away" (The), HN 2153, brown slicker, 1955-59 .... 275.00

Figurine, "Orange Lady" (The), HN 1759, pink skirt, 1936-75...... 183.00

Figurine, "Orange Lady" (The), HN 1953, yellow dress, green shawl, 1940-75 .... 196.00

Figurine, "Organ Grinder" (The), HN 2173, green jacket, 1956-65 ....550.00 to 575.00

Figurine, "Owd Willum," HN 2042, brown jacket, 1949-59 .... 215.00

Figurine, "Paisley Shawl," M 4, yellow-green dress, rose colored shawl, 1932-45 .... 278.00

Figurine, "Pantalettes," M 16, red skirt, red tie on hat, 1932-45 ..... 250.00

Figurine, "Pantalettes," M 31, green skirt, red tie on hat, 1932-45 ..... 184.00

Figurine, "Pantalettes," HN 1362, green skirt, red tie on hat, 1929-38 .... 320.00

Figurine, "Pantalettes," HN 1412, pink skirt, green tie on hat, 1930-49 .... 355.00

Figurine, "Parisian," HN 2445, 1972-75 .... 140.00

Figurine, "Polly Peachum," HN 549, red dress, deep curtsey, 1922-49.. 290.00

Figurine, "Pretty Lady," HN 70, pale blue dress, 1916-38 .... 673.00

Figurine, "Priscilla," M 14, blue ruffled dress, 1932-45 ......225.00 to 250.00

Figurine, "Priscilla," HN 1337, pale lavender & yellow dress, 1929-38 .... 348.00

Figurine, "Priscilla," HN 1340, red dress, purple collar, 1929-49 ..... 310.00

Figurine, "Prudence," HN 1883, blue dress, 1938-49 .... 840.00

Figurine, "Regal Lady," HN 2709, 1975-83 .... 125.00
Figurine, "Rhapsody," HN 2267, green dress, 1961-73 .... 215.00
Figurine, "Rita," HN 1448, yellow & pink dress, 1931-38 .... 650.00
Figurine, "Rita," HN 1450, blue dress, 1931-38 .... 675.00
Figurine, "Rosabell," HN 1620, 1934-38 .... 660.00
Figurine, "Rosamund," HN 1320, pink jacket, pale green skirt, 1929-38 ....1,350.00
Figurine, "Roseanna," HN 1921, green dress, 1940-49 .... 270.00
Figurine, "Rosebud,"HN 1580, pink dress, 1933-38 .... 625.00
Figurine, "Rowena," HN 2077, 1951-55 .... 495.00
Figurine, "Royal Governor's Cook," HN 2233, black dress, white apron, 1960-83 .... 215.00
Figurine, "Rustic Swain" (The), HN 1746, green suit, 1935-49.....2,100.00
Figurine, "Sleep," HN 24, pale blue-green dress, 1931-38 ....1,950.00
Figurine, "Snake Charmer" (The), HN 1317, 1929-38 .... 990.00
Figurine, "Stitch in Time" (A), HN 2352, 1966-80 ....120.00 to 150.00
Figurine, "Stop Press," HN 2683, 1977-80 .... 150.00
Figurine, "Sunshine Girl," HN 1344, green & black bathing suit, 1929-38 ....1,750.00
Figurine, "Sweet Anne," M 5, cream to red skirt, shaded red & blue jacket, 1932-45.........215.00 to 250.00
Figurine, "Sweet Lavender," HN 1373, 1930-49 .... 465.00
Figurine, "Sweet Maid," HN 1504, blue gown, 1932-38 .... 750.00
Figurine, "Tailor," HN 2174, orange vest, 1956-59 .... 655.00
Figurine, "Thanksgiving," HN 2446, blue overalls, 1972-76 .... 200.00
Figurine, "This Little Pig," HN 1794, purple & blue striped blanket, 1936-49 .... 495.00
Figurine, "Vanessa,"HN 1836, purple bodice, green skirt, 1938-49 .. 815.00
Figurine, "Verena," HN 1835, rose & green dress, 1938-49 ....1,500.00
Figurine, "Virginia," HN 1694, green dress, 1935-49 .... 975.00
Figurine, "Wandering Minstrel" (The), HN 1224, purple, pink & red costume, 1927-38 ....1,200.00
Figurine, "Wardrobe Mistress," HN 2145, 1954-67 .... 390.00
Flask, King's Ware, Bonnie Prince Charlie 195.00
Flask, King's Ware, bust of Night Watchman, 8"..................... 225.00
Game plates, each w/different game bird depicted in a rustic woodland setting, within elaborate scroll-molded border heightened in gilding, artist-signed, Doulton-Burslem, ca. 1893, set of 12 .... 825.00
Humidor, cov., court jester, "Welcome is the Best Cheer," signed Noke 150.00
Jardiniere, gold "tapestry" decoration, cobalt blue pierced border, enameled flowers, Doulton-Lambeth, 7 x 7½" 200.00
Jardiniere, flow blue, Babes in Woods series, boy & children playing Blindman's Buff under tree, gold trim, 9½" d., 9½" h. .. 465.00
Jug w/handle, applied floral & beaded decoration on incised brown & cobalt blue ground, artist-signed, Doulton Lambeth, 9¾" h. 225.00
Jug, Bayeux Tapestry series, "The Battle of Hastings," warriors on horses, green top & bottom bands, 4" d., 6 3/8" h. 150.00
Jug, Coronation of Elizabeth II, 1953, sepia, 7" h. 95.00
Jug, flow blue, cats standing at each side of motto "May we never break a joke to crack a reputation," band of cats at rim, 5" d., 8¼" h. 195.00
Jug, lightly embossed Dutch children in colors against natural color ground w/windmill, 4" d., 6¼" h. 140.00
Model of a bird, Throated Warbler, yellow, K 27 .... 35.00
Model of a dog, Terrier w/ball, HN 1103 .... 60.00
Model of a duck, sitting, Rouge Flambe glaze, 7½" h. 35.00
Model of horses, Chestnut mare w/foal, HN 2522 .... 425.00
Pitcher, 2½" h., 1½" d., Dutch series, colorfully garbed elderly man w/cane, girl, boy & boats, lemon yellow to cream to green base, top edged w/green, green handle 67.00
Pitcher, 4¾" h., 4" d., Moorish Gateway series, embossed scene, natural colors 85.00
Pitcher, 5½" h., jug-type, Corinth shape, Gleaners series 90.00
Pitcher, 6" h., Arabian Nights series 225.00
Pitcher, 7" h., Robin Hood series, "The Jovial Friar Joins Robin Hood" 165.00
Plaque, pierced to hang, "Dr. John-

son at the Cheshire Cheese," signed, 13" d. 130.00

Plate, 7¼" d., Nursery Rhyme series, "Simple Simon," dated 1920 .... 45.00

Plate, 8¾" d., flow blue Babes in Woods series, mother playing w/daughter 230.00

Plate, 9" d., intricate floral decoration w/floral & vine border in gold, ruffled & fluted edge, completely traced in gold 98.00

Plate, 9" d., Shakespeare series, "Merry Wives of Windsor" 65.00

Plate, 9" d., Shakespeare series, Anne Page in red dress on pastel ground 65.00

Plate, 10" d., rack-type, "The Mayor" 65.00

Plate, 10" d., rack-type, Night Watchman series, Town Official w/pike & lantern 60.00

Plate, 10½" d., Golfers series, "Every Dog Has His Day" 175.00

Plate, 11" d., Eglington Tournament series, "Knights in Sword Combat" 70.00

Plates, 10½" d., center w/gilt-decorated wide border, cavetto w/gilt foliate scrolls in ivory, outer border w/foliate medallions reserved on cobalt blue ground heightened in gilt w/floral sprays, scalloped gilt rim, early 20th c., set of 12 .... 1,760.00

Soap dish, stoneware, gold, pink, green & brown moth on blue & grey ground, Doulton Lambeth, 5½ x 4" 80.00

Teapot, cov., fisherwoman series, fisherwoman w/sailboats in background, decoration, 9 x 4", 5½" h. 195.00

Teapot, cov., Castles & Churches series, Cawdor Castle 115.00

Tea set: cov. teapot, creamer & cov. sugar bowl; lavender & blue florals w/gold scrolling decoration, ca. 1895, 3 pcs. 200.00

Toothpick holder, square, Welsh Ladies series, two Welsh ladies & children on two sides, natural colors, 2" d., 2" h. 69.00

Vase, 3" h., Silicon Ware, coffee color w/embossed blue & white flowers, marked "1379" 65.00

Vase, 4" h., Babes in Woods series, flow blue, little girls (2) under umbrella 200.00

Vase, 5½" h., 4 x 2" flattened shape, Robin Hood series, Robin Hood slays Gus of Gisbourne on front 100.00

Vase, 7" h., Shakespeare series, "Ophelia" 140.00

Vase, 7¾ x 6½", Titanian Ware, rust, blue & brown heavily plumed bird outlined in metallic gold, in flight against grey-green ground, brown ink stamp mark "Made in England - Royal Doulton - England - Titanian," die-stamped "7794 - 5 - 26," ca. 1915 .... 450.00

Vase, 8½" h., 4½" w., Sung Ware, cylindrical w/shoulder sloping to neck opening, "flambe" orange, red & shocking pink flowers w/green-blue leaves & stems against violet ground, ink stamped "Royal Doulton - England - Flambe," marked in black vertically "Sung - Noke" 550.00

Doulton Lambeth Vases

Vases, 17½" h., baluster-form, leafed branches of maple & beech used to form impressed & sgraffitoed tan & rust design on olive & blue low-relief twig patterned ground, Doulton Lambeth, 1880's, pr. (ILLUS.) 715.00

DRESDEN

Dresden porcelain has been produced since the type now termed Dresden was made at the nearby Meissen Porcelain Works early in the 18th century. "Dresden" and "Meissen" are often used interchangeably for later wares. "Dresden" has become a generic name for the kind of porcelains produced in Dresden and certain other areas of Germany but perhaps should be confined to the wares made in the city of Dresden.

Bowl, 6½" w., open latticework sides, applied florettes exterior, painted floral interior $115.00

Candelabra, one w/the figure of an elderly seamstress, other of a shoemaker, each seated on a barrel chair beneath an arching bough applied w/a flowering vine, supporting 2 leaf-tip-molded nozzles, decorated in tones of pink, blue, green & brown, late 19th c., 10 3/8" h., pr. 550.00

Candlesticks, double, applied pink & yellow roses, marked F/Crown/N (WeitschFurstenberg), 8" w., 5" h., pr. 250.00

Compote, 5 x 8½", ribbed circular base, open latticework bowl w/multicolored floral decor 250.00

Cup & saucer, demitasse, yellow floral panels alternating w/lady & gentleman in landscape scenes, lacy gold trim, scalloped rims, Augustus Rex, Dresden 90.00

Dresser tray, cupid w/beautiful maidens within medallion center on cobalt blue ground, ornate gold trim, Crown Mark, Dresden, Prussia, 10¾ x 6½" 65.00

Ewers, Satyr handle, scrolling spout, sides w/continuous frieze of playful putti at various pursuits, 15" h., pr. 1,100.00

Figure of Colonial gentleman, 6" h. 295.00

Figure of a lady wearing ornate "lace" gown applied w/florettes, 8" w., 6" h. 425.00

Figure groups depicting Autumn & Winter, Autumn portrayed as a youth eating grapes w/an infant fawn by his side, Winter as a bearded elderly man in a cloak w/a youth at his side chopping wood, each on scrolled gilt highlighted base, 7½" & 7¾" h., pr... 825.00

Plates, 8¼" d., cupid & nymphs on terraces center within gilt scroll & foliage surrounds, blue border enriched in gilt w/foliage, ca. 1900, set of 19 ....2,530.00

Plate, 10" d., central bust portrait of Cleopatra within a powder blue shading to navy blue border enriched w/gilt scrolling foliage, signed Wagner, late 19th c. 935.00

Teacup & saucer, cup interior w/h.p. pastel scene of children at play, monogram on saucer 165.00

Tea set: cov. teapot, creamer, sugar bowl & 6 c/s; embossed female busts at base, overall red roses & green foliage, Carl Thieme Potschappel mark, 15 pcs. 850.00

Tray, center scene of ladies boating on lake & feeding swans near shore w/distant hills & chateau, ornate border, ca. 1840, 15" l..... 260.00

Tureen, cov., 3 scroll feet & scroll handles enriched in gilding, birds on branches, butterflies & insects w/ozier borders, pear finial, Dresden Potschappel mark, 13" oval .. 440.00

Vase, 8½" h., center medallion w/h.p. courting scene, cobalt blue ground w/gold beading in relief .. 305.00

Dresden "Schneeballen" Vase

Vases, cov., 20¼" h., "Schneeballen," ovoid, each w/a profusion of tiny white florettes w/yellow centers, applied pompons composed of similar florettes edged in blue & growing from an arrangement of stems & branches, w/supporting birds, cover further applied w/fruit, each w/extensive losses & repairs, late 19th c., pr. (ILLUS. of one) ..1,870.00

FIESTA WARE

Fiesta dinnerware was made by the Homer Laughlin China Company of Newell, West Virginia, from the 1930's until the early 1970's. The brilliant colors of this inexpensive pottery have attracted numerous collectors and though it was not even out of production for a decade, it merits inclusion in our price guide. On February 28, 1986, Laughlin reintroduced the popular Fiesta line with minor changes in the shapes of a few pieces and a contemporary color range. The effect of this new production on the Fiesta collecting market is yet to be determined.

Ashtray, ivory, turquoise or yellow, each $18.00

Ashtray, red 24.00

Bowl, individual fruit, 4¾" d., light green 9.00
Bowl, individual fruit, 5½" d., cobalt blue 12.00
Bowl, 6" d., light green or turquoise, each 15.00
Bowl, 6" d., yellow 12.00
Bowl, individual salad, 7½" d., red 40.00
Bowl, nappy, 8½" d., cobalt blue 21.00
Bowl, nappy, 8½" d., red 30.00
Bowl, salad, 9½" d., medium green 16.00
Bowl, salad, 9½" d., red 37.00
Bowl, cream soup, red 24.00
Bowl, cream soup, turquoise 16.50
Bowl, salad, large, footed, cobalt blue 125.00
Bowl, salad, large, footed, ivory 73.00
Bowl, salad, large, footed, red 175.00
Candleholder, bulb-type, red (single) 23.00
Candleholders, bulb-type, yellow, pr. 20.00
Candleholders, tripod-type, ivory, pr. 195.00
Carafe, cov., light green 80.00
Carafe, cov., red 115.00
Casserole, cov., two-handled, grey, 10" d. 80.00
Casserole, cov., two-handled, red, 10" d. 95.00
Coffee pot, cov., demitasse, stick handle, medium green 98.00

Fiesta Coffee Pot

Coffee pot, cov., chartreuse (ILLUS.) 98.00
Comport, 12" d., low, footed, cobalt blue 44.00
Comport, 12" d., low, footed, red 105.00
Compote, sweetmeat, high stand, red 45.00
Creamer, stick handle, yellow 11.00
Creamer, individual size, red 50.00
Cup & saucer, demitasse, stick handle, cobalt blue 23.00
Cup & saucer, ring handle, chartreuse 25.00
Egg cup, medium green 22.00
Gravy boat, cobalt blue 24.00
Marmalade jar, cov., light green 68.00
Mixing bowl, nest-type, turquoise, size No. 2, 6" d. 28.00
Mixing bowl, nest-type, forest green, size No. 4, 8" d. 28.00
Mixing bowl, nest-type, ivory, size No. 7, 11½" d. 65.00
Mug, chartreuse, cobalt blue, light green or medium green, each .... 25.00 to 40.00
Mustard jar, cov., cobalt blue, ivory or yellow, each .... 45.00 to 60.00
Onion soup bowl, cov., ivory, light green or red, each .... 145.00 to 195.00
Pitcher, jug-type, cobalt blue or turquoise, 2 pt., each 30.00
Pitcher, juice, disc-type, turquoise or yellow, 30 oz., each 30.00

Fiesta Ware Pitcher

Pitcher w/ice lip, globular, light green, 2 qt. (ILLUS.) 85.00
Pitcher, water, disc-type, chartreuse, forest green or rose, each 65.00
Plate, 6" d., cobalt blue, ivory or turquoise, each 4.00
Plate, 7" d., cobalt blue or red, each 5.00
Plate, 9" d., cobalt blue 8.00
Plate, 10" d., chartreuse or red, each 18.00
Plate, compartment, 10½" d., light green, rose, turquoise or yellow, each .... 8.00 to 12.00
Plate, chop, 13" d., rose 24.00
Plate, chop, 15", cobalt blue, light green or turquoise, each .... 15.00 to 18.00
Platter, 12" oval, rose 22.00
Platter, 13" oval, chartreuse, grey or rose, each 20.00
Refrigerator jar, stacking-type, yellow 20.00
Relish tray w/five multicolored in-

serts, cobalt blue or yellow base, each set ....95.00 to 120.00
Salt & pepper shakers, chartreuse, forest green or red, each pr........................18.00 to 22.00
Soup plate w/flange rim, cobalt blue, medium green, red or yellow, 8" d., each..........15.00 to 20.00
Sugar bowl, cov., forest green, ivory, medium green or yellow, each 15.00
Syrup pitcher w/original lid, medium green or turquoise, each...85.00 to 95.00
Teapot, cov., chartreuse or rose, medium size (6 cup), each 110.00
Teapot, cov., ivory, light green or turquoise, large (8 cup), each ....60.00 to 75.00
Tidbit tray, 3-tier, medium green or red, each....................... 95.00
Tumbler, juice, red, 5 oz. 19.50
Tumbler, water, light green, red or turquoise, 10 oz., each ....22.00 to 30.00
Utility tray, red 28.00
Vase, bud, 6½" h., red 35.00
Vase, 10" h., cobalt blue........... 280.00

FLOW BLUE

Flowing Blue wares, usually shortened to Flow Blue, were made at numerous potteries in Staffordshire, England, and elsewhere. They are decorated with a blue that smudged lightly or ran in the firing. The same type of color flow is also found in certain wares decorated in green, purple and sepia. Patterns were given specific names, which accompany the listings here.

ALDINE (W. H. Grindley, ca. 1891)
Bowl, 5" d. $16.00
Platter, large 75.00
Teapot, cov. 95.00

ALEXANDRA (S. Hancock & Sons, ca. 1910)
Gravy boat, 7½" l. 30.00
Plate, 8" d. 10.00
Plate, 10" d. 12.00
Plate, 11" d. 25.00
Platter, 10½ x 8½" 35.00
Platter, 14 x 11½" 60.00
Tureen, cov., 11 x 7", 6" h. 70.00

AMOY (Davenport, dated 1844)
Bowl, 5 1/8" d. 95.00
Cup & saucer, handleless 80.00
Cup plate ....60.00 to 75.00
Dinner service for six w/creamer & sugar bowl, 38 pcs. 2,400.00
Plate, 7" d. (ILLUS.) 55.00

Amoy Plate

Plate, 8" d. 62.00
Plate, 9" d. 85.00
Plate, 10½" d. 95.00
Platter, 9¾" l. 110.00
Platter, 13½" l. 180.00
Sauce dish 40.00
Soup plate w/flange rim 75.00
Sugar bowl, cov. (professional repair) 135.00

ARGYLE (W. H. Grindley, ca. 1896)

Argyle Platter

Cup & saucer 48.00
Gravy boat w/attached underplate............................ 150.00
Plate, 7" d. 25.00
Platter, 15 x 10" (ILLUS.) 115.00
Vegetable bowl, cov., oval 165.00

ASHBURTON (W. H. Grindley, ca. 1891)
Bowl, cereal, 6¼" d. 20.00
Cup & saucer, demitasse 45.00
Plate, 6¾" d. 25.00
Plate, 9" d. 40.00
Soup tureen, cov. (professional repair to finial) 175.00

BLOSSOM (G. L. Ashworth & Bros., ca. 1865)
Dish, 9½" d. 30.00
Soup plate w/flange rim, 9" d. 20.00
Syllabub cup 50.00

BRAZIL (W. H. Grindley, ca. 1891)
Plate, 9" d. 25.50
Soup plate w/flange rim 42.00
Soup tureen, cov., 10½" d., 5¾" h. 175.00

CALIFORNIA (Podmore Walker & Co., marked Wedgwood (Enoch) & dated 1849)
Plate, 7¾" d. 48.00
Plate, 9¾" d. 55.00
Tea set, cov. teapot, creamer & cov. sugar bowl, 3 pcs. 295.00

CASHMERE (Ridgway & Morley, G. L. Ashworth, et al., 1840's on)
Bowl, 10½" d. 138.00
Cup, handleless, miniature 50.00
Cup & saucer 105.00
Plate, 10½" d. ....95.00 to 110.00
Platter, 15" l. 425.00
Platter, 17½ x 14¼" 495.00
Sugar bowl, cov. 350.00

CHAPOO (John Wedge Wood, ca. 1850)
Bowl, soup, 7¼" d. 85.00
Cup & saucer 95.00
Plate, 8" d. 65.00
Plate, 9" d. 80.00
Plate, 10½" d. 110.00
Saucer 35.00
Soup plate w/flange rim, 10½" d. .. 100.00
Teapot, cov. (professional repair to finial) 335.00

CHEN-SI (John Meir, ca. 1835)
Platter, 16 x 12" octagon........... 325.00
Platter, 17½ x 14" 225.00
Soup plate w/flange rim, 10¼" d. .. 90.00
Waste bowl........................ 125.00

CHISWICK (Ridgways, ca. 1900)
Cup & saucer 40.00
Plate, 7¾" d. 85.00
Plate, 9" d. 100.00
Plate, 9½" d. 115.00
Platters, 14" & 16", pr. 140.00
Sugar bowl, open 35.00

CLARENCE (W. H. Grindley, ca. 1900)
Bone dish 30.00
Bowl, dessert 30.00
Pitcher, water, 8" h. 130.00
Plate, 9" d. 40.00
Saucer 15.00
Soup plate w/flange rim 35.00
Vegetable bowl, cov., 12½" oval ... 150.00

CLAYTON (Johnson Bros., ca. 1902)
Bowl, 9½ x 7¼" oval............. 40.00
Cake plate, 10¼" d. 85.00
Plate, 7" d. (ILLUS.) 28.00
Platter, 14¼" l. 110.00
Vegetable tureen, cov. 155.00

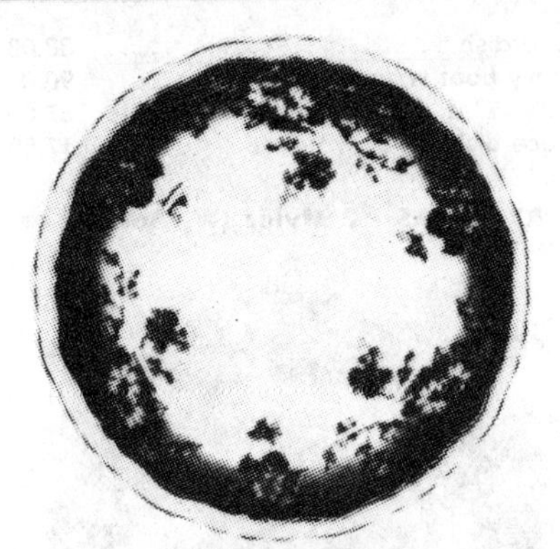

Clayton Plate

CONWAY (New Wharf Pottery, ca. 1891)
Butter pat 30.00
Creamer 125.00
Plate, 6" d. 22.00
Plate, 9" d. 45.00
Platter, 10¼" l. 65.00
Sauce dish, 5" d. 28.00
Soup plate w/flange rim 45.00
Vegetable bowl, open, 9" d. 48.50
Wash basin & pitcher, 2 pcs. 325.00

CRUMLIN (Myott, Son & Co., ca. 1900)
Butter dish, cover & drain insert 125.00
Gravy boat w/underplate 100.00
Plate, 6" d. 22.00
Plate, 9" d. 28.00
Sauce dish, 5" d. 20.00

DELAWARE (J. & G. Meakin, ca. 1890)
Dinner service for 12.............2,450.00
Plate, 10½" d. 45.00
Platter, 20" l. 250.00

DEL MONTE (Johnson Bros., ca. 1900)
Creamer 85.00
Plate, 9" d. 30.00
Sauce ladle 85.00

DOROTHY (Johnson Bros., ca. 1900)

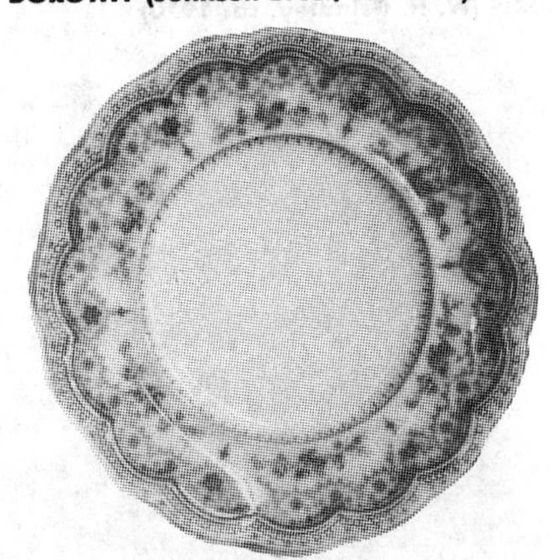

Dorothy Plate

Bone dish 38.00
Gravy boat w/underplate 90.00
Plate, 9" d. (ILLUS.) 67.00
Sauce dish, 6" d. 17.50

FAIRY VILLAS - 3 styles (W. Adams, ca. 1891)

Fairy Villas III Plate

Bowl, 10" d. 75.00
Plate, 8" d. 35.00
Plate, 9" d. 40.00
Plate, 9¾" d. (ILLUS.) ...... 60.00 to 70.00
Sauce dish, 5¼" d. 23.00
Vegetable bowl, open, 10" 70.00

GRECIAN (Ford & Sons Ltd., ca. 1908)

Plate, 10" d. 35.00
Platter, 15" l. 55.00
Soup plate w/flange rim, 9½" d. ... 25.00

HOLLAND (Johnson Bros., ca. 1891)

Egg cup 48.00
Plate, 10" d. 22.00
Platter, 12" l. 112.50
Platter, 18" l. 150.00
Sauce dish, 5" d. 15.00
Toast cover 125.00

IDRIS (W. H. Grindley, ca. 1910)

Idris Cup & Saucer

Bone dish 45.00
Creamer & sugar bowl, pr. 145.00
Cup & saucer (ILLUS.) 55.00
Tureen, cov., open handles, 9" d. ... 265.00
Vegetable tureen, open 110.00

INDIAN JAR (Jacob & Thos. Furnival, ca. 1843)

Platter, 10¾" l. 135.00
Platter, 14" l. 195.00
Soup plate w/flange rim, 10¼" d. ... 120.00
Teapot, cov., octagonal 200.00

JEWEL (Johnson Bros., ca. 1900)

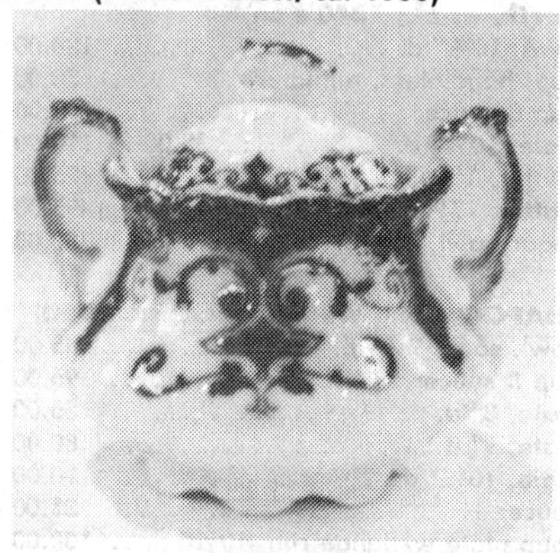

Jewel Sugar Bowl

Gravy boat 65.00
Platter, 14¼" l. 75.00
Sugar bowl, cov., 5" h. (ILLUS.) .. 120.00
Vegetable dish, individual, oval 35.00

KENWORTH (Johnson Bros., ca. 1900)

Butter dish, cov. 150.00
Plate, 10" d. 45.00
Saucer 10.00

KNOX (New Wharf Potteries, ca. 1891)

Plate, 9" d. 48.00
Platter, 10½" l. 95.00
Sauce dish, 5" d. 22.00

LA BELLE (Wheeling Pottery, ca. 1900)

La Belle Chop Plate

Bowl, 13" d., scalloped rim 75.00
Compote, loop handle, scalloped . . . 155.00
Pitcher, 6½" h. . . . . .145.00 to 160.00
Pitcher, milk 215.00
Pitcher, 2½ qt. 250.00
Plate, 8½" d. 35.00
Plate, chop, 11½" d. (ILLUS.) 75.00
Platter, 14½ x 10" oval 195.00
Serving tray 155.00
Syrup jug w/original lid 175.00

LAKEWOOD (Wood & Sons, ca. 1900)
Butter pat 25.00
Plate, 7¾" d. 27.00
Platter, 12" l 85.00

LORNE (W. H. Grindley, ca. 1900)
Bowl, 10" d. 45.00
Butter pat 20.00
Creamer 95.00
Dinner service, four each, 6", 8", 9" & 10" d. plates,, soup bowls, sauce dishes & cups & saucers, 32 pcs. 950.00
Gravy boat 75.00
Plate, 8" to 9" d. 30.00
Plate, 10" d. 40.00
Platter, 12" l. 85.00
Platter, 14" oval 85.00
Sauce dish, 5½" d. 20.00
Teacup & saucer 65.00
Vegetable bowl, cov., round 165.00
Vegetable bowl, open, 9" 75.00
Vegetable bowl, open, 10" 85.00

LOTUS (W. H. Grindley, ca. 1910)
Creamer, 4" h. 95.00
Platter, 16 x 12" 125.00
Soup plate w/flange rim 85.00

MADRAS (Doulton & Co., ca. 1900)
Plate, 10" d. 65.00
Platter, large 205.00
Vegetable bowl, cov. 230.00

MARQUIS, THE (W. H. Grindley, ca. 1906)
Bowl, cereal (worn gold) 10.00
Cup & saucer 42.00
Plate, 6" to 8" d. . . . . .15.00 to 25.00

MELBOURNE (W. H. Grindley, ca. 1900)
Creamer & cov. sugar bowl, pr. 250.00
Egg cups, pr. 95.00
Gravy boat w/underplate, two-handled . . . . .150.00 to 195.00
Marmalade jar, cover w/spoon slot & attached underplate 175.00
Plate, 8¾" d. 45.00
Plate, 10" d. 55.00
Platter, 11" l. (crazing) 95.00
Platter, 14" l. 125.00
Platter, 18" l. (back chip) 165.00
Vegetable bowl, open, 10" d. (ILLUS.) 85.00

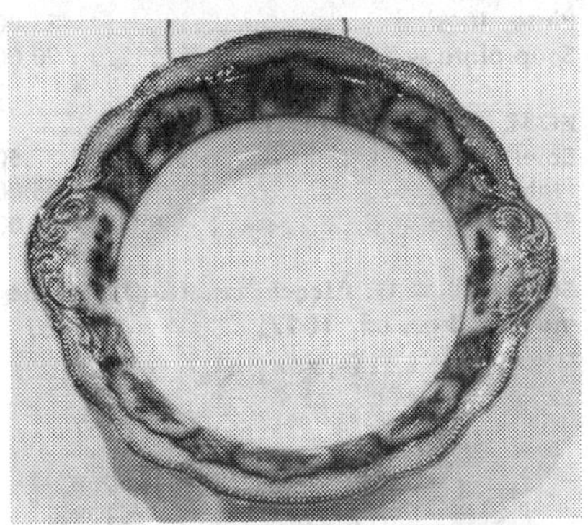

Melbourne Vegetable Bowl

MILAN (W. H. Grindley, ca. 1893)
Gravy boat w/underplate 85.00
Plate, 7" d. 35.00
Sugar bowl, cov. 75.00
Vegetable bowl, pierced handles . . . 45.00

MONGOLIA (Johnson Bros., ca. 1900)
Plate, 7" d. 28.00
Plate, 9" to 10" d. . . . . .25.00 to 35.00
Vegetable bowl, open, 10" oval 65.00

MURIEL (Upper Hanley Potteries, ca. 1895)
Creamer 65.00
Plate, 10" d. 60.00
Sugar bowl, cov. 135.00

NON PAREIL (Burgess & Leigh, ca. 1891)
Pitcher, jug-type, milk, 5¾" h. 125.00
Plate, 7½" d. 40.00
Plate, 9¾" d. 40.00
Platter, 12¼" l. 95.00
Platter, 16" l. 245.00
Sauce dish 10.00
Soup plate w/flange rim 45.00
Vegetable bowl, open, 9½" oval . . . 85.00
Vegetable tureen, cov. 210.00
Waste bowl 75.00

OSBORNE (W. H. Grindley, ca. 1900)
Butter dish, cover & drain insert 215.00
Cup & saucer 55.00
Gravy boat w/underplate (slight damage to underplate) 95.00

OSBORNE (Ridgways, ca. 1905)
Gravy boat 55.00
Platter, 14" l. 65.00
Platter, 16" l. 85.00

PARIS (New Wharf Pottery and Stanley Pottery Co., ca. 1891)
Bowl, 10" d. 35.00
Platter, 14" l. 110.00
Vegetable bowl, cov. 110.00

RICHMOND (Burgess & Leigh, ca. 1904)
Bowl, 8" d. 28.00

Plate, 10½" d. 35.00
Soup plate w/flange rim, 8" d. 20.00

ROSE (Ridgways, ca. 1910)
Bowl, 7¼" d., 1¼" h. 37.50
Plate, 7" d. 35.00
Plate, 8" to 9" d. ....38.00 to 42.00

SCINDE (J. & G. Alcock, ca. 1840 and Thomas Walker, ca. 1847)

Scinde Plate

Bowl, 12" d., low 195.00
Creamer, 5½" h. 250.00
Cup & saucer 110.00
Cup & saucer, handleless 95.00
Gravy boat, 8 x 3½" 125.00
Plate, 7" d. 53.00
Plate, 9" d. (ILLUS.) 95.00
Platter, 15" l. 265.00
Platter, 16" l. 450.00
Vegetable bowl, open, 8½" d. (glaze wear) 125.00
Vegetable bowl, open, 8¾ x 7" oblong 165.00
Vegetable bowl, open, 10¼" oblong 225.00

SHANGHAI (W. & T. Adams, ca. 1870)
Bowl, cereal 35.00
Plate, 10" d. 75.00
Soup plate w/flange rim, 9½" d. ... 70.00

TOURAINE (Henry Alcock, ca. 1898 and Stanley Pottery, ca. 1898)
Bone dish 53.00
Cup & saucer ....55.00 to 65.00
Gravy boat w/underplate 130.00
Pitcher, water 300.00
Plate, 7½" to 8½" d. ....35.00 to 45.00
Platter, 13 x 9" 95.00
Platter, 15 x 10½" oval (small chip) 150.00
Vegetable bowl, cov., 11½" oval ... 250.00
Waste bowl 95.00

TURIN (Johnson Bros., date unknown)
Creamer 45.00
Dinner service, eight each 7" & 9" d. plates, 5¼" d. bowls, cups & saucers plus cov. vegetable bowl, open oval bowl & round bowl, 14" l. platter, creamer & cov. sugar bowl, 46 pcs. 800.00
Plate, 6" d. 45.00

VERONA (Ford & Sons, Ltd., ca. 1908)
Plate, 7" d. 20.00
Plate, 9½" to 10½" d. ....25.00 to 35.00
Platters, nest-type, set of 3 .... 235.00

WATTEAU (Doulton, ca. 1900)
Bacon platter, 11 x 9" 65.00
Compote, 6½" d., reticulated edge 60.00
Pitcher, 6½" h. 75.00
Plates, 7¾" to 8¾" d. ....25.00 to 35.00
Plate, 10" d. 55.00
Platter, 13½ x 11" 95.00
Sauce tureen w/underplate 125.00
Soup plate w/flange rim, 10" d. 70.00
Vegetable bowl, open, 9" d. 75.00
Vegetable bowl, open, pedestal base, 10½" d. 95.00

(End of Flow Blue Section)

FRANKOMA POTTERY

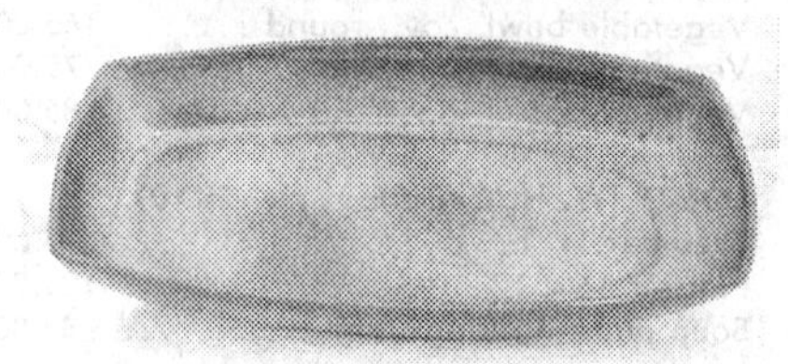

Westwind Pattern Steak Plate

John Frank began producing and selling pottery on a part-time basis during the summer of 1933 while he was still teaching art and pottery classes at the University of Oklahoma. In 1934, Frankoma Pottery became an incorporated business that was successful enough to allow him to leave his teaching position in 1936 to devote full-time to its growth. The pottery was moved to Sapulpa, Oklahoma in 1938 and a full range of art pottery and dinner wares were eventually offered. Since John Frank's death in 1973, the pottery has been directed by his daughter, Joniece. The early wares and limited editions are becoming increasingly popular with collectors today.

Ashtray, model of a walking elephant w/trunk up on rim, black glaze, 6½" d. $30.00
Book ends, model of a rearing Clydesdale horse, No. 431, 8½" h., pr. 125.00

Book ends, model of a walking ocelot, black glaze, incised "Taylor," No. 424, 7" l., 3" h., pr. 370.00
Bottle-vase, 1970, turquoise blue glaze, signed John Frank, 12" h... 35.00
Bottle-vase, 1972, black & terra cotta glaze, signed John Frank, 12" h. 38.00
Bottle-vase, 1974, celadon (greyish green) w/black base, signed Grace Lee Frank, 13" h. 27.00
Bottle-vase, 1976, Freedom red & white w/red stopper, signed Joniece Frank, 13" h. 32.50
Bottle-vase, 1978, morning glory blue w/white interior, or coffee brown w/white interior, signed Joniece Frank, 11½" h., each 27.50
Candleholders, low domed form w/molded line design, green glaze, No. 300, pr. 20.00
Christmas card, 1976 (The Bicentennial) or 1977 (The Book & Resting Hands), white sand glaze, each... 15.00
Console set: bowl & pr. candleholders; mottled green & brown glaze, 3 pcs. 25.00
Creamer, Wagon Wheel patt., brown & cream glaze, 4½" h. 4.50
Figure, "Dreamer Girl" or "Weeping Lady," black glaze, 5 3/8" h. 125.00
Figure, "Indian Bowl Maker," bright orange glaze, 6" h. 85.00
Figures, "Gardener Boy" & "Gardener Girl," prairie green glaze, 7" & 5¾" h., pr. 150.00
Masks, Indian Chief wearing 2-feathered headdress & Indian Maiden wearing headband, dark blue glaze, 5" & 4 1/8" h., pr. 75.00
Model of a horse, green & brown glaze, miniature, unmarked 15.00
Model of a swan, prairie green glaze, 3" h. 35.00
Mug, 1968 (Republican) elephant, white glaze (first in "Political" Mug Series) 55.00
Mug, 1970 elephant, blue glaze..... 30.00
Mug, 1971 elephant, black glaze.... 40.00
Mug, 1973 elephant, "Nixon-Agnew," desert gold glaze 22.50
Mug, 1977 (Democratic) donkey, "Carter-Mondale," dusty pink glaze 9.50
Mug, 1979 elephant, brown satin glaze 12.00
Plate, 7" d., 1973, limited edition Wildlife Series, "White-tailed Deer," prairie green 27.00
Plate, 7" d., 1977, limited edition Wildlife Series, "Gray Squirrel," prairie green 27.00
Plate, 8½" d., Madonna Series, Grace Madonna, rubbed bisque (wood tones) finish, No. 1, 1977 .. 17.50
Plate, 8½" d., Bicentennial commemorative, sand white glaze, 1972 through 1976, each 10.00
Salt & pepper shakers, model of a black panther, pr. 35.00
Steak plate (or shallow platter), Westwind patt., peach glow (mottled peach & brown), 13¼ x 7", 1¾" h. (ILLUS.) 12.00
Tea set: 4¾" h. cov. teapot, creamer, sugar bowl & 2½" h. salt & pepper shakers; Wagon Wheel patt., prairie green, 5 pcs. 35.00
Vase, 5½" h., model of ram's head, black glaze, Ada clay 20.00
Vase, 18" h., 2-handled, green shaded to brown glaze 45.00
Wall pocket, model of an Acorn, brown or green glaze, 6" h., each 17.50

FULPER

Fulper Ovoid Vase

The Fulper Pottery was founded in Flemington, N.J., in 1805 and operated until 1935, although operations were curtailed in 1929 when its main plant was destroyed by fire. The name was changed in 1929 to Stangl Pottery, which continued in operation until July of 1978, when Pfaltzgraff, a division of Susquehanna Broadcasting Company of York, Pennsylvania, purchased the assets of the Stangl Pottery, including the name.

Book blocks, "Ramses II," 8½", paper label, verte antique green glaze $650.00
Book end, model of a book, green & grey decoration, 4¾" l., 4¾" h. (single) 45.00
Bowl, 8½" d., rolled rim, green & grey streaks on glossy finish 85.00
Bowl, 9" d., green, grey & brown "mirror" glaze 55.00

Bowl-vase, bulbous round body w/curved-in rim opening, silvery-green crystalline flambe glaze dripping unevenly onto butterscotch lustre at base, vertical black printed mark, 6½" d., 5¾" h. 165.00
Candleholder, canopy-type, verte antique green w/three pieces of slag glass inset above the opening, early rectangular ink stamp, 6" d., 10¾" h. 1,650.00
Chamberstick, arched candle shield w/loop handle on round shallow dish, ca. 1915, signed, 7" h. 60.00
"Effigy" bowl, grey matte figures & base, gold & copper dust on blue "flambe" glaze (tight hairline) 425.00
Flower frog, figural nude lady, white glaze 100.00
Flower frog, model of lily pad, green & brown glaze, 3" d. 35.00
Jar, w/pedestal base, green to blue glaze, 9 x 8" 400.00
Jug, musical, green crystalline glaze 75.00
Model of a cat, glossy ochre glaze (superb repair of ear chip) 525.00
Perfume lamp, figural parrot, blue w/orange wing tips, 9" h. 465.00
Pitcher, 4" h., grey brown & blue high glaze 50.00
Powder jar, cov., Art Deco figural lady w/purple dress & black hair w/top knot cover 150.00
Powder jar, cov., Art Deco style Egyptian woman figural cover 250.00
Urn-vase, three-handled, green shaded to mauve, embossed mark, 8 x 6½" 95.00
Urn-vase, Grecian urn form w/short scrolled handles flanking neck at top of shoulder, mirrored gunmetal glaze ending unevenly over copperdust finish, round edged ink mark, 8" d., 15½" h. 770.00
Vase, 4" h., chocolate brown to mustard "flambe" glaze 40.00
Vase, bud, 5½" h., black "mirror" glaze 95.00
Vase, 7 x 6", bulbous, silvery green "flambe" dripping unevenly over a silver brown textured semi-gloss finish, incised oval mark 275.00
Vase, 7½" h., broad ovoid, mustard crystalline glaze shading to beige, fuchsia & navy, signed (ILLUS.) ... 440.00
Vase, 14" h., 7½" d., squatty bulbous form w/long flared cylindrical neck, streaky flowing black glaze ending unevenly over a silvery green "flambe," early rectangular mark 990.00
Water cooler, cov., tall swollen

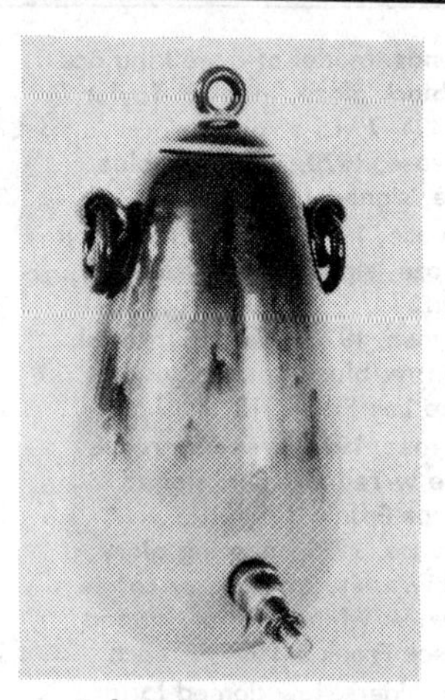

Fulper Water Cooler

cylindrical form w/molded loop handles & metal spigot, blue "flambe" over green glaze, obscured signature, early 20th c., 15" h. (ILLUS.) 60.00

GALLE' POTTERY

Galle' Pottery Pieces

Fine pottery was made by Emile Galle', the multi-talented French designer and artisan, who is also famous for his glass and furniture. The pottery is relatively scarce.

Basket, handled, 13 x 8" $750.00
Dish, fleur-de-lis shape, h.p. underglaze scene of Victorian lady & gentleman meeting in front of a monument in the park, signed, 9½" l. 225.00
Dish, *vide poche*, faience, model of a standing rooster w/wide ruff

perched on side of shield-shaped dish w/thistle decoration, mustard, rust, lime green & midnight blue w/gilt highlights, signed, late 19th c., 11¾" l. 990.00

Jug, squat body on flared foot, flared neck, strap handle, earth tones lotus leaves on dark brown ground, 20th c., 7¼" h. (ILLUS. right) 467.50

Model of a wise old owl, faience, green glass eyes, ochre, beige & grey drip glaze, Chinese red round base, signed, original paper labels, ca. 1895, 13" h. 3,300.00

Pitcher, 5¾" h., pinched gourd form, tall elongated upright spout, h.p. organic forms & stems in earth tones of green, orange, off-white & yellow against brown ground, highlighted w/gilt tracery, applied handle, recessed base, signed "E. Galle', Nancy" (minor glaze chips) 385.00

Pitcher, 15" h., tapering reeded & molded cylinder w/waved rim, twisted strap handle, exotic insect & flowering plant on turquoise blue dripped over brown ground, whole highlighted w/gilt, w/most of original label, late 19th c. (ILLUS. left) 1,540.00

Vase, 11" h., flower-shaped, Nancy faience, blue & white castle & field decoration, marked "Delvaux, Rue Royal Paris" 565.00

GAUDY DUTCH

Grape Pattern Plate

This name is applied to English earthenware and ironstone wares with designs copied from Oriental patterns. Production began in the 18th century. These copies flooded into this country in the early 19th century. The incorporation of the word "Dutch" derives from the fact that it was the Dutch who first brought these Oriental wares into Europe. The ware was not, as often erroneously reported, made specifically for the Pennsylvania Dutch.

Cup & saucer, handleless, Butterfly patt. (minor damage & wear).....$325.00

Cup & saucer, handleless, Single Rose patt. (stains, hairlines) ....200.00 to 300.00

Plate, 6¼" d., Single Rose patt. 325.00

Plate, 6½" d., Flower Basket patt... 185.00

Plate, 6 7/8" d., Single Rose patt. (minor wear) 495.00

Plate, 7 1/8" d., Grape patt. (minor wear & small glaze flakes) 225.00

Plate, 7¼" d., Urn patt. w/sectional border (minor wear & scratches).. 500.00

Plate, 7½" d., Single Rose patt. (wear & scratches) 250.00

Plate, 8¼" d., Grape patt., minor wear & repairs (ILLUS.) 300.00

Plate, 8¼" d., War Bonnet patt. (minor stains & touch-up) 325.00

Plate, 9¾" d., Grape patt. (minor flaking) 250.00

Teapot, cov., boat-shaped, Grape patt., 6½" h. (minor wear, nicks & stains) 500.00

Waste bowl, Double Rose patt., 6½" d., 3" h. (stains, repair) 275.00

GAUDY WELSH

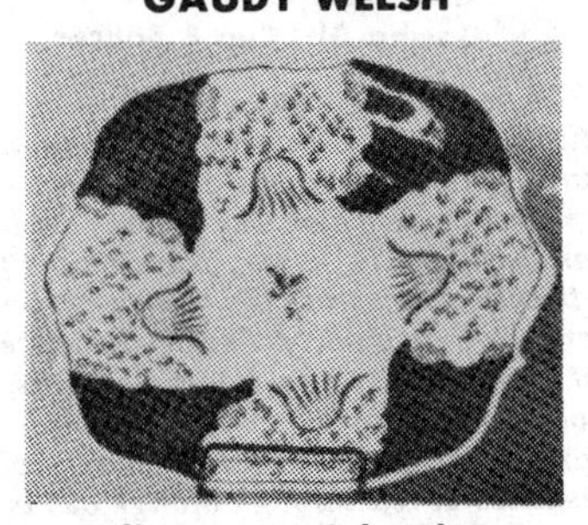

Tulip Pattern Cake Plate

This is a name for wares made in England for the American market about 1830 to 1845. Decorated with Imari-style flower patterns, often highlighted with copper lustre, it should not be confused with Gaudy Dutch wares whose colors differ somewhat.

Bowl, 9½" d., 4" h., footed, bold floral pattern, underglaze blue,

rust & copper lustre (small edge chips) $135.00
Cake plate, molded handles, Tulip patt., 10" (ILLUS.) 90.00
Cream jug, Oyster patt., ca. 1820, 3¾" h. 80.00
Cup & saucer, Oyster patt. 50.00
Cup & saucer, Tulip patt. 40.00
Mug, child's, Grape II patt., cobalt blue florals, orange petals, light green leaves, 2 1/8" d., 2 3/8" h. 75.00
Mug, Oyster patt., strap handle, 4 1/8" h. (crazing & minor wear) 105.00
Pitcher, 5" h., Oyster patt. 45.00
Pitcher, 6" h., Dogwood patt., English registry mark 105.00
Plate, 5½" d., Wagon Wheel patt. .. 32.00
Teacup & saucer, Wagon Wheel patt. 52.00
Tea set: cov. teapot, creamer, cov. sugar bowl; 10½" sq. cake plate & eight cups & saucers; cobalt blue w/h.p. florals, 20 pcs. 600.00

GEISHA GIRL WARES

Geisha Girl Cup & Saucer

The beautiful geisha, a Japanese girl specifically trained to entertain with singing or dancing, is the featured decoration on this Japanese china which was cheaply made and mass-produced for export. Now finding favor with collectors across the United States, the ware varies in quality. The geisha pattern is not uniform-Butterfly, Paper Lanterns, Parasol, Sedan Chair and other variations are found in this pattern that is usually colored in shades of red through orange but is also found in blue and green tones. Collectors try to garner the same design in approximately the same color tones.

Celery dish, 12" l. $35.00
Chocolate set: cov. chocolate pot & three cups & saucers; scene of pink bushes on pale blue mountain background, orange-red w/gold trim, Kutani mark, 7 pcs. 100.00
Chocolate set: cov. chocolate pot & four cups & saucers; red trim, marked "Made in Japan," 9 pcs. .. 80.00
Cracker jar, cov., child & adults (2) scene, cobalt blue trim 65.00
Cracker jar, cov., scene of pink bushes on pale blue mountain background, orange-red w/gold trim, Kutani mark 60.00
Creamer & sugar bowl, scene of pink bushes on pale blue mountain background, orange-red w/gold trim, Kutani mark, pr. 40.00
Cup & saucer, scene of two geishas in boat w/lanterns overhead, orange trim (ILLUS.) 15.00
Match holder, wall-type, rust trim .. 18.00
Nut set: master bowl w/nut spoon & three individual nut bowls; scene of pink bushes on pale blue mountain background, Kutani mark, 5 pcs. 60.00
Rose bowl, scene of pink bushes on pale blue mountain background, orange-red w/gold trim, Kutani mark 25.00
Salt & pepper shakers, cobalt blue trim, 3½" h., pr. 15.00
Tea set: cov. teapot & four cups & saucers; red trim, 9 pcs. 139.00
Tea set: cov. teapot, creamer, sugar bowl & five cups & saucers; green trim, marked "Japan," 13 pcs. 80.00
Tea set: cov. teapot, creamer, five cups & saucers (one cup chipped) & six 7" d. plates; lithophane bottoms w/mountain & lake scene, Kutani mark, 18 pcs. 135.00

GIBSON GIRL PLATES

"She Longs For Seclusion"

The artist Charles Dana Gibson produced

a series of 24 drawings entitled "The Widow and Her Friends," and these were reproduced on plates by the Royal Doulton works at Lambeth, England. The plates were copyrighted by Life Publishing Company in 1900 and 1901. The majority of these plates usually sell within a price range of $75.00 to $90.00 today.

A Message from the Outside World (No. 1) $85.00
And Here Winning New Friends (No. 2) 95.00
A Quiet Dinner with Dr. Bottles (No. 3) 85.00
Failing to Find Rest and Quiet in the Country She Decides to Return Home (No. 4) 75.00
Miss Babbles Brings a Copy of the Morning Paper (No. 5) 95.00
Miss Babbles, the Authoress, Calls and Reads Aloud (No. 6) 85.00
Mrs. Diggs is Alarmed at Discovering... (No. 7) 85.00
Mr. Waddles Arrives Late and Finds Her Card Filled (No. 8) 90.00
She Becomes a Trained Nurse (No. 9) 80.00
She Contemplates the Cloister (No. 10) 85.00
She Decides to Die in Spite of Dr. Bottles (No. 11) 85.00
She Finds Some Consolation in Her Mirror (No. 12) 90.00
She Finds That Exercise Does Not Improve Her Spirits (No. 13) 80.00
She Goes into Colors (No. 14) 75.00
She Goes to the Fancy Dress Ball as "Juliet" (No. 15) 85.00
She is Disturbed by a Vision (No. 16) 80.00
She is Subject to More Hostile Criticism (No. 17) 85.00
She Longs for Seclusion, No. 18 (ILLUS.) 90.00
She Looks for Relief Among Some of the Old Ones (No. 19) 78.00
Some Think that She has Remained in Retirement Too Long (No. 20) 80.00
The Day After Arriving at Her Journey's End (No. 21) 80.00
They All Go Skating (No. 22) 80.00
They All Go Fishing (No. 23) 85.00
They Take a Morning Run (No. 24) 75.00

GOLDSCHEIDER

The Goldscheider firm manufactured porcelain and faience in Austria between 1885 and 1953. Founded by Friedrich Goldscheider and carried on by his widow, the firm came under the control of his sons, Walter and Marcell, in 1920. Fleeing their native Austria at the time of World War II, the Goldscheiders set up an operation in the United States. They were listed in the Trenton, New Jersey, City Directory from 1943 through 1950 and their main production seems to have been art pottery figurines.

Busts of Chinese boy & girl, 8" h., pr. $70.00
Candlestick, double socket, Art Deco-style couple kissing, 11" h. (single) 350.00
Figure of lady w/new bonnet, 6" h. 35.00
Figure, "Lady Rose," 7" h. 50.00
Figure, "Love Letter," 7½" h. 55.00
Figure of "Lorenzl," lady in lace dress, marked "Austria," 8" h. 400.00
Figure of a Southern Belle, No. 802, marked "U.S.A.," 8" h. 32.00
Figure of a Southern Belle, No. 804, marked "U.S.A.," 8" h. 32.00
Figure of a lady, dressed in beige, pale yellow & lavender gown, 8½" h. 45.00
Figure of a Colonial lady wearing yellow hat, American, 10½" h. 50.00
Figure of a Chinese girl with fan, 12" 150.00
Figure of Juliet w/doves, 12" h. 125.00
Figure of "Venice," standing lady in long gown, 12" h. 150.00
Figure of an Art Deco-style lady dancer holding the hem of her Empire-style gown & wearing a bonnet, 15" h. 250.00
Figure of "Lady Chrysanthemum" 55.00
Lamps, figural gentleman & lady, w/paper label marked "U.S.A.," 9" h., pr. 165.00
Model of a Russian Wolfhound, marked "U.S.A.," 10 x 11" 135.00
Model of a Siamese cat 35.00
Model of a Spaniel 15.00
Plaque, Art Nouveau lady, signed "A. Zehle," Vienna, Austria, 8" 125.00

GOUDA

While tin-enameled earthenware has been made in Gouda, Holland, since the early 1600's, the productions of modern factories are attracting increasing collector attention. The art pottery of Gouda is easily recognized by its brightly colored peasant-style decoration with some types having achieved a "cloisonne" effect. Pottery workshops located in, or near, Gouda include Regina, Zenith, Plazuid, Schoonhoven, Arnhem and others.

Their wide range of production included utilitarian wares, as well as vases, miniatures and large outdoor garden ornaments.

Bowl, 6" d., 1¾" h., unusual shape, green ground w/rust & cobalt blue scrolls, house mark & "Gouda Holland" $45.00
Bowl, 10" d., Primrose Ivora patt. .. 100.00
Candlestick, flaring base, deep drip pan beneath candle socket, multicolored geometric decor & bands of Greek Key design, marked "Gouda, Holland," 9¾" h. (single) 50.00
Candlesticks, red, gold & blue design on black matte ground, marked "Swaro, Gouda Holland," original paper label marked "Royal Pottery," 6" h., pr. 125.00
Dish, boat-shaped, 2-handled, colorful decor on black satin ground, 3" w., 8" l., 3¼" h. 35.00
Humidor, cov., tan, blue & green decor on matte ground, house mark 125.00
Inkwell, cov., w/clear insert & hole for pen, yellow, royal blue, turquoise, brown & rust decor, 3¾" d., 4" h. 95.00
Jug, w/stopper, marked "Gerla Gouda Holland," 11" h. 175.00
Model of a Dutch shoe, marked "Regina" w/a crown, 5" 79.00
Mug, green vines & fruit on high glaze finish, Royal Zuid mark, 3½" h. 50.00
Pitcher, 3" h., double-pierced handle, peacock feather decor on black matte finish, Zwaro mark .. 35.00
Vase, 5" h., 2-handled, tulip decor, Royal Zuid mark 45.00

Gouda Vase

Vase, 7" h., black, grey & green stylized decor, house mark (ILLUS.) 80.00
Vase, 16" h., bulbous form tapering towards footed base, elongated neck, flared rim, white & green Art Nouveau florals on dark brown & burnt orange ground, marked "Herat, Gouda Holland AR" (hairline in rim) 165.00
Wall pocket, model of a Dutch Shoe, Regina house mark 85.00

GRUEBY

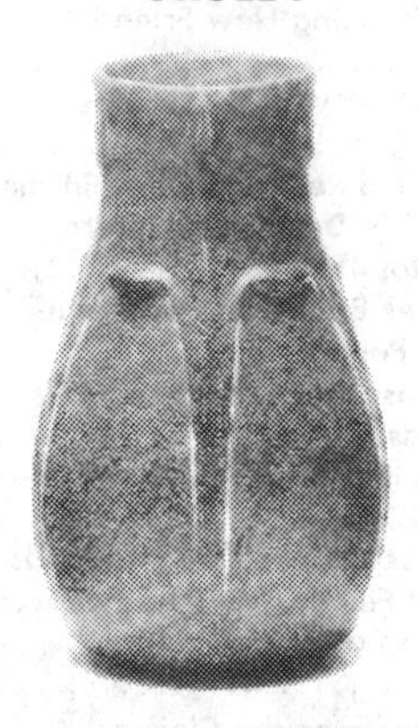

Grueby Vase with Molded Leaves

Some fine art pottery was produced by the Grueby Faience and Tile Company, established in Boston in 1891. Choice pieces were created with molded designs on a semi-porcelain body. The ware is marked and often bears the initials of the decorators. The pottery closed in 1907.

Fireplace mantel, frieze of eight tiles, 48" l. $13,200.00
Vase, 4¼" h., squat bulbous form w/cylindrical neck & rolled rim w/ridges, ca. 1905 .... 412.50
Vase, 4½" h., ovoid, molded broad leaves & slender stems in matte dark green glaze & cattails in light green glaze 880.00
Vase, 5¼" h., ovoid, five molded broad leaves, matte cucumber green glaze, artist-signed 495.00
Vase, 7½" h., flared cylinder w/vertical ribbing, matte cucumber green glaze, artist-signed 440.00
Vase, 7 5/8" h., oviform, alternating molded leaves w/curved tips at the shoulder & slender stems & buds at the neck, matte cucumber green glaze, impressed "Grueby Faience Co. Boston U.S.A." (ILLUS.) 770.00
Vase, 8½" h., broad baluster form, molded wide petals w/curved tips, textured matte green glaze, artist-signed 2,420.00

Vase, 9½" h., spherical w/flared cylindrical neck, molded parallel curved lines reaching an angular band at the shoulder, matte cucumber green glaze, artist-signed 990.00

Vase, 10" d., melon-shaped, molded broad angular leaves & long slender stems ending w/small yellow buds, matte green glaze, artist-signed 4,400.00

Vase, 11 1/8" h., waisted baluster form, molded w/seven broad ribbed leaves w/curled tops, leaves separated by deep grooves that continue to form small curved handles, designed by George P. Kendrick (restoration to one handle) 13,200.00

HAVILAND

Princess Pattern on Ranson Blanks

Haviland porcelain was originated by Americans in Limoges, France, shortly before mid-19th century and continues in production. Some Haviland was made by Theodore Haviland in the United States during the last World War. Numerous other factories also made china in Limoges, which see.

Bone dish, Ranson blank $11.00

Bowl, fruit, Princess patt. 10.00

Butter pat, Princess patt., Haviland & Co. 12.00

Butter pat, Ranson patt. 5.00

Casserole, cov., Old Blackberry patt. 65.00

Casserole & cover w/anchor finial, braided handles, Haviland & Co., Limoges 40.00

Chocolate set: cov. chocolate pot & five cups & saucers; h.p. roses, Ranson blank, 11 pcs. 325.00

Chocolate set: cov. chocolate pot & six cups & saucers; Wedding Band patt., 13 pcs. 295.00

Coffee pot, cov., Ganga patt. 135.00

Cracker jar, cov., pink & yellow roses w/coiled ribbon handles & finial, 1890's, artist-signed 89.00

Creamer, Ganga patt. 29.00

Creamer & sugar bowl, Old Carnation patt., large, ca. 1885, pr. 47.50

Creamer & sugar bowl, Princess patt., pr. 95.00

Cup & saucer, demitasse, Norma patt. 30.00

Cup & saucer, Autumn Leaf patt., w/gold trim 22.00

Cup & saucer, Ganga patt. 29.00

Cup & saucer, Marseille blank, all white 37.50

Cup & saucer, Princess patt., Ranson blank, Haviland & Co. (ILLUS. right) 25.00

Cup & saucer, Ranson blank 22.50

Cup & saucer, Rosalinde patt., Theodore Haviland, Limoges 30.00

Silver Anniversary Pattern

Cup & saucer, Silver Anniversary patt., Silver blank (ILLUS. right) 30.00

Cup & saucer, Trellis patt. 28.00

Cup & saucer, butterfly handle, pink, Haviland & Co. 75.00

Dinner service for 8: dinner plates, luncheon plates, salad & bread & butter plates, individual vegetable bowls, cups & saucers, two serving bowls, gravy boat, 10" open vegetable bowl, 8" cov. creamer & sugar bowl & two platters; Schleiger Patt. 278, 64 pcs. 695.00

Dish, fruit, Old Blackberry patt., square 15.00

Dish, pink florals all around, scalloped edge, 8½" d. 50.00

Dresser tray, gold scalloped edge, h.p. roses decor on shaded green ground, Haviland, France, 11¼ x 8 7/8" oval 52.50

Fish platter, h.p. fish center, 24 x 10" 275.00

Gravy boat, Ganga patt. 98.00
Gravy boat, Spring Bouquet patt. 29.00
Ice cream set: 15 x 8¾" tray & twelve 7½" serving plates; enameled floral decor, Haviland & Co., Limoges, 13 pcs. 175.00
Luncheon set: four salad plates & four cups & saucers; Moss Rose patt., Haviland & Co., 12 pcs. 100.00
Mustard pot, ribbed, conventional green & yellow border, Theodore Haviland, w/unmarked porcelain ladle 45.00
Planter, ovoid basket form w/three open-lobed sides, scalloped edges, underglaze floral decoration, Haviland, Limoges, France, late 19th c., 11" h. 165.00
Plate, 5" d., bread & butter, Ganga patt. 10.00
Plate, 5" d., bread & butter, Rosalinde patt., Theodore Haviland, Limoges 15.00
Plate, 7½" d., salad, Apple Blossom patt. 12.50
Plate, 7½" d., salad, Chalfonte patt. 22.00
Plate, 7½" d., salad, Chrysanthemum No. 86 patt. 30.00
Plate, 7½" d., salad, Old Blackberry patt. 12.00
Plate, 7½" d., salad, Princess patt. 12.00
Plate, 7½" d., salad, "coupe," Princess patt., Haviland & Co. 14.00
Plate, 8½" d., luncheon, Ganga patt. 17.00
Plate, 8½" d., luncheon, Princess patt., Star blank 16.00
Plate, 8½" d., luncheon, pink, white & aqua flowers, gold double border, Romeo blank, Theo. Haviland 20.00
Plate, 9½" d., dinner, Autumn Leaf patt. 10.00
Plate, 9½" d., dinner, Ganga patt. 26.00
Plate, 9½" d., dinner, Princess patt. 15.00
Plate, 9½" d., dinner, Rosalinde patt., Theodore Haviland, Limoges 25.00
Plate, 9½" d., Princess patt., Ranson blank (ILLUS. left) 30.00
Plate, 9½" d., Silver Anniversary patt., Silver blank (ILLUS. left) 15.00
Plate, chop, 12½" d., embossed gold rim w/embossed "plume"-shaped tab handles, pink floral sprays 40.00
Plate, oyster, pink, blue & yellow flowers, Presidential blank 50.00
Platter, 11" l., Old Blackberry patt., Haviland & Co., Limoges 35.00
Platter, 16", Ganga patt. 89.00
Platter, 18 x 12", Moss Rose patt., Haviland & Co. 65.00
Relish, Princess patt., 14" 40.00
Sauce dish, Princess patt., Haviland & Co., 5" d. 9.00
Soup set: cov. soup tureen (3 qt.), tray & 11 wide lip soups; Blank No. 9 w/salmon colored asters, 13 pcs. 235.00
Sugar bowl, cov., Ganga patt. 39.00
Tea set: cov. teapot, creamer, sugar bowl, waste bowl & eight individual plates; purple flowers on white ground, Theo. Haviland, 12 pcs. 400.00
Tureen, cov., ornate handles, Moss Rose patt., ornate finial, gold trim, marked "CFH," 10" across handles, 6" h. 65.00
Vase, 7½" h., ewer-shaped, h.p. butterfly, large poppies, a daffodil & foliage w/pastel shades & delicate touches of enamel, round bulbous bottom crowned w/3" d. neck w/handle attached, half eggshell white w/other half creamy lustre ground, bottom marked "Persian" in gold 90.00
Vegetable dish, cov., Princess patt., Haviland & Co., 7½" d. 62.00
Vegetable dish, cov., Ranson patt., 7¼" d. 60.00
Vegetable dish, open, Princess patt., 10" oval 36.00

HISTORICAL & COMMEMORATIVE

Landing of Lafayette Plate

Numerous potteries, especially in England and the United States, made various porcelain and earthenware pieces to com-

memorate persons, places and events. Scarce English historical wares with American views command high prices. Objects listed here are alphabetically by title of views.

American Eagle on Urn cup & saucer, flowers & urns border, dark blue (Clews) $225.00
Battle Monument, Baltimore plate, long-stemmed roses border, pink, 9" d. (Jackson) 85.00
Castle w/flag, boats in foreground platter, border w/names of fifteen states in festoons separated by 5-point stars, dark blue, 12¾" l. (Clews) 1,100.00
Catskill Mountain House, U.S. plate, flowers, shells & scrolls border, pink, 10¼" d. (Adams) 115.00
City Hall, New York plate, spread eagles amid flowers & scrolls border, dark blue, 6½" d. (Stubbs) .. 150.00
City Hall, New York plate, flowers within medallions border, dark blue, 10" d. (Ridgway) 175.00
Fairmount, Hudson River cup plate, birds, flowers & scrolls border, black (Clews) 65.00
Headwaters of the Juniata, U.S. soup plate, flowers, shells & scrolls border, pink, 10½" d. (Adams) 100.00
Hendrick Hudson plate, rolled edge, vignettes border, dark blue, 10½" d. (Rowland & Marsellus) ... 42.00
Hoboken in New Jersey plate, spread eagles amid flowers & scrolls border, dark blue, 7¾" d. (Stubbs) 175.00
Junction of the Sacandaga & Hudson Rivers plate, birds, flowers & scrolls border, brown, 7" d. (Clews) 125.00
Landing of General Lafayette at Castle Garden, New York, 16 August, 1824 plate, floral & vine border, dark blue, 5½" d. (Clews) ... 325.00
Landing of General Lafayette at Castle Garden, New York, 16 August, 1824, plate, floral & vine border, dark blue, 9" d., Clews (ILLUS.) .... 185.00 to 200.00
Landing of General Lafayette at Castle Garden, New York, 16 August, 1824, sauceboat & tray, floral & vine border, dark blue, 2 pcs. (Clews) 1,100.00
Landing of General Lafayette at Castle Garden, New York, 16, August, 1824, soup plate, floral & vine border, dark blue, 10" d. (Clews) 295.00
Landing of General Lafayette at Castle Garden, New York, 16 August, 1824, covered sugar bowl, floral & vine border, dark blue, 6¼" h. (Clews) 385.00
Landing of General Lafayette at Castle Garden, New York, 16 August, 1824, covered vegetable dish, floral & vine border, dark blue, 6" h. (Clews) 1,320.00
Mount Vernon, The Seat of the Late Gen'l. Washington cov. sugar bowl, rectangular w/domed lid, two scrolled handles, floral border, dark blue, 6½" h. 495.00
Near Sandy Hill, Hudson River cup plate, birds, flowers & scrolls border, pink, 3 7/8" d. (Clews) 150.00
Niagara Falls plate, fruit & floral border, dark blue, 10" d. (Rowland & Marsellus) 22.50

Texian Campaigne Soup Tureen

Texian Campaigne - Battle of Resaca de La Palma soup tureen, cover, underplate & ladle, symbols of war & goddess-type border, light blue, 14½" l. tray, overall 10" h., Shaw (ILLUS.) 4,290.00
Transylvania University, Lexington plate, shell border, dark blue, 9" d. (Wood) 250.00
Valentine (The) plate, Wilkie series, flowers & scrolls border, dark blue, 10" d. (Clews) 170.00
Washington Standing at His Tomb, Scroll in Hand cup & saucer, floral border, dark blue (Enoch Wood) .. 286.00
West Point, Hudson River plate, birds, flowers & scrolls border, purple, 8" d. (Clews) 95.00

HULL

This pottery was made by the Hull Pottery Company, Crooksville, O., beginning in 1905. Art Pottery was made until 1950 when the company was converted to utilitarian wares. All production ceased in 1986.

Ashtray, deer center decor, brown glaze $10.00
Bank, Corky Pig 22.50
Basket, center handle, Bow Knot patt., 6½" 58.00
Basket, tri-handle, Butterfly patt., white glaze, 10½" 40.00
Basket, Ebb Tide patt., heavy gold decor, 16½" 65.00
Basket, Magnolia Matte patt., blue & pink, 10½" 125.00
Basket, Royal Woodland patt., 10½" 55.00
Bon bon, basket-shaped, Serenade patt. 38.00
Bowl, 7" d., low, Dogwood patt. 40.00
Bowl, 10" d., Water Lily patt., brown & yellow 22.00
Candleholders, Open Rose patt., white doves w/flowers decor, pr. 40.00
Candleholders, Serenade patt., blue, 6½" h., pr. 40.00
Candlesticks, Parchment & Pine patt., pr. 20.00
Candy dish, cov., Serenade patt. 34.00
Canister, cov., cereal, coffee, flour, sugar or tea, Little Red Riding Hood patt., each 250.00
Casserole, cov., model of chicken on nest, brown glaze, 8" 15.00
Console bowl, Bow Knot patt., 13½" d. 56.00
Console bowl, Ebb Tide patt., 15¾" 40.00
Console bowl, Magnolia patt., pink glossy finish, 13" 35.00
Console set: 12" l. console bowl & pr. bird candleholders; Open Rose patt., 3 pcs. 165.00
Cookie jar, cov., Goldilocks 85.00
Cornucopia-vase, Open Rose patt., 8½" h. 35.00
Cornucopia-vases, facing right & left, Parchment & Pine patt., 12" h., pr. 55.00

Woodland Cornucopia-Vase

Cornucopia-vase, Woodland patt., green & pink glossy finish, 11" (ILLUS.) 27.50
Creamer, Little Red Riding Hood patt., w/ruffled skirt 75.00
Creamer & sugar bowl, Serenade patt., yellow, pr. 30.00
Ewer, Butterfly patt., 13" h. 42.00
Ewer, Dogwood patt., 11½" h. 70.00
Ewer, Rosella patt., 6½" 18.00
Flower pot w/attached saucer, Bow Knot patt., 6½" 52.00
Jardiniere, Water Lily patt., 5" 18.00
Jardiniere, Wildflower patt., 4" h. 17.00
Jardiniere, Woodland patt., 5½" 36.00
Lamp base, Little Red Riding Hood patt. 700.00
Lamp base, Open Rose patt. 150.00
Lamp base, Wildflower patt., pink & blue, 12½" h. 85.00
Lavabo, Butterfly patt., 3 pcs. 45.00
Marmalade jar, Little Red Riding Hood patt., basket at feet 150.00
Pitcher, milk, 7" h., Little Red Riding Hood patt. 125.00
Pitcher, 8½" h., Woodland patt. 45.00
Pitcher, 10½" h., Serenade patt. 25.00
Planter, Butterfly patt. 25.00
Planter, model of a duck w/polka dot bandana, 4" 9.00
Planter, model of a Dachshund dog, 14" 28.50
Planter, model of a kitten, pink glaze, 7½" h. 15.00
Planter, model of a Poodle's head, matte finish 35.00
Planter, model of a rooster, white strutting bird w/high arched tail, red comb & wattle 25.00
Rose bowl, Iris patt., pink shaded to blue, 7" 50.00
Rose bowl, Open Rose patt., 7" 25.00
Spice set, Little Red Riding Hood patt., 6 pcs. 1,950.00
Sugar bowl, open, Wildflower patt., pink shaded to blue, 4¾" 35.00
Sugar bowl, cov., Woodland patt., glossy finish 18.00
Teapot, cov., Butterfly patt. 45.00
Teapot, cov., Little Red Riding Hood patt. 105.00
Teapot, cov., Open Rose patt., white 56.00
Teapot, cov., Water Lily patt., pink glaze 88.00
Tea set: cov. teapot, creamer & cov. sugar bowl; Ebb Tide patt., 3 pcs. 85.00
Tea set: cov. teapot, creamer & cov. sugar bowl; Woodland patt., glossy finish, 3 pcs. 65.00
Vase, 4" h., bulbous, Poppy patt. 35.00
Vase, 4¾" h., Dogwood patt., peach 29.00
Vase, 5" h., Calla Lily patt., pink to green 20.00
Vase, 5¼" h., hat-shaped, Serenade patt., yellow 30.00

Vase, 6" h., Tulip patt., blue & pink matte 35.00
Vase, 6¼" h., Magnolia Matte patt., yellow 24.00
Vase, 7" h., Thistle patt. 20.00
Vase, 8½" h., Iris patt. 45.00
Vase, 9½" h., Bow Knot patt. 42.00
Vase, 10" h., Dogwood patt., peach 55.00
Vase, 10½" h., Mardi Gras patt. 52.00
Vase, 12½" h., Water Lily patt. 45.00
Vase, 14½" h., Continental patt. 27.00

Magnolia Matte Vase

Vase, 15" h., Magnolia Matte patt. (ILLUS.) 135.00
Wall pocket, Rosella patt. 35.00
Wall pocket, Sunglow patt., model of a cup & saucer 22.50

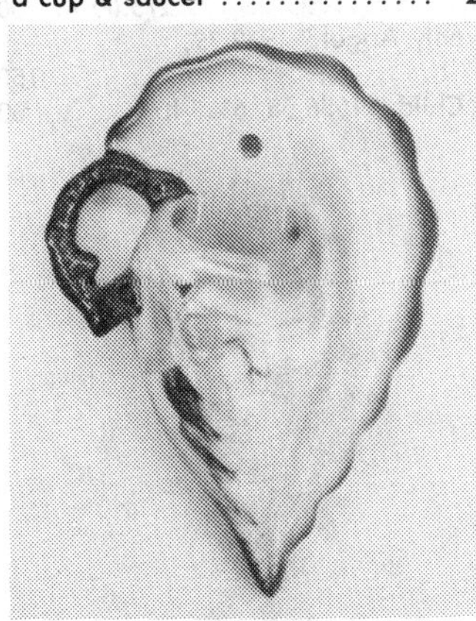

Woodland Wall Pocket

Wall pocket, Woodland patt., pink, 7½" h. (ILLUS.) 28.00

HUMMEL FIGURINES

The Goebel Company of Oeslau, Germany, first produced these porcelain figurines in 1934 having obtained the rights to adapt the beautiful pastel sketches of children by Sister Maria Innocentia (Berta) Hummel. Every design by the Goebel artisans was approved by the nun until her death in 1946. Though not antique, these figurines, with the "M.I. Hummel" signature, especially those bearing the Goebel Company factory mark used from 1934 and into the early 1940's, are being sought by collectors though interest may have peaked about 1980.

"Boots"

"Accordion Boy," full bee mark, 1940-57, 5" h. $135.00
"Accordion Boy," last bee mark used, 1972-79, 5" h. 57.00
"Angel Duet," stylized bee mark, 1956-68, 5" h. 135.00
"Angel Duet," three line mark, 1963-71, 5" h. 225.00
"Angelic Sleep," 1956-68, 3½ x 5" 99.00
"Angel Serenade," 1940-57, 5½" h. 325.00
"Angel with Trumpet," 1972-79, 2" h. 35.00
"Apple Tree Boy," crown mark, 1934-49, 4" h. 220.00
"Apple Tree Boy," 1940-57, 4" h. 105.00
"Apple Tree Boy," 1940-57, 6" h. 170.00
"Apple Tree Boy," 1963-71, 10" h. 500.00
"Apple Tree Girl," 1940-57, 4" h. 140.00
"Apple Tree Girl," 1956-68, 4" h. 60.00
"Apple Tree Girl," 1972-79, 4" h. 45.00
"Apple Tree Girl," 1963-71, 10" h. 480.00
"Auf Wiedersehen," 1940-57, 5" h. 190.00
"Baker," 1940-57, 4¾" h. 120.00
"Band Leader," 1956-68, 5" h. 110.00
"Band Leader," 1972-79, 5" h. 75.00
"Barnyard Hero," 1940-57, 5½" h. 325.00

"Begging His Share," 1934-49, 5½" h. 425.00
"Begging His Share," 1940-57, 5½" h. 310.00
"Be Patient," 1940-57, 4¼" h. 205.00
"Be Patient," 1940-57, 6¼" h. ....195.00 to 215.00
"Birthday Serenade," reverse mold, 1940-57, 5¼" h. 600.00
"Book Worm," 1940-57, 4" h. 175.00
"Book Worm" book ends, 1972-79, 5½" h., pr. 180.00
"Boots," 1940-57, 5½" h. (ILLUS.) 150.00
"Boots," 1972-79, 5½" h. 55.00
"Boots," 1940-57, 6½" h. 450.00
"Boy with Toothache," 1940-57, 5½" h. 170.00
"Brother," 1934-49, 5½" h. 300.00
"Candlelight," long candle, 1940-57, 6¾" h. 740.00
"Celestial Musician," 1940-57, 7" h. 325.00
"Celestial Musician," 1972-79, 7" h. 115.00
"Chicken-Licken," 1972-79, 4¾" h. 110.00
"Chick Girl," 1934-49, 3½" h. 275.00
"Chick Girl," 1940-57, 3½" h. 130.00
"Chimney Sweep," 1956-68, 5½" h. 110.00
"Coquettes," 1934-49, 5" h. 500.00
"Culprits," 1940-57, 6¼" h. 190.00
"Culprits," 1972-79, 6¼" h. 80.00
"Doll Bath," 1972-79, 5" h. 75.00
"Doll Mother," 1934-49, 4¾" h. ....350.00 to 400.00
"Easter Time," 1956-68, 4" h. 105.00
"Farewell," 1940-57, 4¾" h. 280.00
"Farm Boy," 1934-49, 5" h. 400.00
"Farm Boy," 1940-57, 5" h. 212.00
"Feeding Time," 1956-68, 4¼" h. 70.00
"Feeding Time," 1940-57, 5½" h. 268.00
"Flower Vendor," 1956-68, 5¼" h. 90.00
"Follow the Leader," 1956-68, 7" h. 350.00
"Follow the Leader," 1972-79, 7" h. 425.00
"For Father," 1940-57, 5½" h. 170.00
"For Father," 1956-68, 5½" h. 100.00
"For Father," 1972-79, 5½" h. 80.00
"Friends," 1972-79, 10¾" h. 500.00
"Girl with Fir Tree," candlestick, 1956-68, 3½" h. 35.00
"Girl with Trumpet," 1972-79, 2¼" h. 35.00
"Globe Trotter," 1940-57, 5" h. 108.00
"Globe Trotter," 1956-68, 5" h. 82.00
"Globe Trotter," 1972-79, 5" h. 75.00
"Good Friends," 1934-49, 4" h. 450.00
"Good Friends," 1940-57, 4" h. 175.00
"Good Friends," 1956-68, 4" h. 108.00
"Good Hunting," 1963-71, 5" h. 133.00
"Good Shepherd," 1940-57, 6¼" h. 128.00
"Goose Girl," 1956-68, 4" h. 77.00
"Goose Girl," 1934-49, 4¾" h. ....350.00 to 400.00
"Goose Girl," 1940-57, 4¾" h. 186.00
"Goose Girl," 1956-68, 4¾" h. 125.00
"Goose Girl," 1956-68, 7½" h. 375.00
"Happy Days," 1972-79, 6¼" h. 225.00
"Happy Pastime," 1940-57, 3½" h. 170.00
"Happy Pastime," 1956-68, 3½" h. 99.00
"Happy Traveler," 1940-57, 5" h. 95.00

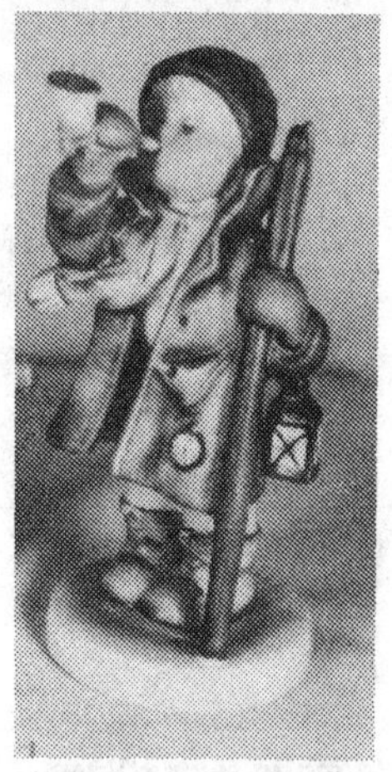

"Hear Ye, Hear Ye"

"Hear Ye, Hear Ye," 1956-68, 5" h. (ILLUS.) 118.00
"Hear Ye, Hear Ye," 1956-68, 7" h. ....275.00 to 300.00
"Heavenly Angel," 1972-79, 8¾" h. 150.00
"Holy Child," 1956-68, 6¾" h. 80.00

"Home From Market"

"Home From Market," 1956-68, 4¼" h. (ILLUS.) ....80.00 to 100.00
"Joyful," 1940-57, 4" h. 100.00
"Just Resting," 1940-57, 4" h. 115.00

"Just Resting," 1963-71, 4" h. 95.00
"Just Resting," 1956-68, 5" h. 92.00
"Kiss Me," 1956-68, 6" h. 85.00
"Kiss Me," 1963-71, 6" h. 125.00
"Knitting Lesson," 1963-71, 7½" h. . . 245.00
"Latest News," 1940-57, 5" h. 205.00
"Latest News," 1956-68, 5" h. 190.00
"Let's Sing," 1972-79, 4" h. 72.00
"Letter to Santa Claus," 1956-68, 7¼" h. 110.00
"Little Cellist," 1940-57, 6" h. 188.00
"Little Cellist," 1956-68, 6" h. 150.00
"Little Cellist," 1972-79, 6" h. 69.00
"Little Fiddler," plaque, 1972-79, 4½ x 5" 62.00
"Little Gardener," 1956-68, 4" h. . . . . .80.00 to 100.00
"Little Goat Herder," 1940-57, 4¾" h. 210.00
"Little Helper," 1940-57, 4" h. 127.00
"Little Hiker," 1940-57, 4½" h. 71.00
"Little Hiker," 1940-57, 6" h. 148.00
"Little Hiker," 1956-68, 6" h. 97.00
"Little Pharmacist," 1963-71, 6" h. 85.00
"Little Scholar," 1972-79, 5½" h. 69.00
"Little Shopper," 1940-57, 4¾" h. . . . 125.00
"Little Thrifty," bank, 1972-79, 5" h. 59.00
"Lost Sheep," 1940-57, 5½" h. 300.00
"Lost Sheep," 1972-79, 5½" h. 58.00
"Madonna," no halo, w/color, 1956-68, 11¼" h. 60.00
"Madonna," seated, color, 1940-57, 12" h. 1,825.00
"The Mail is Here," 1963-71, 4¼ x 6" 325.00
"March Winds," 1956-68, 5" h. 64.00
"Max & Moritz," 1934-49, 5" h. 280.00
"Max & Moritz," 1940-57, 5" h. 162.00
"Max & Moritz," 1956-68, 5" h. 72.00
"Meditation," 1972-79, 4¼" h. 45.00
"Meditation," 1940-57, 5½" h. . . . . .150.00 to 200.00
"Meditation," 1956-68, 5½" h. 120.00
"Meditation," 1972-79, 7" h. 160.00
"Merry Wanderer," 1940-57, 4¼" h. 125.00
"Merry Wanderer," 1956-68, 4¼" h. 71.00
"Merry Wanderer," 1972-79, 4¼" h. 48.00
"Merry Wanderer," 1934-49, 4¾" h. 310.00
"Merry Wanderer," 1956-68, 4¾" h. 70.00
"Merry Wanderer," 1972-79, 4¾" h. 56.00
"Merry Wanderer," 1972-79, 6¼" h. 77.00
"Merry Wanderer," 1940-57, 9½" h. 750.00
"Mother's Darling," 1934-49, 5½" h. . . . . .325.00 to 375.00
"Mother's Darling," 1940-57, 5½" h. 245.00
"Mother's Helper," 1934-49, 5" h. . . . 400.00
"Mountaineer," 1963-71, 5" h. 117.00
"Out of Danger," 1940-57, 6¼" h. . . 195.00
"Out of Danger," 1956-68, 6¼" h. . . 100.00
"Photographer," 1940-57, 5¼" h. . . . 230.00
"Photographer," 1956-68, 5¼" h. . . . 120.00
"Photographer," 1963-71, 5½" h. . . . 130.00
"Playmates," 1956-68, 4" h. 72.00
"Prayer Before Battle," 1956-68, 4¼" h. 110.00
"Retreat to Safety," 1956-68, 5½" h. 185.00
"School Boy," 1956-68, 4" h. 75.00
"School Boy," 1972-79, 4" h. 50.00
"School Boy," 1940-57, 5" h. 125.00
"Schoolboys," 1940-57, 10¼" h. . . . . .1,200.00 to 1,500.00
"School Girl," 1940-57, 4¼" h. 97.00
"School Girl," 1956-68, 4¼" h. 59.00
"School Girl," 1972-79, 4¼" h. 50.00
"School Girl," 1940-57, 5" h. 145.00

"School Girl"

"School Girl," 1956-68, 5" h. (ILLUS.) 120.00
"Schoolgirls," 1963-71, 7½" h. 495.00
"Searching Angel," plaque, 1972-79, 4¼" h. 70.00
"Sensitive Hunter," 1934-49, 4¾" h. . . . . .350.0 to 450.00
"Sensitive Hunter," 1940-57, 4¾" h. 155.00
"Sensitive Hunter," 1972-79, 4¾" h. 80.00
"Serenade," 1934-49, 4¾" h. 198.00
"Serenade," 1956-68, 4¾" h. 70.00
"She Loves Me," 1940-57, 4¼" h. . . . 175.00
"She Loves Me," 1956-68, 4¼" h. . . . 135.00
"Singing Lesson," 1940-57, 2¾" h. . . 140.00
"Sister," 1956-68, 5½" h. 105.00
"Sister," 1972-79, 5½" h. 65.00
"Skier," 1940-57, 5" h. 252.00
"Soldier Boy," 1963-71, 6" h. 85.00
"Soloist," 1934-49, 4¾" h. 190.00
"Soloist," 1940-57, 4¾" h. 110.00

"Soloist," 1972-79, 4¾" h. 55.00
"Spring Cheer," yellow dress, 1940-57, 5" h. ....230.00 to 290.00
"Spring Cheer," 1956-68, 5" h. 72.50
"Spring Cheer," 1963-71, 5" h. 65.00

"Spring Dance"

"Spring Dance," 1963-71, 6¾" h. (ILLUS.) ....200.00 to 250.00
"Spring Dance," 1972-79, 6¾" h..... 280.00
"Star Gazer," 1934-49, 4¾" h. ....400.00 to 450.00
"Stitch in Time," 1972-79, 6¾" h. ... 80.00
"Stormy Weather," 1934-49, 6¼" h. ....525.00 to 625.00
"Stormy Weather," 1956-68, 6¼" h. 246.00
"Street Singer," 1940-57, 5" h. 118.00
"Strolling Along," 1940-57, 4¾" h. .. 152.00
"Strolling Along," 1956-68, 4¾" h. .. 80.00
"Surprise," 1940-57, 4" h. 115.00
"Surprise," 1934-49, 5½" h. 365.00
"Surprise," 1940-57, 5½" h. 265.00
"Sweet Music," 1940-57, 5¼" h. 145.00
"Telling Her Secret," 1956-68, 5" h. 95.00
"Telling Her Secret," 1963-71, 5" h. 155.00
"Telling Her Secret," 1940-57, 6½" h. 500.00
"Telling Her Secret," 1972-79, 6½" h. 130.00
"To Market," 1940-57, 4" h. 175.00
"To Market," 1940-57, 5½" h. 210.00
"To Market," 1956-68, 5½" h. 110.00
"Trumpet Boy," 1940-57, 4¾" h. 105.00
"Umbrella Boy," 1956-68, 4¾" h. ... 310.00
"Umbrella Boy," 1963-71, 4¾" h. ... 295.00
"Umbrella Boy," 1956-68, 8" h. 620.00
"Umbrella Boy," 1972-79, 8" h. 640.00
"Umbrella Girl," 1956-68, 4¾" h. ....425.00 to 450.00
"Umbrella Girl," 1963-71, 4¾" h. ... 300.00
"Umbrella Girl," 1972-79, 4¾" h. ... 225.00
"Umbrella Girl," 1940-57, 8" h. ....550.00 to 600.00
"Umbrella Girl," 1963-71, 8" h. 630.00
"Umbrella Girl," 1972-79, 8" h. ....650.00 to 700.00
"Vacation Time" plaque, 1972-79, 4¾ x 4" 83.00
"Valentine Gift," 1972-79, 5¾" h ... 325.00
"Village Boy," 1940-57, 4" h. 85.00
"Village Boy," 1956-68, 4" h. 65.00
"Village Boy," 1972-79, 4" h. 39.50
"Village Boy," 1940-57, 6" h. 165.00
"Village Boy," 1956-68, 6" h. 118.00
"Village Boy," 1972-79, 6" h. 130.00
"Village Boy," 1956-68, 7¼" h. 225.00
"Village Boy," 1972-79, 7¼" h. 135.00
"Visting an Invalid," 1972-79, 5" h... 75.00
"Volunteers," 1972-79, 6½" h 250.00
"Waiter," 1940-57, 6" h. 150.00
"Wash Day," 1956-68, 6" h. 100.00
"Watchful Angel," 1972-79, 6¾" h. 115.00
"Wayside Devotion," 1934-49, 7½" h. ....600.00 to 650.00
"Wayside Devotion," 1940-57, 7½" h. ....350.00 to 400.00
"Wayside Harmony," 1934-49, 4" h. 195.00
"Wayside Harmony," 1940-57, 4" h. 125.00
"Wayside Harmony," 1956-68, 4" h. 110.00
"Wayside Harmony," 1934-49, 5" h. 380.00
"Wayside Harmony," 1940-57, 5" h. 165.00
"We Congratulate," 1940-57, 4" h. .. 168.00
"We Congratulate," 1956-68, 4" h. .. 125.00
"Which Hand?" 1956-68, 5½" h. 60.00
"White Angel," font, 1956-68, 3½ x 1¾" 35.00

"Whitsuntide"

"Whitsuntide," 1940-57, 7" h. (ILLUS.) ....600.00 to 650.00
"Worship," 1940-57, 5" h. 185.00
"Worship," 1956-68, 5" h. 125.00

IMARI

Imari Bowl

This is a multicolor ware that originated in Japan, was copied by the Chinese, and imitated by the English and European potteries. It was decorated in overglaze enamel. Made in the Hizen and Arita areas of Japan, much of it was exported through the port of Imari. Arita Imari often has brocade patterns.

Bowl, 9¾" d., interior & exterior w/iron-red, green & underglaze-blue trailing florals, gilt highlights, 19th c., minor hairline & firing defect (ILLUS.) $550.00

Bowl, 10¾" d., central garden scene w/flower vases, underglaze-blue & iron-red w/gilt-enriched floral motif border, late 19th c. 165.00

Bowl, 11 7/8" l., oval, scalloped edge, painted w/a central oval medallion of potted flowers enclosed by alternating shaped reserves of birds & flowers 495.00

Bowl, 12 5/8" w., octagonal, underglaze-blue budding branches radiating from circular pine tree medallion w/iron-red & gilt highlights, late 19th c. 495.00

Bowl, 13½" d., shaped rim, interior & exterior decorated w/floral & bird designs, blue & white, ca. 1880 .... 302.50

Charger, central underglaze-blue floral medallion enclosed by landscape reserves w/large insect separated by shaped reserves of *kiku* against wave pattern & brocade bands, 19th c., 16" d. 550.00

Charger, decorated at left w/large figure of *Tokiwa Gozen* w/her three chidlren, at right a village rendered in underglaze-blue & autumn colors above a vignette w/peasants in a rainstorm, all below a snow-capped Mt. Fuji silhouetted against a gilt-painted sky, Meiji period, 16½" d. 467.50

Chargers, central underglaze-blue stylized blossom surrounded by three dragons emerging from stylized clouds chasing elusive flaming pearls & alternating w/large floral *mon*, underside painted w/underglaze-blue dragons, 19th c., 18" d., pr. 1,210.00

Jardiniere, slightly rounded sides, fruit blossoms & wisteria in shades of brown & blue on white ground, 18" d., 12¼" h. 350.00

Jardiniere, slightly rounded sides, continuous scene of mountains, water & trees under a cloud-filled sky in shades of brown, blue & black on white ground, 18" d., 12¾" h. 290.00

Pitcher, 9½" h., bands of diapering & flowers, late 19th c. 600.00

Plate, 9¼" d., "Pronk" style, after design by Cornelius Pronk, "La dame au parasol," w/two *meiren* observing birds in a marsh, honeycomb band w/eight reserves, iron-red, underglaze-blue & gilt, seven pencilled insects reverse, ca. 1740 .... 1,430.00

Serving bowl, paneled circular form, gilt rim, border of enameled circular medallions on blue ground, centering similar conjoined underglaze-blue & enameled medallions on white ground, 19th c., 12½" d., 2¾" h. 375.00

Umbrella stand, cylindrical, decorated in monochromatic blue w/an exotic flower in a landscape, floral borders at base & rim, late 19th c., 24" h. 357.50

Impressive Imari Vase

Vase, 49 5/8" h., baluster form w/applied bas-relief dragon on either side, decorated w/floral, fan & bird motifs in iron-red, underglaze-blue, green & gold, dull brown slip around rim, 19th c., minor glaze chips (ILLUS.) 4,600.00

IRONSTONE

The first successful ironstone was patented in 1813 by C.J. Mason in England. The body contains iron slag incorporated with the clay. Other potters imitated Mason's ware and today much hard, thick ware is lumped under the term ironstone. Earlier it was called by various names, including graniteware. Both plain white and decorated wares were made throughout the 19th century. We include the Tea Leaf pattern and its variants here.

GENERAL

Ironstone Cornucopia-Vase

Bowl, 8½" octagonal, brown & white transfer, Mason's $35.00
Butter pat, Moss Rose patt., Alfred Meakin Ltd...................... 15.00
Chamber pot, cov., Asia shape, all white, large pod finial, Wooliscroft 90.00
Cornucopia-vases, tapering faceted vase w/tapering lip, terminating in acanthus on rectangular cushion base w/chamfered corners, decorated w/reserves of prunus in pots on blue ground, base w/red & green diamond pattern (one base chipped), Mason's, 8" h., pr. (ILLUS. of one) 1,210.00
Creamer, Grenade shape, all white, T. & R. Boote, 5½" h. 60.00
Creamer, octagonal, flat base, angled handle, high arched spout, "gaudy," Strawberry patt. (edge wear, small flakes).............. 350.00
Cup, Moss Rose patt., Alfred Meakin........................... 6.00
Cup & saucer, handleless, Wheat patt., all white, W.E. Corn, ca. 1860 .... 30.00
Cup & saucer, barrel-shaped, Moss Rose patt., Meakin 28.00
Ewer, Corn & Oats patt., all white, J. Wedgwood, ca. 1863, 12¾" h. 150.00
Gravy boat, Fuchsia patt., all white, George Jones & J. & G. Meakin .. 30.00
Gravy boat, Hyacinth patt., all white, Wedgwood & Co., ca. 1860 .... 22.00
Gravy boat, Moss Rose patt., Alfred Meakin......................... 30.00
Gravy boat, Vintage shape, all white, E. & C. Challinor, ca. 1865 .... 22.00
Pitcher, 5½" h., h.p. "gaudy," Mason's, 1825-27.................. 90.00
Pitcher, jug-type, 6½" h., Japan patt., Mason's, ca. 1815.......... 275.00

Mason's "Japan" Pattern

Pitcher, 6 5/8" h., octagonal jug-type, serpent handle, "Japan" patt., Mason's, ca. 1850 (ILLUS.) .. 95.00
Pitcher, 7¼" h., "gaudy," embossed bust portrait of trumpeter, underglaze-blue & purple lustre .. 45.00
Pitcher, 8¼" h., octagonal, "gaudy," Morning Glory patt., underglaze-blue, purple lustre trim 115.00
Pitcher, 8 3/8" h., Moss Rose patt... 100.00
Pitcher, 8¾" h., "gaudy," embossed scene of children w/bird nest, underglaze-blue & purple lustre .. 65.00
Pitcher, 9¼" h., Hyacinth patt., all white, Wedgwood & Co., ca. 1860 .... 55.00
Pitcher, 9¾" h., Full Ribbed patt., all white, J.W. Pankhurst & Co., 1852-82.......................... 80.00
Pitcher, 12" h., brown design of birds, nest, eggs, blossoms, branches, leaves over front of bulbous body, marked "S.P. Co., Ironstone China" 35.00
Pitcher, milk, 6" h., "gaudy," willow tree, florals, birds & architectural detail 95.00

Pitcher, milk, 8" h., Panelled Grape patt., all white, Charles Meigh & Son, 1851-61 .... 75.00
Pitcher, milk, 8¼" h., medium white w/copper lustre trim, Livesley Powell 60.00
Pitcher, milk, "gaudy," ivy decor 165.00
Pitcher, milk, octagonal, Lily of the Valley patt., all white 65.00
Pitcher, wash, Ceres patt., all white, Elsmore & Forster 115.00
Pitcher, wash, Wheat & Blackberry patt., all white, Thomas Hughes, 1860-94 .... 100.00
Plate, child's, Forget-Me-Not patt., all white, Henry Alcock & Co. 16.00
Plate, 6¾" d., Moss Rose patt., Alfred Meakin 12.00
Plate, 7½" d., "gaudy," Wagon Wheel patt. 75.00
Plate, 8" d., luncheon, Moss Rose patt., Alfred Meakin 7.00
Plate, 8" d., 12-sided, "gaudy," underglaze dark blue leaves interspersed w/strawberries 65.00
Plate, 8¼" d., "gaudy," nine flowers w/five petals each outlined in copper lustre 85.00
Plate, 8½" d., "gaudy," Blackberry patt., underglaze-blue, polychrome enameling & purple lustre trim, impressed registry mark & "B. Walley, Niagara Grape" 50.00
Plate, 8½" d., flow blue & "gaudy," Dahlia patt. 45.00
Plate, 8 7/8", 12-sided, "gaudy," Flower Basket patt. 95.00
Plate, 9" d., Ceres shape, Wheat patt., all white, Elsmore & Forster 20.00
Plate, 9" d., Tulip design, English, set of 4 .... 200.00
Plate, 9¼" d., 12-sided, "gaudy," Urn patt. 75.00
Plate, 9½" d., dinner, Moss Rose patt., Alfred Meakin 15.00
Plate, 9¾" d., Lustre Band patt., blue & white, Elsmore & Forster .. 25.00
Plate, 10" d., Moss Rose patt., Powell & Bishop 20.00
Plates, 10" d., shaped rims, Imari patt., gilt trim, Mason's, set of 12 .... 990.00
Plate, 10½" d., scalloped rim, bright multicolor birds, flowers & insects, Mason's 25.00
Plates, 10¼" d., Imari-style decoration, polychrome florals on cobalt blue border centering iron-red & polychrome floral spray, mid-19th c., set of 12 .... 350.00
Platter, 11½ x 9½", Ashworth's Mandalay patt., Mason's Patent .. 35.00
Platter, 12 x 9", Moss Rose patt., Alfred Meakin 25.00
Platter, 13", "gaudy," nine flowers w/five petals each outlined in copper lustre 150.00
Platter, 13½ x 10¾", Double Landscape patt., ca. 1883, Mason's 250.00
Platter, 15½", Moss Rose patt., Alfred Meakin 35.00
Platter, 16½", Wheat patt., all white, Alfred Meakin 35.00
Platter, oval, Sydenham shape, all white, T & R Boote, large size 50.00
Punch bowl w/handles, berry cluster decoration, all white, Jacob Furnival & Co. 125.00
Punch bowl, Scrolled Bubble patt., all white, J.W. Parkhurst & Co.... 195.00
Relish dish w/reticulated handles, Fluted Pearl patt., John Wedgwood 40.00
Relish dish, Vineyard patt., all white, Davenport 45.00
Sauce dish, flat, low, Moss Rose patt., Alfred Meakin 8.00
Sauce dish, Moss Rose patt., Johnson Bros. 10.00
Sauce tureen & cov., Columbia shape, all white, Goodwin, 2 pcs. 125.00
Sauce tureen, cover & ladle, Baltic shape, all white, Hulme & Sons, 3 pcs. 95.00
Sauce tureen, cover & undertray, Imari-type design w/polychrome floral enameling & underglaze blue, impressed "Patent Ironstone China," Mason's, England, ca. 1850, 7¾" l., 3 pcs. 275.00
Sauce tureen, cover & ladle, Prairie shape, all white, Joseph Clementson, 3 pcs. 125.00
Soup plate w/flange rim, Panelled Grape patt., Furnival, 8 7/8" d. .. 12.00
Soup plate w/flange rim, Niagara shape, all white, 9 5/8" d., Edward Walley 15.00
Soup tureen, cov., Lily of the Valley patt., all white, Anthony Shaw ... 225.00
Soup tureen, cover & ladle, Hyacinth patt., all white, 3 pcs. 215.00
Soup tureen, cover & ladle, Canada shape, Wheat & Poppy patt., all white, ca. 1877, 3 pcs. 225.00
Soup tureen, cover & ladle, Fig shape, all white, large, 3 pcs. 425.00
Soup tureen, cover & underplate, Vista patt., rose decoration, 3 pcs. 290.00
Soup tureen, cover & underplate, dragon handles, "gaudy," multicolor floral decoration, "Stone China No. 13" w/lion & unicorn mark, 13½" h., 3 pcs. 550.00

Soup tureen, cover, underplate & ladle, Ceres shape, all white, Wm. Adams & Sons, 4 pcs. . . . 675.00
Sugar bowl, cov., six-sided body on high six-sided base, flared, arched loop handles w/"earred" tops, six-sided "pagoda" style lid w/rosette finial, h.p. morning-glory blossoms & leaves in underglaze blue, 8¼" h. (minor stains) . . . 145.00
Sugar bowl, cov., Wheat & Blackberry patt., all white . . . 65.00
Syrup pitcher w/pewter lid, Moss Rose patt., ca. 1872 . . . 80.00
Teapot, cov., Berlin Swirl patt., all white, T.J. & J. Mayer . . . 165.00
Teapot, cov., Ceres shape, Wheat patt., all white w/copper lustre trim, Elsmore & Forster . . . 225.00
Teapot, cov., Fig shape, all white . . . 135.00
Teapot, cov., Pearl patt., Sydenham shape, J & G Meakin . . . 165.00
Toddy cup, Columbia shape, all white . . . 25.00
Toilet set: bowl, pitcher, soap dish & cov. chamber pot; vines & hackberries patt. on blue & white ground, Alfred Meakin, 5 pcs. . . . 450.00
Toothbrush holder, w/lid, Hyacinth patt., horizontal, all white, Wedgwood . . . 60.00
Vegetable dish, cov., Berlin Swirl patt., large apple finial, Mayer & Elliot . . . 115.00
Vegetable dish, cov., Ceres patt., all white, rope embossment in center of lid, Elsmore & Forster, small . . . 150.00
Vegetable dish, cov., Ivy Wreath patt., all white, John Meir . . . 70.00
Vegetable dish, cov., Ribbed Bud patt., all white, J.W. Pankhurst & Co., 1852-82 . . . 190.00
Vegetable dish, cov., Sydenham shape, all white, T. & R. Boote, small . . . 150.00
Vegetable dish, cov., Sydenham shape, T. & R. Boote, medium . . . 175.00
Vegetable dish, cov., Wheat, Clover & Bowknot patt., all white, Turner & Tomkinson, large . . . 75.00
Waste bowl, cov., Forget-Me-Not patt. all white, Elsmore & Forster . . . 25.00

TEA LEAF

Bacon rasher, Wilkinson . . . 40.00
Baker, Alfred Meakin, 7¾" sq. . . . 37.50
Baker, Anthony Shaw, large . . . 40.00
Bone dish, Alfred Meakin . . . 37.00
Bone dishes, scalloped edge, Alfred Meakin, pr. . . . 90.00
Bowl, 6" sq., ribbed, Mellor, Taylor & Co. . . . 30.00
Bowl, 7" sq., Alfred Meakin . . . 35.00
Bowl, 8" sq., Alfred Meakin . . . 45.00
Bread plate, closed handles, square, Alfred Meakin . . . 55.00
Bread tray, square, Bamboo patt., Alfred Meakin . . . 40.00
Butter dish, cover & liner, J. & E. Mayer . . . 70.00
Butter dish, cover & liner, Bamboo patt., Alfred Meakin . . . 65.00
Butter dish, cover & liner, Bamboo patt., Wedgwood . . . 120.00
Butter pat, round, Alfred Meakin . . . 12.00
Butter pat, square, Alfred Meakin . . . 9.00
Butter pats, round, Mellor, Taylor & Co., set of 8 . . . 60.00
Butter pat, hexagonal, Anthony Shaw . . . 15.00
Butter pat, square, Anthony Shaw . . . 9.00
Butter pat, square, Wedgwood, 2¾" . . . 12.00
Butter pat, Wilkinson . . . 8.00
Cake plate, Furnival . . . 75.00
Cake plate, pedestal base, copper band, Livesley-Powell (some crazing) . . . 155.00
Cake plate, Bamboo patt., Alfred Meakin . . . 55.00
Cake plate, oval, Mellor, Taylor & Co. . . . 65.00
Cake plate, Basketweave patt., Anthony Shaw . . . 135.00
Chamber pot, cov., Bishop & Stonier . . . 155.00
Chamber pot, cov., Alfred Meakin . . . 150.00
Coffeepot, cov., Bamboo patt., Alfred Meakin . . . 120.00
Coffeepot, cov., Fish Hook patt., Alfred Meakin . . . 95.00
Coffeepot, cov., Fish Hook patt., Alfred Meakin, large . . . 120.00
Coffeepot, cov., Wilkinson . . . 45.00
Creamer, East End Pottery . . . 50.00
Creamer, Furnival . . . 100.00
Creamer, W. H. Grindley & Co. . . . 40.00
Creamer, J. & E. Mayer . . . 65.00
Creamer, Alfred Meakin . . . 112.00
Creamer, Basketweave patt., Anthony Shaw . . . 72.50
Creamer, Chinese shape, Anthony Shaw . . . 270.00
Creamer, Lily-of-the-Valley patt., Anthony Shaw . . . 125.00
Creamer, Arthur J. Wilkinson (late Alcock) . . . 90.00
Cup & saucer, ribbed, W. & E. Corn . . . 55.00
Cup & saucer, handled, Davenport . . . 50.00
Cup & saucer, handleless, Elsmore & Forster . . . 55.00
Cup & saucer, handled, barrel-shaped, Alfred Meakin . . . 40.00
Cup & saucer, handled, Chelsea patt., Alfred Meakin . . . 60.00

Cup & saucer, handleless, cone-shaped, Alfred Meakin 45.00
Cup & saucer, handled, Cable & Ring patt., Anthony Shaw.............. 80.00
Cup & saucer, handleless, Lily-of-the-Valley patt., Anthony Shaw... 75.00
Doughnut stand, Alfred Meakin, 7" sq. 255.00
Gravy boat, Victory patt., dolphin handle, John Edwards 55.00
Gravy boat, Alfred Meakin......... 35.00
Gravy boat w/attached undertray, Bamboo patt., Alfred Meakin..... 80.00
Gravy boat w/underplate, Mellor, Taylor & Co. 80.00
Honey dish, Lily-of-the-Valley patt., Anthony Shaw 140.00
Mug, Chinese shape, Anthony Shaw (hairline) 80.00
Oyster bowl, individual size, round, J. & E. Mayer 55.00
Pitcher, 6" h., Alfred Meakin 80.00
Pitcher, milk, 6½" h., Chinese shape, Anthony Shaw 125.00
Pitcher, hot water, 7½" h., Lily-of-the-Valley patt., Anthony Shaw... 325.00
Pitcher, milk, 8 1/8" h., Victory (Dolphin) patt., Edwards 150.00

Blanket Stitch Milk Pitcher

Pitcher, milk, 8 3/8" h., Blanket Stitch patt., Alcock (ILLUS.)....... 120.00
Pitcher, milk, 8½" h., Fish Hook patt., Alfred Meakin............ 150.00
Pitcher, water, 9" h., Alfred Meakin......................... 90.00
Pitcher, milk, 9" h., ribbed, Mellor, Taylor & Co. 315.00
Pitcher, milk, 10" h., Morning Glory shape, Wileman & Co. 160.00
Pitcher, milk, Bullet patt., Anthony Shaw 85.00
Pitcher, water, Lion's Head patt., Mellor, Taylor & Co. 95.00
Plate, child's, 4¼" d., Alfred Meakin............................ 50.00
Plate, luncheon, 7¾" d., Lily-of-the-Valley patt., Anthony Shaw 12.00
Plates, luncheon, 7¾" d., Chinese shape, Anthony Shaw, set of 4 ... 60.00
Plate, 8" d., Anthony Shaw 17.50
Plate, 8½" d., Clementson 18.00
Plate, 9" d., Mellor, Taylor & Co. ... 20.00
Plates, luncheon, Niagara shape, Edward Walley, set of 4 .... 50.00
Platter, 11½" oval, Mellor, Taylor & Co. 50.00
Platter, 12" oval, pierced handles, Anthony Shaw 50.00
Platter, 12 x 8½", Alfred Meakin ... 15.00
Sauce dish, rectangular, Alfred Meakin........................ 20.00
Sauce dish, square, Alfred Meakin.. 16.00
Sauce dishes, square, scalloped edge, Mellor, Taylor & Co., set of 3 .... 50.00
Sauce dish, round, Chinese shape, Anthony Shaw 18.00
Sauce dish, round, Hanging Leaves patt., Anthony Shaw........... 26.00
Sauce dish, round, plain, Anthony Shaw 24.00
Sauce tureen, cover & ladle, Bamboo patt., Alfred Meakin, 3 pcs... 375.00
Sauce tureen, cov., Fish Hook patt., Alfred Meakin, 2 pcs. 140.00
Sauce tureen, cov., w/underplate, Lily-of-the-Valley patt., Anthony Shaw, 3 pcs.................... 245.00
Shaving mug, W.H. Grindley & Co... 100.00
Shaving mug, Fish Hook patt., Alfred Meakin 110.00
Shaving mug, Lily-of-the-Valley patt., Anthony Shaw............ 155.00
Soup plate w/flange rim, L. Burgess, Burslem, 9" d. 20.00
Soup plate w/flange rim, Alfred Meakin....................... 26.00
Soup plate w/flange rim, Wilkinson 15.00
Sugar bowl, cov., J. & E. Mayer 60.00
Sugar bowl, cov., child's, Mellor, Taylor & Co. 230.00
Sugar bowl, cov., Bamboo patt., Alfred Meakin 55.00
Sugar bowl, cov., Powell & Bishop .. 75.00
Sugar bowl, cov., Lily-of-the-Valley patt., Anthony Shaw............ 175.00
Teapot, cov., Square Ridged patt., Mellor, Taylor & Co. (ILLUS.) 125.00
Teapot, cov., Chinese shape, late 1850's, Anthony Shaw 255.00
Teapot, cov., Wedgwood 120.00
Teapot, cov., bulbous, Wilkinson ... 145.00
Vegetable dish, open, Alfred Meakin, 8" sq. 20.00
Vegetable dish, cov., Hexagon patt., Anthony Shaw 120.00
Wash bowl & pitcher, Bamboo patt., Alfred Meakin 290.00

Square Ridged Teapot

Wash bowl & pitcher, Chinese shape, Anthony Shaw 465.00

TEA LEAF VARIANTS

Baker, Pepper Leaf, Elsmore & Forster, 9 x 7" oval, 2" h. 80.00
Coffeepot, cov., Morning Glory, Elsmore & Forster ....225.00 to 250.00
Creamer, Cinquefoil, Paneled Grape shape, 6½" h. 110.00
Cup, Teaberry (or Coffeeberry) 50.00
Cup & saucer, handleless, Pepper Leaf, Elsmore & Forster 60.00
Pitcher, milk, 8" h., Tobacco Leaf, Elsmore & Forster 110.00
Plates, 7½" d., Pepper Leaf, Elsmore & Forster, pr. 22.00
Plates, saucers & handleless cups, Pin Wheel, Walley, 12 pcs. 225.00
Shaving mug, Cloverleaf, Knowles, Taylor & Knowles 32.50
Soup plate w/flanged rim, Teaberry, Clementson 25.00
Sugar bowl, cov., Teaberry, Clementson, 7¼" h. 110.00

JASPER WARE
(Non-Wedgwood)

Jasper Ware Cheese Dish

Jasper ware is fine-grained exceedingly hard stoneware made by including barium sulphate in the clay and was first devised by Josiah Wedgwood, who utilized it for the body of many of his fine cameo blue-and-white and green-and-white pieces. It was subsequently produced by other potters in England and Germany, notably William Adams & Sons, and is in production at the present. Also see WEDGWOOD - JASPER.

Book ends, white relief cameos w/columns & sphinx on blue, impressed "4005," 5 x 4 x 4", pr. ... $85.00
Box, cov., white relief winged lady on cover, white relief lady, flowers, garlands & cherub head around sides on blue, Germany, 3 7/8 x 2½", 2 1/8" h. 59.00
Box, cov., white relief cupid & nymph on blue, Schafer & Vater, Germany, 5" oval 35.00
Cheese dish, cov., white relief classical figures as actors, musicians & scholars on mulberry ground center w/fruiting grapevine borders on cover & base, white relief anthemia & palmettes on cover w/acorn finial, England, late 19th c., 8½" h. (ILLUS.) 357.00
Clock, white relief cupids, foliage & flowers on sage green, 7" d., 9 1/8" h. (clock needs repair) 151.00
Cracker jar, bulbous, white relief hunting scene on dark blue, silver plate cover, rim & handle, Adams, England, 6" d., 6" h. 135.00
Cup & saucer, bucket-shaped cup w/white relief classical figures & saucer w/formal foliage & engine-turning on blue, Turner, England, ca. 1800 .... 176.00
Hair receiver, cov., white relief ladies & flowers on blue, white relief cupids on lid, Germany, 3 3/8" d., 3½"h. 64.00
Pitcher, 5½" h., white relief Grecian figures on green, Copeland, England 75.00
Pitcher, 7½" h., 5" d., ivory relief dancing nymphs on blue, Copeland, late Spode, England ... 95.00
Plaque, pierced to hang, white relief child & cupid w/angels & flowers at edge on sage green, 5" d. 80.00
Plaque, pierced to hang, white relief cupid pushing other cupid on sleigh holding umbrella, surrounded by raised white dots on green, Germany, 5" d. 75.00
Plaque, pierced to hang, white relief children (2) climbing on heron, two children in water & white relief lilies-of-the-valley border on green, Germany, 5½" d. 70.00

Plaque, pierced to hang, white relief cupid aiming bow & arrow at lady & flowers at edge on sage green, 6" d. 80.00
Plaque, pierced to hang, white relief young man w/fishing pole saying goodbye to girl on dock & border of roses on blue ground, green, Germany, 6" d. 80.00
Plaque, pierced to hang, white relief young man w/fishing pole saying goodbye to girl on dock & border of roses on blue ground, Germany, 8 x 6½" oval 118.00

Jasper Ware Sugar Bowl

Sugar bowl, cov., white relief classical figure garlanding an urn on one side & playful putti reverse & rim w/interlocking circlets on blue, lower part w/basketweave border, Neale & Co., England, ca. 1800, 4¾" oval (ILLUS.) 660.00
Sugar bowl, cov., two-handled, white relief sacrifice scene on both sides on blue, cover w/swan finial, Adams, ca. 1800, 6" w. 1,045.00
Syrup pitcher w/pewter lid, white relief ladies (6), tree, bushes on dark blue, handle & 1" base grey, glazed, Copeland, late Spode, England, 6" h. 87.00
Urn, white relief hunting scene on cobalt blue, Adams, Tunstall, England, 8" d., 8" h. 195.00
Vase, 7½" h., bulbous, white relief birds, insects & flowers on dark green, marked, "Dudson Bros., Hanley, England" 75.00
Vase, 7¾" h., two-handled, white Art Nouveau woman's face w/flowing hair w/two white swans below on lilac ground, handles are topiary trees in green, A. Radford Pottery, Ohio (1896-1912) 850.00

JEWEL TEA AUTUMN LEAF PATTERN

Though not antique, this ware has a devoted following. The Hall China Company of East Liverpool, Ohio, made the first pieces of Autumn Leaf pattern ware to be given as premiums by the Jewel Tea Company in 1933. The premiums were an immediate success and thousands of new customers, all eager to acquire a piece of the durable Autumn Leaf pattern ware, began purchasing Jewel Tea products. Though the pattern was eventually used to decorate linens, glasswares and tinwares, we include only the Hall China Company items in our listing.

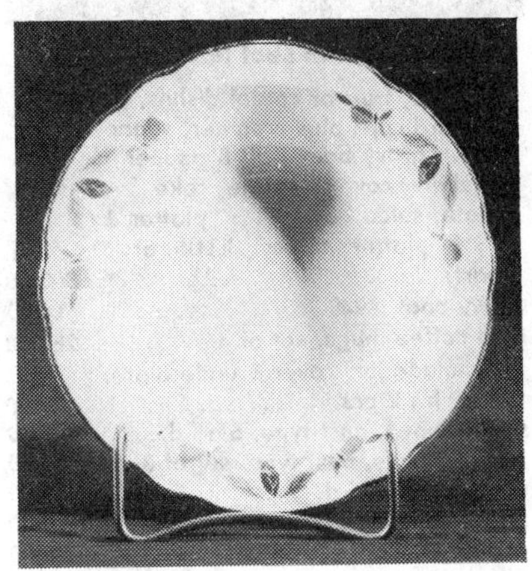

Autumn Leaf Cereal Bowl

Baking dish, 4" d. $6.00
Baking dish, swirl form, 10 oz. 20.00
Bean pot, cov., 2-handled 75.00
Bouillon cup 18.00
Bowl, cereal, 6" d. (ILLUS.) 8.00
Bowl, cov., 6½" d. 30.00
Bowl, salad, 9" d. 12.00
Bowl, cream soup 16.00
Butter dish & cover w/scalloped handle, ¼ lb. 132.00
Butter dish, cov., 1 lb. 185.00
Cake plate, 9½" d. 11.00
Candy dish w/"Goldenray" metal base 250.00
Casserole, cov., round, 2 qt. 25.00
Casserole, open, handled, 10" oval 15.00
Clock, electric, wall model, 9½" d. 310.00
Coffee perculator, all-china w/china insert, 1941-45 .... 75.00
Coffeepot (or casserole) warmer, oval 110.00
Cookie jar, cov., large earred handles, 1957-69 .... 88.00
Creamer & cov. sugar bowl, post-1940, pr. 15.00
Cup, St. Denis style 13.00
Custard cup 4.50
Dinner service, six each 7" d. salad plates, 10" d. dinner plates, cups,

Autumn Leaf Pattern

saucers, fruit or cereal dishes, & custard cups plus creamer, sugar bowl, gravy boat, salt & pepper shakers, cov. casserole, cake plate, salad bowl, 11½" platter & 13½" platter, 46 pcs. (ILLUS. of part) 300.00
Gravy boat, 1940-76 .... 14.00
Irish coffee mugs, set of 4 .... 280.00
Marmalade jar, cover & underplate, 3½" h., 2 pcs. 39.00
Mixing bowl, nest-type, 6½" d. 9.00
Mixing bowls, nest-type, set of 3 .... 35.00
Pie baker, 9½" d. 15.00
Pitcher, utility, 2½ pt. 18.00
Pitcher w/ice lip, 5½ pt. 18.00
Platter, 11½" l. 14.00
Platter, 13½" l. 15.00
Range top set, cov. grease jar & salt & pepper shakers, 3 pcs. 30.00
Salt & pepper shakers, bell-shaped, small, pr. 15.00
Salt & pepper shakers, handled, range size, pr. 17.50
Teapot, cov., Aladdin lamp shape 40.00
Tidbit tray, 3-tier ....45.00 to 50.00
Vase, bud ....125.00 to 160.00
Vegetable bowl, cov., 2-handled, 10½" oval 40.00
Vegetable bowl, open, 9" d. 44.00
Vegetable bowl, open, 10" oval 12.00

JUGTOWN POTTERY

This pottery was established by Jacques and Juliana Busbee in Jugtown, North Carolina, in the early 1920's in an attempt to revive the skills of the diminishing North Carolina potter's art as Prohibition ended the need for locally crafted stoneware whiskey jugs. During the early years, Juliana Busbee opened a shop in Greenwich Village in New York City to promote the North Carolina wares that her husband, Jacques, was designing and a local youth, Ben Owen, was producing under his direction. Owen continued to work with Busbee from 1922 until Busbee's death in 1947 at which time Juliana took over management of the pottery for the next decade until her illness (or mental fatigue) caused the pottery to be closed in 1958. At that time, Owen opened his own pottery a few miles away, marking his wares "Ben Owen - Master Potter." The pottery begun by the Busbee's was reopened in 1960, under new management, and still operates today using the identical impressed mark of the early Jugtown pottery the Busbee's managed from 1922 until 1958.

Jugtown Pottery Vase

Bowl, 7" d., 4½" h., closed form, frothy white over olive green flambe' glaze $220.00
Creamer, orange glaze, small 40.00
Jar, stoneware, ovoid w/four pinched strap handles, brownish olive green glaze, marked "Jugtown Ware," 10½" h. 45.00
Pitcher, 8" h., clear glaze w/good orange color, impressed "Jugtown" (some wear & small chips) 55.00
Vase, 4" h., Chinese blue glaze 75.00
Vase, 10¾" h., 7¼" widest d., bulbous w/corset neck & flaring rim, turquoise matte finish w/burgundy blotches, professionally repaired hole in bottom, impressed circular mark (ILLUS.) 522.50

KAUFFMANN, ANGELICA

Angelica Kauffmann (Marie Angelique Catherine Kauffmann) was an accomplished Swiss artist who lived from 1741 until 1807. Colored decals copied from her original works often embellish late 19th century porcelain and pieces carrying her facsimile signature are quite collectible.

Stein with Kauffmann Scene

Coffee set: cov. demitasse pot, 6 c/s & tray; various classical scenes, signed "Kauffmann," 14 pcs. $950.00

Condensed milk can holder, cover & underplate, classical maiden after Kauffmann reserved on green ground w/gold tracery........... 85.00

Cracker jar, cov., scenic front panel after Kauffmann w/three ladies & gentleman in pastel colors, alternating green & maroon panels w/gold trim around body, silver plate rim, handle & lid, 5" d., 7" h.......................... 141.00

Cup & saucer, classical scene after Kauffmann reserved on royal blue ground, beehive mark blank 100.00

Cup & saucer, footed, typical Kauffmann scene reserved on teal green ground w/gold trim 48.00

Cup & saucer, demitasse, footed, scene of classical ladies after Kauffmann interior, various types of fruit alternating w/gold banding exterior, beehive mark....... 55.00

Marmalade jar, cov., "Three Graces" scene after Kauffmann... 60.00

Plate, 10" d., scene of 2 maidens & cupid after Kauffmann center, gilt roses on green & cream border... 65.00

Stein, classical scene of Venus entitled "Schmukung der Venus," w/further scenes on top & inside inlaid porcelain lid, signed "Kauffmann," beehive mark, 5 liter, 6½" h. (ILLUS.)..................1,650.00

Vase, 20" h., classical scene of 4 maidens on cobalt blue ground, signed "Angelica Kauffmann" 395.00

LEEDS

The Leeds Pottery in Yorkshire, England, began production about 1758. It made, among other things, creamware that was highly competitive with Wedgwood's. In the 1780's it began production of reticulated and punched wares. Little of its production was marked. Most readily available Leeds ware is that of the 19th century during which time the pottery was operated by several firms.

Leeds Model of a Horse

Basket & undertray, shaped basket w/handles, lattice-cut border, swag base border, w/conforming undertray, Leeds Pottery, England, ca. 1780, basket 9" l., tray 9¼" l. (rim chip) $1,320.00

Bowl, 5¾" d., King's Rose patt., rust-colored rose (minor hairlines) 138.00

Bowl w/flower arranger top, creamware, embossed floral swags, twisted handles & rose finial, impressed "Leeds Pottery," 7" d., 8" h. (chip on base foot, minor damage to finial)............... 265.00

Centerpiece, three-tier, creamware, each tier w/five scallop shells divided by foliage supported on double C-scroll supports & surmounted by a figure of Venus flanked by Cupid & a dolphin, on a rockwork base, ca. 1775, 24" h. (three shells restored, crack to base, chips) 10,450.00

Coffeepot, cov., pear-shaped, painted on either side & extending over domed cover w/a wide diagonal band of iron-red diamond-shaped devices centering purple flowerheads & reserved on a ground of *oeil-de-perdrix* panels in iron-red & black enamel within wavy green borders edged in black enamel, the band intersected by a narrower band of purple chevrons on a black-dotted ground within similar iron-red wavy borders edged in black, acanthus-molded spout & ribbed intertwined loop handle w/flower & leaf terminals painted w/alternating black & iron-red enamel stripes, possibly painted in the workshop of David Rhodes, 1775-80, 10" h. (repair to spout, cover restored)..........2,860.00

Model of a horse, pearlware, standing white stallion w/black mane & tail, black eyes, spotted muzzle, rose mouth & nostrils, wearing an ochre bridle, standing on a chamfered rectangular base, its top painted w/streaky-green enamel within a molded foliate border painted in deep rose enamel & bordered on the sides w/a band of stiff leaves between ochre, rose & underglaze-blue lines, ca. 1820-30, 16 5/8" h. (ILLUS.) 23,100.00

Pitcher, jug-type, 5¾" h., h.p. pink roses, blue & rust flowers (chip) .. 220.00

Plates, 8" d., h.p. "Pansy" pattern in purple & yellow on cream color ground, slightly scalloped rim, early 19th c., set of 6 ....3,700.00

Plates, 8½" d., King's Rose patt., rust-colored rose, yellow buds & green leaves, pr................ 352.00

Plate, dinner, King's Rose patt., rust-colored rose, pink border 193.00

Sauce tureen on attached stand, cov., creamware, lobed bowl affixed to a serrated leaf incised w/a network of veining & forming the stand, its handle joining that of the tureen at one end, lobed oval cover w/two pierced zones flanking a melon sprig knop, ca. 1785, 8 5/8" l. (repaired rim chips) 2,750.00

Teapot, cov., creamware, cylindrical, transfer-printed in black on either side with "The Prodigal Son in Excess" or "The Prodigal Son in Misery" w/the details picked out in iron-red, green, yellow & pink enamel between panels painted w/iron-red blossoms & green ovals reserved on sponged-pink ground, shoulder & acanthus-molded spout w/further pink details, cover transfer-printed & painted w/two cherubs flanking sponged-pink panel w/flower knop, rims w/molded key border w/traces of gilding, ca. 1780, 5½" h. (repairs to knop & spout, hair crack in base)..........................2,200.00

LIMOGES

Limoges Chocolate Set

Numerous factories produced china in Limoges, France, with major production in the 19th century. Some pieces listed below are identified by the name of the maker or the mark of the factory. Although the famed Haviland Company was located in Limoges, wares bearing their marks are not included in this listing. Also see HAVILAND.

Box, cov., heavy & wide floral gold borders on cover & base, pale blue ground, apricot tea roses & buds decorate center medallion, artist-signed, 8"...............$250.00

Butter pats, pink roses w/gold trim decor, set of 5................. 45.00

Butter tub, half-barrel shape, ornate iridescent gold interior & exterior decor, 3 x 5", T & V (Tresseman & Vogt)........................ 85.00

Charger, h.p. lavender, tan & green pansies overall, 16" d............ 160.00

Chocolate set: cov. chocolate pot & six cups & saucers; cascading purple flowers w/ornate gold trim on pale green ground, 13 pcs. (ILLUS.)........................ 275.00

Coffeepot, cov., white w/ornate gold handle, curving spout & pierced finial, 10¾" h. 55.00

Cracker jar, cov., overall floral sprays, light blue around bottom & on lid, heavy gold trim, 7½" h.......................... 125.00

Creamer & sugar basket, purple flowers w/scrolling trim, pr., T & V France 60.00

Demitasse set: cov. pot & ten cups & saucers; relief-molded tiny pink floral medallions & ribbons, gold trim, 21 pcs.................... 350.00

Dessert set: 10½" d. master bowl, six 6" d. bowls & 10" d. plate; overall relief-molded rococo scallops & plumes, bright green border between tiny pink roses & heavy gold trim, 8 pcs. 125.00

Dish, red berries & green leaves accentuated w/gold flowers on edge, 9 x 13", marked "Patented 1906 J. P. France" (J. Pouyat) 75.00

Dresser set: 9¾ x 12½" tray, pin tray, pair candlesticks, three cov. boxes, ring tree & pair matching perfume cruets w/original stoppers; teal blue edges shading to white w/white & pink flowers & gooseberries decor, ornate gold floral trim around edges, 10 pcs. 305.00

Ferner, gold feet, paneled lavender flowers w/green & gold accents, A.K. Co. (Kittel & Klingenberg, exporters) 90.00

Fish plates, each naturalistically painted w/a fish swimming among coral & marine plants, within a gros bleu border w/gilt branches bearing lavender blossoms, tooled gilt shaped outer border, 8¾" d., set of 8, O. Gutherz 935.00

Fish set: 17" platter & eight 9" d. plates; each plate w/h.p. fish of various species, blue-green wave ground w/gold trim, ca. 1910, 9 pcs. 320.00

Game plaques, pierced to hang, deer (2) decor, green brown & orange w/blue sky, gold rococo edges, artist-signed, 10¼" d., pr. 385.00

Game plates, pierced to hang, pastel natural settings w/four quail on one, four pheasants on the other, heavy rococo gold edge, artist-signed, 12½" d., pr. 505.00

Game platter, quail in foreground w/flowers, grasses, trees & pond in background, irregular edge w/gold edging, artist-signed, 14¼ x 20" 385.00

Game set: platter & twelve 8½" d. plates; h.p. stylized birds, light green borders w/gold trim, artist-signed, 13 pcs. 650.00

Hair receiver, roses decor, artist-signed, J.P.L. 45.00

Mug, Dutch girls decoration, green glaze, T & V 30.00

Nappy, handled, maple leaf-shaped, large pink roses, Elite, Limoges, France (William Guerin), 10" d. ... 55.00

Pitcher, 5½" h., h.p. dancing couple on each side, gold trim, dated 1890 .... 190.00

Pitcher, water, 8" h., apple in foliage decoration, artist-signed 75.00

Pitcher, tankard, 9" h., h.p. grape clusters, molded band around base (Delinieres & Co.) 125.00

Pitcher, tankard, 12" h., embossed decoration on handle & base, h.p. three-color grape cluster decoration, T & V (Tressemann & Vogt) .. 150.00

Pitcher, tankard, 12" h., ornate handle, h.p. mauve, green & rose apples & leaves decoration, J.P.L. (Jean Pouyat, Limoges) 149.00

Limoges Tankard Pitcher

Pitcher, tankard, 12" h., h.p. two-color grape decoration on dark brown blended to yellow blended to rust ground, J.P.L. (ILLUS.) 175.00

Pitcher, tankard, 13½" h., h.p. full figure cavalier decoration 450.00

Pitcher, tankard, 14¾" h., h.p. berries, blossoms & leaves decoration, T & V 235.00

Pitcher, tankard, 15" h., h.p. large grapes & leaves around body, stylized hearts border, signed "Xmas 1898, to Ernst Marie," WG & Co. (William Guerin & Co.) 295.00

Plaque, pierced to hang, h.p. Dutch harbor scene w/people & boats, ornate rococo border w/gold rim, artist-signed, C et J (exporter mark), 10" d. 115.00

Plaque, pierced to hang, h.p. tame rabbits w/feeding dish decoration, artist-signed, 10" d. 150.00

Plaque, pierced to hang, bust of beautiful lady against green ground w/rococo gold border, artist-signed, 10¼", Coronet 162.00

Plaque, pierced to hang, h.p. game birds (2) in center w/gold rococo rim, artist-signed, 11½" d., Coronet (ILLUS.) 155.00

Plaque with Game Birds

Plate, 8" d., Queen Louise portrait w/gold trim, Elite, Limoges, France 45.00
Plate, 8½" d., h.p. raspberries & leaves decoration, gold scalloped rim, artist-signed 40.00
Plate, 9¼" d., h.p. gold "spider web" design on emerald green ground, gold rococo border 55.00
Plate, 9¼" d., h.p. kitten w/butterfly scene, artist-signed, Coronet .. 45.00
Plate, 10" d., h.p. portrait of American Indian, artist-signed, Coronet 62.00
Plates, 10" d., h.p. portrait of Art Nouveau-type women, artist-signed, pr. 225.00
Plate, 11" d., holly berries w/gold trim, ornate gold border, A. Lanternier & Cie.................. 50.00
Plate, 12" d., portrait of woman w/poppies in her long flowing black hair within a border of poppy blossoms, ornate gold rim, T & V (Tressemann & Vogt) 120.00

Limoges Scenic Plate

Plate, 13" d., h.p. scene of lady & gentleman in colonial dress walking arm in arm w/dog at side, soft tones of blue, green & brown, artist-signed (ILLUS.)............. 260.00
Platter, 16", red, pink & purple grapes decoration, J.P.L. (Jean Pouyat, Limoges) 70.00
Platter, 17½ x 11¾" oval, h.p. center scene of mother dog & four puppies on grassy knoll w/cloud-filled blue sky, gold scalloped rim 605.00
Punch bowl, h.p. Art Deco style purple grape clusters w/green & gold leaves on cream ground, artist-signed, 15" d., 6¼" h., T & V 275.00
Sardine dish, shell-shaped, pale pink & green decoration 165.00
Smoking set: tobacco jar, pipe rest & 11¼" tray; h.p. stylized florals in brown tones w/gold, 3 pcs..... 135.00
Soup plates, center petaled well painted w/gilt turtle on white ground, gilt lambrequin border on cobalt blue, gilt rim, ca. 1900, 8½" d., set of 12................137.50
Syrup jug, cov., handled, h.p. corn decoration, 1906, 6" h. 125.00
Tea set: cov. square teapot, creamer, sugar bowl & 12" cake plate; clusters of berries & foliage on deep green shading to pale green, cream & orange ground, gold trim, 4 pcs................ 120.00
Tray, kidney-shaped, h.p. large purple & yellow iris, rococo border w/gold trim, 12¾" l., WG & Co. (William Guerin & Co.) 70.00
Tray, detailed center group of musical instruments & sheet music w/dainty pink roses & small blue & yellow flowers on shaded pastel salmon pink ground, embossed border w/heavy gold trim, 16½ x 9" 273.00
Tumbler, h.p. purple grapes, pink flower w/green & brown leaves on soft yellow ground, 2 5/8" d., 3½" h.................................. 16.00
Tureen, 3-handled, gold touches on handles & base, rose drape & dainty rose garlands decoration, 12" w., 6" h.................... 60.00
Vase, cov., 8¾" h., h.p. portrait of young woman w/wavy brown hair gazing upward over one shoulder, wearing a white cloak w/hood, leafy sprigs on her shoulders, within floral spray-tooled gilt borders reserved on a burgundy ground molded & decorated in gilt w/foliate scrolls, medallions & feathered trellis motifs, spiral

molded pierced lid, signed "Wagner," late 19th c. 660.00
Vase, 11" h., 3¼" d., cylindrical, Art Nouveau style large red-orange poppies w/trailing stems on ebony ground, wide gold band near top & base, WG & Co. 100.00
Vase, 12½" h., elaborate twined handles, floral decoration w/green & gold accents 280.00
Vase, 14¾" h., tapering cylinder, portrait of young woman clad in a fluid pink gown blending into deep burgundy ground, late 19th c. 220.00

LONGWY

Cylindrical Longwy Vase

This faience factory was established in 1798 in the town of Longwy, France and is noted for its enameled pottery which resembles cloisonne. Utilitarian wares were the first production here but by the 1870's an Oriental style art pottery that imitated "cloisonne" was created through the use of heavy enamels in relief. By 1912, a modern Art Deco style became part of Longwy's production and these wares, together with the Oriental style pieces, have made this art pottery popular with collectors today. As interest in Art Deco has soared in recent years, values of Longwy's modern style wares have risen sharply.

Bowl, 8½ x 9¼", cobalt blue handles, enameled red & blue floral interior, cobalt blue basketweave exterior $255.00
Bowl, double-handled, enameled blue basketweave exterior, interior enameling in red & blue flowers 235.00
Box, hexagonal, Art Deco style decoration, 8" 300.00
Candlesticks, colorful pottery base, brass standards & eight crystal prisms on each, 9¾" h., pr. 185.00
Plate, 9" d., colorful enameled bird in center 55.00
Vase, 5½" h., cylindrical, enameled stylized bands of flower & leaf sprigs in yellow & red on turquoise ground, impressed mark (ILLUS.) 40.00
Vase, 7" h., 3" w., cylindrical, enameled florals & bird on white beach w/palm trees on turquoise ground 295.00
Whimsey, shoes, enameled bright turquoise w/flowers overall decoration, 6", pr. 100.00

LUSTRE WARES

Copper Lustre Pitcher

Lustred wares in imitation of copper, gold, silver and other colors were produced in England in the early 19th century and onward. Gold, copper or platinum oxides were painted on glazed objects which were then fired, giving them a lustred effect. Various forms of lustre wares include plain lustre—with the entire object coated to obtain a metallic effect, bands of lustre decoration and painted lustre designs. Particularly appealing is the pink or purple "splash lustre" sometimes referred to as "Sunderland" lustre in the mistaken belief it was confined to the production of Sunderland area potteries. Objects decorated in silver lustre by the "resist" process, wherein parts of the objects to be left free from lustre decoration were treated with wax, are referred to as "silver resist."

Wares formerly called "Canary Yellow Lustre" are now referred to as "Yellow-Glazed Earthenwares," which see.

COPPER

Bowl, 6" d., wide blue band on copper lustre body $25.00

Cup, footed, figural satyr-mask body w/enameled face & lustre trim, scroll handle, figural frog inside, 5" h. 95.00

Goblet, copper lustre body w/Sunderland pink lustre inset over cream, 4½" h. 45.00

Mug, copper lustre body w/blue band, 2¾" h. 40.00

Pitcher, 4½" h., copper lustre body w/enameled flowers 47.50

Pitcher, 4½" h., copper lustre body w/two yellow bands, one w/squiggly lustre design 48.00

Pitcher, 5½" h., bulbous copper lustre body below wide rim band of canary yellow decorated w/black transfer clock face & "Riddle & Bryan, Longton," early 19th c. (chips at spout) 105.00

Pitcher, 5½" h., copper lustre bulbous body on wide foot, C-scroll handle, decorated w/blue bands decorated w/lustre squiggles (ILLUS.) 125.00

Pitcher, 6½" h., copper lustre body w/white, blue & yellow florals, marked "Allerton" 75.00

Pitcher, 7½" h., copper lustre body w/cherubs in relief 165.00

Shaker, figural standing Toby w/hat, copper lustre body, 4¾" h. 75.00

Teapot, cov., copper lustre body w/floral enamels 75.00

Toby jug, copper lustre body w/outstretched hands holding jug, 7" h. 110.00

SILVER & SILVER RESIST

Creamer, silver lustre body w/paneled Loop & Rib patt. around base, gadroon top border, 4 x 5" 85.00

Creamer, pedestal base, silver lustre body w/garland design around top, 5¾" h. 85.00

Pitcher, 6¼" h., baluster-form, pulled spout, applied handle, silver resist trailing grape & vintage band above iron-red vintage wreath encircling the initials "W I" flanked by two black transfer-printed scenes w/enameled highlights, one depicting a farmer feeding his chickens, other depicting a farmer & his wife centering a coat-of-arms beneath a banner inscribed "The Farmer's Arms, God Speed the Plough," early 19th c. (minor chips) 550.00

Pitcher, silver lustre body w/mulberry transfer scene 165.00

SUNDERLAND PINK & OTHERS

Cup & saucer, demitasse, pink lustre, House patt. 45.00

Cup & saucer, handleless, h.p. florals in medallion connected by swagged fern fronds in pink lustre 45.00

Mug, pink lustre, House patt., 3" h. 85.00

Mug, transfer-printed in black heightened in green, yellow & iron-red one side w/inscribed view of the Iron Bridge over the Wear, other side w/poem entitled "Friendship, Love and Truth" within a flower & foliate border highlighted in colors & beneath the spout w/Masonic verses & symbols within a similar floral & leaf enameled vine, surrounded by pink lustre squiggles, rim, spout & handle w/lustre bands, first half 19th c., 8¾" h. 605.00

Sunderland Lustre Mustard Pot

Mustard pot, cov., bulging cylindrical form w/small molded base, applied ribbed double-twist handle w/leaf-molded terminals, domical lid w/a cylindrical knop, decorated overall w/pink splash lustre, rim chip, 3½" h. (ILLUS.) .. 99.00

Pitcher, 6½" h., vase-shaped, pulled spout, applied handle, pink lustre stylized floral band above inscription "Joseph and Alice Leech 1816" flanked by two circular reserves each w/black transfer-printed scenes depicting birds in a flowering tree & pastoral landscape w/enameled highlights 715.00

Pitcher, 7¼" h., ovoid w/flaring spout, applied C-scroll handle, transfer-printed w/two romantic sailor's verses & two lovers before a ship, on marbleized pink lustre ground, early 19th c. 715.00

Pitcher, 8" h., white reserves w/polychrome enameled scenes of "Sailor's Farewell" & "John Abraham, Dorey, 1844," pink

splash lustre ground (some wear & scratches) 375.00
Pitcher, 8¾" h., bas-relief strawberry & vine decoration, pink lustre trim, Georgian handle, 1810-30 ... 325.00
Plaque, pierced to hang, round, black transfer of "Thou God Seest Me," on pink splash lustre ground w/copper lustre trim, impressed "Dixon & Co.," 19th c., 8 3/8" d. (wear, minor stains, hairline) 65.00
Plaque, pierced to hang, "Thou God Seest Me" in black within floral & leaf garland centered at top w/an eye, molded rectangular border in pink splash lustre, ca. 1850, 8½ x 7½" 137.50
Plaques, pierced to hang, transfer-printed in black & highlighted w/polychrome enamels, one w/scene of building w/Grecian columns, the other w/landscape w/stream, bridge & castle in background, pink splash lustre border, 7¾ x 8½", pr. 280.00
Plates, 7½" d., deep, each border painted in iron-red w/large pinwheel flowerheads flanked by pink lustre, yellow & green foliate sprigs, pink lustre rim, 1820-30, pr. 88.00
Plate, 7¾" d., 1½" h., "Shepherd Boy" center transfer scene, pink lustre border, 1820-40 .... 65.00
Sauce boat & tray, black transfer w/"The Mariner's Compass," pink splash lustre ground, 7½" h., 2 pcs. (wear & scratches) 360.00

Pink Lustre-Trimmed Tea Service

Tea service: boat-shaped cov. teapot, cov. sugar bowl & creamer w/ten cups & saucers, two cake plates, waste bowl & stand; teapot, sugar & creamer each w/gadroon-molded footrim, all pieces enameled in iron-red, blue & yellow w/flowerheads outlined in black on a pale pink lustre band highlighted w/dark pink lustre foliate forms on a white ground, pink lustre borders & highlighting, early 19th c., 27 pcs. (ILLUS. of part) 440.00

MAASTRICHT

Petrus Regout founded a company in Maastricht, Holland in the early 1830's and in 1836 he expanded the operation by including De Sphinx Pottery. This pottery went on to produce good quality ironstone wares decorated with many transfer-printed designs, including the famous "Willow" pattern. In the late 19th century multi-colored printing was used and many pieces were given a tan lustre glazing.

Production continues today although the pottery became part of an English conglomerate in 1974.

Charger, scalloped edge, transfer-printed w/children skating on frozen canal, w/windmill, boat & house scene, signed "T. Sonneville," 15½" d. $65.00
Cup & saucer, demitasse, brushed green, black & orange decoration 35.00
Cup & saucer, Blue Willow patt. 18.00
Pitcher, milk, Canton patt., polychrome Oriental decoration 40.00
Plates, 7" d., stick spatter rim pattern of small round blossoms & three h.p. large abstract florals, center h.p. design of abstract florals, all in polychrome colors, marked "Maastricht," pr. 50.00
Plate, 8" d., Abbey patt., blue transfer 20.00
Plate, 8" d., Elvire patt. 60.00
Plate, 9" d., Blue Willow patt. 11.00

MAJOLICA

Majolica, a tin-enameled-glazed pottery, has been produced for centuries. It originally took its name from the island of Majorca, a source of figuline (potter's clay). Subsequently it was widely produced in England, Europe and the United States. Etruscan majolica, now avidly sought, was made by Griffen, Smith & Hill, Phoenixville, Pa., in the last quarter of the 19th century. Most majolica advertised today is 19th or 20th century. Once scorned by most collectors, interest in this colorful ware so popular during the Victorian era has now revived and prices have risen dramatically in the past two years. Also see MINTON and WEDGWOOD.

ETRUSCAN

Bowl, 9¾" d., Classical series, putti riding lion center scene, interwoven leafy vines border decoration, sepia coloring $100.00
Bread tray, embossed fern leaves &

stocks of wheat around rim, 11½" d. 250.00
Butter pat, Begonia Leaf patt. 19.00
Butter pat, Geranium Leaf patt. 35.00
Cake stand, pedestal base, Maple Leaf patt., pink 135.00

Daisy Pattern Compote

Compote, salad, Daisy patt., 9" d., 5" h. (ILLUS.) 175.00

Bamboo Pattern Cup & Saucer

Cup & saucer, Bamboo patt. (ILLUS.)........................... 150.00
Dessert dish, Leaf patt., four molded leaves in brown, yellow, blue & green 85.00
Mug, Acorn patt., green oak leaves & brown & yellow acorns on yellow basketweave ground, pink interior, 3½" h. 175.00
Pitcher, 4½" h., Hawthorne patt., mottled blues, greens & pink 165.00
Pitcher, 4½" h., Wild Rose patt., tan, brown & green, butterfly lip 130.00
Plate, 7" d., Rose patt. 69.00
Plate, 8" d., Albino, Shell & Seaweed patt. 65.00
Plate, 8½" d., Albino Shell & Seaweed patt., yellow coral center w/gold rim 90.00
Plate, 9" d., Begonia Leaves patt. .. 100.00
Plate, 9" d., Cauliflower patt. 80.00
Plate, 9" d., Maple Leaves patt., white & yellow decor 50.00
Plate, Bamboo patt. 95.00
Spooner, Bamboo patt. 150.00
Sugar bowl, cov., Albino Shell & Seaweed patt., pink interior 125.00
Sugar bowl, cov., Cauliflower patt. 145.00

Syrup pitcher w/pewter lid, Sunflower patt., realistic sunflower on cobalt blue ground 225.00
Tea set: cov. teapot, cov. sugar bowl, spooner & creamer; Shell & Seaweed patt., 4 pcs. 825.00

Shell & Seaweed Tea Set

Tea set, Shell & Seaweed patt., 23 pcs. (ILLUS. of part) 1,850.00
Tray, oval w/loop "twig" handles, Geranium patt., polychrome flowers, 12" l. 100.00

GENERAL

Palissy-type Dish

Bank, model of dog w/hat & bow, brown & blue, 6" h. 65.00
Bank, man's face, brown, 3" h. 47.50
Basket, pale blue handle w/molded pink ribbon, sprays of florals on sides, white rim w/beaded & folded-out panels, 6½" h......... 225.00
Basket, lily bud on handle, turquoise ground w/pond lilies & lavender decor, lavender interior, small 115.00
Bowl, 11½" d., Lettuce Leaf patt., Wannopee Pottery Company, New Milford, Connecticut 125.00
Bowl, 12" d., pedestal base, florals & reeds 135.00
Bowl, 19" w., 10" h., urn-shaped, cupids decor 295.00
Bread tray, Pond Lily patt., 13" l. ... 150.00
Butter dish, cov., daisies & various florals decor, 7½".............. 127.50
Butter dish, cov., Flower & Wheat patt., ice liner, twig handle 98.00
Cake stand, pedestal base, Pineapple patt., yellow, brown, green & tan, Wardle & Co., Hanley, England, 9¾" 240.00
Cake stand, Begonia Leaf patt., green, brown & yellow decor..... 90.00

Cake stand, overlapping fans on tan ground, S. Fielding & Co., Ltd., Stoke, England 140.00

Chamber pot, w/handle, magenta grapes & leaves on white ground 110.00

Charger, pierced to hang, white crane in flight w/nude cherub clutching bird, florals & scrolls across bottom & up side, cream, deep pink, blue, green & brown, 12½" d. 200.00

Cheese keeper, cov., embossed shield front w/"Mrs. Elrick 1890," mottled cobalt blue, brown, green & cream, 10" d., 8" h. 390.00

Cheese keeper, ivory basketweave ground w/red lattice border, W.T. Copeland (& Sons, Ltd.), England 695.00

Cheese keeper, Sunflower & Classical Urn patt., Samuel Leaf, Hanley, England, ca. 1881 .... 275.00

Clock, decorated majolica disc surrounds clock face, Avalon Faience, Baltimore, Maryland 200.00

Compote, 9½" d., cobalt blue rim, yellow, brown, red, green & blue bluebird w/holly, "Merry Xmas & Happy New Year" decor 275.00

Compote, Begonia Leaf patt. 140.00

Cookie jar, cov., deep roses, white leaves & flowers decor on brown ground 160.00

Creamer, crimped edge, Lettuce Leaf patt., Wannopee Pottery Company, New Milford, Connecticut 60.00

Creamer & sugar bowl, Rose & Rope patt., aqua blue ground, pr....... 150.00

Dish, Palissy-type, molded & applied leaves, insects & snakes centering a group of three fish, late 19th century (damages), 9¾" d. (ILLUS.) 935.00

Majolica Garden Seat

Garden seat, spreading cylinder w/relief lily & leaf decor painted white & green on blue basketweave ground, pierced circular top molded to resemble rush seat, late 19th c. (rim chip), 12" d., 17¾" h. (ILLUS.) 1,045.00

Humidor & cover w/pipe finial, scalloped foot, Dutch children portrait decor, 4½" l., 3¼" deep, 4" h.... 55.00

Humidor & cover w/pipe finial, lady smoking on front, 5½" l., 3¾" deep, 5¼" h. 62.00

Humidor, cover inscribed "Take a Pipe," Art Nouveau florals in relief decor 110.00

Jardiniere, blackberries & pink flowers on white ground, gold twisted rope around top rim, 5½ x 6" 175.00

Oil lamp, applied leaves on mottled ground, cast metal base, 12½" h. without chimney 230.00

Pitcher, 4" h., Corn patt., lavender interior 65.00

Pitcher, 5½" h., Basketweave patt., pink flowers & green leaves on brown ground, 1" gold top 70.00

Pitcher, 6" h., Bird & Fan patt. 150.00

Running Elephant Pitcher

Pitcher, 7½" h., Running Elephant patt. (ILLUS.) 190.00

Pitcher, 8" h., Robin on Branch patt. 135.00

Pitcher, 8½" h., Dragon-handled Floral patt. 190.00

Pitcher, Conch Shell shape, marked "Wedgwood," England 1,650.00

Plaque, pierced to hang, elaborately detailed gentleman in blue & green waistcoat astride horse w/finely detailed saddle against green ground & castle, back impressed "Elliott," 11 x 9" 450.00

Plate, 6½" d., grape cluster decoration, Germany 20.00

Plate, 8" d., Floral & Three Leaf patt. 45.00
Plate, 8½" d., Greek Key reticulated border, green, brown & yellow mottled center, Wedgwood, England 125.00
Plate, 9" d., Bamboo & Basketweave patt., Banks & Thorley, England .. 57.00
Plate, 10" d., Bird & Fan patt., Wardle & Co., England 45.00
Plate, 10½" d., Blackberry & Basketweave patt. 75.00
Platter, 11" d., Wild Rose & Rope patt., aqua ground, cobalt center 110.00
Platter, 11½ x 8½" oval, Dragonfly on Leaf patt., green & brown decoration 90.00

Bird & Fan Platter

Platter, 12 x 11½" oval, Bird & Fan patt., Wardle & Co., England (ILLUS.) 295.00
Platter, 13" oval, Blackberry patt., Clifton Decor, D.F. Haynes, Baltimore, Maryland 110.00
Platter, 14" oval, Fern, Floral & Bow patt., Banks & Thorley, England .. 225.00
Punch bowl, footed, Sunflower & Classical Urn patt., Samuel Lear, England 1,210.00
Sardine box, cov., Cobalt & Seaweed patt., two fish finial, 7½ x 6½ x 5" 325.00
Sauce dish, Begonia Leaf patt. 35.00
Syrup pitcher, 6" h., w/pewter lid, Pineapple patt. 235.00
Teapot, cov., Wild Rose & Rope patt., aqua blue ground 150.00
Tea set: cov. teapot, cov. sugar bowl, milk jug, four cups & saucers & platter; molded floral sprays & stylized key-pattern design, polychrome on white, Brownfield & Co., England, 12 pcs. 303.00
Tureen, cov., molded bands of formal foliage enriched in green on a pale lavender ground w/yellow rims, cover naturalistically modeled in high relief w/fish on seaweed, enriched in colors, England, ca. 1870, 8½" l. 770.00
Vase, 11¼" h., girl in wooden shoes holding bowl of fish stands beside vase w/boat, draped green vines for handles & flower trim, multicolored 155.00

MARBLEHEAD

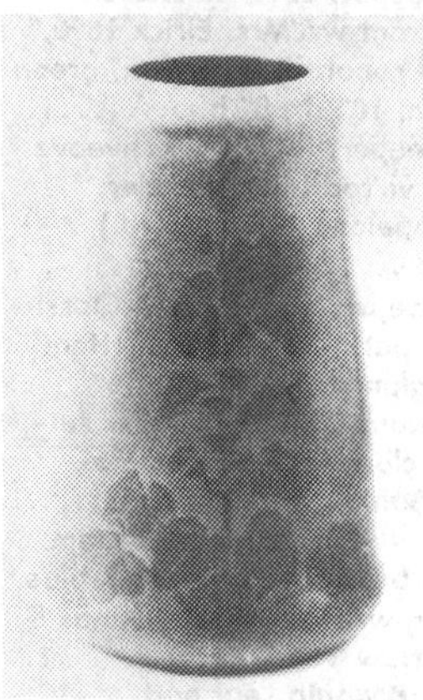

Marblehead Pottery Vase

This pottery was organized in 1904 by Dr. Herbert J. Hall as a therapeutic aid to patients in a sanitarium he ran in Marblehead, Massachusetts. It was later separated from the sanitarium and directed by Arthur E. Baggs, a fine artist and designer, who bought out the factory in 1916 and operated it until its closing in 1936. Most wares were hand-thrown and decorated and carry the company mark of a stylized sailing vessel flanked by the letters "M" and "P."

Bowl, 7¾" d., angled on side, black spades & drips over dark green ground, ca. 1910 ....$357.50
Plaque, dark green silhouettes of trees on lighter green, ca. 1910, framed, overall 6 1/8 x 6" 1,210.00
Tea tile, five color floral decor, framed 475.00
Vase, 3" h., 6" d., squatty, blue glaze, incised mark & paper sticker 175.00
Vase, 3½ x 3½", stylized grape decor on yellow ground 450.00
Vase, 4½" h., cylindrical, incised cinnamon, olive & navy apples on matte green ground 770.00
Vase, 6" h., swelling cylinder w/wide rolled rim, band & squares w/long stems, brown on green ground, ca. 1905 ....1,540.00

Vase, 6¼" h., bulbous, blue glaze 85.00
Vase, 6¼" h., oviform, matte mauve glaze 176.00
Vase, 9¼" h., cylinder w/wide mouth, dark forest green glaze, paper label, ca. 1915 .... 412.50
Vase, 12¾" h., cylinder flattened on three sides, flaring towards base & w/rolled rim, three sides w/tall hollyhock fronds in two-color grey-greens on pale green ground, artist-signed, 1905-10 (ILLUS.) 6,325.00

MARTIN BROTHERS POTTERY

Martin Brothers Bird Jar

Martinware, the term used for this pottery, dates from 1873 and is the product of the Martin brothers - Robert, Wallace, Edwin, Walter and Charles - often considered the first British studio potters. From first to final stages, their hand-thrown pottery was completely the work of the team. The early wares may be simple and conventional, but the Martin brothers built up their reputation by producing ornately engraved, incised or carved designs on their wares. The amusing face-jugs are considered some of their finest work. After 1910, the work of the pottery declined and can be considered finished by 1915, though some attempts were made to fire pottery as late as the 1920's.

Jar, cov., model of a grotesque bird, standing bird w/mean visage & downward pointed beak, webbed feet, glazed in ochre, navy blue, chocolate brown & olive green, head incised "Martin Bros. - London - Southall," base inscribed "Martin B. - London," w/black circular wood base, 8 5/8" h. (ILLUS.) $2,090.00
Pitcher, 5" h., blue foliage decoration, monogram mark 50.00
Pitcher, 11" h., peacock decoration 300.00
Tile, fish decoration, unglazed, 3" .. 50.00
Vase, 2½" h., fish decoration, unglazed 65.00
Vase, 3" h., frog decoration, unglazed 85.00
Vase, 5" h., grotesque fish decoration 225.00
Vase, 7" h., square, grotesque fish decoration 325.00
Vase, 7" w., squash decoration on red lustre ground 155.00
Vase, 8½" h., 3¾" w., cylindrical tapering to small foot, overall incised w/white & brown fish outlined in black, beige seaweed against brown & cream undulating linear ground, incised "RW Martin & Bros. - London & Southall- 9-1886" 900.00
Vase, 9¾" h., 3" w., footed oviform w/thin cylindrical neck, decorated w/leafy stalks w/blue berries & a brown butterfly against cream ground, incised "RW Martin - London & Southall - 6-11-79 - 333".... 475.00
Vase, 10" h., palmettes decoration 135.00

MC COY

Covered Wagon Cookie Jar

Collectors are now beginning to seek the art wares of two McCoy potteries. One was founded in Roseville, Ohio, in the late 19th century as the J.W. McCoy Pottery, subsequently becoming Brush-McCoy Pottery Co., later Brush Pottery. The other was founded also in Roseville in 1910 as Nelson McCoy Sanitary Stoneware Co., later becoming Nelson McCoy Pottery. In 1967 the pottery was sold to D.T. Chase of the Mount Clemens Pottery Co., who sold his interest to the Lancaster Colony Corp. in 1974. The pottery shop closed in 1985 and the pottery sold to people in New Jersey in 1986. Reportedly they will reopen the plant.

Bank, model of pig, brown & white spotted $27.50
Bean pot, cov., beans in pods decor on brown glaze 15.00
Bowl, 9", shoulder-type, blue, ringed, rectangular base 22.00
Bowl, Amaryllis patt., pastel coloring, large 20.00
Bowl, shoulder-type, pink & blue stripes, 1930's 18.00
Coffee server, El Rancho patt. 30.00
Cookie jar, Apple on Basketweave, 1957 .... 30.00
Cookie jar, Asparagus, 1977 .... 25.00
Cookie jar, Basket of Fruit, 1961 .... 30.00
Cookie jar, Betsy Baker, 1975-76 .... 30.00
Cookie jar, Chinese Lantern ("Fortune Cookies"), 1965-68 .... 22.00
Cookie jar, Cookie Boy, 1940-43 .... 58.00
Cookie jar, Cookie Churn, 1977-87 .... 25.00
Cookie jar, Cookie House, 1960 .... 44.00
Cookie jar, Cookie Jug, 2-handled, 1967 .... 16.00
Cookie jar, Cookie Pot, 1964-74 .... 22.00
Cookie jar, Cookie Safe, black, 1962-63 .... 28.00
Cookie jar, Covered Wagon, 1959-62 (ILLUS.) 36.00
Cookie jar, Davy Crockett, 1957 .... 150.00 to 200.00
Cookie jar, Donkey with Cart, Brush-McCoy 80.00
Cookie jar, Drum, 1959-60 .... 27.00
Cookie jar, Duck on Basketweave, 1956 .... 40.00
Cookie jar, Dutch Boy, 1946 .... 23.00
Cookie jar, Dutch Treat Barn, 1968-73 .... 24.00
Cookie jar, Elephant, split trunk, 1945 .... 50.00 to 75.00
Cookie jar, Elephant w/baby hat, Brush-McCoy 110.00
Cookie jar, Football (Boy on Football), 1983 .... 22.00
Cookie jar, Globe, 1960 .... 70.00
Cookie jar, Grandfather Clock, 1962-64 .... 38.00
Cookie jar, Hound Dog (Thinking Puppy), 1977-79 .... 15.00
Cookie jar, Indian, 1954-56 .... 100.00 to 125.00
Cookie jar, Jack-O-Lantern (Pumpkin), 1955 .... 150.00 to 175.00
Cookie jar, Kitten on Basketweave, 1956-69 .... 26.00
Cookie jar, Kookie Kettle, 1960-77 .... 17.00
Cookie jar, Lamb on Basketweave, white w/brown, 1956-57 .... 25.00
Cookie jar, Lantern (Lamp), 1962-63 .... 38.00
Cookie jar, Lollipops, 1958-60 .... 20.00
Cookie jar, Lunch Bucket, 1978-87 .... 25.00
Cookie jar, Mammy, "Cookies" only, 1948-57 .... 50.00 to 75.00
Cookie jar, Milk Can, white or brown, 1972-75, each 20.00
Cookie jar, Monk ("Thou Shalt Not Steal"), 1968-73 .... 30.00
Cookie jar, Monkey on Stump, 1970 .... 16.00
Cookie jar, Mouse on Clock (Time For Cookies), 1968-73 .... 25.00
Cookie jar, Peter Pumpkin Eater, Brush-McCoy 46.00
Cookie jar, Picnic Basket, 1962-63 .... 30.00
Cookie jar, Pineapple, natural colors, 1955-57 .... 30.00
Cookie jar, Pine Cones on Basketweave, 1957 .... 25.00
Cookie jar, Pot Belly Stove (Country Stove), black, 1963-69 .... 16.00
Cookie jar, Rabbit w/cookie on Stump, 1971 .... 30.00
Cookie jar, Raggedy Ann, 1972-75 .... 30.00
Cookie jar, Smiling Bear, Brush-McCoy 125.00
Cookie jar, Snow Bear, 1965 .... 26.00
Cookie jar, Turkey, white or brown, 1960, each .... 65.00 to 75.00
Cookie jar, Wishing Well, 1961-70 .... 20.00
Cookie jar, Wren House w/bird on top, 1958-60 .... 42.00
Cuspidor, lady's, Nurock line, mottled yellow & brown Rockingham-type glaze, 1916, 3½" h. 21.00
Decanter set, model of an early train engine, coal car & two passenger cars, created by B. Harness for McCormick, 1969, set of 4 .... 200.00
Grease jar, cov., model of a head of cabbage, 1954 .... 30.00
Jardiniere, four-footed, h.p. tulip decoration, Loy-Nel-Art, 11¾ x 9" 160.00
Jardiniere, Sylvan patt., molded gnarled trees w/leaves forming top edge, glossy green, marked "Brush-McCoy," 1916, 12" h. 75.00
Jardiniere & pedestal base, diamond-quilted w/molded leaves at rim, white glaze, 1950's, 2 pcs. 90.00
Jug, Onyx glaze in rust, beige & dark brown, 5" h. 32.00
Lamp base, model of cowboy boots, brown, 6¾" h. 22.00

Mug, Corn patt., pale yellow kernels, green husk, ca. 1910 .... 60.00
Mug, embossed scene of buccaneer w/parrot, green glaze, Nelson McCoy Sanitary Stoneware Company, ca. 1926 .... 12.00
Mug, figural Little Boy Blue, Brush-McCoy 38.00
Mug, figural Peter Pan, Brush-McCoy 38.00
Mug, figural Little Red Riding Hood, Brush-McCoy 38.00
Pitcher, 9½" h., embossed reserve of grapes & leaves on wood grain green & brown ground, 1920's 47.50
Pitcher, embossed scene of a buccaneer w/parrot, green glaze, Nelson McCoy Sanitary Stoneware Company, 1926 .... 70.00
Pitcher, model of a fish 15.00
Pitcher, water, model of a turtle ... 18.00
Planter, bird dog before a fence w/"No Hunting" sign, 1954, 12" l., 8½" h. 55.00
Planter, model of a carriage w/parasol, ca. 1955 .... 37.50
Planter, model of a duck with umbrella 35.00
Planter, model of Dutch shoes, white w/red rose, pr. 25.00
Planter, model of a gondola, green glaze, 11" l. 10.00
Planter, footed, heart-shaped w/embossed blossoms & leaves at top, 1941 .... 12.00
Planter, model of a pelican, 1941 ... 15.00

McCoy Quail Planter

Planter, molded figural quail (3) against leafy background, 1955 (ILLUS.) 25.00
Planter, molded scene of a rodeo cowboy roping a calf, 1950's 25.00
Planter, scoop w/Mammy on handle, 1953 .... 38.50
Planter, model of Scottie dog head 17.50
Planter, model of a Spinning Wheel 22.00
Planter, model of a Wishing Well, 6" h. 12.00
Pretzel jar, cov., embossed scene of a buccaneer w/parrot, green glaze, Nelson McCoy Sanitary Stoneware Company, 1920's 70.00
Soup tureen w/sombrero cover, El Rancho Bar-B-Que patt., 1960 .... 52.00
Teapot, cov., Parchment & Pine patt. 18.00
Teapot, cov., Pine Cone patt. 20.00
Vase, 8" h., 10" w., pillow-shaped, h.p. daisies, marked "Loy-Nel-Art" 275.00
Vase, 10" h., cylindrical, h.p. pale yellow & cream narcissus on brown ground, Greek Key border, marked "Loy-Nel-Art" 125.00
Vase, 10" h., Springwood patt., pink glaze, 1961 .... 20.00
Vase, 13" h., h.p. wild roses decoration, artist-signed, Loy-Nel-Art ... 325.00

McCoy Mailbox Wall Pocket

Wall pocket, model of a mailbox embossed "Letters," green glaze, 1951 (ILLUS.) 15.00
Water set: pitcher & six mugs; molded center reserve of grape cluster & leaves on embossed wood grain ground, 1920's, 7 pcs. 70.00

MEISSEN

The secret of true hard-paste porcelain, known long before to the Chinese, was "discovered" accidently in Meissen, Germany, by J.F. Bottger, an alchemist, working with E.W. Tschirnhausen. The first European true porcelain was made in the Meissen Porcelain Works, organized about 1709. Meissen marks have been widely copied by other factories. Some pieces listed here are recent.

Bowl, cov., 4½" d., cylindrical bowl

Meissen Covered Bowl

w/domed cover, each painted w/two oblong landscape panels in shades of brown & green w/blue & violet highlights depicting hunters & their hounds, one with stag, another w/stone ruin, brown line borders, white ground, bud-form finial w/green stem (chip to leaf), Marcolini Period, 1774-1814 (ILLUS.) $770.00

Bowl, 4¾" d., 3¼" h., Blue Onion patt., scalloped top 123.00

Bowl, 6 x 9" oval, reticulated, Blue Onion patt. 160.00

Bowl, cereal, 7" d., Blue Onion patt., mid-20th c. 40.00

Bowl, 10½" d., Blue Onion patt. 95.00

Bowl, 10½" d., 2" h., white leaf decor around relief-molded gold border, cobalt blue ground 169.00

Bowl, 11" d., 2½" h., Blue Onion patt., gold trim, 19th c. 165.00

Bowl, 11 x 13", 3¼" h., leaf-shaped w/overall "coralene" beaded decoration, h.p. scene of bird hovering over nest w/eggs amidst array of colorful flowers, ferns & leaves trimmed in gold, gold banding on ten-lobe petal rim, applied porcelain branch handle w/gold, blended pink & light blue ground 675.00

Box, cov., domed cover painted in colors w/riverscape spanned by an arched bridge & the city of Dresden in the distance, within scrolling foliate borders reserved on a white ground decorated w/gilt scrollwork, late 19th c., 3 3/8" d. 220.00

Cake plate, center polychrome floral bouquet, gilt gadrooned border, late 19th c., 11" d. 99.00

Candleholders, double, tree trunk form w/two figures on each & round mirrors in center, applied porcelain flowers, 13½" h., pr. . . . 575.00

Candle snuffer, Blue Onion patt. 75.00

Chargers, swirled Neuozier-molded & gilt-edged border centering colorful spray of *deutsche Blumen* & scattered floral sprigs, 19th c., pr. 825.00

Coffeepot, cov., oviform, painted w/views of Dresden & Schandau, named in black script on the base, within rectangular gilt dot & band cartouches, gilt handle w/acanthus terminals, gilt grotesque head spout, bud finial, on spreading gilt foot, ca. 1815, 7½" h. 718.00

Meissen Coffee Pot

Coffeepot & domed cover w/flower bud finial, baluster form, entwined branch handle, shaped blue bands edged w/gilt foliage & suspending flower sprays w/scattered insects, ca. 1770 (finial restuck), 10½" h. (ILLUS.) 550.00

Creamer & sugar bowl, Blue Onion patt., gold trim, ca. 1900, pr. 175.00

Cup & saucer, figures in extensive landscapes within black & gilt shell & foliage scroll cartouches enclosing a trellis w/gilt rims, cup w/two *Holzschnittblumen*, ca. 1740 . . . . 1,045.00

Dinner service: place settings plus numerous large serving pieces; Blue Onion patt., late 19th c., 123 pcs. 7,900.00

Dish, bouquets of *deutsche Blumen* within ozier border, gilt rim, ca. 1745, 13½" d. 495.00

Ecuelle, cov., entwined branch handles w/flowering foliage terminals, bouquets of flowers divided by panels of molded flower sprays, cover w/lemon finial, ca. 1745, 7½" w. 825.00

Figure of a boy in an Oriental costume, w/his left hand held in front of him & his right hand on his hip, wearing pink bonnet, yellow jacket, flowered chemise & pink pantaloons, standing on scroll-molded tree stump base enriched in gilding, ca. 1750, 4¾" h. (chips to left hand fingers) 550.00

Figures, Malabar musicians, he playing the guitar & she the hurdy-gurdy, wearing brightly colored striped & flowered fur-lined clothes, on scroll-molded pad bases, after the models by J.J. Kaendler, 20th c., 7" h., pr. 1,210.00

Figures, "Taste" & "Smell," each a classical maiden attended by a putto w/various attributes emblematic of her sense, scrolling gilt-edged base centering a cartouche shaped panel modeled w/either a mouth for "taste" or a nose for "smell," 19th c., 11 1/8" & 10½" h., pr. (minor losses & repair).........................2,310.00

Figure group, female playing the mandolin, her companion w/his hat filled w/flowers by her side, a young boy holding a floral wreath behind her, on oval rockwork base w/applied tree, base molded w/foliage wreath, mid-19th c., 10½" h. (some chips)........... 990.00

Fish platter, Blue Onion patt., 22 x 10½" w/20 x 7½" insert......... 375.00

Hors d'oeuvres fork w/pistol grip, 2-tine, Blue Onion patt........... 40.00

Knife rests, Blue Onion patt., set of 4.......................... 150.00

Mantel clock, cartouche form case surmounted by a figure of a seated putto playing the harp, flanked below by two other seated putti holding a garland entwining a pair of gilt wings, the circular enamel clock face w/numeric chapters separated by a garland, the case encrusted w/colorful flowerheads, on four scroll feet, further raised on a rectangular flower-encrusted & gilt plinth, late 19th-early 20th c., 21" h. 2,640.00

Mirror, hanging-type, cartouche-shaped mirror frame encrusted w/blue & white porcelain florals & leaves, scrolled crest at top center w/bust of a lady's head, full-figure cupids at center sides, three-socket candleholder at base, 19th c. 1,540.00

Model of gulls, incised feather markings enriched in grey, blue & black, their heads turned to the left & right respectively, on circular bases applied w/reeds enriched in turquoise, after models by J.J. Kaendler, 11¼" h., pr. ...1,650.00

Pastry crimper, Blue Onion patt..... 60.00

Pitcher, 7" h., Blue Onion patt., ca. 1860 .... 125.00

Plate, 6" d., Blue Onion patt., gold trim, 19th c. 28.00

Plates, 9¼" d., specimen birds center, basketwork molded border enriched w/insects, ca. 1745, set of 12 ....3,850.00

Plate, 9½" d., h.p. harbor scenes within pierced gilt scroll cartouches within a gilt line rim on turquoise ground, ca. 1880 .... 385.00

Platter, 14 x 10", Blue Onion patt. .. 150.00

Salt dip, Blue Onion patt., gold trim, 4" w., 1¼" h.................. 195.00

Salt dips, interiors w/birds perched on branches or under arbors, rococo scrolled exterior w/shaped bands enclosing blue-scale pattern & puce checkered pattern, ca. 1770, 4½" w., set of 4........... 935.00

Sauce boat w/attached undertray, Blue Onion patt., gold trim, 8 x 4 7/8", 3½" h.................. 164.00

Soup plates, h.p. scattered *deutsche Blumen* within ozier border, gilt rim, ca. 1750, 9" d., set of 10....2,090.00

Soup tureen, cover w/cut lemon finial & stand, branch handles terminating in flowers, bouquets of *deutsche Blumen* within ozier bands, stand w/scroll handles, ca. 1750, 17¼" w. stand, 2 pcs. 2,970.00

Sugar bowl, cov., landscape vignettes within gilt scroll & foliage surrounds divided by flower sprays, cover w/knob finial, ca. 1738, 3½" d. (minor rim chips to cover) 2,420.00

Meissen Sugar Shaker

Sugar shaker, baluster form, h.p. bouquet of *deutsche Blumen* beneath an ozier band, cover edged in puce, ca. 1750, finial chipped & rim repair, 6½" h. (ILLUS.) 440.00

Sweetmeat dishes, each formed as a

Meissen Figural Sweetmeat Dish

reclining figure, he w/a powdered wig, she provocatively draped, each holding in front a quatrefoil lobed dish, both the dishes & their costumes decorated w/puce flowers highlighted w/gilt, raised on a shaped scrolled edge base, 12¾" l., 7" h., pr. (ILLUS. of one) 1,760.00

Teabowl & saucer, exterior molded w/fruiting vine, white, ca. 1725 .. 1,430.00

Teabowls & saucers, h.p. bouquets of *deutsche Blumen*, butterflies & insects, gilt rims, ca. 1750, pr. 550.00

Tea caddy & cover w/cone finial, cylindrical neck, overall molded fruiting vine, white, ca. 1735, 5" h. (chips to neck) 2,530.00

Teacup & saucer, horsemen in combat after Rugendas, within elaborate gilt *Laub und Bandelwerk* cartouches, ca. 1740 (repair to handle) 1,320.00

Teapot, cov., swan form, white-glazed w/beak, eyes & feet highlighted in black, late 19th c., 4¼" h. 302.50

Trembleuse cup & saucer, cup w/putti on cloud scrolls, one holding a torch, the other a bow & arrow, saucer w/musical instruments within gilt scroll surrounds, blue ground enriched w/gilding, ca. 1765 .... 1,100.00

Tureen & cover w/ornate finial, Blue Onion patt., ca. 1860, 12 x 10", 5½" h. 495.00

Tureen, cov., modeled as a cockerel w/incised feather markings enriched in green, blue, yellow, iron-red & brown, circular base, 8¾" w. 275.00

Vase, cov., 8" h., painted both sides w/court figures seated in a garden landscape playing musical instruments within a flowering foliage surround, cover similarly painted, ca. 1750 .... 1,430.00

Vases, 8 5/8" h., fluted campana form, everted rim, petal-molded base, molded & highlighted in gilt w/C-scrolls, painted colorful sprays, early 20th c., pr. 247.50

Vases w/covers & stands, 34¾" h., ovoid, panel depicting maidens entertained by their swain playing musical instruments, reverse w/panel of full-blown summer blossoms within an elaborate border of applied colorful flowers, fruits & insects, each base applied w/figure of a maiden or cupid holding a basket of flowers, third quarter 19th c., pr. (minor losses & repairs) 10,175.00

METTLACH

Mettlach Plaque No. 2697

Ceramics with the name Mettlach were produced by Villeroy & Boch and other potteries in the Mettlach area of Germany. Villeroy and Boch's finest years of production are thought to be from about 1890 to 1910.

For listings of Mettlach steins see the "Steins" category.

Beaker, shield w/rearing horse & band at top w/legend "Stadt Stuttgart," No. 1200/2327, ¼ liter..... $60.00

Beaker w/handle, printed under glaze boy w/arm raised & "Join Health and Cheer - Drink Hires Rootbeer," (No. 2327), ¼ liter 75.00

Plaque, pierced to hang, Delft-type, h.p. musician, No. 5041, 12" d. .. 231.00

Plaque, pierced to hang, etched scene of knight carrying flag, signed Schultz, No. 1384, 14½" d. 600.00

Plaque, pierced to hang, etched

scene w/young girl reclined in bed of flowers, signed Mangum, No. 2546, 16 x 9½" 990.00

Plaque, pierced to hang, printed under glaze drinking scene, No. 1044/1206, 17" d. 335.00

Mettlach Plaque No. 2698

Plaques, pierced to hang, etched scene of dwarf eating porridge in field of mushrooms on one, the other w/dwarf reading book in field of mushrooms, signed Schlitt, No. 2697 & No. 2698, 17" d., pr. (ILLUS.) 22,500.00

Plaque, pierced to hang, etched castle scene, dated 1895, No. 1108, 17" d. 870.00

Plate, 7" d., six-sided, Art Deco stylized floral decoration, royal blue flowers separated from each other by tan ground 50.00

Plates, 7¼" d., white relief bust of Wagner on grey on one, white relief Beethoven on grey on other, pr. 65.00

Plate, 10¼" d., pierced to hang, boat scene on matte ground, shield mark.................... 95.00

Punch set: punch bowl & 12 cups; incised grape & leaf decoration, diamond geometric border, 10" d., 13" h. bowl, 13 pcs. 990.00

Sugar bowl, cov., blue & tan stylized trees on ivory ground, 3½" h. 95.00

Vase, 9" h., bulbous body w/wide flat center band decorated w/reserves of seated musician & birds, domed foot, tall slender flaring neck w/reserves, overall incised decoration of leaf bands, No. 1591 .... 200.00

Vase, 9½" h., ovoid body w/short flaring neck, decorated w/wide middle band of incised & painted leaf scrolls & medallions on light ground, No. 1829................ 310.00

Vase, 9½" h., 6" d., etched orange & blue florals w/green & gold leaves on grey ground, floral band at top & base edged in gold, shell pink lining, No. 1844 .... 345.00

Mettlach Vase

Vase, 10½" h., terra cotta body w/raised, molded classical winged women's heads w/swags & ribbons in color, blue trim, sea green interior, No. 1898 (ILLUS.) .. 695.00

Vases, 12¾" h., 6" d., center scenes around body w/young boys playing flute, picking flowers, w/bow & arrow & playing mandolin, floral designs above scenes, green & gold ground, No. 1591, pr. 675.00

Vases, 14" h., 5 3/8" d., brown, blue & white ornate geometric borders, cherubs portraying one of four seasons, each within four panels on sides, soft pink interior, No. 1537, pr. 650.00

MINTON

Minton Garden Seats

The Minton factory in England was established by Thomas Minton in 1793. The factory made earthenware, especially the blue-

printed variety and Thomas Minton is sometimes credited with invention of the blue "Willow" pattern. For a time majolica and tiles were also an important part of production, but bone china soon became the principal ware. Mintons, Ltd., continues in operation today.

Bottle w/stopper, partially draped putti sitting on bottle, masks & swags of fruit, neck w/stylized foliate motif & prunus within a banded border, pale blue ground w/naturalistic polychrome coloring, dated 1867, 13¾" h. $957.00

Centerpiece, floriform base divided into six segmented compartments & w/six feet of rounded triangular shape w/molded leaves, surmounted by a fox's head & paws, a swag going behind the fox's head & running around the base backed by a latticework decor w/daisies, base surmounted by a tiered column w/garlanded stags' heads supporting a scalloped dish, green, pale blue & ochre ground w/naturalistic polychrome coloring, dated 1865, 14¼" h. 4,785.00

Compote, 6½" h., modeled as two winged putti w/mating doves in between them holding a shaped oval dish on their wings, putti holding a ribboned garland of leaves, naturalistic polychrome coloring, dated 1870 ....1,037.00

Condiment holder, modeled as a pair of embracing putti w/conch shell on either side of them, shells w/bulrushes, on shaped oval base, dated 1864, 6½" h. ... 319.00

Creamer, Genevese patt., blue & white decoration 75.00

Cup & saucer, pate-sur-pate, white enameled birds & insects on green ground, artist-signed 200.00

Figure group of Ariadne seated on the back of a panther, parian, 14" h. 440.00

Game pie dish & cover w/recumbent hound on bed of ferns & gun & shooting pouch as finial, four lion's paw feet, body molded w/basketweave design adorned w/holly branches, pheasant in flight one side, running hare on other, each depicted against naturalistic background within oval cartouche, dated 1862, 17" oval 2,871.00

Garden seats, majolica, molded band of stylized honeysuckle alternating w/stylized passion flower above bands of stiff stylized leaves & guilloche pattern, on three block feet w/key pattern decor, tops w/band of passion flower w/naturalistic polychrome glaze, dated 1875, 18" h., pr. (ILLUS.) 6,135.00

Jardiniere w/underplate, bearded ram's head handles w/suspended garlands of flowers & fruit each side, egg-and-dart border top, ribboned laurel wreath at foot, aubergine ground w/naturalistic polychrome coloring, dated 1851, 14" h. 1,276.00

Jug, parian, ribbed w/yellow & gold Greek Key pattern at neck, ca. 1852, 6½" h. 90.00

Plaque, relief-molded classical maiden w/cornucopia center, border w/alternating winged angels' heads & satyrs' heads w/cornucopia, ochre & cobalt blue on turquoise ground, dated 1873, 20" oval 829.00

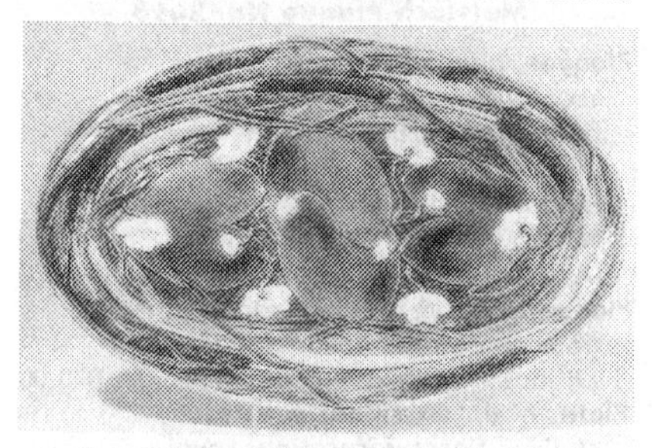

Minton Majolica Platter

Platter, 24" oval, majolica, four bracket feet, relief-molded white waterlilies among lily pads within border of intertwining bulrushes, glazed in green, yellow, brown & white, dated 1862 (ILLUS.) 1,595.00

Teapot, cov., gourd-shaped, leafy stem feet which spread to form handle & decorate the body, lid formed as a mushroom cap surmounted by a mushroom, yellow body w/naturalistic polychrome coloring, dated 1862, 5¾" h. 638.00

Wine coolers, rams' heads handles, molded narrative frieze of satyrs, goats & fawns, foot w/vines, naturalistic polychrome coloring, dated 1859, 10" h., pr. 1,276.00

MOCHA

Mocha decoration is found on basically utilitarian creamware or yellowware articles and is achieved by a simple chemical reaction. A color pigment of brown, blue, green or black is given an acid nature by infusion of tobacco or hops. When this acid nature colorant is applied in blobs to an alkaline ground color, it reacts by spreading in feathery seaweed designs. This type of decoration is usually accompanied by horizontal bands of light color slip. Produced in numerous Staffordshire potteries from the late 18th until the late 19th centuries, its name is derived from the similar markings found on mocha quartz.

Mocha Bowl with Seaweed Decor

Bowl, 4¾" d., 2¾" h., wide blue band & narrow black pin stripe bands each side $45.00
Bowl, 8¾" d., 4" h., Earthworm & Cat's Eye patt., brown & greenish grey bands w/black stripes (stained & badly cracked) 200.00
Bowl, 12" d., Seaweed patt. (ILLUS.) 175.00
Butter dish, cov., cream slip band w/green feathering seaweed on yellowware, 6½" d. underplate, overall 5½" h. 160.00
Cup & saucer, marbleized decor w/black & white geometric border, embossed white ribbed band 425.00

Mocha Mug with Marbleized Decor

Mug, applied handle, marbleized brown, orange & white, brown & white geometric border, 3¾" h. (ILLUS.) 325.00
Mug, applied handle, green & brown bands w/narrow white wavy lines on embossed ribbing, 4 5/8" h. 405.00
Mug, leaf-embossed handle, Earthworm patt. between blue & grey bands w/black & white striping, 4 7/8" h. (hairlines & small chips) 350.00
Mug, brown band w/black & blue stripes & seaweed, incised crown mark, initialed, dated, 5" h. 145.00
Mug, applied handle, brown & green bands w/narrow white striping over embossed ribbing, 6 7/8" h. (hairlines, small edge chips) 295.00
Pitcher, 7" h., leaf-molded handle, barrel-shaped, dark brown-black feathering seaweed on deep orange w/black, white & green striping, embossed shoulder designs (stains, chips & small hairline) 525.00
Pitcher, cov., 8½" h., Earthworm patt. on blue band w/dark brown striping (crazing, stains & poorly executed repair on lid & spout) . . . 425.00
Pitcher, 9¾" h., white slip band w/blue feathering seaweed on yellowware, East Liverpool, Ohio (stains & hairlines) 425.00
Stein w/domed pewter lid w/name in script & date "1864," Earthworm patt. on blue ground w/upper & lower band of dark brown, England, 19th c., 7 7/8" h. 522.50

MOORCROFT

William Moorcroft became a designer for James Macintyre & Co. in 1897 and was put in charge of their art pottery production. Moorcroft developed a number of popular designs, including Florian Ware, *while with Macintyre and continued with that firm until 1913 when they discontinued the production of art pottery.*

After leaving Macintyre in 1913, Moorcroft set up his own pottery in Burslem and continued producing the art wares he had designed earlier as well as introducing new patterns. After William's death in 1945, the pottery was operated by his son, Walter.

Bowl, cov., 5½" d., hibiscus decoration $75.00
Bowl, 8" d., 4¼" h., green iridescent glaze w/sterling silver trim . . 45.00
Bowl, cov., 9" d., leaf & berry decoration on colored matte ground, 1930 . . . . 285.00

Box, cov., round, Pansy patt., rose & purple pansies on deep cobalt blue ground 250.00
Creamer, Hazledene Ware, landscape w/trees 225.00
Dish, Florian Ware, red & blue poppies decoration on blue-green ground, 8½" d., 1⅛" h. 145.00
Dish, Pomegranate patt., 8½" d. ... 90.00
Jar, cov., wisteria decoration on green ground, 5" h. 135.00
Lamp base, floral, red flambe glaze, brass mounts, 6" h., 1919-40 ..... 285.00
Lamp base, bulbous, hibiscus decoration on cobalt blue ground, signed, impressed mark, paper label, 13½" h. 275.00
Pin tray, hibiscus decoration on olive green ground, 1946-73, 9 x 6" 35.00
Pitcher, 5" h., bulbous, orchids decoration on cobalt blue ground, signed "Potter to HM Queen, Made in England" 85.00
Pitcher, 7" h., w/pewter lid, Aurelian patt., 1898 .... 275.00
Plate, 9" d., "Moonlit Blue" glaze, w/brass handle 355.00
Tazza, ceramic base, Pomegranate patt., 7" d. 200.00
Teapot, cov., blue flowers on green ground, Macintyre Period, 1897-1913........................ 300.00
Teapot, cov., w/stand, Aurelian patt., Macintyre Period, the set... 450.00
Tea set: cov. teapot, creamer & sugar bowl; floral decoration on green & cobalt blue ground, script signed, 3 pcs. (small repair to tip of spout) 250.00
Vase, 4¾" h., ovoid, broad band of purple, red, yellow & white iris blossoms & green leaves & smaller blue-shaded white blossoms, all outlined in slip, on shaded green & cobalt blue ground, impressed "Moorcroft/Made in England" 110.00
Vase, 6" h., three-handled, Aurelian patt., Macintyre Period 300.00
Vase, 7" h., bulbous, Florian Ware, green & pearl poppies decoration....................... 185.00
Vase, 10" h., Honeycomb patt. 125.00
Vase, 14¾" h., baluster-shaped, Hazledene Ware, landscape w/trees, impressed "Moorcroft 85 O D Made in England"........... 770.00
Vase, 15" h., Fairy Rings patt....... 150.00

NEWCOMB COLLEGE POTTERY

This pottery was established in the art department of Newcomb College, New Orleans, La., in 1897. Each piece was hand-thrown and bore the potter's mark and decorator's monogram on the base. It was always a studio business and never operated as a factory and its pieces are therefore scarce, with the early wares being eagerly sought. The pottery closed in 1940.

Newcomb College Jardiniere

Bowl-vase, floral decor, signed Sadie Irvine.....................$475.00
Coaster, floral decor, signed A.F. (Anna Frances) Simpson, paper label, 4" d. 325.00
Coaster, repeating lily of the valley, green border on matte blue, 1926, paper label 247.50
Jardiniere, h.p. decor of large leaves & stems on light ground, high glaze, signed Irene Borden Keep, 1901 (ILLUS.) 4,950.00
Vase, 3" h., 5½" d., floral border .. 550.00
Vase, 3½" h., blue-grey glossy decor 175.00
Vase, 5½" h., scenic decor on shaded blue ground, signed Sadie Irvine/Kenneth Smith 750.00
Vase, 6¼" h., ovoid, light yellow & blue magnolias amongst green leaves on matte blue ground, signed Anna Frances Simpson ...1,320.00
Vase, 6½" h., broad oviform, molded large trees & hanging moss, dark blue glaze, signed Sarah Irvine, 1913 .... 495.00
Vase, 6½" h., swollen cylinder, opening crocus of joining leaves banding, blue-green glossy glaze, ca. 1930 ....1,650.00
Vase, 6 5/8" h., ovoid, four small blue handles at the shoulder, molded broad light red & blue petals in a matte glaze, signed Sarah Irvine, 1917 (small chip & hairline at rim) 330.00
Vase, 11¾" h., flared cylinder, yellow-centered pale blue flowers & green stems on matte blue ground, signed Anna Frances Simpson ...2,420.00

NILOAK

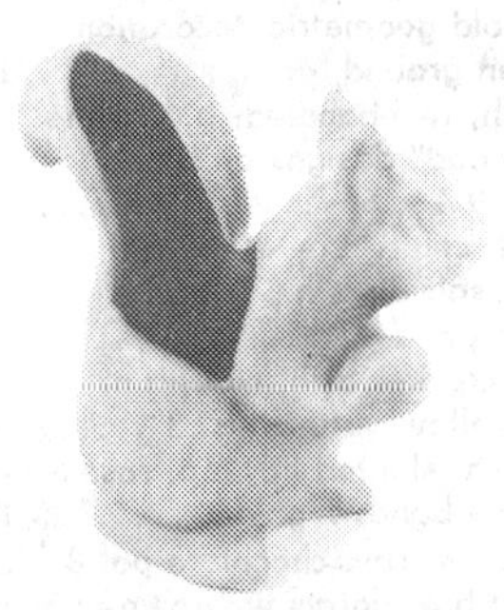

Niloak Squirrel Planter

This pottery was made in Benton, Arkansas, and featured hand-thrown vari-colored swirled clay decoration in objects of classic forms. Designated Mission Ware, this line is the most desirable of Niloak's production which was begun early in this century. Less expensive to produce, the cast Hywood line, finished with either high gloss or semi-matte glazes, was introduced during the economic depression of the 1930's. The pottery ceased operation about 1946.

Candlestick, Mission Ware, marbleized swirls, 8" h. (single) $95.00
Candlestick, three turned rings on shaft, blue, brown & cream, 8" h. (single) 60.00
Dish, cream, brown, blue & rust, 4" d., 2" h. (small chips inside rim) 20.00
Lamp base, Mission Ware, blue, cream, grey & brown marbleized swirls, 11½" 200.00
Match holder, model of a cannon ... 35.00
Model of a bullfrog, white 25.00
Model of a dog, hand-formed, rusty glaze, 2½" 125.00
Model of a donkey, white 45.00
Model of a swan, green 18.50
Pitcher, 7" h., bulbous, Hywood line, rose glaze 15.00
Pitcher, 6" d., 10¼" h., Mission Ware, cylindrical body slightly flared at base, strap handle, swirled light blue, cream & terra cotta colored clays, stamped "Niloak" 302.50
Planter, Hywood line, model of a camel, blue glaze 25.00
Planter, Hywood line, model of a canoe, white glaze, 11" 28.00
Planter, Hywood line, model of a deer, pink glaze 12.00
Planter, Hywood line, model of an elephant 18.00
Planter, Hywood line, model of a kangaroo, brown glaze 22.00
Planter, Hywood line, model of a squirrel (ILLUS.) 25.00
Planter, Mission Ware, marbleized swirls, 5½" d., 4" h. 50.00
Powder jar, cov., Mission Ware, marbleized swirls, small 325.00
Toothpick holder, Mission Ware, marbleized swirls 25.00
Vase, 3" h., Mission Ware, marbleized swirls, signed 30.00

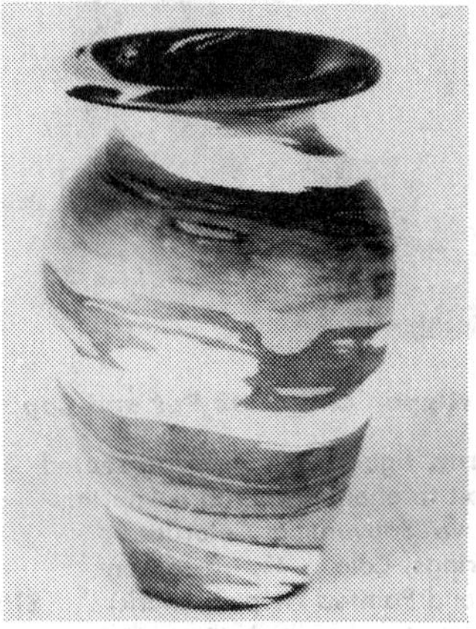

Mission Ware Vase

Vase, 5½" h., Mission Ware, blue, brown & mauve marbleized swirls (ILLUS.) 55.00
Vase, bud, 6" h., model of leaf, Hywood line, blue glaze 18.00
Vase, 6" h., Mission Ware, tapering to 1" bowl lip, blue, brown & rust marbleized swirls 75.00
Vase, 6½" h., 6" d., Mission Ware, bulbous, wide flared neck, blue, rust, cream & brown marbleized swirls 100.00
Vase, 7½" h., Mission Ware, cream, terra cotta, green & blue marbleized swirls 85.00
Vase, 8" h., four open flowers on grey shaded to pink ground 30.00
Vase, 8" h., Hywood line, aqua-green glaze, paper label 17.00
Vase, 10" h., Mission Ware, marbleized swirls 110.00
Vase, 12" h., Mission Ware, marbleized swirls 200.00
Vase, wing handles, blue glaze, paper label 16.00

NIPPON

This colorful porcelain was produced by numerous factories in Japan late last century and until about 1921. There are numerous marks on this ware, identifying the producers or decorating studios. The hand-painted pieces of good quality have shown a dramatic price increase within the past three years.

Nippon Chocolate Pot and Cup

Ashtray, figural "Nipper" dog seated next to phonograph horn imprinted w/"Souvenir of Colorado Springs, Colo.," 4½" l. (green "Hand Painted Nippon" mark) $150.00

Ashtray, two-handled, Moriage trim, red, brown, black & green sailboat scene w/windmill, 4¼" d. (green "M" in Wreath mark) 75.00

Ashtray-matchbox holder, relief-molded forepart of long-eared dog sits on edge of bowl, 5 x 4" (green "M" in Wreath mark) 495.00

Bowl, 7", self-handled, pastel scenic decoration, matte finish (green "M" in Wreath mark) 35.00

Bowl, 8 x 2½", deep, four-sided w/1" flat edge, top flat edge w/relief gold filigree w/flowers on black ground, interior scene of two barns near water w/birch trees (green "M" in Wreath mark) 175.00

Bowl, 10" d., 2½" h., band of large yellow & pink flowers on deep red ground, overall gold dot trim, gold scalloped edge (Royal Kinran mark) 80.00

Bowls, cereal, floral decor on white ground, set of 6 (Rising Sun mark) 30.00

Butter dish, cov., h.p. pink & blue flowers w/green leaves.......... 45.00

Cake set: master cake plate & six individual serving plates; h.p. black & gold cottage scene decor on white ground, 7 pcs. (blue Maple Leaf mark) 85.00

Candle lamp, h.p. white doves in flight decor on cobalt blue ground (green "M" in Wreath mark) 780.00

Candlesticks, squared pyramidal form, gold geometric decoration on green ground, pr. 180.00

Candy dish, two-handled, h.p. white "Wedgwood" designs on blue ground, 9½ x 6" 205.00

Celery set: celery tray & six individual salt dips; h.p. floral decor, 7 pcs..................... 80.00

Cheese & cracker dish, cov., h.p. blue & yellow butterflies, 8"..... 49.00

Cheese dish, slanted lid, h.p. roses on yellow band w/gold 100.00

Chocolate set: cov. chocolate pot & five c/s; h.p. florals w/brown leaves outlined in gold on shaded brown ground, ornate gold trim, 11 pcs. (ILLUS. of pot & one cup) 175.00

Compote, open, 8½" d., 4¾" h., h.p. white "Wedgwood" scrolls on wide blue rim bands, h.p. colored florals on white on inside & on pedestal base (green "M" in Wreath mark) 225.00

Condiment set: six small low bowls fitting around center bowl, on lazy Susan; h.p. sailing ship scene, in original lacquer box, 7 pcs. 85.00

"Gaudy" Nippon Cracker Jar

Cracker jar, cov., footed, melon-ribbed, "gaudy," h.p. red & pink roses w/ornate gold trim on cobalt blue ground, 7¾" h. (ILLUS.)........................ 350.00

Cracker jar, cov., three-handled, three-footed, orange & yellow florals w/green foliage around top of lid, main body w/gold trim........................... 80.00

Creamer & sugar shaker, h.p. orange chrysanthemums w/green leaves & gold lustre trim, 6" h. shaker, pr. (Cherry Blossom mark) 48.00

Demitasse set: cov. coffeepot & six

cups & saucers; h.p. Satsuma-like decoration w/scenes of people in reserves surrounded by diapered designs, 13 pcs. 210.00

Dresser set: 11½ x 8" tray, 6 1/8" d. tray, open footed compote, open hatpin holder, cov. powder jar, hair receiver w/tall legs & two small cov. jars; looped beading & encrusted gold florals & jewelling w/cobalt banding, 8 pcs. 160.00

Egg warmer w/jewelled handle, four-egg, h.p. overall rural scene (green "M" in Wreath mark) 115.00

Ferner, triangular, h.p. woodland scene, 5" h. (green "M" in Wreath mark) 130.00

Fruit bowl, two-piece, pedestal base w/three gold legs, h.p. scene inside bowl of trees & rowboat by lake, blue & gold trim, 5¼" h. (green "M" in Wreath mark) 250.00

Hair receiver, cov., three-footed, h.p. roses, leaves & swags, gold beading & trim (green Maple Leaf mark) 65.00

Humidor, cov., squatty bulbous shape & bulbous finial on cover, h.p. cottage scene, 4" h. (green "M" in Wreath mark) 165.00

Humidor, cov., creamy relief-molded scene of lion & serpent surrounding body, brown ground, artist-signed, 6¾" h. (green "M" in Wreath mark) 600.00

Juice reamer, white w/heavy gold trim 45.00

Lamp, boudoir-type, h.p. peacock & florals on black ground, 9½" h. . . 45.00

Lemonade set: pitcher & five 3" h. mugs; h.p. sunset colors w/sailboat decoration, pitcher w/decorated ice lip, 6 pcs. 185.00

Model of a bird, blue, 4¼" h. (green "M" in Wreath mark) 350.00

Nippon Mug

Mug, slightly ovoid, h.p. dark red band around middle w/h.p. round reserve of a tall stein, dice, cards & a pipe on red ground, h.p. mottled background, green "M" in Wreath mark, 5" h. (ILLUS.) 195.00

Napkin ring, h.p. holly berries decoration 35.00

Nut bowl, relief-molded flower, nut & leaf, surrounded by chestnuts & leaves, brown matte finish, 8" d. (green "M" in Wreath mark) 100.00

Pen rest, h.p. florals on cobalt blue ground, 6½" 45.00

Pin tray, relief-molded florals in earth tones, bisque finish 45.00

Pitcher, tankard, 11½" h., h.p. roses w/relief-molded gold beading 450.00

Pitcher, tankard, 16" h., h.p. large pink florals w/green centers, gold in relief decor on gold ground (Royal Moriye mark) 295.00

Plaque, pierced to hang, h.p. colored fox hunt scene, 10" d. (green "M" in Wreath mark) 175.00

Plaque, pierced to hang, relief-molded & h.p. buffalo, 10½" d. (green "M" in Wreath mark) 1,200.00

Plaque, pierced to hang, relief-molded (3) dogs' faces center, 10½" d. (green "M" in Wreath mark) 1,400.00

Plaque, pierced to hang, rectangular,. h.p. scene of Indians (3) wrapped in blankets & w/head-dresses riding horses across the prairie in the moonlight, border has Indian symbols, 10½ x 8¼" (green "M" in Wreath mark) 245.00

Plate, 10" d., h.p. white & delicate lavender wisteria blossoms, narrow gold border 50.00

Powder box, cov., footed, h.p. small pink florals, 3¾" (blue Rising Sun mark) 35.00

Ramekin w/underplate, h.p. roses w/heavy gold trim, 2 pcs. 38.00

Salt & pepper shakers, h.p. butterflies, pr. 20.00

Smoking set: large & small tray, cov. tobacco humidor, cigar & cigarette jars, match holder & cigarette rolling-paper cup; green bisque finish, h.p. Arab astride camel scene, 7 pcs. . . . . .750.00 to 775.00

Stein, straight sides, relief-molded dogs' heads (6) around body, rope-twist handle, 7" h. (green "M" in Wreath mark) 750.00

Tea set: cov. teapot, creamer & cov. sugar bowl; h.p. detailed Moriage dragon w/jeweled eyes decoration, 3 pcs. 85.00

Toothpick holder, three-handled, h.p. pyramids & palm tree scene (green "M" in Wreath mark) 40.00

Tray, oval, open-handled, h.p. floral center on white & h.p. white "Wedgwood" designs on wide blue rim band, 10½" l. (green "M" In Wreath mark) 175.00

Trinket box, cov., relief-molded Campbell Kid face 75.00

Vase, 3" h., flared base tapering to bulbous top, h.p. early airplane in flight decoration (green "M" in Wreath mark) 125.00

Vase, 5½" h., ovoid footed body w/short ruffled neck & loop handles at shoulder, h.p. oval reserve w/river scene in center, overall gold trim, all on cobalt blue ground (blue Maple Leaf mark) ... 145.00

Ornate Nippon Vase

Vase, 7" h., round bulbous body on three short gold legs, narrow short neck w/two S-curved gold handles curving to top of body, h.p. reserve of pink roses on yellow ground, surrounded by h.p. turquoise beading & roses on gold ground, blue Maple Leaf mark (ILLUS.) 200.00

Vase, 8" h., tall ovoid body w/small short neck & long loop handles on shoulder, "tapestry" finish w/large h.p. pink & yellow roses & green leaves (blue Maple Leaf mark) 450.00

Vase, 10" h., ovoid body w/short narrow neck & flared rim, short scroll handles on shoulder, "tapestry" finish w/h.p. grape clusters & leaves, gold trim, blue Maple Leaf mark (ILLUS.) 350.00

Vase, 12" h., tall slightly waisted cylinder w/two short scroll handles at top, h.p. cowboy on horseback 'silhouette' against colored desert sunset scene (blue Imperial Nippon mark) 550.00

Nippon Tapestry Vase

Vase, 16" h., 8½" w., bulbous form, floral border decoration on turquoise blue ground at top, overall white, pink, blue, orange & green florals w/black butterflies on deep yellow ground, 1900-1910, paper label 625.00

Whiskey jug w/stopper, round body w/shaped neck & loop handle, mushroom stopper, h.p. windmill & house scene trimmed w/enameled flowers & jewels, 7½" h. (blue Maple Leaf mark) ... 350.00

NORITAKE

Noritake Figural Dresser Box

Noritake china, still in production in Japan, has been exported in large quantities to this country since early in this century. Though the Noritake Company first registered in 1904, it did not use "Noritake" as part of their backstamp until 1918. Interest in Noritake has escalated as collectors now seek out pieces made between the "Nippon" era and World War II (1921-41). The Azalea pattern is also popular with collectors.

Ashtray, figural lady, half-figure of young lady sits on edge of dish holding fan, red skirt forms exterior of dish w/yellow interior forming bowl (green "M" in Wreath - Made in Japan mark) . . . $195.00
Ashtray, spade-shaped w/red heart & black club in center . . . 25.00
Bacon platter, Tree in Meadow patt., 10" l. . . . 95.00
Basket, handled, Tree in Meadow patt., small . . . 70.00
Bonbon, ring handle center, orange & blue florals, 5" d. . . . 20.00
Bowl, 5¼" d., Azalea patt. . . . 12.00
Bowl, 6¾" l., boat-shaped w/pointed prow, figural duck finial on side handle, green & orange w/colorful florals (green "M" in Wreath - Made in Japan mark) . . . 65.00
Bowl, 7" d., three open handles, two large peony-type flowers in center, much greenery, cobalt blue trim w/relief gold beading (green "M" in Wreath mark) . . . 45.00
Bowl, soup, 7 1/8" d., Azalea patt., w/gold . . . 16.00
Butter dish, cov., Tree in Meadow patt. . . . 30.00
Cake plate, pierced handles, Tree in Meadow patt. . . . 20.00
Candlesticks, blue lustre w/gold overlay florals & central bird on branch, 7½" h., pr. . . . 68.00
Candlestick lamp, tapering cylindrical shape w/flared socket & wide, flared base, purple glaze, 5¾" h. . . . 75.00
Candy jar, cov., Azalea patt. . . . 550.00
Celery tray, Art Deco style trees, florals & pagoda decor on orange border, blue lustre ground, 13" l. . . . 20.00
Centerpiece bowl, double handle on pedestal base, exterior w/Wedgwood-type jasper ware decoration, interior w/riverside scene, 8" d. plus handles, 5" h. . . . 225.00
Cigarette holder, bell-shaped, ship scene, bird finial, 5" h. . . . 100.00
Coffeepot, cov., demitasse, Azalea patt. . . . 398.00
Cologne bottles w/original gold stoppers, hexagonal, heavy gold decoration, pr. . . . 95.00
Condiment set: covered mustard jar w/spoon, salt & pepper shakers & tray; Azalea patt., 5 pcs. . . . 49.00
Cracker jar, Mosaic patt., blue, red, yellow, black, gold & cream, silver plate lid & handle (blue Tree Crest mark) . . . 125.00
Creamer & cov. sugar bowl, scenic decor on brown ground, beaded trim, pr. . . . 65.00
Creamer & sugar shaker, Bird of Paradise patt., heavy gold, pr. . . . 75.00
Cup & saucer, demitasse, Azalea patt. . . . 60.00
Dresser box, cover w/half-figure of young woman wearing mob cap, gown forms base of box, gold lustre finish, 5½" h., green "M" in Wreath - Made in Japan & number mark (ILLUS.) . . . 160.00
Egg cup, Azalea patt. . . . 30.00
Humidor, cov., colorful portrait of Turkish lady on front, beige lustre ground, figural pipe on cover . . . 110.00
Humidor, cov., tree-stump form w/loop branch handles & domed cover w/large knob finial, relief-molded racoon on side (green "M" in Wreath mark) . . . 450.00
Humidor, cov., bulbous paneled shape w/domed cover w/large knob finial, h.p. Art Deco designs of narrow white & black scroll bands on red ground w/large panel of two black owls on white ground (green "M" in Wreath mark) . . . 135.00
Inkwell, cov., figural Art Deco-style clown lady w/cover formed by head w/wide collar & pointed hat, red w/floral trim (red "M" in Wreath mark) . . . 250.00
Lemon dish, oval w/large relief-molded yellow lemon & molded white blossoms at one end, h.p. green & yellow leaves (red "M" in Wreath mark) . . . 32.00
Marmalade jar, cov., w/underplate & ladle, h.p. blue trees, pagoda, pink cherry trees, birds & sailboats on water scene on green lustre ground, 4" h. . . . 25.00
Match holder, cov., beehive shape, gold lustre decoration, cover lifts off to conical grooved striker, 3¾" h. . . . 47.00
Mayonnaise bowl, underplate & ladle, Azalea patt., 3 pcs. . . . 32.00
Model of a swan, gold beak & legs, gold floral decoration, black features on white body, orange interior, 3¼" l., 2¾" h. . . . 45.00
Napkin rings, h.p. Art Deco-style man in top hat & cape on one &

Art Deco "flapper" lady on other (red "M" in Wreath mark), pr. 95.00
Nut bowl, shell-shaped, Azalea patt., 7¾" 175.00

Noritake Nut Bowl

Nut bowl, tri-lobed bowl w/figural squirrel seated at side of dish eating nut, 7½" w. (ILLUS.) 85.00
Peanut set: 6½" l. master relief-molded peanut-shaped bowl w/six 3" l. individual peanut-shaped bowls; each h.p. w/peanuts & leaves on the interiors, 7 pcs. (green "M" in Wreath mark) 125.00
Pin tray, hexagonal, h.p. pastel flowers & scenes w/heavy gold trim & beading 25.00
Pitcher, milk, Azalea patt. 188.00
Plate, 6 3/8" d., Azalea patt. 7.00
Plate, cake, 9¾" d., Azalea patt. 35.00
Plate, bread & butter, Baroda patt. 4.00
Platter, 16", Alberta patt. 15.00
Playing card holder, h.p. Art Deco-style girl w/red flower in hair 115.00
Powder box, cov., h.p. roses on blue ground, 4" d. (green "M" in Wreath mark) 65.00
Spoon tray, two-handled, h.p. yellow florals w/black & green leaves on orange ground w/gold trim, 7¾" l. (red "M" in Wreath mark) 24.00
Sugar bowl, cov., Tree in Meadow patt. 12.00
Teapot, cov., Azalea patt. 75.00
Toothpick holder, Tree in Meadow patt., marked "Made in Japan" ... 35.00
Trinket dish, round w/center loop handle, h.p. blue & white stripes, 2¼" d. 23.00
Vase, 5" h., two-handled, bulbous, h.p. pastel flowers & scenes w/heavy gold trim & beading 35.00
Vase, 5¼" h., rockwork base w/small yellow-breasted bluebird sitting next to small cylindrical vase w/flaring rim & blue iridized finish, 5¼" h. 150.00
Vase, 7½" h., ovoid body tapering to short flaring neck, gold loop handles on shoulder, h.p. plush pink & white roses & green leaves on shaded brown ground 95.00
Vegetable bowl, open, Baroda patt. 20.00
Wall pocket, cone-shaped, h.p. house & trees landscape band at top above blue lustre base 65.00
Wall pocket, red poppy decor on blue lustre ground, 8½" l. 55.00
Whipped cream set: 4½" d. bowl, ladle & plate; Azalea patt., 3 pcs. 30.00

NORTH DAKOTA SCHOOL OF MINES POTTERY

All pottery produced at the University of North Dakota School of Mines was made from North Dakota clay. In 1910, the University hired Margaret Kelly Cable to teach pottery making and she remained at the school until her retirement. Julia Mattson and Margaret Pachl were other instructors between 1923 and 1970. Designs and glazes varied through the years ranging from the Art Nouveau to modern styles. Pieces were marked "University of North Dakota - Grand Forks, N.D. - Made at School of Mines, N.D." within a circle and also signed by the students until 1963. Since that time, the pieces bear only the students' signatures. Items signed "Huck" are by the artist Flora Huckfield and were made between 1923 and 1949. We list only those pieces made prior to 1963.

Book end-bowl combination, signed "M.C." (Margaret Kelly Cable), pr. $150.00
Coaster, oxen & wagon in relief, 4" 195.00
Creamer, four-color floral decoration, dated 1947, 3½" h. 155.00
Creamer & sugar bowl, blue mottled glaze, pr. 55.00
Curtain pull, figural, bright yellow glaze 45.00
Lamp, incised cowboys on horses decoration, 7½ x 7" 500.00
Model of Red River ox cart, light blue to cream galze, 8 x 5" 125.00
Pitcher, 7½ x 4½", Red River ox cart scene, blue-grey glaze, signed "Cable" 115.00
Pitcher, 8½" h., maroon glaze 110.00
Pitcher, ball-type, blue glossy glaze 40.00
Pitcher, ball-type, mottled blue glaze 100.00
Pitcher, shaded magenta to pink glaze, artist-signed 135.00

Plate, 10" d., ruffled, buff glaze 48.00
Tile, colorful carved scene, signed "Julia Mattson," dated 1928 .... 350.00
Vase, 2½" h., 3" d., reddish-brown matte glaze, marked 75.00
Vase, 3 x 2", tan glaze 55.00
Vase, 3" h., squatty, shoulder drip decoration 150.00
Vase, 3" h., yellow glaze, early U.N.D. stamp 60.00
Vase, 4" h., blue & rust concentric rings 55.00
Vase, 4" h., incised floral decoration on green ground 195.00
Vase, 4" h., handled, mustard glaze, artist-signed 35.00
Vase, 4½" h., blue glaze, signed "McCarthy," dated 1928 .... 74.00
Vase, 6 x 5", blue drip on blue glaze, signed "McCarthy," dated "11/20/28" 65.00
Vase, 6½" h., cobalt blue glaze 85.00
Vase, 7" h., lavender & pink glaze, signed "FW" 95.00
Vase, 7 3/8" h., three-ring tapered body, signed "Mattson" 90.00
Vase, 7½" h., turquoise incised rings 100.00
Vase, 8" h., bulbous, hand-thrown, made by Flora Huckfield, dated 1927 .... 130.00
Vase, 8" h., carved abstract decoration on brown high gloss ground 135.00
Vase, 9" h., butterfly & flowers slip decoration, wheel-thrown, incised "Seim 1953" & cobalt stamp 185.00
Vase, haystacks decoration on brown ground, signed "Cable".... 295.00
Water bottle, cov., Sioux calendar decoration 225.00

OHR (George) POTTERY

Log Cabin Inkwell

George Ohr, the eccentric potter of Biloxi, Mississippi, worked from about 1883 to 1906. Some think him to be one of the most expert throwers the craft will ever see. The majority of his works were hand thrown, exceedingly thin-walled items, some of which have a crushed or folded appearance. He considered himself the foremost potter in the world and declined to sell much of his production, instead accumulated a great horde to leave as a legacy to his children. In 1972, this collection was purchased for resale by an antiques dealer.

Bank, potato-shaped, orange-brown clay, signed, 3 1/8 x 2¼" $357.50
Bowl, 5" d., 2 5/8" h., notched rim, in-body twist, bisque-fired, signed & dated 1906 .... 385.00
Goblet, flared foot, straight cylindrical sides, bisque finish w/incised lines & squiggles, incised script mark, 3½" d., 6¾" h. 110.00
Inkwell, model of a hand-built log cabin w/pen hole in roof, metallic black glaze, die-stamped "Biloxi" three times, 3¼ x 2 5/8" h. (ILLUS.)......................... 385.00
Mug, angular handle, bulbous base w/ten round indentations encircling it below straight cylindrical upper section incised with "Here's to your good health and your family's and may they all live long and prosper. J. Jefferson," high-gloss black glaze over mustard yellow, die-stamped "G.E. Ohr, Biloxi, Miss.," incised "3-18-1896," 4" d., 5" h. 715.00

George Ohr Pitcher

Pitcher, 5 x 3", oval & squat w/oval dimples on either side & a loop handle, rim folded over & pinched to form spout, glossy metallic black-brown glaze, die-stamped "GEOHR" & "Biloxi Miss" (ILLUS.)......................... 715.00
Pitcher, 5¼ x 3", swirling form w/wildly ruffled rim, medium & grey-brown clays, bisque-fired, signed 1,210.00
Pitcher, 5½ x 4", swirling form, ruffled rim, pinched & folded handle, bisque-fired, orange-pink to light orange clay, signed 495.00
Pitcher, 8" h., 6¼" widest d., ewer form, bulbous bottom w/in-body twist at midsection, scrolled handle, incised chevrons around bottom & near top, vibrant blood

red glaze w/green accents & w/sheets of feathered white, signed....................13,200.00

Plaque, green high glaze w/applied pallid green hand holding a deep burgundy bird, signed, 5½" d. ... 880.00

Puzzle jug, articulated snake handle, incised leaves & flowers, false screw & eight reticulations, green-brown "flambe" glaze on golden yellow ground, signed, 4¼" d., 7¼" h.......................8,525.00

Puzzle mug, rabbit head handle, metallic orange-brown glaze w/gun-metal splotches, signed, 5¼ x 3¼"..................... 220.00

Vase, 3½" h., 3" d., squat bulbous form w/rim rolled on three sides & body pinched five times on one side, dark brown & red speckled high-gloss glaze on the outside, speckled gold, green & brown high-gloss glaze on inside, die-stamped "G.E. Ohr, Biloxi, Miss."........................660.00

Vase, 4½" h., 2½" d., footed cylinder w/tapered neck ending in jagged plated rim, wild pink, orange & cream textured "flambe" glaze, signed....................1,760.00

Vase, 7 x 6", wide angular bulbous bottom w/footed base & bulbous top ending in a crimped opening, bisque-fired, incised "March 1, 1902" & "Elam Erma Lopez Julia Lopez Eva" on side, incised "GEOHR" in script on base & "Mary had a little lamb. Ohr has a little pottery. That's no joke".......... 302.50

OLD IVORY

Old Ivory Pattern No. 16

Old Ivory china was produced in Silesia, Germany, in the late 1800's and takes its name from the soft white background coloring. A wide range of table pieces was made with most patterns identified by a number rather than a name.

Berry set: master bowl & four sauce dishes; No. 69, 5 pcs.............$150.00

Berry set: master bowl & six sauce dishes; No. 11, 7 pcs............ 195.00

Berry set: master bowl & six sauce dishes; No. 84, 7 pcs............ 225.00

Bowls, 6½" d., No. 28, set of 6..... 120.00

Bowl, master berry, 9½" d., No. 15 .... 58.00

Bowl, 10" d., No. 10.............. 70.00

Bowl, 10" d., No. 75.............. 65.00

Bowl, 10¼" d., No. 15............ 75.00

Cake plate, pierced handles, No. 63, 10" d.......................... 65.00

Cake plate, pierced handles, No. 10, 11" d.......................... 60.00

Cake plate, No. 16, 11" d..................100.00 to 125.00

Cake plate, No. 75, 11½" d. 90.00

Cake set: master plate w/pierced handles & six serving plates; No. 73, 7 pcs................ 200.00

Cake set: master plate w/pierced handles & six 6¼" d. serving plates; No. 84, 7 pcs............ 225.00

Celery tray, No. 16................ 95.00

Celery tray, No. 84, 11 x 5½"...... 80.00

Chocolate cup & saucer, No. 28..... 45.00

Chocolate cup & saucer, No. 73..... 50.00

Chocolate pot, cov., No. 11 .... 325.00

Chocolate pot, cov., No. 15 .... 262.00

Chocolate pot, cov., No. 84 .... 295.00

Chocolate pot, cov., Thistle patt. ... 180.00

Chocolate set: cov. chocolate pot & six cups & saucers; No. 16, 13 pcs.......................... 650.00

Cracker jar & cover w/fleur de lis finial, No. 16 (ILLUS.) 375.00

Cracker jar, cov., No. 84........... 265.00

Creamer, No. 11 .... 60.00

Creamer, No. 75 .... 35.00

Creamer & cov. sugar bowl, No. 15, pr............................ 115.00

Creamer & cov. sugar bowl, No. 84, pr............................ 125.00

Cup & saucer, demitasse, No. 11 ... 45.00

Cup & saucer, No. 10.............. 45.00

Cup & saucer, No. 15.............. 45.00

Cup & saucer, No. 16.............. 55.00

Cup & saucer, No. 33.............. 45.00

Pickle dish, 6½ x 4½", No. 84 ..... 38.00

Plate, 6¼" d., Thistle patt.......... 14.00

Plate, fluted, 6½" d., No. 84....... 25.00

Plate, 7½" d., No. 7.............. 42.50

Plate, 7¾" d., No. 11, Clarion patt........................... 28.00

Plate, 7¾" d., No. 16.............. 25.00

Plate, 7¾" fluted, No. 33 .... 25.00
Plate, 7¾" d., No. 75 .... 32.00
Plate, 7¾" d., No. 84 .... 25.00
Plate, cake, 11" d., pierced handles, No. 16 .... 95.00
Platter, 11½", No. 16 .... 125.00
Sugar bowl, cov., No. 16 .... 60.00
Teacup & saucer, No. 16 .... 45.00
Tea set: cov. teapot, cov. sugar bowl, creamer & five cups & saucers; No. 84, 13 pcs. 560.00
Vegetable dish, open, No. 7 .... 20.00

OLD SLEEPY EYE

Sleepy Eye Salt Bowl

Sleepy Eye, Minn., was named after an Indian Chief. The Sleepy Eye Milling Co. had stoneware and pottery premiums made at the turn of the century first by the Weir Pottery Company and subsequently by Western Stoneware Co., Monmouth, Ill. On these items the trademark Indian head was signed beneath "Old Sleepy Eye." The colors were Flemish blue on grey. Later pieces by Western Stoneware to 1937 were not made for Sleepy Eye Milling Co. but for other businesses. They bear the same Indian head but "Old Sleepy Eye" does not appear below. They have a reverse design of teepees and trees and may or may not be marked Western Stoneware on the base. These items are usually found in cobalt blue on cream and are rarer in other colors.

Bowl (salt bowl), 6½" d., 4" h., Flemish blue on grey stoneware, Weir Pottery, 1903 (ILLUS.) $435.00
Butter jar, Flemish blue on grey stoneware, Weir Pottery, 1903.... 410.00
Creamer & sugar bowl, blue on white, stamped "Western Stoneware Co., Monmouth, Ill.," 4" h., pr. 450.00
Mug, cobalt blue on white, small Indian head on handle, Western Stoneware Co., 1906-37 .... 180.00
Mugs, convention, 1976-1981, set of 6 .... 300.00
Paperweights, brown, 1979......... 15.00
Pitcher, 4" h., cobalt blue on white, w/small Indian head on handle, Western Stoneware Co., 1906-37 (half-pint) ....150.00 to 175.00
Pitcher, 5¼" h., cobalt blue on grey, w/small Indian head on handle, Western Stoneware Co., World War I era, 1914-18 (pint) ... 155.00
Pitcher, 5¼" h., cobalt blue on white, w/small Indian head on handle, Western Stoneware Co., 1906-37 (pint) 220.00
Pitcher, 7½" h., "Standing Indian," w/wigwams, Flemish blue on grey stoneware 1,025.00
Pitcher, 7¾" h., cobalt blue on white, w/small Indian head on handle, Western Stoneware Co., 1906-37 (half-gallon) 195.00
Pitcher, convention, "Old Sleepy Eye 1984-9th Annual Collectors Convention" 40.00
Stein, blue on white, Western Stoneware Co., 1906-37, 7¾" h. 450.00
Stein, chestnut brown, 1952, 22 oz. size 325.00
Stein, Flemish blue on grey stoneware, Weir Pottery Co., 1903 ..... 450.00
Stein, tan & brown, Limited Edition, No. 126 .... 250.00
Vase, 9" h., Flemish blue on grey stoneware, Indian head signed, dragonfly, frog & bullrushes reverse, Weir Pottery Co., 1903 .... 313.00

OYSTER PLATES

Union Porcelain Works Oyster Plate

Oyster plates intrigue a few collectors. Oysters were shucked and the meat served in wells of these attractive plates specifically designed to serve oysters. During the late 19th century, they were made of fine china and majolica. Some plates were decorated in the realistic "trompe l'oeil" technique while others simply matched the pattern of a dinner service. Following is a random sampling of oyster plates that were sold in the past eighteen months.

Austrian china, yellow florals on green ground, "Victoria Austria," set of 6 .... $250.00

German porcelain, five molded shells around center well, two small shell wells, white, green & pale lavender lustre ground, embossed florals, scalloped edges, 9" d. 50.00

Haviland china, five wells, salmon pink w/dark green & brown trim, some gold, Limoges mark, 8 5/8" d. 60.00

Haviland china, six wells, rich yellow w/brown, much gold trim, Limoges mark, 8¾" d. 53.00

Haviland china, green flower bordered edge, impressed "T.H." (Theodore Haviland) 37.50

Limoges china, scalloped, shaped rim painted in tones of mulberry, beige ground w/shell motifs painted in the interiors, late 19th c., 8" d., set of 12 .... 385.00

Majolica, green drip glaze on brown ground 60.00

Majolica, half-moon shape, Seaweed patt. 155.00

Minton china, Shell & Seaweed patt., set of 12 .... 1,980.00

Union Porcelain Works, Brooklyn, New York, china, "trompe l'oeil" technique, clam shell form holding four realistic oyster shell wells & single seashell sauce well separated by molded shellfish & seaweed, ca. 1880, 8½ x 6¾" (ILLUS.) ....75.00 to 85.00

PARIAN

Parian is unglazed porcelain in the biscuit stage, and takes its name from its resemblance to Parian marble used for statuary. Parian wares were made in this country and abroad through much of the last century and continue to be made.

Bust of Mendelssohn, 5½" h. $90.00

Bust of Rev. C.H. Spurgeon, Robinson & Leadbeater, dated 1878, 13" h. 140.00

Bust of Queen Victoria, wearing lace mantle, lace gown, jewelry & sash below which hangs a medallion of Prince Albert, on waisted socle base above a fluted columnar pedestal w/classical motifs on an octagonal plinth, Robinson & Leadbeater, ca. 1887, overall 27" h. (minor firing cracks) 3,300.00

Figure of Hygeia, goddess on throne, w/brass snake, Hellman, Austria, 8" h. 125.00

Figure of man, "Grape Harvester," Robinson & Leadbeater, late 19th c., 9" h. 90.00

Figure of Rebecca at the Well, outstretched arms holding urn, 9" h. 55.00

Figure of a mother w/child on her shoulders, Art Union of Great Britain, 19th c., 14" h. 200.00

Figure group, owls sitting on branch, "Match Making," rectangular base, registry mark for 1871, 4½ x 5½", 7" h. 250.00

PARIS & OLD PARIS

Old Paris Figure Group

China known by the generic name of Paris and Old Paris was made by several Parisian factories from the 18th through the 19th century; some of it is marked and some is not. Much of it was handsomely decorated.

Bowl, 8" d., gilt stepped foot & rim, pastel marbleized exterior ground painted in brown w/various soldiers & a princess within gothic niches, ca. 1820 .... $880.00

Cornucopia-vase, coral handle & foot, fluted, gilt trim, ca. 1820, 4" h. on marbled wood stand 550.00

Figural mantel clock, eight-day movement w/a white enameled porcelain dial w/Roman numerals, indistinctly inscribed "? Debain a la Haye," set in a scroll-molded rococo porcelain case decorated w/an oval panel enameled w/Cupid in clouds reserved on a *bleu-de-roi* ground enriched w/gilt scrolling foliage & highlighted in white, yellow & puce w/gilt, the case surmounted by a figural group molded w/a young woman on the arm of a soldier, standing on a brown & green base molded w/tree-stumps w/applied leaves, mid-19th c., 18" h. together w/a serpentine carved giltwood plinth base 522.50

Figure group, white biscuit maiden holding a gilt shell & seated next to an urn & behind a green glazed seated greyhound, both raised on a cobalt blue & gilt rectangular plinth, formed as an inkstand, ca. 1820, 7¼" h. (ILLUS.) 1,320.00

Plates, 9¼" d., center w/basket or vase of flowers on ledge, within dark blue border richly gilt w/trefoils, quatrefoils & trellis pattern between gilt bands, ca. 1820, pr. (some minor retouching to enamels)..................... 605.00

Potpourri vase & pierced cover, rococo scroll-molded form, lower part w/gilt scrolls & florals on claret ground, cover w/alternate purple & white bands painted w/flowers, on foliage-molded & green rockwork base, ca. 1840, 12¼" h. 825.00

Paris Porcelain Vases

Vases, 11" h., campana form w/elongated neck & everted rim, decorated w/a flower-filled basket & sprigs within gilt C-scroll & flowerhead borders, the neck w/elaborate floral bisque bands, square black slate plinth base, second half 19th c., pr. (ILLUS.)... 935.00

Vases, 12" h., oviform w/two gilt winged lion form handles on spreading circular foot & square base, gilt neck, panel depicting a young lad in the street, green ground w/gilt bands of neoclassical motifs, ca. 1830, pr. 1,980.00

Vases, 14¾" h., baluster form, h.p. grey standing classical figure, orchid glaze w/gold banding, mid-19th c., pr. 357.50

Vases, 22" h., flattened baluster form, painted w/scenes of a mother, daughter & child in a landscape within a blue & gold border, 19th c., pr.....................1,980.00

PAUL REVERE POTTERY

Saturday Evening Girls Bowl & Plate

This pottery was established in Boston, Mass., in 1906, by a group of philanthropists seeking to establish better conditions for underprivileged young girls of the area. Edith Brown served as supervisor of the small "Saturday Evening Girls Club" pottery operation which was moved, in 1912, to a house close to the Old North Church where Paul Revere's signal lanterns had been placed. The wares were mostly hand decorated in mineral colors and both sgraffito and molded decorations were employed. Although it became popular, it was never a profitable operation and always depended on financial contributions to operate. After the death of Edith Brown in 1932, the pottery foundered and finally closed in 1942.

Bowl, 3 x 7½", undulating shape, black glaze, marked "S.E.G." (Saturday Evening Girls) $90.00

Bowl, 5½" d., rolled sides, w/flower frog, yellow, marked "S.E.G."...................... 40.00

Bowl, 5½" d., green w/band of white roosters facing each other, interior motto "Harriet - early to bed and early to rise makes a

child healthy, wealthy and wise," marked "S.E.G." & dated 1909 (ILLUS. left) 605.00
Bowl, 6" d., white w/yellow roosters facing each other, marked "S.E.G." & dated 1912 .... 880.00
Bowl, 8¼" d., olive green, marked "S.E.G., 714 L.M." 35.00

Saturday Evening Girls Bowl

Bowl, 11½" d., 5" h., repeating trees on blue & brown band, green ground, marked "S.E.G." & dated 1914 (ILLUS.) 1,870.00
Cereal bowl & underplate, rabbit borders, mauve pink ground, marked "S.E.G.," 2 pcs........... 250.00
Plate, 6 3/8" d., blue band w/white hen & chick border, motto "O Don' bother me said the hen with one chick," marked "S.E.G." & dated 1912 (ILLUS. right) 1,320.00
Plates, 7¾" d., white band w/initials "H.O.S.," centering rooster medallion on forest green ground, 1929, set of 4 .... 660.00
Plate, 8½" d., eight pigs w/curly tails on brown, yellow & green border, marked "S.E.G." & dated, 1910...........................1,540.00
Plate, 8½" d., pine cone decor, marked "S.E.G." & dated 250.00
Salt dip, grey w/yellow & black lines around rim, marked "S.E.G.," 1¾" d. 35.00
Tea tile, white goose w/elongated neck against stylized green & blue landscape, blue border, marked "S.E.G.," ca. 1918, 5½" 275.00

PETERS & REED

In 1897, John D. Peters and Adam Reed formed a partnership to produce flower pots in Zanesville, Ohio. Formally incorporated as Peters and Reed in 1901, this type of production was the mainstay until after 1907 when they gradually expanded into the art pottery field. Frank Ferrell, a former designer at the Weller Pottery, developed the "Moss Aztec" line while associated with Peters and Reed and other art lines followed. Though unmarked, attribution is not difficult once familiar with the various lines. In 1921, Peters and Reed became Zane Pottery which continued in production until 1941.

Bowl, 4" d., 2" h., Moss Aztec line, dragonfly decoration $20.00
Candlesticks, Black Mirror patt., pr.............................. 18.00
Invalid server, grape & leaf garland around spout, glossy brown glaze 27.00
Jug, bulbous, mottled light & dark brown glaze w/grapes & leaves in colored relief, 6½" h. 68.00
Pitcher, 17" h., grape & leaf decoration, brown glaze 150.00
Vase, 6 x 4", hexagonal, floral medallion decoration, brown glaze 45.00
Vase, 6" h., Landsun Line 22.00
Vase, 7¾" h., Moss Aztec line, large embossed flowers, signed "Ferrell"........................ 48.00
Wall pocket, Egyptian Ware, green glaze 75.00
Wall pocket, figural Art Nouveau nude, Moss Aztec line, 9 x 7" 55.00
Wall pocket, figural Egyptian man, green matte glaze............... 50.00

PEWABIC POTTERY

Pewabic Vase

Mary Chase Perry (Stratton) and Horace J. Caulkins were partners in this Detroit, Michigan pottery. Established in 1903, Pewabic Pottery evolved from their Revelation Pottery, "Pewabic" meaning "clay with copper color" in the language of Michigan's Chippewa Indians. Caulkins attended to the clay for-

mulas and Mary Perry Stratton was the artistic creator of forms & glaze formulas, eventually developing a wide range of colors for her finely textured glazes. The pottery's reputation for fine wares and architectural tiles enabled it to survive the depression years of the 1930's. After Caulkins died in 1923, Mrs. Stratton continued to be active in the pottery until her death, at age ninety-four, in 1961. Her contributions to the art pottery field are numerous.

Charger, mottled metallic green w/blue rim, signed, 15¾" d. $325.00
Cup & saucer, plum over tan glaze, artist-signed 105.00
Tile, relief-molded Oriental dolphin in burgundy & turquoise iridescent glaze, 5" sq. 120.00
Tile, owl decoration, 3 x 3" 55.00
Vase, 2½" h., red & green iridescent glaze 200.00
Vase, 3¾ x 4½", squatty bulbous form, sky blue & black speckled glaze, signed 165.00
Vase, 4½ x 2¾", bulbous w/cylindrical neck & flared rim, iridescent blue & gold flambe' glaze, signed 440.00
Vase, 5¾" h., 6½" w., closed-bowl form w/bulbous body & collar rim, rich, iridescent grey-blue flambe' glaze, impressed mark (ILLUS.) ... 715.00
Vase, 6" h., orange semi-gloss drip glaze over brown clay 140.00
Vase, 6½" h., bulbous, heavy mottled orange & khaki glaze over brown clay, lower part unglazed, glossy glazed khaki interior 265.00
Vase, 9¾" h., 6½" d., flared w/bulbous top, carved stylized flowers & leaves, flowing turquoise matte glaze 1,540.00
Vase, 15½" h., 6" d., bottle form, textured iridescent gold glaze over 2/3 of its surface, dripping unevenly over a smooth, uniform midnight blue iridescent glaze 1,430.00

PHOENIX BIRD or FLYING TURKEY

The phoenix bird, a symbol of immortality and spiritual rebirth, has been handed down through Egyptian mythology as a bird that consumed itself by fire after 500 years and then rose again, renewed, from its ashes. This bird has been used to decorate Japanese porcelain designed for export for more than 100 years. The pattern incorporates a blue design of the bird, variously known as the "Flying Phoenix," the "Flying Turkey" or the "Ho-o," stamped on a white ground. It became popular with collectors because there was an abundant supply since the ware was produced for a long period of time. Pieces can be found marked with Japanese characters, with a "Nippon" mark, or a "Made in Japan" or "Occupied Japan" mark. Though there are several variations to the pattern and border, we have lumped them together since values seem to be quite comparable. A word of caution to the collectors, Phoenix Bird pattern is still being produced.

Phoenix Bird Salt & Pepper Shakers

Bowl, cereal, Phoenix Bird $7.00
Chocolate pot, Phoenix Bird (replaced lid) 80.00
Creamer, Phoenix Bird ..... 10.00 to 15.00
Creamer & sugar bowl, Phoenix Bird, pr. 45.00
Cup, demitasse, Phoenix Bird 6.00
Cup & saucer, Phoenix Bird 12.00
Cup & saucer, Phoenix Bird, marked "Japan" 16.00
Cups & saucers, Flying Turkey, set of 5 ..... 24.50
Dinner service for nine: plates, cups, saucers, creamer, sugar bowl & oval & round vegetable bowls; Flying Turkey, 31 pcs. 300.00
Egg cups, Phoenix Bird, set of 4 ..... 35.00
Plate, 7½" d., Phoenix Bird 8.00
Plate, 8" d., Flying Turkey ... 10.00 to 15.00
Plate, 8½" d., Phoenix Bird, marked "Noritake" 16.00
Plate, 9¾" d., Phoenix Bird 12.00
Plate, dinner, 10" d., Phoenix Bird, marked "Noritake" 30.00
Platter, 12¼ x 8½", Phoenix Bird .. 35.00
Rice bowl, Phoenix Bird 10.00
Salt & pepper shakers, Phoenix Bird, pr. (ILLUS.) 20.00
Sauce dish, Flying Turkey, 6" d. 12.00
Saucer, Phoenix Bird 4.00
Teacup, Phoenix Bird 6.00
Teapot, cov., Phoenix Bird, 7" w., 2¾" h. 60.00
Tea tile, Phoenix Bird 45.00
Tumbler, Phoenix Bird, 2½" h. 15.00

PICKARD

Pickard, Inc., making fine china today in Antioch, Illinois, was founded as a china decorating company by Wilder A. Pickard in Chicago in 1894. The company now makes its own blanks but once bought them from other potteries, primarily from the Havilands and others in Limoges, France.

Basket, center gold handle & gold interior, exterior w/gold tracery on mauve ground, 5¼" w., 4" h. $75.00

Berry set: 9" d. master bowl & four 6" d. sauce dishes; ornate gold borders, h.p. clover on white ground, Limoges, France blank, 5 pcs. 115.00

Bowl, 8½" d., footed, four large scallops, bulging sides, gooseberries interior & exterior, gold trim, artist-signed 145.00

Card plate, heart-shaped, h.p. floral decoration w/gold, 1910 mark, 5 x 4" 55.00

Celery tray, open handled, overall gold-etched decoration, 11" l. 40.00

Chocolate pot, cov., floral decoration, artist-signed, 12" h. 175.00

Coffeepot, cov., demitasse, Christmas Poinsettia decoration, artist-signed, 1910 mark 195.00

Creamer & sugar bowl, h.p. fruit decoration w/gold bands, pr. 250.00

Creamer & sugar bowl, bisque finish, Dutch girl decoration, artist-signed, 3¾ x 4¾", pr. 110.00

Cup & saucer, demitasse, gold & blue bands, gold handle & interior, embossed florals, ca. 1919 .... 35.00

Ewer, bulbous, green matte finish w/gold grapes & trim, artist-signed, 1905 mark 195.00

Fruit bowl, footed, currants, leaves & vines, deep scrolled gold rim, Limoges blank, artist-signed, 1895-98 mark, 9½" d., 4½" h. 285.00

Mayonnaise dish w/attached underplate, h.p. day lilies, gold border 165.00

Pitcher, juice, 5" h., 4" top d., ornate gold on handle & rim, poppies & leaves on cream ground, artist-signed, Limoges blank 215.00

Plate, 5½" sq., gazebo, trees & moonlit landscape scene, matte finish 149.00

Plate, 6¾" d., goldenrod & daisy decoration, wide gold rim, artist-signed 55.00

Plate, 7¾" d., flower decoration in iridescent colors w/gold & red tracery, artist-signed 55.00

Plate, 8¼" d., scalloped, pink, florals in gold ovals, gold leaves & trim on ivory ground, artist-signed 55.00

Plate, 8½" d., moon over lake & trees landscape scene, blue ground 150.00

Plate, 8½" d., violets & gold trim, artist-signed 62.50

Plates, 11" d., decorated w/6" garden scenes, artist-signed, set of 12 different scenes 3,995.00

Salt & pepper shakers, gold band w/clusters of pink & blue flowers on a mother-of-pearl ground, 1910, pr. 45.00

Syrup pitcher, cov., w/matching underplate, Art Nouveau shape around the gold band rim, small groupings of pastel flowers & foliage w/gold trim, mostly white ground, Limoges blank, 5" h., 2 pcs. 80.00

Tea set: cov. teapot, cov. sugar bowl, creamer & tray; each w/overall gold-etched design, 4 pcs. 225.00

Tray, rectangular, decorated w/violets & gold border, 8½ x 4½" 42.50

Vase, 6½" h., Deserted Garden scene on gold ground, artist-signed 195.00

Vase, 7" h., garden columns w/bridge, moon & trees landscape scene, gold handles, artist-signed 250.00

Vase, 7½" h., harbor scene w/four sailboats in background, artist-signed 175.00

Vase, 8" h., wide top w/royal blue stripe decorated w/Phoenix birds & gold dotting, narrow black & white stripe on base w/another wide stripe of royal blue below, heavy gold scrolling, artist-signed 235.00

Vase, 17½" h., tall cylinder swelling towards top w/wide mouth, arched scroll handles at neck, decorated w/large bright red poinsettias, artist-signed, 1905-10 .... 640.00

Vase, 9¾" h., curved gold handles & also gold trim w/red tracery, pastel iridescent floral decoration 130.00

Vegetable bowl, cov., Cinderella patt. 55.00

Whiskey jug, w/stopper, ears of Indian corn on shaded ground, artist-signed, 6" w., 6½" h. 230.00

PICTORIAL SOUVENIRS *"Special Focus"*

Souvenir Plates and Related Wares

by Arene Burgess

Although some souvenir plates are now over one hundred years old, few collectors seem to be taking them seriously. Only two books have been written on the subject, and few in-depth articles have appeared in the collector magazines. Many antiques collectors look upon these plates as a poor imitation of the early nineteenth century Staffordshire wares which were studied and collected as far back as the 1890's. Except for the border treatments the two types of plates are really nothing alike. The early Staffordshire pieces were made to be used. Nearly all were made for dinner or tea sets. They were made cheaply, meant for the emerging middle class of the young United States. The later (souvenir) plates were unabashedly commercial. Each city and/or scenic plate was designed to show how "up-to-date" or beautiful that particular place was. They also were cheap and meant to sell as an impulse item. Most cost thirty cents or less. Unlike the earlier Staffordshire ware, these pieces were not meant to be used. They were to be displayed on a plate rail or in a china cabinet; evidence that some member of the family had "traveled."

The first true souvenir plates were made by Wedgwood who, incidentally, did not make the "old" blue wares. All were scenes of Eastern scenic places such as the Great Stone Face. Davenport was also among the earliest to make "picture" plates. Their plates, however, were "Western" scenes of places such as Indianapolis and St. Louis. The souvenir plate craze really got underway in 1893 when the Rowland and Marsellus Importing Company of New York commissioned Hancock (and some other English potteries) to make views commemorating the World's Columbian Exposition in Chicago. The most popular piece was the large tankard-type pitcher depicting the exploits of Christopher Columbus. Wedgwood also made plates for this event. They were a rather uninspiring pale pink or blue with views of the Fair buildings.

In the early 1890's, the Jones, McDuffee, and Stratton Importing Company of Boston had commissioned Wedgwood to make small square calendar tiles with a view on the back. These were "give-aways." The firm was so impressed with their popularity that they asked Wedgwood to make a series of blue plates with scenes of Boston and vicinity. The first ones date to 1895. By 1910 there were over one hundred different views (from Maine to California). The company continued to import plates until 1955 when they merged with another firm and stopped importing commemoratives. Jones, McDuffee, and Stratton also used items made by Adams, Wood, and others.

Two other firms also imported Wedgwood views. They were Mellon and Hewes of Hartford, Connecticut and the Van Heusen Charles Company of Albany, New York. The early Wedgwood plates all had the same border — a full-blown cabbage rose design taken from an old Staffordshire pattern. They were all a deep, rich blue and were approximately nine inches in diameter. Later views were sometimes larger and also had different borders. In the 1930's college views became very popular. They were made in sets, generally six or twelve plates, each showing a different campus building. Unlike many other firms, Wedgwood always marked each piece with the firm name and date of manufacture (in code). This code can be found in any book about English ceramics.

Wedgwood's most aggressive competitor in distributing the souvenir plates was the Rowland and Marsellus Company of New York, New York. This firm's method of backstamping led most people to believe that "R and M" was an English pottery. They were only importers. Even today some price guides (and writers) continue to perpetuate this myth. The earliest plates had a fruit and flower border design which the firm continued to use during the life of the business. Rowland and Marsellus also introduced the rolled edge plate. Generally there would be seven equal-sized views covering the edge with a large central view. They also used a rimless coupe shape design. Just about every city in the United States and Canada was commemorated, as well as historic sites, statues, schools, churches, etc. The company evidently ceased operation about 1933 which is the last year their name appears in the New York City business directory. In addition to the plates, the firm imported cups and saucers, tumblers, pitchers, vases and platters. They also used colors such as green, black, brown and multicolor decorations.

Beginning in the 1930's the Jonroth Importing Company of Peoria, Illinois was the leading importer of English souvenir plates. The company actually dates back to 1909. At that time they were importing miniature porcelain novelties made in Germany. For their English wares the firm used Adams, Ridgways, British Anchor and others. In 1970 the firm moved their headquarters to Florida and as of 1980 were still active in the importing business.

The short-lived firm of Frank Beardmore and Company (1904-1913) made an interesting line of souvenir ware. Their special design was an eight inch plate with seven equal-sized views separated by scrolls and flowers. This design was later copied by several other firms.

Royal Doulton also made a line of souvenir plates. They are probably best remembered for their Gibson Girl series.

The prestigious Royal Worcester firm made a few souvenir plates in the Teen years for the "carriage" trade. The known examples are all of St. Augustine, Florida.

The leading importer of blue souvenir plates today is the ENCO firm based in New York. Other importers and their dates of operation are listed at the end of this article.

Several American firms also made souvenir plates. The most important one was the Buffalo Pottery Company of Buffalo, New York. Another American company which made a large number of commemorative and souvenir-type plates was the Vernon Kilns of Vernon, California. The company was in business from 1930 to 1955.

Two English firms, Crown Ducal and Johnson Brothers, made dinner sets with historic views. They are often mistaken for souvenirs when an odd piece turns up. The Crown Ducal set called "Colonial Times" was made in 1932 to commemorate the 200th anniversary of the birth of George Washington. Each piece has the same border with four views — an Indian on horseback, the Mayflower, a Pilgrim couple and Plymouth Rock. Each major piece has a different center scene. The Johnson Brothers set was made about 1950 and was called "Historic America." Each scene is of an event in American history.

The Homer Laughlin Company of Newell, West Virginia, made a dinnerware set in 1942. The pattern name was "Historical America." It also showed scenes of significance in American history.

Much harder to find than plates are platters and bowls (rare), cups and saucers, tumblers, sugars and creamers. The majority of such pieces will be backstamped by Rowland and Marsellus, although Wedgwood did make cups and saucers and a few platters.

The following lists are of English and American manufacturers and their dates of operation. Another list includes American importers as sometimes only their mark appears on some of the earlier pieces.

English Manufacturers and Their Dates of Operation:

William Adams and Company - 1789 to present
Ambassador Ware, Simpson's Limited - 1944 to present
Frank Beardmore and Company - 1904 to 1913
Bedford Works (Ridgways Ltd.) - 1920 to 1962
Sampson Bridgwood and Son, Ltd., Anchor Pottery - 1804 to ?
British Anchor Pottery Company, Ltd. - 1884 to present
Cauldon Ltd. - 1905 to 1962
Coalport Ltd. - 1795 to present
W.T. Copeland and Sons, Ltd. - 1847 to present
Crown Ducal - 1916 to 1975
Davenport - 1793 to 1897
(Royal) Doulton - 1882 to present
Wallis Gimson and Co. - 1884 to 1890
Johnson Brothers - 1899 to present
John Maddock and Sons - 1855 to ?
Alfred Meakin Ltd. - 1875 to present
J. and G. Meakin - 1851 to present
Minton - 1793 to present (now part of Royal Doulton)
Ridgways - 1879 to present
Royal Crown Staffordshire - 1952 to 1957
Royal Fenton (no dates or location found)
Royal Staffordshire Pottery - 1885 to ?
Royal Worcester - 1862 to present
Stoke Grimwades, Ltd. - 1900 to 1960's
Swinnerton's Ltd. - 1900 to ?
Upper Hanley Pottery Company, Ltd. - 1895 to 1910
Josiah Wedgwood and Sons - 1759 to present
F. Winkle and Company - 1890 to 1931
Wood and Sons - 1861 to present

American Manufacturers and Their Dates:

Edwin Bennett Pottery Company, Baltimore, Maryland - 1890 to ?
Buffalo Pottery, Buffalo, New York - 1901 to present

Carr China Company, Grafton, West Virginia - 1916 to 1952
East Liverpool Pottery Company, East Liverpool, Ohio - 1843 to 1911
Glasgow Pottery Company, Trenton, New Jersey - 1863 to 1908
Hall China Company, East Liverpool, Ohio - 1903 to present
Hampshire Pottery, Keene, New Hampshire - 1871 to 1916
George S. Harker and Company, East Liverpool, Ohio - 1890 to ?
Kettlespring Kilns, Alliance, Ohio - presently in business
LaBelle China, Wheeling, West Virginia - 1879 to 1900
Lamberton-Scammell, Trenton, New Jersey - 1893 to 1954
Homer Laughlin China Company, Newell, West Virginia - 1874 to present
Lenox China Company, Trenton, New Jersey - 1889 to present
Limoges China Company, Sebring, Ohio - 1894 to 1928?
Thomas Maddock and Sons, Trenton, New Jersey - 1869 to 1893
D.E. McNicol and Company, East Liverpool, Ohio - 1892 to 1954
Mellor and Company, Trenton, New Jersey - 1884 to ?
Mercer Pottery Company, Trenton, New Jersey - 1868 to ?
Pope-Gosser, Coshocton, Ohio - 1902-1958
Sebring Pottery Company, Trenton, New Jersey - 1887 to 1930's
Shenango Pottery, Trenton, New Jersey - 1955 to present
(formerly Lamberton-Scammell)
Sterling China Company, East Liverpool, Ohio - 1890 to 1920
Steubenville Pottery Company, Steubenville, Ohio - 1879 to 1900
Vernon Kilns, Vernon, California - 1930 to 1955
Wellsville China Company, Wellsville, Ohio - 1879 to ?

American Importers of Souvenir Wares:

Bawo and Dotter, New York, New York - 1864 to 1910
A.C. Bosselman and Company, New York, New York - 1904 to 1930
George Bowman and Company, New York and Cleveland - 1888 to 1932
ENCO National, New York, New York - 1909 to present
French Mitchell Woodbury Company - 1901 to 1905
Jonroth (John Roth and Company), Peoria, Illinois - 1909 to 1970
Jones, McDuffee, and Stratton, Boston, Massachusetts - 1810 to 1955
Mellon & Hewes, Hartford, Connecticut
Rowland and Marsellus, New York, New York - 1893 to 1933
Van Heusen Charles Company, Albany, New York - 1900 to 1930?
C.E. Wheelock and Company, South Bend, Indiana and Peoria, Illinois - 1888 to 1971
Wright, Tyndale and Van Roden, Philadelphia, Pennsylvania - 1818 to 1960

ABOUT THE AUTHOR

Arene Burgess is a long-time collector of souvenir wares and a well-known authority in this field. In 1978 she authored the book, "Souvenir Plates – A Collector's Guide," which has become a standard reference. Mrs. Burgess has a few copies of this book still available and interested persons may contact her at Route 1, Box 26, Bethalto, IL 62010. Please include a stamped, self-addressed envelope with all inquiries.

For those wishing to learn more about the collecting of souvenir wares there is a collecting club. The Souvenir China Collectors Society, Box 562, Great Barrington, MA 01230, also publishes a newsletter for members, "Souvenir Collectors News."

Illustrated Listings:

The following listings are arranged alphabetically by the name of the manufacturer or importing firm.

Adams Souvenir Series: "Robert L. Stevenson Cottage, Saranac Lake, N.Y.;" 7¾" d., bright blue, imported by Jones, McDuffee, and Stratton, 1920's (very collectible, though late; not made in as large a quantity as many items of this period) $12.00

Bawo and Dotter (importer): "Souvenir of Jacksonville, Florida;" 10" d., bright blue, ca. 1915. Archetypical; a plate of this type was made for almost every city of any consequence in the U.S.. The center scene is always a courthouse or city hall. The surrounding scenes were generally of schools, churches, parks, etc. 30.00

Beardmore and Company (imported by Bowman): "Balanced Rock, Garden of the Gods, Colo.;" 7¾" d., slate blue, ca. 1910. Stylized tulips border was a "trademark" of Beardmore, although sometimes used by others. (Note: value is only for Beardmore examples, not later imitators) 16.00

A.C. Bosselman and Co. (importers), made by Ridgways: "Souvenir of Plymouth, Mass.;" 10" d., bright blue, ca. 1910. Center scene is taken from an old print. Lots of detail, good impression. (Early Bosselman examples are not com-

mon) 45.00

Similar later examples 30.00

British Anchor Pottery: "Snowball Dining Room in Mammoth Cave, Ky.," Picturesque Mammoth Cave National Park, Kentucky; 10" d., deep blue, ca. 1940. Late example of a border that was popular for more than thirty years. It is generally called "fruit and flower" 20.00

Buffalo Pottery: The White House, Washington; 10¼" d., medium blue, ca. 1915. Many of these were made and it is one of the easier Buffalo commemoratives to find 40.00

Caulden, Ltd.: Admiral George Dewey, hero of the Spanish-American War; 10¾" d., bright blue, ca. 1900 . . . . 35.00

If the same piece is back-stamped, "Souvenir of the dinner given for Adm. and Mrs. Dewey by the Union League Club of Brooklyn" 80.00

W.T. Copeland and Sons: John Alden and Priscilla(?), a Pilgrim couple; 10½" d., bright blue, no date, probably about 1920. The gadroon border rim is associated with Spode-Copeland 40.00

Crown Ducal: "The Spirit of '76;" 10¼" d., light blue, ca. 1930.

Made for Sternes of Boston and *not* part of Crown Ducal dinner set 15.00

Davenport, Ltd.: Compton Hill Water Tower, St. Louis, Missouri; 10" d., soft blue, ca. 1900 or earlier. This is a scarce, early souvenir plate . . 45.00

French, Mitchell, Woodbury and Co. (importer): "Yankee Doodle, Spirit of '76;" 10½" d., bright blue, ca.

1903, made by Adams. French, Mitchell, et al. was in business for less than five years. This is an interesting mark to look for 35.00
Later examples 25.00

(Royal) Doulton: Mt. Vernon; (imported by Bowman), 10" d., deep blue, ca. 1905. Many different views were made with this border. Also note the railing and side porch on the building. They have been removed. Details such as this sometimes help to date unmarked plates 40.00

Jonroth (John Roth and Company) (importers): "Lincoln's New Salem, Illinois;" 10" d., bright blue, ca. 1965. This piece was made by Adams but many other firms were used by this company 6.00

Minton's: 200th Anniversary of the Town of Salem, Massachusetts; 10½" d., deep blue, ca. 1920. This plate has everything — color, de-

sign and a limited issue for a specific event 50.00

Pope-Gosser: Lafayette, Indiana, 100th Anniversary; 10" d., bright blue, 1925, semi-porcelain. Anyone collecting American-made views would consider this a cornerstone of the collection. It carries the poem, "On the Banks of the Wabash," and was designed by a Lafayette resident 40.00

Ridgways: Martha Washington, from an original miniature by Robertson; 10" d., deep blue, ca. 1920. It was probably part of a series . . 40.00

Rowland and Marsellus (importers): DeSoto's Discovery of the Mississippi River; 10" d., deep blue, ca. 1910 . . . . 45.00

Rowland and Marsellus: Lewis and Clark Centennial, Portland, Oregon; 10" d., deep blue, 1905 . . . . . 55.00

Royal Worcester: "Old City Gates," St. Augustine, Florida; 10" d., bright blue, 1915. The dates on Royal Worcester items were indicated by a peculiar system of dots and circles 50.00

Van Heusen Charles Company (importer): New Capitol, Albany, New York; 9½" d., blue, floral border, made by Ridgways, 1933 (Not Illus.) 35.00

Van Heusen Charles Company (importers): Residence of Major-General Philip Schuyler; 9¼" d., deep blue, ca. 1920, made by Wedgwood, one of a set of nineteen, all with views of Albany, New York 25.00

Wedgwood: Old Town Square, Plymouth, Massachusetts; 8" d., medium blue, ca. 1880. The first Wedgwood souvenir plates, about eight different views, were of this style and size. Also made was a pitcher with a view of "Old Man of the Mountain" 35.00

Wedgwood: Ruins of Old Spanish Mission, New Smyra, Florida;

9¼" d., deep blue, ca. 1930. Prototype of Jones, McDuffee and Stratton, importers. Note the cabbage rose border. It is decorated with rich color 30.00

Wheelock (importer): Lincoln's Home, Springfield, Illinois; 9" d., bright blue, ca. 1910. Many Lincoln plates were issued about 1909-1910 to commemorate the one hundredth anniversary of his birth 20.00

F. Winkle and Company: "Souvenir of Gettysburg, General Mead's Headquarters;" 10" d., deep blue, ca. 1930 .... 30.00

Ye Old Historical Pottery: "Souvenir of Plymouth;" 10" d., bright blue, undated but probably post-World War II, made by British Anchor ... 12.00

Related Wares:

Beardmore and Company, (imported by Bowman): "Souvenir of Salt Lake City;" tumbler, 3¾" tall, slate blue, ca. 1910. Tumblers are not common although quite a few were made 25.00

Deep blue examples by "R and M" are considerably more ....40.00 and up

Crown Ducal: Colonial Times patt.; teapot, Boston Tea Party scene;

teal blue, 1932, lid finial is head of Pilgrim man. Colonial Times dinner set was also made in pink 65.00

Rowland and Marsellus: creamer and sugar, Plymouth, Mass., Pilgrim scenes (Plymouth Rock, etc.); bright blue, ca. 1905, the set 85.00

Rowland and Marsellus: cup and saucer, souvenir of Minneapolis, Minnesota; deep blue, ca. 1910... 60.00

Rowland and Marsellus: World's Columbian Exposition (Chicago World's Fair), 1893; pitcher, made in blue, green, and sepia with lustre. This was probably the first item imported by Rowland and Marsellus; deep blue, 85.00; green, 70.00; sepia 60.00

Rowland and Marsellus: "Plymouth in 1822;" platter, 13 x 17", deep blue, ca. 1905.................. 125.00

Rowland and Marsellus: vase, St. Louis World's Fair (Louisiana Purchase Exposition), 1904; deep blue. This has a mate, similar except it has one handle and a spout 75.00

Arthur J. Wilkinson: Capitol, Washington, D.C.; bowl, exceedingly rare, 9¾" d., 3" deep, dark blue, ca. 1907 .... 75.00

(End of Special Focus)

MISCELLANEOUS

Ashtray, "Aerial Bridge, Duluth, Minnesota," star-shaped, Germany, 5" w. $35.00
Bell, figural girl in bonnet w/green dress, W. H. Goss 22.00
Candy dish, "Washington D.C.," h.p. center scene of Capitol Building within a dotted framework superimposed on cherry blossoms & branches, stylized landscape borders, blue IC Nippon mark, 6½" l. 65.00
Creamer, "Bushkill Falls, Pennsylvania" scene, Germany 10.00
Creamer, w/seal of Windsor Castle, W. H. Goss 17.00
Cup & saucer, demitasse, "Bradford Academy, Haverhill, Massachusetts," pink lustre 20.00
Cup & saucer, demitasse, "Miles City, Montana," ranch scene 40.00
Dish, "Congress Springs Monument, Saratoga, New York," Wheelock, Austria, 7½" d. 12.50
Dish, "YMCA Building, Temple, Texas," scalloped shell, pierced, made in Germany for the Fair, Temple, 6" 22.50
Model of Robert Burns' Cottage, Ayr, night light, W. H. Goss, 6" .. 140.00
Model of First and Last House in England, W. H. Goss 130.00
Model of Huer's House, Newquay, W. H. Goss 190.00
Model of Manx Cottage, W. H. Goss 100.00
Model of a skull, "Alas poor Yorick," W. H. Goss 110.00
Sauce dish, "Randolph-Macon Woman's College, Lynchburg, Virginia" scene, 6" d. 12.50
Sugar bowl, open, "St. Joseph, Michigan, Pavilion," Germany, made for Drake & Wallace 25.00
Toothpick holder, "Adams Memorial Building, Derry, New Hampshire," cobalt blue, rectangular 15.00
Tumbler, "Detroit, Michigan," shades of blue, red, green & pink w/gold trim, Victoria, Austria 22.00
Vase, 4½" h., "Incline Railway, Duluth, Minnesota," Germany 28.00

PISGAH FOREST

Walter Stephen experimented with making pottery shortly after 1900 with his parents in Tennessee. After their deaths in 1910, he eventually moved to the foot of Mt. Pisgah in North Carolina where he became a partner of C.P. Ryman. Together they built a kiln and a shop but this partnership was dissolved in 1916. During 1920 Stephen again began to experiment with pottery and by 1926 had his own pottery and equipment. Pieces are usually marked and may also be signed "W. Stephen" and dated. Walter Stephen died in 1961 but work at the pottery still continues, although on a part-time basis.

Pisgah Forest Vase

Beaker, blue & plum glaze, 5¼" h. $40.00
Beaker, brown & green glaze, 6" h. 40.00
Bowl, 7" d., 2½" h., cameo-like white relief pioneer scenes all around 280.00
Candlesticks, handled, green glaze, pr. 30.00
Creamer, pink glaze, 3¾" h. 15.00
Creamer & sugar bowl, maroon & turquoise glaze, pr. 22.00
Jar, cov., turquoise glaze, signed "Stephen," dated 1941, 4½" h. 20.00
Mug, cameo-like white relief on sky blue ground, 3½" h. 195.00
Mug, cameo-like white relief designs, signed "Stephen" 210.00
Mug, cameo-like white relief scene of dancing couple on platform 285.00
Teapot, cov., cameo-like white relief scenes of Indians, teepees, fiddler & pioneers, turquoise & moss green glaze, dated 1931 .... 720.00
Vase, 3" h., blue, green & pink glaze 30.00
Vase, 3" h., frothy turquoise glaze, dated 1936 .... 38.00
Vase, 3" h., light green glaze, dated 1941 .... 30.00
Vase, 4¼" h., squat, bulbous, cameo-like white relief scene of covered wagon pulled by oxen on matte olive ground around center, high-gloss green glaze around base, signed "Stephen" (ILLUS.) 330.00
Vase, 4½" h., bulbous, brown glossy glaze, dated 1933 .... 50.00
Vase, 4½" h., 6" d., white to tan glaze w/crystals, signed "Stephen," dated 1946 .... 105.00

Vase, 5" h., flared, turquoise to plum glaze 35.00

Vase, 5½" h., buff classic style, plum drip interior crystalline glaze, plum exterior glaze, signed "Stephen, 49" 125.00

Vase, 6¼" h., green exterior glaze, yellow interior glaze, dated 1950 .... 22.50

Vase, 7" h., Chinese Crackle glaze 75.00

Vase, 8" h., flared top, crystalline glaze 125.00

Vase, 9" h., navy blue glaze, dated 1928 .... 75.00

Vase, 9½" h., Chinese Crackle glaze, signed "Stephen" 65.00

Vase, pink w/molded flowers, experimental glaze, signed "Nancy Jones," dated 1940 .... 335.00

POT LIDS

Collectible pot lids are decorated ceramic lids for commercial pots and jars originally containing soaps, shaving creams, hair pomade, and so on. The best-known lids were made by F. & R. Pratt in Fenton, England, from about the middle of the 19th century.

"Bazin's Premium Shaving Cream, Philadelphia," black transfer, w/jar, 3" d. (small chips & large chip inside flange) $275.00

Benjamin Franklin profile bust portrait center, "Jules Hauel Perfumer, 120 Chestnut St., Philadelphia," purple transfer, w/jar, 3½" d. (small edge chips) 330.00

Benjamin Franklin profile bust portrait center, "Jules Hauel Perfumer, 120 Chestnut St., Philadelphia," red transfer, w/jar, 3½" d. (base chips) 225.00

Cow standing center, "Beef Marrow, Jules Hauel, Perfumer, Philadelphia," black transfer, w/jar, 3" d. (small edge chips) 350.00

Pratt, "Charity," black frame 70.00

Pratt, "Prince of Wales at Tomb of Washington" 175.00

Pratt, "Revenge" 75.00

Pratt, "The State House in Philadelphia," in giltwood frame, 8½" d. 175.00

"Washington Crossing the Delaware" center, "H.P. & W. C. Taylor, Perfumers, Philadelphia," black transfer, w/jar, 3 3/8" d.... 425.00

PRATT WARES

Early 19th Century Pratt Lion

The earliest ware now classified as Pratt ware was made by Felix Pratt at his pottery in Fenton, England from about 1810. He made earthenware with bright glazes, relief sporting jugs, toby mugs and commercial pots and jars whose lids bore multicolored transfer prints. The F. & R. Pratt mark is mid-19th century. The name Pratt ware is also applied today to mid and late 19th century English ware of the same general type as that made by Felix Pratt.

Figure of a clergyman, wearing a white wig, white bands, brown robes & holding a small book w/an orange cover in his right hand, white oval base, ca. 1790, 6 5/8" h. (arm repaired)........$2,200.00

Flask, naturalistically modelled as a scallop shell w/three tiers of ribbing picked out in alternating ochre enamel or underglaze-blue divided by wavy brown bands, rims & spout outlined in brown enamel, ca. 1800, 4 3/8" l. 1,210.00

Models of a lion & lioness, each w/a white coat enriched w/brown & ochre spots, the head & tail w/brown & ochre markings, front paw resting on an ochre ball above a rectangular base sponged in green & decorated on the sides w/a stylized floral band painted in blue, green & ochre, footrim (chip to one corner) w/an ochre line border, early 19th c., 7¼" l., pr. (ILLUS. of one) 34,100.00

Mug, molded as the head of a satyr w/brown hair & beard, wearing a wreath of underglaze-blue grapes & green leaves, brown eyes, cheeks heightened in ochre, all below an ochre band at the rim, applied at the back of the head & neck w/a ribbed handle, w/foliate-molded terminals, ca.

1800, 4" h. (repaired rim chips) 412.00

Pitcher, 6 7/8" h., jug-type, "Union" motif (emblematic of the Commonwealth of Great Britain), molded on either side w/a spray of flowers comprising a large ochre rose (England) & four blue, ochre & brown thistles amid numerous green leaves (Scotland), further molded below the rim w/a band of ochre & blue shamrocks on brown vines (Ireland), ca. 1825 (cracks & discoloration) 385.00

Pitcher, 10" h., pewter lid, seashells & water plants decoration, 1810-20........................ 200.00

Tazza, "Spanish Dancers," ornate scrolled gold border, 1850, 11" ....155.00 to 170.00

Tea caddy, double, rectangular, molded on either side w/hunting motifs & painted in ochre, green, brown & underglaze-blue within beaded ochre borders, top molded at the edge w/a foliate border, ca. 1810, 4½" h. (cracked & restored) 1,870.00

QUIMPER

Henriot - Quimper Egg Cup

This French earthenware pottery has been made in France since the end of the 17th century and is still in production today. Because the colorful decoration on this ware, predominantly of Breton peasant figures, is all hand-painted and each piece is unique, it has become increasingly popular with collectors in recent years. Most pieces offered today date from about the mid-19th century to the present. Modern potteries continue to operate today and contemporary examples are available in gift shops.

Book ends, figural, seated baby in cap & long gown on each, artist-signed by Berthe Savigny, Grande Maison HB Quimper, ca. 1920's, pr. $1,000.00

Book ends, figural, seated Breton boy in hat & vest w/one *sabot* on & one off, & seated Breton girl in cap & aproned skirt, signed by artist Berthe Savigny, Grande Maison "Modern Movement," ca. 1925, pr.........................1,200.00

Bowl, 8¼" d., mermaids in water, clouds in sky, artist-signed by Louis Garin, Grande Maison HB Quimper, ca. 1920's 650.00

Candlestick, model of a horse in "folk art" style w/head down & tail forming loop handle, socket in middle of back, decorated w/h.p. florals, Grande Maison HB Quimper, ca. 1920's, 8½" l. (single) ... 125.00

Cruet, two crossed flagons on base, peasant decoration, Grande Maison HB Quimper, ca. 1920's, 6¼" h. 48.00

Egg cup, h.p. rooster decoration, Henriot - Quimper, 3 5/8" h. (ILLUS.)......................... 75.00

Figures, sad-faced standing boy in cap, jacket & button vest & standing sad-faced girl w/cap & long dress, artist-signed by Berthe Savigny, Grande Maison HB Quimper, undecorated faience, ca. 1920's, boy, 10" h., girl, 10¼" h., pr.............................. 800.00

Jar, cov., round, peasant w/basket decoration, Grande Maison HB Quimper, 4½" h................ 95.00

Pitcher, 8" h., figural Breton girl's head w/tall, rounded bonnet forming spout & hooped scarf forming handle, Grande Maison HB Quimper 175.00

Crest of Brittany Quimper Plate

Plate, 9¼" d., h.p. Crest of Brittany in center, wide band of scrolls & florals at slightly scalloped rim, HR Quimper, ca. 1890 (ILLUS.) 250.00
Plates, 10¼" h., peasant man & woman decor, marked "Henriot-Quimper France 99," pr. 95.00
Platter, large, pastel florals, birds & insect decor, HB Quimper 650.00
Porringer, floral decoration, HR Quimper, pre-1922 .... 32.00
Salt dip, double, model of *sabots* (wooden shoes), center handle, h.p. trim, Grande Maison HB Quimper, ca. 1920's 46.00
Serving dish, peasant girl decoration, yellow glaze, HB Quimper, 10½ x 7" oval 175.00
Soup tureen, cov., pedestal base, foliage & stripes decoration, Henriot-Quimper, large 265.00
Tray, cut-out handles, fluted w/scalloped edges, red & blue flower center, Grande Maison HB Quimper 165.00
Vase, 7½"h., diamond-shaped, stylized birds & florals, brown & green, P. Fouillen, Quimper, after 1928 .... 70.00

REDWARE

Redware Apple Butter Jar

Red earthenware pottery was made in the American colonies from the late 1600's. Bowls, crocks and all types of utilitarian wares were turned out in great abundance to supplement the pewter and handmade treenware. The ready availability of the clay, the same used in making bricks and roof tiles, accounted for the vast production. The lead-glazed redware retained its reddish color, though a variety of colors could be obtained by adding various metals to the glaze. Interesting effects occurred accidentally through unsuspected impurities in the clay or uneven temperatures in the firing kiln which sometimes resulted in streaks or mottled splotches.

Apple butter jar w/flared lip & strap handle, clear glaze, 9¼" d., 7¼" h. (ILLUS.) $235.00
Bottle, keg-shaped w/burn hole in top, grey glaze w/brown & greenish spots, 5½" l. (hairlines & minor chips) 250.00
Bowl, 5¼" d., 3 1/8" h., crown-like form w/molded tab handles at upper sides, mottled brownish black glaze (minor wear & flakes)...... 375.00
Bowl, cov., 4" h., greenish clear glaze, attributed to Schwinford ... 305.00
Bowl, 12" d., 5" h., protruding lip & tooled line band, sponged brown rim & three vertical sponged bands 185.00
Bowl, 15½" d., 2½" h., shallow w/coggled edge & three & four-line bands of yellow slip decoration (minor wear) 1,800.00
Charger, coggled edge, brown glaze w/lattice design of yellow slip, 12" d. (old hairlines & small edge chips) 450.00
Charger, coggled edge, ornate yellow slip monogram, beautiful condition, 14" d. 1,000.00
Cup, waisted sides w/flared lip & applied handle, clear glaze w/mottled amber color, 3¾" h. (minor wear) 85.00
Cuspidor, round, w/straight sides w/tooled bands, flaring lip w/side drainage hole, brown & green running glaze w/brown dashes at bottom, 8" d., 4¼" h. (some wear & edge chips) 250.00

Redware Flower Pot

Flower pot, finger-crimped rim above two incised lines, brown speckled glaze, 6" d. opening, 5¾" h. (ILLUS.) 85.00

Flower pot w/attached saucer base, yellow slip stripes & sponged brown w/clear glaze, 4¼" h. (chip on bottom edge) 135.00

Jar, cov., low, bulbous body narrowing slightly to top rim, sloped lid w/button finial, mottled green glaze w/white slip, 3½" h. (minor edge chips) 230.00

Jar, cov., ovoid, incised lines at shoulder, cover w/finial & further incised line design, red-orange glaze w/manganese splotches, America, 19th c., 9¼" h. 495.00

Jar, slightly waisted cylinder w/sloping shoulder to raised neck opening, embossed bands, green glaze w/red highlights, 6¼" h. 375.00

Jar, semi-ovoid w/sloping shoulder & tooled lip, rich dark green glaze w/brown splotching, bottom incised "Pickle," 7" h. (wear, small chips) 425.00

Jug, fat ovoid body w/narrow opening & strap handle, greenish glaze w/orange spots & brown splotches, 9" h. (small old chips) 800.00

Jug, ovoid, strap handle, running yellow slip, European, 10½" h. (wear & chips) 95.00

Loaf pan, rectangular w/rounded corners, coggled edge, four combed lines of yellow slip decoration, 9½ x 13½" (wear & flakes) 852.00

Milk bowl, tooled dot band around center of slightly flared sides, bulbous lip, brown sponged glaze, minor wear, 7" d., 3¼" h. 225.00

Mixing bowl, glazed, tapering circular body w/raised lip, the interior partially glazed, late 19th c., 14¼" d. 99.00

Model of a bird, molded w/simple details, some white slip & amber glaze, edge wear, 1½" h......... 70.00

Model of recumbent lion, molded & hand-finished w/tooled mane, bottom initialed "R.L.W.," greenish glaze, 12½" l. (minor edge chips) 75.00

Mug, green glaze w/brown flecks, 4 1/8" h. (rim chips & minor edge wear) 85.00

Pie plate, coggled edge, stylized double tulip in yellow slip highlighted in rich green, 7 5/8" d. (old chips) 1,625.00

Pie plate, pairs of yellow slip wavy lines crossing at center, impressed "W. Smith, Womelsdorf," Pennsylvania, 19th c., 8 1/8" d. (rim chips) 500.00

Pitcher, 4 5/8" h., ovoid w/wide top opening, applied strap handle, pinched spout, dark brown splotches on orange body (minor glaze wear)..................... 345.00

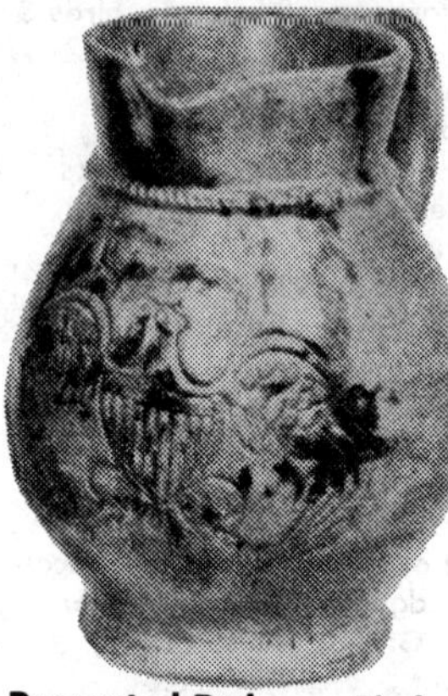

Decorated Redware Pitcher

Pitcher, 6 7/8" h., ribbed strap handle, flared rim w/incised rope band around neck, incised American eagle w/shield & banner on front, mottled amber glaze w/brown & green sponging, made by Mettinger (ILLUS.) 700.00

Pitcher, 6 7/8" h., bulbous body w/high flaring spout, wide ribbed strap handle, tooled band at top of shoulder, clear lead glaze w/brown splotches 475.00

Porringer, round shallow bowl w/rounded handle at one side, clear interior glaze on good orange color, dark patina on handle & back, 5½" w. (edge chips, 1 glued flake) 185.00

Preserving jar, straight sides w/sloping shoulder & protruding lip, tooled lines just below shoulder, black fleck glaze w/three vertical bands of brown sponging, 6" h. (some wear & chips) 145.00

Preserving jar, ovoid, applied ear handles, rust glaze w/manganese splotching, ca. 1800, 3 qt......... 360.00

Washboard, wooden frame w/corrugated redware scrubbing surface, 7 x 13" (frame worn & has damage) 235.00

RED WING

Various potteries operated in Red Wing, Minnesota, from 1868, the most successful be-

ing the Red Wing Stoneware Co., organized in 1878. Merged with other local potteries through the years, it became known as Red Wing Union Stoneware Co. in 1894, and was one of the largest producers of utilitarian stoneware items in the United States. After a decline in the popularity of stoneware products, an art pottery line was introduced to compensate for the loss and this was reflected in a new name for the company, Red Wing Potteries, Inc., in 1930. Stoneware production ceased entirely in 1947, but vases, planters, cookie jars and dinnerwares of art pottery quality continued in production until 1967 when the pottery ceased operation altogether.

Red Wing Figure of a Monk

Ashtray, wing-shaped, marked "Red Wing Pottery - 75th - 1878-1953" on bottom, red glaze $24.00
Bean pot, cov., single handle, white ribbed base, brown-glazed top, bail handle, marked "Red Wing Union Stoneware Co.," 1 qt....... 90.00
Beater jar, ribbed sides, blue banding on white-glazed stoneware, 1930's 52.50
Bowl, 6" d., paneled sides, spongeware, blue & rust daubing on tan stoneware, unmarked 67.00
Bowl, 7" d., ridged sides, red & blue banding on grey stoneware, w/advertising 32.50
Bowl, 12" d., ridged sides, blue banding on white-glazed stoneware 45.00
Bread tray, dinnerware, Bob White patt., 24" l. 85.00
Butter churn, salt-glazed stoneware, cobalt blue slip-quilled birch leaves, 5 gal. (no lid)........... 140.00
Butter churn, cov., stoneware, 1913 patent date, 6 gal. 165.00
Butter crock, cov., Gray Line w/Spongeband, bail handle, 3 lb. 210.00
Console bowl w/figural deer flower frog, art pottery line, ivory, 2 pcs. 25.00
Cookie jar, cov., Bob White patt. ....30.00 to 40.00
Cookie jar, cov., figural French Chef, blue or yellow glaze, h.p. details, stamped wing mark & "Red Wing Pottery," each ..35.00 to 50.00
Cookie jar, cov., figural Katrina (or Dutch Girl), blue or yellow glaze, impressed "Red Wing U.S.A.," each 45.00
Cookie jar, cov., model of a pear, high-gloss turquoise glaze, impressed "Red Wing U.S.A." 25.00
Cookie jar, cov., Saffron Ware 55.00
Crock, straight sides, salt-glazed stoneware w/brown lining, "target," Minnesota Stoneware, 2 gal. 100.00
Crock, straight sides, salt-glazed stoneware, "target," 3 gal........ 175.00
Crock, straight sides, cobalt blue butterfly design, marked "Red Wing Stoneware Company," 12 gal. 300.00
Cuspidor, salt-glazed stoneware 250.00
Figure of a cowgirl, reddish-brown monochrome glaze, No. B1414, 10½" h. 45.00
Figure of a man in "Gay 90's" attire, pink, No. 1350, 10¾" h. 55.00
Figure of a monk playing the accordion, grey glaze, 12" h. (ILLUS.) .. 45.00
Fruit jar w/screw-on lid, "Stone Mason Fruit Jar, Union Stoneware Co., Red Wing, Minn." printed in black on stoneware, qt. ..98.00 to 125.00
Hors d'oeuvre holder, dinnerware, Bob White patt., model of a bird pierced for picks 40.00
Jug, brown glazed shoulder & white glazed base, advertising, marked "Aleda Vinegar - For Pickling and Table, Milwaukee Vinegar," 1/8 pt. 85.00
Jug, stoneware, w/advertising, "Henry Bosquet," 1/8 pt. 100.00
Jug, cone-top w/"unattached handle," blue bands around top & bottom of straight sides, 1 gal. (small repair) 250.00
Jug, beehive shape, white glaze, large red "wing" decal & oval "Red Wing Union Stoneware Co." mark, 5 gal. 155.00
Jug, standard shoulder, white glaze, large red "wing" & oval "Red Wing Union Stoneware Co." mark, 5 gal. 75.00
Jug, standard shoulder w/brown

glaze, white glazed base, large red "wing" decal & oval "Red Wing Union Stoneware Co." mark, 5 gal. 190.00

Mixing bowls, Saffron Ware, tapering circular vessel w/wide lip over a fluted body, decorated overall in blue & brown on a yellow ground to simulate marbleing, one stamped "Red Wing Saffron Ware," 9 5/8" d. & 6¾" d., 2 pcs. 192.50

Model of a badger on football, stump base, signed "Red Wing Potteries" & dated 1939 . . .75.00 to 100.00

Red Wing Cherry Band Pitcher

Pitcher, 6" h., blue & grey stoneware, Cherry Band patt., blue at borders fading to grey (ILLUS.) . . . 145.00

Pitcher, 12" h., Bob White patt. 15.00

Pitcher, water, Saffron Ware, advertising, marked "Anton Hommerberg, Ballaton, Minnesota" 135.00

Plate, 6½" d., Bob White patt. 4.00

Plates, dinner, square, Magnolia patt., set of 6 . . . . 29.00

Plate, 10½" d., Morning Glory patt., pink 6.00

Platter, 13½" oval, Bob White patt. 14.00

Platter, 19", Round Up patt. 35.00

Platter, Capistrano patt., large 12.00

Salt & pepper shakers, Bob White patt., pr. 25.00

Slop jar, cov., blue stripe band w/lily on front (sl. repair on lid) . . 120.00

Tidbit tray, double, Bob White patt. 24.00

Vase, 10¾" h., bulbous, brushed ware, embossed floral branches decoration 36.00

Vase, 12½" h., Bamboo patt., green & yellow 40.00

RIDGWAY

Oriental Pattern Plate

There were numerous Ridgways among English potters. The firm J. & W. Ridgway operated in Shelton from 1814 to 1930 and produced many pieces with scenes of historical interest. William Ridgway operated in Shelton from 1830 to 1865. Most wares marked Ridgway that have been offered in this country were made by one of these two firms, or by Ridgway Potteries, Ltd., still in operation.

Ale set: tankard pitcher & six tankard mugs on matching round tray; Coaching Days & Ways series, black transfer on caramel ground, silver lustre trim, 8 pcs. $310.00

Bowl, 8½" d., "Henry the VIII" portrait 40.00

Bowl, 13" oval, "A Christmas Visit" scene 75.00

Compote, cov., 9 x 8", Oriental patt. w/gold trim, light blue transfer . . . 70.00

Creamer, Oriental patt. w/gold trim, light blue transfer, 5" h. 60.00

Feeding dish, Jolly Jinks patt., three bears playing at beach center scene, bears, rabbits & squirrels on border 48.00

Mug, barrel-shaped, Coaching Days & Ways series, black transfer on caramel ground, silver lustre band at rim & on handle, 2¾" d., 4½" h. 39.00

Pitcher, 5½" h., 5" d., jug-type, Coaching Days & Ways series, black transfer on caramel ground, gold lustre trim 80.00

Pitcher, 7" h., Tam-O-Shanter design, blue & white registery date "Oct. 1, 1835" 120.00

Pitcher, cider, 7¼" h., 5" d., barrel-shaped, Coaching Days & Ways series, black transfer on caramel ground, silver lustre trim 80.00

Pitcher, 7½" h., relief-molded knights on horseback design, registry date "Sept. 1, 1840" 125.00

Pitcher, tankard, 9½" h., Coaching Days & Ways series, black transfer on caramel ground, silver lustre trim 98.00

Pitcher, tankard, 12½" h., Famous Paintings series - "Two Strings to Her Box" 175.00

Pitcher, jug-type, Bacchus & Pan design, ca. 1830 ..... 160.00

Plate, 7¾" d., Coaching Days & Ways series - "Charles Recognized," silver lustre rim 45.00

Plate, 8" d., Coaching Days & Ways series - "A Clandestine Interview" 30.00

Plate, 8" d., Royal Vista patt., "The Rainbow" 15.00

Plate, 9" d., Capitol, Washington, D.C. pictured 42.00

Plate, 9¼" d., Oriental patt., green transfer (ILLUS.) 30.00

Plate, 10" d., Coaching Days & Ways series - "A Snapped Pole" 35.00

Platter, 17½ x 13", sprigs of rust colored roses w/foliage sprigs from the flow blue rim, trimmed w/gold 60.00

Punch bowl, painted & printed in colors w/spreading peonies & scrolling foliage enriched in blue & burnt orange & outlined w/gilding, raised on circular base, 15" d. 220.00

Sugar bowl, cov., Oriental patt., w/gold trim, light blue transfer, 5" h. 60.00

Tureen, open, Oriental patt. w/gold trim, interior & exterior pattern, light blue transfer, 6" h., 10" d. 75.00

Urn, "Burns at the Plow" scene, 5½" wide, 5½" h. 65.00

Water set: pitcher & six mugs; Coaching Days & Ways series, 7 pcs. ..... 150.00 to 200.00

ROCKINGHAM

An earthenware pottery was first established on the estate of the Marquis of Rockingham in England's Yorkshire district about 1745 and occupied by a succession of potters. The famous Rockingham glaze of mottled brown, somewhat resembling tortoise shell, was introduced about 1788 by the Brameld Brothers, and was well received. During the 1820's, porcelain manufacture was added to the production and fine quality china was turned out until the pottery closed in 1842. The popular Rockingham glaze was subsequently produced elsewhere, including Bennington, Vermont, and at numerous other U.S. potteries. We list herein not only wares produced at the Rockingham potteries in England, distinguishing porcelain wares from the more plentiful earthenware productions, but also include items from other potteries with the Rockingham glaze.

"Rebecca at the Well" Teapot

Bowl, 5¼" d., 3" h., canted sides w/embossed decoration, mottled brown glaze $55.00

Bowl, 5¾" d., canted sides, mottled brown glaze 65.00

Bowl, 6½" d., 3½" h., rounded flaring sides, diamond-quilted embossed band near base, mottled brown glaze 60.00

Bowl, 11" d., 3¼" h., canted sides, mottled dark brown glaze 65.00

Bowl, 12" d., canted sides, mottled brown glaze, 19th c. 82.50

Bowl, 12" d., 3 3/8" h., canted sides, mottled brown glaze 105.00

Candlesticks, flaring base, cylindrical stem w/embossed ring at base & beneath flaring candle socket, mottled brown glaze, 8½" h., pr. (one w/lip repair) 250.00

Coffeepot, cov., Rebecca at the Well patt., mottled brown glaze, 1 gal. 145.00

Creamer, ovoid body w/flat-topped embossed rim band w/long spout, loop handle, mottled brown glaze, 4 5/8" h. (small edge chips) 45.00

Dish, embossed ring of hearts at base, mottled brown glaze, 6 7/8" d. 55.00

Dish, oval, mottled brown glaze, 8¼" l. 45.00

Figural bottle, model of a rotund bearded man w/turban, mottled brown glaze, 5" h. (minor chip on bottom edge) 95.00

Figural bottle, incised "Jem Crow" & "2," mottled brown glaze, 8 7/8" h. 85.00
Flask, morning glory & eagle embossed, mottled brown glaze, 7¼" h. (minor kiln damage) 255.00
Jar, cov., wide embossed band w/vintage decoration around center, applied ear handles, flat cover w/knob finial, brown mottled glaze, 7½" h. (small flakes, crow's foot in base) 115.00
Milk pan, canted sides, mottled brown glaze, 12½" d., 3½" h. 50.00
Mixing bowl, mottled brown glaze, 10½" d., 4¼" h. 55.00
Mixing bowl w/spout, mottled brown glaze, 16" d. (hairline) 95.00
Model of a Spaniel in seated position, well-detailed tooling, freestanding front legs, irregular oblong base, mottled brown glaze, 10¼" h. 175.00
Model of a Spaniel in seated position, well-detailed tooling, freestanding front legs, irregular rectangular base w/rounded corners, mottled brown glaze, 11¼" h. (hairlines & chips in base) 195.00
Mug, applied strap handle, embossed band at rim, mottled brown glaze, 2 7/8" h. 45.00
Mug, waisted form w/bands around base & strap handle, good mottled brown glaze, 3 3/8" h. 135.00
Mug, Acanthus Leaf patt., mottled brown glaze, 5" h. 150.00
Pie plate, mottled brown glaze, 7 5/8" d. 70.00
Pie plate, scalloped rim, embossed ribs, mottled brown glaze, 7 7/8" d. 60.00
Pie plate, mottled brown glaze, 9" d. 75.00
Pie plate, mottled brown glaze, 10" d. 115.00
Pie plate, mottled brown glaze, 11¼" d. 130.00
Pitcher, 8¼" h., cylindrical shape w/embossed peacock design, mottled medium brown glaze (chips on base edge) 55.00
Pitcher, 8¾" h., embossed scene of sleeping children, mottled brown glaze (shallow flake on base) 65.00
Pitcher, milk, embossed oak leaves & acorns, mottled brown glaze 75.00
Soap dish w/six drain holes, 12 panels on lower half, mottled brown glaze, 4 1/8" d., 2" h. 60.00
Soap dish, rectangular w/rounded corners, mottled light brown glaze, 4¾" h. 48.00
Teapot, cov., figural duck, neck & head form spout, simple embossed detail, mottled brown glaze, rectangular cover, 9¾" l. (minor cover flakes) 195.00
Teapot, cov., Rebecca at the Well patt., mottled brown glaze, 9" (ILLUS.) .... 100.00 to 125.00
Washboard insert, yellowware w/mottled brown glaze, no frame, 11 x 10¾" (edge chips) 140.00

ROOKWOOD

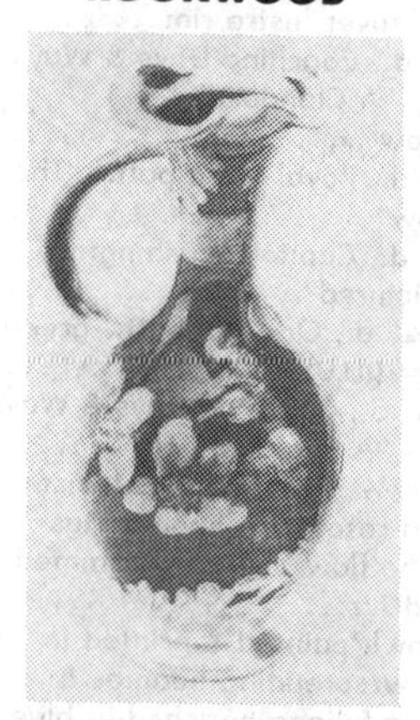

Rookwood Ewer with Silver Overlay

Considered America's foremost art pottery, the Rookwood Pottery Company was established in Cincinnati, Ohio in 1880, by Mrs. Maria Longworth Storer. To accurately record its development, each piece carried the Rookwood insignia, or mark, was dated, and, if individually decorated, was usually signed by the artist. The pottery remained in Cincinnati until 1959 when it was sold to Herschede Hall Clock Company and moved to Starkville, Mississippi, where it continued in operation until 1967.

Ashtray, model of a rook perched at one side, green high glaze, 1949 .... $85.00
Book end, model of a horse's head, No. 6014, white glaze, 1934, W.P. McDonald, 6¼" h. 135.00
Book ends, model of a flower, white glaze, 1932, pr. 160.00
Book ends, model of an owl, brown high glaze, 1948, pr. 125.00
Book ends, model of a Sphinx, blue glaze, 1920, pr. 135.00
Bowl, 8½" d., 2½" h., straight sides, wide mouth w/ruffled rim, apple blossoms on shaded pink to brown ground, 1890 .... 100.00

Bowl, 10" d., 3" h., No. 2875, stippled green interior w/flower bud & stem, 1928 .... 150.00
Box, cov., bust of an Art Deco woman, green glaze, 1927, 4 x 3" 155.00
Candleholder, "Aladdin's Lamp" form, underglaze slip-painted florals, standard glaze (single) ... 185.00
Candleholders, three-section, floral relief in dark & light blue, 1920, 2 x 5", pr. 75.00
Chamberstick, shield-back type, pink shaded to olive green matte finish, 1915, 7¾" h. 60.00
Cigarette box, cov., fluted cylinder, "Western & Southern Life Insurance Co.," green glaze, 3½" h. .. 85.00
Console bowl w/figural bird w/lily pad flower frog, purple matte glaze, 1925, bird 6" h., bowl 11" d., 2 pcs. 165.00
Console bowl w/flower frog, turquoise glaze, 1930, 8" 75.00
Creamer, cylindrical ovoid w/pinched spout & angled handle, bird & catkins on variegated yellow ground, 1893, Olga Geneva Reed, 4¼" h. 192.50
Creamer, underglaze slip-painted florals & foliage, standard glaze, 1891, Mary Louella Perkins 200.00
Ewer, underglaze slip-painted yellow primroses, standard glaze, w/sterling silver loop handle, pinched rim & floral overlay, 1893, Sallie Elizabeth Coyne, silver by Gorham, 6½" h. (ILLUS.) 2,310.00
Ewer, bisque, ruffled rim, scrolled handle, rust & green leaves & blueberries in relief on pale blue to peach ground, 1888, Matthew A. Daly, 16¾" h. 1,540.00
Jug, underglaze Limoges-style decoration of brown butterfly, green, white, gold & black ground, standard glossy glaze, 1884, Martin Rettig, 4¾" h. 585.00
Lamp base, model of a seahorse, dark glaze, 1926, Edward T. Hurley, 20" h. 850.00
Lamp base, embossed fuchsia blossoms, celadon green glaze, mounted on metal lion's feet, No. 6045, 1937 .... 150.00
Loving cup, cylindrical, three loop handles, underglaze slip-painted pastel moonlit landscape scene, Vellum glaze, Frederick Rothenbusch (1896-1931), 6" d., 7¼" h. 1,000.00
Model of Cocker Spaniel, brown glaze 125.00
Model of pheasant, glossy green glaze 195.00
Mug, slant handle, underglaze slip-painted Japanese monk w/his arms outstreched, shaded golden brown to dark brown standard glaze, 1890, Anna Marie Valentien, 6 x 4" 990.00
Oil lamp, underglaze slip-painted oak leaves, standard brown glaze, original metal fittings, 1899, Sallie Toohey, 10" d., 25½" h. 605.00
Paperweight, model of a donkey, No. 6241, cinnamon colored glaze, Louise Abel 125.00
Paperweight, model of duck, white glaze, w/original paper label, No. 6064, 1965 .... 65.00
Paperweight, model of a ladybug w/nursery rhyme, yellow matte glaze, No. 108, 1937, Louise Abel 115.00
Paperweight, model of an owl, 1946 .... 100.00
Paperweight, model of a rook, green glaze, 1923 .... 110.00
Pin tray, shallow edge w/slight flute, underglaze slip-painted yellow mouse, standard brown glaze, 1888, Anna Marie Valentien, 7" d. 250.00
Pin tray, dandelion leaves on yellow matte ground, 1904, Anna Marie Valentien 185.00
Pitcher, 6¼ x 6", painted white roses & rust stems & leaves on grey to light pink ground, bisque finish, 1887, Harriet Wilcox 330.00
Plaque, underglaze slip-painted pastel green, blue, violet, rose, yellow & cream waterscape at sunset w/trees & bush in the foreground & hills in the distance, 1914, Charles J. McLaughlin, 9¼ x 5" ..1,045.00
Plaque, underglaze slip-painted pastel dark to medium blue impressionistic scene of sailboats on light blue to cream ground, Vellum glaze, Carl Schmidt (1875-1959), original black frame, 8 5/8 x 8 5/8" 2,200.00
Plaque, scene w/blue, dark green, grey & pink inlet w/brush & trees & hills in the distance, 1917, Frederick Rothenbusch, 7¼ x 9¼" 1,210.00
Plaque, blue-green & blue shoreline & lake w/further landscape & range of trees in the distance & a blue, rose & green-tinted ivory sky, Vellum glaze, 1915, Lorinda Epply, 8¾ x 11" 1,100.00
Plaque, pastel shades w/scene of swans swimming on quiet lake w/trees in background, Vellum

Rookwood Swan Plaque

glaze, wide, flat wood frame (ILLUS.) 2,145.00

Plate, 10" d., relief-molded rim, grapes & foliage center decoration, 1885, William Purcell McDonald 375.00

Ramekin, slip-painted birds flying through clouds decoration, 1883, Martin Rettig 285.00

Smoking set: hexagonal cov. jar, hexagonal ashtray-match holder & 12-sided tray; red & yellow mums on deep burgundy to rose ground, Wax Matte glaze, 1925, Elizabeth Lincoln, 3 pcs. 495.00

Stein, underglaze slip-painted berries, standard brown glaze, inlaid lid w/frog finial & ram's head thumblift, 1896, Sallie Toohey, 1 liter 1,155.00

Tile, No. 2351, white seagulls w/turquoise background, 1929 . . . . 110.00

Tile, No. 3077, violet parrot, green vines & purple flowers on white background, 1927 . . . . 120.00

Trivet, standard glossy glaze, No. 3210, 1925 . . . . 105.00

Umbrella stand, bulbous w/long cylindrical neck, underglaze slip-painted gaggle of five startled geese in various stages of flight, shaded dark to medium brown standard glaze, 1891, Artus Van Briggle, 11" d., 25½" h. 2,090.00

Vase, 4" h., Goldstone, 1954 . . . . 40.00

Vase, 4½" h., bulbous, modeled fruit & leaves on matte blue ground, 1928 . . . . 42.00

Vase, 4½" h., underglaze slip-painted apple green-veined blue leaves on plum ground, 1924, Kataro Shirayamadani 695.00

Vase, 5" h., ginger jar-shape, incised bird w/foliage in ivory matte glaze, 1934 . . . . 35.00

Vase, 5" h., pine cone decoration, Vellum glaze, 1910, Katherine VanHorne 160.00

Vase, 5¾" h., baluster form, underglaze slip-painted floral decoration, cream band at shoulder, deep blue glaze, 1917, Caroline Frances Steinle 264.00

Vase, 6" h., wide-mouthed swollen cylinder tapering towards base, underglaze slip-painted chrysanthemums, shaded pink glaze, Amelia Browne Sprague (ca. 1888) 302.50

Vase, 6½" h., expanding conical shape, sides grey shaded to cherry, base w/poppies & leafage decoration, matte glaze, 1926, Elizabeth N. Lincoln 275.00

Rookwood Jewelled Porcelain Vase

Vase, 7" h., spherical form w/short neck, underglaze painted maroon tulips & teal blue overlapping leaves on turquoise ground, Jewelled Porcelain body, 1924, Kataro Shirayamadani (ILLUS.) . . . 1,400.00

Vase, 8" h., 4¼" d., cylindrical w/bulbous top, underglaze slip-painted pastel grey-blue galleon silhouettes against light blue to peach-cream horizon, Vellum glaze, 1918, Ed Diers 1,320.00

Vase, 8½" h., underglaze slip-painted scene of two crows flying under a full moon, 1907, Carl Schmidt (ILLUS.) 1,430.00

Vase, 9" h., 5" d., violet & cream dogwood blossoms & dark green leaves on feathered brown to orange-brown ground, Wax Matte glaze, 1927, Margaret McDonald . . 522.50

Vase, 10" h., two-handled, large stylized flowers on salmon

ground, high glaze, 1924, William E. Hentschel 425.00

Rookwood Vase with Crows

Vase, 11" h., underglaze slip-painted bough laden w/pink apple blossoms against greyish blue shaded to pink ground, Vellum glaze, 1910, Edward Timothy Hurley 700.00

Vase, 12¼" h., 4¾" d., cylindrical, purple-blue wisteria & grey-green leaves on black to green to cream ground, Iris glaze, 1906, Carl Schmidt 3,795.00

Vase, 14" h., spherical, 2 brown & white birds & a black & brown bird in a gilt-enhanced brown & green landscape against a blue sky, 1881 (minor flakes at foot) 1,320.00

Vase, 14 1/8" h., swollen cylinder, purple-blue wisteria pendant from olive green leaves & stems, Vellum glaze, 1913, Edward George Diers 825.00

Vase, 14¼" h., swollen cylinder divided into 4 vertical panels, dark blue Venetian boats w/blue, fuchsia, pastel green & grey-green sails, Vellum glaze, 1926, Carl Schmidt 7,150.00

Vase, 14¾" h., 5½" d., cylindrical w/collared neck, carved & painted white & dark green stylized dandelions & leaves on mint green to cream ground, 1904, Albert Valentien 1,320.00

Vase, 20½" h., oviform, bordered by gilded bands, w/beige, brown & olive chrysanthemums on matte powder blue ground, 1886, Matthew Andrew Daly 1,540.00

ROSEMEADE

Laura Taylor was a ceramic artist who supervised Federal Works Projects in her native North Dakota during the Depression era and later demonstrated at the potter's wheel during the 1939 New York World's Fair. In 1940, Laura Taylor and Robert J. Hughes opened the Rosemeade-Wahpeton Pottery, naming it after the North Dakota county and town of Wahpeton where it was located. Rosemeade Pottery was made on a small scale for only about twelve years with Laura Taylor designing the items and perfecting colors. Her animal and bird figures are popular among collectors. Hughes and Taylor married in 1943 and the pottery did a thriving business until her death in 1959. The pottery closed in 1961 but stock was sold from the factory salesroom until 1964.

Rosemeade Salt & Pepper Shakers

Ashtray, souvenir, "Pennsylvania" or "South Dakota," each $22.00

Bank, model of a buffalo 92.00

Bank, model of a hippopotamus 85.00

Basket, pastel blue & pink glaze, miniature 15.00

Bell, model of an elephant 73.00

Bell, model of a tulip 55.00

Book ends, model of a dog, black glaze, large, pr. 160.00

Flower frog, model of a fish 25.00

Jug, applied handle, blue glaze, 4½" h. 15.00

Model of a pheasant, original paper label, 14" l. 175.00

Model of a sleigh 45.00

Pie bird, model of a peacock, blue & green glaze, original paper label, 4½" h. 45.00

Pitcher, souvenir, pinched handle, swirled clay exterior, aqua glaze interior, miniature 27.00

Planter, model of a horse, black or cinnamon brown glaze, each 40.00

Plaque, pierced to hang, mountain goat in relief 185.00

Salt & pepper shakers, model of a Boston Terrier, pr. 55.00

Salt & pepper shakers, model of a fighting cock, rust & black glaze w/red comb, 4" l., 3" h., pr. (ILLUS.) 18.00

Salt & pepper shakers, model of an elephant, rose glaze, pr. 32.00

Salt & pepper shakers, model of a

fish, pink or green glaze, each pr. 25.00
Television lamp, model of a horse, black glaze 185.00
Trivet, souvenir, "Minnesota Centennial" 40.00
Vase, 5" h., bronze lustre finish 27.00
Wall pocket, figural Indian God of Peace 85.00

ROSE MEDALLION - ROSE CANTON

Rose Medallion Platter

The lovely Chinese ware known as Rose Medallion was made through the past century and into the present one. It features alternating panels of people and flowers or insects with most pieces having four medallions. The ware is called Rose Canton if flowers and birds or insects fill all the panels. Unless otherwise noted, our listing is for Rose Medallion ware.

Bowls, soup, set of 6 . . . . . $225.00
Bowl, 10" d., 4½" h. 375.00
Bowl, 12" d., shallow, 1900 . . . . . 60.00
Candlestick, 3¾" d., 8½" h. (single) 145.00
Charger, 12" d. 175.00
Charger, 14" d. 200.00
Cup & saucer, octagonal 60.00
Cup & saucer, scalloped rim, unmarked 38.00
Plate, 7" d. 30.00
Plates, 8 1/8" d., ca. 1830, set of 13 . . . . . 1,210.00
Plate, 9½" d., 19th c. 125.00
Plate, 10¼" d. 75.00
Platter, 18" l. (ILLUS.) 300.00
Punch bowl, late 19th c., 14¾" d., 6 1/8" h. 550.00
Soap dish w/drain insert 175.00
Tea cup & saucer, marked "China" . . 25.00
Teapot, cov., w/basket holder 160.00
Teapot, cov., early 19th c., miniature 80.00
Tea set, cov. teapot & 2 handleless cups in fitted wicker basket, 4 pcs. 175.00
Vase, 3¾" h.., Rose Canton 55.00
Vase, 18" h. 725.00

ROSENTHAL

The Rosenthal porcelain manufactory has been in operation since 1880 when it was established by P. Rosenthal in Selb, Bavaria. Tablewares and figure groups are among its specialties.

Bonbon, on sterling base, Winifred patt., pink Moss Rose decoration, 5¼ x 2½" $25.00
Bowl, fruit, 9" d., two gold handles, grapes & leaves decoration on cream ground 165.00
Bowl, deep, lavender sides, h.p. winter scene w/bridge in center . . 25.00
Cake plate, varied colored roses, leaves & stems center, cobalt blue & gold border, 10" d. 50.00
Clock, circular drum form cast w/gilt chapter ring, surmounted by a nude female figure w/length of drapery flowing about her limbs, flanked one side by young boy blowing a horn, on other w/posy, rectangular base w/scrolled ends above an apron cast w/flowers & leafage, on four outward flaring feet, white body heightened in lime green, lemon yellow, dusty rose, turquoise & gilt, designed by Gustav Oppel, decorated by Kurt Severin, ca. 1925, 14¼" h. 3,850.00
Figure of a child feeding pigeons, 4¼" h. 75.00
Figure of a girl feeding flowers to a fawn, artist-signed, 6½" h. 145.00
Figure of a naked boy holding a goat, 6½" h. 135.00
Figure of a girl w/braids holding a bouquet & hat, artist-signed, 7¾" h. 160.00
Figure of man playing pipe w/sitting dog nearby, 8" 325.00
Model of a frog, 3 x 2" 65.00
Model of a horse, grey & white, artist-signed, 10¼ x 9¾" 200.00
Model of peacock, w/tail feathers open, large 265.00
Nut set: master nut bowl & six 3½" d. bowls; ornate gold scrolled rim, Pompadour patt. on creamy ground, 7 pcs. 50.00
Plate, 9" d., slightly scalloped at rim, 2" border of rich cobalt blue w/gold tracery frames center portrait of a huge ivory & rose col-

ored rose w/foliage on green ground 45.00
Vase, 5" h., fluted, cobalt blue w/white gold, Selb, Bavaria 75.00
Vase, 9½" h., tulip-shaped, h.p. overall flowers in pastel colors, artist-signed 78.00

ROSEVILLE

Roseville Pottery Company operated in Zanesville, Ohio., from 1898 to 1954 after having been in business for six years prior to that in Muskingum County, Ohio. Art wares similar to those of the Owens and Weller Potteries were produced. Items listed here are by patterns or lines.

ANTIQUE MATT GREEN (pre-1916)

Bowl, 4" d., 4" h., matte green glaze w/burnished highlights $45.00
Jardiniere, 2-handled, matt green glaze w/burnished highlights, 14" across handles 165.00
Urn-vase, matt green glaze w/burnished highlights, 5" h. 40.00

APPLE BLOSSOM (1948)

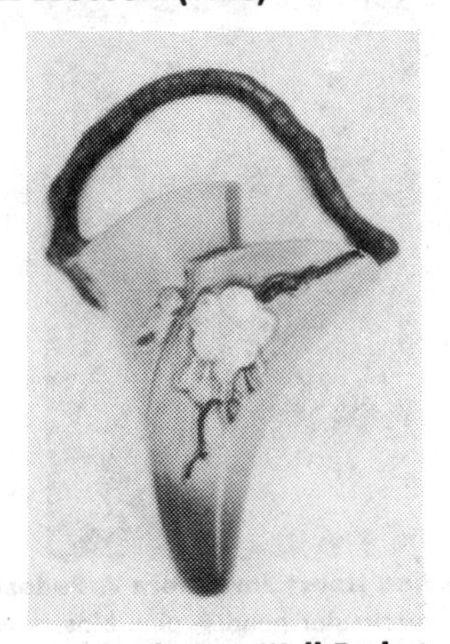

Apple Blossom Wall Pocket

Basket w/overhead branch handle, apple blossoms in relief on rose, 10" h. 70.00
Book ends, apple blossoms in relief on blue, pr. 95.00
Bowl, 4" d., apple blossoms in relief on green 32.00
Candleholders, apple blossoms in relief on green, 4½" h., pr. 59.00
Cornucopia-vase, apple blossoms in relief on blue, 6" h. 35.00
Ewer, apple blossoms in relief on blue, 15" h. 160.00
Jardiniere, apple blossoms in relief on green, 11" d., 8½" h. 115.00
Teapot, cov., apple blossoms in relief on green 75.00
Vase, 6" h., apple blossoms in relief on blue or pink, each 26.00
Vase, bud, 7" h., apple blossoms in relief on green 30.00
Vase, 9" h., asymmetrical branch handles, apple blossoms in relief on blue 50.00
Wall pocket, apple blossoms in relief on rose, 8" h. (ILLUS.) 65.00
Window box, branch handles, apple blossoms in relief on green, 10½" l., 2½" h. 32.50

AZTEC (1916)

Lamp base, yellow & white slip geometric design on blue, 11" h. 295.00
Pitcher, 5" h., wide mouth, light blue & white slip geometric design on blue 195.00
Vase, 9½" h., cylindrical, blue & white slip geometric design on black 350.00
Vase, 10¼" h., white slip geometric design on blue 325.00

BANEDA (1933)

Baneda Vase

Bowl, 8½" d., 2-handled, band of embossed pods, blossoms & leaves on green 45.00
Urn, 2-handled, band of embossed pods, blossoms & leaves on raspberry pink, 7" h. 65.00
Vase, 4" h., small rim handles, band of embossed pods, blossoms & leaves on raspberry pink 34.00
Vase, 6" h., 2-handled, tapering body, band of embossed pods, blossoms & leaves on green, paper label 55.00
Vase, 7" h., 2-handled, cylindrical w/short collared neck, band of

embossed pods, blossoms & leaves on green, paper label 70.00
Vase, 10" h., shoulder handles, bulbous, band of embossed pods, blossoms & leaves on raspberry pink 220.00
Vase, 12" h., band of embossed pods, blossoms & leaves on raspberry pink (ILLUS.) 295.00

BANKS & BOTTLES (early 1900's)
Bank, bust of Uncle Sam, 4" h. ....85.00 to 125.00
Bank, model of a reclining buffalo, 6" l., 3" h. ....85.00 to 110.00
Bank, model of an eagle's head, 2½" h. 175.00
Bank, model of a frog w/open mouth, 3" w., 4" h. ....80.00 to 95.00
Bank, model of a standing spotted pig, 5" l., 2½" h. ....70.00 to 90.00
Bank, model of a spotted pig on base, 5½" l., 4" h. ....80.00 to 100.00
Bottle, model of a monkey seated w/elbows on knees, green glaze, 5½" h. 85.00

BITTERSWEET (1940)
Basket w/pointed overhead handle, orange bittersweet pods & green leaves on grey or yellow bark-textured ground, 6" h., each ....38.00 to 45.00
Bowl, 6" w., orange bittersweet pods & green leaves on green bark-textured ground 30.00
Console bowl, twig handles, orange bittersweet pods & green leaves on green bark-textured ground, 14" l., 6" h. 40.00
Cornucopia-vase, double, orange bittersweet pods & green leaves on green bark-textured ground, 4½" h. 40.00
Planter, shaped sides, orange bittersweet pods & green leaves on yellow bark-textured ground, 10½" l. 55.00
Vase, 5" h., twig handles, sloping rim, orange bittersweet pods & green leaves on grey bark-textured ground................ 32.00
Vase, 6" h., asymmetrical twig handles, orange bittersweet pods & green leaves on yellow bark-textured ground................ 30.00
Vase, 8" h., curved handles rising from mid-section to shaped rim, orange bittersweet pods & green leaves on grey bark-textured ground 40.00

BLACKBERRY (1933)
Basket w/round overhead handle, tapering body w/flared mouth, band of blackberries & leaves in relief on green textured ground, 7" h. 375.00
Bowl, 9 x 6", 4" h., small handles below rim, band of blackberries & leaves in relief on green textured ground 155.00
Candlesticks, curved handles rising from domed base to candle nozzle, blackberries & leaves in relief on base, green textured candle nozzle, 4½" h., pr. 170.00
Jardiniere, slender handles, band of blackberries & leaves in relief on green textured ground, 6" h. 155.00
Vase, 4" h., 2-handled, globular, band of blackberries & leaves in relief on green textured ground .. 75.00
Vase, 5" h., canted sides, band of blackberries & leaves in relief on green textured ground........... 110.00
Vase, 6" h., 2-handled, band of blackberries & leaves in relief on green textured ground.......... 145.00
Vase, 10" h., curved handles at mid-section, waisted cylinder, band of blackberries & leaves in relief on green textured ground.......... 250.00

BLEEDING HEART (1938)

Bleeding Heart Jardiniere & Pedestal

Basket w/circular handle, pink blossoms & green leaves on shaded blue or green, 10" h., each 75.00
Candleholders, pink blossoms & green leaves on shaded blue, 2½" h., pr. 35.00
Ewer, pink blossoms & green leaves on shaded blue or pink, 6" h., each 45.00
Flower frog, pink blossoms & green leaves on shaded blue or pink, each ....30.00 to 35.00
Jardiniere & pedestal base, pink blossoms & green leaves on shad-

ed pink, overall 25" h. (ILLUS.) ....350.00 to 400.00

Vase, double bud, 4½" h., bridge form, pink blossoms & green leaves on shaded green 45.00

Vase, 6" h., 7" widest d., globular, pink blossoms & green leaves on shaded green 65.00

Vase, 8½" h., base handles, canted sides, pink blossoms & green leaves on shaded pink 45.00

Vase, 10" h., pink blossoms & green leaves on shaded green 65.00

BUSHBERRY (1948)

Bushberry Vase

Basket w/overhead branch handle, berries & leaves on blue or russet bark-textured ground, 8" h., each 65.00

Basket w/overhead branch handle, berries & leaves on green bark-textured ground, 12" h. 115.00

Candleholders, berries & leaves on blue bark-textured ground, 2" h., pr. 30.00

Cornucopia-vase, berries & leaves on blue bark-textured ground, 8" h. 38.00

Ewer, berries & leaves on green or russet bark-textured ground, 15" h., each 120.00

Flower pot w/underplate, berries & leaves on green bark-textured ground, 5" h. 45.00

Jardiniere & pedestal base, berries & leaves on blue bark-textured ground, small, 2 pcs. 350.00

Planter, branch handle rising from rim at one end, berries & leaves on green bark-textured ground, 6" l. 35.00

Vase, 4" h., berries & leaves on russet bark-textured ground (ILLUS.) 28.00

Vase, 9" h., 2-handled, berries & leaves on blue bark-textured ground 37.50

Vase, 12½" h., asymmetrical angular handles, berries & leaves on brown bark-textured ground 115.00

CAPRI (late line)

Ashtray, shell form, cactus green, 9" w. 10.00

Basket w/angular overhead handle, shell form body, cactus green, 8" h. 65.00

Basket w/overhead branch handle, molded leaf design, sandlewood yellow, 10" h. 47.00

Bowl, 7" w., quadrilobed, sandlewood yellow 22.00

Vase, 10" h., cylindrical w/flared serrated rim, ribbed body, sandlewood yellow 36.00

CARNELIAN I (1910-15)

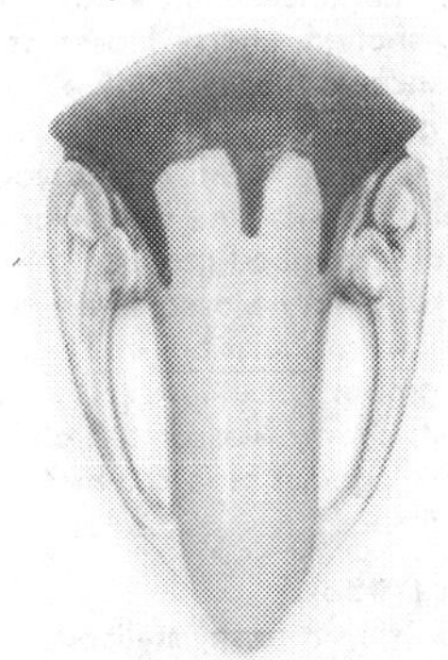

Carnelian I Wall Pocket

Bowl, 8" d., 2¾" h. 2-handled, medium blue drip glaze over light blue 22.00

Bowl, 11 x 5" oval, 2-handled, turquoise drip glaze over aqua 26.00

Candleholders, turquoise drip glaze over aqua, 3" h., pr. 38.00

Urn, 2-handled, medium blue drip glaze over light blue, 6" h. 65.00

Vase, 5" h., pillow-shaped, antique gold drip glaze over green 35.00

Vase, 6" h., fan-shaped, turquiose drip glaze over aqua 30.00

Vase, 8" h ., 5" w., fan-shaped, turquoise drip glaze over aqua 40.00

Wall pocket, medium blue drip glaze over light blue, 8" h. (ILLUS.) 48.00

CERAMIC DESIGN (before 1916)

Flower arranger, creamware w/colorful molded design at rim, 2" h., 2 pcs. 65.00

Wall pocket, creamware w/molded spring green stylized leaves on slender stems, 10" h. 100.00

Wall pocket, creamware w/molded

heart-shaped devices on swirling stems, 17" h. 300.00
Water set: 6½" h. pitcher & four 4" h. tumblers; creamware w/molded colorful design, 5 pcs. 450.00

CHERRY BLOSSOM (1933)

Basket, hanging-type, cherry blossoms & ivory fencework against brown combed ground, 8" 250.00
Jardiniere, cherry blossoms & ivory fencework against brown combed ground, 4" h. 95.00
Jardinere, cherry blossoms & pink fencework against blue combed ground, 6" h. 135.00
Pedestal base, cherry blossoms & pink fencework against blue combed ground, 15" h. 335.00
Vase, 4" h., angular shoulder handles, jug-shaped, cherry blossoms & pink fencework against blue combed ground 115.00
Vase, 7½" h., 2-handled, cylindrical, cherry blossoms & pink fencework against blue combed ground 115.00
Vase, 12" h., cherry blossoms & ivory fencework against brown combed ground 325.00
Wall pocket, cherry blossoms & pink fencework against blue combed ground, 8" h. 275.00

CLEMANA (1934)

Candlestick, flared base, stylized blossoms & embossed latticework on green ground, 4½" h. (single)........................ 35.00
Vase, 6" h., angular pierced handles, stylized blossoms & embossed latticework on green ground 75.00
Vase, 12" h., pierced handles, stylized blossoms & embossed latticework on tan ground 210.00

CLEMATIS (1944)

Basket w/circular handle, clematis blossoms on green textured ground, 7" h. (ILLUS.)............ 45.00
Bowl, 4" d., clematis blossoms on brown textured ground 22.00
Candleholders, angular handles at shoulder, bulbous, clematis blossoms on green textured ground, 2½" h., pr. 35.00
Cornucopia-vase, clematis blossoms on green textured ground, 8" h. .. 35.00
Creamer & sugar bowl, clematis blossoms on blue textured ground, pr. 55.00
Ewer, clematis blossoms on blue or green textured ground, 6" h., each 35.00

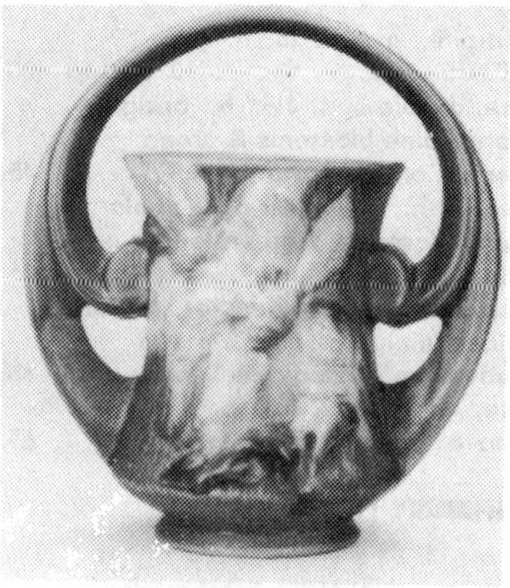

Clematis Basket

Ewer, clematis blossoms on green or brown textured ground, 10" h., each 55.00
Jardiniere & pedestal base, clematis blossoms on blue textured ground, 2 pcs. 350.00
Vase, 4" h., clematis blossoms on blue textured ground 22.50
Vase, bud, 7" h., angular pierced handles, clematis blossoms on blue or green textured ground, each 30.00
Vase, 10" h., 2-handled, clematis blossoms on blue or green textured ground, each 60.00
Vase, 15" h., 2-handled, clematis blossoms on brown or green textured ground, each 125.00
Window box, clematis blossoms on blue textured ground, 10½" l. across handles 40.00

COLUMBINE (1940's)

Basket w/overhead handle, columbine blossoms in relief on shaded tan ground, 8" h. 68.00
Basket w/pointed handle rising from footed base, columbine blossoms in relief on shaded blue ground, 12" h. 115.00
Bowl, 14" d., columbine blossoms in relief on shaded pink ground..... 38.00
Console set: 8" d. bowl, flower frog & pair 4½" h. candlesticks; columbine blossoms in relief on shaded pink ground, 4 pcs.............. 125.00
Ewer, columbine blossoms in relief on shaded blue ground, 7" h. 50.00
Flower frog, columbine blossoms in relief on shaded tan ground...... 20.00
Jardiniere, columbine blossoms in relief on shaded blue ground, 4" h. 42.50
Jardiniere, columbine blossoms in relief on shaded pink ground, 5" h. 65.00

Vase, 6" h., two-handled, columbine blossoms in relief on shaded tan ground 50.00

Vase, 10" h., two-handled, ovoid, columbine blossoms in relief on shaded pink ground 65.00

COSMOS (1940)

Cosmos Vase

Basket w/overhead handle, realistic cosmos blossoms in relief on ivory band, shaded blue ground, 10" h. 105.00

Basket, hanging-type, realistic cosmos blossoms in relief on blue band, shaded green ground 75.00

Bowl, 4" h., two-handled, compressed sphere, realistic cosmos blossoms in relief on ivory band, shaded blue ground 30.00

Jardiniere, two-handled, realistic cosmos blossoms in relief on green band, shaded tan ground, 3" h. 35.00

Vase, 4" h., two-handles rising from mid-section to rim, globular w/slender neck, realistic cosmos blossoms in relief on blue band, shaded green ground 22.00

Vase, 5" h., loop handles at footed base, chalice form, realistic cosmos blossoms in relief on ivory band, shaded blue ground 30.00

Vase, 7" h., two large handles at mid-section, globular w/slender neck, realistic cosmos blossoms in relief on ivory band, shaded blue ground 50.00

Vase, 8" h., realistic cosmos blossoms in relief on blue band, shaded green ground 37.50

Vase, 12" h., realistic cosmos blossoms in relief on green band, shaded tan ground (ILLUS.) 75.00

DAHLROSE (1924-28)

Bowl, 10" oval, two-handled, ivory blossoms in relief on mottled tan shaded to green 45.00

Jardiniere, angular rim handles, ivory blossoms in relief on mottled tan shaded to green, 6" h. 50.00

Dahlrose Jardiniere & Pedestal

Jardiniere & pedestal base, ivory blossoms in relief on mottled tan shaded to green, overall 30½" h., 2 pcs. (ILLUS.) 550.00

Vase, triple bud, 6½" h., expanding cylinder flanked by tusk form tubes, ivory blossoms in relief on mottled tan shaded to green 46.50

Vase, 9" h., ivory blossoms in relief on mottled tan shaded to green .. 60.00

Vase, 10" h., ivory blossoms in relief on mottled tan shaded to green 55.00

Wall pocket, angular rim handles, ivory blossoms in relief on mottled tan shaded to green, 9" h. ... 77.50

Window box, band of ivory blossoms in relief beneath rim, mottled tan shaded to green, 11½ x 6" 110.00

DEALER SIGNS

"Roseville," block lettering, green shaded to tan, 6 x 2" 400.00

"Roseville," script lettering, pink or blue, 8 x 5", each ....425.00 to 550.00

"Roseville Pottery," block lettering, aqua, 10 x 4½" ....450.00 to 600.00

DOGWOOD I (1916-18)

Basket, hanging-type, dogwood blossoms on textured green ground, 7" d. 95.00

Vase, 7" h., ovoid, dogwood blossoms on textured green ground .. 85.00

Vase, 8" h., dogwood blossoms on textured green ground 70.00

Vase, 10" to 12" h., dogwood blossoms on textured green ground, each ....90.00 to 110.00

DOGWOOD II (1928)

Dogwood II Vase

Basket w/overhead handle, dogwood blossoms on matte green ground, 8" h. 55.00
Planter, rim handles, tub-shaped, dogwood blossoms on matte green ground, 7" d., 4" h. 30.00
Planter, boat-shaped, dogwood blossoms on matte green ground, 11 x 6" 55.00
Vase, 14½" h., dogwood blossoms on matte green ground (ILLUS.) 140.00
Wall pocket, angular side handles, dogwood blossoms on matte green ground, 10" h. 75.00

DONATELLO (1915)

Donatello Vase

Bowl, 6½" d., cherubs in light relief on tan band, green & ivory fluted body 45.00
Bowl w/flower frog, 7½" d., 3½" h., cherubs in light relief on tan band, green & ivory fluted body, 2 pcs. 58.00
Candlestick, ring handle at flaring base, 6" h. (single) 65.00
Compote, 5" h. 45.00
Flower pot w/attached saucer, 5" h. 77.50
Jardiniere, 9" d., 8" h. 90.00
Jardiniere & pedestal base, overall 23½" h., 2 pcs. ....345.00 to 425.00
Plate, 8" d. ....175.00 to 225.00
Powder jar, cov., 5" d., 2" h. 290.00
Vase, double bud, 5" h., 8" w., gate form ....35.00 to 45.00
Vase, 8" h., cylindrical 35.00
Vase, 12" h. (ILLUS.) 175.00
Wall pocket, 9" h. 95.00

EARLAM (1930)

Candlesticks, angular base handles, mottled green blending to tan glaze, 6" h., pr. 55.00
Chamberstick, deep saucer base w/loop handle, mottled green glaze, 4" h. 125.00
Vase, 4" h., two-handled, globular, mottled green glaze 40.00
Vase, 5½" h., two handles rising from mid-section to rim, bulbous w/short wide neck, mottled blue & green glaze 42.50
Urn-vase, mottled blue & green glaze, 6" h. 62.50
Vase, 6" h., 10" w., fan-shaped, mottled green glaze 55.00
Wall pocket, mottled green glaze, 6½" h. 180.00

EARLY EMBOSSED PITCHERS (pre-1916)

"The Boy," 7½" h. (chip & hairline crack at spout) 150.00
"Landscape," 7½" h. 55.00
'The Owl," 6½" h. 250.00
"Tulip," 7½" h. ....50.00 to 65.00
"Wild Rose," 9" h. 72.50

FERRELLA (1930)

Candlestick, chalice form w/slender nozzle rising from shell-molded reticulated bowl, mottled brown, 4½" h. (single) 125.00
Console bowl w/attached flower frog, shell-molded reticulated rim, mottled red & turquoise, 10" d., 4" h. 155.00
Vase, 4" h., angular handles rising from mid-section to base of neck, shell-molded base & rim, mottled brown 125.00
Vase, 5½" h., drooping side handles, urn-shaped, shell-molded reticulated base & rim, mottled red & turquoise 185.00
Vase, 6" h., two-handled, shell-molded reticulated base & rim, mottled brown 135.00
Vase, 8" h., ovoid, shell-molded reticulated base & rim, mottled red & turquoise 275.00
Vase, 9" h., slender side handles,

shell-molded reticulated base & rim, mottled brown or red & turquoise, each............175.00 to 200.00
Vase, 10½" h., 2-handled, mottled brown........................ 380.00

FLORANE I (1920's)
Basket w/overhead handle, flaring cylinder, shaded rust, 8½" h. 65.00
Bowl, 5" d., shaded rust 40.00
Bowl w/flower frog, 8" d., shaded rust........................ 90.00
Vase, 6" h., rim handles, cylindrical, shaded rust.................... 45.00
Vase, 10" h., shaded rust 100.00
Wall pocket, pierced crest, shaded rust to green, 9" h.............. 47.50
Wall pocket, side handles, shaded rust to green, 10½" h............ 115.00

FLORENTINE (1924-28)
Basket, hanging-type, bark-textured panels alternating w/embossed garlands of cascading fruit & florals, ivory, tan & green........ 75.00
Bowl, 9" d., bark-textured panels alternating w/berries & foliage, brown tones 50.00
Candlesticks, flaring base, bark-textured panels alternating w/embossed pendant garlands of fruit & florals, brown tones, 10½" h., pr............................ 110.00
Console bowl, bark-textured panels alternating w/garlands of cascading fruit & florals, dark brown tones, 10" d.................... 60.00
Jardiniere, bark-textured panels alternating w/berries & foliage, brown tones, 9" h. 80.00
Rose bowl, rim handles, bark-textured panels alternating w/embossed pendant garlands of fruits & florals, dark brown tones, 4" h.......................... 35.00

Florentine Double Bud Vase

Vase, double bud, 4½" h., 9" w., two cylinders w/flaring bases joined by reticulated gate w/central pendant garland of fruit, brown tones (ILLUS.)............ 38.00
Vase, 6" h., squatty, bark-textured panels alternating w/pendant garlands of fruit & florals, dark brown tones 22.00
Vase, 8½" h., two-handled, bark-textured panels alternating w/cascading garlands of florals & fruit, ivory, tan & green 40.00
Wall pocket, overhead handle, central bark-textured panel flanked by pendant floral garlands, brown tones, 7" h. ....45.00 to 55.00
Wall pocket, central bark-textured panel flanked by pendant floral garlands, dark brown tones, 12½" h........................ 115.00

FORGET-ME-NOT (before 1916)
Creamer & cov. sugar bowl, decal band of clusters of tiny blue flowers on creamware, pr............ 135.00
Dresser tray, decal band of clusters of tiny blue flowers on creamware.......................... 125.00
Ring tree, decal band of clusters of tiny blue flowers on creamware, 3½" h.......................... 65.00

FOXGLOVE (1940's)

Foxglove Vase

Basket w/overhead handle, white foxglove spray on shaded blue ground, 12" h. 110.00
Console bowl, white foxglove spray on shaded green ground, 10" d. ... 35.00
Candlesticks, flat base, pierced handles rising from base to rim, white foxglove spray on shaded green ground, 4½" h., pr. 27.00
Pedestal base, white foxglove spray on shaded pink ground 140.00
Tray, pierced rim handles, white foxglove spray on shaded blue ground, 11" l. oval 50.00
Jardiniere, two-handled, white foxglove spray on shaded pink or blue ground, 4" d., each...20.00 to 25.00
Vase, 4" h., white foxglove spray on shaded green ground........... 25.00
Vase, 8½" h., two handles rising from base to mid-section, fan-

shaped, white foxglove spray on shaded pink ground 45.00

Vase, 10" h., angular side handles, white foxglove spray on shaded green ground (ILLUS.)............ 125.00

Vase, 14" h., four handles at base, flaring mouth, white foxglove spray on shaded green ground ... 165.00

FREESIA (1945)

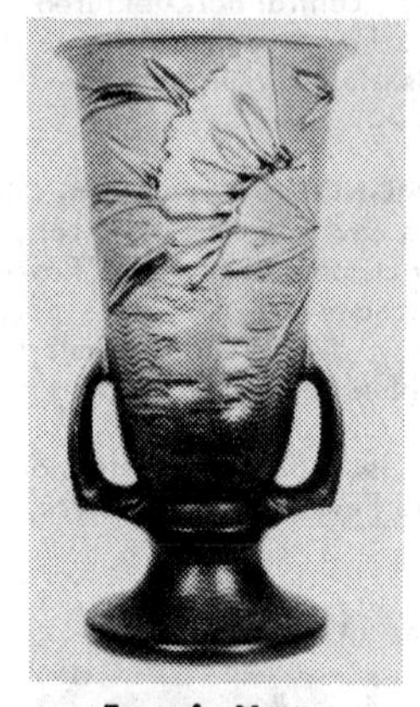

Freesia Vase

Basket w/pointed overhead handle, white to yellow blossoms & green leaves on shaded tangerine textured ground, 10" h.............. 60.00

Book ends, open book form, white blossoms & green leaves on shaded green textured ground, pr..... 45.00

Bowl, 4" d., small pierced handles at rim, white to yellow blossoms & green leaves on shaded tangerine textured ground 40.00

Console bowl, two-handled, shaped rim, white blossoms & green leaves on shaded green textured ground, 16½" l.................. 50.00

Cornucopia-vase, white blossoms & green leaves on shaded green textured ground, 8" h............ 25.00

Ewer, white to yellow blossoms & green leaves on shaded tangerine textured ground, 6" h........... 65.00

Tea set: cov. teapot, sugar bowl & creamer; white blossoms & green leaves on shaded textured green ground, 3 pcs. 90.00

Urn-vase, two-handled, white to yellow blossoms & green leaves on shaded tangerine textured ground, 8" h. 50.00

Vase, bud, 7" h., two-handled, white to yellow blossoms & green leaves on shaded tangerine textured ground 52.50

Vase, 9½" h., two handles at midsection, white blossoms & green leaves on shaded green textured ground 45.00

Vase, 10½" h., low foot, two handles rising from base, white to yellow blossoms on shaded tangerine textured ground (ILLUS.)... 45.00

Vase, 18" h., white blossoms & green leaves on shaded blue textured ground 220.00

FUCHSIA (1939)

Fuchsia Cornucopia-Vase

Basket w/overhead handle, footed, pendant fuchsia blossoms on green w/terra cotta highlights, w/flower frog, 8" h., 2 pcs. 110.00

Bowl, 5" d., two-handled, pendant fuchsia blossoms on blue w/cream highlights 45.00

Bowl-vase, two-handled, pendant fuchsia on tan w/gold highlights, 3" d. 32.00

Console bowl, two-handled, pendant fuchsia blossoms on tan w/gold highlights, 12½" l. 65.00

Cornucopia-vase, pendant fuchsia blossoms on blue w/cream highlights, 6" h. (ILLUS.) 45.00

Ewer, pendant fuchsia blossoms on green w/terra cotta highlights, 10" h. 175.00

Flower pot, pendant fuchsia blossoms on blue w/cream highlights, 5" h. (no saucer) 46.00

Vase, 6" h., large handles rising from mid-section to rim, pendant fuchsia blossoms on blue w/cream highlights 48.00

Vase, 9" h., pendant fuchsia blossoms on blue w/cream highlights 62.50

FUTURA (1928)

Bowl, 12 x 5 x 3½", footed, sharply canted sides, blended earth tones, w/flower frog................. 225.00

Vase, bud, 6" h., two slender handles rising from sharply canted base to rim of cone-shaped body, relief-molded stylized green vine & foliage on shaded sandy beige ground 125.00

Vase, 6" h., Art Deco style, rectangular stepped base, flat body w/stepped reeded sides, relief-molded branch w/blossom rising from base to rim, pale cream flecked w/blue glaze 115.00

Vase, 7" h., ovoid, ring-molded upper section, blended earth tones 85.00

Vase, 8" h., high square marbleized blue base w/sharply inclined sides & four short projections supporting globular blue body w/narrow neck & flaring mouth, overlapping pale blue & cream circles of varying sizes around upper portion & on side 325.00

Vase, 9" h., angular handles rising from bulbous base to rim, sharply stepped neck, green high-gloss glaze 345.00

GARDENIA (1940's)

Gardenia Console Bowl

Basket w/overhead handle, scalloped rim, white gardenia blossom on shaded green, 8" h. 58.00

Basket, hanging-type w/insert & chain, white gardenia blossom on shaded green or grey, 5", each ....75.00 to 95.00

Console bowl, canoe-shaped, white gardenia blossom on shaded grey, 12" l. (ILLUS.) ....50.00 to 60.00

Ewer, white gardenia blossom on shaded grey, 6" h. 35.00

Vase, 6" h., two-handled, white gardenia blossom on shaded tan 33.00

Vase, 10½" h., two-handled, white gardenia blossom on shaded green 65.00

Wall pocket, two-handled, white gardenia blossom on shaded tan, 9½" h. ....85.00 to 100.00

HOLLAND (before 1916)

Ale set: tankard pitcher & four mugs; embossed & colorfully painted figures of Dutch children on oatmeal ground, deep green base & rim, 5 pcs. 350.00

Ale set: tankard pitcher & six mugs; embossed & colorfully painted Dutch men, women & children, 7 pcs. 450.00

Holland Mug

Mug, embossed & colorfully painted Dutch girl, 4" h. (ILLUS.) 40.00

IMPERIAL I (1916)

Basket w/rounded overhead handle, pretzel-twisted vine & grape leaves in relief on green & brown textured ground, 6" h. 35.00

Basket w/slanted overhead handle, slanted rim, pretzel-twisted vine & grape leaves in relief on green & brown textured ground, 8" h. 56.00

Basket w/tall overhead handle, slanted rim, pretzel-twisted vine & grape leaves in relief on green & brown textured ground, 13" h. 65.00

Basket, hanging-type, pretzel-twisted vine & grape leaves in relief on green & brown textured ground 105.00

Umbrella stand, pretzel-twisted vine & grape leaves in relief on green & brown textured ground 225.00

Vase, triple bud, 8" h., pretzel-twisted vine & grape leaves in relief on green & brown textured ground 58.00

Wall pocket, pretzel-twisted vine & grape leaf in relief on green & brown textured ground, 10" h. 100.00

IMPERIAL II (1924)

Bowl, 8" d., ring-molded sides, mottled turquoise glaze 115.00

Bowl, 9½" d., blue glaze w/yellow splotches 130.00

Vase, 4" h., globular w/flattened sides, greyish-green matte glaze w/bright yellow rim 90.00

Vase, 10" h., blue glaze w/mottled white & yellow collar 175.00

Wall pocket, narrow band of horizontal ribbing at center, mottled lavender & pink glaze, 6½" h. 175.00

Wall pocket, three-prong, horizontal ridges, mottled orange & green glaze, 6½" h. 225.00

IRIS (1938)

Iris Vase

Basket, hanging-type, iris & leaves on shaded blue ground 135.00
Bowl, 4" d., iris & leaves on shaded tan ground 45.00
Console bowl, iris & leaves on shaded pink ground, 14" l. 125.00
Console set: 10" l. console bowl & pair 4" h. candlesticks; iris & leaves on shaded pink ground, 3 pcs. 110.00
Ewer, iris & leaves on shaded pink ground, 10" h. 150.00
Jardiniere, iris & leaves on shaded pink ground, 8" h. 95.00
Vase, 4" h., base handles, iris & leaves on shaded blue ground 24.00
Vase, 5" h., iris & leaves on shaded pink ground (ILLUS.) 35.00
Vase, 7" h., iris & leaves on shaded tan ground 45.00
Vase, bud, 7" h., iris & leaves on shaded blue ground 40.00
Vase, 12" h., angular shoulder handles, iris & leaves on shaded pink ground 125.00

IXIA (1930's)

Ixia Centerpiece

Candlesticks, lavender floral cluster on shaded green, 4½" h., pr. 45.00
Centerpiece, one-piece console set w/candleholders attached to center bowl, lavender floral cluster on shaded green, 13" l. (ILLUS.) 110.00
Flower pot w/saucer, white floral cluster on shaded pink, 5" h. 48.00
Jardiniere, base handles, lavender floral cluster on shaded green, 4" h. 30.00
Vase, 7" h., white floral cluster on shaded pink 38.00
Vase, 8" h., lavender floral cluster on shaded green 45.00

JONQUIL (1931)

Basket w/overhead handle, jonquil blossoms & leaves in relief against textured tan ground, 8" h. 185.00
Bowl, 5½" h., small handles at rim, jonquil blossoms & leaves in relief against textured tan ground 60.00
Candlestick, domed base, jonquil blossoms & leaves in relief against textured tan ground, 4" h. (single) 70.00
Console bowl, jonquil blossoms & leaves in relief against textured tan ground, 10 x 6", 3½" h. 115.00
Crocus pot w/attached saucer, elongated handles, jonquil blossoms & leaves in relief against textured tan ground, 7" h. 150.00
Plate w/attached flower frog, jonquil blossoms & leaves in relief against textured tan ground, 10" d. 165.00
Pot w/attached flower frog, flaring cylinder, jonquil blossoms & leaves in relief against textured tan ground, 5½" h. 85.00
Vase, 6½" h., two-handled, bulbous, jonquil blossoms & leaves in relief against textured tan ground 82.00
Vase, 8" h., two-handled, ovoid, jonquil blossoms & leaves in relief against textured tan ground 95.00
Wall pocket, jonquil blossoms & leaves in relief against textured tan ground, 8½" h. 220.00

JUVENILE (1916 on)

Juvenile Pitcher

Bowl, 6½" d., chicks 55.00
Egg cup, chicks, 3½" h. 75.00

Egg cup, sitting rabbits, 3½" h. . . . . .90.00 to 110.00
Feeding dish w/rolled edge, chicks, 7" d. 45.00
Feeding dish w/rolled edge, chicks, 8" d. 55.00
Feeding dish w/rolled edge, nursery rhyme "Tom, The Piper's Son," 8" d. 35.00
Feeding dish w/rolled edge, sitting rabbits, "Baby's Plate," 7" d. 30.00
Feeding dish w/rolled edge, sitting rabbits, "Baby's Plate," 8" d. 55.00
Feeding dish w/rolled edge, sunbonnet girl, 8" d. 45.00
Mug, chicks, 3½" h. 50.00
Mug, two-handled, duck w/hat, 3" h. 65.00
Mug, sitting rabbits, 3" h. 45.00
Pitcher, 3" h., side-pour, chicks 35.00
Pitcher, 3" h., chicks 40.00
Pitcher, 3½" h., side-pour, fat puppy 85.00
Pitcher, 3½" h., seated dog (ILLUS.) 65.00
Pitcher, 3" h., side-pour, sitting rabbits 55.00
Pitcher, 3½" h., sitting rabbits 47.50
Plate, 8" d., sunbonnet girl 40.00

LANDSCAPE (1910)

Custard cup, creamware w/sailboats decal, in original silver server 55.00
Planter, square, creamware w/windmill decal, 4½" h. 65.00
Tea set: cov. teapot, creamer & cov. sugar bowl; creamware w/windmill decal, 3 pcs. . . . . .275.00 to 350.00

LAUREL (1934)

Laurel Vase

Urn-vase, laurel branch & berries in low relief, reeded panels at sides, terra cotta, 6" h. 44.00
Vase, 6" h., angular shoulder handles, laurel branch & berries in low relief, reeded panels at sides, green 40.00
Vase, 7" h., angular shoulder handles, short stepped neck, laurel branch & berries in low relief, reeded panels at sides, deep yellow 85.00
Vase, 8" h., footed, laurel branch & berries in low relief, reeded panels at sides, green (ILLUS.). . . . 75.00
Vase, 9½" h., closed handles rising from top of bulbous base to middle of stepped neck, green. 67.00
Vase, 10" h., low foot, closed angular handles rising from base to mid-section, deep yellow 70.00

LOMBARDY (1924)

Bowl, 8" d., low, three-footed, melon-ribbed, blue-grey matte glaze 135.00
Vase, 6" h., three-footed, acorn-shaped, melon-ribbed, mottled pink & grey matte glaze 100.00
Wall pocket, straight lip, melon-ribbed, blue-grey matte glaze, 8" h. . . . . .225.00 to 250.00

LUFFA (1934)

Vase, 5" h., angular handles, relief-molded ivy leaves & blossoms on shaded green wavy horizontal ridges 50.00
Vase, 6" h., angular rim handles, relief-molded ivy leaves & blossoms on shaded green wavy horizontal ridges 47.50

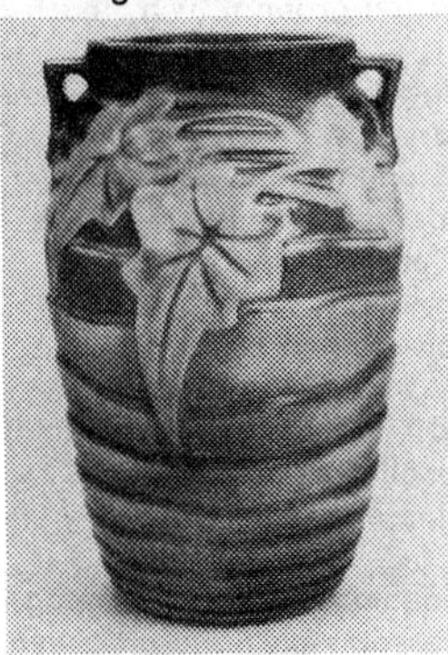

Luffa Vase

Vase, 7" h., swollen cylinder, angular rim handles, relief-molded ivy leaves & blossoms on shaded green wavy horizontal ridges (ILLUS.) 65.00
Vase, 8" h., expanding cylinder, angular rim handles, relief-molded ivy leaves & blossoms on shaded green wavy horizontal ridges 82.50
Vase, 8½" h., angular handles rising from shoulder to middle of

short collared neck, relief-molded ivy leaves & blossoms on shaded green wavy horizontal ridges 80.00

MAGNOLIA (1943)

Magnolia Vase

Basket w/overhead handle, magnolia blossoms on textured blue or tan ground, 7" h., each ....45.00 to 60.00
Basket w/angular overhead handle, cornucopia form, magnolia blossoms on textured tan ground, 12" h. 85.00
Book ends, magnolia blossoms on textured green or tan ground, each pr.....................65.00 to 85.00
Candlesticks, angular handles rising from circular base to mid-section, magnolia blossoms on textured green or tan ground, 5" h., each pr. 33.00
Cornucopia-vase, magnolia blossoms on textured green ground, 6" h. .. 30.00
Creamer & open sugar bowl, magnolia blossoms on textured blue ground, pr. 55.00
Ewer, magnolia blossoms on textured tan ground, 10" h. 80.00
Jardiniere, magnolia blossoms on textured blue ground, 4" d. 50.00
Mug, magnolia blossoms on textured blue or green ground, each 45.00
Planter, angular end handles, magnolia blossoms on textured green ground, 8½" l. 30.00
Rose bowl, magnolia blossoms on textured blue or green ground, 4" widest d., each 27.50
Vase, 6" h., bulbous w/short wide neck, angular handles, magnolia blossoms on textured blue or green ground, each ....35.00 to 45.00
Vase, 8" h., two-handled, magnolia blossoms on textured blue or tan ground, each ....55.00 to 65.00
Vase, 9" h., two-handled, magnolia blossoms on textured blue ground (ILLUS.) 70.00
Vase, 12" h., magnolia blossoms on textured green ground........... 90.00

MING TREE (1949)

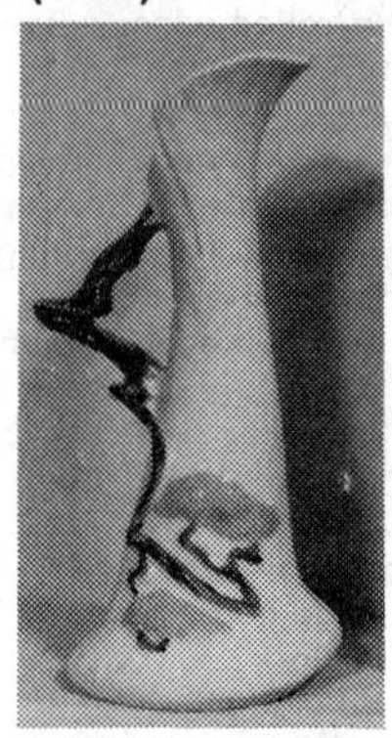

Ming Tree Ewer

Ashtray, oriental branches in relief on blue ground, 6" w. 20.00
Basket w/overhead branch handle, footed, globular body w/irregular rim, oriental branches in relief on blue ground, 8" h. 55.00
Book ends, oriental branches in relief on blue or white ground, 5½" h., each pr. ....80.00 to 95.00
Bowl, branch handle at each end, oriental branches in relief on blue ground, 11½ x 4" 43.00
Console bowl, branch handle at each end, irregular rim, oriental branches in relief on green ground, 10" l. 57.50
Ewer, angular branch handle, oriental branches in relief on white ground, 10" h. (ILLUS.) 80.00
Planter, irregular rim, oriental branches in relief on blue or white ground, 8½ x 4", each 38.00
Window box, oriental branches in relief on white ground, 11 x 4" ... 85.00

MOCK ORANGE (1950)

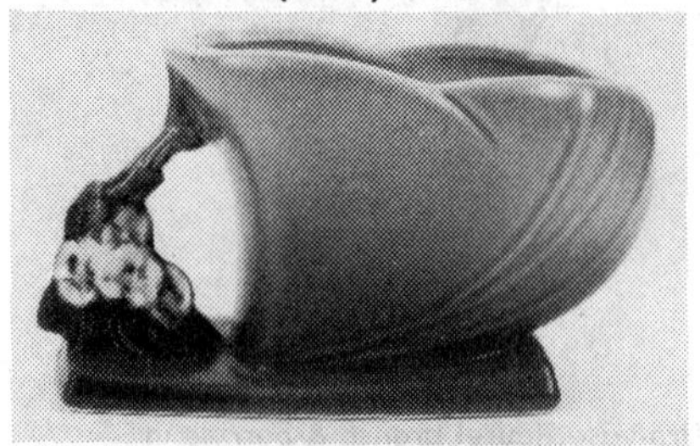

Mock Orange Planter

Basket, hanging-type, white blossoms & green leaves on green ground 75.00

Bowl, 11" w., three-footed, white blossoms & green leaves on green ground 37.00
Bowl, 12" d., white blossoms & green leaves on green or pink ground, each 50.00
Ewer, white blossoms & green leaves on pink ground, 16" h. 160.00
Planter, oblong base, cluster of white blossoms & green leaves at base of handle, green body, 7" l., 4" h. (ILLUS.) 38.00
Vase, 7" h., white blossoms & green leaves on pink ground 35.00

MONTACELLO (1931)
Basket w/pointed overhead handle, white stylized trumpet flowers w/black accents on band, mottled tan ground, 6½" h. 165.00
Bowl-vase, two-handled, white stylized trumpet flowers w/black accents on band, mottled blue & tan ground, 7" d., 5" h. 95.00
Candlesticks, white stylized trumpet flowers w/black accents on band, mottled turquoise shaded to tan ground, 4½" h., pr. 80.00
Vase, 5" h., globular, two-handled, white stylized trumpet flowers w/black accents on band, mottled tan ground 45.00
Vase, 6" h., two-handled, white stylized trumpet flowers w/black accents on band, mottled blue & tan ground 65.00
Vase, 9" h., two handles rising from mid-section to wide mouth, white stylized trumpet flowers w/black accents on band, mottled blue & tan ground 125.00

MORNING GLORY (1935)
Console bowl, small angular handles, stylized pastel morning glories in low relief on green ground, 11½ x 4½" 170.00
Urn-vase, two-handled, stylized pastel morning glories in low relief on green ground, 6½" h. 225.00
Vase, 6" h., waisted cylinder, two-handled, stylized pastel morning glories in low relief on white ground ....135.00 to 150.00
Vase, 8" h., angular handles rising from shoulder to rim, stylized pastel morning glories in low relief on white ground 200.00
Vase, 9" h., angular handles, stylized pastel morning glories in low relief on green ground....... 295.00

MOSS (1930's)
Bowl-vase, globular, angular handles rising from base to mid-section, pendant moss on pink shaded to blue ground........... 70.00
Console bowl, angular end handles, pendant moss on pink shaded to green ground, 13" l. 50.00
Jardiniere, angular rim handles, pendant moss on pink shaded to green ground, 8" h. 175.00
Vase, 9" h., two-handled, pendant moss on pink shaded to blue or green ground, each ......60.00 to 70.00

Moss Wall Pocket

Wall pocket, two-handled, pendant moss on pink shaded to blue ground (ILLUS.).................. 110.00

MOSTIQUE (1915)

Mostique Jardiniere

Bowl, 6" d., handles rising from base to under everted rim, glossy brown, yellow, blue & green geometric design on pebbled grey ground 55.00
Bowl, 9½" d., 3" h., multicolored geometric design on glossy beige ground 65.00
Jardiniere, glossy designs in brown, yellow, blue & green on pebbled grey ground, 12" d., 9½" h. (ILLUS.)......................... 80.00
Vase, 9" h., tapering cylinder w/wide mouth, two-handled, panels of glossy orange squares & white triangles on blue bands on pebbled grey ground 93.50

Vase, 12" h., 8" d., two-handled, glossy multicolored floral designs on pebbled tan ground 105.00
Wall pocket, glossy square & band design on pebbled grey ground w/incised heart-shaped leaves, 9½" h. 135.00

ORIAN (1935)

Vase, 7" h., slender handles rising from compressed globular base to middle of long wide neck, glossy yellow w/green lining 65.00
Vase, 7½" h., squatty ringed base, slender handles rising from shoulder to rim of short wide neck, glossy burgundy w/turquoise lining or turquoise w/orange lining, each ....80.00 to 95.00
Vase, 8" h., 7" widest d., slender handles, glossy burgundy w/turquoise lining 85.00
Vase, 9½" h., slender handles, glossy brown w/green lining 70.00
Vase, 10½" h., urn-form, slender handles rising from foot to shoulder, glossy burgundy w/turquoise lining or turquoise w/brown lining, each ....80.00 to 95.00
Vase, 12½" h., footed, slender handles rising from globular base to rim of long neck, turquoise w/orange lining 95.00

PANEL (1920)

Vase, 6" h., fan-shaped, panel w/nude lady on brown-black ground ....140.00 to 175.00
Vase, 7" h., panels of florals on dark green ground 53.00
Vase, 10" h., baluster form, panels of naturalistic leaves on brown-black or dark green ground, each 55.00
Wall pocket, panel of florals on brown-black ground, 9" h. 120.00
Wall pocket, tapering body, panel of naturalistic leaves on dark green ground, 9" h. 95.00

PEONY (1942)

Basket w/angular overhead handle, irregular rim, peony blossoms in relief against textured pink ground, 10" h. 57.00
Bowl, 11" l., two-handled, shaped rim, peony blossoms in relief against textured gold ground 40.00
Bowl-vase, globular, tiny rim handles, peony blossoms in relief against textured pink ground, 6" d. 35.00
Ewer, peony blossoms in relief against textured gold or pink ground, 10" h., each ....50.00 to 65.00
Pitcher w/ice lip, 7½" h., peony blossoms in relief against textured gold ground 80.00
Teapot, cov., peony blossoms in relief against textured gold ground 82.00
Vase, 4" h., base handles, peony blossoms in relief against textured green ground 28.00
Vase, 6" h., large angular handles, peony blossoms in relief against textured gold ground 40.00
Vase, bud, 7" h., peony blossoms in relief against textured gold ground 35.00
Vase, 8" h., two-handled, peony blossoms in relief against textured green or pink ground, each ....30.00 to 40.00

Peony Vase

Vase, 10" h., two-handled, peony blossoms in relief against textured green ground (ILLUS.) 50.00
Wall pocket, two-handled, irregular rim, peony blossoms in relief against textured gold ground, 8" h. 68.00

PINE CONE (1931)

Basket w/overhead handle, realistic pine cones in relief on shaded blue or brown ground, 6" h., each .... 105.00 to 125.00
Basket w/overhead branch handle, realistic pine cones in relief on shaded green ground, 13 x 9" 175.00
Basket, hanging-type, realistic pine cones in relief on shaded brown or green ground, 5", each ....115.00 to 140.00
Book ends, realistic pine cones in relief on shaded brown ground, pr. 105.00
Bowl, 4½" h., twig handles, realistic pine cones in relief on blue or brown ground, each ....50.00 to 65.00
Centerpiece, one-piece console set w/candleholders attached to cen-

ter bowl, pine cones in relief on brown ground, 6" 185.00
Cornucopia-vase, pine cones in relief on brown or blue ground, 8" h., each ....90.00 to 120.00
Dish, boat-shaped w/single curving handle, pine cones in relief on green ground, 9" l.............. 85.00
Jardiniere, twig handles, pine cones in relief on blue ground, 3" h..... 38.00
Jardiniere & pedestal base, pine cones in relief on green ground, overall 30" h., 2 pcs. 600.00
Pitcher, 9½" h., globular, branch handle at shoulder, pine cones in relief on green ground 150.00
Planter, cylindrical, single handle rising from base to rim, pine cones in relief on brown ground, 5" 110.00
Plate, 7½" d., pine cones in relief on green ground 145.00
Sand jar, pine cones in relief on green ground 525.00
Tray, double, center handle in the form of pine needles & cone, blue, 10" 150.00
Urn-vase, square foot, twig handles, pine cones in relief on blue or brown ground, 7½" h., each ....110.00 to 135.00
Vase, bud, 7½" h., single handle in the form of pine needles & cone rising from base to mid-section, brown 50.00
Vase, 8" h., pillow-shaped, pine cones in relief on brown ground .. 85.00
Vase, 10" h., expanding cylinder, small branch handles, pine cones in relief on brown or green ground, each ....100.00 to 125.00

Pine Cone Wall Pocket

Wall pocket, double, overhead handle in the form of pine needles & cone, brown, 8½" h. (ILLUS.) 135.00

POPPY (1930's)

Bowl, 4" h., two-handled, poppies on shaded pink ground (ILLUS.)... 40.00

Poppy Bowl

Bowl, 10" d., two-handled, poppies on turquoise blue shaded to white ground 60.00
Ewer, cylindrical, poppies on shaded pink ground, 10" h. 80.00
Jardiniere, ring handles at rim, poppies on shaded pink ground, 6½" 75.00
Vase, 8" h., two-handled, poppies on shaded pink ground 35.00
Vase, 10½" h., two-handled, poppies on turquoise blue shaded to white ground 60.00
Vase, 18" h., large handles below rim, cylindrical, poppies on shaded pink ground 175.00

RAYMOR (1952)

Ashtray, Beach gray 8.00
Bean pot, cov., individual size, Avocado green................ 25.00
Bowl, fruit, handled, Terra Cotta ... 55.00
Coffee pot, cov., Autumn brown (no stand) 75.00
Coffee pot, cov., Terra Cotta, w/Autumn brown swinging-type stand 135.00
Creamer, cov., & cov. sugar bowl, Terra Cotta, pr. 35.00
Cup & saucer, Beach gray 10.00
Dish, fruit, Avocado green 12.00
Gravy boat, Avocado green, 9½" l. 15.00
Mustard jar, cov., Autumn brown ... 25.00
Plate, dinner, Avocado green 8.00
Plate, salad, Terra Cotta 4.00
Platter, 14" l., Contemporary white 15.00
Soup bowl, lug handles, Terra Cotta 20.00
Vegetable bowl, divided, Avocado green, 13" l. 30.00

ROSECRAFT (1916)

Bowl, 6" d., glossy black........... 16.50
Vase, 6" h., two-handled, glossy blue 24.00
Vase, 7½" h., glossy black ..45.00 to 60.00
Vase, bud, 8" w., gate-form, glossy yellow 25.00
Vase, 9" h., two handles rising from shoulder to rim, globular w/wide neck, glossy black................. 50.00

Vase, 10" h., two-handled, glossy black 50.00
Wall pocket, two-handled, flaring rim, glossy yellow, 10½" h. 110.00

ROSECRAFT HEXAGON (1924)

Bowl, 7½" w., small rim handles, bleeding hearts on dark matte green finish ....70.00 to 85.00
Candlesticks, bleeding hearts on dark green matte finish, 8" h., pr. 250.00
Vase, 5" h., bleeding hearts on dark brown matte finish, burnt orange lining 95.00
Vase, 6" h., dark brown or green matte finish, each ....85.00 to 95.00

ROSECRAFT VINTAGE (1924)

Rosecraft Vintage Vase

Vase, 5" h., curving band of brown & yellow grapevine w/fruit & foliage at shoulder, dark brown matte ground (ILLUS.)............ 40.00
Vase, 7" h., curving band of brown & yellow grapevine w/fruit & foliage below rim, dark brown matte ground 45.00
Vase, 8½" h., angular rim handles, expanding cylinder, curving band of brown & yellow grapevine w/fruit & foliage at shoulder, dark brown matte ground 155.00
Wall pocket, two handles rising from mid-section to rim, brown & yellow grapevine w/fruit & foliage, dark brown matte ground, 9" h. 115.00
Window box, band of brown & yellow grapevine w/fruit & foliage, dark brown matte ground, 11½ x 6" 225.00

ROZANE (early 1900's)

Ewer, fluted rim, underglaze slip-painted florals, standard brown glaze, artist-signed, 7½" h. 95.00
Ewer, underglaze slip-painted berries & foliage, standard brown glaze, 9½" h. 225.00
Mug, flared base, underglaze slip-painted florals, standard brown glaze, 4" h. 145.00
Mug, underglaze slip-painted cherries & foliage, standard brown glaze, 4½" h. ....110.00 to 125.00
Pitcher, tankard, 15" h., underglaze slip-painted yellow & green ears of corn, standard brown glaze 425.00
Pitcher, 16" h., underglaze slip-painted golden pears, standard brown glaze, artist-signed 350.00
Vase, 4" h., two-handled, underglaze slip-painted pansies, standard brown glaze 150.00
Vase, 7" h., two-handled, pillow-shaped, ruffled rim, underglaze slip-painted yellow jonquils & green foliage, standard brown glaze ....250.00 to 265.00

Rozane Vase

Vase, 9" h., pillow-shaped, underglaze slip-painted scene of dog w/pheasant, standard brown glaze (ILLUS.) ....1,400.00 to 1,500.00
Vase, 9½"h., bulbous, underglaze slip-painted orange florals & green foliage, shaded tan to dark brown standard glaze 290.00
Vase, 14" h., underglaze slip-painted portrait of an Indian in full headdress, standard brown glaze (restored) 1,300.00

ROZANE (1917)

Basket w/rounded overhead handle, clusters of delicately tinted pink, lavender & yellow roses w/green leaves against stippled ivory ground, 8" h. 65.00
Bowl, 3½" h., cluster of pink, lavender & yellow roses w/green leaves against stippled pink ground 45.00
Candlesticks, cluster of pink, lavender & yellow roses w/green leaves against stippled ivory ground, 7" h., pr. 55.00
Compote, 6½" h., cluster of pink,

lavender & yellow roses w/green leaves against stippled ivory ground 75.00

Cuspidor, cluster of pink, lavender & yellow roses w/green leaves against stippled ivory ground, 5" h. 90.00

Jardiniere, cluster of pink, lavender & yellow roses w/green leaves against stippled mint green ground, 5" h. 55.00

Jardiniere, cluster of pink, lavender & yellow roses w/green leaves against stippled pale pink ground, 8" h. ....70.00 to 85.00

Jardiniere, cluster of pink, lavender & yellow roses w/green leaves against stippled ivory ground, 14" d., 12" h. ....200.00 to 250.00

Rozane Jardiniere & Pedestal

Jardiniere & pedestal base, clusters of pink, lavender & yellow roses w/green leaves against stippled ivory ground, overall 28½" h., 2 pcs. (ILLUS.) ....350.00 to 450.00

Vase, 6½" h., cone-shaped, cluster of pink, lavender & yellow roses w/green leaves against stippled ivory ground 40.00

Wall pocket, cluster of pink, lavender & yellow roses w/green leaves against stippled ivory ground, 7½" h. 70.00

RUSSCO (1930's)

Cornucopia-vase, narrow vertical ribbon panels, blue matte lustre glaze, 8" h. 30.00

Vase, 6" h., urn-shaped, octagonal rim, narrow vertical ribbon panels, gold w/metallic gold trim 55.00

Vase, 7" h., two-handled, urn-shaped, octagonal rim, narrow vertical ribbon panels, gold w/metallic gold trim 70.00

Vase, 8" h., footed, handles rising from base of cone-shaped body to just beneath flaring octagonal rim, narrow vertical ribbon panels, turquoise matte finish 65.00

Vase, 10" h., octagonal rim, gold matte finish w/crystalline overlay 75.00

SILHOUETTE (1940's)

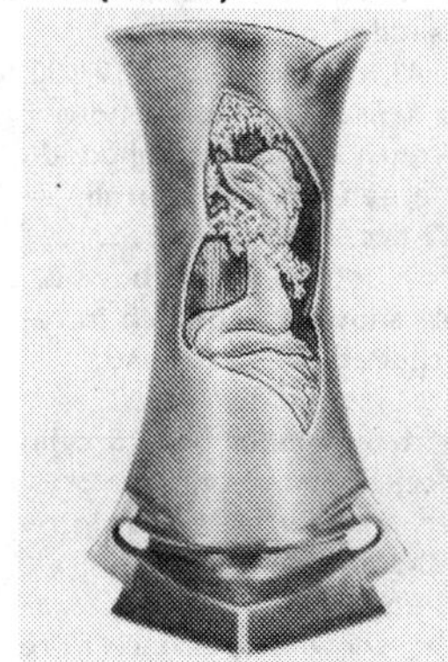

Silhouette Vase

Basket w/asymmetrical overhead handle, silhouette floral panel, shaded tan, 10" h 75.00

Basket, hanging-type, silhouette floral panel, shaded rose, 4" h. ....40.00 to 50.00

Rose bowl, silhouette panel of a nude, white w/turquoise blue, 6" widest d. 100.00

Vase, 6" h., silhouette floral panel, shaded tan 25.00

Vase, 7" h., fan-shaped, silhouette panel of a nude, shaded rose 160.00

Vase, 8" h., squared body on wave-form base, silhouette floral panel, shaded turquoise blue 30.00

Vase, 10" h., waisted cylinder on square base, small handles between base & body, silhouette panel of a nude, shaded turquoise blue (ILLUS.) 150.00

Wall pocket, silhouette floral panel, shaded turquoise blue, 8" h. 55.00

SNOWBERRY (1946)

Ashtray, snowberry branch in relief on shaded green ground 40.00

Basket w/asymmetrical overhead handle, snowberry branch in relief on shaded blue ground 45.00

Basket w/asymmetrical overhead handle, shaped rim, snowberry branch in relief on shaded blue ground, 12½" h. 75.00

Bowl, 5" d., pointed handles at

shoulder, snowberry branch in relief on shaded green ground 35.00
Console bowl, 10" l., pointed pierced end handles, snowberry branch in relief on shaded blue or rose ground, each ....40.00 to 50.00
Ewer, snowberry branch in relief on shaded blue ground, 6" h. 25.00
Flower pot, snowberry branch in relief on shaded green ground, 5" h. 32.50
Jardiniere, snowberry branch in relief on shaded green or rose ground, 4" h., each ....27.00 to 35.00
Jardiniere & pedestal base, snowberry branch in relief on shaded blue or green ground, overall 24" h., 2 pcs., each set 425.00
Tea set: cov. teapot, sugar bowl & creamer; snowberry branch in relief on shaded green ground, 3 pcs. 150.00
Vase, 7½" h., globular base & cylindrical neck, pointed handles at shoulder, snowberry branch in relief on shaded blue or green ground, each 55.00
Vase, 8" h., snowberry branch in relief on shaded green ground 48.00
Vase, 15" h., snowberry branch in relief on shaded blue ground..... 125.00

Snowberry Wall Pocket

Wall pocket, angular handles rising from base, snowberry branch in relief on shaded green ground, 8" w., 5½"h. (ILLUS.) ....55.00 to 65.00

STEIN SETS (before 1916)

Ale set: tankard pitcher & six mugs; creamware, Shrine emblem & "Osman Temple," ca. 1913, 7 pcs. 685.00
Mug, Fraternal Order of Eagles (F.O.E.), creamware, brown spread-winged eagle & rock decal decoration, 5" h. 75.00
Mug, creamware, decal portrait of Indian w/full headdress, 5" h. 80.00
Mug, Knights of Pythias, creamware, colorful decal of heroic scene, 5" h. 150.00
Mug, creamware, Quaker men motif, 5" h. 150.00
Mug, creamware, Shrine emblem & "Osman Temple, Feb. 14, 1916," 5" h. 85.00
Pitcher, tankard, 12" h., F.O.E., creamware, brown spread-winged eagle & rock decal decoration 175.00
Pitcher, tankard, 12" h., Knights of Pythias, colorful decal scene entitled "Friendship" 425.00

SUNFLOWER (1930)

Sunflower Vase

Basket, hanging-type, chrysanthemum-type yellow sunflowers on mottled green ground 225.00
Console bowl, chrysanthemum-type yellow sunflowers on mottled green ground, 12½" l., 3" h. 90.00
Jardiniere, chrysanthemum-type yellow sunflowers on mottled green ground, 6" d. 87.00
Vase, 4" h., two-handled, chrysanthemum-type yellow sunflowers on mottled green ground (ILLUS.) 47.50
Vase, 6" h., angular rim handles, chrysanthemum-type yellow sunflowers on mottled green ground 60.00
Vase, 7" h., flaring cylinder, chrysanthemum-type yellow sunflowers on mottled green ground 95.00
Vase, 8" h., two-handled, globular, everted rim, chrysanthemum-type yellow sunflowers on mottled green ground 95.00
Window box, two-handled, chrysanthemum-type yellow sunflowers on mottled green ground, 11" l., 3½" h. 115.00

THORN APPLE (1930's)

Bowl, 8" d., trumpet-like flower one side & prickly burr reverse on shaded pink ground 100.00
Candlesticks, trumpet-like flower & prickly burr on shaded brown ground, 4½" h., pr. 75.00

Cornucopia-vase, trumpet-like flower & prickly burr at base on shaded brown ground, 6" h. 35.00
Flower pot w/attached saucer, trumpet-like flower one side & prickly burr reverse on shaded blue ground 75.00
Vase, 4" h., squatty body w/short narrow neck, angular pierced handles rising from mid-section, trumpet-like flower one side & prickly burr reverse on shaded blue ground 40.00
Vase, 6" h., trumpet-like flower one side & prickly burr reverse on shaded blue or pink ground, each 30.00
Vase, 8" h., goblet form on low foot, slender cylindrical column rising from base to rim at each side, trumpet-like flower one side & prickly burr reverse on shaded pink ground 85.00
Vase, 10" h., two-handled, trumpet-like flower one side & prickly burr reverse on shaded blue ground... 50.00

TOPEO (1934)
Bowl, 6" d., four areas of relief-molded beading, glossy deep red glaze 75.00
Bowl, 11½" d., 3" h., four areas of relief-molded beading, glossy deep red glaze.................. 125.00
Console bowl, irregular fluted rim, four areas of relief-molded beading, blue shaded to green glaze, 13" l., 4" h. 60.00
Vase, 6" h., four areas of relief-molded beading, glossy deep red glaze 110.00
Vase, 7" h., four areas of relief-molded beading, blue shaded to green 55.00
Vase, 7" h., four areas of relief-molded beading, glossy deep red glaze 85.00
Vase, 9" h., globular base w/wide flaring mouth, four areas of relief-molded beading, blue shaded to green.................... 80.00

TOURMALINE (1933)
Ginger jar, cov., mottled terra cotta & yellow 300.00
Urn, hemispherical, embossed design around short neck, semi-gloss medium blue glaze, 4½" h. 55.00
Vase, 5" h., semi-gloss medium blue glaze 60.00
Vase, 5" h., mottled turquoise blue 40.00
Vase, 6" h., bulbous base, wide neck, handles rising from mid-section to rim, streaked powder blue 50.00
Vase, 8" h., waisted cylinder on low foot, streaked powder blue 55.00

TUSCANY (1927)
Candleholders, conical base w/open handles rising from embossed clusters of grapes & leaves to mid-section of nozzle, mottled pink, 3" h., pr. 38.00
Console bowl, rectangular w/rounded ends, mottled pink, 11" l. 35.00
Flower arranger, pedestal base, flaring body, open handles terminating in clusters of grapes & leaves, mottled pink, 5" h. 50.00
Vase, 4" h., two-handled, mottled grey 35.00
Vase, 7" h., open handles terminating in clusters of grape leaves, mottled pink 32.00
Vase, 9" h., globular base, short wide mouth, open handles rising from clusters of grapes & leaves at shoulder, mottled pink 55.00

VELMOSS SCROLL (1916)
Bowl, 8" d., incised stylized red roses & green leaves, creamy ivory matte glaze 30.00
Bowl, 9" d., 2½" h., incised stylized red roses & green leaves, creamy ivory matte glaze 40.00
Candlesticks, incised stylized red roses & green leaves, creamy ivory matte glaze, 8" h., pr. 70.00
Candlesticks, incised stylized red roses & green leaves, creamy ivory matte glaze, 9" h., pr. 80.00
Candlesticks, incised stylized red roses & green leaves, creamy ivory matte glaze, 10" h., pr. 145.00
Jardiniere, incised stylized red roses & green leaves, creamy ivory matte glaze, 10" d., 8" h. 170.00
Vase, 10" h., baluster form w/wide mouth, incised stylized red roses & green leaves, creamy ivory matte glaze.................... 70.00
Wall pocket, incised stylized red roses & green leaves, creamy ivory matte glaze, 12" h. 125.00

WATER LILY (1943)
Basket w/overhead handle, water lilies in relief on textured blue ground, 8" h. 54.00
Basket w/pointed overhead handle, water lilies in relief on textured blue ground, 10" h. 73.00
Basket, hanging-type, angular rim

handles, water lilies in relief on textured blue ground, 9" 110.00

Book ends, water lilies in relief on pink shaded to green ground, pr. 80.00

Bowl, 6" d., water lilies in relief on pink shaded to green ground 35.00

Water Lily Bowl

Bowl, 8½" d., 5" h., two-handled, water lilies in relief on brown shaded to tan ground (ILLUS.) 45.00

Candlesticks, flat circular base, angular handles, water lilies in relief on textured blue ground, 5" h., pr. 60.00

Console bowl, angular end handles, water lilies in relief on pink shaded to green ground, 12" l. 45.00

Ewer, flattened base, water lilies in relief on blue or brown shaded to tan ground, 6" h., each ....30.00 to 42.00

Flower arranger, fan-shaped, angular handles rising from base to rim, water lilies in relief on blue or brown shaded to tan ground, 4½" h., each ....30.00 to 40.00

Model of a conch shell, water lilies in relief on pink shaded to green ground, 6" h. 50.00

Pedestal base, water lilies in relief on blue ground, 16" h........... 165.00

Rose bowl, water lilies in relief on pink shaded to green ground, 4" d. 18.00

Vase, 6" h., cylindrical w/large angular side handles, water lilies in relief on pink shaded to green ground 34.00

Vase, 7" h., compressed base, swollen cylindrical body, angular handles rising from mid-section to rim, water lilies in relief on blue ground 60.00

Vase, 14" h., two-handled, water lilies in relief on brown shaded to tan ground 150.00

Vase, 15" h., angular handles, water lilies in relief on blue ground 145.00

WHITE ROSE (1940)

Basket w/overhead handle, white roses in relief on brown shaded to green ground, 8" h. 65.00

Basket w/circular handle rising from base & curling under opposite rim, white roses in relief on brown or pink shaded to green ground, 12" h., each 75.00

Basket, hanging-type, white roses in relief on brown shaded to green ground, 5" 100.00

Candleholder, two-light, white roses in relief on shaded blue ground, 4" h. 25.00

White Rose Ewer

Ewer, bulbous base, white roses in relief on shaded blue ground, 15" h. (ILLUS.) 127.50

Flower frog w/overhead handle, white roses in relief on brown shaded to green ground 20.00

Jardiniere, white roses in relief on pink shaded to green ground, 4" h. 38.00

Jardiniere, white roses in relief on brown shaded to green ground, 7" h. 47.50

Vase, 6" h., cylindrical w/short collared neck, angular handles at shoulder, white roses in relief on brown shaded to green ground ... 35.00

Vase, 7" h., two-handled, white roses in relief on shaded blue ground 34.00

Vase, 9" h., two-handled, white roses in relief on brown shaded to green ground 40.00

Wall pocket, conical w/flaring rim, curving handle rising from base to mid-section of opposite side, white roses in relief on brown shaded to green ground, 6½" h. 70.00

Wall pocket, fan-shaped top, large loop handles rising from mid-section to rim, white roses in relief on shaded blue ground, 8½" h. 90.00

WINCRAFT (1948)

Wincraft Cornucopia-Vase

Basket w/low overhead handle, florals & foliage in relief on glossy shaded blue ground, 8" h. 45.00
Book ends, teardrop shape, florals in relief on glossy dark blue ground, 6½" h., pr. ....40.00 to 50.00
Candleholders, square base, glossy lime green, 1" h., pr............ 22.00
Cornucopia-vase, florals in relief on glossy shaded green ground, 8" h. (ILLUS.)........................ 35.00
Creamer & sugar bowl, florals in relief on glossy shaded blue ground, pr........................... 25.00
Ewer, branch handle, glossy shaded blue, 6" h...................... 25.00
Vase, 6" h., urn-shaped, relief florals & foliage on glossy shaded blue ground 35.00
Vase, 8" h., pine cones & needles in relief on glossy shaded green ground 55.00
Window box, florals & foliage in relief on glossy shaded blue ground, 13" l. 70.00

WISTERIA (1933)

Jardiniere & pedestal base, lavender wisteria & green vines on textured brown ground, overall 24½" h., 2 pcs. 650.00
Console bowl, angular end handles, lavender wisteria & green vines on textured blue to brown ground, 9 x 5" 80.00
Vase, 4" h., lavender wisteria & green vines on textured brown ground 55.00
Vase, 6" h., lavender wisteria & green vines on textured blue to brown ground.................. 75.00
Vase, 7" h., wisteria & vines on textured blue to brown ground 125.00
Vase, 8" h., two-handled, wisteria & vines on textured brown ground . . 150.00
Vase, 8½" h., base handles, wisteria & vines on textured brown ground 135.00
Vase, 10½" h., two-handled, wisteria & vines on textured brown to green ground 195.00
Wall pocket, flaring rim, wisteria & vines on textured brown ground, 8" h. 285.00

ZEPHYR LILY (1946)

Zephyr Lily Wall Pocket

Basket w/asymetrical handle, yellow lilies on brown shaded to green ground w/impressed oval swirls, 8" h. 60.00
Basket, hanging-type, two-handled, yellow lilies on brown shaded to green ground w/impressed oval swirls, 7½" widest d............ 65.00
Console bowl, white & yellow lilies on blue ground w/impressed ovals, 10" l. 55.00
Candlesticks, two-handled, white & yellow lilies on blue ground w/impressed ovals, 4½" h., pr. 40.00
Cookie jar, cov., yellow lilies on brown shaded to green ground ... 125.00
Creamer, white & yellow lilies on blue ground 22.00
Flower pot & saucer, yellow lilies on brown shaded to green ground, 5" h. 37.50
Jardiniere, yellow lilies on brown shaded to green ground, 8" d. ... 85.00
Jardiniere & pedestal base, rose & yellow lilies on green ground, overall 25" h., 2 pcs. 395.00
Tray, leaf-shaped, rose & yellow lilies on green ground, 14½" l. ... 57.00
Vase, 6½" h., fan-shaped, base handles, white & yellow lilies on blue ground 24.00

Vase, 8" h., cylindrical, base handles, rose & yellow lilies on green ground 35.00
Vase, 12" h., conical, base handles, yellow lilies on brown shaded to green ground 125.00
Vase, 15" h., rose & yellow lilies on green ground 165.00
Wall pocket, two-handled, yellow lily on green ground, 8" h. (ILLUS.) 55.00

(End of Roseville Section)

ROYAL BAYREUTH

Good china in numerous patterns and designs has been made at the Royal Bayreuth factory in Tettau, Germany, since 1794. Listings below are by the company's lines, plus miscellaneous pieces. Interest in this china remains at a peak and prices continue to rise. Pieces listed carry the company's blue mark except where noted otherwise.

CORINTHIAN

Creamer, bulbous shape, classical figures on green ground, 4½" h. $70.00
Creamer, classical figures on black ground 50.00
Creamer & open sugar bowl, classical figures on red ground w/black trim, small, pr. 60.00
Dresser tray, classical figures on black ground, yellow band w/leaf decoration around edge, 10" l. 95.00
Pitcher, milk, classical figures on red ground 75.00
Toothpick holder, model of a coal hod w/overhead handle, classical figures on black ground 295.00

MOTHER-OF-PEARL FINISH

Creamer, grape cluster mold, pearlized pink 125.00
Match holder, hanging-type, Murex Shell patt. 95.00
Pitcher, water, grape cluster mold, pearlized white w/lavender tints 325.00

ROSE TAPESTRY

Ashtray, pink & white roses, 4¾" square 155.00
Basket, apricot roses w/two inside basket, rope band around base, gold rope handle, 7 3/8 x 4", 6¾" h. 395.00
Bell, w/original wooden clapper, three-color roses, gold handle, circle of relief beading in gold 695.00
Box, cov., rounded one end, squared other end, three-color roses 235.00
Creamer, gold square spout & handle, pink roses, 3" h. 125.00
Dish, palette-shaped, embossed self-handle, 4½ x 4" 135.00
Dresser tray, diagonal bands of alternating pink roses & yellow & white roses repeated across tray w/green foliage bands between the rows, 11 x 7¾" 300.00
Dresser tray, pink roses, small white daisies & green leaves, 11 1/8 x 7 7/8" 295.00
Picture frame, 5½ x 4¼" 495.00
Toothpick holder, footed, three-color roses, gold handles 495.00

SUNBONNET BABIES

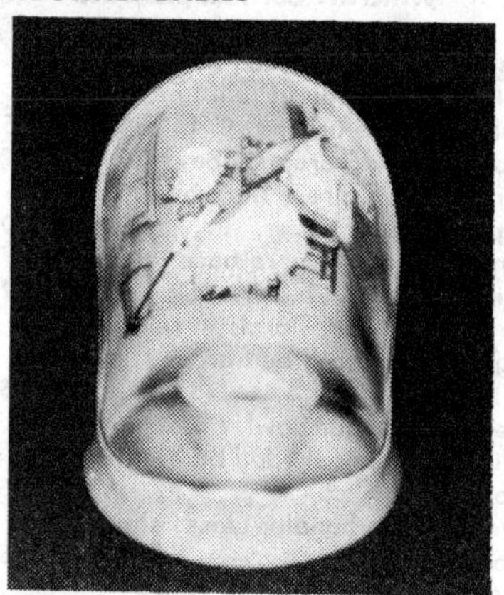

Sunbonnet Babies Chamberstick

Candlesticks, babies fishing, sewing or washing, 4½" h., each pr. 325.00
Candlestick, saucer-shaped, squat handle, babies sweeping (single) 250.00
Cereal bowl w/matching underplate, 7" d. plate, babies washing, set 385.00
Chamberstick, shield-back type, handled, babies cleaning (ILLUS.) 295.00
Chamberstick, shield-back type, handled, babies washing .... 425.00 to 450.00
Creamer, 3¼" h., babies ironing 185.00
Creamer, tankard, 4" h., 3" d., babies cleaning 195.00
Creamer, 4½" h., babies sweeping 210.00
Creamer, child's, bulbous, babies sewing, unmarked 140.00
Creamer, squat form, bulbous, babies sweeping 150.00
Creamer, tankard, cylinder-shaped, babies sewing or washing, each 150.00

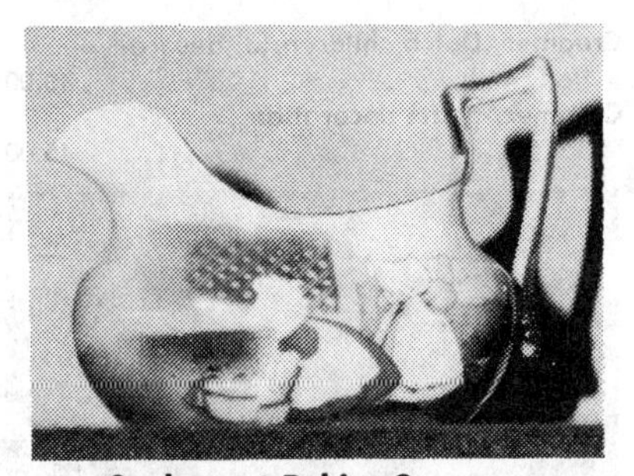

Sunbonnet Babies Creamer

Creamer & sugar bowl, boat-shaped, babies cleaning, pr. (ILLUS. of creamer) 300.00
Cup & saucer, babies cleaning, large 155.00
Cup & saucer, babies fishing 125.00
Cup & saucer, babies sewing 145.00
Dish, club-shaped, babies sewing, 4½" ....125.00 to 150.00
Dish, diamond-shaped, babies sewing 155.00
Dish, heart-shaped, babies gardening 155.00
Dish, spade-shaped, babies cleaning, fishing or sweeping, each.... 155.00
Feeding dish, babies sewing (slight wear) 165.00
Hair receiver, cov., babies cleaning 325.00
Mug, babies cleaning, 3" h. 210.00
Mug, babies sewing 150.00
Nappy, handled, babies cleaning or sewing, each 155.00
Pitcher, milk, bulbous w/lip turned in on two sides, babies fishing ... 175.00
Pitcher, milk, pinched spout, babies washing 235.00
Plate, 5" d., babies ironing.......... 145.00
Plate, 6½" d., babies ironing or sweeping, each ....100.00 to 120.00
Plate, 7" d., babies cleaning or washing, each ....100.00 to 140.00
Relish dish, open handles, babies fishing or washing, 8" l., each.... 175.00
Teapot, cov., babies sewing, unmarked, 3¾".......... 150.00
Toothpick holder, three-footed, three-handled, basket-shaped, babies cleaning 425.00

MISCELLANEOUS

Ashtray, three square feet, two sheep & girls on mountainside scene 75.00
Bell, Jack & the Beanstalk decoration, unmarked 285.00
Bowl, cereal, 6" d., w/plate, Jack & Jill decoration, 2 pcs. 125.00
Bowl, fruit, 8½" to 9" d., figural pansy w/pearlized purple glaze, yellow center, each .....225.00 to 285.00
Bowl, 10" d., pastoral scene w/cattle 85.00
Bowl, 10½" d., pink roses on pastel shaded ground, gold trimmed rim 195.00
Box, cov., round, hunting scene w/horseman & man in horse-drawn cart, 2½" d., 1½" h. 60.00
Cake plate, pierced handles, cherries decoration, 10½" d. 30.00
Candleholder, black & white storks on chartreuse ground, 6½" h. 65.00
Candleholder, figural dog, black w/orange trim around ears & holder, tail forms handle, satin finish, 4 x 2½", 4¼" h. (single) .. 130.00
Candlestick, figural basset hound ... 140.00
Candlestick, Little Bo Peep decoration, 4" h. 65.00
Candlestick, saucer-type w/ring handle, Cavalier musicians decoration (single) ....150.00 to 200.00
Celery tray, figural red lobster, 12 3/8" l. 90.00
Chamberstick, shield-back type, Cavalier musicians decoration 150.00

Hunt Scene Chamberstick

Chamberstick, shield-back type, hunt scene decoration in greens (ILLUS.) 245.00
Chamberstick, shield-back, pansies & roses decoration 68.00
Chocolate cup & saucer, figural poppy, apricot matte finish 135.00
Chocolate pot, cov., figural poppy .. 550.00
Cracker jar, cov., enameled, "Ivory" 290.00
Cracker jar, cov., figural lobster 250.00
Cracker jar, cov., figural poppy, pearlized lustre glaze w/touch of pale orange (tiny chip underside lid) 400.00

Creamer, figural alligator 175.00
Creamer, figural apple 70.00
Creamer, figural bellringer......... 235.00
Creamer, figural Bird of Paradise ... 258.00
Creamer, figural butterfly w/open wings 265.00
Creamer, figural cat, black......... 110.00
Creamer, figural cat, calico 220.00
Creamer, figural clown 175.00
Creamer, figural coachman wearing red coat........................ 180.00
Creamer, figural crow, black 110.00
Creamer, figural Dachshund dog.... 143.00

Figural Eagle Creamer

Creamer, figural eagle (ILLUS.) 158.00
Creamer, figural elk head, shades of brown & cream, 3½" d., 4¼" h. 77.00
Creamer, figural melon w/morning glory 140.00
Creamer, figural monkey, brown ... 265.00
Creamer, figural mouse............ 650.00
Creamer, figural oak leaf 85.00
Creamer, figural Old Man of the Mountain 75.00
Creamer, figural orange 225.00
Creamer, figural orchid 395.00
Creamer, figural owl 285.00
Creamer, figural parakeet 220.00
Creamer, figural platypus 375.00
Creamer, figural Poodle dog 168.00
Creamer, figural poppy, red........ 83.00
Creamer, figural red fox 475.00
Creamer, figural rooster 180.00
Creamer, figural St. Bernard dog ... 185.00
Creamer, figural sea horse, unmarked 95.00
Creamer, figural seal 148.00
Creamer, figural squirrel, unmarked 115.00
Creamer, figural turtle............. 250.00
Creamer, figural water buffalo, black w/orange horns & trim, 3½ x 6", 4" h. 135.00
Creamer, figural water buffalo, overall red glaze 115.00
Creamer, pinched spout, Cavalier musicians decoration, 4" h. 70.00
Creamer, Dutch children (3) decoration, 4" h. 40.00
Creamer, goats decoration, 3¼" h. 45.00

Creamer with Hunting Scene

Creamer, hunter & dogs decoration, green ground, 4" h. (ILLUS.)...... 100.00
Creamer, orchid & pink & yellow pansy decoration, 4" h. 65.00
Creamer, Ring Around the Rosie decoration, 3" h. 95.00
Creamer, pinched spout, sheep in meadow decoration, 4" h. 115.00
Creamer, pinched spout, swans on lake decoration, 4" h. 45.00
Creamer, "tapestry," corset-shaped, pinched spout, goats decoration .. 165.00
Creamer, "tapestry," pinched spout, three dogs & swimming stag decoration, 4" h. 195.00
Creamer & sugar bowl, pink roses decoration, pr.................. 95.00
Creamer & cov. sugar bowl, figural pink & yellow rose, pr. 344.00
Cup, child's, Jack & The Beanstalk decoration 68.00
Cup & saucer, demitasse, figural apple 110.00
Cup & saucer, demitasse, figural pansy 135.00
Cup & saucer, demitasse, figural pear 135.00
Cup & saucer, Little Jack Horner decoration..................... 150.00
Dish, clover-shaped, hunting scene w/horseman & hounds.......... 40.00
Dish, figural pink rose, small....... 170.00
Dish, figural red clown 260.00
Dish, figural red lobster, oval 47.00
Dish, figural strawberry leaf w/handle, flowers decoration 70.00
Dish, maple leaf-shaped, Little Bo Peep decoration................. 65.00
Dish, stirrup-shaped, handled, por-

trait of lady & horse decoration, artist-signed 55.00
Dresser tray, "tapestry," Christmas cactus decoration 450.00
Dresser tray, "tapestry," scene w/raging stream, house, castle & train on bridge in distance 185.00
Ewer, "tapestry," portrait of peasant woman w/horse, ornate gold trim, 2½" h. 130.00
Ewer, white swans (two) in lake scene on blue, green & yellow ground, 3½" d., 5¼" h. 75.00
Feeding dish, girl w/dog decoration 135.00
Feeding dish, Ring Around the Rosie decoration 125.00
Hair receiver, cov., "tapestry," turkeys decoration 195.00
Hatpin holder, figural penguin 495.00
Hatpin holder, figural poppy, red 275.00
Hatpin holder, figural poppy, satin finish, 4¼" h. 350.00
Hatpin holder, "tapestry," Christmas cactus decoration 395.00
Hatpin holder w/saucer base, Cavalier musicians decoration, signed "Dixon" 250.00
Humidor, cov., figural bellringer, plate inside for moistener, unlisted 750.00
Humidor, open handled lid, scene of farmer & two horses 150.00
Marmalade jar, cov., w/ladle & underplate, figural red lobster 79.00
Match holder, double w/center handle, one side w/man on horse w/dogs, other side w/lady on horse w/dogs 110.00
Match holder, hanging-type, Cavalier musicians decoration 185.00
Match holder, hanging-type, figural chimpanzee 295.00
Match holder, hanging-type, figural clown 190.00
Match holder, hanging-type, figural mountain goat 310.00
Mug, Jack & the Beanstalk decoration, 3" h. 45.00
Mustard jar, cov., figural poppy, red 75.00
Nut set: master nut bowl & six individual nut dishes; almonds in relief, impressed "Deponiert," 7 pcs. 90.00
Pitcher, 3¼" h., 2" d., double-handled, hunting scene w/horseman & man in horse-drawn cart 55.00
Pitcher, 3¾" h., goats decoration in pink & white w/gold handle 65.00
Pitcher, 4" h., "tapestry," pinched spout, nudes, forest lake & castle scene 285.00
Pitcher, 4¼" h., scene of three playful bears, gold handle, brown, yellow & green ground 95.00
Pitcher, 5" h., fighting cocks decoration 65.00
Pitcher, 5" h., fisherman in sailboat decoration, dark grey ground 85.00
Pitcher, 5¼" h., 2½" d., English coaching scene at top, green base 65.00
Pitcher, 9" h., scene of cows in pasture 185.00
Pitcher, lemonade, figural apple 395.00
Pitcher, lemonade, figural lemon 625.00
Pitcher, milk, figural fish head 168.00
Pitcher, milk, figural milkmaid 225.00
Pitcher, water, figural coachman 495.00
Pitcher, water, figural frog, red trim 525.00
Pitcher, water, figural moose, qt. 175.00
Plaque, pierced to hang, scene of man w/two horses, one brown & one white that's rearing, heavy rococo scrolled gold rim, 9¾" d. 125.00
Plate, 6" d., Goose Girl decoration 70.00

Royal Bayreuth Tapestry Plate

Plate, 9½" d., "tapestry," multicolored scene of sheep in meadow (ILLUS.) 295.00
Plate, 10" d., scene of lady w/donkey center, relief-molded gold trim 125.00
Salt dip, figural pansy 32.00
Salt & pepper shakers, figural grape cluster, purple, pr. 95.00
Salt & pepper shakers, figural grape cluster, yellow to green, pr. 85.00
Salt & pepper shakers, nursery rhyme decoration, one w/Jack & Jill, other w/Little Boy Blue, pr. 195.00
Sugar bowl, cov., figural lobster 125.00
Sugar bowl, cov., figural turtle 195.00
Teapot, cov., figural apple 145.00
Tea tile, girl w/dog decoration 65.00
Toothpick holder, coal hod-shaped

w/overhead handle, "tapestry," portrait of woman w/horse 395.00
Toothpick holder, "tapestry," peasant woman w/horse decoration .. 165.00
Tray, sheep in meadow decoration, 11 x 8" 295.00
Vase, 2¾" h., 2½" d., ball-shaped, footed, lady on horse w/farm couple 52.00
Vase, 3 3/8" h., 2 3/8" d., two-handled, Colonial man & woman on pastel blue, pink & green ground, hallmarked silver top rim 44.00
Vase, 5" h., "tapestry," polar bear decoration 195.00
Wall pocket, figural grapes, pink ... 165.00
Wall pocket, figural peach, 9" h. ... 350.00

ROYAL BONN & BONN

Royal Bonn Scenic Vase

Bonn and subsequently Royal Bonn china were produced in Bonn, Germany, in a manufactory established in 1755. Later wares made there are often marked Mehlem or bear the initials FM or a castle mark. Most wares were of the hand-painted type. Clock cases were also made in Bonn.

Bowl, 8½" d., silver plate rim, h.p. florals, artist-signed & numbered $145.00
Cheese dish, cov., multicolored iris on white ground w/gold trim, castle mark 85.00
Cracker jar, overall lavender, pink, yellow & blue florals w/green leaves outlined in heavy gold on satin finish ground enriched w/gilding, silver plate cover, rim & handle, 5½" d., 6" h. 95.00
Cracker jar, pink & blue florals w/green leaves on beige ground, brass cover, rim & handle, 5¼" d., 7" h. 105.00
Ewer, multicolored florals on turquoise & ivory ground, 13" h. 110.00
Urn, portrait of lovely woman reserved on shaded green ground, artist-signed, 12" h. 395.00
Vase, 6" h., 2-handled, squatty, Art Nouveau style florals w/gold trim on green ground 150.00
Vase, 6½" h., 3" d., colorful rooster, hen & chicks w/inscription "Nach Melch D. Hondecoeter, F. Sticher artist" on green ground .. 150.00
Vases, 8" h., 4" widest d., ovoid, blue banding at neck, delicate pink & white orchids w/ornate gold trim on spring green ground, pr. 225.00
Vase, 9" h., portrait of Art Nouveau style lady, artist-signed 265.00
Vase, 10" h., h.p. maroon florals on gold ground 235.00
Vase, 10½" h., chrysanthemums decor w/intricate raised gold border, artist-signed 249.00
Vase, 11" h., 13½" w., 4-handled, h.p. portrait of beautiful young maiden reserved on cobalt blue ground within gilt border 595.00
Vase, 11¾" h., tapering cylinder, profile portrait of a woman w/flowing hair surrounded by pink iris blossoms in a wooded setting, relief-molded trim of pods & florals 275.00
Vase, 13½" h., portrait of lovely maiden w/long brown hair, landscape scene reverse, artist-signed 595.00
Vase, 24" h., scene of children at the seashore gazing into the water at a toy sail boat, pastel tones w/gilt scrolling vines on neck & base, artist-signed, late 19th c. (ILLUS.) 880.00

ROYAL COPENHAGEN

This porcelain has been made in Copenhagen, Denmark, since 1715. The ware is hardpaste.

Bottle w/stopper, Frederiksburg Castle decor $85.00
Coffee cans & saucers, cylindrical, Flora Danica patt., specimen flower named at the base, gilt rims, set of 6 .... 1,760.00

Dinner service for 12: 7 pc. place settings w/serving pieces; fluted, Open Lace patt., blue 4,500.00
Figure of girl feeding cat, 5¼" 128.00
Figure of Pan playing with bear, No. 648, 5½ x 3", 6½" h. 232.00
Figure of Jan Hansen Schmidt, 1800's, 13" h. 320.00
Ice cream dish w/reticulated cover & stand, Flora Danica patt., botanical specimen within gilt dentil border, domed cover formed by an arrangement of overlapping leaves above wide latticework mid-section reserving 4 flower panels, lavender & pale yellow tulip form knop, 12¾" d. stand, 10¼" h. to top of cover 3,025.00
Model of European pheasant, 13½" l., 7½" h. 150.00
Model of a penguin, No. 417, 9" h. 200.00
Model of a recumbent lioness, shaded grey & white, 12½" l. 220.00
Plates, 10¾" d., Flora Danica patt., botanical specimen within border heightened by pink enamel & gilding, set of 12 .... 6,600.00
Plate, dinner, fluted, Half Lace patt., blue 60.00
Sugar box, cov., oval, Flora Danica patt., botanical specimen within pink & gold molded beadwork borders, 6½" l. 1,430.00
Vase, 14¼" h., oviform, large brick red, salmon & gilt flowers on a crazed grey-white ground, artist-signed, 1938 .... 605.00
Vegetable dish, cov., Flora Danica patt., various botanical specimen within a border heightened by pink enamel & gilding, 9 3/8" d. 2,750.00

Flora Danica Pattern Wine Cooler

Wine cooler, applied double twig handles w/spray of flowerheads & leaves at each terminal, Flora Danica patt., botanical specimen beneath pink & gold molded beadwork border, gilt dentil rim, 6 3/8" h. (ILLUS.) 1,760.00

ROYAL DUX

Royal Dux Figure Group

These wares were made in Bohemia and many were imported to the United States around the turn of the century. Although numerous pieces were originally inexpensive, collectors have taken a fancy to the ware and the prices of the better pieces continue to rise.

Bust of Shakespeare, edge of base has mask w/dagger, pink triangle mark $325.00
Candlestick, figural boy wearing knickers, ivory glaze, 13" h. (single) 155.00
Centerpiece, central flared vase w/striped decoration flanked by two nude women kneeling, one on each side, creamy white w/cobalt blue & gold trim, 11 x 4¼", 7¾" h. 395.00
Centerpiece, figures of maiden & two cherubs holding up shell bowl, matte finish, 12 x 15 x 20" h. 875.00
Centerpiece, basket flanked by 8" h. figures of girls, one standing on each side, pink triangle mark 350.00
Figure of man, seated, decorating pottery jugs, 6 x 4" base, 7½" h. 415.00
Figure of a woman potting, shaded green, pink & purple decoration, pink triangle mark, 8" h. 450.00
Figure of an Art Deco-style lady dressed in blue iridized satin finish gown w/green trim, green hat, satin flesh tones, 4 x 5½", 9" h. 265.00
Figure of a woman standing in front of a large shell mounted on a pedestal base, 8½" w., 10½" h. .. 465.00
Figures, peasant boy & peasant girl,

pink, green & gold garments w/matte finish flesh tones, pink triangle mark & "Bohemia," 11½" h., pr. 550.00
Figure of a female snake charmer reclining, playing her pipe for the gilt-spotted blue-glazed snake entwined about her legs, on shaped plinth, pink triangle mark, 12½" l. 550.00
Figure of a lady holding her blue glazed dress up at the sides, wearing gilt high heels, on socle base, pink triangle mark, 12¾" h. 550.00
Figures, Art Nouveau-style maiden filling lamp & companion holding hourglass, 15" h., pr. 450.00
Figure of peasant boy carrying a basket on his shoulder, rose colored breeches, tan boots & hat, green & gold, matte finish, pink triangle mark, 16" h. 450.00
Figure of a lady carrying two water jugs, earth tones, 18½" h. 295.00
Figure group, shepherdess & goats, she wearing rose toga, beige sheepskin robe & green turban, white & tan goats, semi-gloss finish, 4½" d., 14¾" h. 575.00
Figure group, young bearded man in Arab garb seated astride a camel & holding a pipe in one hand as he looks down at his young servant boy who struggles w/their bags, ivory glaze trimmed in dusty rose, pale blue, olive & gilt, ca. 1900, pink triangle mark, 24¼" h. (ILLUS.) 825.00
Model of standing bear w/guitar, pink triangle mark, 4" h. 55.00
Model of a cockatiel, 15" h. 395.00
Model of an elephant, 4 x 3", pink triangle mark 45.00
Model of a polar bear, white, 13" l., 8" h. 265.00
Pin tray, figural Art Nouveau-style maiden on wave 300.00
Vase, 10" h., relief-molded cyclamens 105.00
Vase, 14" h., peach-colored Art Nouveau stylized florals & leaves w/gold tracery decoration on yellow ground, large band of molded green foliage at base 240.00

ROYAL RUDOLSTADT

This factory began as a faience pottery established in 1720. E. Bohne made hard paste porcelain wares from 1852 to 1920, when the factory became a branch of Heubach Brothers. The factory, still producing in East Germany, was nationalized in 1960.

Bowl, 8 3/8" d., footed, h.p. poppies $65.00
Bust of lovely lady, on pedestal, beige tones, No. 1714 . . . . 150.00
Cake plate, open handles, pink & white roses on cream & light blue ground, gold rim & handles, 10" d. 40.00
Cake plate, open handles, scalloped rim, peach-colored poppies & foliage on pastel ground, gold border, 10" d. 39.00
Celery, open handled, pink & yellow roses w/gold trim, 12½ x 5½" . . . 70.00
Chocolate pot, cov., pink roses w/green leaves, 10" h. 95.00
Creamer, pastel grape leaves, worn gold handle, 5½" 32.00
Dresser set: hatpin holder, hair receiver & tray; pastel florals w/gold, 3 pcs. 225.00
Dresser tray, bluebirds on branches decoration, blue border, 12½ x 7¾" 120.00
Pitcher, 10 x 4½", h.p. pansies on soft beige ground, silver plate rim & underplate marked "Derby" 135.00
Pitcher, 15½" h., bulbous, gold floral designs & jeweled flowers on off-white ground 285.00
Plate, 8 3/8" d., spray of pink roses at top, scene of man & woman in boat w/lake & mountains in background 60.00
Syrup pitcher w/underplate, roses decoration, 2 pcs. 27.00
Tray, open handles, scalloped rim, Day Lily patt., 12" l. 47.50
Vase, 8" h., floral decoration w/gold & brown leaves, reticulated neck, heavy gold trim 90.00
Vase, 9½" h., bulbous base, narrow neck w/flaring & ruffled rim, sides embossed w/tree bark pattern, large bouquet of flowers trail up sides, pastel ground, flowers outlined & highlighted in gold 60.00
Vase, 12" h., florals w/leaves & fronds in relief, yellow shaded to beige ground 80.00
Vase, 16" h., orange flowers on cream ground 150.00

ROYAL VIENNA

The second factory in Europe to make hard-

paste porcelain was established in Vienna in 1719 by Claud Innocentius de Paquier. The factory underwent various changes of administration through the years and finally closed in 1865. Since then, however, the porcelain has been reproduced by various factories in Austria and Germany, many of which have reproduced also the early beehive mark. Early pieces, naturally, bring far higher prices than the later ones or the reproductions.

Royal Vienna Portrait Vases

Bowl, 9" d., shallow, scalloped edge, h.p. apple blossom decoration, signed "Wheelock Vienna" .. $32.00

Box, cov., cushioned rectangular lid w/scene depicting "The Judgment of Paris" within gilt & claret borders, front panel w/three playful putti resting on clouds, sides w/panels w/gilt squirrel & snake or snail & urn on pale yellow ground, ca. 1900, 4¾" l., 3" h. ... 330.00

Chargers, transfer-printed reserve w/figural group in a landscape, wide border w/bands of light blue & dusty pink interrupted by three claret cartouches & a narrow black band w/conforming scrolls, all highlighted w/gilding, early 20th c., 25" d., pr. 220.00

Demitasse set: cov. pot, sugar bowl, six cups & saucers & tray; sepia polychrome Watteau scenes on cobalt blue ground, ornate gold trim, gold interior cups, 15 pcs. .. 275.00

Ewer, portrait of ladies (two) w/five cherubs surrounding them, dark blue ground, ornate gold trim, 9 x 7" 150.00

Ewer, portrait decoration w/gold striped ground, iridescent "Tiffany" finish, blue beehive mark, 9½" h. 375.00

Jar, cov., central gold-leaf panel w/color portrait of a Roman lady, surrounded by overall gold pine cones & laurel leaves on cobalt blue ground, 3¾" d., 7½" h. 201.00

Plate, 9 3/8" d., "unter Bluthen," maiden & cupid standing in a clearing surrounded by flowering trees, within a jeweled deep green & brown border heightened by gilding, artist-signed, ca. 1900 .... 880.00

Plate, 9½" d., scene of candle girl, gold beaded border, signed "Wagner" 450.00

Plate, 9½" d., mermaid bidding her lover farewell on the banks of a river, within lustrous salmon-colored, brown, pale yellow & blue paneled border enriched by gilding, late 19th c. 1,100.00

Plate, 9½" d., bust portrait of "Kaiserin Elisabeth" within a cobalt blue border heightened in elaborate gilding & jeweling, artist-signed, late 19th c. 825.00

Plate, 10" d., bust portrait of Princess Louise within a cobalt blue border heightened in gilding w/alternating panels of royal emblems, signed "Wagner," late 19th c. 935.00

Teapot, cov., globular, stylized florals & rocks w/double line border below, scalloped border at inverted mouth & on the cover which has an applied pear finial, blue & white, 2nd half 18th c., 4" h. (restoration to spout) 220.00

Vase, 9" h., front oval portrait of Daphne w/foliate wreath in her upswept hair, wearing a rose colored drape within a gilt-tooled floral spray border, reverse w/two cupids in flight & a cupid playing the mandolin below, all before an extensive landscape, everted neck w/gilt rim, late 19th c. 935.00

Vase, 9½" h., urn-shaped, central color scene of cherub & woman, royal red ground w/gold applied trim, artist-signed, ca. 1880, blue beehive mark 210.00

Vase, 9½" h., "Pilgrim flask" form, everted pinched rim, scene of a scantily clad maiden in a forest setting within gilt-bordered cartouche reserved on a metallic aqua ground, artist-signed 550.00

Vase, 12½" h., baluster form, central portrait of a lovely lady w/short dark wavy hair & white robe, seated in a pensive pose w/head resting on one arm, a book under the other, entitled

"Inspiration," within gilt-tooled borders reserved on an ivory ground w/burgundy median band, socle base, artist-signed, late 19th c. 825.00

Vase, 14½" h., cylindrical, h.p. large pink roses & leaves on pale green ground, artist-signed, late 19th c. 175.00

Vases, 14¾" h., urn-shaped, central portrait reserve, one w/young woman, "Lilien," other w/young woman, "Clematis," within gilt-tooled Greek key, palmette & floral spray border on lavender ground elaborately decorated w/three foliate scrolled registers, molded on either side w/gold scrolled handles w/classical female bust terminals, raised on socle base, signed "Wagner," late 19th c., blue beehive mark, one handle restored, 14¾" h., pr. (ILLUS.) 4,400.00

Vases, cov., 17¾" h., waisted ovoid urn-shaped, scrolled handles w/lion-head terminals, oval three-quarter length portrait of a maiden, one entitled "Mandolinenspielerin" & the other "Inspiration," within trellis & gilt band borders reserved on ivory & pale blue grounds, gilded flaming urns & foliate scrolls, cover w/flaming urn finial, late 19th c., pr. 3,850.00

ROYAL WORCESTER

Royal Worcester Ewer

This porcelain has been made by the Royal Worcester Porcelain Co. at Worcester, England, from 1862 to the present. For earlier porcelain made in Worcester, see WORCESTER. Royal Worcester is distinguished from those wares made at Worcester between 1751 and 1862 that are referred to as only Worcester by collectors.

Bowl, 9½ x 9½", 2" h., square w/fluted edges, sprays of purple thistle, fuchsia & bellflowers, gold rim $125.00

Candle snuffer, figural monk 75.00

Candle snuffer, figural woman warming hands 65.00

Candleholder, chamberstick-type, cream-colored board base w/border handle, large gold mouse sits by base, satin finish, 1892, 3½ x 5¾", 2½" h. 403.00

Candlestick, figures of boy & girl in Empire outfits w/pug dog lean against gnarled tree, branches hold three candlesockets fitted w/silver plated cups & bobeches, late 19th c., 11½" h. (glaze slightly dull on girl's cheek) 275.00

Cracker jar, cov., straight sides, Bamboo patt., w/h.p. floral decoration, 5½" h. 350.00

Cracker jar, cov., embossed swirl ribs, h.p. pink flowers, yellow & blue small florals & green leaves on beige satin finish, silver plate top, rim & handles, 5¾" d., 7¼" h. 303.00

Creamer & sugar bowl, Watteau patt., pr. 45.00

Cup & saucer, Coral patt., blue & white w/gold trim, cup 4¼" d., 2¼" h., saucer, 6" d. 59.00

Cup & saucer, Blue Willow patt., large 30.00

Dish, leaf-shaped, gold scalloped & ribbed edge, one end curled upward, beige & tan decoration, ca. 1908, 4 x 3" 50.00

Ewer, burnished gold handle, top & base, center w/pink rose one side & pink & yellow rose on other, beige satin finish, 1907, 2½" d., 3½" h. 100.00

Ewer, bundle of branches handle, branches & flowers in relief w/overall gold tracery, ca. 1887, 8" h. 195.00

Ewer, scrolled molded handle issuing from dolphin's mask & terminating at side w/satyr's mask, compressed ovoid body h.p. w/flock of swans flying above bulrushes & gilt foliage on matt blue ground, ca. 1895, 17" h. (ILLUS.) 1,210.00

Figure, "Babes in Woods," young girl w/her older sister dressed in blue & pink, 1930, 2½" d., 6" h. 235.00

Figure of Sambo, wearing white shirt, blue pants, gold hat & shoes, black hair, green base, early 1930's, 2 5/8" d., 6½" h. . . . 450.00

Figure of Anne Boleyn, blue gown w/cream & gold coat, beaded headdress, 8½" h. 350.00

Figure, "Tuesday's Child," dancing girl dressed in yellow ballerina dress, 8½" h. 130.00

Figure, "April," modeled by Doughty 95.00

Figure group, boy & girl getting water from a cistern, 1882, artist-signed, 6½" w., 7½" h. 350.00

Fish plates, each w/different species of fish swimming amid aquatic plants, within pale yellow border edged w/gilding, 1926, 9¼" d., set of 12 . . . . 1,045.00

Flower holder, green pedestal foot & top rim, h.p. red & pink roses w/green leaves, gold trim, original brass flower holder insert, artist-signed, 1911, 5¼" d., 5¼" h. 302.00

Gravy boat w/underplate, Watteau patt. 45.00

Lamp, figural gilded 13" woman playing lute by 18" gilded tree, brass arm atop tree holds two glass Cricklites w/fabric shades, all lamp parts marked "Clarke," base marked "Worcester" & "Clarke," ca. 1898, overall 25" h. 2,900.00

Model of ducks (2), porcelain, white & gold, artist-signed 35.00

Model of goldfinch, No. 3239 . . . . 50.00

Model of parakeet, ca. 1930, 7" 80.00

Pitcher, 5" h., flat back, ivory w/floral gold handle, base & rims 40.00

Pitcher, 6" h., tusk-form, horn handle, decorated w/vines, firs, berries & leaves on cream ground, Shape No. 1116, ca. 1885 . . . . 160.00

Pitcher, 7" h., gilt outlined pink, red & blue florals & green & rust leaves, ca. 1892 . . . . 175.00

Pitcher, hot milk, cov., 8" h., floral decoration, metal cover 175.00

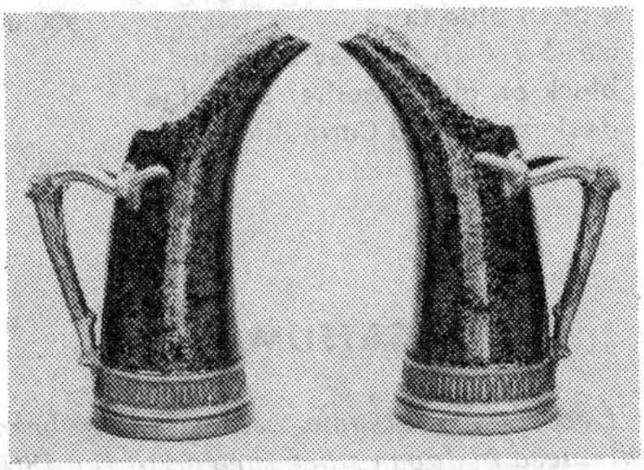

Royal Worcester Tusk-Form Pitchers

Pitchers, 8" h., tusk-form, overall decoration in gilt w/floral sprigs on a cobalt blue ground, gilt egg-and-dart frieze around base, applied gilt antler-form handle, 1888, minor chip to one spout, pr. (ILLUS.) 330.00

Pitcher, 8¾" h., blue, pink & orange flowers, green leaves & two butterflies, w/gilding, gilded handle, ca. 1884 . . . . 175.00

Pitcher, 9" h., 7" across body to handle, bulbous, floral sprays (five different) w/gold trim 250.00

Pitcher, 10¼" h., lighthouse shape, gold flowers & branches in high relief around top, deep horizontal gold ribbing around body from top & bottom of handle, red trim w/random threading of the red around gold handle 235.00

Plate, 9" d., white chrysanthemums & foliage in glossy center w/wide olive matte border, artist-signed . . 100.00

Plates, 10¾" d., each w/different h.p. English countryside scene, gilt border, artist-signed, reverse w/scene identification, marked "Royal Worcester," set of 6 . . . . . . 660.00

Plate, chop, Watteau patt. 45.00

Soup bowl, Blue Willow patt. 35.00

Table centerpiece, figure of a young boy & girl leaning over a large woven basket, Shape No. 1174, artist-signed, 10¾" w., 6½" deep, 10" h. 900.00

Teapot, cov., hexagonal, exotic bird on blue scale ground 150.00

Vase, 5¾" h., footed, gold handle, h.p. roses, artist-signed 165.00

Vase, 7" h., 3½" d., h.p. roses & lilies w/small blue flowers, beige satin finish, gold trim 130.00

Vase, 10¾" h., gold dolphin handles, molded face on neck, fluted top, h.p. wild flowers on cream ground, Shape No. 1327 . . . . 265.00

Vase, cov., 14¾" h., ovoid, two lion's mask handles, molded at shoulder w/floral panels w/pendant garlands & centering a mask, green, brown, russet, mauve, grey & brown woodland scene w/two rabbits, 1890 (cover repaired & missing finial) 605.00

SALTGLAZED WARES

This whitish ware has a pitted surface texture, which resembles an orange skin as a result of salt being thrown into the hot kiln to produce the glaze. Much of this ware was sold in the undecorated state, but some pieces were decorated. Decorative pieces have been produced in England and Europe since at least the 18th century with later production in the United States. Most pieces are unmarked.

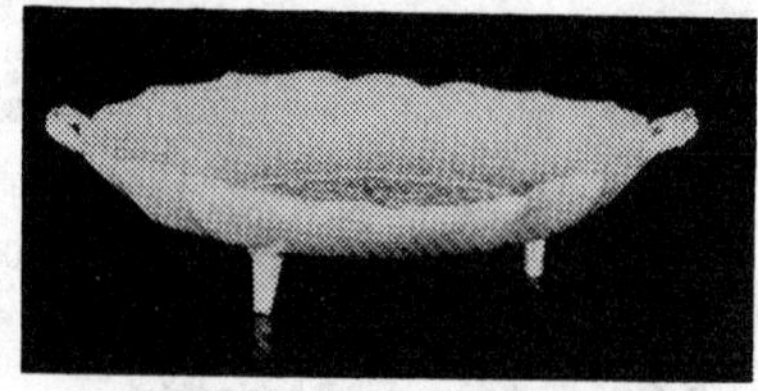

Saltglazed Vegetable Strainer

Dish, deep, scalloped rim, reticulated panel w/basketwork fillers, England, mid-18th c., 10½" d. $220.00
Dish, molded basketweave & diaper cartouches within foliate scrollwork beneath pierced rim, Staffordshire, ca. 1760, 11 7/8" (rim chips, firing crack) 264.00
Pitcher, cov., 15" h., 6½" d., overall grapevines & figures in relief on mocha ground, Villeroy & Boch Raised Shield mark 175.00
Teapot, cov., octagonal, sides molded w/panels enclosing animals, figures & crests, curved spout w/flowering foliage, cover w/disc finial, Staffordshire, ca. 1760, 7½" w. 660.00
Teapot & cover w/green button finial, branch-molded handle & spout, painted w/bouquets within yellow scrolls on a later pink ground, Staffordshire (restored) 1,210.00
Vegetable strainer, oval, three applied legs, applied loop handles, molded decoration w/pierced bottom, Staffordshire, ca. 1750, 11¼ x 8¾" (ILLUS.) . . . . 700.00 to 750.00

SAN ILDEFONSO (Maria) POTTERY

A thin-walled and crudely polished blackware has been made at most Rio Grande Pueblos. Around 1918 a San Ildefonso Pueblo woman, Maria Montoya Martinez and her husband, Julian, began making a thicker walled blackware with a finely polished gunmetal black sheen. It was fired in the traditional manner using manure to smother the firing process and produce the black coloration. The following is a chronology of Maria's varied signatures: Marie, mid to late teens-1934; Marie & Julian, 1934-43; Marie & Santana, 1943-56; Maria and Popovi, 1956-71 and Maria Poveka, used on undecorated wares after 1956. Maria died in July of 1980. Rosalia, Tonita, Blue Corn and other signatures might also be found on pottery made at the San Ildefonso Pueblo. Considered a true artistic achievement, early items signed by Maria, or her contemporaries, command good prices. It should be noted that the strong pottery tradition is being carried on by current potters.

Plate Signed Marie & Santana

Bowl, 5" d., 4" h., glossy & matte black on black, signed Marie & Julian, 1934-43 . . . . $425.00
Dish, glossy & matte black on black, signed Santana & Adam (Martinez), 6" d. 110.00
Jar, glossy & matte black on black, signed Marie & Julian, 2½" d., 3" h. 295.00
Jar, glossy & matte black on black, signed Marie & Julian, 6¼" h. . . . 1,650.00
Plate, 5½" d., glossy & matte black on black, signed Marie & Santana, 1943-56 . . . . 687.00
Plate, 6" d., glossy & matte black on black, signed Marie & Santana (ILLUS.) 450.00
Plate, 8 x 7" oval, glossy & matte black on black feather motif, signed Blue Corn 500.00
Vase, 5 7/8" h., glossy & matte black on black feather & wedge designs, signed Carmelita Dunlap 220.00

SATSUMA

Decorated Satsuma wares have been produced in Japan since the end of the 18th century. The early pieces are scarce and high-

priced. Later Satsuma wares are plentiful, affordable and as highly collectible as earlier pieces.

Satsuma Jar and Cover

Bowl, 5½" d., temple scene decoration, Meiji Period, 1880's $475.00

Bowl, 6" d., interior w/figures in a spring landscape encircled by panels w/scattered flowerhead design, exterior w/continuous band of blossoming iris, marked "Senzan" 220.00

Bowl, 12 1/8" d., enamel & gilt scene of Rakan (disciples of Buddha) in a lush landscape interior, exterior w/confronted "asparas" against a patterned black ground, marked "Higashi Shozan-zukuri" . . 192.50

Box, cov., knob finial, varied flying birds in delicate enameling accented w/gold sprays of leaves & blossoms around base, many gold dust clouds, late Edo period, ca. 1840 . . . . 145.00

Charger, 12 7/8" d., birds & flowers in red & black on white ground, gold trim 115.00

Cup & saucer, demitasse, scenes of Samurai warriors on cobalt blue ground, signed "Hozan" 210.00

Dessert set: large circular serving dish, ten demitasse cups & saucers & eleven small dessert plates; enamel & gilt *mille fleur* patt., "Ishiyama," 32 pcs. 275.00

Jar, cov., inner pierced lid, bulbous shoulders, scenes of lords & attendants, Nishikide diapering on garments of panel, Meiji period, ca. 1885, 5" d., 7" h. 125.00

Jar, cov., domed cover w/young seated girl (head reglued) holding dog, baluster-form body decorated w/low relief open fans containing floral or figural scenes, floral accents, diaper pattern borders, 19th c. (chips on rim), 29" h. (ILLUS.) 1,320.00

Koro (incense burner), ball shape, three scalloped feet, openwork brass lift-off top w/mum finial, colorful border pattern, 14 seated Rakan w/heavy beaded gold halos, their clothes an array of colorful enameling of gosu blue, iron-red & turquoise, diapering of heavy gold & bead clouds, attributed to the artist Issan, 5½" d. 675.00

Plaque, pierced to hang, hanging wisteria & other florals & foliage, waterfowls & pond scene, heavy gold trim, narrow gold & red border, Meiji period, ca. 1900, 9½" d. 225.00

Plate, 9" d., 1½" h., two Samurai under a pine tree w/supplicant on his knees, on the shores of the sea w/approaching ships 275.00

Tea bowl, gosu blue & colorful Rakan decor, mid-19th c. 350.00

Teapot, cov., miniature, round body w/low domed cover, decorated w/continuous band of courtesans, gold & red diapering around top rim & on cover, Meiji period, ca. 1910, 2½" h. 325.00

Teapot, cov., overall colorful florals on gold, scalloped reserves depicting family life, Meiji period, ca. 1900, 4½" spout to handle, 3½" h. 275.00

Tea set: cov. teapot, creamer, cov. sugar bowl & four cups & saucers; six Rakan & dragon in a waterway landscape, spout & handle molded in the shape of a dragon, scaly body picked out in raised white enamel w/red & gilt highlights, signed "Da Nihon Satsuma Kuni Kinkoku saku," 11 pcs. 330.00

Urns, bird handle, Geisha Girl scene, ca. 1920, Awata Satsuma, 14" h., pr. 265.00

Urn, winged dragon handles beneath lobed flaring rim, ovoid tapering body, colorful enameled scene of ladies in a garden setting, 50" h. .1,400.00

Vase, 2¾" h., bulbous, paneled scenes of mother & child, gold florals on cobalt blue ground, Meiji period, ca. 1900 . . . . 95.00

Vase, 2¾" h., cobalt blue w/gold florals, scene of woman, wisteria & gold dust clouds, grass & floral

scene reverse, Meiji period, ca. 1910 .... 58.00
Vase, cov., 6 1/8" h., baluster form w/squared shoulder & recessed mouth surmounted by a circular flat-topped cap, painted in enamels & gilt w/figural reserve set against a lavish ground of flowering plants & butterflies, bracketed by abstract & floral patterned bands repeated on the lid, base w/cartouche w/"Yamamoto seizo" 385.00
Vase, 7" h., scene of butterflies & flowers trailing over fence, blue shading to pink 325.00
Vase, 9" h., Thousand Cranes patt., golden cranes on black background 195.00

Satsuma Vase

Vases, 9 5/8" h., waisted form w/domed shoulder & narrow circular rim, Thousand Faces patt., continuously decorated w/numerous figures in gilt robes w/enameled dragons, one w/small crack at rim, pr. (ILLUS. of one) 1,200.00
Vase, 12" h., Samurai decoration w/gold trim on green ground, Taisho period 255.00
Vase, 12½" h., 6½" w., baluster form, rolled rim, haloed Rakan & Kannon in colored, trailed enamels, ca. 1915, pr. 480.00
Vase, 18" h., urn-shaped, h.p. w/two green moriage hawks w/florals on shaded tan, yellow & green ground 300.00
Vase, 18 1/8" h., slender ovoid w/waisted neck & tapering to flared foot, two large enameled polychrome & gilt reserves, one showing Kannon & Rakan in a landscape, other a spring excursion, elaborate brocade ground, rolled rim w/gilt band, Meiji period 770.00

SCHLEGELMILCH

Decorated china marked "R.S. Germany" and "R.S. Prussia" continues to grow in popularity. According to Clifford J. Schlegelmilch in his book "Handbook of Erdmann and Reinhold Schlegelmilch—Prussia—Germany, and Oscar Schlegelmilch—Germany," Erdmann Schlegelmilch established a porcelain factory in the Germanic provinces at Suhl, in 1861. Reinhold, his younger brother, worked with him until 1869 when he established another porcelain factory in Tillowitz, upper Silesia. China bearing the name of this town is credited to Reinhold Schlegelmilch. It customarily bears also the phrase "R.S. Germany." Now collectors seek additional marks including E.S. Germany, R.S. Poland and R.S. Suhl. Prices are high and collectors should beware the forgeries that sometimes find their way to the market. Mold names and numbers are taken from Mary Frank Gaston's books on R.S. Prussia.

R.S. GERMANY

R.S. Germany Berry Bowl

Basket, lily of the valley decor, gold trim, 6¾ x 5½", 4½" h. $155.00
Berry set: master bowl & 4 sauce dishes; pink roses on grey shaded to cream ground, 5 pcs. (ILLUS. of bowl) 110.00
Bonbon dish, pointed ends, loop handle at side, variegated pink & white peonies on a shaded grey satin ground, gold lacy trim, 7¾ x 4½" 48.00
Bowl, 7 5/8" d., cabbage leaf mold, shaded green exterior, white lining 95.00
Bowl, fruit, 9" d., 2-handled, reticulated rim, floral decor on shaded ground 205.00
Bowl, 9½" d., Cottonplant patt., gold trim 150.00
Cake plate, pierced handles, Man

with Horses scene w/house & trees, 10" d. 185.00
Celery set: celery tray & 6 individual salt dips; pink roses decor, 7 pcs. 85.00
Chocolate cup & saucer, white tulips on green ground 30.00
Chocolate pot, cov., pink, yellow & white roses on pale green ground, 10½" h. 150.00
Chocolate set: cov. chocolate pot & 4 c/s; yellow daffodils decor, 9 pcs. 185.00
Chocolate set: cov. chocolate pot & 5 c/s; Art Deco style panel-molded body, white tulips on pale green ground, 11 pcs. 325.00
Condensed milk can holder, cover & underplate, 2-handled, floral decor w/bands of gold on white ground, 5" h. 145.00
Cracker jar, cov., 2-handled, white flowers w/orange centers & green leaves on shaded brown & cream ground, gold trim 125.00
Creamer & sugar bowl, Cottage scene w/cows & sheep, pr. 155.00
Dresser set: tray, hatpin holder, cov. powder box & cov. hair receiver; chrysanthemum decor, gold trim, 4 pcs. 135.00
Ferner, iris mold, feet w/gold outlining, scalloped & beaded rim, pink poppies on light green shaded to light blue ground 165.00
Mustard jar, cover & ladle, yellow roses decor 45.00
Plate, chop, 12½" d., pink & white roses decor, ornate gold trim 75.00
Syrup pitcher w/original top, Mill scene 75.00
Toothbrush holder, floral decor 75.00

R.S. PRUSSIA

Snowbird Winter Scene Bowl

Berry set: 10" d. master bowl & six 5 5/8" sauce dishes; iris mold, pink poppies on shaded green ground, gold trim, 7 pcs. 475.00
Bowl, 6¼" d., 2" h., scalloped rim, lavender & white lilac blossoms on shaded pastel ground, satin finish 130.00
Bowl, 9" d., icicle mold, reflecting water lilies 180.00
Bowl, 9" d., ribbon & jewel mold, roses decor 130.00
Bowl, 9¼" d., scalloped & beaded rim, pink, yellow & white poppies w/green leaves, gold trim 150.00
Bowl, 9½" d., hidden images mold, floral center, pink border w/hidden lady & florals 225.00
Bowl, 9¾" d., pie crust mold, Stag scene 735.00
Bowl, 10" d., leaf mold, lily of the valley decor 250.00
Bowl, 10" d., plume mold, pink roses & white florals decor 175.00
Bowl, 10" d., point & clover mold, roses decor, sapphire jeweling & gold trim 150.00
Bowl, 10" d., pointed border w/notched indentations, roses decor 195.00
Bowl, 10¼" d., violet mold, Cottage scene..........................1,000.00
Bowl, 10½" d., acorn mold, red & pink roses decor 475.00
Bowl, 10½" d., icicle mold, Snowbird winter scene (ILLUS.) 850.00
Bowl, 10½" d., iris mold, wild blackberries & autumn leaves on pale green shaded to white ground (unmarked).............. 120.00
Bowl, 10½" d., 3" h., ripple mold, portrait of Madame Recamier 595.00
Bowl, 10½" d., Swans with Gazebo scene 395.00
Bowl, 12" d., Cottage scene 900.00

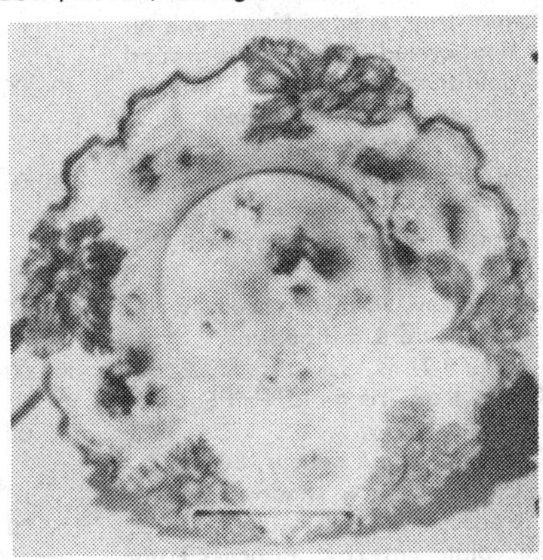

R.S. Prussia Bowl

Bowl, 14½" d., poppy mold, pink

poppies decor, gold trim (ILLUS.) 1,200.00
Bread tray, double domed rim, roses decor on shaded green ground, 13½ x 6½" 165.00
Bun tray, Castle scene on shaded orange to yellow ground, 13 x 8¼" 810.00
Cake plate, pierced handles, carnation mold, pink poppies center decor, pearlized border, 10" d. 165.00
Cake plate, icicle mold, Barnyard Animals with Pheasant scene, 10" d. 775.00

Dice Throwers Cake Plate

Cake plate, pierced handles, point & clover mold, Dice Throwers scene, 11" d. (ILLUS.) 1,050.00
Cake plate, sunflower mold, roses decor, satin finish, 11" d. 225.00
Cake plate, pierced handles, Swans on Lake scene w/water lilies & trees, ornate gold trim, 11" d. 350.00
Celery tray, iris mold, pink & yellow roses on shaded green ground, 12" l. 125.00
Celery tray, Masted Ship scene on light orchid, tan & white ground, gold trim, 12 x 6¼" 400.00
Celery tray, sunflower mold, pink & white roses on shaded green ground, satin finish, 12½" l. 220.00
Celery tray, crimped scalloped rim, snowball & roses decor, 13½" l. 200.00
Celery tray, Farmyard scene w/turkeys, swans & bluebirds, 13½ x 7" 800.00
Celery tray, iris mold, Fall Season portrait 795.00
Chocolate cup & saucer, Swans & Castle scene w/shadowy brown trees 150.00
Chocolate pot, cov., Princess Potocka portrait on green Tiffany-type iridescent ground, 10" h. 900.00
Chocolate pot, cov., icicle mold, Barnyard scene, 10½" h. 375.00
Chocolate pot, cov., Melon Eaters scene on green ground 1,000.00
Chocolate set: 9½" h. cov. chocolate pot & 4 c/s; Castle scene, 9 pcs. 2,495.00
Chocolate set: cov. chocolate pot & 4 c/s; reflecting water lilies on blue & pink ground, 9 pcs. 375.00
Chocolate set: cov. chocolate pot & 6 c/s; swirl mold, white surreal dogwood blossoms on green lustre ground, 13 pcs. 925.00
Cracker jar, cov., Icicle mold, Barnyard scene on white to green ground, 5" h. 450.00
Cracker jar, cov., Point & Clover mold (643), pink poppies decoration, 7½" h. 495.00
Cracker jar, cov., Ribbon & Jewel mold, Melon Eaters scene 1,400.00
Cracker jar, cov., footed, Mold 631, swallows & waterlilies decoration, lustre finish 500.00
Creamer, six-sided, six green feet, pink & white roses w/gold swags near top, green ground 55.00
Creamer & cov. sugar bowl, Mold 501, pearlized Surreal Dogwood Blossoms decoration w/gold trim, pr. 150.00
Creamer & cov. sugar bowl, Mold 510, white w/pink rose garlands w/pink shading, heavy gold trim & stenciling, pr. 275.00
Creamer & cov. sugar bowl, Mold 603, swans decoration, satin finish, unmarked, pr. 525.00
Creamer & sugar bowl, Quiet Cove design w/swan on back, black trim, pr. 850.00
Cup & saucer, demitasse, Iris mold, green shadows w/pink poppies decoration 75.00
Dresser set: 11 x 8" tray, cov. powder box & hair receiver; sweet peas on pink & lavender ground, gold rim, 3 pcs. 175.00
Dresser tray, Iris mold, red roses decoration, 11 x 7½" 184.00
Dresser tray, Barnyard scene, cobalt center (some gold wear on one end) 895.00
Hair receiver, Mold 804, Laurel Chain decoration, 5" d., 3" h. 125.00
Mustard jar, cover & spoon, Mold 642, red & pink roses decoration, green trim, 3 pcs. 175.00
Nut dish, three-footed, Mold 309, white Christmas Roses nestled in green holly & red berries border, white glossy finish, 6 x 3½" 65.00
Pin dish, cov., Hidden Images mold

(827), pink orchids, tiny pink roses & gold trim on shaded blue ground, unmarked, 4¾" l. 135.00

Pitcher, milk, 4 5/8" h., Hidden Images lady profile mold (515), floral decoration, unmarked 175.00

Pitcher, cider, 6½" h., Mold 636, peeled orange & fruit decoration 875.00

Pitcher, lemonade, 9" h., Carnation mold, light & dark pink roses decoration 650.00

Pitcher, tankard, 13" h., Stippled Floral mold, roses decoration 900.00

R.S. Prussia Tankard Pitcher

Pitcher, tankard, Point & Clover mold (643), six flowers decoration, satin finish (ILLUS.) 800.00

Plate, 6" d., Mold 207, Masted Ship decoration, pearlized lustre finish 175.00

Plate, 8" d., Mold 208, purple daisies on green ground 135.00

Plate, 8½" d., Mold 92, peacock in field on green shading w/blue trim & chickens in distant background 800.00

Plate, 8½" d., plain round shape, pink poppies decoration 85.00

Plate, 8¾" d., Plume mold, Reflecting Poppies & Daisies center, blue feathers & pink poppies & roses border w/gold tapestry edge 190.00

Plate, 8¾" d., Mold 301, Swans decoration 190.00

Plate, 9½" d., Gibson Girl in burgundy hat decoration 900.00

Plate, 11¾" d., 1¾" deep, Fall Season scene, 2" cobalt blue band & ¾" gold rim w/small relief-molded flow blue flowers w/gold trim . . . . .2,500.00 to 2,800.00

Relish dish, Carnation mold, pink florals, 9" 110.00

Relish dish, Mold 202, pink & yellow roses, satin finish, 9½ x 4½" 140.00

Relish dish, Icicle mold, Quiet Cove scene, 12" 325.00

Sauce dishes, Surreal Dogwood Blossoms decoration, set of 6 . . . . 225.00

Shaving mug, mirrored, Mold 863, pink poppies on shaded green ground 275.00

Sugar bowl, cov., Mold 704, fleur-de-lis shaped feet, floral decoration w/gold on shaded green ground 125.00

Syrup pitcher, cov., Medallion mold, flowers on one side, Diana the Huntress on other, hanging basket of flowers at bottom 300.00

Teapot, cov., Ball Foot mold (632), pink roses w/yellow, light green & dark green shading, gold feet & trim 225.00

Teapot, cov., Iris mold (628), pink roses on blue ground 300.00

Tea strainer & undercup, pink flowers decoration, 6" l., unmarked . . 150.00

Vase, 5¼" h., tall ovoid shape, cobalt blue w/flowers & leaves decoration 225.00

Vase, 8" h., pedestal base, two-handled, eight jewels decorated as opals, four at top & four on base, Roses & Snowball decoration, green, gold & violet w/gold handles, rim & base 695.00

Vase, 11½" h., tall slender ovoid w/tapering neck to flared rim, two ornate scrolled gold handles at sides, Summer Season portrait on Tiffany ground 850.00

OTHER MARKS

Berry set: 9" master bowl & six sauce dishes; Apple Blossoms w/grey shading, 7 pcs. (Prov. Saxe) 75.00

Bowl, 9 5/8" d., overall fox hunt scene (E.S. Germany) 80.00

Cake plate, Dice Throwers scene, heavy gold border, 11" (C.S. Prussia) 200.00

Candlestick, violets & lily-of-the-valley decoration, 6" h. (R.S. Poland) 110.00

Chocolate pot, cov., overall multicolored roses, gold trim, 8½" h. (E.S. Prov. Saxe) 120.00

Creamer & sugar bowl, pink roses decoration, pr. (R.S. Tillowitz) 55.00

Dish, leaf-shaped, "tapestry," windmill, stream, trees & cloudy sky decoration, 7" l. (E.S. Germany, Prov. Saxe) 55.00

Dresser set: 12" tray, cov. hair receiver & cov. powder box; pink & green florals, 3 pcs. (R.S. Poland) 345.00

Dresser tray, scalloped rim, pierced bow handles, center medallion courting scene w/full figure Cavalier & two ladies w/flowers, maroon ground, gold trim, 11 x 9" (E.S. Germany, Prov. Saxe) 90.00
Dresser tray, red roses decoration (E.S. Germany) 55.00
Hair receiver, violets & lily-of-the-valley decoration (R.S. Poland) 100.00
Humidor, cov., Oriental girl decoration (E.S. Germany, Prov. Saxe) .. 80.00
Nappy, w/handle, four-leaf clover shaped, bluebird on tree limb on purple to green ground (E.S. Germany) 95.00
Nut dish, openwork rim, lavender peonies & snowballs on cream ground, 6" (R.S. Tillowitz) 90.00
Planter, pedestal base, band of pink flowers highlighted w/gold, 6½" d., 6¾" h. (R.S. Poland) 230.00
Plaque, pierced to hang, Indian Chief on spotted horse scene, 6½" d. (E.S. Germany, Royal Saxe) 45.00
Plate, 8" d., Dogwood & Pine decoration (R.S. Poland) 95.00
Plate, 8" d., handled, portrait of beautiful lady on burgundy lustre ground, ornate gold trim (E.S. Germany, Prov. Saxe) 65.00
Plates, 10" d., pierced to hang, portraits of Mme. Recamier & Marie Louise, pr. (E.S. Prov. Saxe) 150.00
Powder jar, cov., bluebird & leaves on green & black ground, 6 x 3½" (E.S. Germany) 85.00
Syrup pitcher, delicate florals on cream to brown ground (R.S. Silesia) 35.00
Teapot, cov., footed pedestal base, roses decoration (R.S. Poland) 95.00
Tea set: cov. teapot, cov. sugar bowl & creamer; footed pedestal base, Angelica Kauffmann scenes on each, double ribbon finials on teapot & sugar bowl covers, wide gold border w/beaded edges around each Kauffmann scene & gold on handles & finials, pearlized light blue-green ground, 3 pcs. (E.S. Prov. Saxe) 375.00
Urn, cov., portrait of lady in pink gown w/peacock in background, 10" h. (E.S. Suhl) 425.00
Vase, 8" h., Pheasants decoration, pr. (R.S. Poland) 495.00
Vase, 10" h., two-handled, portrait of girl w/holly wreath in hair, forest green & yellow ground w/gold trim (E.S. Germany) 175.00

SEVRES

Sevres Jardinieres

Some of the most desirable porcelain ever produced was made at the Sevres factory, originally established at Vincennes, France, and transferred, through permission of Madame de Pompadour, to Sevres as the Royal Manufactory about the middle of the 18th century. King Louis XV took sole responsibility for the works in 1759 when production of hard paste began. Between 1850 and 1900, many biscuit and soft-paste porcelains were again made. Fine early pieces are scarce and high-priced. Many of those available today are late productions. The various Sevres marks have been copied.

Bowl, 6½" d., two reserves, each depicting a putto amid clouds on apple green ground, within gilt borders, interior rim w/gilt trellis border suspending a floral swag, 1753 ....$17,600.00
Box, cov., scroll-molded cartouche-shaped cover painted w/floral swags & a wreath suspending a flower-filled basket in gilt within foliate scrolled borders reserved on a pink ground, sides w/swag panels, interior w/scattered rose sprigs, gilt metal mounts, ca. 1900, 7¾" l. 330.00
Box w/hinged lid, painted in colors depicting an 18th century couple in a forest within a quatrefoliate scroll-embellished border reserved on a *gros bleu* ground, sides w/gilt highlights, gilt mounts, 7½" rectangle 385.00
Cachepots, cylindrical, painted w/reserves of elegant figures in a garden landscape, on pink ground, within gilt scroll borders, 9" h., pr. 880.00
Charger, ormolu rim w/foliate handles & four scroll legs joined by vine swags, central reserve w/three putti holding doves, border w/three elongated oval reserves w/polychrome flowers in elaborate gilt frame, *bleu celeste* ground, late 19th c., 14¾" d. 605.00
Charger, portrait of Louis XVI center, Marie Antoinette on top w/la-

dies of court around edge, names of figures on back, blue & gold, 19" d. 1,025.00

Coffee can & saucer, "Feuille de Choux" (cabbage leaf), flower bunches within cobalt blue & gilt feathered borders, 1768-82 .... 880.00

Compotes, 10" d., wide border painted w/animals amid scrolling acanthus leaves w/Louis Philippe cipher, heightened by gilt motifs, gilt-bronze mounts w/heavily molded collar above a garlanded swag continuing to chamfered base, mid-19th c., pr. 660.00

Ewer, cov., ovoid, gilt-bronze, shell-molded spout, griffin-form handle & pierced base, *bleu de roi* glaze heightened w/scrolling gilt motifs, late 19th c., 25½" h. 2,475.00

Jardinieres, rounded cylindrical body w/18th c. genre scene, one depicting a woman nursing a child w/another child looking on in a kitchen interior, the other depicting a woman scolding while a child feeds a dog, each within gilt foliate scroll & sprig borders, *bleu celeste* ground, reverse w/h.p. floral reserve, molded w/white & gilt shell handles on each side, marked w/pseudo interlaced "L's" enclosing "C," late 19th c., 8½" d., 6 1/8" h., pr. (ILLUS.) 1,320.00

Sevres Pedestals

Pedestals, earthenware, printed & painted w/panels of putti within molded borders trimmed in colorful enamels & reserved on a *bleu-du-roi* ground, ebonized wood top & base, late 19th c., 46½" h., pr. (ILLUS.) 1,210.00

Plate, 8" d., embracing couple in garden scene, yellow decoration, scalloped gold decorated rim, artist-signed, marked "Chateau St. Cloud" 75.00

Plate, 9½" d., Napoleon on a white horse at Battle of Austerlitz, cobalt blue border encrusted w/gold leaves & an "N," artist-signed 250.00

Plate, 9½" d., portrait of Marie Antoinette center, gold trim, chateau mark 135.00

Sevres Botanical Plate

Plates, 9 9/16" d., botanical decoration, each painted in shades of yellow, purple, rose & green, one w/two dahlia blossoms & a spray of *liseron des champs*, the other w/geranium bicolor & azalea sprigs, each floral cluster encircled by a gilt foliate vine, pale blue *fond agate* rim patterned w/gilt florette-centered trelliswork between narrow foliate, dot & band borders, botanical inscriptions on back, inscribed & artist-signed, dated 1836-38, pr. (ILLUS. of one) 7,700.00

Platter, 16¼" l. oval, decorated at the center w/a portrait medallion of Louis XVI, within a gilt scroll & floral border all on pink ground .. 242.00

Tazza, two gilt-lined flat handles molded w/acanthus flanking the gilt foliate rim, exterior painted w/a wide emerald green band, raised on a flat circular foot, ca. 1832, 10 5/8" d. 440.00

Teapot, cov., painted both sides w/figures in extensive landscapes within gilt surrounds on blue ground, shoulder & cover w/band of foliage, 1757, 4¼" h. (minor wear to gilding) 715.00

Tea service: covered teapot, cov. sugar bowl, milk jug, 12 plates (one damaged), 12 teacups & saucers; each piece painted w/a panel depicting couples wearing 18th c. costumes & relaxing in pastoral landscapes, each either reserved on a *bleu celeste* ground or within a *bleu celeste* border reserving small flower or landscape panels, pseudo-Sevres year marks, "Chateau des Tuileries," inventory marks & Louis Philippe marks, late 19th c., teapot 7¾" h., plates 9 5/8" d., 39 pcs. 2,475.00

Trinket jar, cov., floral design interior & exterior, portrait of lady in gold frame forms cover, 4" d. 450.00

Urn, cov., central portrait scene of standing colonial lady, yellow ground w/gold trim & blue forget-me-nots, ormolu handles & foot on pedestal base, ormolu bud finial on cover, 1890's 245.00

Vases, cov., 12" h., fluted body w/scene of a maiden & her suitor in a landscape above gilt foliage & scrolling devices on a *bleu celeste* ground, domed cover w/ornate finial, ormolu side handles & twist-fluted circular base, 19th c., pr. 825.00

Ornate Sevres Vase

Vase, 15 3/8" h., Louis XVI-style, w/gilt-bronze mounts, h.p. w/scene of seated maiden w/pearls in her hair & wearing a red dress, a baton in one outstretched hand, flanked by three cupids on clouds, one holding a laurel wreath & sprigs, another w/a flute before open music sheets, the reverse w/two playful putti, one w/a large harnessed butterfly, raised on a gilt-bronze socle base on a *bleu celeste* lobed porcelain circular base mounted w/ribbon-tied laurel wreath cartouches, foliate scroll handles suspending rings, raised on foliate scroll feet, artist-signed, ca. 1900 (ILLUS.) 1,650.00

Vases, cov., 18¾" h., ovoid, lion's mask handles, scene of lovers attended by cupids near a waterfall or in a woodland clearing near a monument, reverse w/rustic building, gilt-bronze mounts, artist-signed, ca. 1900, pr. 2,750.00

Vase, 26 5/8" h., loop handles issuing from masks, panel w/scene depicting three rustic maidens & a suitor in a bucolic landscape, man presenting a bird in a nest from an empty cage to one maiden while the other two look on wistfully, continuing to a misty landscape view across a tranquil body of water to a small temple beyond, whole between *bleu celeste* borders reserving white panels w/scrolling gilt motifs, gilt-bronze mounts, late 19th c. 1,760.00

Vase, 36" h., oval scene of a maiden beneath inscription "Homere Virgile" & w/a shaped panel depicting a procession of classical figures, each within gilt borders & reserved on a *bleu celeste* ground heightened in gilding & w/various trophies, circular foot set on chamfered gilt-bronze base raised on four bun feet, late 19th c. 3,300.00

SHAWNEE

The Shawnee Pottery operated in Zanesville, Ohio, from 1937 until 1961. Much of the early production was sold to chain stores and mail-order houses including Sears Roebuck, Woolworth and others. Planters, cookie jars and vases, along with the popular "Corn King" oven ware line, are among the collectible items which are plentiful and still reasonably priced. Reference numbers used here are taken from Mark E. Supnick's book, Collecting Shawnee Pottery.

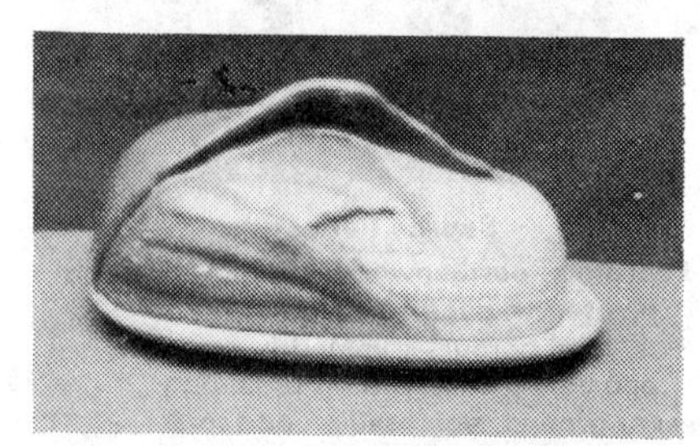

Corn King Butter Dish

Bank-cookie jar combination, figural Smiley Pig, brown glaze $140.00

Bowl, cov., Fruit Basket, small, No. 81 .... 15.00
Butter dish, cov., "Corn King" line, No. 72 (ILLUS.) 30.00
Casserole, cov., "Corn King" line, 1½ qt., No. 74, 11" oval 36.00
Cookie jar, figural Basket of Fruit, No. 84 .... 32.00
Cookie jar, figural Cookie House ... 250.00
Cookie jar, figural Dutch Boy, striped pants 46.00
Cookie jar, figural Dutch Boy, marked "Great Northern" 125.00
Cookie jar, figural Dutch Girl, yellow skirt w/gold trim 90.00
Cookie jar, figural Mugsey the dog, decal decoration & gold trim 105.00
Cookie jar, figural Puss 'n Boots, w/decorations & gold trim 90.00
Cookie jar, figural Smiley Pig, clover leaves & gold trim 80.00
Cookie jar, figural Smiley Pig, red scarf 44.00
Cookie jar, figural Winnie Pig, blue flowers 50.00
Cookie jar, figural Winnie Pig, green collar & cherries decor 65.00
Creamer, "Corn Queen" line 25.00
Creamer, figural Puss 'n Boots, 5" h. 13.00
Creamer & cov. sugar bowl, "Corn King" line, pr. 25.00
Mug, "Corn Queen" line 18.00
Pitcher, 7½" h., figural Bo Peep, No. 47 .... 27.00
Pitcher, figural Chanticleer Rooster, outlined in gold 66.00
Pitcher, "Corn Queen" line 24.00
Pitcher, Fruit decoration, No. 80 .... 30.00
Planter, figural boy at stump, No. 532 .... 8.00
Planter, figural man pushing cart, No. 621 .... 14.00
Planter, figural Polynesian girl's head, blue & maroon, No. 896.... 10.00
Planter, model of doe in shadowbox, white glaze, No. 850 .... 16.00
Planter, model of elf shoe, green glaze, No. 765 .... 6.00
Planter, model of grist mill, No. 769 .... 15.00
Planter, model of a reclining giraffe in front of scrolled background, No. 521 .... 9.00
Planter, model of a shoe w/children molded in relief (Children Who Lived In A Shoe), No. 525 .... 6.50
Planter, model of a skunk on scrolled base, heavy gold trim, No. 512 .... 10.00
Planter, model of watering trough & pump, No. 716 .... 12.00
Plate, salad, 8" oval, "Corn Queen" line 12.50
Platter, 12 x 8" oval, "Corn King" line, No. 96 .... 22.50
Relish tray, oblong, "Corn King" line, No. 79 .... 13.00

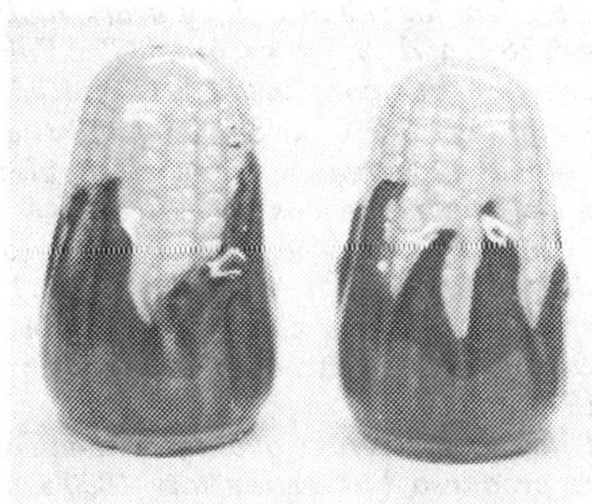

Small Corn King Salt & Pepper

Salt & pepper shakers, "Corn King" line, 3¼" h., No. 76, pr. (ILLUS.) 10.00
Salt & pepper shakers, "Corn King" line, 5½" h., No. 77, pr. 12.00
Salt & pepper shakers, "Corn Queen" line, 5½" h., pr. 22.00
Salt & pepper shakers, figural Puss 'n Boots, small, pr. 14.50
Salt & pepper shakers, figural Swiss children, gold trim, pr. 28.00
Teapot, cov., "Corn King" line, individual size, 10 oz., No. 65 ...... 62.00
Teapot, cov., "Corn King" line, 30 oz., No. 75 .... 32.00
Vase, 9½" h., bulbous base w/tall flared top, green glaze, No. 890 .. 15.00
Vase, model of heads of giraffe & baby, black glaze, No. 841 .... 30.00
Vase, pitcher-form, ribbed sides, single dolphin handle, green glaze, No. 828 .... 12.00

SHELLEY CHINA

Shelley Creamer

Members of the Shelley family were in the pottery business in England as early as the

18th century. In 1872 Joseph Shelley formed a partnership with James Wileman of Wileman & Co. who operated the Foley China Works. The Wileman & Co. name was used for the firm for the next fifty years, and between 1890 and 1910 the words "The Foley" appeared above conjoined "WC" initials.

Beginning in 1910 the Shelley family name in a shield appeared on wares, although the firm's official name was still Wileman & Co. The company's name was finally changed to Shelley in 1925 and then Shelley China Ltd. after 1965. The firm changed hands in the 1960's and became part of the Doulton Group in 1971.

At first only average quality earthenwares were produced but in the late 1890's new shapes and better quality decorations were used.

Bone china was introduced at Shelley before World War I and these fine dinnerwares became very popular in the United States and are increasingly popular today with collectors. Thin "eggshell china" teawares, miniatures and souvenir items were widely marketed during the 1920's and 1930's and are sought-after today.

Bonbon dish, three sections, Blue Rock patt. $40.00

Bowl, cream soup w/underplate, six-flute shape, Begonia patt., 2 pcs. 40.00

Bowl, master berry, Primrose patt. 18.00

Bowls, berry, Butterfly & Berry patt., marigold, set of 7 . . . . 190.00

Breakfast set: cov. teapot, cov. marmalade pot w/underplate, 5½" oval dish, 6½" shell dish, two cups/saucers, two oval plates, salt & pepper shakers, ashtray & cigarette holder; Rosebud patt., 15 pcs. 350.00

Butter dish, cov., Harmony patt., orange & green 115.00

Butter dish w/insert, cov., Rosebud patt. 110.00

Cake set: 9" d. master cake plate & eight individual plates; fluted design w/delicate pink & green flowers, gold trim on edge, marked "The Foley," 1890-1910, 9 pcs. 179.00

Cake set: 9¼" d. handled tray, six 6½" d. plates, six cups/saucers, creamer & block sugar bowl; Rambler Rose patt., 21 pcs. 195.00

Chocolate cup & saucer, Rosebud patt. 29.00

Chocolate pot, cov., Dainty Blue patt. 185.00

Chocolate pot, cov., Queen Anne shape, yellow, green & orange floral decoration on white ground, 4" d., 7" h. 110.00

Chocolate pot, cov., Rosebud patt. . . 95.00

Coffeepot, cov., Begonia patt. 135.00

Coffeepot, cov., Violets patt., 6" h. 115.00

Coffee set: 7½" h. cov. coffeepot, open sugar bowl, creamer & four cups/saucers, orange, yellow & green chrysanthemum-type florals on white, 11 pcs. 295.00

Coffee set, demitasse: cov. coffeepot, sugar bowl & five cups/saucers; Rosebud patt., 12 pcs. 110.00

Compote, 3½" h., 9" w., Blue Rock patt. 45.00

Creamer, Duchess patt. 45.00

Creamer, fluted body w/fan-shaped ribs w/thin embossed ribbing alternating w/plain fan-shaped ribs, gold handle & narrow gold band at rim (ILLUS.) 30.00

Creamer & sugar bowl, Begonia patt., pr. 60.00

Creamer & sugar bowl, Blue Rock patt., pr. 60.00

Creamer & sugar bowl, Campanula patt., small, pr. 42.50

Creamer & sugar bowl, Dainty Green patt., medium, pr. 40.00

Creamer, open sugar bowl & oblong tray, purple pansies on white ground, 3 pcs. 95.00

Cup & saucer, demitasse, Bridal Rose patt. 30.00

Cup & saucer, demitasse, Daffodil Time patt. 29.00

Cup & saucer, demitasse, Dainty Blue patt. 35.00

Cup & saucer, demitasse, Harebell patt. 29.00

Cup & saucer, demitasse, Lily of the Valley patt., fluted 34.00

Cup & saucer, demitasse, Rose Spray patt. 26.00

Cup & saucer, demitasse, Stocks patt. 30.00

Cup & saucer, demitasse, Woodland patt., blue handle 29.00

Cup & saucer, Begonia patt. 25.00

Cup & saucer, Blue Daisy patt. 29.00

Cup & saucer, tulip shape, Blue Lily patt. 35.00

Cup & saucer, Blue Rock patt. 35.00

Cup & saucer, Dainty Blue patt. 28.00

Cup & saucer, Jacobean Ware 35.00

Cup & saucer, Maple Leaf patt. 25.00

Cup & saucer, Maytime patt. 34.00

Cup & saucer, Sheraton patt. 25.00

Cup & saucer, Wildflower patt., extra-large 32.00

Dish, cov., Blue Rock patt., 8" d. 78.00

Dish, handled, Rosebud patt., 4½" square 20.00
Egg cup, Blue Rock patt. 40.00
Egg cup, Bridal Rose patt. 24.00
Egg cup, Forget-Me-Not patt. 32.00
Egg cup, Rose Pansy patt. 32.00
Feeding dish, puppy & elf decoration, artist-signed, 6¼" d. 55.00
Gravy boat w/underplate, six-flute shape, Begonia patt. 50.00
Marmalade jar, cover & underplate, Stocks patt. 50.00
Mayonnaise bowl, cover & underplate, Rosebud patt., 3 pcs. 38.00
Model of "Golden Eagle," Bird Studies No. 5, 7" h. 225.00
Mush set, Red Riding Hood patt., 3 pcs. 175.00
Nut dish, commemorates Queen Elizabeth & Prince Philip's visit to Canada, 1959, 4½" d. 30.00
Pitcher, jug-type, 7 3/8" h., 4 7/8" d., bands of yellow, rust, grey & black running around body from top to base 64.00
Plate, 6" d., Begonia patt. 20.00
Plate, 6" d., Regency patt. 10.00
Plate, 8" d., six-flute shape, Begonia patt. 22.50
Plate, 8" d., Daisy patt., green 20.00
Plate, 8" d., Rock Garden patt. 20.00
Plate, 9¼" d., Forget-Me-Not patt. . . 30.00
Plate, 10½" d., Harebell patt. 30.00
Plate, 11" d., Blue Rock patt. 52.00
Platter, 14" l., Duchess patt. 60.00
Powder box, cov., octagonal Queen Anne shape, butterfly decoration on lilac ground, black trim 65.00
Relish dish, Blue Rock patt., 4¾" d. 47.00
Sugar bowl, demitasse, Rose Pansy patt. 55.00
Sugar bowl, cov., Harebell patt. 30.00
Teapot, cov., Dainty Blue patt. 155.00
Teapot, cov., Duchess patt. 95.00
Teapot, cov., Regency patt., w/silver trim 175.00
Teapot, cov., Stocks patt., green trim, 7¼" w. 75.00
Tea set: cov. teapot, creamer & cov. sugar bowl; Begonia patt., 3 pcs. 185.00
Tea set: cov. teapot, creamer & cov. sugar bowl; six-flute shape, Hibiscus patt., 3 pcs. 150.00
Tray, Begonia patt., 8 x 5" 35.00
Tray, Blue Rock patt., 14 x 5¼" 30.00
Vase, 5" h., cone-shaped, Art Deco blue & green decoration 50.00
Vase, 7" h., Art Deco-style balloons on black ground 65.00
Vegetable dish, cov., Rosebud patt. 65.00

SHENANDOAH VALLEY POTTERY

John Bell Greyhound Figure

The potters of the Shenandoah Valley in Maryland and Virginia turned out an earthenware pottery of a distinctive type. It was the first earthenware pottery made in America with a varied, brightly colored glaze. The most notable of these potters, Peter Bell, Jr., operated a pottery at Hagerstown, Maryland and later at Winchester, Virginia, from about 1800 until 1845. His sons and grandsons carried on the tradition. One son, John Bell, established a pottery at Waynesboro, Pennsylvania in 1833, working until his death in 1880, along with his sons who subsequently operated the pottery a few years longer. Two other sons of Peter Bell, Jr., Solomon and Samuel, operated a pottery in Strasburg, Virginia, a town sometimes referred to as "pot town" for six potteries were in operation there in the 1880's. Their work was also continued by descendants. Shenandoah Valley redware pottery, with its colorful glazes in green, yellow, brown and other colors, and the stoneware pottery produced in the area, are eagerly sought by collectors. Some of the more unique forms can be considered true American folk art and will fetch fantastic prices.

Bank, keg-shaped, reddish buff clay w/green, brown & clear glaze, 4½" h. $400.00
Bank, turnip-shaped, redware w/white slip & brown glaze, 4 1/8" h. 235.00
Bowl, 10" d., 3" h., narow rim, redware w/interior glaze, impressed "John Bell, Waynesboro" 360.00
Cuspidor, embossed eagles, redware w/rich brown running glaze, unmarked, probably John Bell, 7½" w., 4 3/8" h. 85.00
Cuspidor, redware w/white slip & mottled green, brown & clear glaze, 7" d. (edge chips & wear) . . 150.00
Flower pot, unglazed redware w/tooled rim & attached saucer base, white slip & brushed grey-

green glaze "commas," impressed "S. Bell & Sons, Strasburg," 8¼" h. (edge chips) 350.00
Flower pot, redware w/edge tooling on rim & on attached saucer, yellow slip interior w/highlights of yellow slip on exterior w/splotches of brown & green, clear shiny glaze, 8½" h. 500.00
Flower pot w/attached saucer base, canted sides, narrow everted rim, redware w/running brown glaze, impressed "John Bell," 5" h. (edge chips) 200.00
Jar, semi-ovoid, tooled rim, redware w/interior glaze, impressed "John W. Bell, Waynesboro, Pa.," 6¾" h. (rim flakes).............. 155.00
Jar, ovoid, brown interior glaze, unglazed exterior w/good patina, impressed "John W. Bell, Waynesboro, Pa.," 8¼" d., 6¾" h. (minor wear & flakes) 80.00
Jar, ovoid, redware w/interior glaze, impressed "John Bell, Waynesboro," 6¼" d., 7½" h..... 120.00
Models of greyhounds in recumbent position, black collar, on yellow rectangular base, impressed "John Bell, Waynesboro, Pennsylvania," 1833-80, 9½" l., pr. (ILLUS. of one) 5,280.00
Mug, rich brown overall sponging, impressed "John Bell," 4½" h. ... 775.00
Pie plate, redware w/interior glaze, impressed "John W. Bell, Waynesboro, Pa.," 9 5/8" d. 305.00
Pitcher, 6½" h., tall slightly ovoid body w/short strap handle, redware w/yellow slip w/green & brown (wear & short hairlines) ... 500.00
Pitcher, 7" h., slightly ovoid shape w/strap handle & flaring rim, white slip & green glaze (small edge chips)....................... 475.00
Preserving jar, redware w/greenish brown glaze, impressed "John Bell," 5¼" h. (base chip)......... 195.00
Preserving jar, yellowware w/greenish clear glaze, impressed "John Bell," 6½" h. (minor edge flakes) 225.00
Tile, flared end, unglazed redware, impressed "John W. Bell, Waynesboro, Pa.," 8 7/8" l. 85.00
Urn, reddish clay w/white slip & brushed brown & green floral decoration, detailed lion-head handles & coggled rim, drainage hole in bottom, impressed "Solomon Bell, Strasburg, Va.," 14¾" h. (surface repairs & chips, one lion head restored).......... 800.00

SPATTERWARE

Rooster Spatterware Cup & Saucer

This ceramic ware takes its name from the "spattered" decoration, in various colors, generally used to trim pieces hand-painted with rustic center designs of flowers, birds, houses, etc. Popular in the early 19th century, most was imported from England.

Related wares, called "stick spatter," had free-hand designs applied with pieces of cut sponge attached to sticks, hence the name. Examples date from the 19th and early 20th century and were produced in England, Europe and America.

Bowl, 7½" d., piecrust applied rim, yellow & red spatter............$195.00
Creamer, ovoid body w/hoop handle, h.p. peafowl in red, blue, yellow & black, blue spatter band at rim, 4" h. (pinpoint rim flakes) 350.00
Creamer, octagonal paneled form, Peafowl patt., free-hand brown, red, green & black, blue spatter trim, 5½" h. (minor pinpoint on rim)......................... 550.00
Cup & saucer, handleless, Acorn patt. in two shades of green & black & yellow, purple spatter trim (stains) 525.00
Cup & saucer, handleless, red & green spatter in Christmas Ball patt. 500.00
Cup & saucer, handleless, Dove patt., free-hand yellow ochre, green, blue & black on blue spatter ground (minor wear) 750.00
Cup & saucer, handleless, Fort patt., free-hand color center on blue spatter ground (hairlines & pinpoint flakes in cup)............ 225.00
Cup & saucer, handleless, Peafowl patt., free-hand blue, yellow, red & green on green spatter ground (minor stains & wear, blue on saucer flaked) 250.00
Cup & saucer, handleless, Plaid design in blue, red & green spatter (stains & flakes)................ 510.00

Cup & saucer, handleless, Rainbow spatter bands in red, green & blue 325.00

Cup & saucer, handleless, Rooster patt., free-hand red, blue, yellow, ochre & black rooster, blue spatter trim (ILLUS.) 600.00

Cup & saucer, handleless, Rose patt., free-hand red, green & black, blue spatter trim (minor stains & pinpoints) 150.00

Pepper pot, pierced domed top, Peafowl patt., free-hand blue, ochre, rose & black peacock on a branch on yellow spatter ground, Staffordshire, ca. 1840, 4¾" h. (rim chips at neck) 1,100.00

Pitcher, 7¾" h., paneled body, Rose patt., free-hand red, blue, green & black rose on white, blue spatter trim 300.00

Pitcher, 8" h., baluster form w/shaped rim, Peafowl patt., free-hand blue, ochre, green & brown peacock on a branch either side on red spatter ground, applied twisted handle, Staffordshire, ca. 1840 (some enamel flaking & firing imperfections) 880.00

Pitcher, 10 1/8" h., paneled bulbous footed body tapering to high arched spout & high arched strap handle, blue transfer scene of Oriental figures in interior in center surrounded by blue spatter ... 150.00

Pitcher, 12" h., Rainbow spatter stripes in red & blue (hairlines in base) 275.00

Plate, 7 7/8" d., Rooster patt., black outlined free-hand cock w/an ochre body, blue wing & red comb, wattles & tail, standing on a red spatter mound, red spatter trim, Staffordshire, ca. 1840 ...... 467.00

Plate, 8 1/8" d., scalloped edge, Rainbow spatter in red, blue & green, impressed "Adams" 160.00

Plates, 8¼" d., Rose patt., centrally painted in deep red w/a stylized floral sprig surrounded by green leaves on a white ground within a spattered blue border, two plates stamped "T. Walker," set of 6 .....715.00

Plate, 8¼" d., center blue transfer of eagle & shield, blue spatter trim (minor stains) 100.00

Plate, 8 3/8" d., Castle patt., red spatter trim (minor pinpoints) 400.00

Plate, 8½" d., Rooster patt., the stylized red & blue figure of a rooster flanked by green foliage within deep red spatterware border, impressed "JD," factory mark "UC" within blue shield, England, mid-19th c. 99.00

Plate, 9¼" d., Single Rose patt. in red, green & black, blue spatter trim (stains & edge chips) 175.00

Plate, 9 3/8" d., Tulip patt. in red, blue, green & black, blue spatter trim (minor stains & glaze defects) 220.00

Soup plate, Peafowl patt. in free-hand red, blue, green & black, red spatter trim, impressed "Adams," 9½" d. (stains & two hairlines) 105.00

Soup plate, gaudy polychrome tulip in center, coarsely spattered red & blue rim band, impressed "Cotton & Barlow," 10 5/8" d. (hairline) 125.00

Sugar bowl, cov., octagonal paneled form, Peafowl patt., free-hand brown, red, green & black, blue spatter trim, 7½" h. (pinpoint flakes on lid) 500.00

Sugar bowl, cov., Thistle patt., free-hand red & green on yellow spatter ground (stains, hairlines, chips) 315.00

Teapot, cov., Peafowl patt., free-hand red, orange, green & black peafowl on blue spatter ground, 8¾" h. (spout chip & small areas of repair)...................... 300.00

Toddy plate, Peafowl patt., free-hand red, blue, green & black, green spatter trim, 5 1/8" d. (short hairline) 200.00

Waste bowl, Christmas Ball patt. in red, green & yellow spatter (stains & pinpoint flakes) 235.00

STICK SPATTER

Chop plate, gaudy stamped design in center of three large circles w/two three-leaf sprigs below them & pyramid of six small circles w/dots above them, rim design of blossom & leaf band, red, blue & green, 16½" d. (minor stains & crazing, glaze chip)...... 145.00

Creamer, stick spatter decoration of vertical red florette & green leaf bands, blue border stripe, 4½" h. (small chips, hairline in spout).... 85.00

Plate, 8" d., blue stick spatter sprig edge band, polychrome h.p. diamond pattern across center w/h.p. leaves & blossom at very center, marked "France" (slightly faded) 60.00

Plate, 8 1/8" d., gaudy floral free-hand decoration in center in underglaze blue, red & green, rim band of free-hand flower sprigs (minor damage)................. 75.00

Plate, 10" d., gaudy floral free-hand wreath around center in underglaze blue, red & green, outer rim band of free-hand S-scrolls w/leaf sprigs (minor crazing) 115.00

Platter, 10½" oval, blue & red stick spatter edge border of triangular leaf sprigs, h.p. polychrome floral bouquet in center, marked "Auld Heather Ware, Scotland" 65.00

Platter, 11 5/8" l., octagonal w/cut corners, wide border band of diamond & dot pattern in red, green & blue w/florette design at center (rim chips) 125.00

Soup plate, stick spatter red & green zigzag rim, gaudy floral center in polychrome colors, marked "Made in Belgium," 10 7/8" d. 45.00

SPONGEWARE

Spongeware Batter Bowl

Spongeware, a common utilitarian ware of the 19th and early 20th centuries, usually featured boldly daubed colors on a pottery body. A coarse sponge (hence the name) or a piece of cloth was used to apply the colors. Blue on white is most often seen but rusts, browns and greens on yellowware are also abundant. Although related, Spongeware and the earlier Spatterware are distinctly different decorative techniques.

Batter bowl, w/pour spout & molded handle on opposite edge, wire bail handle w/wood handgrip across top, blue on yellowware, 7½ x 4¼" (ILLUS.) ....$125.00 to 150.00

Batter bowl w/lid, blue on white, large 350.00

Bean pot, marked "Beans," blue on white, small 625.00

Beater jar, brown & green on yellowware 85.00

Bowl, 5" d., brown on yellowware .. 20.00

Bowl, 6½" d., blue & rust on cream body 45.00

Bowl, 7" d., light green & brown on cream body 65.00

Bowl, 9½" d., rust on yellowware .. 65.00

Bowl, 10" d., blue & rust 55.00

Bowl, wide blue band, blue & rust, marked "No. 9," Monmouth Pottery 40.00

Butter crock, cov., cover marked "Butter," blue on white 350.00

Casserole, cov., blue & rust on cream body 80.00

Chamber pot, blue on white........ 95.00

Chamber pot w/lid, blue on yellowware, gold trim 85.00

Cuspidor, blue daubing on white ... 115.00

Custard cup, blue daubing on white 60.00

Jar, cov., straight cylindrical sides w/molded rim, flat inset cover w/knob finial, blue daubing on white, 6" h. (wire bail handle missing, edge chips)............. 140.00

Mixing bowl, ribbed sides, blue daubing on white, 11" d., 5¾" h. (stains) 185.00

Mug, straight sides, blue & purple daubing on white, 3½" h. (small lip chips) 35.00

Pie plate, brown & green daubing on cream, 9" d. 50.00

Pitcher, 4½" h., light green & brown daubing on yellowware, embossed ribs w/oblong smooth reserve w/black transfer label "Equity Elev. & Trading Co....Whitman, N. Dakota" 45.00

Pitcher, 5 7/8" h., cylindrical w/strap handle down side & pinched spout, green daubing on white (two chips on base)........ 65.00

Pitcher, 6½" h., rust daubing on yellowware 95.00

Pitcher, tankard, 6¾" h., rectangular handle, blue daubing on white 175.00

Pitcher, 8¾" h., slightly tapering cylinder w/pinched spout & molded strap handle, bands of blue daubing on white (hairlines at spout, small chip on base) 230.00

Pitcher, tankard, 9" h., blue daubing on white (ILLUS.) 192.00

Pitcher, 11" h., 4½" w., brown & blue daubing on cream 185.00

Plate, 8 5/8" d., scalloped edge, blue daubing on white (pinpoint rim flakes) 125.00

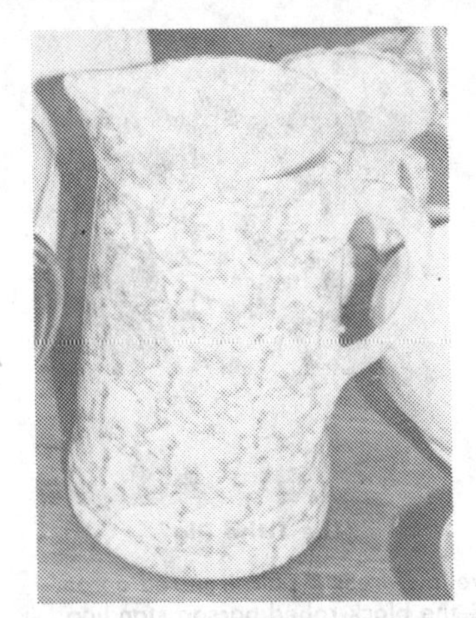

Spongeware Tankard Pitcher

Plate, 10¼" d., embossed scalloped edge, blue daubing on white 175.00

Platter, 10 x 13", Ironstone, blue daubing on white 200.00

Platter, 13¾" l., rectangular w/rounded ends & corners, blue daubing on white (minor stains & pinpoints) 210.00

Salt & pepper shakers, hand-thrown, green & amber daubing on white, pr. 95.00

Salt box, blue daubing & "Salt" on white, arched crest pierced for hanging, 6" w., 6" h. (no lid) 215.00

Soap dish, blue on white, 6" d. 85.00

Teapot, cov., brown & rust on cream body, w/grain elevator advertising 67.50

Vegetable dish, cov., blue on white 175.00

STAFFORDSHIRE FIGURES

Bust of the Rev. George Whitefield

Small figures and groups made of pottery were produced by the majority of the Staffordshire, England potters in the 19th century and were used as mantel decorations or "chimney ornaments," as they were sometimes called. Pairs of dogs were favorites and were turned out by the carload, and 19th century pieces are still available. Well-painted reproductions also abound and collectors are urged to exercise caution before investing.

Bust of the Rev. George Whitefield, pearlware, white hair, face painted in flesh tones, wearing black robes & white bands, reverse w/medallion impressed "The Revd, George Whitfield (sic) Died Sept. 30. 1770, Aged 56-...-Enoch Wood, Sculp. Burslem," raised on a black bow-fronted rectangular base, ca. 1810, 13 1/8" h. (ILLUS.) $1,045.00

Bust of Sir Francis Burdett, creamware, curly hair, wearing a high-necked bow-tied shirt, open waistcoat & coat, on waisted oval base, 1810-15, 15 7/8" h. 385.00

Cat, seated, black spots on white body, ochre ribbon at neck, 3¾" h. (hairlines) 195.00

Cats, white coat w/black spots, wearing green collar & resting on orange cushion, mid-19th c., 5½" l., 5½" h., pr. 1,200.00

Dogs, Greyhounds, each standing opposing, w/chestnut coats & dead hare at the feet, on gilt-lined oval grassy bases, 10" h., pr. 935.00

Dogs, Poodles w/sanded coat, on grassy mound base, 4" h., pr. 150.00

Dogs, Spaniel in seated position, white coat w/copper lustre ears, spots, tail, collar & chain, black nose, brown eyes, 7 x 5", 9¼" h., facing pr. 275.00

Dogs, Spaniels, in seated position, white coat, black muzzle & original glass eyes, even wear to gold collar & trim, 12¼" h., pr. 450.00

Dogs, Spaniel in seated position, white coat w/orange nose & embossed chain at neck, late 19th c., 13" h., pr. 580.00

Dog, Whippet, in seated position, white coat w/polychrome spots & trim, on molded base w/scalloped bottom edge, 8¾" h. (minor wear & small base flake) 350.00

Equestrian figures, "Going to Market" & "Coming Home," each showing couple on horseback, she in a plumed hat, he holding a basket, flatback type, 8" h., pr. .. 550.00

Equestrian figure, Princess Louise, lady riding sidesaddle, "PRINCESS" in raised lettering on base, flat-back type, 10¼" h. 88.00

Figure of a harvester, wearing a pale green dress beneath a light brown bodice, Ralph Wood, ca. 1770, 7 7/8" h. (repair to elbow).. 850.00

Figures of a shepherd & shepherdess, painted in tones of green & brown, Ralph Wood, ca. 1770, 8¾" h. & 9" h., pr. 2,600.00

Figures, woman in country dress carrying a young girl & a man in country dress w/cloak over his shoulder, 9½" h., pr. 357.50

Figure of actor David Garrick as "Richard III," 1860, 10" h. (repaired) 115.00

Figure of Benjamin Franklin holding book in his left hand, his right hand outstretched, standing on a square plinth molded on three sides w/classical portrait medallions within fluted borders, interior glazed, Ralph Wood, ca. 1775, 13 3/8" h. 1,980.00

Figure of Flora standing, draped in white cloak painted w/scattered flower sprays, holding a yellow cornucopia filled w/flowers in her left hand, ca. 1840, 14" h. 275.00

Figure of King Edward VII, by Wm. Kent, 14" h. 160.00

Figures of Queen Victoria & Prince Albert, 18" h., pr. 775.00

Figure of Shakespeare leaning on books & a manuscript on a pedestal molded w/portrait busts, wearing green-lined yellow cloak & brown breeches, on oblong base enriched in black, Enoch Wood, incised P.V. reverse, ca. 1790, 18" h. (some restoration) 1,540.00

Figure group, pearlware, of Obadiah Sheratt-type, centering a school mistress in a blue & russet flowered dress, holding a book & stick, flanked by four diminutive pupils dressed in green & russet, seated on benches & reading within an arched niche molded w/fruiting grapevines & blue & red marbleized pilasters, on a similarly marbled stepped base, ca. 1825, 6 1/8" h. (hairline)..............2,200.00

Figure group, young lady & man in country setting standing before tree branches w/tree trunk forming vase, oblong base, 6¾" h. ... 175.00

Figure group, pearlware, farmer wearing black hat, purple coat & green breeches, holding a staff & piglet, his wife wearing blue cape,

"The Tithe Pig"

yellow dress & pale iron-red apron, & the black-robed parson standing before a green leafy tree, a small pig, basket of blue eggs & sheaves of yellow wheat at their feet on a green mound base molded at the front w/scrollwork heightened in iron-red & blue, chips & repairs, 1810-25, 7¼" h. (ILLUS.) 1,430.00

Figure group, Scotsman standing before oversized sheep w/white "sanded" coat, on gilt-lined oval base, 8¼" h. 235.00

Figure group, Scottish couple standing in sea serpent-shaped boat, gilt-lined oval base w/applied "waves," 8 5/8" h. 250.00

Figure group, "The Lost Sheep," young shepherd wearing dark brown hat & shoes, green coat & yellow waistcoat over olive-green breeches, carrying on his shoulders the tethered sheep, walking by tan gnarled stump on green & tan grassy rockwork base, Ralph Wood, ca. 1770, 8¾" h. 1,870.00

Uncle Tom and Eva Figure Group

Figure group, Princess Royal seated

on the back of a St. Bernard, 1845, 9" h. 250.00

Figure group, Uncle Tom & Eva, Uncle Tom seated on rockwork w/hat in left hand, Eva standing on his knee, oval base inscribed "Uncle Tom," polychrome enameling, 10½" h., stains & hairlines in base (ILLUS.)................... 195.00

Lamb, lying down, 3¼ x 2¼" 65.00

Lion, standing, brown & tan glaze w/black trim, 3¼" h. (hairlines & wear) 165.00

Ram in recumbent position, looking to the left, curly fleece & curved horns, on grassy brown, beige, green & black mound base, Ralph Wood, ca. 1760, 7¼" w..........3,080.00

Stag recumbent before a hollow tree stump applied w/a fox in branches, enriched in yellow, green & brown, on oval base, Ralph Wood, ca. 1770, 5¾" l. (minor repairs to antlers) 4,840.00

STANGL POTTERY BIRDS

Stangl Cockatoo

Johann Martin Stangl, who first came to work for the Fulper Pottery in 1910 as a ceramic chemist and plant superintendent, acquired a financial interest and became president of the company in 1926. The name of the firm was changed to Stangl Pottery in 1929 and at that time much of the production was devoted to a high grade dinnerware to enable the company to survive the Depression years. Around 1940 a very limited edition of porcelain birds, patterned after the illustrations in John James Audubon's "Birds of America," was issued. Stangl subsequently began production of less expensive ceramic birds and these proved to be popular during the war years, 1940-46. Each bird was handpainted and each was well marked with impressed, painted or stamped numerals which indicated the species and the size. Collectors are now seeking these ceramic birds which we list below.

Allen Hummingbird, No. 3634, 3½" h. $42.50

Bird of Paradise, No. 3408, 5½" h... 70.00

Bluebird (Double), No. 3276-D, 8½" h. 125.00

Blue Jay, No. 3715, 10¼" 357.00

Blue Jay, No. 3716, 10¼" 375.00

Bobolink, No. 3595, 4¾" h. 89.00

Canary facing left - Blue Flower, No. 3747, 6¼" h. 145.00

Canary facing right - Rose Flower, No. 3746, 6¼" h. 130.00

Cardinal, No. 3444, 6½" h.......... 55.00

Cockatoo, No. 3484, 11 3/8" h. (ILLUS.)......................... 200.00

Cock Pheasant, No. 3492, 6¼ x 11" 150.00

Double Wren, No. 3401D 50.00

Flying Duck, No. 3443, 9" h......... 225.00

Group of Chickadees, No. 3581, 5½ x 8½" 140.00

Group of Goldfinches, No. 3635, 4 x 11½" 160.00

Hen, No. 3446, 7" h................ 114.00

Hen Pheasant, No. 3491, 6¼ x 11".. 148.00

Indigo Bunting, No. 3589, 3¼" h. 37.50

Kentucky Warbler, No. 3598, 3" h. .. 35.00

Key West Quail Dove, No. 3454, 9" h. 225.00

Kingfisher, No. 3406, 3½" h. 53.00

Kingfisher, No. 3406-S, 3½" h. 45.00

Love Bird, No. 3400, 4" h........... 33.00

Magpie-Jay, No. 3758............... 585.00

Mountain Blue Bird, No. 3453....... 70.00

Oriole, No. 3402, 3¼" h. 37.00

Oriole, No. 3402-S, 3¼" h.......... 35.00

Pair of Hummingbirds, No. 3599, 8 x 10½" 240.00

Pair of Kingfishers, No. 3406-D, 5" h. 125.00

Pair of Parakeets, No. 3582, 7" h. .. 110.00

Pair of Wrens, No. 3401-D, 8" h..... 82.00

Penguin, No. 3274, 5½" h. 280.00

Red-Breasted Nuthatch, No, 3851 ... 58.00

Red-Headed Woodpecker (Double), No. 3752-D, 7¾" h. 350.00

Rooster, grey, No. 3445, 9" h. 96.00

Scarlet Tanager (Double), No. 3750-D, 8" h 296.00

Scissor-Tailed Flycatcher, No. 3757, 11" h. 355.00

Single Wren, No. 3401S 30.00

Swallow, No. 3852 .... 50.00

Titmouse, No. 3592, 2½" h. 35.00

Turkey, No. 3275, 3½" h. 245.00
Western Blue Bird, No. 3815 .... 136.00
White Headed Pigeon, No. 3518, 12½" l., 7½" h. 450.00
Wilson Warbler, No. 3597, 3½" h. 32.00
Wren, No. 3401, 3½" h. 42.00
Yellow Warbler, No. 3447, 5" h. 47.00

STONEWARE

Stoneware Butter Crock

Stoneware is essentially a vitreous pottery, impervious to water even in its unglazed state, that has been produced by potteries all over the world for centuries. Utilitarian wares such as crocks, jugs, churns and the like, were the most common productions in the numerous potteries that sprang into existence in the United States during the 19th century. These items were often enhanced by the application of a cobalt blue oxide decoration. In addition to the coarse, primarily salt-glazed stonewares, there are other categories of stoneware known by such special names as basalt, jasper and others.

Beater jar, wide blue stripe on grey, 5½" h. $30.00

Butter churn, salt glazed, waisted ovoid vessel stenciled in blue "I.A. Bauer Pottery Company, Los Angeles, Manufacturers Bockmon's Quality Pottery and Tile, no. 2," early 20th c., 2 gal., 7¾" d., 13" h. 165.00

Butter churn, ovoid, brushed cobalt blue floral design on grey, impressed "A.D. Whittemore, Havana, N.Y." & "5," 1869-93, 5 gal., 17" h. plus dasher (hairlines & replaced lid) 285.00

Butter churn, ovoid w/applied ear handles, unusual brushed cobalt blue decoration of shield flanked by rampant lion & beaver (?) on grey, attributed to Ohio potters, impressed "6," 18¼" h. (minor lip chips, professional repair) 850.00

Butter crock, cov., low straight sides w/flat cover, applied ear handles, brushed cobalt blue leafy sprigs around sides, at handles & on cover, ca. 1850, chips on cover handle, 8¼" d., 5½" h. (ILLUS.) .. 495.00

Crock, straight sides, earred handles, slip-quilled cobalt blue wreath encircling "2" on grey, impressed "West Troy, N.Y. Pottery," 2 gal., 9¼" h. 135.00

Crock by F.B. Norton & Co.

Crock, straight sides, earred handles, brushed cobalt blue bird perched on branch on grey, impressed "F.B. Norton & Co., Worcester, Mass." & "2," 1865-85, 2 gal. (ILLUS.) 550.00

Crock, straight sides, earred handles, brushed cobalt blue eagle w/banner in its beak inscribed "E Pluribus Unum" on grey, 3 gal., 10¾" h. (old stabilized cracks) ... 825.00

Crock, straight sides, eared handles, slip-quilled cobalt blue long-tailed bird on scrolling branch on grey, impressed "N.A. White & Son, Utica, N.Y. 4," 1882-86, 4 gal., 10¾" h. (hairlines along back near base) 425.00

Crock, straight sides, earred handles, slip-quilled cobalt blue bird on branch, impressed "Ottman Bro's. & Co., Fort Edward, N.Y.," 1872-92, 11¾" h. (small chips & glaze flakes) 275.00

Crock, straight sides, earred handles, slip-quilled cobalt blue stylized fish on grey, impressed "W. Hart, Ogdensburgh" (New York) & "5," 1858-69, 5 gal., 12¾" h. (firing flakes & rim crack) 700.00

Crock, straight sides, stenciled blue ribbon & "Blue Ribbon Brand, Buckeye Pottery Co., Macomb, Ill." on grey, 12 gal. 90.00

Crock, straight sides, rolled lip, double applied handles, stenciled cobalt blue spread-winged eagle & swags on grey, impressed "J. Hamilton and Co., Greensboro, Pa." & "20," 1850-80, 20 gal., 25¾" h. 715.00

Jar, ovoid, stenciled greyish blue "A. P. Donaghho, Fredericktown, Pa." & spread-winged eagle on grey, 7¾" h. 425.00

Jar, ovoid, open earred handles, incised & brushed cobalt blue flower each side on grey, attributed to Jonathan Fenton, Boston, 1794-96, 8 7/8" h. (firing dent in side) 1,075.00

Jar, ovoid, stenciled cobalt blue label "Hamilton & Jones, Greensboro, Pa." & "2," brushed cobalt blue foliate scrolls on grey, 2 gal., 10 3/8" h. (interior lime deposits) 350.00

Jar, ovoid, dark brown glaze shading to black w/green highlights on back, impressed in bold block letters "T. Cartmill," 10½" h...... 130.00

Jar, cov., slightly ovoid, quilled cobalt blue design of abstract three-sprig florals on grey, impressed "Cortland 2," impressed mark highlighted in blue, 2 gal., 10¾" h. (edge chips, rim hairline, minor lid damage) 150.00

Jar, semi-ovoid, stenciled cobalt blue label "Hamilton & Jones, Greensboro, Green Co, Pa." & "2," brushed cobalt blue vining foliage & stripes on grey, 1880-1915, 2 gal., 11¾" h. 225.00

Jar, cov., slightly ovoid, brushed cobalt blue floral spray & "2" on grey, 2 gal., 12½" h............. 325.00

Jar, semi-ovoid, earred handles, slip-quilled cobalt blue bird w/long beak & tail on grey, impressed "A.B. Wheeler & Co., 69 Broad Street, Boston, Mass." & "3," 3 gal., 12¾" h. (chips & hairlines) 260.00

Jar, slightly ovoid, earred handles, tooled lines & brushed cobalt blue florals & "3" on grey, impressed "S. R. Dilliner, New Geneva, Pa." w/eagle, ca. 1854, 3 gal., 13 5/8" h. (cracks in base & side) 975.00

Jar, ovoid, earred handles, impressed w/reeding in imitation of cast iron, brushed cobalt blue tulips on grey, 13¾" h. (hairlines & chips) 725.00

Jar, ovoid, applied ribbed handles, tooled shoulder band, stenciled cobalt blue "Stephen H. Ward, West Brownsville, Pa." & stars on grey, 15¼" h. (crow's foot in side) 450.00

Jar, ovoid, strap handles, brushed cobalt blue flowers each side on grey, splashes of blue at handles, impressed "H. Glazier, Hun--ngd-n, Pa.," 15½" h. 350.00

Jar, ovoid, earred handles, brushed cobalt blue florals & "Tom Suttle" (Perryopolis, Pennsylvania) on grey, impressed "5," 5 gal., 15 5/8" h. 300.00

Jar, slightly ovoid, earred handles, stenciled cobalt blue "Samuel Cooper, Manufacturers Agent No. 7 Diamond, Pittsburgh Eagle Pottery Co." w/brushed eagle & wavy lines on grey, 16¼" h......2,250.00

Jar, straight sides, earred handles w/impressed designs in imitation of cast iron, brushed cobalt blue stylized scene of woman in long dress, trees & other motifs on grey, possibly Morgantown, West Virginia, 17¼" h. (stains, hairlines & small chips) 1,900.00

Jar, ovoid, earred handles, stenciled cobalt blue "Hamilton & Jones, Greensboro, Pa." & "10 gallon" w/brushed lines & foliate scrolls on grey, 20¾" h. 475.00

Jug, miniature, ovoid w/elongated neck & applied strap handle, Albany slip glaze w/resist stenciled advertising label, "Chas. Hogg, 19 Water St.," 3¾" h. 125.00

Jug, semi-ovoid, brushed cobalt blue long-tailed bird looking over shoulder on slender perch on grey, impressed "Whites Utica," 11¾" h. 275.00

Jug, brushed cobalt blue leaves & florals on grey, impressed "New York Stoneware Co., Fort Edward, N.Y.," 1861-91, 1 gal............. 165.00

Jug, brushed cobalt blue butterfly & swirls on grey, impressed "J. & E. Norton, Bennington, Vt.," 1850-61, 1 gal. 215.00

Jug, ovoid, brushed cobalt blue florals on grey, impressed label "Copal Varnish No. 1 from Lucins H. Pratt, general dealer in groceries, paints, oils, etc. No. 163 opposite the Commercial Bank, Main Street, Buffalo, N.Y." & "3," 3 gal., 14½" h. 400.00

Jug, straight sides, slip-quilled cobalt blue backwards looking bird on branch on grey, impressed "F.B. Norton & Co., Worcester,

Mass." & "3," 1865-85, 15¼" h., 3 gal. 700.00

Jug, ovoid, strap handle, brushed cobalt blue floral design, impressed "Cowden & Wilcox, Harrisburg" & "3," 1870-81, 15¾" h., 3 gal. 400.00

Jug, semi-ovoid, slip-quilled stylized floral sprig, impressed label "E. & L.P. Norton, Bennington, Vt., 4," 1861-81, 4 gal., 16" h. (stains, minor firing crack at base) 425.00

Milk bowl, oval, rim spout & applied handles, brushed cobalt blue foliage decoration on grey, 11½" d., 4¼" h. 550.00

Milk bowl, deep sloped sides, applied ear handles, brushed cobalt blue floral decorations around sides, impressed "1" in a circle, 12½" d., 4" h. (shallow rim flakes, hairlines) 650.00

Model of a dog, seated Spaniel, grey salt-glaze w/blue face & ears, 7¾" h. (minor chips & in-the-making hairlines) 1,800.00

Mug, strap handle, brushed blue bands around top & base & initials "G.N.F." on grey, Albany slip interior, 3¾" h. 45.00

Mug, brushed cobalt blue cog design & stripes on grey, 5" h. 30.00

Pitcher, 7 3/8" h., keg-shaped, medallions w/bust portrait of "B. Franklin" one side & other w/scene of two drummers & fife player, each highlighted in cobalt blue on bark-finish ground 150.00

Decorated Stoneware Pitcher

Pitcher, 8¼" h., ovoid, stand-up neck w/applied band picked out in cobalt blue, front w/slip-quilled cobalt blue smiling sunface w/leaves & scrolls on grey, applied strap handle w/cobalt blue stripes, salt glazed finish, America, ca. 1855 (ILLUS.) .2,200.00

Pitcher, 8 5/8" h., cylindrical sides tapering slightly to top, shaped & molded strap handle, blue wash on grey stoneware body w/embossed tavern scenes, marked "Flemish Jugs made for Kinney & Levan, Cleveland, U.S.A." (short rim hairline, spout chip, base crow's foot & small flake) 150.00

Pitcher, 13¼" h., slightly bulbous base, straight collared neck, applied strap handle, brushed cobalt blue bird on a branch on grey, impressed "Chelsea 2" (Loammi Kendall, Chelsea, Massachusetts, 1836-70) 500.00

Preserving jar, stenciled cobalt blue "Greensboro" w/fruit & foliage on grey, 8" h. 250.00

Preserving jar, stenciled cobalt blue shield & brushed wavy & straight lines on grey, 8¼" h. 275.00

Preserving jar, stenciled cobalt blue triangular label w/rose & stenciled lettering, "Conrad, New Geneva, Fayette Co., Pa.," 8¼" h. 230.00

Preserving jar, stenciled cobalt blue "Jas. Benjamin, Wholesale Stoneware Depot, No. 14 Water St., Cincinnati, O." on grey, 1868-95, 8 3/8" h. (minor rim chips) 105.00

Preserving jar, brushed cobalt blue scene of three long-skirted figures w/arms linked on grey, tooled lines, 9½" h. (lip chips) 1,300.00

Tumbler, footed, incised inscription "W. Bane, 1857" highlighted in cobalt blue on grey, Albany slip interior, 4 1/8" h. (rim flakes) 800.00

Stoneware Water Cooler

Water cooler, ovoid, short strap handles at each side of top, bung hole near base, brushed cobalt blue decoration w/random flowers, flourishes & "5," band of blue down-pointing triangles around top rim above "Ice Water" in block letters, 16½" h., 5 gal. (minor rim chips) 2,200.00

Water cooler, jug-type, strap handles, stenciled cobalt blue label "C. Fenton, Pure Cold Water" w/eagle & "E Pluribus Unum" on grey, w/wooden spigot, 18¾" h. 875.00

Water cooler, barrel-shaped, brushed & molded cobalt blue bands & leaves on grey w/painted date "1851," 27" h., minor hairline cracks (ILLUS.) 1,540.00

Water cooler, straight sides, side handles, brushed cobalt blue "24" w/swirl motifs either side over tulip w/foliage & stenciled spread-winged American eagle w/banner, ca. 1850, 24 gal., 32" h. (chip on one handle) 880.00

TECO POTTERY

Teco Pottery Bud Vase

Teco Pottery was actually the line of art pottery introduced by the American Terra Cotta and Ceramic Company of Terra Cotta (Crystal Lake), Illinois in 1902. Founded by William D. Gates in 1881, American Terra Cotta originally produced only bricks and drain tile. Because of superior facilities for experimentation, including a chemical laboratory, the company was able to develop an art pottery line, favoring a matte green glaze in the earlier years but eventually achieving a wide range of colors including a metallic lustre glaze and a crystalline glaze. Though some hand-thrown pottery was made, Gates favored a molded ware because it was less expensive to produce. By 1923, Teco Pottery was no longer being made and in 1930 American Terra Cotta and Ceramic Company was sold.

Aladdin lamp, footed, loop handle & spout, textured purple & orange aventurine semi-gloss glaze, signed, 3 x 5¼" $82.50

Book block, figural woman w/jug beside pool of water, two-color glaze 550.00

Bulb bowl, green glaze, 9" d., 2" h. 175.00

Pitcher, 9" h., cylinder tapering toward base, shaped rim extending to curving handle, early 20th c. . . . 150.00

Vase, bud, 4½" h., 5½" w., squat onion-shaped body flaring toward base & w/short, narrow flared neck, yellow glaze, marked, small stress crack at base (ILLUS.) 375.00

Vase, 6¾ x 5½", double gourd form, four buttressed handles, porous green & gun-metal matte glaze, signed 770.00

Vase, 10¼" h., 5¼" d., bulbous w/rolled rim, six ruffled feet, flowing feathered green matte glaze, signed 1,072.50

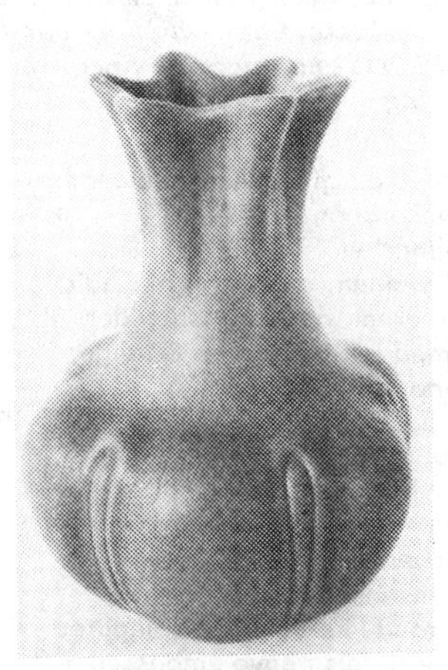

Teco Pottery Fluted Vase

Vase, 10½" h., bulbous base divided into lobes below elongated neck w/rim pinched into six points, marked, ca. 1905, base chips (ILLUS.) 1,200.00

Vase, 13½" h., 4¼" d., flaring cylinder, four oblong openings between each handle, smooth pea green matte glaze, signed 1,980.00

Wall pocket, Indian peace sign design, 6½ x 6½" . . . . .500.00 to 600.00

Wall pocket, spiked leaves design, medium green matte finish, signed & w/remnants of original paper label, 14½ x 7" 715.00

TEPLITZ

Teplitz Ewer

This ware was produced in numerous potteries in the vicinity of Teplitz in the Bohemian area of what is now Czechoslovakia during the late 19th and early 20th centuries. Vases and figures, of varying quality, were the primary productions and most were hand decorated. These items originally retailed in gift shops at prices from 25 cents to around $2. Now collectors are searching out these marked items and prices for finer examples are soaring.

Bowl, 5½" d., girl pulling rooster's tail decoration, marked "Stellmacher - Teplitz" $70.00

Bust of woman, plumes in her hair, apple green ruffles at shoulders, trimmed in pink, green & beige, Amphora mark, "R St K," 7¾" h. 395.00

Ewer, burnished gold trim upper & lower body, lavender & pink florals w/gold outlining, gold branches & leaves, 5" d., 7¼" h. 110.00

Ewer, frond-like handle, variegated purple florals above embossed pebbling around base, ornate gold trim, cream ground, marked "RS & K - Teplitz," 9" h. (ILLUS.) 90.00

Ewer, ornate handle, floriform top, ornate purple flowers on creamy ivory ground, Amphora mark "R St K," 9" h. 225.00

Ewer, pierced work on both sides, creamy yellow florals & green leaves w/gold trim on pale lavender satin ground w/tan & dull Roman gold trim, marked "Turn Vienna," 3 5/8" w., 11 3/8" h. 175.00

Ewers, ornate beige satin handle, ornate orange poppies w/heavy gold outlining & trim on gold burnished green satin ground, marked "Turn-Teplitz" (Wahliss mark), 4½" d., 17¼" h., pr. 475.00

Model of bear, black glaze, marked "Austria," 9" l. 35.00

Vase, 4¾" h., Sunbonnet baby decoration on green ground 135.00

Vase, 6½" h., two-handled, relief-molded colorful flowers on green & pink ground, gold trim, marked "Amphora-Teplitz" 110.00

Vases, 7½" h., four-handled, poppy design, blue glaze, pr. 150.00

Vase, 13½" h., two-handled, orchids w/relief-molded gold outlines, marked "Alexander" 155.00

Vase, 15" h., 7" d., bulbous base, tall slender neck w/two loop handles, cobalt & light blue flowers outlined in gold on cream ground, gold trimmed handles 265.00

Vase, 15¾" h., bulbous base w/loop handles arching to center of waisted neck w/reticulated top opening, applied cupid at center of neck, colored florals on green & lavender ground, ivory handles 375.00

TERRA COTTA

"The Sunflower" by J. S. Hartley

This is redware or reddish stoneware, usually unglazed. All kinds of utilitarian objects have been made for centuries as have statuettes and large architectural pieces.

Bust of a woman w/sunflower hat & wearing sunflower leaves as the embodiment of the "aesthetic" spirit, incised "'The Sunflower' J.S. Hartley, Sc. New York Copyrighted Oct., 1878," 24" h. (ILLUS.) ....$3,000.00 to 3,500.00

Bust of a young girl w/long hair, frilled neckline, original Borghese label on base, 18th c. 200.00

Figure of a girl playing mandolin, ca. 1870, 15" h. 275.00

Figures of archers, classical man & woman, each w/a bow held to one side, raised on square plinth, Continental, artist-signed, 5' 11" h., pr. 4,675.00

Jar, cov., straight sides, disc base, band of enameled geometric shapes at shoulder & on domed cover 60.00

Models of lions in recumbent position, w/wavy mane & open mouth, on rectangular plinth, 31" l., 19" h., pr. 1,540.00

Models of a sphinx in recumbent position, draped figure raised on rectangular base, 27" l., 25½" h., pr. 3,025.00

Syrup pitcher, cov., center band enameled w/geometric shapes, England 65.00

TILES

Decorative Victorian Tile

Tiles have been made by potteries in the United States and abroad for many years. Apart from small tea tiles used on tables, there are also decorative tiles for fireplaces, floors and walls and this is where present collector interest lies, especially in the late 19th century American-made art pottery tiles.

American Encaustic Tiling Co., Zanesville, Ohio, relief-molded young girl in flowing gown playing horn, 6 x 18" $275.00

American Encaustic Tiling Co., Zanesville, Ohio, relief-molded geometric shape w/yellow-green glaze 350.00

Grueby Faience & Tile Company, Boston, Massachusetts, white & brown Viking ship on blue-green ground, ca. 1905, 4 x 4" 137.50

Grueby Faience & Tile Company, Boston, Massachusetts, white polar bear on mottled light blue matte ground, artist-signed, 5½ x 7" 522.50

Grueby Faience & Tile Company, Boston, Massachusetts, bird decoration, Mission-style frame, 6 x 6" 300.00

Grueby Faience & Tile Company, Boston, Massachusetts, floral decoration, Mission-style frame, 6 x 6" 250.00

Grueby Faience & Tile Company, Boston, Massachusetts, mauve tulip w/green leaves on lighter green ground, 6 x 6" 357.50

Grueby Faience & Tile Company, Boston, Massachusetts, white overlapping horses on blue & green ground, early 20th c., 6 x 6" 412.50

Grueby Faience & Tile Company, Boston, Massachusetts, Saint George slaying a dragon, knight in blue armor on white horse, light green dragon, against dark green trees & dark blue sky, all outlined in black, remnants of original paper label, 9 x 9" 1,430.00

International Tile Company, Brooklyn, New York, leafy scroll embossed design, olive green glaze, marked "I.T.Co.," ca. 1880's, 4¼" (ILLUS.) 2.00

Low (J. & J.G.) Art Tile Works, Chelsea, Massachusetts, vertical form w/shepherd leaning on his staff w/his dog standing by, glossy yellow-green glaze, late 19th c., 15 x 7¾" 1,045.00

Marblehead Pottery, Marblehead, Massachusetts, painted seascape w/clouds & ship on horizon, early 20th c., framed, 4½" d.......... 150.00

Marblehead Pottery, Marblehead, Massachusetts, stylized bouquet of flowers in a basket in blue, green & yellow glazes on dark brown ground, framed, 1910, 6" d. 125.00

Moravian Pottery and Tile Works, Doylestown, Pennsylvania, decoration of the clipper ship "Aves," blue & natural, 4" 60.00

Mosaic Tile Co., Zanesville, Ohio, Longfellow's home, 6 x 6" 22.50
Rookwood Pottery Co., Cincinnati, Ohio, Arts & Crafts style, tall brown trees w/dark green leaves, blue lake & dark blue mountains under a sky blue sky, 1910, 12 x 12" 632.50

Teco Pottery Tiles

Teco Pottery, Terra Cotta, Illinois, tiles depicting raised figures emerging from within square frames, 9", pr. (ILLUS.) 1,870.00
Trent Art Tile Co., Trenton, New Jersey, Middle Eastern woman's head, green glaze, 6 x 6" 85.00
Trent Art Tile Co., Trenton, New Jersey, portrait decoration, glossy mustard brown glaze, molded mahogany frame, late 19th c., 9¾ x 7¾" 275.00
Van Briggle Pottery Co., Colorado Springs, Colorado, three cream colored walking geese on green & blue ground, 6 x 6" 385.00

TOBY MUGS & JUGS

Early Staffordshire Toby

The Toby is a figural jug or mug usually delineating a robust, genial drinking man. The name has been used in England since the mid-18th century. Copies of the English mugs and jugs were made in America.

Goebel "Pickwick" Toby, blue full bee mark, 6" h. $60.00
Lenox "William Penn Treaty" Toby, pink w/white Indian head handle 165.00
Royal Doulton "Drake" Toby, large, 1940-60 .... 138.00
Royal Doulton "Huntsman" Toby, Kingsware, designed by Harry Fenton, ca. 1910, 7¼" h. 350.00
Royal Doulton "Old Charlie" Toby, small, 1939-60 .... 135.00
Royal Doulton "Old King Cole" Toby, "A" mark, small, 1939-60 .... 225.00
Royal Doulton "Paddy" Toby, tiny, 1940-60 .... 60.00
Shorter & Sons "Flower Seller" Toby, 1950's 30.00
Staffordshire Toby, seated man holding a frothing jug of ale, in black hat, blue jacket, brown breeches, on green base, chip to hat, handle spring, ca. 1800, 9¾" h. (ILLUS.) 418.00
Staffordshire Toby, seated man wearing a blue glazed coat w/mustard buttons over a white waistcoat w/blue dots & buttons, black-edged mustard breeches, a black tricorn (rim chips, restorations, crown broken), & black shoes w/mustard trim, his white hair lined w/grey & black, holding a blue & black decorated jug, seated on a green enameled chair (repainted) w/white loop handle w/blue leaf decoration applied at the back, Staffordshire, England, 19th c., 9¾" h. 247.50
Wood (Ralph) "Rodney's Sailor" Toby, black hat, green coat & white trousers w/blue stripes, impressed "65" in base, 1765-75, 11¾" h. (lid missing) 5,700.00

VAN BRIGGLE

The Van Briggle Pottery was established by Artus Van Briggle, who formerly worked for Rookwood Pottery, in Colorado Springs, Colorado, at the turn of the century. He died in 1904 but the pottery was carried on by his widow and others. From 1900 until 1920, the pottery was dated. It remains in production today, specializing in Art Pottery. Design numbers are from "A Collector's Guide to

Van Briggle Pottery" by Nelson, Crouch, Demmin & Newton.

Van Briggle Bud Vase

Book ends, model of puppy dog, rust & green glaze, pr. $80.00
Book ends, model of squirrel, Persian Rose (maroon to blue-green) glaze, pr. 85.00
Bowl, Pine Cone patt., 75th Anniversary Edition, dated 1974 .... 150.00
Bowl-vase, leaves in relief encircling body, deep blue shaded to maroon glaze, 1920's 45.00
Candleholder, Turquoise Ming (shaded turquoise blue matte) glaze, 3" h. (single) 25.00
Candlestick, mulberry glaze, 8¾" h. (single) 40.00
Chamberstick, dark blue glaze, 7" h. 100.00
Cigarette box, cov., acorn finial on lid, blue glaze, 1930's 40.00
Console bowl w/seashell flower frog insert, Siren of the Sea, Turquoise Ming glaze, 2 pcs. 325.00
Creamer, melon-shaped, midnight black glaze 35.00
Flower bowl, maroon & dark blue matte glaze, ca. 1945, 5" d. 35.00
Flower frog, three-frog decor, Turquoise Ming glaze 20.00
Flower frog, honey brown & green glaze, 1915 .... 85.00
Lamp, three relief-molded Indian heads around top, Turquoise Ming glaze, original shade w/butterflies & dried flowers encased in celluloid (split on side of shade), signed "AA Colorado Springs," ca. 1915, 11" h. 300.00
Lamp, model of a butterfly, Turquoise Ming glaze, w/original shade 125.00
Lamp base, model of an owl, Persian Rose glaze, 6" h. 140.00
Model of a cat, brown glaze, marked "Anna Van Briggle," 1955-68, 15" 65.00
Model of a conch shell, Persian Rose (maroon to blue-green) glaze, 10" 32.00
Model of a conch shell, Turquoise Ming (shaded turquoise blue matte) glaze, 17" 85.00
Model of a donkey, Turquoise Ming glaze, 4½ x 4½" 35.00
Model of an elephant, jade green glaze, 7" l., 4½" h. 45.00
Model of owl on stump, Persian Rose glaze, 9½" 85.00
Pitcher (or ewer-vase), 9" h., Turquoise Ming glaze 40.00
Plaques, pierced to hang, relief bust of Indian maiden "Little Star" & "Big Buffalo," Persian Rose glaze, pr. .... 80.00 to 110.00
Vase, triple bud, 5" h., Turquoise Ming glaze, signed (ILLUS.) 55.00
Vase, 2 1/8" h., fleur de lis & leaves in low relief, green glaze, signed, 1908-11 .... 40.00
Vase, 2¼ x 3¾", relief-molded mushrooms, Persian Rose glaze .. 26.00

Van Briggle Vase

Vase, 5" h., spherical, relief-molded stylized flowers w/long vertical stems, dark pastel green glaze, signed, 1905 (ILLUS.) 660.00
Vase, 5¾" h., 3¼" d., flaring cylinder w/closed & flared rim, embossed tulips & leaves, textured light green matte finish, dated 1904 .... 2,530.00
Vase, 6¾" h., 3" d., embossed stylized leaves & trefoils, grey-blue & green matte crystalline glaze, 1903 .... 440.00
Vase, 8" h., 3¼" d., cylindrical form tapering to wide collared rim, stylized floral design w/blossoms flaring out at shoulder & encir-

cling body, incised mark & "1912" 275.00
Vase, 8½" h., 3½" d., tall cylindrical body w/bulbous top, blue matte glaze, incised "Van Briggle - X" & "1905" 247.50
Vase, 10" h., 4½" d., "Lorelei," Mountain Craig brown (honey brown & green) glaze, incised "Van Briggle - Colo. Spgs.," late 1920's-early 1930's, No. 17 .... 220.00
Vase, 12" h., swollen cylindrical form tapering towards base, molded petaled flowers on long stem, matte pale blue w/dark blue highlights, early 20th c., signed 150.00
Vase, 13¼" h., elongated form w/iris swelling towards base, two loop handles, darker blue on pale blue, early 20th c., signed 175.00

WARWICK

Warwick Ale Set

Numerous collectors have turned their attention to the productions of the Warwick China Manufacturing Company that operated in Wheeling, West Virginia, from 1887 until 1951. Prime interest would seem to lie in items produced before 1914 that were decorated with decal portraits of beautiful women, monks and Indians. Fraternal Order items, as well as floral and fruit decorated items, are also popular with collectors.

Ale set: tankard pitcher & 7 mugs; elk & clock emblem & "B.P.O.E." (Benevolent & Protective Order of Elks) on shaded brown ground, 8 pcs. (ILLUS. of part) $275.00
Humidor, cov., portrait of beautiful woman on brown ground, IOGA mark 190.00
Mug, portrait of monk .... 40.00 to 50.00
Pitcher, tankard, 13" h., portrait of monk w/mug of ale 245.00
Plate, 9½" d., portrait of monk reading 49.00
Vase, 8" h., two-handled, four ball feet, rectangular, pastel florals on pink shaded to green ground 90.00
Vase, 8" h., footed, portrait of beautiful woman wearing large hat w/peacock feather & holding a rose to her lips on shaded brown to cream ground, IOGA mark 95.00
Vase, 10" h., orange amaryllis blossoms on brown ground, IOGA mark 70.00
Vase, 10" h., red asters on brown ground, IOGA mark 60.00
Vase, 10½" h., twig handles, portrait of gypsy girl on red ground 150.00
Vase, 11" h., two-handled, scalloped rim, portrait of monk on brown ground, IOGA mark .... 160.00 to 195.00
Vase, 11" h., upright loop handles at shoulder, portrait of beautiful blonde woman, artist-signed 300.00
Vase, 11½" h., ring handles, storks on shaded grey ground 195.00
Vase, 11½" h., ring handles, portrait of beautiful woman on reddish brown ground, IOGA mark 250.00
Vase, 11 5/8" h., twig handles, portrait of young lady on brown ground 95.00
Vase, 11¾" h., twig handles, red poinsettias on red ground 98.00

WATT POTTERY

Founded in 1922, in Crooksville, Ohio, this pottery continued in operation until the factory was destroyed by fire in 1965. Although stoneware crocks and jugs were the first wares produced, by 1935 sturdy kitchen items in yellowware were the mainstay of production. Attractive lines like Kitch-N-Queen (banded) wares and the hand-painted Red Apple, Cherries and Pennsylvania Dutch (tulip) patterns were popular throughout the country. Today these hand-painted utilitarian wares are "hot" with collectors.

Bean pot, Pennsylvania Dutch (tulip) patt. $78.00
Bean pot, Red Apple patt. 61.00
Bean pot, Red Leaves patt. 45.00
Bowl, berry, 5½" d., Quilted Morning Glory patt. 35.00
Bowl, 6" d., Red Apple patt. 22.00

Bowl, 7½" d., 6" h., Red Apple patt. 45.00
Bowl, 12" d., Red Apple patt. 38.00
Bowl, onion soup, handled, Red Apple patt. 90.00
Bowl, cereal, Tulip patt., No. 4 .... 20.00
Bowl, cereal, Red Apple patt., No. 4 .... 15.00
Bowl, cereal, Star Flower patt., No. 4 .... 12.50
Bowl, Red Apple patt., w/advertising, No. 6 .... 18.00
Bowl, Red Apple patt., No. 7 .... 32.00
Bowl, Red Leaves patt., No. 7 .... 15.00
Bowl, Kitch-N-Queen, pink & blue bands on yellow ground, No. 8 .... 25.00
Bowl, Star Flower patt., No. 8 .... 28.00
Bowl, Kitch-N-Queen, No. 9 .... 38.00
Bowl, Star Flower patt., No. 18 .... 10.00
Bowl, Tulip patt., No. 62 .... 40.00
Bowl, Red Apple patt., No. 63 .... 32.00
Bowl, Rooster patt., No. 64 .... 48.00
Bowl, Autumn Foliage patt., No. 65 .... 45.00
Bowl, Star Flower patt., No. 67 .... 10.00
Bowl, salad, Red Apple patt., No. 73 .... 30.00
Bowl, Autumn Foliage patt., No. 75 .... 25.00
Bowl, Red Apple patt., No. 96 .... 32.50
Bowl, cov., Tulip patt., No. 110 .... 50.00
Bowl, Autumn Foliage patt., No. 600 .... 20.00
Bowls, Autumn Foliage patt., nest-type, set of 3 .... 52.00
Canister, cov., Star Flower patt., No. 82 .... 100.00
Canister, cov., Tulip patt., 8½ x 10½" 165.00
Casserole, cov., Star Flower patt., No. 18 .... 35.00
Casserole, cov., Red Apple patt., No. 96 .... 58.00
Chip & dip set, Red Apple patt. 55.00
Cookie jar, Tulip patt., large, No. 503 .... 125.00
Creamer, Cherries patt., No. 62 .... 28.00
Creamer, Pennsylvania Dutch (tulip) patt., No. 62 .... 30.00
Creamer, Red Apple patt., No. 62 .... 38.00
Cup, Quilted Morning Glory patt. 55.00
Cup & saucer, Star Flower patt., large 60.00
French casserole, open, Rooster patt. 50.00
Ice bucket w/lid, Red Apple patt. 75.00
Mug, Red Apple patt. 88.00
Mug, Star Flower patt., No. 501 .... 48.00
Pepper shaker, Red Apple patt. (single) 45.00
Pepper shaker, Red Apple patt., w/advertising (single) 75.00
Pitcher, Red Apple patt., No. 15 .... 35.00
Pitcher, Red Leaves patt., No. 15 .... 30.00
Pitcher, Tulip patt., No. 16 .... 48.00
Pitcher w/ice lip, Red Apple patt., No. 17 .... 75.00
Pitcher, Autumn Foliage patt., large, No. 115 .... 49.00
Plate, salad, 7½" d., Quilted Morning Glory patt. 45.00
Platter, 15¼" d., Red Apple patt. 95.00
Popcorn bowls, Mexican interior, No. 603, set of 6 .... 210.00
Salt & pepper shakers, Red Apple patt., pr. 105.00
Salt & pepper shakers, Star Flower patt., pr. 50.00
Spaghetti bowl, Red Apple patt., No. 39 .... 49.00
Spooner, Quilted Morning Glory patt. 85.00
Sugar bowl, open, 2-handled, Red Apple patt. 24.00
Sugar bowl, open, 2-handled, Rooster patt. 55.00

WEDGWOOD

Reference here is to the famous pottery established by Josiah Wedgwood in 1759 in England. Numerous types of wares have been produced through the years to the present.

BASALT

Basalt Teapot

Bust of Sir Francis Bacon, bearded poet in fur-lined cloak & ruff, on a circular spreading socle, late 19th-early 20th c., 16" h. $880.00
Bust of Mercury, marked Wedgwood only, 10¼" d., 17" h. 1,100.00
Bust of Prior, marked Wedgwood only, 8" d., 11½" h. 762.00

Creamer & sugar bowl, Union Emblem patt., 1850, pr. 155.00

Cup & saucer, demitasse, rows of ribs w/fine beading near edge, marked Wedgwood only 95.00

Figures, King Charles I & Oliver Cromwell, both in plumed hats, jackets & breeches, w/swords at their sides, on circular named bases, ca. 1880, 6½" h., pr. 1,320.00

Jardiniere, lions heads w/draping grapes & leaves & classical figures, marked Wedgwood only, 4" d., 3¾" h. 85.00

Model of an egret, yellow glass eyes, perched on rockwork, ca. 1916, 7¾" h. 176.00

Plaque, Death of a Roman Warrior in high relief, mid-19th c., 10¼ x 19" rectangle, wood frame 2,420.00

Teapot & cover w/widow finial, trefoil over-handle, putti w/garlands of vine between bands of engine-turning, ca. 1800 (finial reglued), 10½" h. (ILLUS.) 935.00

Tea set: cov. teapot, creamer & cov. sugar bowl; globular, teapot & sugar bowl w/domed cover w/ball finial, 3rd quarter 19th c., 3 pcs... 412.50

CALENDAR TILES

1895, State House, Boston.......... 65.00

1897, Old Federal Street Theatre ... 65.00

1900, John Hancock House, Reed McDuffee & Stratten Co. 50.00

1908, Harvard Medical School 45.00

1914, Commonwealth Pier.......... 45.00

1920, Mayflower in Plymouth Harbor 1620 .... 75.00

1925, The Flying Cloud (ship) 75.00

CREAMWARE

Creamware Sauce Tureen

Basket & undertray, reticulated basket, undertray w/molded basket-weave design, 19th c., 7 x 8¾" basket, 8½ x 10¼" undertray, 2 pcs. 192.50

Dish, lobed, children in a wooded landscape within an ochre rim, signed "Emile Lessore," ca. 1865, 11½" oval 660.00

Jelly mold, in the form of corn-on-the-cob, 19th c., 7" l. 132.00

Sauce tureen, cover w/flowerhead finial, ladle & stand, loop handles, molded slightly scalloped feather-edge motif trimmed in brown, ca. 1800, one handle repaired, 7½" w. stand, 4 pcs. (ILLUS.) 935.00

Teapot, cov., globular shape, painted in iron-red, puce, green, yellow & black w/panels of stylized geometric devices reserved on a scale ground alternating w/wavy-edged panels enclosed by vertical bands, foliate-molded spout & handle, cover w/similarly painted panels, painted possibly in the workshop of David Rhodes, ca. 1770, 5½" h. (repairs to spout & handle, cover restored) 1,540.00

Teapot, cov., painted Bamboo patt., ca. 1860 .... 95.00

JASPER WARE

Jasper Ware Pitcher

Bowl, 7" d., 3 3/8" h., white relief classical ladies in circle dancing on black, white relief leaf decor around top & bottom, marked "Wedgwood" only 225.00

Box, cov., white relief classical figures & chariot w/white relief roses around edges on cobalt blue, marked "Wedgwood" only, 2 3/8 x 3½", 1½" h. 80.00

Candlesticks, white relief classical figures around sides & white relief acorns & leaves around base on black, marked "Wedgwood" only, 4" d., 6" h., pr. 232.00

Cracker jar, cov., white relief classical ladies in panels on sage green, silver plate rim, handle & top w/ivory finial, 4 7/8" d., 6" h. 175.00

Cracker jar, cov., white relief classical figures on black center band, gold top & bottom bands, silver plate cover, rim & handle, marked "Wedgwood" only, 5" d., 6¾" h. 695.00

Creamer & cov. sugar bowl, white relief classical figures on sage green, marked "Wedgwood, England," pr. 125.00

Medallion, white relief standing cupid grasping a bird in one upraised hand, a nest in the other on blue, within neoclassical style gilt metal frame w/ribbon-tied cresting, 19th c., 3¾" w., 5½" h. 192.50

Mug, three-handled, white relief cameo medallions of Washington, Franklin & Lafayette on olive green, marked "Wedgwood England," 4½ x 4" 450.00

Mustard jar w/silver plate lid w/spoon opening, black relief grape swags & lion's heads w/two white bands around base on yellow, marked "Wedgwood" only, 3½" h. 250.00

Pitcher, 5 3/8" h., 3 3/8" d., cylindrical, white relief classical ladies around sides, white grapes & leaves top border on cobalt blue, marked "Wedgwood England" 100.00

Pitcher, 6" h., cylindrical, rope handle, white relief classical figures w/grape frieze border on green, marked "Wedgwood, England" (ILLUS.) 107.00

Pitcher, 6" h., 4 1/8" d., white relief classical ladies around sides on lavender, marked "Wedgwood" only 200.00

Plaque, white relief cherubs playing Blindman's Buff on light blue, marked "Wedgwood" only, in original black & gold frame, overall 13 3/8 x 7½" 450.00

Portland vase replica, white relief Paris wearing the Phrygian cap on brilliant blue dip, ca. 1875, 10¼" h. (ILLUS.) 1,045.00

Preserve jar w/cover & matching underplate, white relief figures of Muses (4) in cartouches on dark blue, marked "Wedgwood England," 3 pcs. 195.00

Teapot, cov., cylindrical, white relief playful children & dogs on green dip, spout w/classical figure within foliage surrounds, shoulder w/band of S-scrolls, lower part w/band of flowerheads & foliage, cover w/disc finial enriched w/foliage, ca. 1785, 6½" w. 1,210.00

Wedgwood Portland Vase

Vase, 3¾" h., 2 1/8" d., cylindrical, white relief classical figures in panels on cobalt blue around top, relief-molded deep blue stylized leaves around base, gold ground w/fine white bands, marked "Wedgwood" only 442.00

Vase, cov., 8" h., cylindrical w/domed cover, white relief classical figures & urns divided by palm trees beneath a band of scrolling flowers on pale blue, engine-turned cover w/white relief Diana seated on a cloud finial (damaged), ca. 1800 . . . . 462.00

Water bottle w/stopper, white relief Muses on black dip, ca. 1870, 11" h. 565.00

MISCELLANEOUS

Fairyland Lustre Footed Bowl

Bowl, 2¼ x 1½", Dragon Lustre, purple, mother-of-pearl lustre & gold, Model FZ4829 . . . . 150.00

Bowl, 4 7/8" d., 3½" h., footed, Fairyland Lustre, interior w/greenish lustre w/two elves on branch in bottom & leaves & elf on bird, bat, etc., around top outlined in gold, midnight blue exterior w/green grass, leapfrogging elves & fairies & gold stars in sky (ILLUS.) 780.00

Bowl, 5 1/8" w., 2 7/8" h., octagonal, Dragon Lustre, green & maroon dragons outlined in gold, dragons w/gold trim on pearl lustre interior 185.00

Bowl, 7" d., Dantry patt., lustre ground 200.00

Bowl, 7½" w., 3" h., octagonal, Hummingbird Lustre, decorated w/geese & hummingbirds on exterior & hummingbirds on the interior, orange & blue 750.00

Bowl, 7 5/8" w., octagonal, Fruit Lustre, copper-bronze exterior & mother-of-pearl interior printed in gold w/single & clustered fruits painted in tones of blue, lavender, russet, green & yellow beneath gilt rope & "Armagh" borders, gold-printed Portland vase "Wedgwood Made in England" mark, ca. 1930 .... 550.00

Bowl, 8" d., 5" h., footed, majolica, grey & red designs on yellow ground, garland of flowers trim, silver plated rim band 375.00

Bowl, 8½" w., 4" h., octagonal, Fairyland Lustre, interior "Smoke Ribbons" & exterior "Moorish," gold outlining, Portland vase mark 1,800.00

Bowl, 8 5/8" d., 4" h., Fairyland Lustre, interior mottled flame lustre w/medallions of colored pheasants w/gold trim, exterior midnight blue & white bands w/colored pheasants & florals, green band in lustre w/gold trim 1,650.00

Bust of Lord Zetland, parian, marked "No. 23, Registered, 11th Dec. 1868," 21" h. 950.00

Compote & stand: 10¼" l. "Nautilus" shell-form deep bowl & 11¼" l. bivalve-shaped stand; Moonlight Lustre, covered interior & exterior in splashed pink lustre w/tinges of orange, ochre & grey, each impressed "WEDGWOOD" & "W," ca. 1810, 2 pcs. (rim repair) 1,430.00

Dinner service: 18 dinner plates, 19 salad plates, 11 bouillon cups & 12 saucers, 18 teacups & saucers, a pair of circular covered tureens, a pair of bowls, a 15" oval platter, a 13¾" oval platter, a pair of sauceboats, a lozenge-shaped small dish; "Ruby Tonquin" patt., each piece painted w/sprays of pale yellow flowers w/gilt foliage reserved on deep ruby ground, the whole enriched by further gilt sprigs & a gilt border, marked, "Wedgwood, Bone China, Made in England," the set 3,300.00

Wedgwood Pearlware Figures

Figures, Pearlware, shepherd & shepherdess, wearing spotted & flowered clothes, he w/a dog & she w/a lamb on a tree stump, on square bases, ca. 1800, 7½" h., pr. (ILLUS.) 1,320.00

Inkstand & cover w/maroon lustre widow finial, Hummingbird Lustre, mottled blue lustre ground w/colorful Hummingbirds finely outlined in gold, gold geese around edges, lift out porcelain ink cup, flame lustre inside larger pot, square base, marked w/Portland vase mark, 6" d., 3 7/8" h. 595.00

Jardiniere, majolica, three feet molded w/foliage, body reserved w/panels molded w/flowering plants & enriched in colors, alternating w/panels enclosing trellis pattern enriched in yellow & white, rim similarly molded, dated 1888, 16¼" h. 880.00

Model of a polar bear, off-white matte glaze, marked "Wedgwood & Skeaping," 4¼ x 9", 6¾" h..... 325.00

Nut cup, Fairyland Lustre, "Nizami," colorful Persian gentleman center, dark green lustre w/gold trim, 3¾" d., 1 1/8" h. 325.00

Peach melba bowl, Fairyland Lustre, pedestal base, jumping faun interior, Garden of Paradise patt. exterior, Portland vase mark, 8" d., 5½" h. 1,850.00

Plate, 9¾" d., American Yachting series, "The Lillie Off Telegraph Hill," flow blue, 1916 .... 65.00

Plate, 10" d., Ivanhoe series, "Rebecca Repelling the Templar," blue transfer.................... 55.00

Plate, 10¾" d., Fairyland Lustre, multicolor center w/pixies on bridge, one in boat on water, outlined in gold, wide gold border w/lacy overlay of gold designs of flowers & fairies & pixies, Portland vase mark 1,750.00

Vase, 4 3/8" h., 2½" d., Hummingbird Lustre, mottled blue lustre ground w/colorful hummingbirds outlined in gold, mottled Flame Lustre interior 175.00

Vase, 8½" h., Fairyland Lustre, "Candlemas" 650.00

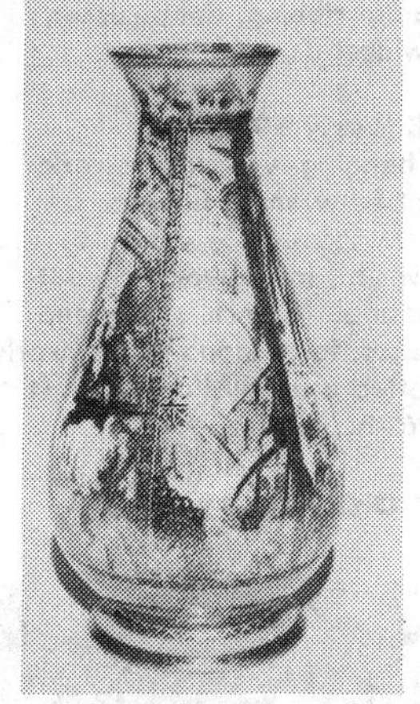

Fairyland Lustre Vase

Vase, 12" h., footed w/rounded, tapered body & flared rim, Fairyland Lustre, Persian-inspired landscape scenes up side between narrow gilt scroll bands (ILLUS.) 1,750.00

WELLER

This pottery was made from 1872 to 1945 at a pottery established originally by Samuel A. Weller at Fultonham, Ohio, and moved in 1882 to Zanesville. Numerous lines were produced and listings below are by the pattern or lines. Most desirable is the Sicardo line.

ARDSLEY (1920-28)

Candleholder, water lily form, green matte glaze, 3" h. (single) $30.00

Console bowl & "Kingfisher" flower frog, 16½" d., 3½" h. bowl molded w/cattails & grasses & 9½" h. flower frog, 2 pcs. 395.00

Umbrella stand, molded water lilies at base, cattails & grasses body, green matte glaze, 19" h. 275.00

Vase, 7" h., globular sides of sword-shaped green leaves forming irregular rim interspersed w/purple iris blossoms .... 60.00 to 75.00

AURELIAN (1898-1910)

Jardiniere & pedestal base, slip-painted florals, glossy brown glaze, overall 38" h. (repairs) 1,200.00

Pitcher, tankard, 12" h., slip-painted berries, glossy brown glaze, artist-signed 275.00

Vase, 12 x 10", 4-footed, pillow-shaped, slip-painted blackberries & vines, glossy brown glaze, artist-signed 345.00

BALDIN (1915-20)

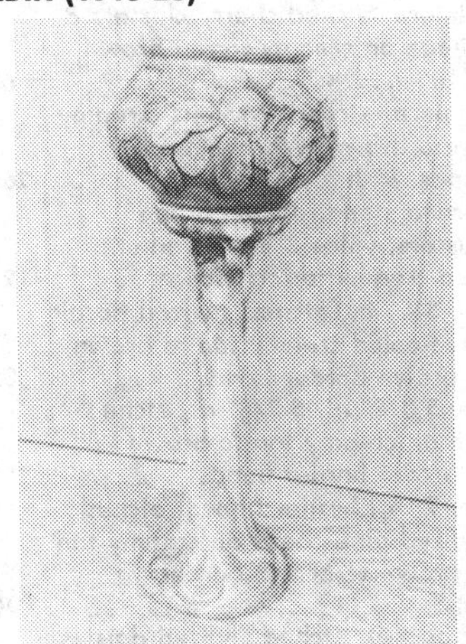

Baldin Jardiniere & Pedestal Base

Bowl, 8" d., 4" h., realistically painted apples & branches molded in low relief against earth tones 80.00

Jardiniere & pedestal base, realistically painted apples & branches molded in low relief against earth tones, overall 34" h. (ILLUS.) 550.00

Vase, 6" h., stick-type, realistically painted apples & branches molded in low relief against earth tones .. 25.00

Vase, 7" h., stick-type, realistically painted apples & branches molded in low relief against earth tones .. 40.00

Vase, 10" h., realistically painted apples & branches molded in low relief against earth tones 95.00

BLUE WARE (pre-1920)

Jardiniere, 3-footed, ivory relief of classical ladies against deep blue ground, 8½" d., 7½" h. 100.00

Vase, 8½" h., expanding cylinder, ivory relief of classical lady hold-

ing cluster of grapes against deep blue ground 85.00
Vase, 8½" h., tapering form, ivory relief of classical lady w/lyre against deep blue ground 130.00

BONITO (1927-33)

Basket, hanging-type, h.p. florals & foliage on cream ground 165.00
Bowl, 5" d., 4" h., pedestal base, h.p. pastel florals on cream ground, artist-signed 40.00
Vase, 7" h., scroll handles at mid-section, h.p. florals & foliage on cream ground................ 55.00
Vase, 9½" h., multicolored floral decor on cream ground, artist-signed 125.00

BURNTWOOD (1910)

Jardiniere, etched cherry clusters & foliage on creamy tan to brown, 4" h........................... 65.00
Jardiniere, etched chickens, creamy tan to brown w/brown border bands, 8" h..................... 265.00
Umbrella stand, etched grape clusters, vines & leaves on stippled creamy tan to brown........ 125.00
Vase, 3½" h., etched stylized florals on stippled creamy tan to brown w/brown border bands 32.00
Vase, 5 3/8" h., 5 7/8" d., etched fish on creamy tan to brown w/brown border bands 55.00
Vase, 9" h., bottle-shaped, etched stylized pine cones on creamy tan to brown w/brown border bands 40.00
Wall pocket, etched stylized daisies on creamy tan to brown w/brown rim, 8" h. 45.00

CAMEO (1935-39)

Basket, hanging-type, scalloped rim, white relief florals on matte powder blue, 5" h................. 40.00
Cornucopia-vase, white relief florals on matte coral, 7" h. 20.00
Ewer, white relief florals on matte powder blue, 10" h. 34.00
Vase, 6½" h., base handles, white relief florals on matte powder blue 18.00
Vase, 7½" h., 2-handled, white relief florals on matte powder blue 27.50
Vase, 13" h., 2-handled, bulbous, slender neck w/flaring mouth, white relief florals on matte soft green 50.00

CLARMONT (1920's)

Candlestick, circular base, vertically ribbed stem topped by band of relief florals & flattened ball-shaped sections w/bands of beading around centers, double looped handles, deep russet, 12" h., pr........................... 195.00
Console bowl w/attached candleholders, band of relief grape clusters & swirling vines between bands of beading, deep russet, 12" d. 150.00
Jar, cov., earred shoulder handles, band of relief grape clusters & swirling vines at mid-section between bands of beading & horizontal ribbing, deep russet, 5½" widest d., 8½" h. 135.00

CLASSIC (early 1930's)

Basket, hanging-type, latticework top dotted w/small flowers, beige 65.00
Vase, 8½" h., latticework top dotted w/small flowers, soft green .. 35.00
Wall pocket, fan-shaped, latticework top dotted w/small flowers, soft blue, 6" h...................... 40.00

COPPERTONE (late 1920's)

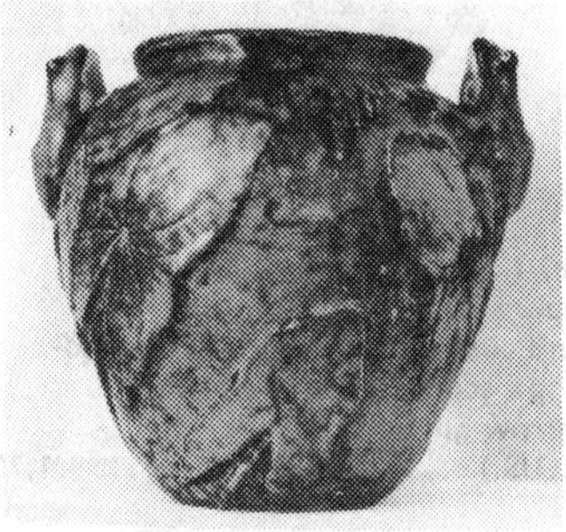

Coppertone Vase

Ashtray, model of a frog seated at one end, blotchy semi-gloss green over brown glaze, 6½" w. ....85.00 to 95.00
Console bowl, overlapping lily pads, w/figural frog flower holder, 12" d., 3" h., 2 pcs. 225.00
Jardiniere-vase, frog on side w/pond, plants & fish decor, 6½" across top, 7" h. 135.00
Model of a frog, 4" h. 85.00
Model of a frog, 4½" h. 130.00
Model of a frog w/hole for water tube, Garden Ware, 15 x 11½"... 450.00
Model of a turtle, 4¼ x 3¼", 1½" h. 75.00
Planter, model of a frog on lily pad holding a flower planter, 4" 95.00
Vase, 8" h., frog handles, lily pads on sides, blotchy semi-gloss green over brown glaze (ILLUS.) 165.00

DICKENSWARE 2ND LINE (1900-05)

Humidor, sgraffito bust portrait of an Indian w/full headdress, artist-signed (no cover) 650.00
Jug, sgraffito scene of men playing checkers, 4¾" h. 375.00
Mug, sgraffito portrait of an Indian, artist-signed, 6" h. 395.00
Mug, sgrafitto portrait of monk drinking 280.00
Pitcher, tankard, 14" h., sgraffito profile portrait of a monk, blending blue high glaze (minor rim flaw) 375.00
Vase, 5½" h., 2-handles at neck, sgraffito scene of 2 men fencing, tan shaded to grey ground 275.00
Vase, 8¾" h., sgraffito scene of golfers 400.00
Vase, 9" h., sgraffito stag's head ... 450.00

2nd Line Dickensware Vase

Vase, 12" h., sgraffito portrait of Indian "Hollow Horn Bear," artist-signed (ILLUS.) 1,300.00
Vase, 12" h., sgraffito scene of cowboys on horseback, cream & rust tones 480.00
Vase, 14" h., ovoid, sgraffito portrait of a monk, glossy blue glaze (flake repair on rim) 375.00

EOCEAN (1898-1918)

Jardiniere, slip-painted yellow wildflower decor on turquoise shading to cream ground, 9½" d., 6¾" h. 135.00
Vase, 6½" h., slip-painted pansy decor on shaded pale blue to grey ground (ILLUS.) 170.00
Vase, 7" h., slip-painted berries & leaves decor on green shaded to blue ground, artist-signed 160.00
Vase, 9" h., slip-painted dark green berries & leaves on grey shaded to cream ground 210.00

Eocean Vase

Vase, 11" h., slip-painted dogwood blossoms decor on grey shaded to white ground 225.00

ETNA (1906)

Etna Vase & Mug

Mug, relief-molded & painted realistic grape cluster on shaded light to dark grey, 6" h. (ILLUS. right) .. 150.00
Pitcher, tankard, 10½" h., relief-molded & painted realistic cherries on shaded light to dark grey 275.00
Vase, 4" h., 2-handled, relief-molded & painted realistic pink clover on shaded green (ILLUS. left) 85.00
Vase, 5" h., 2-handled, relief-molded & painted realistic blue florals on shaded grey 60.00
Vase, 6" h., relief-molded & painted realistic pink florals on shaded grey 105.00
Vase, 14¾" h., relief-molded & painted realistic grape cluster & vine on shaded dark to light grey 250.00

FLEMISH (1915-28)

Basket, hanging-type, roses in relief on tan basketweave ground, 10" 80.00

Bowl, 5" d., florals in relief on tan ground 45.00
Jardiniere, florals in relief on shaded tan ground, 5½" h. 50.00

Flemish Jardiniere

Jardiniere, panels of cream-colored florals in relief on stippled ground, 7" h. (ILLUS.) 65.00
Jardiniere, panels w/single large pink flower amid greenish leaves in relief on tan stippled ground, 7½" h. 80.00
Tub, rim handles, roses in relief on tan basketweave ground, 9" d., 4½" h. 65.00
Umbrella stand, panels of pink flowers, heavy brown branches & green leaves in relief on textured ground, 21½" h. 185.00
Vase, 6½" h., flaring cylinder, blossoms & foliage in relief on shaded tan ground 30.00

FLERON (Late 1920's)

Vase, 4¾" h., everted ruffled rim, ridged body, green shading to lavender-pink glaze 35.00
Vase, 8½" h., waisted cylinder, ruffled rim, ridged body, green glaze 50.00
Vase, 10" h., two-handled, ridged body, green glaze 50.00

FLORAL (Late 1930's)

Basket, floral spray & foliage in relief on blue ground, 6" h. 26.00
Vase, 4½" h., two-handled, squatty, floral branch in relief on blue or green ground, each 25.00
Vase, 6½" h., two handles at midsection, bulbous base, wide neck, florals & foliage in relief on green ground 24.00

FLORETTA (1904)

Pitcher, jug-type, grape cluster in low relief, shaded brown glaze ... 65.00
Pitcher, tankard, 10½" h., grape cluster in low relief, shaded brown glaze 80.00
Vase, 5" h., 5" widest d., bulbous, slip-painted raspberries & swirling vines in low relief on shaded oatmeal grey ground 75.00
Vase, 7½" h., relief-molded handles & mouth, shaded brown glaze 75.00
Vase, 10" h., slip-painted florals in low relief on cream shaded to grey ground 85.00
Vase, 11½" h., slip-painted pink flower in low relief on cream shaded to grey ground 135.00

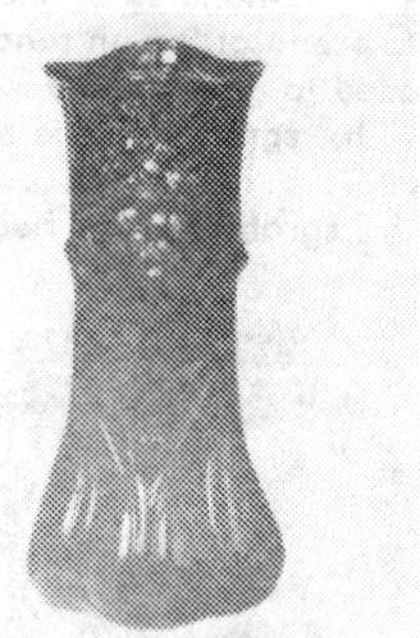

Floretta Vase

Vase, 12" h., slip-painted cluster of green grapes in low relief, shaded brown glaze (ILLUS.) 115.00
Vase, 14" h., slip-painted grape cluster in low relief, shaded brown glaze 165.00

FOREST (1915)

Basket w/overhead handle, realistically molded & painted forest scene, 6 x 4", 9" h. 85.00
Bowl, 7" d., canted sides, realistically molded & painted forest scene 67.50
Jardiniere, realistically molded & painted forest scene, 4½" to 6½" h., each .... 100.00 to 150.00
Teapot, cov., realistically molded & painted forest scene, high-gloss glaze 165.00
Vase, 7" h., cylindrical, realistically molded & painted forest scene ... 60.00
Vase, 8" h., waisted cylinder, realistically molded & painted forest scene 65.00
Window box, realistically molded & painted forest scene, 14½ x 5¼" 165.00

GLENDALE (1920's)

Console set: 16" d. bowl w/rolled rim, flower frog & pair 5½" h. candleholders; birds & nest

w/eggs in low relief, shades of russet, blue & grey, 4 pcs. 240.00
Vase, 6½" h., bird in flight over grassy marsh, shades of blue, tan & beige 145.00
Vase, 11½" h., bird & nest, shades of russet, tan & beige 170.00
Wall pocket, double bud, vase w/bird & nest of eggs flanked by tree trunks, shades of yellow, tan, blue & brown, 7" h. ...65.00 to 85.00
Wall pocket, mother bird & babies on branch, blue, yellow, beige & tan 175.00

HUDSON (1920's-1935)

Hudson Vases

Vase, 6" h., urn-shaped, underglaze slip-painted daisies, signed Sarah Timberlake 250.00
Vase, 6" h., two-handled, underglaze slip-painted band of florals at top, signed Sarah Timberlake .. 195.00
Vase, 6" h., underglaze slip-painted pink & blue dogwood blossoms, artist-signed 175.00
Vase, 7" h., underglaze slip-painted deep pink blossoms & dark green branches, white matte glaze (ILLUS. right) 90.00
Vase, 7" h., underglaze slip-painted colorful florals, pale pink shaded to grey matte glaze, signed M. Ansel (ILLUS. left) 155.00
Vase, 7" h., underglaze slip-painted florals, blue shaded to grey matte glaze, artist-signed 185.00
Vase, 7" h., underglaze slip-painted roses, signed Hester Pillsbury 350.00
Vase, 7½" h., underglaze slip-painted grape clusters, signed Hood 150.00
Vase, 8" h., underglaze slip-painted blackberries & blossoms, signed Sarah McLaughlin 215.00
Vase, 8" h., underglaze slip-painted florals, signed Hood 155.00
Vase, 8½" h., underglaze slip-painted iris blossoms & foliage ... 125.00
Vase, 9" h., underglaze slip-painted florals, artist-signed 245.00
Vase, 9" h., underglaze slip-painted florals, greenish-blue shaded to pink matte ground, artist-signed .. 195.00
Vase, 10" h., underglaze slip-painted apple blossoms 150.00
Vase, 10" h., underglaze slip-painted daffodils, incised mark ... 110.00
Vase, 10" h., underglaze slip-painted milkweed pods & feathery seeds, deep blue matte glaze, signed Hester Pillsbury 295.00
Vase, 10" h., bulbous, underglaze slip-painted florals, signed Hester Pillsbury 425.00
Vase, 11" h., slender cylinder, underglaze slip-painted pink & white poppies 135.00
Vase, 11½" h., underglaze slip-painted mauve & pink wild rose & grey vines, creamy ivory matte glaze 250.00

LA SA (1920-25)

Vase, 3½" h., landscape scene, iridescent glaze 100.00
Vase, 4" h., bullet-shaped, trees & water w/mountains in distance, iridescent glaze 185.00
Vase, 4½" h., landscape scene, iridescent gold glaze 150.00
Vase, 5" h., slender cylinder, landscape scene, iridescent glaze..... 100.00
Vase, 6½" h., landscape scene, iridescent pink & gold glaze 120.00
Vase, 7½" h., landscape w/palm trees, iridescent gold, red & copper glaze 170.00
Vase, bud, 8" h., landscape scene, iridescent glaze ....135.00 to 155.00

La Sa Vase

Vase, 9" h., landscape scene w/trees, mountains & lake, iridescent glaze (ILLUS.)............... 200.00
Vase, 11" h., tapering cylinder, landscape scene w/trees & water, iridescent glaze 245.00

LOUWELSA (1896-1924)

Clock, mantel-type, slip-painted yellow wild roses & green leaves, standard brown shaded to dark green glaze, original face & works, 11 x 10" 795.00

Clock, mantel-type, slip-painted florals, standard brown glaze, original face & works, 12" h. 950.00
Ewer, slip-painted florals, standard brown glaze, signed Hester Pillsbury, 7" h. 425.00
Jardiniere, slip-painted daffodils, standard brown shaded to orange glaze, 6" h. 375.00

Louwelsa Jardiniere & Pedestal

Jardiniere & pedestal base, slip-painted yellow flowers & green leaves, standard brown glaze, overall 31" h., 2 pcs. (ILLUS.) 475.00
Jug, slip-painted red cherries, standard brown glaze, 5" h. 150.00
Mug, slip-painted hummingbird, standard dark brown shaded to green glaze, 6½" h. (rim bruise) 185.00
Mug, slip-painted yellow & green ear of corn, standard brown glaze 90.00
Pitcher, 3" h., 5½" w., squatty, slip-painted yellow jonquil & green foliage, standard brown shaded to rust glaze 140.00
Pitcher, tankard, 17" h., slip-painted florals, standard brown shaded to dark green glaze, artist-signed ... 550.00
Pitcher, 17" h., 6½" base d., 4" top d., slip-painted grape clusters, standard brown glaze, artist-signed 300.00
Vase, 4¼" h., three-footed, squatty, trefoil lip, slip-painted pansies, standard brown glaze, artist-signed 95.00
Vase, 5½" h., bulbous, slip-painted orange flowers, standard brown glaze, artist-signed 95.00
Vase, 5¾" h., slip-painted florals, shaded blue glaze 410.00
Vase, 6" h., bulbous, slip-painted florals, standard brown glaze, artist-signed 185.00
Vase, 6¼" h., 2" top d., bulbous, slip-painted orange & grey-green chrysanthemums, standard brown shaded to gold glaze 125.00
Vase, 8½" h., 4½" d., slip-painted large white flowers w/brown centers, standard brown shaded to green glaze, artist-signed 150.00
Vase, 9" h., slip-painted carnations, standard brown glaze, artist-signed 275.00

LUXOR (Ca. 1910)

Umbrella stand, relief-molded florals on stippled ground shaded brown-black to beige 125.00
Vase, 9½" h., relief-molded florals on stippled ground shaded brown-black to beige 45.00

MAMMY LINE (1935)

Cookie jar, cov., figural Mammy 325.00
Creamer, figural nude boy handle .. 275.00
Syrup pitcher, cov., figural Mammy, 6" h. ....300.00 to 325.00

MANHATTAN (early 1930's)

Vase, 6¼" h., embossed stylized plums & leaves 50.00
Vase, 6½" h., slightly tapered cylindrical shape, embossed band of large leaves around bottom half, green glaze..................... 38.00
Vase, 9" h., cylindrical shape w/long, narrow embossed leaves up side, tan & brown glaze 70.00

MONOCHROME (1903-04)

Compote, open, 9¼" d., round base tapering to support low, round bowl w/inverted rim, green semi-gloss glaze 48.00
Compote, open, 10" d., round base tapering to support low, round bowl w/inverted rim, blue semi-gloss glaze 50.00
Vase, 10" h., four-panel shape, incised grape design, tan semigloss glaze 58.00

MUSKOTA (1920's)

Flower holder, model of a seated boy w/fishing pole 75.00
Flower holder, model of a nude girl seated on rocks 95.00
Model of an elephant, 15½" l., 10" h. (damage to tip of tusk) 650.00
Model of a frog 55.00
Model of a gate w/two seated cats & pots on top, 7" h. 275.00
Planter, model of a log, 10½" l..... 45.00

OAK LEAF (pre-1936)

Console bowl, 11", molded oak leaves on one side, acorns on other side 35.00

Vase, 16" h., ewer-form, molded oak leaves on one side, molded acorns on other 100.00
Wall pocket, cone-shaped, molded oak leaf at base, molded acorns at top, 8½" l. 35.00

ORRIS (1915)

Basket, hanging-type, relief-molded band of flowers, 6" 35.00
Vase, 10" h., relief-molded branches & leaves 55.00
Wall pocket, cone-shaped, serpentine band of relief-molded daisy-like flowers across center 35.00

ROMA (1914 - late 1920's)

Jardiniere, urn-form, cream ground w/applied colored fruit, 11 x 13½" 150.00
Vase, triple bud, 6½" h., footed base, square center column flanked by curving square columns w/trelliswork between each column, ribbon & floral garland in pink & green swags from left to right arm, creamy white ground 30.00
Window box, rectangular, embossed stylized pink daisy-like blossoms & white leaf sprigs on ground of small swirled circles, 13½" l., 5½" h. 55.00

SICARDO (1902-07)

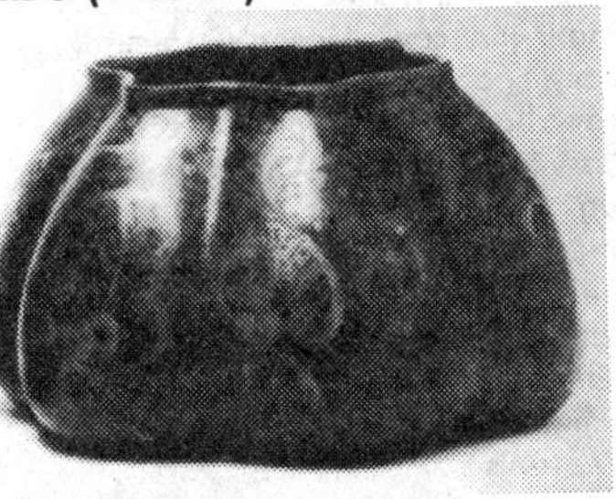

Weller Sicardo Vase

Vase, 4" h., 13" d., bowl shaped, magenta lining, blue-green & gold purple ground, star decoration ... 432.00
Vase, 4¾" h., 8" d., squatty bulbous form w/fluted rim, six lobed sections, overall iridescent floral & scroll design, signed (ILLUS.) 325.00
Vase, 5" h., 3" w., simple ovoid cylinder w/top slightly tapered to three-sided opening, trailing vines w/leaves & berries in metallic gold against an iridescent green & violet ground, surface signed "Weller Sicard" 250.00
Vase, 11" h., 4½" d., cylindrical w/four oval indentations around the opening, silver & crimson leaves & berries 660.00

SILVERTONE (1925-29)

Basket, flattened shape w/small base & widely flared rim, vine loop handle across top, embossed purple grapes & green leaves down side, 8½" h. 80.00
Console bowl w/flower frog, molded pink blossoms, green leaves & brown branches on bluish ground, bowl 12" d., 3½" h., frog, 2½" d., pr. 85.00
Vase, 10" h., slightly bulbous base & straight cylindrical body w/squared handles from top rim to bulbous base, molded pink & white large blossoms, leaves & branches on splotched bluish pink ground 95.00
Vase, beautiful pastels, blue swirl ground, pale lavender lotus, large pale green leaves, shape 17 ..... 295.00

SYDONIA (late 1920's-33)

Cornucopia-vase, slender horn-shaped vase on round base w/molded leaves, green mottled glaze, 7½" h. 45.00
Vase, double, 7½" h., two flaring horn-shaped vases w/ruffled rims joined at round base w/molded leaf design, mottled green glaze 95.00

WOODCRAFT (1920-33)

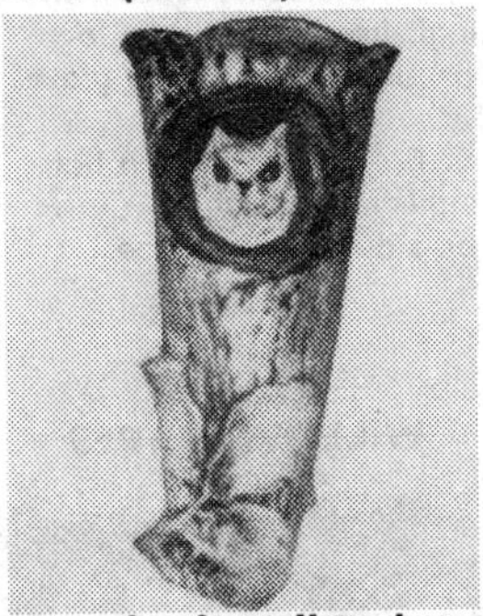

Woodcraft Wall Pocket

Mug, textured tree trunk form w/three relief-molded foxes peeking out of hole in trunk, 6" h. 245.00
Pitcher, tankard, 12½" h., textured tree trunk form w/three relief-molded foxes peeking out of hole in trunk, tree branch handle 395.00
Vase, double bud, 8" h., two slender tree trunk shaped containers joined by arched, criss-crossing tree branches w/molded green leaves & red berries 95.00
Vase, bud, 8½" h., molded tree

trunk shape w/slender vine handle along side, green relief-molded clump of leaves near top 29.00

Vase, 17½" h., molded tree trunk shape w/relief-molded owl & squirrel decoration 400.00

Wall pocket, molded tree trunk shape w/flared top, large relief-molded leaves at base & relief-molded owl head in trunk opening near top, 10" h. (ILLUS.) 80.00

WOODROSE (pre-1920)

Basket, hanging-type, model of an oaken bucket w/pendent red roses & green leaves at front center, brown matte ground (no chain) 115.00

Jardiniere, model of an oaken bucket w/pendent red roses & green leaves at front center, brown matte ground, 7" 100.00

Vase, 9" h., model of an oaken bucket w/pendent red roses & green leaves at front center, brown matte ground 45.00

Wall pocket, fan-shaped, model of an oaken bucket w/pendent red roses & green leaves at front center, brown matte ground 75.00

ZONA (1915-20)

Creamer, h.p. white baby duck strutting, white ground, 3½" h. ... 36.00

Pitcher, 7" h., molded branch handle, kingfisher & cattails in low relief on sides, cobalt blue glaze, ½ gal. 97.00

Pitcher, 8" h., molded branch handle, kingfisher & cattails in low relief on sides, green glaze 125.00

WILLOW WARES

Buffalo Pottery Blue Willow

This pseudo-Chinese pattern has been used by numerous firms throughout the years. The original design is attributed to Thomas Minton about 1780 and Thomas Turner is believed to have first produced the ware during his tenure at the Caughley works. The blue underglaze transfer print pattern has never been out of production since that time. An Oriental landscape incorporating a bridge, pagoda, trees, figures and birds, supposedly tells the story of lovers fleeing a cruel father who wished to prevent their marriage. The gods, having pity on them, changed them into birds enabling them to fly away and seek their happiness together.

Pieces in colors other than blue are also being included in our listings.

Blue Willow

Bowl, 6" d. $8.00

Bowl, serving, Homer Laughlin 20.00

Bowl, soup, English 22.00

Butter pat, Buffalo Pottery 18.00

Creamer, Booth 85.00

Creamer, Ridgway 45.00

Creamer & sugar bowl, Homer Laughlin, pr. 35.00

Cup, oversize, pattern interior & exterior, Japan 10.00

Cup & saucer, Homer Laughlin 12.00

Dinner service for 6: place settings, tureen, platter & gravy boat; child's, original box, the set 200.00

Dish, cov., Japan, 6 x 4 x 2" 40.00

Dish & cover w/recessed knob, Japan, 8 x 6 x 4" 65.00

Ginger jar, cov., Mason's, 16-cup ... 150.00

Gravy boat, Wedgwood & Co. 50.00

Gravy boat w/underplate, rectangular, Staffordshire, England 35.00

Mug, Japan 15.00

Oil & vinegar cruets, Buffalo Pottery, each (ILLUS.) 15.00

Pitcher, 3 5/8" h., Wedgwood & Co., England 25.00

Pitcher, 4¼" h., hexagonal, Mason's 38.00

Pitcher, cov., 6" h., Buffalo Pottery, 1910 .... 75.00

Plate, 10" d., Buffalo Pottery, each (ILLUS. of six) 49.00

Platter, 7 x 6", Allertons 45.00

Platter, 10 x 8", Allertons 20.00

Platter, 10¾" l., 8½" w., Buffalo Pottery (ILLUS.) 32.50

Platter w/well, 12 x 9¼", Ridgway 45.00

Platter, 13" oval, Occupied Japan ... 12.00

Platter, 13 x 10" octagon, marked "Burleigh, England" 35.00

Salt & pepper shakers, pr. 39.00

Sandwich plate, Johnson Bros., England, 8" square 8.00

Sauce dish, Booth 8.00

Sauce dish, Occupied Japan 5.00

Buffalo Pottery Platter

Sauce tureen, underplate & ladle, Japan, 1950's 30.00
Soap dish, Burleigh Ware 35.00
Soup bowl w/flange rim, Allertons, 7¾" d. 15.00
Soup bowl, Maastrich, 9" d. 15.00
Soup bowl w/flange rim, Ridgway, 10½" d. 25.00
Soup tureen & ladle, Davenport, 1840 .... 375.00
Sugar bowl, cov., Booth 110.00
Sugar bowl, cov., Ridgway 52.00
Sugar bowl, cov., Steventon 25.00
Teacup & saucer, Grainger, Worcester 24.00
Teapot, cov., Allertons 110.00
Teapot, cov., "Booth - Real Old Willow" 125.00
Tea set: cov. teapot, cov. sugar bowl, creamer & six cups & saucers; marked "Japan" 125.00
Tea tile, ca. 1910, Wedgwood, 6" d. 55.00
Tidbit tray, two-tier, Japan, ca. 1950 .... 15.00
Toothbrush box, cov., unmarked, possibly Ridgway 130.00
Toothbrush holder, 7½ x 3" 35.00
Tray, marked "Wedgwood, Etruria", 10 x 8" 48.50
Tureen, cov., underplate & ladle, unmarked, 9 x 6½" l., the set 145.00
Tureen, cov., England, ca. 1900, 12 x 8" 350.00
Vegetable bowl, open, Wedgwood, 9 x 7" 35.00
Vegetable bowl, open, Occupied Japan, 10¼" 12.00

Other Colors

Jar w/dome lid, brown, Staffordshire 25.00
Tea set: cov. teapot, creamer, sugar bowl, ten cups & saucers, ten 6¾" d. plates & one 10" d. plate; mulberry, Stanley Pottery Co., Burslem, England, 34 pcs. 450.00

WORCESTER

Worcester Covered Milk Jug

The famed English Worcester factory was established in 1751 and produced porcelains. Earthenwares were made in the 19th century. Its first period is known as the "Dr. Wall" period; that from 1783 to 1792 as the "Flight" period; that from 1792 to 1807 as the "Barr and Flight & Barr" period. The firm became Barr, Flight & Barr from 1807 to 1813; Flight, Barr & Barr from 1813 to 1840; Chamberlain & Co. from 1840 to 1852, and Kerr and Binns from 1852 to 1862. After 1862, the company became the Worcester Royal Porcelain Company, Ltd., known familiarly as Royal Worcester, which see. Also included in the following listing are examples of wares from the early Chamberlains and early Grainger factories in Worcester.

Bowl, 5 7/8" d., reserved w/large & small gilt edge cartouches painted in polychrome enamels w/floral sprays on blue-scale ground, gilt rim $440.00
Bowl, 6 3/8" d., 3" h., fluted, footed, four panels of exotic birds in flowering shrubbery alternating w/underglaze-blue bands w/insects within elaborate gilt framed cartouches, ca. 1770 (some wear, glaze imperfections) 715.00
Compotes, cov., each painted on sides & cover w/various fruits, gilt-rimmed square base, satyr's mask handles heightened w/gilding, Flight, Barr & Barr, ca. 1820, pr. 1,870.00
Cup, saucer & tea bowl, Bengal Tiger patt., ca. 1776, Dr. Wall period, 3 pcs. 425.00
Dish, center painted w/coat-of-arms supported by a lion & a horse &

surmounted by a coronet, suspending a ribbon w/inscription, border w/elaborate foliate scrolls & urns in gilt on pale salmon pink ground, Barr, Flight & Barr period, ca. 1813, 10" oval 3,520.00

Ice pails w/covers, bucket-shaped, Armorial w/twisted foliage handles & painted w/a baronet's arms within a Garter Motto, on a white ground w/a wide band of iron-red enriched w/scrolling flowering branches between gilt bands of oak branches & foliage & gilt-lined rims, Barr and Flight & Barr period, ca. 1802, 11" h., pr. (lacking liners, some rubbing) 7,700.00

Milk jug w/cover, pear-shaped, decorated w/circular river landscape within a turquoise husk border flanked by flowering branches & butterflies beneath a blue border trimmed w/gilt interlaced scrolls, cover w/flower finial, blue crescent mark, ca. 1775, 5¼" h. (ILLUS.) 1,540.00

Mug, h.p. Chantilly Spring patt., random blue blossoms on white, strap handle, ca. 1770, 5" h. 650.00

Plate, 7¾" d., Blind Earl patt., molded budding rose spray enriched in colors & painted w/a butterfly & flower sprays, lobed rim w/gilt scrolls, ca. 1765 (minor rim chips) 1,100.00

18th Century Worcester Plate

Plate, 8½" d., blue-scale ground, reserved w/large & small gilt-edged cartouches painted in polychrome enamels w/scattered flowers & bouquets, within shaped circular gilt rim, pseudo seal mark, ca. 1770 (ILLUS.) 522.50

Platter, 11 5/8" rectangle, chamfered corners edged w/brown line, Sir Joshua Reynolds patt., bird perched on rockwork, Dr. Wall period, ca. 1760 ....2,200.00

Sauce boat, oval, blue & white, painted w/two Orientals in a garden, the reverse w/trailing flowers issuing from rockwork within a triple-arched cartouche, the lower part w/stiff leaves, the interior w/trailing flowers, blue crescent mark, ca. 1758, 5½" w. 418.00

Tea & coffee set: cov. barrel-shaped teapot, four coffee cups, four teacups, five saucers (one damaged) & one similar saucer; colorful trailing flowering plants suspended from apple green border etched w/gilt scrolls, ca. 1770, 15 pcs. 990.00

Tea bowl & saucer, fluted, Japan patt., panels of iron-red, yellow & green florals alternating w/cobalt blue panels w/iron-red flowerhead, Dr. Wall period, ca. 1765... 242.00

Tea caddy, cov., shallowly-fluted oviform, Bengal Tiger patt., ca. 1765, 6½" h. 715.00

Teapot, cov., globular, two flower bunches & scattered sprigs, flower finial edged w/iron-red band, 1775-80, 5 7/8" h. 770.00

Teapot w/cover & stand, each piece painted w/a wide border of large shaded brown leaves & small iron-red blossoms & buds issuing from gilt foliate band at the neck & handle, the cover w/a gilt flame-form finial, stand w/impressed crown above "BFB," Barr, Flight & Barr period, 1807-13, 7½" h. 330.00

Vase, 7" h., baluster-shape, blue-scale ground, painted w/wheat sheaves & flowers within shaped cartouches w/gilt scroll borders, reserved on the blue-scale ground, the neck w/a band of flowers, blue seal mark, ca. 1765 .... 715.00

Wine coolers, Bengal Tiger patt., Chamberlain period, pr. 6,600.00

YELLOW-GLAZED EARTHENWARE

In the past this early English ware was often referred to as "Canary Lustre," but recently a more accurate title has come into use.

Produced in the late 18th and early 19th centuries, pieces featured an overall yellow glaze, often decorated with silver or copper lustre designs or black, brown or red transfer-printed scenes.

Most pieces are not marked and today the

scarcity of examples in good condition keeps market prices high.

Mug, enameled roses, zig-zag rim band & red, black & faded green ship transfer on yellow ground, 5¼" h. (wear & hairlines) $250.00
Pitcher, 7" h., transfer-printed in silver lustre "For the American Trade, Success to the United States of America, Peace and Plenty," w/small eagle on yellow ground 1,925.00
Pitcher, silver lustre transfer of bird & other decorations on yellow ground 1,760.00
Punch bowl, copper lustre designs on yellow ground 852.50

YELLOWWARE

Yellowware is a form of utilitarian pottery produced in the United States from the 1850's onward. Its body texture is less dense and vitreous (impervious to water) than stoneware. Most, but not all, yellowware is unmarked and its color varies from deep yellow to pale buff. In the late 19th and early 20th centuries bowls in graduated sizes were widely advertised. Still in production, yellowware is plentiful and still reasonably priced.

Batter bowl, 11½" d. $65.00
Bowl, 4¾" d., two blue bands & four narrow white bands 40.00
Bowl, 9" d., blue bands 30.00
Bowl, 9" d., three brown bands 25.00
Bowl, 9" d., 5" h., two medium-wide blue bands & two narrow white bands 42.00
Bowl, 10" d., three blue bands 35.00
Bowl, 12" d., narrow white & brown bands 50.00
Bowl, 13" d. 59.00
Butter crock, embossed ribs, round 60.00
Colander 145.00
Custard cup 20.00
Figure of woman pulling dress up over her head, pedestal & vase at her side, greenish-gold trim, base marks, 8½" h. 240.00
Flower pot 85.00
Mixing bowl, two narrow & one wide white band, 11¾" d. 44.00
Mixing bowl, 12" d., 6" deep, wide white band 23.50
Mixing bowl, 15" d., 7½" deep, brown & white bands 45.00
Mixing bowls, tapering cylinder, brown bands, 5¼" to 9½" d., graduated set of 5 .... 66.00
Mug w/loop handle, smeary brown polka dot decoration, sticker reading "Roger Bacon Collection," 3¼" h. (very worn & chipped) 675.00
Pitcher, 5¾" h., three white bands, two of them in relief 110.00
Pitcher, milk, light blue & white bands 75.00
Pitcher, ½ gal. 40.00
Washboard, blue mottled glaze, mounted in pine frame, ca. 1880 .... 475.00

ZSOLNAY

Zsolnay Vase

This pottery was made in Pecs, Hungary, in a factory founded in 1855 by Vilmos Zsolnay. Currently Zsolnay pieces are being made in a new factory.

Box, cov., molded band of chariots & soldiers on side, iridescent green glaze $80.00
Model of a bull, iridescent green glaze 275.00
Model of a recumbent deer, iridescent green glaze, signed A. Sinko, 6" 140.00
Model of goats, signed A. Sinko, 5¾ x 5½", pr. 125.00
Puzzle jug, handled, reticulated roundels & three looped protrusions, multicolored jeweling & iridescent florals on pale beige ground, 6¾" h. (Blue Castle mark) .... 115.00 to 135.00
Puzzle jug, iridescent multicolored florals outlined in gold, reticulated roundels 155.00
Vase, bud, 3¾" h., 2¾" d., double-walled body w/overall reticulated outer wall, brown & green glaze w/gold highlighting 125.00
Vase, 6½" h., double-walled reticulated sides, cobalt blue, beige & gold Persian-style decoration 350.00
Vase, 6¾" h., iridescent cobalt blue glaze 195.00

Vase, 7" h., four-handled, ovoid, iridescent purple-blue blossoms & dots against an iridescent streaking gold ground, ribbed scrolling handles glazed in iridescent chartreuse, ca. 1900, impressed mark (ILLUS.) 715.00
Watering can, floral decoration, 5" h. 90.00

(End of Ceramics Section)

CHALKWARE

Chalkware Stag

So-called chalkware available today is actually made of plaster of Paris, much of it decorated in color and primarily in the form of busts, figurines and ornaments. It was produced through most of the 19th century and the majority of pieces were originally quite inexpensive when made. Today even 20th century "carnival" pieces are collectible but we do not include any of them in this listing.

Bank, model of a dove, worn original paint, 11" h. $300.00
Bank, model of an owl, old red & yellow paint, 6¾" h. 85.00
Figure, Art Nouveau woman wearing clinging sheer blue gown, arms over head, pre-1920, signed "Rigacci, No. 1302," 15" h. 115.00
Figures, angels on half-moon, one playing harp & other playing fife, black, pr. 145.00
Mantel garniture, pineapple on plinth, worn blue paint w/yellow & red, 9½" h. 250.00
Model of a bird seated on tapering plinth, worn old red, yellow & olive green paint, 6" h. 130.00
Model of a dog in seated position, low oblong base, black "smoke" decorated yellowish coat & features picked out in red, 5½" h. 200.00
Model of a dove, original paint, 11" h. 300.00
Model of lovebirds, pair w/beaks touching, worn original red, yellow, green & black paint, 5½" h. 400.00
Model of a parrot, original yellow, green, red & black paint, 10¼" h. (old repair in base between feet) 375.00
Model of a Spaniel dog standing, white coat w/russet spots & brown ears, greenish yellow oval base, 7½" h. 295.00
Model of a squirrel, worn original red, green & black paint, 6" h. (chips on base) 350.00
Model of a stag, hollow figure of reclining stag w/rack of antlers, the body painted a beige-yellow w/markings of red, yellow, black & green (chip in base), Pennsylvania, mid-19th c., 8¼" l., 10" h. (ILLUS.) 1,540.00

CHARACTER COLLECTIBLES

Betty Boop Ukelele Advertisement

Numerous objects made in the likeness of or named after movie, radio, television, com-

ic strip and comic book personalities or characters have abounded since the 1920's. Scores of these are now being eagerly collected and prices still vary widely. Also see ADVERTISING ITEMS, BANKS, BIG LITTLE BOOKS, BROWNIE COLLECTIBLES, BUSTER BROWN COLLECTIBLES, CAMPBELL KIDS COLLECTIBLES, CANDY CONTAINERS, CHRISTMAS TREE LIGHTS, COMIC BOOKS, DISNEY ITEMS, DOLLS, GAMES & GAME BOARDS, KEWPIE COLLECTIBLES, SHEET MUSIC and TOYS.

Amos & Andy book, "Amos' Wedding" $55.00
Amos & Andy figures, bisque, Pfeffer, 4" h., pr. 120.00
Amos & Andy vending machine cards, 5¼ x 3¼", set of 16 .... 75.00
Andy Gump brush & mirror combination 13.00
Andy Gump food mold, plated copper 90.00
Andy Gump & Min toothbrush holder, bisque 85.00
Annie Oakley game, 1950.......... 26.00
Annie Oakley skirt & vest.......... 37.00
Barney Google & Spark Plug game, Milton Bradley, 1923.......... 32.00
Barney Google & Spark Plug paperweight, metal.......... 29.00
Batman bank, ceramic, by National Periodical Publications, 1966, 7" h. 37.50
Batman bubble gum cards, Topps, 1966, assorted set of 207.......... 100.00
Batman helmet & cape, ca. 1966 .... 30.00
Batman "Sanctuary" Bat Cave Playset, Ideal, 1966, 23 pcs. in original Sears & Roebuck box 280.00
Batman toy, friction-type Batmobile, tin & plastic, Japan, 1960's, w/box 125.00
Batman & Robin movie serial poster, "Chapter No. 1 Batman Takes Over," 1949.......... 350.00
Bat Masterson cane 25.00
Beatles book, "Growing Up With the Beatles," Schaumburg, 1976 .... 12.00
Beatles gum cards: Sets 1, 2 & 3, "A Hard's Day's Night" series, Diary set & color cards set; American, 6 full sets together w/white Beatles binder 660.00
Beatles hair brush, plastic 32.50
Beatles nodders, composition, 8" h., set of 4 .... 350.00
Beatles sneakers.......... 225.00
Beatles sweatshirt.......... 45.00
Beatles watercolor set, "Yellow Submarine".......... 67.00
Betty Boop bank, papier mache.......... 75.00
Betty Boop figure, wood-jointed body, Fleischer, 1935, 12½" h. 450.00
Betty Boop mask, cardboard, 1931 .... 40.00
Betty Boop nodder, celluloid 650.00
Betty Boop noise maker, lithographed tin 45.00
Betty Boop ukelele, wooden, 21" (ILLUS. from ad).......... 55.00
Beverly Hillbillies toy, windup car, 1963, 23" l. 400.00
Blondie game, "Blondie Goes to Leisureland," Westinghouse premium, 1940, in original envelope 35.00
Blondie game, "Ring Toss," under glass, 1941 .... 28.00
Blondie jigsaw puzzle, King Features Syndicate, 1933 .... 16.00
Blondie & Dagwood blocks, wooden, interchangeable, Gaston, 1951 .... 36.50
Blondie & Dagwood game, "Race for the Office" 26.00
Blondie & Dagwood game, "Target".......... 49.00
Buck Rogers book, pop-up type, "Spidership Adventures," 1935.......... 150.00
Buck Rogers card game, "All-Fair," Richardson Co., 1936, in box 375.00
Buck Rogers lunch box w/thermos bottle 22.00
Buck Rogers photograph, Dixie Cup premium 75.00
Buck Rogers Punch-Out Rubber-Band gun, 1940 (unpunched).......... 45.00
Buck Rogers rocket ship, Tootsietoy 189.00
Buck Rogers Space Ranger kit, 1942 .... 145.00
Buck Rogers walkie-talkie, original box 45.00
Buffalo Bill mug, milk white glass 6.00
Bugs Bunny alarm clock, Ingraham.......... 45.00
Bugs Bunny bank, chalkware, 24".......... 200.00
Captain Marvel beanbag 15.00
Captain Marvel Club pinback button, "Shazam".......... 28.00
Captain Marvel game, "Shazam," unused 20.00
Captain Marvel tie clip, dated 1946, on original card 110.00
Captain Marvel wrist watch, yellow face, picture & logo, blue leather strap, Swiss, 1948 .... 75.00
Captain Midnight decoder, 1941, Code-O-Graph, Ovaltine premium 37.50
Captain Midnight decoder, 1942, "Photo-matic Code-O-Graph," Ovaltine premium (ILLUS.).......... 40.00 to 50.00
Captain Midnight ring, "Flight Commander Signet," Ovaltine premium 85.00

Captain Midnight Decoder

Captain Midnight "spinner" toy, brass 8.00
Captain Midnight stamp album w/stamps, Skelly Oil premium . . . 60.00
Captain Video Mysto Coder 225.00
Charlie Chaplin book, "The Charlie Chaplin Book," Sam'l. Gabriel Sons Publishers 45.00
Charlie Chaplin card game w/flip movie backs 10.00
Charlie Chaplin figure, articulated carved wood, black & flesh colored paint, 12½" h. (damage to back brim of hat) 90.00
Charlie Chaplin figure, chalkware, 30" h. 100.00
Charlie Chaplin pinback button, 2½" 45.00
Charlie McCarthy book, "So Help Me Mr. Bergen," 1938 . . . . . 30.00
Charlie McCarthy game, "Bingo" 35.00
Charlie McCarthy game, "Question & Answer" 18.00
Charlie McCarthy marionette, lithographed cardboard, 12" 39.00
Charlie McCarthy radio, white Bakelite 445.00
Charlie McCarthy teaspoon, silverplate 15.00
Clarabell the Clown suction cup toy 48.00
Daffy Duck bank, cast iron, Warner Bros. 40.00
Dagwood paint set, 1950's 10.00
Dale Evans figure, Hartland 90.00
Dale Evans jacket 30.00
Dennis the Menace teaspoon, silver plate 15.00
Dennis the Menace water pistol, original box, dated 1954 . . . . . 65.00
Dick Tracy badge, "Secret Service Patrol Sergeant" 35.00
Dick Tracy book, pop-up type, "The Capture of Boris Arson," 1935, published by Pleasure Books, Inc. 80.00
Dick Tracy book, "Celebrated Cases of Dick Tracy," hard cover, 1931-51, 1970 copyright 50.00
Dick Tracy Christmas card, 1940's . . . 20.00
Dick Tracy dart board, metal, dated 1941 . . . . . 25.00
Dick Tracy fingerprint set 75.00
Dick Tracy flashlight, original box, 1940's 35.00
Dick Tracy handcuffs, on original card 47.00
Dick Tracy machine gun, 11" l. 80.00
Dick Tracy magnifying glass 7.50
Dick Tracy playing cards, dated 1934 . . . . . 35.00
Dick Tracy Viewmaster, 4 reels 25.00
Dionne Quintuplets book, "Story of the Dionne Quintuplets," 1935, Whitman No. 937 . . . . . 25.00
Dionne Quintuplets bowl & cup, pottery, marked Photo Copyright N.E.A., 2 pcs. 75.00
Dionne Quintuplets calendar, 1946, "Queens of the Kitchen," painted by Andrew Loomis, 12 x 15" 12.50
Dionne Quintuplets calendar, 1947, "Everybody Helps," painted by Andrew Loomis 16.00
Dionne Quintuplets calendar, 1950, "Sweet Sixteen," painted by Andrew Loomis 16.50
Dionne Quintuplets paper dolls, uncut, "All Aboard for Shut-Eye Town," Palmolive premium, 1937, original mailing envelope 55.00
Dionne Quintuplets prints, 1935, colored, set of 5 . . . . . 45.00
Dionne Quintuplets scrapbook, over 90 pages from the 1930's, 12½ x 10½" 75.00
Dionne Quintuplets teaspoons, silver plate, full figure handles w/names, set of 5 . . . . . 85.00 to 110.00
Dolly Dingle plate, china, h.p. "September Morn," 8" d. 35.00
Elvis Presley band uniform worn in "Frankie and Johnnie," red & white uniform w/gold fringed lapels & a matching hat w/black feather plumes, label w/star's name, designed by Gwenn Wakeling, United Artists, 1966, four pieces together w/two movie stills of Presley in costume 1,210.00
Elvis Presley dog tag anklet, on original card, dated 1956 . . . . . 50.00
Elvis Presley handkerchief, 1956 . . . . 225.00
Elvis Presley perfume bottle, "Teddy Bear," 1957, original box 115.00

Fat Albert & Cosby Kids lunch box w/thermos bottle, 1973 .... 15.00
Felix the Cat bowl, china, U.S.A. China Co., 8½" d. 55.00
Felix the Cat figure, wooden, jointed body, Schoenhut, 4" h. 127.50
Felix the Cat flashlight w/whistle attached to end 65.00
Felix the Cat transfers, sheet of 15 .... 45.00
Flash Gordon Christmas card w/envelope, 1951, King Features (unused) 8.00
Flash Gordon coloring book, 1958 ... 40.00
Flash Gordon compass, on original card 55.00
Flash Gordon rocket fighter, Louis Marx & Co. 240.00
Flash Gordon 2-way telephones, on original card 150.00
Flintstones toy, battery-operated car, 1961 .... 100.00
Flintstones toy, battery-operated yacht, 1961 .... 100.00
Foxy Grandpa jigsaw puzzle 32.00
Foxy Grandpa nodding figure, hand-painted 89.00
Foxy Grandpa toy, mechanical, push his chest & he crashes his cymbals, 1910, 11" h. 250.00
Gabby Hayes target, w/gun & suction darts 100.00
Gene Autry belt, leather 10.00
Gene Autry book, "Redwood Pirates," illustrated, 1946 .... 50.00
Gene Autry coloring book, 1941 .... 15.00
Gene Autry guitar, wooden, regulation size, Supertone 110.00
Gene Autry pinback button, advertising "Sunbeam Bread" 5.00
Gene Autry suspenders, elastic, Champion on clips, sheriff's badge on braces 75.00
Green Hornet lunch box w/thermos bottle ....35.00 to 50.00
Gunsmoke handcuffs, on card 45.00
Happy Hooligan figure, bisque, 9" h. 65.00
Harold Teen ukulele, 1920's, 21" l. .. 175.00
Henry figure, composition, jointed at shoulders, copyright 1934 by Carl Anderson, 8" h. 110.00
Herbie figure, bisque, Japan, 1930, 2¼" h. 17.50
Hopalong Cassidy belt, leather 16.00
Hopalong Cassidy bicycle, girls 20" model, Rollfast 800.00
Hopalong Cassidy bicycle horn, original box 90.00
Hopalong Cassidy book carrying case, split cow hide leather 55.00
Hopalong Cassidy field glasses, metal, black crinkle painted finish w/two multicolor decals, 5" h. (ILLUS.) 45.00

Hopalong Cassidy Field Glasses

Hopalong Cassidy milk bottle, black & red graphics, Dairy-Lee Milk, qt. 45.00
Hopalong Cassidy movie poster, "Strange Gamble," 1947 .... 95.00
Hopalong Cassidy pennant, felt, 1950's, 10 x 8" 20.00
Hopalong Cassidy pogo stick ....85.00 to 95.00
Hopalong Cassidy "Official Bar 20 TV Chair," folding-type, wooden frame w/red, black & white canvas seat & back, 22" h. 65.00
Hopalong Cassidy woodburning set, w/electric tool & wooden plaques, American Toy Co., Chicago, 1950, in original box (ILLUS.) ...95.00 to 125.00

Hopalong Cassidy Woodburning Set

Hopalong Cassidy Zomerang gun, red plastic, shoots paper roll, original box ....150.00 to 185.00
Howdy Doody bank, ceramic, bust of Howdy 55.00
Howdy Doody bath towel 27.50
Howdy Doody chair, folding-type, aluminum & canvas 75.00

Howdy Doody crayon set, Milton Bradley 65.00
Howdy Doody game, "Flub-A-Dub Flip-A-Ring," 1955 .... 19.00
Howdy Doody neckerchief slide 12.50
Howdy Doody playing cards 16.00
Howdy Doody ukulele 75.00
Howdy Doody ventriloquist doll, w/instruction manual, original box 60.00
Huckleberry Hound cartoon cel, Huck riding bucking bronco, black & white 65.00
Ignatz the Mouse figure, wooden, jointed body, copyright by Geo. Herriman, 6" h. 95.00
Jack Armstrong game, "Big 10 Football," 1933, radio premium, original envelope 50.00
Jack Armstrong secret bomb sight 25.00
Jack Webb (Dragnet) badge & whistle, 2 pcs. 15.00
Jack Webb (Dragnet) cap gun, 1955, original box 46.50
James Bond car, white Toyota w/missles in rear, Corgi 45.00
James Bond Electro Drawing set 65.00
James Bond game, "Message From M" 55.00
James Bond wrist watch, Gilbert 165.00

Jeep Figure

Jeep (from Popeye) figure, composition, jointed body, bright yellow w/red nose, King Features Syndicate, 1935, 12¾" h. (ILLUS.) 145.00
Jetson's cartoon cel, Judy, Jane & Rosie the Robot, on original h.p. background, matted 125.00
Jetson's space copter, dated 1962 .... 75.00
Jimi Hendrix felt tip drawing, multicolor on orange poster board, depicts abstract motifs & a staircase, inscribed lower right "up the staircase to midnight, Jimi Hendrix," matted & framed, 24 x 19" 5,500.00
Jimi Hendrix floral shirt & black velvet jacket, 2 pcs. 2,970.00
Joe Palooka punching bag, Ideal 10.00
Junior (Dick Tracy) pinback button, Kellogg's Pep Cereal premium 6.00
Katzenjammer Kids jigsaw puzzle, 1942 .... 20.00
Katzenjammer Kids punch-out game, ca. 1945 .... 15.00
Katzenjammer "Mama" mechanical doll, composition, mouth opens, cloth dress, 1920's, 9" h. 225.00
Kit Carson cap gun, Kilgore 30.00
Krazy Kat pin, enameled, w/banjo 25.00

Krazy Kat Water-Color

Krazy Kat water-color depicting Krazy Kat plucking a flower in a desert w/Ignatz & Officer Pupp, w/personal inscription by the artist, George Herriman, matted & framed, 12" w., 17" h. (ILLUS.) 10,450.00
Kukla sugar spoon, figural handle, silver plate 25.00
Laurel & Hardy figural salt & pepper shakers on tray, 1930's, 3 pcs. 125.00
Li'l Abner suspenders, elastic, 1949 .... 45.00
Li'l Abner Village of Dog Patch construction set, 32 pcs. 35.00
Little Black Sambo dartboard, self-framed tin, 14 x 23" 189.00
Little Black Sambo jigsaw puzzle, signed Fern Bisel Peat, ca. 1930 .... 38.00
Little Lulu cartoon kit, dated 1948, w/box 90.00
Little Lulu clothes line set 50.00
Little Lulu figure, Napco, 1958, 3½" h. 14.00
Little Lulu & Tubby valentine 18.00
Little Nemo postcard, Nemo & Princess at Court, 1907 .... 65.00
Little Red Riding Hood pencil box, wooden, 1920 .... 20.00
Lone Ranger alarm clock 20.00
Lone Ranger badge, "Safety Scout," Silver Cup Bread premium, 1935 .... 30.00
Lone Ranger bank, model of a strong box 55.00
Lone Ranger book, "Lone Ranger & The Texas Rangers," 1938 .... 30.00
Lone Ranger clicker gun, tin, mul-

ticolor decal on black, 1938, 9" l. (ILLUS.) 30.00

Lone Ranger Clicker Gun

Lone Ranger figure, composition head, hands & feet, 1938, 20" h. (gun belt & bandana missing) 200.00
Lone Ranger game, "Guarding Gold Panners" 19.00
Lone Ranger pencil, bullet-shaped .. 8.00
Lone Ranger printing set, 1939 ..... 22.00
Lone Ranger ring, "National Defender" 30.00
Lone Ranger & Tonto figures mounted on horses, plastic, Hartland, pr. 70.00
Lone Ranger & Tonto saddle bag, 1950's 125.00
Lum & Abner badge, "Weather Prophet" 17.50
Lum & Abner Family Almanac, 1938 .... 12.00
Maggie & Jiggs book, "Bringing Up Father," by George McManus, 3rd Series, Cupples & Leon, 1919 ..... 30.00
Maggie & Jiggs paperweight, glass 35.00
Maggie & Jiggs salt & pepper shakers, china, Germany, ca. 1920, pr. 95.00
Major Bowes gong-bell w/chain & hammer, sterling silver, marked T.D.G., 1930's, 5/8" d. 100.00
Mammy Yokum hand puppet 35.00
Man from U.N.C.L.E. radio transmitter 95.00
Melvin Purvis G-Man Corps Manual, 1936 .... 45.00
Mighty Mouse game, "Ring Toss," Terrytoons, 1964 .... 35.00
Monkees ring, flasher-type 10.00
Moon Mullins figure, wooden, jointed body, 6" h. 135.00
Moon Mullins & Kayo salt & pepper shakers, glass, pr. 38.00
Mutt & Jeff bank, cast iron 130.00
Mutt & Jeff book, "Mutt & Jeff," No. 2, cartoon comic book, by Bud Fisher, 1908, 1st edition, H.C. Fisher, complete w/introduction & dedication, hard cover 300.00
Olive Oyl figure, wood-jointed, 1940's, 5" h. 50.00
Orphan Annie bank, wooden 37.00
Orphan Annie book, "In the Circus" 35.00
Orphan Annie book, "Little Orphan Annie and The Haunted House," by Harold Gray, first edition, 1928, Cupples & Leon, 86 pp. 40.00
Orphan Annie book, "Never Say Die" 35.00
Orphan Annie book, "Orphan Annie Gets Into Trouble," Whitman, 1938, 2½ x 3 5/8" 14.00
Orphan Annie booklet, "Secret Society Membership," 1937, 12 pp. ... 27.00
Orphan Annie Coin Collection Folder, 1937 .... 35.00
Orphan Annie coloring book, "Jr. Commando," 1943 .... 45.00
Orphan Annie cup & saucer, h.p. lustre china, 1930's 22.50
Orphan Annie decoder, 1935, Ovaltine premium 23.00
Orphan Annie decoder, 1936, Ovaltine premium, w/Secret Society manual 25.00
Orphan Annie decoder, 1937, Ovaltine premium 26.00

Orphan Annie Telematic Decoder

Orphan Annie decoder, "Telematic," 1938, Ovaltine premium (ILLUS.) .. 25.00
Orphan Annie decoder, 1939, Ovaltine premium 32.00
Orphan Annie decoder, 1940 .... 26.00
Orphan Annie decoder manual, 1935, radio premium 26.00
Orphan Annie decoder manual, 1937 .... 33.00
Orphan Annie game, "Treasure Hunt," Ovaltine premium, 1933, Wander Co. 58.00
Orphan Annie "ID" bracelet, 1930's 29.00
Orphan Annie jigsaw puzzle, Jaymar, 1940's 50.00
Orphan Annie jigsaw puzzle, Jaymar, 1950's 15.00

Orphan Annie knitting machine, wooden 25.00
Orphan Annie mug, plastic, Ovaltine premium, 3" h. 30.00
Orphan Annie nodding figure, bisque, Germany, 4" h. 97.00
Orphan Annie pinback button, celluloid, "Little Orphan Annie Loves Red Cross Macaroni," three-color, 1¼" d. 38.00
Orphan Annie pinback button, Pep premium 10.00
Orphan Annie pull-toy, wooden, Trixey, 12" l. 70.00

Orphan Annie Shake-Up Mug

Orphan Annie "shake-up" mug, Beetleware, w/orange cover, Ovaltine premium, 1935 (ILLUS.) .. 32.00
Orphan Annie sheet music, 1928, Chicago Tribune, 8 pp. 21.00
Orphan Annie token, "Good Luck" coin, "Radio Secret Society" 16.50
Orphan Annie toy electric stove, tin, red, chrome legs 82.00
Orphan Annie toy electric stove, tin, green & tan, 8½ x 9½" 42.00
Orphan Annie & Sandy ashtray, bisque, 1930's 74.00
Orphan Annie & Sandy nodding figures, bisque, impressed names on backs, 3¼" h. Annie & 2" h. Sandy, pr. 175.00
Orphan Annie & Sandy toothbrush holder, bisque .... 100.00 to 150.00
Orphan Annie & Sandy wall pocket vase, china, Annie & Sandy on white ground, tan pearlized trim, marked "Licensed by Famous Artists Syndicate, Made in Japan," 3" top d., 5¼" h. 92.00
Our Gang blotter, advertising "Mikado Pencils" 20.00
Our Gang book, "A Story of Our Gang," Whitman, 1929 .... 20.00
Our Gang coloring book, No. 966, 1938 (unused) 35.00
Our Gang film box & reel 20.00
Our Gang jigsaw puzzle, 11 x 14" .. 58.00
Our Gang pencil box, w/picture of Jackie, Chubby, Farina & dog 18.00
Our Gang pinback button, advertising "Maryland Theatre Komedy Klub" 75.00
Pappy Yokum (Li'l Abner) hand puppet 35.00
Pink Panther cel, Panther walking through empty sports stadium 120.00
Pinky Lee coloring book, "Health & Safety," 80 pp. 25.00
Popeye bagetelle game, 1935 .... 190.00
Popeye bank, dime register, copyright 1929, 2½" sq. 42.00
Popeye beanbags, pr. 15.00
Popeye Big Big Book, "Thimble Theater," 1935 .... 60.00
Popeye book, "Popeye Goes Duck Hunting," Whitman, 1937 .... 20.00
Popeye cereal bowl, 1935 .... 58.00
Popeye chalk crayons, 1954, box of 12 .... 22.50
Popeye Colorforms, set, 1957 .... 20.00
Popeye crayon set, tin box 15.00
Popeye dart board 25.00
Popeye doll, composition, jointed, signed "King Features Syndicate," 1935, 14" 300.00
Popeye egg cup, china, figural 120.00
Popeye figure, chalkware, 1929, 8" h. 35.00
Popeye figure, chalkware, 1933, stamped "K.F.S. Inc.," 10" h. 79.00
Popeye figure, chalkware, 14" h. 575.00
Popeye figure, wood-jointed, 1930's, 5½" h. 63.00
Popeye flashlight, whistling-type 100.00
Popeye fountain pen, King Features Syndicate, 1930's 40.00
Popeye game, "Pipe Toss," Rosebud Art Co., 1935, original box 25.00
Popeye game, "Ring Toss," King Features Syndicate, 1923 .... 45.00
Popeye game, "Skeet Shoot," late 1950's, original box 125.00
Popeye game, "Where's Me Pipe," 1930's, uncut in box 50.00
Popeye guitar 36.00
Popeye gun & holster set, on original card 90.00
Popeye hand puppet, Gund 12.00
Popeye mechanical pencil, 1929 .... 35.00
Popeye paddle wagon, Corgi (no box) 150.00
Popeye paint set, "Presto," Kenner, 1961 .... 32.50
Popeye pen & ink drawing, "Blow Me Down," in color, signed "Segar," 7½ x 10¼" 55.00
Popeye pencil box, cardboard, dated 1934, 4½ x 10½" 28.00

Popeye pencil sharpener, tin, dated 1929 .... 30.00
Popeye pistol, "Popeye Pirate Pistol," tin, by Marx Toy Co., King Features Syndicate, ca. 1935, 9½" l. ....175.00 to 200.00
Popeye pull-toy, Fisher-Price, 1933 .. 60.00
Popeye record player, like new, illustrated case 95.00
Popeye sand pail, lithographed tin, 1929-33 .... 65.00
Popeye soap figure, 1930's, 5" h. 45.00
Popeye tablecloth, paper, Tuttle Press Co., 36 x 72" 15.00
Popeye toothbrush, battery-operated 5.00
Popeye wallet, plastic, 3-D flicker-type 15.00
Popeye vase, bud, glazed ceramic, 1930's 45.00
Popeye wrist watch, Ingersoll 145.00
Popeye & Olive Oyl ball & jacks, 1950's 18.00
Porky Pig book, linen, Saalfield No. 2178, 1938 .... 50.00
Red Ranger clicker gun, tin, Wyandotte 10.00
Red Ranger holster, leather w/"jewel" 6.00
Red Ryder BB gun, Daisy Mfg., 1930's 38.00
Red Ryder game, "Target," Whitman Publishing Co., 1939 .... 25.00
Red Ryder flashlight 35.00
Rin Tin Tin figure, chalkware, 15½" 29.00
Rin Tin Tin hand puzzle, metal, "Rinny & Rusty" 12.50
Rin Tin Tin jigsaw puzzle 25.00
Rin Tin Tin pen, rifle-shaped, original mailer 40.00
Robin (Batman series) bank, ceramic, 1966 .... 45.00
Roy Rogers alarm clock, animated, Ingraham, 1951 .... 110.00
Roy Rogers archery set, w/box 45.00
Roy Rogers badge, "Deputy," star-shaped, copper 8.50
Roy Rogers badge, "Deputy Sheriff," gold-finished, w/secret compartment, mirror & whistle 40.00
Roy Rogers bank, pot metal, model of a cowboy boot on horseshoe base, 6" h 21.00
Roy Rogers belt buckle 65.00
Roy Rogers billfold, leather 35.00
Roy Rogers binoculars 30.00
Roy Rogers bolo tie, "Blinkin Bull," on original store display card 35.00
Roy Rogers book, "Raiders of Sawtooth Ridge," 1946 .... 8.00
Roy Rogers book, "Roy Rogers & The Gopher Creek Gunman," worn dust jacket, 1945 .... 10.00
Roy Rogers book, "Roy Rogers & Rimrod Renegades," 1952 .... 5.00
Roy Rogers book, "Trigger to the Rescue," 1950 .... 20.00
Roy Rogers camera, Herbert George Co., original box 25.00

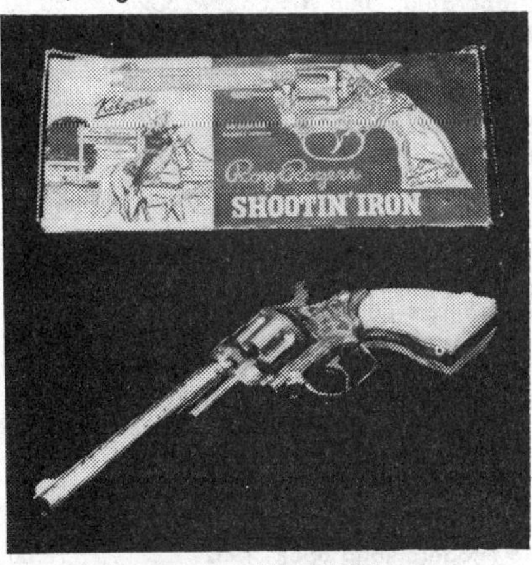

Roy Rogers Shootin' Iron

Roy Rogers cap gun, "Shootin' Iron," Kilgore Inc., Westerville, Ohio, 1953, original box (ILLUS.) 36.00
Roy Rogers cereal bowl, ceramic, Roy & Trigger shown 12.00
Roy Rogers chaps, Trigger shown, pr. 18.50
Roy Rogers cowboy outfit, original box 150.00
Roy Rogers creamer, F & F Mold & Die Works, Dayton, Ohio 15.50

Roy Rogers Flashlight

Roy Rogers flashlight, "Signal Siren," Usalite (ILLUS.) 38.00
Roy Rogers gloves, gauntlet-type, leather, pr. 40.00
Roy Rogers guitar, original case 70.00
Roy Rogers gum trading cards, black & white, set of 24 .... 20.00

Roy Rogers harmonica, on original card 25.00
Roy Rogers holster & gun set, leather holster & guns w/white handle grips, set 47.00
Roy Rogers lantern, tin, battery-operated, Ohio Art Co., w/box 50.00
Roy Rogers lunch box w/thermos bottle, "Double R Bar Ranch" metal box, ca. 1960 .... 22.00
Roy Rogers neckerchief 17.50
Roy Rogers paint book, 1948 .... 25.00
Roy Rogers photograph, autographed 30.00
Roy Rogers playing cards (unopened) 10.00
Roy Rogers pull-toy, lithographed paper on wood "Chuck Wagon," 1950's 145.00
Roy Rogers radio, Louis Marx & Co. 45.00
Roy Rogers repeating cap rifle, 26" 58.00
Roy Rogers rodeo program, 1947 .... 7.00
Roy Rogers song book, 1952 .... 12.00
Roy Rogers tent, 4 x 6 x 4' 150.00

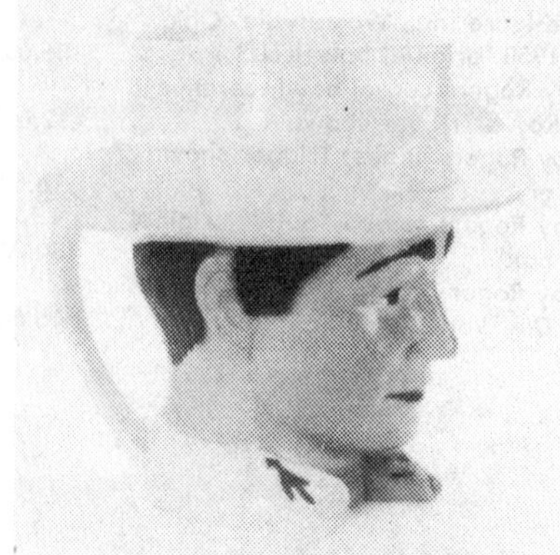

Roy Rogers Toby Mug

Roy Rogers toby mug, "F. & F. Mold & Die Wks, Dayton, Ohio," 4" h. (ILLUS.) 14.00
Roy Rogers toothbrush 25.00
Roy Rogers toy set: horse trailer, jeep & figures; Ideal, the set 95.00
Roy Rogers toy set, "Hartland" 155.00
Roy Rogers wrist watch, green face w/picture of Roy & Trigger, original brown leather band, Ingraham, 1951 .... 65.00
Roy Rogers & Dale Evans book, "River of Peril," 1957, written by Fannin, published by Whitman 45.00
Roy Rogers & Trigger pull-toy .... 150.00 to 200.00
Roy Rogers on Trigger lamp, plastic w/plaster base, very good original shade 136.00

Rudolph the Red-Nosed Reindeer paperweight, snow-type 22.00
Rudolph the Red-Nosed Reindeer rain cape 13.00
Sally Rand (fan dancer) souvenir program & photo 25.00
Sergeant Bilko (TV character) coloring book 15.00
Sergeant Preston whistle, 1949 .... 17.50
Shield G-Man ring, 1940 .... 14.00
Shirley Temple book, "Dimples," 1936 .... 20.00
Shirley Temple book, "Heidi," movie version, 1st edition, 1937 .... 25.00
Shirley Temple book, "How I Raised Shirley Temple," by her mother, 1935, 40 pp. 25.00
Shirley Temple book, "In Starring Roles," 1936 .... 20.00
Shirley Temple book, "The Little Colonel" 20.00
Shirley Temple book, "The Littlest Rebel" 15.00
Shirley Temple book, "Now I Am Eight," Saalfield, 1937 .... 26.00
Shirley Temple book, "On the Movie Lot," 1936 .... 20.00
Shirley Temple book, "Poor Little Rich Girl," 1936 .... 25.00
Shirley Temple book, "Shirley Temple's Favorite Poems," Saalfield Publishing Co., 1936 .... 18.00
Shirley Temple book, "Shirley Temple at Play," Saalfield, 1935, eight full-page color illustrations, 18 pp. 10 x 12½" 30.00
Shirley Temple book, "Shirley Temple in Stowaway," 1937 .... 20.00
Shirley Temple book, "The Shirley Temple Treasury," 1959 .... 18.00
Shirley Temple book, "Spirit of Dragonwood," 1945, w/dust jacket 20.00
Shirley Temple book w/dust jacket, "Susannah of the Mounties," Dowd, Mead Co., Random House, New York, 1936 .... 10.00
Shirley Temple book, "Thru the Day," 1936 .... 27.00
Shirley Temple (cereal) bowl, cobalt blue glass w/decal portrait of Shirley 45.00
Shirley Temple breakfast set: cereal bowl, mug & pitcher; cobalt blue glass, 3 pcs. .... 100.00 to 140.00
Shirley Temple cigarette card, Mitchell, 1935 .... 10.00
Shirley Temple doll carriage, wicker 365.00
Shirley Temple doll's pinback button, "The World's Darling - Genuine Shirley Temple Doll," picture & signature, 1¼" d. 35.00

Shirley Temple dress tag, paper, 1930's, 3 x 5" 10.00
Shirley Temple figure, salt-glazed pottery, 6" h. 32.00
Shirley Temple dress, size 10 .... 45.00
Shirley Temple hair styler, Gabriel .. 50.00
Shirley Temple hanger, wooden, w/head & face, holds 1935 tagged Shirley Temple dress 59.00
Shirley Temple mirror, pocket-type, photo on pink ground, Fox Films, 1935, 1¾" d. 30.00
Shirley Temple pocketbook, 1934, original tags 100.00
Shirley Temple record, "The Good Ship Lollipop," Golden Records, Shirley on cover 18.00
Shirley Temple scrapbook full of 1930's clippings 95.00
Shirley Temple soap figure 52.00
Shirley Temple song album, "Sing with Shirley Temple," 1935, w/pictures 45.00
Shirley Temple stationery box, w/heavy cardboard Shirley cut-out on top, 1936 .... 17.50
Shirley Temple trunk for doll clothes 65.00

CHILDREN'S BOOKS

"The Tale of Johnny Town-Mouse"

The most collectible children's books today tend to be those printed after the 1850's and, while age is not completely irrelevant, illustrations play a far more important role in determining the values. While first editions are highly esteemed, it is the beautifully illustrated books that most collectors seek. The following books, all in good to fine condition, were sold within the past twelve months.

"A Child's Book of Country Stories," illustrated by Jessie Willcox Smith, 1935 .... $18.00
"Adventures of Huckleberry Finn," by Mark Twain (Samuel Clemens), New York, 1885, first American edition 1,500.00
"Billy Whiskers Travels," by Frances Montgomery, six color illustrations by Williams, published by Saalfield, 1907 .... 15.00
"The Black Arrow," by Robert Louis Stevenson, nine color illustrations by N. C. Wyeth, published by Scribners, 1927 .... 25.00
"The Children's Book," by Frances Hodgson Burnett, illustrated, 1915, first edition 19.50
"Daughter of the Land," by Gene Stratton Porter, 1918, first edition 20.00
"Dr. Doolittle's Garden," by Hugh Lofting, 1927 .... 18.00
"Eric of Sweden," by Madeline Brandeis, illustrated, 1938 .... 3.00
"Frawg," by Annie Vaughn Weaver, 1930 .... 125.00
"Hans Brinker," by Mary Mapes Dodge, color illustrations by Alice Carsey, 1917 .... 29.50
"Happy Jack Squirrel Helps Unc' Billy," by Thornton Burgess, 1927 ... 7.50
"Helen's Babies," by John Habberton, illustrated, 1908, engraved cover 12.50
"Jack, the Giant Killer," shape book, published by McLoughlin, 1895 .... 12.00
"The Jolly Jump-Ups See The Circus," pop-up type, published by McLoughlin Bros., 1944, six pop-ups, 7½ x 10½" 45.00
"Koko's Circus," illustrated by Hank Hart, 1942 .... 27.50
"Laddie: A True Blue Story," by Gene Stratton Porter, 1913 .... 12.00
"The Land of Oz," by L. Frank Baum, 1932, w/dust jacket 35.00
"Lightfoot the Deer," by Thornton W. Burgess, 1921, published by Little Brown & Co., Boston, first edition 37.50
"Little Black Sambo," six full page color illustrations by Fern Bisel Peat, 1931, 10 x 13" 45.00
"Little Susie Sunbonnet," eleven color illustrations, published by Cupples & Leon Company, 1907 ...... 125.00
"Mary Poppins," by P.L. Travers, illustrated by Mary Shephard, 1934 .... 15.00
"Nancy Drew & The Clue of the Broken Locket," by Caroline Keene, w/dust jacket 10.00

"Now-A-Days Fairy Book," by Chapin, color illustrations by Jessie Willcox Smith, 12 x 15" 75.00
"Old Dutch Nursery Rhymes," by H. Willebeek Le Mair, England, 1917, dedicated to Royal Highness Juliana Wilhelmina 18.75
"Ozma of Oz," by L. Frank Baum, 1907 .... 35.00
"Peter Pan in Kensington Gardens," by Sir James M. Barrie, 15 color illustrations by Arthur Rackham, published by Scribners, 1912 .... 43.00
"Rebecca of Sunnybrook Farm," by Kate Douglas Wiggin, 1903, first edition 35.00
"Rip Van Winkle," by Washington Irving, 24 color illustrations by Arthur Rackham, 1917 .... 65.00
"Rollo on the Atlantic," by Jacob Abbot, engraved illustrations, 1853 .... 39.50
"Royal Book of Oz," by L. Frank Baum, 12 color illustrations by J. R. Neill, 1921, first edition 100.00
"Sports & Play Times," illustrated by Frances Brundage, published by Saalfield, 1910 .... 25.00
"The Tadwinkle Twins," illustrated by Florence Williams, Saalfield No. 2050, 1920 .... 20.00
"The Tale of Johnny Town-Mouse," by Beatrix Potter, published by F. Warne & Co., Ltd., 1918, 4 x 5¾" (ILLUS.) 28.00
"The Ten Virgins," illustrated by Frances Brundage, published by Raphael Tuck, from Father Tuck's "Parable Series" 65.00
"Three Little Pigs," animated by Julian Wehr, published by Animated Book Co., N.Y., 1944 .... 15.00

"Toby Tyler"

"Toby Tyler or Ten Weeks with a Circus," by James Otis, illustrated by Everett Shinn, 1937 (ILLUS.) 4.50
"Treasure Island," by Robert Louis Stevenson, color illustrations & cover by Edmund Dulac, 1931, 287 pp. 18.00
"The Water Babies," by Charles Kingsley, illustrated by Jessie Willcox Smith, 1916 .... 65.00
"The Wonderful Story Book," illustrations by Frances Brundage, published by Saalfield, 1925 .... 30.00
"Young Folks Travels in Asia & Africa," black & white illustrations, 1889, 304 pp. 9.00

CHILDREN'S DISHES

Bead & Scroll Table Set

During the reign of Queen Victoria, doll houses and accessories became more popular and as the century progressed, there was greater demand for toys which would subtly train a little girl in the art of homemaking. Also see DEPRESSION and PATTERN GLASS.

Baking set, pressed glass, "Glasbake," McKee, 9 pcs. in original box $50.00
Banana boat, pressed glass, Zipper patt., clear 45.00
Banana bowl, pressed glass, Eyewinker patt., clear 22.00
Berry set: master bowl & four sauce dishes; pressed glass, Lacy Daisy patt., clear, 5 pcs. 50.00
Berry set: master bowl & six sauce dishes; pressed glass, Fine Cut Panel patt., clear, 7 pcs. 110.00
Butter dish, cov., pressed glass, Beaded Swirl patt., clear 35.00
Butter dish, cov., pressed glass, Block patt., clear 20.00
Butter dish, cov., pressed glass, Menagerie patt., amber (small chip on inner rim fitting into bottom) 1,100.00
Butter dish, cov., pressed glass, Tappan patt., clear 25.00

Cake stand, pressed glass, Arrowhead in Ovals patt., clear 20.00
Cake stand, pressed glass, Baby Thumbprint patt., clear, 4 1/8" d., 3" h. 125.00
Candlestick, blue opaque glass, Dutch Boudoir patt. (single) 145.00
Canister set: "Rice," "Barley," "Sugar" & "Beans" containers, pitcher & hanging salt; china, gold & white, 6 pcs. 115.00
Celery dish, pressed glass, Lacy Daisy patt., clear 23.00
Chocolate set: 6" h. cov. chocolate pot, creamer & cov. sugar bowl; china, floral decor, probably Germany, 3 pcs. 75.00
Compote, open, carnival glass, 8-panel, clear base, marigold shallow bowl, 4¾" d., 2" h. 150.00
Compote, open, pressed glass, Baby Thumbprint patt., clear 160.00
Condiment & spice set, 3 1/8" h. tea, sugar, flour, rice & oatmeal containers, 2¼" h. cinnamon, nutmeg, allspice, cloves, ginger & pepper containers & one hanging salt box; china, Germany, 12 pcs. 160.00
Creamer, china, Blue Willow patt., Japan 10.00
Creamer, china, elephant decoration, around top, Nippon, 3½" h. 14.00
Creamer & cov. sugar bowl, china, Azalea patt., Noritake, pr. 175.00
Cup, china, Punch and Judy patt., Allertons 14.00
Cup & saucer, china, Garden Sports patt., Staffordshire 20.00
Cup & saucer, china, Happifats decor, Royal Rudolstadt 50.00
Dinner service for 6, plus cov. teapot, sugar, creamer, platter & cov. vegetable dish, china, Blue Willow patt. 200.00
Honey jug, pressed glass, Duncan & Miller No. 42, clear 25.00
Ice cream set: tray & six individual dishes; Frances Ware, 7 pcs. 250.00
Loving cup, pressed glass, Jewel in Heart patt., clear, 2½" h. 30.00
Mustard, pressed glass, Menagerie patt., bear, clear 295.00
Pepper shaker, pressed glass, English Hobnail patt., clear 8.00
Pitcher, pressed glass, Hobnail patt., blue 28.00
Pitcher, water, pressed glass, Nursery Rhyme patt., clear, 4¼" h. 65.00
Plate, ironstone, Forget-Me-Not patt., all white 16.00
Plate, pressed glass, Wee Branches patt., clear, 3 1/8" d. 55.00
Punch set: punch bowl & five cups; pressed glass, Flattened Diamond & Fan patt., clear, 6 pcs. 125.00
Sauce dishes, pressed glass, Patee Cross patt., clear, set of 6 .... 37.00
Spooner, milk white glass, Wild Rose patt. 50.00
Spooner, pressed glass, Arrowhead in Ovals patt., clear 18.00
Spooner, pressed glass, Oval Star patt., clear 20.00
Spooner, pressed glass, Rooster patt., clear 152.00
Sugar bowl, cov., pressed glass, Pert patt., clear 65.00
Sugar bowl, cov., pressed glass, Tappan patt., amber 25.00
Table set: cov. butter dish, creamer & cov. sugar bowl; pressed glass, Buzz Star patt., clear, 3 pcs. 80.00
Table set: cov. butter dish, cov. sugar bowl, creamer & spooner; pressed glass, Bead & Scroll patt., clear, 4 pcs. (ILLUS.) 275.00
Table set, pressed glass, Colonial patt., Cambridge Glass Co., green, 4 pcs. 110.00
Table set, pressed glass, Wee Branches patt., clear, 4 pcs. 355.00
Teapot, cov., china, Boy on Bench decoration, marked "Germany" ... 50.00
Tea set: cov. teapot, cov. sugar bowl, waste bowl & three handleless cups & saucers; white ironstone, J. & G. Meakin, England, 9 pcs. 55.00
Tea set: cov. teapot, cov. sugar bowl, creamer, four cups & saucers & four plates; china, Blue Willow patt., Occupied Japan, 15 pcs. 115.00
Tumbler, pressed glass, Fancy Cut patt., clear 12.00
Tumbler, pressed glass, Wheat Sheaf patt., clear 6.00
Water set: pitcher & four tumblers; pressed glass, Galloway patt., clear, 5 pcs. 40.00
Water set: pitcher & six fluted tumblers; pressed glass, Portland Maiden Blush patt., 7 pcs. 220.00

CHILDREN'S MUGS

The small size mug used by children first attempting to drink from a cup, appeals to many collectors. Because they were made of china, glass, pottery, graniteware, plated silver and silver, the collector is given the opportunity to assemble a diversified collection or to single out one particular type of decoration, such as Franklin Maxims, or a specific material, such as glass, around which to base his collection. Also see PATTERN GLASS.

"Hickory Dickory Dock" Mug

China, alphabet-type, "O" & "P," "O was an organ man leading an ape," "P was a pedlar w/ribbons & tape," corresponding pictures . . $135.00
China, blue transfer scene of boys at play, applied handle, footed, 2½" d., 2 3/8" h. 60.00
China, transfer scene of girl & duck in bonnets w/basket of colored eggs decoration, Nippon, 2½" h. 75.00
China, polychrome transfer of Cowboy scene 140.00
China, polychrome transfer scene of three kittens 140.00
China, transfer print of "Hickory Dickory Dock," young child, mouse & cuckoo clock (ILLUS.) 25.00
China, transfer print of "The Chase," dressed duckling chasing butterfly 25.00
Coin silver, engraved "Eliz. Goldsmith, April 1860" 195.00
Milk white glass, Gooseberry patt., 1 7/8" h. 30.00
Pressed glass, Boy/Girl patt., embossed childrens' faces, girl on one side, boy on other, Findlay Glass, amber 36.00
Pressed glass, Buster Brown & Tige patt., clear, 2¼" h. 45.00
Pressed glass, Cats Fighting patt., clear 32.00
Pressed glass, Daisy & Button w/V Ornament patt., amber 20.00
Pressed glass, Dewey patt., vaseline 35.00
Pressed glass, "Our Boy," w/monkey riding pig patt., amber, 3¼" 42.00
Pressed glass, Thousand Eye patt., amber 55.00
Redware, slant side handle, brown to rust glaze, ca. 1810, 2½ x 3" (fleck on rim) 75.00
Silver plate, embossed border of flowers, beading & vertical ribbing at base, Gorham 28.00
Staffordshire pottery, blue transfer scene of children in woods 38.00
Staffordshire pottery, pearlware, iron-red transfer bust portrait of George Washington flanked by shield-emblazoned eagles bearing ribbons in their beaks inscribed "E Pluribus Unum" beneath 17 stars, rim & handle w/iron-red detail, ca. 1820, 2½" h. 1,760.00
Staffordshire pottery, red transfer harbor scene 29.95
Sterling silver, engraved "Edna," Wood & Hughes 175.00

CHRISTMAS TREE LIGHTS

Along with a host of other Christmas-related items, early Christmas tree lights are attracting a growing number of collectors. Comic characters seem to be the most popular form among the wide variety of figural lights available, most of which were manufactured between 1920 and World War II in Germany, Japan and the United States. Figural bulbs listed are painted clear glass unless otherwise noted.

BULBS

Aviator, milk white, painted $35.00
Ball w/stars, blue 15.00
Bird, 4" l. 14.00
Bird, red, small 9.00
Bluebird 10.00
Candy canes, set of three 45.00
Cat, begging, milk white, painted . . 45.00
Child's face 15.00
Chinese lantern, milk white, painted 10.00
Cross w/star, milk white, painted . . 25.00
Doll head 45.00
Elephant, milk white, painted 25.00
Frog, paint worn 18.00
Girl holding rose 18.00
Girl in flower bud 35.00
Grape cluster 10.00
House, milk white, painted 12.00
King w/two blackbirds, milk white, painted 35.00
Kitten in boot 30.00
Lantern 9.00
Little Boy Blue, milk white, painted 35.00
Little Red Riding Hood, embossed scene on milk white ball 65.00

Moon Mullins, milk white, painted .. 45.00
Old Woman in the Shoe, milk white, painted 25.00
Rose 10.00
Sailor, 2 7/8" h. 5.00
Santa Claus face, 2½" h. 25.00
Santa w/ski poles, Barclay 35.00
Santa on sled, Barclay 30.00
Snowflake, tin reflector w/colored bulb, Nippon 30.00
Snowman w/holly sprig, milk glass 8.00
Star, milk white, painted 11.00
Three Bears, milk white 20.00
Three Men in a Tub, milk white, painted 55.00

SETS

NOMA (National Outfit Manufacturers Association) "Bubble Lites," original box, set of 10 .... 30.00
NOMA "Katzenjammer Kids," set of standard series bulbs w/plastic bell-shaped caps depicting cartoon characters, King Features, original box, the set 90.00
NOMA "Popeye," set of seven standard series bulbs w/plastic bell-shaped caps depicting cartoon characters, King Features, 1930's, original box 80.00
Reliance Toyland Christmas lights, six working bulbs on string, original box 100.00
Sail-Me Company, "Whirl-Glo Shades," revolving paper cone-shaped shades, each depicts different scene including Santa Claus, Chicago, ca. 1936, set of 10 .... 15.00
"Scrappy" set, string of standard series bulbs w/plastic bell-shaped caps depicting cartoon characters, 1930's, original box 185.00
Star reflectors for bulbs, tin, set of six 40.00

CANDLE LIGHTS

Candle light, hanging-type, inverted bell-shaped mold-blown glass, diamond pattern, aqua 50.00
Candle light, hanging-type, inverted bell-shaped mold-blown glass, diamond pattern, cobalt blue ....75.00 to 125.00
Candle light, hanging-type, inverted bell-shaped mold-blown glass, diamond pattern, light amethyst .. 55.00
Candle light, hanging-type, inverted bell-shaped mold-blown glass, broken-swirl ribbed pattern, medium green 125.00

CHRISTMAS TREE ORNAMENTS

Foxy Grandpa Ornament

The German blown glass Christmas tree ornaments and other commercially-made ornaments of wax, cardboard and cotton batting were popular from the time they were first offered for sale in the United States in the 1870's. Prior to that time, Christmas trees had been decorated with homemade ornaments that usually were edible. Now nostalgic collectors who seek out ornaments that sold for pennies in stores across the country in the early years of this century are willing to pay some rather hefty prices for unusual or early ornaments.

Angel, blown glass, painted, German, 1930's $6.50
Angel, wax, w/mohair wig & spun glass wings 45.00
Angel & Santa, angel hair circle w/embossed paper scraps, 5½" d. 90.00
Automobile, coupe, blown glass, silver w/red & gold, 7 7/8" l. 65.00
Baby in buggy, blown glass 220.00
Baby rattle, barrel-shaped, blown glass 35.00
Basket of fruit, blown glass 12.00
Bear w/muff, blown glass 95.00
Bell, milk white glass, embossed figural two-faced Santa 22.00
Bell, Dresden-type cardboard, w/tinsel & sheer tuck trim, Victorian... 45.00
Bird, blown glass, spring clip, Victorian 20.00
Butterfly, composition body, glass wings 75.00
Cat in bag, blown glass 220.00
Cat in shoe, blown glass 65.00
Church, sand pebbled cardboard, paper label, "Made in Czechoslovakia" 35.00

Christmas tree, blown glass, spring clip, Victorian 45.00
Clown face w/pointed hat, blown glass, silver w/red & gold, 3 5/8" h. 35.00
Cockatoo, blown glass 25.00
Cottage, blown glass 10.00
Dove on 6" perch, beaded glass w/hanging loop, apple in mouth, beaded date "1910," 8" 55.00
Ear of corn, blown glass, gold, 3¾" h. ....50.00 to 75.00
Fish, blown glass, gold, large 75.00
Fish, Dresden-type cardboard, 4" 25.00
Flying crane, blown glass, blue wings 50.00
Foxy Grandpa, blown glass (ILLUS.) ....175.00 to 275.00
Girl in beehive, blown glass 55.00
Girl's face in rose, blown glass 50.00
Grape cluster, blown glass, silver, embossed brass hanger, 7" l. 225.00
Grape cluster, Dresden-type cardboard, large 20.00
Hot air balloon, blown glass, w/wire tinsel supports, glass & die-cut cupid 45.00
Hot air balloon, Dresden-type cardboard w/die-cut angel, pink, 6" h. 50.00
Icicle, cotton batting 40.00
Japanese lantern, milk white glass 12.00
Kugel (blown glass ball), amber, 10" d. 260.00
Kugel, gold, 2½" d. 18.00
Kugel, silver, 4" d. 45.00
Kugel, green, 10" 290.00
Mandolin, tinsel & paper scrap trim, Lauscha, Germany 45.00
Mandolin, wax 15.00
Man on bicycle, die-cut paper, tinsel & die-cut flowers trim 15.00
Mushroom, blown glass, tinsel basket, Germany 32.50
Owl, blown glass 55.00
Parrot, milk white glass 20.00
Peach, blown glass, 2¾" l. 40.00
Peacock, blown glass, silver w/polychrome trim & angel hair tail, spring clip, 5" l. 15.00
Pear, cotton, pink & white, 2½" 15.00
Pelican, blown glass 55.00
Rabbit eating carrot, blown glass 50.00
Reindeer, Dresden-type cardboard, pulling crepe paper sleigh 125.00
Rose bud, blown glass, fabric stamen, unsilvered, spring clip 95.00
Sailboat, blown glass, tinsel wire-wrapped, Victorian 50.00
Sailboat, Dresden-type cardboard, pink & silver 20.00
Santa Claus, blown glass, silver face, beard, white sparkle mustache, red hat & jacket, green tree under arm, 3" h. 24.00
Skier, cotton batting 45.00
Snow White & Seven Dwarfs, Snow White painted white, Dwarfs solid colors, original box 500.00
Spatter glass, blown glass ball, blue & white stripes w/silver iridescence in controlled spirals, Corning, New York, 1908, 2" d. 85.00
Spider on a pear, blown glass, silver w/red & gold, 3" h. 75.00

Celluloid Star Ornament

Star, molded celluloid, multicolored trim, Germany, pre-World War II (ILLUS.) 12.50
Teapot, blown glass 8.00
Tomato, Dresden-type cardboard 97.50
Umbrella, closed, blown glass, 10" l. 20.00
Watermelon slice, Dresden-type cardboard 90.00

CIGAR & CIGARETTE CASES, HOLDERS & LIGHTERS

Cigar case, silver plate, hinged three-compartment case, scroll engraving on both sides, gold-washed interior $38.00
Cigar holder, meerschaum, carved full figure hunter w/dog 175.00
Cigar lighter, counter-type, brass base, ruby red glass shade, 9¾" h. (ILLUS.) 285.00
Cigar lighter, counter-type, model of a lamp, "Counsellor" 850.00
Cigarette case, advertising, "Harley Davidson," w/skull & wings logo 55.00

Counter-type Cigar Lighter

Cigarette case, gold, rectangular w/rounded sides, overall reeding, Cyrillic maker's mark "P.P.," Russia, ca. 1910, 3¾" l. 1,870.00

Cigarette case, silver & enamel, oblong w/rounded corners, hinged cover & base mounted w/various charms, monograms & regimental devices, including a horseshoe centering a diamond, elephants & the Imperial Eagle set w/a faceted red stone, I. P. Smirnov, Moscow, ca. 1900, 4" l 1,870.00

Russian Enameled Cigarette Case

Cigarette case, silver-gilt w/shaded enameling in colorful scrolling foliage on sky blue ground, Moscow, ca. 1900, 3 5/8" l. (ILLUS.) 1,320.00

Cigarette case, stainless steel, lid engraved w/map of England, marked "Made in England" 28.00

Cigarette case, sterling silver, marked "Napier" 75.00

Cigarette case, lady's, Art Deco style, hammered sterling silver inlaid w/bands of yellow & pink 14k gold, sterling silver chain link handle, marked "Bliss" 145.00

Cigarette holder, 14k gold & Bakelite, 1930's 30.00

Cigarette holder, ivory, carved florals, 1930's 35.00

Cigarette holder, ivory, carved w/entwined snake, 1930's 30.00

Cigarette lighter, advertising, "Dow Oven Cleaner," can-shaped w/lighter on top 12.00

Cigarette lighter, advertising, "Oscar Mayer Epicure Lard," Zippo . . . 26.50

Cigarette lighter, aluminum, Art Deco style, "Automet," w/original box 100.00

Cigarette lighter, cast iron, model of Boston bulldog, electric, 5" l. 165.00

Cigarette lighter, chrome, Art Deco style airplane on pedestal base . . . 35.00

Cigar lighter, table model, copper, in the form of an Oriental teapot-shaped lamp w/cast dragon handle, reeded domed cover & spout w/wick-holder, applied w/a silver Oriental figure juggling & floral sprig, Gorham Manufacturing Co., Providence, 1882, 5" l., 2 3/8" h. 176.00

CIGAR & TOBACCO CUTTERS

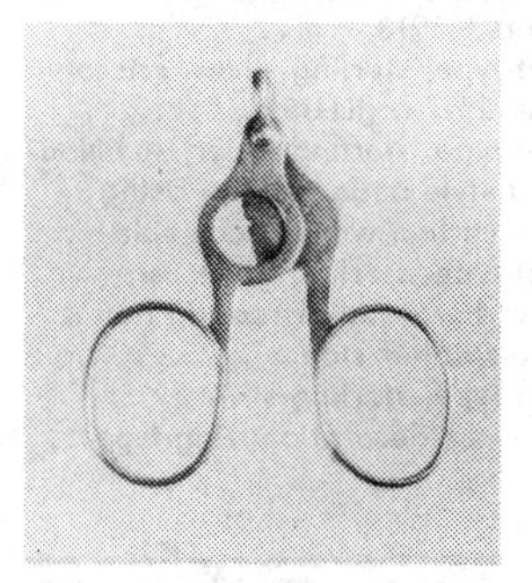

Scissors-type Cigar Cutter

Both counter-type and individual cigar and plug tobacco cutters were in widespread use last century and earlier in this century. Some counter types were made in combination with lighters and vending machines and were used to promote various tobacco packaging companies.

Counter-type, cast iron advertising, "Brown & Williamson" $65.00

Counter-type, cast iron, advertising, "Brown's Mule Tobacco, R.J. Reynolds Tobacco Co." 40.00

Counter-type, cast iron, advertising, "Five Bros. Tobacco Works, John

Finzer & Bros., Louisville, Ky." (minor rust) 68.00
Counter-type, cast iron, advertising, "Robert Burns Cigars" 250.00
Counter-type, cast iron, advertising, "Wilson & McGallay Tobacco Co.," model of a guillotine 150.00
Counter-type, cast iron, advertising, "Wm. Wrigley Jr. & Co.," roller-type 190.00
Counter-type, cast iron, model of a bulldog on stand, "Merriam," 1900, 3 x 5 x 6" 450.00
Counter-type, cast iron, "Standard Cutter" by "Reading Hardware Co." .... 40.00 to 50.00
Counter-type, cast iron, "Tobacco Shaver" by "Enterprise Mfg. Co., Philadelphia," three-footed 36.00
Counter-type, cutter & lighter, cast white metal figure of standing newsboy by street lamp, cigar cutter in base, top burner w/white globe used for "lighting-up," marked "Extra, John Anderson & Co.," worn brass finish, 21¾" h. including globe 650.00
Desk model, "Enterprise Tobacco Co., Philadelphia, Pennsylvania," ca. 1871 .... 45.00
Pocket-type, advertising, "Dodge/Plymouth," 1940's 18.00
Pocket-type, advertising, "El-Roi-Tan Cigars," 1913 .... 32.00
Pocket-type, sterling silver, scissors-type, 2¾" l. (ILLUS.) 38.00
Pocket-type, sterling silver, Art Nouveau style nude maiden rising from curling waves each side 50.00
Pocket-type, sterling silver, engraved w/head of roaring lion & florals either side 48.00
Pocket-type, sterling silver, repousse decoration, ring-type 35.00

CIRCUS COLLECTIBLES

The romance of the "Big Top," stirred by memories of sawdust, spangles, thrills and chills, has captured the imagination of the American public for over 100 years. Though the heyday of the traveling circus is now past, dedicated collectors and fans of all ages eagerly seek out choice memorabilia from the late 19th and early 20th centuries, the "golden age" of circuses.

Book, "The Circus Annual Route Book of Ringling Bros.," 1897 season $50.00
Book, "Cole Bros. Official Route Book," 1937 season 35.00
Book, "Facing The Big Cats," by Clyde Beatty 10.00
Book, "Pictorial History of the American Circus," Durant, 1957 .... 40.00
Book, "Ringling Bros. and Barnum & Bailey Spectacular 'Glittery' Bicentennial," 4-part center spread about Gunther Gebel 23.00
Christmas card, Ringling Bros. and Barnum & Bailey, 12 x 6" 35.00
Magazine, "Magazine of Wonders," Ringling Bros. and Barnum & Bailey, 1928, all photographs, 24 pp. 40.00
Magazine, "Ringling Bros. Circus Magazine," includes full page color ads for Coca-Cola, Borden's 'Elsie,' Philip Morris' 'Johnny,' Chesterfields, 1943 .... 25.00
Pennant, felt, Ringling Bros., 1930's 27.50
Postcard, Ringling Bros. residence, ballroom, in color 8.00
Poster, Christiana Bros., circus logo, 1950's, 41" w., 27" h. 25.00
Poster, Christiana Bros., girls (3) on trapeze, 1950's, 40" w., 55" h. 45.00
Poster, self-framed, Ringling Bros. World's Greatest Shows, pictures "The 4 McCrees, America's Foremost Equestrians" in upper corner on horses & dogs, copyright 1910 by Strobridge Litho Co., 24 x 18" 175.00

P.T. Barnum Circus Print

Print, "P.T. Barnum's New and Greatest Show on Earth coming by Four Special Trains," hand-colored lithograph, published by H.A. Thomas & Co., New York (stained, small tears in margins, two extending into image, laid down), late 19th c., 17¼ x 25½" (ILLUS.) .... 300.00 to 350.00
Program, Barnum & Bailey, 1914, "Wizard Prince of Arabia" 45.00

Uniform: jacket w/"Big Top" patch on shoulder, red & black corded material w/yellow piping and hat w/visor, "Ringling Bros.," 2 pcs. . . 90.00

CLOCKS

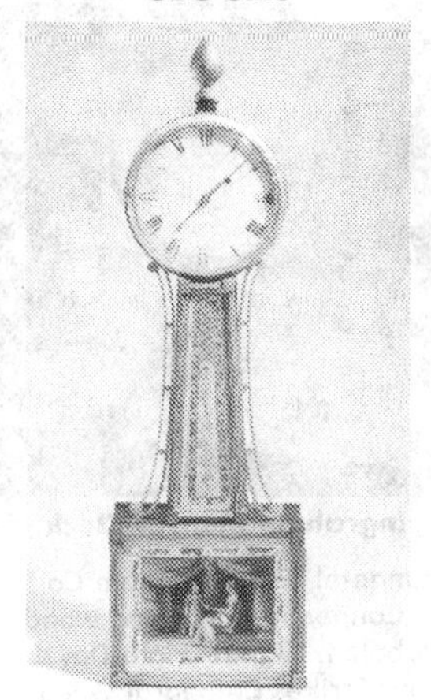

Aaron Willard Banjo Clock

Animated, United Electric Co., Brooklyn, New York, white metal case w/metal figure of Franklin D. Roosevelt standing at helm of ship, 15" h. $138.00

Banjo, Aaron Willard, Boston, Massachusetts, drum clock w/white-painted dial w/inscription "Willard Jr. Boston, No. 1772," surmounted by giltwood pointed ball finial, mahogany case w/"eglomise" panel in throat flanked by brass fillets above "eglomise" panel in lower door depicting young woman & child within drapery surrounds centering an oculus, stamped "A. Willard, Jr. Boston" on front plate of brass works, ca. 1825, 32¾" h. (ILLUS.) 18,700.00

Banjo, Simon Willard, Boston, Massachusetts, mahogany, brass urn finial above brass-hinged glazed door opening to white-painted dial w/faint inscription over tapering mahogany throat centering "eglomise" panel inscribed "Willard's Patent," above rectangular hinged door centering an "eglomise" panel depicting "The Constitution," and "The Guerriere," ca. 1810, 33½" h. (restorations to paint) 1,320.00

Banjo, attributed to Simon Willard, Roxbury, Massachusetts, drum clock w/white-painted dial w/Roman numerals & brass spire finial, w/"eglomise" panel in throat flanked by gilt gesso spandrels & marked "Willard's Patent," lower door w/reverse painting, early 19th c., 39" h. 1,760.00

Bracket, John Grant, Fleet Street, London, circular enamel dial within brass bezel, satinwood paneled arched case surmounted by brass urn finial, w/original bracket, George III period, last quarter 18th c., 9 x 5", 20½" h. 5,000.00

China case, Ansonia Clock Co., Ansonia, Connecticut, "LaVergne" model, No. 630, Royal Bonn china case 500.00

China case, Ansonia Clock Co., Ansonia, Connecticut, time & strike movement, porcelain dial, cobalt blue china case w/gilt florals 600.00

Double dial calendar, Ithaca Calendar Clock Co., Ithaca, New York, H.P. Horton's Patent 1866, 8-day brass weight driven calendar movement, upper dial inscribed "Becker Lathrop" (merchants), walnut case w/broken pediment crest centered by turned urn finial, 45" h. 1,750.00

Grandfather, Elliot, oak case, Westminster & Whittington chimes, retailed by Tiffany & Co., ca. 1890 . . . . 8,360.00

Grandfather, J. Hansell, Philadelphia, white-painted dial w/maker's name, rocking ship, sweep second & calendar dial flanked by spandrels w/cornucopiae, mahogany Empire-style case w/molded swan's neck pediment above glazed arched cupboard door over dial, flanked by spiral reeded colonettes over waisted case w/thumb-molded cupboard door flanked by spiral reeded colonettes above box base, ring-turned feet, 22¼" w., 97" h. . . . 4,620.00

Grandfather, Joseph & John Hollingshead, Burlington, New Jersey, brass dial w/calendar aperture & painted moon dial flanked by gilt spandrels signed by maker, Chippendale-style mahogany hooded case centering three urn-shaped finials above arched door flanked by columns, waist w/cupboard door flanked by fluted quarter columns, molded base, ogee bracket feet, 19" w., 98" h. 12,100.00

Grandfather, John Parry, Philadelphia, white-painted dial w/minute & date registers, phases of the moon & maker's name, mahogany hooded case in Federal style w/swan's neck cresting above arched door flanked by turned columns, waist w/molded door, base w/fluted quarter columns, bracket feet, ca. 1800, 96" h. (restoration to backboard, terminals of hood & paint on dial) 3,850.00

Grandfather, Gustav Stickley, oak, beveled overhanging cornice above square glass door & round brass dial, recessed side panels w/block "S" cut-out over paneled sides, long rectangular glass door revealing pendulum, weights & chime, straight apron & canted feet, branded mark, ca. 1910, 21½" w., 70¾" h. (refinished, numerals 8 & 9 missing) 5,500.00

Grandfather, Aaron Willard, Boston, Massachusetts, white-painted dial w/minute register & maker's name, inlaid mahogany hooded Federal-style case w/arched cresting centering three brass ball & steeple finials & colonettes flanking hinged door to dial, waist w/molded cross-banded door flanked by brass-fitted quarter columns, cross-banded base, bracket feet, ca. 1800, 95" h. (losses & some retouching to paint on dial) 6,875.00

Grandfather, Aaron Willard, Boston, Massachusetts, white-painted dial w/minute register & maker's name & w/painting of lady mourning Washington in arched top, inlaid mahogany hooded Federal-style case w/arched crest centering three brass ball & steeple finials, hinged door to dial flanked by brass-fitted colonettes, waist w/line-inlaid door flanked by fluted brass-fitted quarter columns, line-inlaid base, ogee bracket feet, ca. 1800, 94" h. (restoration to crest & feet) 14,300.00

Jeweler's wall regulator, Gilbert Clock Co., Bristol & Winsted, Connecticut, Model No. 20, oak case, porcelain dial, lyre-form brass pendulum, 6' 11" h. 3,895.00

Jeweler's wall regulator, E.N. Welch Manufacturing Co., Bristol, Connecticut, Model No. 11, 3-day movement, oak case 995.00

Kitchen, Waterbury Clock Co., Waterbury, Connecticut, 8-day time & strike movement, gingerbread-carved golden oak case 175.00

Shelf, or mantel, Gilbert Clock Co., Bristol & Winsted, Connecticut, Mission-style (Arts & Crafts movement) oak case, crest & rectangular top over applied numerals, centered pierced panels lined w/glass, sides flare towards base, early 20th c., 20" w., 12¾" h. 247.50

Ingraham Mantel Clock

Shelf, or mantel, E.E. Ingraham Co., Bristol, Connecticut, painted wood case, labeled "Signet, Eight-Day, Half-Hour Strike, Cathedral Gong and Patent Regulator, E.E. Ingraham Co., Bristol, Conn., U.S.A.," ca. 1900 (ILLUS.) 71.50

Shelf, or mantel, "W. L. Johnson, No. 49 Courtland St., New York" label inside, Double Steeple case, time & strike movement, white-painted metal dial w/Roman numerals, mahogany veneered case w/reverse-painted spread-winged American eagle in lower door, New York City, 1841-61, 24" h. 935.00

Shelf, or mantel, Maniere, Paris, France, circular enamel dial surmounted by ormolu foliate fronds & flanked by two mythological figures on columnar supports above indented rectangular marble plinth mounted w/beading & three plaques depicting frolicking putti, on *toupie* feet, Louis XVI, signed "Maniere a Paris," late 18th c., 22½" h. 1,430.00

Shelf, or mantel, New Haven Clock Co., New Haven, Connecticut, 30-hour weight-driven movement, mahogany veneer ogee-molded case w/transfer-printed scene in lower tablet of door entitled "Branksea Castle, Dorsetshire, England," 26" h. 132.50

Shelf, or mantel, Seth Thomas, Thomaston, Connecticut, Pillar & Scroll case, white-painted dial w/sweep second dial & painted spandrels in upper part of door & painted "eglomise" panel in lower door flanked by freestanding columns, case w/swan's neck pediment centering three brass urn finials above hinged door over dial, shaped apron at base w/French feet, original label of Seth Thomas, 28½" h. (some restorations) 1,760.00

Shelf, or mantel, Jerome Thompson & Co., Bristol, Connecticut, Pillar & Scroll case, wooden movement, white-painted wooden dial, three-section door, central panel w/reverse painting of Mount Vernon, lower section w/florals, 38½" h. (veneer damage, replaced cornice) 475.00

Aaron Willard Case-on-Case Clock

Shelf, or mantel, Aaron Willard, Boston, Massachusetts, mahogany Case-on-Case, Federal-style case w/shaped crest centering brass eagle & ball finial over upper door w/"eglomise" panel centering dished white-painted dial above panel bearing maker's name, projecting lower case w/convex molding below mirror, raised on cast-brass hairy paw feet, unrestored condition w/old finish & replaced feet, ca. 1825, 34" h. (ILLUS.) 8,250.00

Vienna regulator wall clock, carved walnut "hotel" style case w/carved bird below arched crest flanked by turned finials, heavy turned columns down front flank glass panel over dial & pendulum, double side shelves w/mirrored backs, drop-finials at base, ca. 1890 (ILLUS.) 325.00

Vienna Regulator with Ornate Case

Wag-on-wall, unknown maker, white-painted dial w/Roman numerals & polychrome florals, brass works w/wooden plates, wooden case, w/weights & pendulum, 9½" w., 13¾" h. (glued crack on face) 400.00

CLOISONNE & RELATED WARES

Cloisonne Elephant

Cloisonne work features enameled designs on a metal ground. There are several types of this work, the best-known utilizing cells of wire on the body of the object into which the enamel is placed. In the plique-a-jour form of cloisonne, the base is removed leaving translucent enamel windows. The champleve technique entails filling in, with enamels, a design which is cast or carved in the base. "Pigeon Blood" cloisonne includes a type where foil is enclosed within colored enamel walls. Cloisonne is said to have been invented by the Chinese and brought to perfection by the Japanese.

Bowl, scalloped rim, overall floral design on interior & exterior in shades of green, red & ochre on mahogany ground, 10½" d., 3½" h. $225.00

Box, cov., lobed, each lobe decorated w/a *taotie* mask amid multicolored tendrils & swirls on a turquoise ground, gilt-metal stem & branch finial, China, late 19th c., 12" d., 10½" h. 357.50

Charger, intricate Arabesque border, songbird amid chrysanthemums & roses center against a wave-form ground, 12" d. 210.00

Charger, central dragon motif surrounded by stylized floral bands in shades of blue, rust, orchid, yellow & white, back countered in cerulean blue, Japan, late 19th c., 23½" d. (ring base damaged) 1,100.00

Desk set: cov. inkwell w/original porcelain insert, quill holder w/flared base & 6½" l. tray w/irregular edge; colorful florals, varied mons & geometric designs on cobalt blue ground, close spring coil cloisons, Japan, 3 pcs. 325.00

Ice chest, tapered square form, sky blue ground w/overall *wan* fret design & w/rows of differing forms of *shou* characters separated by bats w/auspicious emblems, all in alternating primary colors, cover in two sections, one w/two pierced circular medallions, borders of gilt-copper, case bound by two raised gilt-copper bands inlaid w/cloisonne enamel butterflies & flowers, w/four massive gilt-copper bail handles, interior lined w/tin, 18th c., 32½" w., 18½" h. 27,500.00

Incense box (Kogo), varied pink, red & white florals & butterfly against dark blue ground, green triangle design border, 2¼" d. 50.00

Models of elephants, enameled w/stylized animals & flowers on a turquoise ground, each supporting an ovoid vase & cover on its back, 15" h., pr. (ILLUS. of one) 2,200.00

Model of a zebra, gilded eyes, nostrils, mouth & extremities, black & white stripes w/cloison scrolls, underside in pale green enamel w/wavy cloisons, 36½" h., pr. .. 11,000.00

Pitcher, low set ovoid body tapering to a waisted neck below a wide flaring spout w/gilt metal rim, "S" curve handle issuing from a gilt-metal zoomorphic head, body decorated w/a yellow *ruyi* band between large fronted lotus below a floral & *ruyi* neck band, all on a turquoise ground of multi-colored scrolling tendrils, China, late 18th-early 19th c., 17" h. (ILLUS.) 935.00

Chinese Cloisonne Pitcher

Plate, Phoenix bird in tree on multicolored ground, 5" d. 140.00

Plate, large clump of iris on blue ground center, wide border of Arabesque & floral motifs on alternating black & orchid ground, reverse enameled in cerulean blue, Japan, late 19th c., 12" d. .. 385.00

Urn, globular, four lotus blossoms surrounded by multicolored scrolling tendrils & angular turquoise & brick-red C-scrolls on a blue ground, China, 19th c., 6¼" h. ... 385.00

Vase, small silver & pink flowers & green & brown branches on royal blue foil ground, Japan, 1½" d., 2½" h. 65.00

Vases, ovoid w/waisted neck & tapering towards base, scene of a sparrow perched on a branch of blossoming wisteria above flowering magnolia, peony & *kiku* mon on dark blue ground, Japan, 4¾" h., pr. 302.50

Vase, flaring top & brass base w/incised Japanese characters, Arabesque borders, large white cockatoo perched on blossoming cherry tree branch on deep green ground w/ornate goldstone designs, 5" d., 12" h. 475.00

RELATED WARES

Champleve incense burner (Koro), model of a turtle supporting another turtle on its back, colorful geometric designs on brass, 4¾" l., 2¾" w. 125.00

Champleve urn, baluster-form w/hexagonal body tapering sharply to a high ring foot & decorated w/floral-and animal-patterned band suspending decorated stiff-leaves beneath two animal masks & loose ring handles, the waisted neck w/additional patterned band, Meiji Period, Japan, 17¾" h. (slight wear) 605.00

Plique-a-jour pendant w/chain, dragonfly-shaped, set w/paste rubies & diamonds, marked "935," 3" wingspan 395.00

Plique-a-jour salt dip, three twisted wire feet, multicolored band around cobalt blue bowl, 2 1/8" w., ¾" h. 510.00

Plique-a-jour vase, high shouldered ovoid, "millefleur" pattern on pale green ground below a silver mounted rim, 6" h. 440.00

CLOTHING

Man's 18th Century Formal Coat

Recent interest in period clothing, uniforms and accessories from the 18th, 19th and through the 20th century has compelled us to add this category to our compilation. While style and fabric play an important role in the values of older garments of previous centuries, designer dresses of the 1920's and 30's, especially evening gowns, are enhanced by the original label of a noted couturier such as Worth or Adrian. Prices vary widely for these garments which we list by type, with infant's and children's apparel so designated.

Apron, homespun fabric, simple embroidered design & "1796," 23" w., 30" l. $110.00

Apron, dark blue & cream checked homespun fabric, gored & gathered, long 45.00

Bathing suit, lady's, black wool, one-piece w/peek-a-boo lattice sides, 1920's - early 1930's 35.00

Bathing suit, lady's, red & white wool, Web Foot brand 15.00

Beret, lady's, red mohair, 1915 .... 30.00

Blouse, white voile, embroidered & hemstitched w/lace trim, long sleeves, drawstring waist, ca. 1910, size 10 .... 28.00

Bonnet, baby's, Amish, blue, 1930's 28.00

Camisole, white cotton w/lace inserts, Victorian 28.00

Cap, baby's, hand-crocheted white cotton, Pineapple patt. 15.00

Cap, boy's, black velvet, w/earflaps & plush trim, 1890's 20.00

Cape, lady's, floor-length, fuchsia silk w/fox collar, 1920's 60.00

Cape, lady's, floor-length, hunter green silk velvet w/chinchilla collar, 1920's 50.00

Chinese jacket, lady's, shell pink silk brocade w/dragons & prunus, blue & white embroidered borders, late 19th c., 33½" l. 880.00

Christening dress, white cotton, tuck-pleated bodice & skirt, embroidered florals & openwork on bodice, cuffs & scalloped skirt 35.00

Coat, girl's, white linen, shawl collar w/satin-stitched florals, size 7-8 .... 37.50

Coat, lady's, full-length, black sealskin 100.00

Coat, lady's, white Irish lace, overall floral design, shawl collar, filet lace inserts at sleeves, ca. 1920 .... 418.00

Coat, man's, black, silver-grey & blue patterned velvet embroidered w/floral sprays of pale blue, coral, green & cream silks, last quarter 18th c., France, probably Lyons (ILLUS.) 2,640.00

Dress, child's, Amish, black cotton sateen, two-piece, size 2-3 .... 40.00

Dress, girl's, blue silk w/embroidered accents, size 7 .... 20.00

Dress, Edwardian, Irish lace, skirt & bodice inset w/bands of foliate-embroidered net, w/Fox label, ca. 1905 .... 550.00

Dress, flapper era, black chiffon w/red beading, ca. 1920 .... 275.00

Dress, flapper era, black silk w/beaded ecru bodice, rhinestone belt closure, 1920's 67.50

Dress, flapper era, chemise style, cream & turquoise silk gauze

w/overall gold, white & clear bugle beads worked in scrolling panels, ca. 1925 .... 220.00
Dress, Victorian, ecru silk, tiered skirt, white beadwork trim 165.00
Dress, Victorian, mourning-type, black silk faille, 1890's, size 14 ... 50.00
Evening cape, black silk crepe w/stylized rhinestone & gilt thread motif on the back & feather trim at hem, red charmeuse lining, w/Worth label, 1920's 825.00
Evening coat, three-quarter length, gold, rose, blue & olive green floral design brocade, stand-up collar & long sleeves w/wide band of China mink, Mariano Fortuny fabric by unknown designer 1,760.00
Evening gown, blue cut silk velvet, bias-cut, long fitted sleeves, lined, 1930's, size 13 .... 150.00
Gloves, lady's, black leather, w/white stitched flowers, 1930's, pr. 14.00
Gloves, lady's, black silk, Van Raalte, 23" l., original box, pr. 6.00
Gloves, lady's, green suede w/beadwork at cuffs, long, pr. 12.00
Hat, lady's, black felt w/rhinestone pin, 1920's 25.00
Hat, lady's, black beaver w/narrow rolled brim, ostrich feather trim, Victorian 55.00
Hat, lady's, cloche-type, purple w/ornate beading, 1920's 30.00
Hat, man's, black Derby-type, Knox, size 7 1/8 .... 35.00
Muff, black seal skin, lined, 12 x 14" 35.00
Muff, black velvet 10.00
Nightgown, white cotton w/crocheted bodice 25.00
Nightshirt, man's, white cotton 22.50
Parasol, child's, black silk lace, carved wooden handle........... 75.00
Parasol, white net w/pink silk lining, small 35.00
Petticoat, brown cotton, hand-quilted 125.00
Petticoat, black sateen 36.00
Petticoat, white voile w/tucks & wide crocheted ruffle, full-length, Victorian 35.00
Robe, green velvet, square-cut & gilt-printed w/"Bellini" stylized foliate motif, w/"Fortuny" label ..2,090.00
Rompers, child's, white cotton w/hand-embroidered Sunbonnet Babies 15.00
Shawl, black challis w/black satin stitch embroidery, tri-corner type, Victorian 45.00
Shawl, ecru silk w/embroidered pastel florals, heavy fringe, France, 1930's........................ 275.00
Shirt, man's, natural homespun, 1890's 38.00
Shoes, baby's, high button style, brown leather, pr. 25.00
Shoes, baby's, red leather w/plaid trim, pr. 32.00
Shoes, boy's, kid high lace style, "Goodman, Columbus, Ohio," never worn, size 9, in original box, pr. 35.00
Shoes, lady's, high top style, black brocade tops w/silver heel & toe, hand-sewn black beads across toe forming bow, "Welch Bros. Shoes, F. Dodge, Iowa," pr. 60.00
Shoes, man's, black leather & suede, high button style, never worn 45.00
Skirt, brown felt w/appliqued Poodle, flowers & beads, 1950's, size 12-14 ....9.00 to 14.00
Skirt, white muslin w/deep tucks & ruffled flounce, hand-embroidered, full-length 38.00
Slip, baby's, homespun wool 8.00
Slip, white cotton w/rows of tucks & lace inserts, crocheted top w/self-flowers, full-length 27.50
Smoking jacket, black silk brocade, ornate frog closure, silk-lined, ca. 1900 .... 40.00
Spats, boy's, felt 10.00
Spats, man's, 4-button style, black felt 15.00
Stockings, baby's, pink crocheted, long, pr. 6.00
Stockings, child's, mint green wool w/white scallops at top, hand-knit, Amish, 10" l., pr. 60.00
Stockings, man's, tan wool w/blue geometric border, hand-knit, pr... 44.00
Suit, boy's, wool tweed, long pants, vest, coat & tie, 1920's, size 5, 4 pcs. 20.00
Suit, lady's, smokey grey gabardine, fitted jacket w/triple pleated pockets, padded shoulders, tailored, 1940's, 2 pcs. 25.00
Suit, lady's, Edwardian, black silk shantung, 2 pcs. 80.00
Suit, man's, cream & brown wool tweed, cuffed & pleated pants, 1950's, large, 2 pcs. 30.00
Suit dress, Victorian, taupe satin w/ornate lace inserts & ribbon trim, 1890's, 2 pcs. 85.00
Sunbonnet, brown gingham, ruffled trim 22.50
Sunbonnet, Shaker-type, blue & white checked cotton, ruffled & gathered w/sun-shield & ties, ca. 1830 .... 140.00

Sweater, black wool w/batwing sleeves, trimmed w/pearl flowers w/sequin leaves, oblong pearls & rhinestones, double row of pearls & satin ribbon at neck, w/"Apollo of New York" label, 1940's, size 34 .... 165.00

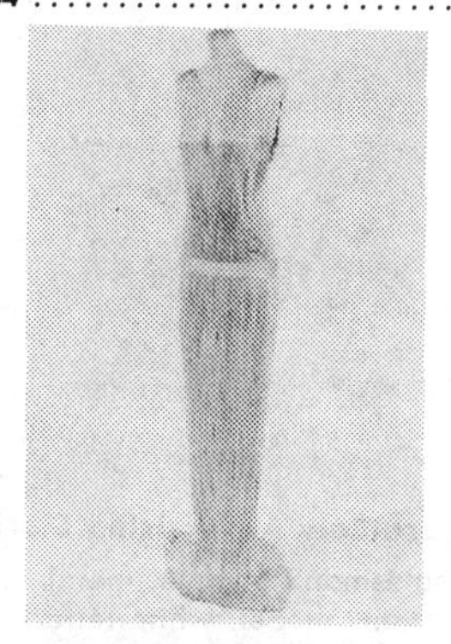

Tea Gown by Fortuny

Tea gown, "Delphos" style, pleated rose silk, sleeveless, sides strung w/translucent Venetian glass beads, matching rose silk belt stamped in geometric designs, by Mariano Fortuny, in original box, late 1920's (ILLUS.) 5,500.00

Teddy, pink silk w/lace trim, 1920-30.......................... 20.00

Top hat, beaver, w/"Lancaster" label, in figured wallpaper-covered box 250.00

Tuxedo trousers, wool, wide leg w/side stripe, 1950's 20.00

Underslip, child's, white linen w/handwork.................... 15.00

Union suit, gentleman's, grey cotton 14.00

Chinese Counted-Stitch Vest

Vest, gauze, worked in front & back w/branches of flowering magnolia in shaded tones of purple w/lime green & blue leaves on a grid pattern, all in counted stitch on thin gauze overlaying couched metallic gold, China, late 19th c., 23¾" l. (ILLUS.) 5,500.00

Wedding gown, Victorian, batiste w/lavish lace trim, high neck, long sleeves, tiered ruffled petticoat w/train, size 5, ca. 1880 ... 210.00

Wedding gown, Victorian, Brussels Point de Gaze lace on net, high neck, demi-train, linen petticoat, ca. 1900 .... 195.00

Wedding gown, Victorian, ecru satin, hand-stitched w/exquisite tucks, ruffles & lace, bustle-back & train, ruffled hem, ca. 1890 .... 650.00

Wedding gown, lightweight cream satin, long train, long sleeves w/buttons, V-neck, fitted waist, 1930's 60.00

COCA-COLA ITEMS

Coca-Cola Bottle Bag

Coca-Cola promotion has been achieved through the issuance of scores of small objects through the years. These, together with trays, signs, and other articles bearing the name of this soft drink, are now sought by many collectors.

Ashtray, aluminum, round, crimped edge, embossed "Drink Coca-Cola" & bottle in center, 1950 .... $15.00

Ballpoint pen, Coca-Cola Bottling Co., Greencastle, Indiana 25.00

Bank, ceramic, "Drink Coca-Cola," Haeger Pottery.................. 65.00

Bank, plastic, model of vending machine, w/original box, 1950's 135.00

Blotter, 1944, three girls w/bottles of Coca-Cola 7.50
Blotter, 1953, Sprite Boy w/bottle & "Good" 4.00
Book, "Alphabet Book of Coca-Cola," 1928 .... 46.00
Book, "When You Entertain," by Ida B. Allen, 1932, 124 pp. 15.00
Bookmark, 1898, celluloid, heart-shaped, beautiful woman w/glass of Coca-Cola in center, 2 x 2¼" .. 250.00
Bottle, 1909, amber, straight-sided w/"Coca-Cola" & embossed arrow 25.00
Bottle, 1957, 1 pt. 10 oz. 35.00
Bottle, "Christmas Coke" marked "Pat'd Dec. 25, 1923," w/original contents, 6 oz. 45.00
Bottle, commemorative, 1961, Hutchinson-stoppered style, multicolored decorations, "75th Anniversary, Engineering Dept., Convention Time" 85.00
Bottle bag, white paper printed w/"Drink Coca-Cola" & other wording, 1932 (ILLUS.) 3.00
Bottle carton-carrier, cardboard, pat'd. 1924, 6-pack 55.00
Bottle carrier, wooden w/wooden slat handle, 1940's 37.00
Bottle case, miniature, plastic, w/24 miniature plastic bottles, yellow case w/red lettering "Drink Coca-Cola in Bottles," 3½ x 2½" case.. 10.00
Bottle holder for shopping cart, two-bottle iron wire rack w/metal plaque "Enjoy Coca-Cola While You Shop - Place Bottles Here," ca. 1940 .... 15.00
Bottle opener, brass, 1910, "Drink Coca-Cola in Bottles" 30.00
Bottle opener, metal, pointed tip, "Drink Coke in Bottles," Milwaukee Bottling Co. 40.00
Bridge score pad, 1942 .... 15.00
Bridge score pad, 1944 .... 15.00
Calendar, 1926, girl seated on picnic table holding glass of Coca-Cola w/tennis racket, tennis balls & bottle of Coca-Cola beside her, complete w/pad 450.00
Calendar, 1935, boy & dog fishing from stump, Norman Rockwell illustration 200.00
Cigarette lighter, model of Coca-Cola can, 1960's, large 12.00
Clock, wall regulator, Gilbert Clock Co., walnut case, dial inscribed "Drink Coca-Cola" & "in bottles - 5c" on door tablet, late 19th c., 30" h. (ILLUS.) 825.00
Cooler, salesman's sample-style, red plastic, "Drink Coca-Cola in Bottles," 1930's, 4 x 5 x 4" 85.00

Coca-Cola Advertising Clock

Cooler, salesman's sample, metal "open front" model, white lettering on red, 1934, 11 x 9 x 8½" ....525.00 to 575.00
Counter display bottle, "Christmas Coke" style marked "Pat'd Dec. 25, 1923," empty, clear, 20" h. ... 115.00
Coupon, w/magazine ad illustrating Lillian Nordica, 1905 .... 150.00
Dinnerware set, china, cup & saucer & three sizes of plates, red & yellow decal of bottle & glass w/"Coca-Cola" logo on plates, logo on cup, white ground, Taylor, Smith & Taylor, 1930's, 5 pcs. ....650.00 to 750.00
Frisbee, round, red plastic w/"Enjoy Coca-Cola" in white, ca. 1970 .... 60.00
Game, cribbage board, wooden, w/pegs, 1930's 45.00
Game, "Dominoes," in original box, 1940's 35.00
Game, Ping Pong set, w/four paddles, ca. 1950, original box, the set 48.00
Ice pick, wooden handle w/script & w/metal bottle opener on end, 1940's 21.00
Key for car, 1950, mint in envelope 20.00
Key chain, red-enameled brass disc w/embossed bottle & design, 1955 .... 6.00
Knife, pocket-type, "Compliments of Coca-Cola Bottling Co.," 1930's ... 85.00
Knife, pocket-type, souvenir of Chicago World's Fair, 1933 .... 27.00
Knife, pocket-type, "Have A Coke," pictures bottle, 1950's 90.00
Lapel pin, "20 Years of Service" 50.00
Lighter, musical, 1950 .... 100.00
Lighter, "50th Anniversary," red w/white bull's eye, "Drink Coca-Cola" 80.00

Magazine, "Pause for Living," 1964-65, 16 pp. 4.00
Marbles, glass swirls in plastic bag, "Free with every carton," 1950 .... 35.00
Mirror, pocket-type, "Memos," 50th Anniversary 1886-1936 .... 60.00
Mirror, pocket-type, 1911, Coca-Cola Girl, "The Whitehead & Hoag Co." etc. on rim, oval 195.00
Money clip w/knife on each side, enameled Coke cup on front w/"Enjoy Coca-Cola" 50.00
Nature Study Cards, Series I through VIII, ca. 1928-1933, 96 cards total 32.00
Neckerchief, Kit Carson, printed cotton, red, white & black, 1950 ..... 40.00
Pencil, mechanical-type, w/mini bottle inside clear plastic top, 1950's 27.00

Coca-Cola Pencil Box and Accessories

Pencil box, red leatherette cover w/"Coca-Cola Delicious... Refreshing" in gilt, ca. 1930 (ILLUS.) 34.00
Ping pong paddles, 1940's, set of 4 .... 65.00
Playing cards, Airline Stewardess, 1943 .... 30.00
Playing cards, Cowgirl bust portrait, 1951 .... 46.00
Playing cards, masquerade ball scenes, 1960, full deck 40.00
Poster, cardboard, colorful scene of bottle of Coca-Cola floating in Arctic waters, 1944, framed 150.00
Poster, paper, "The Answer To Thirst After Play," full color girl waterskiing, matted, 14 x 18" 30.00
Radio, model of a cooler, red Bakelite case, 1949-53 .... 310.00
Radio, model of vending machine, 1963, 3½ x 7½" 125.00
School tablet, two globes on cover, says "Pure as Sunlight" 35.00
Seltzer bottle, blue glass w/original spigot, "Coca-Cola Bottling Co. of Bradford, Pa.," 26 oz. 75.00
Sign, cardboard, pictures Clark Gable & Joan Crawford, w/embossed Coca-Cola bottle, 15½ x 24" 45.00
Sign, cardboard, double sided, blond woman in swimsuit for Summer, majorette for Fall, 1952, 20 x 36" 85.00
Signs, cardboard, U.S. Army Fighter & Bomber Planes series, 1943, set of 20 .... 600.00
Sign, cardboard, "Welcome Friends Have a Coke," bottle pictured, 1947 .... 65.00

Coca-Cola Neon Sign

Sign, neon, three-color in shape of large paper cup w/"Coke With Ice" (ILLUS.) 215.00
Stringholder, "Take Home 'Coca-Cola' in Cartons," w/six-pack of Coca-Cola in center 325.00
Study cards, "America's Fighting Planes in Action" (World War II series), 1943, set of 20 .... 40.00
Thermometer, cigar-shaped, metal, "Drink Coca-Cola - Sign of Good Taste," red & white, 30" h. 90.00
Thimble, glass, red 25.00
Toy, cardboard cut-outs of athletes, "Olympic Games of 1932," uncut .. 45.00
Toy truck, battery-operated, 1950's, original box, 14" l. 130.00
Toy truck, red metal, w/six original wood blocks, made by Smith-Miller, in original box, 1940's 405.00
Tray, change, 1906, "Relieves Fatigue," 4½ x 6¼" oval 306.00
Tray, change, 1909, Beautiful Girl at table w/glass of Coca-Cola (once called St. Louis World Fair Girl), 4¼ x 6" oval 195.00
Tray, change, 1912, Hamilton King Girl 135.00
Tray, change, 1914, Betty, 4¼ x 6" oval 92.00
Tray, 1912, Hamilton King Girl, oval 350.00

Tray, 1914, Betty, 10½ x 13¼" oblong 200.00
Tray, 1914, Betty, 12½ x 15¼" oval 310.00
Tray, 1920, Garden Girl, 13¾ x 16½" oval 400.00

1926 Coca-Cola Tray

Tray, 1926, Sports Couple, 10½ x 13¼" oblong (ILLUS.) 180.00
Tray, 1928, Girl with Bobbed Hair, 10½ x 13¼" oblong 150.00
Tray, 1931, Farm Boy with Dog (by Norman Rockwell), 10½ x 13¼" oblong .... 350.00 to 380.00
Tray, 1936, Hostess, 10½ x 13¼" oblong .... 100.00 to 125.00
Tray, 1941, Girl Ice Skater, 10½ x 13¼" oblong 62.00
Tray, 1957, Umbrella Girl 180.00
Tray, 1976, Indiana University, NCAA 25.00
Vienna Art tin plate, beautiful woman w/flowing brown hair w/red cap, left profile, low draped bosom, produced by Western Coca-Cola Bottling Co., 1905 .... 395.00
Watch fob, metal, girl in large hat drinking bottle of Coca-Cola in relief, 1917, 1¼ x 1½" 175.00

COFFEE GRINDERS

Most coffee grinders collected are lap or table and wall types used in many homes in the late 19th and early 20th centuries. However, large store-sized grinders have recently been traded.

Lap-type, mahogany base w/light wood inlay, dovetailed drawer, nickel-plated brass fittings w/scrolled & reticulated handle, overall 12½" h. $150.00
Lap-type, maple base w/machine dovetailing & drawer, brass hopper, cast-iron handle w/wooden knob 70.00
Lap type, maple base w/machine dovetailing & drawer, pewter hopper, cast-iron handle w/wooden knob 95.00
Lap-type, pine base w/machine dovetailing & drawer, cast-iron hopper & handle w/wooden knob 60.00
Lap-type, wooden base w/machine dovetailing & drawer, "Imperial" by Arcade, 5½" sq. 32.50
Lap-type, wooden base w/machine dovetailing & drawer, "Parker No. 70" 45.00
Store counter model, two-wheel, cast iron, open cup, "Enterprise No. 2," dated 1873, original paint, 8¾" d. wheel, 12½" h. . . 350.00 to 440.00
Store counter model, two-wheel, cast iron, "Enterprise No. 3," 10¾" d. wheels, 15" h. . . 400.00 to 450.00
Store counter model, two-wheel, cast iron, "Enterprise No. 9," 19½" d. wheels, 24" h. 900.00
Store counter model, two-wheel, cast iron, "Enterprise No. 12," 25" d. wheels, 32" h. 975.00
Store counter model, cast iron, "Swift Mill No. 12" by Lane Bros., Poughkeepsie, New York, w/patent date of 1875, original red paint, 14" h. 325.00
Table model, clamp-on type, cast iron, "Universal Coffee Grinder No. 109" by Landers, Frary & Clark, w/patent date of 1905 .... 35.00

Table Model Coffee Grinder

Table model, cast iron, "Landers, Frary & Clark No. 11," dark green

paint w/red decal (ILLUS.) ....275.00 to 295.00
Wall-type, cast iron, "Brighton," 6 x 5" 42.50
Wall-type, cast iron, "Landers, Frary & Clark" 75.00
Wall-type, cast iron, "Charles Parker Co. No. 70" 45.00
Wall-type, cast iron & tin, "American No. 50 Parker," black paint, 6 x 8" 48.00
Wall-type, cast iron & wood, "Telephone Mill - Arcade Manufacturing Co.," replaced lid....200.00 to 250.00
Wall-type, cast iron, "Arcade No. 3," w/clear glass jar marked "Crystal" ....85.00 to 100.00
Wall-type, cast iron w/clear glass jar, "Universal No. 24" 38.00

COMIC BOOKS

Comic books, especially first or early issues of a series, are avidly collected today. Prices for some of the scarce ones have reached extremely high levels. Prices listed below are for copies in fine to mint condition.

Amazing Spider-man, No. 8 .... $32.00
Amazing Spider-man, No. 14 .... 38.00
Animal Comics (Walt Kelly), No. 114 .... 20.00
Batman, No. 69 .... 37.50
Beatles, No. 4 .... 30.00
Ben Casey Films, No. 1 .... 24.00
Bewitched, No. 1 .... 21.00
Boris Karloff, No. 65 .... 9.50
Bringing Up Father, 1919, first edition 50.00
Buck Rogers, No. 2 .... 150.00
Buck Rogers, No. 3 .... 130.00
Bulletman, 1942 premium, 4 x 5" ... 28.00
Captain America, No. 200 .... 9.00
Captain Marvel, 1942 premium, 4 x 5" 28.00
Cow Puncher, No. 7 .... 10.00
Cracker Jack, No. 17, w/Red Ryder, Tom Mix & others, 1939 .... 26.00
The Dark Crystal, Marvel Vol. 1, No. 24 .... 10.00
Defenders, No. 1 .... 8.00
Dick Tracy, the Detective, No. 4, August 1937 .... 150.00
Donald Duck, Deep Sea Diver, Wheaties premium, 1951 .... 12.00
Fantastic Four, No. 18 .... 46.00
Flying Saucers, No. 5 .... 3.00
Forbidden Worlds, No. 36 .... 17.00
Freckles & His Friends in the North Woods 16.00
Frosty the Snowman, No. 950 .... 2.50
Golden Age Comics, No. 28, DC's "Star Spangled," January 1944.... 140.00
Gomer Pyle, No. 1 .... 15.00
Have Gun Will Travel, No. 14 ...... 20.00
"If the Devil Would Talk," 1950 ..... 95.00
Invaders (The), No. 1 .... 14.00
I Spy, No. 1 .... 14.50
Katy Keene, No. 1, 1949 .... 45.00
Katy Keene, No. 17 .... 60.00
Keeping Up With the Joneses, 1920 .... 20.00
King of the Royal Mounted, Zane Grey, No. 9, 1938 .... 80.00
Land of the Giants, No. 3 .... 6.00
Laredo, No. 1 .... 14.00
Lone Ranger, No. 39 .... 38.00
Man From U.N.C.L.E., No. 1 .... 24.00
March of Comics, No. 41, Donald Duck by Carl Barks, "Race to the South Seas," 22 pp. 600.00
March of Comics, No. 45, Mickey Mouse 65.00
Marge's Little Lulu, No. 193 .... 8.00
Mickey Mouse, "Mickey & The 7 Colored Terror," No. 27, 1943 .... 75.00
Mod Squad, Dell, No. 1 .... 9.00
Munsters (The), No. 5 .... 8.00
Mutt & Jeff, No. 7, 1920 .... 35.00
Outer Limits, No. 4 .... 4.00
Peter Porkchops, No. 13 .... 17.00
Rawhide, No. 2 .... 30.00
Rawhide Kid, No. 39 .... 12.00
Rex Allen, No. 14 .... 4.00
Roy Rogers, Dell, No. 153 .... 42.50
Sheena, Jumbo Comics, No. 80 ..... 20.00
Strange Tales, No. 112 .... 35.00
Superman, No. 200 .... 5.00
Tarzan, No. 21 .... 10.00
Three Stooges, No. 6 .... 42.00
Three Stooges, No. 50 .... 10.00
Tom Mix, No. 3, 1941, Ralston premium 60.00
Wagon Train, No. 1 .... 16.00
Walt Disney's Comics & Stories, No. 10 .... 35.00
Whiz, No. 38, 1942 .... 31.00
Wild, Wild West, No. 1 .... 12.00

COMMEMORATIVE PLATES

Limited edition commemorative and collector plates rank high on the list of collectible items. The oldest and best-known of these plates, those of Bing & Grondahl and Royal Copenhagen, retain leadership in the field, but other companies are turning out a variety of designs, some of which have been widely embraced by the growing numbers who have made plate collecting a hobby. Plates listed below are a representative selection of the fine porcelain, glass and sterling silver plates available to collectors.

ANRI
Christmas

1971, St. Jakob in Groden $55.00
1972, Pipers At Alberobello 60.00
1973, Alpine Horn 325.00
1974, Young Man & Girl 77.00
1975, Christmas in Ireland 47.50
1976, Alpine Christmas 175.00
1977, Legend of Heiligenblut 125.00
1978, The Klockler Singers 68.00
1979, The Moss Gatherers of Villnoess 73.00
1980, Wintry Church-going in Santa Christina 95.00
1981, Santa Claus in Tyrol 87.50
1982, Star Singers 93.00
1983, Unto Us a Child is Born 110.00
1984, Yuletide in the Valley 120.00
1985, Good Morning, Good Cheer .. 125.00

Father's Day

1972, Alpine Father & Children 40.00
1973, Alpine Father & Children 85.00
1974, Cliff Gazing 35.00
1975, Sailing 92.50

Mother's Day

1972, Alpine Mother & Children 42.00
1973, Alpine Mother & Children 30.00
1974, Alpine Mother & Children 50.00
1975, Alpine Stroll 50.00
1976, Knitting 48.00

BAREUTHER
Christmas

1971 Bareuther Christmas Plate

1967, Stiftskirche 92.00
1968, Kappl 18.50
1969, Christkindlesmarkt 11.00
1970, Chapel in Oberndorf 10.00
1971, Toys for Sale (ILLUS.) 14.00
1972, Christmas in Munich 37.00
1973, Christmas Sleigh Ride 21.00
1974, Church in the Black Forest 23.00
1975, Snowman 28.00
1976, Chapel in the Hills 19.00
1977, Story Time 21.00
1978, Mittenwald 19.50
1979, Winter Day 20.00
1980, Miltenberg 21.50
1981, Walk in the Forest 18.50
1982, Bad Wimpfen 22.00
1983, The Night Before Christmas ... 21.00
1984, Zeil on the River Main 21.50
1985, Winter Wonderland 25.00
1986, Market Place in Forchheim ... 25.50

Father's Day

1969, Castle Neuschwanstein 31.50
1970, Castle Pfalz 13.50
1971, Castle Heidelberg 15.00
1972, Castle Hohenschwangau 19.50
1973, Castle Katz 20.00
1974, Wurzburg Castle 19.00
1975, Castle Lichtenstein 21.00
1976, Castle Hohenzollern 20.50
1977, Castle Eltz 20.50
1978, Castle Falkenstein 25.00
1979, Castle Rheinstein 24.00
1980, Castle Cochem 23.00
1981, Castle Gutenfels 29.00
1982, Castle Zwingenberg 22.50
1983, Castle Lauenstein 21.50
1984, Castle Neuenstein 28.00
1985, Castle Wartburg Near Eisenbach 28.00
1986, Castle Hardegg 25.00

Mother's Day

1969, Dancing 29.00
1970, Mother & Children 13.50
1971, Doing the Laundry 15.50
1972, Baby's First Step 14.00
1973, Mother Kissing Baby 20.00
1974, Musical Children 16.00
1975, Spring Outing 16.50
1976, Rocking Cradle 18.00
1977, Noon Feeding 19.00
1978, Blind Man's Bluff 23.00
1979, Mother's Love 20.00
1980, First Cherries 21.00
1981, Playtime 25.00
1982, Suppertime 21.00
1983, On Farm 24.00
1984, Village Children 26.00
1985, Sunrise 30.00
1986, Playtime 29.50

BELLEEK
Christmas

1970, Castle Caldwell (ILLUS.) 72.00
1971, Celtic Cross 27.50
1972, Flight of the Earls 37.00
1973, Tribute to W.B. Yeats 46.00
1974, Devenish Island 180.00

1970 Belleek Christmas Plate

1975, The Celtic Cross	50.00
1976, Dove of Peace	45.00
1977, Wren	52.00

Irish Wildlife Christmas

1978, A Leaping Salmon	62.00
1979, Hare at Rest	47.00
1980, Hedgehog	62.00
1981, Red Squirrel	62.00
1982, Irish Seal	62.00
1983, Red Fox	71.50

BING & GRONDAHL
Christmas

1932 Bing & Grondahl Christmas Plate

1895	3,165.00
1896	1,345.00
1897	875.00
1898	450.00
1899	940.00
1900	775.00
1901	260.00
1902	272.00
1903	247.00
1904	97.00
1905	105.00
1906	60.00
1907	75.00
1908	61.00
1909	75.00
1910	64.00
1911	54.00
1912	53.00
1913	54.00
1914	60.00
1915	89.00
1916	65.00
1917	53.00
1918	58.00
1919	51.00
1920	61.00
1921	60.00
1922	57.00
1923	58.00
1924	56.00
1925	58.00
1926	59.00
1927	60.00
1928	42.00
1929	53.00
1930	66.00
1931	54.00
1932 (ILLUS.)	58.00
1933	46.00
1934	46.00
1935	47.00
1936	52.00
1937	51.00
1938	76.00
1939	106.00
1940	103.00
1941	171.00
1942	113.00
1943	108.00
1944	65.00
1945	81.00
1946	49.00
1947	65.00
1948	48.00
1949	48.00
1950	80.00
1951	60.00
1952	49.00
1953	57.00
1954	60.00
1955	60.00
1956	79.00
1957	92.00
1958	69.00
1959	80.00
1960	117.00
1961	68.00
1962	49.00
1963	71.00
1964	40.00
1965	41.00
1966	37.00
1967	35.00
1968	28.00
1969	18.00
1970	16.00

Year	Price
1971	14.00
1972	13.00
1973	16.00
1974	14.50
1975	15.50
1976	19.00
1977	16.50
1978	18.50
1979	21.00
1980	23.00
1981	27.50
1982	29.00
1983	28.00
1984	29.50
1985	30.00

Mother's Day

Item	Price
1969, Dog & Puppies	343.00
1970, Birds & Chicks	19.50
1971, Cat & Kitten	10.50
1972, Mare & Foal	13.00
1973, Duck & Ducklings	13.50
1974, Bear & Cubs	14.00
1975, Doe & Fawns	13.00
1976, Swan Family	13.50
1977, Squirrel & Young	17.00
1978, Heron	16.00
1979, Fox & Cubs	18.00
1980, Woodpecker & Young	23.00
1981, Hare & Young	21.00
1982, Lioness & Cubs	24.00
1983, Raccoon & Young	23.00
1984, Stork & Nestlings	21.00
1985, Bear with Cubs	23.50

Jubilee

Item	Price
1960, Kronborg Castle	92.50
1965, Churchgoers	58.00
1970, Amalienborg Castle	16.50
1975, Horses Enjoying Meal	21.00
1980, Happiness over Yule Tree	23.50
1985, Lifeboat at Work	41.50

FERRANDIZ, JUAN

Christmas - Anri (Wood)

Item	Price
1972, Christ in Manger	148.00
1973, Boy with Lamb	110.00
1974, Nativity	169.00
1975, Flight into Egypt	95.00
1976, Mary & Joseph Pray	127.00
1977, Girl with Tree	45.00
1978, Leading the Way	59.00
1979, Drummer Boy	53.00
1980, Rejoice	50.00
1981, Spreading Word	62.00
1982, Shepherd Family	70.00

Mother & Child - Schmid (Porcelain)

Item	Price
1977, Orchard Mother	76.00
1978, Pastoral Mother	44.00
1979, Floral Mother	51.50
1980, Avian Mother	59.00

Mother's Day - Anri (Wood)

Item	Price
1972, Mother Sewing	84.00
1973, Mother & Child	64.00
1974, Mother & Child	79.00
1975, Mother Holding Dove	79.00
1976, Mother & Child	79.00
1977, Girl with Flowers	89.00
1978, Beginning	43.50
1979, All Hearts	35.00
1980, Spring Arrivals	43.50
1981, Harmony	56.00
1982, With Love	50.00

FRANKLIN MINT (STERLING SILVER)

Norman Rockwell Christmas Series

Item	Price
1970, Bringing Home the Tree	134.00
1971, Under the Mistletoe	97.00
1972, The Carolers	125.00
1973, Trimming the Tree	106.00
1974, Hanging the Wreath	169.00
1975, Home for Christmas	156.00

FRANKOMA

Christmas

1969 Frankoma Christmas Plate

Item	Price
1965, Goodwill Toward Men	222.00
1966, Bethlehem Shepherds	113.00
1967, Gifts for the Christ Child	66.50
1968, Flight into Egypt	12.50
1969, Laid in a Manger (ILLUS.)	10.50
1970, King of Kings	11.00
1971, No Room in the Inn	13.50
1972, Seeking the Christ Child	11.50
1973, The Annunciation	12.00
1974, She Loved & Cared	11.50
1975, Peace on Earth	11.50
1976, Gift of Love	12.00
1977, Birth of Eternal Life	11.50
1978, All Nature Rejoiced	11.50
1979, Star of Hope	10.00
1980, Unto Us a Child Is Born	10.00
1981, O Come Let Us Adore Him	9.50
1982, Wise Men Rejoice	10.00
1983, Wise Men Bring Gifts	13.00
1984, Faith, Hope & Love	10.50
1985, The Angels Watched	12.00

Teenagers of the Bible

Item	Price
1973 Jesus the Carpenter	19.00

1974 David the Musician 14.50
1975 Jonathan the Archer 14.50
1976 Dorcas the Seamstress 18.00
1977 Peter the Fisherman 11.00
1978 Martha the Homemaker 14.50
1979 Daniel the Courageous 14.50
1980 Ruth the Devoted 9.00
1981 Joseph the Dreamer 10.00
1982 Mary the Mother 11.50

GORHAM - NORMAN ROCKWELL
Four Seasons
1971, A Boy & His Dog, set of 4 .... 211.00
1972, Young Love, set of 4 .... 91.00
1973, The Ages of Love, set of 4 .... 190.00
1974, Grandpa & Me, set of 4 ...... 103.00
1975, Me & My Pal, set of 4 .... 93.00
1976, Grand Pals, set of 4 .... 133.00
1977, Going on Sixteen, set of 4 .... 140.00
1978, The Tender Years, set of 4.... 76.00
1979, A Helping Hand, set of 4 ..... 56.00
1980, Dad's Boy, set of 4 .... 77.00

HAVILAND & CO.
Christmas
1970, A Partridge in a Pear Tree.... 85.00
1971, Two Turtle Doves 18.50
1972, Three French Hens 13.50
1973, Four Colly Birds 15.50
1974, Five Golden Rings 16.00
1975, Six Geese A'Laying 14.00
1976, Seven Swans A'Swimming 17.50
1977, Eight Maids A'Milking 21.00
1978, Nine Ladies Dancing 25.00
1979, Ten Lords A'Leaping 22.50
1980, Eleven Pipers Piping 30.00
1981, Twelve Drummers
Drumming 34.00

Mother's Day
1973, Breakfast 12.00
1974, The Wash 15.00
1975, In the Park 12.50
1976, To Market 10.50
1977, Wash Before Dinner 10.00
1978, An Evening at Home 11.00
1979, Happy Mother's Day 18.00
1980, A Child & His Animals........ 9.00

HAVILAND & PARLON
Christmas
1972, Madonna & Child (Raphael) ... 83.50
1973, Madonnina (Feruzzi) 77.50
1974, Cowper Madonna & Child
(Raphael) 43.00
1975, Madonna & Child (Murillo) 30.00
1976, Madonna & Child (Botticelli) .. 38.50
1977, Madonna & Child (Bellini) 31.00
1978, Madonna & Child (Fra Filippo
Lippi) 51.00
1979, Madonna of the Eucharist
(Botticelli) 90.00

Mother's Day
1975, Laura & Child 31.50

1976, Pinky & Baby 19.00
1977, Amy & Snoopy 24.50

Tapestry Series

1971 Tapestry Plate

1971, The Unicorn in Captivity
(ILLUS.) 124.00
1972, Start of the Hunt 45.00
1973, Chase of the Unicorn 99.00
1974, End of the Hunt 84.00
1975, The Unicorn Surrounded 38.00
1976, The Unicorn is Brought to the
Castle 56.50

The Lady & The Unicorn
1977, To My Only Desire 45.00
1978, Sight 32.00
1979, Sound 32.00
1980, Touch 80.00
1981, Scent 38.00
1982, Taste 46.50

HUMMEL (GOEBEL WORKS)
Annual
1971, Heavenly Angel 541.00
1972, Hear Ye, Hear Ye 42.50
1973, Globe Trotter 101.00
1974, Goose Girl 49.00
1975, Ride into Christmas 51.00
1976, Apple Tree Girl 50.00
1977, Apple Tree Boy 62.50
1978, Happy Pastime 41.50
1979, Singing Lesson 26.50
1980, School Girl 42.00
1981, Umbrella Boy 49.00
1982, Umbrella Girl 83.50
1983, The Postman 132.00
1984, Little Helper 51.50
1985, Chick Girl 62.00

Anniversary
1975, Stormy Weather 97.50
1980, Spring Dance 60.00
1985, Auf Wiedersehen 135.00

IMPERIAL (GLASS)
Christmas
1970, Partridge in a Pear Tree,
crystal 11.50

1971 Imperial Christmas Plate

1970, Partridge in a Pear Tree, carnival 18.50
1971, Two Turtle Doves, crystal (ILLUS.) 11.00
1971, Two Turtle Doves, carnival 16.00
1972, Three French Hens, crystal 11.50
1972, Three French Hens, carnival . . 15.00
1973, Four Colly Birds, crystal 12.00
1973, Four Colly Birds, carnival 15.00
1974, Five Golden Rings, crystal 11.50
1974, Five Golden Rings, carnival . . . 15.00
1975, Six Geese A-Laying, crystal . . . 12.00
1975, Six Geese A-Laying, carnival . . 15.50
1976, Seven Swans A-Swimming, crystal 14.50
1976, Seven Swans A-Swimming, carnival 16.50
1977, Eight Maids A-Milking, crystal 11.00
1977, Eight Maids A-Milking, carnival 16.00
1978, Nine Drummers Drumming, crystal 12.50
1978, Nine Drummers Drumming, carnival 19.00
1979, Ten Pipers Piping, crystal 12.50
1979, Ten Pipers Piping, carnival 17.50
1980, Eleven Ladies Dancing, crystal 14.00
1980, Eleven Ladies Dancing, carnival 17.50
1981, Twelve Lords A-Leaping, crystal 10.00
1981, Twelve Lords A-Leaping, carnival 14.00
1981, Twelve Lords A-Leaping, ruby 22.50

KAISER

Christmas

1970, Waiting for Santa Claus 19.50
1971, Silent Night 18.00
1972, Welcome Home 18.50
1973, Holy Night 32.50
1974, Christmas Carolers 20.50
1975, Bringing Home the Christmas Tree 14.50
1976, Christ the Saviour Is Born 16.00
1977, The Three Kings 13.50
1978, Shepherds in the Field 15.00
1979, Christmas Eve 18.50
1980, Joys of Winter 20.50
1981, Most Holy Night 42.00
1982, Bringing Home the Christmas Tree 25.00

Mother's Day

1971, Mare & Foal 17.50
1972, Flowers for Mother 18.50
1973, Cat & Kittens 26.00
1974, Fox & Young 26.50
1975, German Shepherd with Pups . . 38.50
1976, Swan & Cygnets 13.50
1977, Mother Rabbit & Young 22.00
1978, Hen & Chicks 17.00
1979, A Mother's Devotion 23.00
1980, Raccoon Family 35.50
1981, Safe Near Mother 37.00
1982, Pheasant Family 28.00
1983, Tender Care 40.00

LALIQUE (GLASS)

Annual

1967 Lalique Annual Plate

1965, Deux Oiseaux (Two Birds) 1,170.00
1966, Rose de Songerie (Dream Rose) 197.00
1967, Ballet de Poisson, Fish Ballet (ILLUS.) 152.00
1968, Gazelle Fantaisie (Gazelle Fantasy) 55.00
1969, Papillon (Butterfly) 54.00
1970, Paon (Peacock) 45.50
1971, Hibou (Owl) 46.00
1972, Coquillage (Shell) 49.00
1973, Petit Geai (Jayling) 44.00
1974, Sous d'Argent (Silver Pennies) 44.50
1975, Duo de Poisson (Fish Duet) . . . 51.00
1976, Aigle (Eagle) 84.00

LENOX

Boehm Bird Series

1970, Wood Thrush 163.00
1971, Goldfinch 60.00
1972, Mountain Bluebird 44.50
1973, Meadowlark 42.00
1974, Rufous Hummingbird 51.00
1975, American Redstart 42.00
1976, Cardinals 46.00
1977, Robins 40.00
1978, Mockingbirds 47.50
1979, Golden-Crowned Kinglets 48.00
1980, Black-Throated Blue Warblers 63.50
1981, Eastern Phoebes 74.50

Boehm Woodland Wildlife Series

1973, Raccoons 60.00
1974, Red Foxes 49.00
1975, Cottontail Rabbits 54.00
1976, Eastern Chipmunks 51.00
1977, Beaver 57.00
1978, Whitetail Deer 59.00
1979, Squirrels 63.00
1980, Bobcats 72.00
1981, Martens 86.00
1982, Otters 89.00

PORSGRUND

Christmas

1970 Porsgrund Christmas Plate

1968, Church Scene 139.00
1969, Three Kings 9.50
1970, Road to Bethlehem (ILLUS.) 9.00
1971, A Child is Born 7.50
1972, Hark, the Herald Angels Sing 12.00
1973, Promise of the Savior 12.00
1974, The Shepherds 37.50
1975, Jesus on the Road to the Temple 21.00
1976, Jesus & the Elders 22.00
1977, Draught of the Fish 15.00

Traditional Norwegian Christmas

1978, Guests Are Coming 17.50
1979, Home for Christmas 18.00
1980, Preparing for Christmas 18.50
1981, Christmas Skating 17.50
1982, White Christmas 21.00

Father's Day

1971, Fishing 3.50
1972, Cookout 4.50
1973, Sledding 4.00
1974, Father & Son 3.00
1975, Skating 3.50
1976, Skiing 6.00
1977, Soccer 8.50
1978, Canoeing 8.50
1979, Father & Daughter 11.50
1980, Sailing 6.50
1981, Building a Ship 8.50
1982, Father & Daughter 9.00
1983, Father's Day 10.00
1984, Tree Planting 14.00
1985, Father's Day 15.00
1986, Father's Day 15.00

Mother's Day

1970, Mare & Foal 4.00
1971, Boy & Geese 6.50
1972, Doe & Fawn 4.00
1973, Cat & Kittens 3.50
1974, Boy & Goats 3.50
1975, Dog & Puppies 3.50
1976, Girl & Calf 3.50
1977, Boy & Chickens 7.50
1978, Girl & Pigs 7.50
1979, Boy & Reindeer 5.00
1980, Girl & Lambs 11.50
1981, Boy & Birds 11.50
1982, Girl & Rabbits 9.50
1983, Mother & Kittens 17.00
1984, By the Pond 11.00

RED SKELTON

Freddie the Freeloader Series (Crown Parian)

1979, Freddie in the Bathtub 151.00
1980, Freddie's Shack 60.00
1981, Freddie on the Green 61.00
1982, Love That Freddie 33.00

Famous Clown Series (Fairmont)

1976, Freddie the Freeloader 400.00
1977, W. C. Fields 49.00
1978, Happy 60.00
1979, The Pledge 60.00

Freddie's Adventures Series (Crown Parian)

1981, Captain Freddie 36.50
1982, Bronco Freddie 32.00
1983, Sir Freddie 34.50

RORSTRAND

Christmas

1968, Bringing Home the Tree 338.00
1969, Fisherman Sailing Home 27.50
1970, Nils with His Geese 20.00
1971, Nils in Lapland 16.00
1972, Dalecarlian Fiddler 15.00

1973, Farm in Smaland 50.00
1974, Vadstena 47.00
1975, Nils in Vastmanland 11.50
1976, Nils in Uppland 19.50

1977 Rorstrand Christmas Plate

1977, Nils in Varmland (ILLUS.) 16.50
1978, Nils in Fjallbacka 20.00
1979, Nils in Vaestergoetland 17.50
1980, Nils in Halland 30.00
1981, Nils in Gotland 30.00
1982, Nils at Skansen in Stockholm 28.00
1983, Nils in Oland 29.50
1984, Nils in Angermanland 31.00
1985, Nils in Jamtland 39.00
1986, Nils in Karlskrona 33.50

Mothers's Day

1971, Mother & Child 7.00
1972, Shelling Peas 7.00
1973, Old Fashioned Picnic 16.50
1974, Candle Lighting 11.00
1975, Pontius on Floor 7.00
1976, Apple Picking 8.00
1977, Kitchen 8.00
1978, Azalea 15.00
1979, Studio Idyll 15.00
1980, Lisbeth 17.50
1981, Karin with Brita 23.00
1983, Brita 24.00
1983, Little Girl 25.00
1984, Mother & Crafts 27.50
1985, Mother's Day 28.00
1986, Mother's Day 33.00

Father's Day

1971, Father & Child 11.00
1972, Meal at Home 9.50
1973, Tilling Fields 9.00
1974, Fishing 13.50
1975, Painting 12.00
1976, Plowing 7.50
1977, Sawing 7.50
1978, Self-Portrait 20.00
1979, Bridge 15.50
1980, My Etch-Nook 15.75
1981, Esbjorn with Playmate 33.00
1982, House Servants 36.00

ROSENTHAL

Christmas

1968, Christmas in Bremen 135.00
1969, Christmas in Rothenburg 103.00
1970, Christmas in Cologne 108.00
1971, Christmas in Garmisch 71.00
1972, Christmas Celebration in Franconia 69.00
1973, Christmas in Lubeck-Holstein .. 77.00
1974, Christmas in Wurzburg 92.00
1975, Freiburg Cathedral 51.50
1976, Castle Cochem 39.00
1977, Hanover Town Hall 80.00
1978, Cathedral at Aachen 84.50
1979, Cathedral in Luxemburg 100.00
1980, Christmas in Brussels 99.00
1981, Christmas in Trier 110.00
1982, Milan Cathedral 133.00
1983, Church at Castle Wittenberg .. 147.50
1984, City Hall of Stockholm 147.50

Wiinblad Christmas

1971, Maria & Child 1,193.00
1972, King Caspar 454.00
1973, King Melchior 361.00
1974, King Balthazar 237.00
1975, The Annunciation 134.00
1976, Angel with Trumpet 119.00
1977, Adoration of the Shepherds ... 158.00
1978, Angel with Harp 110.00
1979, Exodus from Egypt 114.00
1980, Angel with Glockenspiel 119.00
1981, Christ Child Visits Temple 152.00
1982, Christening of Christ 122.00

ROYAL BAYREUTH

Christmas

1972, Carriage in the Village 58.50
1973, Snow Scene 11.00
1974, Old Mill 12.00
1975, Forest Chalet "Serenity" 10.50
1976, Christmas in the Country 16.00
1977, Peace on Earth 17.50
1978, Peaceful Interlude 25.00
1979, Homeward Bound 25.00

Mother's Day

1973, Consolation 19.50
1974, Young Americans 100.00
1975, Young Americans II 59.00
1976, Young Americans III 36.00
1977, Young Americans IV 22.50
1978, Young Americans V 19.00
1979, Young Americans VI 26.00
1980, Young Americans VII 37.00
1981, Young Americans VIII 26.00
1982, Young Americans IX 30.00

ROYAL COPENHAGEN

Christmas

1908 (ILLUS.) 1,545.00
1909 .... 171.50
1910 .... 134.00
1911 .... 118.00
1912 .... 120.00

1908 Royal Copenhagen Christmas Plate

Year	Price
1913	116.00
1914	100.00
1915	110.00
1916	75.00
1917	70.00
1918	72.00
1919	72.00
1920	70.00
1921	62.50
1922	55.00
1923	57.00
1924	83.00
1925	68.00
1926	67.00
1927	110.00
1928	74.00
1929	69.00
1930	80.00
1931	81.00
1932	72.00
1933	107.00
1934	90.00
1935	122.00
1936	116.00
1937	123.00
1938	191.00
1939	222.00
1940	285.00
1941	245.00
1942	271.00
1943	356.00
1944	152.00
1945	274.00
1946	124.00
1947	177.00
1948	163.00
1949	147.00
1950	157.00
1951	247.00
1952	102.00
1953	99.00
1954	100.00
1955	145.00
1956	123.00
1957	79.00
1958	114.00
1959	92.00
1960	112.00
1961	112.00
1962	167.00
1963	60.00
1964	49.00
1965	49.00
1966	35.00
1967	33.00
1968	20.00
1969	21.00
1970	33.00
1971	15.50
1972	15.00
1973	16.00
1974	17.00
1975	15.50
1976	30.00
1977	17.50
1978	17.00
1979	44.00
1980	26.50
1981	31.00
1982	32.50
1983	30.00
1984	29.00
1985	34.00
1986	31.00

Mother's Day

Plate	Price
1971, American Mother	12.50
1972, Oriental Mother	5.50
1973, Danish Mother	6.50
1974, Greenland Mother	6.50
1975, Bird in Nest	6.50
1976, Mermaids	10.00
1977, The Twins	8.50
1978, Mother & Child	8.00
1979, A Loving Mother	9.00
1980, An Outing with Mother	11.50
1981, Reunion	14.50
1982, Children's Hour	15.50

SCHMID HUMMEL

Christmas

Plate	Price
1971, Angel	40.00
1972, Angel with Flute	46.00
1973, The Nativity	75.00
1974, The Guardian Angel	15.50
1975, Christmas Child	21.00
1976, Sacred Journey	14.00
1977, Herald Angel	13.00
1978, Heavenly Trio	16.00
1979, Starlight Angel	17.00
1980, Parade into Toyland	25.00
1981, A Time to Remember	16.00
1982, Angelic Procession	21.00
1983, Angelic Messenger	21.00
1984, A Gift from Heaven	33.50
1985, Heavenly Light	26.00
1986, Tell the Heavens	25.00

Mother's Day

Plate	Price
1972, Playing Hooky	15.00
1973, Little Fisherman	40.00

1974, Bumblebee 11.00
1975, Message of Love 12.00
1976, Devotion for Mother 12.00
1977, Moonlight Return 18.50
1978, Afternoon Stroll 15.00
1979, Cherub's Gift 16.00
1980, Mother's Little Helpers 19.00
1981, Playtime 26.00
1982, The Flower Basket 30.00
1983, Spring Bouquet 33.50
1984, A Joy to Share 28.00
1985, A Mother's Journey 21.50
1986, Home from School 33.00

SPODE

Christmas

1970, Partridge in a Pear Tree 22.00
1971, In Heaven the Angels Singing 12.50
1972, We Saw Three Ships A'Sailing 14.00
1973, We Three Kings of Orient Are 34.50
1974, Deck the Halls 44.00
1975, Christbaum 22.00
1976, Good King Wenceslas 26.00
1977, The Holly & the Ivy 27.50
1978, While Shepherds Watched 21.50
1979, Away in a Manger 28.50
1980, Bringing in the Boar's Head ... 27.00
1981, Make We Merry 47.00

VAL ST. LAMBERT (GLASS)

Old Masters Series

1968, Rubens & Rembrandt, pr. 76.00
1969, Van Gogh & Van Dyck, pr. ... 51.00
1970, Da Vinci & Michelangelo, pr... 54.00
1971, El Greco & Goya, pr. 36.00
1972, Reynolds & Gainsborough 38.00

WEDGWOOD

Christmas

1969, Windsor Castle 162.00
1970, Christmas in Trafalgar Square 19.50
1971, Picadilly Circus, London 29.00
1972, St. Paul's Cathedral 33.00
1973, Tower of London 27.00
1974, Houses of Parliament 21.00
1975, Tower Bridge 34.00
1976, Hampton Court 21.50
1977, Westminster Abbey 32.50
1978, Horse Guards 22.50
1979, Buckingham Palace 37.50
1980, St. James Palace 29.00
1981, Marble Arch 32.50
1982, Lambeth Palace 20.00
1983, All Souls, Langham Palace 45.00
1984, Constitution Hill 35.50
1985, The Tate Gallery 38.00
1986, Albert Memorial 42.00

Mother's Day

1971, Sportive Love 14.00
1972, Sewing Lesson 19.00
1973, Baptism of Achilles 19.00
1974, Domestic Employment 35.00
1975, Mother & Child 23.00
1976, The Spinner 22.00
1977, Leisure Time 24.00
1978, Swan & Cygnets 27.00
1979, Deer & Fawn 23.50
1980, Birds 22.00
1981, Mare & Foal 29.00
1982, Cherubs with Swing 21.00
1983, Cupid & Butterfly 22.50
1984, Cupid & Music 26.50
1985, Cupid & Doves 38.00
1986, Cupids at Play 26.00

(End of Commemorative Plate Section)

COMPACTS & VANITY CASES

Faberge Gold Compact

Basse-taille compact, green enamel, chrome trim, Girey $65.00

Celluloid compact, advertising, "Kremola Skin Cream," cover pictures girl, w/mirror, ca. 1915 .... 10.00

Enameled compact, cartouche form, painted w/a courting couple in an 18th century style landscape, Continental, 3½" w. 66.00

Gold compact, 14k, octagonal, engine turned decoration w/center monogrammed cartouche 100.00

Gold compact, 14k, round, etched florals, "ECB" monogram, w/mirror, ca. 1915 .... 450.00

Gold compact, rectangular w/rounded sides of plain polished gold, the cover & base engraved w/matted bands of entwined vine, cabochon sapphire thumbpiece & finial, interior w/three compartments, Faberge, workmaster August Hollming, St. Petersburg, Russia, ca. 1900, 3½" l. (ILLUS.)..4,950.00

Marcasite compact, heart-shaped, bells & "V" initial 50.00

Metal compact, lipstick & cigarette

case combination, "Sophisticase," by Volupte 20.00
Sterling silver compact, Art Deco floral motif, 4" d. 60.00
Sterling silver compact, blue enamel portrait on cover 60.00
Sterling silver compact, heart-shaped, w/monogram 25.00
Sterling silver compact, engraved "Corinne," Mary Dunhill, 3 x 2" oval 55.00
Sterling silver compact-money holder-card case combination, adjustable handle, marked "Whiting" 95.00
Sterling silver vanity case w/chain handle, w/monogram, 2½ x 3½" 85.00

COOKBOOKS

Procter & Gamble Cookbook

Cookbook collectors are usually good cooks and will buy important new cookbooks as well as seek out notable older ones. Many early cookbooks were published and given away as advertising premiums for various products used extensively in cooking. While some rare, scarce first edition cookbooks can be very expensive, most collectible cookbooks are reasonably priced.

Advertising, "Arm & Hammer Baking Soda - Good Things to Eat," 1930 ..... $5.00
Advertising, "Walter Baker Choice Recipes," illustrated, 1914 ..... 12.00
Advertising, "Baker's Chocolate," 1931, 60 pp. 20.00
Advertising, "Brer Rabbit Molasses" 4.00
Advertising, "Calumet Baking Powder Recipe Book," 1922, full-color illustrations, 80 pp. 12.00
Advertising, "Cream of Wheat - Diamond Cookbook," 1910 ..... 20.00
Advertising, "Crown Cork & Seal Canning Book," 1936 ..... 5.00
Advertising, "Dr. King's Electric Bitters Cookbook" 20.00
Advertising, "Gold Medal Flour Cookbook," 1904 ..... 15.00
Advertising, "Lowney's (Chocolate) Boston Cookbook," 1912, hardbound, 400 pp. 15.00
Advertising, "Old Dutch Beer Book - 300 Ways to Make Sandwiches," 1945 ..... 3.00
Advertising, "Pebeco Toothpaste 'Gone With the Wind' Famous Southern Recipes Cookbook," Scarlett on cover, blacks inside 30.00
Advertising, "Pillsbury Cookbook," 1914, 126 pp. 14.00
Advertising, "Rumford's Baking Powder Cookbook," 1911, girl on cover 17.00
Advertising, "Vaughn Feed Store - Vegetable Cookbook," 1919 ..... 7.50
Advertising, "Westinghouse Sugar & Spice Cookbook," 1951 ..... 3.00
"All About Baking," 1937, hardbound, 144 pp. 12.50
"American Family Cookbook," Culinary Arts, first edition 25.00
"Blondie (& Dagwood) Soup & Sandwich Cookbook," 1947 ..... 12.00
"Boston Cooking School Cookbook," by Fannie Farmer, 1914 ..... 12.50
"Cook's Oracle Cookbook," by Munroe Francis, 1822, Boston, Massachusetts 95.00
"The Everyday Cookbook," by Miss R. Neil, ca. 1890, 315 pp. 15.00
"Fruit & Flower Mission Cookbook," 1924, Seattle, 393 pp. 10.50
"Household Discoveries, Recipes & Processes," 1917, Morse, 842 pp. 15.00
"The Ideal Cookery Book, 1,349 Recipes," 1891, 402 pp. (spine loose) 15.00
"Mary Arnold's Century Cookbook," 1895 ..... 20.00
"Mrs. Rorer's New Cook Book," 1902, 731 pp. 9.50
"New Recipes for Good Eating," 1949, The Procter & Gamble Company, Cincinnati, Ohio, paperback, 112 pp., 5¾ x 7¾" (ILLUS.) 7.00
"Selected Recipes from Hood College, Maryland," 1940 ..... 4.00
"600 Receipts," by John Marquart, 1890, hardbound, 311 pp. 15.00
"G. Taber's Stillmeadow Cookbook,"

1965, Philadelphia (torn dust jacket) 30.00
"Toll House Recipes," by Ruth Wakefield, 1946, 275 pp. 35.00
"White House Cookbook," 1894 . . . . . 50.00
"Woman's World Salad Book," 1929 . . . . . . 8.00

COOKIE CUTTERS

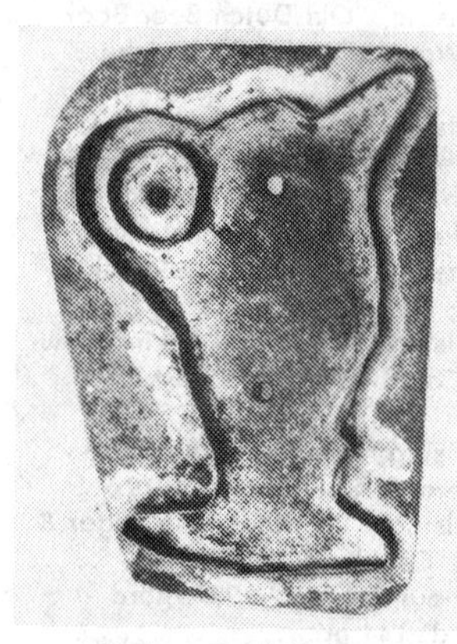

Pitcher Cookie Cutter

Recently there has been an accelerated interest in old tin cookie cutters. For the most part, these were made by tinsmiths who shaped primitive designs of tin strips and then soldered them to a backplate, pierced to allow air to enter and prevent a suction from holding the rolled cookie dough in the form. Sometimes an additional handle was soldered to the back. Cookie cutters were also manufactured in great quantities in an outline form that could depict animals, birds, star and other forms, including the plain round that sometimes carried embossed advertising for flour or other products on the handle. Aluminum cookie cutters were made after 1920. All cutters listed are tin unless otherwise noted.

Advertising, "Pillsbury Company," Winnie Winkle from the Comicooky Cutters series, self-handle, aluminum, in original box w/paper stickers picturing character to be applied to cookie, 1937 . . . . . . $22.00
Advertising, "Robin Hood Flour," figural Robin Hood, clear green plastic 5.00
Bear, flat backplate pierced w/star design, strap handle, 3½ x 2¼" oval 20.00
Bird, flat backplate pierced w/star design 20.00
Bird in flight, flat backplate pierced w/single hole, 4" l. 22.50
Bird w/crimped tail in standing position, flat backplate pierced w/eyehole for bird & three flower-like designs, 6" l. 105.00
Camel, flat backplate pierced w/star design 25.00
Cornucopia w/rolled edges, flat backplate pierced w/single hole, strap handle, 3½" l. 40.00
Diamond, flat backplate pierced w/single hole 7.50
Dog standing, outline w/folded rim, arched handle 44.00
Duck, flat backplate pierced w/single hole, strap handle, 4" h. 12.00
Elephant, flat backplate pierced w/single hole, strap handle, 4" l. 75.00
Fish, flat backplate pierced w/single hole, 5" l. 22.50
Hackney pony prancing, flat backplate, 1830, 6 x 7" 250.00
Hatchet, double strap handles, 7" l. 34.00
Heart, flat backplate pierced w/single hole, strap handle, 2½" h. . . . 25.00
Heart, flat backplate pierced w/single hole, strap handle, 6 x 5" 55.00
Horse standing, flat backplate pierced w/single hole, 4½" l. 105.00
Human head facing left, flat backplate pierced w/two holes, 4½" l. 75.00
Hunter wearing hat w/gun outstretched, flat backplate, 4½" h. 120.00
Lion, flat backplate pierced w/star design 25.00
Multiple-type, round frame enclosing love birds, tulips, stars & other motifs, cuts 10 cookies at once, 8¼" d. 300.00
Pitcher, flat backplate pierced w/three holes (ILLUS.) 24.00
Rabbit sitting, flat backplate pierced w/single hole, strap handle, 4" h. 15.00
Round, crinkled edge, stamped "Fries" on handle, 3" d. . . . .8.00 to 12.00
Santa Claus, flat backplate, 8" h. . . . 130.00
Shamrock, handleless, opaque green plastic 3.00
Star, 6-pointed, flat backplate 8.00
Turkey, flat backplate 20.00
Vegetables, set of nine assorted shapes fitted into 4" d. tin box, attributed to the Watkins Co., New York, ca. 1870, 10 pcs. 27.50

CORKSCREWS

"Old Snifter" Corkscrew

More corkscrews should be available to collectors in years to come since wine sales in the United States have shown a profound increase within the past decade. Today corkscrew collectors seek out those with unique form, with early patent dates, or with desirable handles that are made from a wide variety of materials.

Advertising, brass, "Anheuser-Busch" $15.00
Advertising, brass, leg-shaped, folding-type, "Morgan Distilling Co." 225.00
Advertising, bottle-shaped, "Peebles Old Cabinet Whiskey, Cincinnati, Ohio" 25.00
Advertising, bullet-shaped, "Kammer Whiskey Balt.," 1900 . . . . 23.00
Advertising, bullet-shaped, "Old Forester Whiskey" 25.00
Advertising, chrome-plated, bottle-shaped, "Anheuser-Busch" 26.50
Advertising, metal, pear-shaped, "Mount Vernon Pure Rye," 1890 . . 20.00
Advertising, wooden & metal, "C.D. Kenny Coffee & Tea Co.," 1910 . . . 10.00
Boar's tusk handle w/sterling silver cap 40.00
Brass, cast Bacchus figure w/legs of steel, marked, "Wolfenbutter 1848 Anno" 175.00
Brass, figural Punch & Judy head top, ca. 1840, overall 6" 95.00
Cast iron, figural, "Old Snifter," caricature of Congressman Andrew Volstead, author of Prohibition legislation, w/bottle opener, 6¾" h. (ILLUS.) 72.50
Celluloid, model of a nude mermaid, marked "Geschutz," Germany, 4" l. 320.00
Cow's horn handle, cow etched on each side 45.00
Silver plate, depicts the head of a swan, stamped "L'orfevrerie Christofle," 1930 . . . . 200.00
Stag's horn handle, w/ornate sterling silver cap, 5¾" l. 68.00

COUNTRY STORE COLLECTIBLES

Country store museums have opened across the country in an effort to recreate those slower-paced days of the late 19th and early 20th centuries when the general store served as the local meeting place for much of rural America. Here one not only purchased necessary supplies for upcoming weeks, but caught up on important news events and local gossip. With strong interest in colorful tin cans during the early 1960's came the realization that these stores and neighborhood groceries were fast disappearing, replaced by the so-called supermarkets, and collectors began buying all items associated with these early stores. *Also see CANS & CONTAINERS and CASH REGISTERS.*

Bag rack, iron wire, counter top w/nine graduated sections, 31 x 14 x 10" $125.00
Bag rack - string holder combination, wire, hanging-type w/hoops, wire cup holds string, circular bag clamps below, 12 x 14" 150.00
Broom holder, hanging-type, wire . . 85.00
Cheese cutter w/cleaver, counter-top model 295.00
Coffee bin, lift-lid, tin, "Morning Glory Coffee, Kansas City, Mo.," 19" 149.00
Coffee bin, lift-lid, tin, "Dwinell-Wright Co's. Royal Coffees," 19¼ x 13¼ x 21½" 575.00
Cooler, walk-in type, oak w/milk white glass & mirrored front w/glass doors, solid brass hardware 2,500.00
Counter display, cardboard, Alka-Seltzer multicolored cartoon, 1940's 150.00
Counter display, metal, Prince Albert tobacco pocket tin rack 20.00
Cracker bin, lift-lid, brass front w/glass insert, "Miller Crackers & Biscuits," 10 x 10 x 11½" 65.00
Ribbon dispenser, cast iron w/spool

of ribbon, "Emmons & Dobson, Trunks, Bags, Gloves & Leather Goods," ca. 1870 .... 65.00
Showcase, pine, top well w/three removable pieces of plate glass & one apron w/hinged doors, trestle base w/scalloped ends, worn old brown graining over earlier grey paint, 25 x 80½", 32½" h. 325.00
Spice bin, lift-lid, tin, cloves, "Wallaver & Hoffman Co., Milwaukee, Wisconsin," colored lithographs ... 95.00
Spice bin, six-compartment, part brass w/beveled mirror, "Woolson Spice," 28" l. 475.00

CURRIER & IVES

American Choice Fruits

This lithographic firm was founded in 1835 by Nathaniel Currier with James M. Ives becoming a partner in 1857. Current events of the day were portrayed in the early days and the prints were hand-colored. Landscapes, vessels, sport, and hunting scenes of the West all became popular subjects. The firm was in existence until 1906. All prints listed are hand-colored unless otherwise noted.

American Choice Fruits, large folio, 1869, framed, small tears & discoloration in margins (ILLUS.) $880.00
American Country Life, Summer's Evening, after F.F. Palmer, large folio, N. Currier, 1855 (some staining) ....2,200.00 to 3,080.00
American Frontier Life, On the War Path, after A.F. Tait, large folio, 1863 ....4,510.00
American Winter Sports, Deer shooting "On the Shattagee," after L. Maurer, large folio, N. Currier, 1855 (small margin tear) 6,050.00
Autumn on Lake George, small folio, undated 195.00
Battle of Coal Harbor, Va., June 1st, 1864, small folio, undated 150.00
Cake Walk (De), For Beauty, Grace and Style, de Wimmen takes de Cake, small folio, 1883 .... 245.00
Camping in the Woods, "A Good Time Coming," after A.F. Tait, large folio, 1863, framed (some margin stains & other minor defects) 8,800.00
Catskill Mountains (The), From the Eastern Shore of the Hudson, after F.F. Palmer, large folio, 1860 ....2,090.00
Emily, small folio, N. Currier, undated, framed 55.00
English Winter Scene (An), small folio, undated, framed (stains) 275.00
Fall of Richmond, Virginia (The), small folio, 1865 .... 230.00
Farmer's Home - Summer (The), after F.F. Palmer, large folio, 1864 ....4,400.00
Farm-Yard in Winter (The), after G.H. Durrie, large folio, 1861 ....4,950.00
Frontier Settlement (A), medium folio, undated (stained, few foxmarks) 660.00
Fruits, Autumn Varieties, small folio, 1871, framed 110.00
Gold Mining in California, small folio, 1871 (margin nicks) 2,420.00
Good Shepherdess (The), small folio, N. Currier, 1846, framed 115.00
Good Times on the Old Plantation, small folio, undated, curly maple frame ....300.00 to 375.00
Great West (The), small folio, 1870 ....1,045.00
High Bridge at Harlem, N.Y. (The), small folio, N. Currier, 1849 (creasing, staining in margins) ...1,320.00
Holidays in the Country, Troublesome Flies, large folio, 1868 ....3,850.00
Home in the Wilderness (A), small folio, 1870, framed (slight staining) 588.50
Home of Washington (The), Mount Vernon, Va., medium folio, undated, framed (stains) 200.00
Hunter's Shanty (The), In the Adirondacks, large folio, 1861 (small image crease, slight staining) 1,430.00
James K. Polk, The People's Candidate for President, small folio, N. Currier, 1844, beveled cherry frame 115.00
John L. Sullivan, Champion Pugilist of the World, medium folio, 1883, in shadowbox frame 2,010.00
Lake Memphremagog, Owl's Head, small folio, undated, old giltwood frame 200.00
Landscape, Fruit and Flowers, after F.F. Palmer, large folio, 1862, framed (margins soiled & rust-

stained, reverse staining showing through in places) 10,450.00

Life of a Fireman (The), The Night Alarm - "Start her Lively, boys," large folio, N. Currier, 1854 .....2,640.00

Life of a Sportsman (The), Camping in the Woods, small folio, 1872 (small margin loss & margin abrasions) 385.00

Life on the Prairie, The "Buffalo Hunt," after A.F. Tait, large folio, 1862, framed (some staining to image & margins) 4,125.00

Little Manly, small folio, 1874, beveled mahogany veneer frame (stains, slight damage) 90.00

Major Gen. Benj. F. Butler - of Mass., small folio, black & white 66.00

Maple Sugaring, Early Spring in the Northern Woods, small folio, 1872, framed ....1,000.00 to 1,200.00

Moonlight Promenade (The), small folio, framed 80.00

Morning in the Woods, after F.F. Palmer, large folio, 1865, 14 5/8 x 20½" (reverse discoloration, pale reverse foxing, margin loss, an abrasion & two old tape stains to margins) 2,970.00

My Cottage Home, after F.F. Palmer, large folio, 1866 (reverse surface soiling, small margin nicks)......1,980.00

National Democratic Banner, small folio, framed, 1860 (trimmed, creases, minor stains) 325.00

New England Winter Scene, after G.H. Durrie, large folio, 1861, framed (some overall & vertical line staining)..................6,000.00

New Suspension Bridge - Niagara Falls, small folio 352.00

Old Homestead in Winter (The), after G. H. Durrie, large folio, 1864 (some foxing & soiling)..........4,125.00

Old Manse (The), small folio, framed 375.00

Pasture in Summer (The), The Drinking Trough, large folio, 1867 ..... 770.00

Perry's Victory On Lake Erie, small folio 625.00

The Pursuit

Pretty Story (The), printed on same sheet with Birdie and Pet, small folio, framed, 18 5/8 x 13½" (minor stains & small tear in margin) 265.00

Pursuit (The), after A.F. Tait, large folio, 1856, framed (ILLUS.) 3,575.00

Reading the Scriptures, medium folio, N. Currier, framed........... 105.00

Roadside Mill (The), small folio, 1870, curly maple frame 225.00

Scenery of the Upper Mississippi, An Indian Village, small folio, curly maple frame (slight margin tear extending into image area) 200.00

Season of Blossoms (The), after F.F. Palmer, large folio, 1865, framed (apparent repair to margin)..........................1,320.00

Snowy Morning (A), after F.F. Palmer, medium folio, 1864, framed 2,200.00

Star Spangled Banner (The), small folio, framed 95.00

Summer in the Country, small folio, bird's-eye maple veneer frame (stains) 200.00

Surrender of Lord Cornwallis at Yorktown Va. Oct. 19th 1781, after John Trumbull, large folio, N. Currier, 1852, 15¾ x 24 7/8", framed 4,400.00

"Monitor" and "Merrimac"

Terrific Engagement between the "Monitor" 2 guns, and "Merrimac" 10 guns, in Hampton Roads, March 9th 1862, large folio, 1862 (ILLUS.) 2,420.00

Thomas Jefferson, medium folio, N. Currier, mahogany veneer frame (margins trimmed, tears, wear & stains) 130.00

Trapper's Last Shot (The), medium folio 990.00

View on the Hudson, after F.F. Palmer, large folio, framed (small stain in image, staining & discoloration throughout) 2,090.00

Village Blacksmith (The), after F.F. Palmer, medium folio, N. Currier, framed (some staining) 715.00

Washington's Entry Into New York, medium folio, 1857 .... 700.00
Water Jump (The), large folio, 1884 (backboard stains, margin water stains) 990.00
Wm. Penn's Treaty With the Indians When He Founded the Province of Pennsa, 1661, after N. Sarony, small folio, N. Currier, framed ... 528.00
Winter Evening, medium folio, N. Currier, 1854, framed (somewhat stained & discolored) 1,210.00
Winter Moonlight, after F.F. Palmer, medium folio, 1866, framed 3,850.00
"Wooding up" on the Mississippi, after F.F. Palmer, large folio, 1863 (staining, especially to margin, some pale foxing) 16,500.00
Yosemite Valley - California, The Bridal Veil Fall, after F.F. Palmer, large folio, 1866 ....4,950.00

CUSPIDORS

Blown Glass Cuspidor

The cuspidor, or spittoon, is a bowl-shaped vessel into which tobacco chewers could spit. These containers were a necessity in an era when much of the male population chewed tobacco and even some ladies were known to "take a chew." Made of metal, earthenware pottery, china and glass, they ranged in size from the large barroom floor models to small glass cuspidors designed for the ladies.

Brass, cast, Arcade Mfg. Co. $95.00
Brass, marked "California State House" 80.00
Brass, saloon-style, concave lid, 4 x 9½" 45.00
Cast iron, top hat-shaped, marked "Bott Bro's., Columbus, O., Billard (sic) and Pool Tables," old gold repaint, 6½" h. 155.00
Cast iron w/tin insert, mechanical-type, model of a turtle, step on head to lift cover, 1891 patent, 14" l. 149.00
China, lady's, gold decoration on white ground, 2 1/8" top d., 1½" base d., 1½" h. 40.00
China, lady's, h.p. flowers on white ground, gold borders, Germany, 6¾" d. 110.00
China, lady's, h.p. roses on dark green & gold flared rim, rose garland decoration on white ground on sides, 7 5/8" top d., 6¼" base d., 4¾" h. 65.00
China, lady's, h.p. red & white roses, shaded green leaves on black ground on front & reverse, also around top opening rim, unmarked 45.00
Glass, blown, cobalt blue, w/folded rim, mid-19th c., 9" d., 5" h. (ILLUS.) 275.00
Glass, milk white, red & black stripes, unmarked 50.00
Graniteware, aqua & white swirls .. 60.00
Graniteware, grey 59.00
Ironstone china, lady's, marked "KT & K China," Knowles, Taylor & Knowles, East Liverpool, Ohio, 8" d. 75.00
Pottery, Lily & Plume patt., blue & white 90.00
Pottery, relief-molded grapes on green ground 37.50
Pottery, white, pink & black, Knowles, Taylor & Knowles, East Liverpool, Ohio 135.00
Stoneware, embossed Scroll & Leaf patt. w/blue sponged earthworm designs 180.00

DECOYS

Black-breasted Plovers

Decoys have been utilized for years to lure flying water fowl into target range. They have been made of carved and turned wood, papier-mache, canvas and metal, and some are in the category of outstanding folk art and command high prices.

Black-breasted Plovers, hollow two-piece construction, carved wing detail, original bills, one in spring plumage, other in fall plumage, New England, pr. (ILLUS.) $3,850.00
Black Duck, Mason Challenge Grade, glass eyes, old working repaint, 17" l. (holes in bottom, age cracks & old chips on tail).... 105.00
Black Duck Hen, Armstrong Decoy Co., stuffed canvas body w/original silk screened paint, underside w/worn grey repaint, glass eyes, 14½" l. (shot scars) 60.00
Bluebill, carved wood, body & bill w/original paint, green repaint on head, 10¾" l..................... 120.00
Bluebill Drake, carved wood, glass eyes, original paint, 13¼" l. 175.00
Blue Heron, carved wood, well-shaped cedar body w/whittle marks, original grey paint, inserted ochre beak reglued, stamped "Mackey Collection" on driftwood base, 30" l., 24" h. 675.00
Brant Goose, carved wood, hollow construction, glass eyes, original paint, branded "C.W.," mid-20th c., 18" l. 155.00
Broadbill, wood w/painted canvas covering, glass eyes, 12" l........ 20.00
Bufflehead Drake, attributed to Alvin Gunner Meckins, old paint & tack eyes, 10" l. 185.00
Bufflehead Hen, attributed to Alvin Gunner Meckins, old paint & tack eyes, 10¾" l. 155.00
Canada Goose, pressed paper, movable neck, 24" body 115.00
Canada Goose swimming, carved wood, glass eyes, worn old paint, mid-20th c., 26¼" l. 375.00
Canada Goose, carved wood, tack eyes, two-piece head & neck, short legs, mounted on oblong base, Indian-made, 28" l., 15½" h. 305.00

Canada Goose Swimming Decoy

Canada Goose swimming, by Sam Soper, Barnegat, New Jersey (ILLUS.) 34,100.00
Canvasback Drake, carved wood, original paint, glass eyes, 11¾" l. (shot scars) 105.00
Crows, black sheet iron, stick-up type, ca. 1910, 16½" l., pr. 175.00
Crow, papier-mache, life-size, glass eyes 45.00
Fish, carved wood, tin fins & tail, orange/red paint, 4¼" l. 12.50
Fish, carved wood, well-shaped dorsal fin & large glass eye, original red & yellow paint, 11½" l. (missing tail insert w/hook)........... 25.00
Fish, "Crappies," carved wood, painted, pr...................... 30.00
Fish, "Perch," tin fins & tail, green back, white belly, red chin, unknown maker, 5½" 25.00
Fish, "Pike," carved wood, jointed, nail eyes, tin fins & tail, red & white paint, 7¼" l............... 20.00
Fish, "Pike," w/small decoy in its mouth, carved wood, tin fins & tail, 28" l. 200.00
Fish, "Sturgeon," carved wood, glass eyes, metal fins, old grey & white paint, 36¼" l. 700.00
Geese, waxed cardboard, folding-type decoys in original canvas bag marked "One Dozen Complete Johnson's Folding Goose Decoys," w/metal standards, unused, 17" l., set of 12 .... 275.00
Goldeneye Drake, carved wood, old black & white working repaint, inset head, 13¾" l. (age cracks) ... 85.00
Golden Plover in spring plumage, unknown maker, Massachusetts .. 700.00
Mallard Drake, Evans Duck Decoy Company, Wisconsin, hollow construction, worn repaint, glass eyes, marked "Evans Decoy," 15½" l. 125.00
Mallard Drake, carved wood, painted green, brown, blue, red, black & white, glass eyes, by A. Bennett, Joliet, Illinois area, 16½" l. 192.50
Mallard Drake, Mason Premier Grade, glass eyes, original paint, 17¾" l. (glued break at neck & tail chipped) 475.00
Mallard Hen, carved wood, hollow construction, old worn working repaint, glass eyes, branded "N.A.W.A.," 15¾" l. 195.00
Merganser, carved wood, by F.J. Dobbins, Jonesport, Maine 145.00
Merganser Hen & Drake, carved wood, hollow construction, original paint, mid-20th c., 16½" l., pr. 250.00
Redhead Drake, carved wood, old working repaint & glass eyes, by John Ososkie, Wyandotte, Michi-

gan, 15½" l. (split in neck & age cracks in body block) 55.00

Ruddy Turnstones, carved wood, old colorful repaint, 9" l., 9" & 10" h., on contemporary stands, pr. 210.00

Shorebird, tin, folding-type, original paint w/minor wear & light rust, on contemporary wooden base, 11" h. 130.00

Shoveler Drake, carved wood, original paint, glass eyes, signed "Cliff Reinsager, Muscatine, Iowa, 1959," 14¾" l. 135.00

Whistler Drake, carved wood, inset head & relief carved detail, glass eyes, 14" l. 95.00

DISNEY (Walt) COLLECTIBLES

Davy Crockett Cereal Bowl

Scores of objects ranging from watches to dolls have been created showing Walt Disney's copyrighted animated cartoon characters, and an increasing number of collectors are now seeking these, made primarily by licensed manufacturers. Also see BIG LITTLE BOOKS.

Alice in Wonderland note paper & envelopes, 1951 .... $45.00

Alice in Wonderland wrist watch, U.S. Time, 1950's 60.00

Bambi card game, Vol. 4 .... 10.00

Bambi music box night light 35.00

Bambi napkin ring, sterling silver ... 45.00

Bambi night light w/perfume well, 1950's 200.00

Bambi planter, ceramic, tan, pink & green on beige, glossy, marked "Bambi, Walt Disney Productions" on bottom, 7" l., 7" h. 25.00

Bambi rug, cotton, Bambi & friends in the woods, 60 x 48" 105.00

Bambi vase, china, Goebel & Co., 6" h. 110.00

Big Bad Wolf game, 1933 .... 35.00

Big Bad Wolf pinback button, early 1930's 80.00

Big Bad Wolf sand pail, tin, Ohio Art 65.00

Cinderella planter, ceramic, pastel blue, pink, green & yellow, impressed "WDP," 6½" l., 6½" h. .. 24.00

Cinderella wrist watch, w/glass slipper case, U.S. Time, 1950 .... 90.00

Daisy Duck figure, frosted glass, 4½" h. 29.00

Daisy Duck wrist watch, 1948 .... 110.00

Davy Crockett bank, metal, dime register 25.00

Davy Crockett belt, leather 20.00

Davy Crockett binoculars 30.00

Davy Crockett cereal bowl, milk white glass w/red figures & lettering, Fire King Ovenware, 4¾" d., 2½" h. (ILLUS.) 12.50

Davy Crockett clicker gun, lithographed tin 36.50

Davy Crockett clock, wall-type, Davy on face of pendulum 125.00

Davy Crockett costume & accessories, in original box w/picture of Fess Parker on cover 65.00

Davy Crockett fishing set, on original card 150.00

Davy Crockett flashlight, original box 35.00

Davy Crockett knife, pocket-type, 3-blade, Walt Disney Productions 30.00

Davy Crockett money belt 10.00

Davy Crockett mug, milk white glass, red graphics 10.00

Davy Crockett pencil box 40.00

Disney characters book, "Tomorrowland" 35.00

Disney characters coloring book, "Silly Symphony," Whitman, 1934, 34 pp. 35.00

Disney characters lunch box, school box w/Disney characters, w/thermos bottle, Aladdin Industries 35.00

Disney characters masks, Pinocchio, Figaro, Geppetto, Jiminy Cricket & Cleo, Gilette premium, original envelope 175.00

Disney characters Melody Player music box, w/five paper rolls, J. Chein & Co., 6½ x 7" 115.00

Disney characters toy, wind-up tin "Disneyland Roller Coaster," figure-8 roller coaster w/two passenger cars, J. Chein & Co., 1940's, 10" h. 300.00

Disney characters toy, wind-up tin ferris wheel, J. Chein & Co. 155.00

Donald Duck alarm clock, Bayard Co., France, dated 1956 .... 85.00

Donald Duck bicycle ornament, celluloid, 4½" 65.00
Donald Duck book, "Donald Duck & The Mystery of the Double X," Better Little Book 12.50
Donald Duck booties, pink, original bag, 1940's 12.00
Donald Duck camera, Walt Disney Enterprises, Herbert George Co., 1947 .... 53.00
Donald Duck figure, bisque, long-billed, marked "Walt Disney," 1930's, 3¼" h. 35.00
Donald Duck figure, celluloid, spring-jointed, long-billed, 1930's, 3" h. 40.00
Donald Duck figure, rubber, Seiberling, 5½" h. 95.00
Donald Duck game, "Bean Bag Party," original box, dated 1939 .... 35.00
Donald Duck hand puppet, rubber head, cloth body, 1930's 85.00
Donald Duck "jack-in-the-box," paper-covered wooden box w/papier-mache head Donald wearing blue felt jacket w/stuffed cloth arms inside, marked "Donald Duck W.D.P., A Spear Product," 1930's 900.00
Donald Duck lamp, bisque, figural, 8" h. 75.00
Donald Duck movie cel, Donald closing suitcase, matted, 1950's 125.00
Donald Duck pitcher, ceramic, figural, marked "Donald Duck, Walt Disney, U.S.A.," 6 1/8" h. 40.00
Donald Duck plate, Patriot China, 1930's 60.00
Donald Duck pull toy, Choo-Choo, Fisher Price No. 450 .... 70.00

Donald Duck Straws

Donald Duck straws, multi-color box of 100, Herz Mfg. Co., New York, New York, ¾ x 3¾ x 8¾" box (ILLUS.) 10.00
Donald Duck toothbrush holder, bisque, long-billed Donald, "Walt E. Disney," 5" h. 160.00
Donald Duck toy, wind-up tin drummer, Line-Mar 196.00
Dumbo the Elephant creamer & sugar bowl, W. Disney U.S.A., 1940's, pr. 45.00

Dumbo Movie Cel

Dumbo the Elephant movie cel, Dumbo nestled within his mother's legs, applied to airbrushed ground, 1940, matted, 10¼ x 8¾" (ILLUS.) 1,980.00
Dumbo the Elephant planter, ceramic, 4" l. 15.00
Dwarf Bashful figure, bisque, 3¼" 25.00
Dwarf Doc figure, rubber, Seiberling 25.00
Dwarf Dopey bank, composition, 1938 .... 125.00
Dwarf Dopey carpet sweeper, musical, Fisher Price 95.00
Dwarf Grumpy figure, bisque, 4" h. 38.00
Dwarf Sleepy doll, Ideal, w/original 1937 tag, 12" 90.00
Dwarf Sneezy charm, sterling silver 30.00
"Fantasia" drawing, pastel on colored paper, depicting the Milkweed ballerinas from the "Nutcracker Suite" sequence, 1940, 8 x 10½" 990.00
"Fantasia" movie cel, depicting seven mushrooms below raindrops in the "Nutcracker Suite" sequence, applied to an airbrushed ground, 1940, matted & framed, 6¼ x 7" 2,530.00
"Fantasia" movie program, 1940 .... 42.00
Fantasyland Train Load of Card Games 25.00
Ferdinand the Bull figure, bisque, 3" h. 24.00
Ferdinand the Bull figure, rubber, Seiberling, 1938-40 .... 43.00

Ferdinand the Bull movie cel, Ferdinand's mother grazing on grass, applied to airbrushed & watercolor ground, 1938, framed, matted, 7¾ x 9½" 715.00
Ferdinand the Bull tumbler, glass, 1938 .... 15.00
Figaro (Pinocchio's cat) figure, wood, Multi-Wood Products, 1940's, 3" h. 15.00
Geppetto (Pinocchio's father) figure, standing w/hand on chin, syrocco-type pressed wood, by Multi-Wood Products, 1940's, 5½" h. 35.00
Geppetto soap figure, 1939, 3¾" h. (chipped foot).................. 15.00
Goofy blotter, Sunoco premium, 1939 .... 15.00
Goofy candy container, "Pez" 10.00
Goofy movie cel from "How to Be a Sailor," gouache on full celluloid, depicting Goofy as an admiral w/a torpedo, 1944, framed, 8 x 10" 990.00
Goofy toy, windup, tin, Goofy on unicycle, Line Mar ......300.00 to 350.00
Goofy wrist watch, Bradley 28.00
Goofy & Pluto paint board, Tomart No. P0460 .... 14.00
Huey, Dewey & Louie (Donald Duck's nephews) rug, 1950's, 3½ x 6½" 350.00
Jiminy Cricket (Pinocchio) clicker, metal, Walt Disney Productions ... 10.00
Jiminy Cricket figure, wood, Multi-Wood Products, 1940's, 4½" h. 15.00

Jiminy Cricket Movie Cel

Jiminy Cricket movie cel, from "Pinocchio," depicting Jiminy Cricket sitting on matchbox used as his bed, applied on airbrushed background, Courvoisier Galleries label, matted & framed, 1939, 6¼ x 8½" (ILLUS.) 4,675.00
Lady & the Tramp movie cel, multi-sheet, depicting Lady, Tramp & their two puppies going for a stroll, applied to a hand-prepared ground, 1955, framed, 10 x 13" ..1,540.00
Mickey Mouse alarm clock, animated "wagging head" Mickey, Bayard Co., France, 1930's to 1969, original box ....100.00 to 125.00
Mickey Mouse alarm clock, shaped like oversized pocket watch, Bradley, 1979 .... 35.00
Mickey Mouse animation pan layout drawing, graphite & colored pencil, depicting Mickey thrown from his raft onto land, probably from "Mickey's Man Friday," ca. 1935, 7 x 20" 2,090.00
Mickey Mouse bank, model of a phone, Walt Disney Enterprises ... 25.00
Mickey Mouse barrette, 1940's 10.00
Mickey Mouse blackboard, standing-type w/shelf, folds flat, turning knobs w/animal pictures, 1939, 3½' h. ....125.00 to 175.00
Mickey Mouse blotter, 1930's 8.50
Mickey Mouse book, "Book for Coloring," die-cut, shows Mickey skating, 1936 .... 75.00
Mickey Mouse book, "Here They Are," 1930's 29.00
Mickey Mouse book, "Mickey Mouse & Boy Thursday," Whitman, 1948.. 20.00
Mickey Mouse book, "Mickey Mouse & His Friends," linen, Whitman No. 904, 1936, 12 pp. 75.00
Mickey Mouse book, "Mickey Mouse Circus," pop-up type, 1933 .... 300.00
Mickey Mouse book, "Mickey Mouse, Fifty Happy Years, The Official Birthday Book," Harmony Books, New York, New York, 1977 .... 25.00
Mickey Mouse book, "Mickey Mouse's Misfortune," Wee Little Book, 1934 .... 20.00
Mickey Mouse book, "Mickey Mouse Stories," Book No. 2, Mickey & Pluto on soft cover, Dave McKay Publications, 1934, unused, 3/8 x 6¼ x 8½" 80.00
Mickey Mouse book, "Mickey Mouse Presents Walt Disney's Nursery Stories from Walt Disney's Silly Symphony," Whitman, 1937, 212 pp.......................... 90.00
Mickey Mouse book, "Mickey Sees USA," w/color prints, 1944 ....25.00 to 30.00
Mickey Mouse book, "School Days In Disneyville," 1930's 29.00
Mickey Mouse books, Wee Little Books by Whitman, in original slip-in case, set of 6............ 165.00
Mickey Mouse camera, "Mick-A-Matic," ear actuated............. 40.00
Mickey Mouse card game, "Snap," w/box 60.00
Mickey Mouse ceiling lamp, glass shade 100.00

Mickey Mouse clock-radio, General Electric Youth Electronics 75.00
Mickey Mouse comb & mirror, Loma Plastics, the set 30.00
Mickey Mouse cookie jar, Mickey w/drum 95.00
Mickey Mouse creamer, china, Japan, 4" 60.00
Mickey Mouse croquet set, Withington, West Minot, Maine, original box 48.00
Mickey Mouse doll, stuffed felt, stamped "Steiff" on bottom of foot, 6" h. .... 350.00 to 450.00
Mickey Mouse doll, stuffed, squeak-type, pie wedge eyes, Gund, 14" h. 25.00
Mickey Mouse Easter egg transfers, 1935, unopened package 35.00
Mickey Mouse "Explorers Club" outfit, w/gun, belt, holster, hat & binoculars 70.00
Mickey Mouse feeding dish, silver, cut-out Mickey handle, Mickey riding his horse 95.00
Mickey Mouse figure, bisque, Mickey playing horn, 3½" h. 40.00
Mickey Mouse figure, bisque, w/slouch hat & walking cane, marked "Made in Japan," 1930's, 4¼" h. 80.00
Mickey Mouse figure, chalkware, 1930's, 3" h. 25.00
Mickey Mouse figure, papier-mache, hanging-type w/loop at top of head, bulbous red body & hands & feet on flexible armatures, early pie wedge eyes, 4½" h. 195.00
Mickey Mouse figure, rubber, Sun Rubber Co., 10½" h. 25.00
Mickey Mouse figure, wood, fully jointed, pre-War, mint, 1½" h. 600.00
Mickey Mouse figure, jointed wood, complete w/ears & tail, 1934, 3½" 95.00
Mickey Mouse figure, jointed wood, Borgfeldt, Pat. 8-17/1926, 5" h. 160.00
Mickey Mouse figure, die-cut wood, 13" h. 48.00
Mickey Mouse figure group, bisque, Mickey riding Pluto, 2½" 95.00
Mickey Mouse fork & spoon, baby's, silver plate, pr. 45.00
Mickey Mouse fountain pen, 1930's 125.00
Mickey Mouse game, "Circus" .... 150.00 to 180.00
Mickey Mouse game, "Dominoes," Walt Disney Enterprises, 1938, original box 62.00
Mickey Mouse game, "Pin the Tail on Mickey," oil cloth, Louis Marx, ca. 1935 .... 60.00
Mickey Mouse gumball bank, Hasbro, 1968 .... 18.00
Mickey Mouse Halloween costume, 1950's, original box 35.00
Mickey Mouse handkerchief, Mickey playing football, 1940's, 8½" sq... 9.00
Mickey Mouse iron-on patches, Bondex, Walt Disney Productions, ca. 1945 .... 16.00
Mickey Mouse movie cel, Mickey fishing, from "Plausible Impossible" Walt Disney cartoon 675.00
Mickey Mouse movie cel, Mickey Mouse holding a threaded needle, from "Brave Little Tailor," matted, 1938, 9 x 12" 550.00
Mickey Mouse mug, embossed wrist watch, "Mickey Mouse Time," Enesco 12.00
Mickey Mouse party horn, Louis Marx, 1930's, 7" l. 45.00
Mickey Mouse pencil box, Hasbro Co., red or blue, 1950's, each 22.00
Mickey Mouse pen knife, "Chicago World's Fair, 1933" souvenir 26.00
Mickey Mouse perfume bottle, figural, 4" h. 40.00
Mickey Mouse pinback button, "Penny's Back to School," Walt Disney Enterprises, 1930 .... 22.00
Mickey Mouse planter, ceramic, Mickey as cowboy, multicolored glossy finish, 4 x 7 x 6½" 34.00
Mickey Mouse planter, china, lustre ware, Mickey playing saxophone, 1930's, 4" l. 56.00
Mickey Mouse plate, china, "Happy Birthday Mickey," Schmid, 1978, limited edition 125.00
Mickey Mouse pocket watch, die-debossed back, Ingersoll, 1933 ... 350.00
Mickey Mouse radio, Mickey's head turns dial, 1960's 95.00
Mickey Mouse ring, sterling silver, Walt Disney Productions, 1930's, ¾" h. figure of Mickey 200.00
Mickey Mouse rug, Mickey, train & other Disney characters, 48 x 57" 125.00
Mickey Mouse suspenders, original card 50.00
Mickey Mouse Talky Jecktor, projector-phonograph combination, 13 films, key crank, needles, no record, sold only by Sears, original box .... 200.00 to 225.00
Mickey Mouse toy chest, Odora Co., ca. 1932 .... 285.00
Mickey Mouse toy, Mickey in fire truck, hard rubber w/white rubber tires, Walt Disney Productions, Sun Rubber Co. 50.00
Mickey Mouse toy, pull-type, wooden, Mickey Mouse Choo-Choo,

Walt Disney Productions, Fisher-Price No. 485, 1949-53, 4 x 8½ x 7" (ILLUS.) .... 75.00 to 100.00
Mickey Mouse toy, pull-type, wooden, drummer, Fisher-Price No. 476, 1941-43 & 1946-69 .... 90.00

Mickey Mouse Choo-Choo Toy

Mickey Mouse toy washing machine, Walt Disney Enterprises, 1934, original box 650.00
Mickey Mouse toy, windup, tin, "Mickey Mouse Express," Louis Marx & Co. .... 400.00 to 450.00

Mickey Mouse Handcar

Mickey Mouse toy, windup, tin & composition, handcar w/figures of Mickey & Minnie on each end of center handle, Lionel, ca. 1933, w/original box (ILLUS.) .. 550.00 to 650.00
Mickey Mouse toy, windup, tin, Mickey playing xylophone, Louis Marx & Co. 350.00
Mickey Mouse wallpaper trim, original box 30.00
Mickey Mouse watch fob, original leather strap, 1930's 75.00
Mickey Mouse water-color, Mickey Mouse as the sorcerer, from "Fantasia," w/broom carrying two buckets of water, Walt Disney Studio signature on lower left, 1941, 8 x 10" 2,090.00
Mickey Mouse wrist watch, original model, round dial, yellow-gloved minute & hour hands & three Mickey figures on subsidiary seconds dial, original black band w/Mickey figures, works patented "July '18 - Nov. 14, 1922," made in U.S.A., Ingersoll, 1933 .... 300.00 to 400.00
Mickey Mouse wrist watch, oblong dial, red leather band, U.S. Time, 1948-50's 86.00
Mickey Mouse wrist watch, 50th Birthday, boxed, mint, Bradley, 1978 .... 125.00
Minnie Mouse book, "Minnie Mouse & The Antique Chair," 1948 ..... $12.50
Minnie Mouse charm, sterling silver 34.00
Minnie Mouse doll, black plush, red polka dot bow, yellow shoes, 9" .. 8.00
Minnie Mouse feeding dish, Patriot China 50.00
Minnie Mouse figure, bisque, Minnie w/mandolin, Japan 45.00
Minnie Mouse figure, plastic clothes, Remco, 5½" 24.00
Minnie Mouse figure, wood-jointed, w/cloth skirt, marked "Walt E. Disney," 1934, 3½" h. 95.00
Peter & The Wolf movie cel, Russian bird standing on the limb of a tree in the snow, applied to water-color inkwash background, lower left signed by Walt Disney & stamped "WDP," matted, 1946, 7½ x 9¼" 1,210.00
Pinocchio bank, composition, Pinocchio leaning on tree, signed "Disney Enterprises," 1940's 100.00
Pinocchio bank, plastic, Play Pal, 12" h. 55.00
Pinocchio book, "Pinocchio," Walt Disney, Cocoa Malt ad back cover, 1939 .... 35.00
Pinocchio figure, composition, Ideal, 8" 125.00
Pinocchio ice cream wrapper, 1950's 8.00
Pinocchio mask, paper, Gillette Blue Blades advertising premium, uncut, 1939 .... 25.00
Pinocchio movie cel, gouache on celluloid, depicting Figaro the Cat in Geppetto's workshop, applied to a water-color master pan ground, 1940, 9 x 29" 12,100.00
Pinocchio teaspoon, silver plate, Duchess Silverplate, ca. 1939 ..... 16.00
Pinocchio toy, pull-type, Pinocchio on donkey, Fisher-Price No. 494 .. 30.00
Pluto figure, ceramic, crouching dog, Brayton Laguna, unsigned, 1938-40 .... 50.00
Pluto planter, ceramic, Pluto w/wheelbarrow 25.00
Pluto salt & pepper shakers, china, Walt Disney, pr. 18.50
Pluto toy, windup tin, "Drum Major," Line Mar .... 250.00 to 350.00

Sleeping Beauty movie cel, King Stephan, matted & framed 200.00
Sleeping Beauty paint w/water set, original box 28.00
Snow White drawing, water-color & pencil, inscribed lower left "To My Dearest Friend Yvonne Ingram, Princess Snow White," 1941, 10 x 8" 880.00
Snow White figure, bisque, Japan, 1932-38, 4¼" h. 35.00
Snow White lobby card, 1951 re-release, 11 x 14" 50.00
Snow White movie cel, depicting a frightened Snow White running through the dark forest, applied to an original water-color ground, matted & framed, 1937, 9¼ x 11¼" 4,400.00
Snow White movie poster, 1962 re-release, French 40.00
Snow White souvenir song album, 1938 original, 50 pages, illustrated 45.00
Snow White stove, tin, Wolverine ... 65.00
Snow White Tinkertoy Sand Set, complete in box, Disney Enterprises, 1938.................... 375.00
Snow White & the Seven Dwarfs Big Golden Book, 1952 .... 15.00
Snow White & the Seven Dwarfs booklet, "Mystery of the Missing Magic" 20.00
Snow White & the Seven Dwarfs drawing, pencil & water-color, Snow White and the seven dwarfs hanging up Christmas stockings & decorations at the hearth, signed lower left w/studio signature, "Walt Disney," matted & framed, 1938, 12 x 14½"..................4,675.00
Snow White & the Seven Dwarfs drinking glasses, marked "Walt Disney," set of 8.................. 150.00

Dwarf Happy Movie Cel

Snow White & the Seven Dwarfs movie cel, depicting Dwarf Happy, applied to starred airbrushed background, matted & framed, 1937, 6¾ x 4½" (ILLUS.) 1,870.00
Snow White & the Seven Dwarfs paper dolls, 1938, w/box, cut....... 125.00
Snow White & the Seven Dwarfs valentine, 1930's 15.00
Sword in the Stone Christmas card, pictures Merlin, Mickey & Donald, original Walt Disney Studios card, 1964 .... 175.00
Three Little Pigs bank, Zell Products, 1940's 37.50
Three Little Pigs book, "Three Little Pigs' Picnic," hardcover, Heath, 1939 .... 20.00
Three Little Pigs figures, bisque, Japan, 1932-38, 3½" h., set of 3 .. 70.00
Three Little Pigs jigsaw puzzle, Jaymar, 1940's 25.00
Three Little Pigs plate, Patriot China 125.00
Three Little Pigs playing cards, Walt Disney Silly Symphonies, w/box .. 35.00
Three Little Pigs sheet music, "Who's Afraid of the Big Bad Wolf" 18.00
Three Little Pigs toothbrush holder, bisque, figures of three pigs in front of holder, colored trim, Japan, 4 x 4" 63.00
Three Little Pigs & Big Bad Wolf wall plaques, figurals in original box marked "Walt Disney Character Plaq-Ettes," unused, 7 x 15" box, the set 77.00
Thumper (from Bambi) figure, ceramic, American Pottery 65.00
Thumper planter, ceramic, marked "Disney" 35.00
Tinker Bell figure, ceramic, Goebel, Germany, 1959, 8" 175.00

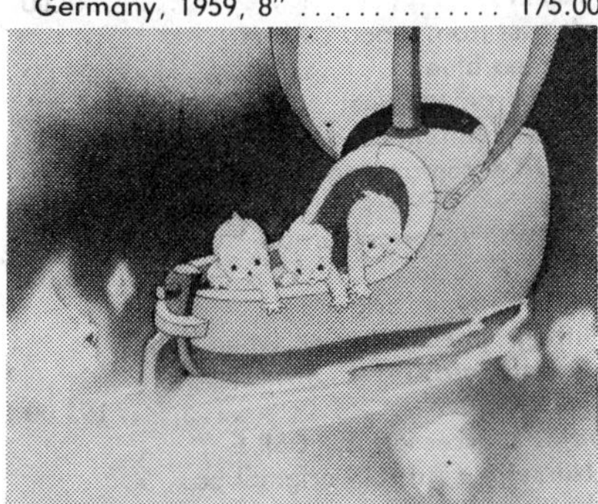

Wynken, Blynken and Nod Movie Cel

Wynken, Blynken & Nod movie cel, depicts the three in a wooden shoe sailboat passing starfish, applied to airbrushed background, matted & framed, 1938, 9½ x 11" (ILLUS.) 5,500.00

Zorro jigsaw puzzle, complete in box, Walt Disney Enterprises No. 8609 .... 10.00
Zorro mask, "Secret Sight Mask," on original store card 22.00
Zorro game, target board, gun & darts, T. Cohn 80.00

DOLL FURNITURE & ACCESSORIES

Doll's Ladder-Back Chair

Armchair, Mission-style, wooden, 7 x 7½ x 12½" $40.00
Bathroom hamper, plastic, "Petite Princess," Ideal Toy Corp. 15.00
Bathtub, plastic, "Petite Princess," Ideal Toy Corp. 45.00
Beater jar w/beater, pressed glass, Taplin 48.00
Bed, cast iron, wood casters, painted blue 25.00
Bed, cherry, tall post, turned posts w/steeple finials, scalloped headboard & conforming footboard, 13½" w., 21¾" l., 18" h. posts 125.00
Bed, iron, Victorian, ornate, 10 x 16" 65.00
Bed, rope-type, original lithographed paper on wood head & footboard, tick mattress, 16 x 7½" 195.00
Bottles & accessories, "Doll-E-Nursette," Amsco, original box, 5 bottles 18.00
Bottle sterilizer w/lid, metal, w/rack for bottles, three bottle scrubbers, cup, funnel & "Doll-E-Nurser" nipple jar w/lid, Amsco, 4" h., 8 pcs. 45.00
Buggy, pot metal, metal wheels, painted green 25.00
Buggy, ornate woven reed, upholstered interior, w/umbrella 295.00
Buggy, wicker, glass windows in hood, "South Bend Toy Co.," 23" h. 120.00
Butter churn, "Dazey," 1922 .... 40.00
Candlestick, pressed glass, Jack-Be-Nimble patt., No. 31, unsigned Heisey (single) 32.00
Canisters, cov., tin, Dutch decor in blue & white, set of 3 .... 40.00
Chair, wooden, blue paint w/red beneath, Adirondack-type, 7¾" h. 145.00
Chair, painted wood, turned uprights & legs, woven cane seat, old red paint, 9¼" h. 115.00
Chair, painted maple w/rush seat, 3-slat back, turned stiles w/shaped finials, turned legs w/stretchers, painted yellow, early 19th c., 15½" h. (ILLUS.) 1,045.00
Chest of drawers, pine, oblong top set w/pair step-back short drawers above case w/three long drawers, porcelain pulls, original red graining, 15½" w., 22¾" h. 650.00
Clothes drying rack, wooden, umbrella-shaped 10.00
Coffee pot, cov., graniteware, white w/black trim, 6" h. 28.00
Cradle, pine, w/original blue & white ticking covered mattress, 19 x 7" 125.00
Cradle, walnut, white-painted side slats, paneled ends w/cut-out finials, cleaned down to original varnish & gold paint, 22¼" l. 135.00
Dollhouse, wooden, Schoenhut, 2-story, grey pressed board "brick" exterior, red shingled roof, covered porch, white-framed windows, opening at the side to reveal upper & lower rooms containing wood furnishings, 1915-20, 14 x 10 x 9" 1,100.00
Dollhouse, 2-story, painted yellow w/grey dormered roof, red "brick" trim & pillared front porch, opening at each end to reveal four rooms, Germany, ca. 1910, 18 x 22½ x 19" 330.00
Dollhouse, Lancaster County farm house, 2-story, painted red "brick" exterior w/hand-split shingled roof, green shutters, dormer, covered porches on three sides & small separate outhouse, rear & side doors open to reveal upper & lower floors, ca. 1890, 34 x 38 x 23" (ILLUS.) 8,250.00
Dollhouse, Marx No. 4739, in box, never assembled 80.00
Dollhouse, wooden, Schoenhut, one-

room bungalow, w/original decal label 249.00

Dollhouse of Lancaster County Home

Dollhouse bathroom set, white-painted wooden bathtub, sink, commode, footstool & mirrored tin medicine cabinet, 5 pcs. 242.00

Dollhouse bedroom set: sleigh bed, four-drawer chest, side chair & side table; yellow w/floral & striped detail, Tynietoy, Providence, Rhode Island, 1930's-40's, 4 pcs. 220.00

Dollhouse candelabra, plastic, "Petite Princess, Royal," Ideal Toy Corp. 12.50

Dollhouse clothes hamper, wicker, pink w/wooden lid 19.00

Dollhouse commode, painted tin, opening top & front, brown wood grain finish, Rock & Grenier, London, 1850-90, 2 3/8" w., 2½" h. .. 220.00

Dollhouse desk, French style w/gold Japanned detail, Germany, late 19th c., 4¾" w., 5 1/8" h. 192.50

Dollhouse doll, lady w/movable limbs, No. 43, Renwal 15.00

Dollhouse dolls, bisque head black butler w/painted features & molded hair, wearing a white shirt & waistcoat w/later black felt suit & bisque head maid w/molded brown topknot, 2 pcs. 605.00

Dollhouse drop-leaf table, painted tin, rectangular w/short leaves, red paint w/stenciled floral detail, Stevens & Brown, Cromwell, Connecticut, 1868-72, 5 7/8" l., 2 7/8" h. 110.00

Dollhouse furniture: day bed, settle, armchair, trestle table & sideboard; Jacobean style, Tynietoy, East Providence, Rhode Island, 1930's-40's, 5 pcs. 1,045.00

Dollhouse furniture, "Little Red Schoolhouse" set, Renwal 125.00

Dollhouse parlor set: loveseat, two side chairs & rocker; white metal, molded scene of Columbus discovering America, pat. 1896, Fairy Furniture, 4 pcs. 175.00

Dollhouse refrigerator, "Kelvinator," Arcade 89.00

Dollhouse sofa, painted tin, Victorian Rococo style, brown wood grain frame w/green upholstery, Rock & Grenier, London, 1850-90, 8¼" l. 1,100.00

Dollhouse table lamp, metal, red, Renwal 5.00

Dollhouse television set, "Petite Princess," Ideal Toy Corp. 55.00

Dress & underclothes, dotted Swiss, scalloped collar, w/Shirley Temple tag, 7½" l. 55.00

Dust pan, graniteware, grey speckled 115.00

Egg beater, tin, "Betty Taplin," 5½" 11.50

Highchair, metal, enameled w/bear decal, Amsco, 24" h. 27.50

Highchair, wicker w/wooden legs & tray, white & green, 18" h. 45.00

Kitchen cabinet w/glass doors, "Hoosier," 20" h. 135.00

Pan, graniteware, two-handled, blue 28.00

Purse, leather, w/delicate rolled leather handles 17.50

Quilt, black & light blue sateen, Amish, 20 x 25" 300.00

Range, electric, "Little Chef," original box, 1940's 48.00

Sad iron, cast iron, twisted handle, w/matching trivet, silver paint, 2¾" 35.00

Soup bowl, white enamel, h.p. red flowers & stems w/blue & green leaves, 3½" d. 15.00

Strainer-ladle combination, graniteware, grey speckled 75.00

Waffle Iron

Stroller, painted steel, four wooden wheels & pusher bar w/steel handle, animal & children decals, marked "Turner," holds dolls to 26" 75.00

Teacart, wooden frame, tin tray w/lithographed Dutch children scene, Wolverine................ 75.00

Waffle iron, cast iron, w/wooden handles (ILLUS. previous page) ... 75.00

DOLLS

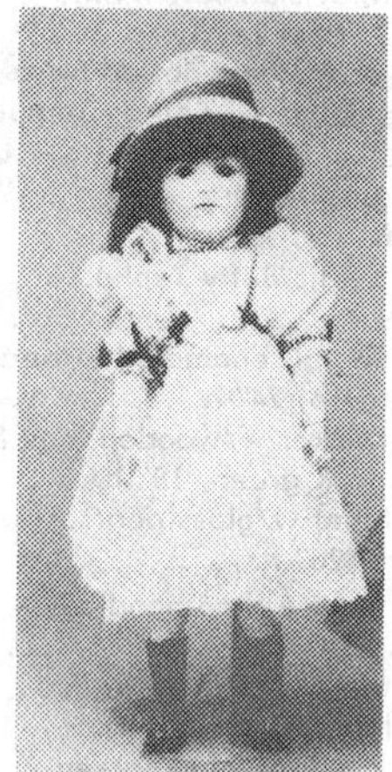

A.M. Doll Made for G.A. Schwarz

A.B.G. (Alt, Beck & Gottschalk) bisque socket head character girl marked "1361," brown glass sleep eyes, open mouth, h.h. (human hair) wig in braids, ball-jointed composition body, dressed, 25" ...$495.00

A.B.G. "Bonnie Babe," all bisque, brown eyes, molded hair in curls, molded shoes, original dress, 6½" 1,050.00

Alexander (Madame) Caroline, all vinyl, blue sleep eyes, open-closed mouth, rooted blonde hair, 1961, dressed, 14".............. 206.00

Alexander (Madame) Dionne Quintuplet toddler, composition, dressed, 19" 260.00

Alexander (Madame) Fisher Quintuplets, vinyl w/hard plastic head, 1964, dressed, set of 5........... 600.00

Alexander (Madame) Jacqueline, hard plastic w/vinyl over plastic arms, 1962, dressed in riding outfit & w/horse, 21" 762.00

Alexander (Madame) Kate Greenaway, composition, blue sleep eyes w/lashes, open mouth w/four teeth, golden red glued on mohair wig, 1940, dressed, 24" 250.00

Alexander (Madame) Shari Lewis, hard plastic w/vinyl over plastic arms, 1959, dressed, 21" 250.00

A.M. (Armand Marseille) bisque socket head "googlie" girl marked "323," blue glass "googlie" sleep eyes, jointed composition body, dressed, 9" 550.00

A.M. bisque socket head girl marked "390," blue sleep eyes, (new) h.h. wig, 11-piece composition body, dressed, 10" 250.00

A.M. bisque socket head lady marked "Armand Marseille Germany 400 A.O.M.," brown sleep eyes, closed mouth, brown hair, ball-jointed composition lady body w/molded bust, stamped in red "Germany," & w/label "Made for G.A. Schwarz Philadelphia made in Germany," dressed, 16" (ILLUS.) 2,310.00

Armand Marseille Character Child

A.M. bisque socket head character child marked "590 A.5 M Germany D.R.G.M.," blue sleep eyes, open-closed mouth, blonde wig, ball-jointed wood & composition body, dressed, 17½" (ILLUS.) 1,045.00

A.M. bisque socket head baby marked "A.M. Kiddie Joy," blue sleep eyes, "pouty" baby mouth, molded & painted hair, cloth body, composition legs, celluloid hands, dressed, 19" 325.00

A.M. bisque socket head character girl marked "G327 B Germany A 10 M," blue glass sleep eyes, auburn h.h. wig & auburn eyelashes, open mouth w/teeth, ball-jointed wood & composition body, dressed, 24" (ILLUS.)...800.00 to 1,000.00

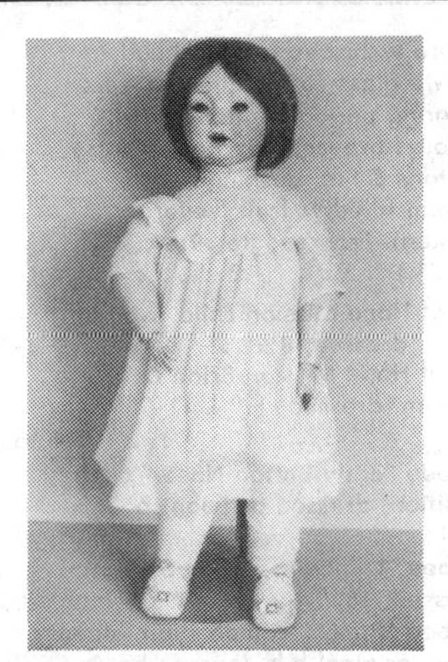

Armand Marseille Character Girl

Amberg (Louis & Son) bisque flange-necked head "New Born Babe," glass sleep eyes, open mouth, cloth body, (repainted) composition arms, 11½" 295.00

Arranbee "Nancy," composition, dressed, 12" 55.00

Belton-type bisque head girl marked "G.K." (Gebruder Kuhnlenz), blue glass stationary paperweight eyes, closed mouth, brown h.h. wig, composition body, straight wrists & legs, dressed, 7½" 475.00

Belton-type bisque head girl marked "204," blue glass threaded paperweight eyes, toddler body, straight wrists, dressed, 10½".... 950.00

Betsy McCall, plastic & vinyl, blue sleep eyes, rooted blonde hair, jointed waist, legs, ankles & wrists, Uneeda, 1961, original dress, 29" 125.00

Bisque bride & groom w/movable arms, dimpled knees, original clothing, Germany, 4½" h., pr.... 150.00

Bisque head girl marked "1," blue glass paperweight eyes, closed mouth, pierced ears, brunette h.h. wig, kid body, (replaced) bisque arms, dressed, 14" 770.00

Bisque socket head girl marked "F 6 G" (F. Gaultier), blue glass paperweight eyes, outlined closed mouth, pierced ears, original wig, dots accenting eye corners & nostrils, ball-jointed wood & composition body, straight wrists, dressed, 15½" 3,575.00

Bisque head girl marked "R.D." (Rabery & Delphieu), blue feathered glass paperweight stationary eyes, closed mouth, pierced ears, brown h.h. wig, original ball-jointed composition body, straight wrists, dressed, 17"............1,800.00

Bisque socket head character baby marked "PM 820" (Otto Reinecke), (replaced) h.h. wig, pink kidoline body w/"Baby Doll" sticker, dressed, 18" 395.00

Bisque head girl marked "Mon Tresor" (Henri Rostal), blue glass stationary eyes, jointed wood body, straight wrists, dressed, 19"...... 895.00

Bisque socket head girl marked "B P 10 G" (Paul Girard of Bru), brown glass paperweight eyes, outlined closed mouth, pierced ears, jointed composition body, straight wrists, dressed, 20" 2,420.00

Rabery & Delphieu French Bisque Doll

Bisque head girl marked "R.3.D." (Rabery & Delphieu), brown glass paperweight eyes, open-closed mouth, pierced ears, dots accenting eye corners & nostrils, ball-jointed composition body, dressed, 25" h. (ILLUS.) 3,025.00

Brookglad "Poor Pitiful Pearl," vinyl, blue sleep eyes, rooted blonde hair, 1957, dressed, 13"... 75.00

Bru bisque shoulder head girl marked "Jne 3," brown glass paperweight eyes, closed mouth, pierced ears, (later) brown h.h. wig, kid body, bisque arms, dressed, 14" (mold cracks near ears, ear flakes)........................4,950.00

Bru bisque head girl, "Circle/Dot" model, paperweight stationary eyes, open-closed mouth, bisque hands, dressed (ILLUS. next page)........................16,000.00

Buddy Lee (trade-mark doll for H.D.

Lee Co.) cowboy, hard plastic, dressed, 12½" 105.00

Rare Bru Girl

Celluloid shoulder head school boy, brown eyes, leather body, dressed, 13" 85.00

Chad Valley "Prince Edward," cloth, glass eyes, dressed, 15"..........1,650.00

Chad Valley "Princess Alexandria," cloth, dressed, 15" 950.00

Chase (Martha) stockinette girl, sateen body, elbow & knee joints, early 1900's, dressed, 16" 350.00

China head lady, pink tint, molded & painted covered wagon hair style w/white part, red line above eyes, red circles in nostrils, white line between lips, dressed, 20" ... 500.00

China head boy, molded & painted blond hair, dressed, 24" 245.00

China head lady, molded flat-top hairstyle, dressed, 31" 425.00

Fruit Vendor Automaton

Clockwork automaton, fruit vendor, figure w/bisque fashion head, brown glass eyes & pierced ears, wearing period beige & red silk pleated breeches, jacket w/brass buttons & hat, pushing a straw basket filled w/fruit (several broken), France, late 19th c., 12" (ILLUS.) 4,125.00

Door of Hope Mission child, wooden head, dressed, 8½" 495.00

Door of Hope Mission Bride & Groom, dressed, 11" & 11½", pr. 1,150.00

Effanbee "Betty Button Nose," composition, dressed as Spanish Girl 125.00

Effanbee "Lambkins," composition, dressed, 16" 205.00

Effanbee "Patsy," composition, sleep eyes, original h.h. (human hair) wig, dressed, 19" 525.00

Fly-Lo Baby, bisque head marked "Copr. by Grace S. Putnam," blue sleep eyes, molded brown hair, bisque hands, costume w/wings w/wire running through the edge, 10" 374.00

French Fashion, bisque swivel head w/cork pate, blue glass eyes, closed mouth, pierced ears, brown wig, gusseted kid body w/individually stitched fingers, incised "11" on left side of shoulderplate, dressed in white silk tafetta dress w/floral embroidery, 13½" 1,210.00

French Fashion, bisque swivel head, blue threaded glass eyes, closed mouth, blonde wig, gusseted kid body w/individually stitched fingers, body stamped in blue "Au Nain Bleu, CHAUVIERE, 27 Bould des Capucines," dressed, 18½" 1,540.00

Frozen Charlotte, parian-type, molded & painted blonde hair, white glazed stockings w/lavender upper bands & lavender lustre boots, 3½" 200.00

Handwerck (Heinrich) bisque socket head girl marked "109," brown glass sleep eyes, dressed, 24".... 550.00

Handwerck (Max) bisque socket head girl marked "Bebe Elite," open mouth, h.h. wig, jointed composition body, dressed, 24" ... 650.00

Heubach (Ernst) - Koppelsdorf bisque socket head toddler marked "320," blue glass sleep eyes, open mouth, composition body, dressed, 14" 360.00

Heubach (Ernst) - Koppelsdorf bisque socket head girl marked "320 8," blue sleep eyes, pierced nostrils, brown h.h. wig, five-piece toddler body, dressed, 23" .. 605.00

Heubach (Gebruder) bisque solid dome head character boy, intaglio eyes, composition body, dressed, 17" 875.00

Ideal Novelty & Toy Co. "Bonnie Braids," vinyl head, blue sleep eyes w/lashes, open mouth w/three painted teeth, one-piece braided saran hair pulled through two holes in the sides of head, hard plastic body, 1951, dressed, 13" 100.00

Ideal Novelty & Toy Co. "Liberty Boy," composition, 1918, dressed 160.00

Jumeau bisque head girl marked "5," brown paperweight eyes, outlined closed mouth, pierced ears, original blonde wig, ball-jointed wood & composition body, dressed, 13" 4,125.00

Jumeau Bisque Head Girl

Jumeau bisque head girl stamped in red "Depose, Tete Jumeau, Bet. S.G.D.G., 7," cork pate, blue paperweight eyes, outlined closed mouth, pierced ears, original blonde wig, ball-jointed wood & composition body stamped in blue "Jumeau, Medaille d'Or, Paris," original white cotton dress w/lace trim labeled "Bebe Jumeau," 16" (ILLUS.) 3,190.00

K (star) R (Kammer & Reinhardt) bisque head character girl marked "114 19," blue intaglio eyes, painted facial features, original wig, jointed composition body, dressed, 7½" 715.00

K (star) R bisque head character girl marked "101," blue intaglio eyes, closed mouth, original brown wig done up as braided buns on each side of head, ball-jointed wood & composition body, dressed, 15" ..1,760.00

K (star) R bisque socket head girl marked "115 A," brown sleep eyes, closed "pouty" mouth, original h.h. wig, chunky toddler body, original clothes, 15½" 3,500.00

Bisque Head "Gretchen"

K (star) R bisque head girl known as "Gretchen" marked "114," original clothes & box, 17" (ILLUS.) 8,200.00

K (star) R bisque head character boy marked "100," painted intaglio eyes, open-closed mouth, painted hair, jointed composition body, jointed wrists, dressed, 17½" 995.00

K (star) R - Simon & Halbig bisque socket head baby marked "122 26," blue sleep eyes, blonde h.h. wig, bent-limb body, dressed, 10" 495.00

Kamkins Boy

Kamkins boy, cloth, painted deep blue eyes w/dot pupils, closed red mouth w/full lower lip, pug nose, brown h.h. wig, body w/seams down legs & arms, flexible limbs, stitched fingers, Louise Kampes, Atlantic City, New Jersey, 1919-25, dressed, 19" (ILLUS.) 1,400.00

Kestner (J.D.) bisque character girl marked "150," all bisque, sleep eyes, open-closed mouth, original h.h. wig, jointed body, dressed, 5¼" 155.00

Kestner (J.D.) bisque socket head character baby marked "152," brown sleep eyes, open mouth w/teeth, bent-limb composition body, dressed in Little Lord Fauntleroy suit, 15"..............475.00

Kestner Bisque Head Girl

Kestner (J.D.) bisque head girl marked "14," brown glass eyes, closed mouth, brown wig, ball-jointed composition body w/straight wrists, wearing maroon cotton dress w/lace shawl & period shoes, 20½" (ILLUS.) 2,090.00

Kestner (J.D.) bisque socket head girl marked "Hilda 1914 16," blue stationary eyes, blonde brush-stroke hair, bent-limb body, dressed, 21" 3,850.00

Kewpie bisque head doll incised, "ges. gesch., O'Neill, J.D.K., 10," glass "googlie" eyes glancing to side, watermelon smile, molded peak of hair, five-piece jointed composition body, undressed, 10" 2,530.00

Kley & Hahn, bisque socket-head girl, marked "Walkure," brown sleep eyes, ball-jointed composition body, antique clothes, 28" (not original wig) 750.00

Lenci boy smoking a pipe, felt, dressed, 11" 770.00

Lenci boy, felt, blue eyes, "pouty" expression, blonde mohair wig, dressed as baseball player, 1929 Sport Series, 17" (lacking hat) ...1,045.00

Lenci, "Amelia Earhart," felt, dressed, 16½" 2,500.00

Lenci, "Contessa Maffei" (Model 165/U), felt, side glancing Victorian figure w/black braided hair, small straw hat, green parasol, burgundy jacket w/black trim over wide skirt w/blue & green criss-cross & red ruffled trim, ca. 1925, 9" h. 215.00

Lenci Felt Dolls

Lenci girl (Model 109/46), felt, early 1920's, dressed, 23" (ILLUS. left) .. 880.00

Lenci girl (Model 109/54), felt, early 1930's, dressed, 23" (ILLUS. right) 935.00

Leo Moss composition black child, sad, crying expression, original clothes, ca. 1912, 19" 9,500.00

Little Lulu (cartoon character), cloth, 7" 55.00

Mae Star phonograph doll, composition head, grey sleep eyes, original h.h. (human hair) wig, cloth body, composition arms & legs, dressed 400.00

Mattel "Charmin' Chatty," plastic body & legs, vinyl arms & head, rooted blonde hair, blue side glancing sleep eyes w/lashes, closed mouth, 1961, w/original metal trunk & clothes, 25" 95.00

Mattel "Cheerful Tearful," vinyl, original clothes, 1966 .... 30.00

Minerva tin shoulder head girl, cloth body, cloth upper arms & legs, wooden lower arms & hands, dressed, 21" 250.00

Nancy Ann Storybook "Debbie," all hard plastic, 11" 60.00

Nippon bisque head character baby,

brown sleep eyes, dark brown h.h. wig, composition body, dressed, 14" 195.00

Papier-mache head boy, glass eyes, mohair wig, original cloth body, china arms, Germany, dressed, 15" 300.00

Papier-mache shoulder head girl, painted black pate, brush strokes around face, brown glass eyes, open mouth inset w/bamboo teeth, kid body, late 19th c., French-type, wearing period style dress, 20" 495.00

Papier-mache Lady Doll

Papier-mache head lady, glass eyes, open mouth w/set teeth, wearing bonnet & long linen gown, ca. 1850, 36" (ILLUS.) 1,100.00

Parian head girl, molded blonde hair w/head band, ca. 1860, dressed, 24" 600.00

Parian head lady, cloth & kid body, dressed, marked "1000," 22" 270.00

Patti Playpal, vinyl head & arms, plastic body, rooted brown hair, blue sleep eyes, closed mouth, original clothes, Ideal, 1960, 36" .. 125.00

Rag-stuffed Black Doll

Rag-stuffed black boy, cotton body w/button nose & embroidered eyes & mouth, button hair, wearing green velvet shirt & dark blue velvet pants w/green velvet pockets, ca. 1930, 13½" (ILLUS.) 302.50

Rag-stuffed "Philadelphia" baby, molded & painted features, brown hair, J.B. Sheppard & Co., 22" ...1,850.00

R&B (Arranbee) Nanette, glued-on Saran braided wig, blue sleep eyes, closed mouth, fully jointed hard plastic body, original clothes, 1953, 21" 125.00

Rohmer (Mlle. Marie Antoinette) fashion girl, china swivel neck, painted blue eyes, china arms, stamped kid body, Paris, France, 1857-80, 14" (small repair to one hand)..........................3,500.00

Schmidt (Franz & Co.) bisque head character girl marked "1272," blue glass sleep eyes, open mouth w/two upper teeth & tongue, dark blonde h.h. wig, ball-jointed composition body, straight wrists, dressed, 17" (nose w/hairline) ... 425.00

Schoenau & Hoffmeister bisque head girl marked "1906," brown sleep eyes, long h.h. wig, ball-jointed composition body, dressed in four layers of lace & cotton clothing, 18" (½ of one finger missing).... 550.00

Schoenhut toddler boy, wooden, dressed in rompers, 11" 575.00

Schoenhut girl, wooden, carved hair w/blue band & bow, dressed in original teddy, 14½" 2,250.00

S.F.B.J. (Societe Francaise de Fabrication de Bebes et Jouets) bisque head character girl marked "252," "pouty" expression w/puffy cheeks, glass eyes, short blond wig, ball-jointed, composition body, dressed, 13½"............4,950.00

S.F.B.J. bisque head character girl marked "236," brown stationary eyes, open-closed mouth, brown mohair wig, ball-jointed composition toddler body, dressed, 15"..............................1,430.00

S.F.B.J. bisque head girl marked "60 Paris," brown glass stationary eyes, open mouth w/molded upper row of teeth, black h.h. wig, ball-jointed composition adult body, jointed wrists, dressed, 20" 850.00

Shirley Temple, vinyl, Montgomery Ward, 1972, mint in box, 14" 140.00

Shirley Temple, vinyl, all original in Heidi dress w/pin & wrist booklet, 1957, 17", mint in box 350.00

Simon & Halbig bisque head character baby marked "1428," blue paperweight eyes, open-closed mouth, dark blonde h.h. wig, original jointed curved limb body, dressed, 14" 1,395.00

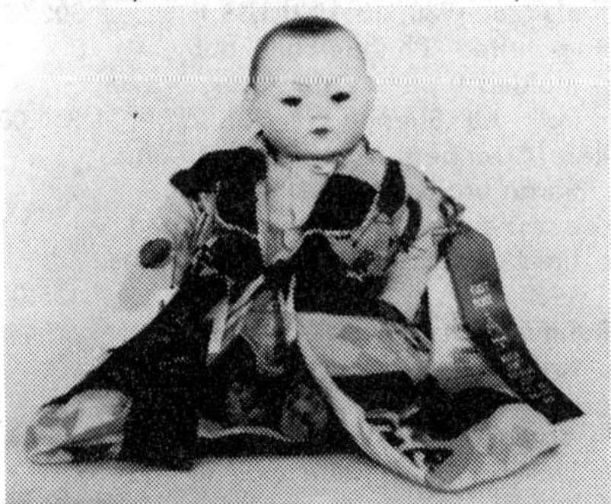

Simon & Halbig Oriental Baby

Simon & Halbig bisque head Oriental baby, dressed, 18" (ILLUS.) 2,600.00

Simon & Halbig bisque head lady marked "1159, S&H, DEP, 7, Germany," brown wig, blue glass eyes, pierced ears, open mouth w/teeth, wood & composition lady body w/molded bust & slim arms, dressed, 19" 1,320.00

Skeezix (cartoon character), oil cloth, 13" 68.00

Skipper, Mattel, vinyl, in original case w/clothes & accessories, 1964 . . . . 55.00

Skookum composition head Indian squaw w/papoose, dressed, 12" . . 60.00

Steiner (Jules) bisque head girl marked "Steiner, Paris, Fre A.9," cork pate, original blond wig, blue paperweight eyes, pierced ears, closed mouth, composition body w/jointed elbows & straight wrists & legs, dressed in original beige silk dress trimmed in lace w/embroidered floral designs, 16" 3,850.00

Steiner (Jules) bisque head girl marked "C, J. Steiner Bte S.G.D.G., Paris," blue paperweight eyes, blushed eyelids, molded pierced ears, dots at eye corners & nostrils, outlined closed mouth, composition jointed body, dressed, 24" h. 4,400.00

Toni, American Character, marked "P91," brunette wig, 15" 85.00

Vogue "Ginny," sleep eyes, painted eyebrows, hard plastic w/bendable knees, dressed, 8" 140.00

Vogue "Ginny Coronation Queen," hard plastic, 1950's, dressed, 8" . . 1,100.00

Wax over composition head girl, glass eyes, mouth opens by lever, jointed composition body, dressed, 8" 150.00

Wellings (Norah) felt girl, blonde braids, wrist label, 15" 195.00

Wellings (Norah) Royal Canadian Mountie, velvet, 14½" 165.00

Wooden man, articulated black man w/well-carved face, original brown paint w/black & red, 14" h. 225.00

Wooden woman, hand-carved black woman made in seated position w/movable arms, fine detail w/realistic paint & glass eyes, dressed in white satin dress w/lace & metallic thread embroidery w/sequins, seated in primitive ladder-back chair, 10" h. (one hand & forearm missing, dress worn) 325.00

DOORSTOPS

Figural Doorstops

All doorstops listed are flat-back cast iron unless otherwise noted. Most names are taken from "Doorstops - Identification & Values," by Jeanne Bertoia (Collector Books, 1985).

Angel, standing figure holding wreath above her head, marked "8," England, 7½ x 16½" $350.00

Ann Hathaway's Cottage, w/flowers & shrubs in front, original polychrome paint, Hubley, 8 3/8" w., 6 3/8" h. 65.00

Aunt Jemima (Small Mammy), full figure, worn polychrome paint, 4¾ lbs., 8¾" h. 168.00

Basket of Daisies, colorful polychrome paint, marked "No. 344," 6½" h. 95.00

Basket of Flowers, large polychrome blossoms in tall, tightly woven basket w/high loop handle, stepped base, Hubley, 7 x 5" 85.00

Basket of Flowers, ribbed basket

w/round base & high arched handle w/twisted pattern holding arched, overflowing bouquet of flowers, old polychrome paint, 8½" h. 45.00

Basket of Zinnias, polychrome paint, 10½ x 8" 250.00

Bathing Girls, two "flappers" seated under umbrella, worn original polychrome paint, marked "Copyright Fish," & "Hubley," 10 7/8" h. (ILLUS. left) 285.00

Bird by Urn, cast brass, standing crane-like bird w/beak in tall ewer, England, 10" h. 70.00

Bobby Blake, standing chubby boy, polychrome paint, signed "Grace Drayton," 9½ x 5¼" 500.00

Buccaneer, full figure, pirate w/one arm extended holding sword pointed toward ground, other hand on hip, wearing a cape & seven-league boots, old gold repaint, 6 7/8" h. 45.00

Camel, full figure, single-hump animal on oval base, worn black repaint, 5 5/8" h. 45.00

Cape Cod, yellow cottage w/red roof, marked "LACS," 8¾ x 5½" 175.00

Cardinal, full figure, red bird on base, 5" h. 250.00

Carpenter, full figure, orange shirt, blue pants & hat, 5½" h. 200.00

Cat, seated animal w/ovoid head & rounded shoulders & haunches, original black paint w/green eyes, 6¾" h. 95.00

Cat, seated animal, old black & white repaint, glass eyes, 9¾" h. 85.00

Cats, Basket of Kittens (3), original polychrome paint, marked "M. Rosenstein, Copyright 1932, Lancaster, PA USA," 10 x 7" (ILLUS. right) 235.00

Cherubs, two standing blond babies, one holding a bunch of grapes, rounded base, 10 x 6 3/8" 175.00

Church, steepled w/painted stained glass look windows, marked "12562," 5½" w., 7½" h. 325.00

Cockatoo, white bird sitting on flowering branch, 11¼ x 9½" 500.00

Colonial Pilgrim, chubby standing figure w/one arm out to side, brown suit w/white collar & cuffs, 8¾ x 5 3/8" 475.00

Cottage in Woods, polychrome paint, 8¼ x 7¼" 215.00

Delphinium, ribbed vase w/blue ribbon holds overflowing bouquet of colorful flowers, stepped base, Hubley, 8¾ x 7¼" 140.00

Dog, Bird Dog, standing setter w/bird in mouth, rectangular flat base, National Foundry, 6 x 11¾" 215.00

Dog, Boston Terrier, full figure, standing animal w/head turned, worn original black & white paint, 9" h. 75.00

Dog, Cairn Terrier, seated animal on base, Bradley & Hubbard, 9 x 6" 325.00

Dog, Sealyham, full figure, standing white animal, Hubley, 14" l., 9" h. 425.00

Dog, Terrier, standing animal on base, old worn polychrome paint, marked "Spencer, Guilford, Conn.," wedge in back, 5¼ x 6" .. 110.00

Dog, Welsh Corgi, seated animal, traces of old paint, marked "B & H," Bradley & Hubbard, 8¼" h. .... 250.00 to 300.00

Doll on Base, full figure, doll wearing bonnet & long ruffled dress, 5½ x 4 7/8" 85.00

Drum Major, full figure, solid bright blue jacket & hat, 13½" h. 345.00

Duck with Top Hat, worn old polychrome paint, 7½" h. 165.00

Elephant, full figure, walking animal w/trunk raised, original pearl white paint, Hubley, 8¼ x 12" ... 145.00

Fisherman, full figure, man in light colored two-piece slicker & dark rain hat w/arms at side & legs together, original polychrome paint, 8" h. 55.00

Flower Basket, roses, daisies & other flowers in stave-constructed basket w/flared foot & shaped overhead handle on stepped base, original polychrome paint, 6½ x 5¾" 85.00

Flower Basket, low, compact basket w/single loop handle containing compact bouquet of colorful flowers, 10 x 6" 140.00

Football Player, full figure, running athlete w/ball under one arm & the other extended ahead, bronze finish, 5½" h. 55.00

Fox, curled up sleeping, worn old red paint, 7" l. 65.00

Frog, low, squat animal w/legs spread out, green & yellow paint, 7½" l., 1½" h. 125.00

Fruit Basket, simple staved basket w/ribbon around center & round loop handle holds overflowing grapes, bananas & other fruits, marked "cJo 1252," 9 5/8 x 6¼" .. 225.00

Game Cock, full figure, polychrome paint, 7 x 5 3/8" 275.00

Gate, Gothic style gate w/stone

Gothic Gate Doorstop

piers, green w/tan doors (ILLUS.) 145.00
Geisha, full figure, seated Japanese lady w/string instrument, Hubley, 7 x 6" .... 150.00 to 200.00
Girl holding Bouquet, full figure, chubby girl in bonnet & long dress, polychrome paint, Albany Foundry Co., 4¾" w., 7 5/8" h. 200.00
Gnome, full figure, walking figure w/beard & wearing pointed red cap, black coat, green leggings & black & green shoes, original paint, 5" w., 11" h. 170.00
Horse, full figure, standing animal w/original bay paint, black mane & tail, Hubley, 10½ x 12" 136.00
Horse on Base, prancing animal on step-down rectangular pedestal base, white w/gilt bridle & girth, flat hollow back, 10½ x 12¼" 225.00
House, modern style one-story cottage w/floral vines across front, marked "cJo 1288," 8 1/8 x 4½" 178.00
Jonquil, three large yellow & orange flowers w/green stems & leaves, rectangular base, Hubley, 7 x 6" 185.00
Knight, full figure, standing figure in full armor, marked "LVL Pat Pend," 6" w., 13¼" h. 240.00
Lighthouse, tapering structure w/stone foundation stands on rock-form rectangular base, polychrome paint, marked "cJo 1290," 7¾ x 5" 225.00
London Royal Mail Coach, coach w/figures pulled by two horses, original polychrome paint marked "Pat. Pending," 12" l., 7" h. 110.00
Mad Hatter, full figure, square base, polychrome paint, 2 7/8" w., 6 5/8" h. 340.00
Nasturtium, ovoid pot holding colorful bunch of flowers & leaves, green base, Hubley, 7¼ x 6" 100.00
Naval officer, standing figure in uniform wearing Napoleonic hat, one arm down leaning on sword, other hand on hip, traces of old paint, 16" h. (pitted surface) 70.00

DRUGSTORE & PHARMACY ITEMS

The old-time corner drugstore, once a familiar part of every American town, has now given way to the modern, efficient pharmacy. With the streamlining and modernization of this trade many of the early tools and store adjuncts have become outdated and now fall into the realm of "collectibles." Listed here are a variety of tools, bottles, display pieces and other ephemera once closely associated with the druggist's trade.

Cork press, pin-striped oak base, ornate $70.00
Counter dispenser, "Alka-Seltzer," w/bottle w/original paper label on top 135.00
Counter dispenser, "Bromo-Seltzer," blue glass base 195.00
Counter display case, "Parke Davis Vitamins," tin & glass, "If You Don't Know Your Vitamins, Know the Maker," 18 x 11", 22½" h. 85.00
Counter screen, frosted glass w/walnut frame, "Prescriptions Carefully Compounded," Victorian, 66" w. 1,100.00
Display jar, cov., "Dr. King's New Life Pills," black & white label w/gold trim, 5" w., 13" h. 505.00
Display jar, hanging-type, egg-shaped w/ornate cast-iron hanger, 16" 185.00
Dose glass, embossed "Butler & Evans, Druggists, West Side of Square, Yate's Center, Kan." 25.00
Pill roller, walnut & brass, ca. 1880, America, 13 x 5" 195.00
Prints, "Parke Davis History of Pharmacy in Pictures," 40 pictures, original portfolio (slightly soiled) 210.00
Scale, beam-type, brass, single beam, single drawer in front, made by Henry Troemner, w/weights, overall 13" h. 90.00
Scale, beam-type, brass, single beam, w/two pans, made by W. Jones, New York, 28" h. 206.00
Scale, hanging-type, brass & iron, single beam, made by August Sauter Ebinger, Germany, 3" d. pans, 7¼" l. beam 60.00
Show globe, etched glass, w/cork, 17" h. 200.00
Show globe, blown glass, one piece blown body appears as three sec-

tions, two narrow sections are faceted all around, three bulbous areas w/cross-cuts in an attractive pattern, 8½" cut & faceted stopper, overall 22" h. 1,210.00

Sign, reverse-painted glass, electric, "Prescriptions" in white lettering w/gold highlights on burgundy ground, red metal case, 24" l. (plug missing) 165.00

Syrup bottles, cobalt blue glass, "SYR: TOLUT:" & "SYR: SCILLE," black on white label w/red & gold trim, 9½" h., pr. 175.00

ENAMELS

Russian Enamel Cup & Saucer

Enamels have been used to decorate a variety of substances, particularly metals. The best-known small enameled wares such as patch and other small boxes and napkin rings are the Battersea Enamels made by the Battersea Enamel Works in the last half of the 18th century. However, the term is often loosely applied to other English enamels. Russian enamels, usually on a silver or gold base, are famous and expensive. Early 20th century French enamel on copper wares and those items produced in China at the turn of the century in imitation of the early Russian style are also drawing dealer and collector attention.

Battersea box w/divided lid, enameled one side w/portrait of George II, other w/portrait of Queen Charlotte, box enriched w/flower sprays, ca. 1775, 2¾" w. $990.00

Battersea snuff box, w/hinged lid, in the form of a peach, enriched in yellow & puce, ca. 1775, 1¼" h. 418.00

Bowl, silver-gilt, eight-panel, enameled interior & exterior w/colorful peacocks & foliage on gilded stippled ground, central boss w/florals on a white ground, Maria Semyenova, Moscow, ca. 1900, 5¼" d. 4,125.00

Cup & saucer, silver-gilt, enameled w/multicolored foliage within geometric borders, scroll handle, Nicholai Alexeev, Moscow, 1892, saucer 4¾" d. (ILLUS.) 1,430.00

Jewel box, oblong w/cut corners, enameled w/multicolored foliage & geometric designs, cover w/a plique-a-jour panel, border set w/four carnelian cabochons, ornate end handles, bracket feet, The Sixth Artel, Moscow, ca. 1910, 5½" l. 3,575.00

Snuff box in the form of a recumbent King Charles Spaniel, black hair markings, lying on a pink cushion, cover painted in colors w/a flower spray, Staffordshire, ca. 1765, 2" l. 1,430.00

Sugar basket & spoon, enameled w/panels of colorful flowering foliage on sky blue, Chinese red, sea green or cream ground, each panel topped by an onion dome enameled aubergine, w/swing handle, matching spoon w/hook handle, Maria Semyenova, Moscow, ca. 1900, 4½" d. basket 2,420.00

Tea set: 4½" h. cov. teapot, cov. sugar bowl & creamer; silver-gilt, enameled w/colorful scrolling flowering foliage w/borders of white beads, Vasily Agafonov, Moscow, also w/pseudo-Faberge marks, ca. 1900, 3 pcs. 2,200.00

Vase, oviform, Art Deco style enameled violet, crimson, white, lavender & black spiral design, signed "C. Faure Limoges," France, 12" h. 4,070.00

Whiskey shot glass, silver, enameled w/multicolored geometric designs, marked 84 & initialed, Russia, 1¼" d., 1 7/8" h. 356.00

EPERGNES

Epergnes were popular as centerpieces on tables of last century. Many have receptacles of colored glass for holding sweetmeats or other edible items or for flowers or fruits. Early epergnes were made entirely of metal including silver.

Blue cased glass, single lily, interior of bowl-base & stem w/enameled

yellow & white flowers w/green & gold leaves, applied clear edging, ormolu foot & mountings, 5¼" d., 10¾" h. $175.00
Blue cased glass, single lily, applied blue rigaree, 20½" h. 380.00
Clear cut glass, 4-lily, ornate silver base, 15" h. 225.00
Clear glass w/deep blue edging, 3-lily, center lily w/two curved side lilies & two hanging baskets, crimped & ruffled rims w/applied clear trim, in crimped & ruffled bowl, 20¾" h. 800.00
Cranberry glass, single lily, applied clear leaves around top, 12" h. ... 225.00
Cranberry glass, 3-lily, center lily w/two curved side lilies & two hanging baskets, ruffled rims w/applied clear trim, in ruffled bowl, 22" h. 800.00
Cranberry glass, 7-lily, applied clear spiraling rigaree, in 11" d. fluted bowl, 22" h. 625.00
Cranberry shading to pink to opalescent to clear blown glass, 3-lily, applied clear spiraling rigaree, in matching 9" d. bowl w/turned in rim, 21½" h. 295.00
Green glass, 3-lily, square lilies w/folded rims, in square bowl, 20" h. 680.00

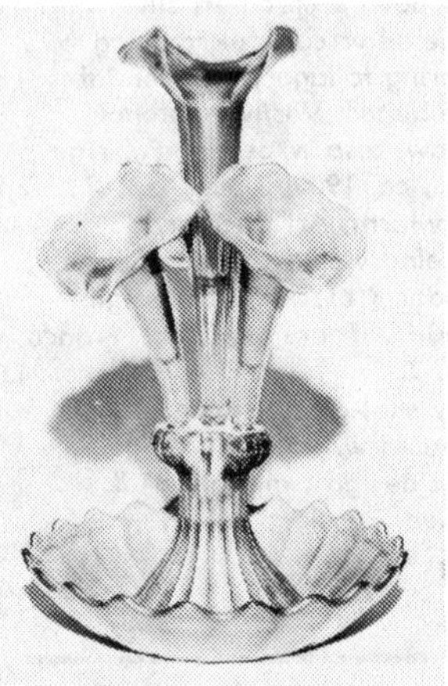

Carnival Glass Epergne

Green Carnival glass, 4-lily, in scalloped bowl (ILLUS.) 875.00
Green opalescent glass, 4-lily, applied rigaree, 21" h. 585.00
Pastel pink opalescent glass, single lily, Swirl patt., ormolu mountings & swan form handles, 17" d. bowl, 23" h. 450.00
Rubina Verde glass, single lily, applied rigaree, 16" h. 295.00
Sterling silver, trumpet form center vase w/four scrolled arms supporting four shaped circular baskets, stepped circular weighted base, monogrammed "B," Reed & Barton, 13½" h. (lacking base plate) 275.00
Turquoise glass, single lily, applied turquoise rigaree, 10½" h. 185.00
White opalescent glass, single lily, Hobnail patt., 10" h. 65.00
White Satin glass, single lily, applied pink trim, 18" h. 275.00

FABERGE

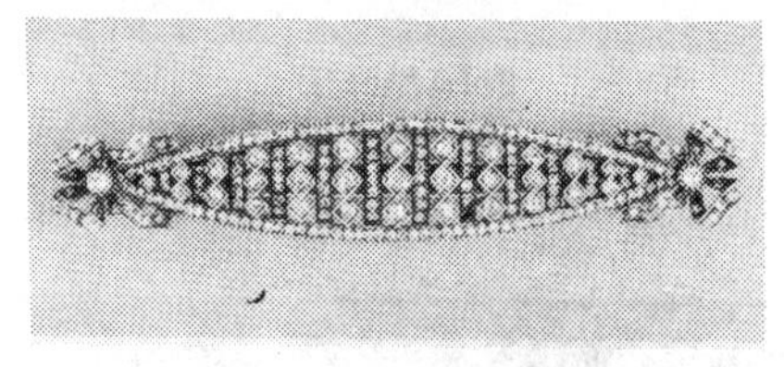

Faberge Barrette

Carl Faberge (1846-1920) was goldsmith and jeweler to the Russian Imperial Court and his creations are recognized as the finest of their kind. He made a number of enamel fantasies, including Easter eggs, for the Imperial family and utilized precious metals and jewels in other work.

Barrette, gold & diamonds, oblong openwork ovoid shape tapering to bows at each end, the whole set w/diamonds in a geometric pattern, workmaster August Holmstrom, St. Petersburg, ca. 1900, 3" l. (ILLUS.) $6,050.00
Bonbonniere, moss agate, in the form of an Easter egg, carved translucent green agate body w/gold mount enameled opaque white & w/gold circles at intervals, diamond thumbpiece, workmaster Erik Kollin, St. Petersburg, ca. 1890, 1 1/8" l. 9,350.00
Cane handle, gold & translucent enamel, waisted cylindrical shape enameled translucent amber over a *guilloche* ground & applied w/neo-rococo scrolls & flowers, lower border of diamonds & cabochon ruby finial, mounted as riding crop, workmaster Michael Perchin, St. Petersburg, ca. 1885, 2 3/8" l. 15,400.00
Cigar box, table model, silver & translucent enamel, rectangular form enameled w/translucent steel blue over *guilloche* ground,

the front & back applied w/anthemion & laurel wreaths, the hinged cover w/reserve containing miniature of a palace, the border of the reserve enameled translucent sky blue over a *guilloche* ground, raised on four feet, workmaster Karl Gustav Hjalmar Armfeldt, "Faberge" in Cyrillic & 88 standard, St. Petersburg, ca. 1910, 6¾" l. 55,000.00

Cup, silver-gilt & translucent enamel, tapering round shape enameled translucent lime green over a *guilloche* ground, raised on three ball feet, workmaster Anders Nevalainen, "Faberge" in Cyrillic & 88 standard, St. Petersburg, ca. 1900, 1 5/8" h. 4,125.00

Desk clock, gold, silver & translucent enamel, octagonal, enameled translucent purple over an engine-turned sunburst ground & applied w/garlands of gold flowers, dial edged by seed pearls, w/ribbon-tied reeded border, ivory back & silver strut, signed in Cyrillic, workmaster Michael Perchin, St. Petersburg, ca. 1890, 4 3/8" h. . .22,000.00

Fob seal, gold & citrine, chased w/leaves, the quartz matrix engraved w/initials, marked w/Cyrillic initials "K.F." on each loop, Russia, late 19th c., 1½" h. 2,200.00

Gum pot, gold & translucent enamel, compressed round shape enameled translucent oyster over a *guilloche* ground, the spreader w/cabochon garnet finial, workmaster Henrik Wigstrom, St. Petersburg, ca. 1900, 1¾" d. 6,050.00

Faberge Crystal Jar

Jar, cov., crystal w/silver-gilt mounts, shaped tapered rectangular section raised on four silver-gilt paw feet, top corners w/satyr masks, sides hung w/swags (lacks cap), workmaster Julius Rappoport, Moscow, ca. 1900, 6¼" h. (ILLUS.) 2,750.00

Kovsh, silver-gilt, enameled w/foliate scrolls & geometric designs on grounds of cream, brick red, sky blue & black, high hook handle, workmaster Fyodor Ruckert, Moscow, ca. 1900, 4 1/8" l. 1,760.00

Model of a frog, bowenite, carved in a crouching position, cabochon ruby eyes, St. Petersburg, ca. 1900, 2¼" l. 19,800.00

Model of a Pug dog, carved purpurine, model of a seated dog in attentive posture w/broad back & tightly curled tail, diamond-set eyes, St. Petersburg, ca. 1900, 1½" h. 26,400.00

Necklace, carved nephrite & gold, formed as carved nephrite "batons" joined by diamond-set circles, the lozenge-shaped pendant applied w/a diamond-set arrow piercing a wreath set w/diamonds & rubies, marked w/Cyrillic initials "K.F.," Moscow, ca. 1900, 17" l. (in fitted case) . .37,400.00

Pencil, palisander wood w/silver mounts, cylindrical shape, applied w/silver swags of flowers pendant from ribbons, top & bottom w/reeded borders, workmaster Anders Nevalainen, St. Petersburg, ca. 1900, 4¾" h. 4,620.00

Tea glass holder, silver, partly gilded & 'jeweled,' plain matted finish, the borders gilded, front set w/coin, the finial mounted w/a cabochon red hardstone, workmaster Theodore Ringe, St. Petersburg, ca. 1895, 3¼" h. 1,650.00

Vase, silver & translucent enamel, baluster shape enameled translucent royal blue over a *guilloche* ground, foot chased w/border of acanthus leaves, workmaster Anders Nevalainen, & 88 standard, & scratched inventory mark, St. Petersburg, ca. 1910, small 3,300.00

FANS

Advertising, "Bell Coffee," cardboard, Victorian lady pictured & "Are You a Bell Fan?" $8.00

Advertising, "New Home Sewing Machines," cardboard 18.50

Celluloid, h.p. feathers & peacock feather points, large 45.00

Faberge Fan

Gold & enamel-mounted, guards enameled translucent rose pink over a *guilloche* ground & w/cartouche-shaped reserve enameled translucent pale blue over a sunburst ground & bordered by diamonds; body of fan painted w/courting scenes & embroidered w/gilt foliate motifs Faberge, marked w/Cyrillic initials of workmaster Michael Perchin & 56 standard, St. Petersburg, Russia, ca. 1900, 8¼" l. (ILLUS.) 7,700.00

Ostrich feather, black, tortoise shell sticks, large 50.00

Ostrich feather, orange, tortoise shell sticks, 20" l. 75.00

Painted cloth, black painted on gauze, mourning-type, w/moon & stars motif...................... 26.00

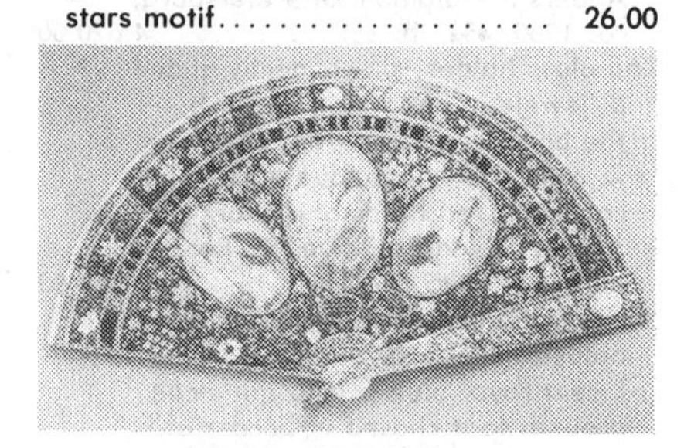

Painted Ivory Fan

Painted ivory, mythological scenes & flowers, guards set w/turquoise & red stones mounted on flower heads, Continental, third quarter 19th c., 8½" l. (ILLUS.)........... 880.00

Painted satin, pink florals & bluebird on fuchsia ground, Victorian, 29 x 13½" 75.00

Painted silk, Art Nouveau style, black, grey & white silk poppy on black net w/black sequins, 13½" l. 75.00

Painted silk, center scene of maiden, young men, mother & child beneath cherry tree, side ovals of flower baskets, sprays of sequins form floral arrangement in between, framing of colorful sequins, pierced ivory sticks engraved w/gold & silver flowers, some jeweling, 10½" l., opening to 20" 150.00

Colorful Paper Fan

Paper, folding-type, lithographed & h.p. center scene of an 18th century musical gathering in a garden setting, two oval reserves of floral bouquets, overall background of scrolling florals, pierced ivory sticks, 10½" l., opening to 18 3/8" (ILLUS.) 135.00

Printed paper, six wide sections printed in color w/1900 calendar entitled "Bright Buds" & alternating designs of lovely little girls & landscapes, lavender, purple & pink floral impressed borders, 3" w., 7" l. 35.00

FIREARMS

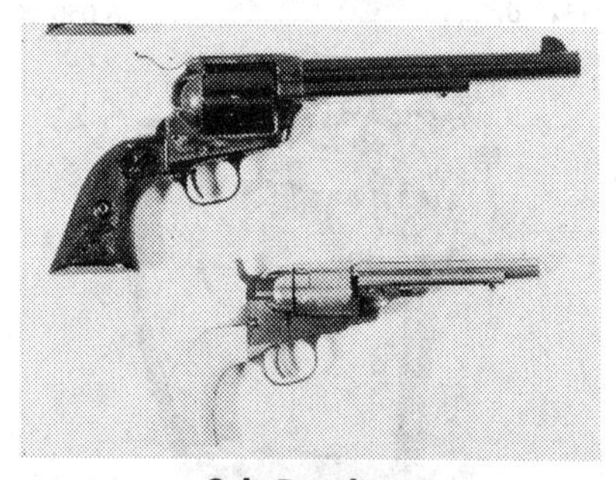

Colt Revolvers

Carbine, Sharps Model 1853, breech loading percussion, brass barrel band, crescent buttplate, brass patch box engraved "Martha E. Cannary," SN 22898, .52 caliber, 21½" l. barrel..................$1,150.00

Carbine, Spencer Repeating contract model, manufactured by Burnside Rifle Co., 1865, iron barrel band, short forend, brass plate on buttstock engraved "Chief Gall Hunkpapas" & eye-in-cross symbol, SN 9330A, .52 caliber, 20" l. barrel (very good condition) 800.00

Handgun, single-shot, nickel-plated, walnut grip, marked "J. Stevens & Co. Chicopee, Mass., Patented 1864," 6½" l. 100.00

Handgun, single-shot, brass & iron, made in Springfield, Massachusetts, Ser. #707, octagonal barrel, wood grips, marked "Patent Pending," ca. 1870, 7" l. 100.00

Musket, percussion smooth bore model, barrel w/side mounted bayonet lug, lockplate w/crowned "V" proofer mark, half-stock w/brass trigger guard, buttplate & forend cap stamped "3444," buttstock stamped "64 Th Y.C.," lock screw escutcheon plate engraved "Joseph N. Nichollet," .69 caliber, 23 3/8" l. barrel (overall poor condition) 200.00

Powder tester, flintlock pistol grip type w/brass gauging device mounted in front of lock, 5½" l. . . . 450.00

Revolver, Colt 1862 Pocket Navy model, .38 caliber rimfire (ILLUS. bottom) 1,375.00

Revolver, Colt Single Action Army model, .45 caliber, new condition in original box (ILLUS. top) 715.00

Rifle, Kentucky half-stock, curly maple stock w/percussion back, brass patch box w/star, heart & circle inlay, 42½" l. barrel, overall 58" l. (some replacements) 325.00

Rifle, Kentucky full stock, curly maple stock, 17 silver inlays including deer, eagle, star, etc., breech lock, 32¾" l. barrel, overall 49" l. (old repairs to stock) 650.00

Rifle, Kentucky full stock, curly maple stock, percussion-type, brass patch box w/twelve silver inlays & engraved w/flowers & fish, barrel & percussion lock signed "I. Keller," 39" l. barrel, overall 56" l. (several silver inlays missing) 2,500.00

Rifle, Winchester Model 66, brass framed lever action, full magazine, brass forend cap, crescent buttplate, stock refinished, left side of action engraved, "Thomas Howard," in script & scroll motif, SN 37127, .44 caliber rimfire, 44" l. octagonal barrel 300.00

Shotgun-rifle, swivel-breech type, curly maple half-stock, engraved silver patch box w/twelve engraved silver inlays, attributed to Leonard, an Ohio gunsmith, 32" l. barrel, overall 47½" l. 3,900.00

FIRE EXTINGUISHERS

Harden's Hand Grenade

Various types of fire extinguishers intended primarily for use in extinguishing small fires were made in the 19th and early in the 20th centuries and are now being collected.

"All State," tin, tubular-type $10.00

"American LaFrance Foamite Corp.," copper cylinder, brass name plate & instructions, bronze screw-off top & handles, 20 lbs., 7" d., 24" h. 47.50

"AutoFyrStop" glass grenade, w/hanger, 5 lbs. 38.00

"Fire Killer," tin, tubular-type 35.00

"Fyr Fyter," brass, tubular-type, 16" l. 10.00

"Harden's Hand Grenade," cobalt blue glass, bulbous w/vertical ribbing & embossed star, 6½" h. (ILLUS.) 60.00

"Harden's Hand Grenade," peacock blue glass, bulbous w/vertical ribbing & embossed star, 6¾" h. 55.00

"Hayward's Hand Fire Grenade," clear glass, pleated, small size ... 125.00

"Hazelton High Pressure Fire Keg," dark amber glass, large wire bail, 11" h. 140.00

"Hero," tin, tubular-type 10.00

"Invincible Fire Killer," tin, tubular-type, 22" l. 15.00

"Jiffy," tin, tubular-type 10.00

"Kerotest Fire Extinguisher," metal, double tank, w/wood case, red w/yellow letters, early 1900's 175.00

"Liberty," tin, tubular-type 18.00

"London Fire Appliance," amber glass, zinc head cap, 9¼" h. 425.00
"Presto," brass cylinder, red flame logo & black lettering on shiny brass, 5½" l. 10.00
"Pyrene," copper cylinder, 5 gal. ... 90.00
"Quick Aid," brass cylinder, w/wall bracket 18.00
"Red Comet," red metal canister w/red glass bulb inside 30.00
"Rockford-Kalamazoo," cobalt blue glass 350.00
"Safety First Fire Dust," tin, tubular-type, New Begin Fire Appliance Co., Oakland, Calif., 2½" d., 15" l. 45.00
"Stop-Fire Inc.," brass plated cylinder, pressure gauge, 9 lb. commercial-type 45.00

FIRE FIGHTING COLLECTIBLES

Early Fire Bucket

Badge, silver-tone metal, shield-shaped, "Advance H.L. & E. Co. - 1 Bellmore," Cairns & Bros., New York, ca. 1880, 2" l. $21.00
Badge, silver-tone metal, simple cross-form, "B.F.D.1," ca. 1889, 2" l. 20.00
Badge, "35th Annual Convention Delegate, Elmira, N.Y. Firemen's Assn., Aug. 21-23, 1907" 27.50
Belt, parade-type, felt-covered leather, "Dublin," belt slide w/large "No. 1," ca. 1910 .... 60.00
Book, "Fire Dept., Haverhill, Ma., Complete History," 1897, photographs & advertisements, hard cover, 8 x 10", 148 pp. 75.00
Book, "Fire Dept., Syracuse, New York," souvenir, 27th Convention of International Association of Fire Chiefs, 1899, 14 fire apparatus photographs, 6 x 9½", 112 pp. 55.00
Booklet, "Fire Service of Portland, Maine," 1888, w/advertising, fire members listed, equipment, horsedrawn steam pumper on cover 60.00
Bucket, leather, green ground w/scene depicting a flaming house w/firemen in foreground, all within scrolling frame, "No. 2" below rim, "City Fire Society" in white band above scene & "Benjn. Dodd" in white band below scene, lower section dated "1822," America, 1822, handle detached, minor paint loss, 12½" h. (ILLUS.) 9,350.00
Bucket, leather, cylindrical w/bail handle, red-painted, centering a gilt foliate cartouche w/painted American eagle & shield & inscriptions "E.P. Pike" & "1829 W.F. Club," 13½" h. (minor paint losses, handle broken) 418.00
Dress coat, parade-type, tan w/navy blue trim & piping, two rows of silver buttons front & four buttons on tails 65.00
Engine bell, bronze, "La France," w/eagle 450.00
Fire alarm call box, cast iron, architectural form w/pediment & raised letters "Fire Alarm Telegraph Station," heavily alligatored red paint & polished brass numbers, 16¾" h. 85.00
Fire alarm rattle, wooden w/brass ends 62.00
Fire bell, brass, from horse-drawn fire wagon, 8" d. 250.00
Fire mark, cast iron, "Fire Association of Philadelphia, B U No. 90," 7 5/8 x 10 13/16" 225.00
Fire mark, cast iron, relief-cast design of four clasped hands & "No 906," 7¼ x 10½" 300.00
First aid kit, "Detroit Fire Dept.," pre-1923 .... 58.00
Helmet, aluminum, high eagle crest on front, painted black, "Engine No. 1 C F D," Cairns, pat. 1889 .. 165.00
Helmet, leather, high eagle crest on front, black leather frontpiece w/red background, white letters "Washington R F D," w/large applied hook & ladder, lined, painted blue underneath, marked "Cairns" & dated 1855 on brim ... 300.00
Helmet, leather, high eagle crest on front, silvered metal frontshield

embossed "Rex York, Pa. 1886" w/applied hook & ladder, scroll-work on top of plate, lined, marked "Cairns" 350.00

Hose cart, wooden frame, two 5' h. iron wheels, pulled by eight men, ca. 1871 .... 1,500.00

Hose nozzle, brass, marked "Powhatan B & I Works, Ranson, W. Va.," red cord wrapping, 30" l. 45.00

Lantern, "Dietz Little Giant," tin, marked "Property of Jacksonville" (Florida Fire Dept.), molded lettering, three round red glass eyes surrounded by tin 50.00

Newspaper, *Harpers Weekly,* July 29, 1865, "Barnum's Museum Fire," matted on museum board, 16 x 20" 55.00

Oil Painting of Firehouse

Painting, oil on canvas, primitive scene of a fireman standing in front of fire wagon, firehouse in background w/"Neptune Hose No. 2" above doorway, 19th c., 18 x 25" (ILLUS.) 4,510.00

Photograph, fireman in dress uniform, no hat or helmet, wearing large parade ribbon from Junior Fire Co. of Reading, Pa., 5 x 7" .. 6.00

Photograph, firehouse w/horse-drawn steamers, 1907, Pittsburgh, Pa., 11 x 8¼" 3.00

Postcard, "Central Fire Station, Glens Falls, N.Y.," colored, ca. 1915 .... 3.00

Pumper wagon, hand-pulled, tank & hose, American La France & Foanite Corp. No. S7659 .... 460.00

Ribbon, "Compliments of Chamberlain Fire Department, 42nd Annual Tournament at Rapid City, June 15 to 18, 1926," printed silk, equipment pictured 4.50

Ribbon, "Good Will Steam Fire Eng. Co., East York Pa., Sesquicentennial, Sept. 3-6, 1899," red, white, blue & gold 49.00

Trumpet horn, brass, red tassel, ca. 1880, 17" l. 430.00

Trumpet horn, presentation-type, Britannia metal, steamer & other engraving, marked "Simpson, Hall Miller Co., Wallingford, Conn.," 19 x 9" 785.00

Trumpet horn, presentation-type, silver plate, New York City, 1908, 20" l. 1,250.00

Watch fob, advertising, "Franklin Fire Insurance," brass, Franklin bust & old fire pumper embossed on front, reverse says, "Finders Please Attach Postage & Drop in Mailbox" 30.00

FIREPLACE & HEARTH ITEMS

Baseball Player Andirons

Andirons, bell metal, Chippendale style, double urn-turned finial, flaring columnar standard, spurred arched legs w/shod slipper feet, similarly turned log stops, 22¾" h., pr. $880.00

Andirons, brass, ball finial above turned standard, on spurred arch legs w/shod slipper feet, w/turned log stops, early 19th c., 16½" h., pr. 440.00

Andirons, brass, Federal style, double lemon-turned finial, ring-turned columnar standard, spurred arched legs w/disc feet, America, 1800-20, 14¼" h., pr. ... 462.00

Andirons, cast iron, molded in the half round, one modeled in the form of a baseball batter holding his bat over his shoulder, the other in the form of a pitcher grasping a baseball, each in uniform of the 1900 era, some repaint, America, ca. 1900, 19½" h., pr. (ILLUS.) ... 6,600.00

Bellows, painted & decorated wood, original yellow paint w/green & black striping & red, green & black floral decoration, worn leather sides, brass nozzle, 16" l. (glued repair to back handle) 60.00

Bellows, painted & decorated wood, turtle-back style, original green paint w/yellow striping & gilt stenciled floral design, releathered sides, brass nozzle, 16¾" l. 100.00

Clock jack, meat roasting rack on clockwork mechanism, brass, embossed "Geo. Salter & Co. warranted," 13" h. 85.00

Ember carrier, wrought iron pan & handle shaped to accept additional wooden handle, overall 17¼" l. (pitted) 95.00

Dated Pennsylvania Fireback

Fireback, cast iron, arched molded crest & frame centering three tulips above a flowerhead & the date "1794," Pennsylvania, 22½" h. (ILLUS.) 3,410.00

Fireback, cast iron, scrolling leafage centering a rectangular panel pressed w/swags, Pennsylvania, 18th c., 30" w., 23" h. 770.00

Fireplace fender, brass, three panels cast w/stylized swans & separated by turned spindles w/flame finials, 20th c., 42" l. 225.00

Fireplace fender, brass, overall reticulated design, scalloped feet, large urn finials, 43" l., 14" h. 90.00

Fireplace screen, tulipwood & fabric, serpentine cresting above fabric-lined panel & hinged wooden writing surface, raised on trestle supports, Louis XVI, France, late 18th c., 29" w., 43" h. (ILLUS.) 605.00

Fireside food warmer, tin & wrought iron, case w/slightly rounded top & conforming door at front, old black repaint w/gold & white geometric floral decoration, on wrought iron cabriole legs terminating in penny feet, original brass bail handle, 28¼" h. 725.00

French Fireplace Screen

Fish broiler, cast iron, made like toaster but rigid tapered spikes hold fillet, rotating-type, step up closed ring handle, forged feet & arched foot under handle, 18th c. 650.00

Hearth broiler, rotary-type, wrought iron, radiating spokes & lacy design within circular rim, tapering handle w/hook end, 23½" l. 400.00

Hearth broom, birch splint, ca. 1810, 55" l. 95.00

Hearth fry pan, brass, on three legs, 4" handle, 18th c., 3¾" d. 85.00

Hearth griddle for crane, iron, arched solid tubular handle w/swivel ring top center handle, 14½" d. 57.00

Hearth shovel & tongs, wrought iron w/brass steeple finials, 31½" l., 2 pcs. 550.00

Kettle lifter, wrought iron, wishbone-shaped, hinged bail, 18th c., 14" l. 57.00

Trammel, wrought iron, sawtooth-type, suspended from a hook & terminating in a large heart, together w/griddle w/bail handle & hook, Pennsylvania, 1750-1800, 35" h., 2 pcs. 880.00

FISHER (Harrison) GIRLS

The Fisher Girl, that chic American girl whose face and figure illustrated numerous magazine covers and books at the turn of the century, was created by Harrison Fisher. A professional artist who had studied in England and was trained by his artist father, he was able to capture an element of refined, cultured elegance in his drawings of beautiful women. They epitomized all that every American girl longed to be and catapulted their creator into the ranks of success. Harrison Fisher, who was born in 1877, worked as a commercial artist full time until his death in 1934. Today collectors seek out magazine covers, prints, books and postcards illustrated with Fisher Girls.

Book, "American Beauties," illustrations by Harrison Fisher, 1909 .... $165.00
Book, "Bachelor Belles," illustrations by Harrison Fisher, published by Grosset & Dunlap, 1908 .... 175.00
Book, "Beverly of Graustark," by George Barr McCutcheon, illustrations by Harrison Fisher 5.00
Book, "Cowardice Court," by George Barr McCutcheon, illustrations by Harrison Fisher, 1906 .... 25.00
Book, "Day of the Dog," by George Barr McCutcheon, illustrations by Harrison Fisher, 1904 .... 38.00
Book, "The Harrison Fisher Book," published by Scribners, 1908 ...... 175.00
Book, "Heart & Masks," by Harold MacGrath, illustrations by Harrison Fisher, 1905 .... 25.00
Book, "The Lure of the Mask," by Harold MacGrath, illustrations by Harrison Fisher, published by Grosset & Dunlap, 1908 .... 7.50
Book, "What's His Name?" by George Barr McCutcheon, illustrations by Harrison Fisher, 1911 .... 25.00
Postcards, "The Greatest Moments of a Girl's Life" series, set of 6 ... 65.00
Postcards, "The Senses" series, set of 6 in original frame 130.00
Print, "The End of the Season," artist's proof, 11½ x 16¾" 65.00
Print, "The Evening Hour," original frame, 8 x 11" 45.00
Print, "The King of Hearts," original frame, 11 x 13" 65.00
Print, "The Only Pebble," Colliers Publishing Co., 1908, 10 x 15" 20.00
Print, "Sparring For Time," The Star Co., 1916, framed, 8½ x 12½" ... 155.00

FOOD, CANDY & MISC. MOLDS

Cake, bundt-type, redware w/light rust & green glaze, 7" d. $130.00
Cake, rabbit, cast iron, marked "Griswold," 11" h. .... 175.00 to 225.00
Cake, Santa Claus, cast iron, two-part, 10" h. 275.00
Candle, single redware tube, greenish interior glaze, 9" h. 55.00
Candle, 18 pewter tubes in pine frame, 21½ x 7", 16" h. 600.00
Candle, floor standing type, 24 pewter tubes in pine frame, old worn patina, 21½" l., 17¾" h. 675.00
Chocolate, bears (12), tin 95.00
Chocolate, creches (2), tin, 1900's ... 225.00
Chocolate, deer, tin, two-part, 6¼" h. 97.50
Chocolate, Easter bunny & chick on egg, tin, marked "Germany," 5¾" h. 75.00
Chocolate, hen on nest, pewter, 9 x 9" 125.00
Chocolate, rabbit, tin, two-part, marked "Made in Germany," 3 7/8" h. 25.00
Chocolate, rabbit on bicycle, pewter, 7" w., 6" h. 125.00
Chocolate, Santa Claus, full-face, tin, 7½ x 3½" 25.00

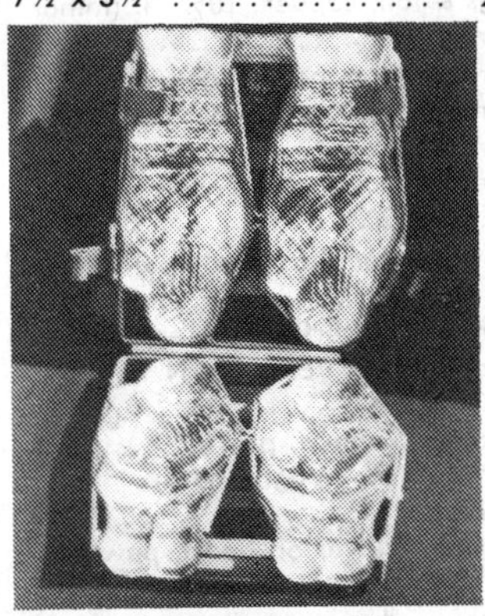

Tin Chocolate Mold

Chocolate, Santa Clauses (2), tin, 8" w., 8½" h. (ILLUS.) 125.00
Chocolate, Santa Clauses (6), tin, marked "Anton Reiche 1900 Dresden," 3 x 5" 65.00
Chocolate, sheep (5), tin, 1900's 85.00
Chocolate, squirrel w/bushy tail eating acorn, tin, hinged, three-part, 12" h. .... 95.00 to 110.00
Chocolate, Teddy Bear, tin, two-part, 1930's 165.00
Chocolate, witches (4), metal, hinged, three-part 75.00
Chocolate, Zeppelin, tin, stamped "Germany, H. Walter Berling," 4½ x 2" 70.00
Food, eagle center, fluted sides, copper w/tinned interior, 7¾" d. 175.00
Food, ear of corn, ironstone 55.00
Food, fish, tin, w/original ring for hanging, 11½" l. 95.00
Food, fruit center, deeply fluted

sides, copper w/tinned interior, 13½ x 11½" oval 165.00
Food, Gothic arch design sides, copper, ring handle, 5½" d. 39.00
Food, heart-shaped w/relief of spirited horseman center, redware, marked "R. Schmidt, Medford, Pa.," 1823 .... 285.00
Food, rabbit, ironstone, 8½ x 5½" 60.00
Food, seashell, copper w/tinned interior, curved & scalloped rim, 5" w. 47.50
Food, Turk's turban, graniteware, turquoise & white marbleized 200.00
Food, Turk's turban, redware, scalloped rim, rich green glaze, 10¾" d. 110.00
Food, Turk's turban, mottled brown Rockingham glaze pottery, 6" d. .. 175.00
Food, turtle, turtle-shaped body w/projections for animal's head, legs & tail, copper, 10½" l. (minor dents) 165.00
Ice cream, banana, pewter 32.00
Ice cream, basket, pewter, three-part, 4" 95.00
Ice cream, bassinet, pewter, S & Co., No. 203 .... 35.00
Ice cream, Buddha, pewter, S.B. & S., No. 476 .... 40.00
Ice cream, butterfly, pewter, two-part, marked "E. & Co. N.Y.," 4¼" 20.00
Ice cream, cannon, pewter 35.00
Ice cream, champagne bottle, pewter 45.00
Ice cream, clover on heart, pewter, No. 572 .... 22.00
Ice cream, dog, seated, pewter, No. 390 .... 65.00
Ice cream, eagle w/head turned & wings raised within semi-circular wreath, pewter, 3¾" d. 105.00
Ice cream, engagement ring, pewter 55.00
Ice cream, football, pewter, No. 381 .... 45.00
Ice cream, hand, pewter, No. 289 .. 35.00

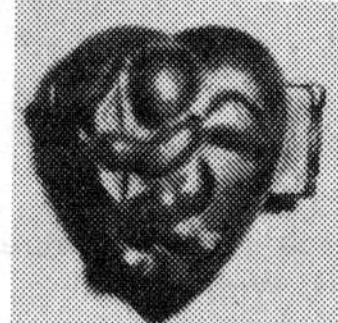

Heart Ice Cream Mold

Ice cream, heart w/molded cupid w/bow, pewter, two-part, marked "E. & Co., Pat. Apd. For," 3¾" (ILLUS.) 50.00
Ice cream, lobster, pewter, marked "E. & Co.," 5½" l. 100.00
Ice cream, locomotive, pewter 65.00
Ice cream, monkey, pewter 45.00
Ice cream, shell, pewter, No. 524 ... 35.00
Ice cream, soldier boy, pewter 65.00
Ice cream, U.S. shield, pewter...... 45.00
Ice cream, figure of George Washington standing, pewter, marked "F. C. Cassel," 5 5/8" h... 30.00
Ice cream, witch figure, pewter, marked "IVWP. Son," 4¾" h...... 85.00
Jelly, conch shell, white ironstone .. 55.00
Jelly, oval, rimmed tin, ca. 1880 .... 65.00
Maple sugar candy, diamond & spade, carved wood w/handle, 16½ x 4" 55.00
Maple sugar candy, reindeer w/flowered coat, carved wood, two-part, 5 x 5" 65.00
Maple sugar candy, rooster, carved pine, 8½" sq. 240.00
Maple sugar candy, strawberry, carved pine, ca. 1830, 9 x 5 x 1½" 150.00
Maple sugar candy, swan, carved wood w/well-defined feathers, two-part, 4 5/8 x 3 1/8" 210.00
Pudding, acorn, copper w/brass pedestal & lid ring, pewter lining, marked "FW Co., 1700-1" 40.00
Pudding, melon, tin, two-part, w/rings, ca. 1900 .... 35.00
Pudding, oval open ring, early pattern, copper w/tinned interior, 3 x 5½ x 9" 130.00
Pudding, star-shaped (five-point), tin, 8" w. 50.00

FOOT & BED WARMERS

Pierced Tin Foot Warmer

Bed warmer, brass pan w/perforated cover & simple engraved design, turned wood handle, 41½" l. $225.00
Bed warmer, brass, deep pan w/perforated & incised line decoration, stylized floral designs, gadrooned rim, well-turned maple

handle w/old finish, England or America, late 18th c., 42½" l. 302.50

Bed warmer, brass pan w/engraved "pinwheel" scrolls, turned wood handle w/traces of old graining, 42½" l. (some edge damage on handle) 250.00

Bed warmer, brass pan w/circular pierced lid engraved w/foliate decoration, turned wood handle, 45½" l. 176.00

Bed warmer, brown-glazed stoneware, dome-shaped, arched small open handle top, vent hole, signed "Jager Co.," 7½ x 9½" 220.00

Bed warmer, copper pan w/stamped & pierced brass cover, long turned wood handle, 19th c., 42" l. 302.50

Bed warmer, copper pan w/tooled starflower design on lid, turned wood handle, 42" l. 175.00

Bed warmer, copper pan w/pierced circular brass lid chased w/bird & foliate decoration, turned wood handle, 19th c., 42½" l. 286.00

Foot warmer, cherry, pierced body w/wire bail handle, a ring pull on sliding front panel opening to reveal pierced tin box w/inner coal pan, branded on base "D.W.C.," probably England, 19th c. (wear, slight warping) 275.00

Foot warmer, oak, Friesian-style carving on all sides & top, door carved w/Dutch inscription & dated "1829," brass bail handle, good old dark finish, 8" h. (pin for door bolt & pan missing) 250.00

Foot warmer, pierced tin & wood, mortised wood frame w/turned corner posts holds pierced tin panels w/heart & circle designs, simple metal swing handle on top, 9 1/8" w., 6" h. (ILLUS.) 192.50

Foot warmer, pierced tin & wood, mortised wood frame w/turned corner posts holds pierced tin panels in compass star pattern, old worn brown finish, 9" l. 135.00

Foot warmer, pierced tin & wood, mortised wood frame w/turned corner posts holds pierced tin sides & top w/heart & circle designs, door in one end, interior pan, old worn red stain, large size, 17¾" l. (some light rust) 250.00

Foot warmer, stoneware, impressed "Doulton-Lambeth," black transfer on side 55.00

Foot warmer, walnut dovetailed box w/slide-up door, drilled air holes & brass bail handle at top, old dark finish, 8¾ x 8¾", 6" h. (minor damage) 305.00

Foot warmer, wood, tin & glass, wood & tin case w/oval glass sides w/wire guards & interior kerosene burner w/heat shield, top folds back to form carpet-covered footrest, original dark paint w/red striping & indistinct stenciled label "Patented by H.L. J---, March 14, 1863," iron bail handle on lid & four celluloid buttons, 8" l. 205.00

FRAKTUR

Parrot in Tree Fraktur

Fraktur paintings are decorative birth and marriage certificates of the 18th and 19th centuries and also include family registers and similar documents. Illuminated family documents, birth and baptismal certificates, religious texts and rewards of merit, in a particular style, are known as "fraktur" because of the similarity to the 16th century type-face of that name. Gay water-color borders, frequently incorporating stylized birds, angels, animals or flowers surrounded the hand-lettered documents, which were executed by local ministers, school masters or itinerant penmen. Most are of Pennsylvania Dutch origin.

Baptismal record for Ewald Arader, water-color & ink, red & yellow angels, birds & flowers centering a reserve w/brown ink German inscription, w/lower heart-shaped reserve w/inscription, Northampton County, Pennsylvania, 1804, framed, 12½ x 26½" $2,200.00

Birth record for Amos Bauer, pen & ink & water-color, vital statistics in ornamental calligraphy in center surrounded by large heart w/peacocks, tulips, compass stars & large parrots around the edge, in shades of red, green, blue, brown, yellow & black, large signature at bottom edge, "H. Seller," framed, 16 x 19¼" (minor tears, stains & holes) 12,000.00

Birth record, printed & hand-colored, design of three angels among printed boxes for recording statistics, records 1821 birth, printed by Ebner & Comp., Allentown, Pennsylvania, bright colors, matted & framed, 16 x 21" (creases, short tear, corner hole) 65.00

Bookplate, pen & ink & water-color, double size decorated w/stylized floral decoration by John Spangenborg for "Catharina Haupt," rich colors of red, blue, green, yellow & brown, gilt frame, overall 8½ x 10½" (some satins, fading & folds) 3,500.00

Drawing, water-color, figure of a parrot w/bright green head, red & blue wings & red & blue spotted body perched in the branches of a flowering tulip tree, anonymous, Pennsylvania, ca. 1800, in early frame, 5¾ x 7¼" (ILLUS.) 1,210.00

Religious text, pen & ink, ornate calligraphic text w/"Elizabeth Richterin" above religious text, all surrounded by heart surrounded by stylized flowers & a small crowned face at top center, dark shades of brown, olive & reddish brown on laid paper, framed, overall 10¾ x 11½" (glued on lined paper, minor stains) 1,650.00

Vorschrift (writing specimen), pen & ink & water-color, ornamental calligraphy, English inscriptions w/religious verse & "Laura Dickinson" within large central heart surrounded by eagle, stylized flowers & foliage in shades of red, yellow, green, blue & black, poplar frame w/painted graining, 10¼ x 12½" 1,250.00

FRAMES

Aventurine quartz & 18k gold, rectangular, the border set w/panels of emerald green aventurine quartz overlaid w/gold latticework, retailed by Pasque, Paris, 12 5/8" h. $6,050.00

Bird's-eye maple veneer, ogee style w/flat liner, 19th c., 25 x 28½" w/3 5/8" w. edges (minor damage) 105.00

Brass, w/tin back, easel & hanging-type, beautiful design on edges, dated 1908, 4¼ x 5½" oval 55.00

Cherry, w/silver painted inner liner, 1¼" w. reeded framework, 10¼ x 7 3/8" 45.00

Giltwood, rectangular surround carved w/flowering vines & acanthus leaves, within a ribbon-tied cluster border, the shield-shaped crest carved w/buckles & pelicans, George II period, England, mid-18th c., 34" w., 40" h. 3,575.00

Glass, Art Deco painted black & silver designs w/chrome corners, 7 x 9" 20.00

Painted & decorated poplar, original black paint & gold stenciled decoration, fine condition, 9¾ x 11¾", 1¼" w. edge 245.00

Silver & shaded enamel, enameled w/flowering foliage in the Old Russian style on grounds of apricot, avocado & deep green, Fyodor Ruckert, Moscow, Russia, ca. 1910, 6½" h. 3,300.00

Sterling silver, swollen rectangle, two large repousse peacocks perched on flowering branches, bordering a rising sun, England, 8 5/8" h. 550.00

Walnut, figural shield, open heart cut-out for photo, ca. 1865, 4 x 5" 95.00

Walnut, hexagonal shape w/round center opening, carved from single piece of wood w/foliage & gadrooning, old finish, holds mirror, 11" d. (two cracks) 65.00

Walnut, criss-cross corners w/applied leaves, 17 x 20" 30.00

Ornate Victorian Walnut Frame

Walnut, ornately open-carved w/scrolling grapevines along sides & central top crest of basket of fruit, Victorian, large size (ILLUS.) 3,500.00

FRATERNAL ORDER COLLECTIBLES

Masonic Tie Clip

B.P.O.E. (Benevolent & Protective Order of Elks) card case, sterling silver, inscribed & dated 1913, 1½ x 2" $95.00

B.P.O.E. pitcher, china, elk's head & clock emblems on purple shaded to white ground, National Art China, Trenton, N.J., 12" h. 95.00

B.P.O.E. plate, china, clock emblem, Warwick China, 9½" d. 40.00

B.P.O.E. shaving mug, porcelain, large h.p. elk's head w/"B.P.O.E." between antler prongs above "J.H. Briggs" in gold lettering (worn gold) 60.00

B.P.O.E. shot glass, "B.P.O. Elks No. 895 Martins Ferry, Ohio" 12.00

B.P.O.E. spoon, sterling silver, enameled clock emblem, "Chanute, Kansas," 6" l. 55.00

B.P.O.E. stein, china, h.p. elk & clock emblems, purple w/gold trim, artist-signed, Pickard, 7" h. 125.00

F.O.E. (Fraternal Order of Eagles) straight razor, imitation ivory handle inset w/red, white & blue spread-winged eagle center, Aerial Cutlery Co., Marinette, Wisconsin (hairline crack) 16.00

G.A.R. (Grand Army of the Republic) badge, celluloid, "Mauston, Wisconsin," memorial 15.00

G.A.R. medallion, bronze, commemorating "Lincoln's 100th Birthday," 1909, 3" 60.00

I.O.O.F. (Independent Order of Odd Fellows) checkerboard, painted wood, rectangular w/rounded corners centering yellow & black squares highlighted w/gilt striping, flanked by rectangular reserves, one containing the "all seeing eye," "links of fellowship," four comic character heads & inscription "The Odd Fellows," the other w/clasped hands & two character heads, all within a black & yellow striped border, 20th c., 15 x 26" (surface blistering) 770.00

I.O.O.F. shaving mug, interlocking links & heart in hand symbols 75.00

L.O.O.M. (Loyal Order of Moose) pencil clip, figural moose w/red eye 5.00

L.O.O.M. straight razor, blade etched w/gold bridge, green swirled handle w/inlaid red & gold enameled emblem, "Old Dutch," Aerial Cutlery Co. 36.00

Masonic book, "Universal Masonic Library, Vol. IV: Antiquities of Freemasonry & Harris's Discourses," 1856, over 400 pp. (rebound) 22.50

Masonic book box w/sliding drawer, wooden, relief carved Masonic symbols, original black & gold paint, 7 7/8" l. 50.00

Masonic pendant, 14k gold, in the form of an armorial shield applied w/a silver compass flanked by an eagle & lion, back inscribed, late 19th c., 1½" h. 715.00

Masonic plate, china, fraternal symbols around scalloped rim, polychrome center scene of teams of oxen, back inscribed to commemorate the 64th Annual Conclave of Toledo Commandery in 1906, Knowles, Taylor & Knowles, 8¼" d. 35.00

Masonic shaving mug, porcelain, bright gold name, "Geo. F. Clider," above Masonic emblem around "G" flanked by gold scrolls, bottom marked "Royal China International" & signed "Leo C. Benitz" 125.00

Masonic straight razor, blade etched w/bridge, rounded brown swirled handle w/inlaid blue & gold enameled emblem, Aerial Cutlery Co. 36.00

Masonic tie clip, emblem set w/small diamonds, marked "Sterling" (ILLUS.) 35.00

Masonic tumbler, milk white glass, "Landmark Lodge No. 127, Baltimore, 1866-1916" 38.00

O.E.S. (Order of the Eastern Star) compact, emblem in center of lid 20.00

O.E.S. ring, 14k white gold band, enameled star & gold gavel centering ¼ carat zircon 80.00

Shrine 1897 tumbler, clear glass, one side a crying Victorian lady in gold, "I want to be a Shriner," other side w/full figure Shriner

holding a glass in gold, "Pittsburgh to Detroit 1897" 110.00
Shrine 1899 goblet, clear glass, "Pittsburgh," w/scimitar, crescent & lion 50.00
Shrine 1902 champagne, clear glass, "San Francisco" 65.00
Shrine 1904 mug, clear glass, "Atlantic City," fish handle 65.00
Shrine 1905 3-handled mug, clear glass, "Pittsburgh" 65.00
Shrine 1906 plate, clear glass, "Los Angeles" & "May" 50.00
Shrine 1908 goblet, ruby-flashed glass, "St. Paul" 60.00
Shrine 1909 champagne, clear glass, "Louisville, Kentucky," swords & horseshoes 50.00
Shrine 1911 champagne, clear glass, colorful man w/camera in relief & "Rochester" one side, man w/camel & "Pittsburgh" reverse .. 80.00
Shrine humidor, metal Art Nouveau style cover w/ornate finial composed of various emblems, paneled clear glass body, "Yaarab Temple, Atlanta" 75.00
Shrine mug, china, "Zagazig Temple, Des Moines" & "Atlantic City 1904" 35.00
Shrine pendant, gold & silver, scimitar-shaped, lava cameo w/enameled headdress set in gold-mounted lion's claws suspending a gold, jet & enameled cross set w/mine-cut diamonds 235.00

FRUIT JARS

Atlas E-Z Seal Quart

Acme, clear, qt. $2.50
Adlam's Patent, Boston, Mass. on base, aqua, pt. 85.00
African Nag Co. (The), porcelain lined, midget 125.00
Atlas E-Z Seal, amber, qt. 32.00
Atlas E-Z Seal, aqua, qt. (ILLUS.) ... 2.00
Atlas Good Luck, clear, ½ pt. 8.00
Ball Ideal, aqua, ½ pt. 30.00
Ball Mason, olive, qt. 25.00
Ball Perfect Mason, olive, pt. 35.00
Ball Sure Seal, blue, ½ pt. 45.00
Brighton, clear, qt. (no lid or clamp) 35.00
Chamber's (A & D H) Union Fruit Jar, Pittsburgh, Pa., aqua, qt. 65.00
Chief (The), aqua, qt. (repro lid) 195.00
Dandy (The) Trade Mark, amber, qt. 120.00
Doolittle, clear, pt. (lid embossing only) 60.00
Franklin Dexter Fruit Jar, aqua, qt. 32.00
Gem (The), aqua, ½ gal. 25.00
Gem (The), aqua, gal. 450.00
Gilberds Jar w/star, aqua, pt. (clear repro wire) 150.00
Globe, clear, ¼ pt. 375.00
Globe, amber, pt. 75.00
Griffen's Patent Oct 7, 1862, aqua, qt. (some haze) 100.00
Hamilton Glass Works, blue, qt. (repro clamp) 125.00
Kerr Anniversary, gold, qt. 22.00
Knowlton Vacuum Fruit Jar, w/matching lid, aqua, qt. 20.00
"L G CO" on base, wax sealer, aqua, ½ gal. 20.00
Lafayette, applied lip & matching glass lid w/metal fastener, aqua, qt. 87.50
Leader (The), amber, pt. 225.00
Leotric, apple green, qt. 20.00
Lightning, amber, pt. 37.00
Lightning, brilliant yellow, ½ gal. .. 70.00
Lightning Trade Mark, amber, qt. 35.00
Lyman (W.W.), Patd. Aug. 5th 1862, aqua, pt. 125.00
Magic (The) Fruit Jar, w/star, amber, qt. 550.00
Mason's Improved, aqua, qt. 3.25
Mason's Patent Nov. 30th, 1858, amber, midget 1,200.00
Mason's Patent Nov. 30th, 1858, aqua, pt. 6.00
Mason's Patent, Nov. 30th, 1858, cobalt blue, qt. 32.50
Mason's, stoneware, ½ gal. 150.00
McKee (F. & J.), Pittsburgh, Pa., ground lip & top, open pontil, clear, 1½ qt. 450.00
Middleby (Joe.), Jr., Inc., clear, ½ gal. 14.00
Premium, Coffeyville, Kas., clear, qt. 20.00
Spencer's, C.F., Patent Rochester, N.Y., lift top, aqua, qt. 80.00
Standard, W. McC & Co., dark aqua, qt. 55.00
United Drug Co., clear, qt. 10.00
Wax sealer, folded lip, iron pontil, whittled, aqua, ½ gal. 215.00

FURNITURE *Special Focus*

Rocking Chairs

by Connie Morningstar

America has been rocking since colonial times. In fact, every section of the country, save the Spanish Southwest, has introduced or adapted some version of the rocking chair.

Legend has it that Benjamin Franklin invented the piece. At any rate, Franklin, ever the comfort-loving pragmatist, seems to have raised rocking to acceptable respectability. In the beginning there were cradles for infants and adult cradles for the old and infirm. Others were expected to sit erect in a straight chair, four-square on the floor. Sometime in the 1740's, rockers appear to have been added to upholstered "easy" chairs. Still the piece was intended for use only by the less than able.

It was an idea whose time had come, however, and soon rockers were being added to ordinary side chairs—attached to the inside or outside of the legs and extending equal distance fore and aft. This produced an abrupt, jolting movement that was eased by the subsequent extension of the rockers some ten inches to the rear. With this, the rocking chair as it is known today was born.

Slat-back rockers were being made in the early 1800's. By the 1820's, spindle-back Windsors had appeared. Probably based on sites of origin, Windsor rockers with contoured, S-profiled seats are called "Boston" while similar pieces with flat seats are known as "Salem." Both have enduring popularity. Various sizes of Boston rockers were produced during the 1830's by Lambert Hitchcock's firm in Hitchcocksville, Connecticut, one of the first assembly-line factories in the furniture industry. These were painted and stenciled in the customary Hitchcock manner.

Of interest also are the "Cape Cod" rocking settees, now commonly called Mammy Benches, turned out by Hitchcock's plant in the late 1830's. These pieces are identified by a removable fence across half the seat front that is anchored by removable posts set into the seat top. This arrangement allowed the mother or nurse to rock the baby while freeing her hands for other work. Some pieces have a fence on each side to accommodate twins.

Mammy benches were made at least as late as the mid-19th century and novelty, child/doll pieces were sold in the 1940's. All in the country genre, backs might be spindle or splat or a combination of both. The fence will likely have two or three horizontal slats or a solid panel. Early pieces probably will have narrow "carpet-cutter" rockers set into the leg ends. Mammy benches are particularly desirable at this time. Prices in the past year have ranged from $400 to $1,800.

The Grecian rocker was an exceedingly popular chair that first appeared during the 1830's, became especially popular in the late 19th century, and is being reproduced today. Caned Grecians might have scrolled arms or, in the case of "nurse" or sewing rockers, be armless or have hip-hugging brackets. Backs are contoured; seats are flat and convex at the front. Because of the contoured stiles, the piece is sometimes referred to as a gooseneck rocker.

Upholstered Grecians have been called "Lincoln" rockers because of the chair in which President Lincoln was sitting when he was assassinated. Early examples have an exposed mahogany frame, often with a carved crest. Later pieces most likely are black walnut. Other features include an upholstered spring seat, tufted back and padded arm tops. Carved swans occasionally grace the ends of scrolled arm supports.

Michael Thonet put his famous bentwood rocking Chair No. 1 into mass-production in Koritschan, Moravia (now Czechoslovakia), in 1860. Although rocking chairs had long since been taken to heart in America, the concept was virtually unknown in central Europe at that time. Thonet's production of rockers increased slowly to over 20,000 pieces annually in the 1890's. Made of some 27 feet of steam-bent birch wood, various versions of the original have been produced since by the Thonet firm and several competitors—principally Jacob and Josef Kohn. By 1904, 24 variations of this rocker with caned seat and back were shown in the Thonet catalog. At that time, only Model No. 1 appeared available with plush upholstered seat and back and fringed upholstered arm tops. Antique Thonet rockers can be expected to bring between $1,000 and $1,200 today.

A platform rocker of sorts made its debut at the London Crystal Palace Exhibition in 1851. This was an ornate piece whose fringed skirt concealed the centripetal spring that allowed the chair to tilt and rotate. The "platform" consisted of four bracket-type legs. The piece was patented by the American Chair Company, Troy, New York, and was, in fact, the precursor of the office desk chair rather than the parlor-oriented true platform rocker which did not rotate.

During the 1870's and 1880's, particularly, hundreds of patents were issued for devices that allowed a chair to swing, glide or rock on a platform. P. C. Lewis, Catskill, New York, patented his Rip van Winkle reclining/rocking chair, the "most wonderful chair in the world," in 1887-1888. Manufacturer as well as patentee, Lewis claimed some 15 pieces of furniture were combined in this one remarkable chair and noted that more than 200 changes of position were possible.

Most platform rockers were considerably more prosaic. Many were overstuffed and fringed in the Turkish mode. Others had elaborately carved exposed frames. Combinations of flat-cut scrolls and pressed designs appeared in the Golden Oak era. From the 1880's into the early 20th century, the platform rocker together with the settee and armchair made up the popular three-piece parlor suite.

Rockers turned out by the Shaker communities were as simple and unadorned as the contemporary platforms were complicated and fussy. The Shaker furniture factory at Mt. Lebanon, New York, was established in 1863 by Elder Robert M. Wagan and continued to produce furniture until about 1940, operating in later years as R.M. Wagan & Company. Most production pieces (those intended for sale on the outside rather than within the society) were marked; but a general rule-of-thumb identification would be that backs are not spindled and rockers are set into leg ends.

During the 1870's, the Mt. Lebanon factory turned out eight models of production rockers in graduated sizes, numbered and marked from No. 0 (child's) to No. 7, a large adult piece. At that time, prices ranged from $3.50 for No. 0 to $8.50 for No. 7. In the summer of 1987, a No. 7 rocker was show-priced at $1,650 and a child-size No. 1 brought $3,190 at auction.

Rocking chairs lent themselves well to designs carved by machines such as those made by the Union Carving and Embossing Machine Company of Indianapolis, Indiana. During the 1890's, pressed or patterned chair back designs were legion. Designs might depict anything from simple cord-like outlining of a scroll-cut crest to shells, birds, fish, "North Wind," or Admiral Dewey's victorious fleet. A rocker with the last design, incidentally, brought $247.50 at auction in Ohio last October. Competition decreed that designs be changed frequently, and retooling every six months was not unusual for most factories.

In 1904, a new line of embossed work in which the motif was raised in the wood was brought out by the Union firm. This style was deemed appropriate for chairs, tabourets, tables, etc. Illustrated in the company's ad was the "Tavern" rocker with an embossed back design depicting monks drinking around a table. The chairs were exhibited at the Louisiana Purchase Exposition in St. Louis that year.

Montgomery Ward's 1895 catalog showed 44 models of pressed-back rockers—spindle and splat-back Bostons with cane, flat, or scrolled ("swell") seats; armless "nurse" rockers with upholstered spring seats; open-arm rockers with upholstered seats; and patent McLean Swing Rockers. All had pressed designs on the crest. All were priced under $8.50.

Interest in Mission-style rockers is warming up with recent auction prices of labeled Gustav Stickley pieces, particularly, exceeding their pre-sale estimates. One such piece, a high-back, open-arm rocker with leather-cushioned seat and inlaid metal decoration on the three vertical back slats, brought $13,200 ($4,400 over estimate) at auction last November. The rocker was designed by Harvey Ellis. A spindle-back "nurse" rocker bearing the red Gustav Stickley decal went for $1,320. On the other hand, a similar "nurse" rocker made by Elbert Hubbard's Roycrofters brought only $247.50—$82.50 below the *low* pre-sale estimate.

Clearly the message in antique rockers is that the name's the thing. And it's best if that name is Stickley, or Thonet, or Shaker.

(Editor's Note: *Connie Morningstar, author of several books on furniture, including* Early Utah Furniture, *has also written numerous articles for various periodicals and is a regular columnist for* THE ANTIQUE TRADER WEEKLY *newspaper. Delving into the records of early cabinetmakers, furniture shops and factories, she has become respected for her thorough research which enables her to write with accuracy, clarity and authority about American furniture styles and trends.*)

A specialized book, just on rocking chairs,

was written by Ellen and Bert Denker several years ago. The Rocking Chair Book *was published by Main Street Press, New York, New York, in 1979.*

ILLUSTRATED PRICE LISTINGS:

Boston-Windsor rocker, scrolled seat, inset rockers, metal rod arm support reinforcement, painted black w/stenciled design on crest & seat front $225.00

"Nurse" or sewing rocker w/splat back, scrolled seat, inset rockers, painted & w/gold stenciled decoration, labeled "1840 Germantown, Pa." 400.00

Hitchcock-type armless rocker, splat & arrow banister back, rolled crest, slightly scrolled plank seat, short rockers attached to outside of legs, painted black w/gold

stenciling & striping, ca. 1840 .... 240.00

Youth rocker, grain-painted & striped, round seat w/scooped center, splayed turned legs, inset rockers, spindle back, Williamsburg, New York, ca. 1850, 17" w., 30" h. 395.00

Child's slat-back rocker, oak, rush

seat, inset rockers, 12" w., 25" h. 65.00

Slat-back rocker, pine, woven rush seat, arm supports pass through seatrail & attach to top stretcher, inset short rockers, 40" h. 495.00

Slat or "ladder-back" armchair rocker, painted wood, four wide, rounded-top curved slats flanked by sausage-turned stiles, flat arms supported by turned posts above wide woven rush seat, turned front legs w/one turned & one plain rung, worn dark brown paint over old red, early 19th c., minor repairs, one rocker replaced, one old addition (Not illus.)...................... 300.00

"Nurse" or sewing rocker, pine, spindle back, plank seat, inset rockers, 19th c. 189.00

Victorian open-arm rocker, mahogany frame, gondola-shaped stiles, leaf-carved motif on crest & inside

arm supports, concave front legs, burl veneer on skirt, maroon velvet tufted upholstery, mid-19th c. 595.00

Victorian "Grecian" caned rocker, maple, refinished & recaned, late 19th c. 195.00

Victorian "Grecian" rocker w/upholstered back, maple, caned seat, concave front stretcher, late 19th c. 225.00

Victorian "patent" rocking chair, walnut, rectangular cloth strap back & seat in turned wood frame, signed & dated, George Hunzinger, New York, New York, ca. 1875, 31½" h. (Not illus.)..... 357.50

Victorian Eastlake substyle platform rocker, black walnut frame w/incised carving on crest, stiles, arm supports, skirt, siderails & platform, cutwork under arms, four metal casters, gold velvet upholstery, ca. 1880 .... 275.00

Victorian "nurse" or sewing rocker, walnut, keystone-shaped back w/walnut burl panel on crest, hip brackets, recaned, ca. 1885, 19" w., 35" h.................... 175.00

Victorian Eastlake substyle "nurse" or sewing rocker, walnut, cut-out

crest panel, caned back panel & caned seat, applied burl panels, incised carving on stiles, hip brackets, ca. 1880 .... 110.00

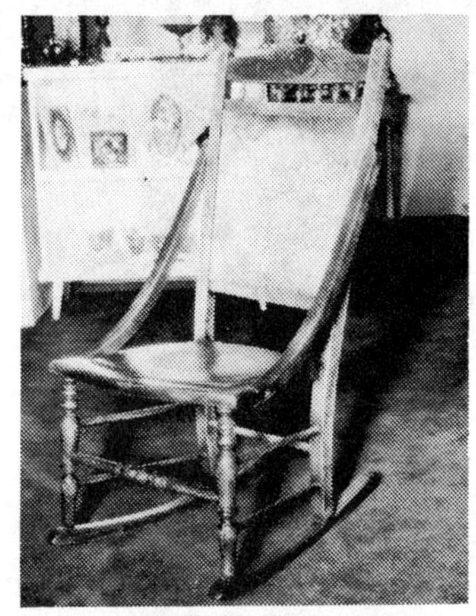

Victorian "nurse" or sewing rocker, maple, gondola-shaped sides, decorated plywood panel seat & back, ca. 1890 .... 98.00

Child's rocking armchair, bentwood, arched top rail above spindled splats, bentwood arms & woven seat above a spindled apron, raised on stick legs on a bentwood rocker base, late 19th c. (Not illus.)..................... 330.00

Bentwood rocker, rounded rectangular caned back & rectangular caned seat conjoined by an oval bentwood open section between scrolling bentwood arms continuing into elaborately scrolling sides & raised on two rockers joined by two simple turned stretchers, manufactured & retailed by Mundus, w/paper label, ca. 1910 (Not illus.) 550.00

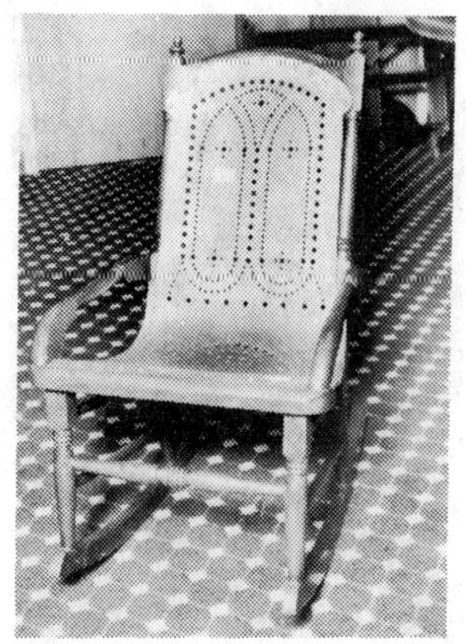

Victorian child's rocker, walnut, perforated laminated seat, 1870's 121.00

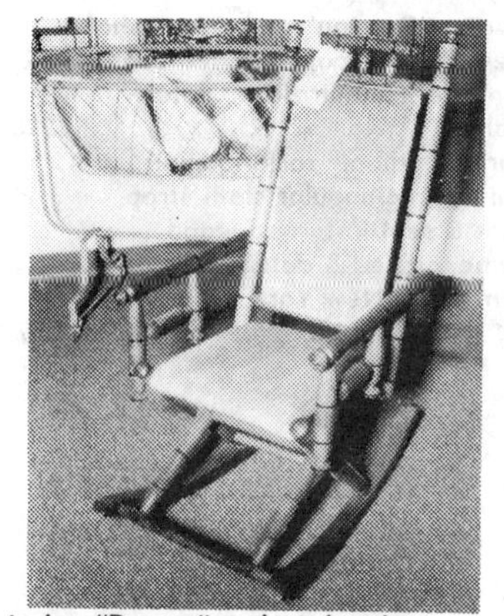

Victorian "Dexter" rocker, bamboo-turned frame, blue velvet upholstery, ca. 1885 . . . . 215.00

Child's bentwood rocker, rustic construction w/tied joints, 27" h. 145.00

Golden Oak pressed-back youth rocker, pressed crest, turned spindle back, recaned seat, ca. 1900 . . 285.00

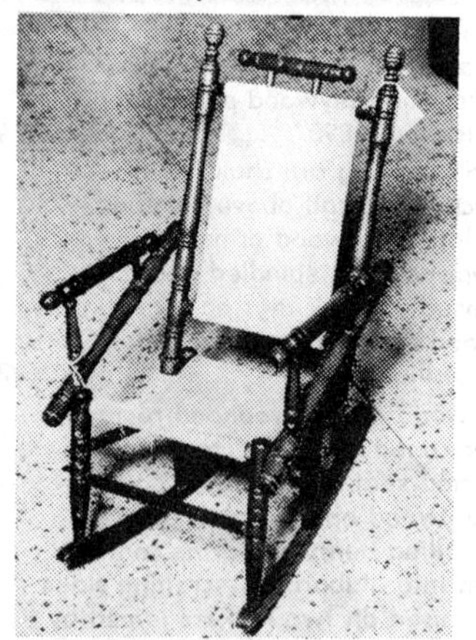

Child's "Dexter" rocker, spool-turned walnut frame, replaced fabric seat & back, ca. 1885, 15" w., 26" h. 265.00

Golden Oak rocker, arrow banisters in back, stiles continuing to form scrolled arms, brass medallions on finials, saddle seat, ca. 1900 . . . . 175.00

Golden Oak pressed-back "nurse" or sewing rocker, pressed design in crest, spindle back, caned seat insert, metal brackets, ca. 1900 .. 125.00

Golden Oak rocker, spindle back, plain crest, scrolled upholstered seat, ca. 1900 .... 325.00

Oak platform rocker, plain crest, shaped arms, concentric circle springs in base, metal casters on platform front only, new leather tufted upholstery, ca. 1900 .... 550.00

Art Nouveau style parlor rocker, fumed finish, saddle seat, ca. 1900 .... 225.00

Art Nouveau armless rocker, oak, carved & pierced back panel & front stretcher, incised line carving on stiles, carved & incised rockers mounted on outside legs, pink velvet upholstery, ca. 1900 .. 275.00

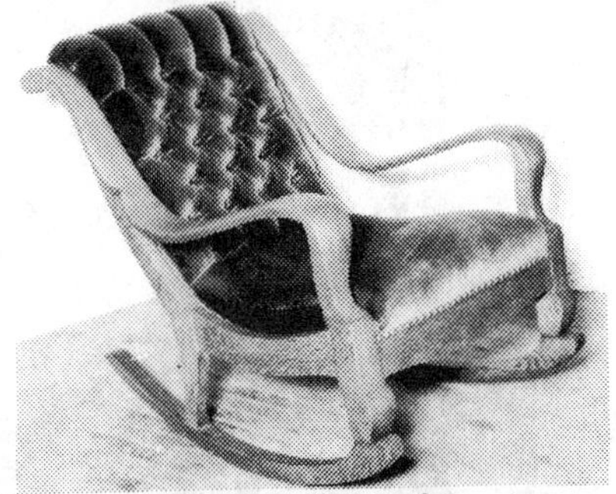

Victorian open-arm rocker, oak, gondola-shaped stiles, open shaped arms, brown velvet tufted upholstery, ca. 1900 .... 595.00

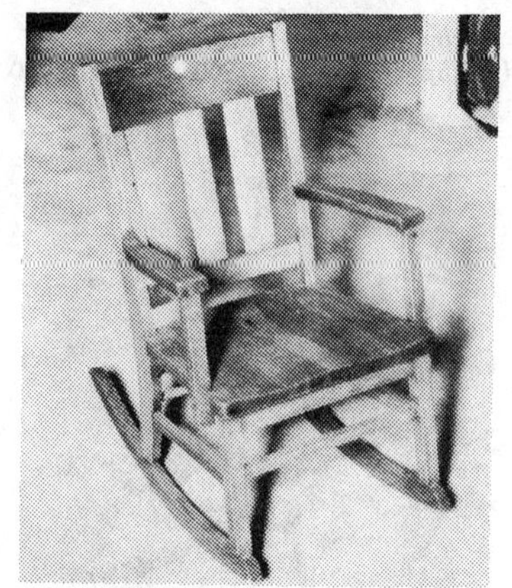

Mission Oak rocker, child's, banister back, shaped seat, ca. 1910, 28" h. 140.00

Mission Oak lady's rocker, nine slender spindles in back, five below the seat on each side, new black leather seat & relatively new brown finish, red decal mark of Gustav Stickley, ca. 1900, 36 x 16 x 14" 1,320.00

Mission Oak armless rocker, five vertical slats in back, new thick canvas seat, dark brown nearly new finish, branded orb trademark on front, Roycroft Shops, ca. 1900, 35 x 18 x 31" 247.50

Mission style inlaid lady's rocker, curly maple w/three vertical back slats inlaid w/stylized Arts & Crafts-Art Nouveau pewter & green wood designs, curved skirt under front & sides of drop-in leather seat, designed by Harvey Ellis for Gustav Stickley, unmarked, ca. 1900, 34 x 17 x 25¾" 3,850.00

Mission Oak rocker, high back w/eleven spindles, nine spindles under each arm, drop-in leather seat, original brown color w/new lightly oiled finish, red decal Gustav Stickley mark, 45 x 27½ x 22½" 9,900.00

Wicker rocker, high arched back, woven continuous arms, ornate curliques in back, caned seat,

painted white, ca. 1890 . . 600.00 to 650.00

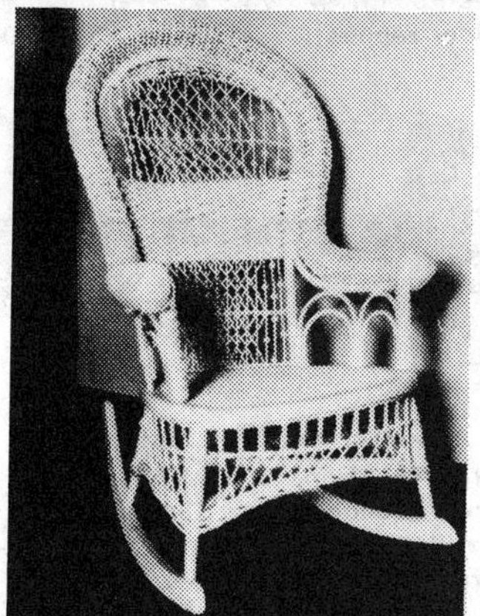

Wicker rocker, high rounded back continuing down to form arms, criss-cross weaving in back, caned seat, painted white, ca. 1890 .300.00 to 350.00

Wicker rocker, high squared back w/curlique & criss-cross woven back, wrapped frame, refinished paint, ca. 1900 . . . . 360.00

Wicker rocker, child's, high squared

back, tightly woven back & seat, painted brown, ca. 1910, 17" w., 26" h. 250.00

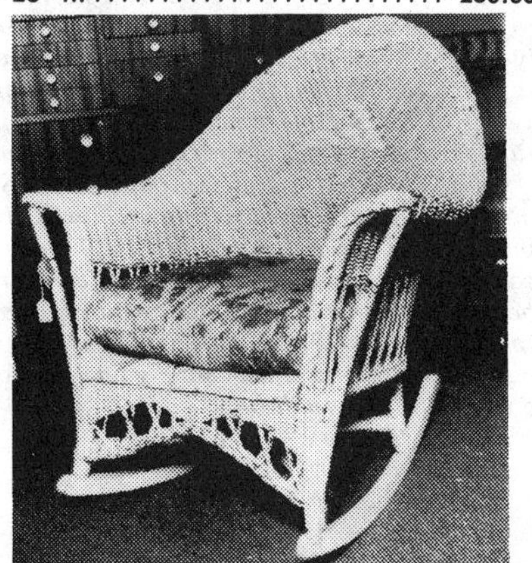

Woven fibre rocker, arched, pointed back, cushion seat, painted white, 1920's 75.00

Federal-style child's rocker, mahogany, carved crest, needlepoint seat, 20th c., 22" h. 145.00

(End of Special Focus)

FURNITURE

Furniture made in the United States during the 18th and 19th centuries is coveted by collectors. American antique furniture has a European background, primarily English, since the influence of the Continent usually found its way to America by way of England. If the style did not originate in England, it came to America by way of England. For this reason, some American furniture styles carry the name of an English monarch or an English designer. However, we must realize that, until recently, little research has been conducted and even less published on the Spanish and French influences in the areas of the California missions and New Orleans.

After the American Revolution, cabinetmakers in the United States shunned the prevailing styles in England and chose to bring the French styles of Napoleon's Empire to the United States and we have the uniquely named "American Empire" style of furniture in a country that never had an emperor.

During the Victorian period, quality furniture began to be mass-produced in this country with its rapidly growing population. So much walnut furniture was manufactured, the vast supply of walnut was virtually depleted and it was of necessity that oak furniture became fashionable as the 19th century drew to a close.

For our purposes, the general guidelines for dating furniture will be:

Pilgrim Century - 1620-85
William & Mary - 1685-1720
Queen Anne - 1720-50
Chippendale - 1750-85
Federal - 1785-1820
Hepplewhite - 1785-1800
Sheraton - 1800-20
American Empire - 1815-40
Victorian - 1840-1900
Early Victorian - 1840-50
Gothic Revival - 1840-90
Louis XV (rococo) - 1845-70
Louis XVI - 1865-75
Eastlake - 1870-95
Renaissance - 1860-85
Jacobean & Turkish Revival - 1870-90
Art Nouveau - 1890-1918
Turn-of-the-Century - 1895-1910
Mission (Arts & Crafts movement) - 1900-15
Art Deco - 1925-40

All furniture included in this listing is American unless otherwise noted. Also see MINIATURES (Replicas.)

BEDS

Biedermeier daybed, fruitwood veneer, two outscrolled well-figured solid sides & curved side rails, interior veneered w/pale fruitwood, on square plinths, after a design by Josef Danhauser, Vienna, Austria, early 19th c., 85" l $4,400.00

Campaign bed, folding-type, painted finish, shaped headboard flanked by square posts w/button finials, turned legs, old red & black grain-painted finish w/yellow & green striping, old red paint on rails, 52" w., 73" l., 39½" h. 900.00

Empire, American, country-style bunk beds, heavy posts w/turnings & paneled spire finials, shaped one-board headboards, original side rails, old white over green paint, 44 x 73", 85½" h. (minor repairs) 900.00

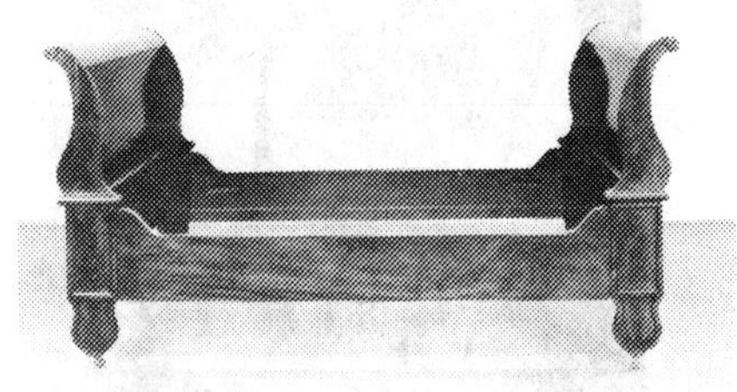

American Empire "Sleigh" Bed

Empire, American, "sleigh" bed, carved mahogany, ca. 1840, double size (ILLUS.) 1,800.00

Empire, French, *"lit à bateau"* (boat-form bed), mahogany, head & footboard w/round section crestrail over plain panel, fronted by detached column w/ormolu base & capital surmounted by applied ormolu swan, the two ends joined by concave front rail w/later mounts, France, early 19th c., 41½" h. (imperfections) 2,310.00

Federal Low Poster Bed

Federal country-style low poster bed, painted maple, arched headboard flanked by vase- and ring-turned low posts & vase-turned tapering legs ending in disc feet, rope-type side rails & conforming legs at foot w/flattened finials, painted blue-green, New England, ca. 1810, 53" w., 74" l., 37" h. (ILLUS.) 2,860.00

Federal country-style low poster bed, painted finish, "rolling pin" crest on boldly shaped headboard flanked by turned posts w/spire finials, turned foot rail flanked by conforming posts, rope-type, original side rails, old red paint, 53½" w., 70¼" l., 46" h. 375.00

Federal tall poster bed, maple, headboard w/leaf-carved crest centering a carved fruit basket above two inset panels, four leaf-carved & turned posts w/pineapple finials, 52" w., 75" l., 80" h. 1,320.00

Federal tall poster bed, curly maple & pine, simple pine head- and footboards flanked by baluster-turned curly maple posts on blocked supports, Connecticut, ca. 1810, 57½" w., 84" h. posts (side rails lengthened) 935.00

Sheraton tester bed, birch, shaped headboard w/pine insert flanked by faceted headposts & reeded, leaf-carved ring- and baluster-turned footposts, original rope side rails, 55" w., 73" l., 65" h. posts, w/(repaired) tester 5,000.00

Turn-of-the-Century Brass Bed

Turn-of-the-Century brass bed, rounded tubular headboard w/five straight, round slats & conforming lower footboard, ca. 1910, three-quarter size (ILLUS.) 200.00

Victorian half-tester bed, Renaissance Revival substyle, mahogany & mahogany veneer, serpentine half-tester w/beaded band & urn finials at front corners & scrolled crest at center front w/pleated upholstery interior above tall headboard w/scroll-carved crest center-

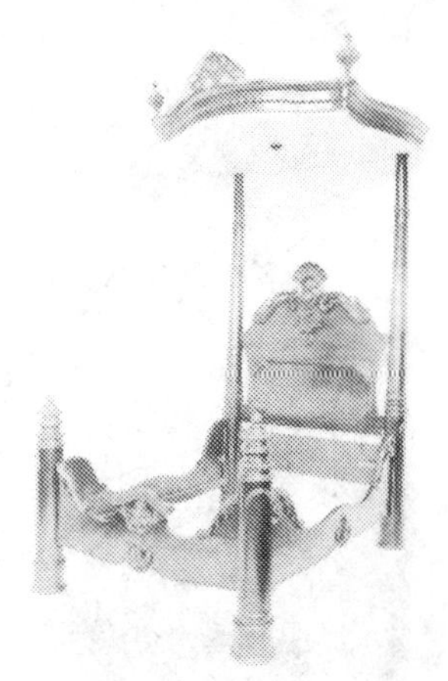

Mallard Half-Tester Bed

ed by shell-carved finial all above recessed panel, low arched footboard w/scrolling leaf-carved trim & floral-carved pendant, shaped & carved side rails join round, carved columnar corner posts, by Prudent Mallard, New Orleans, Louisiana, 1850's (ILLUS.) 5,500.00

Renaissance Revival Bed

Victorian bed, Renaissance Revival substyle, walnut & burl walnut, tall headboard w/arched, paneled crest topped by scroll-carved finial above raised burl panels around center recessed panel all flanked by side posts topped w/carved finials above half-round drop-finials, arched footboard w/raised burl panels around recessed center panel & rounded corner panels w/line-incised decoration, ca. 1875, double size (ILLUS.) 880.00

Victorian bed, Renaissance Revival substyle, walnut, tall headboard w/ornate shield-shaped crest open-carved w/scrolls & pomegranates

Ornate Victorian Bed

above raised panels over three arches w/raised borders & half-round fruit drops all flanked by side posts w/finials above raised panels & scroll- and fruit-carved drops, low footboard w/pedimented crest above shield & scroll-carved raised panel & w/rounded corner panels w/carved scrolls, ca. 1875, double size (ILLUS.) 2,500.00

Youth's bed, painted hardwood, spindle-sided sleigh-shaped, raised on legs, rope-type, flattened head, foot & side rails above squared spindles, original finish, 1830's 495.00

BEDROOM SUITES

Empire-Style Bed

Empire-Style: bed, commode & side table; gilt-bronze mounted mahogany; "sleigh" style bed w/outswept head- and footboard raised on plinth base & fitted w/mounts depicting mermaids, trumpets, scrolls & masks; the commode w/rectangular marble top & overhanging frieze drawer above four long drawers flanked by columns; the bedside table w/single frieze drawer, raised on columnar supports, late 19th c., 3 pcs. (ILLUS. of bed) 8,800.00

Victorian, Cottage "Bamboo" style: bed, dresser & bookcase; maple & bird's-eye maple, each piece carved to simulate bamboo, ca. 1890, 3 pcs. 4,400.00

Victorian, Cottage style: bed, chest of drawers w/wishbone mirror, side table w/spool-turned legs, three spindle-back side chairs & spindle-back nursing rocker; light painted overall decoration w/painted scroll decorations and line trim, 1850-60, 7 pcs. 1,900.00

Victorian Eastlake substyle: high-back bed, three-drawer chest w/mirror, three-drawer commode stand; cherry w/pink marble tops & backsplashes, typical incised carvings, original brass pulls, 3 pcs. 3,000.00

Victorian Renaissance Revival substyle: high-backed bed, wardrobe, marble top washstand w/mirror & marble top dresser w/mirror; walnut, ornately carved scrolled crests w/wide band of leafy swags above wide panels of burl walnut, ca. 1880, 4 pcs. 4,510.00

Carved Rosewood Half-Tester Bed

Victorian Renaissance Revival substyle: half-tester bed, double-door armoire, tall marble top dresser & washstand; carved rosewood w/leaf & scroll-carved trim & framed & raised panels, bed head- and foot-boards w/arched crests, ca. 1860, 4 pcs. (ILLUS. of bed) . . 11,000.00

BENCHES

Church pew, oak, solid-board back,

Oak Church Pew

plank seat, shaped ends w/simple carved designs (ILLUS.) 250.00

Cobbler's bench, pine, dovetail construction, oblong work tray w/three-quarter gallery & drawer below, round leather-covered seat, whittled legs, 49" l. 425.00

Empire country-style bench, painted & decorated, flat crestrail above narrow cross-rail continuing under turned arms, plank seat, turned legs w/flat stretchers, old black paint w/traces of yellow & gold striping & painted decoration, 82" l. 550.00

Federal country-style bench, painted & decorated, flat narrow rectangular crestrail decorated w/foliate devices, scrolled arms, plank seat above eight turned legs joined by flat front stretchers, painted yellow & highlighted w/pinstriping & leafy devices in green & black, Pennsylvania, ca. 1830, 76" l., 32½" h. 2,800.00

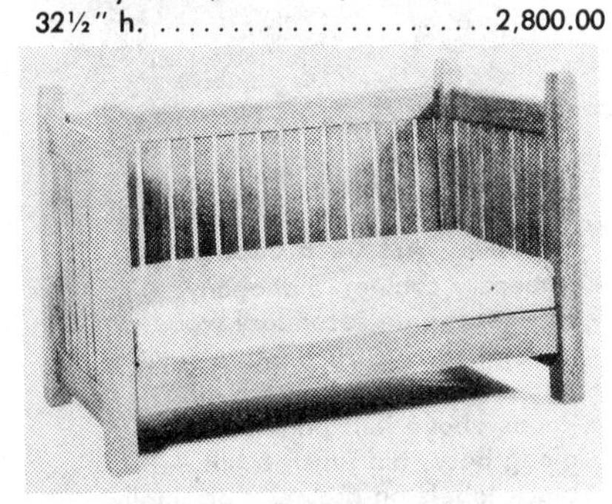

Mission Style Bench by Stickley

Mission-style (Arts & Crafts movement) slat-back bench, oak, plain crestrail above multiple flat slats, square arms above seven-slat sides, leather seat, Model No. 221, w/L. & J. G. Stickley red hand-clamp label, 5' l., 39" h. (ILLUS.) 8,800.00

Primitive pine bench, one-board top, plain apron, mortised construction, cut-out sides forming feet, old worn green paint over white, 31" l., 11" deep, 18" h. 170.00

Settle bench, painted, primitive construction w/cut-out ends, slightly curving paneled back w/matching seat, old red paint, 19th c., 51½" w., 52" h. (old repairs) 625.00

Settle bench, painted & decorated, half spindle back w/angel wing cresting, scrolled arms, plank seat, turned legs, old olive green repaint w/stenciled florals highlighted w/black & yellow striping, 72½" l. 500.00

Wagon seat, painted & decorated pine, worn old dark grey paint w/black, red & yellow striping, 30" l. (edge wear & damage) 100.00

Water bucket bench, painted pine, two-tier, oblong top w/three-quarter gallery, single board sides forming cut-out feet, old worn white paint over greyish blue, 54½" w., 16" deep, 34½" h. 250.00

Window bench, Federal, mahogany, square end supports each surrounding three reeded columns flanking half-upholstered seat, reeded square tapering legs, 44½" l., 31½" h. 2,640.00

Work bench, painted pine, square nail construction, rectangular divided top w/galleried sides above pull-out drawer & tray on each side to allow two people to work, tapering legs, old grey paint, 24 x 34", 32" h. 350.00

BOOKCASES

Majorelle Art Nouveau Bookcase

Art Nouveau bookcase, carved walnut & bronze, flat-top w/cove molding above three-section cabinet consisting of tall end sections w/glazed cabinet doors w/violet glass & bronze foliate devices above paneled base section flanking step-down center cabinet section w/two glazed cabinet doors w/bronze foliate devices; flat plinth base carved w/ginko leaves, "Majorelle Nancy" inlaid within lozenge, Louis Majorelle, Nancy, France, ca. 1900, 86½" w., 78½" h. (ILLUS.) 13,200.00

Mission-style (Arts & Crafts movement) bookcase, oak, flat three-quarter gallery above rectangular top over case w/pair 8-pane glazed doors opening to shelves, solid side w/four chamfered tenons in each, Model No. 716, red decal mark of Gustav Stickley, ca. 1905, 42¾" w., 56¼" h. 4,400.00

Turn-of-the-Century bookcase, mahogany, four-stack type w/glass-fronted doors lifting to shelves, "Globe Wernicke" label, ca. 1900 .... 310.00

Turn-of-the-Century Bookcase

Turn-of-the-Century bookcase, oak, plain flat top above pair glazed doors opening to four shelves, bracket base, on casters (ILLUS.) 375.00

Victorian bookcase, Eastlake substyle, walnut, rectangular bowed cornice w/oak leaf carved frieze above bowed glazed door flanked by two rectangular glazed doors, base w/central bowed drawer flanked by two short drawers, platform base, late 19th c., 70" w., 7' h. 2,970.00

Victorian bookcase, Renaissance Revival substyle, oak, flat cornice centered by scroll-carved bonnet crest w/center carved cartouche & w/fan-carved finials at each end above wide scroll-carved three-section band over three glazed cabinet doors w/rounded tops opening to shelves & flanked by carved panels at sides, all above base section **w/three narrow drawers w/carved grotesque face pulls, above base panel of carved serpentine vines across bottom, large, flat bun feet, 19th c. (ILLUS.) 3,630.00**

Carved Victorian Bookcase

CABINETS

Art Deco Cabinet

Apothecary cabinet, mahogany facade w/pine secondary wood, dovetailed construction, 46 dovetailed drawers w/wood button knobs above four paneled doors along base, old finish & gilt & black labels on drawers, originally built-in, 73¾" w., 50¼" h. (new plywood back, base molding added) 1,650.00

Art Deco cabinet, mahogany w/brass mounts, rectangular form w/rounded front corners, the inset top above a molded edge continuing to two cupboard doors each set w/a large rectangular brass escutcheon, raised on stepped base, designed by Victor Zoonens, ca. 1935, 46¾" w., 4' h. (ILLUS.) 990.00

Art Nouveau cabinet, walnut & mahogany, in the Clementine pattern, narrow upright form w/oblong molded top above open cabinet centered w/narrow upright cupboard w/arch-glazed cupboard door enhanced w/floral & vine carvings & flanked by six oval shelves, outward flaring legs, by Louis Marjorelle, France, ca. 1900, 36½" w., 63" h. 7,700.00

Oak China Cabinet

China cabinet, Turn-of-the-Century, golden oak, serpentine shaped top w/gadrooned edge above conforming frame w/stamped scrolls at top center above single curved glass door opening to two glass shelves, gadrooned band at base above shallow apron, cabriole legs w/claw feet, ca. 1900 (ILLUS.) 715.00

Chippendale cabinet, mahogany, rectangular top w/molded cornice above pair of cupboard doors opening to interior fitted w/shelves & small drawers, molded base continuing to cabriole legs ending in claw-and-ball feet, Massachusetts, ca. 1780, 42½" l., 12¼" deep, 24½" h. 3,300.00

Dental cabinet, Victorian Renaissance Revival substyle, walnut & walnut burl, half-round form w/shaped front consisting of wide flat center section flanked by rounded side sections each w/numerous small drawers & cabinet doors trimmed

Ornate Victorian Dental Cabinet

in burl veneer, with label reading, "Dr. Charles Essig's Dental Cabinet," ca. 1868 (ILLUS.) 2,750.00

Federal cabinet, cherry, rectangular top w/molded edge above pair of panelled cupboard doors opening to interior fitted w/compartments & two small drawers, bracket feet, 19½" w., 9¾" deep, 21¾" h. (restoration to interior & feet) ...1,320.00

Oak Filing Cabinets

Filing cabinets, Turn-of-the-Century, golden oak, plain vertical-stack five-drawer cabinet w/original brass nameplates & pulls, ca. 1910, pr. (ILLUS.) 795.00

Hardware store bolt cabinets, oak, 96-drawer octagon, original porcelain knobs, brass index frames & original finish, pr. 1,395.00

Kitchen cabinet, Turn-of-the-Century "Hoosier" type, oak, 2-part construction: plain top above three short cupboard doors over pair of cupboard doors resting on base w/three graduated drawers beside cupboard door, refinished ... 475.00

Sewing cabinet, Mission-style (Arts & Crafts movement), oak & metal, galleried top above door, sides w/exposed tenons secured by pins, interior fitted w/sliding sectioned trays to hold thread, "R" insignia of Charles Rohlfs & "1907" carved in door, 17¼" w., 25" h. 3,080.00

Side cabinets, Regency, ebonized wood w/parcel-gilt gilt-bronze trim, rectangular *faux* marble top above frieze mounted w/figures above a pair of brass grillwork-inset doors, reeded ball feet, England, early 19th c., 36½" w., 35½" h., pr....9,350.00

CANDLESTANDS

Mahogany Tilt-Top Candlestand

Chippendale tilt-top candlestand, mahogany, round dished top tilting above turned column w/swirled fluting, downswept tripod, snake feet, 19½" top d., 28" h. 6,300.00

Empire, American, tilt-top candlestand, mahogany, oblong top w/crossbanded edge tilting above vase- and drum-turned standard, downswept acanthus-carved legs ending in foliate-cast brass casters, attributed to Charles Honore' Lannuier, New York, ca. 1815, 18½ x 23¾" top, 29½" h. (ILLUS.) 2,750.00

Federal tilt-top candlestand, inlaid cherry, octagonal top tilting above ring- and vase-turned chip-carved standard, arched tripod, spade feet, New England, probably Connecticut, ca. 1800, 21" w. top, 27½" h. 3,850.00

Federal candlestand, inlaid cherry, rectangular top centering an oval

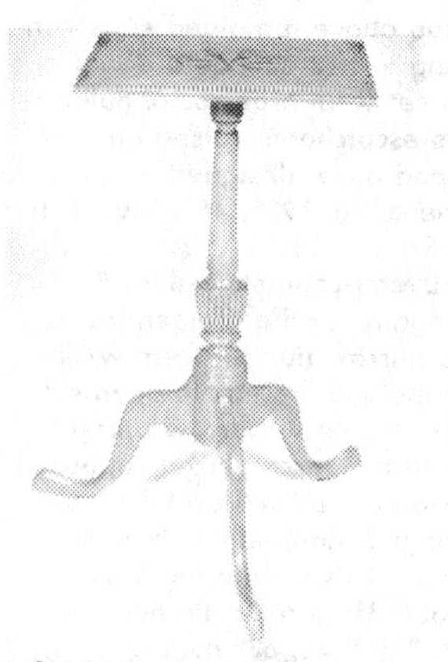

Inlaid Cherry Candlestand

patera & bordered w/diamond pattern stringing, flaring columnar pedestal above vertically-reeded urn turning, over horizontal reeding, downswept cabriole tripod, slipper feet, Connecticut River Valley, 1790-1810, 14¾ x 17" top, 26¾" h. (ILLUS.) 13,200.00

Federal country-style candlestand, maple, round top, ring- and baluster-turned standard, downswept cabriole tripod, snake feet, ca. 1845, 24" d., 29½" h. 330.00

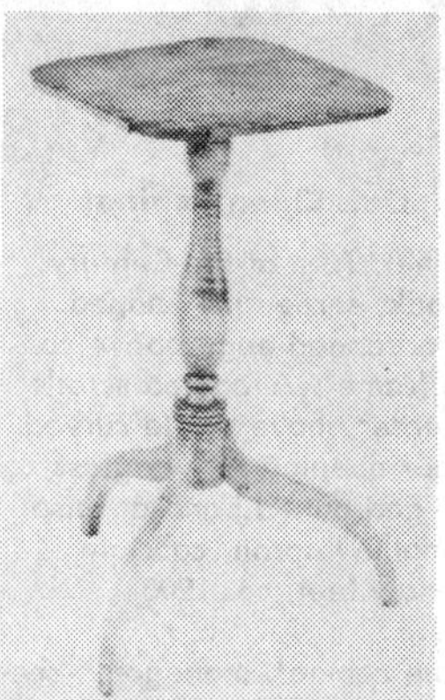

Tiger Stripe Maple Candlestand

Federal country-style candlestand, tiger stripe maple, one-board rectangular top w/oval notched corners, vase- and ring-turned standard, downswept spider-legged tripod, New England, ca. 1810, 15 x 15½" top, 28¼" h. (ILLUS.) 2,090.00

Hepplewhite candlestand, cherry, well-figured one-board top, baluster-turned & fluted standard, spider legs, 16¼ x 16½" top, 26¾" h. 950.00

Queen Anne country-style candlestand, walnut, round top, baluster-turned standard, downswept tripod, snake feet, 17" d., 29" h. 750.00

CHAIRS

Art Deco Armchair

American Colonial "ladder back" rocker w/arms, painted finish, five-slat back flanked by turned uprights w/turned finials, rush seat arms w/shaped handgrips on baluster-turned supports continuing to turned legs w/ball feet on rockers, bulbous-turned frontal stretcher, old worn dark green paint....... 1,050.00

Art Deco armchair, laminated birch, upholstered square back & rectangular seat between wide scrolling arms continuing into sled-form feet, designed & signed by "Artec A. Aalto," ca. 1935 (ILLUS.)...... 1,430.00

Art Nouveau side chairs, carved walnut, pierced arching crest carved w/two clusters of berries on entwined stems above rectangular panel back, flared seat raised on tapering square legs, upholstered, pr. 440.00

Barber's chair, oak frame, simple carving, hydraulic base, marked "Koken" 550.00

"Barcelona" Side Chair & Ottoman

"Barcelona" side chairs w/matching ottomans, chrome & leather, each set w/button-upholstered tan leather cushions & raised on S-form supports, designed by Ludwig Mies van der Rohe for the Barcelona Exhibition of 1929, retailed by Knoll Associates, Inc., ca. 1970, 2 sets, 4 pcs. (ILLUS. of one set) 3,850.00

Bentwood rocker w/arms, caned oblong back w/rounded corners & conforming square seat set between sides formed of elaborate bentwood scrolls, w/integral rockers, attributed to Thonet, ca. 1915 .... 770.00

Biedermeier side chairs, birch & ebonized birch, slightly curving crestrail above pierced ebonized splat w/stylized acanthus carving, over-upholstered seat, square tapering sabre legs, Germany, 1825-50, set of 4 .... 4,950.00

Child's armchair, Mission-style (Arts & Crafts movement) "Morris" style, oak, adjustable back, original cushions 225.00

Child's armchair, painted pine & hardwood, shaped crestrail above four-spindle back, turned arms w/shaped grips on baluster-turned upright, plank seat, splayed turned legs, original red finish, 19th c. 150.00

Child's Slat-Back Highchair

Child's highchair, Early American slat-back style, back w/turned & splayed stiles centering two horizontal slats flanked by turned arms above splint seat, turned & splayed front legs joined by double box stretcher, New England, early 19th c., 36½" h. (ILLUS.).... 715.00

Child's arrow back side chair, bamboo turned legs, worn brown paint over old decoration, 14½" h. seat 60.00

Child's side chair, Sheraton, curly maple, original rush seat w/old worn yellow paint, 24" h. 215.00

Chippendale country-style side chair, walnut, ox-yoke crest above pierce-cut shaped back splat, square wood seat, square legs w/molded corner & inside chamfer joined by "H" stretcher, old dark finish 500.00

Chippendale side chair, mahogany, cupid's bow crestrail w/scrolling ears above pierced tassel-carved splat w/gadrooned shoe, slip seat, plain seatrail w/gadrooned lower edge above acanthus-carved cabriole legs, claw-and-ball feet, Philadelphia, ca. 1770 (restorations)..........................4,675.00

Elizabethan Revival side chair, walnut & laminated walnut, tall, narrow back w/open-cut arched scroll-cut crest above scroll & urn carved wide back flanked by columnar turned styles, upholstered seat on trumpet-turned front legs flanking arched, open-cut scrolled front rung, labelled "Shaw Furniture Co., Cambridge, Mass.," early 20th c. 350.00

Empire, American, armchair, mahogany, rectangular crestrail above swan-carved splat, down-scrolled arms, upholstered seat, sabre legs, New York, 1830-40 (old break to arms) 209.00

Empire, American, side chairs, tiger stripe maple, ring-turned cylindrical crest above three horizontal spindles over a rush seat, baluster-and ring-turned legs w/turned feet joined by box stretchers, New England, ca. 1830, 33" h., set of 4.................. 495.00

Federal cane-seat side chairs, curly maple, plain crestrail over pierce-carved foliate stayrail, caned seat, ring-turned legs w/flaring feet joined by stretchers, Catskill, New York, pr. 600.00

Federal "fancy" side chairs, painted & decorated, shaped crestrail above center splat over four half-spindles, shaped plank seats above turned, splayed legs joined by box stretchers, original green paint w/black & yellow striping, stenciled fruit & foliage on crests & seat fronts, minor wear, early 19th c., set of 6 ....2,100.00

Federal wing armchair, mahogany, serpentine crest above shaped wings over scrolled arms, trapezoidal seat, Marlborough legs joined by H-stretcher, 47" h. 3,740.00

Federal Revival dining chairs, mahogany, flat crest above lyre-form splat flanked by out-curving stiles, upholstered seats, sabre-form front legs, ca. 1900, 2 armchairs & 6 side chairs, the set..................3,850.00

Folding camp chair, "Union" type, painted & decorated, painted blue w/red, white & blue cut-out shield-shaped splat, ca. 1864, 18¼" w., 32" h. (minor damage & paint wear) 450.00

Hepplewhite "Martha Washington" armchair, mahogany frame w/line inlay at front of square tapering legs, H-stretcher, pale blue upholstery, early 19th c. 2,600.00

17th Century Chinese Armchair

Huanghuali style horseshoeback armchair, gently curving splat carved w/recessed cloud medallion flanked by narrow flanges on a hard cane seat, outscrolled arms joined to cylindrical legs through the seat frame & framed by beaded side flanges w/scroll-carved apron, on low box stretcher, reduced in height, seat transverses replaced, China, 17th c. (ILLUS.)...........4,950.00

Mission-style (Arts & Crafts movement) armchair, oak, tall back w/straight crest over four vertical slats, open arms, spring cushion seat, stamped No. 836, L. & J.G. Stickley, 28" w., 43½" h. 550.00

Mission-style (Arts & Crafts movement) "Morris" armchair, oak, oblong back w/five horizontal slats adjusting between flattened, bent arms above five flat slats, Model No. 369, red decal mark of Gustav Stickley, ca. 1909 ....6,600.00

Armchair Designed by Frank Lloyd Wright

Mission-style (Arts & Crafts movement) reclining armchair, oak, angled back w/wide single slat resting against back framework, wide flat arms above stile set at right angles to back stile, backrest set into seat which slides forward, designed by Frank Lloyd Wright, probably executed by John W. Ayers Co. for the Francis W. Little House, Peoria, Illinois, ca. 1902, 31¾" w., 40" h. (ILLUS.) 60,500.00

Mission-style (Arts & Crafts movement) swivel office chair, oak, upholstered leather back, shaped curving open arms, upholstered seat on cross-base, No. 535, Limbert's branded label, ca. 1910, 29" w., 42" h. 495.00

Queen Anne corner armchair, mahogany, horseshoe-shaped back w/cushion-molded crest above pair pierced beaker-form splats & three turned uprights, slip seat, plain seatrail, cabriole front leg & three turned legs w/padded pad feet, Massachusetts, ca. 1770 ...17,600.00

Queen Anne country-style corner armchair, walnut, horseshoe-shaped back w/cushion-molded crest above three baluster turned uprights, rush seat, block- and ring-turned legs w/baluster- and ring-turned stretchers, Spanish feet 1,950.00

Queen Anne wing armchair, maple, upholstered arched back, shaped wings & outscrolled arms, seat w/loose cushion, cabriole legs w/turned stretchers, pad feet, New England, ca. 1760 ....5,500.00

Queen Anne side chair, walnut, yoked crestrail above vase-form

Queen Anne Side Chair

splat & slip seat, lambrequin-carved cabriole legs joined by shaped stretchers ending in stocking pad feet, Philadelphia, ca. 1750, repair to rear left foot & crest (ILLUS.) 5,500.00

Queen Anne "rush-seat" side chairs, curly maple, yoked crestrail above vase-form splat in "spooned" back, rush seat, blocked & turned legs w/stretchers, Spanish feet, New England, 1740-60, pr. 12,650.00

Turn-of-the-Century dining chairs, golden oak, pressed pattern back, die-stamped crest w/scrolling design above flattened spindle back, caned seat, turned legs w/numerous stretchers, set of 6 (refinished & newly caned seats) 1,000.00

Turn-of-the-Century "swivel-seat" office chair w/arms, golden oak, pressed pattern back, die-stamped crest above seven flattened spindles, flattened bentwood arms on baluster-turned spindles, seat swiveling on downswept quadruped support on casters 350.00

Victorian (early) dining chairs, maple & tiger stripe maple, serpentine crestrail above diamond-pierced shaped splat over arched & shaped stayrail, balloon-shaped caned seat, sabre legs w/concave flat frontal stretcher, 1860-80, set of 4 .... 500.00

Victorian parlor armchair, Eastlake substyle, walnut, rectangular upholstered back w/line incised wood sides & open-cut panel w/turned cross-spindles below, arms w/open-cut panels w/turned cross-spindles & padding, front arm supports w/line incised decor continue to form front legs, deep-

Victorian Eastlake Armchair

ly padded upholstered seat, ca. 1885 (ILLUS.) 82.50

"Rosalie" Pattern Armchair

Victorian parlor open armchair, Rococo substyle, laminated & carved rosewood, crest carved w/floral sprigs & fruit, voluted armrests, carved apron on serpentine seat, demi-cabriole legs on casters, "Rosalie" pattern attributed to John Henry Belter, New York, New York, ca. 1855 (ILLUS.) 3,520.00

Victorian parlor side chair, Gothic Revival substyle, walnut, pierce-carved scrolling crest above arrangement of graduated oval gothic arched medallions flanked by spiral-turned stiles w/turned finials, over-upholstered seat, seatrail w/arch-scalloped edge, spiral-turned legs & baluster-turned feet on casters, Philadelphia, ca. 1850.................. 660.00

Victorian parlor side chair, Renaissance Revival substyle, walnut,

Renaissance Revival Parlor Chair

upholstered balloon back w/arched crest w/raised burl panel, scrolled skirt guards join back to seat frame, round upholstered seat, simple cabriole front legs, ca. 1870 (ILLUS.) 85.00

Victorian "patent" folding chairs, Renaissance Revival substyle, painted to imitate bamboo turnings, folding seat w/cut-velvet squab cushion, attributed to George Hunzinger, New York, New York, ca. 1869, pr. 1,210.00

Victorian "slipper-seat" chair, Rococo substyle, piece-carved rosewood, floral-carved arched crest above pierce-carved back centering grape cluster, over-upholstered round seat w/conforming seatrail, demi-cabriole legs, attributed to John Meeks & Co., New York, New York, ca. 1860 .... 990.00

Wallace Nutting signed Windsor "continuous arm brace-back" armchair, 9-spindle back style (early repair) 900.00

Stickley Wicker Armchair

Wicker armchair, tall back w/shallow

wings, flat arms, square caned seat, deep apron w/four rectangular piercings at front & four piercings at each side, green stain, **Model No. 88, by Gustav Stickley, ca. 1913, 39¼" h. (ILLUS.)** 1,430.00

Wicker **"boardwalk" chair, woven reed, flat crest w/rounded corners continuing down to form rounded arms which continue down to** form footrest platform at front; two large wheels at back & two small wheels at front, painted white, 1900-20 ....150.00

William & Mary "Bannister-Back" Chair

William & Mary **"bannister-back" side chair, carved maple, pierced-cut & C-scroll carved crest flanked by baluster-turned stiles w/ball-**turned finials over three split-baluster spindles over rush seat, ring-turned legs joined by stretchers, probably Massachusetts, 1725-50 (small brace on rear of crest), 40½" h. (ILLUS.)..................990.00

Windsor "birdcage" side chairs, birdcage crest w/three carved medallions above 7-spindle back, shaped seats, splayed legs w/stretchers, Massachusetts, ca. 1800, pr.........................1,760.00

Windsor "bow-back" armchair, bowed crestrail above 7-spindle back, arms w/shaped handgrips on vase- and ring-turned supports, shaped seat, ring- and vase-turned tapering splayed legs w/"bobbin" stretchers, old refinishing 600.00

Windsor "bow- and brace-back" side chair, bowed crestrail above

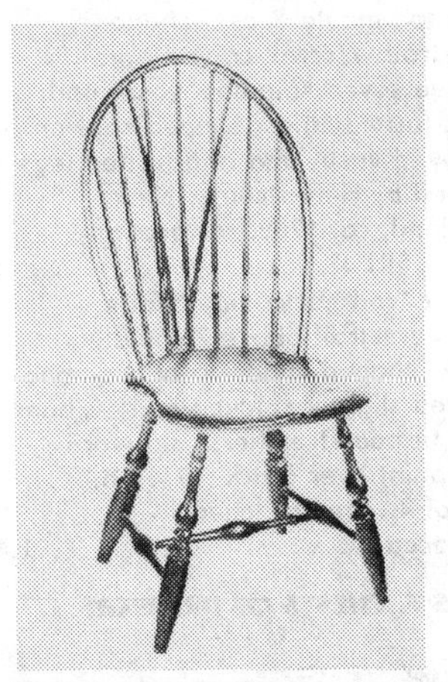

Windsor Bow-Back Chair with Braces

7-spindle (one replaced) back, shaped saddle seat, vase- and ring-turned legs joined by swelling H-stretchers, painted black, Rhode Island, ca. 1790, slightly reduced in height (ILLUS.) 600.00

Windsor "brace-back" continuous armchair, bowed crestrail above 8-spindle back continuing to form arms w/braced back, vase- and ring-turned arm supports, shaped saddle seat, bulbous-turned splayed legs, New England, 1780 (refinished & w/one replaced spindle)........................1,430.00

Windsor "comb-back" armchair, shaped crestrail w/volute-carved terminals above nine tapering spindles & shaped hand-holds, eliptical shaped seat, turned legs joined by turned stretchers, blunt arrow feet, painted green, Pennsylvania, ca. 1770...............9,900.00

Windsor Fan-Back Side Chair

Windsor "fan-back" side chair,

painted maple & ash, shaped crestrail w/scroll-carved ears above seven spindles, vase- and ring-turned stiles, shaped seat on splayed vase- and ring-turned legs joined by H-stretchers, New England, ca. 1780, restoration, 35" h. (ILLUS.) 660.00

Windsor "rod back" side chairs, plain crestrail above 7-spindle back, shaped saddle seat, bamboo-turned slightly splayed legs w/bamboo turned stretchers, old worn red paint over black, 17½" h., set of 4 (one stretcher replaced) 1,680.00

CHESTS & CHESTS OF DRAWERS

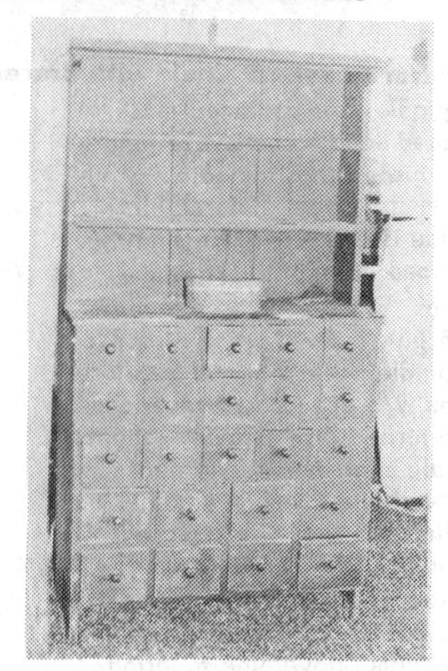

Early Apothecary Chest

Apothecary chest, painted wood, flat top cornice above open hutch w/two shelves above lower section of 23 small drawers w/wood knobs, old green paint (ILLUS.)..11,550.00

Biedermeier Chest of Drawers

Biedermeier chest of drawers, birch & marquetry, rectangular top cross banded in rosewood above three long drawers, the central drawer inlaid w/a mourning picture, ebonized lockplates, bracket feet, probably Swedish, first quarter 19th c., 33½" w., 34" h. (ILLUS.) 4,180.00

Blanket chest, Chippendale country-style, painted pine, rectangular top w/molded edge lifting to deep well w/till w/secret drawer in dovetailed case w/pair overlapping short drawers below w/original brass bail handles, scalloped bracket feet, worn dark paint w/light blue on one end, 48½ x 20½", 28½" h. (repaired breaks in front feet brackets) 950.00

Blanket chest, painted & decorated pine, rectangular lift-top above wide single-board sides & ends, original red flame-graining in "herringbone" pattern, original wrought-iron lock, strap hinge & end handles, flat, molded base, 37" w., 19½" h. (minor wear) 350.00

Blanket chest, painted & decorated pine & poplar, rectangular top w/molded edge lifting to deep well w/till in dovetailed case, applied base molding, turned feet, original finger graining in reddish brown on yellow ground, back signed "C. Gerberich, Wooster, Wayne Co., Ohio," 38¼ x 19", 23¼" h. 1,100.00

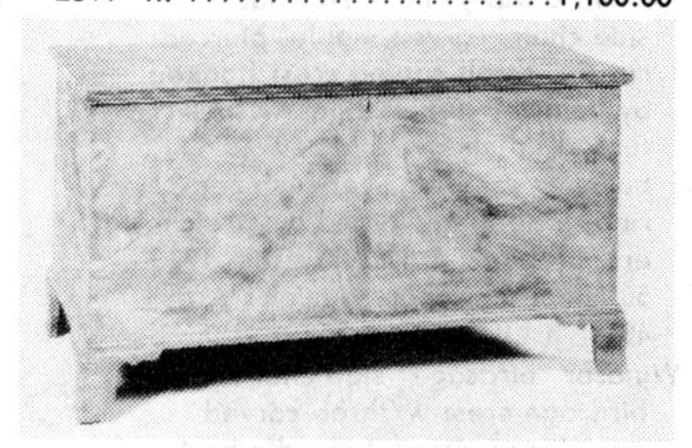

Painted Blanket Chest

Blanket chest, painted & decorated, rectangular molded top lifting above a compartment w/till above conforming dovetailed case over molded base on ogee bracket feet, grain-painted decoration, probably Mid-Atlantic States, early 19th c., 28" h. (ILLUS.).......715.00

Cedar chest, Renaissance Style, "antiqued" yellow finish, pressed bands of design, bun feet, labeled "Ed Roos Co., Forest Park, Ill.,"

Renaissance Style Cedar Chest

early 20th c., 47½" l., 22" h. (ILLUS.) 35.00

Cellarette (wine chest), Classical, brass-mounted & inlaid mahogany, coffered & crossbanded hinged lid opening to an interior w/bottle compartments, inward tapering sides brass-mounted & supported on turned feet, New York or Boston, ca. 1810, 25" l., 20½" h. 4,675.00

Charles II Chest of Drawers

Charles II chest of drawers, oak, rectangular top above four molded long drawers, each fitted w/brass pendant drawer pulls, block feet, England, ca. 1665, 33½" w., 33½" h. (ILLUS.) 3,850.00

Chippendale "block-front" chest of drawers, mahogany, rectangular top w/thumb-molded edge & blocked front above case of conforming outline within cockbeaded surrounds, molded conforming base, bracket feet, Boston area of Massachusetts, ca. 1765, 36" w., 31½" h. (feet restored) 16,500.00

Chippendale "bombe" chest of drawers, mahogany, rectangular top w/thumb-molded edge & serpentine front above conformingly shaped case w/swollen sides & four graduated serpentine & blocked drawers within cockbeaded surrounds, molded base,

Chippendale "Bombe" Chest of Drawers

angular short cabriole legs, claw-and-ball feet, Boston, Massachusetts, ca. 1765 (missing side handles), 36 1/8" w., 31¼" h. (ILLUS.) 660,000.00

Chippendale chest of drawers, maple w/some curl, oblong top w/molded edge above case w/two short drawers over four long graduated drawers, bracket feet, original brass bat's wing handles, 37½" w., 42½" h. 2,700.00

Chippendale chest on chest, maple, top section w/projecting molded cornice above three short drawers w/central fan carving & four graduated long drawers set into base of four graduated long drawers, carved claw & ball feet centering fan-carved pendant, Massachusetts, ca. 1780, 38" w., 78½" h. (replaced brasses, some restorations & imperfections) 9,625.00

Chippendale Chest of Drawers

Chippendale serpentine-front chest of drawers, mahogany, molded serpentine overhanging top above conforming cockbeaded case of four graduated drawers on ogee bracket feet, New England, ca. 1780, refinished, replaced pulls, minor restoration, 38¼" w., 32½" h. (ILLUS.) 5,500.00

Chippendale Tall Chest of Drawers

Chippendale tall chest of drawers, walnut, rectangular top w/applied molding over case w/arrangement of three short drawers over five graduated long thumb-molded drawers, molded base, bracket feet, Pennsylvania, ca. 1780 (repairs to feet), 40½" w., 61" h. (ILLUS.) 3,575.00

Chippendale Style tall chest of drawers, mahogany, bonnet-top w/molded swan's neck pediment ending in carved floral rosettes centering flame finials above three short drawers, the center fan-carved, over four graduated long drawers flanked by fluted quarter columns, above a molded mid-band over one long & three short drawers, the center fan-carved, flanked by fluted quarter columns above shaped shirt, cabriole legs w/pad feet, made by Drexel, 20th c., 38½" w., 82" h. 1,210.00

Empire, American, chest of drawers, cherry, rectangular top w/molded edge above an outset deep drawer over three recessed long drawers, flanked by half-round baluster-turned stiles, raised on turned cylindrical legs, second quarter 19th c., 42¼" w., 47" h. 275.00

Empire, American, chest of drawers, mahogany w/flame veneer facade, rectangular top w/three-quarter gallery w/scrolling crest set w/two recessed short drawers over case w/two short drawers & three long drawers flanked by free-standing ring- and foliage-carved columns continuing to ring-turned legs & high feet, carved apron detail, 41" w., overall 52" h. (replaced turned wood drawer pulls) 850.00

Empire, American, country-style chest of drawers, curly maple, rectangular top over a row of three small drawers over deep, long drawer all overhanging three long, graduated drawers flanked by half-round columnettes, short turned legs, turned wood drawer knobs, 42¾" w., 47½" h. (refinished, feet replaced) 375.00

Empire, American, country-style chest of drawers, painted pine, rectangular top set w/three short recessed drawers & scrolling backsplash above case w/long drawer over three slightly recessed drawers flanked by free-standing turned columns continuing to turned feet, original black & red flame graining w/green & yellow striping, replaced brass rosette handles, 43¾" w., 50" h. 3,600.00

Empire, American, country-style chest of drawers, walnut w/curly maple drawer fronts, rectangular top w/plain backsplash above case w/deep central drawer flanked by two pair short drawers above three slightly recessed graduated long drawers flanked by ring- and ball-turned columns continuing to ball feet, 46½" w., 41¼" h. plus backsplash (refinished) 450.00

Empire Revival Chest of Drawers

Empire Revival chest of drawers, mahogany veneer, rectangular swivel mirror in wood frame above rectangular top over two drawers above two long drawers, slightly scrolled sides continue down to C-scroll front feet, wooden mushroom drawer knobs, 1900-25 (ILLUS.) 40.00

Federal Bow-Front Chest of Drawers

Federal "bow-front" chest of drawers, mahogany, bowed top w/patterned string inlay above a conforming case w/four graduated drawers w/string inlay around edges, French feet (pieced), Massachusetts, 1800-1815, 40¾" w., 39¾" h. (ILLUS.) 1,100.00

Federal chest-on-chest, maple, two-part construction: upper section w/projecting molded cornice above five graduated drawers & w/upper drawer faced to resemble three short drawers w/central carved fan; lower section w/three graduated drawers & w/lower drawer faced to resemble two narrow drawers w/central carved fan above base, molded base above bandy legs, on duck feet w/turned pads, Dunlap School, Connecticut, 35¾" w., 76½" h. (refinished & replaced brasses, repair to back foot, molding between sections replaced) 5,750.00

Hepplewhite country-style chest of drawers, cherry, rectangular top above four graduated drawers w/oval bail brasses & brass keyhole escutcheons, banded inlay around top & base & around each drawer, shaped skirt w/French feet, 43½" w., 33½" h. (refinished, replaced brasses) 1,000.00

Hepplewhite chest of drawers, cherry & cherry veneer, rectangular top w/bowfront edge above conforming case w/four long graduated drawers w/oval brass pulls & brass keyhole escutcheons, shaped apron & French feet, Connecticut River Valley, late 18th c. 2,475.00

Mission-Style Tall Chest of Drawers

Mission-style (Arts & Crafts movement) tall chest of drawers, oak, low crest above rectangular top overhanging case w/six half drawers above three long slightly graduated drawers, round wooden knobs on drawers, gently bowed sides & arched apron, designed by Harvey Ellis, branded signature of Gustav Stickley, Model No. 913, ca. 1912. 36" w., 51" h. (ILLUS.) 7,700.00

Mule chest, (box chest w/one or more drawers below storage compartment), six-board construction w/sides continuing to cut-out feet, rectangular top w/molded edge opening to deep well w/till in case w/drawer below, original dark red paint, 43½ x 19", 35½" h. 800.00

Mule chest, Chippendale, country-style, painted pine, rectangular lift-top above two graduated fake drawers over two dovetailed overlapping drawers, all with wooden knobs, scrolled bracket feet, original red paint, 38 3/8" w., 41½" h. 1,800.00

Mule chest, Federal country-style, painted wood, hinged rectangular top opening to a storage well over two long drawers, raised on bracket feet (front left foot replaced, back lacking one board), old red paint, New England, first quarter 19th c., 41" w., 36½" h. 660.00

Queen Anne chest-on-frame, cherry, two-part construction: upper section w/cove-molded cornice above two short & four long graduated drawers; frame w/shaped skirt, cabriole legs, pad feet, probably Connecticut, ca. 1760, 37" w., 46" h. (restored) 2,310.00

Sheraton country-style chest of drawers, cherry, rectangular top above two drawers w/beaded edges & stamped oval brasses w/bails over three long drawers w/beaded edges & stamped oval brasses w/bails, simple reeded bands flank drawers at sides, short turned legs, 41¾" w., 44" h. (refinished, repairs, replaced brasses) 630.00

Sugar chest, cherry, dovetailed construction, narrow flat top above sloping lift lid opening to two-section interior w/two drawers, base molding, boldly ring- and ball turned feet, refinished, Kentucky, 36½" w., 33½" h. 1,000.00

Victorian cottage-style chest of drawers, primitive pine, rectangular top above pair short drawers over four long drawers w/turned wood pulls, ca. 1850 ....350.00

Victorian Eastlake Chest of Drawers

Victorian chest of drawers w/mirror, Eastlake substyle, golden oak, undulating crest w/line incised decor at top of frame surrounding rectangular swivel mirror, rectangular case top above three long drawers w/incised leaf sprig decor & stamped brass & bail pulls, slightly shaped apron, ca. 1890 (ILLUS.) 250.00

Victorian chest of drawers w/mirror, Golden Oak substyle, rectangular tall back w/wide crest board w/applied scroll carving frames swiveling rectangular mirror, rectangular serpentine chest top w/molded edge overhangs conforming case w/two short drawers w/brass rosette pulls above two long drawers w/stamped brass & bail pulls, slightly shaped legs, ca. 1900 (ILLUS.) 250.00

Golden Oak Chest of Drawers

Victorian Renaissance Revival Chest

Victorian chest of drawers, Renaissance Revival substyle, walnut, tall back w/flaring crest w/center pediment & decorated w/raised burl panels frames swiveling rectangular mirror, candle shelves & burl panels along sides above rectangular chest top w/set-back center section above three small drawers & small white marble shelf above three long drawers w/shaped raised panels w/black pear-shaped pulls, scrolled apron & bracket feet, ca. 1885 (ILLUS.) 275.00

Victorian chest of drawers w/mirror, Renaissance Revival substyle, tall back w/scrolling machine-carved details & crowned cartouche-shaped crest frames large rectangular mirror, candle shelves at sides, rectangular chest top w/raised center section w/red marble shelf flanked by lower red marble sections, all above three narrow drawers w/burl bands, the center drawer forming a lift-top jewelry case, above two long drawers w/wide burl bands, all drawers w/brass ring pulls, short square legs, ca. 1880 .... 600.00

Victorian chest of drawers w/mirror, Rococo substyle, rosewood w/white marble top, superstructure w/ornate crest above arch-top mirror flanked by three tiers of shelves on spindle supports, marble slab top w/serpentine front & outset rounded front corners above case of conforming outline w/four graduated long drawers centered w/applied rococo carvings & flanked by carved stiles, plinth base w/applied C-scroll & S-scroll carved lower edge, possibly by Mitchell & Rammelsberg, Cinncinnati, Ohio, ca. 1860 ....4,950.00

William & Mary Chest of Drawers

William & Mary chest of drawers, oyster-veneered walnut, rectangular top w/molded edge above two short & three long drawers, foliate-scroll inlay of later date, raised on later bracket feet, England, 39½" w., 38" h. (ILLUS.) 5,500.00

William & Mary chest of drawers, maple & pine, rectangular top above case w/two short & three long overlapping drawers w/brass bat's wing handles & keyhole escutcheons, molded base, turned bun feet, old dark brown painted finish, 35¼" w., 40½" h.........6,250.00

COMMODES

Louis XV commode, kingwood & tulipwood marquetry w/ormolu mounts, mottled marble rectangular top w/serpentine edge above case w/two quarter-veneered drawers w/ormolu handles & keyhole escutcheons, splayed legs w/ormolu "chutes," stamped "P. Roussel MJE," France, mid-18th c., 36½" w., 32" h. 11,000.00

Louis XVI commode, mahogany w/ormolu mounts & marble slab top, molded grey-veined marble top w/canted corners above case w/three drawers banded w/ormolu beading & mounted w/circular beaded & ribbon-tied lockplates flanked by canted sides mounted w/conforming ormolu panels, high bracket feet, France, late 18th c., 37½" w., 34" h. 3,080.00

Victorian commode, country-style, painted & decorated pine, rectangular lift-top opens to deep well, one drawer at left side of top section above medial band above base w/single paneled door, scalloped apron, original red flame graining in pristine condition, 19th c., 30½" w., 30" h. 325.00

Victorian Eastlake Commode

Victorian commode, Eastlake substyle, walnut, burl walnut & white marble, high white marble backsplash w/two candle shelves above rectangular white marble slab top above one long drawer w/raised line incised panel & brass ring pulls above two cabinet doors w/raised burl panels, all flanked by sides w/raised burl panels and small line incised carved fans, plinth base, ca. 1880 (ILLUS.) 525.00

Victorian demi-commode, Renaissance Revival substyle, walnut & burl walnut, square white marble slab top w/canted front corners

Renaissance Revival Demi-Commode above conformingly shaped cabinet w/one small drawer w/raised burl panel & scroll carved pull above single door w/raised burl center panel & wood knob flanked by heavy block & scroll carved ornaments on canted front corners, plinth base, ca. 1875 (ILLUS.) 467.50

CRADLES

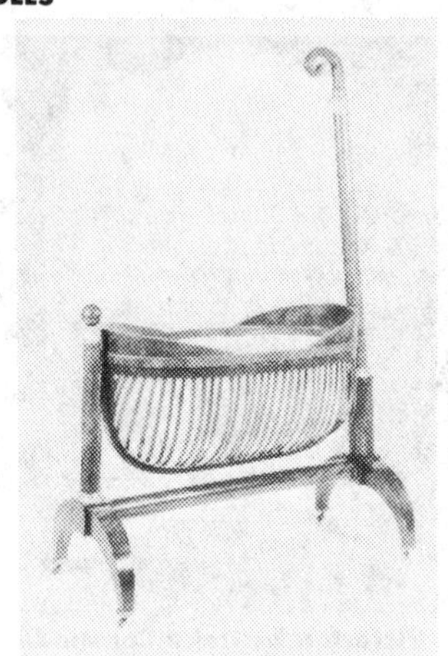

French Empire Cradle

Country-style low cradle on rockers, walnut, dovetail construction, arched head- and footboards w/cut-out heart in foot & cut-out trefoil in head, scalloped, canted sides, shaped rockers, old finish, 39½" l. (minor cracks, repaired split in one rocker) 200.00

Country-style low cradle on rockers, grain-painted finish, canted sides, square corner posts w/turned finials, shaped rockers, early 19th c., 40" l. 352.00

Hooded cradle on rockers, grain-painted & decorated, arched hood, canted sides, shaped footboard, original rosewood graining w/gold stenciled decoration, light blue interior, New England, ca. 1840 .... 425.00

Hooded cradle on rockers, pine, dovetail construction, shaped hood, canted sides, cut-out rockers, exterior w/brown grained repaint, white interior, 40½" l. ... 170.00

Suspended-type cradle, bentwood elm, rectangular cradle w/arched fronts having inverted U-shaped bands, tall overhead crook, U-shaped support on twin legs, Thonet, ca. 1904, 41" l., 43" h. ... 275.00

Suspended-type cradle, French Empire, mahogany w/ormolu mounts, oval cradle w/rounded end crests & ribbed sides on gimbels between two columnar supports, one w/scroll top supporting a baldachin, trestle base w/arched legs w/casters, France, first quarter 19th c. (ILLUS.)......3,300.00

Wicker low cradle on rockers, woven splint, oval w/arched back, 37" l. 265.00

CUPBOARDS

Federal Cherry Corner Cupboard

Corner cupboard, painted & decorated pine, one-piece construction, cove-molded cornice above two paneled cupboard doors each opening to shelves, scalloped apron continuing to cut-out bracket feet, original red & black painted graining, 36" w. at cornice, 71" h. 4,050.00

Corner cupboard, Federal country-style, pine, one-piece construction, applied cove molding above paneled cupboard door opening to two shelves over a paneled cupboard door above a molded base, bracket feet, early 19th c., 41" w., 78" h. 2,090.00

Corner cupboard, Federal country-style, cherry, one-piece construction, reeded flat cornice above a band of sawtooth dentilling over double paneled door w/scalloped inner edge opening to three shelves above short drawer flanked by two small square drawers over another paneled & scalloped door, scalloped apron, shaped continuous stile feet, probably Ohio or Kentucky, 1800-30, 43" w., 78½" h. (ILLUS.) 6,050.00

Corner cupboard, Federal country-style, curly maple, one-piece construction, cove molding above pair 10-pane glazed cupboard doors above medial raised banding over pair paneled cupboard doors, scalloped apron, bracket feet, good curl to wood, old refinish, early 19th c., 42¾" w., 82¾" h. (ends of cornice replaced) 5,800.00

Corner cupboard, Chippendale, cherry & poplar, two-part construction: upper section w/narrow cove molding above pair double raised-panel cabinet doors opening to three shelves; lower section w/applied molded edge over two paneled cupboard doors opening to single shelf, scrolled apron, bracket feet, late 18th c., 52" w., 91" h. (restorations) 2,090.00

Corner cupboard, Federal country-style, curly maple, two-part construction: upper section w/flat cornice above pair 6-pane glazed cabinet doors above pie shelf; lower section w/three small drawers w/wooden knobs over pair paneled cupboard doors, scalloped apron, bracket feet, early 19th c., 55" w., 83" h. 2,800.00

Hanging cupboard, primitive poplar, square nail construction, board & batten door w/original brass thumb latch, original tan paint, 24" w., 7½" deep, 36¼" h. 275.00

Jelly cupboard, walnut, rectangular top above pair short drawers over pair paneled cupboard doors opening to shelves, paneled ends, scalloped apron, turned feet, 39¼" w., 19½" deep, 43¾" h. ... 375.00

Jelly cupboard, walnut, oblong top above pair paneled doors opening to shelves, one-board sides, cut-out feet, 50½" w., 44" h. 325.00

Jelly cupboard, country-style, pine & cherry, shaped backboard crests at back & sides around flat rectangular top above two long drawers w/chamfered edges above two paneled cupboard doors flanked by simple side pilasters, scroll bracket feet, mid-19th c. (ILLUS.) 600.00

Country-style Jelly Cupboard

Chippendale Linen Press

Linen press, Chippendale, poplar, two-part construction: upper part w/molded cornice above patterned frieze over two arched paneled doors opening to four shelves, flanked by fluted pilasters; lower part w/three long graduated drawers w/thumb-molding above molded & gadrooned base, straight bracket feet, New Jersey, 1760-90, 46¼" w., 75½" h. (ILLUS.) 5,500.00

Pewter cupboard, stained poplar, one-piece construction, step-back upper section w/flat, wide cornice w/slightly shaped edges above four open shelves flanked by wide, flat pilasters w/notched edges, lower section w/two open shelves flanked by wide, flat pilasters similar to those on upper section, flat base, old reddish brown stain, early 19th c., 40" w., 69" h. 900.00

Pie safe, painted poplar, oblong top above pair cupboard doors w/three punched tin stylized pot of flowers in each & w/three conforming panels in each side, turned front feet, old red painted finish, 39¼" w., 17¼" deep, 45½" h. 725.00

Pie safe, walnut & poplar, rectangular top above case w/long drawer over pair cupboard doors w/three pierced tin stylized floral panels in each, one-board ends w/cut-out feet, refinished, 43 x 15¼", 55" h. 650.00

Walnut Wall Cupboard

Wall cupboard, Federal country-style, walnut, two-part construction: upper part w/stepped ogee-molded cornice above pair 6-pane glazed cupboard doors opening to shelves; lower section w/oblong top above three short drawers over pair paneled cupboard doors, flat base w/molding (minor repairs, replaced brasses), 61½" w., 83½" h. (ILLUS.) 4,600.00

Wall cupboard, Oriental, elmwood, sides tapering to double-cushioned molded top above pair of long doors w/finely molded borders opening to interior w/pair of short drawers, doors above recessed rectangular panel, chamfered rectangular legs, original brass mounts on doors, interior retains original cinnamon-colored lacquer surface, China, 17th c., 35" w., 66" h. 3,575.00

DESKS

Chippendale desk-on-legs, walnut, rectangular hinged slant lid lifting to fitted interior w/two short drawers above thumb-molded long drawer, on square quarter molded legs w/block feet, Pennsylvania, 1760-80, 35" w., 43" h. 6,600.00

Chippendale reverse-serpentine slant-front desk, mahogany, rectangular top above a molded & hinged slant lid enclosing an interior w/two long drawers over four short drawers & eight valanced pigeonholes centering an inlaid prospect drawer, above four reverse-serpentine cockbeaded long drawers, ball & claw feet, Massachusetts, 1760-1790, 41¾" w., 44¼" h. (restoration to lid) 5,280.00

Chippendale Slant-Front Desk

Chippendale slant-front desk, tiger stripe maple, thumb-molded slant lid opening to fitted interior w/eight pigeonholes above four short drawers centering a fan-carved drawer over one shaped & one plain short drawer, the case w/four thumb-molded long drawers, bracket feet, 18th c., 31" w., 39¼" h. (ILLUS.) 5,280.00

Federal butler's desk, inlaid mahogany, rectangular top above a pull-out writing section fitted w/small drawers over pigeonholes centering a hinged prospect drawer opening to two small drawers, a pair of cupboard doors below, each centering oval inlaid reserves flanked by satinwood inlaid dies, on bracket feet, Pennsylvania, ca. 1810, 41½" w., 43¼" h. (slight repairs to feet) 8,800.00

Federal cylinder-top desk, mahogany & cherry, rectangular top above three short cockbeaded drawers over a cylinder top opening to fitted interior w/two valanced pigeonholes over four short drawers centering a prospect door flanked by document drawers above a sliding writing surface, above case w/three cockbeaded & banded long drawers, shaped apron, French feet, partial label "Adams...Stonington, Ct," Stonington, Connecticut, 1800-10, 44½" w., 47" h. (minor repairs) 3,850.00

Federal lady's writing desk, curly maple & mahogany, two-part construction: upper section w/three drawers above pair of cupboard doors opening to small drawers over valanced pigeonholes; lower section w/hinged baize-lined writing flap above three cockbeaded graduated drawers, reeded tapering legs, vase-form feet, eastern New England, ca. 1810, 40½" w., 56½" h. 4,950.00

Federal slant-front desk, inlaid mahogany, thumb-molded slant lid w/line inlay opening to a fitted interior w/four long drawers over eight pigeonholes centering a prospect door, the case w/four line-inlaid long drawers above a banded, shaped skirt, French feet, New York, 1790-1810, 47" w., 43½" h. (top reset, veneer loss) 1,650.00

Mission-style (Arts & Crafts movement) drop-front desk, oak, low crest at rectangular top above drop-front writing surface opening to fitted interior over single drawer, flat sides w/bootjack ends & lower medial shelf, L. & J.G. Stickley, No. 613, ca. 1910, 32" w., 40½" h. 715.00

Mission-style (Arts & Crafts movement) writing desk, oak, rectangular leather top attached w/large metal buttons above kneehole surmounted by single drawer flanked by two drawers either side, Gustav Stickley, Model No. 709, ca. 1904, 47½" w., 30¼" h. 1,980.00

Partner's desk, pedestal style, Yumu & Huamu, in three sections, 'cracked ice' parquetry top w/arrangement of hexagonal cells joined by florets, arranged around a large boxwood-outlined burl elm rectangular panel, above a pair of pedestals w/working drawers on both sides faced w/burl elm panels, short bracket feet (reduced in height), China, 18th c., 62½" l., 31¾" h. 18,700.00

Plantation desk, cherry, two-piece construction: upper section w/rectangular top w/wide flared molded cornice above pair of cupboard doors w/white porcelain knobs & three large horizontal panes opening to two interior shelves; lower section w/rectangular top w/slant-front writing surface opening to simple fitted interior, porcelain keyhole escutcheon on front of apron, bold vase & ring-turned legs w/porcelain casters, 38¾" w., 73" h. (refinished, small repairs) 1,000.00

Queen Anne slant-front desk-on-frame, maple, rectangular hinged lid opening to interior fitted w/valanced pigeonholes over small drawers over four graduated long drawers; on base w/shaped skirt w/pendant continuing to short cabriole legs w/pad feet, New England, ca. 1765, 34" w., 43½" h. (base restored & some restoration to desk interior) 4,950.00

Schoolmaster's desk, country-Hepplewhite, walnut, narrow flat top above wide sloping lift-top opening to fitted interior w/two dovetailed drawers, center door & four pigeonholes, above one long, narrow drawer w/turned wood knobs flanked by pull-out supports for lid, square tapered front legs & square back legs, old finish, 31¼" w., 39½" h. (repairs to lid & hinge rails) 425.00

Schoolmaster's desk, grain-painted pine, slant lift-top opens to interior w/five open compartments, the case w/two drawers, square legs, old red ground color, black graining, New England, ca. 1830, 3' w., 3' h. (backboard missing) 825.00

Victorian "Davenport" Desk

Victorian "Davenport" desk, walnut

& burl walnut, rectangular superstructure w/three-quarter gallery & inlaid medallion over slant writing lid, the side w/four sham drawers & four working drawers, S-form supports at front ending in ball feet, England, mid-19th c., 21" l., 33" h. (ILLUS.) 2,090.00

Victorian "patent" desk, Wooton Standard Grade, walnut & burl veneer, hinged doors opening to cubbyholes & drop-front writing surface 8,000.00

Victorian "patent" desk, Wooton rotary desk, walnut, S-roll top opening to small drawers & cubbyholes, paneled door on left pedestal & swing-out section of filing slots in right pedestal, late 19th c. 4,000.00

Wooton Patent Rotary Desk

Victorian "patent" desk, Wooton rotary desk, walnut, low C-scroll top opening to small drawers & cubbyholes, left pedestal w/swing-out section of small drawers & right pedestal of swing-out section of filing slots, labeled "Wooton's Rotary Desk, 1875," 60" w. (ILLUS.) 3,850.00

Victorian Pine Desk

Victorian pine desk, rectangular top w/molded edge over a bank of four drawers on one side & a single drawer over a cupboard door on the other, Marysville, Utah, ca. 1860, 4'4" l., 31" h. (ILLUS.) 715.00

Victorian rolltop desk, mahogany, three-quarter gallery w/scroll-carved sides on top above fold-down rectangular panel over

Victorian Rolltop Desk

C-scroll roll opening to fitted interior, base w/three rounded drawers over two sections of three small drawers flanking recessed center kneehole w/paneled door, block feet, ca. 1890, 50" w. (ILLUS.) 2,750.00

DRY SINKS

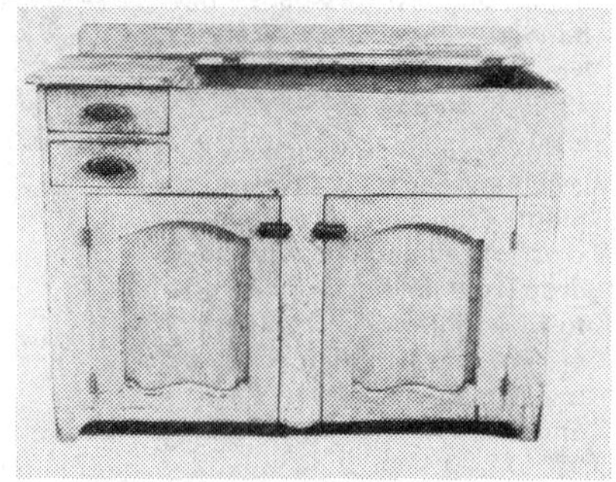

Grain-Painted Dry Sink

Curly maple dry sink, rectangular work well w/work surface to right above short drawer over case w/pair of paneled cupboard doors, short bracket feet, all curly except for poplar door panels, hardwood edge strips & board over drawer, 55" l., 34½" h. (refinished, drawer front replaced, door latches removed, top edge of well recut) 2,200.00

Double-folded dry sink, painted wood, double-hinged rectangular top opening to a flared basin over two cupboard doors enclosing shelves, raised on simple bracket feet, painted overall in ochre, Missouri, first quarter 19th c., 4' ¼" l., 40" h. 1,100.00

Grain-painted dry sink, rectangular top w/tin-lined well & rounded splashboard over two small drawers, two cupboard doors below enclosing shelves, the stiles continuing to form bracket feet, painted overall in brown & yellow pine graining, New England, 19th c., 4' 1" l., 38" h. (ILLUS.) 770.00

Painted wood dry sink, dished rectangular top above two paneled cupboard doors enclosing a shelf, painted overall in pale brown, first half 19th c., 4' 5½" l., 33" h. 357.50

Painted wood dry sink, rectangular top w/gallery & sloping sides over two paneled cupboard doors opening to a plain interior, raised on simple arched feet, painted overall in pale green, New England, early 19th c., 4' 7" l., 38" h. (some flaking to paint) 1,540.00

Pine & poplar dry sink, back crest w/rounded corners above long rectangular well w/small top work area at one end above single narrow drawer, lower case w/two double-paneled doors, plain apron w/short bracket feet, refinished, 62½" w., 34" h. 700.00

Poplar dry sink, tall backboard w/upper shelf above rectangular well w/work surface & dovetailed drawer at one end above pair of paneled cupboard doors, simple cut-out feet, 48" w., 48¾" h. (worn refinishing, some edge damage) 1,076.00

GARDEN & LAWN FURNITURE

Lacy Style Victorian Settee

(Cast iron unless otherwise noted)

Chairs, wire mesh, rounded back, circular seat, curving legs w/scrolled feet, painted black, pr. 430.00

Settee, Victorian Rococo substyle, cast w/lacy C- and S-scrolls at crest above pierced interlaced ovals & rosettes in back, lacy seat, pierced apron joining cabriole legs w/foliate motif, New York, ca. 1850-60, 32½" h. (ILLUS.) 1,100.00

Settee, cast w/scrolling foliage, urn & garland detail, old dark green paint, 37¾" l. 550.00

Settees, cast openwork back in Vintage patt. above reticulated oval seat w/grape & leaf vine skirt, leaf-form legs & feet joined by cross stretcher, John McLean, New York, late 19th c., 38" l., 30" h., pr. 1,760.00

Settees, semi-circular w/openwork leaf-form back & scrolled seat, griffon-form legs, painted black, 19th c., 41" l., 30" h., pr. 2,090.00

Settees, Branch patt., cast w/arched crestrail above openwork interconnecting branches continuing to arched armrests, openwork seat w/branches, curved legs w/branch-form brackets, 19th c., 50" l., pr. 2,420.00

Settees, Victorian Rococo substyle, shaped floral & foliate scroll crest above a back composed of interlocking horseshoes flanked by C-scroll arms over a pierced scroll seat, C-scroll legs, late 19th c., 62" l., pr. 2,640.00

Table, cast w/lacy scrollwork top & foliate scrolling legs, painted green, 41½" d., 27" h. 200.00

Table, ornately scrolling base & legs, multicolored marble mosaic design top, 35½ x 24½", 30" h. 300.00

ICE CREAM PARLOR SETS

Child's Ice Cream Parlor Set

Child's ice cream parlor set: table & four chairs; round table w/wire mesh top & bent iron frame & chairs w/round wood seats & bent

iron backs in heart design & bent iron legs & rungs, 18" d., 21½" h. table, 5 pcs. (ILLUS.) 200.00
Ice cream parlor chair, bentwood, signed Thonet, ca. 1889 .... 100.00
Ice cream parlor set: table & four chairs; round table w/oak top & bent iron frame & chairs w/round wood seats & bent iron frames, ca. 1890, 5 pcs. 600.00
Ice cream parlor stool, round wood seat & bent iron frame, 30" h. 60.00

LOVE SEATS, SOFAS & SETTEES

Chinese Export Chaise Longue

Chaise longue, bentwood, long curved adjustable back & seat raised on scrolling rockers, Austria, ca. 1900, 66½" l. 770.00
Chaise longue, Chinese Export, carved hardwood, removable backrest carved w/a flowerhead & scroll motif centering a cane panel, outscrolled headrest above a caned seat on lotus petal carved circular legs, mid-19th c., 78" l. (ILLUS.) 2,860.00
Day bed, Mission-style (Arts & Crafts movement), oak, four vertical slats at each end, Model No. 292, by L. & J.G. Stickley, ca. 1910, 80½" l., 27 7/8" h. 3,520.00
Love seat, Victorian Rococo substyle, walnut, serpentine crestrail & finger-molded frame w/floral & foliate-carved cresting above upholstered back & serpentine-fronted seat w/conforming finger-molded seatrail, demi-cabriole legs (original finish & worn upholstery) 535.00
Meridienne, Victorian Rococo substyle, carved & laminated rosewood, ornately pierce-carved back crest w/leaves, fruits, flowers, C- and S-scrolls, tufted upholstered back & upholstered seat, demi-cabriole legs, attributed to John Henry Belter, New York, ca. 1850-60 (ILLUS.) 9,075.00

Victorian Meridienne

Settee, bentwood, shaped back w/scrolling bentwood lobes filled w/caning & continuing to scrolled arms, shaped caned seat, turned legs w/flaring feet joined by bentwood box stretcher, by J. & J. Kohn, Austria, ca. 1900, 44" l. 550.00
Settee, Mission-style (Arts & Crafts movement), oak, back w/shaped ears & straight crestrail w/three vertical slats, open arms fitting into curving front posts, unsigned, attributed to Stickley Brothers, Grand Rapids, Michigan, No. 3578, ca. 1908, 40" w., 36" h. 990.00
Settee, wicker, flat back crestrail dropping to armrest, overall latticework back & sides, label of Heywood-Wakefield, ca. 1910, 84" w., 33½" h. (painted, cushion missing) 825.00
Settee, Windsor, painted finish, cushion-molded crestrail & shaped terminals above broad plank seat supported on bamboo-turned outward flaring legs joined by turned stretchers, old dark green paint, Pennsylvania, ca. 1780, 75" l. (one arm repaired) 12,100.00
Settle, Mission-style (Arts & Crafts movement), oak, flat backcrest above narrow vertical slats cut-out w/repeating arches, even arms on slightly canted sides, cushion seat on slats, attributed to Stickley Brothers, Grand Rapids, Michigan, No. 905-3865, ca. 1910, 84" w., 36" h. 3,630.00
Settle, wicker, flat topped back continues to wide, flat arms of the same height, all above vertical piercings in back & sides, wide apron also w/piercings, Gustav Stickley, No. 70, ca. 1913, 86" w., 32" h. 4,400.00

Sofa, American Empire, mahogany, shaped crest carved w/flowerheads above upholstered back & scrolled arms, seat w/loose cushion, shaped seatrail continuing to face arms & ending in carved rosettes, winged animal paw feet, attributed to Samuel Field McIntire, Salem, Massachusetts, ca. 1825, 87" l. 6,600.00

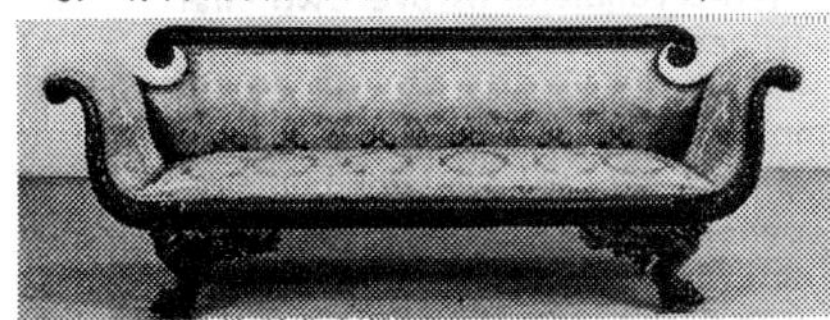

American Empire Sofa

Sofa, American Empire, carved mahogany, cylindrical crestrail w/scrolled leaf-carved terminals, outscrolled arms w/leaf-carved supports continuing to plain seatrail, raised on wing-shaped leaf-carved legs ending in hairy animal feet, ca. 1825 (ILLUS.) 2,200.00

Sofa, Biedermeier, ashwood, rectangular padded back topped by arched serpentine crest panel flanked by S-scrolls, padded sides w/cylindrical arms supported by free-standing ebonized columns, upholstered in light blue striped cotton, possibly Swedish, early 19th c., 79½" w. 4,180.00

Sofa, Federal, mahogany, upholstered arched back & sides w/molded sloping arms on ring-turned reeded supports, string-inlaid & paneled legs continuing to turned & reeded feet, New England, 69" l., 36" h. 880.00

Federal Sofa

Sofa, Federal, mahogany, molded crestrail centering a fluted rectangular reserve, the molded fluted arms above a slightly bowed upholstered seat, flowerhead dies flanking, on square reeded legs ending in brass spade feet, on brass casters, New York, ca. 1805, some restorations, 73" l. (ILLUS.) 6,875.00

Sofa, Louis XV "canape," beechwood, serpentine crestrail w/trailing flowers & vines above upholstered back continuing to downswept arms, seat w/loose cushion, vine-and floral-carved seatrail, short cabriole legs, France, mid-18th c., 77¾" l. 6,875.00

1950's Modern Sofa

Sofa, 1950's Modern style, vinyl-upholstered, high angled form of two long collapsible cushions about long rectangular seat upholstered in grey vinyl, raised on two U-form chrome-plated legs, designed by Charles Eames, ca. 1954, 6' l. (ILLUS.) 1,100.00

Sofa, Victorian, Hunzinger 'lollipop' style, oak, back composed of graduated rows of 'lollipop' shaped turnings surrounding center rectangular upholstered panel & continuing to form sides, padded upholstered seat above apron composed of short turned spindles, late 19th c. 1,500.00

Victorian Renaissance Revival Sofa

Sofa, Victorian Renaissance Revival substyle, walnut, arched crestrail w/burl panels & carved palmette center finial, low, out-scrolled upholstered arms w/carved front supports, seatrail w/narrow burl band at center above carved drop, short turned legs, ca. 1875, 72" l. (ILLUS.) 600.00

Sofa, Victorian Rococo substyle, carved & laminated rosewood, high back w/undulating open-carved crestrail composed of florals & vines w/three fruit & flower carved finials, crestrail continuing down to

"Fountain Elms" Belter Sofa

form curved arm supports & short cabriole front legs w/fruit & floral carved knees, undulating seatrail w/finely carved floral & scroll reserves, "Fountain Elms" patt. by John Henry Belter, New York, ca. 1850-60 (ILLUS.) 36,300.00

MIRRORS

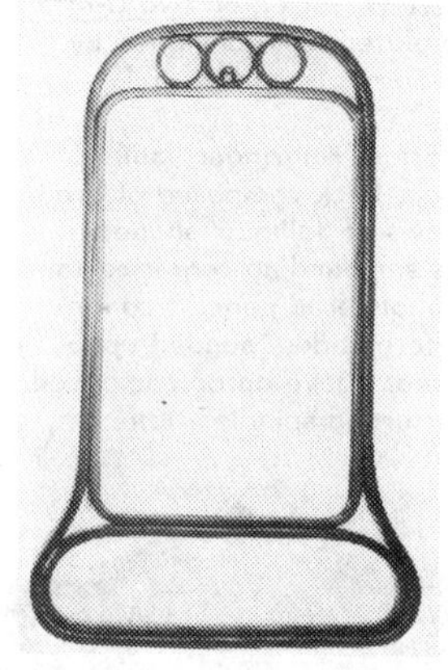

Bentwood Wall Mirror

Bentwood wall mirror, rectangular beveled mirror plate within an outer arched support surmounted by three pierced circles, bulbous pierced base enclosing a pierced oval, in the manner of Koloman Moser, ca. 1902, 41½" h. (ILLUS.) 1,650.00

Chippendale wall mirror, mahogany veneer, ornately scrolling crests at top & base w/long scrolling ears at corners enclosing original rectangular mirror plate, original paper label for "S. Cariss & Co., Baltimore," 20" w., 35½" h. (two minor reglues) 1,100.00

"Courting" mirror, shaped crest w/"eglomise" insert at top, original rectangular mirror plate below, scrolled edges w/applied molding, old heavily alligatored red paint, back labeled "this looking glass was brought to Dover from Temple, N.H.....in the year of 1803," 11½" w., 16½" h. 825.00

Empire, American, "girandole" mirror, carved giltwood, crest centering a carved seahorse flanked by two eagles above a circular frame w/applied stars, gilt spherules centering convex mirror flanked by two candle-arms over two intertwined carved dolphins, 1825-1835, 45" h. 20,900.00

Empire, American, two-part wall mirror, giltwood, reverse-painted panel at top of dancing girl w/swirling draperies edged w/painted leaves & blossoms above rectangular (replaced) mirror plate flanked by ring- and spool-turned applied half columns w/corner blocks, 17½" w., 34" h. 400.00

Federal convex mirror, ebonized & giltwood gesso, spread-winged black-painted American eagle on carved rockwork above circular convex mirror plate within molded framework hung w/gilt spherules, acanthus-carved pendant below, early 19th c., 24" w., overall 48" h. 18,700.00

Federal Cheval Mirror

Federal cheval mirror, mahogany, rectangular mirror plate within ring-turned framework surmounted by ball finials & applied w/brass roundels, base w/turned traverse-reeded down-curving legs, brass animal paw feet on brass casters, Philadelphia, ca. 1820, 31" w., 79" h. (ILLUS.) 7,700.00

George III-style Chinese Chippendale overmantel mirror, giltwood, shaped mirror plate w/pagoda

Ornate Overmantel Mirror

cresting centering a Chinese servant, the frame carved w/C-scrolls & flowerheads, some losses, England, third quarter 19th c., 4' 11" w., 6' 3" h. (ILLUS.) 5,500.00

Queen Anne girandole mirror, giltwood, shell-shaped crest carved w/panels & a crown, rectangular mirror plate engraved w/three stars & surmounted by a scalloped ruby glass panel, base mounted w/two candle-arms, first quarter 18th c., 18¾" w., 37½" h. 2,750.00

Queen Anne wall mirror, walnut veneer, scrolled pediment above shaped rectangular mirror frame enclosing double plate mirror, early 18th c., 18¾" w., 48" h. ...3,740.00

Victorian overmantel mirror, carved walnut, shaped rectangular mirror plate set within conforming carved & pierced frame decorated overall w/trailing grapevines & summer flowers surmounted by bird in scrolled cartouche, mid-19th c., 69" w., 52" h. 1,430.00

Victorian pier mirror, Renaissance Revival substyle, walnut, baroque cartouche crest flanked by scrolling foliage above arch-top mirror plate flanked by baluster-turned & reeded pilasters above white marble scalloped shelf raised on turned legs, ca. 1860 .... 935.00

PARLOR SUITES

Edwardian: two-seat settee, pr. of side chairs & open armchair; inlaid rosewood, each w/railed slat back centered by panel splats inlaid w/urns & scrolls suspending husks, green velour seats, raised on

Edwardian Settee

square tapering legs ending in spade feet, England, ca. 1900, 4 pcs. (ILLUS. of settee) 1,210.00

Empire-style: settee, pr. open armchairs & two side chairs; each w/slightly scrolled rectangular back, the settee & armchairs w/downswept arms on gilt-bronze sphinx-form supports, raised on winged lion-form front legs ending in animal paw feet, upholstered in Napoleonic bee pattern red silk, France, ca. 1900, 5 pcs. 9,350.00

Carved & Ebonized Oriental Settee

Oriental: settee, four armchairs & table; carved hardwood, each carved & colored w/flowers, foliage & birds in profusion, resting on slightly cabriole legs, late 19th c., 6 pcs. (ILLUS. of settee) . .1,870.00

Steer's horn eclectic style: settee & armchair; each w/shaped interlacing horn back & arms above upholstered seat, raised on horn legs, ca. 1890, 2 pcs............2,860.00

Victorian, Overstuffed style: settee & two armchairs; each w/an outswept upholstered square back w/padded armrest above an upholstered seat w/a trellis woven

Victorian Overstuffed Armchair

apron, ca. 1860, 3 pcs. (ILLUS. of one armchair) 1,320.00

Victorian, Renaissance Revival sub-style: settee, armchair & pr. side chairs; walnut, each w/a shaped upholstered back within a walnut frame decorated at the crestrail w/a carved female bust flanked by flowerheads, above an upholstered seat, the armchair & settee w/arm support carved as male busts, turned legs, in the manner of John Jeliff, ca. 1870, 4 pcs. 4,400.00

SCREENS

Victorian Folding Screen

Fire screen, Art Deco, "Les Plumes," wrought iron, border w/bombe' sides, scalloped top w/shell at crest, interior w/dancer surmounting a fan amidst ostrich feathers, Edgar Brandt, ca. 1925, 29" w., 39¼" h. 10,450.00

Fire screen, George II, mahogany & needlepoint, gros and petit-point panel depicting the discovery of Moses in the bullrushes, framed in blue, green, yellow, red & brown scrolls, rectangular frame carved w/leaf scrolls, acanthus & cabochons on leaf-carved trestle supports, England, 18th c., 31" w., 44" h. . . 1,650.00

Fire screen, William & Mary style, walnut, scrolled top & frame enclosing an octagonal gros and petit-point tapestry panel depicting figures in contemporary dress in a shallow landscape setting within a scrolled border, raised on cabriole legs ending in pad feet, partially composed of 18th c. elements, 32" w., 4' 10" h. 550.00

Folding screen, 4-fold, marble & rosewood, each double-hinged oblong panel set w/grey mottled white marble plaques within rosewood framework, the upper portion carved w/"scholar's implements" & the lower w/scenes of birds & flowers in high relief, each panel 13½" w., 71½" h. 1,320.00

Folding screen, 4-fold, Victorian, rosewood & papier-mache, each panel decorated both sides w/decoupage incorporating children, animals, flowers & architectural scenes, last half 19th c., each panel 26" w., overall 72" h. (ILLUS.) 3,300.00

Folding screen, 6-fold, paper panels h.p. w/continuous scene of cat-like tiger walking on a path lined w/bamboo sheltered by large pine trees, executed in shades of ink wash & line on gold-flecked paper ground, Japan, Meiji period, each panel 24¼" w., overall 68" h. . . . 1,100.00

Folding screen, 12-fold, Coromandel lacquer, colorfully decorated both sides, one w/continuous scene of figures in gardens & pavilions, other w/scene of exotic birds perched among rocky crags & leafy branches, within borders of scrolling dragons, florettes & keyfret, on bracket feet, green, coral, brown & yellow, 18th-19th c., each panel 14½" w., 98" h., overall 8' 2" x 14' 6" (losses & restoration to surface) 16,500.00

Pole screens, Victorian, rosewood & papier-mache, adjustable scrolled panel painted w/large floral sprays & exotic birds within gilt scrolled borders, swelling acanthus-carved support raised on shaped triangular base on scrolled feet, ca. 1840, 5' h., pr. 935.00

SECRETARIES

Biedermeier "Patent" Secretary

Biedermeier "patent" secretary, parcel-ebonized birch, arched pediment above a rectangular fall-front enclosing a writing surface & fittings, between columnar supports on square pedestals over an incut rectangular base, possibly Vienna, Austria, ca. 1820, 26½" w., 51" h. (ILLUS.) 6,600.00

Chippendale secretary-bookcase, mahogany, two-part construction: upper part w/projecting dentil-molded cornice above pair scalloped & molded doors opening to an arrangement of shelves & eight drawers, flanked by fluted pilasters; lower part w/hinged slant-front lid opening to fitted interior w/valanced compartmented eight drawer interior, above cockbeaded case w/four graduated drawers, bracket feet, Massachusetts, ca. 1780, 34" w., 76" h. 15,400.00

Chippendale Secretary-Bookcase

Chippendale secretary-bookcase, birch, two-part construction: upper section w/molded cornice above two geometrically glazed cupboard doors opening to a partitioned interior; lower section w/a slant-lid opening to a fitted interior w/four shell-carved short drawers above eight pigeonholes over five blocked drawers centering a shell-carved prospect door, the case w/four graduated long drawers, bracket feet w/minor patches, New England, 1770-90, 38½" w., 80" h. (ILLUS.) 8,800.00

Classical (American Empire) secretary-bookcase, stenciled mahogany, two-part construction: upper section w/angular cornice above an arched frieze over a geometrically-glazed cupboard door opening to shelves, flanked by free-standing columns w/brass capitals; lower section w/veneered long drawer above a gilt-stenciled paneled cupboard door flanked by free-standing columns w/brass capitals, leaf-carved ball feet, New York, ca. 1820-30, 23" w., 88" h........9,350.00

Empire, American, "secretaire à abattant," ormolu-mounted mahogany, molded cornice above a concave arched long drawer flanked by figural ormolu mounts above a fall-front lid w/fielded panels & figural mounts, enclosing a fitted interior w/four vertical document compartments flanked by four pigeonholes over two drawers over two cupboard doors opening to a shelved interior, the case flanked by brass-mounted columns, tapering hexagonal feet, Philadelphia, 1815-25, 42" w., 59½" h. (feet probably restored) 2,200.00

Federal Mahogany Secretary

Federal secretary, inlaid mahogany,

two-part construction: upper section w/rectangular top & patterned inlaid edge above two cupboard doors w/patterned line inlay opening to a fitted interior w/four short drawers flanked by four pigeonholes; lower section w/line-inlaid hinged writing flap above two cockbeaded drawers flanked by line-inlaid maple reserves & cuffs, minor repair to one door, Massachusetts, 1790-1810, 35½" w., 53" h. (ILLUS.) 1,540.00

Federal country-style secretary-bookcase, walnut, two-part construction: upper section w/cove-molded cornice above two glazed cupboard doors opening to two interior shelves above pigeonholes; lower section w/slant lid opening to fitted interior w/pigeonholes & two drawers above single long drawer over pair paneled doors, corner posts extending to form feet, paneled ends, 35¾" w., 78¾" h. 950.00

Federal lady's secretary-bookcase, inlaid mahogany, two-part construction: upper section w/shaped cornice fitted w/three turned urn-form finials above pair of glazed & mullioned doors opening to shelves; lower section w/hinged writing flap above four cockbeaded & graduated long drawers, molded base continuing to flaring bracket feet, Massachusetts, ca. 1800, 40" w., 77½" h. 12,100.00

Federal secretary-bookcase, mahogany, three-part construction: upper section w/shaped cornice w/ball- and urn-turned ivory finials & veneered frieze; middle section w/glazed arched cupboard doors opening to two adjustable shelves over three cockbeaded short drawers; lower section w/hinged writing flap above three cockbeaded long drawers, all w/ring-turned ivory pulls, tapering reeded legs, ball-turned feet, Massachusetts, 1800-10, 40¾" w., 77" h. (minor repairs, losses to veneer) 6,600.00

Federal secretary-bookcase, inlaid mahogany, two-part construction: upper section w/shaped pediment centering three brass ball finials above pr. of glazed doors opening to adjustable shelves over small drawers & valanced pigeonholes; lower section w/baize-lined hinged writing flap over four cockbeaded drawers, shaped skirt continuing

Federal Secretary-Bookcase

to bracket feet, North Shore, Massachusetts, ca. 1805, 40½" w., 79" h. (ILLUS.) 14,300.00

George II Secretary-Bookcase

George II secretary-bookcase, inlaid walnut, two-part construction: upper section w/flat top w/flared cornice above pr. arch-paneled cupboard doors opening to shelves; lower section w/slant-top hinged lid opening to interior fitted w/slots, small drawers & center prospect door above three long graduated drawers, bracket feet, England, first half 18th c. (ILLUS.) 2,640.00

Louis XVI "secretaire a'abattant," mahogany w/ormolu mounts, shaped rectangular mottled grey marble top above long drawer & a fall-front above three long drawers, circular tapered legs, ormolu banding, drawer handles, keyhole escutcheons & *sabots*, France, last quarter 18th c., 38¼" w., 4' 7" h. 4,950.00

Oak Side-by-Side Secretary

Turn-of-the-Century "side-by-side" secretary-cabinet, oak, stepped, shaped back crest w/applied carving above long curved-glass cupboard door on left side next to shaped beveled mirror above open shelf over hinged fall-front lid opening to fitted interior all above ogee-fronted drawer over two drawers, each drawer fitted w/brass bail pulls, short cabriole front legs, ca. 1900 (ILLUS.) 425.00

Eastlake Ebonized Secretary

Victorian Eastlake substyle secretary, ebonized wood, three-quarter galleried shelf superstructure above a slant-front centered by a ceramic plaque above two shelves flanked by cupboard doors, sabre feet, overall line-incised & gilt decoration, attributed to Kimbel & Cabus, New York, ca. 1880, 35½" w., 68" h. (ILLUS.) 41,800.00

Victorian Eastlake substyle cylinder-roll secretary-bookcase, walnut & burl walnut, two-part construction:

Victorian Eastlake Secretary-Bookcase

upper section w/molded cornice w/center raised crown panel w/raised panel w/incised florals flanked by two similar raised panels above frieze of carved & incised floral decoration over pr. glazed cupboard doors opening to shelves & flanked by reeded stiles; lower section w/cylinder rolling back to fitted interior above case w/three short drawers flanked by cabinet doors, all above long drawer on reeded base, ca. 1875, 40¾" w., 95" h. (ILLUS.)......... 2,090.00

SHELVES

Victorian Carved Shelf

Clock shelf, cherrywood, shaped simple crest above single shelf w/reeded front edge, old worn finish, 17¼" w., 9½" deep, overall 26" h. 95.00

Floor standing shelves, pine, three-tier, dovetail construction, single board sides form bootjack feet, 29" w., 10½" deep, 29¼" h. 250.00

Floor standing shelves, pine, three-tier, dovetail construction, natural finish w/good patina, 27" w., 12" deep, overall 54" h. 400.00

Floor standing shelves, primitive pine, four-tier, fishtail-carved cornice above open shelves raised on bootjack ends, blue paint, Scandinavian influence 395.00

Hanging shelf, primitive pine, two-tier, upper shelf w/dovetailed apron above shaded sides joined by narrower lower tier, layers of worn paint, 24½" l. 125.00

Hanging shelf, Victorian Rococo substyle, carved walnut, bowed top above vigorously carved bird & nest on leafy tapering limb, late 19th c., 10½" l. (ILLUS.) ....375.00 to 425.00

Hanging shelf, walnut, arched top over cut-out Masonic emblem flanked by turned posts, ornate cut-out work below shelf, 9½" w., 16½" h. 95.00

Hanging shelf, Zoar, Ohio, poplar, single shelf supported on shaped braces, 12" l. 120.00

Hanging shelves, corner type, pine, three-tier, graduated quarter-round tiers pinned to chamfered backpost & diagonal side posts, original old red finish, attributed to Shaker craftsmen, 21¼" w., 37½" h. 700.00

Hanging shelves, Victorian, walnut, galleried top w/pierced & carved medallion surmounted by ball finials, shaped back w/carved panels flanking burl walnut panel, square reeded supports, ca. 1880, 60" w., 8½" deep shelves, 29" h. 275.00

SIDEBOARDS

Federal Grain-Painted Server

Classical (American Empire) sideboard, mahogany, rectangular top surmounted by a splashboard above three drawers & two pair of cupboard doors centering fluted pilasters w/acanthus-carved capitals, tapered spade feet w/brass waterleaf-form caps, New York, ca. 1820, 72½" w., 48½" h. (lacks brass gallery & brass casters) 9,350.00

Empire, American, sideboard, grain-painted, shaped three-quarter gallery & recessed shelf above rectangular top above conforming case w/central short drawer & arched kneehole section w/three drawers on left & two on the right, eight turned feet, mahogany burnt sienna graining, ca. 1830, 45" w., 42" h. 1,430.00

Federal hunt board, Sheraton country-style, tiger maple, rectangular pine top w/tiger maple edge veneer above case w/two deep drawers, turned legs w/brass casters, replaced brasses, 45 x 21", 36¾" h. 4,250.00

Federal server, grain-painted, rectangular top w/scrolled backboard fitted w/two corner shelves over a long drawer, scrolled side supports joined by a platform stretcher, turned cylindrical legs, painted overall in red & black to simulate graining, further stenciled w/fruit & floral sprays, New England, ca. 1840, 35¼" w., 39½" h. (ILLUS.) .. 715.00

Federal server, inlaid mahogany, bowed rectangular top w/outset-rounded corners & a pattern-inlaid edge over a conforming case w/two long drawers, each centering a flame birch panel surrounded by patterned inlay & banding & flanked by line-inlaid panels, the case w/spool-turned corner columns on reeded tapering cylindrical legs w/turned feet, early 19th c., 36½" w., 33" h. 2,640.00

Federal sideboard, inlaid mahogany, rectangular top above three drawers over pair recessed cupboard doors flanked by bottle drawers & cupboard doors, all line-inlaid & centering inlaid diamond & elliptical dies, line inlaid square tapering legs w/cross-banded cuffs, Southern, ca. 1810, 71¾" l., 41½" h. (restorations) 3,300.00

Federal sideboard, inlaid mahogany, rectangular top w/serpentine front above conforming case w/bow-fronted drawer flanked by concave small drawers over pr. of cupboard doors flanked by deep drawers all outlined w/stringing, inlaid square tapering legs ending in crossbanded

Federal Mahogany Sideboard

cuffs, New York, ca. 1800, 73¾" l., 30" h. (ILLUS.) 12,650.00

French Canadian Sideboard

French Canadian sideboard, carved pine, rectangular top w/molded edge above two drawers & two raised diamond paneled cupboard doors, carved end panels, large bun feet (replaced), Saint-Vallier, Canada, 18th c., 58" w., 51" h. (ILLUS.) 1,100.00

Mission Oak Sideboard

Mission-style (Arts & Crafts movement) sideboard, oak, plate rail over vertical slats centering mirrored panel above case w/recesssed top over two central drawers & cabinet doors over long drawer, side stretchers in base, branded mark of Charles P. Limbert Co., No. 1453, ca. 1910, 48" w., 58½" h. (ILLUS.) 522.50

Mission-style (Arts & Crafts movement) sideboard, oak, open plate rack w/five vertical central slats above rectangular top over two upper drawers w/swing pulls & strap hardware over open lower shelf & two lower drawers, Stickley Bros. Co., Grand Rapids, Michigan, stamped No. 861, ca. 1908, 53¾" w., 46" h. 825.00

Mission-style (Arts & Crafts movement) sideboard, oak, rectangular top above three drawers flanked by cabinet doors surmounting a long drawer, exposed tenons on the legs, copper hardware, red decal mark of Gustav Stickley, Model No. 814, ca. 1904, 66" w., 49" h. 3,960.00

Golden Oak Sideboard

Turn-of-the-Century Golden Oak sideboard, tall paneled superstructure w/scrolled crest & applied scroll carving over wide shelf w/cove molding supported by carved winged beasts flanking long rectangular mirror, case w/two round-fronted drawers w/brass knobs over two paneled cupboard doors w/carved cartouche & scroll designs above long drawer across bottom, leaf scrolls at base front above carved claw feet, ca. 1900 (ILLUS.) 550.00

Victorian Aesthetic Movement sideboard, inlaid walnut, raised backboard at center w/crenelated top flanked by florette finials & decorated w/incised line bands & arched panel w/inlaid & ebonized florals & urn, stepped rectangular top at center above single drawer &

Victorian Aesthetic Sideboard

flanked by canted shelves above inlaid bands over canted open side shelves, large triple-paneled cupboard door at center below inlaid band & featuring two vertical burl panels over narrow horizontal inlaid panel at base of door, turned front legs, attributed to Herter Bros., ca. 1875 (ILLUS.) 1,320.00

Victorian Renaissance Revival substyle sideboard, walnut, very tall back w/high arched crest open-carved w/leaves, scrolls & fruit pendants above open shelf w/ornately scroll-carved supports framing a rectangular mirror w/ovolu corners above a second open shelf above an identical mirror arrangement, this superstructure above a curved front white marble-topped cabinet base w/wide rounded corners w/highly carved fruit & nut pendants in panels framing two long drawers over two cabinet doors, all carved w/matching scroll & fruit carvings, stenciled "A.C. Richards," Cincinnati, Ohio, ca. 1860-70 .... 8,800.00

STANDS

Candlestand, painted & decorated maple, rectangular top w/notched corners above bulbous & ring-turned standard on three cabriole legs, top painted w/stylized yellow & red star motif (paint early 19th c.), New England, 1775-1800, 13½ x 12½", 26" h. 660.00

Magazine stand, Mission-style (Arts & Crafts movement), oak, gallery top over two shelves over arched toe board, marked w/Limbert's brand, No. 301, ca. 1910, 16" w., 29" h. 467.50

Magazine stand, Mission-style (Arts & Crafts movement), oak, rectangular top above three open shelves framed by solid sides, square legs, Model No. 72, designed by Harvey Ellis, produced by Gustav Stickley, ca. 1904, 21½" w., 41¾" h. 2,640.00

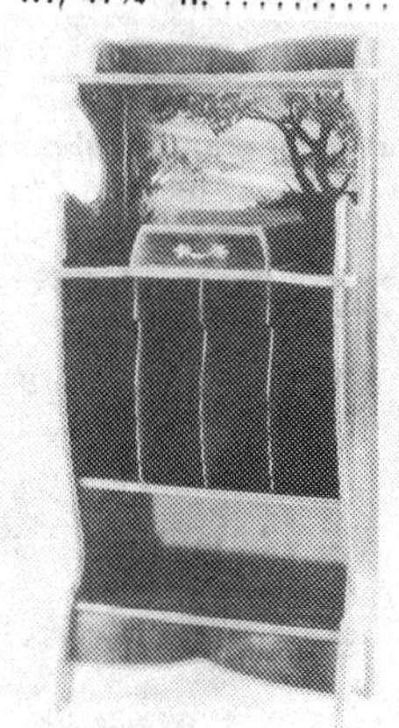

Art Nouveau Music Stand

Music stand, Art Nouveau, carved mahogany & fruitwood marquetry, upright rectangular form w/a V-crest above a shelf w/lobed sides, continuing to scooped-out edges carved at the edges w/waves & centering a low shelf w/central short drawer & a panel at rear, inlaid in various woods w/a view of a boat sailing on a lake; lower section divided into four compartments above an open shelf & raised on lug feet, designed by Louis Majorelle, France, ca. 1900, 31 3/8" w., 4' 8¼" h. (ILLUS.) 3,025.00

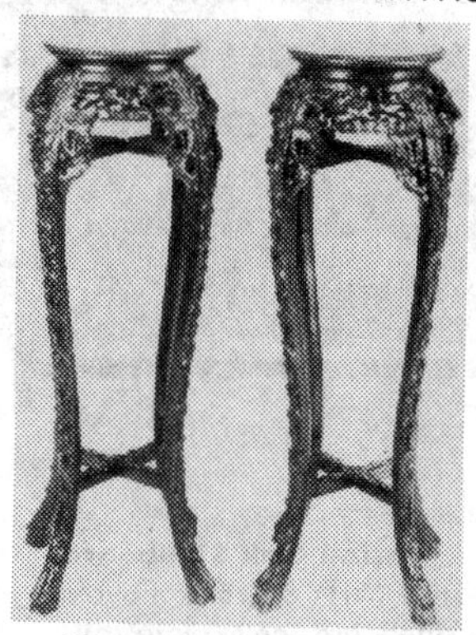

Chinese Plant Stands

Plant stands, Oriental, hardwood w/marble inset, circular top inlaid w/marble w/pierced apron carved w/flowering vines on four flowering vine-carved cabriole legs joined by an X-stretcher, China, mid-19th c., 35¾" h., pr. (ILLUS.) 550.00

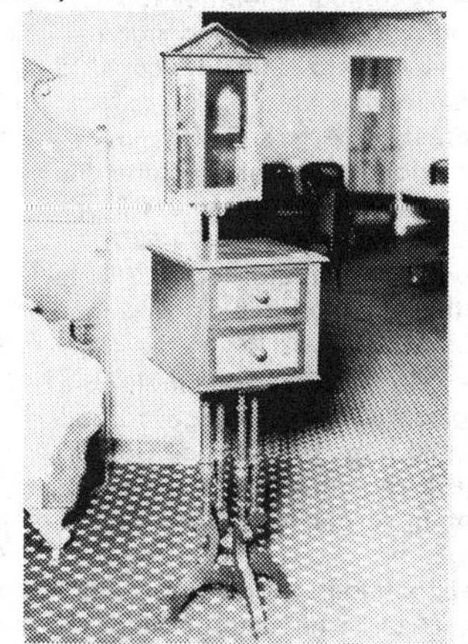

Victorian Shaving Stand

Shaving stand, Victorian, walnut & burl walnut, adjustable rectangular mirror in burl frame w/pedimented top above square topped stand w/two small drawers w/burl veneer, base composed of four slender turned legs resting on four section arched base w/central turned finial, ca. 1875 (ILLUS.) 385.00

Umbrella stand, cast iron, model of seated Terrier painted white forms base of upright umbrella rack, tray base on small feet, old black & white repaint over green, 24½" h. 150.00

Umbrella stand, Mission-style (Arts & Crafts movement), oak, four tapering posts w/side rails w/copper pan at base, paper label of Gustav Stickley, Model No. 54, 1904-06, 25½" w., 53½" h. 440.00

Washstand, Victorian cottage-style, grain-painted finish, rectangular top surmounted by shaped wide splashboard at back w/towel bars extending from each end supported at front by S-scroll brackets, base w/single long drawer w/two wooden knobs above two paneled cupboard doors, scalloped apron, good red-over-yellow finish, ca. 1870 .... 450.00

Washstand, late Federal-style, painted & decorated pine, shaped superstructure above top fitted w/a hole for a basin, a lower shelf fitted w/a drawer, turned legs, painted & grained in pale yellow

Late Federal Painted Washstand

& brown w/green highlights, ca. 1835, 17" w., 38" h. (ILLUS.) 660.00

Empire, American, country-style 2-drawer stand, cherry, oblong top above case w/two ogee front drawers w/turned wood pulls, top drawer divided into four compartments, ring-turned & blocked legs, turned feet, 24 x 20¼" top, 30" h. 300.00

Federal country-style, 1-drawer stand, curly maple, oblong top, apron w/single drawer, ring- and vase-turned legs, 23¾ x 24¼" top, 30½" h. 550.00

Louis XV-Style, gilt-bronze mounted mahogany *"gueridon"* (three-legged stand), round parquetry & brass bordered top above frieze fitted w/foliate mounts, cabriole legs topped by shell & sea-form mounts & ending in *sabots*, France, late 19th c., 21" d., 30" h. 3,025.00

Sheraton-style 2-drawer stands, mahogany & pine, square top w/shaped corners, reeded tapering legs, signed by Wallace Nutting, early 20th c., 18¼" sq. top, 29" h., pr. 850.00

Victorian *"gueridon,"* cast iron, molded circular marbleized top supported on three griffin monopodia joined by reticulated trefoil form shelf, late 19th c., 24" d., 29½" h. 495.00

STOOLS

Broom maker's stool, splayed turned legs w/mid-way shelf, wood & wrought iron clamps, worn original grey paint, 36" h. 200.00

Empire, American, footstool, pine, slip seat w/floral petit point upholstery, ogee-molded frame, bracket feet, 12½" sq. top, 7½" h. 187.50

Empire, American, stool, mahogany, upholstered shaped seat w/tasseled corners above C-scroll sides joined by single stretcher brace, Boston, 1830-40 .... 385.00

George II stool, walnut, oval (modern) needlepoint upholstered drop-in seat, straight shell-carved seatrail, hipped cabriole legs carved at the knees w/shells & acanthus, claw-and-ball feet (legs spliced) 3,300.00

18th Century Chinese Stool

Hongmu stools, square top inset w/soft cane seat w/a waisted frame, on rectangular legs joined by a high shaped rectangular stretcher w/two vertical struts, hoof feet, China, 18th c., 19¾" w., 18½" h., pr. (ILLUS.) 2,420.00

Louis XV Footstool

Louis XV footstool, giltwood, square upholstered top, serpentine siderails centered by carved shell motifs & incised w/crosshatching, cabriole legs w/shell-carved knees & acanthus-carved scrolled toes, France, mid-18th c., 19" w., 16½" h. (ILLUS.) 1,760.00

Mission-style (Arts & Crafts movement) footstool, oak, short flaring legs, rectangular leather top, Model No. 302, branded signature, by Gustav Stickley, ca. 1912, 12½" w., 4½" h 605.00

Mission-style (Arts & Crafts movement) footstool, oak, rectangular frame w/narrow stretchers & upholstered insert, No. 674-5265, "Quaint" line metal tag of Stickley Brothers, Grand Rapids, Michigan, ca. 1912, 18" w., 12" h. 192.50

Painted & decorated footstool, oblong top w/beveled edge, turned splayed legs, old red paint on base & repainted top w/graining forming corner fans, 9¾ x 13" top, 8" h. 65.00

Shaker footstool, hardwood, square top w/cut corners, turned legs w/two rungs, original dark finish, Mt. Lebanon, New York, 11½" sq. 250.00

Windsor Footstools

Windsor footstools, similar w/oval top, splayed bamboo-turned legs w/stretchers, painted red, each branded "Raymond Warntd." on underside, early 19th c., 2 pcs. (ILLUS.) 935.00

Windsor country-style footstool, wooden w/upholstered top, splayed legs w/old red paint over black, floral patterned linen top, 6½ x 12" oval 50.00

Windsor stool, slightly oval scooped seat, splayed bamboo-turned legs w/H-stretcher, stamped "M. Cane" on underside of seat, New England, 1800-15, 10¾" w. seat, 11¼" h. 330.00

Piano stool, cast iron claw & glass ball feet 125.00

TABLES

Art Deco coffee table, burr walnut & ivory, circular top finely veneered w/radiating sections of burr walnut, stepped edge w/dentil band of ivory, four square legs w/bronze feet join the top to the lower shelf decorated w/radiating

Art Deco Coffee Table

sections of burr walnut, branded "Ruhlmann," & insignia "B," Emile-Jacques Ruhlmann, Paris, France, ca. 1925, 27½" d., 18½" h. (ILLUS.) 14,300.00

Art Deco console table, mirrored-glass & mahogany, elongated D-shaped top set w/mirrored glass above two scrolling arms centering an angular block-form support, w/label of Jules Leleu, France, ca. 1936, 63" l., 16½" h. 1,925.00

Art Deco circular low table, Colonette patt., rosewood, inset circular top edged in ivory raised on five supports formed of pairs of tapering square columns & centering a lower circular shelf & raised on five wide feet ending in ivory sabots, designed by Emile-Jacques Ruhlmann & so branded, ca. 1920, 26¾" d., 18" h. 13,200.00

Art Nouveau nest of tables, fruitwood marquetry, oblong tops on trestle legs, inlaid w/gulls flying over rocky coast w/sailing ships in distance, also houses, ladies (3) on shore & man rowing in boat, signed "Galle" in marquetry, ca. 1900, 14" to 23" w., 25" to 27½" h., set of 4 . . . . 3,300.00

Chinese Export sewing table, black lacquer, shaped rectangular hinged top opening to a fitted compartment w/ivory fittings over conforming frieze decorated w/mother-of-pearl inlaid Chinese landscape, supported on lyre-form legs joined by stretcher, paw feet, ca. 1840, 16¼ x 25" (lacquer distressed) 550.00

Chippendale drop-leaf dining table, walnut, rectangular top w/rectangular drop leaves, apron w/single drawer & scalloped edge, six cabriole legs (two swinging as supports), claw-and-ball feet, New York, ca. 1770, opening to 48 x 47", 28½" h. (some restoration to top & skirt) 5,775.00

Chippendale tilt-top tea table, walnut, round dished top tilting & revolving above bird-cage support, ring-turned & compressed ball-form standard, cabriole tripod base w/snake feet, Pennsylvania, ca. 1780, 32" d., 29" h. 2,860.00

Country-style work table, painted pine, removable one-board top overhangs mortised & pinned apron w/molded edge, square, tapered legs w/outward-curved feet, old worn brown paint on base & green on top, 23 x 68½", 30" h. (some worm holes, some cracks, some pins replaced) 375.00

Empire, American (Classical), card table, mahogany, rounded rectangular hinged top swivelling above bolection-molded frieze w/carved flowers above a baluster over a flaring leaf-carved pedestal above a shaped base on leaf-carved lion's-paw feet w/leaf & scroll knee brackets & casters, attributed to Anthony Quervelle, Philadelphia, ca. 1825, 36¼" w., 29½" h. 1,320.00

American Empire Side Table

Empire, American, side table, curly maple, rectangular top flanked by rectangular drop leaves w/rounded corners above apron w/one drawer w/ogee front, round ball drops at each corner of apron, octagonal pedestal on hexagonal platform raised on three C-scroll legs w/casters, Midwestern, ca. 1840, 16½" w., 27 3/8" h. (ILLUS.) 450.00

Empire, American, sewing table, rosewood, rectangular top above two rounded drawers supported on plain cylindrical column on coved square platform raised on carved mahogany paw feet w/porcelain casters, case underside stamped "W. Alexander," William Alexander, Boston, Massachusetts, 1820-30, 21" w., 29½" h. 660.00

Empire, American, work table, mahogany & mahogany veneer, oblong top flanked by D-shaped drop leaves, apron w/two drawers, upper fitted w/writing surface & compartments & lower drawer fitted w/work bag w/maroon silk-covered exterior & decorative tack & gilt rosette border, tapering columnar legs on square arched-front platform stretcher & sabre legs below ending in hairy paw feet on casters, original cast brass drawer pulls, signed "Spooner & Trask, Washington Street, Boston, Massachusetts," ca. 1830, 29½" w., 29" h. 4,950.00

Federal banquet table, two-part, cherry, each part w/trapezoidal top w/wide single-board drop-leaf on inner long side, ogee-shaped apron, rope-turned legs w/ring-turnings at top & bottom, swing-out fifth leg, 22¾ x 45¾" w/21½" leaves, 29" h. (one leg repaired) 900.00

Federal card table, mahogany w/flame-birch inlay, shaped rectangular hinged top w/outset rounded corners above conforming apron inlaid w/checkered-line reserve flanked by inlaid dies on reeded tapering legs on tapering feet, Eastern New England, ca. 1805, 37" w., 30" h. (minor repairs to inlay) 12,650.00

Federal card table, inlaid mahogany, serpentine hinged top folding over a conforming apron centering a veneered panel flanked by inlaid astragals, square tapering legs w/inlaid cuffs, Philadelphia, Pennsylvania, 1790-1810, 36" w., 29¼" h. 8,800.00

Federal card table, Sheraton-style, mahogany w/flame birch inlay, hinged rectangular top w/bowed front & outset shaped corners above conforming apron reserved w/flame birch rectangular central panel, fluted tapering legs, tapering feet, ca. 1810 (leg repair) 2,200.00

Federal drop-leaf "breakfast" table, mahogany, rectangular top w/two shaped drop leaves above one sham & one cockbeaded drawer flanked by carved paterae over molded scrolled supports w/carved rosettes, molded & leaf-carved sabre legs w/brass paw feet, early 19th c., 42" w., 29" h. 1,430.00

Federal sewing table, mahogany & curly maple, rectangular top w/outset rounded corners above apron w/two drawers, the upper w/compartments & the lower w/a slide w/work bag below, w/outset three-quarter spool-turned corners above ring-turned & reeded tapering legs, branded "C. Briggs," Cornelius Briggs, Boston, Massachusetts, on the frame, ca. 1810, 19¼ x 15½" top, 29" h. 6,600.00

Federal side table, mahogany, rectangular top above apron w/single long drawer & original brass oval drop ring handles, ring-turned tapering legs, w/tapering feet, Delaware or Pennsylvania, 1800-20, 29½" w., 28¼" h. 935.00

Federal Sofa Table

Federal sofa table, inlaid mahogany, rectangular top w/D-shaped flaps over two frieze drawers, two false drawers on the other side, raised on trestle supports joined by a turned stretcher ending in downswept legs on brass casters (restoration to legs), probably New York, ca. 1800, 4' 10" l., 28½" h. (ILLUS.) 1,540.00

Federal work table, mahogany & bird's-eye maple, rectangular mahogany top w/ovolo corners above conforming bird's-eye maple apron w/two cockbeaded drawers w/inlaid ivory diamond-shape keyhole escutcheons & turned handles, ring-turned stiles continuing to fluted tapering legs, peg feet, Massachusetts, ca. 1815, 19½ x 17" top, 29½" h. 4,675.00

George III writing table, mahogany, rectangular leather-inset top above three frieze drawers opposed by two false drawers, circular turned tapering legs ending in top-form feet w/casters, England, ca. 1780, 32½ x 54" top, 29" h. 5,500.00

Hepplewhite country-style card table, solid curly maple, hinged D-shaped top above conforming apron, square tapering legs, swing-leg supports top, 17½" w., 29¼" h. (refinished, old age cracks) 11,250.00

Hepplewhite country-style drop-leaf dining table, curly maple, rectangular one-board top w/drop leaves, plain apron, square tapered legs, all curly maple, soft, warm patina w/excellent grain, 20 x 40¾" w/12" leaves, 28" h. (warped top & leaves, minor damage & replacements) 800.00

Hepplewhite country-style Pembroke table, mahogany, rectangular top flanked by D-shaped drop leaves w/cut corners, apron w/single drawer w/original brass bail, square tapering legs, old rubbed finish, top opening to 38 x 32", 28¾" h. 575.00

Huanghuali low table, square top w/inset panel & an apron composed of three pierced rectangular panels joined to the cylindrical legs, underside w/extensive lacquer remaining, (formerly tall center table), China, 17th c., 36½" w., 19¼" h. 7,425.00

Grain-painted Hutch Table

Hutch (or chair) table, grain-painted, round two-board top tilting above simple rectangular arms on chamfered supports, square seat above rectangular panels, arms continuing to form the feet, painted overall in red & dark brown graining (wear to paint), Massachusetts, late 18th c., 47½" d., 26¾" h. (ILLUS.) 1,980.00

Hutch table, Hepplewhite country-style, hardwood & pine, two-board round top pinned to chair base w/square posts w/tapering feet, worn old red paint, 48" d., 26¾" h. (feet ended out w/metal caps) 1,950.00

Hutch table, pine w/oak posts, three-board rectangular top w/breadboard ends pinned to chair base w/two dovetailed overlapping drawers beneath, original brass bail handles, old nut brown finish, 42 x 29½", 28" h. 575.00

Louis XV Provincial writing table, fruitwood, rectangular top w/low three-quarter gallery & inset leather writing surface above scalloped apron w/single small drawer, cabriole legs now w/ormolu *sabots*, France, mid-18th c., 27¾ x 20", 27¾" h. 2,090.00

Louis XVI drop-leaf dining table, fruitwood, rectangular divided top w/rounded ends flanked by D-shaped drop leaves, raised on tapering octagonal legs fitted w/ormolu thimble *sabots* & casters, France, last quarter 18th c., 50 x 48" w/four 19" w. leaves, 29" h. 6,875.00

Louis XVI-Style Center Table

Louis XVI-Style center table, ormolu-mounted marquetry & parquetry, foliate-crossbanded octagonal top inlaid w/lozenge trellis-pattern above lozenge-inlaid frieze, cabriole legs w/basket X-stretcher, France, late 19th c., 36" d. (ILLUS.) 2,860.00

Mission-style (Arts & Crafts movement) book table, oak, square top over four-sided alternating bookcases, signed "The Work of L & JG Stickley," No. 516, ca. 1912, 27" w., 29" h. 4,400.00

Mission-style (Arts & Crafts movement) chess table, oak, rectangular top w/original leather showing traces of printed chess board, large tacks attach leather along sides of top, square legs joined by heavy H-stretcher w/exposed tenons & keys, red logo of Gustav Stickley, Model No. 419, ca. 1902, 38" w., 26" h. 3,300.00

Mission Oak Library Table

Mission-style (Arts & Crafts movement) library table, oak, rectangular top overhanging paneled apron w/two drawers w/metal plates w/oval bails, heavy square legs w/curved braces under apron, wide medial shelf below w/through-tenons into end stretchers, stretchers w/through-tenons into legs, attributed to Gustav Stickley (ILLUS.) 990.00

Mission-style (Arts & Crafts movement) serving table, oak, gallery top, three short drawers over long drawer, open shelf space above arched toe board, wrought-iron swing pulls, red decal of Gustav Stickley, Model No. 808, 1904-06, 48 x 18", 40" h. 13,500.00

Mission-style (Arts & Crafts movement) telephone table, oak, rectangular top w/hinged drop leaf & four exposed tenons w/key, lower shelf w/four exposed tenons, solid slab sides, hand holes at top sides, red decal mark of Gustav Stickley, Model No. 721, ca. 1911, 29 7/8" w., 37¾" h. 1,870.00

Pool or billiard table, mother-of-pearl & ivory inlaid walnut, the playing surface w/six leather pockets bordered in rosewood, raised on six flared square-form legs inlaid w/geometric patterns of ebony & mother-of-pearl, Brunswick, "The Kling," ca. 1916, together w/cues, 10' 1" l., 5' 6" w., 32" h. 8,250.00

Potter's table, pine, three-board rectangular top w/slatted superstructure, over two drawers, raised on tapering turned cylindrical legs ending in turned feet, painted red overall, central Vermont, mid-19th c., 5' 5½" l., 28¼" h. (top scrubbed, retains majority of original red paint) 935.00

Queen Anne card table, turret-top, walnut, shaped top opening to a baize-lined playing surface w/circular candlerests & oval counters above an inlaid shaped skirt, molded cabriole legs ending in pointed trifid feet, mid-18th c., 35½" l., 27½" h. (restoration to one leg) 6,050.00

Queen Anne dressing table, walnut, rectangular top w/thumb-molded edge above one long & three short molded drawers, center drawer fan-carved, on angular cabriole legs ending in pad feet, New England, ca. 1765, 40" w., 30½" h. (possibly highboy base, slight restoration) 5,225.00

Queen Anne drop-leaf dining table, walnut, top w/rounded ends flanked by drop leaves above a skirt w/shaped apron, cabriole legs w/pad feet, New England, ca. 1760, 44½" l., 28" h. (top reset) 3,300.00

Queen Anne drop-leaf dining table, maple, rectangular top w/two D-shaped leaves above plain skirt on tapered circular legs ending in pad feet, New England, ca. 1765, top opening to 56½" w., 27" h. (minor foot repair) 5,500.00

Queen Anne country-style tea table, painted oak & maple, oval one-board top above straight skirt joining block- and ring-turned legs, button feet, red-brown painted finish, New England, 18th c., 27¾ x 33½" top, 26½" h. (crack in top) 7,260.00

Queen Anne "porringer top" tea table, maple, rectangular top w/outset rounded porringer corners, shaped apron, tapering turned legs, pad feet, New England, mid-18th c., 36 x 24" top, 27¾" h. (top not original to base) 1,210.00

Queen Anne tilt-top tea table, cherry, circular dished top tilting & revolving on birdcage support, vase-turned standard, cabriole tripod, snake feet, Pennsylvania or New York, ca. 1785, 32" d., 28" h. (some restoration to top) 1,320.00

Queen Anne tilt-top tea table, walnut, circular dished top tilting & revolving above birdcage support, vase-turned standard, cabriole tripod w/snake feet, Pennsylvania, ca. 1775 (repair to two feet) 3,300.00

Regency breakfast table, mahogany, rectangular top w/rounded corners & molded edge, ring-turned columnar standard w/four downswept reeded supports ending in brass paw feet w/casters, England, ca. 1810, 40 x 52" top, 28½" h. 4,125.00

"Sawbuck" table, rectangular one-board top raised on X-form legs joined by median shelf stretchers, painted overall in red, New England, late 18th c., 10' 9" l., 28" h. 2,090.00

Sheraton Breakfast Table

Sheraton breakfast table, mahogany, rectangular top flanked by D-shaped drop leaves w/shaped corners, acanthus leaf-spiral carved legs, original brass casters, New England, ca. 1820, 36" l., 29½" h. (ILLUS.) 900.00

Sheraton country-style drop-leaf table, cherry, rectangular top w/13¼" w. drop leaves on each side, on round legs w/turned feet, underside signed "P.H. Powers, Hydetown, Pa.," 40½" l., 29" h. 500.00

Sheraton country-style Pembroke table, cherry, rectangular top, two wide drop leaves w/decorative cut-outs at corners, dovetailed drawer at one end, turned, tapered legs, original red finish, 18 x 38" w/13¼" leaves, 29¾" h. 850.00

Sheraton country-style work table, cherry & tiger maple, rectangular top above conforming case of three cockbeaded drawers w/turned pulls & tiger maple fronts, the bottom shallow drawer fitted w/bag frame, four ring-turned, tapering legs w/ball feet, stencil on drawer bottom reads "Albert A. Downing Cabinet and Chair Manufacturers, Main St. Opposite the old Mo. Bank St. Louis," old finish, St. Louis, Missouri, ca. 1830, 26" w., 30" h. 1,540.00

Tavern table, Federal-style, rectangular top w/rounded corners above a plain frieze, raised on tapering flared legs joined by stretchers, painted red, New England, ca. 1790, 36¼"l., 29" h. (top scrubbed & possibly of a different origin, losses to paint) .. 330.00

Tavern table, painted, oval unpainted overhanging top on Windsor-style vase- and ring-turned legs w/turned stretchers at the apron & base, wafer feet, never painted mellow worn surface on top, base painted black at later date, possibly Rhode Island, ca. 1780, 21¼ x 28" top, 25¾" h. 6,600.00

Tavern table, Queen Anne country-style, maple, oval top over shaped skirt, block-turned tapering legs, pad feet w/exaggerated platforms, base w/old brown stippled paint over mustard yellow, possibly Rhode Island, ca. 1740, 27 x 33" top, 25¾" h. (minor repairs to top) 9,350.00

Tavern table, Queen Anne country-style, maple w/pine one-board top w/breadboard ends, oblong top w/wide overhang, apron w/single long (re-constructed) drawer, turned legs w/box stretchers, 45¾ x 24" top, 26" h. 1,600.00

Tavern table, Sheraton country-style, painted poplar, rectangular top w/breadboad ends, plain apron w/single drawer, ring- and baluster-turned legs, original red-painted flame graining, 36 x 25¾" top, 30" h. 550.00

Tavern table, William & Mary, maple & pine, rectangular top w/breadboard ends & wide overhang, apron w/single long drawer, vase- and ring-turned & blocked legs w/box stretcher, turned feet, old grey paint & later red paint on surface, New England, ca. 1730 (damage to lower edge of drawer) 1,760.00

Turn-of-the-Century dining table, Golden Oak, extension-type round top, shell- and foliate-carved apron, fluted, turned & gadrooned pedestal w/four vigorously-carved lion's head & lion's paw feet, signed "R.J. Horner Furniture Co., New York" 1,925.00

Turn-of-the-Century extending library table, stripped walnut, rectangular top w/molded edge above a single catch which separates top panels, raised on baluster-turned legs on a trestle base, ca. 1900, 4' l., 29½" h. (lacking leaves) 357.50

20th Century Coffee Table

Twentieth Century coffee table, walnut, rectangular removable tray top w/glass insert over carved eagle design, scroll-carved apron, flat cabriole legs w/incised lines, 1920-40 (ILLUS.) 75.00

Victorian parlor center table, Renaissance Revival substyle, inlaid walnut w/brass mounts, rectangular banded top w/bowed ends & conforming inset panel inlaid w/central musical trophy in framed reserve surrounded by leafy arabesques & scrolls, above conforming floral inlaid skirt mounted w/shaped & incised trophy panels, raised on tapering incised & parcel gilt legs joined by molded & scrolled stretchers centering elaborate incised urn finial, probably New York, ca. 1870, 52" w., 30½" h. (minor veneer imperfections) 1,980.00

Renaissance Revival Parlor Table

Victorian parlor center table, Renaissance Revival substyle, rosewood, oval top w/inlaid marble center above wide apron w/line-incised decoration, four turned & scrolled legs joined by X-stretcher centered by turned, flattened urn, ca. 1880 (ILLUS.) 2,860.00

Victorian parlor center table, Rococo substyle, walnut, serpentine white marble slab top above conforming base w/molded scrolled feet joined by serpentine shaped stretchers w/center finial, ca. 1860, 26" h. 550.00

Victorian parlor center table, Rococo substyle, pierce-carved rosewood w/white marble turtle-shaped slab top, apron pierce-carved w/grapevines & grape clusters, cabriole legs joined by serpentine cross-stretcher centered w/fruit-filled bowl, attributed to John Henry Belter, New York, New York, ca. 1860, 46" l., 29½" h. 10,450.00

Belter Rosewood Center Table

Victorian parlor center table, Rococo substyle, pierce-carved rosewood w/white marble turtle-shaped slab top, solid apron w/carved leaf scrolls, four finely carved dolphin-form legs joined by serpentine cross-stretcher centered w/fruit-filled bowl, attributed to John Henry Belter, New York, New York, ca. 1850 (ILLUS.) 14,000.00

Victorian parlor center table, Rococo substyle, rosewood w/white marble turtle-shaped slab top, elaborately carved in the manner of Prudent Mallard, New Orleans, Louisiana, large size 4,125.00

Victorian parlor table, Eastlake substyle, walnut, molded rectangular top over incised pendants raised on carved tripartite base w/turned incised pedestal supported by similarly decorated splayed legs w/knob mounts, ca. 1870, 20½" w., 32½" h. 220.00

Victorian parlor table, Renaissance Revival substyle, ebonized wood, rectangular top w/marquetry inlay consisting of rectangular bands w/scrolls & a center reserve of florals, gadrooned apron w/scroll carved trim, four legs w/block & urn turnings w/out-curved square feet joined by flat wide stretcher w/two panels of inlay, ca. 1875 .. 715.00

Wicker Table with Bookcase Base

Wicker table, round wood top above rounded wicker apron, wicker-wrapped legs w/arched apron supports framing revolving book-case in base w/scrolling wicker trim, ca. 1900 (ILLUS.) 550.00

William & Mary "gate-leg" table, maple, rectangular top flanked by D-shaped drop leaves above two heavy baluster-turned supports, w/attached swinging gate supports, shoe foot base, New England, ca. 1740, top opening to 46½ x 37", 28" h. 15,400.00

William IV Japanned Tea Table

William IV tilt-top tea table, japanned wood, round piecrust top tilting above baluster support, raised on S-form legs w/casters, overall decorated w/lacquer & painted Chinoiserie pavillions & courtesans, England, ca. 1840, 33" d., 29" h. (ILLUS.) 2,640.00

Windsor side table, painted wood, rectangular top w/breadboard sides on four block- and ring-turned legs, joined by double turned stretchers at skirt, old worn red paint, possibly New Hampshire, ca. 1800, 17¾ x 23¾", 28¼" h. 825.00

Work table, pine, two-board rectangular top w/rounded corners & blue-painted edge, over a simple rectangular apron, raised on tapering square legs, the base painted in pale green, probably Midwestern, 19th c., 4' 10" l., 29" h. (top scrubbed) 275.00

WARDROBES & ARMOIRES

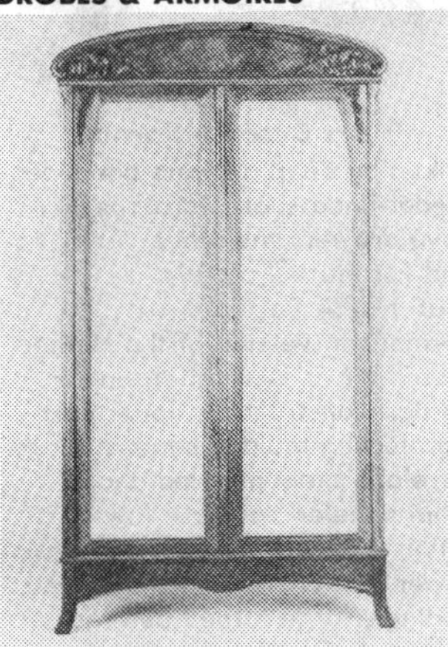

Art Nouveau Armoire

Armoire, Art Nouveau, walnut, arched crestrail carved w/blossom & leafage above two rectangular cupboard doors set w/mirrors & opening to a shelved interior, continuing to a scrolling apron & raised on four lug feet, w/keys, France, ca. 1910, 45½" w., 7' 5¼" h. (ILLUS.) 770.00

Armoire, Louis Philippe bird's-eye maple & stained maple faux bamboo, molded cornice above two doors opening to shelves, two short drawers below, the whole w/stained maple bamboo-turned supports & split faux bamboo borders, France, second quarter 19th c., 4' 8" w., 7' 5½" h. 1,980.00

Armoire, South German Baroque, walnut, large molded cornice above pair of well-figured doors w/raised molded panels, w/similar base, bun feet, Germany, probably Bayern, first quarter 18th c., 84" w., 85" h. 18,700.00

Chifforobe, Art Deco, waterfall design veneered door & drawer fronts, narrow center mirror

Art Deco Chifforobe

flanked by deep drawers one side & cedar-lined short wardrobe above drawers the other, "Tri-Bond Furniture," ca. 1940 (ILLUS.) 225.00

Kas (American version of the Netherlands *Kast* or wardrobe), poplar, two-part construction: upper part w/projecting molded cornice above pair elaborately paneled doors within paneled sections; lower section w/shallow dovetailed drawer & applied diamond-shaped moldings, large turned bun feet, old dark finish, 74¾" w., 78½" h. 4,500.00

William & Mary Kas

Kas, William & Mary, gumwood, two-part construction: upper part w/elaborately molded cornice above two paneled cupboard doors enclosing shelved interior w/one small drawer & centering three pilasters w/double vertical molded panels & three horizontal applied short moldings, lower section w/single long drawer paneled to resemble two drawers, w/flanking diamond-molded panels, large ball-turned feet, New York, 1725-55, 54" w., 74" h. (ILLUS.)...........4,180.00

Wardrobe, Federal country-style, painted & decorated, ogee-molded cornice above pair paneled cupboard doors over single long drawer, molded base, bracket feet, doors w/free-hand floral bouquets & "1865" on grain-painted ground, blue painted base & marbleized cornice, 52" w., 78½" h. 770.00

Gustav Stickley Wardrobe

Wardrobe, Mission-style (Arts & Crafts movement), oak, flat rectangular top above two long paneled doors opening to reveal two compartments & eight narrow drawers over two shelves, lower arched toe board, No. 920, red decal mark & remnants of paper label of Gustav Stickley, 1905-07, 33¼" w., 59¾" h. (ILLUS.) 5,500.00

Wardrobe, Victorian, early country-style, grain-painted finish, line-molded cornice & side stiles flanking single paneled door, cut-out feet, worn original red flame graining, 30" w., 71" h. 400.00

Wardrobe, Victorian, early country-style, poplar w/cherry-colored finish w/some brushed graining, cove-molded cornice above four-panel door, flat base w/molding, one interior shelf & clothes hooks, 49¼" w., 79½" h. 350.00

(End of Furniture Section)

GAMES & GAME BOARDS

A Trip Through Puzzleland

Acrobat set, Crandalls, box top warped $175.00
Addams Family card game, original box, 1960's 17.00
All Star Baseball board game, 1943, original box 35.00
Alphabet & Numbers wheel-type, Cress Board, 1916, original box ... 36.00
All Star Comic, King Features card game, 1934 .... 45.00
Ambuscade, Constellations & Bounce, McLoughlin Bros., 1877, original box 50.00
Bagatelle board game, 1914 .... 60.00
Baseball Marble Game, colorful cartoon wooden playing board w/standup back panel, spring action plunger shoots marbles up into backboard pockets to score runs, w/unopened bag of 28 marbles 45.00
Batman & Robin board game, 1965 .. 22.00
Beatles - Flip Your Wig board game, 1964 .... 50.00
Bingo, Milton Bradley, 1936 .... 10.00
Blackout military board game, Milton Bradley, original box 45.00
Boom or Bust board game, Parker Bros., 1951 .... 15.00
Calling All Cars board game, Parker Bros., ca. 1930 .... 28.00
Carom game board, wooden w/pieces & instructions, 1920's ... 38.00
Checkerboard, reverse-painted glass & tinsel, red, blue, yellow & green, framed, 19¾" sq. 75.00
Checkerboard, slate w/worn painted surface, 20 x 20" (1 corner chipped) 90.00
Checkerboard, wooden, relief-carved pattern of 64 squares on one side, 144 on other, old black paint & varnish finish, 17 x 26" (minor age cracks) 250.00
"Chinker Chek" Chinese Checkers marble game, 1937 .... 20.00
Clown Ring Toss, Parker Bros., 1912, original box 10.00
Clyde Beatty & His Animals cut-out game, 1945 .... 15.00
"Confucius Say," Chinese Fortune Sticks, celluloid & wood, 1940's ... 15.00
Cootie, lithograph of World War I battlefield, 1920, 4 x 5 x 1" box .. 15.00
Cribbage board, tin w/brass ball feet, worn original red, blue & yellow striping on black ground, small door in base for pegs, 10 x 2 3/8", 1/8" h. 105.00
Dominoes, ebony w/inlaid ivory dots, set of 26 .... 35.00
Educator card game, John Train, 1936, original box 7.50
"Fire Fighters," Milton Bradley, 1909, lithograph of fire engine on lid of box 25.00
Fish Pond, McLoughlin Bros., 1890 .... 75.00
Flowers card game, Cincinnati Game Co., 1899 .... 10.00
Game of Boy Scouts card game, Parker Bros., 1912 .... 55.00
Game of the Pilgrims Progress board game, McLoughlin Bros., 1875 .... 50.00
Hasko Mystic Tray, original surrealistic graphics box, Haskelite Co., Chicago, Illinois, 1930-40 .... 28.00
Hearts card game, Parker Bros., 1914 .... 12.00
Illya Kuryakin card game, Milton Bradley, 1966 .... 16.00
Katzenjammer Kids punch-out game, ca. 1945, original envelope 15.00
Limited Mail & Express board game, Parker Bros., 1895, large 150.00
Logomachy card game, McLoughlin Bros., 1874, original box w/instructions 85.00
Max & Maurice board game, McLoughlin Bros., 1905 .... 10.00
Monopoly, Parker Bros., 1961 edition, original box, complete 7.00
Moon Mullins Gets the Run Around board game, Milton Bradley, 1925 .... 46.00
Movie-Land Keeno card game, Wilder Mfg. Co., eight large cards w/large picture of star on back w/small pictures on front, deck of cards w/picture on each showing star, w/lithographed box w/caricatures of the actors, 1929 .... 75.00
Our National Life card game, Cincinnati Game Co., 1903 .... 45.00
Palmistry, McLoughlin Bros., 1887, original box 110.00
Rook card game, Parker Bros., 1910 .... 8.50
Soldier Ten Pins, McLoughlin Bros., 1890 .... 45.00

Thornton W. Burgess Animal Board game, Saalfield, 1925 .... 20.00

Trip Through Puzzleland (A) puzzle game, complete w/color preview litho & pieces to fit together, ca. 1900, original box (ILLUS.) 35.00

Uncle Jim's Question Bee radio board game, N.B.C. Blue Network, 1938 .... 50.00

Wings Airmail card game, Parker Bros., 1920 .... 22.00

Words and Sentences Game

Words and Sentences, crossword-style game, Milton Bradley, ca. 1885, original wooden box (ILLUS.) 52.00

GARDEN FOUNTAINS & ORNAMENTS

Figural Garden Fountain

Ornamental garden or yard fountains, urns and figures often enhanced the formal plantings on spacious lawns of mansion-sized dwellings during the late 19th and early 20th century. While fountains were usually reserved for the lawns of estates, even modest homes often had a latticework arbor or cast iron urn in the yard. Today garden enthusiasts look for these ornamental pieces to lend an aura of elegance to their landscaping.

Bird bath, cast iron, cast as three scallop shells, 20th c., 32" w., 5" h. $2,200.00

Figure, lead, modelled as a young rustic boy playing a reed flute, on a coved circular base, 19th c., 26" h. 440.00

Figures, lead, modelled as scantily-clad putti, each emblematic of a season, on octagonal bases, late 18th-early 19th c., 25½" h., set of 4 .... 1,320.00

Fountain, lead, cast in the form of two speckled fish w/tails up forming a circle, raised on a rectangular plinth, 38" h. (ILLUS.) 2,750.00

Ornament, model of rabbit in seated position w/ears up, cast iron, traces of black paint, 12" h. (minor rust) 325.00

Ornaments, model of whippet, cast iron, seated animal on oval base, 20th c., 17½" h., pr. 3,300.00

Urn, cast iron, compressed urn form w/everted leaf-molded rim over a fluted & leaf-bordered body above a domed circular foot, square stepped plinth, 19th c., 28" d., 24" h. 330.00

Urn, cast iron, ornate side handles, reeded rim, low standard on square stepped base, mounted on high square plinth, flaking white paint, 49" h. to top of handles.... 350.00

Urns, cast iron, flared scalloped rim above reeded sides & band of florals & foliage, low standard on circular reeded foot, square base, worn white repaint, 21¼" d., 15½" h., pr. 350.00

Urns, cov., cast iron, urn finial above fluted domed cover over a fluted urn form body w/drapery swag border, on a spreading circular bead-molded foot, 24" h., pr. 1,980.00

GLASS

AGATA

Agata was patented by Joseph Locke of the New England Glass Co., in 1887. The application of a mineral stain left a mottled effect on the surface of the article. It was applied chiefly to the Wild Rose (Peach Blow) line but

sometimes was applied as a border on pale opaque green. In production for a short time, it is scarce. Items listed below are of the Wild Rose line unless otherwise noted.

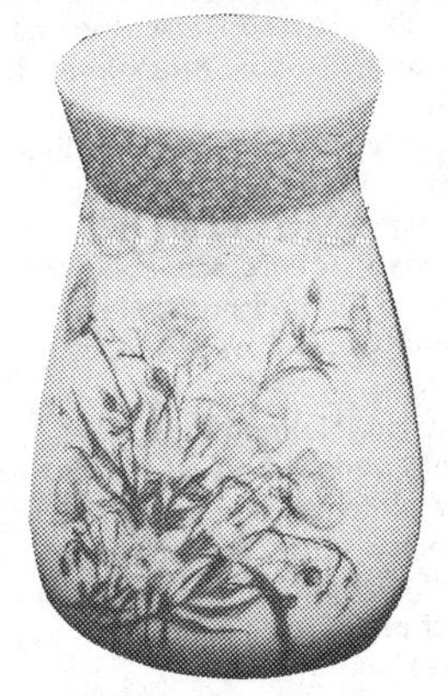

Green Opaque Agata Vase

Bowl, 5½" d., 2½" h., ruffled rim . . $700.00
Cruet w/original stopper, green opaque 1,185.00
Tumbler, 3¾" h. . . . . 550.00 to 685.00
Tumbler, green opaque 495.00
Tumbler, green opaque, 12 optic ribs 685.00
Vase, 6" h., lily form 525.00
Vase, 6¼" h., green opaque, buttercups decor (ILLUS.) 1,500.00

AKRO AGATE

Akro Agate Ashtray

This marbled ware was made by the Akro Agate Company in Clarksburg, West Va., between 1932 and 1951 and most articles bear on the reverse side the likeness of a crow flying through a capital letter A. The majority of these pieces were small.

Ashtray, shell-shaped, marbleized orange swirls in white opaque (ILLUS.) $12.50
Creamer, child's playtime item, Interior Panel patt., blue opaque . . . 25.00
Cup & saucer, child's playtime item, Chiquita patt., green opaque 5.00
Cup & saucer, child's playtime item, Stippled Band patt., green transparent 11.00
Pitcher, water, child's playtime item, Octagonal patt., blue opaque 11.00
Pitcher, water, child's playtime item, Stacked Disc & Panel patt., green transparent 9.00
Plate, 3¼" d., child's playtime item, Interior Panel patt., topaz transparent 2.75
Plate, 3¼" d., child's playtime item, Stacked Disc & Panel patt., green transparent 5.00
Powder jar, Colonial Lady cover, cobalt blue 150.00
Powder jar, Colonial Lady cover, white opaque 58.00
Powder jar, Scottie dog cover, white opaque top, pale pink opaque base 80.00
Sugar bowl, cov., child's playtime item, Interior Panel patt., blue opaque 35.00
Sugar bowl, cov., child's playtime item, Interior Panel patt., topaz transparent 19.00
Teapot, cov., child's playtime item, open handle, Octagonal patt., blue opaque w/white lid 15.00
Tea set, child's playtime item: cov. teapot, creamer & sugar bowl; Chiquita patt., powder blue opaque, 3 pcs. 65.00
Tea set, child's playtime item: Chiquita patt., cobalt blue, 12 pcs. . . . 125.00
Toothpick holder, marbleized orange swirls in white opaque 12.00
Tumbler, child's playtime item, Stacked Disc patt., pink opaque . . 6.00
Tumbler, child's playtime item, Stacked Disc & Panel patt., green transparent 7.00
Water set, child's playtime item: pitcher & 6 tumblers; Stippled Band patt., green transparent, 7 pcs. in original box 75.00

ALEXANDRITE

This glass, shading from a yellowish color to rose to blue, was produced by Thomas Webb & Sons and Stevens & Williams of England. A somewhat similar ware was made by Moser of Carlsbad.

Compote, 5 11/16" d., 1 5/8" h., Expanded Diamond patt., amber in-

terior, rosy pink rim w/sapphire blue, honey colored wafer base & tiny connecting post $985.00
Custard cup & underplate, Moire patt., 2 pcs. 975.00
Plate, 6" sq., Empress patt., signed 35.00
Plate, 7½" d., Empress patt., signed 55.00
Tazza, pedestal foot, Honeycomb patt., 5½" d., 2" h. 795.00
Tumbler, juice, 3" h. 365.00
Vase, 2¾" h., Honeycomb patt. base 1,250.00
Vase, 13" h., round bulbous base w/tall slender neck ending in ruffled, flared neck, Honeycomb patt., Webb 1,750.00
Wine, Honeycomb patt., 4½" h. 750.00

AMBERINA

Plated Amberina Cruet

Amberina was developed by the New England Glass Company, and pressed Amberina was made by Hobbs, Brockunier & Company (under a license from the former) and by other glass factories. A similar ware called Rose Amber was made by Mt. Washington Glass Works. The glass shades from amber to red. Cut and plated Amberina also were made. About the turn of this century and again in the 1920's, the Libbey Glass Co. made some Amberina.

Basket, squat form on fluted foot, wide ruffled rim, applied ribbed handle, enameled gold & blue florals, late 19th c., 8" d., 5¾" h. $440.00
Basket, cylindrical form swelling toward base, ruffled wide mouth, loop handle, late 19th c., 6¼" h. 550.00
Basket, tapered, flared rolled rim, upright handle, early 20th c., 13" h. 1,430.00
Bowl, 8" d., 3" h., Plated Amberina, crimped rim 4,500.00
Bread tray, pressed Daisy & Button (101) patt., Hobbs, Brockunier & Co., 13 x 9" 135.00
Carafe, Reverse Amberina, bulbous Inverted Thumbprint patt. base, tall neck w/flared rim, 7½" h. . . . 210.00
Celery vase, square scalloped top, Diamond Quilted patt., New England Glass Co., 3 7/8" d., 6¼" h. 325.00
Celery vase, Hobnail patt., Mt. Washington Glass Co., in Aurora silver plate holder, overall 9" h. . . 495.00
Centerpiece bowl, amber wafer foot, Swirl patt., enameled gold branches, berries & flowers, ground pontil, 10½" d., 7 5/8" h. 395.00
Condiment set, 3-bottle, Inverted Thumbprint patt., Mt. Washington Glass Co., original silver plate handled frame marked Pairpoint 395.00
Creamer, ribbed, triangular rim, flaring toward base, applied amber ribbed handle, New England Glass Co., ca. 1880, 2½" h. 247.50
Creamer, applied clear reeded handle, Inverted Thumbprint patt., 4½" h. 375.00
Cruet w/original stopper, Inverted Thumbprint patt., Mt. Washington Glass Co. 225.00
Cruet w/clear cut faceted stopper, applied clear reeded handle, Reverse Amberina, Diamond Quilted patt., 3½" d., 6½" h. 175.00
Cruet, Plated Amberina, bulbous melon-ribbed body (ILLUS.) 3,400.00
Cup, Plated Amberina, ribbed squat form swelling toward base, New England Glass Co., ca. 1886, 2½" d., 2½" h. 880.00
Decanter w/amber stopper w/cranberry bubble center, applied amber handle, enameled white florals & leaves, 4¾" d., 9" h. 275.00
Finger bowl, fluted, New England Glass Co., 5½" d., 2¾"h 225.00
Ice cream dish, square, pressed Daisy & Button (101) patt., Hobbs, Brockunier & Co. 125.00
Lemonade set: 10" h. fluted pitcher & four tumblers; enameled red holly berries & green leaves, 5 pcs. 795.00
Mustard pot, cov., Inverted Thumbprint patt., Mt. Washington Glass Works, 3" h. 275.00

Pitcher, 6½" h., square mouth, reeded handle, Inverted Thumbprint patt., New England Glass Co. 485.00
Pitcher, tankard, 7½" h., applied amber reeded handle 275.00
Pitcher, water, 7½" h., 5" d., bulbous w/round mouth, applied amber handle, Inverted Thumbprint patt. 175.00

Reverse Amberina Pitcher

Pitcher, 7¾" h., bulbous melon-ribbed body w/round mouth, applied clear reeded handle, Inverted Thumbprint patt. (ILLUS.) 265.00
Pitcher, water, 7¾" h., applied amber handle, pressed Hobnail patt., Hobbs, Brockunier & Co. 465.00
Pitcher, water, 7¾" h., 5 3/8" d., bulbous w/round mouth, applied clear reeded handle, Reverse Amberina, enameled lacy green leaves & pink & blue florals w/red or green stems 245.00
Pitcher, 8" h., bulbous body, straight neck w/triangular mouth, applied amber handle, shades from cranberry to medium amber, Inverted Thumbprint patt. 210.00
Pitcher, 8¼" h., squared body w/straight neck & small spout, applied pale blue reeded handle, shades from deep red to cranberry to amber, Inverted Thumbprint patt. 210.00
Pitcher, water, braided handle ending in two large rosettes, Honeycomb patt., New England Glass Co. 495.00
Punch cup, applied amber handle, Baby Thumbprint patt., Libbey 75.00
Punch cup, applied amber handle, Expanded Diamond patt. 85.00
Punch set: bowl & eight punch cups; Inverted Thumbprint patt., 9 pcs. 625.00

Salt & pepper shakers, enameled decoration, Inverted Thumbprint patt., pr. 225.00
Spooner, square scalloped top, Diamond Quilted patt., New England Glass Co., 3 1/8" d., 4½" h. 235.00
Toothpick holder, tricornered top, Baby Thumbprint patt., New England Glass Co., 2" 375.00
Toothpick holder, Inverted Thumbprint patt. 400.00
Toothpick holder, Reverse Amberina, Raised Diamond patt. 265.00
Tumbler, Baby Thumbprint patt. 87.50
Tumbler, Expanded Diamond patt., Mt. Washington 275.00
Tumbler, Inverted Thumbprint patt. 95.00
Tumbler, Reverse Amberina, 4½" h. 125.00
Vase, 4¾" h., 4½" w., free-form wide lip, applied thin amber "crackle," marked "C" on lip 250.00
Vase, 6" h., jack-in-pulpit shaped . . . 175.00

Reverse Amberina Vase

Vase, 7½" h., pear-shaped body tapering to short, straight neck, band of applied "icicles" around base of neck, Reverse Amberina, Inverted Thumbprint patt. (ILLUS.) 225.00
Vase, 7 5/8" h., 3 7/8" d., cylindrical, Swirl patt., enameled w/soft pink florals & green leaves 138.00
Vase, 8¼" h., 6 3/8" d., fan-shaped top, applied amber wishbone feet, Swirl patt. 135.00
Vase, 9½" h., 4" d., fluted top, enameled blue & pale pink daisies, small white flowers, green leaves & green bow ribbon 165.00
Vases, 10 1/8" h., 3 3/8" d., cylindrical, applied amber feet, Swirl patt., enameled turquoise blue &

white florals w/green branch & gold leaves, applied amber spiral trim around base, pr. 325.00

Vase, 10½" h., amber scalloped top, six applied amber feet, Swirl patt., enameled florals & bird 650.00

Vases, 12½" h., 7" d., three applied amber foot w/raised lion's head at top of each foot, fluted top, amber edging, Swirl patt., enameled gold bird, bamboo & green leaves w/small blue & white florals, gold trim, facing pr. 595.00

Vase, 13 7/8" h., 4 1/8" d., lily-shaped, pedestal foot, applied amber spiral trim, Swirl patt., enameled gold florals & foliage . . 245.00

Water set: pitcher & four tumblers; Diamond Quilted patt., 5 pcs. 750.00

Whiskey shot glass, Venetian Diamond patt., New England Glass Co., 2¾" h. 125.00

Wine decanter w/matching stopper, pedestal foot, enameled pink & white florals w/blue centers & green leaves, 4½" d., 14" h. 245.00

ANIMALS

Heisey Donkey

Americans evidently like to collect glass animals and, for the past fifty years, American glass manufacturers have turned out a wide variety of animals to please the buying public. Some were produced for long periods and some were later reproduced by other companies, while others were made for only a short period of time and are rare. We have not included late productions in our listings and have attempted to date the productions where possible. Evelyn Zemel's book, "American Glass Animals A to Z" *(now out of print), will be helpful to the novice collector. Also see STEUBEN in Glass.*

Angel Fish book end, clear, A. H. Heisey & Co., 3½ x 2¼" wave base, 7" h. (single) $85.00

Asiatic Pheasant, clear, A. H. Heisey & Co., 1944-45, 7¼" l., 10¼" h. 275.00

Baby Bear w/cart, clear, New Martinsville Glass Mfg. Co., 4¼" l. bear, 5¼" l. cart, 2 pcs. 70.00

Baby Seal candlestick, clear, New Martinsville Glass Mfg. Co., 4¾" h. (single) . . . . .45.00 to 55.00

Chinese Pheasant, blue, Paden City Glass Mfg. Co., 13¾" l., 5¾" h. . . 97.50

Clydesdale Horse, clear, A. H. Heisey & Co., 1942-48, 8" l., 8" h. 335.00

Deer finial powder dish, marigold sprayed-on finish, Jeannette Glass Co., 6" h. 12.50

Deer standing, clear, Fostoria Glass Co., 2 x 1" base, 4½" h. 38.50

Donkey standing, clear, Duncan & Miller Glass Co., 4½" l., 4½" h. . . 150.00

Donkey standing, clear, A. H. Heisey & Co., 1944-53, 4¼" l. base, 6½" h. (ILLUS.) . . . .215.00 to 245.00

Duck family: 3¼" l., 4¼" h. mama, 2½" h. duckling looking back, 2 1/8" h. duckling looking forward & 1¼" h. duckling looking down; amber, Fostoria Glass Co., 4 pcs. . . . . .50.00 to 70.00

Eagle book ends, clear, New Martinsville Glass Mfg. Co., 8" h., pr. 150.00

Elephant book ends, clear, Fostoria Glass Co., 1938-44, 5¾ x 3" base, 7¾" h., pr. . . . . .125.00 to 135.00

Fish vase on wave base, clear, A. H. Heisey & Co., 9" h. 150.00

Gazelle, clear, A. H. Heisey & Co., 1927-49, 11" h. 1,150.00

Gazelle book ends, clear, New Martinsville Glass Mfg. Co., 8½" h., pr. . . . . .135.00 to 165.00

Goose (The Fat Goose), clear, Duncan & Miller Glass Co. . . . . .200.00 to 250.00

Goose (or Mallard) w/wings down, clear, A. H. Heisey & Co., 1942-53, 5¾" h. 265.00

Hen, clear, A. H. Heisey & Co., 1948-49, 2¾ x 2½" base, 4½" h. . . . . .375.00 to 400.00

Hen, clear, New Martinsville Glass Mfg. Co., 2¾" base d., 5" h. . . . . .45.00 to 50.00

Horse rearing book end, black, Fostoria Glass Co., 3 x 5" base, 6" l., 7½" h. (single) 85.00

Horse rearing book end, clear, L. E. Smith, 1940's, 3 x 5½" base, 5¾" l., 8" h. (single) 22.00

Horse rearing book end, dark green, L. E. Smith, 1940's, 3 x 5½" base, 5¾" l., 8" h. (single) 45.00

Pelican, clear, Fostoria Glass Co., 1938-44, 3" sq. base, 4½" w., 4½" h. 80.00

Penguin, clear, Fostoria Glass Co., 1938-44, 2" sq. base, 1½" w., 4½" h. 31.00

Penguin head stopper for decanter, clear, A.H. Heisey & Co. 60.00

Pheasant w/turned head, light blue, Paden City Glass Mfg. Co., 2½ x 2¾" base, 12" l., 7" h. 95.00

Plug Horse Sparky, amber, A.H. Heisey & Co., 1941-46, 3½" l., 4¼" h. 565.00

Plug Horse Sparky, clear, A.H. Heisey & Co., 1941-46, 3½" l., 4¼" h. 95.00

Police Dog (German Shepherd) book end, amethyst w/frosted base, New Martinsville Glass Mfg. Co., 1937-50, 5 1/8" h. (single) 125.00

Pony, long-legged, clear, New Martinsville Glass Mfg. Co., 5¼ x 3¼" oval base, 4¼" l., 12" h. 92.50

Pony standing, clear, A.H. Heisey & Co., 1940-52, 2¼ x 1½" base, 3" l., 5" h. 95.00

Pony standing, chocolate (caramel slag), Imperial Glass Co., Heisey mold 25.00

Pony standing, clear, Paden City Glass Mfg. Co., 5½ x 3" base, 12" h. 52.50

Poodle finial powder dish, marigold sprayed-on finish, Jeannette Glass Co., 6" h. 14.50

Pouter Pigeon, clear, A.H. Heisey & Co., 1947-49, 6½" h. ....450.00 to 525.00

Pouter Pigeon book end, clear, Cambridge Glass Co., 4 x 5" base, 6" h. (single) 68.00

Pouter Pigeon book ends, clear, Paden City Glass Mfg. Co., 3 x 3¾" base, 6½" h., pr. 82.50

Puppy dog electric night lamp, milk white on black base 210.00

Rooster fighting, clear, A.H. Heisey & Co., 1940-46, 8½" h. 140.00

Sea Horse book end, clear, Fostoria Glass Co., 1938-44, 8" h. (single) ....75.00 to 85.00

Seal, lilac, Fostoria Glass Co., 1938-44, 3¼" sq. base, 3¾" h. (ILLUS.) 80.00

Show Horse, clear, A.H. Heisey & Co., 7 3/8" h. 1,200.00

Sparrow, clear, A.H. Heisey & Co., 1942-45, 4" l., 2¼" h. ......65.00 to 75.00

Star Fish book end, clear, New Martinsville Glass Mfg. Co., 6¼ x 2¾" base, 7¾" h. (single) 29.00

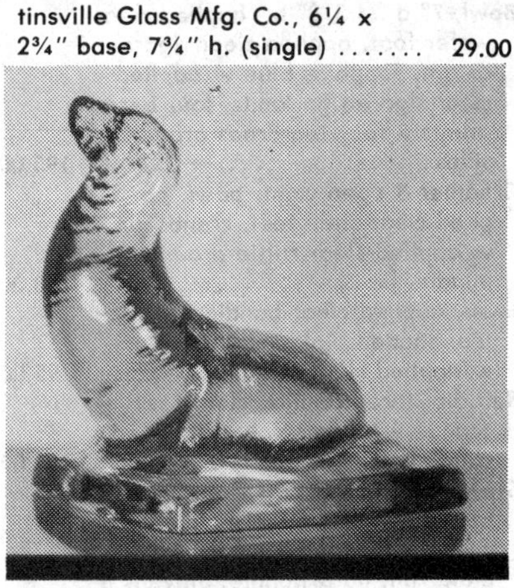

Fostoria Seal

Swan candlesticks, Sahara (yellow), double swan bodies form a graceful heart, A.H. Heisey & Co., 6½" h., pr. 275.00

Swan w/spread wings, clear, Duncan & Miller Glass Co., 12" w., 11" h. 30.00

Swan family, clear, A.H. Heisey & Co., 7" h. mother, 1947-53 & two 2¼" h. cygnets, 1947-49, 3 pcs. 585.00

APPLIQUED

Simply stated, this is an art glass form with applied decoration. Sometimes master glass craftsmen applied stems or branches to an art glass object and then added molded glass flowers or fruit specimens to these branches or stems. At other times a button of molten glass was daubed on the object and a tool pressed over it to form a prunt in the form of a raspberry, rosette or other shape. Always the work of a skilled glassmaker, applied decoration can be found on both cased (two-layer) and single layer glass. The English firm of Stevens and Williams is renowned for the appliqued glass they produced.

Basket, applied clear twisted thorn handle, vaseline opalescent Diamond Quilted patt. w/applied pink flowers & clear leaves, 6¾ x 5¾", 7" h. $185.00

Basket, applied clear twisted thorn handle, deep royal blue shading to lighter blue w/two applied white opal flowers & clear leaves, 7½ x 4½", 8½" h. 225.00

Bowl, 6½" d., 3¼" h., 8-crimp top, deep cranberry w/applied clear leaves & branch 265.00

Bowl, 7" d., 4 3/8" h., applied clear wafer foot, applied clear rigaree at rim, sapphire blue w/applied clear rigaree garlands, four berry prunts & four teardrops around sides 195.00

Creamer & open sugar bowl, applied clear shell feet, cranberry w/applied clear ruffle around middle, pr. 150.00

Ewer, applied clear handle, ruffled top, shaded pink cased in clear w/applied clear branch & leaves .. 95.00

Salt dip, three applied clear feet, orange w/double row of applied clear shells, 3¼" d., 2 3/8" h..... 85.00

Sweetmeat jar, cov., cased, cream opaque w/three applied amber & green leaves, pink lining, silver plate rim, lid & handle, Stevens & Williams, 3½" d., 6" h. 195.00

Vase, 8" h., 2¾" d., coiled stem, applied vaseline petal feet, ruffled top, cranberry shading to vaseline opalescent w/applied vaseline spiral trim 110.00

Vase, 8¾" h., 4 3/8" d., cased, rich pink w/applied clear flower & branch, white lining 118.00

Vase, 9¾" h., swirled cylinder w/fluted mouth, applied five-petal foot, lime green shading to clear w/applied white flower & twisted leaves 150.00

ART GLASS BASKETS

Popular in the late Victorian era, these ornate hand-crafted glass baskets were often given as gifts. Sometimes made with unusually tall handles and applied feet, these fragile ornaments usually command a good price when they survive intact.

Amethyst, squared fluted shape w/wide vaseline opalescent edge & applied vaseline handle, 4¾" d., 7 3/8" h. $175.00

Blue opalescent, tri-cornered, Seaweed patt., applied thorn handle, 6 x 6", 7" h. to top of handle 145.00

Cased, creamy opaque exterior, deep rose interior, amber edging around ruffled rim, applied amber twisted handle, 6" d., 8" h. 150.00

Cased, opaque white exterior w/Hobnail patt., heavenly blue interior, tightly ruffled edge, applied sapphire blue thorn handle, 5¼ x 6", 5¼" h. 165.00

Cased, opaque white exterior w/Hobnail patt., shaded apricot interior, applied clear thorn handle, 5½" d., 6¼" h. 175.00

Cased, pink exterior, white interior, fluted top edge, applied clear wide edge & reeded handle, 3 5/8" d., 7½" h. 165.00

Cased, pink w/green spatter w/clear casing, applied clear twisted handle, embossed rosettes around sides, 5" d., 6¾" h. 135.00

Cobalt blue, applied insects, in golden metal frame, Moser, 8" d., 5" h. 1,750.00

Cranberry, round body w/applied clear reeded handle, applied clear feet & applied clear leaves around rim, 4½" d., 7¼" h. 175.00

Cranberry, reversed poke bonnet shape, Paneled Optic patt., applied clear edging, handle & trim, 6 1/8 x 8 3/8", 12" h............. 295.00

Cranberry, Swirl patt., applied clear handle, top edging & "drippings," 6 3/8 x 8½", 14 1/8" h........... 325.00

Creamy opaque, rose bowl shape w/applied amber edging around ribbon candy rim, applied amber twisted handle, appled amber branches w/pink & amber leaves, applied white & pink spatter flower, 4¼" d., 7" h. 148.00

Green shading to opalescent, flower form rim, applied clear twisted handle, 4" w., 6" h. 85.00

Lemon yellow satin overlay, square ruffled shape, applied frosted, braided handle, 5" w., 6" h. 145.00

Pink candy stripe cased exterior w/embossed swirl design, white interior, ruffled rim, applied square clear thorn handle, 5" d., 6½" h. 195.00

Pink opalescent shaded to amber, applied pink twisted handle, transparent cranberry edging, embossed circular design, 5 5/8" d., 5" h. 110.00

Pink opalescent to greenish vaseline w/half circle designs, vaseline edging, applied vaseline twisted rope handle, 7½" sq., 10" h...... 375.00

Pink opaque exterior w/dimpled sides & tiny brown string-like designs under outer clear casing, pink interior, ruffled top, applied clear thorn handle, 5¼" d., 6½" h. 125.00

Spangled pink w/gold mica flecks, crimped top, applied clear thorn handle, 4½" w., 6" h. 210.00

Spatter, aqua & white, crimped top, applied aqua thorn handle, 5½" w., 5½"h. 195.00

Vaseline opalescent "overshot," hobnailed edge, applied vaseline twisted handle, 8 x 9¼", 6½" h. 185.00

BACCARAT

Baccarat Inkstand

Baccarat glass has been made by Cristalleries de Baccarat, France, since 1765. The firm has produced various glasswares of excellent quality and paperweights. Baccarat's Rose Tiente is often referred to as Baccarat's Amberina.

Bobeche, Rose Tiente Paneled Zipper Swirl patt., 3 3/8" d. $40.00
Bowl, 8" d., scalloped foot, Rose Tiente Swirl patt., signed 95.00
Celery tray, Rose Tiente Swirl patt., signed, 3½ x 9½" 55.00
Cologne bottle w/matching stopper, Rose Tiente Paneled Zipper Swirl patt., 2¼" d., 5¾" h. 65.00
Cologne bottle, clear to cranberry, one jewel in screw-on cap, 6" h. 145.00
Cologne bottle w/matching stopper, Rose Tiente Paneled Laurel Leaves patt., 2½" d., 6 3/8" h. 65.00
Cologne bottle w/matching stopper, Rose Tiente Swirl patt., 3" d., 7 1/8" h. 65.00
Cologne bottle w/matching stopper, Rose Tiente Swirl patt., 3¾" d., 8½" h. 75.00
Compote, 4 1/8" d., 4" h., Rose Tiente Swirl patt. 85.00
Goblet, D'Assas patt., clear 40.00
Inkstand, cast as a clear breaking wave w/a gilt-bronze mermaid languishing on the crest, flanked by two inkwells, one w/gilt-bronze cover cast as a seashell & the other a porthole cover, gilding rubbed, ca. 1900, 14¼" l. (ILLUS.) 4,125.00
Perfume bottle, made for "Houbigant," 4" h. 65.00
Perfume bottle w/original stopper, Rose Tiente Swirl patt., 5½" h. 65.00
Perfume bottle w/original stopper, Rose Tiente Sunburst Swirl patt., 6½" h. 90.00
Pitcher, water, Harcourt patt., clear 145.00
Wine, cobalt blue bowl, clear stem, signed, 7¾" 49.00
Wine, D'Assas patt., clear 55.00

BLOWN THREE MOLD

Blown Three Mold Decanter

This type of glass was entirely or partially blown in a mold from about 1820 in the United States. The object was formed and the decoration impressed upon it by blowing the glass into a metal mold, usually of three but sometimes more sections, hinged together. Mold-blown glass actually dates back to ancient times. Recent research reveals that certain geometric patterns were reproduced in the 1920's and collectors are urged to read all recent information available. McKearin reference numbers are to George L. and Helen McKearin's book, "American Glass."

Basket, flaring rim w/applied handle, rayed base, iron pontil, 3½" h. (GV-24) $145.00
Carafe, flared mouth, alternating horizontal & vertical bands of ribbing, rayed base w/pontil, rare dark yellow-green, attributed to the Mount Vernon Glass Company, qt., 9¼" h. 2,300.00
Decanter w/slightly mismatched stopper, geometric, clear, half pint (GII-24) 850.00
Decanter w/original stopper, geometric, clear, qt., 8" h. plus stopper (GIII-5) 245.00
Decanter (no stopper), geometric, olive amber, pt., 6¾" h., GIII-16 (ILLUS.) 300.00

Decanter w/original stopper, geometric, rayed base, clear, qt. (GIII-24) 235.00

Decanter w/original stopper, geometric w/round reserves w/large sunburst star on sides surrounded by vertical ribbing & same pattern on stopper, pale yellow-green, Boston and Sandwich Glass Company, qt. (GV-10) 375.00

Hat shape, geometric, clear (GIII-4) 145.00

Pitcher, flared mouth, geometric, clear, applied handle, 6½" h. (GIII-5) 775.00

Pitcher, blown in Gothic Arch decanter mold w/word "Gin" embossed in reverse, applied hollow handle w/curl ending, flaring mouth, clear, rare, possibly unique, pt. (GIV-7) 3,700.00

Tumbler, geometric, clear, Boston and Sandwich Glass Company, Sandwich, Massachusetts, two small chips on interior of lip (GIV-2) 350.00

BOHEMIAN

Bohemian Glass Vase

Numerous types of glass were made in the once-independent country of Bohemia and fine colored, cut and engraved glass was turned out. Flashed and other inexpensive wares also were made and many of these, including amber- and ruby-shaded glass, were exported to the United States last century and in the present one. One favorite pattern in the late 19th and early 20th centuries was Deer and Castle. Another was Deer and Pine Tree.

Bowl, 9" d., footed, Deer & Castle patt., amber cut to clear $85.00

Bowl, 10" d., 4 3/8" h., Vintage patt., engraved grape clusters & vines, ruby, frosted & clear 50.00

Cologne bottle w/matching steeple stopper, Vintage patt., alternating clear & ruby panels, 3" d., 6¾" h. 125.00

Compote, open, 7½" d., 9½" h., white cut to green w/multicolor enameled floral designs 80.00

Cruet w/original stopper, Deer & Castle patt., ruby & clear 85.00

Decanter w/original stopper, Deer & Castle patt., ruby cut to clear, 15" h. ....75.00 to 100.00

Decanter w/original faceted stopper, faceted neck & base, Vintage patt., ruby & clear 125.00

Dressing table box w/hinged bronze lid, rectangular, clear & frosted overlaid in cobalt blue & cut on four sides w/hunting hound or game in a forest, applied bronze handles, ca. 1900, 10¾" l. 605.00

Goblet, Deer & Castle patt., amber & clear ....35.00 to 50.00

Lamp, Deer & Castle patt., ruby & clear, brass & marble base 250.00

Pitcher, 5½" h., Deer & Castle patt., amber, frosted & clear, gold trim 115.00

Salt dip, tab handles, clear & ruby w/squiggly designs, gold trim, 1½ x 2 7/8" oval, 1 1/8" h. 65.00

Vase, 5" h., flared Diamond & Oval patt., cranberry cut to clear 145.00

Vase, 9½" h., lower half w/elongated cut ovals, upper half w/frosted engraved deer in woodland design, amber cut to clear (ILLUS.) .. 225.00

Vase, 12" h., footed, flared rim, etched birds & trees design, ruby & clear 75.00

BREAD PLATES & TRAYS

Memorial Hall Tray

Scores of special bread plates were

produced last century and early in this one, of pattern glass and as commemorative pieces. Also see CUT and PATTERN GLASS.

Ball & Swirl patt. plate, factory scene center, "The Tiffin Glass Co. Incorporated, Apr. 24, 1888," clear, 10 7/8" d. $285.00

Cupid's Hunt patt. platter w/Virginia Dare center, clear 65.00

Dolphin patt. platter, oval, clear frosted center w/dolphin pattern, pattern on handles, clear frosted dolphin feet 225.00

Memorial Hall tray, hand holding baton handles, "Continental - 1776 - 1876" motto border, clear, 13 x 9" (ILLUS.) 65.00

Old Statehouse tray, shows Independence Hall above "Old Statehouse, Philadelphia, Erected 1739," sapphire blue.............. 195.00

Sheaf of Wheat patt. platter, maple leaf handles, sheaf in center & motto border, 13 x 9 5/8 x 2½" deep 75.00

Stork plate, clear frosted 85.00

BRIDE'S BASKETS & BOWLS

Cased Glass Bride's Basket

These are berry or fruit bowls, once popular as wedding gifts, hence the name.

Butterscotch bowl, ruffled & fluted rim, ornate silver plate pedestal base w/four floral embossed arms, overall 10½" h. $375.00

Cased bowl, shaded rose interior, white exterior w/enameled blue, peach & white florals & green leaves outlined in gold, ormolu frame, 7 3/8 x 5", 6½" h......... 135.00

Cased bowl, soft heavenly blue interior w/enameled white leaves & florals w/yellow centers, applied light sapphire blue ruffled rim, white exterior, ormolu basket frame, 8 3/8 x 6 5/8", 7¼" h..... 265.00

Cased bowl, shaded deep pink interior w/gold band & enameled white florals w/green leaves, white exterior, fluted rim w/applied clear edging, silver plate basket frame w/applied flowers at sides, marked "Pairpoint," 10¾" d., 12" h. 325.00

Case bowl, deep raspberry pink interior, opaque white exterior, enameled multicolored florals, applied light amber scalloped rim, silver plate frame marked "Tufts," 11¼" d., overall 10¾" h. 225.00

Cased bowl, heavenly blue interior w/deeper blue applied edging, enameled white & yellow florals w/green foliage, creamy white exterior, brass chain link overhead handle & footed base, 11¼ x 7¼", 12¼" h. (ILLUS.)..... 750.00

Cased bowl, gold interior w/enameled white florals w/pink leaves & foliage, white exterior, original silver plate frame, 13½" d., 11½" h. 550.00

Green opalescent bowl, silver plate frame marked "Rogers," 9¾" d., 7¾" h. 90.00

Opalescent bowl w/applied Amberina Verde rim, enameled decoration, ornate silver plate frame w/high figural pedestal in the shape of a standing lady, Barbour Silver Co. frame 1,350.00

Pale to dark pink scalloped bowl w/raised gold florals, signed "Webb," 12" d. 195.00

Pink shading to blue then to white overlay bowl, ruffled rim, enameled yellow, pink & white flowers & two large gold heart-shaped reserves w/enameled blue & white flowers, ornate silver plate stand, 10½" d., 8¾" h. (stand resilvered) 195.00

Robin's egg blue overlay bowl w/applied clear frilly rim, painted bust portrait of a lady, enameled floral decoration, 12" d., 3¾" base d. .. 200.00

Vaseline opalescent footed bowl, deep scalloped top, threaded dimpled body, ca. 1880, 4" w., 7" h. 125.00

White opaline ruffled bowl w/blue enameling & pink trim, ornate silver plate frame w/blackberry clusters marked "Pairpoint" 225.00

BRISTOL

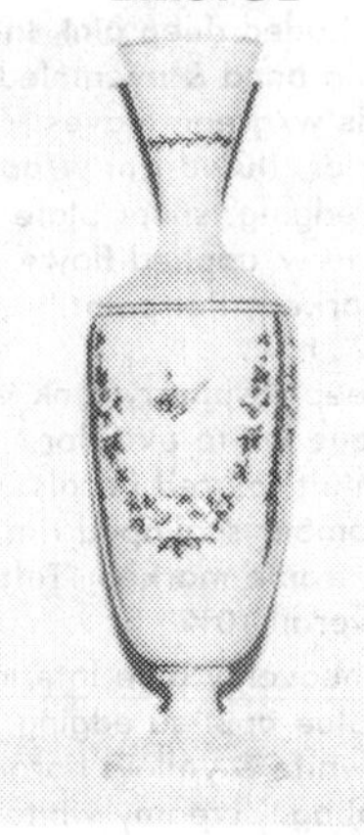

Bristol Vase

While glass was made in several glasshouses in Bristol, England, the generic name Bristol glass is applied today by collectors to a variety of semi-opaque glasses, frequently decorated by enameling, and made both abroad and in United States glasshouses in the 19th and 20th centuries.

Box w/hinged lid, ormolu feet, opaque white w/soft blue to cream scenes of ladies & lady w/man on lid, lavender florals on sides, 3¾" d., 3¾" h. $100.00

Box w/hinged lid, ormolu feet, opaque white w/heavenly blue scenes of cupids outlined in white, gold enamel scrollwork, 3¼" d., 4 3/8" h. 165.00

Cracker jar, lavender-pink w/enameled white florals & leaves & blue forget-me-nots decor, silver plate rim, cover & bail handle, 5 1/8" d., 6" h. 145.00

Cracker jar, grey-brown w/enameled ostrich one side & stork other, silver plate rim, cover & bail handle, 4¼" d., 7" h....... 265.00

Cruet w/blue ball stopper, applied blue handle, 3-petal top, heavenly blue opaque w/enameled yellow florals & leaves, 2½" d., 6½" h... 75.00

Dresser set: cov. box, perfume bottle, ring tree & tray; pastel green opaque w/pink, blue, white & yellow florals & gold latticework, gold trim, 4 pcs. 275.00

Flower pot on matching stand, square, turquoise blue w/enameled yellow, blue, white & rust florals, green leaves, insects & birds, 5½" w., 7¼" h., 2 pcs. .. 198.00

Perfume bottle w/stopper, blue w/white, yellow & orange florals & green leaves, 6¼" h. 65.00

Urn, cov., pink opaque, oval gold medallion enhanced w/white scrollwork enclosing scene of boy & girl w/lamb, overall white dots & gold bands w/blue dots & enameled blue & white trim, 5" d., 17" h. 595.00

Urn, cov., footed, cinnamon & white w/enameled bust of drummer boy in gilt wreath-like surround, 18½" h. 375.00

Vases, 7" h., robin's egg blue w/enameled white egrets & foliage, pr. 65.00

Vases, 8¼" h., 3" d., 2-handled, pedestal base, turquoise blue w/gilt panels of enameled white, yellow & gold florals & leaves, pr. 165.00

Vase, 10 1/8" h., 5½" d., bulbous, rectangular pedestal foot, turquoise blue w/enameled white & cream florals & green leaves w/birds perched on branch, gold trim 165.00

Vase, 11" h., footed, pink w/enameled floral swag & butterfly (ILLUS.) 95.00

Vase, 11¾" h., 5¾" d., applied black handles w/gold trim, opaque light beige w/four brown birds, grasses & blue cornflowers, gold trim w/white enamel dots ... 165.00

Vase, 13" h., tannish pink matte w/enameled pastel florals, leaves, bird & butterfly, gold trim 85.00

BURMESE

Burmese is a single-layer glass that shades from pink to pale yellow. It was patented by Frederick S. Shirley and made by the Mt. Washington Glass Co. A license to produce the glass in England was granted to Thomas Webb & Sons, which called its articles Queen's Burmese. Gunderson Burmese was made briefly about the middle of this century.

Bell, rigaree top loop, Mt. Washington Glass Co., 5¾" h. $225.00

Berry set: two master bowls & eight sauce dishes; crimped rims, satin finish, Mt. Washington Glass Co., 10 pcs. 3,500.00

Bottle-vase, h.p. fern fronds, unsigned, 4" d., 8½" h. 395.00

Bowl, 2¾" d., 2¼" h., piecrust rim, satin finish, signed "Thos. Webb & Sons Queen's Burmese Ware" 210.00

Bowl, 6¼" d., 3¾" h., scalloped top w/applied edging, h.p. florals, Thomas Webb & Sons 1,100.00

Bowl-vase, fluted, satin finish, h.p. green ivy leaves & vines, unsigned Webb, 3¾" d., 2¾" h. 325.00

Cologne bottle w/hallmarked sterling silver screw-on lid, enameled multicolored butterfly hovering over spray of diminutive amber flowers w/gold foliage, Thomas Webb & Sons, 4" h. 725.00

Creamer, pear-shaped, satin finish, Mt. Washington Glass Co. 385.00

Creamer & open sugar bowl, applied pale yellow handles, satin finish, Mt. Washington Glass Co., pr. 785.00

Creamer & open sugar bowl, 6-sided top, satin finish, h.p. grapes & green leaves, unsigned Webb, in silver plate frame, 3 pcs. 795.00

Crocus bowls, set of four joined in a line, satin finish, h.p. five-petal flowers w/green & brown leaves, frosted berry prunts each end, Thomas Webb & Sons, overall 9¼ x 2¼", 2¼" h. 550.00

Cruet w/original stopper, bulbous ribbed body 595.00

Cruet w/original stopper, satin finish, Mt. Washington Glass Co..... 695.00

Finger bowl, nine-scallop top, satin finish, Mt. Washington Glass Co., 6" d., 2¾" h. 285.00

Jar, cov., enameled butterfly & blossoms, signed "Thos. Webb Queen's Burmese," silver plate lid & bail handle, 3¾" 575.00

Marmalade jar, satin finish, unsigned Webb, in original silver plate frame w/lid & spoon, 5¾" d., 5" h. 265.00

Mustard jar w/silver plate lid, glossy 175.00

Pitcher, squat form, satin finish, Mt. Washington Glass Co., 2 qt....... 585.00

Pitcher, tankard, tightly crimped top & refined spout, two heavily enameled artistically presented orchids on front, one on reverse, applied handle, gold detail on handle, base & edge of the crimped top & spout 635.00

Pitcher, water, bulbous w/applied square yellow handle, satin finish,

Burmese Pitcher

Mt. Washington Glass Co. (ILLUS.) 985.00

Rose bowl, 6-crimp top, satin finish, enameled white & blue florals w/brown leaves, unsigned Webb, 2½" d., 2¼" h. 295.00

Rose bowl, 8-crimp top, enameled blossoms & leaves on vine, signed "Queen's Burmese Ware Thos. Webb & Sons," 4" d., 3½" h. 450.00

Salt & pepper shakers w/original tops, Mt. Washington Glass Co., pr. 235.00

Salt dip, open, footed, enameled bittersweet-colored blossoms on branches of shiny gold, signed "Thos. Webb & Sons, Queen's Burmese Ware Patent" 445.00

Sweetmeat dish, glossy exterior w/applied yellow shell trim around middle, satin finish, interior band of enameled florals & green leaves, in silver plate basket frame, unsigned Webb, overall 6¼" d., 7" h. 335.00

Toothpick holder, bulbous w/lobes & ribs & star-shaped rim, satin finish, ca. 1885, 1 7/8" h. 220.00

Toothpick holder, refired yellow edge, enameled blue & pink florals, Mt. Washington Glass Co., 2" h. 465.00

Toothpick holder, tricorner top curls inward, Diamond Quilted patt., Mt. Washington Glass Co., 2" h... 315.00

Diamond Quilted Burmese Toothpick

Toothpick holder, cylindrical w/squared rim, Diamond Quilted patt. (ILLUS.) 225.00

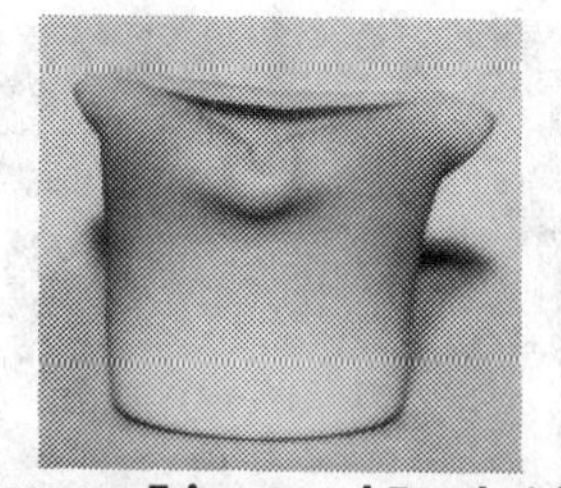

Burmese Tricornered Toothpick

Toothpick holder, yellow tricornered rim (ILLUS.) 185.00
Tumbler, satin finish, probably Mt. Washington Glass Co., 3¾" h. ... 190.00
Tumbler, glossy finish, Mt. Washington Glass Co. 285.00
Tumbler, whiskey, satin finish, Diamond Quilted patt., small enameled blue & white forget-me-nots & green leaves, original Mt. Washington label, 2 7/8" h., 2¼" d. 325.00
Vase, 2¾" h., 3" d., flower petal top, satin finish, enameled red berries w/green & tan leaves, signed "Thos. Webb Queen's Burmese Ware" 410.00
Vase, 3½" h., 2 7/8" d., flower petal top, glossy finish, enameled brown pine cones & green pine needles, signed "Thos. Webb Queen's Burmese Ware" 350.00
Vase, 3 5/8" h., 3¾" d., wide flared fluted top, dimpled sides, satin finish, slightly raised yellow ribs, unsigned Webb 195.00
Vase, 4" h., 2 5/8" d., ruffled top, ruffled yellow pedestal foot, satin finish, enameled lavender five-petal flowers w/green & brown leaves, unsigned Webb 300.00
Vase, 4 3/8" h., 3½" d., flower petal top, three applied yellow feet, satin finish, enameled green maiden hair ferns, signed "Thos. Webb Queen's Burmese Ware" ... 525.00
Vase, 5 1/8" h., 2 7/8" d., applied yellow handles, satin finish, enameled lavender five-petal flowers w/green & brown leaves, signed "Thos. Webb Queen's Burmese Ware" 685.00
Vase, 7 5/8" h., 4" d., bottle-shaped, satin finish, enameled red flowers, brown leaves, smaller clusters of yellow flowers, brown bird in flight & small butterfly at back, signed "Thos. Webb & Sons Queen's Burmese Ware" 895.00
Vase, 9" h., 4¾" widest d., elongated egg shape w/short, narrow flared neck, enameled shaded gold daisy-like blossoms & foliage outlined in raised gold, Mt. Washington Glass Co. 787.00
Vase, 11½" h., 6¾" widest d., bulbous w/6" slender neck w/h.p. gold oak leaf, body w/stylized enameled oak leaves, acorns & other adornments outlined in raised gold, Mt. Washington Glass Co. 1,250.00

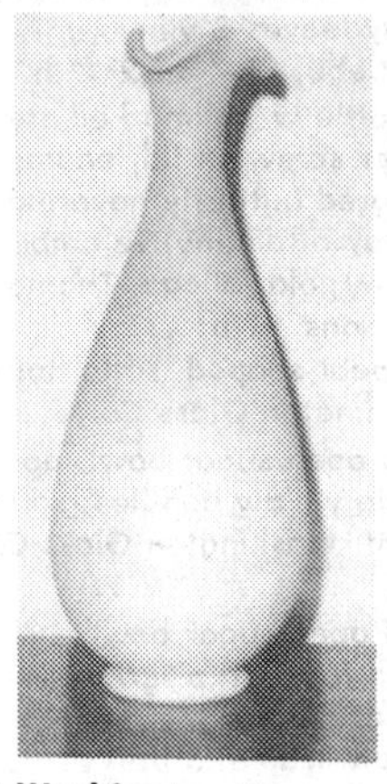

Mount Washington Burmese Vase

Vase, 12½" h., bowling pin shape w/trefoil top, satin finish, Mt. Washington Glass Co. (ILLUS.) 685.00
Vase, 12½" h., 6" d., pear-shaped w/stick neck, satin finish, Mt. Washington Glass Co. 950.00
Waste bowl, crimped rim, Thomas Webb & Sons, 5¾" w., 2¾" h. ... 225.00
Water set: pitcher & six tumblers; satin finish, Mt. Washington Glass Co., 7 pcs. 2,250.00

CAMBRIDGE

Crown Tuscan Compote

The Cambridge Glass Company was founded in Ohio in 1901. Numerous pieces are now sought, especially those designed by Arthur J. Bennett, including Crown Tuscan. Other productions included crystal animals, "Black Amethyst," "blanc opaque," and other types of colored glass. The firm was finally closed in 1954. It should not be confused with the New England Glass Co., Cambridge, Massachusetts.

Ashtray, etched Rose Point patt., crystal, 2½" sq. $55.00
Ashtray, pressed Caprice patt., blue, 5" 20.00
Book ends, model of an eagle, crystal, 6" h., pr. 155.00
Bowl, 10" d., Decagon patt., amber 25.00
Bowl, 10" d., footed, Honeycomb patt., Amberina (ruby top delicately blending off to amber) 66.00
Bowl, 13" d., etched Appleblossom patt., blue 48.00
Bowl, cream soup, etched Diane patt., crystal 45.00
Bowl, Ram's Head handles, Rubina (ruby top blending to blue, then to green) 900.00
Butter dish, cov., etched Appleblossom patt., crystal 90.00
Butter dish, cov., etched Rose Point patt., crystal, ¼ lb. 285.00
Cake plate, footed, pressed Caprice patt., blue, 11½" 42.00
Cake plate, handled, Heatherbloom (delicate orchid) 45.00
Candleholders, three-light, pressed Caprice patt., crystal, pr. 130.00
Candlesticks, etched Portia patt., keyhole stem, gold encrusted, pr. 66.00
Candlesticks, Twist patt., Jade (blue-green opaque), 8½" h., pr. 95.00
Candlesticks, two-light, Everglade patt., amber, pr. 140.00
Candy box, cov., three-part, etched Rose Point patt., crystal 40.00
Candy dish, cov., three-footed, Caprice Alpine patt., blue, 6" 135.00
Candy jar, cov., Martha Washington patt., pink, 10" 55.00
Centerpiece bowl, ruffled & fluted rim, four-footed, pressed Caprice patt., ice blue, 12" d. 45.00
Centerpiece bowl, Everglade patt., Moonlight (delicate pastel blue), 13" d., 6" h. 195.00
Champagne, etched Elaine patt., crystal 22.50
Cigarette box, cov., pressed Caprice patt., blue 45.00
Cocktail, Carmen (clear brilliant ruby red) bowl, clear Nude Lady stem 100.00
Cocktail, etched Elaine patt., crystal 22.50
Cocktail, pressed Caprice patt., crystal 14.00
Cocktail shaker, etched Chantilly patt., crystal 122.00
Cocktail shaker, etched Portia patt., crystal 79.00
Compote, 6½", Honeycomb patt., Rubina 120.00
Compote, 7" d., 5½" h., Tomato (yellow-green at top, blending into red & yellow-green at bottom) 85.00
Compote, 7" d., 7½" h., Seashell patt., Nude Lady stem 120.00
Console set: 13½" console bowl & pair 4" candlesticks; pressed Caprice patt., crystal w/gold overlay, 3 pcs. 38.00
Cordial, etched Chantilly patt., crystal 78.00
Cordial, etched Rose Point patt., crystal, 1 oz. 45.00
Creamer & sugar bowl, Everglade patt., crystal, pr. 35.00
Creamer & sugar bowl, etched Lily of the Valley patt., crystal, pr. 150.00
Creamer & sugar bowl, individual size, etched Rose Point patt., crystal, pr. 48.00
Crown Tuscan bowl, 10" d. 95.00
Crown Tuscan candy dish, footed, ruffled 40.00
Crown Tuscan cocktail, Nude Lady stem 75.00
Crown Tuscan compote, open, 5½", gold trim, Nude Lady stem (ILLUS.) 145.00
Crown Tuscan compote, cov., 6" d., 6½" h., Seashell patt., gilt trim, unsigned 49.00
Crown Tuscan compote, open, 8" d., 5½" h., crimped, Hobnail patt. 45.00
Crown Tuscan cornucopia-vase, 10" h. 75.00
Crown Tuscan dish, four-footed, 8" oval 50.00
Crown Tuscan ivy ball 45.00
Crown Tuscan urn, cov., 12" .... 275.00 to 300.00
Cruet w/original stopper, loop handle, etched Rose Point patt., crystal, 6 oz. 70.00
Cruet w/original stopper, etched Wildflower patt., crystal, 6 oz. 115.00
Cup & saucer, pressed Caprice patt., blue 32.00
Cup & saucer, Decagon patt., pink 16.00
Decanter w/stopper, Mt. Vernon patt., crystal, 40 oz. 68.00
Decanter, etched Rose Point patt., crystal, 28 oz. 295.00

Figure flower holder, "Bashful Charlotte," Moonlight, 6½" h. 425.00
Figure flower holder, "Bashful Charlotte," pink, 6½" h. 85.00
Figure flower holder, "Bashful Charlotte," emerald green, 13" h...... 350.00
Figure flower holder, "Draped Lady," amber, 8½" h. 175.00
Figure flower holder, "Draped Lady," crystal, 8½" h. 75.00
Figure flower holder, "Draped Lady," crystal, 12½" h. 150.00
Figure flower holder, "Draped Lady," light emerald green, 13" h. 280.00
Figure flower holder, "Mandolin Lady," green 275.00
Figure flower holder, "Rose Lady," green frosted 115.00
Figure flower holder, "Two-Kid," amber frosted 230.00
Figure flower holder, "Two-Kid," crystal 92.00
Figure flower holder, "Two-Kid," green 195.00
Flower holder, Bird (Blue Jay), crystal 77.00
Flower holder, Sea Gull, crystal, 8" 32.00
Goblet, pressed Caprice patt., blue 32.00
Goblet, etched Rose Point patt., crystal 24.00
Ice bucket, Decagon patt., amber... 22.00

Cambridge Liqueur Set

Liqueur set: decanter & six liqueurs; amethyst, in Farberware tray, 8 pcs. (ILLUS. of partial set) 125.00
Nut cups, pedestal base, Peach-Blo (light transparent pink), ca. 1920, 3", set of 6 .... 55.00
Pitcher, ball-shaped, Heatherbloom, 80 oz. 225.00
Pitcher, etched Chantilly patt., crystal, 76 oz. 145.00
Pitcher, tankard, Tally Ho patt., crystal, 74 oz. 95.00
Plate, 9" d., pressed Caprice patt., crystal 25.00
Plate, 10½" d., needle-etched Willow Blue patt., crystal 120.00
Plate, 12" d., etched Rose Point patt., crystal 60.00
Plate, dinner, etched Elaine patt., crystal 25.00
Punch bowl, Tally Ho patt., red, w/clear ladle, 2 pcs. 125.00
Relish, three-part, etched Diane patt., crystal, 8" 26.00
Relish, three-part, pressed Caprice patt., blue 35.00
Salt & pepper shakers w/sterling silver tops & bases, etched Chantilly patt., crystal, 3½" h., pr. 20.00
Sherbet, Cascade patt., crystal 6.00
Sherbet, etched Rose Point patt., forest green 77.00
Stein, Tally Ho patt., Carmen 45.00
Swan, Ebony (opaque black), 4½" .. 95.00
Swan, green, 3½" 28.00
Swan, Mandarin Gold (very light golden yellow), 6" 89.00
Swan, Moonlight, 5" 22.00
Tray w/center handle, Decagon patt., amber 12.00
Tray w/center handle, etched Diane patt., Heatherbloom 90.00
Vase, 10" h., trumpet-shaped, Tomato 98.00
Vase, 12" h., keyhole stem, etched Rose Point patt., crystal 125.00
Wine, clear bowl, Ebony, Nude Lady stem 75.00

CAMPHOR

All types of objects were made in so-called Camphor glass, which has a cloudy appearance as a result of exposure to acid fumes. It somewhat resembles gum camphor, from which it takes its name. It was pressed, blown and blown-molded.

Candlesticks, gold ring trim, 4½" base, 6¼" h., pr. $38.50
Candy dish, cov., Art Deco style nude women at base, green 80.00
Goblet, twisted stem & foot, yellow bowl w/medallion of enameled gold filigree around blue cabochon "jewel" circled by nine deep red cabochon "jewels," 7" h. 75.00
Goblet, plain, large 15.00
Plate, relief-molded kitten 37.50
Powder jar, cov., relief-molded irregular pattern, elephant on lid, green or pink, 1930's, each ....25.00 to 38.00
Toothpick holder, scalloped rim, Button Arches patt., Minnesota souvenir 17.50
Toothpick holder, barrel-shaped, green, metal rim at base & top ... 18.00

CARNIVAL GLASS

Earlier called Taffeta glass, the Carnival glass now being collected was introduced early in this century. Its producers gave it an iridescence that attempted to imitate that of some Tiffany glass. Collectors will find available books by leading authorities Donald E. Moore, Sherman Hand, Marion T. Hartung and Rose M. Presznick.

ACANTHUS (Imperial)

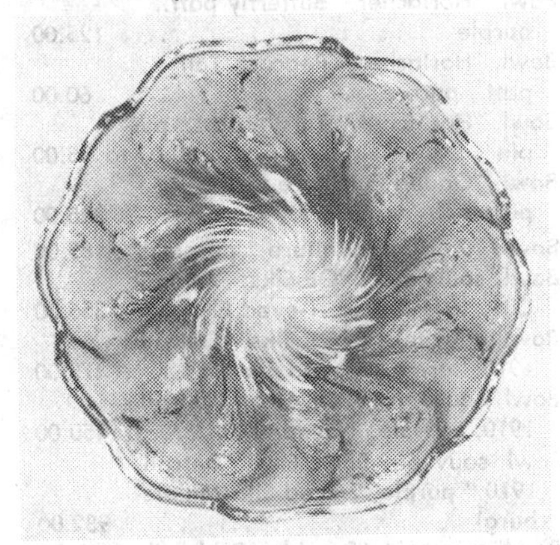

Acanthus Bowl

Bowl, 7" d., green $20.00
Bowl, 8" to 9" d., green 62.50
Bowl, 8" to 9" d., marigold (ILLUS.) 52.50
Bowl, 8" to 9" d., purple 60.00
Bowl, 8" to 9" d., smoky 65.00
Plate, 9" to 10" d., marigold 166.00
Plate, 9" to 10" d., smoky 182.00

ACORN (Fenton)

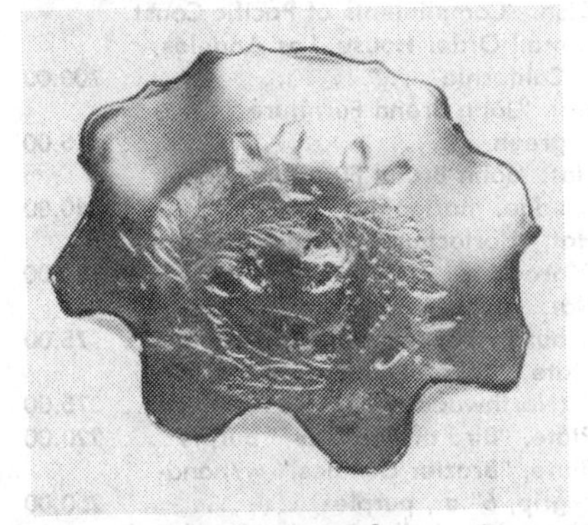

Acorn Bowl

Bowl, 5" d., ribbon candy rim, blue 60.00
Bowl, 5" d., marigold over milk white 300.00
Bowl, 7" d., ruffled, amber 110.00
Bowl, 7" d., aqua opalescent 103.00
Bowl, 7" d., blue 45.00
Bowl, 7" d., green 65.00
Bowl, 7" d., ice blue 150.00
Bowl, 7" d., marigold 30.00
Bowl, 7" d., marigold over milk white 155.00
Bowl, 7" d., purple 47.50
Bowl, 7" d., red 456.00
Bowl, 7" d., ruffled, vaseline 95.00
Bowl, 8" to 9" d., blue 60.00
Bowl, 8" to 9" d., marigold w/opalescent rim 300.00
Bowl, 8" to 9" d., ribbon candy rim, purple 50.00
Bowl, 8" to 9" d., ruffled, red (ILLUS.) 525.00
Bowl, ice cream shape, aqua 100.00
Bowl, ice cream shape, red slag 550.00
Bowl, ruffled, aqua 65.00
Bowl, ruffled, peach opalescent 375.00
Compote, vaseline (Millersburg) .... 1,250.00 to 2,000.00

ACORN BURRS (Northwood)

Acorn Burrs Tumbler

Berry set: master bowl & 4 sauce dishes; green, 5 pcs. 260.00
Berry set: master bowl & 6 sauce dishes; marigold, 7 pcs. 208.00
Bowl, master berry, 10" d., marigold 80.00
Bowl, master berry, 10" d., purple 130.00
Butter dish, cov., green .... 150.00 to 185.00
Butter dish, cov., marigold 150.00
Butter dish, cov., purple 225.00
Creamer, green 100.00
Creamer, marigold 80.00
Creamer, purple 125.00
Pitcher, water, marigold 315.00
Pitcher, water, purple 450.00
Punch bowl, marigold 400.00
Punch bowl base, ice blue 175.00
Punch bowl base, ice green 100.00
Punch bowl & base, ice green, 2 pcs. 1,800.00

Punch bowl & base, purple, 2 pcs. . . 450.00
Punch cup, green 32.50
Punch cup, ice blue 65.00
Punch cup, ice green 65.00
Punch cup, marigold 20.00
Punch cup, purple 32.00
Punch cup, white 67.00
Punch set: bowl, base & 4 cups; marigold, 6 pcs. 525.00
Punch set: bowl, base & 6 cups; green, 8 pcs. 975.00
Punch set: bowl, base & 6 cups; ice blue, 8 pcs. 3,750.00
Punch set: bowl, base & 6 cups; purple, 8 pcs. 775.00
Punch set: bowl, base & 6 cups; white, 8 pcs. 3,200.00
Punch set: bowl, base & 12 cups; white, 14 pcs. 2,850.00
Sauce dish, green 38.00
Sauce dish, marigold 20.00
Sauce dish, purple 58.00
Spooner, green 80.00
Spooner, marigold 67.50
Spooner, purple 87.50
Sugar bowl, cov., marigold 95.00
Sugar bowl, open, purple 125.00
Table set: cov. sugar bowl, creamer, spooner & cov. butter dish; green, 4 pcs. 475.00
Table set: cov. sugar bowl, creamer, spooner & cov. butter dish; purple, 4 pcs. 685.00
Tumbler, green (ILLUS.) 62.00
Tumbler, marigold 42.00
Tumbler, purple 55.00
Water set: pitcher & 4 tumblers; green, 5 pcs. 525.00
Water set: pitcher & 4 tumblers; marigold, 5 pcs. 450.00
Water set: pitcher & 6 tumblers; purple, 7 pcs. 785.00

ADVERTISING & SOUVENIR ITEMS

Brooklyn Bridge Unlettered Bowl

Ashtray, souvenir, "Cleveland Memorial," purple (Millersburg) . . 1,400.00
Basket, "John H. Brand Furniture Co., Wilmington, Del.," marigold 46.00
Basket, "Miller's Furniture," marigold 85.00
Bell, souvenir, BPOE Elks, "Atlantic City, 1911," blue 1,190.00
Bowl, 6¼" d., "Isaac Benesch," purple (Millersburg) 172.00
Bowl, "Burnheimer," blue 625.00
Bowl, "Horlacher," Butterfly patt., purple 125.00
Bowl, "Horlacher," Peacock Tail patt., purple 60.00
Bowl, "Horlacher," Thistle patt., purple . . . . 80.00 to 95.00
Bowl, "Ogden Furniture Co.," purple 225.00
Bowl, "Sterling Furniture," purple . . . 185.00
Bowl, souvenir, BPOE Elks, "Atlantic City, 1911," blue, 1-eyed Elk 356.00
Bowl, souvenir, BPOE Elks, "Detroit, 1910," green, 1-eyed Elk 475.00
Bowl, souvenir, BPOE Elks, "Detroit, 1910," purple, 1-eyed Elk 450.00
Bowl, souvenir, BPOE Elks, "Detroit, 1910," purple, 2-eyed Elk (Millersburg) 932.00
Bowl, souvenir, "Brooklyn Bridge," marigold 270.00
Bowl, souvenir, "Brooklyn Bridge," unlettered, marigold (ILLUS.) 550.00
Bowl, souvenir, "Millersburg Courthouse," purple 435.00
Bowl, souvenir, "Millersburg Courthouse," unlettered, purple 965.00
Card tray, "Fern Brand Chocolates," turned-up sides, 6¼" d., purple . . 175.00
Card tray, "Isaac Benesch," Holly Whirl patt., marigold 65.00
Dish, "Compliments of Pacific Coast Mail Order House, Los Angeles, California" 700.00
Hat, "John Brand Furniture," green 65.00
Hat, "John Brand Furniture," open edge, marigold 40.00
Hat, "Horlacher," Peacock Tail patt., green 100.00
Hat, "Miller's Furniture - Harrisburg," basketweave, marigold 75.00
Plate, "Ballard, California," purple (Northwood) 375.00
Plate, "Bird of Paradise," purple 220.00
Plate, "Brazier Candies," w/handgrip, 6" d., purple 250.00
Plate, "Cambell & Beasley," w/handgrip, purple 420.00
Plate, "Davidson Chocolate Society," 6¼" d., purple 215.00
Plate, "Driebus Parfait Sweets," 6¼" d., purple 175.00

Plate, "Eagle Furniture Co.," purple 225.00
Plate, "Fern Brand Chocolates," 6" d., purple 210.00
Plate, "Gervitz Bros., Furniture & Clothing," w/handgrip, 6" d., purple 350.00
Plate, "Greengard Furniture Co.," purple 625.00
Plate, "E.A. Hudson Furniture Co.," 7" d., purple (Northwood) 225.00
Plate, "Jockey Club," w/handgrip, 6" d., purple 255.00
Plate, "Morris N. Smith," purple 250.00
Plate, "Old Rose Distillery," Grape & Cable patt., 9" d., stippled, green 240.00

Roods Chocolates, Pueblo Plate

Plate, "Roods Chocolates, Pueblo," purple (ILLUS.) 750.00
Plate, "Season's Greetings - Eat Paradise Soda Candies," 6" d., purple 188.00
Plate, "Spector's Department Store," Heart & Vine patt., 9" d., marigold 300.00
Plate, "Utah Liquor Co.," w/hand-grip, 6" d., purple 300.00
Plate, "We Use Brocker's," 7" d., purple 495.00
Plate, souvenir, BPOE Elks, "Atlantic City, 1911," blue 475.00
Plate, souvenir, BPOE Elks, "Parkersburg, 1914," 7½" d., blue 785.00

AGE HERALD

Bowl, 8" to 9" d., collared base, straight edge, purple 750.00
Plate, 9½" d., purple 1,200.00

AMARYLLIS (Northwood)

Compote, marigold 143.00
Compote, purple 98.00

APPLE BLOSSOMS

Bowl, 7" d., collared base, marigold (ILLUS.) 30.00

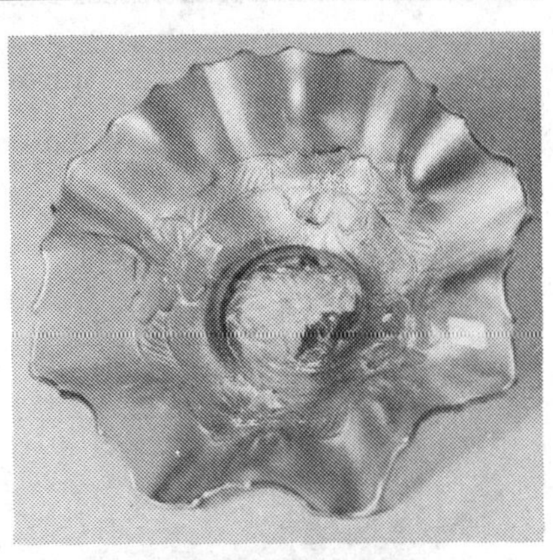

Apple Blossoms Bowl

Bowl, 7" d., collared base, peach opalescent ....75.00 to 110.00
Bowl, 7" d., collared base, purple .. 70.00
Bowl, 7" d., ribbon candy rim, white 125.00
Rose bowl, marigold 35.00

APPLE BLOSSOM TWIGS

Banana boat, ruffled, peach opalescent 175.00
Bowl, 8" to 9" d., marigold 50.00
Bowl, 8" to 9" d., peach opalescent 125.00
Bowl, 8" to 9" d., purple 125.00
Bowl, 8" to 9" d., white 90.00
Bowl, 10" d., purple 250.00
Plate, 9" d., blue 175.00
Plate, 9" d., marigold 85.00
Plate, 9" d., ruffled, marigold 50.00
Plate, 9" d., peach opalescent 215.00
Plate, 9" d., purple 258.00
Plate, 9" d., ruffled, smoky 350.00
Plate, 9" d., ruffled, white 130.00

APPLE TREE

Pitcher, water, marigold 150.00
Pitcher, water, white 350.00
Tumbler, amber 55.00
Tumbler, blue 48.00
Tumbler, marigold 32.00
Tumbler, white 140.00
Water set: pitcher & 1 tumbler; white, 2 pcs. 275.00
Water set: pitcher & 5 tumblers; marigold, 6 pcs. 435.00
Water set: pitcher & 6 tumblers; blue, 7 pcs. 820.00

AUSTRALIAN

Bowl, 9" to 10" d., Emu, marigold .. 145.00
Bowl, 9" to 10" d., Kangaroo, marigold 100.00
Bowl, 9" to 10" d., Kangaroo, purple 125.00

Bowl, 9" to 10" d., Kingfisher, purple ... 110.00
Bowl, 9" to 10" d., Kiwi, ruffled, marigold ... 250.00

Kiwi Bowl

Bowl, 9" to 10" d., Kiwi, purple (ILLUS.) ... 225.00
Bowl, 9" to 10" d., Kookaburra, marigold ... 98.00
Bowl, 9" to 10" d., Kookaburra, purple ... 100.00
Bowl, 9" to 10" d., Swan, purple ... 98.00
Bowl, 9" to 10" d., Thunderbird, purple ... 165.00
Bowl, ice cream, 11" d., Kookaburra, marigold ... 135.00
Bowl, ice cream, 11" d., Kookaburra, purple ... 300.00
Bowl, pin-up, purple ... 65.00
Compote, Butterflies & Waratah, aqua ... 135.00
Compote, Butterflies & Waratah, purple ... 210.00
Compote, Butterfly & Bush, purple ... 110.00
Sauce dish, Emu, marigold ... 75.00
Sauce dish, Kangaroo, purple ... 52.50
Sauce dish, Kingfisher, marigold ... 50.00
Sauce dish, Kingfisher, purple ... 45.00
Sauce dish, Kookaburra, marigold ... 30.00
Sauce dish, Kookaburra, purple ... 45.00
Sauce dish, Thunderbird, purple ... 73.00

AUTUMN ACORNS (Fenton)

Bowl, 7" d., blue ... 40.00
Bowl, 8" to 9" d., amber ... 65.00
Bowl, 8" to 9" d., blue ... 75.00
Bowl, 8" to 9" d., green ... 40.00
Bowl, 8" to 9" d., marigold ... 50.00
Bowl, 8" to 9" d., purple ... 45.00
Bowl, 8½" d., ice cream shape, Persian blue ... 750.00
Plate, green ... 825.00

BASKET (Northwood)

Aqua opalescent, 4½" d., 4¾" h. ... 305.00
Clambroth ... 400.00
Cobalt blue ... 105.00
Green ... 200.00
Ice blue ... 383.00
Ice green ... 220.00
Lavender ... 95.00
Lime green opalescent ... 900.00
Marigold ... 65.00
Purple ... 100.00
Smoky ... 250.00
White ... 160.00

BASKETWEAVE (Fenton)

Basket w/clear handle, marigold ... 27.50
Basket, 2-handled, green ... 190.00
Hat shape, Jack-in-pulpit style, red ... 225.00
Hat shape, 2-sides turned up, red ... 200.00
Vase, 5" h., purple ... 45.00
Vase, 5" h., white ... 85.00
Vase, 8½" h., marigold ... 20.00

BASKETWEAVE CANDY DISH (Fenton's Hat)

Amber ... 65.00
Aqua ... 65.00
Blue ... 30.00
Green ... 55.00
Ice green ... 70.00
Marigold ... 45.00
Red ... 220.00

BEADED BULL'S EYE (Imperial)

Vase, green ... 35.00
Vase, marigold ... 30.00
Vase, purple ... 45.00

BEADED CABLE (Northwood)

Bowl, 7" d., 3-footed, ruffled, marigold ... 30.00
Candy dish, green ... 65.00
Candy dish, marigold ... 32.00
Candy dish, purple ... 55.00
Loving cup, marigold ... 125.00
Rose bowl, aqua ... 345.00
Rose bowl, aqua opalescent ... 275.00
Rose bowl, blue ... 125.00
Rose bowl, green ... 78.00
Rose bowl, ice blue ... 1,000.00
Rose bowl, marigold ... 75.00
Rose bowl, purple ... 78.00
Rose bowl, white ... 600.00

BEADED SHELL (Dugan or Diamond Glass Co.)

Berry set: master bowl & 3 footed sauce dishes; purple, 4 pcs. ... 185.00
Creamer, marigold ... 60.00
Creamer, purple ... 45.00 to 70.00
Mug, blue ... 110.00
Mug, marigold ... 140.00
Mug, purple ... 75.00
Mug, white ... 1,000.00
Pitcher, water, purple ... 530.00
Rose bowl, green ... 40.00
Spooner, footed, marigold ... 37.50
Sugar bowl, cov., marigold ... 65.00
Table set, marigold, 4 pcs. ... 245.00
Table set, purple, 4 pcs. ... 525.00

Tumbler, blue 42.50
Tumbler, lavender 95.00
Tumbler, marigold 55.00
Tumbler, purple 55.00
Water set: pitcher & 1 tumbler; purple, 2 pcs. 550.00

Beaded Shell Water Set

Water set: pitcher & 6 tumblers; marigold, 7 pcs. (ILLUS.) 700.00

BEADS & BELLS

Beads & Bells Bowl

Bowl, 7" d., peach opalescent (ILLUS.) 60.00
Bowl, 7" d., purple 40.00

BEAUTY BUD VASE

Marigold, 8" h. .... 25.00 to 35.00
Purple, 8" h. 36.00
Marigold, 9½" h. 20.00

BIG FISH BOWL (Millersburg)

Green 325.00
Green, square 87.00
Marigold 250.00
Marigold, ruffled 425.00
Marigold, square 435.00
Purple, ice cream shape 620.00
Purple, ruffled (ILLUS.) 575.00
Purple, square 700.00
Vaseline w/marigold, tricornered 2,250.00

Big Fish Bowl

BIRDS & CHERRIES

Bonbon, blue 55.00
Bonbon, green 65.00
Bonbon, marigold 38.00
Bonbon, purple 70.00
Bowl, 8" to 9" d., blue 400.00
Bowl, 10" d., blue 450.00
Compote, green 65.00
Compote, marigold 45.00
Compote, purple 50.00
Plate, chop, marigold 385.00

BIRD WITH GRAPES

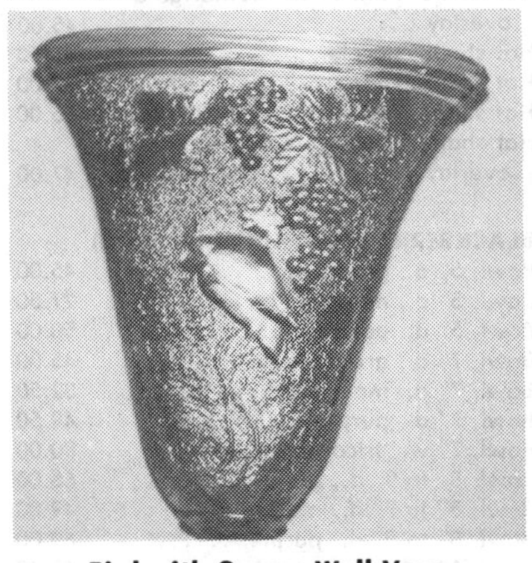

Bird with Grapes Wall Vase

Wall vase, marigold, 8" h., 7½" w. (ILLUS.) 75.00

BLACKBERRY (Fenton)

Basket, blue 40.00
Basket, red 240.00
Bowl, 8" to 9" d., ruffled, green 90.00
Bowl, 8" to 9" d., ruffled, purple 58.00
Compote, miniature, blue 65.00
Compote, miniature, green 40.00
Compote, miniature, marigold 50.00
Compote, miniature, purple 55.00

Compote, miniature, white 425.00
Plate, openwork rim, white 400.00

BLACKBERRY BLOCK (Fenton)

Pitcher, water, green 1,000.00
Pitcher, water, marigold 465.00
Pitcher, water, purple 1,000.00
Pitcher, water, vaseline 5,000.00
Tumbler, blue 52.50
Tumbler, green 150.00
Tumbler, marigold 50.00
Tumbler, purple 85.00
Water set: pitcher & 4 tumblers; purple, 5 pcs. 1,300.00

BLACKBERRY BRAMBLE

Compote, ruffled, green 40.00
Compote, ruffled, marigold 47.50
Compote, ruffled, purple 42.50

BLACKBERRY SPRAY

Bonbon, marigold 30.00
Compote, 5½" d., green 42.00
Compote, 5½" d., purple 45.00
Hat shape, amber 45.00
Hat shape, Amberina 200.00
Hat shape, amethyst opalescent 295.00
Hat shape, aqua 60.00
Hat shape, aqua opalescent 350.00
Hat shape, blue 30.00
Hat shape, ice green opalescent 300.00
Hat shape, marigold 40.00
Hat shape, milk white w/marigold overlay 145.00
Hat shape, purple 45.00
Hat shape, red 272.00
Hat shape, red slag ....375.00 to 425.00
Hat shape, vaseline w/marigold overlay 47.00

BLACKBERRY WREATH (Millersburg)

Bowl, 5" d., green 45.00
Bowl, 5" d., marigold 27.50
Bowl, 5" d., purple 50.00
Bowl, 7" d., green 45.00
Bowl, 7" d., marigold 32.50
Bowl, 7" d., purple 42.50
Bowl, 7" w., tricornered, purple 80.00
Bowl, 8" to 9" d., green 65.00
Bowl, 8" to 9" d., marigold 49.00
Bowl, 8" to 9" d., purple 69.00
Bowl, 10" d., green 65.00
Bowl, 10" d., marigold 67.50
Bowl, 10" d., purple 155.00
Bowl, ice cream, large, marigold ... 110.00

BLOSSOM TIME COMPOTE

Compote, marigold 135.00

BLUEBERRY (Fenton)

Pitcher, water, blue 515.00
Tumbler, blue 95.00
Tumbler, marigold 33.00
Tumbler, white 200.00

Water set: pitcher & 6 tumblers; blue, 7 pcs. 975.00
Water set: pitcher & 6 tumblers; marigold, 7 pcs. 375.00

BO PEEP

Mug, marigold 183.00
Plate, marigold 275.00

BOUQUET

Pitcher, water, blue 372.00
Pitcher, water, marigold 179.00
Tumbler, blue 45.00
Tumbler, marigold 25.00
Water set: pitcher & 1 tumbler; blue, 2 pcs. 400.00
Water set: pitcher & 4 tumblers; marigold, 5 pcs. 425.00

BROKEN ARCHES (Imperial)

Broken Arches Punch Set

Punch bowl, purple, 12" d. 500.00
Punch bowl & base, marigold, 12" d., 2 pcs. 198.00
Punch cup, marigold 22.00
Punch cup, purple 25.00
Punch set: bowl, base & 6 cups; marigold, 8 ps. (ILLUS.) 335.00

BUTTERFLIES

Bonbon, blue 45.00
Bonbon, green 60.00
Bonbon, marigold 43.00
Bonbon, purple 52.00
Bonbon, smoky 85.00
Nappy, marigold 15.00
Nappy, 2-handled, purple, 7" 35.00

BUTTERFLY & BERRY (Fenton)

Berry set: master bowl & 6 sauce dishes; blue, 7 pcs. 400.00
Berry set: master bowl & 6 sauce dishes; marigold, 7 pcs. 200.00
Bowl, 8" to 9" d., footed, blue 70.00
Bowl, 8" to 9" d., footed, marigold 65.00
Bowl, 8" to 9" d., footed, purple 95.00
Bowl, master berry or fruit, 4-footed, blue 110.00

Bowl, master berry or fruit, 4-footed, green 115.00
Bowl, master berry or fruit, 4-footed, marigold 50.00
Bowl, master berry or fruit, 4-footed, purple.................. 128.00
Bowl, master berry or fruit, 4-footed, white 200.00
Butter dish, cov., blue 155.00
Butter dish, cov., marigold 105.00
Centerpiece bowl, purple 500.00
Creamer, green 110.00
Creamer, marigold 56.00
Creamer, purple 110.00
Hatpin holder, blue................. 700.00
Nut bowl, blue....................... 725.00
Nut bowl, purple..................... 185.00
Pitcher, water, marigold 190.00
Sauce dish, blue 42.00
Sauce dish, green 45.00
Sauce dish, marigold 25.00
Sauce dish, purple 95.00
Spooner, green 70.00
Spooner, marigold.................... 55.00
Sugar bowl, cov., green 95.00
Sugar bowl, cov., marigold.......... 67.50
Table set: cov. butter dish, cov. sugar bowl & creamer; blue, 3 pcs. 450.00
Table set, marigold, 4 pcs. 250.00
Tumbler, blue........................ 36.00
Tumbler, green 50.00
Tumbler, marigold.................... 27.50
Tumbler, purple...................... 125.00
Vase, 6" h., blue..................... 55.00
Vase, 8" h., blue..................... 65.00
Vase, 8" h., marigold................ 30.00
Vaes, 9" h., blue..................... 75.00
Vase, 9" h., marigold................ 30.00
Water set: pitcher & 6 tumblers; marigold, 7 pcs. ....300.00 to 425.00

BUTTERFLY & FERN (Fenton)

Pitcher, water, blue ....300.00 to 450.00
Pitcher, water, green 425.00
Pitcher, water, marigold 250.00
Tumbler, blue......................... 40.00
Tumbler, green 45.00
Tumbler, marigold.................... 40.00
Tumbler, purple...................... 45.00
Water set: pitcher & 1 tumbler; blue, 2 pcs........................ 410.00
Water set: pitcher & 5 tumblers; purple, 6 pcs...................... 575.00
Water set: pitcher & 6 tumblers; green, 7 pcs. 625.00
Water set: pitcher & 6 tumblers; marigold, 7 pcs.................... 500.00

BUTTERFLY & TULIP

Bowl, 9" w., 5½" h., footed, marigold (ILLUS.) 230.00
Bowl, 9" w., footed, purple 700.00
Bowl, 10½" square flat shape, footed, marigold 342.00

Butterfly & Tulip Bowl

Bowl, 10½" square flat shape, footed, purple ....1,000.00 to 2,000.00
Bowl, 12" d., upturned sides, footed, marigold 338.00
Bowl, vaseline 394.00

BUZZ SAW - See Double Star Pattern

CAPTIVE ROSE

Bonbon, 2-handled, blue, 7½" d. ... 55.00
Bonbon, 2-handled, marigold, 7½" d. 45.00
Bonbon, 2-handled, purple, 7½" d. 55.00
Bowl, 8" to 9" d., amber 65.00
Bowl, 8" to 9" d., blue.............. 45.00
Bowl, 8" to 9" d., green 47.50
Bowl, 8" to 9" d., ruffled rim, marigold 35.00
Bowl, 8" to 9" d., ribbon candy rim, green 37.00
Bowl, 8" to 9" d., ribbon candy rim, purple 44.00
Compote, blue 82.50
Compote, green...................... 50.00
Compote, purple 45.00
Compote, white 95.00
Plate, 9" d., amber 200.00
Plate, 9" d., blue.................... 170.00
Plate, 9" d., green ....175.00 to 225.00
Plate, 9" d., marigold 150.00
Plate, 9" d., purple.................. 192.00

CARNIVAL HOLLY - See Holly Pattern

CAROLINA DOGWOOD

Bowl, 8½" d., aqua opalescent 350.00
Bowl, 8½" d., blue opalescent 240.00
Bowl, 8½" d., marigold on milk white 290.00
Bowl, 8½" d., peach opalescent 125.00
Plate, 8½" d., peach opalescent 450.00

CAROLINE

Basket w/applied handle, peach opalescent........................ 346.00
Bowl, 8" to 9" d., peach opalescent........................ 46.00

Bowl, 8" to 9" w., tricornered, peach opalescent 82.50
Plate, w/handgrip, peach opalescent 80.00

CATTAILS & WATER LILY - See Water Lily & Cattails Pattern

CHATELAINE
Pitcher, purple 2,000.00
Tumbler, purple 275.00

CHECKERBOARD
Goblet, marigold 310.00
Goblet, purple 150.00
Punch cup, marigold 95.00
Tumbler, purple 370.00

CHERRY
Bowl, 6" d., Jeweled Heart exterior, purple 32.00
Bowl, 7" d., 3-footed, crimped rim, peach opalescent 60.00
Bowl, 8" to 9" d., 3-footed, marigold 54.00
Bowl, 8" to 9" d., 3-footed, peach opalescent 82.00
Bowl, 8" to 9" d., 3-footed, purple .. 72.00
Bowl, large, peach opalescent 240.00
Dish, ruffled, purple, 6" d. 38.00
Plate, ruffled, purple 132.00
Sauce dish, peach opalescent 64.00
Sauce dish, purple 60.00

CHERRY or CHERRY CIRCLES (Fenton)
Bonbon, 2-handled, aqua 280.00
Bonbon, 2-handled, blue 55.00
Bonbon, 2-handled, marigold 42.00
Bonbon, 2-handled, purple 50.00
Bonbon, 2-handled, red 1,700.00
Bowl, 5" d., fluted, blue 18.00
Bowl, 7" d., 3-footed, peach opalescent w/plain interior 77.50
Bowl, 8" to 9" d., marigold 30.00
Bowl, 8" to 9" d., white 70.00
Bowl, 10" d., vaseline w/marigold overlay 70.00
Card tray, aqua 125.00
Plate, 6" d., marigold 40.00

CHERRY or HANGING CHERRIES (Millersburg)
Banana compote (whimsey), purple 1,300.00
Bowl, 5" d., ruffled, blue satin 600.00
Bowl, 5" d., ruffled, marigold 50.00
Bowl, 5" d., piecrust rim, purple 49.00
Bowl, 7" d., green 70.00
Bowl, 7" d., marigold 55.00
Bowl, 7" d., purple 100.00
Bowl, 8" to 9" d., dome-footed, marigold 65.00
Bowl, 8" to 9" d., purple 60.00
Bowl, ice cream, 10" d., green ....75.00 to 90.00
Bowl, ice cream, 10" d., marigold .. 94.00
Bowl, ice cream, 10" d., purple 125.00
Bowl, ice cream, 10" d., teal blue .. 850.00
Butter dish, cov., green 250.00
Butter dish, cov., marigold 150.00
Butter dish, cov., purple 175.00
Creamer, green 62.50
Creamer, marigold 55.00
Creamer, purple 90.00
Pitcher, milk, marigold 600.00
Pitcher, milk, purple 437.00
Pitcher, water, green 700.00
Pitcher, water, marigold 200.00

Millersburg Cherries Pattern

Pitcher, water, purple (ILLUS.) 545.00
Plate, 6" d., purple 165.00
Plate, 7" d., purple 225.00
Plate, 8" d., green 475.00
Spooner, green 75.00
Spooner, marigold 60.00
Spooner, purple 75.00
Sugar bowl, cov., green 85.00
Sugar bowl, cov., marigold 85.00
Sugar bowl, cov., purple 125.00
Table set, marigold, 4 pcs. 375.00
Table set, purple, 4 pcs. ....500.00 to 700.00
Tumbler, green 145.00
Tumbler, marigold 310.00
Tumbler, purple (ILLUS.) 320.00

CHERRY CHAIN (Fenton)
Bonbon, 2-handled, marigold 42.50
Bowl, 5" d., blue 35.00
Bowl, 5" d., Orange Tree exterior, marigold 26.00
Bowl, 8" to 9" d., blue 55.00
Bowl, 8" to 9" d., white 90.00
Bowl, ice cream, 10" d., vaseline ... 175.00
Bowl, 10" d., Orange Tree exterior, blue 68.00
Bowl, 10" d., Orange Tree exterior, marigold 42.00
Bowl, 10" d., Orange Tree exterior, white 120.00

Plate, 6" to 7" d., blue .....95.00 to 135.00
Plate, 6" to 7" d., marigold 50.00
Plate, chop, white 605.00

CHERRY CIRCLES - See Cherry (Fenton) Pattern

CHRISTMAS COMPOTE

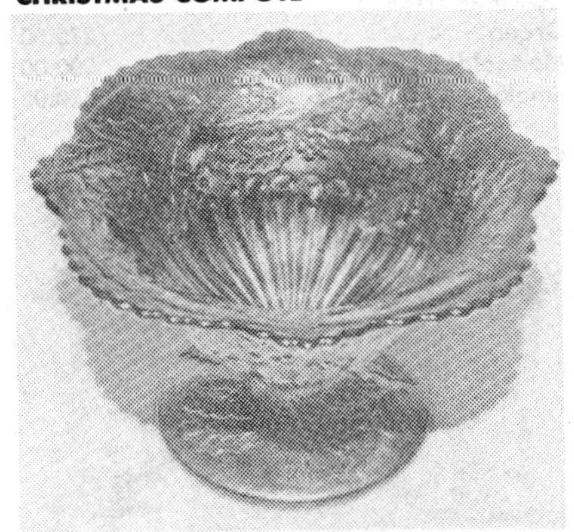

Christmas Compote

Marigold ....1,500.00 to 2,100.00
Purple (ILLUS.) ....2,100.00 to 2,750.00

CHRYSANTHEMUM or WINDMILL & MUMS

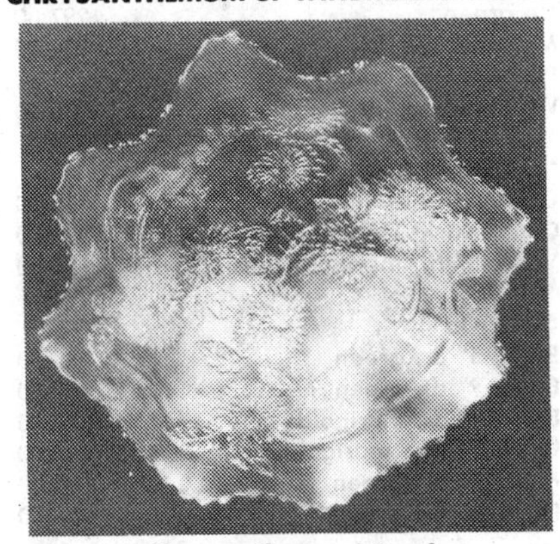

Chrysanthemum Bowl

Bowl, 8" to 9" d., 3-footed, blue 100.00
Bowl, 8" to 9" d., 3-footed, green... 80.00
Bowl, 8" to 9" d., 3-footed, marigold 43.00
Bowl, 10" d., 3-footed, blue 145.00
Bowl, 10" d., 3-footed, marigold (ILLUS.) 60.00
Bowl, 10" d., 3-footed, purple 75.00
Bowl, 10" d., collared base, red 950.00
Bowl, collared base, green 225.00
Bowl, collared base, marigold 45.00
Bowl, orange, footed, vaseline 350.00

CIRCLED SCROLL (Dugan or Diamond Glass Co.)

Creamer, marigold 51.00
Pitcher, water, marigold 1,400.00
Spooner, marigold................. 125.00
Tumbler, marigold................. 250.00
Tumbler, purple 1,050.00
Vase, 7½" h., purple 52.50
Vase, 9" h., marigold.............. 85.00
Vase, hat-shaped, marigold 60.00
Vase, hat-shaped, purple 85.00

COBBLESTONES BOWL (Imperial)

Green, 9" d...................... 37.50
Purple, 9" d...................... 55.00

COIN DOT (Northwood)

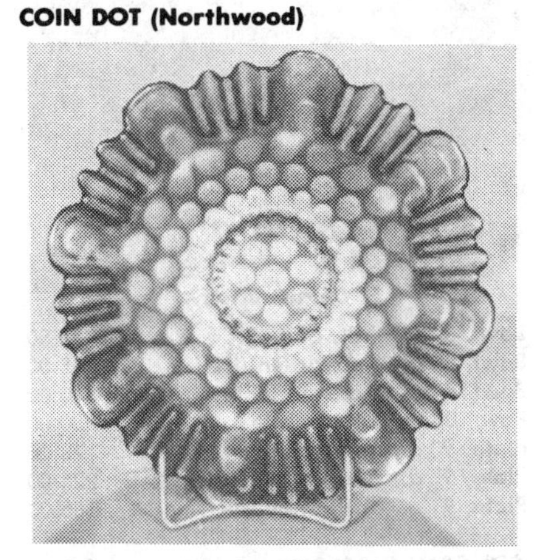

Coin Dot Bowl

Bowl, 6" d., green 20.00
Bowl, 7" d., blue................. 30.00
Bowl, 7" d., ribbon candy rim, green (ILLUS.)........................ 35.00
Bowl, 7" d., marigold............. 36.00
Bowl, 7" d., purple 28.00
Bowl, 7" d., red..........675.00 to 750.00
Bowl, 8" to 9" d., stippled, aqua.... 55.00
Bowl, 8" to 9" d., blue............ 35.00
Bowl, 8" to 9" d., green 37.50
Bowl, 8" to 9" d., marigold......... 25.00
Bowl, 8" to 9" d., purple 40.00
Bowl, 8" to 9" d., ruffled, vaseline.. 55.00
Pitcher, water, marigold 150.00
Plate, purple...................... 55.00
Rose bowl, green 52.00
Rose bowl, marigold............... 50.00
Tumbler, marigold................. 50.00
Water set: pitcher & 6 tumblers; marigold, 7 pcs................. 425.00

COIN SPOT (Dugan)

Compote, 4½" d., peach opalescent...................... 60.00
Compote, 7" d., blue 125.00
Compote, 7" d., marigold 30.00
Compote, 7" d., fluted, peach opalescent...................... 50.00
Plate, 9" d., aqua 295.00
Plate, 9" d., purple................ 35.00

Syrup pitcher, applied handle, plated lid, 9-panel, green, 6" h. 77.50
Syrup pitcher, pear-shaped, applied handle, plated lid, blue, 7" h. 77.50

COMET or RIBBON TIE (Fenton)

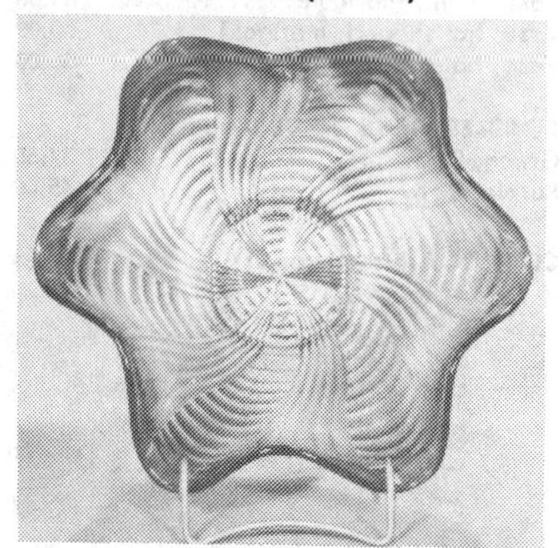

Comet Bowl

Bowl, 8" to 9" d., blue 52.50
Bowl, 8" to 9" d., green (ILLUS.) 45.00
Bowl, 8" to 9" d., marigold 40.00
Bowl, 8" to 9" d., purple 50.00
Plate, 9" d., ruffled, blue 173.00
Plate, 9" d., ruffled, marigold 225.00
Plate, 9" d., ruffled, purple 185.00

CONCAVE DIAMOND - **See Diamond Concave Pattern**

CONCORD (Fenton)

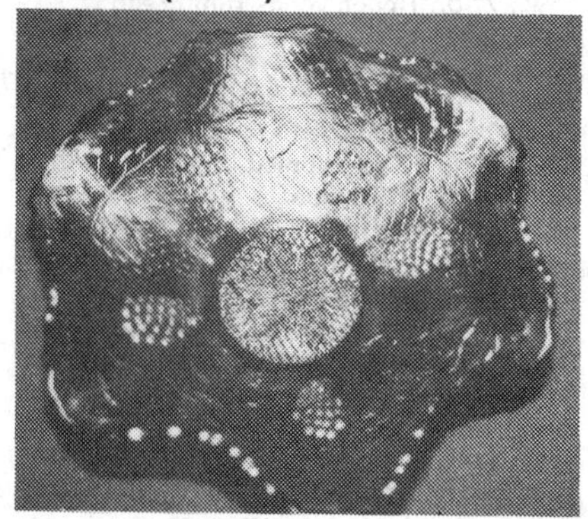

Concord Bowl

Bowl, blue 134.00
Bowl, green 125.00
Bowl, marigold (ILLUS.) 90.00
Plate, green 275.00
Plate, marigold 250.00

CONSTELLATION (Dugan)
Compote, marigold 44.00
Compote, white 95.00

CORAL (Fenton)
Bowl, 8" to 9" d., collared base, green 135.00
Bowl, 8" to 9" d., collared base, marigold 77.50
Plate, 9" d., marigold 600.00

CORN BOTTLE
Green 275.00
Marigold 200.00
Smoky 220.00

CORN VASE (Northwood)

Corn Vases

Blue, pastel (ILLUS. center) 375.00
Green (ILLUS. left) 400.00
Ice blue 1,250.00
Ice green 297.00
Marigold 550.00
Purple (ILLUS. right) 432.00
White 275.00

CORNUCOPIA
Candlestick, white (single) 85.00
Candlesticks, ice blue, pr. 115.00
Vase, 5" h., marigold 30.00

COSMOS
Bowl, 5" d., green 42.00
Bowl, 9" d., green 62.00
Bowl, 9" d., marigold 40.00
Bowl, 10" d., marigold 45.00
Plate, 6" d., green 90.00
Plate, 9" d., green 65.00

COSMOS & CANE

Cosmos & Cane Butter Dish

Bowl, 8" to 9" d., marigold 50.00
Bowl, 8" to 9" sq., white 118.00
Bowl, 10" d., white 130.00
Butter dish, cov., marigold 215.00
Butter dish, cov., purple 100.00
Butter dish, cov., white (ILLUS.)..... 295.00
Compote, amber 500.00
Compote, marigold 150.00
Compote, white 150.00
Creamer, honey amber 85.00
Creamer, marigold 110.00
Pitcher, white 1,000.00
Rose bowl, Headdress interior, marigold 400.00
Sauce dish, green 40.00
Sauce dish, marigold 30.00
Sauce dish, white 60.00
Sugar bowl, cov., honey amber 85.00
Tumbler, amber 95.00
Tumbler, marigold.................. 50.00
Tumbler, white..................... 175.00

COUNTRY KITCHEN (Millersburg)
Bowl, 5" d., ruffled, marigold 97.50
Butter dish, purple 325.00
Spooner, marigold.................. 100.00

CRAB CLAW (Imperial)

Crab Claw Water Set

Bowl, 8" to 9" d., marigold......... 35.00
Bowl, 8" to 9" d., fluted, smoky 45.00
Tumbler, marigold.................. 45.00
Water set: pitcher & 6 tumblers; marigold, 7 pcs. (ILLUS.) 300.00

CRACKLE
Automobile vase w/bracket, marigold 25.00
Plate, 9½" d., purple 40.00
Tumbler, dome-footed, marigold 15.00
Vase, fan-shaped, marigold 20.00
Water set: cov. pitcher & 5 tumblers; marigold, 6 pcs............ 90.00

CRUCIFIX
Candlesticks, marigold, pr.......................295.00 to 375.00

CURVED STAR
Bowl, 9" d., marigold............... 25.00
Chalice, blue 105.00
Chalice, marigold 90.00
Compote, marigold 20.00
Epergne, single lily, blue 54.00
Epergne, 2-lily, marigold, small..... 35.00
Epergne, 3-lily, marigold 190.00
Rose bowl, blue.................... 450.00

CUT ARCS
Bowl, 9" d., marigold............... 16.50

CUT COSMOS
Tumbler 222.00

DAHLIA (Dugan or Diamond Glass Co.)

Dahlia Pitcher

Berry set: master bowl & 4 sauce dishes; white, 5 pcs. 640.00
Berry set: master bowl & 5 sauce dishes; purple, 6 pcs............. 275.00
Bowl, master berry, 10" d., footed, white 170.00
Butter dish, cov., marigold 140.00
Butter dish, cov., white 350.00
Creamer, marigold 60.00
Creamer, purple 125.00
Creamer, white 125.00
Creamer & cov. sugar bowl, white, pr.............................. 275.00
Pitcher, water, marigold (ILLUS.).... 250.00
Pitcher, water, purple 685.00
Pitcher, water, white 550.00
Sauce dish, marigold 40.00
Sauce dish, purple 45.00
Sauce dish, white 40.00
Spooner, marigold.................. 60.00
Spooner, purple.................... 75.00
Sugar bowl, cov., purple 100.00
Table set: cov. sugar bowl, cov. butter dish & spooner; marigold, 3 pcs. 200.00
Table set: cov. sugar bowl, creamer, spooner & cov. butter dish; purple, 4 pcs...............825.00 to 850.00

Table set: cov. sugar bowl, creamer, spooner & cov. butter dish; white, 4 pcs. 900.00
Tumbler, amber 95.00
Tumbler, marigold 125.00
Tumbler, pastel marigold 150.00
Tumbler, purple 195.00
Tumbler, white 165.00
Tumbler, white w/blue flower 275.00
Tumbler, white w/gold flower 195.00
Tumbler, white w/red flower 275.00
Tumbler, white w/silver band 300.00
Water set: pitcher & 1 tumbler; white, 2 pcs. 700.00
Water set: pitcher & 6 tumblers; marigold, 7 pcs. 1,025.00

DAISIES & DRAPE VASE (Northwood)

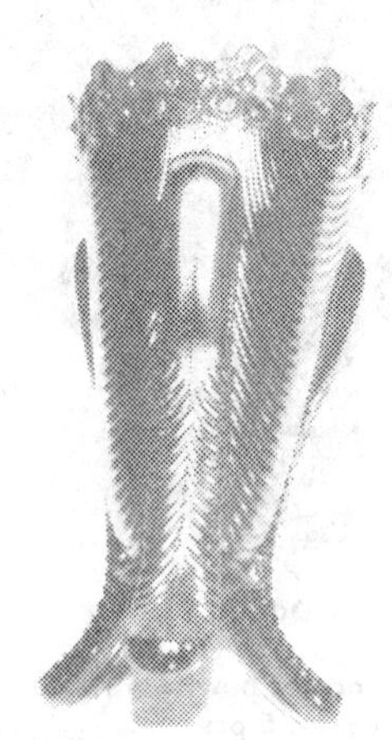

Daisies & Drape Vase

Aqua opalescent 450.00
Blue (ILLUS.) 350.00
Marigold 255.00
Purple 300.00
White 170.00

DAISY & LATTICE BAND or LATTICE & DAISY

Pitcher, tankard, marigold .. 90.00 to 125.00
Tumbler, blue 50.00
Tumbler, marigold 25.00
Water set: pitcher & 4 tumblers; marigold, 5 pcs. 215.00

DAISY & PLUME

Candy dish, footed, green 48.00
Candy dish, footed, marigold 50.00
Candy dish, footed, peach opalescent 60.00
Candy dish, footed, purple 80.00
Compote, green 50.00
Compote, marigold 31.00
Compote, purple 45.00
Rose bowl, 3-footed, green (ILLUS.) 65.00
Rose bowl, 3-footed, ice blue 800.00

Daisy & Plume Rose Bowl

Rose bowl, 3-footed, ice green 675.00
Rose bowl, 3-footed, marigold 42.00
Rose bowl, 3-footed, purple 98.00

DAISY BASKET

Marigold 42.00

DAISY BLOCK ROWBOAT

Marigold, 12" l., 4" w., 3¼" h. 189.00
Purple 300.00

DAISY CUT BELL

Marigold 400.00

DAISY SQUARES

Bowl, 6" d., clear w/marigold 425.00
Compote, amber 265.00
Compote, marigold 425.00
Goblet, green 275.00
Rose bowl, stemmed, green 375.00

DAISY WREATH (Westmoreland)

Bowl, 8" to 9" d., blue opalescent .. 365.00
Bowl, 8" to 9" d., milk white w/marigold overlay .... 150.00 to 200.00
Bowl, 8" to 9" d., peach opalescent 70.00
Plate, 9" d., ruffled, aqua 350.00

DANDELION (Northwood)

Mug, aqua opalescent 495.00
Mug, blue 412.00
Mug, green 695.00
Mug, ice blue opalescent 895.00
Mug, marigold 285.00
Mug, purple 280.00
Mug, Knight's Templar, ice blue 1,050.00
Mug, Knight's Templar, ice green 895.00
Mug, Knight's Templar, marigold 495.00
Pitcher, water, tankard, green 750.00
Pitcher, water, tankard, marigold (ILLUS.) 375.00
Pitcher, water, tankard, purple .... 450.00 to 590.00
Pitcher, water, tankard, white 2,000.00

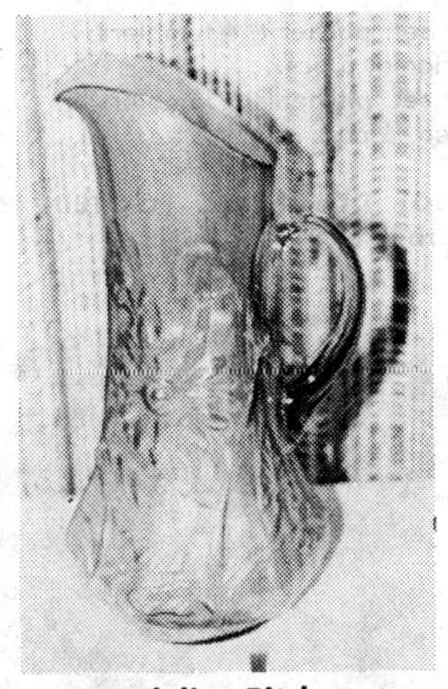

Dandelion Pitcher

Tumbler, green 90.00
Tumbler, ice blue 187.00
Tumbler, lavender................. 225.00
Tumbler, marigold.................. 44.00
Tumbler, purple.................... 45.00
Tumbler, smoky.................... 250.00
Tumbler, white.................... 142.00
Water set: pitcher & 6 tumblers; marigold, 7 pcs.................. 600.00
Water set: pitcher & 6 tumblers; purple, 7 pcs.................... 882.00

DANDELION, PANELED (Fenton)

Paneled Dandelion Pitcher

Pitcher, water, blue ....325.00 to 375.00
Pitcher, water, green 325.00
Pitcher, water, marigold 265.00
Pitcher, water, purple (ILLUS.) 625.00
Tumbler, blue...................... 36.00
Tumbler, green 40.00
Tumbler, marigold.................. 37.50
Tumbler, purple.................... 35.00
Water set: pitcher & 5 tumblers; blue, 6 pcs....................... 812.50
Water set: pitcher & 5 tumblers; marigold, 6 pcs.................. 375.00

Water set: pitcher & 6 tumblers; green, 7 pcs. 624.00
Water set: pitcher & 6 tumblers; purple, 7 pcs.................... 650.00

DIAMOND & RIB VASE

Vase, 10" h., blue.................. 40.00
Vase, 10" h., green 32.00
Vase, 10" h., marigold............. 20.00
Vase, 10" h., purple............... 30.00
Vase, 11" h., green 24.00
Vase, 11" h., ice green 65.00
Vases, 11" h., purple, pr. 80.00
Vase, 19" h., purple.............. 450.00
Vase, 20" h., marigold............ 300.00

DIAMOND & SUNBURST

Decanter w/stopper, marigold...... 60.00
Wine, marigold..................... 27.50
Wine, purple....................... 45.00
Wine set: decanter w/stopper & 6 wines; marigold, 7 pcs. 275.00
Wine set: decanter w/stopper & 6 wines; purple, 7 pcs. 495.00

DIAMOND CONCAVE or CONCAVE DIAMOND

Pitcher w/cover, vaseline 550.00
Tumbler, ice blue 25.00
Tumbler, vaseline 168.00
Tumble-up (water carafe w/tumbler top), ice blue 325.00

DIAMOND LACE (Imperial)

Diamond Lace Tumbler

Bowl, 5" d., marigold.............. 16.00
Bowl, 5" d., purple 22.00
Bowl, 8" to 9" d., marigold......... 30.00
Bowl, 8" to 9" d., purple........... 50.00
Bowl, 10" d., purple 72.00
Pitcher, water, purple 235.00
Tumbler, marigold................. 425.00
Tumbler, purple (ILLUS.) 45.00
Water set: pitcher & 6 tumblers; purple, 7 pcs.................... 366.00

DIAMOND POINT COLUMNS

Bowl, 5" d., 2½" h., marigold 22.00
Creamer, marigold 35.00
Vase, 6" h., marigold.............. 30.00
Vase, 7" h., purple 40.00

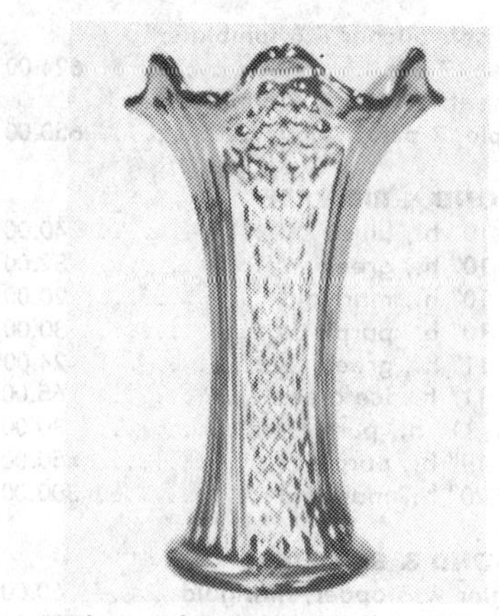

Diamond Point Columns Vase

Vase, 8" h., green (ILLUS.) 40.00
Vase, 10" h., white 65.00
Vase, 16" h., blue 365.00

DIAMOND RING (Imperial)

Diamond Ring Bowl

Berry set: master bowl & 4 sauce dishes; smoky, 5 pcs. 40.00
Bowl, 8" to 9" d., marigold 30.00
Bowl, 8" to 9" d., smoky (ILLUS.) ... 28.00
Rose bowl, marigold 300.00

DIAMONDS (Millersburg)

Pitcher, water, green 178.00
Pitcher, water, marigold 138.00
Pitcher, water, purple 175.00
Punch bowl & base, marigold, 2 pcs. 1,600.00
Punch bowl & base, purple, 2 pcs. ... 900.00
Tumbler, amber 42.50
Tumbler, green 60.00
Tumbler, marigold 45.00
Tumbler, purple 55.00
Water set: pitcher & 1 tumbler; purple, 2 pcs. 250.00
Water set: pitcher & 4 tumblers; marigold, 5 pcs. 350.00
Water set: pitcher & 5 tumblers; green, 6 pcs. 400.00

DIVING DOLPHINS FOOTED BOWL (Sowerby)

Diving Dolphins Bowl

Marigold, embossed scroll interior .. 120.00
Marigold 175.00
Purple (ILLUS.) 173.00

DOGWOOD SPRAYS

Bowl, 8" to 9" d., dome-footed, peach opalescent 95.00
Bowl, 8" to 9" d., dome-footed, purple 65.00

DOLPHINS COMPOTE (Millersburg)

Blue, Rosalind interior 2,500.00
Purple, Rosalind interior ... 675.00 to 800.00

DOUBLE DUTCH BOWL

Marigold, 7" d. 20.00
Purple, 7" d. 42.00
Green, 8" to 9" d., footed 55.00
Marigold, 8" to 9" d., footed 35.00
Purple, 8" to 9" d., footed 80.00

DOUBLE STAR or BUZZ SAW (Cambridge)

Cruet w/stopper, green, small, 4" .. 425.00
Cruet w/stopper, green, large, 6" .. 435.00
Cruet w/stopper, marigold, large, 6" 300.00
Pitcher, water, green 350.00
Pitcher, water, marigold ... 425.00 to 500.00
Tumbler, green 52.00
Water set: pitcher & 1 tumbler; green, 2 pcs. 425.00

DOUBLE STEM ROSE

Bowl, 8" to 9" d., dome-footed, blue 325.00
Bowl, 8" to 9" d., dome-footed, lavender 160.00
Bowl, 8" to 9" d., dome-footed, marigold 30.00

Bowl, 8" to 9" d., dome-footed, peach opalescent 75.00
Bowl, 8" to 9" d., dome-footed, purple 50.00
Bowl, 8" to 9" d., dome-footed, white 117.00
Plate, dome-footed, white 150.00

DRAGON & LOTUS (Fenton)

Dragon & Lotus Bowl

Bowl, 7" to 9" d., 3-footed, blue 55.00
Bowl, 7" to 9" d., 3-footed, green . . . 70.00
Bowl, 7" to 9" d., 3-footed, marigold 40.00
Bowl, 7" to 9" d., 3-footed, peach opalescent 510.00
Bowl, 7" to 9" d., 3-footed, purple . . 66.00
Bowl, 8" to 9" d., collared base, amber 150.00
Bowl, 8" to 9" d., collared base, aqua opalescent 650.00
Bowl, 8" to 9" d., collared base, green 100.00
Bowl, 8" to 9" d., collared base, lime green opalescent 684.00
Bowl, 8" to 9" d., collared base, ruffled, peach opalescent 580.00
Bowl, 8" to 9" d., milk white w/marigold iridescence 850.00
Bowl, 8" to 9" d., red 775.00
Bowl, ice cream shape, 9" d., collared base, amber 200.00
Bowl, ice cream shape, 9" d., collared base, blue (ILLUS.) 53.00
Bowl, ice cream shape, 9" d., collared base, green 55.00
Bowl, ice cream shape, 9" d., collared base, marigold 38.00
Plate, collared base, blue 668.00
Plate, collared base, ruffled, marigold 350.00
Plate, spatula footed, marigold 638.00

DRAGON & STRAWBERRY BOWL (Fenton)

Bowl, 9" d., blue 438.00
Bowl, 9" d., green 442.00
Bowl, 9" d., marigold 233.00

DRAPERY (Northwood)

Candy dish, tricornered, aqua opalescent 150.00
Candy dish, tricornered, ice blue . . . 112.00
Candy dish, tricornered, ice green . . 110.00
Candy dish, tricornered, marigold . . 62.50
Candy dish, tricornered, purple 120.00
Candy dish, tricornered, white 120.00
Rose bowl, aqua opalescent 260.00
Rose bowl, blue 250.00
Rose bowl, ice blue 550.00
Rose bowl, lavender 110.00
Rose bowl, marigold 325.00
Rose bowl, purple 234.00
Rose bowl, white 320.00
Vase, 4" h., ice blue 170.00
Vase, 7" h., aqua opalescent 150.00
Vase, 7" h., blue 75.00
Vase, 7" h., ice green 69.00
Vase, 7" h., marigold 46.00
Vase, 8" h., ice green 100.00
Vase, 8" h., white 52.50

EMBROIDERED MUMS (Northwood)

Embroidered Mums Bowl

Bowl, 8" to 9" d., ruffled, aqua opalescent 1,400.00
Bowl, 8" to 9" d., blue (ILLUS.) 260.00
Bowl, 8" to 9" d., ice blue 650.00
Bowl, 8" to 9" d., ice green 650.00
Bowl, 8" to 9" d., ruffled, marigold 210.00
Bowl, 8" to 9" d., purple 260.00
Plate, ice green . . . . . 775.00 to 875.00

ESTATE (Westmoreland)

Creamer, marigold opalescent 45.00
Creamer, peach opalescent 75.00
Creamer & sugar bowl, aqua, pr. . . . 150.00
Mug, marigold 85.00

FAN (Dugan)

Pitcher, milk, marigold 50.00
Sauceboat, peach opalescent 85.00
Sauceboat, purple 65.00

FANCIFUL (Dugan)

Fanciful Ruffled Bowl

Bowl, 8" to 9" d., blue 82.50
Bowl, 8" to 9" d., peach opalescent 204.00
Bowl, 8" to 9" d., ruffled, purple (ILLUS.) 110.00
Bowl, 8" to 9" d., ruffled, white 112.00
Plate, 9" d., blue 190.00
Plate, 9" d., marigold 85.00
Plate, 9" d., peach opalescent 400.00
Plate, 9" d., purple .... 175.00 to 225.00
Plate, 9" d., white 175.00

FANTAIL

Bowl, 9" d., footed, blue 86.00
Bowl, 9" d., shallow, footed, w/Butterfly & Berry exterior, blue 95.00
Bowl, 9" d., footed, green 80.00
Bowl, 9" d., footed, marigold 100.00

FARMYARD (Dugan)

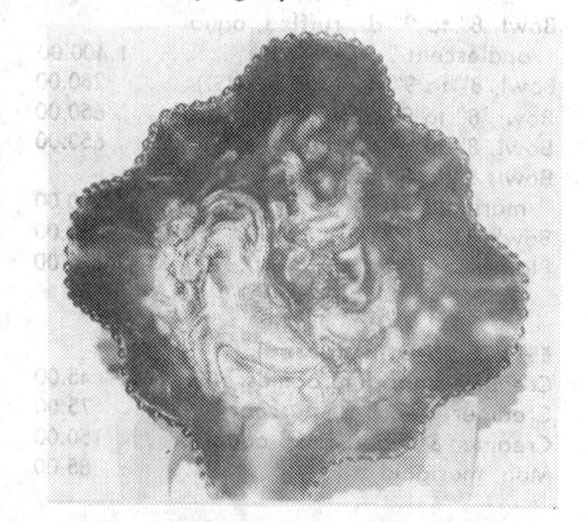

Farmyard Bowl

Bowl, purple (ILLUS.) 2,600.00
Bowl, ribbon candy rim, purple 2,350.00
Plate, 10" d., purple 8,125.00

FASHION (Imperial)

Fashion Punch Set

Bowl, 9" d., clambroth 30.00
Bowl, 9" d., marigold 18.00
Bowl, 9" d., ruffled, smoky 48.00
Bowl, 10" d., marigold 45.00
Creamer, marigold 22.50
Creamer & sugar bowl, marigold, pr. 60.00
Pitcher, water, marigold 105.00
Pitcher, water, purple 825.00
Pitcher, water, smoky 335.00
Punch bowl & base, marigold, 12" d., 2 pcs. 120.00
Punch cup, marigold 12.00
Punch cup, smoky 30.00
Punch set: 12" d. bowl, base & 6 cups; marigold, 8 pcs. (ILLUS.) 190.00
Rose bowl, marigold, 7" d. 83.00
Sugar bowl, marigold 20.00
Sugar bowl, smoky 90.00
Tumbler, marigold 25.00
Tumbler, smoky 65.00
Water set: pitcher & 6 tumblers; marigold, 7 pcs. 250.00
Water set: pitcher & 6 tumblers; smoky, 7 pcs. 400.00

FEATHER & HEART

Feather & Heart Water Pitcher

Pitcher, water, green (ILLUS.) 450.00
Pitcher, water, marigold 375.00
Pitcher, water, purple 475.00
Tumbler, green 150.00
Tumbler, marigold.................. 48.00
Tumbler, purple.................... 92.50
Water set: pitcher & 1 tumbler; green, 2 pcs. 500.00
Water set: pitcher & 5 tumblers; marigold, 6 pcs. ....550.00 to 700.00

FEATHERED SERPENT

Berry set: master bowl & 6 sauce dishes; marigold, 7 pcs. 195.00
Berry set: master bowl & 6 sauce dishes; purple, 7 pcs............. 160.00
Bowl, 8" to 9" d., green 70.00
Bowl, 8" to 9" d., marigold......... 40.00
Bowl, 8" to 9" d., purple 60.00
Bowl, 10" d., fluted, green 48.00
Bowl, 10" d., marigold.............. 45.00
Bowl, 10" d., flared, purple 69.00
Sauce dish, blue 20.00
Sauce dish, green 26.00

FEATHER STITCH BOWL

Aqua 225.00
Blue 65.00
Marigold 40.00
Purple 55.00

FENTONIA

Fentonia Water Set

Berry set: master bowl & 4 sauce dishes; marigold, 5 pcs. 185.00
Bowl, master berry, blue 95.00
Butter dish, cov., footed, blue 150.00
Butter dish, cov., footed, marigold . . 150.00
Creamer, blue 50.00
Creamer, marigold 65.00
Pitcher, water, blue 700.00
Pitcher, water, marigold 225.00
Spooner, marigold................. 60.00
Sugar bowl, cov., blue 125.00
Table set: creamer, cov. sugar bowl & spooner; blue, 3 pcs. 350.00
Table set, marigold, 4 pcs. 350.00
Tumbler, blue 40.00
Tumbler, marigold................. 35.00

Water set: pitcher & 1 tumbler; marigold, 2 pcs. 200.00
Water set: pitcher & 6 tumblers; blue, 7 pcs. (ILLUS.) 800.00

FENTON'S (OPEN EDGE) BASKET

Aqua 64.00
Aqua, 2 sides turned up 80.00
Black 365.00
Blue 50.00
Green............................ 53.00
Ice blue, w/three rows of lace 150.00
Ice green.................125.00 to 150.00
Lavender 75.00
Marigold 20.00
Purple 50.00
Red 250.00
Vaseline 53.00
White, square.................... 75.00

FENTON'S FLOWERS or FLOWERS ROSE BOWL

Rose bowl, blue.................. 62.50
Rose bowl, clambroth.............. 88.00
Rose bowl, green 81.00
Rose bowl, ice green opalescent.... 650.00
Rose bowl, marigold............... 40.00
Rose bowl, purple 102.00
Rose bowl, white................. 275.00

FERN

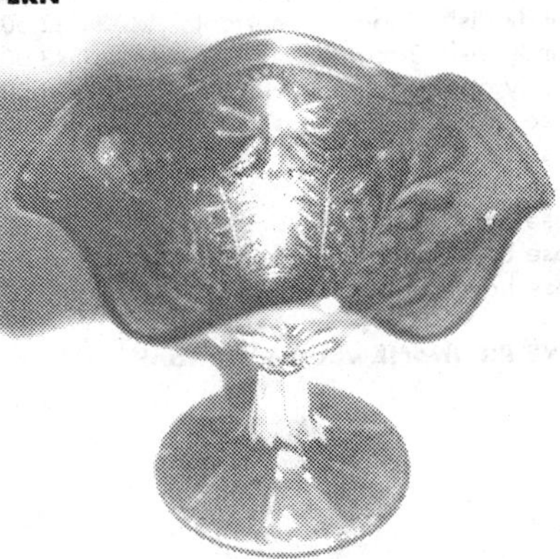

Fern Compote

Compote, w/Daisy & Plume exterior, green, Northwood (ILLUS.) 45.00
Compote, w/Daisy & Plume exterior, marigold (Northwood) 75.00
Compote, w/Daisy & Plume exterior, purple (Northwood) 60.00
Dish, hat-shaped, marigold (Fenton) 17.50
Dish, hat-shaped, red (Fenton) 375.00

FIELD FLOWER (Imperial)

Pitcher, water, amber 250.00
Pitcher, water, green 236.00
Pitcher, water, marigold 118.00
Pitcher, water, purple 390.00

Pitcher, water, teal blue 285.00
Tumbler, green 70.00
Tumbler, marigold ....20.00 to 35.00
Tumbler, purple 70.00
Water set: pitcher & 1 tumbler; green, 2 pcs. 350.00
Water set: pitcher & 6 tumblers; marigold, 7 pcs. 275.00

FIELD THISTLE (English)

Bowl, 10" d., marigold 50.00
Butter dish, cov., marigold 75.00
Pitcher, water, marigold 250.00
Plate, 6" d., marigold 110.00
Plate, 9" d., marigold 395.00
Spooner, marigold 55.00
Table set: cov. butter dish, creamer & spooner; marigold, 3 pcs. 175.00
Tumbler, marigold 45.00
Vase, 7" h., marigold 45.00

FILE & FAN

Compote, blue opalescent 495.00
Compote, peach opalescent 85.00

FINECUT & ROSES (Northwood)

Candy dish, 3-footed, amber 55.00
Candy dish, 3-footed, aqua opalescent 425.00
Candy dish, 3-footed, green 60.00
Candy dish, 3-footed, ice blue 175.00
Candy dish, 3-footed, marigold 32.50
Candy dish, 3-footed, purple 43.00
Candy dish, 3-footed, white 118.00
Rose bowl, aqua opalescent 900.00
Rose bowl, green 128.00
Rose bowl, ice blue 250.00
Rose bowl, marigold 76.00
Rose bowl, purple 75.00
Rose bowl, white 250.00

FINE RIB (Northwood & Fenton)

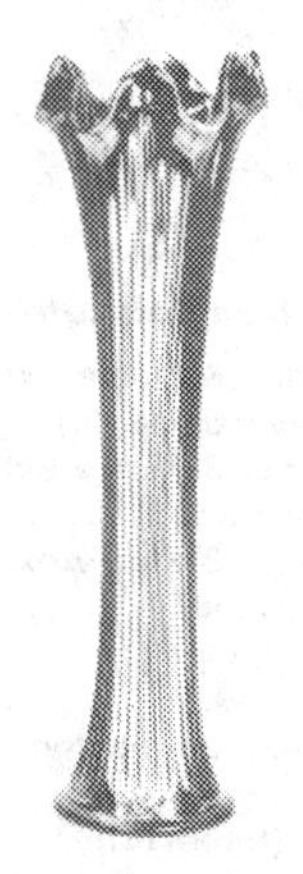

Fine Rib Vase

Vase, 6½" h., 5" d., marigold 32.00
Vase, 7" h., green 40.00
Vase, 7½" h., white 55.00
Vase, 8" h., aqua 49.00
Vase, 9" h., fluted rim, ice green ... 40.00
Vase, 9" h., red (Fenton) 215.00
Vase, 9½" h., vaseline (Fenton) 47.00
Vase, 10" h., amber (Fenton) 27.00
Vase, 10" h., aqua (Northwood) ....70.00 to 80.00
Vase, 10" h., red (Fenton) 250.00
Vase, 11" h., aqua 50.00
Vase, 11" h., blue (ILLUS.) 36.00
Vase, 11" h., ice green (Northwood) 65.00
Vase, 11" h., red (Fenton) 200.00
Vase, 12" h., blue 35.00
Vase, 14" h., marigold 38.00
Vase, 15" h., blue 50.00
Vase, 15" h., purple 65.00
Vase, 16" h., red (Fenton) 350.00

FISHERMAN'S MUG

Fisherman's Mug

Marigold 196.00
Peach opalescent (ILLUS.)..........1,250.00
Purple 84.00

FISHSCALE & BEADS

Banana boat, peach opalescent, 7" l. 35.00
Bonbon, marigold, 6" 35.00
Bonbon, peach opalescent, 6" 52.00
Plate, 7" d., marigold 52.00
Plate, 7" d., ruffled rim, peach opalescent 95.00
Plate, 7" d., purple 300.00
Plate, 7" d., white 80.00
Plate, 7½" d., purple 150.00

FLEUR DE LIS (Millersburg)

Bowl, 8" to 9" d., dome-footed, purple (ILLUS.) 205.00
Bowl, 10" d., green 190.00
Bowl, 10" d., marigold 150.00
Bowl, 10" d., purple 225.00
Bowl, tricornered, marigold 170.00

Fleur de Lis Bowl

Flowers & Frames Bowl

FLORAL & GRAPE (Dugan or Diamond Glass Co.)

Pitcher, water, blue 215.00
Pitcher, water, green 275.00
Pitcher, water, marigold 104.00
Pitcher, water, purple 140.00
Pitcher, water, white 289.00
Tumbler, blue 32.50
Tumbler, green 60.00
Tumbler, marigold 21.00
Tumbler, purple 34.00
Tumbler, white 60.00
Water set: pitcher & 1 tumbler; blue, 2 pcs. 170.00
Water set: pitcher & 4 tumblers; white, 5 pcs. 635.00
Water set: pitcher & 5 tumblers; purple, 6 pcs. 325.00
Water set: pitcher & 6 tumblers; marigold, 7 pcs. 212.00

FLORAL & WHEAT COMPOTE (Dugan)

Blue 50.00
Clambroth 35.00
Marigold 25.00
Peach opalescent 75.00
White 70.00

FLOWERS & BEADS

Card tray, tricornered, purple, 7" w. 62.00
Plate, 7½" w., 6-sided, peach opalescent ....95.00 to 145.00

FLOWERS & FRAMES

Bowl, 7" d., dome-footed, purple ... 100.00
Bowl, 9" d., dome-footed, peach opalescent 65.00
Bowl, 9" d., dome-footed, fluted, purple (ILLUS.) 120.00

FLOWERS ROSE BOWL (Fenton) - See Fenton's Flowers Pattern

FLUTE (Imperial)

Berry set: master bowl & 6 sauce dishes; purple, 7 pcs. 200.00
Bowl, 8" to 9" d., purple 70.00
Creamer, marigold 29.00
Creamer, purple 68.00
Pitcher, water, marigold 300.00
Pitcher, water, purple 293.00
Punch cup, green 12.50
Punch cup, marigold 35.00
Punch cup, purple 28.00
Punch set: bowl, base & 5 cups; purple, 7 pcs. 535.00
Sauce dish, green 34.00
Sauce dish, marigold 22.00
Sugar bowl, cov., green 35.00
Sugar bowl, open, green 35.00
Sugar bowl, open, purple 60.00
Table set: creamer, sugar bowl & toothpick holder; purple, 3 pcs.... 200.00
Toothpick holder, green 50.00
Toothpick holder, marigold 48.00
Toothpick holder, purple 67.00
Tumbler, aqua 175.00
Tumbler, cobalt blue 400.00
Tumbler, marigold 35.00
Tumbler, purple 80.00
Tumbler, smoky 425.00
Vase, 17" h., green 65.00
Water set: pitcher & 1 tumbler; purple, 2 pcs. 175.00

FLUTE (Northwood)

Pitcher, water, clambroth 175.00
Salt dip, master size, blue 45.00
Tumbler, cranberry 575.00
Tumbler, dark marigold 95.00
Tumbler, marigold 60.00

FLUTE & CANE

Goblet, marigold 65.00
Pitcher, milk, marigold 111.00

Pitcher, tankard, marigold 365.00
Tumbler, marigold 1,500.00

FOUR FLOWERS - See Pods & Posies Pattern

FOUR SEVENTY FOUR (Imperial)

Four Seventy Four Pitcher

Compote, green 90.00
Goblet, water, marigold 81.00
Pitcher, milk, green 208.00
Pitcher, milk, marigold 168.00
Pitcher, milk, purple 200.00
Pitcher, water, green (ILLUS.) .... 225.00 to 400.00
Pitcher, water, marigold 143.00
Pitcher, water, purple ..... 425.00 to 600.00
Punch cup, green 28.00
Punch cup, marigold 18.00
Punch cup, purple 46.00
Punch set: bowl, base & 4 cups; marigold, 6 pcs. 175.00
Tumbler, green 125.00
Tumbler, marigold 25.00
Tumbler, purple 114.00
Vase, 16" h., green 1,925.00
Vase, 16" h., marigold 525.00
Water set: pitcher & 4 tumblers; marigold, 5 pcs. 325.00
Water set: pitcher & 6 tumblers; purple, 7 pcs. 1,800.00
Wine, marigold 165.00

FROLICKING BEARS (U.S. Glass)

Pitcher, green .... 5,000.00 to 7,000.00

FROSTED BLOCK

Bowl, 8" to 9" d., scalloped & fluted, clambroth 26.50
Compote, clambroth 65.00
Plate, 9" d., clambroth 32.50
Plate, 9" d., marigold 50.00
Rose bowl, clambroth 60.00
Rose bowl, marigold 35.00
Rose bowl, white 45.00
Sugar bowl, clambroth 20.00
Vase, smoky 35.00

FRUIT SALAD

Punch bowl & base, purple, 2 pcs. .. 650.00
Punch cup, marigold 15.00
Punch cup, peach opalescent 100.00

FRUITS & FLOWERS (Northwood)

Berry set: master bowl & 6 sauce dishes; purple, 7 pcs. 230.00
Bonbon, stemmed, 2-handled, aqua opalescent 380.00
Bonbon, stemmed, 2-handled, blue 94.00
Bonbon, stemmed, 2-handled, green 70.00
Bonbon, stemmed, 2-handled, ice blue 450.00
Bonbon, stemmed, 2-handled, lavender 195.00
Bonbon, stemmed, 2-handled, marigold 40.00
Bonbon, stemmed, 2-handled, purple 60.00
Bonbon, stemmed, 2-handled, white 325.00
Bowl, 7" d., purple 65.00
Bowl, 7" d., ruffled, ice green 300.00
Bowl, master berry, 10" d., green .... 65.00 to 110.00
Bowl, master berry, 10" d., ice green 750.00
Bowl, master berry, 10" d., marigold 35.00
Bowl, master berry, 10" d., purple .. 78.00
Bowl, 10" d., ruffled, ice green 475.00
Card tray, green 125.00
Plate, 6" d., marigold 168.00
Plate, 7" d., blue 320.00
Plate, 7" d., green 115.00
Plate, 7" d., marigold .... 80.00 to 95.00
Plate, 7" d., purple 120.00
Plate, 7½" d., hand-grip, pastel marigold 185.00
Plate, 7½" d., hand-grip, purple 200.00
Sauce dish, marigold 29.00
Sauce dish, purple 36.00

GARDEN PATH

Berry set: master bowl & 6 sauce dishes; white, 7 pcs. 350.00
Bowl, 8" to 9" d., marigold 45.00
Bowl, 10" d., ruffled, marigold 75.00
Bowl, 10" d., ruffled, peach opalescent 200.00
Bowl, 10" d., ruffled, white 200.00
Bowl, variant, white 50.00
Plate, 6" d., white 260.00
Plate, 7" d., peach opalescent 500.00
Plate, chop, 11" d., peach opalescent 4,200.00
Plate, chop, 11" d., purple (ILLUS.) 1,750.00

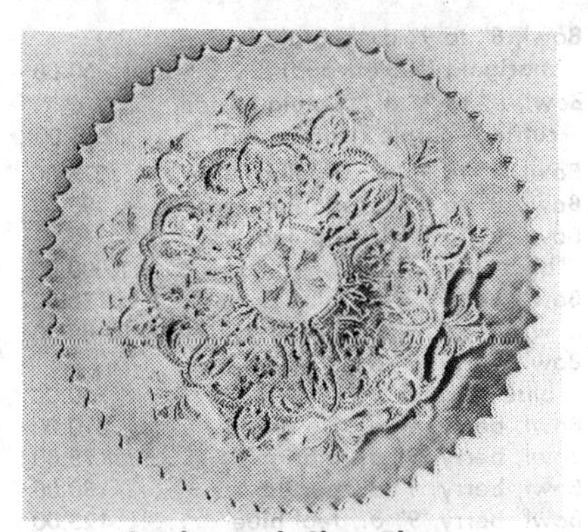

Garden Path Chop Plate

Sauce dish, peach opalescent 115.00
Sauce dish, purple 75.00

GARLAND ROSE BOWL (Fenton)

Blue 60.00
Marigold 40.00

GAY NINETIES (Millersburg)

Pitcher, amethyst 7,500.00
Pitcher, green . . . . 5,550.00 to 8,000.00
Tumbler, purple . . . . 600.00 to 1,000.00

GOD & HOME

Pitcher, blue 1,130.00
Tumbler, blue 225.00
Water set: pitcher & 6 tumblers; blue, 7 pcs. 2,400.00

GODDESS OF HARVEST (Fenton)

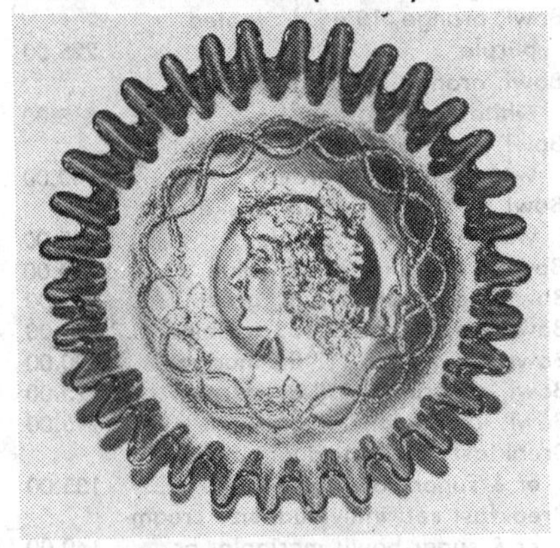

Goddess of Harvest Bowl

Bowl, blue (ILLUS.) 3,100.00
Bowl, marigold 4,200.00

GOLDEN HARVEST or HARVEST TIME (U.S. Glass)

Decanter w/stopper, marigold 95.00
Decanter w/stopper, purple . . . . 150.00 to 175.00
Wine, marigold 18.00

GOOD LUCK (Northwood)

Bowl, 7" d., ruffled, blue 245.00
Bowl, 7" d., ruffled, green 303.00
Bowl, 7" d., ruffled, purple 167.00
Bowl, 8" to 9" d., piecrust, aqua opalescent 1,250.00

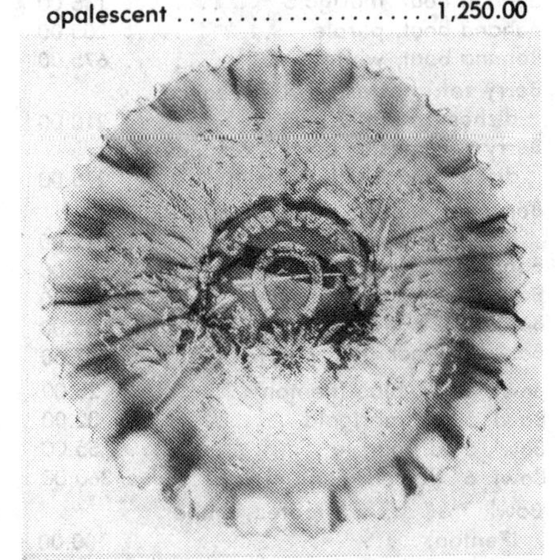

Good Luck Bowl

Bowl, 8" to 9" d., piecrust, blue (ILLUS.) 240.00
Bowl, 8" to 9" d., piecrust, clambroth 450.00
Bowl, 8" to 9" d., piecrust, green . . . 290.00
Bowl, 8" to 9" d., piecrust, lavender 700.00
Bowl, 8" to 9" d., piecrust, marigold 112.00
Bowl, 8" to 9" d., piecrust, purple . . 158.00
Bowl, 8" to 9" d., piecrust, teal blue (Northwood) 700.00
Plate, 9" d., blue 425.00
Plate, 9" d., green 425.00
Plate, 9" d., marigold 215.00
Plate, 9" d., purple 300.00
Plate, 9" d., white 1,600.00

GRAPE & CABLE

Grape & Cable Bowl

Banana boat, blue.................. 330.00
Banana boat, green 275.00
Banana boat, stippled, green 400.00
Banana boat, ice blue 550.00
Banana boat, ice green 590.00
Banana boat, marigold 146.00
Banana boat, purple................ 205.00
Banana boat, white 675.00
Berry set: master bowl & 6 sauce dishes; green, 7 pcs. 210.00
Berry set: master bowl & 6 sauce dishes; marigold, 7 pcs. 275.00
Berry set: master bowl & 6 sauce dishes; purple, 7 pcs.............. 312.00
Bonbon, 2-handled, blue 65.00
Bonbon, 2-handled, green............ 40.00
Bonbon, 2-handled, marigold 35.00
Bonbon, 2-handled, purple 47.50
Bowl, 5" d., blue (Fenton)........... 25.00
Bowl, 5" d., marigold............... 32.00
Bowl, 5" d., purple 55.00
Bowl, 6" d., red (Fenton)........... 360.00
Bowl, 7½" d., ball-footed, amber (Fenton) 100.00
Bowl, 7½" d., ball-footed, aqua (Fenton) 96.00
Bowl, 7½" d., ball-footed, blue (Fenton) 65.00
Bowl, 7½" d., ball-footed, green (Fenton) 40.00
Bowl, 7½" d., ball-footed, marigold (Fenton) 25.00
Bowl, 7½" d., ball-footed, purple (Fenton) 52.00
Bowl, 7½" d., ball-footed, red (Fenton)............................ 425.00
Bowl, 7½" d., ball-footed, vaseline (Fenton) 80.00
Bowl, 7½" d., ruffled, ice blue 875.00
Bowl, 7½" d., spatula-footed, marigold (Northwood) 26.00
Bowl, 7½" d., spatula-footed, purple (Northwood) 60.00
Bowl, ice cream shape, 8" d., footed, celeste blue (ILLUS.) 600.00
Bowl, 8" to 9" d., aqua opalescent (Northwood) 950.00
Bowl, 8" to 9" d., ball-footed, blue (Fenton) 58.00
Bowl, 8" to 9" d., ball-footed, celeste blue (Fenton) 550.00
Bowl, 8" to 9" d., ball-footed, green (Fenton) 52.00
Bowl, 8" to 9" d., ball-footed, purple (Fenton) 45.00
Bowl, 8" to 9" d., ball-footed, red (Fenton) 1,200.00
Bowl, 8" to 9" d., ball-footed, white (Fenton) 70.00
Bowl, 8" to 9" d., spatula-footed, blue (Northwood) 55.00
Bowl, 8" to 9" d., spatula-footed, green (Northwood) 70.00
Bowl, 8" to 9" d., spatula-footed, marigold (Northwood) 60.00
Bowl, 8" to 9" d., spatula-footed, ruffled, purple (Northwood) 55.00
Bowl, 8" to 9" d., stippled, blue 275.00
Bowl, 8" to 9" d., stippled, green ... 95.00
Bowl, 8" to 9" d., stippled, ice blue 1,000.00
Bowl, berry, 9" d., blue............ 175.00
Bowl, berry, 9" d., green ....60.00 to 85.00
Bowl, berry, 9" d., stippled, ice blue 750.00
Bowl, berry, 9" d., ice green 810.00
Bowl, berry, 9" d., marigold........ 75.00
Bowl, berry, 9" d., purple 80.00
Bowl, berry, 9" d., teal blue 125.00
Bowl, orange, 10½" d., footed, Persian Medallion interior, blue (Fenton)........................... 250.00
Bowl, orange, 10½" d., footed, Persian Medallion interior, green (Fenton)....................... 235.00
Bowl, orange, 10½" d., footed, Persian Medallion interior, marigold (Fenton)....................... 90.00
Bowl, orange, 10½" d., footed, Persian Medallion interior, purple (Fenton)....................... 195.00
Bowl, orange, 10½" d., footed, blue 225.00
Bowl, orange, 10½" d., footed, green 185.00
Bowl, orange, 10½" d., footed, ice blue 1,100.00
Bowl, orange, 10½" d., footed, marigold 115.00
Bowl, orange, 10½" d., footed, purple 225.00
Bowl, orange, 10½" d., footed, white 815.00
Bowl, 10½" d., ruffled, Basketweave exterior, green 80.00
Bowl, 10½" d., ruffled, Basketweave exterior, purple 135.00
Bowl, ice cream, 11" d., blue....... 600.00
Bowl, ice cream, 11" d., green 135.00
Bowl, ice cream, 11" d., ice blue ...2,050.00
Bowl, ice cream, 11" d., marigold .. 90.00
Bowl, ice cream, 11" d., purple..... 125.00
Bowl, ice cream, 11" d., white 295.00
Breakfast set: individual size creamer & sugar bowl; green, pr. 135.00
Breakfast set: individual size creamer & sugar bowl; marigold, pr. ... 140.00
Breakfast set: individual size creamer & sugar bowl; purple, pr. 160.00
Butter dish, cov., green............ 165.00
Butter dish, cov., marigold 148.00
Butter dish, cov., purple 180.00
Candle lamp, green 530.00
Candle lamp, marigold ....395.00 to 550.00
Candle lamp, purple................ 385.00
Candle lamp shade, marigold 210.00
Candle lamp shade, purple.......... 235.00

Candlestick, green (single) 85.00
Candlestick, marigold (single) 60.00
Candlestick, purple (single) 120.00
Candlesticks, marigold, pr. 155.00
Candlesticks, purple, pr. 250.00
Card tray, marigold 65.00
Centerpiece bowl, blue 625.00
Centerpiece bowl, green ... 225.00 to 400.00
Centerpiece bowl, ice blue 850.00
Centerpiece bowl, ice green 650.00
Centerpiece bowl, marigold 185.00
Centerpiece bowl, purple 350.00
Centerpiece bowl, white 585.00
Cologne bottle w/stopper, green ... 210.00
Cologne bottle w/stopper, marigold 145.00
Cologne bottle w/stopper, purple ... 185.00
Cologne bottles w/stoppers, marigold, pr. 450.00
Compote, cov., large, marigold 1,250.00
Compote, cov., small, purple 245.00
Compote, cov., large, purple 350.00
Compote, open, large, green 385.00
Compote, open, large, marigold 310.00
Compote, open, small, purple 300.00
Compote, open, large, purple 375.00
Cookie jar, cov., blue 500.00
Cookie jar, cov., marigold 285.00
Cookie jar, cov., purple 295.00
Cookie jar, cov., white 1,010.00
Creamer, green 90.00
Creamer, purple 110.00
Creamer, individual size, green .... 50.00 to 65.00
Creamer, individual size, marigold .. 75.00
Creamer, individual size, purple 65.00
Creamer & cov. sugar bowl, purple, pr. .... 225.00 to 400.00
Cup & saucer, green 365.00
Cup & saucer, marigold 265.00
Cuspidor, purple .... 4,000.00 to 7,000.00
Decanter w/stopper, whiskey, marigold 450.00
Decanter w/stopper, whiskey, purple 825.00
Dresser set, purple, 7 pcs. 2,500.00
Dresser set, marigold, 8 pcs. 1,200.00
Dresser tray, green 255.00
Dresser tray, marigold 115.00
Dresser tray, purple 180.00
Fernery, marigold 980.00
Fernery, white .... 700.00 to 1,000.00
Hatpin holder, green 195.00
Hatpin holder, ice blue 1,600.00
Hatpin holder, marigold 135.00
Hatpin holder, purple 175.00
Hat shape, green 75.00
Hat shape, marigold 35.00
Hat shape, purple 45.00
Humidor (or tobacco jar), cov., blue 915.00
Humidor, cov., marigold 220.00
Humidor, cov., purple 375.00
Ice cream dish, celeste blue 600.00
Ice cream dish, ice green 625.00
Ice cream set, purple, 7 pcs. 530.00
Nappy, single handle, green 70.00
Nappy, single handle, marigold 45.00
Nappy, single handle, purple 90.00
Perfume bottle w/stopper, marigold .... 350.00 to 450.00
Perfume bottle w/stopper, purple .. 575.00
Pin tray, green 125.00
Pin tray, marigold .... 100.00 to 150.00
Pin tray, purple 175.00
Pitcher, water, 8¼" h., green 350.00
Pitcher, water, 8¼" h., marigold ... 160.00
Pitcher, water, 8¼" h., purple 250.00
Pitcher, tankard, 9¾" h., green 1,500.00
Pitcher, tankard, 9¾" h., ice green 2,400.00
Pitcher, tankard, 9¾" h., marigold 468.00
Pitcher, tankard, 9¾" h., purple 585.00
Plate, 5" to 6" d., purple (Northwood) 110.00
Plate, 7½" d., turned-up hand grip, green 85.00
Plate, 7½" d., turned-up hand grip, marigold 50.00
Plate, 7½" d., turned-up hand grip, purple 85.00
Plate, 8" d., footed, green (Fenton) .... 65.00 to 110.00
Plate, 8" d., footed, purple 72.00
Plate, 9" d., blue 250.00
Plate, 9" d., green 85.00
Plate, 9" d., spatula-footed, green .. 90.00
Plate, 9" d., spatula-footed, ice green 1,000.00
Plate, 9" d., marigold 65.00
Plate, 9" d., spatula-footed, marigold 68.00
Plate, 9" d., purple 100.00
Plate, 9" d., spatula-footed, purple 88.00
Plate, 9" d., Basketweave exterior, green 85.00
Plate, 9" d., Basketweave exterior, marigold 70.00
Plate, 9" d., Basketweave exterior, purple 75.00
Plate, 9" d., stippled, blue 485.00
Plate, 9" d., stippled, green 250.00
Plate, 9" d., stippled, ice blue 1,700.00
Plate, 9" d., stippled, marigold 70.00
Plate, 9" d., stippled, purple 192.00
Plate, 9" d., stippled, teal blue 1,200.00
Powder jar, cov., green 95.00
Powder jar, cov., marigold 58.00
Powder jar, cov., purple 90.00
Punch bowl & base, blue, 11" d., 2 pcs. 395.00
Punch bowl & base, purple, 11" d., 2 pcs. 360.00
Punch bowl & base, purple, 14" d., 2 pcs. 525.00
Punch cup, aqua opalescent 260.00

Punch cup, blue ... 35.00
Punch cup, stippled, blue ... 60.00
Punch cup, green ... 36.00
Punch cup, stippled, green ... 40.00
Punch cup, ice blue ... 60.00
Punch cup, ice green ... 55.00 to 75.00
Punch cup, marigold ... 19.00
Punch cup, purple ... 21.00
Punch cup, white ... 58.00
Punch set: bowl, base & 3 cups; purple, 5 pcs. ... 585.00
Punch set: 11" bowl & 6 cups; marigold, 7 pcs. ... 425.00
Punch set: 14" bowl & 6 cups; white, 7 pcs. ... 1,700.00
Punch set: 14" bowl, base & 6 cups; marigold, 8 pcs. ... 595.00
Punch set: 14" bowl, base & 10 cups; blue, 12 pcs. ... 4,200.00

Grape & Cable Punch Set

Punch set: 14" bowl, base & 12 cups; purple, 14 pcs. (ILLUS.) ... 1,400.00
Punch set: 17" bowl, base & 6 cups; marigold, 8 pcs. ... 895.00
Punch set: 17" bowl, base & 8 cups; purple, 10 pcs. ... 1,350.00
Sauce dish, green ... 30.00
Sauce dish, marigold ... 32.50
Sauce dish, purple ... 35.00
Sherbet or individual ice cream dish, green ... 35.00
Sherbet or individual ice cream dish, marigold ... 30.00
Sherbet or individual ice cream dish, purple ... 45.00
Spooner, green ... 90.00
Spooner, ice green ... 200.00
Spooner, marigold ... 50.00
Spooner, purple ... 90.00
Sugar bowl, cov., green ... 125.00
Sugar bowl, cov., marigold ... 75.00
Sugar bowl, cov., purple ... 96.00
Sugar bowl, individual size, green ... 50.00
Sugar bowl, individual size, marigold ... 40.00
Sugar bowl, individual size, purple ... 50.00
Sweetmeat jar, cov., marigold ... 750.00
Sweetmeat jar, cov., purple ... 195.00
Table set: cov. sugar bowl, creamer, spooner & cov. butter dish; green, 4 pcs. ... 500.00
Table set: cov. sugar bowl, creamer, spooner & cov. butter dish; marigold, 4 pcs. ... 450.00
Table set: cov. sugar bowl, creamer, spooner & cov. butter dish; purple, 4 pcs. ... 475.00
Tumbler, green ... 50.00
Tumbler, marigold ... 25.00
Tumbler, purple ... 35.00
Tumbler, smoky ... 30.00
Tumbler, stippled, marigold ... 68.00
Tumbler, stippled, purple ... 75.00
Tumbler, tankard, green ... 200.00
Tumbler, tankard, marigold ... 65.00
Tumbler, tankard, purple ... 35.00
Water set: pitcher & 6 tumblers; green, 7 pcs. ... 460.00
Water set: pitcher & 6 tumblers; ice green, 7 pcs. ... 2,400.00
Water set: pitcher & 6 tumblers; marigold, 7 pcs. ... 325.00
Water set: pitcher & 6 tumblers; purple, 7 pcs. ... 425.00
Water set: tankard pitcher & 6 tumblers; marigold, 7 pcs. ... 825.00
Water set: tankard pitcher & 6 tumblers; purple, 7 pcs. ... 850.00
Whimsey compote (sweetmeat base), green ... 175.00
Whimsey compote (sweetmeat base), purple ... 245.00
Whimsey teacup, purple ... 115.00
Whiskey set: whiskey decanter w/stopper & 1 shot glass; marigold, 2 pcs. ... 750.00
Whiskey shot glass, marigold ... 160.00
Whiskey shot glass, purple ... 150.00
Wine, marigold ... 35.00

GRAPE & GOTHIC ARCHES (Northwood)

Grape & Gothic Arches Table Set

Berry set: master bowl & 4 sauce dishes; blue, 5 pcs. ... 150.00
Berry set: master bowl & 6 sauce dishes; blue, 7 pcs. ... 185.00
Bowl, master berry, blue ... 60.00
Butter dish, cov., green ... 225.00
Creamer, blue ... 68.00
Creamer & spooner, blue, 2 pcs. ... 90.00
Pitcher, water, blue ... 250.00 to 300.00
Pitcher, water, green ... 235.00
Pitcher, water, marigold ... 150.00
Sauce dish, aqua ... 25.00
Sauce dish, marigold ... 15.00

Spooner, blue 60.00
Spooner, marigold 28.00
Sugar bowl, cov., blue 75.00
Sugar bowl, cov., green 67.50
Sugar bowl, cov., marigold 45.00
Table set: creamer, cov. sugar bowl & spooner; blue, 3 pcs. 280.00
Table set, marigold, 4 pcs. (ILLUS.) .... 175.00 to 195.00
Tumbler, amber 35.00
Tumbler, blue 45.00
Tumbler, green 38.50
Tumbler, marigold 30.00
Water set: pitcher & 6 tumblers; blue, 7 pcs. 475.00
Water set: pitcher & 6 tumblers; marigold, 7 pcs. 375.00

GRAPE & LATTICE

Tumbler, blue 36.00
Tumbler, marigold 22.00
Water set: pitcher & 6 tumblers; marigold, 7 pcs. 300.00

GRAPE ARBOR (Northwood)

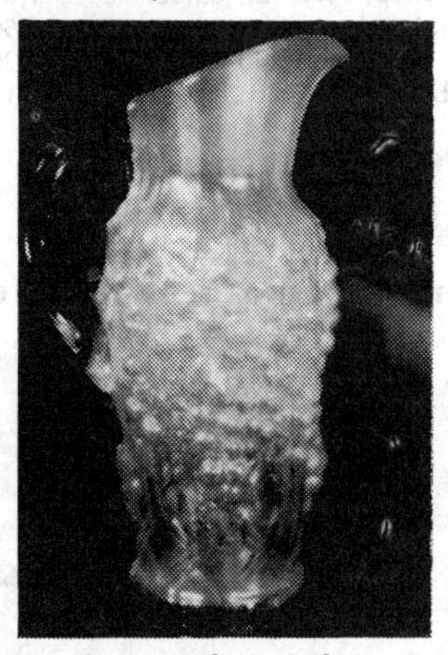

Grape Arbor Pitcher

Bowl, 10" d., footed, blue (Dugan) .. 210.00
Bowl, 10" d., footed, marigold (Dugan) 90.00
Hat shape, blue 80.00
Hat shape, ice green 375.00
Pitcher, water, ice green (ILLUS.) 3,250.00
Pitcher, water, marigold 350.00
Pitcher, water, purple 540.00
Pitcher, water, white 475.00
Tumbler, blue 175.00
Tumbler, ice blue 145.00
Tumbler, ice green 515.00
Tumbler, marigold 40.00
Tumbler, purple 50.00
Tumbler, white 90.00
Water set: pitcher & 5 tumblers; marigold, 6 pcs. 315.00

Water set: pitcher & 6 tumblers; purple, 7 pcs. 695.00
Water set: pitcher & 6 tumblers; white, 7 pcs. 1,460.00

GRAPE DELIGHT

Nut bowl, 6-footed, blue 78.00
Nut bowl, 6-footed, marigold 55.00
Nut bowl, 6-footed, purple 52.00
Nut bowl, 6-footed, white 95.00
Rose bowl, 6-footed, blue 78.00
Rose bowl, 6-footed, clambroth 60.00
Rose bowl, 6-footed, marigold 65.00
Rose bowl, 6-footed, purple 75.00
Rose bowl, 6-footed, white 75.00
Wine, purple 23.00

GRAPEVINE LATTICE

Grapevine Lattice Plate

Bowl, 7" d., ruffled, marigold 28.00
Bowl, 7" d., ruffled, white 42.50
Hat shape, white 65.00
Pitcher, water, blue .... 225.00 to 410.00
Pitcher, water, marigold ... 160.00 to 230.00
Pitcher, water, white 850.00
Plate, 6" to 7" d., blue 80.00
Plate, 6" to 7" d., marigold 55.00
Plate, 6" to 7" d., peach opalescent 140.00
Plate, 6" to 7" d., purple (ILLUS.) ... 190.00
Plate, 6" to 7" d., white 80.00
Tumbler, marigold 40.00
Tumbler, purple 40.00
Tumbler, white 85.00
Water set: pitcher & 6 tumblers; marigold, 7 pcs. 525.00

GREEK KEY (Northwood)

Bowl, 8" to 9" d., blue 250.00
Bowl, 8" to 9" d., fluted, green 90.00
Bowl, 8" to 9" d., ruffled, marigold 70.00
Bowl, 8" to 9" d., purple 96.00
Pitcher, water, green 700.00
Pitcher, water, marigold 700.00
Pitcher, water, purple (ILLUS.) 875.00

Greek Key Water Pitcher

Plate, 9" d., green 350.00
Plate, 9" d., marigold 370.00
Tumbler, green 80.00
Tumbler, marigold.................. 65.00
Tumbler, purple.................... 75.00
Water set: pitcher & 6 tumblers; purple, 7 pcs. 1,400.00

HAMMERED BELL

Hammered Bell Shade

Chandelier shade, white (ILLUS.).... 80.00

HANGING CHERRIES - See Cherry (Millersburg) Pattern

HARVEST FLOWER (Dugan or Diamond Glass)

Pitcher, tankard, marigold.........1,600.00
Tumbler, marigold.................. 90.00

HARVEST TIME - See Golden Harvest Pattern

HATTIE (Imperial)

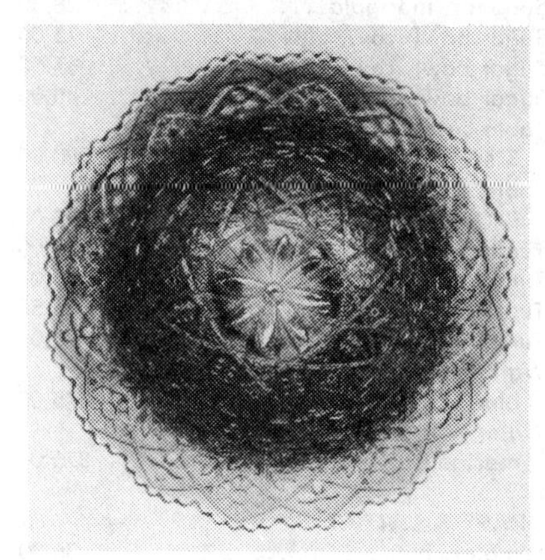

Hattie Bowl

Bowl, 8" to 9" d., marigold......... 32.00
Bowl, 8" to 9" d., purple........... 65.00
Bowl, 8" to 9" d., smoky (ILLUS.) ... 50.00
Plate, chop, 10½" d., amber.......1,000.00
Plate, chop, green 500.00
Plate, chop, marigold.............. 200.00
Rose bowl, marigold................ 110.00

HEADDRESS BOWL (Imperial)

Blue 55.00
Marigold 37.50

HEART & HORSESHOE (Fenton's Good Luck)

Heart & Horseshoe Bowl

Bowl, marigold (ILLUS.) 925.00

HEART & VINE (Fenton)

Bowl, 8" to 9" d., ribbon candy rim, blue (ILLUS.) 75.00
Bowl, 8" to 9" d., green 65.00
Bowl, 8" to 9" d., marigold......... 40.00
Bowl, 8" to 9" d., purple........... 75.00
Plate, 9" d., blue.................. 280.00

Heart & Vine Bowl

Plate, 9" d., marigold 250.00
Plate, 9" d., purple 225.00

HEARTS & FLOWERS (Northwood)

Hearts & Flowers Plate

Bowl, 8" to 9" d., aqua w/opalescent tips 1,100.00
Bowl, 8" to 9" d., piecrust rim, blue 425.00
Bowl, 8" to 9" d., ruffled, blue 450.00
Bowl, 8" to 9" d., ribbon candy rim, green 710.00
Bowl, 8" to 9" d., ruffled, ice blue .. 275.00
Bowl, 8" to 9" d., ruffled, ice green 535.00
Bowl, 8" to 9" d., ruffled, marigold 245.00
Bowl, 8" to 9" d., piecrust rim, purple 440.00
Bowl, 8" to 9" d., ruffled, purple ... 320.00
Bowl, 8" to 9" d., ruffled, white 185.00
Compote, 6¾" h., aqua opalescent 385.00
Compote, 6¾" h., blue 215.00
Compote, 6¾" h., green 550.00
Compote, 6¾" h., ice blue 500.00
Compote, 6¾" h., ice green 710.00
Compote, 6¾" h., marigold 120.00
Compote, 6¾" h., purple 365.00
Compote, 6¾" h., white 125.00
Plate, green 1,600.00
Plate, ice green 1,000.00
Plate, marigold 292.00
Plate, purple (ILLUS.) 600.00
Plate, white 695.00

HEAVY GRAPE (Dugan, Diamond Glass or Millersburg)

Heavy Grape Ice Cream Bowl

Bowl, master berry, 10" d., peach opalescent 650.00
Bowl, master berry, 10" d., purple .. 400.00
Bowl, ice cream, purple, Millersburg (ILLUS.) 600.00
Compote, purple (Millersburg) 850.00

HEAVY GRAPE (Imperial)

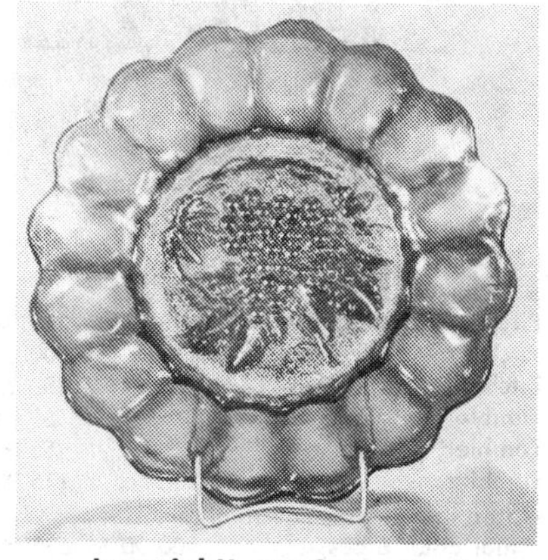

Imperial Heavy Grape Bowl

Bowl, 5" d., 2" h., marigold 30.00
Bowl, 5" d., 2" h., purple 32.50
Bowl, 6" d., marigold 30.00
Bowl, 7" d., fluted, green 30.00
Bowl, 7" d., purple 42.50
Bowl, 8" to 9" d., green 55.00
Bowl, 8" to 9" d., marigold 40.00
Bowl, 10" d., purple (ILLUS.) 125.00
Compote, green 850.00

Nappy, handled, green 35.00
Nappy, handled, marigold 28.00
Nappy, handled, purple 35.00
Plate, 7" to 8" d., amber 75.00
Plate, 7" to 8" d., blue 65.00
Plate, 7" to 8" d., green 55.00
Plate, 7" to 8" d., marigold 50.00
Plate, 7" to 8" d., purple 78.00
Plate, chop, 11" d., amber 165.00
Plate, chop, 11" d., green 250.00
Plate, chop, 11" d., marigold 175.00
Plate, chop, 11" d., purple 285.00
Platter, 11 x 7½", green 65.00
Punch bowl, green 225.00
Punch bowl & base, marigold, 2 pcs. 285.00
Punch bowl & base, purple, 2 pcs. .. 285.00
Punch cup, green 20.00
Punch cup, marigold 20.00
Punch cup, purple 38.00
Punch set: bowl, base & 5 cups; marigold, 7 pcs. 195.00
Punch set: bowl, base & 5 cups; purple, 7 pcs. 450.00
Punch set: bowl, base & 6 cups; green, 8 pcs. 250.00

HEAVY IRIS (Dugan or Diamond Glass)

Heavy Iris Water Set

Pitcher, water, marigold (ILLUS.) 368.00
Pitcher, water, peach opalescent ... 1,000.00
Pitcher, water, white 1,250.00
Tumbler, marigold (ILLUS.) 65.00
Tumbler, purple 55.00
Tumbler, white 175.00
Water set: pitcher & 5 tumblers; marigold, 6 pcs. .... 500.00 to 635.00
Water set: pitcher & 6 tumblers; purple, 7 pcs. 1,800.00

HERON MUG (Dugan)

Marigold 75.00
Purple 225.00

HOBNAIL (Millersburg)

Butter dish, cov., marigold 350.00

Millersburg Hobnail Butter Dish

Butter dish, cov., purple (ILLUS.) 625.00
Cuspidor, marigold 475.00
Cuspidor, purple .... 460.00 to 600.00
Pitcher, water, blue 1,500.00
Pitcher, water, marigold 1,500.00
Pitcher, water, purple 1,500.00
Rose bowl, marigold 150.00
Rose bowl, purple 315.00
Sugar bowl, cov., marigold 300.00
Tumbler, blue 1,000.00
Tumbler, marigold 750.00
Tumbler, purple 600.00

HOBNAIL, SWIRL - See Swirl Hobnail Pattern

HOBSTAR (Imperial)

Hobstar Pickle Castor

Butter dish, cov., marigold 62.50
Compote, marigold 45.00
Cookie jar, cov., marigold 135.00
Creamer, marigold 30.00
Creamer, purple 50.00
Pickle castor, cov., marigold, complete w/silver plate frame (ILLUS.) 450.00
Spooner, marigold 45.00

Spooner, purple 85.00
Sugar bowl, cov., green 50.00
Sugar bowl, cov., marigold 40.00
Table set, marigold, 4 pcs. 110.00

HOBSTAR & FEATHER (Millersburg)

Hobstar & Feather Rose Bowl

Punch cup, green 28.50
Punch cup, marigold ....20.00 to 45.00
Punch cup, purple 56.00
Punch set: bowl, base & 12 cups; marigold, 14 pcs. 1,525.00
Rose bowl, green, 7½" top d., 13" h. (ILLUS.) 1,235.00
Vase, 13" h., purple 4,500.00

HOBSTAR BAND

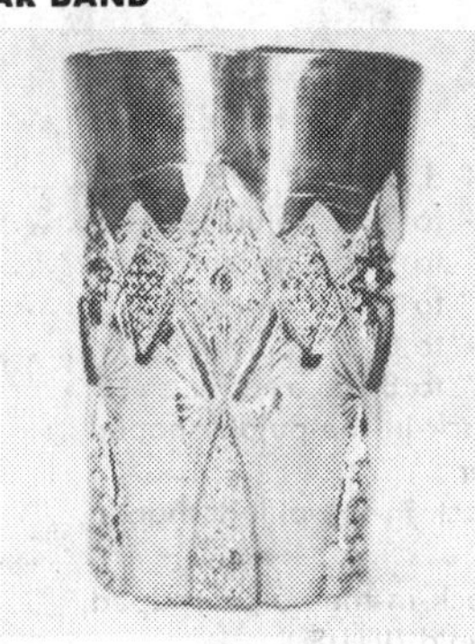

Hobstar Band Tumbler

Celery vase, 2-handled, marigold ... 75.00
Pitcher, marigold 167.00
Tumbler, marigold (ILLUS.) 45.00
Water set: pitcher & 6 tumblers; marigold, 7 pcs. 395.00

HOLLY, HOLLY BERRIES & CARNIVAL HOLLY

Bonbon, 2-handled, blue 65.00
Bonbon, 2-handled, green 55.00
Bonbon, 2-handled, marigold 45.00
Bonbon, 2-handled, purple 60.00
Bowl, 5" d., marigold 25.00
Bowl, 7" d., marigold 35.00
Bowl, 7" d., fluted, peach opalescent (Dugan) 45.00
Bowl, 8" to 9" d., blue 48.00
Bowl, 8" to 9" d., green 53.00
Bowl, 8" to 9" d., marigold 45.00
Bowl, 8" to 9" d., purple 55.00

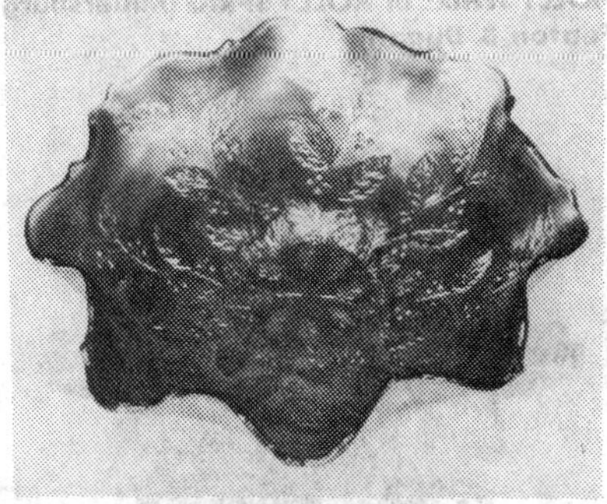

Holly Bowl

Bowl, 8" to 9" d., red, Fenton (ILLUS.) 688.00
Bowl, 8" to 9" d., vaseline 80.00
Bowl, 8" to 9" d., white 95.00
Bowl, 10" d., aqua 195.00
Bowl, 10" d., fluted, green 78.00
Bowl, 10" d., fluted, marigold 90.00
Bowl, 10" d., ribbon candy rim, vaseline (Fenton) 193.00
Bowl, ruffled, white 100.00
Compote, small, aqua w/marigold overlay 45.00
Compote, small, blue 35.00
Compote, small, green 32.00
Compote, small, marigold 25.00
Compote, small, purple 57.50
Compote, small, red (Fenton) 335.00
Compote, small, vaseline 75.00
Dish, hat-shaped, amber, 5¾" 28.00
Dish, hat-shaped, aqua, 5¾" 55.00
Dish, hat-shaped, blue, 5¾" 28.00
Dish, hat-shaped, green, 5¾" 28.00
Dish, hat-shaped, marigold, 5¾" ... 22.00
Dish, hat-shaped, milk white w/marigold overlay 70.00
Dish, hat-shaped, red, 5¾" 276.00
Dish, hat-shaped, vaseline, 5¾" 48.00
Goblet, green 75.00
Goblet, marigold 30.00
Goblet, red (Fenton) 382.00
Plate, 9" to 10" d., blue 200.00
Plate, 9" to 10" d., clambroth 100.00
Plate, 9" to 10" d., green 375.00
Plate, 9" to 10" d., marigold 85.00
Plate, 9" to 10" d., purple 250.00
Plate, 9" to 10" d., white 150.00
Sauceboat, handled, peach opalescent (Dugan) 75.00
Sauceboat, handled, purple 52.00
Sherbet, red (Fenton) 380.00

HOLLY SPRIG - See Holly Whirl Pattern

HOLLY STAR PANELED or HOLLY STAR (Northwood)

Bonbon, green 50.00
Bonbon, marigold 20.00

HOLLY WHIRL or HOLLY SPRIG (Millersburg, Fenton & Dugan)

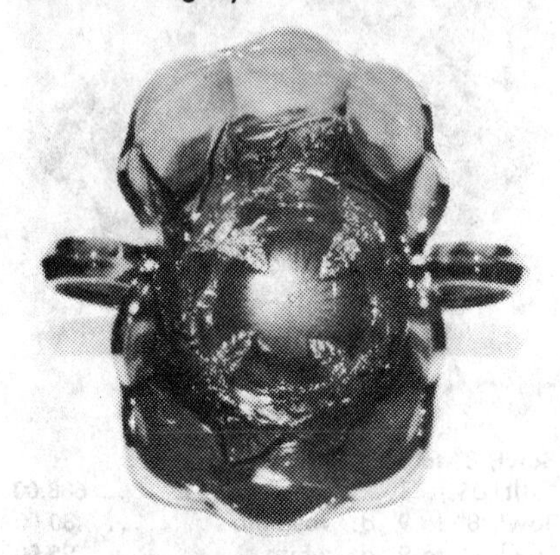

Holly Whirl 2-Handled Nappy

Bowl, 7" d., marigold 65.00
Bowl, 8" to 9" d., ruffled, blue 55.00
Bowl, 8" to 9" d., green 58.00
Bowl, 8" to 9" d., marigold 42.00
Bowl, 8" to 9" d., purple 50.00
Nappy, single handle, peach opalescent (Dugan) 49.00
Nappy, single handle, purple (Dugan) 35.00
Nappy, tricornered, green (Dugan) .. 60.00
Nappy, tricornered, marigold (Millersburg) 125.00
Nappy, tricornered, purple (Dugan) 75.00
Nappy, 2-handled, amethyst, Millersburg (ILLUS.) 65.00
Nappy, 2-handled, green 120.00
Nut dish, 2-handled, green 69.00
Nut dish, 2-handled, purple 68.00
Sauceboat, peach opalescent (Dugan) 50.00
Sauce dish, purple, 5½" d. (Millersburg) 145.00
Sauce dish, marigold, 5¾" d. 125.00
Sauce dish, green, 6½" d., (Millersburg) 165.00

HOMESTEAD (Imperial)

Plate, amber 680.00
Plate, blue 1,125.00
Plate, green 845.00
Plate, marigold 325.00
Plate, purple 585.00
Plate, white 600.00

HONEYCOMB

Honeycomb Rose Bowl

Rose bowl, marigold 110.00
Rose bowl, peach opalescent (ILLUS.) 195.00

HORSE HEADS or HORSE MEDALLION (Fenton)

Horse Heads Bowl

Bowl, 5" d., footed, marigold 55.00
Bowl, 7" to 8" d., blue 110.00
Bowl, 7" to 8" d., green 130.00
Bowl, 7" to 8" d., marigold 72.00
Bowl, 7" to 8" d., purple 118.00
Bowl, 7" to 8" d., red 800.00
Bowl, jack-in-the-pulpit shaped, amber 195.00
Bowl, jack-in-the-pulpit shaped, blue 135.00
Bowl, jack-in-the-pulpit shaped, marigold (ILLUS.) 75.00
Bowl, jack-in-the-pulpit shaped, vaseline 125.00
Nut bowl, 3-footed, blue 146.00
Nut bowl, 3-footed, marigold 75.00
Nut bowl, 3-footed, red 970.00
Nut bowl, 3-footed, vaseline 210.00
Plate, 7" to 8" d., blue 500.00
Plate, 7" to 8" d., marigold 128.00
Rose bowl, blue 215.00
Rose bowl, marigold 110.00

HORSESHOE CURVE - See Twins Pattern

ILLINOIS SOLDIER'S & SAILOR'S PLATE

Blue 600.00
Marigold 550.00

ILLUSION (Fenton)

Illusion Bonbon

Bonbon, 2-handled, blue (ILLUS.) 68.00
Bonbon, 2-handled, marigold 70.00
Bonbon, 2-handled, purple 150.00

IMPERIAL GRAPE (Imperial)

Basket, marigold 88.00
Basket, smoky 102.00
Berry set: master bowl & 6 sauce dishes; green, 7 pcs. 200.00
Berry set: master bowl & 6 sauce dishes; marigold, 7 pcs. . . . . . . 150.00 to 200.00
Bowl, 7" d., 2½" h., green 40.00
Bowl, 7" d., 2½" h., marigold 21.00
Bowl, 7" d., 2½" h., ruffled, purple 35.00
Bowl, 8" to 9" d., aqua 50.00
Bowl, 8" to 9" d., green 40.00
Bowl, 8" to 9" d., marigold 26.00
Bowl, 8" to 9" d., purple 48.00
Bowl, 8" to 9" d., white 55.00
Bowl, 10" d., clambroth 40.00
Bowl, 10" d., green 50.00
Bowl, 10" d., marigold 32.50
Bowl, 10" d., purple 68.00
Bowl, 10" d., white 45.00
Bowl, 11" d., ruffled, purple 130.00
Compote, marigold 55.00
Compote, purple 25.00
Compote, smoky 40.00
Cup & saucer, green 86.00
Cup & saucer, marigold 62.00
Decanter w/stopper, green 120.00
Decanter w/stopper, marigold 72.00
Decanter w/stopper, purple . . . . . . 120.00 to 150.00
Goblet, clambroth 45.00
Goblet, green 50.00
Goblet, marigold 30.00
Goblet, purple 55.00
Goblet, smoky 90.00
Pitcher, water, green 250.00
Pitcher, water, marigold 89.00
Pitcher, water, purple 250.00
Pitcher, smoky 275.00
Plate, 6" d., amber 160.00
Plate, 6" d., green 50.00
Plate, 6" d., marigold 40.00
Plate, 6" d., purple 82.00
Plate, 7" d., green 30.00
Plate, 7" d., marigold 25.00
Plate, 8" d., green 75.00
Plate, 8" d., marigold 42.00
Plate, 8" d., purple 85.00
Plate, 9" d., ruffled, clambroth . . . . . . 50.00 to 85.00
Plate, 9" d., ruffled, green 105.00
Plate, 9" d., flat, marigold 100.00
Plate, 9" d., ruffled, marigold 35.00
Plate, 9" d., ruffled, purple 70.00
Plate, 9" d., purple 310.00
Plate, 9" d., ruffled, white 50.00
Rose bowl, amber 175.00
Sauce dish, amber 20.00
Sauce dish, green 20.00
Sauce dish, ruffled, marigold 14.00
Tumbler, green 25.00
Tumbler, marigold 15.00
Tumbler, purple 38.00
Tumbler, smoky 75.00
Water bottle, green 100.00
Water bottle, marigold 75.00
Water bottle, purple 125.00
Water bottle, smoky 180.00
Water set: pitcher & 1 tumbler; amber, 2 pcs. 850.00
Water set: pitcher & 6 tumblers; green, 7 pcs. 345.00
Water set: pitcher & 6 tumblers; marigold, 7 pcs. 190.00
Water set: pitcher & 6 tumblers; purple, 7 pcs. 610.00
Wine, green 28.00
Wine, marigold 22.00
Wine, purple 32.00
Wine, vaseline 40.00
Wine set: decanter w/stopper & 6 wines; green, 7 pcs. 165.00
Wine set: decanter w/stopper & 6 wines; marigold, 7 pcs. 200.00
Wine set: decanter w/stopper & 6 wines; purple, 7 pcs. 325.00

INVERTED FEATHER (Cambridge)

Inverted Feather Cookie Jar

Cookie jar, cov., green (ILLUS.) 180.00
Cookie jar, cov., purple 750.00
Parfait, marigold 65.00
Pitcher, milk, marigold 750.00
Pitcher, water, tankard, marigold . . 4,000.00
Tumbler, green . . . . 450.00 to 500.00
Tumbler, marigold . . . . 450.00 to 500.00

INVERTED STRAWBERRY (Cambridge)

Inverted Strawberry Water Set

Berry set: master bowl & 6 sauce dishes; purple, 7 pcs. 320.00
Bowl, 7" d., green 70.00
Bowl, master berry, 10" d., purple . . 155.00
Candlestick, marigold (single) 135.00
Candlesticks, green, 7" h., pr. 225.00
Candlesticks, marigold, 7" h., pr. . . . 380.00
Celery, blue 1,200.00
Compote, open, 5" d., 6" h., green 525.00
Compote, open, giant, marigold 200.00
Compote, open, giant, purple 400.00
Creamer & sugar bowl, purple, pr. . . 325.00
Cuspidor, green 600.00
Cuspidor, marigold 600.00
Decanter, green, marked Near-Cut 3,550.00
Pitcher, milk, purple 1,300.00
Pitcher, tankard, green . . . 850.00 to 1,200.00
Pitcher, tankard, purple 800.00
Powder jar, cov., green 170.00
Powder jar, cov., marigold 90.00
Spooner, green 225.00
Sugar bowl, cov., green 100.00
Table set: creamer, sugar bowl & spooner; marigold, 3 pcs. 550.00
Tumbler, marigold 190.00
Tumbler, purple 176.00
Water set: pitcher & 6 tumblers; marigold, 7 pcs. (ILLUS.) 1,500.00

IRIS

Compote, 6¾" d., blue 160.00
Compote, 6¾" d., green 76.00
Compote, 6¾" d., marigold 40.00
Compote, 6¾" d., purple 60.00
Compote, 6¾" d., white 285.00
Goblet, buttermilk, green 75.00
Goblet, buttermilk, marigold 48.00
Goblet, buttermilk, marigold, souvenir 80.00
Goblet, buttermilk, purple 75.00

JARDINIERE (THE)

Marigold 325.00
Purple 600.00

JEWELED HEART (Dugan or Diamond Glass)

Jeweled Heart Water Pitcher

Bowl, master berry, 10½" d., fluted, peach opalescent 145.00
Dish, two turned-up sides, peach opalescent 25.00
Pitcher, marigold (ILLUS.) . . 650.00 to 850.00
Plate, 7" d., ruffled, peach opalescent 38.00
Sauce dish, peach opalescent . . . . 22.50 to 30.00
Sauce dish, purple 41.00
Tumbler, marigold 56.00

KITTENS (Fenton)

Bowl, cereal, blue 210.00
Bowl, cereal, marigold 110.00
Bowl, ruffled, marigold 140.00
Bowl, 4-sided, ruffled, aqua 225.00
Bowl, 4-sided, blue 240.00
Bowl, 4-sided, ruffled, marigold 90.00
Bowl, 6-sided, ruffled, marigold 140.00
Cup, marigold 90.00
Cup & saucer, marigold 225.00
Dish, turned-up sides, blue 315.00
Dish, turned-up sides, marigold 112.00
Plate, 4½" d., marigold 150.00
Saucer, marigold 90.00
Spooner, blue 262.00
Spooner, marigold 133.00
Toothpick holder, blue 300.00
Toothpick holder, marigold 120.00
Vase, blue 215.00
Vase, marigold 125.00

LATTICE & DAISY - See Daisy & Lattice Band Pattern

LATTICE & GRAPE (Fenton)
Pitcher, water, blue 250.00
Pitcher, water, marigold 112.00
Tumbler, blue 38.00
Tumbler, marigold 20.00
Water set: pitcher & 1 tumbler; white, 2 pcs. 850.00
Water set: pitcher & 2 tumblers; marigold, 3 pcs. 225.00
Water set: tankard pitcher & 6 tumblers; blue, 7 pcs. 700.00
Water set: tankard pitcher & 6 tumblers; marigold, 7 pcs. 250.00

LATTICE & POINSETTIA (Northwood)

Lattice & Poinsettia Bowl

Bowl, cobalt blue (ILLUS.) 315.00
Bowl, ice blue 1,200.00
Bowl, marigold 175.00
Bowl, purple . . . . 185.00 to 210.00

LATTICE & POINTS
Bowl, 6" d., low, ruffled, hat-shaped, clambroth 28.00
Bowl, 6" d., low, ruffled, hat-shaped, pastel marigold 30.00
Hat shape, marigold 30.00
Hat shape, white 30.00
Vase, 5" h., white 32.00
Vase, 8½" h., marigold 28.00

LEAF & BEADS (Northwood)

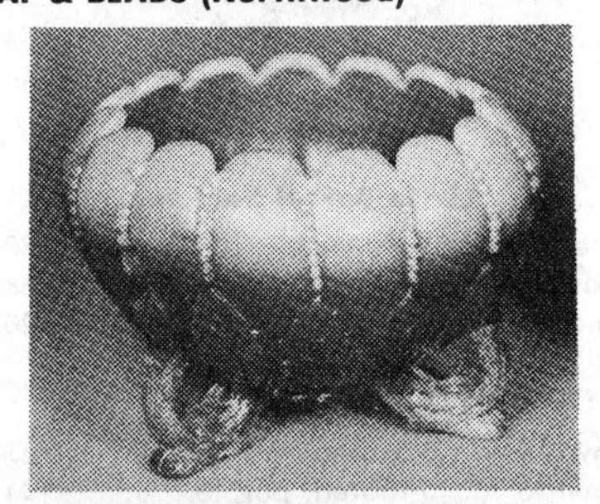

Leaf & Beads Rose Bowl

Candy bowl, footed, aqua opalescent 500.00
Candy bowl, footed, green 70.00
Nut bowl, aqua opalescent 550.00
Nut bowl, handled, green 45.00
Nut bowl, handled, marigold 32.00
Nut bowl, handled, purple 65.00
Rose bowl, aqua 275.00
Rose bowl, aqua opalescent (ILLUS.) 270.00
Rose bowl, blue 100.00
Rose bowl, electric blue 175.00
Rose bowl, green 68.00
Rose bowl, ice blue 1,200.00
Rose bowl, ice green opalescent 1,600.00
Rose bowl, lavender 500.00
Rose bowl, marigold 68.00
Rose bowl, purple 82.00
Rose bowl, interior pattern, teal blue 1,000.00
Rose bowl, white 920.00

LEAF & FLOWERS or LEAF & LITTLE FLOWERS (Millersburg)
Compote, miniature, green 298.00
Compote, miniature, marigold 280.00
Compote, miniature, purple 280.00

LEAF CHAIN (Fenton)

Leaf Chain Bowl

Bowl, 7" d., aqua 115.00
Bowl, 7" d., marigold 42.00
Bowl, 7" d., red 500.00
Bowl, 7" d., vaseline w/marigold overlay 60.00
Bowl, 7" d., white 58.00
Bowl, 8" to 9" d., aqua 165.00
Bowl, 8" to 9" d., blue (ILLUS.) 45.00
Bowl, 8" to 9" d., clambroth 45.00
Bowl, 8" to 9" d., green 45.00
Bowl, 8" to 9" d., marigold 35.00
Bowl, 8" to 9" d., purple 68.00
Bowl, 8" to 9" d., vaseline 110.00
Bowl, 8" to 9" d., white 75.00
Plate, 7" to 8" d., blue 92.00
Plate, 7" to 8" d., marigold 58.00
Plate, 7" to 8" d., white 250.00
Plate, 9" d., clambroth 80.00

Plate, 9" d., green 110.00
Plate, 9" d., marigold 95.00
Plate, 9" d., white 125.00

LEAF RAYS NAPPY

Leaf Rays Nappy

Marigold 18.00
Peach opalescent.................. 40.00
Purple (ILLUS.) 35.00
White 48.00

LEAF SWIRL

Compote, purple 45.00
Compote, teal blue 75.00
Compote, vaseline 95.00

LEAF TIERS

Berry set: 9" d. master bowl & 4 sauce dishes; marigold, 5 pcs. 68.00
Butter dish, cov., marigold 135.00
Creamer, marigold 42.50
Cuspidor, marigold 3,000.00
Pitcher, footed, marigold 300.00
Sauce dish, footed, marigold 21.50
Shade, marigold opalescent 90.00
Tumbler, marigold.................. 70.00
Water set: pitcher & 1 tumbler; marigold, 2 pcs. 500.00

LILY OF THE VALLEY (Fenton)

Lily of the Valley Pitcher & Tumbler

Pitcher, water, blue (ILLUS.) ....3,900.00 to 4,500.00
Tumbler, blue (ILLUS. front) 325.00
Tumbler, marigold.................. 400.00

LINED LATTICE VASE

Marigold 25.00
Purple 40.00
White 50.00

LION (Fenton)

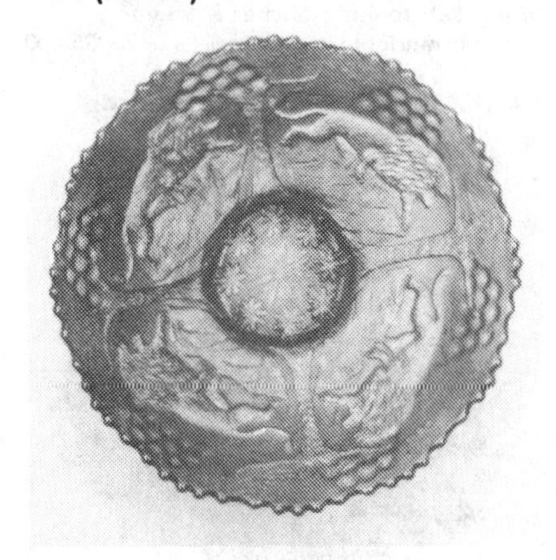

Lion Bowl

Bowl, 5" d., marigold.............. 110.00
Bowl, 7" d., blue (ILLUS.) 305.00
Bowl, 7" d., marigold............... 102.00
Plate, 7" d., marigold 575.00

LITTLE BARREL PERFUME

Little Barrel Perfume

Green (ILLUS.) 80.00
Marigold 68.00
Smoky ....85.00 to 120.00

LITTLE FISHES (Fenton)

Bowl, 6" d., 3-footed, marigold 47.50
Bowl, 6" d., 3-footed, purple 144.00
Bowl, 8" to 9" d., 3-footed, blue 185.00
Bowl, 8" to 9" d., 3-footed, marigold 135.00

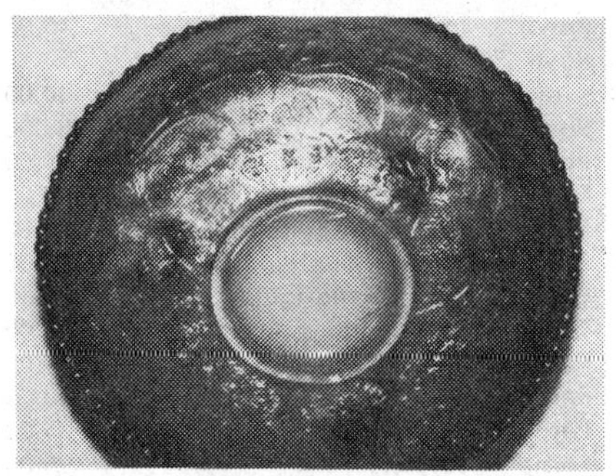

Little Fishes Bowl

Bowl, 10" d., 3-footed, blue (ILLUS.) 200.00
Bowl, 10" d., 3-footed, marigold 118.00
Sauce, 5" d., footed, aqua 195.00

LITTLE FLOWERS (Fenton)

Little Flowers Chop Plate

Berry set: master bowl & 3 sauce dishes; blue, 4 pcs. ......75.00 to 100.00
Berry set: master bowl & 6 sauce dishes; green, 7 pcs. 235.00
Bowl, 5" d., aqua 100.00
Bowl, 5" d., blue 32.00
Bowl, 5" d., green 20.00
Bowl, 5" d., marigold 23.00
Bowl, 8" to 9" d., blue 82.50
Bowl, 8" to 9" d., green 50.00
Bowl, 8" to 9" d., purple 75.00
Bowl, 8" to 9" d., red 1,500.00
Bowl, 10" d., purple 65.00
Bowl, 10" d., spatula-footed, red ... 850.00
Nut bowl, blue 75.00
Nut bowl, marigold 65.00
Plate, 6" d., marigold .....150.00 to 180.00
Plate, chop, marigold (ILLUS.) ....350.00 to 600.00

LITTLE STARS BOWL (Millersburg)

Bowl, 7" d., green 125.00
Bowl, 7" d., fluted, marigold 107.00
Bowl, 7" d., purple 82.00
Bowl, 8" d., ruffled, marigold 82.00
Bowl, 8" d., ruffled, purple 125.00
Bowl, ice cream, 8" d., marigold ... 110.00

LOGANBERRY VASE (Imperial)

Amber 300.00
Clambroth 225.00
Green 255.00
Marigold 125.00
Purple 360.00
Smoke 225.00

LONG THUMBPRINTS

Creamer, marigold 20.00
Creamer & sugar bowl, marigold, pr. 40.00
Sugar bowl, marigold 20.00
Vase, 7" h., green 36.00

LOTUS & GRAPE (Fenton)

Bonbon, 2-handled, blue 25.00
Bonbon, 2-handled, celeste blue 300.00
Bonbon, 2-handled, green 53.00
Bonbon, 2-handled, marigold 39.00
Bonbon, 2-handled, purple 50.00
Bonbon, 2-handled, red 1,100.00
Bowl, 5" d., footed, blue 40.00
Bowl, 5" d., footed, green 75.00
Bowl, 5" d., footed, marigold 45.00
Bowl, 8" to 9" d., green 105.00
Bowl, 8½" d., ice cream shape, Persian Blue 400.00

Lotus & Grape Plate

Plate, 9" d., blue (ILLUS.) 580.00
Plate, 9" d., green 650.00

LOUISA (Westmoreland)

Bowl, 8" to 9" d., 3-footed, green... 45.00
Bowl, 8" to 9" d., 3-footed, marigold 45.00
Bowl, 8" to 9" d., 3-footed, peach opalescent 500.00
Bowl, 8" to 9" d., 3-footed, purple .. 45.00
Bowl, 8" to 9" d., 3-footed, teal blue 40.00
Nut bowl, footed, green 40.00

Nut bowl, footed, marigold 28.00
Nut bowl, footed, purple 31.00
Plate, 9½" d., footed, marigold 146.00
Plate, 9½" d., footed, teal blue 98.00

Louisa Rose Bowl

Rose bowl, footed, green (ILLUS.) ... 68.00
Rose bowl, footed, lavender 68.00
Rose bowl, footed, marigold 60.00
Rose bowl, footed, purple 60.00
Salt & pepper shakers, marigold, pr. 22.50

LUSTRE FLUTE (Northwood)

Breakfast set: individual size creamer & sugar bowl; marigold, pr. ... 50.00
Breakfast set: individual size creamer & sugar bowl; green, pr. 85.00
Creamer, green 49.50
Hat shape, fluted, green, 5" d. 35.00
Hat shape, fluted, marigold, 5" d. .. 25.00
Nappy, green 35.00
Nappy, marigold 20.00
Punch cup, green 16.00
Sugar bowl, green 35.00
Sugar bowl, marigold 15.00
Tumbler, marigold 20.00

LUSTRE ROSE (Imperial)

Lustre Rose Bowl

Bowl, 7" d., 3-footed, marigold 40.00
Bowl, 7" d., 3-footed, vaseline 75.00
Bowl, 8" to 9" d., 3-footed, amber .. 72.00
Bowl, 8" to 9" d., 3-footed, blue (ILLUS.) 65.00
Bowl, 8" to 9" d., 3-footed, clambroth 30.00
Bowl, 8" to 9" d., 3-footed, green ... 45.00
Bowl, 8" to 9" d., 3-footed, marigold 40.00
Bowl, 8" to 9" d., 3-footed, purple .. 108.00
Bowl, 10½" d., 3-footed, marigold .. 50.00
Bowl, 10½" d., 3-footed, purple 400.00
Bowl, 10½" d., 3-footed, smoky 83.00
Bowl, fruit, red 2,300.00
Butter dish, cov., marigold 50.00
Creamer, marigold ....30.00 to 40.00
Fernery, amber 75.00
Fernery, blue 80.00
Fernery, marigold 35.00
Fernery, purple 95.00
Fernery, smoky 70.00
Pitcher, water, clambroth 70.00
Pitcher, water, marigold 52.50
Plate, 9" d., amber 85.00
Plate, 9" d., marigold 51.00
Plate, 9" d., purple 95.00
Rose bowl, amber 85.00
Rose bowl, green 45.00
Sauce dish, green 24.00
Sauce dish, marigold 9.00
Spooner, amber 50.00
Spooner, green 40.00
Spooner, marigold 35.00
Spooner, purple 25.00
Sugar bowl, cov., amber 75.00
Sugar bowl, cov., marigold 45.00
Table set, marigold, 4 pcs. 160.00
Tumbler, green 35.00
Tumbler, marigold 15.00
Tumbler, purple 32.50
Water set: pitcher & 4 tumblers; purple, 5 pcs. 538.00
Water set: pitcher & 6 tumblers; marigold, 7 pcs. 193.00

MANY FRUITS (Dugan)

Many Fruits Punch Bowl

Punch bowl, 9¾" d., marigold 180.00
Punch bowl, 9¾" d., purple 245.00
Punch bowl & base, purple, 2 pcs. (ILLUS.) 475.00

Punch cup, blue 50.00
Punch cup, white 65.00
Punch set: bowl, base & 6 cups; blue, 8 pcs. 500.00
Punch set: bowl, base & 6 cups; purple, 8 pcs. 730.00
Punch set: bowl, base & 10 cups; white, 12 pcs. 1,600.00

MANY STARS (Millersburg)
Bowl, 8" to 9" d., ruffled, green 400.00
Bowl, 8" to 9" d., ruffled, marigold 338.00
Bowl, 10" d., ruffled, purple 494.00
Bowl, ice cream, 10" d., green 386.00
Bowl, ice cream, 10" d., marigold .. 342.00

MAPLE LEAF (Dugan)

Maple Leaf Water Set

Berry set: master bowl & 6 small berry bowls; pedestaled, purple, 7 pcs. 225.00
Bowl, 6" d., small berry, purple 22.50
Bowl, master berry or fruit, marigold 100.00
Butter dish, cov., blue 85.00
Creamer, blue 60.00
Creamer, marigold 42.00
Spooner, marigold 42.50
Spooner, purple 54.00
Sugar bowl, cov., marigold 40.00
Table set: cov. sugar bowl, creamer & spooner; purple, 3 pcs. 235.00
Table set, marigold, 4 pcs. 222.00
Tumbler, clambroth 75.00
Tumbler, marigold 22.50
Water set: pitcher & 6 tumblers; marigold, 7 pcs. 215.00
Water set: pitcher & 6 tumblers; purple, 7 pcs. (ILLUS.) 375.00

MARILYN (Millersburg)
Pitcher, water, green 675.00
Pitcher, water, purple 750.00
Tumbler, green 327.00
Tumbler, marigold 150.00
Tumbler, purple 100.00
Water set: pitcher & 5 tumblers; marigold, 6 pcs. 700.00
Water set: pitcher & 6 tumblers; purple, 7 pcs. 1,325.00

MARY ANN VASE (Dugan)
Marigold 50.00

Purple 105.00
Vaseline 350.00

MAYAN (Millersburg)
Bowl, 8" to 9" d., green 67.00
Bowl, 8" to 9" d., purple 65.00

MEMPHIS (Northwood)
Fruit bowl & base, cobalt blue, 2 pcs. 2,300.00
Punch bowl, 11½" d., purple 190.00
Punch bowl & base, green, 2 pcs.... 400.00
Punch bowl & base, ice green, 2 pcs. 2,950.00
Punch bowl & base, marigold, 2 pcs. 175.00
Punch cup, green 35.00
Punch cup, ice blue 60.00
Punch cup, ice green 60.00
Punch cup, white 54.00
Punch set: bowl, base & 4 cups; ice blue, 6 pcs. 2,000.00
Punch set: bowl, base & 6 cups; marigold, 8 pcs. 388.00

MIKADO (Fenton)
Compote, 10" d., blue 376.00
Compote, 10" d., marigold 121.00
Compote, 10" d., purple 302.00

MILADY (Fenton)

Milady Pitcher & Tumbler

Pitcher, water, blue (ILLUS.) 750.00
Pitcher, water, marigold 475.00
Tumbler, blue (ILLUS.) 62.00
Tumbler, marigold 72.00
Tumbler, purple 123.00
Water set: pitcher & 2 tumblers; blue, 3 pcs. 1,000.00

MILLERSBURG PIPE HUMIDOR - See Pipe Humidor Pattern

MILLERSBURG TROUT & FLY - See Trout & Fly Pattern

MIRRORED LOTUS

Bonbon, blue 55.00
Bowl, 7" d., blue 65.00
Bowl, 7" d., ice green 250.00
Bowl, 7" d., marigold 55.00
Rose bowl, marigold 450.00
Rose bowl, white 525.00

MITERED OVALS (Millersburg)

Vase, green 1,700.00
Vase, marigold 2,450.00

MORNING GLORY (Millersburg)

Morning Glory Pitcher

Pitcher, tankard, green 9,000.00
Pitcher, tankard, marigold 5,350.00
Pitcher, tankard, purple (ILLUS.) .... 6,350.00 to 7,500.00
Tumbler, green 1,125.00
Tumbler, purple 1,000.00

MULTIFRUITS & FLOWERS (Millersburg)

Multifruits & Flowers Pitcher

Pitcher, water, green ... 5,250.00 to 7,500.00
Pitcher, water, marigold 4,400.00
Pitcher, water, purple (ILLUS.) 3,000.00

Punch bowl & base, marigold, 2 pcs. 600.00
Punch bowl & base, purple, 2 pcs. 850.00
Punch cup, green 60.00
Punch set: bowl, base & 3 cups; purple, 5 pcs. 950.00
Punch set: bowl, base & 4 cups; marigold, 6 pcs. 700.00
Punch set: bowl, base & 5 cups; green, 7 pcs. 1,675.00

MY LADY

Powder jar, cov., marigold 75.00

NAUTILUS (Dugan)

Creamer, peach opalescent 185.00
Creamer, purple 167.00
Sugar bowl, open, peach opalescent 250.00
Sugar bowl, open, purple 245.00

NESTING SWAN (Millersburg)

Bowl, 10" d., amber 225.00
Bowl, 10" d., green 225.00
Bowl, 10" d., marigold 175.00
Bowl, 10" d., purple 225.00

NIGHT STARS (Millersburg)

Bonbon, green 308.00
Card tray, purple 300.00

NIPPON (Northwood)

Bowl, 8" to 9" d., 2¼" h., ice blue .. 175.00
Bowl, 8" to 9" d., ice green 148.00
Bowl, 8" to 9" d., marigold 50.00
Bowl, 8" to 9" d., purple 143.00
Bowl, 8" to 9" d., fluted, white 152.00
Plate, 9" d., marigold 360.00
Plate, 9" d., white 600.00

NU-ART

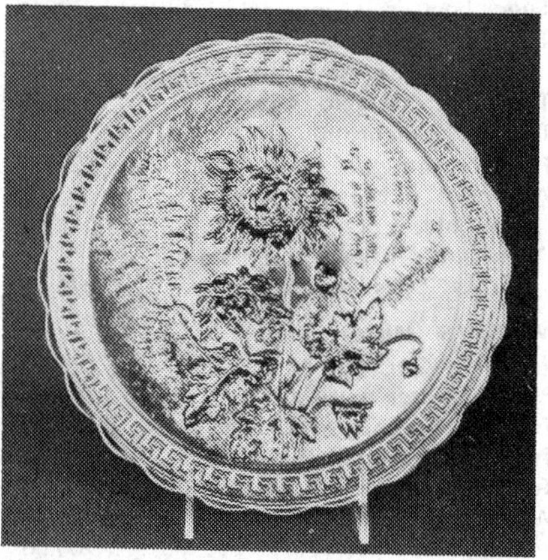

Nu-Art Plate

Plate, Chrysanthemum, amber 600.00
Plate, Chrysanthemum, green 350.00
Plate, Chrysanthemum, marigold 450.00

Plate, Chrysanthemum, purple (ILLUS.) 985.00
Plate, Chrysanthemum, smoky 530.00

OCTAGON (Imperial)

Bowl, 10" sq., green 49.00
Bowl, 11½" d., marigold 45.00
Butter dish, cov., marigold 110.00
Compote, jelly, green 75.00
Compote, jelly, marigold 50.00
Creamer, marigold 30.00
Decanter w/stopper, marigold 77.00
Goblet, water, marigold 35.00
Pitcher, water, 8" h., marigold 80.00
Pitcher, water, 8" h., purple 445.00
Pitcher, water, tankard, 9¾" h., marigold 100.00
Pitcher, water, tankard, 9¾" h., purple 300.00 to 400.00
Spooner, marigold 45.00
Sugar bowl, cov., marigold 50.00
Table set, marigold, 4 pcs. 225.00
Toothpick holder, marigold 170.00
Tumbler, green 80.00
Tumbler, marigold 26.00
Tumbler, purple 75.00
Vase, 8" h., marigold 55.00
Water set: pitcher & 1 tumbler; marigold, 2 pcs. 185.00
Water set: pitcher & 1 tumbler; purple, 2 pcs. 425.00
Wine, marigold 34.00
Wine, purple 50.00
Wine set: decanter & 1 wine; marigold, 2 pcs. 90.00 to 125.00
Wine set: decanter & 1 wine; purple, 2 pcs. 450.00

OHIO STAR (Millersburg)

Compote, jelly, marigold 525.00
Vase, marigold 300.00
Vase, purple 725.00

OPEN ROSE (Imperial)

Berry set: master bowl & 4 sauce dishes; amber, 5 pcs. 60.00
Berry set: master bowl & 6 sauce dishes; marigold, 7 pcs. 85.00
Bowl, 5" d., marigold 16.00
Bowl, 7" d., footed, green 65.00
Bowl, 7" d., footed, marigold 35.00
Bowl, 7" d., footed, purple 45.00
Bowl, 8" to 9" d., amber 50.00
Bowl, 8" to 9" d., aqua 52.00
Bowl, 8" to 9" d., green 42.00
Bowl, 8" to 9" d., marigold 30.00
Bowl, 8" to 9" d., purple 95.00
Bowl, 8" to 9" d., smoky 65.00
Bowl, 10" d., marigold 50.00
Bowl, 10" d., purple 325.00
Plate, 9" d., amber 150.00
Plate, 9" d., clambroth 110.00
Plate, 9" d., green 70.00
Plate, 9" d., marigold 55.00
Plate, 9" d., purple 168.00
Plate, chop, purple 375.00
Rose bowl, amber 59.00
Rose bowl, green 52.00
Rose bowl, purple 325.00
Spooner, marigold 29.00
Tumbler, marigold 20.00
Vase, marigold 45.00
Water set: pitcher & 6 tumblers; marigold, 7 pcs. 200.00
Water set: pitcher & 6 tumblers; purple, 7 pcs. 375.00

ORANGE TREE (Fenton)

Orange Tree Loving Cup

Berry set: master bowl & 4 sauce dishes; white, 5 pcs. 165.00
Berry set: master bowl & 6 sauce dishes; marigold, 7 pcs. 220.00
Bowl, 7" d., white 64.00
Bowl, 8" to 9" d., amber 60.00
Bowl, 8" to 9" d., blue 60.00
Bowl, 8" to 9" d., clambroth 45.00
Bowl, 8" to 9" d., green 65.00
Bowl, 8" to 9" d., marigold 35.00
Bowl, 8" to 9" d., purple 75.00
Bowl, 8" to 9" d., red 1,455.00
Bowl, 8" to 9" d., white 94.00
Bowl, 10" d., 3-footed, blue 148.00
Bowl, 10" d., 3-footed, green 265.00
Bowl, 10" d., 3-footed, marigold 79.00
Bowl, 10" d., 3-footed, white 150.00
Bowl, ice cream, marigold 25.00
Bowl, ice cream, green 150.00
Bowl, milk glass w/marigold overlay 1,400.00
Breakfast set: individual size creamer & cov. sugar bowl; blue, pr. 124.00
Breakfast set: individual size creamer & cov. sugar bowl; marigold, pr. 70.00
Breakfast set: individual size creamer & cov. sugar bowl; purple, pr. 98.00
Compote, 5" d., blue 65.00
Compote, 5" d., green 85.00
Compote, 5" d., marigold 25.00
Creamer, footed, blue 50.00

Creamer, footed, marigold 35.00
Creamer, footed, white 50.00
Creamer, individual size, blue 52.50
Creamer, individual size, marigold . . 37.50
Creamer, individual size, purple 44.00
Creamer & sugar bowl, footed, blue, pr. 115.00
Dish, ice cream, footed, blue 45.00
Dish, ice cream, footed, marigold . . . 20.00
Goblet, aqua 110.00
Goblet, blue 55.00
Goblet, green 138.00
Goblet, marigold 25.00
Goblet, marigold, w/advertising 60.00
Hatpin holder, blue 187.00
Hatpin holder, green 335.00
Hatpin holder, marigold 125.00
Hatpin holder, purple 165.00
Loving cup, blue 213.00
Loving cup, green 200.00
Loving cup, marigold (ILLUS.) 125.00
Loving cup, purple 200.00
Loving cup, white 200.00
Mug, amber 125.00
Mug, Amberina 300.00
Mug, aqua 213.00
Mug, blue 45.00
Mug, green 400.00
Mug, marigold 25.00
Mug, marigold w/blue base 157.00
Mug, marigold w/green base 120.00
Mug, marigold w/vaseline base . . . . 140.00 to 175.00
Mug, purple 90.00
Mug, red 318.00
Mug, teal blue 275.00
Mug, vaseline 95.00
Pitcher, water, blue 325.00
Pitcher, water, marigold 275.00
Pitcher, water, white . . . . . . 300.00 to 425.00
Plate, 9" d., flat, blue 278.00
Plate, 9" d., flat, clambroth 104.00
Plate, 9" d., flat, green 275.00
Plate, 9" d., flat, marigold 112.00
Plate, 9" d., flat, white 136.00
Powder jar, cov., blue 65.00
Powder jar, cov., green 375.00
Powder jar, cov., marigold 60.00
Powder jar, cov., purple 85.00
Powder jar, open, peach opalescent 195.00
Punch bowl & base, blue, 2 pcs. 225.00 to 275.00
Punch bowl & base, marigold, 2 pcs. 154.00
Punch bowl & base, white, 2 pcs. . . . 325.00
Punch cup, blue 25.00
Punch cup, marigold 13.00
Punch cup, purple 20.00
Punch cup, white 45.00
Punch set: bowl, base & 4 cups; blue, 6 pcs. 375.00
Punch set: bowl, base & 4 cups; marigold, 6 pcs. 365.00

Rose bowl, blue 60.00
Rose bowl, marigold 42.00
Rose bowl, purple 110.00
Rose bowl, red 575.00
Rose bowl, white 250.00
Sauce dish, footed, blue 32.00
Sauce dish, footed, marigold 18.00
Shaving mug, amber 125.00
Shaving mug, blue 55.00
Shaving mug, green 850.00
Shaving mug, marigold 32.00
Shaving mug, purple . . . . . . 110.00 to 200.00
Shaving mug, red 450.00
Spooner, blue 75.00
Sugar bowl, blue 65.00
Sugar bowl, white 50.00
Sugar bowl, open, individual size, marigold 20.00
Sugar bowl, open, individual size, white 50.00
Tumbler, blue 50.00
Tumbler, marigold 48.00
Tumbler, white 100.00
Water set: pitcher & 6 tumblers; blue, 7 pcs. 395.00
Wine, blue 40.00
Wine, green 175.00
Wine, marigold 23.00

ORANGE TREE ORCHARD (Fenton)

Pitcher, marigold 165.00
Pitcher, white 515.00
Tumbler, blue 50.00
Tumbler, marigold 32.00
Tumbler, white 308.00
Water set: pitcher & 4 tumblers; white, 5 pcs. 1,025.00
Water set: pitcher & 6 tumblers; blue, 7 pcs. 750.00
Water set: pitcher & 6 tumblers; marigold, 7 pcs. 500.00

ORANGE TREE SCROLL

Orange Tree Scroll Tumbler

Pitcher, marigold 130.00
Pitcher, white 325.00
Tumbler, blue 70.00
Tumbler, marigold (ILLUS.) 65.00

Water set: pitcher & 6 tumblers; blue, 7 pcs. 900.00

ORIENTAL POPPY (Northwood)

Oriental Poppy Water Set

Pitcher, water, green 725.00
Pitcher, water, marigold 290.00
Pitcher, water, purple 500.00
Pitcher, water, white . . . . 895.00 to 1,200.00
Tumbler, blue 216.00
Tumbler, green 48.00
Tumbler, ice blue 175.00
Tumbler, marigold 35.00
Tumbler, purple 45.00
Tumbler, white 132.00
Water set: pitcher & 1 tumbler; marigold, 2 pcs. 225.00
Water set: pitcher & 6 tumblers; ice green, 7 pcs. 4,000.00
Water set: pitcher & 6 tumblers; purple, 7 pcs. (ILLUS.) 650.00

PALM BEACH (United States Glass Co.)

Palm Beach Rose Bowl

Bowl, 5" d., 4 turned-in sides, marigold 90.00
Butter dish, cov., white 195.00
Creamer, marigold 70.00
Creamer, white 80.00
Pitcher, water, marigold 450.00
Pitcher, water, white 725.00
Rose bowl, amber (ILLUS.) 125.00
Rose bowl, white 75.00
Sauce dish, white 38.00
Spooner, marigold 85.00
Spooner, white 85.00
Tumbler, amber 80.00
Tumbler, marigold 210.00
Tumbler, white 155.00
Water set: pitcher & 5 tumblers; amber, 6 pcs. 405.00
Whimsey banana boat, marigold, 6" . . . . . 75.00 to 90.00
Whimsey banana boat, purple, 6" . . . 115.00
Whimsey vase, white 190.00

PANELED DANDELION - See Dandelion, Paneled Pattern

PANSY and PANSY SPRAY

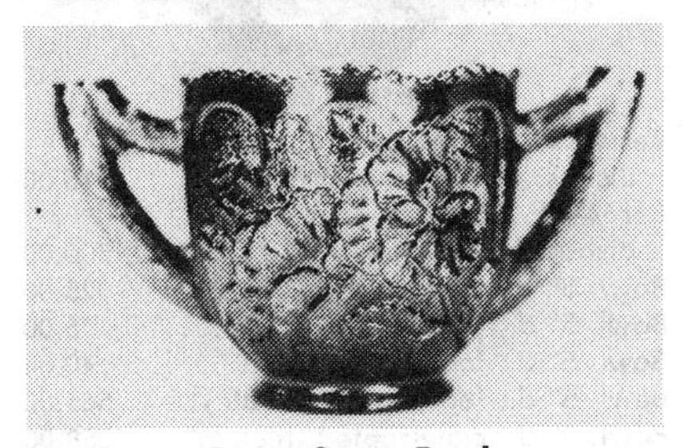

Pansy Sugar Bowl

Bowl, 8" to 9" d., amber 20.00
Bowl, 8" to 9" d., green 45.00
Bowl, 8" to 9" d., marigold 27.00
Bowl, 9" d., fluted, purple 42.00
Compote, white 160.00
Creamer, amber 35.00
Creamer, marigold 19.00
Creamer, purple 30.00
Creamer & sugar bowl, green, pr. . . 39.00
Dresser tray, green 55.00
Dresser tray, marigold 40.00
Nappy, amber 38.00
Nappy, green 18.00
Nappy, lavender 25.00
Nappy, marigold 20.00
Pickle (or relish) dish, amber, 9 x 6" 47.50
Pickle (or relish) dish, blue, 9 x 6" . . 25.00
Pickle (or relish) dish, clambroth, 9 x 6" 20.00
Pickle (or relish) dish, green, 9 x 6" 43.00
Pickle (or relish) dish, marigold, 9 x 6" 20.00
Pickle (or relish) dish, purple, 9 x 6" 35.00
Pickle (or relish) dish, smoky, 9 x 6" 48.00
Plate, 9" d., ruffled, smoky 65.00
Sugar bowl, amber 35.00
Sugar bowl, marigold 25.00
Sugar bowl, smoky 35.00
Sugar bowl, breakfast size, purple (ILLUS.) 54.00

PANTHER (Fenton)

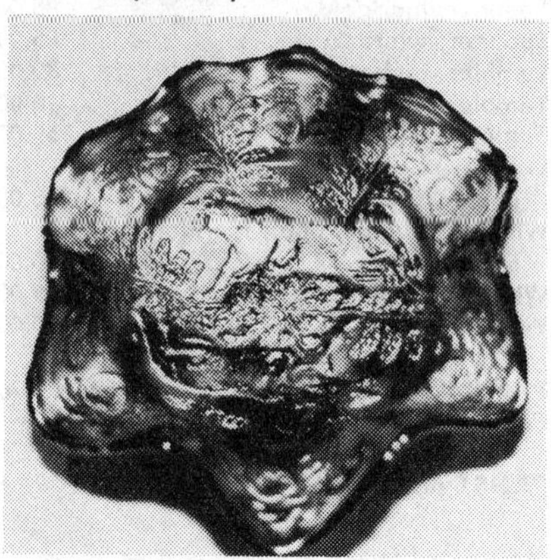

Panther Bowl

Berry set: master bowl & 4 sauce dishes; marigold, 5 pcs. 215.00
Berry set: master bowl & 6 sauce dishes; blue, 7 pcs. 700.00
Bowl, 5" d., footed, aqua 325.00
Bowl, 5" d., footed, blue 76.00
Bowl, 5" d., footed, marigold 40.00
Bowl, 5" d., footed, red (ILLUS.) 565.00
Bowl, 9" d., claw-footed, blue 258.00
Bowl, 9" d., claw-footed, green 585.00
Bowl, 9" d., claw-footed, marigold .. 125.00
Bowl, 9" d., claw-footed, purple 150.00
Bowl, 9" d., claw-footed, white 625.00
Centerpiece bowl, blue 900.00
Centerpiece bowl, marigold 600.00

PEACH (Northwood)

Peach Water Pitcher

Berry set: master bowl & 4 sauce dishes; white, 5 pcs. 395.00
Bowl, 9" d., white 150.00
Butter dish, cov., white 300.00
Pitcher, water, blue (ILLUS.) 1,250.00
Pitcher, water, white 450.00
Sauce dish, white 42.50
Spooner, white 90.00
Sugar bowl, cov., white ....90.00 to 125.00
Table set, white, 4 pcs. 575.00
Tumbler, blue 75.00
Tumbler, marigold 2,100.00
Tumbler, white 125.00
Water set: pitcher & 6 tumblers; blue, 7 pcs. ....900.00 to 1,200.00
Water set: pitcher & 6 tumblers; white, 7 pcs. ....550.00 to 850.00

PEACH & PEAR OVAL FRUIT BOWL

Marigold 75.00
Purple 80.00

PEACOCK, FLUFFY (Fenton)

Fluffy Peacock Water Set

Pitcher, water, blue 650.00
Pitcher, water, green 585.00
Pitcher, water, marigold 325.00
Pitcher, water, purple 500.00
Tumbler, blue 56.00
Tumbler, green 75.00
Tumbler, marigold 45.00
Tumbler, purple 74.00
Tumbler, violet 75.00
Water set: pitcher & 4 tumblers; blue, 5 pcs. 900.00
Water set: pitcher & 6 tumblers; purple, 7 pcs. (ILLUS.) 925.00

PEACOCK & DAHLIA (Fenton)

Bowl, 7" d., ruffled, aqua opalescent 126.00
Bowl, 7" d., ruffled, blue 110.00
Bowl, 7" d., marigold 53.00
Bowl, 7" d., vaseline 185.00
Bowl, 8" d., footed, green 49.00
Plate, 8½" d., marigold 312.00

PEACOCK & GRAPE (Fenton)

Bowl, 7" d., marigold 10.00
Bowl, 7" d., purple 32.00
Bowl, 7" d., red 975.00
Bowl, 8" to 9" d., flat, ribbon candy rim, blue 68.00
Bowl, 8" to 9" d., flat, ribbon candy rim, lavender 75.00
Bowl, 8" to 9" d., 3-footed, amber .. 100.00

Bowl, 8" to 9" d., 3-footed, blue 45.00
Bowl, 8" to 9" d., 3-footed, green... 60.00
Bowl, 8" to 9" d., 3-footed, ice green opalescent................ 515.00
Bowl, 8" to 9" d., 3-footed, lavender 125.00
Bowl, 8" to 9" d., 3-footed, marigold 36.00
Bowl, 8" to 9" d., 3-footed, purple .. 58.00
Bowl, 8" to 9" d., 3-footed, red 604.00
Bowl, 8" to 9" d., 3-footed, vaseline 125.00
Bowl, 8" to 9" d., 3-footed, vaseline opalescent..................... 400.00
Bowl, 8" to 9" d., collared base, blue 58.00
Bowl, 8" to 9" d., collared base, marigold 42.00
Bowl, 8" to 9" d., collared base, peach opalescent................ 590.00
Bowl, 8" to 9" d., collared base, purple 50.00
Bowl, 8" to 9" d., collared base, ruffled, red 920.00
Bowl, 8" to 9" d., collared base, smoky 588.00
Plate, 9" d., collared base, blue 325.00
Plate, 9" d., collared base, marigold 260.00
Plate, 9" d., 3-footed, green 200.00
Plate, 9" d., 3-footed, marigold..... 182.00
Plate, 9" d., 3-footed, purple 260.00

PEACOCK & URN

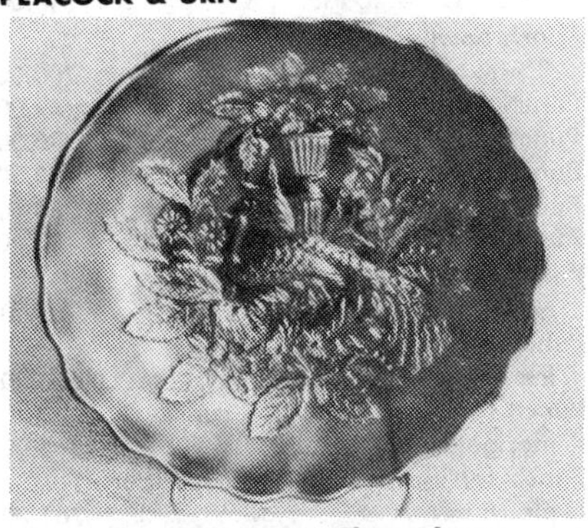

Peacock & Urn Chop Plate

Berry set: master bowl & 4 sauce dishes; marigold, 5 pcs. 225.00
Berry set: master bowl & 5 sauce dishes; purple, 6 pcs............ 750.00
Bowl, 7" d., ruffled, green (Millersburg) 250.00
Bowl, 7" d., ruffled, marigold (Millersburg).................... 375.00
Bowl, 7" d., ruffled, purple (Millersburg) 265.00
Bowl, 7½" d., "shotgun," ruffled, green 425.00
Bowl, 8" to 9" d., blue (Fenton)..... 95.00
Bowl, 8" to 9" d., green (Fenton) ... 200.00
Bowl, 8" to 9" d., green (Millersburg) 382.00
Bowl, 8" to 9" d., marigold (Fenton)........................ 66.00
Bowl, 8" to 9" d., marigold (Millersburg) 145.00
Bowl, 8" to 9" d., purple (Fenton)... 130.00
Bowl, 8" to 9" d., purple (Millersburg) 265.00
Bowl, 8" to 9" d., red (Fenton) 3,500.00
Bowl, 8" to 9" d., white (Fenton) ... 150.00
Bowl, 10" d., fluted, green (Millersburg) 214.00
Bowl, 10" d., marigold (Millersburg) 90.00
Bowl, ice cream, 10" d., blue (Northwood) 300.00
Bowl, ice cream, 10" d., green (Northwood) ....900.00 to 1,000.00
Bowl, ice cream, 10" d., ice blue (Northwood) 750.00
Bowl, ice cream, 10" d., ice green (Northwood) 775.00
Bowl, ice cream, 10" d., marigold (Millersburg).................. 262.00
Bowl, ice cream, 10" d., marigold (Northwood) 193.00
Bowl, ice cream, 10" d., purple (Northwood) 550.00
Bowl, ice cream, 10" d., white (Northwood) 502.00
Bowl, 10½" d., ruffled, blue (Millersburg) 1,325.00
Bowl, 10½" d., ruffled, green (Millersburg).................. 260.00
Bowl, 10½" d., ruffled, marigold (Millersburg).................. 225.00
Bowl, 10½" d., ruffled, purple...... 225.00
Bowl, 10½" d., ruffled, vaseline (Millersburg) 1,900.00
Bowl, ice cream shape, blue (Fenton).......................... 135.00
Bowl, ice cream shape, green (Fenton).......................... 200.00
Compote, 5½" d., 5" h., aqua (Fenton)......................... 325.00
Compote, 5½" d., 5" h., blue (Fenton)......................... 105.00
Compote, 5½" d., 5" h., marigold (Fenton)....................... 45.00
Compote, 5½" d., 5" h., purple (Fenton)....................... 55.00
Compote, 5½" d., 5" h., red (Fenton) ....695.00 to 1,000.00
Compote, 5½" d., 5" h., vaseline (Fenton)....................... 160.00
Compote, 5½" d., 5" h., white (Fenton)......................... 300.00
Compote, blue (Millersburg Giant) .. 475.00
Compote, green (Millersburg Giant) 1,200.00
Compote, marigold (Millersburg Giant)......................... 500.00

Compote, purple (Millersburg Giant) 845.00
Goblet, marigold (Fenton) 65.00
Ice cream dish, aqua opalescent, small (Northwood) 1,500.00
Ice cream dish, blue, small (Northwood) 73.00
Ice cream dish, green, small 145.00
Ice cream dish, ice blue, small 240.00
Ice cream dish, marigold, small 50.00
Ice cream dish, purple, small 60.00
Ice cream dish, white, small 134.00
Ice cream set: large bowl & 2 small dishes; blue, 3 pcs. 525.00
Ice cream set: large bowl & 4 small dishes; purple, 5 pcs. 525.00
Ice cream set: large bowl & 6 small dishes; marigold, 7 pcs. 500.00
Ice cream set: large bowl & 6 small dishes; white, 7 pcs. 1,250.00
Plate, 6½" d., marigold 168.00
Plate, 6½" d., purple 235.00
Plate, 9" d., blue 260.00
Plate, 9" d., marigold 165.00
Plate, 9" d., white 250.00
Plate, chop, 11" d., marigold (Millersburg) 2,800.00
Plate, chop, 11" d., marigold (Northwood) 350.00
Plate, chop, 11" d., purple (Millersburg) 670.00
Plate, chop, 11" d., purple, Northwood (ILLUS.) 350.00
Sauce dish, blue (Millersburg) 123.00
Sauce dish, blue (Northwood) 72.00
Sauce dish, ice green, 6" d. (Northwood) .... 170.00 to 200.00
Sauce dish, marigold (Millersburg) 65.00
Sauce dish, marigold (Northwood) 40.00
Sauce dish, purple (Millersburg) .... 150.00 to 195.00
Sauce dish, purple (Northwood) 52.00
Sauce dish, white (Northwood) 125.00
Whimsey sauce dish, 5¼" d., purple 135.00

PEACOCK AT FOUNTAIN (Northwood)

Peacock at Fountain Creamer & Sugar Bowl

Berry set: master bowl & 6 sauce dishes; marigold, 7 pcs. 200.00
Berry set: master bowl & 6 sauce dishes; purple, 7 pcs. 215.00
Bowl, master berry, ice blue 290.00
Bowl, master berry, marigold 125.00
Bowl, master berry, purple 145.00
Bowl, master berry, white 275.00
Bowl, orange, 3-footed, aqua opalescent 2,000.00
Bowl, orange, 3-footed, blue 280.00
Bowl, orange, 3-footed, green 525.00
Bowl, orange, 3-footed, lavender 325.00
Bowl, orange, 3-footed, marigold 162.00
Bowl, orange, 3-footed, purple 288.00
Butter dish, cov., purple 210.00
Butter dish, cov., white 380.00
Compote, aqua opalescent 3,400.00
Compote, blue 500.00
Compote, ice blue .... 900.00 to 1,200.00
Compote, ice green 650.00
Compote, marigold 408.00
Compote, purple 750.00
Compote, white 870.00
Creamer, marigold 62.50
Creamer, purple (ILLUS. left) 82.00
Pitcher, water, blue 360.00
Pitcher, water, green .... 1,500.00 to 1,750.00
Pitcher, water, ice blue 1,600.00
Pitcher, water, marigold 150.00
Pitcher, water, purple 305.00
Pitcher, water, white 600.00
Punch bowl, marigold 125.00
Punch bowl, purple 375.00
Punch bowl & base, ice blue, 2 pcs. 2,350.00
Punch bowl & base, marigold, 2 pcs. 340.00
Punch bowl & base, purple, 2 pcs. .... 500.00 to 700.00
Punch cup, blue 42.00
Punch cup, ice blue 90.00
Punch cup, marigold 32.50
Punch cup, purple 30.00
Punch cup, white 60.00
Punch set: bowl, base & 1 cup; green, 3 pcs. 2,250.00
Punch set: bowl, base & 6 cups; ice blue, 8 pcs. 2,650.00
Punch set: bowl, base & 6 cups; marigold, 8 pcs. 365.00
Punch set: bowl, base & 6 cups; purple, 8 pcs. 765.00
Punch set: bowl, base & 6 cups; white, 8 pcs. 2,100.00
Sauce dish, blue 35.00
Sauce dish, ice blue 70.00
Sauce dish, marigold 16.00
Sauce dish, purple 28.00
Sauce dish, teal blue 110.00
Sauce dish, white 65.00
Spooner, blue 125.00
Spooner, marigold 55.00
Spooner, purple 80.00
Spooner, white 103.00
Sugar bowl, cov., marigold 75.00
Sugar bowl, cov., purple (ILLUS. right) 85.00

Sugar bowl, cov., white 180.00
Table set, marigold, 4 pcs. 395.00
Table set, purple, 4 pcs. 545.00
Tumbler, blue 40.00
Tumbler, green 350.00
Tumbler, ice blue 200.00
Tumbler, marigold 32.00
Tumbler, purple 39.00
Tumbler, white 185.00
Water set: pitcher & 1 tumbler; ice blue, 2 pcs. 1,800.00
Water set: pitcher & 5 tumblers; marigold, 6 pcs. 410.00
Water set: pitcher & 6 tumblers; blue, 7 pcs. 555.00
Water set: pitcher & 6 tumblers; purple, 7 pcs. 550.00

PEACOCKS ON FENCE (Northwood Peacocks)

Peacocks on Fence Plate

Bowl, 8" to 9" d., aqua opalescent .. 640.00
Bowl, 8" to 9" d., piecrust rim, blue 385.00
Bowl, 8" to 9" d., piecrust rim, green 900.00
Bowl, 8" to 9" d., piecrust rim, ice blue 700.00
Bowl, 8" to 9" d., piecrust rim, ice green 740.00
Bowl, 8" to 9" d., piecrust rim, marigold 165.00
Bowl, 8" to 9" d., piecrust rim, purple 425.00
Bowl, 8" to 9" d., piecrust rim, white ....275.00 to 375.00
Bowl, 8" to 9" d., ruffled rim, blue .. 340.00
Bowl, 8" to 9" d., ruffled rim, green 525.00
Bowl, 8" to 9" d., ruffled rim, marigold 158.00
Bowl, 8" to 9" d., ruffled rim, purple 325.00
Plate, 8" d., blue (ILLUS.) 578.00
Plate, 9" d., green 900.00
Plate, 9" d., ice blue 1,400.00
Plate, 9" d., ice green 340.00
Plate, 9" d., lavender 395.00
Plate, 9" d., marigold 245.00
Plate, 9" d., purple 405.00
Plate, 9" d., white 375.00

PEACOCK STRUTTING (Westmoreland)

Breakfast set: individual size creamer & open sugar bowl; purple, pr. 75.00
Creamer, cov., individual size, purple 40.00
Sugar bowl, cov., individual size, purple 50.00

PEACOCK TAIL (Fenton)

Peacock Tail Bonbon

Bonbon, 2-handled, blue .....18.00 to 35.00
Bonbon, 2-handled, green 35.00
Bonbon, 2-handled, marigold (ILLUS.) 30.00
Bonbon, tricornered, green 70.00
Bonbon, tricornered, marigold 25.00
Bonbon, tricornered, purple 38.00
Bowl, 5" d., ruffled, marigold 22.50
Bowl, 5" d., ruffled, purple 30.00
Bowl, 7" d., ribbon candy rim, amber 40.00
Bowl, 7" d., green 30.00
Bowl, 7" d., purple 35.00
Bowl, 7" d., red 575.00
Bowl, 9" d., blue 47.50
Bowl, 9" d., green 50.00
Bowl, 9" d., crimped, green 65.00
Bowl, 9" d., crimped, marigold 34.00
Bowl, 9" d., ribbon candy rim, purple 50.00
Bowl, ice cream, red 600.00
Compote, 6" d., 5" h., green 45.00
Compote, 6" d., 5" h., marigold 55.00
Compote, 6" d., 5" h., purple 70.00
Plate, 6" d., marigold 28.00
Plate, 9" d., marigold 350.00
Whimsey, hat-shaped, purple 25.00

PERFECTION (Millersburg)

Pitcher, water, marigold 2,700.00
Pitcher, water, purple ..2,000.00 to 3,000.00
Tumbler, green 500.00
Tumbler, purple 288.00

PERSIAN GARDEN (Dugan)

Persian Garden Plate

Berry set: master bowl & 6 sauce dishes; peach opalescent, 7 pcs. . . 400.00
Berry set: 11½" d. fruit bowl & 4 sauce dishes; peach opalescent, 5 pcs. . . . 650.00
Bowl, 5" d., white 55.00
Bowl, ice cream, 11" d., peach opalescent 900.00
Bowl, ice cream, 11" d., purple 775.00
Bowl, ice cream, 11" d., white 188.00
Fruit bowl (no base), marigold, 11½" d. . . . . 70.00 to 85.00
Fruit bowl (no base), peach opalescent, 11½" d. 210.00
Fruit bowl (no base), purple, 11½" d. 135.00
Fruit bowl (no base), white, 11½" d. 205.00
Fruit bowl & base, peach opalescent, 2 pcs. 385.00
Fruit bowl & base, purple, 2 pcs. . . . 300.00
Ice cream dish, white, small 55.00
Ice cream set: 11" d. master ice cream bowl & 4 small dishes; white, 5 pcs. 675.00
Plate, 6" to 7" d., blue 80.00
Plate, 6" to 7" d., marigold 60.00
Plate, 6" to 7" d., peach opalescent (ILLUS.) 260.00
Plate, 6" to 7" d., purple . . 175.00 to 200.00
Plate, 6" to 7" d., white 96.00
Plate, chop, 11" d., peach opalescent 4,200.00
Plate, chop, 11" d., purple . . . . 1,400.00 to 2,000.00
Plate, chop, 11" d., white 900.00

PERSIAN MEDALLION (Fenton)

Bonbon, 2-handled, amber 60.00
Bonbon, 2-handled, Amberina 250.00
Bonbon, 2-handled, aqua 100.00
Bonbon, 2-handled, blue 52.00
Bonbon, 2-handled, green 60.00
Bonbon, 2-handled, marigold 30.00
Bonbon, 2-handled, purple 35.00
Bonbon, 2-handled, red 450.00
Bonbon, 2-handled, vaseline 115.00
Bowl, 5" d., blue 32.00
Bowl, 5" d., green 28.00
Bowl, 5" d., marigold 28.00
Bowl, 5" d., purple 22.50
Bowl, 5" d., red 250.00
Bowl, 7" d., green 60.00
Bowl, 7" d., marigold 55.00
Bowl, 8" to 9" d., fluted, blue . . . . 45.00 to 65.00
Bowl, 8" to 9" d., ribbon candy rim, blue 95.00
Bowl, 8" to 9" d., ribbon candy rim, green 52.00
Bowl, 8" to 9" d., marigold 45.00
Bowl, 8" to 9" d., ribbon candy rim, purple 65.00
Bowl, 8" to 9" d., ruffled rim, red . . . . 900.00 to 1,175.00
Bowl, 10" d., 3-footed, blue 130.00
Bowl, 10" d., 3-footed, purple 185.00
Compote, 6½" d., 6½" h., blue 75.00
Compote, 6½" d., 6½" h., green . . . 45.00
Compote, 6½" d., 6½" h., marigold 37.50
Compote, 6½" d., 6½" h., purple . . 110.00
Compote, 6½" d., 6½" h., white . . . 400.00
Hair receiver, blue 68.00
Hair receiver, marigold 50.00
Hair receiver, white 97.00

Persian Medallion Plates

Plate, 6½" d., blue (ILLUS. left) 68.00
Plate, 6½" d., marigold 58.00
Plate, 6½" d., purple 80.00
Plate, 6½" d., white 75.00
Plate, 9" d., blue 118.00
Plate, 9" d., marigold 115.00
Plate, 9" d., white 395.00
Plate, chop, 10½" d., blue (ILLUS. right) 335.00
Plate, chop, 10½" d., white 225.00
Rose bowl, blue 65.00
Rose bowl, marigold 50.00
Rose bowl, white 143.00

PETAL & FAN (Dugan)
Berry set: master bowl & 4 sauce dishes; peach opalescent, 5 pcs. . . 270.00
Bowl, 5" d., peach opalescent 35.00
Bowl, 5" d., purple 42.00
Bowl, 11" d., peach opalescent 125.00
Bowl, 11" d., ruffled, purple. 125.00
Bowl, 11" d., fluted, white 350.00
Plate, 6" d., ribbon candy edge, purple 225.00

PETALS (Northwood)

Petals Compote

Compote, green (ILLUS.) 60.00
Compote, marigold 45.00
Compote, purple 70.00
Plate, 7" d., purple 25.00

PETER RABBIT (Fenton)

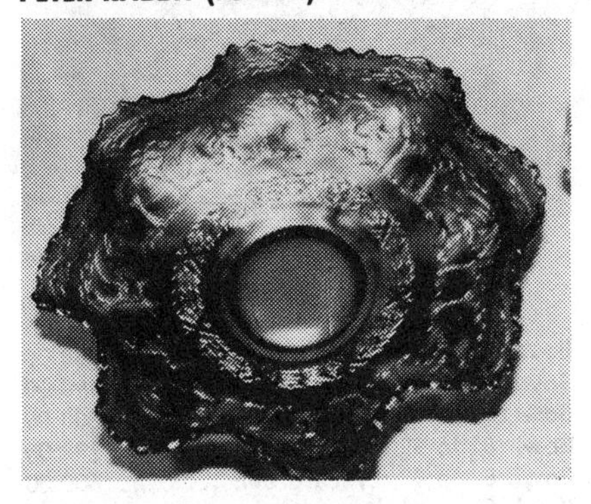

Peter Rabbit Bowl

Bowl, 8" d., blue 1,100.00
Bowl, 8" d., green 800.00
Bowl, 8" d., marigold (ILLUS.) 1,000.00
Plate, blue 2,000.00
Plate, green 3,000.00
Plate, marigold 1,200.00

PILLOW & SUNBURST (Westmoreland)
Bowl, marigold. 25.00
Bowl, purple 43.00
Plate, 8" d., aqua 38.00
Wine, marigold 25.00
Wine, purple. 50.00

PINEAPPLE (Sowerby, England)
Bowl, 5" d., marigold. 30.00
Bowl, 8" d., marigold. 38.00
Compote, purple 45.00
Creamer, marigold, 4½" h. 29.00
Creamer & sugar bowl, purple, pr. . . 50.00
Plate, 8" d., purple 135.00
Rose bowl, marigold. 45.00
Sugar bowl, aqua 215.00

PINE CONE (Fenton)

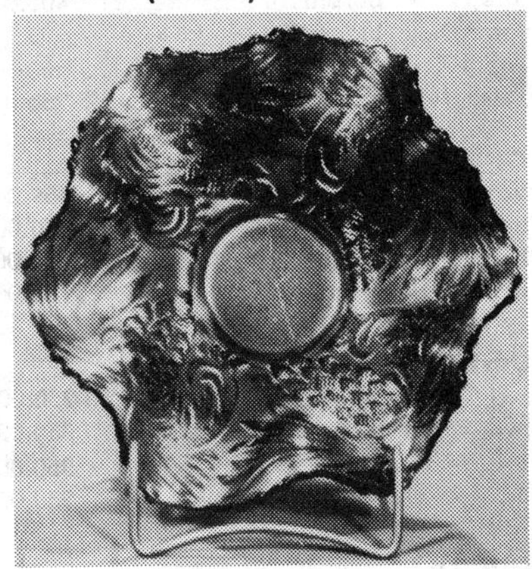

Pine Cone Bowl

Bowl, 5" d., aqua 75.00
Bowl, 5" d., blue 36.00
Bowl, 5" d., marigold 22.50
Bowl, 5" d., purple 35.00
Bowl, 7" d., ruffled, blue (ILLUS.) . . . 52.00
Bowl, 7" d., ruffled, green 35.00
Bowl, 7" d., marigold. 30.00
Bowl, 7" d., ruffled, purple. 40.00
Plate, 5" d., aqua 95.00
Plate, 6½" d., amber 400.00
Plate, 6½" d., blue. 64.00
Plate, 6½" d., green 112.00
Plate, 6½" d., marigold 45.00
Plate, 6½" d., purple 126.00
Plate, 7½" d., blue. 150.00
Plate, 7½" d., marigold 75.00

PIPE HUMIDOR (Millersburg)
Green 3,375.00
Marigold. 3,200.00

PLAID (Fenton)
Bowl, 9" d., marigold. 70.00
Bowl, ice cream, 10" d., blue. 145.00
Bowl, ice cream, 10" d., green 275.00

PLUME PANELS VASE (Fenton)
Blue 35.00
Marigold 30.00
Red 425.00

PODS & POSIES or FOUR FLOWERS (Dugan)
Bowl, 6" d., peach opalescent 36.00
Bowl, 6" d., purple 48.00

Bowl, 8" to 9" d., marigold 45.00
Bowl, 8" to 9" d., purple 50.00
Bowl, 10" d., shallow, ruffled, lavender 225.00
Bowl, 10" d., peach opalescent 190.00
Bowl, 10" d., purple 145.00
Plate, 6" d., green 250.00
Plate, 6" d., peach opalescent 82.00
Plate, 6" to 7" d., Basketweave exterior, peach opalescent 102.00
Plate, 9" d., purple 400.00
Plate, chop, 11" d., peach opalescent 400.00
Plate, chop, 11" d., purple 750.00

POINSETTIA (Imperial)

Pitcher, milk, amber 59.00
Pitcher, milk, green 250.00
Pitcher, milk, marigold 70.00
Pitcher, milk, smoky 105.00

POINSETTIA & LATTICE

Bowl, aqua opalescent 3,250.00
Bowl, cobalt blue 350.00
Bowl, marigold 350.00
Bowl, purple 250.00

POND LILY

Bonbon, blue 65.00
Bonbon, green 75.00
Bonbon, marigold 60.00
Bonbon, white 90.00

PONY

Bowl, 8" to 9" d., aqua 400.00
Bowl, 8" to 9" d., marigold 56.00
Bowl, 8" to 9" d., purple 120.00
Plate, marigold 475.00

POPPY (Millersburg)

Poppy Compote

Compote, green 525.00
Compote, marigold 350.00
Compote, purple (ILLUS.) 1,000.00

POPPY (Northwood)

Northwood's Poppy Pickle Dish

Pickle dish, blue (ILLUS.) 56.00
Pickle dish, green 200.00
Pickle dish, ice blue 300.00
Pickle dish, marigold 55.00
Pickle dish, white 225.00

POPPY SHOW (Northwood)

Poppy Show Bowl

Bowl, 8" to 9" d., blue (ILLUS.) 388.00
Bowl, 8" to 9" d., clambroth 190.00
Bowl, 8" to 9" d., green 1,300.00
Bowl, 8" to 9" d., ice blue 792.00
Bowl, 8" to 9" d., ice green 600.00
Bowl, 8" to 9" d., marigold 210.00
Bowl, 8" to 9" d., purple 295.00
Bowl, 8" to 9" d., white 282.00
Plate, blue 624.00
Plate, green 1,200.00
Plate, ice blue 705.00
Plate, ice green 340.00
Plate, marigold 424.00
Plate, purple 578.00
Plate, white 458.00

POPPY SHOW VASE (Imperial)

Green 495.00
Marigold 304.00

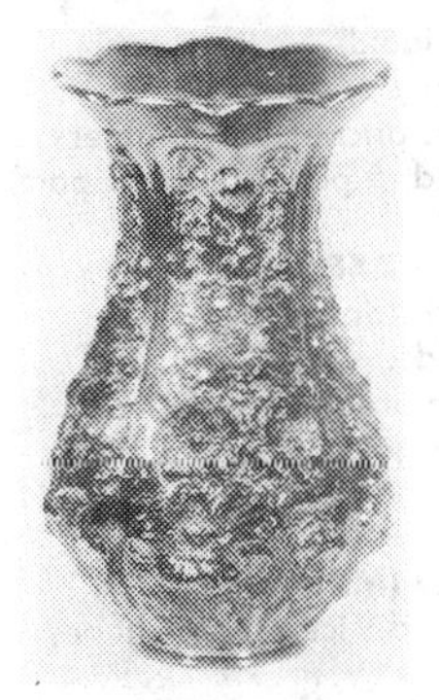

Imperial's Poppy Show Vase

Purple (ILLUS.) 755.00
Smoky ....275.00 to 550.00

PRIMROSE BOWL (Millersburg)

Green 120.00
Marigold 57.00
Purple 82.00

PRINCESS LAMP

Purple, complete 1,000.00
Purple, base only 225.00

PRISMS

Compote, 7¼" d., 2½" h., 2-handled, marigold 50.00
Compote, 7¼" d., 2½" h., 2-handled, purple 55.00

PULLED LOOP

Vase, 5½" h., marigold 28.00
Vase, 9½" h., peach opalescent 52.00

PUZZLE

Bonbon, stemmed, peach opalescent 52.00
Compote, peach opalescent 36.00

QUESTION MARKS

Bonbon, footed, marigold, 6" d., 3¾" h. 32.00
Bonbon, footed, pastel marigold, 6" d., 3¾" h. 35.00
Bonbon, footed, peach opalescent, 6" d., 3¾" h. 64.00
Bonbon, footed, purple, 6" d., 3¾" h. 33.00
Bonbon, footed, white, 6" d., 3¾" h. 120.00
Plate, dome-footed, Georgia Peach exterior, purple 100.00

QUILL (Dugan or Diamond Glass Co.)

Pitcher, water, marigold (ILLUS.) 2,500.00

Quill Water Pitcher

Tumbler, marigold 275.00
Tumbler, purple 400.00

RAINDROPS (Dugan)

Bowl, 9" d., dome-footed, peach opalescent 62.00
Bowl, 9" d. , dome-footed, purple .. 58.00

RAMBLER ROSE (Dugan)

Pitcher, water, marigold 115.00
Pitcher, water, purple 325.00
Tumbler, blue 33.00
Tumbler, marigold 20.00
Water set: pitcher & 4 tumblers; blue, 5 pcs. 400.00
Water set: pitcher & 6 tumblers; marigold, 7 pcs. 295.00
Water set: pitcher & 6 tumblers; purple, 7 pcs. 525.00

RANGER

Pitcher, milk, marigold 145.00
Sherbet, marigold 17.50
Tumbler, marigold 105.00
Whiskey shot glass, marigold 95.00

RASPBERRY (Northwood)

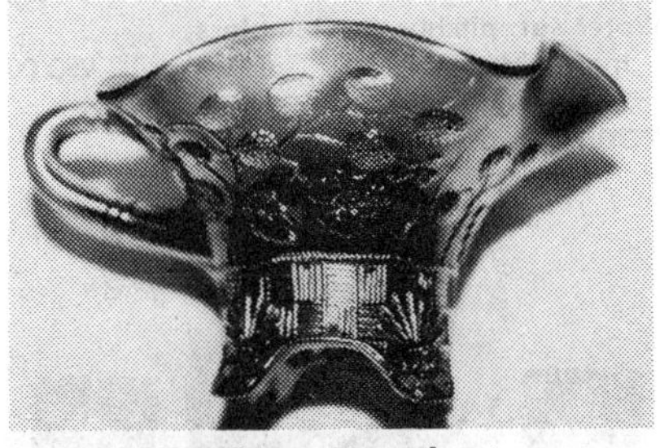

Raspberry Sauceboat

Pitcher, milk, green 195.00
Pitcher, milk, marigold 117.00
Pitcher, milk, purple 172.00
Pitcher, water, green 250.00

Pitcher, water, ice green 2,275.00
Pitcher, water, marigold 129.00
Pitcher, water, purple 227.00
Sauceboat, green (ILLUS.) 155.00
Sauceboat, marigold 65.00
Sauceboat, purple 65.00
Tumbler, green 50.00
Tumbler, ice blue 162.00
Tumbler, ice green 875.00
Tumbler, marigold 28.00
Tumbler, purple 36.00
Water set: pitcher & 2 tumblers; green, 3 pcs. 290.00
Water set: pitcher & 3 tumblers; purple, 4 pcs. 375.00
Water set: pitcher & 6 tumblers; marigold, 7 pcs. 340.00

RAYS & RIBBONS (Millersburg)

Banana boat, green 850.00
Bowl, 8" to 9" d., green 65.00
Bowl, 8" to 9" d., purple 70.00
Bowl, 10" d., green 66.00
Bowl, 10" sq., green ......250.00 to 275.00
Bowl, 10" d., ice cream shape, turned-down rim, green 135.00
Bowl, 10" d., marigold 78.00
Bowl, 10" d., purple 65.00

RIBBED FUNERAL VASE

Marigold, 9¼" h. 35.00
Marigold, 18" h. 100.00
Sapphire blue, 15½" h. 250.00

RIBBON TIE - **See Comet Pattern**

RIPPLE

Vase, 7¼" h., marigold 85.00
Vase, 9½" h., marigold 20.00
Vase, 11½" h., amber 55.00
Vase, 18¾" h., green 163.00
Vase, 20" h., marigold 68.00
Vase, purple 49.00

RISING SUN

Pitcher, water, pedestal base, marigold 488.00
Tumbler, marigold 346.00
Water set: pitcher & 4 tumblers; marigold, 5 pcs. 2,950.00

ROBIN (Imperial)

Robin Water Set

Mug, marigold 47.00
Mug, smoky 65.00
Water set: pitcher & 4 tumblers; marigold, 5 pcs. (ILLUS. of part) .. 300.00

ROCOCO VASE

Bowl, 6" d., dome-footed, marigold 20.00
Vase, clambroth 40.00
Vase, marigold 51.00
Vase, smoky 62.50

ROSALIND (Millersburg)

Bowl, 8¾" d., ice cream shape, green 425.00
Bowl, 10" d., ruffled, green 157.00
Bowl, 10" d., marigold 142.00
Bowl, 10" d., purple 160.00
Compote, 6" d., small, ruffled, purple 485.00
Compote, 6" d., tall, ruffled, marigold 650.00
Compote, 6" d., tall, ruffled, purple 1,000.00
Plate, 9" d., green 575.00

ROSE COLUMNS VASE

Rose Columns Vase

Amethyst 1,500.00
Amethyst, experimental, factory-painted roses decoration (ILLUS.) 3,250.00
Green 1,350.00
Marigold 1,200.00

ROSE SHOW

Bowl, 9" d., amber 750.00
Bowl, 9" d., aqua opalescent 657.00
Bowl, 9" d., blue 538.00
Bowl, 9" d., green 1,050.00
Bowl, 9" d., ice blue 363.00
Bowl, 9" d., ice green 563.00
Bowl, 9" d., marigold 231.00
Bowl, 9" d., purple 354.00
Bowl, 9" d., white 292.00
Plate, 9" d., blue 562.00
Plate, 9" d., green 600.00

Plate, 9" d., ice blue 1,000.00
Plate, 9" d., ice green 525.00
Plate, 9" d., marigold 456.00
Plate, 9" d., purple 355.00
Plate, 9" d., white 446.00

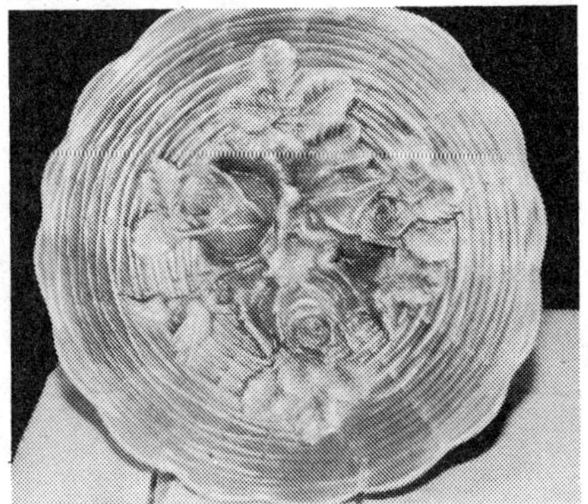

Rose Show Plate

Plate, milk white w/marigold overlay (ILLUS.) 2,500.00

ROUND UP (Dugan)

Round Up Plate

Bowl, 9" d., low, fluted, blue 70.00
Bowl, 9" d., marigold 50.00
Bowl, 9" d., peach opalescent 300.00
Bowl, 9" d., purple 80.00
Bowl, ice cream shape, peach opalescent 200.00
Bowl, ice-cream shape, white 158.00
Plate, 9" d., blue (ILLUS.) 232.00
Plate, 9" d., ruffled, marigold 220.00
Plate, 9" d., flat, peach opalescent 150.00
Plate, 9" d., ruffled, peach opalescent 325.00
Plate, 9" d., purple 292.00
Plate, 9" d., white 375.00

RUSTIC VASE

Blue, 9" h. 40.00
Blue, 16" h. 55.00
Blue, 19" h. 165.00
Blue, 21" h. 244.00
Blue, 23½" h. 270.00
Blue, elephant base 425.00
Green, 11" h. 40.00
Green, 14" h. 45.00
Green, 16" h. 52.00
Green, 18" h. 350.00
Marigold, 11" h. 30.00
Marigold, 16" to 20" h. 150.00
Purple, 9" h. 40.00
Purple, 16" h. 100.00
Purple, elephant base 400.00
White, 6" h. 52.00
White, 18" h. 225.00
White, 20" h. 410.00

SAILBOAT (Fenton)

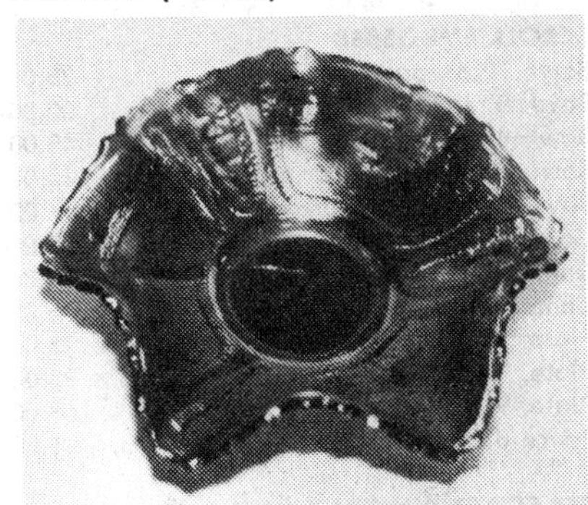

Sailboat Bowl

Bowl, 5" d., aqua 109.00
Bowl, 5" d., ruffled, blue 52.00
Bowl, 5" d., clambroth 40.00
Bowl, 5" d., marigold 25.00
Bowl, 5" d., purple 70.00
Bowl, 5" d., ruffled, red 470.00
Bowl, 6" d., ruffled, green (ILLUS.) .. 105.00
Compote, blue 220.00
Compote, marigold 65.00
Goblet, water, green 300.00
Goblet, water, marigold 170.00
Goblet, water, purple 350.00
Plate, 6" d., blue 350.00
Plate, 6" d., marigold 224.00
Wine, aqua ....195.00 to 225.00
Wine, marigold 30.00
Wine, vaseline 125.00

SCALE BAND

Pitcher, marigold 85.00
Plate, 6" d., flat, marigold 22.00
Water set: pitcher & 6 tumblers; marigold, 7 pcs. 175.00

SCALES

Bowl, 5" d., purple 25.00
Bowl, 7" d., marigold 22.50
Bowl, 7" d., peach opalescent 55.00

Bowl, 7" w., tricornered, peach opalescent 155.00
Bowl, 7" d., purple 40.00
Bowl, 8" to 9" d., aqua opalescent 308.00
Bowl, 8" to 9" d., milk white w/marigold overlay 160.00
Bowl, 8" to 9" d., peach opalescent 110.00
Plate, 6½" d., marigold 40.00
Plate, 6½" d., peach opalescent 31.00
Plate, 6½" d., purple 40.00

SCOTCH THISTLE COMPOTE
Blue 57.00
Green 57.00
Marigold 48.00
Purple 45.00

SCROLL EMBOSSED
Bowl, 7" d., purple 28.00
Bowl, 8" to 9" d., aqua 60.00
Bowl, 8" to 9" d., green 48.00
Bowl, 8" to 9" d., marigold 35.00
Bowl, 8" to 9" d., purple 44.00
Compote, green 55.00
Compote, marigold 28.00
Compote, purple 85.00
Plate, 9" d., green ..... 55.00 to 75.00
Plate, 9" d., marigold 95.00
Plate, 9" d., purple 168.00
Sauce dish, purple, 5½" d. 11.50

SEACOAST PIN TRAY (Millersburg)
Green 325.00
Marigold 290.00
Purple 330.00

SEAWEED (Millersburg)
Bowl, 6" d., purple 475.00
Bowl, 10" d., blue 900.00
Bowl, 10" d., ruffled, green ..... 175.00 to 200.00
Bowl, 10" d., ruffled, marigold 220.00
Bowl, 10" d., ruffled, purple 268.00
Plate, 9" d., green 550.00
Plate, 9" d., marigold 500.00

SHELL (Imperial)
Bowl, footed, marigold 18.00
Bowl, footed, purple 35.00
Bowl, ruffled, green 32.50
Plate, smoky 213.00

SHELL & JEWEL
Creamer, cov., marigold 25.00
Creamer & cov. sugar bowl, green, pr. 55.00
Sugar bowl, cov., green 28.00
Sugar bowl, cov., marigold 20.00

SHELL & SAND
Bowl, 7" d., marigold 30.00
Bowl, 7" d., purple 55.00
Bowl, 8" to 9" d., ruffled, purple 57.00
Mug, purple 75.00
Plate, green 80.00

SHELL & WILD ROSE
Bowl, 8½" d., marigold 13.50
Bowl, small, purple 25.00
Dish, open heart-shaped rim, footed, green 32.50
Dish, open heart-shaped rim, footed, purple 41.00
Rose bowl, in-curved points, green 54.00

SINGING BIRDS (Northwood)

Singing Birds Mug

Berry set: master bowl & 6 sauce dishes; green, 7 pcs. 335.00
Berry set: master bowl & 6 sauce dishes; purple, 7 pcs. 270.00
Bowl, master berry, marigold 75.00
Bowl, master berry, purple 90.00
Butter dish, cov., green 230.00
Butter dish, cov., marigold 138.00
Butter dish, cov., purple 172.00
Creamer, marigold 49.00
Creamer & sugar bowl, purple, pr. 160.00
Mug, aqua opalescent 957.00
Mug, blue 110.00
Mug, green 140.00
Mug, ice blue 850.00
Mug, lavender 125.00
Mug, marigold 52.00
Mug, stippled, marigold 123.00
Mug, purple (ILLUS.) 76.00
Mug, purple, w/advertising, "Hotel Vendome" 133.00
Mug, purple, w/advertising, "Amazon Hotel" 125.00
Mug, white 667.00
Pitcher, green 275.00
Pitcher, marigold 210.00
Pitcher, purple 275.00
Sauce dish, green 28.00
Sauce dish, marigold 32.00
Sauce dish, purple 30.00
Spooner, marigold 50.00
Spooner, purple 85.00
Sugar bowl, cov., green 185.00
Sugar bowl, cov., marigold 80.00
Table set: cov. butter dish, cov.

sugar bowl, creamer & spooner; green, 4 pcs. 425.00
Table set, marigold, 4 pcs. 375.00
Table set, purple, 4 pcs. 865.00
Tumbler, green 40.00
Tumbler, marigold 25.00
Tumbler, purple 40.00
Water set: pitcher & 5 tumblers; purple, 6 pcs. 708.00
Water set: pitcher & 6 tumblers; marigold, 7 pcs. 557.00
Water set: pitcher & 8 tumblers; green, 9 pcs. 750.00

SINGLE FLOWER
Bowl, 9" d., peach opalescent 50.00
Plate, crimped rim, peach opalescent 80.00

SIX PETALS (Dugan)
Bowl, 5" d., marigold 20.00
Bowl, 7" d., crimped, peach opalescent 38.00
Bowl, 7" w., tricornered, peach opalescent 78.00
Bowl, 7" w., tricornered, purple 51.00
Bowl, 8" d., peach opalescent 46.00
Bowl, 8" d., purple 65.00
Bowl, 8" d., white 74.00

SKI STAR (Dugan)
Banana bowl, peach opalescent 132.00
Banana bowl, purple 92.00
Basket, peach opalescent 395.00
Berry set: master bowl & 4 sauce dishes; peach opalescent, 5 pcs. 264.00
Bowl, 5" d., peach opalescent 35.00
Bowl, 5" d., fluted, peach opalescent 65.00
Bowl, 5" d., ruffled, peach opalescent 55.00
Bowl, 5" d., ruffled, purple 52.00
Bowl, 7" d., ruffled, purple 75.00
Bowl, 8" to 9" d., dome-footed, peach opalescent 80.00
Bowl, 8" to 9" d., dome-footed, purple 70.00
Bowl, 10" d., peach opalescent 135.00
Bowl, 11" d., peach opalescent 80.00
Bowl, 11" d., purple 190.00
Bowl, tricornered, dome base, peach opalescent 107.00
Plate, 6" d., crimped rim, peach opalescent 125.00
Plate, 8½" d., dome-footed, w/handgrip, peach opalescent 150.00
Plate, 8½" d., dome-footed, w/handgrip, purple 240.00

SNOW FANCY
Creamer, marigold 40.00
Sauce dish, marigold 30.00
Sugar bowl, marigold 37.50

SODA GOLD (Imperial)

Soda Gold Water Set

Basket, marigold, small 22.00
Bowl, 9" d., marigold 48.00
Candlesticks, marigold, 7½" h., pr. 45.00
Candlesticks, smoky, 7½" h., pr. 50.00
Console set: bowl & pr. candlesticks; marigold, 3 pcs. 45.00
Cuspidor, marigold .... 45.00 to 60.00
Pitcher, milk, marigold 195.00
Pitcher, water, marigold .... 125.00 to 160.00
Pitcher, water, smoky 375.00
Tumbler, marigold .... 25.00 to 40.00
Tumbler, smoky 62.00
Water set: pitcher & 6 tumblers; marigold, 7 pcs. (ILLUS.) 250.00
Water set: pitcher & 6 tumblers; smoky, 7 pcs. 650.00

SOUTACHE (Dugan)

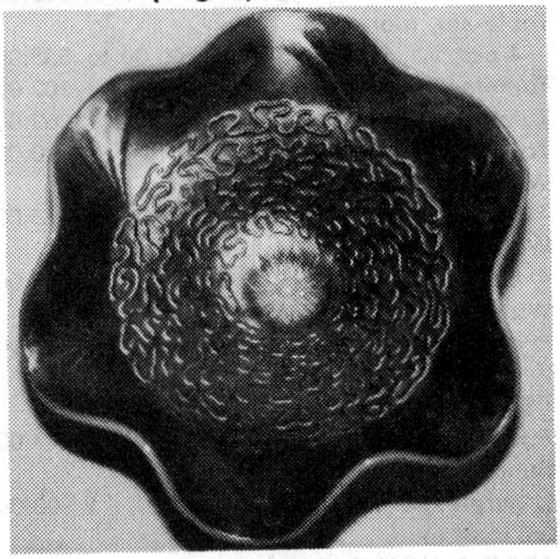

Soutache Bowl

Bowl, 8" d., dome-footed, ruffled, peach opalescent (ILLUS.) 85.00
Bowl, 8" to 9" d., dome-footed, piecrust edge, peach opalescent 87.00
Plate, 9½" d., dome-footed, peach opalescent 350.00

SPRINGTIME (Northwood)
Berry set: master bowl & 6 sauce dishes; green, 7 pcs. 280.00

Bowl, 5" d., green 45.00
Bowl, 5" d., marigold 25.00
Bowl, 5" d., purple 40.00
Bowl, master berry, green 150.00
Bowl, master berry, marigold 75.00
Butter dish, cov., green 400.00

Springtime Butter Dish

Butter dish, cov., marigold (ILLUS.) .. 195.00
Butter dish, cov., purple 225.00
Creamer, marigold 85.00
Creamer, purple 103.00
Pitcher, green 495.00
Pitcher, marigold 414.00
Pitcher, purple 625.00
Spooner, green 150.00
Spooner, marigold 90.00
Spooner, purple 83.00
Sugar bowl, cov., purple 120.00
Table set, green, 4 pcs. 1,600.00
Table set, marigold, 4 pcs. .... 500.00 to 535.00
Tumbler, green 102.00
Tumbler, marigold 62.00
Tumbler, purple 120.00
Water set: pitcher & 3 tumblers; green, 4 pcs. 525.00
Water set: pitcher & 4 tumblers; purple, 5 pcs. 865.00
Water set: pitcher & 6 tumblers; marigold, 7 pcs. 690.00

"S" REPEAT (Dugan)

Punch cup, purple 118.00
Punch set: bowl, base & 13 cups; purple, 15 pcs. 2,900.00

STAG & HOLLY (Fenton)

Bowl, 7" d., spatula-footed, blue ... 107.00
Bowl, 7" d., spatula-footed, green .. 125.00
Bowl, 7" d., spatula-footed, marigold 49.00
Bowl, 7" d., spatula-footed, red 1,050.00
Bowl, 8" to 9" d., spatula-footed, blue 112.00
Bowl, 8" to 9" d., spatula-footed, green 150.00
Bowl, 8" to 9" d., spatula-footed, marigold 70.00
Bowl, 8" to 9" d., spatula-footed, purple 112.00
Bowl, 10" to 11" d., 3-footed, amber 432.00
Bowl, 10" to 11" d., 3-footed, Amberina 838.00
Bowl, 10" to 11" d., 3-footed, aqua 480.00

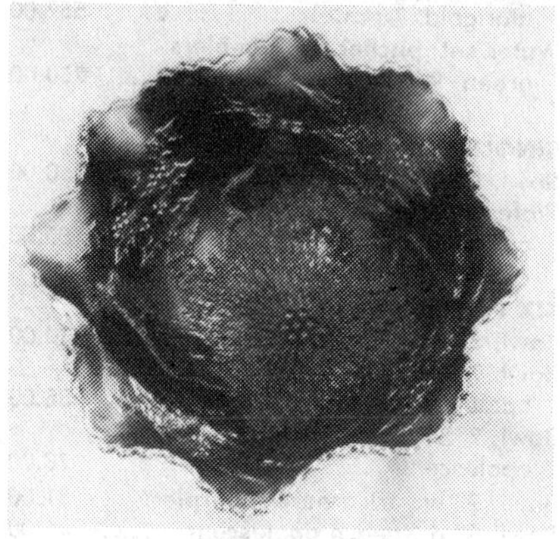

Stag & Holly Bowl

Bowl, 10" to 11" d., 3-footed, blue (ILLUS.) 200.00
Bowl, 10" to 11" d., 3-footed, green 425.00
Bowl, 10" to 11" d., 3-footed, marigold 104.00
Bowl, 10" to 11" d., 3-footed, vaseline 273.00
Bowl, 11" d., flat, amber 450.00
Bowl, 11" d., flat, marigold 125.00
Bowl, spatula-footed, red .... 1,325.00 to 1,375.00
Plate, 9" d., marigold 360.00
Plate, chop, 12" d., 3-footed, marigold 525.00
Rose bowl, blue, large 595.00
Rose bowl, marigold, large 212.00

STAR & FILE (Imperial)

Bowl, 5" d., marigold 25.00
Bowl, 7" d., marigold 20.00
Bowl, 8" to 9" d., marigold 35.00
Card tray, 2 turned-up sides, marigold, 6¼" d. 22.50
Celery vase, 2-handled, marigold ... 27.50
Compote, jelly, clambroth 50.00
Compote, jelly, marigold 55.00
Compote, large, marigold 25.00
Creamer, marigold 23.00
Creamer & sugar bowl, marigold, pr. 47.50
Pitcher, milk, smoky 40.00
Pitcher, water, marigold 120.00
Plate, 6" d., marigold 50.00
Punch cup, marigold 35.00
Relish tray, 2-handled, marigold 45.00

Rose bowl, marigold 51.00
Sugar bowl, marigold 15.00
Tumbler, marigold 46.00
Water set: pitcher & 6 tumblers; marigold, 7 pcs. 255.00
Wine, marigold 38.00
Wine set: decanter w/stopper & 7 wines; marigold, 8 pcs. 350.00

STARFISH

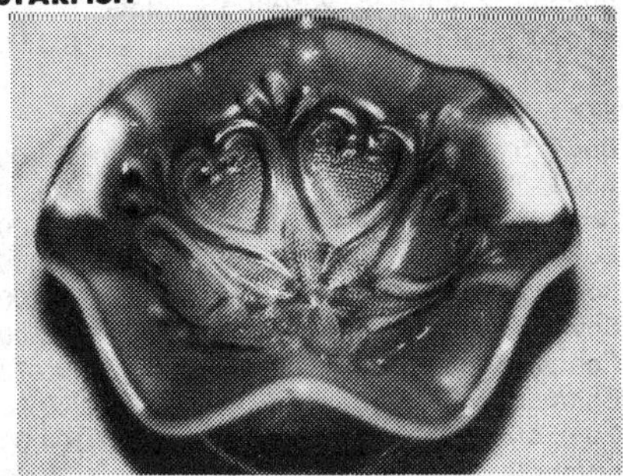

Starfish Compote

Compote, peach opalescent (ILLUS.) 60.00
Compote, purple 45.00

STAR MEDALLION

Bowl, 5" sq., marigold 25.00
Bowl, 7" d., clambroth 15.00
Bowl, 7" d., smoky 22.50
Bowl, 8" d., marigold 30.00
Bowl, 8" d., smoky 26.00
Celery vase, footed, clambroth 38.00
Goblet, marigold 30.00
Pitcher, milk, clambroth 35.00
Pitcher, milk, marigold 35.00
Pitcher, milk, smoky 76.00
Plate, 9" to 10" d., clambroth 50.00
Plate, 9" to 10" d., marigold 35.00
Punch cup, marigold 15.00
Rose bowl, marigold 35.00
Sherbet, stemmed, marigold 25.00
Tumbler, marigold 30.00
Tumbler, tall, tankard form, marigold 35.00

STAR OF DAVID (Imperial)

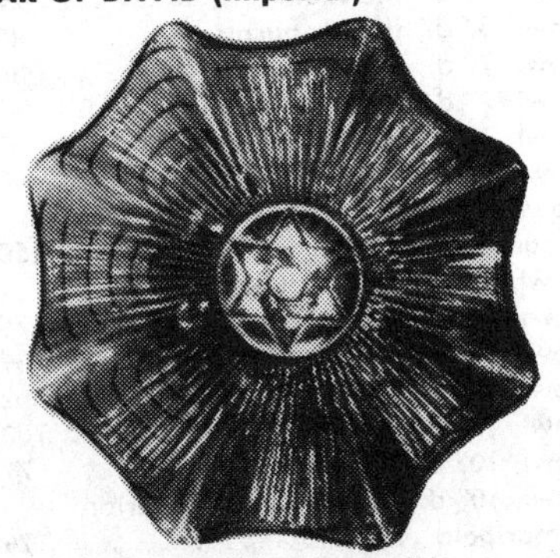

Star of David Bowl

Bowl, 8" to 9" d., collared base, green (ILLUS.) 55.00
Bowl, 8" to 9" d., collared base, marigold 50.00
Bowl, 8" to 9" d., collared base, purple 54.00
Bowl, 9" d., flat, ruffled, purple 88.00

STAR OF DAVID & BOWS (Northwood)

Bowl, 7" d., dome-footed, blue 90.00
Bowl, 7" d., dome-footed, green 60.00
Bowl, 7" d., dome-footed, marigold 53.00
Bowl, 7" d., dome-footed, purple 50.00
Bowl, 8" to 9" d., dome-footed, fluted, purple 74.00

STIPPLED PETALS

Bowl, peach opalescent 82.00
Bowl, purple 87.00
Bowl, white 60.00

STIPPLED RAYS

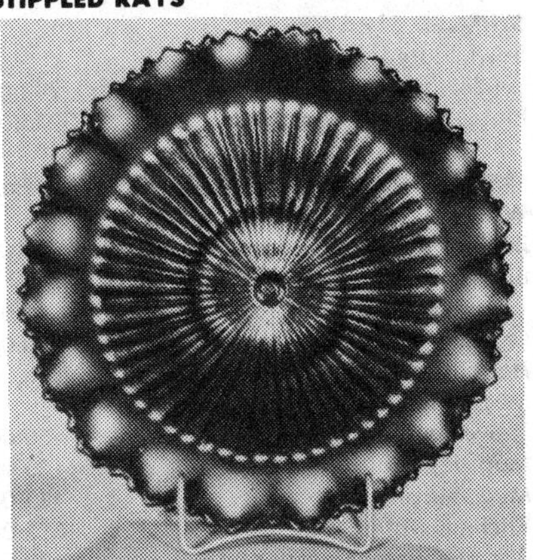

Stippled Rays Bowl

Berry set: master bowl & 4 sauce dishes; green, 5 pcs. 150.00
Bonbon, 2-handled, green 36.00
Bonbon, 2-handled, ice green 80.00
Bonbon, 2-handled, marigold 30.00
Bonbon, 2-handled, purple 25.00
Bonbon, 2-handled, red 260.00
Bowl, 5" d., amber 25.00
Bowl, 5" d., blue 40.00
Bowl, 5" d., green 30.00
Bowl, 5" d., purple 37.50
Bowl, 5" d., red 312.00
Bowl, 6" d., Amberina 100.00
Bowl, 7" d., blue 35.00
Bowl, 7" d., dome-footed, green 25.00
Bowl, 7" d., marigold 25.00
Bowl, 7" d., ruffled rim, red 374.00
Bowl, 8" to 9" d., amber 97.50
Bowl, 8" to 9" d., green 50.00
Bowl, 8" to 9" d., ribbon candy rim, green 57.50
Bowl, 8" to 9" d., marigold 36.00

Bowl, 8" to 9" d., ribbon candy rim, marigold 33.00
Bowl, 8" to 9" d., purple 40.00
Bowl, 8" to 9" d., ribbon candy rim, purple 42.50
Bowl, 8" to 9" d., teal blue 20.00
Bowl, 10" d., green 60.00
Bowl, 10" d., ruffled, marigold 44.00
Bowl, 10" d., purple (ILLUS.) 55.00
Bowl, 10" d., red slag 450.00
Bowl, 10" d., white ....275.00 to 300.00
Bowl, ruffled, red 330.00
Creamer, green 40.00
Creamer, footed, marigold 12.00
Creamer & sugar bowl, marigold, pr. 38.00
Plate, 6" to 7" d., blue 40.00
Plate, 6" to 7" d., marigold 32.00
Plate, 6" to 7" d., red 375.00
Sugar bowl, open, blue 27.50
Sugar bowl, open, marigold 22.00
Sugar bowl, open, red 320.00

STIPPLED STRAWBERRY
Bowl, fluted, ice green (Northwood) 790.00
Plate, 8" d., green 275.00

STORK & RUSHES (Dugan or Diamond Glass Works)
Basket, handled, marigold 90.00
Bowl, master berry or fruit, marigold 40.00
Creamer, marigold 70.00
Hat shape, marigold 25.00
Mug, aqua base w/marigold overlay 450.00
Mug, marigold 35.00
Mug, purple 125.00
Pitcher, water, blue 375.00
Pitcher, water, purple 400.00
Punch bowl & base, marigold, 2 pcs. 200.00
Punch cup, marigold 16.00
Punch cup, purple 19.00
Punch set: bowl, base & 7 cups; marigold, 9 pcs. 340.00
Sauce dish, marigold 18.50
Sauce dish, purple 26.00
Spooner, marigold 63.00
Table set: butter dish, spooner & sugar bowl; marigold, 3 pcs. 250.00
Tumbler, aqua 210.00
Tumbler, blue 30.00
Tumbler w/lattice band, blue 55.00
Tumbler, marigold 19.00
Tumbler, marigold w/pale blue base 128.00
Tumbler, purple 35.00
Vase, marigold 22.00
Water set: pitcher & 6 tumblers; blue, 7 pcs. 1,050.00
Water set: pitcher & 6 tumblers; marigold, 7 pcs. 400.00

STRAWBERRY (Fenton)
Bonbon, Amberina 200.00
Bonbon, 2-handled, blue 50.00
Bonbon, 2-handled, green 59.00
Bonbon, 2-handled, ice green opalescent 450.00
Bonbon, 2-handled, marigold 28.00
Bonbon, 2-handled, purple 29.00
Bonbon, 2-handled, red 285.00
Bonbon, 2-handled, vaseline w/marigold iridescence 133.00

STRAWBERRY (Millersburg)
Bowl, 5" d., green 55.00
Bowl, 5" d., marigold 20.00
Bowl, 5" d., purple 50.00
Bowl, 7" d., green 110.00
Bowl, 8" to 9" d., purple 242.00
Bowl, 8" to 9" d., vaseline 450.00
Compote, amber 45.00
Compote, green 250.00
Compote, marigold 104.00
Compote, purple 178.00
Compote, vaseline 640.00

STRAWBERRY (Northwood)

Strawberry Plate

Berry set: master bowl & 4 sauce dishes; marigold, 5 pcs. 165.00
Bowl, 5" d., fluted, blue 35.00
Bowl, 5" d., marigold 27.50
Bowl, 5" d., fluted, purple 40.00
Bowl, 7" d., green 56.00
Bowl, 7" d., marigold 48.50
Bowl, 7" d., purple 33.00
Bowl, 8" to 9" d., stippled, blue 90.00
Bowl, 8" to 9" d., stippled, ribbon candy rim, green 150.00
Bowl, 8" to 9" d., ruffled, Basketweave exterior, green 75.00
Bowl, 8" to 9" d., marigold 39.00
Bowl, 8" to 9" d., purple 62.00
Bowl, 10" d., ice green 700.00
Bowl, 10" d., marigold 71.00
Bowl, 10" d., Basketweave exterior, marigold 79.00
Bowl, 10" d., purple 102.00

Bowl, 10" d., Basketweave exterior, purple 135.00
Plate, 6" to 7" d., w/handgrip, green 140.00
Plate, 6" to 7" d., w/handgrip, marigold 67.00
Plate, 6" to 7" d., w/handgrip, purple 102.00
Plate, 9" d., green 160.00
Plate, 9" d., lavender 135.00
Plate, 9" d., marigold 77.00
Plate, 9" d., purple (ILLUS.) 118.00

STRAWBERRY SCROLL (Fenton)

Strawberry Scroll Pitcher

Pitcher, water, blue (ILLUS.) 1,990.00
Pitcher, water, marigold 1,325.00
Tumbler, blue 200.00
Tumbler, marigold 184.00

SUNFLOWER BOWL (Northwood)

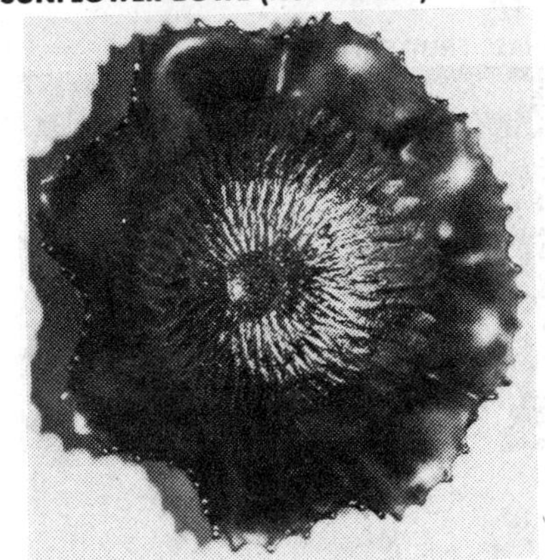

Sunflower Bowl

Bowl, 8" d., footed, blue (ILLUS.) 450.00
Bowl, 8" d., footed, clambroth 350.00
Bowl, 8" d., footed, green 50.00
Bowl, 8" d., footed, marigold 37.00
Bowl, 8" d., footed, purple 60.00

SUNFLOWER PIN TRAY (Millersburg)

Clambroth 195.00
Green 195.00
Marigold 350.00
Purple 210.00

SWAN PASTEL NOVELTIES (Dugan)

Salt dip, ice blue 37.00
Salt dip, ice green 32.00
Salt dip, marigold 116.00
Salt dip, peach opalescent 220.00
Salt dip, pink 25.00
Salt dip, purple 140.00
Salt dip, vaseline 58.00

SWIRL HOBNAIL (Millersburg)

Swirl Hobnail Cuspidor

Cuspidor, marigold 495.00
Cuspidor, purple (ILLUS.) 487.00
Rose bowl, marigold 225.00
Rose bowl, purple 288.00
Vase, green 195.00
Vase, marigold .... 220.00 to 250.00
Vase, purple 210.00

SWIRL RIB

Pitcher, tankard, marigold 150.00
Tumbler, marigold 25.00
Vase, 5½" h., peach opalescent 46.00
Vase, 9½" h., peach opalescent 37.00
Vase, 14½" h., peach opalescent 48.00
Vase, marigold 35.00

TARGET VASE (Fenton)

6" h., white 55.00
11½" h., peach opalescent 52.00

TEN MUMS (Fenton)

Bowl, 8" to 9" d., ribbon candy edge, blue 80.00
Bowl, 8" to 9" d., ribbon candy edge, green 110.00
Bowl, 8" to 9" d., ribbon candy edge, marigold 60.00
Bowl, 10" d., ruffled, blue 155.00
Bowl, 10" d., footed, green 78.00
Bowl, 10" d., footed, marigold 210.00
Bowl, 10" d., ribbon candy edge, purple 83.00
Pitcher, water, blue 800.00
Pitcher, water, marigold 360.00
Pitcher, water, white 1,200.00
Tumbler, blue 70.00

Tumbler, marigold . . . 54.00
Tumblcr, purple . . . 65.00
Tumbler, white . . . 210.00

Ten Mums Pitcher

Water set: pitcher & 5 tumblers; blue, 6 pcs. (ILLUS. of pitcher only) . . . 1,400.00
Water set: pitcher & 6 tumblers; marigold, 7 pcs. . . . 850.00

TEXAS HAT

Marigold . . . 25.00

THIN RIB VASE

6" h., bud, green . . . 45.00
7½" h., ice green (Northwood) . . . 80.00
8" h., aqua . . . 60.00
9" h., aqua opalescent . . . 90.00
9" h., blue . . . 45.00
9" h., green . . . 25.00
9" h., red . . . 150.00
9½" h., aqua . . . 30.00
10" h., vaseline . . . 45.00
11" h., aqua opalescent . . . 140.00
11" h., red . . . 155.00
11¼" h., marigold . . . 40.00
12" h., aqua . . . 50.00
12" h., white . . . 110.00
13" h., ice blue . . . 125.00

THISTLE

Banana boat, amber . . . 170.00
Banana boat, blue . . . 162.00
Banana boat, green . . . 325.00
Banana boat, marigold . . . 115.00
Banana boat, purple . . . 200.00
Bowl, 8" to 9" d., ribbon candy edge, blue . . . 52.00
Bowl, 8" to 9" d., ruffled, blue . . . 40.00
Bowl, 8" to 9" d., flared, green . . . 36.00
Bowl, 8" to 9" d., ribbon candy edge, green . . . 36.00
Bowl, 8" to 9" d., ribbon candy edge, marigold (ILLUS.) . . . 37.00
Bowl, 8" to 9" d., ribbon candy edge, purple . . . 37.00

Thistle Bowl

Bowl, 8" to 9" d., ruffled, purple . . . 50.00
Bowl, aqua . . . 450.00
Plate, 9" d., green . . . 1,800.00
Plate, 9" d., purple . . . 1,400.00
Plate, marigold (Fenton) . . . 1,650.00
Vase, 6" h., marigold . . . 30.00

THISTLE & THORN (Sowerby's, England)

Bowl, 5" to 6" d., footed, marigold . . . 52.00
Bowl, 9" d., footed, marigold . . . 40.00
Creamer, marigold . . . 30.00
Creamer & open sugar bowl, marigold, pr. . . . 60.00
Plate, 9" d., 4-footed, ruffled, scalloped rim, marigold . . . 54.00
Plate, 3-footed, marigold . . . 90.00
Sugar bowl, footed, marigold, 5¼" h. . . . 29.00

THREE FRUITS (Northwood)

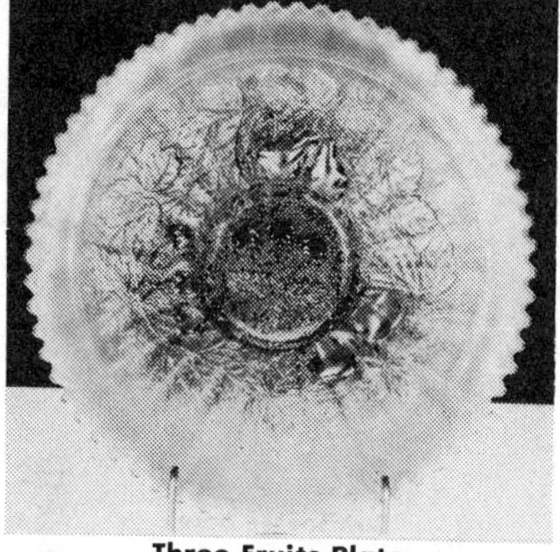

Three Fruits Plate

Bowl, 5" d., purple . . . 27.00
Bowl, 8½" d., piecrust rim, marigold . . . 45.00
Bowl, 8½" d., piecrust rim, purple . . . 85.00
Bowl, 9" d., dome-footed, basketweave & grapevine exterior, green . . . 78.00

Bowl, 9" d., dome-footed, basketweave & grapevine exterior, ice green 750.00
Bowl, 9" d., dome-footed, basketweave & grapevine exterior, marigold 70.00
Bowl, 9" d., dome-footed, basketweave & grapevine exterior, purple 110.00
Bowl, 9" d., dome-footed, basketweave & grapevine exterior, white 203.00
Bowl, 9" d., spatula-footed, aqua opalescent 435.00
Bowl, 9" d., spatula-footed, blue 100.00
Bowl, 9" d., spatula-footed, ruffled, green 60.00
Bowl, 9" d., spatula-footed, ice green 385.00
Bowl, 9" d., spatula-footed, marigold 42.00
Bowl, 9" d., spatula-footed, pastel marigold ....40.00 to 60.00
Bowl, 9" d., spatula-footed, purple.. 60.00
Bowl, 9" d., spatula-footed, white .. 250.00
Bowl, 10" d., purple 67.00
Bowl, collared base, aqua opalescent 750.00
Bowl, collared base, stippled, white 530.00
Plate, 9" d., stippled, aqua opalescent (ILLUS.) 2,250.00
Plate, 9" d., blue 152.00
Plate, 9" d., stippled, blue 400.00
Plate, 9" d., clambroth 100.00
Plate, 9" d., green 118.00
Plate, 9" d., lavender 250.00
Plate, 9" d., marigold 66.00
Plate, 9" d., stippled, marigold 118.00
Plate, 9" d., purple 97.00
Plate, 9" d., stippled, purple 152.00
Plate, 9½" w., 12-sided, blue (Fenton) 130.00
Plate, 9½" w., 12-sided, clambroth (Fenton) 60.00
Plate, 9½" w., 12-sided, green (Fenton) 153.00
Plate, 9½" w., 12-sided, marigold (Fenton) 112.00
Plate, 9½" w., 12-sided, purple (Fenton) 100.00
Plate, teal blue 1,200.00

TIGER LILY (Imperial)

Pitcher, water, green (ILLUS.) 155.00
Pitcher, water, marigold 100.00
Pitcher, water, purple 365.00
Tumbler, aqua 204.00
Tumbler, blue 87.50
Tumbler, clambroth 65.00
Tumbler, green 28.00
Tumbler, marigold 21.00

Tiger Lily Water Pitcher

Tumbler, purple 58.00
Water set: pitcher & 4 tumblers; marigold, 5 pcs. 225.00
Water set: pitcher & 5 tumblers; green, 6 pcs. 300.00
Water set: pitcher & 6 tumblers; aqua, 7 pcs. 2,205.00
Water set: pitcher & 6 tumblers; purple, 7 pcs. 900.00

TORNADO VASE (Northwood)

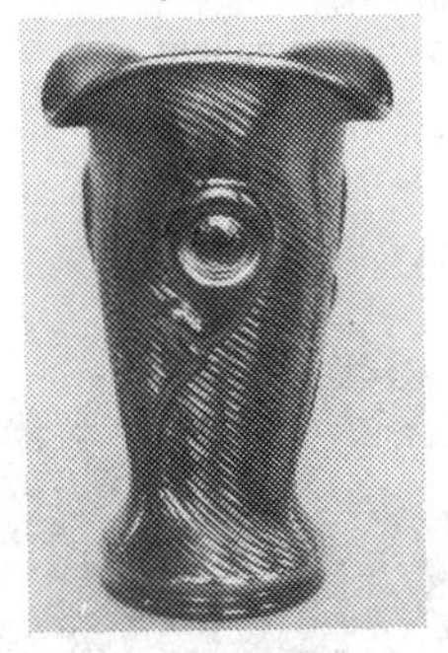

Tornado Vase

Green 242.00
Marigold 242.00
Marigold, small, ribbed 600.00
Purple, ribbed (ILLUS.) 245.00

TOWN PUMP NOVELTY (Northwood)

Marigold ....1,300.00 to 1,375.00
Purple ....600.00 to 650.00

TRACERY (Millersburg)

Tracery Bonbon

Bonbon, handled, square, green (ILLUS.) 900.00

TREE TRUNK VASE (Northwood)

7" h., ice green 134.00
8" h., blue 45.00
8" h., green 30.00
9" h., aqua 95.00
9" h., aqua opalescent 275.00
9" h., green 160.00
9" h., purple 35.00
9" h., white 110.00
10" h., aqua 125.00
10" h., aqua opalescent 385.00
10" h., blue 70.00
10" h., ice blue 168.00
10" h., ice green 204.00
10" h., marigold 25.00
10" h., purple 35.00
11" h., ice green 220.00
11½" h., green 122.50
12" h., aqua opalescent 350.00
12" h., green 35.00
12" h., ice blue 175.00
12" h., 5" d., ice green 350.00
13½" h., blue 425.00
13½" h., green 100.00
15" h., purple, w/elephant foot .... 325.00 to 375.00
18" h., green 550.00
18" h., purple 362.00

TROUT & FLY (Millersburg)

Trout & Fly Bowl

Bowl, ice cream shape, green 504.00
Bowl, ice cream shape, lavender 950.00
Bowl, ice cream shape, marigold 374.00
Bowl, ice cream shape, purple 474.00
Bowl, ruffled, green 425.00
Bowl, ruffled, lavender 780.00
Bowl, ruffled, marigold 334.00
Bowl, ruffled, marigold, satin finish 370.00
Bowl, ruffled, purple (ILLUS.) 402.00
Bowl, square, marigold 550.00
Bowl, square, purple 467.00

TWINS or HORSESHOE CURVE (Imperial)

Bowl, 6" d., green 36.00
Bowl, 6" d., marigold 17.50
Fruit bowl, marigold 85.00
Fruit bowl & base, marigold, 2 pcs. 82.00

TWO FLOWERS (Fenton)

Two Flowers Bowl

Bonbon, stemmed, blue 87.00
Bowl, 6" d., footed, aqua 155.00
Bowl, 6" d., footed, marigold 27.50
Bowl, 6" d., footed, purple 65.00
Bowl, 6" d., footed, vaseline 140.00
Bowl, 7" to 8" d., footed, blue 55.00
Bowl, 7" to 8" d., footed, marigold 35.00
Bowl, 7" to 8" d., footed, fluted, purple 47.00
Bowl, 7" to 8" d., footed, red 2,247.00
Bowl, 10" d., footed, scalloped rim, blue 62.00
Bowl, 10" d., footed, scalloped rim, green 69.00
Bowl, 10" d., footed, scalloped rim, marigold (ILLUS.) 43.00
Bowl, 10" d., footed, scalloped rim, purple 72.50
Bowl, 10" d., footed, aqua 237.00
Bowl, 10" d., footed, vaseline 200.00
Bowl, 10" d., footed, white 334.00
Bowl, 11" d., aqua 295.00
Bowl, 11½" d., footed, blue 150.00
Plate, 6½" d., marigold 125.00
Plate, 9" d., footed, marigold 425.00
Plate, chop, 11½" d., 3-footed, marigold 350.00
Plate, chop, 13" d., 3-footed, marigold 550.00
Rose bowl, 3-footed, blue 102.00
Rose bowl, 3-footed, marigold 96.00
Rose bowl, 3-footed, purple 257.00

TWO FRUITS

Bonbon, divided, blue 85.00
Bonbon, divided, green 135.00
Bonbon, divided, marigold 60.00

VENETIAN GIANT ROSE BOWL (Cambridge)

Venetian Giant Rose Bowl

Green (ILLUS.) 784.00
Marigold 963.00

VICTORIAN

Bowl, 11" d., purple 227.00

VINEYARD

Pitcher, water, marigold 100.00
Pitcher, water, peach opalescent 800.00
Tumbler, marigold 16.00
Tumbler, purple 45.00
Water set: pitcher & 6 tumblers; marigold, 7 pcs. 235.00
Water set: pitcher & 6 tumblers; purple, 7 pcs. 550.00

VINTAGE or VINTAGE GRAPE

Vintage Epergne

Berry set: master bowl & 5 sauce dishes; green, 6 pcs. (Fenton) 110.00
Bonbon, 2-handled, blue (Fenton) ... 60.00
Bonbon, 2-handled, green (Fenton) 47.00
Bonbon, 2-handled, marigold (Fenton) 29.00
Bonbon, 2-handled, purple (Fenton) 27.00
Bowl, 6" d., blue (Fenton) 26.00
Bowl, 6" d., green (Fenton) 40.00
Bowl, 6" d., purple (Fenton) 35.00
Bowl, 7" d., fluted, green (Fenton) .. 30.00
Bowl, 7" d., fluted, purple (Fenton) 28.00
Bowl, 7" d., purple (Millersburg) 60.00
Bowl, 8" to 9" d., footed, blue (Fenton) 41.00
Bowl, 8" to 9" d., green (Fenton) ... 48.00
Bowl, 8" to 9" d., marigold (Fenton) 32.00
Bowl, 8" to 9" d., footed, purple (Fenton) 35.00
Bowl, 8½" d., fluted, Persian blue .. 630.00
Bowl, 9" d., red (Fenton) 850.00
Bowl, 10" d., marigold, Hobnail exterior (Millersburg) 440.00
Bowl, 10" d., ruffled, purple 50.00
Bowl, ice cream shape, 10" d., red (Fenton) 920.00
Bowl, ice cream shape, 11" d., blue (Fenton) 190.00
Bowl, ice cream shape, 11" d., peach opalescent 650.00
Compote, 7" d., blue (Fenton) 42.00
Compote, 7" d., fluted, green (Fenton) 38.50
Compote, 7" d., marigold (Fenton) .. 37.00
Compote, 7" d., purple (Fenton) 50.00
Epergne, blue (Fenton) 123.00
Epergne, green (Fenton) 140.00
Epergne, marigold (Fenton) 150.00
Epergne, purple, small 110.00
Epergne, purple, Fenton (ILLUS.) 130.00
Fernery, footed, blue (Fenton) 50.00
Fernery, footed, green (Fenton) 96.00
Fernery, footed, marigold (Fenton) .. 44.00
Fernery, footed, purple (Fenton) 50.00
Fernery, footed, red (Fenton) .... 275.00 to 350.00
Nut dish, footed, blue, 6" d. (Fenton) 49.00
Nut dish, footed, green, 6" d. (Fenton) 47.00
Nut dish, footed, marigold, 6" d. (Fenton) 48.00
Nut dish, footed, purple, 6" d. (Fenton) 55.00
Nut dish, footed, red 430.00
Nut dish, footed, white 95.00
Plate, 5" d., blue 74.00
Plate, 6" d., green 90.00
Plate, 6" d., purple 62.00
Plate, 6½" d., stippled, marigold ... 50.00
Plate, 7" d., blue (Fenton) 80.00
Plate, 7" d., green (Fenton) 120.00
Plate, 7" d., marigold (Fenton) 87.50
Plate, 7" d., purple (Fenton) 110.00
Plate, 8" d., blue 110.00
Powder jar, cov., marigold (Fenton) 65.00
Powder jar, cov., purple (Fenton) ... 120.00
Sandwich tray, handled, marigold .. 23.00
Sandwich tray, handled, purple 30.00
Sauce dish, blue, Hobnail exterior (Millersburg) 450.00

Sauce dish, marigold (Fenton) 20.00
Wine, marigold (Fenton) 20.00
Wine, purple (Fenton) 25.00

VINTAGE BAND
Mug, marigold 25.00
Pitcher, water, marigold 175.00
Tumbler, marigold.................. 695.00

VINTAGE GRAPE - See Vintage Pattern

WAFFLE BLOCK
Basket w/tall handle, clambroth, 10" h. 44.00
Basket w/tall handle, marigold, 10" h. 42.00
Basket w/tall handle, turquoise, 10" h. 100.00
Bowl, 8½" d., clambroth 55.00
Compote, clambroth 135.00
Creamer, clambroth 28.00
Pitcher, water, marigold 125.00
Punch bowl & base, clambroth...... 165.00
Punch cup, marigold 16.00
Punch set: bowl, base & 5 cups; marigold, 7 pcs................. 115.00
Punch set: bowl, base & 6 cups; marigold, 8 pcs................. 125.00
Sugar bowl, clambroth 25.00
Sugar bowl, marigold 30.00
Tumbler, marigold.................. 150.00

WATER LILY (Fenton)
Bonbon, blue, 7½" d. 75.00
Bonbon, marigold, 7½" d. 25.00
Bowl, 6" d., aqua 130.00
Bowl, 6" d., ruffled, aqua 85.00
Bowl, 6" d., blue 27.00
Bowl, 6" d., green 58.00
Bowl, 6" d., footed, marigold....... 15.00
Bowl, 6" d., footed, red........... 500.00
Bowl, 6" d., footed, red opalescent....................... 900.00
Bowl, 6" d., vaseline w/marigold overlay........................ 84.00
Bowl, 10" d., footed, fluted, blue ... 100.00
Bowl, 10" d., footed, marigold...... 46.00
Tumbler, marigold.................. 45.00

WATER LILY & CATTAILS
Banana boat, blue ....150.00 to 185.00
Banana boat, marigold 140.00
Bonbon, 2-handled, marigold, large........................... 43.00
Bowl, 5" d., marigold 26.00
Dish, 3 turned up sides, marigold, 6" d. 29.00
Pitcher, water, marigold (ILLUS.).... 548.00
Plate, 6" d., marigold 70.00
Sauce dish, marigold 17.50
Sauce dish, footed, vaseline w/marigold overlay 75.00
Spooner, marigold.................. 50.00
Tumbler, blue 2,700.00
Tumbler, marigold.................. 30.00

Water Lily & Cattails Pitcher

Water set: pitcher & 6 tumblers; marigold, 7 pcs.................. 725.00
Whimsey, marigold 39.00

WHEAT SHEAF NO. 2660 (Cambridge)
Cologne bottle w/stopper, green, 8½" h. 450.00
Cologne bottle w/stopper, marigold, 8½" h. 650.00
Cookie jar, cov., purple............ 950.00
Decanter w/stopper, green, 12" h. 2,500.00

WHIRLING LEAVES BOWL (Millersburg)
Green, 9" d........................ 65.00
Marigold, 9" d. 52.00
Purple, 9" d........................ 62.00
Green, 9½" w., tricornered 200.00
Marigold, 9½" w., tricornered...... 132.00
Purple, 9½" w., tricornered 175.00
Vaseline, 9½" w., tricornered 635.00
Green, 10" d....................... 93.00
Purple, 10" d....................... 103.00

WHITE OAK TUMBLERS
Tumbler, marigold................. 153.00

WIDE PANEL
Bowl, 8" to 9" d., marigold......... 19.00
Bowl, 12" d., marigold 45.00
Epergne, 4-lily, green ....800.00 to 1,200.00
Epergne, 4-lily, marigold 615.00
Epergne, 4-lily, purple 950.00
Epergne, 4-lily, white 1,500.00
Goblet, marigold 20.00
Goblet, red 100.00
Plate, 8" d., marigold 30.00
Plate, chop, 14" d., marigold 53.00
Rose bowl, clambroth 12.00
Salt dip, marigold 40.00
Vase, 9½" h., red 140.00
Vase, 13" h., ice blue 45.00
Vase, 18½" h., green 125.00

WILD ROSE
Bowl, 7" d., 3-footed, open heart rim, green, Northwood (ILLUS.) ... 44.00

Wild Rose Bowl

Bowl, 7" d., 3-footed, open heart rim, marigold (Northwood) 32.00
Bowl, 7" d., 3-footed, open heart rim, purple (Northwood) 72.00
Bowl, 8" to 9" d., marigold (Northwood) 35.00
Candy dish, open edge, blue, 5¾" d. 70.00
Lamp, w/original burner & etched chimney shade, marigold, small (Millersburg) 1,250.00
Lamp, w/original burner & etched chimney shade, purple (Millersburg) 500.00
Syrup pitcher, marigold 550.00

WILD STRAWBERRY (Northwood)

Bowl, 6" d., green 55.00
Bowl, 6" d., purple 40.00
Bowl, 10" d., ice green 1,325.00
Bowl, 10" d., marigold 87.00
Bowl, 10" d., purple 108.00
Plate, 6" to 7" d., w/handgrip, green 135.00
Plate, 6" to 7" d., w/handgrip, marigold 76.00
Plate, 6" to 7" d., w/handgrip, purple 94.00

WINDFLOWER

Bowl, 8" to 9" d., blue 42.00
Bowl, 8" to 9" d., marigold 30.00
Bowl, 8" to 9" d., purple 39.00
Plate, 9" d., blue 134.00
Plate, 9" d., marigold 62.00
Sauceboat, marigold 34.00
Sauceboat, purple 35.00
Tumbler, marigold 210.00

WINDMILL or WINDMILL MEDALLION (Imperial)

Bowl, 7" d., green 45.00
Bowl, 7" d., marigold (ILLUS.) 36.00
Bowl, 7" d., purple 43.00
Bowl, 8" to 9" d., green 40.00
Bowl, 8" to 9" d., ruffled, marigold . 95.00
Bowl, 8" to 9" d., ruffled, purple ... 42.50
Bowl, 8" to 9" d., ruffled, vaseline .. 65.00
Bowl, 9" d., ribbon candy edge, milk white w/marigold overlay 145.00

Windmill Bowl

Dresser tray, oval, marigold 40.00
Dresser tray, oval, purple 47.50
Pickle dish, green 50.00
Pickle dish, marigold 32.00
Pickle dish, purple 45.00
Pitcher, milk, clambroth 45.00
Pitcher, milk, ice green 110.00
Pitcher, milk, marigold 62.00
Pitcher, milk, purple 315.00
Pitcher, milk, smoky 132.00
Pitcher, water, marigold 90.00
Plate, 8" d., marigold 18.00
Sauce dish, clambroth 30.00
Sauce dish, marigold 18.00
Sauce dish, purple 24.00
Tumbler, green 38.00
Tumbler, marigold 25.00
Tumbler, purple 90.00
Water set: pitcher & 1 tumbler; green, 2 pcs. 150.00
Water set: pitcher & 2 tumblers; purple, 3 pcs. 1,200.00
Water set: pitcher & 6 tumblers; marigold, 7 pcs. 225.00

WINDMILL & MUMS - See Chrysanthemum Pattern

WINDMILL MEDALLION - See Windmill Pattern

WINE & ROSES

Wine & Roses Goblet

Goblet, blue (ILLUS.) 75.00
Goblet, marigold 35.00
Pitcher, water, marigold ...285.00 to 425.00
Water set: pitcher & 6 tumblers; marigold, 7 pcs. 362.00
Wine, blue 55.00
Wine, marigold 32.00
Wine set: decanter & 6 wines; marigold, 7 pcs. ....325.00 to 390.00

WISHBONE (Northwood)

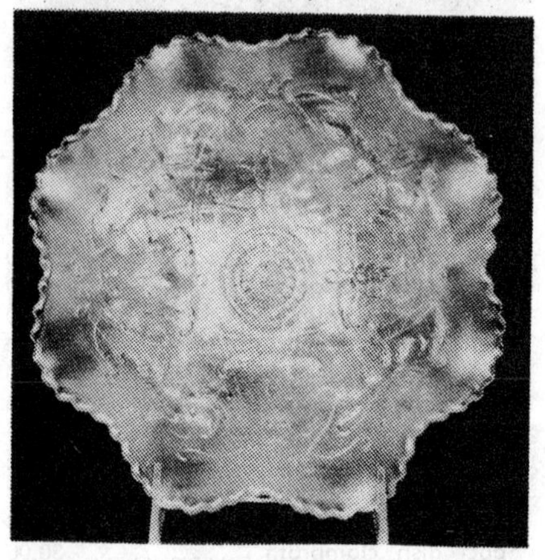

Wishbone Bowl

Bowl, 8" to 9" d., footed, blue..... 75.00
Bowl, 8" to 9" d., footed, green 65.00
Bowl, 8" to 9" d., footed, ice blue (ILLUS.) 950.00
Bowl, 8" to 9" d., footed, ice green 1,850.00
Bowl, 8" to 9" d., footed, lavender 185.00
Bowl, 8" to 9" d., footed, lime green 80.00
Bowl, 8" to 9" d., footed, marigold 65.00
Bowl, 8" to 9" d., footed, purple 80.00
Bowl, 8" to 9" d., footed, white 470.00
Bowl, 10" d., footed, blue.......... 500.00
Bowl, 10" d., piecrust rim, green ... 125.00
Bowl, 10" d., piecrust rim, marigold 75.00
Bowl, 10" d., ruffled, marigold 150.00
Bowl, 10" d., piecrust rim, purple 148.00
Bowl, 10" d., footed, ruffled, purple 124.00
Bowl, 10" d., footed, piecrust rim, white 650.00
Bowl, footed, clambroth 115.00
Epergne, green 265.00
Epergne, marigold.................. 495.00
Epergne, purple.................... 443.00
Epergne, white..................... 950.00
Pitcher, water, purple ..1,150.00 to 1,250.00
Plate, 6½" d., purple............. 85.00
Plate, 8½" d., 3 sides turned up, marigold 140.00
Plate, 8½" d., footed, marigold 225.00
Plate, 8½" d., footed, purple....... 240.00
Plate, 8½" d., footed, tricornered, purple 375.00
Plate, chop, 11" d., marigold 500.00
Plate, chop, 11" d., purple 638.00
Tumbler, green 130.00
Tumbler, marigold.................. 100.00
Tumbler, purple.................... 150.00
Water set: pitcher & 4 tumblers; green, 5 pcs. 1,450.00
Water set: pitcher & 4 tumblers; purple, 5 pcs. 1,300.00
Water set: pitcher & 6 tumblers; marigold, 7 pcs. 1,500.00

WISHBONE & SPADES

Banana bowl, ruffled, peach opalescent, 10" l. 175.00
Bowl, 5" d., purple 40.00
Bowl, 6" d., ruffled, peach opalescent........................ 60.00
Bowl, ice cream shape, 9" d., peach opalescent........................ 175.00
Plate, 6½" d., purple 145.00
Plate, chop, 11" d., purple 850.00
Sauce dish, peach opalescent 70.00
Sauce dish, purple 55.00

WREATHED CHERRY (Dugan)

Berry set: master bowl & 4 sauce dishes; marigold, 5 pcs. 140.00
Berry set: master bowl & 4 sauce dishes; white, 5 pcs. 575.00
Bowl, 8" d., 3-footed, marigold 35.00
Bowl, berry, 12 x 9" oval, marigold 82.00
Bowl, berry, 12 x 9" oval, peach opalescent........................ 250.00
Bowl, berry, 12 x 9" oval, purple ... 106.00
Bowl, berry, 12 x 9" oval, white 172.00
Creamer, blue 55.00
Creamer, marigold 55.00
Creamer, purple 65.00
Pitcher, water, purple 275.00
Pitcher, water, white w/red cherries 350.00
Sauce dish, oval, marigold 34.00
Sauce dish, oval, peach opalescent........................ 68.00
Sauce dish, oval, purple 46.00
Sauce dish, oval, white 47.50
Spooner, marigold.................. 55.00
Spooner, purple.................... 60.00
Spooner, white..................... 100.00
Table set: creamer, cov. sugar bowl, spooner & cov. butter dish; marigold, 4 pcs. 175.00
Tumbler, marigold.................. 45.00
Tumbler, purple.................... 70.00
Tumbler, white..................... 105.00

Water set: pitcher & 4 tumblers; marigold, 5 pcs. 400.00
Water set: pitcher & 4 tumblers; white, 5 pcs. 450.00

WREATH OF ROSES

Bonbon, 2-handled, blue, 8" d. 45.00
Bonbon, 2-handled, green, 8" d. 54.00
Bonbon, 2-handled, marigold, 8" d. 32.00
Bonbon, 2-handled, purple, 8" d. . . . 150.00
Compote, 6" d., blue 45.00
Compote, 6" d., fluted, green 43.00
Compote, 6" d., marigold 25.00
Compote, 6" d., fluted, purple 45.00
Punch bowl, Persian Medallion interior, blue 200.00
Punch bowl, Vintage interior, purple 145.00
Punch bowl & base, Persian Medallion interior, marigold, 2 pcs. 175.00
Punch bowl & base, purple, 2 pcs. . . 255.00
Punch cup, Persian Medallion interior, amber 25.00
Punch cup, blue 24.00
Punch cup, Persian Medallion interior, blue 32.00
Punch cup, Vintage interior, blue . . . 25.00
Punch cup, green 27.50
Punch cup, Persian Medallion interior, green 30.00
Punch cup, marigold 12.00
Punch cup, Persian Medallion interior, marigold 14.00
Punch cup, Vintage interior, marigold 35.00
Punch cup, purple . . . . . 15.00 to 25.00
Punch cup, Persian Medallion interior, purple 20.00
Punch cup, Vintage interior, purple . 18.00
Punch set: bowl, base & 2 cups; green, 4 pcs. 425.00
Punch set: bowl, base & 4 cups; Persian Medallion interior; marigold, 6 pcs. 395.00
Punch set: bowl, base & 4 cups; purple, 6 pcs. 505.00
Punch set: bowl, base & 6 cups; blue, 8 pcs. 695.00
Punch set: bowl, base & 6 cups; purple, 8 pcs. 392.00
Rose bowl, marigold (Dugan) 36.00
Rose bowl, purple (Dugan) 50.00
Whimsey, tricornered, marigold (Dugan) 32.00

ZIG ZAG (Millersburg)

Bowl, 9½" d., marigold 140.00
Bowl, 9½" d., green 375.00
Bowl, 10" d., marigold 163.00
Bowl, 10" d., purple 240.00
Bowl, 10" w., tricornered, marigold 275.00
Bowl, 10" w., tricornered, purple . . . 432.00
Bowl, ribbon candy edge, purple . . . 185.00

ZIPPERED HEART

Berry set: master bowl & 5 sauce dishes; purple, 6 pcs. 188.00
Bowl, berry, 10" d., purple 130.00
Rose bowl, green 450.00
Sauce dish, purple, 5" d. 25.00
Vase, 9" h., green 1,975.00

ZIPPERED LOOP LAMP (Imperial)

Zippered Loop Lamp

Lamp, hand, marigold, 4½" h. 800.00
Lamp, marigold, small 325.00
Lamp, marigold, medium 350.00
Lamp, smoky, medium 600.00
Lamp, marigold, large (ILLUS.) 480.00
Lamp, marigold, 5½" d., 9" h. 435.00

(End of Carnival Glass Section)

CHOCOLATE

Dolphin Covered Dish

This glass is often called Caramel Slag. It was made by the Indiana Tumbler and Gob-

let Company of Greentown, Ind., and other glasshouses, beginning at the turn of this century. Various patterns were produced, highly popular among them being Cactus and Leaf Bracket. Also see GREENTOWN Special Focus.

Animal covered dish, Cat on Tall Hamper, Greentown $335.00
Animal covered dish, Dolphin, beaded top rim, Greentown (ILLUS.) ... 200.00
Animal covered dish, Dolphin, sawtooth rim 410.00
Animal covered dish, Hen on Nest, Greentown 375.00
Bowl, 4½" d., Beaded Triangle patt. 400.00
Butter dish, cov., Dewey patt., Greentown 150.00
Butter dish, cov., File patt. 2,200.00

Melrose Compote

Compote, open, 6" d., Melrose patt., scalloped rim (ILLUS.) 230.00
Creamer, child size, Austrian patt... 250.00
Creamer, Geneva patt. 182.00
Cruet w/original stopper, Wild Rose with Bowknot patt. ......350.00 to 400.00
Dresser tray, Wild Rose with Bowknot patt., 10½ x 8" 305.00

Orange Tree Hatpin Holder

Hatpin holder, Orange Tree patt., Fenton (ILLUS.) 400.00
Lamp, kerosene-type, Wild Rose with Bowknot patt., rare 695.00
Mug, Herringbone patt., Greentown 76.00
Mug, Serenade patt., 3½" d., 5" h. 180.00
Nappy, handled, Cactus patt., Greentown 135.00

Serenade Plate

Plate, 8¼" d., Serenade patt. (ILLUS.) 175.00
Relish, Leaf Bracket patt., Greentown, 8" l. 78.00
Spooner, Cactus patt., Greentown .. 88.00
Spooner, Leaf Bracket patt. 87.00
Spooner, Wild Rose with Bowknot patt. 135.00

Uneeda Biscuit Tumbler

Tumbler, advertising "Uneeda Milk Biscuit," Greentown (ILLUS.) 135.00
Tumbler, Geneva patt. 103.00
Tumbler, Indoor Drinking Scene, Greentown 375.00
Tumbler, Leaf Bracket patt., Greentown 58.00

CHRYSANTHEMUM SPRIG, BLUE

Some collectors of off-white to near yellow

Custard Glass have referred to this blue opaque glass in the Chrysanthemum Sprig pattern as "blue custard." This misnomer is being replaced and this scarce glassware, produced by the Northwood Glass Company at the turn of the century, deserves a classification of its own. Also see CUSTARD GLASS.

Blue Chrysanthemum Sprig Butter Dish

Berry set, master berry or fruit bowl & 6 sauce dishes, 7 pcs. ... $1,00.00 to 1,250.00
Bowl, berry, individual, w/gold trim ... 145.00
Bowl, master berry or fruit ... 395.00
Butter dish, cov. (ILLUS.) ... 950.00
Celery vase ... 950.00
Compote, jelly ... 390.00
Creamer ... 310.00
Cruet w/original stopper ... 600.00
Pitcher, water ... 750.00
Salt & pepper shakers, pr. ... 450.00
Sauce dish ... 112.00
Spooner ... 235.00
Sugar bowl, cov. ... 312.00
Table set, cov. butter dish, cov. sugar bowl, creamer & spooner, 4 pcs. ... 1,750.00
Toothpick holder ... 310.00
Tumbler ... 180.00
Water set, pitcher & 6 tumblers, 7 pcs. ... 1,300.00

CONSOLIDATED

The Consolidated Lamp and Glass Company of Coraopolis, Pennsylvania was founded in 1894 and for a number of years was noted for its lighting wares but also produced popular lines of pressed and blown tablewares. Highly collectible glass patterns of this early era include the Cone, Florette and Guttate lines.

Lamps and shades continued to be good sellers but in 1926 a new "art" line of molded decorative wares was introduced. This "Martele" line was developed as a direct imitation of the fine glasswares being produced by Rene Lalique of France and many Consolidated patterns resembled their French counterparts. Other popular lines produced during the 1920's and 1930's were the "Dance of the Nudes" (originally called "Dancing Nymph"), the delightfully Art Deco "Ruba Rombic," introduced in 1928, and the "Catalonian" line, imitating 17th century Spanish glass, which debuted in 1927.

Although the factory closed in 1933, it was reopened under new management in 1936 and prospered through the 1940's. It finally closed in 1967. Collectors should note that many later Consolidated patterns closely resemble wares of other competing firms, especially the Phoenix Glass Company. Careful study is needed to determine the maker of pieces from the 1920-40 era.

EARLY LINES (Ca. 1894-1920):

Cone

Butter dish, cov., pink, glossy ... $110.00
Cruet w/original stopper, pink ... 295.00
Cruet w/original stopper, cased yellow, glossy ... 175.00
Pitcher, water, cased pink satin ... 175.00
Pitcher, water, yellow satin ... 90.00
Sugar shaker w/original top, blue, glossy, tall ... 75.00 to 85.00
Sugar shaker w/original top, green, tall ... 98.50
Sugar shaker w/original top, pink, tall ... 92.00
Sugar shaker w/original top, pink satin, squatty ... 110.00
Syrup pitcher w/original top, pink ... 295.00
Tumbler, yellow satin ... 25.00
Water set: pitcher & six tumblers; yellow satin, 7 pcs. ... 265.00

Consolidated's Criss-Cross (Opalescent)

Butter dish, cov., cranberry ... 275.00
Tumbler, white ... 55.00

Florette

Bowl, berry, pink ... 45.00
Butter dish, cov., pink satin or glossy ... 150.00 to 175.00
Condiment set: salt & pepper shakers & mustard jar w/original tops in handled holder; light blue cased, the set ... 125.00
Cracker jar w/original silver plate lid & bail handle, pink satin ... 250.00 to 300.00
Cruet w/clear cut stopper, pink satin ... 260.00
Humidor, silver plate lid, pink satin ... 295.00
Pitcher, 7½" h., pink satin ... 275.00
Toothpick holder, blue ... 48.00

Toothpick holder, green, glossy 50.00
Toothpick holder, pink opaque 60.00

Florette Tumbler

Tumbler, pink satin (ILLUS.) 45.00
Water set: pitcher & six tumblers; pink satin, 7 pcs. 425.00

Guttate

Guttate Tumbler

Butter dish, cov., white w/gold 50.00
Condiment set: salt & pepper shakers & mustard jar in fitted glass holder; pink 175.00
Salt & pepper shakers, pink, pr. 85.00
Sugar shaker, cased cranberry 150.00
Syrup pitcher, cased cranberry 150.00
Tumbler, cased pink, glossy (ILLUS.) 50.00
Tumbler, pink satin 35.00
Water set: pitcher & six tumblers; white w/gold, 7 pcs. 155.00

LATER LINES (Ca. 1920-1967):

Bowl, 8¼" d., Dance of the Nudes line 29.00
Compote, 6" d., 3" h., sculpted fish, light green 70.00
Console bowl, Dance of the Nudes line, deep blue, 17" d. 345.00
Cup, Dance of the Nudes line, clear 20.00
Pitcher, water, tankard, Catalonian line, tricornered, green 60.00
Plate, 7½" d., Dance of the Nudes line, pink 75.00
Plate, 10" d., Dance of the Nudes line, clear 40.00
Puff box, cov., Martele line, Hummingbird patt., frosted green, 7" 75.00
Sauce dish, Dance of the Nudes line, clear 20.00
Vase, 6½" h., Martele line, sculpted blue florals & green vines on cream ground, original label 65.00
Vase, 7" h., 5" d., bulbous, sculpted poppies & leaves on milk white opalescent ground w/touch of blue tint 75.00
Vase, 7" h., Martele line, Love Bird patt., clear w/red staining 55.00
Vase, 7" h., Martele line, Love Bird patt., light green frosted 75.00
Vase, 7" h., sculpted poppies, opalescent w/bluish stain 48.00
Vase, 8½" h., clear w/etched calla lily design 65.00
Vase, 9¼" h., sculpted orange peonies & bluish green leaves on custard yellow opaque ground 95.00
Vase, 9½" h., 4" flared rim, bulbous shoulders, sculpted tangerine peonies & bluish green leaves on custard ground 140.00
Vases, 9¾" h., sculpted vines, berries & leaves, original paper labels, pr. 175.00
Vase, 10" h., Martele line, Fish patt., smoky blue ground 150.00
Vase, 10" h., Martele line, Love Bird patt., white birds on green ground 190.00
Vase, 11 x 10", Martele line, Fairy patt., white & gold, original paper label 150.00
Vase, 12¼" h., 5¾" w., bulbous shoulders, sculpted brilliant yellow peonies, bluish green leaves & brown vines on white ground .. 185.00
Vase, Martele line, Cockatoo patt., opaque ivory w/burnt orange birds ....200.00 to 240.00

CORALENE

Coralene is a method of decorating glass, usually Satin glass, with the use of a beaded-type decoration customarily applied to the glass with the use of enamels, which were melted. Coralene decoration has been faked with the use of glue.

Bowl, 8" d., 4½" h., six-scallop top, applied base w/six feet, yellow mother-of-pearl Diamond Quilted patt., two coralene butterflies hovering over a bunch of blue wild asters, robin's egg blue interior $685.00

Coralene Pitcher

Pitcher, water, 7¾" h., applied frosted handle, square mouth, yellow coralene seaweed design on shaded pink satin, Hobbs, Brockunier & Co. (ILLUS.) 750.00

Sugar shaker w/original top, orange coralene seaweed design on frosted white ground 165.00

Tumbler, yellow coralene design on shaded blue satin, white lining, 2¾" d., 3¾" h. 245.00

Vase, 5 1/8" h., 4" d., yellow coralene stars at diamond intersections on shaded rose mother-of-pearl satin Diamond Quilted patt., white lining 425.00

Vase, 6¾" h., 3½ x 5½" flattened oval, coralene wheat design on deep pink to white ground, white lining 450.00

Vase, 8 1/8" h., lobed tapering form w/short neck, coralene design on blue mother-of-pearl satin Herringbone patt., probably Mt. Washington Glass Co., late 19th c. 660.00

Vase, 10½" h., ovoid base w/tall slender neck w/ruffled rim, blue coralene seaweed design on rainbow mother-of-pearl satin ground 295.00

COSMOS

A pattern of Cosmos flowers applied to milk-white glass gives this ware its name. The flowers are stained with various colors.

Cosmos Creamer

Butter dish, cov., pink band decor . . $190.00

Cologne bottle w/original stopper, pink band decor 95.00

Creamer, pink band decor (ILLUS.) . . 160.00

Pickle castor, double, pink band decor, original silver plate frame marked "Racine S.P. Co. Triple Plate" . . . . .500.00 to 525.00

Pitcher, water, 8½" h., 7" d., pink band decor . . . . .225.00 to 295.00

Powder box, cov., pink band decor 155.00

Salt shaker w/original top, blue band decor, short (single) 65.00

Salt & pepper shakers w/original tops, pink band decor, pr. . . . . .150.00 to 200.00

Sugar bowl, cov., pink band decor . . . . .150.00 to 185.00

Syrup pitcher w/original top, pink band decor 215.00

Table set: cov. butter dish, cov. sugar bowl, creamer & spooner; pink band decor, 4 pcs. 550.00

Tumbler, blue band decor 55.00

Water set: pitcher & 5 tumblers; pink band decor, 6 pcs. 560.00

CRANBERRY

Gold was added to glass batches to give this glass its color on reheating. It has been made by numerous glasshouses for years and is currently being reproduced. Both blown and molded articles were produced. A less expensive type of cranberry was made with the substitution of copper for gold.

Basket, applied clear ruffled top &

handle, Diamond Quilted patt., 4½" d., 7½" h. $225.00

Basket, applied clear wishbone feet, clear handle & clear trim, 8 3/8 x 6 1/8", 12" h. 275.00

Bowl, 5" d., 8¼" h., rose bowl shape w/four crimp top, "Arboresque," in ormolu holder 245.00

Bowl, 6½" d., 3¼" h., 8-crimp top, applied clear leaves 265.00

Bowl, 6¾" d., 3" h., footed, wide ruffled band of applied clear trim at rim, clear foot w/berry pontil .. 225.00

Cranberry Enameled Box

Box w/hinged lid, enameled blue & white florals & green leaves on top, blue & white florals around base, 5" d., 3½" h. (ILLUS.) 175.00

Box w/hinged lid, gold panels w/enameled white flowers & green leaves, 5" d., 3½" h. 265.00

Box w/hinged lid, peach, yellow, white & blue dot enameled berry sprays w/small lavender dots, brass rings on sides, ormolu feet, 4 7/8" d., 6" h. 325.00

Box w/lift-off lid, white enameled dots in form of stars on lid, gold bands & white design around sides, 2¾" d., 2" h. 79.00

Box w/lift-off lid, enameled white dots, blue butterfly & flowers & foliage decoration, 4 3/8" d., 2½" h. 135.00

Compote, open, 9¼" d., 9" h., scalloped edge, "overshot" finish 275.00

Condiment set: cov. mustard pot, cov. pepper pot & open salt in silver plate holder; embossed Swirl patt., 5¼" h., 5" d., 4 pcs. (silver in fair condition) 138.00

Cracker jar, cov., enameled scroll & plume design, ornate silver plate rim band, bail handle & cover w/bear finial 235.00

Creamer, applied clear handle, Hobnail patt. 50.00

Creamer & open basin-shaped sugar bowl, applied clear handle on creamer & clear pedestal foot on sugar, enameled small blue & gold florals & gold leaves, 2½" h. creamer, 2" h. sugar, pr. 165.00

Cruet w/clear cut faceted stopper, applied clear handle w/gold trim, clear wafer foot, enameled gold leaves & small flowers, 2 5/8" d., 5" h. 125.00

Cruet w/clear blown stopper w/teardrop-shaped interior bubble, clear wafer base w/gold trim stripes, clear handle w/gold trim stripes, acid-etched scrolls, blossoms & geometrics filled in w/gold, gold trim stripe around spout, 7½" h. 485.00

Cruet w/vaseline blown stopper, vaseline handle & wafer foot, Swirl patt., enameled gold scrolls & floral decoration, 3 1/8" d., 7¾" h. 165.00

Cruet w/clear cut faceted stopper, applied clear spun rope handle, squared bulbous shape, 3¼" d., 8" h. 88.00

Cup & saucer, applied clear handle w/gold trim, enameled lacy gold florals & leaves, gold trim 125.00

Decanter w/clear blown stopper, clear applied shell handle, paneled shape, enameled white & gold trim, 12" h. 155.00

Dresser set: two candlesticks, cov. powder jar, cov. puff box & tray; enameled gold floral decoration, 5 pcs. 295.00

Dresser tray, white, peach & blue enameled florals w/green leaves around edge, gold trim, 6½ x 9½" rectangle 110.00

Finger bowl, enameled lacy gold leaves, several butterflies & lavender florals, 4 1/8" d., 2 7/8" h. 135.00

Jam dish, open, applied vaseline ruffled edge, applied vaseline shell trim around center, Swirl patt., in silver plate footed basket holder w/engraved flowers, 5½" d., 5½" h. 125.00

Jar, cov., applied clear rigaree around neck & ball finial on cover, Inverted Thumbprint patt., 4" d., 6½" h. 125.00

Lamps, banquet-style, hollow-blown foot tapers to melon-ribbed font w/original burner, tulip-form shade; font ornately enameled w/colorful blossoms & leaves, shade ornately enameled w/floral wreath surrounding oval portrait

Ornate Cranberry Lamps

of man in military uniform, pr. (ILLUS.) 1,250.00

Liqueur cruet w/pewter figural cherub stopper, flattened bulbous shape, encased in pewter, 4" d., 8¾" h. 195.00

Pitcher, 2 5/8" h., 2¼" d., bulbous w/round mouth, applied clear handle, enameled green & white leaves, small yellow leaves, gold bands & applied red jewel each side 118.00

Pitcher, 2 7/8" h., 2 1/8" d., applied clear handle, tiny enameled clusters of blue, white & coral flowers & lacy gold foliage 125.00

Pitcher, 5½" h., applied amber handle, Inverted Thumbprint patt., w/gilded floral decoration 68.00

Pitcher, 5¾" h., 5¼ x 8¼", tricornered ruffled rim, clear pedestal foot w/hollow stem, applied clear handle, applied clear ruffled leaf each side 295.00

Pitcher, 6¼" h., 3¾" d., six-sided top, applied clear handle, slight ribbing 75.00

Pitcher, 6¾" h., 5" d., applied clear reeded handle, Inverted Thumbprint patt. 140.00

Pitcher, milk, tankard, 7 1/8" h., 3¾" d., applied clear reeded handle, "overshot" finish 135.00

Pitcher, water, 7 3/8" h., 5" d., bulbous w/round mouth, applied clear rope around neck & braided handle 245.00

Rose bowl, three-footed, applied clear drapery & prunts 325.00

Salt dip, applied clear shell trim around middle, in fluted silver plate holder, w/spoon, 3¾" d., 1¾" h. 100.00

Salt dip, master size, Optic patt., applied clear wishbone-shaped feet, w/old silver salt spoon, 2¼" d., 2 1/8" h. 60.00

Salt dip, applied Vaseline leaves & clear rigaree, polished pontil, 4" d. 55.00

Cranberry Sugar Shaker

Sugar shaker w/silver plate screw-on top, paneled sides, 2 3/8" d., 5¾" h. (ILLUS.) 60.00

Syrup pitcher w/pewter lid, applied clear handle, Baby Thumbprint patt. 125.00

Syrup pitcher w/original pewter top, Hobnail patt., Hobbs, Brockunier & Co. (hinge broken) 265.00

Toddy cup, cover & saucer, applied clear handle, lid w/cranberry bubble finial, engraved w/gold garlands of flowers & leaves w/bow ribbons, 3 pcs. 195.00

Toothpick holder, crimped top, white enamel floral clusters w/gold tracery, 2½" d., 2" h. 135.00

Tumbler, juice, gold band around top w/enameled pink & white flowers & green leaves, lower part w/gold flowers, leaves & scrolls, 2 1/8" d., 3¾" h. 58.00

Tumble-up set: carafe & tumbler; Inverted Thumbprint patt. 80.00

Vase, 3½" h., 2¾" d., garland of blue enameled flowers w/yellow centers, white leaves, white dots & scrolls, gold rim band 59.00

Vase, 4 5/8" h., 2 5/8" d., w/applied clear "icicles" dripping down sides from top rim, Inverted Thumbprint patt. 250.00

Vase, 6" h., 2 1/8" d., flower petal-shaped top, clear stem & pedestal base 60.00

Vase, 8¼" h., 5¼" d., "overshot" finish, applied clear rigaree around top & neck, three applied clear feet, three applied clear flower shapes around middle w/flower prunts in centers 275.00

Vase, 9½" h., 3" d., ewer-shaped, applied clear handle, gold leaves outlined in white enamel, white enameled florals & branches 148.00

Vase, 16¼" h., 2¾" d., four clear square feet, enameled lacy gold scrolls, leaves & dainty blue forget-me-nots 135.00

Water set: pitcher & four tumblers; enameled decoration, 5 pcs. 350.00

Wine decanter, cruet-type, w/clear cut faceted stopper, applied clear handle & wafer foot, engraved florals & leaves, 3 7/8" d., 9½" h. 158.00

CROWN MILANO

Crown Milano Cracker Jar

This glass, produced by Mt. Washington Glass Company late last century, is opal glass decorated by painting and enameling. It appears identical to a ware termed Albertine, also made by Mt. Washington.

Bowl, cov., 5½" d., 2½" h., melon-ribbed, beaded rim, glossy pink roses on cream satin ground, signed $390.00

Bowl, 8½" d., 3½" h., squat round form w/square wide rim w/cut edge, orange & yellow florals w/gilt highlights on yellow ground, ca. 1893, signed 550.00

Bowl, enameled peach, lavender, gold & blue random bouquets & single flower pansies, gold chain border 1,275.00

Cracker jar, gold acorns, rosy brown & green leaves outlined in raised gold on soft pink to white satin ground, original silver plate cover, rim & handle, marked under lid, 5" d., 6¼" h. (ILLUS.) 595.00

Cracker jar, melon-ribbed, pastel & gold enameled oak leaves & acorns on satin finish ground, silver plate cover, rim & bail handle, 6¾" h. 465.00

Cracker jar, enameled bouquets of pansies, roses, asters, wild roses, buds & leaves w/overall gold & shadow tracery, encrusted gold trim, original silver plate cover, rim & bail handle ....800.00 to 950.00

Creamer & sugar bowl, shaded lavender violets on white satin ground w/blush of pink around edge & trimmed w/gold, pr. 910.00

Ewer-vase, footed, ovoid body w/short spout at upper side, short neck at top continuing to form round open-loop handle, large gold chrysanthemums & ornate scrolling outlined in gold, signed, 12" h. 875.00

Mustard jar, cov., overall florals & gold, silver plate cover engraved w/florals & marked "M.W." 563.00

Pitcher, 5¼" h., squat bulbous form w/small neck & flared spout, twisted scroll handle, florals w/gilt & latticework on glossy white ground, ca. 1893, signed ... 522.50

Pitcher, short bulbous body w/long tapered spout, rope-twist scrolled handle, ornately decorated overall w/florals, signed 1,275.00

Salt dip, open, decorated w/roses & other florals, shiny finish 100.00

Sweetmeat jar, melon-ribbed, gold-decorated body, repousse' metal cover & handle, 4½" d. 475.00

Toothpick holder, beaded rim, white satin raised spider web background w/enameled pine cone decoration 210.00

Vase, 8" h., square w/rounded corners, two applied handles, pastel earthtone geometric designs .. 645.00

Vase, 9¼" h., decorated w/maidenhair ferns & gold medallions 450.00

Vase, 11" h., two raised gold cherubs w/arms entwined, encircled by gold ribbon, framed by wreath, reverse w/smaller wreath encircling centered crown, overall scattered stylized blossoms, shiny finish, signed 585.00

Vase, 11¾" h., tall tapered form w/slightly scalloped narrow rim, decorated w/overall fleur de lys & floral designs surrounding two vignettes outlined in heavy gilding, one vignette of young boy & girl examining flowers, other small vignette of river w/houses, signed in violet "CM" and crown w/"589" 750.00

Vase, 12½" h., squatty bulbous base w/tall slender neck, enameled dot design on orange florals & scrolls on cream ground 930.00

CRUETS

Inverted Thumbprint Pattern Cruet

We list here a random sampling of the many cruets advertised for sale within the past year.

Amber, blown, trefoil lip, ribbed, applied blue reeded handle, blue faceted stopper, 3¼" d., 7 5/8" h. $65.00

Amber, blown, enameled pink, blue, yellow & white florals & green leaves, applied blue handle, blue ball stopper, overall enameled white dot trim, 3¾" d., 9" h. 150.00

Blue, blown, enameled multicolored florals & foliage, matching stopper, 8" h. 160.00

Clear, blown, flattened bulbous shape, engraved branches & leaves, applied blue handle, blue facet-cut stopper, 3¾" d., 6¾" h. 135.00

Cranberry, mold-blown, Inverted Thumbprint patt., fluted trefoil lip, applied clear reeded handle, clear stopper, 7" h. (ILLUS.) 125.00

Cranberry, blown, bulbous w/round mouth, enameled blue & white florals, leaves & gold branches, applied clear handle, original clear ball stopper, 3 5/8" d., 7¼" h. 165.00

Green, pressed, Beaded Ovals in Sand patt., original stopper 135.00

Lavender stained, bulbous, trefoil lip, enameled white florals & foliage, applied straw-colored stained reeded handle, original straw-colored stained blown hollow ball stopper, 3 3/8" d., 7¾" h. 100.00

Lime green, blown, enameled pink & white florals, small orange florals & pink branches, applied green handle, matching blown hollow ball stopper, 3½" d., 8" h. 88.00

Milk white, mold blown, pink-lined trefoil lip, ribbed base, pink & blue florals w/green foliage, original tear drop stopper, marked "1000," 6½" h. 285.00

Milk white, pressed, Challinor's Forget-Me-Not patt., original stopper .... 55.00 to 65.00

Pink opaline, blown, body applied w/clear leaves, applied clear handle, clear blown hollow ball stopper 97.50

Sapphire blue, blown, overall gold enameled lacy designs, applied amber handle, amber facet-cut stopper, 2 3/8" d., 6 5/8" h. 125.00

Vaseline, pressed, Riverside's Ranson patt., original stopper 140.00

White cut to cranberry, blown, enameled florals w/gold trim, applied clear handle, white cut to clear stopper 92.50

White opalescent, pressed, Paneled Sprig patt., original stopper 60.00

CUP PLATES

Lacy "Valentine" Cup Plate

Produced in numerous patterns beginning

some 150 years ago, these little plates were designed to hold a cup while the tea or coffee was allowed to cool in a saucer. Cup plates were also made of ceramics. Where numbers are listed below, they refer to numbers assigned these plates in the book, "American Glass Cup Plates," by Ruth Webb Lee and James H. Rose. Plates are of clear glass unless otherwise noted. A number of cup plates have been reproduced. Also see STAFFORDSHIRE CUP PLATES under Ceramics.

L & R No. 28 .... $9.50
L & R No. 36, opalescent opaque ... 475.00
L & R No. 40, peacock blue 180.00
L & R No. 48 .... 40.00
L & R No. 52 .... 30.00
L & R No. 90, opalescent opaque ... 110.00
L & R No. 98 .... 87.50
L & R No. 100, rare 60.00
L & R No. 134-A 30.00
L & R No. 157-B 65.00
L & R No. 177 .... 27.00
L & R No. 225-C, rare 50.00
L & R No. 234 .... 210.00
L & R No. 255-A 55.00
L & R No. 259, rare 75.00
L & R No. 310-B, extremely rare 70.00
L & R No. 319, very rare 90.00
L & R No. 343-A 25.00
L & R No. 362, scarce 25.00
L & R No. 379 .... 15.50
L & R No. 390-A 20.00
L & R No. 399, rare 50.00
L & R No. 410 .... 11.00
L & R No. 433, scarce 60.00
L & R No. 440-B, grey-blue, rare, scallop flakes (ILLUS.) 90.00
L & R No. 445, cloudy, very rare 235.00
L & R No. 447-B 15.00
L & R No. 455 .... 30.00
L & R No. 465-F 20.00
L & R No. 517 .... 12.00
L & R No. 565 .... 45.00
L & R No. 568, scarce 40.00
L & R No. 580-B, extremely rare 275.00
L & R No. 595, amber, extremely rare 230.00
L & R No. 596 .... 45.00
L & R No. 614 .... 150.00
L & R No. 631 .... 40.00
L & R No. 659 .... 50.00
L & R No. 691-A, extremely rare 400.00
L & R No. 808 .... 55.00

CUSTARD GLASS

This ware takes its name from its color and is a variant of milk-white glass. It was produced largely between 1890 and 1915 by the Northwood Glass Co., Heisey Glass Company, Fenton Art Glass Co., Jefferson Glass Co., and a few others. There are 21 major patterns and a number of minor ones. The prime patterns are considered Argonaut Shell, Chrysanthemum Sprig, Inverted Fan and Feather, Louis XV and Winged Scroll. Most custard glass patterns are enhanced with gold and some have additional enameled decoration or stained highlights. Unless otherwise noted, items in this listing are fully decorated.

ARGONAUT SHELL (Northwood)

Argonaut Shell Cruet

Berry set, master bowl & 6 sauce dishes, 7 pcs. $500.00
Bowl, master berry or fruit, 10½" l., 5" h. 150.00
Butter dish, cov. 228.00
Compote, jelly, 5" d., 5" h. 110.00
Creamer 108.00
Cruet w/original stopper (ILLUS.) ... 445.00
Pitcher, water 316.00
Salt & pepper shakers w/original tops, pr. 350.00
Sauce dish 45.00
Spooner 115.00
Sugar bowl, cov. 155.00
Table set, cov. butter dish, cov. sugar bowl, creamer & spooner, 4 pcs. 625.00
Toothpick holder 278.00
Tumbler 66.00
Water set, pitcher & 4 tumblers, 5 pcs. 575.00

BEADED CIRCLE (Northwood)

Berry set, master bowl & 5 sauce dishes, 6 pcs. 495.00
Bowl, master berry or fruit 185.00
Butter dish, cov. 272.00
Creamer (ILLUS.) 170.00
Cruet w/original stopper 650.00
Pitcher, water 428.00
Salt & pepper shakers w/original tops, pr. 255.00

Beaded Circle Creamer

Sauce dish 55.00
Spooner 84.00
Sugar bowl, cov. 165.00
Tumbler 75.00
Water set, pitcher & 4 tumblers, 5 pcs. 850.00

BEADED SWAG (Heisey)

Beaded Swag Sauce Dish

Goblet . . . . 40.00 to 50.00
Goblet, souvenir 80.00
Pickle dish (or tray) 250.00
Sauce dish, souvenir (ILLUS.) 35.00
Wine, w/advertising 75.00
Wine, souvenir 60.00

CARNELIAN - See Everglades Pattern

CHERRY & SCALE or FENTONIA (Fenton)

Cherry & Scale Butter Dish

Berry set, master bowl & 4 sauce dishes, 5 pcs. 280.00
Berry set, master bowl & 6 sauce dishes, 7 pcs. 325.00
Bowl, master berry or fruit 115.00
Butter dish, cov. (ILLUS.) 225.00
Creamer 110.00
Pitcher, water 325.00
Spooner 90.00
Sugar bowl, cov. 125.00
Tumbler 44.00
Water set, pitcher & 6 tumblers, 7 pcs. 600.00

CHRYSANTHEMUM SPRIG (Northwood)

Chrysanthemum Sprig Cruet

Berry set, master bowl & 4 sauce dishes, 5 pcs. 375.00
Bowl, master berry or fruit, 10½" oval 145.00
Bowl, master berry or fruit, 10½" oval (undecorated) 135.00
Butter dish, cov. 242.00
Celery vase 525.00
Compote, jelly 95.00
Compote, jelly (undecorated) 36.00
Condiment set, tray, cruet w/original stopper & salt & pepper shakers w/original tops, 4 pcs. 900.00
Condiment tray 575.00
Creamer 98.00
Cruet w/original stopper (ILLUS.) . . . 295.00
Pin tray 20.00
Pitcher, water 368.00
Salt & pepper shakers w/original tops, pr. 200.00
Sauce dish 75.00
Spooner 92.00
Sugar bowl, cov. 200.00
Sugar bowl, cov. (undecorated) 110.00
Table set, 4 pcs. 582.00
Toothpick holder 250.00
Tumbler 54.00
Water set, pitcher & 6 tumblers, 7 pcs. 696.00

DIAMOND WITH PEG (Jefferson)

Berry set, master bowl & 6 sauce dishes, 7 pcs. 600.00
Bowl, master berry or fruit 225.00

Butter dish, cov. 200.00
Creamer 75.00
Creamer, souvenir 40.00
Mug, souvenir 45.00
Napkin ring, souvenir 145.00
Pitcher, 5½" h. 140.00
Pitcher, tankard, 7½" h. 125.00
Pitcher, water, tankard 375.00
Punch cup 60.00
Salt & pepper shakers w/original
tops, souvenir, pr 90.00
Sauce dish 35.00
Sauce dish, souvenir 32.00
Spooner 95.00
Sugar bowl, cov. 165.00
Sugar bowl, cov., souvenir 105.00
Sugar bowl, open 95.00
Toothpick holder 60.00
Tumbler 49.00
Tumbler, souvenir 42.00
Vase, 6" h., souvenir 50.00
Water set, pitcher & 6 tumblers,
7 pcs. 480.00

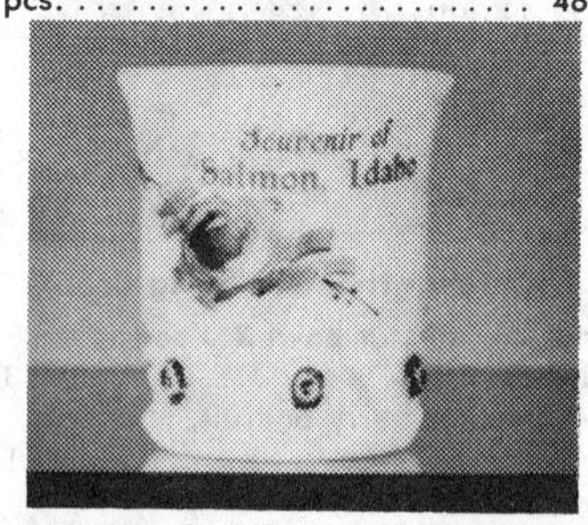

Diamond with Peg Shot Glass

Whiskey shot glass, souvenir
(ILLUS.) 45.00
Wine 50.00
Wine, souvenir 45.00

EVERGLADES or CARNELIAN (Northwood)

Everglades Butter Dish

Berry set, master bowl & 6 sauce
dishes, 7 pcs. 585.00
Bowl, master berry or fruit, footed
compote 195.00
Butter dish, cov. (ILLUS.) 370.00
Compote, jelly 350.00
Creamer 135.00
Cruet w/original stopper 750.00
Pitcher, water 650.00
Salt shaker w/original top (single) .. 150.00
Salt & pepper shakers w/original
tops, pr. 450.00
Sauce dish 65.00
Spooner 135.00
Sugar bowl, cov. 150.00
Tumbler 105.00

FAN (Dugan)

Fan Creamer

Berry set, master bowl & 6 sauce
dishes, 7 pcs. 450.00
Bowl, master berry or fruit 180.00
Butter dish, cov. 215.00
Creamer (ILLUS.) 90.00
Ice cream dish 42.00
Ice cream set, master bowl & 6
individual ice cream dishes,
7 pcs. 500.00
Pitcher, water ....255.00 to 285.00
Sauce dish 55.00
Spooner 72.00
Sugar bowl, cov. 95.00
Table set, cov. butter dish, cov.
sugar bowl & spooner,
3 pcs. ....350.00 to 450.00
Table set, 4 pcs. ....550.00 to 700.00
Tumbler 50.00
Water set, pitcher & 6 tumblers,
7 pcs. ....550.00 to 650.00

FENTONIA - See Cherry & Scale Pattern

FLUTED SCROLLS

Bowl, master berry or fruit,
footed 145.00
Creamer 50.00
Cruet w/original stopper 185.00
Pitcher, water, footed 250.00
Salt & pepper shakers w/original
tops, pr. 95.00
Sauce dish 42.50
Spooner 50.00
Sugar bowl, cov. 135.00
Tumbler 38.50
Water set, pitcher & 6 tumblers,
7 pcs. 475.00

FLUTED SCROLLS WITH FLOWER BAND - See Jackson Pattern

GENEVA (Northwood)

Banana boat, four-footed, 11" oval . . 138.00
Berry set, oval master bowl & 6 sauce dishes, 7 pcs. 335.00
Bowl, master berry or fruit, 8½" oval, four-footed 102.00
Bowl, master berry or fruit, 8½" d., three-footed 102.00
Butter dish, cov. 122.50
Compote, jelly 92.50
Creamer 72.00
Cruet w/original stopper 250.00
Pitcher, water 200.00

Geneva Salt Shaker

Salt shaker w/original top, single (ILLUS.) 75.00
Sauce dish, oval 32.50
Sauce dish, round 35.00
Spooner 70.00
Sugar bowl, cov. 125.00
Syrup pitcher w/original top 250.00
Table set, 4 pcs. 395.00
Toothpick holder 150.00
Tumbler 48.00

GEORGIA GEM or LITTLE GEM (Tarentum)

Georgia Gem Cruet

Berry set, master bowl & 6 sauce dishes, 7 pcs. 275.00
Bowl, master berry or fruit 72.00
Butter dish, cov. 175.00
Butter dish, cov. (undecorated) 100.00
Celery vase 160.00
Creamer 40.00
Creamer & cov. sugar bowl, souvenir, pr. 125.00
Creamer & open sugar bowl, breakfast size, pr. (undecorated) 72.00
Cruet w/original stopper (ILLUS.) . . . 250.00
Hair receiver, souvenir 55.00
Pitcher, water 310.00
Pitcher, water (undecorated) 200.00
Powder jar, cov. 45.00
Powder jar, cov., souvenir 54.00
Salt & pepper shakers w/original tops, pr. 75.00
Sauce dish 28.00
Spooner 63.00
Spooner, souvenir 60.00
Sugar bowl, cov. 110.00
Sugar bowl, cov. (undecorated) 45.00
Sugar bowl, open, breakfast size, souvenir 42.50
Table set, 4 pcs. 375.00
Toothpick holder 62.50
Toothpick holder, souvenir 35.00
Tumbler 48.00
Water set, pitcher & 4 tumblers, 5 pcs. 435.00

GRAPE & CABLE - See Northwood Grape Pattern

GRAPE & GOTHIC ARCHES (Northwood)

Grape & Gothic Arches Goblet

Berry set, master bowl & 6 sauce dishes, 7 pcs. 475.00
Bowl, master berry or fruit 175.00
Butter dish, cov. 200.00
Creamer 90.00
Goblet (ILLUS.) 50.00
Pitcher, water 285.00
Sauce dish 37.50
Spooner . . . . 70.00 to 85.00
Sugar bowl, cov. 110.00

Tumbler 58.00
Vase, 10" h. ("favor" vase made from goblet mold) 60.00
Vase, ruffled hat shape ......60.00 to 85.00
Water set, pitcher & 6 tumblers, 7 pcs. ....550.00 to 650.00

GRAPE & THUMBPRINT - See Northwood Grape Pattern

INTAGLIO (Northwood)

Intaglio Tumbler

Berry set, 9" d. footed compote & 6 sauce dishes, 7 pcs. 495.00
Bowl, fruit, 7½" d., footed compote 200.00
Bowl, fruit, 9" d. footed compote ....300.00 to 375.00
Butter dish, cov. 225.00
Compote, jelly 95.00
Creamer 102.00
Cruet w/original stopper 315.00
Pitcher, water 325.00
Salt & pepper shakers w/original tops, pr. 175.00
Sauce dish 52.00
Spooner 92.00
Sugar bowl, cov. 105.00
Table set, 4 pcs. 550.00
Tumbler (ILLUS.) 54.00
Water set, pitcher & 4 tumblers, 5 pcs. 550.00

INVERTED FAN & FEATHER (Northwood)

Berry set, master bowl & 6 sauce dishes, 7 pcs. 565.00
Bowl, master berry or fruit, 10" d., 5½" h., four-footed (ILLUS.) 210.00
Butter dish, cov. ....275.00 to 365.00
Compote, jelly 350.00
Creamer 125.00
Cruet w/original stopper 630.00
Pitcher, water 435.00
Punch cup 210.00
Salt & pepper shakers w/original tops, pr. 468.00
Sauce dish ....45.00 to 65.00
Spooner 110.00

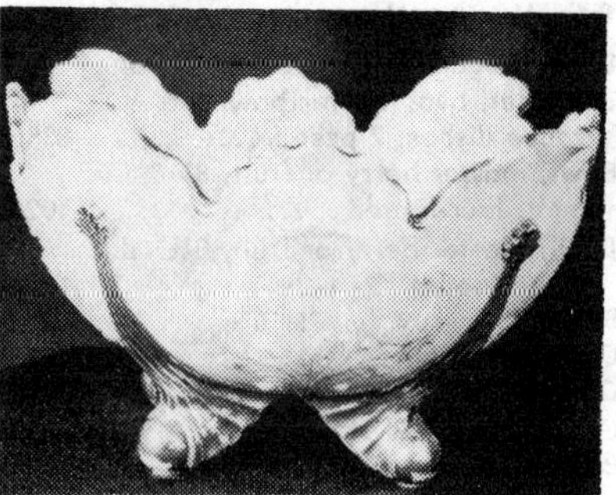

Inverted Fan & Feather Bowl

Sugar bowl, cov. 175.00
Table set, 4 pcs. 800.00
Toothpick holder ....500.00 to 550.00
Tumbler 75.00
Water set, pitcher & 6 tumblers, 7 pcs. 750.00

IVORINA VERDE - See Winged Scroll Pattern

JACKSON or FLUTED SCROLLS WITH FLOWER BAND (Northwood)

Jackson Creamer

Creamer (ILLUS.) 56.00
Salt shaker w/original top, undecorated (single) 45.00
Salt & pepper shakers w/original tops, pr. 135.00
Tumbler 30.00
Water set, pitcher & 4 tumblers, 5 pcs. 390.00

LITTLE GEM - See Georgia Gem Pattern

LOUIS XV (Northwood)

Berry set, master bowl & 6 sauce dishes, 7 pcs. 360.00
Bowl, berry or fruit, 10 x 7¾" oval 145.00
Butter dish, cov. 147.00
Creamer 80.00
Cruet w/original stopper 275.00
Pitcher, water 169.00
Salt shaker w/original top (single) .. 60.00
Salt & pepper shakers w/original tops, pr. 215.00

Louis XV Tumbler

Sauce dish, footed, 5" oval 44.00
Spooner 65.00
Sugar bowl, cov. 85.00
Table set, 4 pcs. 465.00
Tumbler (ILLUS.) 46.00
Water set, pitcher & 4 tumblers, 5 pcs. 325.00

MAPLE LEAF (Northwood)

Maple Leaf Butter Dish

Banana bowl 195.00
Berry set, master bowl & 6 sauce dishes, 7 pcs. 800.00
Bowl, master berry or fruit 265.00
Butter dish, cov. (ILLUS.) 230.00
Compote, jelly 400.00
Creamer 92.00
Cruet w/original stopper 1,100.00
Pitcher, water 350.00
Salt & pepper shakers w/original tops, pr. 500.00
Sauce dish 85.00
Spooner 87.00
Sugar bowl, cov. 185.00
Table set, 4 pcs. 568.00
Toothpick holder 475.00
Tumbler 87.00
Water set, pitcher & 6 tumblers, 7 pcs. 750.00

NORTHWOOD GRAPE, GRAPE & CABLE or GRAPE & THUMBPRINT (Northwood)

Banana boat 375.00
Berry set, master bowl & 6 sauce dishes, 7 pcs. 300.00
Bowl, 7½" d., ruffled rim . . . . 50.00 to 70.00
Bowl, master berry or fruit, 11" d., flat rim, footed 298.00
Butter dish, cov. 225.00
Cologne bottle w/original stopper . . . . 400.00 to 500.00
Cracker jar, cov., two-handled 525.00
Creamer 100.00
Creamer & open sugar bowl, breakfast size, pr. 115.00
Dresser tray . . . . 195.00 to 275.00
Ferner, footed, 7½" d., 4½" h. 150.00
Hatpin holder 450.00
Humidor, cov. 550.00
Nappy, two-handled 47.50
Pin dish 134.00
Pitcher, water 385.00
Plate, 7" d. 49.00
Plate, 8" w., six-sided 70.00
Plate, 8" d. 48.00

Northwood Grape Punch Bowl

Punch bowl & base, 2 pcs. (ILLUS.) . . 800.00
Punch cup 40.00
Sauce dish, flat 38.00
Sauce dish, footed 45.00
Spooner 95.00
Sugar bowl, cov. 125.00
Sugar bowl, open, breakfast size . . . 55.00
Table set, cov. butter dish, cov. sugar bowl & creamer, 3 pcs. 475.00
Tumbler 70.00
Vase, 3½" h. 46.00
Water set, pitcher & 5 tumblers, 6 pcs. . . . . 600.00 to 700.00

PRAYER RUG (Imperial)

Nappy, two-handled, ruffled, 6" d. . . 55.00
Plate, 7½" d. 12.50
Tumbler 80.00
Vase 50.00

PUNTY BAND (Heisey)

Creamer, individual size, souvenir . . 45.00

Punty Band Tumbler

Mug, souvenir 55.00
Salt & pepper shakers w/original tops, souvenir, pr. 80.00
Toothpick holder, souvenir 65.00
Tumbler, floral decor, souvenir (ILLUS.) 38.00
Vase, 5½" h., souvenir 75.00
Wine, souvenir 50.00

RIBBED DRAPE (Jefferson)

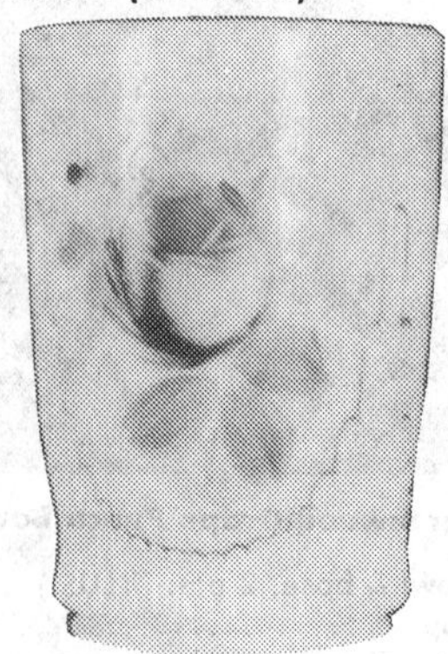

Ribbed Drape Tumbler

Butter dish, cov. 265.00
Compote, jelly 180.00
Creamer 110.00
Cruet w/original stopper 250.00
Pitcher, water 255.00
Salt & pepper shakers w/original tops, pr. 175.00
Sauce dish 40.00
Spooner 75.00
Sugar bowl, cov. 145.00
Toothpick holder 95.00
Tumbler (ILLUS.) 75.00

RING BAND (Heisey)

Berry set, master bowl & 6 sauce dishes, 7 pcs. 275.00
Bowl, master berry or fruit 115.00
Butter dish, cov. 150.00
Celery vase 300.00

Ring Band Jelly Compote

Compote, jelly (ILLUS.) ....155.00 to 200.00
Condiment set, condiment tray, jelly compote, toothpick holder & salt & pepper shakers, 5 pcs. 429.00
Condiment tray ....70.00 to 110.00
Creamer 80.00
Cruet w/original stopper 300.00
Mug, souvenir 45.00
Nappy 40.00
Pitcher, water 235.00
Punch cup 60.00
Punch cup, souvenir 26.00
Salt shaker w/original top, undecorated (single) 38.00
Salt & pepper shakers w/original tops, souvenir, pr. 115.00
Sauce dish 40.00
Spooner 89.00
Sugar bowl, cov. 136.00
Syrup pitcher w/original top ....200.00 to 300.00
Table set, 4 pcs. 410.00
Toothpick holder, 2½" h. ...85.00 to 110.00
Toothpick holder, souvenir 44.00
Tumbler 52.00
Tumbler, souvenir 35.00
Water set, pitcher & 6 tumblers, 7 pcs. 495.00
Whimsey, hat shape (from tumbler mold) 295.00

VICTORIA (Tarentum)

Victoria Creamer

Berry set, master bowl & 5 sauce dishes, 6 pcs. 575.00
Bowl, master berry or fruit 165.00
Butter dish, cov. 285.00
Celery vase 225.00
Creamer (ILLUS.) 85.00
Pitcher, water 350.00
Sauce dish 50.00
Spooner 85.00
Spooner (undecorated) 45.00
Sugar bowl, cov. 165.00
Tumbler 60.00

WINGED SCROLL or IVORINA VERDE (Heisey)

Winged Scroll Water Set

Berry set, master bowl & 4 sauce dishes, 5 pcs. (undecorated) 200.00
Berry set, master bowl & 6 sauce dishes, 7 pcs. 320.00
Bowl, fruit, 8½" d. 170.00
Bowl, master berry, 11" l., boat-shaped 100.00
Butter dish, cov. 164.00
Cake stand 325.00
Celery vase 312.00
Cigarette jar .... 135.00 to 175.00
Cologne bottle w/original stopper 245.00
Compote, 10¾" d., 6¾" h. 495.00
Creamer 85.00
Creamer (undecorated) 55.00
Cruet w/original stopper 188.00
Custard cup 45.00
Dresser tray 150.00
Hair receiver 125.00
Match holder .... 100.00 to 150.00
Nappy, folded side handle, 6" 50.00
Pitcher, water, 9" h., bulbous 235.00
Pitcher, water, tankard 238.00
Pitcher, water, tankard (undecorated) 140.00
Powder jar, cov. 80.00
Powder jar, cov., souvenir 55.00
Salt & pepper shakers w/original tops, pr. 165.00
Sauce dish, 4½" d. 35.00
Spooner 68.00
Sugar bowl, cov. 185.00
Sugar bowl, cov. (undecoratd) 95.00
Syrup pitcher w/original top 285.00
Table set, 4 pcs. 425.00
Toothpick holder 95.00
Tumbler 65.00
Vase, 9" h. 190.00
Water set, tankard pitcher & 6 tumblers, 7 pcs. (ILLUS.) .... 450.00 to 550.00

MISCELLANEOUS PATTERNS

Delaware

Bowl, 5½" (hat-shaped) 45.00
Creamer w/rose decoration 58.00
Pin tray w/rose stain, 4½" 37.00
Pin tray w/blue decoration 62.00
Ring tree, 4" h. 54.00
Sauce dish w/rose stain 65.00
Sauce dish w/blue decoration 45.00
Tumbler, green decoration 50.00

Harvard

Toothpick holder 35.00
Toothpick holder, green decoration 80.00
Toothpick holder, souvenir 26.00
Vase, 5½" h., w/enameled decoration 35.00

Heart with Thumbprint

Creamer 40.00
Finger lamp, green decoration 250.00
Sugar bowl, individual, green decoration 55.00

Peacock and Urn

Peacock and Urn Ice Cream Bowl

Berry bowl, master 110.00
Ice cream bowl, master, w/nutmeg stain, 9¾" d. (ILLUS.) 210.00
Ice cream dish, individual, w/nutmeg stain 62.00
Sauce dish 38.00

Vermont

Berry bowl, master 125.00
Card basket, 7½" d. 95.00
Creamer, green & pink florals 90.00

Pickle tray 30.00
Pitcher, blue trim w/enameled decoration 250.00
Spooner 78.00
Toothpick holder, green decoration 110.00
Toothpick holder, blue trim w/enameled decoration 88.00
Tumbler, blue decoration 55.00
Table set, cov. butter, creamer & spooner, 3 pcs. 195.00
Vase 25.00
Vase w/enameled decoration 70.00

Wild Bouquet

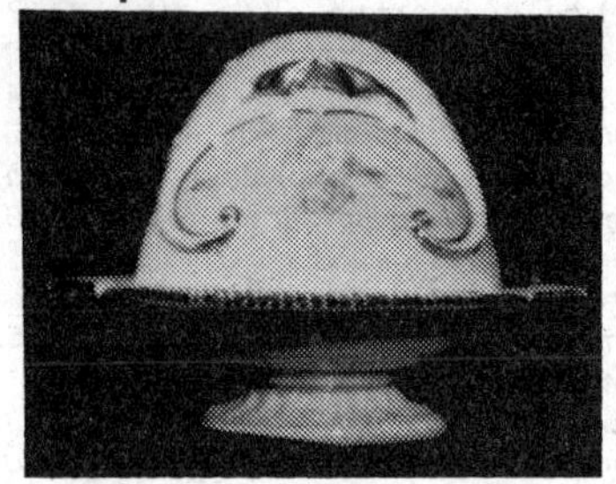

Wild Bouquet Butter Dish

Butter dish, cov. (ILLUS.) 325.00
Creamer 125.00
Cruet w/original stopper, enameling & gold trim 570.00
Sauce dish 50.00
Spooner (undecorated) 65.00
Spooner w/gold trim & colored decoration 145.00
Toothpick holder 475.00
Tumbler (undecorated) 37.50

(End of Custard Glass Section)

CUT GLASS

Cut glass most eagerly sought by collectors is American glass produced during the so-called "Brilliant Period" from 1880 to about 1915. Pieces listed below are by type of article in alphabetical order.

BASKETS

Cane, bull's eye, notched prism & step-cutting, applied handle, overall 11" h. $550.00
Harvard patt. & other cutting, applied double-twist handle, 9½" d. (ILLUS.) 575.00
Mitre cutting, fans & stars, 10 x 7", overall 9½" h. 225.00
Pinwheels (4) separated by bars of cane above strawberry diamond & stars, triple honeycomb handle, 5¼ x 3¼", overall 5" h. 275.00

Brilliant Period Basket

Straus' Songbird with Flowers patt., intaglio-cut birds amidst florals & foliage, applied overhead handle, 12" l. 425.00

BOTTLES

Cut Glass Whiskey Bottle

Peppersauce, Fry signed, hobstars & leaf sprays, octagonal neck w/fine horizontal step cutting, original hollow stopper, 3" base d., 8½" h. 195.00
Water, bull's eye & other cutting . . . 125.00
Water, Hawkes signed, Brilliant Period cutting, 8½" h. 130.00
Water, notched prism & crossed ellipticals, large hobstar base 95.00
Whiskey, chain of hobstars, diamond point & fan, w/sterling silver whiskey shot glass top, ca. 1900, 7¾" h. (ILLUS.) 575.00
Whiskey, Hawkes signed, Brilliant Period cutting, matching stopper, 12½" h. 220.00
Whiskey, Hawkes signed, vertical line cutting, sterling silver collar & stopper, pr. 450.00
Whiskey, Hawkes signed, straw-

berry diamond & fan, sterling silver collar & whiskey shot glass top 300.00
Worcestershire sauce, Brilliant Period cutting, 8" h., pr. 295.00
Worcestershire sauce, Hawkes signed, Brunswick patt., chain of hobstars, zipper-type beading & flute, original stopper, 8" h. 165.00

BOWLS

Cut Glass Fruit Bowl

Berry, pinwheel, hobstar & strawberry diamond, 8" d., 3½" h. 75.00
Caviar, intaglio-cut vintage motif, 3-handled, sterling silver cover, 7" d. 155.00
Eggnog, Hawkes signed, Harvard patt., matching base, 9" d., overall 9½" h., 2 pcs. 475.00
Eggnog, Hawkes signed, hobstars, vesicas & other cutting, matching base, 10½" d., 8½" h., 2 pcs. 750.00
Eggnog, notched prism, hobstars, flashed fan, tiny hobstar clusters & crosshatching, large lapidary-cut knob above scalloped hobstar base, 10¾" d., 9" h. 1,350.00
Fruit, Hoare, hobstars & other cutting, scalloped & serrated base & rim, 2 pcs. (ILLUS.) 650.00
Fruit, Libbey signed, oblong, Brilliant Period cutting, 7½" l. 170.00
Fruit, overall floral cutting, straight sides w/everted rim, 12" d., 4½" h. 245.00
Ice cream, Libbey signed, Brilliant Period cutting, 14" d. 210.00
Mayonnaise, Hawkes signed, Princess patt., hobstars separated by overlapping bull's eyes, bottom cut in 24-point hobstar within 16-point hobstar, 4 3/8" d., 3" h. 110.00
Mayonnaise, Tuthill signed, flashed hobstars 90.00
Brilliant Period cutting w/border of hobstars at base, sterling silver engraved rim w/pierced handles, 8" w. across handles, 2½" h. 165.00
Comet-type patt., 6 swirls w/four hobstars each, 3 w/five stars each & 3 w/strawberry diamond, large 24-point hobstar center, 9¼" d., 3¾" h. 475.00
Dorflinger's Kalana Lily patt., 9 1/8" d., 3 5/8" h. 95.00
Dorflinger's Jubilee patt., 10" d., 4" h. 475.00
Egginton signed, Lotus patt., serrated rim, 8" d. 165.00
Flashed stars & other cutting, 8" d. 100.00
Geometric cutting, shallow, 8" d. 135.00
Harvard patt. sides, large 20-point hobstar center, 9" d., 4¼" h. 195.00
Hawkes signed, hobstars, strawberry diamond & fan, 8" d., 5" h. 210.00
Hawkes signed, Lattice & Rosettes patt., scalloped & serrated rim, 9" d., 4" h. 1,500.00
Hawkes' Chrysanthemum patt., deep, 9" d. 485.00
Hawkes' Venetian patt., chain of hobstars, fan, star & strawberry diamond split vesica, shallow, 9" sq. 850.00
Hoare signed, hobstars & other cutting, 8" d., 2" h. 160.00
Hobstars & pinwheel, 7" d., 3" h. 200.00
Hobstars (6) above strawberry diamond vesicas w/triple cross-cut vesicas of hobstars w/hobnail between, 6-lobed form, 7¾" d., 2¾" h. 165.00
Hobstars (large 20-point) at each corner w/four 12-point hobstars at each side, beading & strawberry diamond, 4 cane vesicas & notched fans radiating from center, 8¼" sq., 3 1/8" h. 275.00
Hobstars, cane & crosshatching, Gorham sterling silver rim, 9" d. 295.00
Hobstars (large & small), cane, strawberry diamond & fan, 18-point hobstar center, 10 1/8" d., 4 3/8" h. 225.00
Libbey signed, Brilliant Period cutting, 6" d. 95.00
Libbey signed, Regis patt., 8 1/8" d. 250.00
Libbey signed, intaglio-cut grapes & vining leaves, 9" d., 2" h. 150.00
Libbey signed, Aztec patt., hobnail vesicas & hobstars, flared, 9¾" d., 3" h. 2,095.00
Libbey's Gloria patt., hobstars, strawberry diamond, beading &

star, hobstar center, 8 1/8" d., 3½" h. 235.00
Libbey's Kimberly patt., fan, hobstar & strawberry diamond, tri-cornered w/turned in sides, 10" w. 350.00
Meriden's Alhambra (Greek Key) patt., 9" d. 1,500.00
Monroe (C.F.) Co. signed, Brilliant Period cutting, sterling silver rim, 8" d. 235.00
Notched prism, crosshatching & fan, Gorham sterling silver rim dated 1897, 9" d. 250.00
Pitkin & Brooks' Plymouth patt., chain of hobstars & notched prism flairs, 9" d. 350.00
Sinclaire signed, Fuchsia patt. w/Russian patt. panels, 8" d. 265.00
Sinclaire signed, Lace, Hobnails & Cornflowers patt., columns of hobstars in a triple mitre checkerboard arrangement & other cutting, 11" octagon, 2½" h. 750.00
Straus signed, Brilliant Period cutting, 8¼" d., 2¼" h. 350.00
Straus, cane vesicas (6) each surrounded by ferns on strawberry diamond field & swirling fans, hobstar center, ruffled rim, 11 1/8" d., 3¾" h. 995.00
Tuthill signed, intaglio-cut border, large geometric 8-point star w/hobstar center, 6" d. 200.00
Tuthill signed, Vintage patt., intaglio-cut grape clusters & vines, pedestal base, rolled rim, 9¾" d., 5" h. 595.00

BOXES

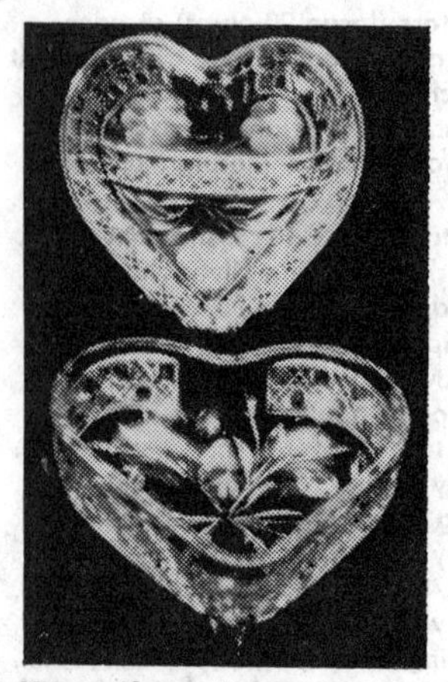

Heart-Shaped Dresser Box

Dresser, Hawkes signed, Brilliant Period cutting on hinged lid & base, silver plate fittings, 5" d. 285.00
Dresser, five 12-point hobstars separated by cross-cut vesicas of strawberry diamond on hinged lid, ridged sides, star-cut base, silver plate fittings, 5 1/8" d., 2¾" h. 250.00
Dresser, intaglio-cut florals on hinged lid, thumbprint band around base, 32-point star-cut bottom, 5½" d., 3" h. 325.00
Dresser, heart-shaped, intaglio-cut florals & foliage w/Harvard patt., 6 x 5½", 3" h. (ILLUS.) 200.00
Dresser, cross-cuts & mitred cross-cuts surrounding an 8-petal flower & foliage on hinged lid, trailing foliage around sides, star-cut base, silver plate fittings, 6¼" d., 3½" h. 200.00
Dresser, Hawkes signed, Brilliant Period cutting on lift-off lid & sides, 6½" d., 3½" h. 265.00
Dresser, hobstar on hinged lid, sterling silver fittings, 7½" d., 4" h. 400.00
Glove, intaglio-cut florals within Harvard border on hinged lid, sterling silver fittings 750.00
Jewelry, large 12-point hobstar w/fans between strawberry diamond points on hinged lid, sides cut w/chain of bull's eye above chain of cross-hatching between rows of bull's eyes, star-cut base, silver plate fittings, 6 7/8" sq., 3 1/8" h. 1,100.00
Jewelry, 4 double cross-cut vesicas of hobstar & strawberry diamond separated by hobstars & fans on hinged lid, sides cut w/ovals, silver plate fittings, 7 7/8" sq. base tapering to 6¾" sq., 5¼" h. 1,500.00
Powder, Brilliant Period cutting on sides, Gorham sterling silver lid w/embossed Art Nouveau woman's head, 5" d. 175.00
Powder, Hawkes signed, Brilliant Period cutting on hinged lid & base, silver plate fittings, 7" d. 165.00
Powder, Brilliant Period cutting, hinged lid, sterling silver rim, 9" d., 6½" h. 600.00
Powder, notched prism & ovals on sides, silver plate lid 65.00

BUTTER DISHES & TUBS

Covered dish, Hawkes signed, Brilliant Period cutting, dome lid & 8" d. underplate 265.00
Covered dish, hobstars, cross-cut vesicas & other cutting, dome lid w/lapidary-cut knob & underplate 295.00
Covered dish, Libbey signed, hobstars, fan & other cutting, 5¼" d., 6" h. dome lid & 8" d. underplate 425.00

Cut Glass Butter Tub

Tub, hobstars, fan & diagonal slashes, tab handles extending from scalloped & serrated rim, 5" d., 3¾" h. plus tab handles (ILLUS.) .. 195.00
Tub, cov., Diamond & Fans patt. 225.00
Tub, cov., Russian patt., matching underplate 2,000.00

CANDLESTICKS & CANDLEHOLDERS

Cane base, cylindrical prism-cut stem, 7¼" h., pr. 275.00
Red cut to clear, open base cut w/moon border, 8-panel stem w/cut ovals at mid-section, overlapping rim w/red interior cut to clear w/chain of ovals above a moon border, 5 1/8" base d., 10 5/8" h. (single) 175.00
Green cut to clear, Sinclaire signed, floral cutting, 12" h. (single) 98.00
Hawkes signed, thumbprint base, stem w/elongated teardrop, strawberry diamond socket, pr. .. 450.00
Strawberry diamond & fan, chamberstick-type w/saucer base & ring handle 550.00

CARAFES

Brilliant Period cutting, 8½" h. 95.00
Hawkes signed, Chrysanthemum patt. 275.00
Hawkes' Imperial patt., 6" d., 9½" h. 200.00
Hawkes' Venetian patt., fan, star & split strawberry diamond vesicas 285.00
Hoare's Croesus patt. 350.00
Hobstars, notched prism & other cutting 110.00
Hobstars & other cutting 105.00
Niland Cut Glass Company's Butterfly & Flowers patt., designed by Thomas Mortensen 180.00
Pinwheel, hobstars & diamond 95.00
Red cut to clear, hobstars, strawberry diamond & fan, mushroom-shaped, notched panel-cut neck, 6¾" d., 6 7/8" h. 650.00
Straus' Drape patt. 180.00

CELERY TRAYS & VASES

Brilliant Period Celery Tray

Tray, Hawkes signed, pinwheels & hobstars, 4½" w., 12" l. 120.00
Tray, hobstars & other cutting, 14" l. (ILLUS.) 175.00
Tray, Libbey signed, Spillane patt., cross-cut vesicas, notched prism, fan & hobstars, 11" l. 100.00
Vase, hobstars, strawberry diamond & fan, 6½" h. 185.00
Vase, Meriden patt., beading, cross-cut diamond & fan, 6½" h. 125.00

CHAMPAGNES, CORDIALS & WINES

Hawkes' Grecian Pattern

Champagne, Brilliant Period cutting, double teardrop stem 35.00
Champagne, Electric (Angulated Ribbon) patt. 50.00
Champagne, Hoare's Monarch patt., cross-cut vesica w/split, hobstars & other cutting, set of 12 .... 900.00
Cordial, Hawkes' Louis XIV patt., w/monogram 60.00
Wine, Clark signed, Baker's Gothic patt., fan, hobstar & strawberry diamond, notch-cut stem, cut base, 3½" d., 4" h., set of 8 ..... 400.00
Wine, Hawkes' Grecian patt., set of 3 (ILLUS. of two) 1,125.00
Wine, hobstars, fan, fine-cut & diamond 30.00
Wine, Russian patt., knobbed stem, set of 4 .... 350.00

Wine, Sherry-type, Hawkes signed, Brilliant Period cutting, clear bowl, green stem 48.00

CHEESE DISHES

Cut Glass Cheese Dish

Hobstars overall, dome lid w/lapidary-cut finial & underplate 375.00

Hobstars, strawberry diamond, fan & sunburst, dome lid & underplate..................350.00 to 375.00

Hobstars & other cutting, dome lid & underplate w/scalloped & serrated rim, large 450.00

Pairpoint's (Mt. Washington) Wheeler patt., dome lid & underplate... 200.00

Pinwheel, fan, strawberry diamond & other cutting, dome lid w/faceted knob & underplate w/scalloped & serrated rim (ILLUS.)........... 475.00

CLOCKS

Boudoir, Cane patt. sides, intaglio-cut florals & leaves around face, 6½" h......................... 255.00

Boudoir, steeple case, Harvard patt. & intaglio-cut chrysanthemum blossoms, 9" h. 850.00

Boudoir, Harvard patt. sides & top, intaglio-cut florals around face ... 165.00

COMPOTES

Brilliant Period cutting, cut stem w/teardrop, 9½" h. 215.00

Cane patt. clusters alternating w/intaglio-cut 10-petal daisies, horizontal step-cut stem, 7" oval, 5½" h.......................... 110.00

Clark signed, Brilliant Period cutting, 6" d., 9" h. 165.00

Clark signed, hobstars & other cutting, 6" h. 185.00

Cross-cut diamond & fan, star-cut base, 6" d., 3" h. 117.00

Hawkes signed, Brilliant Period cutting, teardrop in stem, 7" h. 145.00

Hawkes signed, Brilliant Period cutting, notched prism stem, 8" h.... 175.00

Hawkes signed, chain of triple cross-cut diamond w/ridging above & strawberry diamond & zipper below, panel-cut stem w/double teardrop, hobstar base, 4 5/8" d., 4¾" h. 135.00

Hoare signed, Brilliant Period cutting & etching on bowl, stem & base, scalloped rim, 7" d., 8½" h.......................... 175.00

Hoare signed, Steuben patt., 5" h... 135.00

Compote with Teardrop Stem

Hobstars & flashed stars, double-notched stem w/teardrop, 24-point hobstar base, 7" d., 7¾" h. (ILLUS.) 225.00

Hobstars & other cutting on bowl & base, notched prism tapering stem, 11½" h. 250.00

Hobstars, cane, strawberry diamond, beading & fan on 3" h. tulip-shaped bowl, notched prism panel-cut stem w/teardrop, star-cut base, 6½" d., 9½" h. 175.00

Hobstars, fan & cane, 6" d., 9" h.... 145.00

Hobstars, strawberry diamond & other cutting, teardrop in stem, 9" d., 9" h. 250.00

Hobstars (24- & 16-point), strawberry diamond, star & fan, notched prism panel-cut stem, serrated hobstar base, 10 3/8" w., 13" h... 850.00

Libbey signed, Brilliant Period cutting, petticoat base, 7" d., 7" h. .. 425.00

Pinwheel, cane & fan, notch- & panel-cut stem, cross-hatched foot w/star-cut base, 10" d. 105.00

Tuthill signed, intaglio-cut primrose buds w/polished & matte foliage, flute-cut stem w/teardrop, blazed star motif on base, 6¾" h....... 200.00

Tuthill signed, Rosemere patt., intaglio-cut wild rose blossoms & foliage w/cross-hatched strawberry diamond banding, 8" d., 3" h.......................... 795.00

CREAMERS & SUGAR BOWLS

Brilliant Period cutting, miniature, pr. . . . 225.00

Clark's Prima Donna (Triple Square) patt., square enclosed within 2 squares & chain of hobstars, right angle serrated rim, 4¾" h. creamer, pr. . . . 330.00

Harvard patt., pr. . . . 95.00

Hawkes signed, Brilliant Period cutting, pr. . . . 185.00

Hoare signed, Brilliant Period cutting, 4½" h., pr. . . . 165.00

Hobstars & other cutting, 3" h., pr. . 150.00

Hobstars, fan & other cutting, eight-point hobstar base, pr. . . . 90.00

Hobstars, strawberry diamond & star cutting overall, notched handles, large, pr. . . . 145.00

Hunt's Royal patt., Russian patt. w/hobstar button, pentagonal strawberry diamond lozenge & large hobstars, creamer w/step-cutting under spout, triple-notched handles, pr. . . . 285.00

Libbey signed, blazed motif, pr. . . . 195.00

Libbey signed, Brilliant Period cutting, pr. . . . 110.00

Libbey signed, panel & pinwheel, pr. . . . 175.00

Straus' Ulysses patt., covered sugar bowl, pr. . . . 475.00

Tuthill signed, Brilliant Period cutting, pr. . . . 125.00

CRUETS

Brilliant Period Cruet

Brilliant Period cutting, original stopper, 7" h. . . . 75.00

Brilliant Period cutting, petticoat shape . . . 65.00

Brilliant Period cutting, notched handle, original stopper, pr. . . . 165.00

Hawkes signed, Brilliant Period cutting . . . 75.00

Hawkes signed, intaglio-cut strawberries, original stopper . . . 115.00

Hawkes' Yale patt., fan, hobstar & strawberry diamond, original stopper . . . 165.00

Hobstar panels alternating w/fan cutting, original faceted stopper . . 125.00

Pairpoint's Butterfly & Daisy patt., 7" h. . . . 83.00

Russian patt. . . . 250.00

Russian patt., St. Louis Diamond handle . . . 375.00

St. Louis Diamond patt., applied handle, matching stopper . . . 200.00

Strawberry diamond & fan, loop handle, faceted stopper, 12½" h. (ILLUS.) . . . 200.00

Thumbprint & notched prism, 6½" h. . . . 95.00

DECANTERS

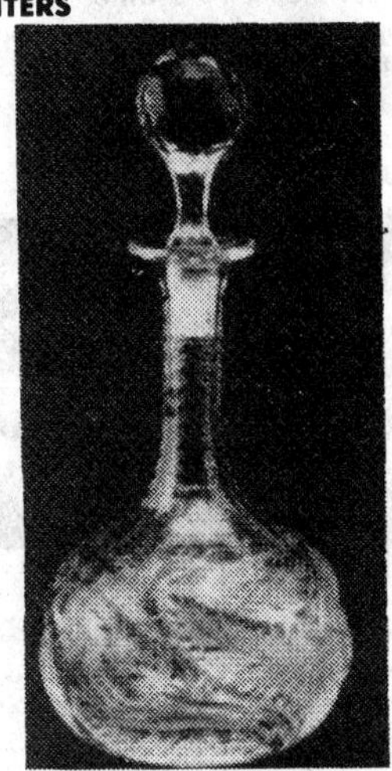

Cut Glass Decanter

Champagne, Hawkes signed, hobstar, strawberry diamond, fan & beading, 24-point hobstar foot, notched spout & handle, original matching stopper, 15" h. . . . 7,500.00

Cordial, Hawkes signed, Brilliant Period cutting, faceted stopper, 8½" h. . . . 235.00

Whiskey, notched prism & chain of stars swirl motif . . . 425.00

Wine, Clark signed, strawberry diamond & other cutting, 13" h. . . . 190.00

Wine, cross-cut diamond & fan . . . 175.00

Wine, Hawkes signed, Brilliant Period cutting, 11½" h. . . . 195.00

Dorflinger's Marlboro patt., hobstars, strawberry diamond & fan, notched panel-cut neck, hobstar base, original lapidary-cut stopper, 5" d., 10" h. . . . 225.00

Flute-cut, original mushroom-shaped stopper 85.00
Hawkes' Design No. 7, large squares of crosscut diamond separated by intersecting clear convex bands, six-panel petticoat-shaped neck, scalloped star-cut pedestal base, original lapidary-cut stopper, 4½" d., 12 5/8" h., pr. 595.00
Hawkes' Grecian patt., vesicas, fan & Russian patt., pedestal base, 19" h. 7,250.00
Hoare signed, Brilliant Period cutting, matching cone-shaped stopper, 12" h. 135.00
Hobstars & other cutting, original faceted stopper, 12" h. (ILLUS.) ... 195.00
Hunt's Royal patt., Russian motif w/hobstar button, five-sided strawberry diamond lozenge & large hobstars 475.00
Tuthill signed, Primrose patt., intaglio-cut blossoms & other cutting, applied handle, 12" h. 400.00
Wheat patt., matching stopper, 11" h. 225.00

DISHES, MISCELLANEOUS

Relish Dish

Boat-shaped, Clark signed, Brilliant Period cutting, 11½" l. 165.00
Boat-shaped, Hawkes signed, Harvard patt., 12½" l. 195.00
Candy, three-compartment, hobstars & other cutting, 7" l. 295.00
Candy, two-handled, four-compartment, hobstars, hobnail, flashed fan, strawberry diamond & star, double bull's eye handles, 9 7/8" w. across handles, 2 3/8" h. 125.00
Candy, two-handled, four-compartment, hobstars & other cutting, 10" d. plus handles 135.00
Candy, two-handled, four-compartment, Brilliant Period cutting, 10½" w. across handles 150.00
Candy, two-handled, four-compartment, hobstars, zipper & arcs, cut loop handles, serrated rim, 12½" l. across handles 205.00
Hobstars & pinwheel alternating around large six-point star, serrated rim, 11½" d. 65.00
Relish, Button & Star patt., 6" l. 45.00
Relish, Harvard patt., 4" w., 8" l. 235.00
Relish, Hawkes signed, Queens patt., chain of hobstars & bull's eye 250.00
Relish, hobstars & cane vesicas, 8½" l. 55.00
Relish, hobstars, strawberry diamond, fan & other cutting, scalloped & serrated rim, 9" l. (ILLUS.) 95.00
Relish, hobstars & cane, serrated rim, 11" l. 45.00
Relish, Libbey signed, Brilliant Period cutting, 6" d., 2½" h. 150.00
Relish, Libbey signed, Brilliant Period cutting, 12" l., 4" h. 175.00
Russian patt., 11" d. 350.00

FERNERS

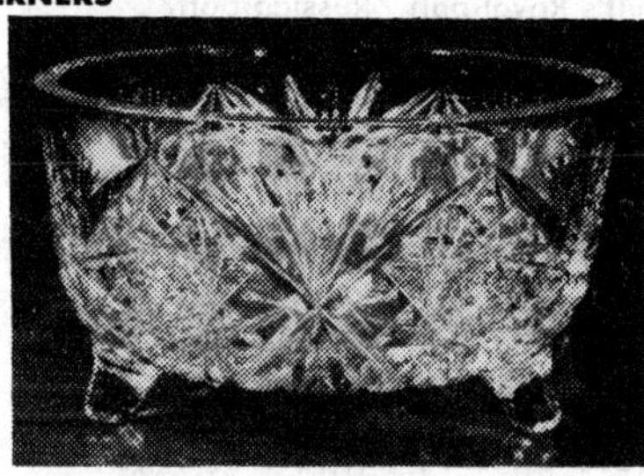

Brilliant Period Ferner

Brilliant Period cutting overall, footed, 7" d., 4" h. 125.00
Hobstars & fan, three-footed, 7½" d. (ILLUS.) 160.00
Hunt's Royal patt., Russian motif w/hobstar button, five-sided strawberry diamond lozenge & large hobstars, three-footed...... 195.00
Meriden's Cutting No. 215, flashed hobstar w/strawberry diamond points, three-footed 225.00

GOBLETS

Cut Glass Goblet

Cross-cut diamond & fan, notched stem, rayed base (ILLUS.) 70.00

Double Lozenge patt., fan, hobstar & strawberry diamond, set of 9 ... 695.00
Hawkes signed, Brilliant Period cutting, square base, set of 6 .... 240.00
Libbey signed, Corinthian patt., cross-cut diamond, fan, hobstar & strawberry diamond, notch-cut stem, cut base, set of 7 .... 400.00
Strawberry patt., intaglio-cut strawberries & leaves 35.00

ICE BUCKETS & TUBS

Bucket, Clarks' Jewel patt., cross-cut diamond, fan, hobstar & strawberry diamond, cut handles, w/matching underplate 590.00
Bucket, Hawkes signed, Brilliant Period cutting, 7" d. 195.00
Bucket, Hawkes signed, Brilliant Period cutting, sterling silver mountings, 8½" h. 425.00
Bucket, Hawkes signed, chain of hobstars, prism flairs & other cutting, triple-notched handles, scalloped & serrated rim, w/matching underplate 1,000.00

JARS

Brilliant Period Tobacco Jar

Cigarello, Maple City Glass Company signed, Brilliant Period cutting 515.00
Cracker, Hawkes signed, Brilliant Period cutting, w/matching 8" d. underplate, 8" h. 1,950.00
Dresser, Florence Star alternating w/fan & cross-cut diamond, hobstar base, sterling silver cover, 5" widest d., 3¾" h. 125.00
Horseradish, hobstars separated by rows of ladder cutting, original cut bulbous hollow stopper, 5½" h. 135.00
Mustard, hobstars & strawberry diamond, matching cover, 3¼" h. ... 50.00
Mustard, strawberry diamond & fan, metal hinged lid & handle 45.00
Mustard, vertical notched prism, rayed base, cover w/faceted knob, w/matching underplate 65.00
Tobacco, hobstars, strawberry diamond, fan & other cutting, lid w/cut knob, 9" h. (ILLUS.) 525.00

KNIFE RESTS

Brilliant Period cutting overall, dumbbell shape, 3½" l.... 18.00 to 25.00
Brilliant Period cutting, sterling silver mountings 65.00
Faceted ball ends, panel-cut bar, 5" l. 42.50
Faceted ball ends, serrated bar, 4½" l. 40.00
Notched prism ball ends & bar, 1½" d. ends, 4" l. 35.00

MISCELLANEOUS

Florence Pattern Coffeepot

Berry set: master bowl & six sauce dishes; Egginton's Cluster patt., hobnail, hobstar, star & strawberry diamond, 7 pcs. 475.00
Cake stand, prism cutting 1,000.00
Canoe, Brilliant Period cutting, 11½" l. 250.00
Canoe, Harvard patt., 2" l. 65.00
Canoe, Harvard patt. sides, hobstar bottom, 11¼" l. 175.00
Centerpiece bowl, Hawkes signed, Brilliant Period cutting overall w/hobstars around scalloped rim, 24-point hobstar base, 4" d. base flaring to 9" d. top, 5" h. 395.00
Centerpiece set: 12" d. footed bowl w/wide flat rim & pair 9 1/8" h. baluster-form candlesticks; cross-hatched diamond & flute, 3 pcs. .. 525.00
Cocktail shaker, Hawkes signed, strawberry diamond & fan, sterling silver top w/pouring spout ... 275.00
Coffeepot, cov., ovoid body, Florence patt., ca. 1890, 12" h. (ILLUS.) 1,980.00

Cordial set: 9" h. ring-necked decanter w/original stopper & eight 4" h. cordial glasses; green cut to clear, Dorflinger's Flute patt., 9 pcs. 875.00

Desk set: inkwell w/insert, pen tray & letter rack; Hawkes signed, Brilliant Period cutting, the set 250.00

Finger bowls, strawberry diamond & fan, set of 4 .... 175.00

Finger bowl & underplate, Libbey signed, Brilliant Period cutting, 2 pcs. 75.00

Flower center, hobstars w/strawberry diamond points & fan, 16-point rayed base, flute- and notch-cut neck, 5½" d., 4¼" h. 285.00

Flower center, Hoare signed, hobstars, checkered motif & fan, step-cut neck, 10" d., 7½" h...... 875.00

Flower center, hobstars, pinwheel, diamond & fan, 10" d. 275.00

Flower center, hobstars, fan & diamond, horizontal step-cut neck, scalloped rim, large hobstar bottom, 10" d. 575.00

Flower center, Libbey's Empress patt., cross-cut diamond, fan, hobstar & strawberry diamond, ring neck, 10" d. 795.00

Ice cream set: tray & ten plates; Pineapple & Fan patt., 11 pcs..... 120.00

Mayonnaise bowl, cover & underplate, bull's eye & flashed pinwheel, the set 135.00

Petit four stand, hobstars alternating w/fields of cane & diamond, pedestal base w/hobstar bottom, 7½" d., 5" h. 225.00

Picture frame, Hawkes signed, intaglio-cut roses & strawberries, 7 x 5" oval 525.00

Punch ladle, Harvard patt. handle, ornate Pairpoint silver plate stem & double spout bowl, 5¼" w. bowl, overall 14" l. 325.00

Punch ladle, notched prism, hobstars & fan handle, Wallace sterling silver twisted handle & scroll-engraved bowl w/inscription dated "1902," overall 15" l. 295.00

Salad bowl & underplate, Libbey signed, Spillane (Trefoil & Rosette) patt., cross-cut vesicas, notched prism, hobstars & fan, 10" d., 6" h. bowl, 11½" d. underplate, the set 1,950.00

Serving bowl & undertray, Hawkes' Venetian patt., chain of hobstars, fan, star & strawberry diamond split vesicas, 8" d. bowl & 12¼" d. tray, the set 1,500.00

Sherbets, Butterfly & Daisy patt., set of 6 .... 135.00

Sherbet, Egginton signed, Brilliant Period cutting 35.00

String holder, notched prism, ornate pierced Gorham sterling silver top 125.00

Sugar shaker, hobstars, diamond, cane & other cutting, sterling silver top 150.00

Table garniture: tall, slender tapering cylindrical vase w/scalloped & serrated everted mouth, raised on scalloped circular foot, w/four bud vases of similar form & four small canoe-shaped bowls, all mounted w/silver plate bands or hooks to form a radiating centerpiece; Hawkes signed, hobstar cutting overall, late 19th c., overall 16¼" h., 9 pcs...............1,320.00

Cut Glass Umbrella Stand

Umbrella stand, chain of hobstars, notched prism, bull's eye & other cutting, 24" h. (ILLUS.) 1,600.00

Urns, cov., campana-shaped body, crosshatching, fan & stop-fluting, covers w/swirled mushroom-shaped finials, w/liners, 19½" h., pr. 1,870.00

Whiskey jug, Dorflinger's Hob & Lace patt. 350.00

Whiskey shot glass, Russian patt. ... 65.00

Wine set: 10½" h. ewer-form decanter w/faceted teardrop stopper & six flared wine glasses; hobstar, fan & diamond, 7 pcs. 495.00

NAPPIES

Brilliant Period cutting, ring handle, 7½ x 6½" 75.00

Cane vesicas center surrounded by hobstars & further cane cutting, scalloped & serrated rim, two-handled, 9" d. 410.00

Chrysanthemum patt. variant, square, two-handled............. 90.00

Clifford patt., vesicas of cross-cut diamond & prism w/hobstars & other cutting, single handle 95.00

Harvard Pattern Nappy

Harvard patt., loop handle, 6" w. (ILLUS.) 170.00

Hawkes signed, Brilliant Period cutting, single handle, 5" d. 65.00

Hawkes signed, Brilliant Period cutting, 8" d. 135.00

Hoare signed, Brilliant Period cutting, two-handled, 8" d. 145.00

Hobstars & other cutting, single handle, 6" d. 120.00

Hobstars, cross-cut diamond, cane & fan, three-handled 95.00

Hobstars, feathered leaves & other cutting, scalloped & serrated rim, double thumbprint handle, 7½" across handle 60.00

Tuthill signed, Primrose & Hobstars patt., 6" d. 145.00

PERFUME & COLOGNE BOTTLES

Cologne, bulbous, Cane patt., long slim flute-cut neck, pointed stopper, 3½" base d., 7" h. 95.00

Cologne, bulbous, green cut to clear, overall Brilliant Period cutting, faceted stopper, 7" h. 235.00

Cologne, cranberry cut to clear, overall Cane patt., atomizer top .. 250.00

Cologne, intaglio-cut florals, faceted stopper 135.00

Perfume, six-sided, alternating panels of Harvard patt. & engraved florals, matching faceted stopper, rayed base, 3" d., 5½" h. 75.00

Perfume, bulbous, Brilliant Period cutting, original stopper, 6½" h... 200.00

Perfume, cranberry, Art Deco style, deeply cut opposing triangles & crosshatching, tall stopper, 6½" h. 125.00

Perfume, panel-cut body, mushroom-shaped stopper, small 65.00

Perfume, Brilliant Period cutting, diamond-cut stopper 85.00

Perfume, lay-down type, cranberry, ten panel, ornate engraved silver ends, one w/screw-on lid, the other hinged, 5¼" l. 185.00

Perfume, lay-down type, Russian patt. 185.00

Perfume atomizer, Hawkes, overall intaglio cutting, marked DeVilbiss, 4½" h. 100.00

Perfume atomizer, Brilliant Period cutting, marked DeVilbiss, 6¼" h. 115.00

Perfume atomizer, Harvard patt., 2½" sq., 4" h., w/gold-washed atomizer top overall 8" h. 100.00

PITCHERS

Brilliant Period Champagne Pitcher

Buttermilk, Libbey signed, Brilliant Period cutting, 7½" h. 175.00

Champagne, Russian patt., applied angular notched handle, 12" h. ..1,250.00

Champagne, Cane patt. & other cutting, sterling silver rim, 12½" h. 350.00

Champagne, hobstars, fan & strawberry diamond, 24-point hobstar base, triple-notched handle, 12½" h. (ILLUS.) 350.00

Champagne, Fry signed, Brilliant Period cutting overall, 24-point star-cut base, triple-notched handle, scalloped & serrated rim, 13 5/8" h. 325.00

Cider, Hoare signed, Brilliant Period cutting, 5" base d., 7½" h. 185.00

Cocktail, Hawkes' block motif, silver rim 235.00

Milk, tankard, Dorflinger signed, hobstars & notched prim, 5" h. ... 125.00

Milk, Hawkes signed, overall 8-point hobstars, tiny Harvard patt. in diamond fields & fan, rayed base, serrated rim, 5½" w. across rim, 5" h. 190.00

Milk, Clark signed, Brilliant Period cutting, 8" h. 190.00

Tankard, Libbey signed, hobstars, fan & other cutting, star-cut base, notched handle, serrated rim, 7½" h. 225.00

Tankard, Cane patt., notched handle, 9½" h. 225.00
Tankard, vertical notched prism, rayed base, double-notched handle, sterling silver collar w/narrow "repousse" band, 10" h. 185.00
Tankard, Meriden Cut Glass Company's Alhambra (Greek Key) patt., wide sterling silver top & lip, 12½" h. 1,850.00
Tankard, Hawkes' Grecian patt., vesica, fan & Russian patt., 18" h. 7,000.00
Water, nailhead diamond, prism & flute, triple notched handle, salesman's sample, 2¼" h. 145.00
Water, Libbey signed, hobstars, cane & other cutting, double thumbprint handle, 5½" base d., 8¼" h. 250.00
Water, Hawkes signed, Queens patt., chain of hobstars & bull's eye, 8½" h. 1,075.00
Water, Fry signed, Brilliant Period cutting, 9½" h. 190.00
Water, panels of Harvard patt. & intaglio-cut sprays of florals & foliage, 9½" h. 150.00
Water, panels of hobstars, cane & cross-cut diamond, 9½" h. 350.00
Water, Fry signed, Brilliant Period cutting, 6" base d., 10" h. 185.00
Water, Hawkes signed, hobstars & other cutting, 10" h. 195.00

PLATES

Shell Pattern Plate

6½" d., Wheeler patt., cross-cut diamond, star, strawberry diamond & fan 85.00
7" d., Hawkes signed, Gladys patt. 125.00
7" d., Hawkes signed, Orpheus patt., fan, flashed star & hobstar 250.00
7" d., hobstars & other cutting, scalloped & serrated rim 50.00
7" d., Lotus patt. 135.00
7" d., Shell patt., notched prism radiants, hobstars & other cutting (ILLUS.) 135.00
7" d., Tuthill signed, Brilliant Period cutting 245.00
8½" d., advertising, "Libbey, This Trade Mark Cut on Every Piece" center bordered by chain of hobstars & other cutting, scalloped & serrated rim 1,675.00
10" d., Tuthill signed, Brilliant Period cutting 1,000.00
10 x 9¼", leaf-shaped, overall cross-cut diamond 225.00

PUNCH BOWLS & SETS

Silver-Mounted Punch Bowl

Clark's Prima Donna (Triple Square) patt. 2,100.00
Dorflinger's Colonial patt., matching base, 12" d., 9½" h., 2 pcs. 495.00
Hoare signed, Newport patt., scalloped rim, matching compote base, 12½" d., 13" h., 2 pcs. 1,500.00
Hobstars & fan, w/matching base, 10" d., 2 pcs. 595.00
Hobstars, cross-cut vesicas & other cutting, serrated rim, matching base, 12½" d., 12" h., 2 pcs. 775.00
Irises & foliage forming a serpentine design around pyriform bowl, silver everted brim w/relief flowers & scrolls, engraved w/a stylized monogram, ca. 1900, marked "Gorham," 17" d., 7½" h. (ILLUS.) 3,520.00
Maple City Glass Company's Temple patt., Arcadia-type pentagonal strawberry diamond lozenge, hobstars & other cutting, serrated rim, matching flared base, 12" d., 2 pcs. 850.00
Panels of graduated hobstars, hobnail & starred hobnail buttons, serrated rim, bell-shaped, matching flared base, 14½" d., 21" h., 2 pcs. 3,850.00
Vesicas of strawberry diamond & hobnail alternating w/panels of small & large hobstars, notched prism baluster-form standard, flaring scalloped & serrated rim, circular stepped base cut w/large hobstar & crosshatching, serrated rim, 11¾" d., 17½" h., 2 pcs. 2,200.00

Punch set: 14" d., 13" h. bowl, base & 12 cups; Fry signed, Frederick patt., flashed hobstar, crossed squares & fan, 14 pcs. 3,000.00

Punch set: bowl & seven cups; Libbey signed, Colonna patt., chain of hobstars, cross-hatched triangle, star, strawberry diamond & fan, 8 pcs. 540.00

ROSE BOWLS

Brilliant Period Rose Bowl

Bergen's Electric patt., chain of hobstars, fan & strawberry diamond, three-handled 135.00

Hawkes' Brazilian patt., fan, star & strawberry diamond, 6" d., 5" h. 350.00

Hawkes' Venetian patt., chain of hobstars, fan, star & strawberry diamond, 6" d., 5" h. 350.00

Hobstars & other cutting, 3" widest d. 85.00

Libbey signed, Colonna patt., chain of hobstars, cross-hatched triangle, star, strawberry diamond & fan, 7" widest d., 5½" h. 450.00

Meriden's Florence hobstar, footed 245.00

Notched prism & fan, 7" d., 6" h. (ILLUS.) 140.00

Russian patt., 6" d. 450.00

Straus' Americus patt., fan, hobstar, star & strawberry diamond, 5" d. 225.00

SALT & PEPPER SHAKERS

Hawkes signed, Brilliant Period cutting, sterling silver tops, pr. 50.00

Irregular notched prism, sterling silver tops, 3 7/8" h., pr. 36.00

Notched prism, sterling silver swirl-molded top, pr. 35.00

Starred hobnail & opposing fans, bulbous, sterling silver beaded top, 3½" h., pr. 36.00

SALT DIPS

Libbey signed, Brilliant Period cutting, pedestal base 30.00

Notched panel, square, set of 6 . . . . 35.00

Russian patt., banana boat shape w/turned-in sides, pr. 125.00

Russian patt. w/clear button, oval w/turned-up sides, 4 x 2" 110.00

Zipper patt., set of 6 . . . . 60.00

Cut Glass Salt Dips

Zipper patt. & diamond panels, set of 4 (ILLUS.) 50.00

SPOONERS

Arlington Pattern Spooner

Brilliant Period cutting, two-handled 120.00

Hobstars overall 175.00

Pinwheel & other cutting, two-handled 80.00

Unger Brothers' Arlington patt., 4½" h. (ILLUS.) 200.00

SYRUP PITCHERS & JUGS

Brilliant Period cutting, silver plate hinged lid 125.00

Vertical irregular band of notched prism, metal hinged lid & handle, 4" h. 58.00

Vertical notched prism, sterling silver hinged lid . . . . .110.00 to 125.00

TOOTHPICK HOLDERS

Brilliant Period cutting 125.00

Chain of hobstars, strawberry diamond & fan, pedestal base, rayed foot 135.00

Fluted diamonds . . . . .35.00 to 45.00

Hobstars overall, barrel-shaped 70.00

TRAYS

Cut Glass Bread Tray

Bread, Brilliant Period cutting, 11½ x 8", pr. 950.00
Bread, hobstars, ring of cane & strawberry diamond, serrated rim, 12 x 4½" (ILLUS.) 300.00
Bread, hobstars overall, 12 x 8" 400.00
Bread, intaglio-cut center, Harvard patt. sides, 13½ x 8½" 115.00
Bread, Libbey's Star & Feather patt., 12 x 7½" 275.00
Brilliant Period cutting, serrated rim, 17½ x 10" 1,100.00
Dorflinger's Marlboro patt., chain of hobstars, strawberry diamond & fan, 15½" l. 795.00
Dresser, Hawkes signed, Sheraton patt., engraved medallions against triple mitre-cut bands alternating w/strawberry diamond bands, 10 x 7" oval.............. 195.00
Hawkes signed, Venetian patt., chain of hobstars, star, strawberry diamond split vesicas & fan, 12" d...1,250.00
Hobstars, vesicas & fan, 12" d. 470.00
Hobstars & strawberry diamond, open handles, 13¼ x 8½" 600.00
Ice cream, Brilliant Period cutting, 11½ x 8" 175.00
Ice cream, Brilliant Period cutting, 14" oval 205.00
Intaglio-cut orange & foliage, 13" d. 475.00
Libbey signed, Brilliant Period cutting center, engraved edge, 12" d. 700.00
Libbey signed, Colonna patt., chain of hobstars, crosshatched triangle, star, strawberry diamond & fan, 10 x 7½" 375.00
Mt. Washington's Corinthian patt., 11½ x 8" oval 550.00
Sandwich, Tuthill signed, intaglio-cut grapes & vines, center handle w/intaglio-cut grape leaves, 10" d., 6" h. handle 425.00

TUMBLERS

Juice, Hawkes signed, Brunswick patt., chain of hobstars, zipper-type beading & flute, 3 7/8" h. 75.00
Juice, hobstars, cross-cut diamond & fan, 3½" h., set of 4 .... 160.00
Juice, Libbey signed, Brilliant Period cutting, set of 6 .... 175.00
Juice, Libbey's Harvard patt., cross-cut diamond, strawberry diamond & fan 40.00
Juice, pinwheel w/central hobstar, diamond point & fan, rayed base 20.00
Juice, pinwheel, hobstars, fan & mitre-cutting, flaring rim, 4" h.... 25.00
Juice, strawberry diamond & fan ... 15.00
Water, Hoare signed, Brilliant Period cutting overall, 24-point star-cut base, set of 4 .... 240.00
Water, Libbey signed, Brilliant Period cutting, set of 6 .... 265.00
Water, pinwheel, set of 9 .... 225.00
Water, starbursts & hobstars, set of 6 .... 175.00

VASES

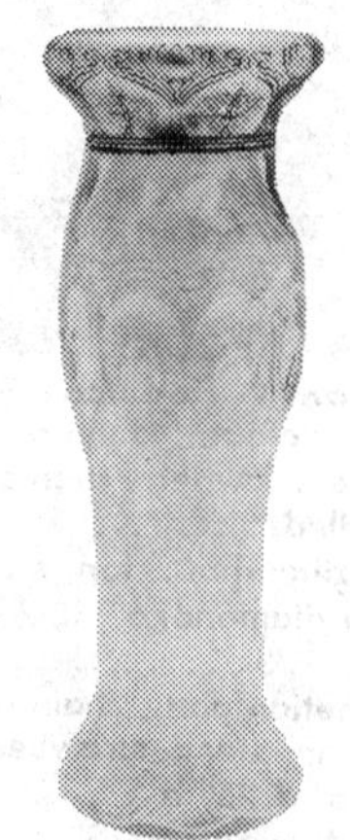

Silver-Mounted Cut Glass Vase

Amethyst cut to clear, grape clusters & leaves, footed, serrated rim, 3¾" base d. flaring to 4¾", 5¼" h. 345.00
Apple green cut to clear, floral sprays above ring of diamond & star-cut lozenges, baluster form, ca. 1900, 12" h. 800.00
Brilliant Period cutting, corset-shaped, scalloped & serrated rim, 12-point rayed base, 8" h. 100.00
Brilliant Period cutting, bud, sterling silver base, 8½" h............... 68.00
Bull's-eye, crosshatching, fan & mitre cutting, flared thumbprint rim, 7" d., 10" h................ 75.00
Clark signed, Carolyn patt., 12" h. .. 375.00
Clark signed, Harvard patt. alternating w/three panels of intaglio-cut flowers, 7½" d. top, 14½" h. 225.00
Clark signed, cane, bull's-eye, hobstars & other cutting, 8½" d., 20" h. 2,800.00
Cranberry cut to clear, cylindrical, full-blown roses w/buds, leaves & thorny branches, scalloped & serrated rim, 12" h. 395.00

Egginton's Lotus patt., chain of hobstars, flashed fan, St. Louis diamond, star, strawberry diamond & fan, 12" h. 395.00
Green cut to clear, vesicas & crosshatching, 5" h. 200.00
Green cut to clear, Libbey's Harvard patt., cross-cut diamond, fan & strawberry diamond, 12" h. 650.00
Harvard patt. & large hobstars, star-cut base, 12" h. 350.00
Hawkes signed, Brilliant Period cutting, 12" h. 225.00
Hawkes signed, Navarre patt., chain of hobstars, bull's-eye & other cutting, 16" h. 1,000.00
Hawkes signed, Queens patt., chain of hobstars & bull's-eye, lapidary-cut knob above base, pedestal foot w/hobstar, 18" h. 1,200.00
Hawkes signed, Gravic Iris, 20" h. 2,000.00
Hawkes' Easter patt., hobnail, flute & fan, trumpet-shaped, 16" h. 500.00
Hoare's Nassau patt., engraved flowers w/cane, hobstar, star & strawberry diamond motifs, 20" h. 1,600.00
Hobnail, large hobstars, strawberry diamond & fan, flattened bulbous form, panelled neck, scalloped rim, 14½" h. 2,090.00
Hobstars alternating w/crosshatching between pairs of fans, squat bulbous form, hobstar & fan base, panel-cut neck, scalloped rim, 9½" h. 1,540.00
Hobstar panels alternating w/fan cutting, baluster form, notched prism neck, scalloped & serrated rim above chain of hobstars, 12½" h. 385.00
Hobstar & sunburst motif, 14" h. 575.00
Hobstars, notched prism, strawberry diamond & other cutting, chalice form, lapidary-cut knob above cut foot, scalloped & serrated rim, 6" widest d., 14 1/8" h. 890.00
Hobstar motif & other cutting, trumpet-shaped, circular foot, scalloped rim, 15" h. 275.00
Notched prism, waisted cylinder, 12" h., pr. 60.00
Pinwheel, hobstar & other cutting, rayed base, serrated rim, 10" h. .. 150.00
Pitkin & Brooks signed, Derby patt., 19" h. 2,000.00
Ruby cut to clear, Libbey's Harvard patt., cross-cut diamond, fan & strawberry diamond, 12" h. 750.00
Russian & Pillar patt., Russian patt. w/star button & swirl, 12" h. 900.00
Stars & mitre cutting, footed, 5¾" d. flared rim, 16" h. 265.00
Stylized flowerheads w/vertical bands of hobnail & hobstars, waisted cylinder, two-handled, scalloped & serrated rim, 18" h. 1,430.00
Tuthill signed, intaglio-cut grapes, 12" h. 295.00
Vesicas of hobstars & strawberry diamond in spiraling panels, urn-shaped body, square base cut w/hobstars, panelled standard, flaring petal-form rim, 14" h. 605.00
Waterlily blossoms above a stylized waterline over stems ending at the spreading base, baluster form, flaring silver rim engraved w/waterlilies & lily pads, Tiffany & Company, New York, 1907-10, 11" h. (ILLUS.) 1,320.00

WATER SETS

Queens Pattern Water Set

Pitcher & three tumblers, Butterfly & Daisy patt., 4 pcs. ....245.00 to 265.00
Pitcher & three tumblers, pinwheels w/central hobstars, fan & other cutting, 10½" h. corset-shaped pitcher, 4 pcs. 195.00
Pitcher & four tumblers, Libbey signed, Brilliant Period cutting, 5 pcs. 495.00
Pitcher & six 3¾" h. tumblers, hobstars & crosshatching, 9" h. pitcher w/double bull's-eye handle, 7 pcs. 250.00
Pitcher & six tumblers, hobstars, vesicas, fan & fields of strawberry diamond, 9¼" h. pitcher w/applied double notched handle, rayed bases, 7 pcs. 325.00
Pitcher & six tumblers, pinwheel, hobstars, vesicas & fan, 10½" h. pitcher w/applied double notched handle & 24-point rayed base, 7 pcs. 270.00
Pitcher & nine tumblers, Hawkes' Queens patt., chain of hobstars, bull's-eye & fan, 10 pcs. (ILLUS. of part) 1,325.00

(End of Cut Glass Section)

CZECHOSLOVAKIAN

Iridescent Gold Czechoslovakian Vase

At the close of World War I, Czechoslovakia was declared an independent republic and immediately developed a large export industry. Czechoslovakian glass factories produced a wide variety of colored and hand-painted glasswares from about 1918 until 1939, when the country was occupied by Germany at the outset of World War II. Between the wars, fine quality blown glasswares were produced along with a deluge of cheaper, vividly colored spatterwares for the American market. Subsequent production was primarily limited to cut crystal or Bohemian-type etched wares for the American market. Although it was marked, much Czechoslovakian glass is mistaken for the work of Tiffany, Loetz, or other glass artisans it imitates. It is often misrepresented and overpriced.

Basket, cased, black exterior, bright orange interior, 10" $150.00

Book end, model of a bear standing, clear, 9" 35.00

Bowl, 12" d., 2" h., scalloped rim, iridescent deep blue, signed 75.00

Dish, cov., cased, blue mottled, 6½" d., 4" h. 48.00

Perfume bottle w/frosted floriform stopper, rosey amber w/overall etched design, 4¼" h. 60.00

Perfume bottle w/steeple-shaped stopper, clear w/etched design, 3" d., 6" h. 65.00

Pitcher, 8" h., square top, applied white opalescent handle, Hobnail patt., blue opalescent 65.00

Scent bottle w/enameled stopper, lay-down type, multicolored jewels 95.00

Vase, 5" h., applied clear rigaree, pink opalescent, signed 30.00

Vase, 7" h., Bohemian-type, Deer & Castle patt., ruby cut to clear 75.00

Vase, 7½" h., 9" w., fan-shaped, mottled yellow, multicolored spatter base 55.00

Vase, 8" h., low foot, Tiffany-type, iridescent gold w/blue highlights, signed (ILLUS.) 115.00

Vase, 10" h., 5" w., applied black rim, mottled pink & white w/green spatter 65.00

Vase, 10 1/8" h., orange w/silver peacock 75.00

D'ARGENTAL

D'Argental Cameo Lamp

Glass known by this name is so-called after its producer, who fashioned fine cameo pieces in France late last century.

Box w/lid, round, branch w/flowers & leaves decoration covers lid, band of matching leaves around center of bottom, 5¼" d., 4¼" h. $835.00

Cameo bowl-vase, carved navy blue to soft yellow scene w/rowboat moored at shore, hills & tree landscape against soft pink translucent frosted ground, 3½" d., 3½" h., signed 550.00

Cameo lamp, conical shade & baluster base in lemon yellow overlaid in medium & deep crimson & cut w/stylized foliate fiddleheads, the foot further carved w/scrolls & circles, gilt-bronze fittings, ca. 1920, signed, rim chips, 10¼" d., 20¼" h. (ILLUS.) 6,600.00

Cameo vase, 5" h., carved rocky shore w/lighthouse in distance, three colors, signed 675.00

Cameo vase, 7" h., carved brown pine cones & mushrooms against light amber ground, outer layer polished 950.00

Cameo vase, 9 5/8" h., 4 1/8" d., carved brown to rose brown scene w/trees, hills & lake against frosted gold ground, signed 895.00

Cameo vase, 11 5/8" h., 4 3/8" d., carved deep brown to rose brown to frosted scene w/tree landscape along coast w/two small boats on water, moon & clouds in sky, signed 995.00

DAUM NANCY

Daum Nancy Vase

This fine glass, much of it cameo, was made by Auguste and Antonin Daum, who founded a factory in 1875 in Nancy, France. Most of their cameo and enameled glass was made from the 1890's into the early 20th century.

Cameo atomizer, carved & enameled branches hanging w/brown pine cones against mottled frosted yellow to clear ground, signed, 2½" d., 8¼" h. . . $250.00

Cameo boudoir lamp, domical shade, baluster form base w/circular foot, top & base acid-etched, carved & enameled in The Rain Scene springtime landscape against pink & green mottled ground, 14" h. . . 14,300.00

Cameo bowl, 6" w., 2¾" h., carved barren forest scene w/snow-laden trees & snow-covered ground against gold ground, signed 700.00

Cameo bowl, 7½" d., 3" h., carved green scene w/trees reflecting on lake against orange ground, signed 1,245.00

Cameo bowl-vase, carved & enameled green & maroon trees & grass against frosted pink opalescent ground, signed, 5¾ x 4½" oval, 4¼" h. 650.00

Cameo lamp, carved winter scene, signed, 18" h. 5,000.00

Cameo perfume bottle, flared raised rim, globular body w/conforming stopper, acid-cut & wheel-engraved spring flowers & leaves highlighted w/gold tracery, matching bands of elaborate floral & geometric enameling around neck & stopper, all against a fiery opalescent yellow w/swirls of orange, green & white, signed "Daum Nancy" & cross of Lorraine, 4½" h. 1,540.00

Cameo salt dip, carved winter scene against yellow-orange ground, 2 x 1¼" oval, 1" h. 580.00

Cameo vase, 1 5/8" h., 1 x 2¼" flattened oval, carved & enameled barren forest scene w/snow-laden trees & snow-covered ground against mottled gold frosted ground, signed 450.00

Cameo vase, 3½" h., 3¼" d., rose bowl shape, carved & enameled two white swans swimming on lake & white birch trees w/green trim against ice blue frosted mottled ground, signed 1,295.00

Cameo vase, 4" h., 2 1/8 x 4 3/8" flattened oval, carved & enameled leafy green forest tree landscape, signed 750.00

Cameo vase, 5" h., rounded rectangle w/turn-in rim, carved orange & dark green poppies against hammered opalescent ground, signed (ILLUS.) 3,740.00

Cameo vase, 5 7/8" h., slender cylinder w/bulbous base & everted rim, carved tomato red & olive green w/brown sprays of small flowers against striated grey & yellow ground, ca. 1900, signed .. 385.00

Cameo vase, 7" h., 3" d., crescent cut top, carved & enameled blue cornflowers & green leaves against mottled translucent shell pink to green & blue frosted ground, signed 1,150.00

Cameo vase, 8½" h., cylindrical, carved spring green splashed w/yellow & emerald green arrowroot blossoms & leafage growing in a pond against mottled mint green to violet ground, applied wheel-carved body of a dragonfly, its wings carved in cameo, ca. 1900, signed 6,875.00

Cameo vase, 10" h., flattened globular form w/tapered neck & elliptical rim, carved & enameled snowy Dutch landscape w/birch trees in foreground & town w/windmills & church spire in background, early 20th c., signed 800.00

Cameo vase, 15" h., bulbous, carved

Daum Nancy Vase with Stylized Flowers
seafoam green stylized bellflowers, berries & leafage against clear mottled w/grey & pale ochre ground, ca. 1925, signed (ILLUS.) 4,400.00

Cameo vase, 19 3/8" h., flaring cylinder w/incurvate rim & spreading circular pad foot, carved deep brown scene w/boats at sail on a lake against mottled light lemon yellow & burnt orange ground, ca. 1915, signed 1,100.00

Cameo vase, 23¼" h., attenuated baluster form, carved burnt orange & brown undulating trumpet blossoms & leaves against mottled orange & dusty rose ground, ca. 1900, signed 1,045.00

Cologne bottle w/ball finial stopper w/fluted band fitting into everted circular neck, rectangular, stylized pineapple decoration on acid roughened ground, early 20th c., signed, 8½" h.................. 165.00

Powder jar, domed circular mottled purple-blue lid on square, slightly bulbous mottled jar, early 20th c., signed, 6" w., 3½" h. 522.50

Vase, 8" h., enameled black bird on branch against frosty white ground, signed.................. 350.00

Vase, 10" h., globular w/circular flared neck, squared Greek form handles, orange & red spatter w/foil inclusions, signed 357.50

Vase, 10½" h., 8" widest d., urn-shaped, Art Deco style, cranberry internally decorated in designs going to deep purple at the bottom & w/gold foil inclusions throughout, signed 1,250.00

Vase, 13" h., outward tapering cylinder, foamy light pink overlaid w/clear invested w/scattered fragments of light grape & turquoise, vertically ribbed iron frame w/panels of scrollwork, ca. 1925, unsigned 522.50

DE LATTE

De Latte Cameo Vase

This ware, chiefly opaque and cameo glass, was made by Andre de Latte in Nancy, France, from 1921. His firm also made light fixtures, but it is chiefly his cameo glass that is now sought.

Bottle w/matching stopper, enameled blue diamond & circle design w/pearl-like dots within window pane divisions on tan ground, signed, 16" h. $950.00

Cameo atomizer, carved dark brown acorns & leaves against peach ground, signed, 6¾" h. 375.00

Cameo sweetmeat jar, carved brown ferns & mushrooms against pale orange ground, silver plate rim, lid & handle, 4¼" d., 5" h. to top of handle 520.00

Cameo vase, 7½" h., bulbous, carved & polished burgundy leaves & florals against pumpkin orange ground 450.00

Cameo vase, 9¼" h., 5 3/8" d., maroon pedestal foot, eared handles, carved maroon to rose river scene w/trees along bank against white mottled satin finish ground w/traces of pink, signed 975.00

Cameo vase, 10" h, pear-shaped, sienna foot, carved light & dark brown thistle branches against mottled cream & orange ground, signed 995.00

Cameo vase, 13¼" h., carved purple sprays of magnolia blossoms & foliage against mottled grey & maroon ground, signed (ILLUS.) 1,400.00

DEPRESSION GLASS

The phrase "Depression Glass" is used by collectors to denote a specific kind of transparent glass produced primarily as tablewares, in crystal, amber, blue, green, pink, milky-white, etc., during the late 1920's and 1930's when this country was in the midst of a financial depression. Made to sell inexpensively, it was turned out by such producers as Jeannette, Hocking, Westmoreland, Indiana and other glass companies. We compile prices on all the major Depression Glass patterns. Collectors should consult Depression Glass references for information on those patterns and pieces which have been reproduced.

ADAM (Process-etched)

Adam Candy Jar

Ashtray, clear, 4½" d. $6.50
Ashtray, green, 4½" d. 15.00
Ashtray, pink, 4½" d. 18.50
Bowl, nappy, 4¾" sq., green or pink 9.00
Bowl, nappy, 5¾" sq., green 29.50
Bowl, nappy, 5¾" sq., pink 22.00
Bowl, nappy, 7¾" sq., green 13.00
Bowl, nappy, 7¾" sq., pink 15.50
Bowl, cov. vegetable, 9" sq., green 55.00
Bowl, cov. vegetable, 9" sq., pink .. 35.00
Bowl, 9" sq., green 27.50
Bowl, 9" sq., pink 17.50
Bowl, 10" oval vegetable, green 16.00
Bowl, 10" oval vegetable, pink 14.00
Butter dish, cov., green 205.00
Butter dish, cov., pink 63.00
Cake plate, green, 10" sq. 15.00
Cake plate, pink, 10" sq. 11.50
Candlesticks, green, 4" h., pr. 70.00
Candlesticks, pink, 4" h., pr. 52.00
Candy jar, cov., green 72.00
Candy jar, cov., pink (ILLUS.) 51.50
Coaster, clear 15.00
Coaster, green 12.00
Coaster, pink 13.50
Creamer & cov. sugar bowl, green, pr. 43.00
Creamer & cov. sugar bowl, pink, pr. 32.50
Creamer & open sugar bowl, green, pr. 23.00
Creamer & open sugar bowl, pink, pr. 18.50
Cup & saucer, green or pink 20.00
Pitcher, 8" h., 32 oz., cone-shaped, clear 34.50
Pitcher, 8" h., 32 oz., cone-shaped, green 29.00
Pitcher, 8" h., 32 oz., cone-shaped, pink 23.00
Plate, sherbet, 6" sq., green or pink 3.50
Plate, salad, 7¾" sq., green 7.00
Plate, salad, 7¾" sq., pink 8.00
Plate, salad, round, pink 55.00
Plate, dinner, 9" sq., green 13.00
Plate, dinner, 9" sq., pink 15.00
Plate, grill, 9" sq., green 11.50
Plate, grill, 9" sq., pink 14.50
Platter, 12" l., green 12.50
Platter, 12" l., pink 10.50
Relish, 2-part, green or pink, 8" oblong 10.00
Salt & pepper shakers, footed, green, 4" h., pr. 67.00
Salt & pepper shakers, footed, pink, 4" h., pr. 42.00
Sherbet, green 25.00
Sherbet, pink 15.50
Tumbler, cone-shaped, green, 4½" h., 7 oz. 13.00
Tumbler, cone-shaped, pink, 4½" h., 7 oz. 15.50
Tumbler, cone-shaped, green, 5½" h., 9 oz. 29.00
Tumbler, cone-shaped, pink, 5½" h., 9 oz. 45.00
Vase, 7½" h., green 32.50
Vase, 7½" h., pink 165.00
Water set: pitcher & 4 tumblers; green, 5 pcs. 79.50

AMERICAN SWEETHEART (Process-etched)

Berry set: 9" bowl & 6 sauce dishes; Cremax, 7 pcs. 50.00
Bowl, berry, 3½" d., pink 24.00
Bowl, cream soup, 4½" d., Monax .. 43.00
Bowl, cream soup, 4½" d., pink 25.50
Bowl, cereal, 6" d., Cremax 6.00
Bowl, cereal, 6" d., Monax 9.50
Bowl, cereal, 6" d., Monax "smoke" w/black edge 25.00
Bowl, cereal, 6" d., pink 8.00
Bowl, 9" d., Cremax 29.00
Bowl, 9" d., Monax 34.50

Bowl, 9" d., pink 18.00
Bowl, soup w/flange rim, 10" d., Monax 34.00
Bowl, soup w/flange rim, 10" d., pink 26.50
Bowl, 11" oval vegetable, Monax ... 40.00
Bowl, 11" oval vegetable, pink 29.50
Console bowl, Monax, 18" d. 305.00
Console bowl, ritz blue, 18" d. 850.00
Creamer, Monax 5.50
Creamer, pink 8.50
Creamer, ritz blue 90.00
Cup & saucer, Monax 9.00
Cup & saucer, pink 10.50
Cup & saucer, ritz blue 121.00
Cup & saucer, ruby red 110.00
Lamp shade, Monax 310.00
Pitcher, 7½" h., 60 oz., jug-type, pink 357.00
Pitcher, 8" h., 80 oz., pink 325.00
Plate, bread & butter, 6" d., Monax 3.00
Plate, bread & butter, 6" d., pink ... 2.00
Plate, salad, 8" d., Monax 5.00
Plate, salad, 8" d., pink 6.00
Plate, salad, 8" d., ruby red 56.00
Plate, luncheon, 9" d., Monax 6.50
Plate, dinner, 10" d., Monax 13.00
Plate, dinner, 10" d., pink 14.50
Plate, chop, 11" d., Monax 10.00
Plate, salver, 12" d., Monax 10.00

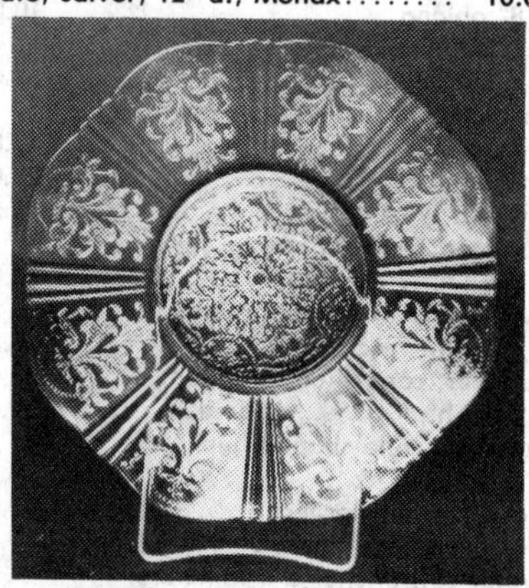

American Sweetheart Plate

Plate, salver, 12" d., pink (ILLUS.) .. 9.00
Plate, salver, 12" d., ritz blue or ruby red 155.00
Plate, 15½" d., w/center handle, Monax 163.50
Plate, 15½" d., w/center handle, ruby red 242.00
Platter, 13" oval, Monax 33.50
Platter, 13" oval, pink 17.50
Salt & pepper shakers, Monax, pr. .. 217.50
Salt & pepper shakers, pink, pr. 286.00
Sherbet, low foot, Monax, 4¼" h. ... 13.00
Sherbet, low foot, pink, 4¼" h. 9.00
Sherbet, ice cream in metal holder, clear 3.00
Sugar bowl, cov., Monax 162.00
Sugar bowl, open, Monax 4.50
Sugar bowl, open, pink 7.50
Sugar bowl, open, ruby red 64.00
Tidbit server, 3-tier, Monax 175.00
Tidbit server, 3-tier, ruby red 545.00
Tumbler, pink, 3½" h., 5 oz. 35.00
Tumbler, pink, 4" h., 9 oz. 36.00
Tumbler, pink, 4½" h., 10 oz. 46.00

BLOCK or Block Optic (Press-mold)

Block Sherbet

Bowl, berry, 4¼" d., green 4.50
Bowl, cereal, 5¼" d., green 7.50
Bowl, cereal, 5¼" d., pink 5.50
Bowl, salad, 7" d., green 15.00
Bowl, salad, 7" d., pink 11.00
Bowl, large berry, 8½" d., green ... 11.50
Butter dish, cov., oblong, green 34.50
Butter dish, cov., round, green 32.00
Candlesticks, green, pr. 50.00
Candlesticks, pink, pr. 31.50
Candy jar, cov., green, 2¼" h. 28.50
Candy jar, cov., pink, 2¼" h. 25.00
Candy jar, cov., yellow, 2¼" h. 34.00
Candy jar, cov., clear, 6¼" h. 19.50
Candy jar, cov., green, 6¼" h. 35.50
Candy jar, cov., pink, 6¼" h. 46.50
Compote, 4" d., cone-shaped, green 16.50
Creamer, green or yellow 8.00
Creamer, pink 7.00
Cup & saucer, clear 4.00
Cup & saucer, green 9.00
Cup & saucer, pink or yellow 7.50
Goblet, wine, clear, 4" h., 2 oz. 8.00
Goblet, wine, green or pink, 4" h., 2 oz. 17.50
Goblet, clear, 6" h., 9 oz. 5.50
Goblet, green, 6" h., 9 oz. 15.00
Goblet, pink, 6" h., 9 oz. 13.00
Goblet, clear, 7¼" h., 9 oz. 7.50
Goblet, green, 7¼" h., 9 oz. 15.50
Goblet, pink, 7¼" h., 9 oz. 10.50
Goblet, yellow, 7¼" h., 9 oz. 16.50
Ice tub, clear 13.00

Ice tub, green 25.00
Ice tub, pink 54.00
Mug (or cup), green 26.00
Pitcher, 7 5/8" h., 68 oz., green 46.00
Pitcher, 8" h., 80 oz., clear 14.00
Pitcher, 8" h., 80 oz., green or pink 37.00
Pitcher, 8½" h., 54 oz., clear 16.00
Pitcher, 8½" h., 54 oz., green 25.00
Pitcher, 8½" h., 54 oz., pink 29.00
Plate, 6" d., clear or pink 1.00
Plate, 6" d., green or yellow 1.50
Plate, luncheon, 8" d., clear, green or pink 2.50
Plate, luncheon, 8" d., yellow 3.00
Plate, dinner, 9" d., clear 4.00
Plate, dinner, 9" d., green 12.00
Plate, dinner, 9" d., yellow 20.00
Plate, grill, 9" d., clear 4.50
Plate, grill, 9" d., green 10.00
Plate, sandwich, 10" d., clear 7.00
Plate, sandwich, 10" d., green 13.00
Plate, sandwich, 10" d., pink 12.00
Salt & pepper shakers, squat, green, pr. 33.00
Salt & pepper shakers, footed, clear, pr. 25.00
Salt & pepper shakers, footed, green, pr. 23.50
Salt & pepper shakers, footed, pink, pr. 43.00
Sandwich server w/center handle, green 32.50
Sandwich server w/center handle, pink 25.50
Sherbet, cone-shaped, footed, green (ILLUS.) 3.00
Sherbet, stemmed, clear, 3¼" h. 2.50
Sherbet, stemmed, green, 3¼" h. 3.50
Sherbet, stemmed, pink or yellow, 3¼" h. 4.50
Sherbet, stemmed, clear, 5" h. 5.00
Sherbet, stemmed, green or yellow, 5" h. 9.50
Sherbet, stemmed, pink, 5" h. 8.00
Sugar bowl, clear 4.00
Sugar bowl, green or pink 7.00
Sugar bowl, yellow 8.50
Tumbler, whiskey, clear, 2½" h. 5.50
Tumbler, whiskey, green, 2½" h. 17.00
Tumbler, whiskey, pink, 2½" h. 25.00
Tumbler, juice, clear, 3" h., 5 oz. 5.50
Tumbler, juice, green or pink, 3" h., 5 oz. 9.50
Tumbler, juice, footed, green, 4" h., 5 oz. 12.50
Tumbler, juice, footed, pink, 4" h., 5 oz. 10.00
Tumbler, clear, 9 oz. 4.50
Tumbler, green, 9 oz. 11.00
Tumbler, pink, 9 oz. 8.00
Tumbler, footed, clear, 9 oz. 6.50
Tumbler, footed, green or yellow, 9 oz. 11.50
Tumbler, footed, pink, 9 oz. 9.50
Tumbler, iced tea, clear, 10 oz. 5.50
Tumbler, iced tea, green, 10 oz. 12.00
Tumbler, iced tea, pink, 10 oz. 8.50
Tumbler, iced tea, footed, green or pink, 6" h., 10 oz. 14.00
Tumbler, iced tea, footed, yellow, 6" h., 10 oz. 15.00
Tumbler, green, 14 oz. 18.50
Tumble-up: bottle & 3" h. tumbler; green, set 43.50
Water set: pitcher & 6 footed tumblers; green, 7 pcs. 125.00

BUBBLE (Press-mold)

Bubble Creamer & Sugar Bowl

Berry set: master bowl & 8 sauce dishes; clear, 9 pcs. 17.50
Bowl, 4" d., blue 8.50
Bowl, 4" d., clear 2.00
Bowl, 4" d., pink 15.00
Bowl, fruit, 4½" d., blue or green 5.50
Bowl, fruit, 4½" d., clear or milk white 2.00
Bowl, fruit, 4½" d., ruby red 4.00
Bowl, cereal, 5¼" d., blue 6.00
Bowl, cereal, 5¼" d., clear 3.00
Bowl, cereal, 5¼" d., green 5.00
Bowl, soup, 7¾" d., blue 7.00
Bowl, soup, 7¾" d., clear 5.00
Bowl, 8 3/8" d., blue 8.00
Bowl, 8 3/8" d., clear or milk white 4.00
Bowl, 8 3/8" d., green 10.00
Bowl, 9" d., flanged, milk white 30.00
Candlesticks, clear, pr. 9.00
Creamer, blue 18.50
Creamer, clear 5.50
Creamer, green (ILLUS. right) 6.00
Creamer, milk white 1.75
Cup & saucer, blue, green or pink 4.00
Cup & saucer, clear 2.50
Cup & saucer, ruby red 6.50
Lamp, clear 35.00
Pitcher w/ice lip, 64 oz., clear 41.00
Pitcher w/ice lip, 64 oz., ruby red 32.00
Plate, bread & butter, 6¾" d., blue or clear 1.50
Plate, bread & butter, 6¾" d., green 2.50
Plate, dinner, 9¼" d., blue 4.00
Plate, dinner, 9¼" d., clear 2.50
Plate, dinner, 9¼" d., green 5.00
Plate, dinner, 9¼" d., ruby red 6.00

Plate, grill, 9¼" d., blue 8.50
Plate, grill, 9¼" d., clear 4.00
Platter, 12" oval, blue 7.50
Platter, 12" oval, clear 12.50
Sugar bowl, open, blue 13.50
Sugar bowl, open, clear 5.00
Sugar bowl, open, green (ILLUS. left) 6.00
Sugar bowl, open, milk white 2.00
Tidbit server, ruby red 27.00
Tumbler, juice, clear or ruby red, 6 oz. 5.50
Tumbler, water, clear or ruby red, 9 oz. 5.00
Tumbler, iced tea, clear, 12 oz. 5.50
Tumbler, iced tea, ruby red, 12 oz. 7.00
Tumbler, lemonade, clear or ruby red, 16 oz. 11.50
Water set: pitcher & 8 tumblers; ruby red, 9 pcs. 70.00

CAMEO or Ballerina or Dancing Girl (Process-etched)

Cameo Cup & Saucer

Bowl, cream soup, 4¾" d., green 49.00
Bowl, cereal, 5½" d., clear 6.50
Bowl, cereal, 5½" d., green 18.50
Bowl, cereal, 5½" d., yellow 22.00
Bowl, salad, 7" d., green 26.50
Bowl, large berry, 8¼" d., green 21.00
Bowl, soup w/flange rim, 9" d., green 28.50
Bowl, 10" oval vegetable, green 16.50
Bowl, 10" oval vegetable, yellow 31.50
Butter dish, cov., green 134.00
Cake plate, footed, green, 10" d. 13.00
Cake plate, handled, green, 10½" d. 55.00
Candlesticks, green, 4" h., pr. 68.00
Candy jar, cov., green, 4" h. 38.50
Candy jar, cov., yellow, 4" h. 55.00
Candy jar, cov., green, 6½" h. 79.00
Compote, mayonnaise, 4" h., cone-shaped, green 19.00
Console bowl, 3-footed, green, 11" d. 39.50
Console bowl, 3-footed, pink, 11" d. 20.50
Console bowl, 3-footed, yellow, 11" d. 52.50
Cookie jar, cov., green 34.00
Creamer, green, 3" h. 15.00
Creamer, yellow, 3" h. 10.50
Creamer, green, 4" h. 15.00
Creamer, pink, 4" h. 62.50
Cup & saucer, green 12.00
Cup & saucer, pink or yellow 7.50
Cup & saucer w/ring, green (ILLUS.) 95.00
Domino tray, green, 7" d. 87.00
Domino tray, pink, 7" d. 185.00
Goblet, wine, green, 4" h. 47.00
Goblet, green, 6" h. 37.50
Goblet, pink, 6" h. 130.00
Ice bowl, green, 3½" h. 112.50
Ice bowl, pink, 3½" h. 425.00
Jar, cov., closed handles, green, 2" 102.00
Juice set: pitcher & 6 tumblers; green, 7 pcs. 162.50
Pitcher, syrup or milk, 5¾" h., 20 oz., green 130.00
Pitcher, juice, 6" h., 36 oz., green 40.50
Pitcher, 8½" h., 56 oz., jug-type, clear or green 35.00
Plate, sherbet, 6" d., clear, green or yellow 2.00
Plate, 7" d., clear 3.50
Plate, luncheon, 8" d., green or yellow 6.50
Plate, luncheon, 8" d., pink 20.00
Plate, salad, 8½" sq., green 26.00
Plate, dinner, 9½" d., green 11.50
Plate, dinner, 9½" d., pink 31.00
Plate, dinner, 9½" d., yellow 6.00
Plate, sandwich, 10" d., green 9.00
Plate, sandwich, 10" d., pink 29.50
Plate, grill, 10½" d., closed handles, green 39.50
Plate, grill, 10½" d., closed handles, yellow 5.50
Plate, grill, 10½" d., green or yellow 6.00
Plate, 11½" d., closed handles, green 8.00
Platter, 10½" oval, green 12.50
Platter, 10½" oval, yellow 34.50
Platter, 12", closed handles, green 13.00
Platter, 12", closed handles, yellow 25.00
Relish, footed, 3-part, green, 7½" 18.00
Salt & pepper shakers, green, pr. 50.00
Sherbet, green, 3" 9.50
Sherbet, pink, 3" 26.00
Sherbet, yellow, 3" 20.00
Sherbet, thin, high stem, green, 4 7/8" h. 22.50
Sherbet, thin, high stem, yellow, 4 7/8" h. 27.00
Sugar bowl, open, green or yellow, 3" h. 9.00
Sugar bowl, open, green, 4" h. 14.50

Sugar bowl, open, pink, 4" h. 50.00
Tumbler, juice, footed, green, 3 oz. 41.50
Tumbler, juice, green, 3¾" h., 5 oz. 18.50
Tumbler, juice, footed, green, 5 oz. 42.00
Tumbler, juice, footed, pink, 5 oz. ... 45.00
Tumbler, clear, 4" h., 9 oz. 8.00
Tumbler, green, 4" h., 9 oz. 17.00
Tumbler, pink, 4" h., 9 oz. 55.00
Tumbler, footed, green, 5" h., 9 oz. 18.00
Tumbler, footed, pink, 5" h., 9 oz. ... 45.00
Tumbler, footed, yellow, 5" h., 9 oz. 11.00
Tumbler, green, 4¾" h., 10 oz. 19.50
Tumbler, green, 5" h., 11 oz. 18.50
Tumbler, yellow, 5" h., 11 oz. 49.50
Tumbler, footed, green, 6" h., 11 oz. 43.50
Tumbler, green, 5¼" h., 14 oz. 36.00
Vase, 5¾" h., green 100.00
Vase, 8½" h., green 17.00
Water bottle w/stopper, green, 10" h. 87.00
Water bottle, dark green "White House Vinegar" base, 8½" h. 15.50
Water set: pitcher & 6 tumblers; green, 7 pcs. 200.00

CHERRY BLOSSOM (Process-etched)

Cherry Blossom Mug

Berry set: master bowl & 6 sauce dishes; Delfite, 7 pcs. 84.00
Berry set: master bowl & 7 sauce dishes; green, 8 pcs. 75.00
Bowl, berry, 4¾" d., Delfite 9.50
Bowl, berry, 4¾" d., green or pink 10.00
Bowl, cereal, 5¾" d., green 25.00
Bowl, cereal, 5¾" d., pink 19.00
Bowl, soup, 7¾" d., green 36.50
Bowl, soup, 7¾" d., pink 37.50
Bowl, berry, 8½" d., Delfite 35.50
Bowl, berry, 8½" d., green 22.50
Bowl, berry, 8½" d., pink 18.00
Bowl, 9" d., handled, clear 15.00
Bowl, 9" d., handled, Delfite 13.00
Bowl, 9" d., handled, green 19.00
Bowl, 9" d., handled, pink 22.00
Bowl, 9" oval vegetable, green 21.50
Bowl, 9" oval vegetable, pink 19.00
Bowl, fruit, 10½" d., 3-footed, green 42.50
Bowl, fruit, 10½" d., 3-footed, pink 36.50
Butter dish, cov., green 70.00
Butter dish, cov., pink 56.00
Cake plate, 3-footed, green, 10¼" d. 16.50
Cake plate, 3-footed, pink, 10¼" d. 20.00
Coaster, green 9.00
Coaster, pink 11.00
Creamer & cov. sugar bowl, green, pr. 30.50
Creamer & cov. sugar bowl, pink, pr. 27.00
Creamer & open sugar bowl, Delfite, pr. 29.00
Creamer & open sugar bowl, green, pr. 18.00
Creamer & open sugar bowl, pink, pr. 20.00
Cup & saucer, Delfite 15.50
Cup & saucer, green 17.00
Cup & saucer, pink 14.50
Mug, green, 8 oz. (ILLUS.) 158.00
Mug, pink, 8 oz. 158.00
Pitcher, 6½" h., 36 oz., jug-type, overall patt., green 34.00
Pitcher, 6½" h., 36 oz., jug-type, overall patt., pink 26.00
Pitcher, 8" h., 36 oz., cone-shaped, patt. top, Delfite 69.00
Pitcher, 8" h., 36 oz., cone-shaped, patt. top, green 32.50
Pitcher, 8" h., 36 oz., cone-shaped, patt. top, pink 37.00
Pitcher, 8" h., 42 oz., straight side, patt. top, green 34.00
Pitcher, 8" h., 42 oz., straight side, patt. top, pink 31.00
Plate, sherbet, 6" d., Delfite 7.00
Plate, sherbet, 6" d., green or pink 4.00
Plate, salad, 7" d., green 13.00
Plate, salad, 7" d., pink 11.50
Plate, dinner, 9" d., Delfite or pink 11.00
Plate, dinner, 9" d., green 14.50
Plate, grill, 9" d., green 17.00
Plate, grill, 9" d., pink 15.00
Platter, 11" oval, Delfite 34.00
Platter, 11" oval, green 23.00
Platter, 11" oval, pink 20.00
Platter, 13" oval, green 32.00
Platter, 13" oval, pink 30.50
Platter, 13" oval, divided, green 34.50
Platter, 13" oval, divided, pink 26.00
Salt & pepper shakers, green, pr. ... 950.00

Sandwich tray, handled, Delfite, 10½" d. 14.00
Sandwich tray, handled, green, 10½" d. 15.50
Sandwich tray, handled, pink, 10½" d. 12.50
Sherbet, Delfite 11.00
Sherbet, green 12.00
Sherbet, pink 10.00
Tumbler, juice, footed, overall patt., Delfite, 3½" h., 4 oz. 12.00
Tumbler, juice, footed, overall patt., green, 3½" h., 4 oz. 13.00
Tumbler, juice, footed, overall patt., pink, 3½" h., 4 oz. 10.50
Tumbler, patt. top, green, 3½" h., 4 oz. 15.00
Tumbler, patt. top, pink, 3½" h., 4 oz. 10.00
Tumbler, patt. top, green, 4" h., 9 oz. 16.00
Tumbler, patt. top, pink, 4" h., 9 oz. 12.50
Tumbler, footed, overall patt., Delfite, 4½" h., 9 oz. 13.50
Tumbler, footed, overall patt., green, 4½" h., 9 oz. 26.00
Tumbler, footed, overall patt., pink, 4½" h., 9 oz. 21.00
Tumbler, patt. top, green, 5" h., 12 oz. 48.00
Tumbler, patt. top, pink, 5" h., 12 oz. 37.50
Water set: pitcher & 6 tumblers; Delfite, 7 pcs. 157.50
Water set: pitcher & 6 tumblers; pink, 7 pcs. 120.00

JUNIOR SET:
Creamer, Delfite 25.00
Creamer, pink 22.50
Cup & saucer, Delfite 26.50
Cup & saucer, pink 22.00
Plate, 6" d., Delfite 7.00
Plate, 6" d., pink 6.00
Sugar bowl, Delfite 24.50
Sugar bowl, pink 23.00
14 pc. set, Delfite 188.50
14 pc. set, pink 194.00

CLOVERLEAF (Process-etched)

Ashtray w/match holder in center, black, 4" d. 51.00
Ashtray w/match holder in center, black, 5¾" d. 71.00
Bowl, dessert, 4" d., green 11.00
Bowl, dessert, 4" d., pink 8.00
Bowl, dessert, 4" d., yellow 18.00
Bowl, cereal, 5" d., green 14.00
Bowl, cereal, 5" d., yellow 18.00
Bowl, 7" d., green 24.50
Bowl, 7" d., yellow 35.50
Bowl, 8" d., green 42.00
Candy dish, cov., green 36.50
Candy dish, cov., yellow 82.00
Creamer, black 10.00
Creamer, green 6.50
Creamer, yellow 9.00
Cup & saucer, black 13.00
Cup & saucer, clear 5.00
Cup & saucer, green 7.00
Cup & saucer, pink 6.00
Cup & saucer, yellow 13.00
Plate, sherbet, 6" d., black 24.50
Plate, sherbet, 6" d., green 3.00
Plate, sherbet, 6" d., yellow 4.50
Plate, luncheon, 8" d., black 11.00
Plate, luncheon, 8" d., clear 3.50
Plate, luncheon, 8" d., green or pink 4.50
Plate, luncheon, 8" d., yellow 8.00
Plate, grill, 10" d., green 16.00
Plate, grill, 10" d., yellow 12.50
Salt & pepper shakers, black, pr. 61.00
Salt & pepper shakers, green, pr. 22.00
Salt & pepper shakers, yellow, pr. 77.00
Sherbet, footed, black, 3" 14.00
Sherbet, footed, clear, green or pink, 3" 4.00
Sherbet, footed, yellow, 3" 8.00
Sugar bowl, open, footed, black or yellow, 3 5/8" 10.00

Cloverleaf Sugar Bowl

Sugar bowl, open, footed, green, 3 5/8" (ILLUS.) 6.50
Tumbler, green, 4" h., 9 oz. 25.00
Tumbler, flared, green, 3¾" h., 10 oz. 25.50
Tumbler, flared, pink, 3¾" h., 10 oz. 15.00
Tumbler, footed, green, 5¾" h., 10 oz. 15.50
Tumbler, footed, yellow, 5¾" h., 10 oz. 18.00

COLONIAL or Knife & Fork (Press-mold)

Bowl, berry, 4" d., clear 4.00
Bowl, berry, 4" d., green 7.50
Bowl, berry, 4" d., pink 19.50
Bowl, cream soup, 4½" d., green 32.00
Bowl, cream soup, 4½" d., pink 28.00

Bowl, nappy, 4½" d., clear 5.50
Bowl, nappy, 4½" d., green 7.50
Bowl, nappy, 4½" d., pink 6.00
Bowl, nappy, 5½" d., pink 31.00
Bowl, soup, 7" d., clear 13.50
Bowl, soup, 7" d., green 33.00
Bowl, soup, 7" d., pink 32.00
Bowl, 9" d., green 16.50
Bowl, 9" d., pink 13.50
Bowl, 10" oval vegetable, clear 12.00
Bowl, 10" oval vegetable, green 19.00
Bowl, 10" oval vegetable, pink 15.00
Butter dish, cov., clear 22.50
Butter dish, cov., green 42.00
Butter dish, cov., pink 250.00
Celery or spooner, clear 35.50
Celery or spooner, green 82.00
Celery or spooner, pink 88.00
Creamer, clear 6.50
Creamer, green 11.00
Creamer, pink 18.00
Cup & saucer, clear 7.00

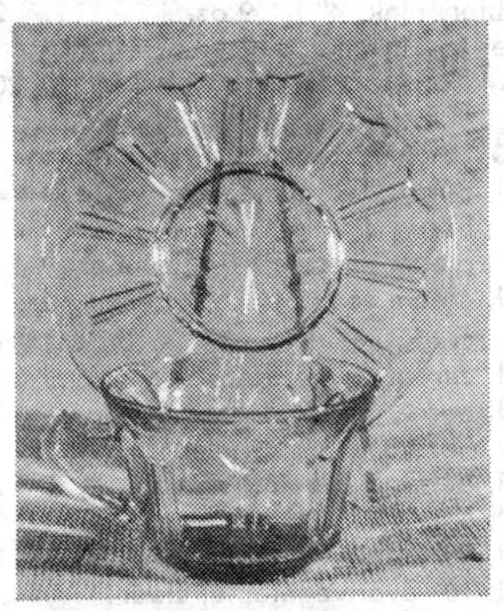

Colonial Cup & Saucer

Cup & saucer, green (ILLUS.) 10.50
Cup & saucer, milk white 12.00
Cup & saucer, pink 8.50
Goblet, cordial, clear, 3¾" h., 1 oz. 10.00
Goblet, cordial, green, 3¾" h., 1 oz. 21.00
Goblet, cordial, pink, 3¾" h., 1 oz. 15.50
Goblet, wine, clear, 4½" h., 2½ oz. 6.50
Goblet, wine, green, 4½" h., 2½ oz. 18.50
Goblet, cocktail, clear, 4" h., 3 oz. 7.00
Goblet, cocktail, green, 4" h., 3 oz. 16.50
Goblet, claret, clear, 5" h., 4 oz. . . . 8.00
Goblet, claret, green, 5" h., 4 oz. . . 18.00
Goblet, clear, 5¾" h., 8½ oz. 10.00
Goblet, green, 5¾" h., 8½ oz. 20.50
Goblet, pink, 5¾" h., 8½ oz. 16.50
Pitcher, 7" h., 54 oz., clear 18.00
Pitcher, 7" h., 54 oz., green 32.50
Pitcher, 7" h., 54 oz., pink 30.50
Pitcher, 7½" h., 67 oz., clear 21.50
Pitcher, 7½" h., 67 oz., green 45.00
Pitcher, 7½" h., 67 oz., pink 36.00
Plate, sherbet, 6½" d., clear 1.50
Plate, sherbet, 6½" d., green or pink 3.00
Plate, luncheon, 8½" d., clear 3.00
Plate, luncheon, 8½" d., green 6.00
Plate, luncheon, 8½" d., pink 5.00
Plate, dinner, 10" d., clear 14.00
Plate, dinner, 10" d., green 42.00
Plate, dinner, 10" d., milk white 10.50
Plate, dinner, 10" d., pink 25.00
Plate, grill, 10" d., clear 11.50
Plate, grill, 10" d., green 19.00
Plate, grill, 10" d., pink 15.50
Platter, 12" oval, clear 9.00
Platter, 12" oval, green 14.50
Platter, 12" oval, pink 17.50
Salt & pepper shakers, clear, pr. . . . 40.50
Salt & pepper shakers, green, pr. . . . 111.00
Salt & pepper shakers, pink, pr. 105.00
Sherbet, clear 4.00
Sherbet, green 9.00
Sherbet, pink 5.50
Sugar bowl, cov., clear 13.00
Sugar bowl, cov., green 22.50
Sugar bowl, cov., pink 25.00
Sugar bowl, open, clear or pink 5.50
Sugar bowl, open, green 9.50
Tumbler, whiskey, clear, 2½" h., 1½ oz. 3.50
Tumbler, whiskey, green, 2½" h., 1½ oz. 9.00
Tumbler, whiskey, pink, 2½" h., 1½ oz. 5.50
Tumbler, cordial, footed, clear, 3¼" h., 3 oz. 6.50
Tumbler, cordial, footed, green, 3¼" h., 3 oz. 12.50
Tumbler, cordial, footed, pink, 3¼" h., 3 oz. 10.00
Tumbler, juice, clear, 3" h., 5 oz. . . . 4.00
Tumbler, juice, green, 3" h., 5 oz. . . 18.00
Tumbler, juice, pink, 3" h., 5 oz. . . . 9.00
Tumbler, claret, footed, clear, 4" h., 5 oz. 6.50
Tumbler, claret, footed, green, 4" h., 5 oz. 19.00
Tumbler, claret, footed, pink, 4" h., 5 oz. 11.50
Tumbler, clear, 4" h., 9 oz. 5.50
Tumbler, green, 4" h., 9 oz. 17.50
Tumbler, pink, 4" h., 9 oz. 8.50
Tumbler, cordial, footed, clear, 5¼" h., 10 oz. 8.50
Tumbler, cordial, footed, green, 5¼" h., 10 oz. 34.50
Tumbler, cordial, footed, pink, 5¼" h., 10 oz. 19.00
Tumbler, green, 10 oz. 29.00
Tumbler, pink, 10 oz. 19.00
Tumbler, iced tea, green, 12 oz. 33.50

Tumbler, iced tea, pink, 12 oz. 28.50
Tumbler, lemonade, clear, 15 oz. 10.50
Tumbler, lemonade, green, 15 oz. 68.00
Tumbler, lemonade, pink, 15 oz. 40.00

COLUMBIA (Press-mold)

Bowl, cereal, 5" d., clear 9.00
Bowl, soup, 8" d., clear 10.00
Bowl, salad, 8½" d., clear 10.00
Bowl, salad, 8½" d., pink 12.00
Bowl, 10½" d., ruffled rim, clear 11.50
Bowl, 10½" d., ruffled rim, pink 12.50
Butter dish, cov., clear 12.00
Butter dish w/metal lid, clear 10.00
Cup & saucer, clear 4.50
Plate, bread & butter, 6" d., clear 1.50
Plate, luncheon, 9½" d., clear 4.00
Plate, luncheon, 9½" d., pink 9.50
Plate, chop, 11¾" d., clear 6.00
Plate, chop, 11¾" d., pink 8.50
Snack plate, handled, clear 23.00

CUBE or Cubist (Press-mold)

Cube Creamer & Sugar Bowl

Bowl, dessert, 4½" d., green or pink 4.00
Bowl, 4½" d., deep, clear 3.50
Bowl, 4½" d., deep, green or pink 4.00
Bowl, salad, 6½" d., clear 3.50
Bowl, salad, 6½" d., green 9.50
Bowl, salad, 6½" d., pink 6.00
Bowl, 7 3/8" d., scalloped rim, clear 9.00
Bowl, 7 3/8" d., scalloped rim, green 12.50
Bowl, 7 3/8" d., scalloped rim, pink 9.50
Butter dish, cov., green 45.00
Butter dish, cov., pink 36.50
Candy jar, cov., green, 7½" h. 21.50
Candy jar, cov., pink, 7½" h. 17.50
Coaster, green or pink, 3¼" d. 4.00
Creamer, clear, 3" h. 1.50
Creamer, green, 3" h. 5.00
Creamer, pink, 3" h. 4.50
Creamer & open sugar bowl, clear, 2" h., pr. (ILLUS.) 4.00
Creamer & open sugar bowl, green, 2" h., pr. 8.00
Creamer & open sugar bowl, pink, 2" h., pr. 5.00
Cup & saucer, green 7.00
Cup & saucer, pink 5.00
Pitcher, 8¾" h., 45 oz., green 156.00
Pitcher, 8¾" h., 45 oz., pink 125.00
Plate, sherbet, 6" d., clear 1.00
Plate, sherbet, 6" d., green 2.50
Plate, sherbet, 6" d., pink 1.50
Plate, luncheon, 8" d., green 4.00
Plate, luncheon, 8" d., pink 3.00
Powder jar, cov., 3-footed, clear 8.00
Powder jar, cov., 3-footed, green 15.50
Powder jar, cov., 3-footed, pink 13.00
Salt & pepper shakers, clear, pr. 16.00
Salt & pepper shakers, green, pr. 23.50
Salt & pepper shakers, pink, pr. 21.00
Sherbet, clear 2.00
Sherbet, green or pink 5.50
Sugar bowl, cov., green, 3" h. 12.50
Sugar bowl, cov., pink, 3" h. 10.00
Sugar bowl, open, clear, 2" h. 1.00
Sugar bowl, open, green, 2" h. 11.00
Sugar bowl, open, pink, 2" h. 2.00
Tray for 3" h. creamer & sugar bowl, clear, 7½" 3.00
Tumbler, green, 4" h., 9 oz. 36.50
Tumbler, pink, 4" h., 9 oz. 22.50
Water set: pitcher & 4 tumblers; pink, 5 pcs. 200.00

DAISY or Number 620 (Press-mold)

Bowl, berry, 4½" d., amber 5.50
Bowl, berry, 4½" d., clear 3.50
Bowl, cream soup, 4½" d., amber 5.00
Bowl, cream soup, 4½" d., clear 3.50
Bowl, cereal, 6" d., amber 19.50
Bowl, cereal, 6" d., clear 9.00
Bowl, berry, 7 3/8" d., amber 19.00
Bowl, berry, 7 3/8" d., clear 3.50
Bowl, berry, 9 3/8" d., amber 18.00
Bowl, berry, 9 3/8" d., clear 9.50
Bowl, 10" oval vegetable, amber 10.50
Bowl, 10" oval vegetable, clear 5.00
Creamer, footed, amber 5.50
Creamer, footed, clear 3.50
Cup & saucer, amber 5.00
Cup & saucer, clear 3.50
Plate, sherbet, 6" d., amber or clear 1.50
Plate, salad, 7 3/8" d., amber 5.00
Plate, salad, 7 3/8" d., clear 2.00
Plate, luncheon, 8 3/8" d., amber 4.00
Plate, luncheon, 8 3/8" d., clear 3.00
Plate, dinner, 9 3/8" d., amber 5.00
Plate, dinner, 9 3/8" d., clear 3.50
Plate, grill, 10 3/8" d., amber 8.50
Plate, grill, 10 3/8" d., clear 3.00
Plate, 11½" d., amber 8.00
Plate, 11½" d., clear 4.50
Platter, 10¾", amber 9.00
Platter, 10¾", clear 5.50
Relish, 3-part, amber, 8 3/8" 14.00
Relish, 3-part, clear, 8 3/8" 6.50
Sherbet, amber 6.00
Sherbet, clear 4.00
Sugar bowl, open, footed, amber 5.00
Sugar bowl, open, footed, clear 3.00
Tumbler, footed, amber, 9 oz. 12.50

Tumbler, footed, clear, 9 oz. 6.50
Tumbler, footed, amber, 12 oz. 27.50
Tumbler, footed, clear, 12 oz. 12.00

DIAMOND QUILTED or Flat Diamond (Press-mold)

Bowl, cream soup, 4¾" d., blue 14.00
Bowl, cream soup, 4¾" d., green ... 8.00
Bowl, cream soup, 4¾" d., pink 6.50
Bowl, cereal, 5" d., pink 5.00
Bowl, 5½" d., single handle, black 11.00
Bowl, 5½" d., single handle, green or pink 6.00
Bowl, 7" d., black 18.00
Bowl, 7" d., blue 13.00
Bowl, 7" d., green or pink 7.50
Candlesticks, black or blue, pr. 22.50
Candlesticks, green, pr. 11.50
Candlesticks, pink, pr. 9.00
Candy jar, cov., footed, pink 60.00
Coaster, pink, 3" d. 4.00
Console bowl, rolled edge, pink 28.00
Creamer, black 12.50
Creamer, blue 11.50
Creamer, green 8.00
Creamer, pink 7.00
Cup & saucer, black 11.50
Cup & saucer, pink 5.50
Ice bucket, blue 47.50
Mayonnaise set: 3-footed dish, plate & ladle; green, 3 pcs. 27.00
Mayonnaise set: 3-footed dish, plate & ladle; pink, 3 pcs. 45.00
Plate, sherbet, 6" d., black 6.00
Plate, sherbet, 6" d., blue 3.50
Plate, sherbet, 6" d., green 2.50
Plate, sherbet, 6" d., pink 3.00
Plate, salad, 7" d., black or green .. 5.00
Plate, salad, 7" d., pink 2.00
Plate, luncheon, 8" d., black 10.50
Plate, luncheon, 8" d., blue 10.00
Plate, luncheon, 8" d., green or pink 4.00
Plate, 14" d., green 21.00
Punch bowl w/stand, green, 2 pcs. 275.00
Sherbet, black 8.00
Sherbet, blue 10.00
Sherbet, green or pink 4.50
Sugar bowl, open, black 10.00
Sugar bowl, open, blue 10.50
Sugar bowl, open, green or pink ... 6.00
Tumbler, whiskey, green, 1½ oz. ... 6.50
Tumbler, footed, pink, 6 oz. 6.00
Tumbler, footed, clear, 9 oz. 3.00
Tumbler, iced tea, green, 12 oz. 10.00

DIANA (Press-mold)

Bowl, cereal, 5" d., amber 4.50
Bowl, cereal, 5" d., clear or pink ... 3.00
Bowl, cream soup, 5½" d., amber .. 8.00
Bowl, cream soup, 5½" d., clear ... 4.00
Bowl, cream soup, 5½" d., pink 3.00
Bowl, salad, 9" d., amber or pink ... 7.50
Bowl, salad, 9" d., clear 6.00
Bowl, 12" d., scalloped rim, amber 7.00
Bowl, 12" d., scalloped rim, clear ... 6.00
Bowl, 12" d., scalloped rim, pink 9.50
Candy jar, cov., round, amber 24.00
Candy jar, cov., round, clear 11.00
Candy jar, cov., round, pink 21.50
Coaster-ashtray, amber or clear, 3½" d. 6.50
Coaster-ashtray, pink, 3½" d. 3.00
Console bowl, amber, 11" d. 9.50
Console bowl, clear, 11" d. 5.00
Console bowl, pink, 11" d. 7.00
Creamer, oval, amber 4.00
Creamer, oval, clear 3.50
Creamer, oval, pink 5.00
Cup & saucer, demitasse, amber 7.50

Demitasse Cup & Saucer

Cup & saucer, demitasse, clear (ILLUS.) 4.00
Cup & saucer, demitasse, pink 12.50
Cup & saucer, amber 8.00
Cup & saucer, clear 4.50
Cup & saucer, pink 11.00
Plate, bread & butter, 6" d., amber 2.50
Plate, bread & butter, 6" d., clear or pink 1.50
Plate, dinner, 9½" d., amber or pink 6.00
Plate, dinner, 9½" d., clear 4.00
Plate, 11¾" d., amber or pink 6.50
Plate, 11¾" d., clear 3.50
Platter, 12" oval, amber 8.00
Platter, 12" oval, clear or pink 6.50
Salt & pepper shakers, amber, pr. .. 65.00
Salt & pepper shakers, clear, pr. ... 20.00
Salt & pepper shakers, pink, pr. 38.00
Sherbet, amber 7.50
Sherbet, pink 9.50
Sugar bowl, open, oval, amber or clear 3.50
Sugar bowl, open, oval, pink 4.50
Tumbler, amber, 4 1/8" h., 9 oz. ... 14.00
Tumbler, clear, 4 1/8" h., 9 oz. 13.50

Tumbler, pink, 4 1/8" h., 9 oz. 16.00
Junior set: 6 cups, saucers & plates w/round rack; clear, set 39.00

DOGWOOD or Apple Blossom or Wild Rose (Process-etched)

Dogwood Cup & Saucer

Bowl, cereal or dessert, 5½" d., green 16.00
Bowl, cereal or dessert, 5½" d., pink 13.00
Bowl, nappy, 8½" d., Cremax 32.50
Bowl, nappy, 8½" d., green 56.00
Bowl, nappy, 8½" d., pink 35.00
Bowl, fruit, 10¼" d., Cremax 60.00
Bowl, fruit, 10¼" d., green 95.00
Bowl, fruit, 10¼" d., pink 197.50
Cake plate, green, 13" d. 59.00
Cake plate, pink, 13" d. 71.00
Creamer, thin, green, 2¾" h. 35.50
Creamer, thin, pink, 2¾" h......... 11.50
Creamer, thick, pink, 3¼" h........ 12.00
Cup & saucer, Cremax 32.50
Cup & saucer, green (ILLUS.) 19.00
Cup & saucer, pink 11.50
Dinner service for 6, pink, 46 pcs. .. 450.00
Pitcher, 8" h., jug-type, green 39.00
Pitcher, 8" h., jug-type, hand-decorated, clear 170.00
Pitcher, 8" h., jug-type, hand-decorated, green 420.00
Pitcher, 8" h., jug-type, hand-decorated, pink 110.00
Plate, bread & butter, 6" d., green or pink 4.00
Plate, luncheon, 8" d., clear........ 3.00
Plate, luncheon, 8" d., green or pink 4.00
Plate, dinner, 9¼" d., pink 16.00
Plate, grill, 10½" d., overall patt., green 18.00
Plate, grill, 10½" d., overall patt., pink 12.50
Plate, grill, 10½" d., border patt., green 9.50
Plate, grill, 10½" d., border patt., pink 11.00
Plate, salver, 12" d., Monax or pink 19.00
Platter, 12" oval, pink 270.00

Sherbet, low foot, pink 16.50
Sugar bowl, open, thin, green, 2½" h. 27.00
Sugar bowl, open, thin, pink, 2½" h. 10.00
Sugar bowl, open, thick, green, 3¼" h. 30.00
Sugar bowl, open, thick, pink, 3¼" h. 9.50
Tidbit server, 2-tier, pink 43.50
Tumbler, decorated, pink, 3½" h., 5 oz. 175.00
Tumbler, plain, pink, 3½" h., 5 oz. 4.50
Tumbler, decorated, green, 4" h., 10 oz. 67.50
Tumbler, decorated, pink, 4" h., 10 oz. 24.00
Tumbler, plain, green, 4" h., 10 oz. 4.00
Tumbler, plain, pink, 4" h., 10 oz. .. 5.00
Tumbler, decorated, green, 4¾" h., 11 oz. 135.00
Tumbler, decorated, pink, 4¾" h., 11 oz. 30.00
Tumbler, plain, pink, 4¾" h., 11 oz. 5.50
Tumbler, decorated, pink, 5" h., 12 oz. 34.00
Tumbler, plain, pink, 5" h., 12 oz. ... 7.00
Water set: decorated pitcher & 6 decorated tumblers; pink, 7 pcs... 275.00
Water set: plain pitcher & 6 plain tumblers; green, 7 pcs. 80.00
Water set: plain pitcher & 6 plain tumblers; pink, 7 pcs. 175.00

DORIC (Press-mold)

Doric Sugar Bowl

Bowl, nappy, 4½" d., green or pink 5.00
Bowl, cereal, 5½" d., green........ 41.00
Bowl, cereal, 5½" d., pink 19.50
Bowl, nappy, 8¼" d., clear 10.00
Bowl, nappy, 8¼" d., green 15.00
Bowl, nappy, 8¼" d., pink 11.50

Bowl, 9" d., handled, green 12.00
Bowl, 9" d., handled, pink 11.00
Bowl, 9" oval vegetable, green 12.00
Bowl, 9" oval vegetable, pink 13.00
Butter dish, cov., green 63.00
Butter dish, cov., pink 51.00
Cake plate, green, 10" d. 12.50
Cake plate, pink, 10" d. 11.50
Candy dish, 3-section, Delfite or pink, 6" 4.00
Candy dish, 3-section, green, 6" 6.50
Candy jar, cov., green, 8" h. 30.50
Candy jar, cov., pink, 8" h. 27.50
Coaster, green, 3" d. 13.00
Coaster, pink, 3" d. 9.00
Creamer, green 9.50
Creamer, pink 8.00
Cup & saucer, green 8.50
Cup & saucer, pink 7.50
Pitcher, 5" or 6" h., 36 oz., jug-type, green 31.50
Pitcher, 5" or 6" h., 36 oz., jug-type, pink 29.00
Pitcher, 7" h., 47 oz., pink 200.00
Plate, sherbet, 6" d., green or pink 2.50
Plate, salad, 7" d., green 12.00
Plate, salad, 7" d., pink 10.00
Plate, dinner, 9" d., green 9.50
Plate, dinner, 9" d., pink 8.00
Plate, grill, 9" d., green 10.50
Plate, grill, 9" d., pink 8.00
Platter, 12" oval, green or pink 13.50
Relish, clear, 4 x 4" 7.50
Relish, green, 4 x 4" 8.50
Relish, pink, 4 x 4" 6.00
Relish, green, 4 x 8" 9.50
Relish, pink, 4 x 8" 6.50
Relish, green, 8 x 8" 10.00
Relish, pink, 8 x 8" 8.50
Relish, square inserts in metal holder, green 37.00
Relish, square inserts in metal holder, pink 44.50
Relish, 4-part, handled, green 32.50
Relish, 4-part, handled, pink 29.00
Salt & pepper shakers, clear, pr. 22.00
Salt & pepper shakers, green, pr. 29.50
Salt & pepper shakers, pink, pr. 25.00
Sandwich tray, handled, green, 10" d. 10.00
Sandwich tray, handled, pink, 10" d. 12.50
Sherbet, Delfite 4.50
Sherbet, green or pink 8.50
Sugar bowl, cov., green 26.50
Sugar bowl, cov., pink (ILLUS.) 22.00
Tumbler, green, 4½" h., 9 oz. 57.00
Tumbler, pink, 4½" h., 9 oz. 29.00
Tumbler, footed, green, 4" h., 10 oz. 47.00
Tumbler, footed, pink, 4" h., 10 oz. 25.50
Tumbler, footed, pink, 5" h., 13 oz. 35.50

DORIC & PANSY (Press-mold)

Doric & Pansy Cup & Saucer

Bowl, 4½" d., clear, green or pink 6.00
Bowl, 4½" d., ultramarine 8.50
Bowl, 8" d., clear 16.00
Bowl, 8" d., pink 17.50
Bowl, 8" d., ultramarine 60.00
Bowl, 9" d., handled, clear 16.50
Bowl, 9" d., handled, green or ultramarine 20.00
Butter dish, cov., ultramarine 467.50
Creamer, ultramarine 150.00
Cup & saucer, clear 9.50
Cup & saucer, ultramarine (ILLUS.) .. 15.00
Plate, sherbet, 6" d., green 8.00
Plate, sherbet, 6" d., pink 5.50
Plate, sherbet, 6" d., ultramarine 6.50
Plate, salad, 7" d., ultramarine 23.50
Plate, dinner, 9" d., green or ultramarine 19.00
Salt & pepper shakers, ultramarine, pr. 362.50
Sugar bowl, open, ultramarine 182.50
Tray, handled, clear, 10" 15.00
Tray, handled, green, 10" 9.00
Tray, handled, ultramarine, 10" 16.50
Tumbler, green, 4½" h., 9 oz. 31.00
Tumbler, ultramarine, 4½" h., 9 oz. 38.00

PRETTY POLLY PARTY DISHES

Creamer, pink 24.50
Creamer, ultramarine 29.00
Cup, pink 18.50
Cup, ultramarine 29.50
Plate, pink 5.50
Plate, ultramarine 7.50
Saucer, pink 3.50
Saucer, ultramarine 4.50
Sugar bowl, pink 25.00
Sugar bowl, ultramarine 29.50
14 piece set, pink 156.00
14 piece set, ultramarine 210.00

ENGLISH HOBNAIL (Handmade - not true Depression)

Ashtray, clear, 4½" d. 20.00

Bowl, nappy, 4½" d., clear 5.00
Bowl, nappy, 4½" d., green 7.00
Bowl, nappy, 4½" d., pink 10.00
Bowl, nappy, 4½" sq., clear 2.00
Bowl, nappy, 4½" sq., pink 14.00
Bowl, cream soup, 4¾" d., clear ... 8.00
Bowl, cream soup, 4¾" d., pink 11.00
Bowl, mayonnaise, 6" d., clear or green 10.00
Bowl, nappy, 6½" d., clear 7.00
Bowl, nappy, 6½" d., pink 8.00
Bowl, nappy, 6½" sq., green 14.00
Bowl, 6¾" d., turquoise 22.50
Bowl, fruit, 8" d., 2-handled, footed, amber 35.00
Bowl, fruit, 8" d., 2-handled, footed, clear 24.00
Bowl, fruit, 8" d., 2-handled, footed, green 36.00
Bowl, fruit, 8" d., 2-handled, footed, pink 28.00
Bowl, fruit, 8" d., 2-handled, footed, turquoise 34.00
Bowl, nappy, 8" d., clear 10.00
Bowl, nappy, 8" d., green 27.00
Bowl, 12" d., canted (bell) sides, turquoise 77.00
Bowl, 12" d., flared, clear or green 23.00
Bowl, 12" d., flared, turquoise 30.00
Candlesticks, amber, 3½" h., pr. ... 19.50
Candlesticks, blue, 3½" h., pr. 36.50
Candlesticks, clear, 3½" h., pr. 16.50
Candlesticks, green, 3½" h., pr. 27.50
Candlesticks, pink, 3½" h., pr. 29.00
Candlesticks, turquoise, 3½" h., pr. 67.50
Candlesticks, amber or green, 8½" h., pr. 75.00
Candlesticks, clear, 8½" h., pr. 36.50
Candlesticks, pink, 8½" h., pr. 41.00
Candlesticks, turquoise, 8½" h., pr. 49.00
Candy dish, cov., amber 30.00
Candy dish, cov., clear 23.00
Candy dish, cov., cobalt blue 252.50
Candy dish, cov., green 38.50
Candy dish, cov., pink 40.50
Celery tray, clear, 9" l. 12.00
Celery tray, clear, 12" l. 7.50
Cigarette jar, cov., clear 13.00
Cigarette jar, cov., pink 23.50
Coaster, clear, 5½" d. 3.50
Cologne bottle, blue or turquoise ... 37.50
Cologne bottle, clear or pink 24.00
Cologne bottle, green 27.00
Cologne bottles w/stoppers, cobalt blue, pr. 100.00
Cologne bottles w/stoppers, turquoise, pr. 125.00
Compote, 5" d., canted (bell) sides, clear 18.50
Compote, 5" d., rounded sides, clear 13.50

Creamer, green 17.50
Creamer & open sugar bowl, amber, pr. 21.50
Creamer & open sugar bowl, clear, pr. 14.00
Creamer & open sugar bowl, pink or turquoise, pr. 20.00
Cruet, oil, clear, 2 oz. 25.50
Cruet, oil, clear or pink, 6 oz. 25.00
Cup & saucer, clear 7.00
Cup & saucer, green 35.00
Cup & saucer, pink 22.50
Decanter w/stopper, clear, 20 oz. .. 29.50
Dish, cov., 3-footed, blue 14.00
Dish, cov., 3-footed, clear 37.50
Dish, cov., 3-footed, green 41.00
Dish, cov., 3-footed, pink 47.50
Dresser set: cov. puff box & 2 cologne bottles; turquoise, 3 pcs. 120.00
Egg cup, clear 13.50
Finger bowl, clear, 4½" d. 4.50
Finger bowl, pink, 4½" d. 9.00
Flip jar, cov., amber 207.50
Goblet, cordial, clear, 1 oz. 10.50
Goblet, wine, clear, 2 oz. 8.50
Goblet, cocktail, clear, 3 oz. 7.50
Goblet, cocktail, green or pink, 3 oz. 15.00
Goblet, claret, blue, 5 oz. 27.00
Goblet, claret, clear, 5 oz. 6.00
Goblet, claret, cobalt blue, 5 oz. ... 18.00
Goblet, claret, green, 5 oz. 20.00
Goblet, amber, 6¼" h., 8 oz. 12.00
Goblet, blue, 6¼" h., 8 oz. 30.00
Goblet, clear, 6¼" h., 8 oz. 7.50
Goblet, green, 6¼" h., 8 oz. 17.50
Goblet, pink, 6¼" h., 8 oz. 19.50
Goblet, turquoise, 6¼" h., 8 oz. 44.00
Ivy ball, clear 17.50
Lamp, clear, 6¼" h. 33.00
Lamp, green, 6¼" h. 86.00
Lamp, pink, 6¼" h. 65.00
Lamp, amber, 9¼" h. 97.50
Lamp, clear, 9¼" h. 26.00
Lamp, green, 9¼" h. 75.00
Lamp, pink, 9¼" h. 67.50
Lamp, turquoise, 9¼" h. 120.00
Marmalade jar, cov., clear 17.50
Marmalade jar, cov., pink 25.50
Nut cup, individual size, footed, amber 7.00
Nut cup, individual size, footed, blue 11.00
Nut cup, individual size, footed, clear 5.50
Nut cup, individual size, footed, green or pink 12.00
Nut cup, individual size, footed, turquoise 25.00
Pickle dish, clear, 8" oblong 5.00
Pitcher, 38 oz., clear 38.00
Pitcher, 38 oz., pink 250.00

Pitcher, ½ gal., straight sides, amber 125.00
Plate, sherbet, 6" d., clear or pink .. 3.00
Plate, luncheon, 8" d., blue 11.00
Plate, luncheon, 8" d., clear 4.50
Plate, luncheon, 8" d., green 6.50

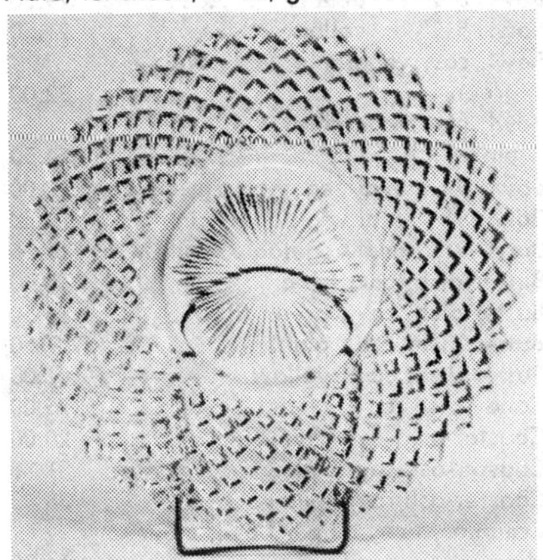

English Hobnail Luncheon Plate

Plate, luncheon, 8" d., pink (ILLUS.) 6.50
Plate, luncheon, 8" d., turquoise 15.00
Plate, luncheon, 8" sq., clear 4.00
Plate, luncheon, 8" sq., green 7.50
Plate, luncheon, 8" sq., turquoise ... 16.00
Plate, dinner, 10" d., blue 30.00
Plate, dinner, 10" d., clear 7.00
Plate, dinner, 10" d., green 18.50
Plate, 10" d., clear 15.50
Puff box, cov., blue 38.00
Puff box, cov., clear 30.00
Puff box, cov., green 27.00
Puff box, cov., pink 28.00
Puff box, cov., turquoise 45.00
Relish, 3-part, clear, 8" d. 18.00
Relish, 5-part, clear, 10" d. 25.00
Rose bowl, clear, 4" 15.00
Rose bowl, clear, 6" 16.00
Salt & pepper shakers, amber, pr. .. 54.00
Salt & pepper shakers, clear, pr. 20.00
Salt & pepper shakers, green, pr. 52.00
Salt & pepper shakers, pink, pr. 62.00
Salt & pepper shakers, turquoise, pr. 138.00
Sherbet, low foot, blue 18.00
Sherbet, low foot, clear 5.00
Sherbet, low foot, green 12.00
Sherbet, low foot, pink 11.50
Sherbet, high foot, clear 7.00
Sugar bowl, open, green 13.00
Tidbit server, 2-tier, amber 42.00
Tidbit server, 2-tier, clear 20.00
Tumbler, whiskey, clear, 3 oz. 10.50
Tumbler, clear, 3¾" h., 5 oz. 4.00
Tumbler, footed, clear, 7 oz. 6.50
Tumbler, amber, 3¾" h., 8 oz. 6.00
Tumbler, clear, green or pink, 3¾" h., 8 oz. 8.00
Tumbler, footed, clear, 9 oz. 5.00
Tumbler, clear, 4" h., 10 oz. 8.00
Tumbler, clear, 5" h., 12 oz. 6.00
Tumbler, pink, 5" h., 12 oz. 12.00
Tumbler, footed, clear, 12½ oz. 8.50
Tumbler, footed, green, 12½ oz. 15.00
Vase, 5¾" h., clear 22.50
Vase, 7¼" h., green 55.00
Vase, 7¼" h., pink 48.50

FLORAL or Poinsettia (Process-etched)

Floral Candy Jar

Bowl, berry, 4" d., green 14.00
Bowl, berry, 4" d., pink 10.00
Bowl, nappy, 7½" d., green 13.00
Bowl, nappy, 7½" d., pink 15.00
Bowl, cov. vegetable, 8" d., green .. 31.00
Bowl, cov. vegetable, 8" d., pink ... 25.00
Bowl, 9" oval vegetable, green 13.00
Bowl, 9" oval vegetable, pink 11.50
Butter dish, cov., green 71.50
Butter dish, cov., pink 69.00
Candlesticks, green, pr. 63.50
Candlesticks, pink, pr. 55.00
Candy jar, cov., green (ILLUS.) 29.50
Candy jar, cov., pink 26.50
Coaster, green or pink, 3¼" d. 7.00
Creamer & cov. sugar bowl, green, pr. 26.50
Creamer & cov. sugar bowl, pink, pr. 24.00
Creamer & open sugar bowl, green, pr. 16.00
Creamer & open sugar bowl, pink, pr. 15.00
Cup & saucer, green 13.50
Cup & saucer, pink 12.00
Ice tub, oval, pink, 3½" h. 495.00
Pitcher, 5½" h., 24 oz., green 402.50
Pitcher, 8" h., 32 oz., cone-shaped, green 24.00
Pitcher, 8" h., 32 oz., cone-shaped, pink 19.50
Pitcher, lemonade, 10¼" h., 48 oz., jug-type, green 225.00

Pitcher, lemonade, 10¼" h., 48 oz., jug-type, pink 185.00
Plate, sherbet, 6" d., green 3.50
Plate, sherbet, 6" d., pink 3.00
Plate, salad, 8" d., green 7.00
Plate, salad, 8" d., pink 6.50
Plate, dinner, 9" d., green 12.00
Plate, dinner, 9" d., pink 10.00
Platter, 10¾" oval, green 11.50
Platter, 10¾" oval, pink 10.00
Powder jar, cov., green 197.50
Refrigerator dish, cov., green 46.00
Refrigerator dish, cov., Jadite 15.00
Refrigerator dish, cov., pink 8.50
Relish, 2-part, green 10.00
Relish, 2-part, pink 9.50
Rose bowl, footed, green 385.00
Salt & pepper shakers, footed, green, 4" h., pr. 36.00
Salt & pepper shakers, footed, pink, 4" h., pr. 32.00
Salt & pepper shakers, green, 6" h., pr. 34.50
Salt & pepper shakers, pink, 6" h., pr. 32.50
Sherbet, green 10.50
Sherbet, pink 9.00
Tray, handled, green, 6" sq. 13.50
Tray, handled, pink, 6" sq. 13.00
Tumbler, footed, green, 4" h., 5 oz. 12.50
Tumbler, footed, pink, 4" h., 5 oz. 11.00
Tumbler, footed, green, 4¾" h., 7 oz. 13.00
Tumbler, footed, pink, 4¾" h., 7 oz. 10.00
Tumbler, footed, green, 4½" h., 9 oz. 152.50
Tumbler, footed, green, 5¼" h., 9 oz. 32.50
Tumbler, footed, pink, 5¼" h., 9 oz. 29.50
Vase, 6 7/8" h., octagonal, green 405.00
Water set: cone-shaped pitcher & 6 footed tumblers; pink, 7 pcs. 86.00

(OLD) FLORENTINE or Poppy No. 1 (Process-etched)

Florentine Butter Dish

Ashtray, green, 5½" 14.50
Bowl, berry, 5" d., clear 6.00
Bowl, berry, 5" d., cobalt blue 16.00
Bowl, berry, 5" d., green, pink or yellow 9.50
Bowl, nappy, 6" d., green 29.00
Bowl, nappy, 6" d., pink 14.00
Bowl, 8½" d., green 22.50
Bowl, 8½" d., pink 29.50
Bowl, 8½" d., yellow 21.50
Bowl, cov. vegetable, 9½" oval, green 32.00
Bowl, cov. vegetable, 9½" oval, pink 44.50
Bowl, 9½" oval vegetable, green 17.00
Bowl, 9½" oval vegetable, pink 21.50
Bowl, 9½" oval vegetable, yellow 16.00
Butter dish, cov., clear 115.00
Butter dish, cov., green (ILLUS.) 96.50
Butter dish, cov., pink 127.50
Butter dish, cov., yellow 107.00
Candy dish, cov., clear 75.00
Coaster-ashtray, green 20.00
Coaster-ashtray, pink 31.50
Coaster-ashtray, yellow 30.00
Creamer & cov. sugar bowl, clear, pr. 16.00
Creamer & cov. sugar bowl, green, pr. 27.50
Creamer & cov. sugar bowl, pink, pr. 32.50
Creamer & cov. sugar bowl, yellow, pr. 31.50
Creamer & open sugar bowl, plain rims, cobalt blue, pr. 12.00
Creamer & open sugar bowl, plain rims, green, pr. 15.00
Creamer & open sugar bowl, plain rims, pink, pr. 19.50
Creamer & open sugar bowl, plain rims, yellow, pr. 16.50
Creamer & open sugar bowl, ruffled rims, clear, pr. 38.00
Creamer & open sugar bowl, ruffled rims, cobalt blue, pr. 94.00
Creamer & open sugar bowl, ruffled rims, pink, pr. 40.00
Cup & saucer, clear 6.00
Cup & saucer, green 8.00
Cup & saucer, pink or yellow 9.00
Pitcher, 6½" h., 36 oz., jug-type, clear 29.50
Pitcher, 6½" h., 36 oz., jug-type, green 33.00
Pitcher, 6½" h., 36 oz., jug-type, pink or yellow 39.00
Pitcher, 7½" h., 54 oz., clear 42.00
Pitcher, 7½" h., 54 oz., green 69.50
Pitcher, 7½" h., 54 oz., pink 98.00
Pitcher, 7½" h., 54 oz., yellow 138.00
Plate, sherbet, 6" d., clear 2.50
Plate, sherbet, 6" d., green or pink 4.00
Plate, sherbet, 6" d., yellow 3.00
Plate, luncheon, 8" d., clear 4.00
Plate, luncheon, 8" d., green 5.50
Plate, luncheon, 8" d., pink 8.50

Plate, luncheon, 8" d., yellow 7.00
Plate, dinner, 9¾" d., clear 6.50
Plate, dinner, 9¾" d., green 10.50
Plate, dinner, 9¾" d., pink 16.00
Plate, dinner, 9¾" d., yellow 12.00
Plate, grill, 9¾" d., clear 6.50
Plate, grill, 9¾" d., green 9.00
Plate, grill, 9¾" d., pink 11.00
Plate, grill, 9¾" d., yellow 10.50
Platter, 11½" oval, clear 9.00
Platter, 11½" oval, green 16.00
Platter, 11½" oval, pink or yellow .. 13.50
Salt & pepper shakers, clear, pr. ... 26.00
Salt & pepper shakers, green, pr. ... 30.50
Salt & pepper shakers, pink, pr. ... 44.00
Salt & pepper shakers, yellow, pr. .. 38.00
Sherbet, clear 4.50
Sherbet, green or pink 6.50
Sherbet, yellow 7.00
Tumbler, juice, footed, clear, 3¼" h., 5 oz. 8.00
Tumbler, juice, footed, green, 3¼" h., 5 oz. 12.00
Tumbler, juice, footed, pink, 3¼" h., 5 oz. 10.50
Tumbler, juice, footed, yellow, 3¼" h., 5 oz. 13.50
Tumbler, water, footed, clear, 4" h., 9 oz. 7.50
Tumbler, water, footed, green, 4" h., 9 oz. 14.00
Tumbler, water, footed, pink, 4" h., 9 oz. 16.00
Tumbler, water, footed, yellow, 4" h., 9 oz. 15.00
Tumbler, iced tea, footed, clear, 5" h., 12 oz. 8.50
Tumbler, iced tea, footed, green, 5" h., 12 oz. 15.00
Tumbler, iced tea, footed, pink, 5" h., 12 oz. 20.50
Tumbler, iced tea, footed, yellow, 5" h., 12 oz. 18.00

FLORENTINE or Poppy No. 2 (Process-etched)

Florentine Plates

Bowl, berry, 4½" d., clear or green 8.00
Bowl, berry, 4½" d., pink 6.00
Bowl, berry, 4½" d., yellow 12.50
Bowl, cream soup, plain rim, 4¾" d., clear 6.00
Bowl, cream soup, plain rim, 4¾" d., green or pink 8.00
Bowl, cream soup, plain rim, 4¾" d., yellow 14.00
Bowl, 5½" d., clear 22.50
Bowl, 5½" d., green 50.00
Bowl, 5½" d., yellow 27.50
Bowl, cereal, 6" d., clear 15.00
Bowl, cereal, 6" d., pink 10.00
Bowl, cereal, 6" d., yellow 25.50
Bowl, nappy, 8" d., clear 5.50
Bowl, nappy, 8" d., green 14.50
Bowl, nappy, 8" d., pink 16.50
Bowl, nappy, 8" d., yellow 18.00
Bowl, cov. vegetable, 9" oval, clear 26.50
Bowl, cov. vegetable, 9" oval, green 33.50
Bowl, cov. vegetable, 9" oval, yellow 41.00
Bowl, 9" oval vegetable, clear 16.00
Bowl, 9" oval vegetable, green 20.00
Bowl, 9" oval vegetable, yellow 18.50
Butter dish, cov., clear 87.50
Butter dish, cov., green 90.00
Butter dish, cov., pink 80.00
Butter dish, cov., yellow 110.00
Candlesticks, clear, 3" h., pr. 32.50
Candlesticks, green, 3" h., pr. 45.00
Candlesticks, yellow, 3" h., pr. 43.00
Candy dish, cov., clear 67.00
Candy dish, cov., green 85.50
Candy dish, cov., pink 90.00
Candy dish, cov., yellow 136.00
Coaster, green, 3¼" d. 8.50
Coaster, pink or yellow, 3¼" d. 14.50
Coaster-ashtray, clear, 3¾" d. 12.00
Coaster-ashtray, green, 3¾" d. 17.50
Coaster-ashtray, yellow, 3¾" d. 16.00
Coaster-ashtray, clear, 5½" d. 12.00
Coaster-ashtray, green, 5½" d. 19.00
Coaster-ashtray, yellow, 5½" d. 23.00
Compote, 3½" d., clear 12.00
Compote, 3½" d., cobalt blue 45.00
Compote, 3½" d., green 22.00
Compote, 3½" d., pink 8.50
Condiment set: creamer, sugar bowl, salt & pepper shakers & 8½" d. tray; yellow, 5 pcs. 115.00
Creamer, clear 4.50
Creamer, green 6.50
Creamer, pink 3.00
Creamer, yellow 7.50
Cup & saucer, clear 6.00
Cup & saucer, cobalt blue 50.00
Cup & saucer, green 8.00
Cup & saucer, pink or yellow 9.00
Custard cup, clear 29.00
Custard cup, green 55.00
Custard cup, yellow 57.00

Custard cup w/underplate, yellow, 2 pcs. 105.00
Gravy boat, yellow 33.00
Gravy boat w/platter, pink, 11½" oval 75.00
Gravy boat w/platter, yellow, 11½" oval 67.00
Nut dish, handled, ruffled rim, clear 16.50
Nut dish, handled, ruffled rim, cobalt blue 32.00
Nut dish, handled, ruffled rim, green 41.50
Nut dish, handled, ruffled rim, pink 8.00
Nut dish, handled, ruffled rim, yellow 19.00
Pitcher, 6" h., 24 oz., cone-shaped, yellow 90.00
Pitcher, 7¼" h., 30 oz., cone-shaped, clear 17.00
Pitcher, 7¼" h., 30 oz., cone-shaped, green or yellow 19.00
Pitcher, 7½" h., 36 oz., footed, cone-shaped, clear 17.50
Pitcher, 7½" h., 36 oz., footed, cone-shaped, green 25.50
Pitcher, 7½" h., 36 oz., footed, cone-shaped, yellow 21.50
Pitcher, 7½" h., 54 oz., straight sides, clear 38.00
Pitcher, 7½" h., 54 oz., straight sides, green 47.00
Pitcher, 7½" h., 54 oz., straight sides, pink 110.00
Pitcher, 7½" h., 54 oz., straight sides, yellow 112.50
Pitcher, 8" h., 76 oz., jug-type, clear 77.00
Pitcher, 8" h., 76 oz., jug-type, green 82.50
Pitcher, 8" h., 76 oz., jug-type, pink 187.50
Pitcher, 8" h., 76 oz., jug-type, yellow 180.00
Pitcher, 80 oz., bulbous, clear 44.00
Pitcher, 80 oz., bulbous, green 150.00
Pitcher, 80 oz., bulbous, pink 190.00
Plate, sherbet, 6" d., clear 2.00
Plate, sherbet, 6" d., green 2.50
Plate, sherbet, 6" d., pink 4.00
Plate, sherbet, 6" d., yellow 3.00
Plate, 6¼" d., w/indentation, clear 7.00
Plate, 6¼" d., w/indentation, green 3.00
Plate, 6¼" d., w/indentation, pink 4.00
Plate, 6¼" d., w/indentation, yellow 22.00
Plate, luncheon, 8½" d., clear 4.00
Plate, luncheon, 8½" d., cobalt blue 10.00
Plate, luncheon, 8½" d., green 5.00
Plate, luncheon, 8½" d., yellow (ILLUS. left) 6.00
Plate, dinner, 10" d., clear 7.00
Plate, dinner, 10" d., green 9.00
Plate, dinner, 10" d., yellow (ILLUS. right) 10.50
Plate, grill, 10½" d., clear 6.50
Plate, grill, 10½" d., green 12.00
Plate, grill, 10½" d., yellow 8.50
Platter, 11" oval, clear 7.50
Platter, 11" oval, green 12.50
Platter, 11" oval, yellow 11.00
Relish, clear, 10" 10.00
Relish, green, 10" 15.00
Relish, yellow, 10" 16.00
Relish, 3-part, clear 12.00
Relish, 3-part, green 14.50
Relish, 3-part, pink 13.50
Relish, 3-part, yellow 18.00
Salt & pepper shakers, clear or green, pr. 30.00
Salt & pepper shakers, yellow, pr. 37.00
Sherbet, clear 4.50
Sherbet, green or pink 5.50
Sherbet, yellow 7.00
Sugar bowl, cov., clear 13.50
Sugar bowl, cov., green 18.00
Sugar bowl, cov., yellow 22.00
Sugar bowl, open, clear 4.50
Sugar bowl, open, green 6.00
Sugar bowl, open, yellow 7.00
Tray, yellow, 8½" d. 60.50
Tumbler, clear or pink, 3½" h., 5 oz. 7.00
Tumbler, green, 3½" h., 5 oz. 8.50
Tumbler, yellow, 3½" h., 5 oz. 12.00
Tumbler, footed, clear, 3½" h., 5 oz. 7.50
Tumbler, footed, green, 3½" h., 5 oz. 8.50
Tumbler, footed, pink, 3½" h., 5 oz. 8.00
Tumbler, footed, yellow, 3½" h., 5 oz. 9.50
Tumbler, clear, 4" h., 9 oz. 7.50
Tumbler, cobalt blue, 4" h., 9 oz. 50.50
Tumbler, green, 4" h., 9 oz. 9.50
Tumbler, pink, 4" h., 9 oz. 8.00
Tumbler, yellow, 4" h., 9 oz. 14.00
Tumbler, footed, clear, 4½" h., 9 oz. 11.50
Tumbler, footed, green, 4½" h., 9 oz. 15.50
Tumbler, footed, pink, 4½" h., 9 oz. 9.00
Tumbler, footed, yellow, 4½" h., 9 oz. 18.00
Tumbler, iced tea, clear, 5" h., 12 oz. 17.50
Tumbler, iced tea, green, 5" h., 12 oz. 23.50
Tumbler, iced tea, pink, 5" h., 12 oz. 25.00

Tumbler, iced tea, yellow, 5" h., 12 oz. 32.50
Tumbler, footed, clear, 5" h., 12 oz. 15.50
Tumbler, footed, green, 5" h., 12 oz. 17.50
Tumbler, footed, yellow, 5" h., 12 oz. 22.00
Vase (or parfait), 6" h., clear 19.00
Vase (or parfait), 6" h., green 33.50
Vase (or parfait), 6" h., yellow 48.00
Water set: cone-shaped pitcher & 6 tumblers; yellow, 7 pcs. 80.00

GEORGIAN or Lovebirds (Process-etched)

(All items in green only.)

Bowl, berry, 4½" d. 4.50
Bowl, cereal, 5¾" d. 12.50
Bowl, 6½" d. 42.50
Bowl, berry, 7½" d. 42.00
Bowl, 9" oval vegetable 43.00
Butter dish, cov. 61.00
Creamer & cov. sugar bowl, 3" h., pr. 38.50
Creamer & cov. sugar bowl, 4" h., pr. 36.50
Creamer & open sugar bowl, 3" h., pr. 16.50
Creamer & open sugar bowl, 4" h., pr. 15.00
Cup & saucer 9.50
Hot plate, center design, 5" d. 34.50
Plate, sherbet, 6" d. 2.50
Plate, luncheon, 8" d. 6.00
Plate, dinner, 9¼" d. 17.50
Plate, 9¼" d., center design only . . . 15.00
Platter, 11" oval 44.00
Sherbet 8.00
Tumbler, 4" h., 9 oz. 41.00
Tumbler, iced tea, 5¼" h., 12 oz. . . . 62.00

HOLIDAY or Buttons and Bows (Press-mold)

(All items in pink only. Later iridescent pieces not included.)

Holiday Pitcher

Bowl, berry, 5 1/8" d. 6.50
Bowl, cereal or flat soup, 7¾" d. . . . 30.50
Bowl, fruit, 8½" d. 14.50
Bowl, 9½" oval vegetable 13.50
Butter dish, cov. 30.00
Cake plate, footed, 10½" d. 55.50
Candlesticks, 3" h., pr. 53.00
Console bowl, 10" d. 67.50
Creamer 5.50
Cup & saucer, plain base 7.50
Cup & saucer, rayed base 7.00
Pitcher, milk, 4½" h., 16 oz. 46.00
Pitcher, 6¾" h., 52 oz. (ILLUS.) 22.00
Plate, sherbet, 6" d. 2.50
Plate, dinner, 9" d. 9.00
Plate, chop, 13 5/8" d. 64.00
Platter, 11 3/8 x 8" 11.50
Sandwich tray, 10½" d. 9.00
Sherbet 5.00
Sugar bowl, cov. 15.50
Sugar bowl, open 6.00
Tumbler, footed, 4" h., 5 oz. 23.00
Tumbler, footed, 6" h., 9 oz. 69.00
Tumbler, 4" h., 10 oz. 14.00
Water set, pitcher & 6 tumblers, 7 pcs. 125.00

HOMESPUN or Fine Rib (Press-mold)

Bowl, 4½" d., closed handles, pink 5.00
Bowl, cereal, 5" d., clear 5.00
Bowl, cereal, 5" d., pink 10.00
Bowl, berry, 8¼" d., pink 9.00
Butter dish, cov., clear 25.50
Butter dish, cov., pink 38.50
Coaster-ashtray, pink 5.00
Creamer & sugar bowl, footed, pink, pr. 12.50
Cup & saucer, pink 6.00
Pitcher, 96 oz., ball tilt type, pink . . 61.00
Plate, sherbet, 6" d., pink 2.00
Plate, dinner, 9¼" d., pink 8.50
Platter, 13", closed handles, pink . . . 12.50
Sherbet, clear 3.00
Sherbet, pink 6.00
Tumbler, juice, footed, clear, 4" h., 5 oz. 4.00
Tumbler, juice, footed, pink, 4" h., 5 oz. 5.00
Tumbler, water, pink, 4" h., 9 oz. . . 10.00
Tumbler, footed, pink, 6¼" h., 9 oz. 9.00
Tumbler, iced tea, clear, 5¼" h., 13 oz. 7.00
Tumbler, iced tea, pink, 5¼" h., 13 oz. 17.50
Tumbler, footed, clear, 6½" h., 15 oz. 13.50
Tumbler, footed, pink, 6½" h., 15 oz. 20.00

CHILD'S TEA SET

Cup & saucer, clear 17.50
Cup & saucer, pink 28.00
Plate, clear 5.50

Plate, pink 7.50
Teapot, pink 69.00
Teapot cover, pink 42.50
14 piece set, pink 197.50

IRIS or Iris & Herringbone (Press-mold)

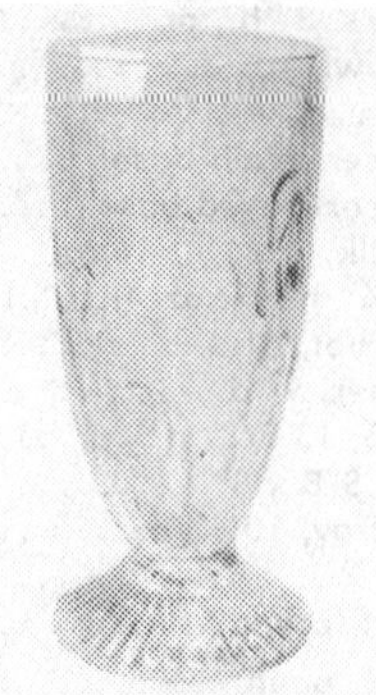

Iris Tumbler

Bowl, fruit, 4½" d., amber iridescent 7.00
Bowl, fruit, 4½" d., clear 32.00
Bowl, sauce, 5" d., ruffled rim, amber iridescent 5.50
Bowl, sauce, 5" d., ruffled rim, clear 5.00
Bowl, cereal, 6" d., amber iridescent 10.00
Bowl, cereal, 6" d., clear 39.00
Bowl, soup, 7½" d., amber iridescent 28.50
Bowl, soup, 7½" d., clear 77.00
Bowl, fruit, 8" d., beaded rim, amber iridescent 12.50
Bowl, fruit, 8" d., beaded rim, clear 50.50
Bowl, fruit, 8" d., ruffled rim, amber iridescent 7.50
Bowl, fruit, 8" d., ruffled rim, clear 9.50
Bowl, salad, 9½" d., amber iridescent or clear 7.50
Bowl, fruit, 11" d., ruffled rim, amber iridescent 6.50
Bowl, fruit, 11" d., ruffled rim, clear 7.50
Bowl, fruit, 11" d., straight sides, clear 32.00
Butter dish, cov., amber iridescent 29.00
Butter dish, cov., clear 27.00
Candlesticks, 2-branch, amber iridescent, pr. 21.50
Candlesticks, 2-branch, clear, pr. 16.00
Candy jar, cov., clear 83.50
Coaster, clear 35.00
Creamer & cov. sugar bowl, amber iridescent, pr. 19.00
Creamer & cov. sugar bowl, clear, pr. 18.00
Creamer & open sugar bowl, amber iridescent, pr. 12.50
Creamer & open sugar bowl, clear, pr. 11.00
Cup & saucer, demitasse, amber iridescent 112.50
Cup & saucer, demitasse, clear 71.50
Cup & saucer, demitasse, ruby 92.50
Cup & saucer, amber iridescent 11.00
Cup & saucer, clear 13.00
Goblet, wine, amber iridescent, 4" h., 3 oz. 15.00
Goblet, wine, clear, 4" h., 3 oz. 12.50
Goblet, wine, amber iridescent, 4½" h., 3 oz. 12.50
Goblet, wine, clear, 4½" h., 3 oz. 12.00
Goblet, amber iridescent, 5¾" h., 4 oz. 15.00
Goblet, clear, 5¾" h., 4 oz. 14.50
Goblet, clear, 5¾" h., 8 oz. 14.50
Lamp shade, blue 35.00
Lamp shade, clear 22.50
Lamp shade, pink frosted 33.00
Lamp shade, pink 32.00
Nut bowl w/metal insert, frosted w/pink roses, 11½" 49.50
Nut set: bowl w/metal holder, cracker & picks; clear, set 37.50
Pitcher, 9½" h., jug-type, amber iridescent 25.50
Pitcher, 9½" h., jug-type, clear 18.50
Plate, sherbet, 5½" d., amber iridescent 5.00
Plate, sherbet, 5½" d., clear 8.00
Plate, luncheon, 8" d., amber iridescent 7.00
Plate, luncheon, 8" d., clear 33.50
Plate, dinner, 9" d., amber iridescent 18.50
Plate, dinner, 9" d., clear 30.50
Plate, sandwich, 11¾" d., amber iridescent 12.50
Plate, sandwich, 11¾" d., clear 16.00
Sherbet, amber iridescent, 2½" h. 8.50
Sherbet, clear, 2½" h. 15.50
Sherbet, amber iridescent, 4" h. 9.00
Sherbet, clear, 4" h. 10.00
Tumbler, clear, 4" h. 49.00
Tumbler, footed, amber iridescent, 6" h. 11.00
Tumbler, footed, clear, 6" h. 10.50
Tumbler, footed, clear, 7" h. (ILLUS.) 13.50
Vase, 9" h., amber iridescent 11.50
Vase, 9" h., clear 13.00
Vase, 9" h., pink 48.00
Water set: pitcher & 6 tumblers; amber iridescent, 7 pcs. 79.00
Water set: pitcher & 6 tumblers; clear, 7 pcs. 93.00

LACE EDGE or Open Lace (Press-mold)

Bowl, cereal, 6½" d., clear 6.50
Bowl, cereal, 6½" d., pink (ILLUS. left) 11.50
Bowl, salad, 7¾" d., plain, pink 14.00
Bowl, 7¾" d., ribbed, pink 37.50

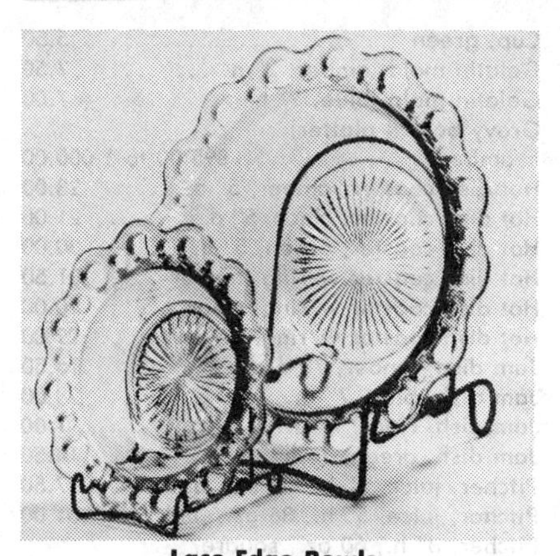

Lace Edge Bowls

Bowl, 9½" d., plain, clear 11.50
Bowl, 9½" d., plain, pink (ILLUS. right) 12.50
Butter dish (bonbon or preserve), cov., pink 41.00
Candlesticks, pink, pr. 148.00
Candlesticks, pink frosted, pr. 43.00
Candy jar, cov., ribbed, clear, 4" h. 31.00
Candy jar, cov., ribbed, pink, 4" h. 35.00
Candy jar, cov., ribbed, pink frosted, 4" h. 27.50
Compote, cov., 7" d., pink 32.00
Compote, open, 7" d., pink 16.00
Console bowl, 3-footed, pink, 10½" d. 114.00
Console bowl, 3-footed, pink frosted, 10½" d. 54.00
Cookie jar, cov., clear, 5" h. 32.50
Cookie jar, cov., pink, 5" h. 46.00
Creamer & open sugar bowl, pink, pr. 30.50
Cup & saucer, clear 18.50
Cup & saucer, pink 23.00
Fish bowl, clear, ½ gal. 14.00
Flower bowl w/crystal block, pink 19.00
Flower bowl w-o/crystal block, pink 17.00
Plate, bread & butter, 7¼" d., pink 12.50
Plate, salad, 8½" d., clear 3.50
Plate, salad, 8½" d., pink 11.50
Plate, dinner, 10½" d., clear or pink 17.00
Plate, grill, 10½" d., pink 12.50
Platter, 12¾" oval, clear 10.00
Platter, 12¾" oval, pink 17.00
Platter, 12¾" oval, 5-part, clear 17.50
Platter, 12¾" oval, 5-part, pink 16.50
Relish, pink, 7½" d. 45.50
Relish, 3-part, clear, 10½" d. 12.50
Relish, 3-part, pink, 10½" d. 15.00
Relish, 4-part, pink, 13" d. 22.50
Sherbet, pink 45.50
Tumbler, pink, 4½" h., 9 oz. 9.00
Tumbler, footed, pink, 5" h., 10½ oz. 45.50
Vase, 7" h., pink 350.00
Vase, 7" h., pink frosted 55.00

LORAIN or Basket or Number 615 (Process-etched)

Lorain Creamer & Sugar Bowl

Bowl, cereal, 6", green 37.50
Bowl, cereal, 6", yellow 44.50
Bowl, salad, 7¼", green 27.00
Bowl, salad, 7¼", yellow 40.50
Bowl, berry, 8", green 55.00
Bowl, berry, 8", yellow 124.00
Bowl, 9¾" oval vegetable, green 24.00
Bowl, 9¾" oval vegetable, yellow 40.00
Cake plate, yellow, 11½" 30.00
Creamer & open sugar bowl, footed, green, pr. 22.50
Creamer & open sugar bowl, footed, yellow, pr. (ILLUS.) 30.00
Cup & saucer, clear 9.50
Cup & saucer, green 11.50
Cup & saucer, yellow 15.00
Plate, sherbet, 5½", clear 4.00
Plate, sherbet, 5½", green 3.00
Plate, sherbet, 5½", yellow 6.00
Plate, salad, 7¾", clear 5.00
Plate, salad, 7¾", green 7.00
Plate, salad, 7¾", yellow 10.00
Plate, luncheon, 8 3/8", green 12.00
Plate, luncheon, 8 3/8", yellow 18.50
Plate, dinner, 10¼", green 28.50
Plate, dinner, 10¼", yellow 42.00
Platter, 11½", green 19.00
Platter, 11½", yellow 28.50
Relish, 4-part, clear, 8" 8.00
Relish, 4-part, green, 8" 14.00
Relish, 4-part, yellow, 8" 22.50
Sherbet, clear 10.00
Sherbet, green 12.00
Sherbet, yellow 22.00
Tumbler, footed, clear or green, 4¾" h., 9 oz. 14.50
Tumbler, footed, yellow, 4¾" h., 9 oz. 17.50
Tumbler, footed, green, 5 1/8" h., 12 oz. 17.00
Tumbler, footed, yellow, 5 1/8" h., 12 oz. 24.00

MADRID (Process-etched)

Ashtray, green, 6" sq. 107.00
Bowl, cream soup, 4¾" d., amber 9.00

Bowl, cream soup, 4¾" d., blue 8.50
Bowl, cream soup, 4¾" d., clear ... 7.00
Bowl, cream soup, 4¾" d., green... 11.00
Bowl, cream soup, 4¾" d., pink 4.00
Bowl, nappy, 5" d., amber 4.50
Bowl, nappy, 5" d., blue 6.00
Bowl, nappy, 5" d., clear 3.00
Bowl, nappy, 5" d., green or pink .. 5.00
Bowl, soup, 7" d., amber 7.50
Bowl, soup, 7" d., blue 8.50
Bowl, soup, 7" d., clear............ 7.00
Bowl, soup, 7" d., green 10.00
Bowl, 8" d., amber 13.50
Bowl, 8" d., blue 46.00
Bowl, 8" d., clear 9.50
Bowl, 8" d., green 16.00
Bowl, 8" d., pink 15.00
Bowl, fruit, 9 3/8" d., amber 14.50
Bowl, fruit, 9 3/8" d., green........ 19.00
Bowl, fruit, 9 3/8" d., pink 12.50
Bowl, salad, 9½" d., amber 19.50
Bowl, salad, 9½" d., blue 67.00
Bowl, salad, 9½" d., green 20.00
Bowl, 10" oval vegetable, amber ... 12.00
Bowl, 10" oval vegetable, blue 26.00
Bowl, 10" oval vegetable, clear..... 8.00
Bowl, 10" oval vegetable, green 13.50
Bowl, 11¾" d., blue 40.00
Bowl, 11¾" d., green 13.00
Bowl, 11¾" d., pink 20.00
Butter dish, cov., amber 48.00
Butter dish, cov., clear 135.00
Butter dish, cov., green............ 64.00
Cake plate, amber, 11½" d. 10.50
Cake plate, clear, 11½" d.......... 14.50
Cake plate, pink, 11½" d. 9.50
Candlesticks, amber, 2" h., pr. 13.50
Candlesticks, carnival, 2" h., pr..... 13.00
Candlesticks, clear, 2" h., pr. 12.00
Candlesticks, pink, 2" h., pr. 14.50
Console bowl, flared, amber, 11" d. 10.50
Console bowl, flared, carnival, 11" d. 10.00
Console bowl, flared, clear, 11" d... 13.50
Console bowl, flared, pink, 11" d. .. 9.00
Console set: bowl & pair candlesticks; amber, 3 pcs. 35.50
Console set: bowl & pair candlesticks; carnival, 3 pcs. 18.00
Console set: bowl & pair candlesticks; pink, 3 pcs. 23.00
Cookie jar, cov., amber............ 32.00
Cookie jar, cov., clear 24.00
Cookie jar, cov., pink 26.50
Creamer, amber 5.00
Creamer, blue 13.00
Creamer, carnival 15.00
Creamer, clear..................... 4.00
Creamer, green 7.50
Creamer, pink 5.00
Cup, amber........................ 4.50
Cup, blue.......................... 10.50
Cup, clear 4.00
Cup, green 5.50
Gelatin mold, amber, 2" h. 7.50
Gelatin mold, blue, 2" h. 7.00
Gravy boat & platter, amber ....895.00 to 1,000.00
Hot dish coaster, amber, 5" d. 23.00
Hot dish coaster, clear, 5" d........ 21.00
Hot dish coaster, green, 5" d. 30.00
Hot dish coaster w/ring, amber 31.50
Hot dish coaster w/ring, clear...... 20.00
Hot dish coaster w/ring, green 29.00
Jam dish, amber, 7" d. 15.50
Jam dish, blue, 7" d. 28.00
Jam dish, clear, 7" d............... 7.00
Jam dish, green, 7" d............... 14.50
Pitcher, juice, 5" h., 36 oz., amber.. 27.50
Pitcher, juice, 5" h., 36 oz., pink.... 31.00
Pitcher, 8" h., 60 oz., square, amber 35.00
Pitcher, 8" h., 60 oz., square, blue.. 130.00
Pitcher, 8" h., 60 oz., square, clear 22.00
Pitcher, 8" h., 60 oz., square, green 95.00
Pitcher, 8" h., 60 oz., square, pink.. 34.00
Pitcher, 8½" h., 80 oz., jug-type, amber 50.00
Pitcher, 8½" h., 80 oz., jug-type, green 170.00
Pitcher w/ice lip, 8½" h., 80 oz., amber 44.00
Plate, bread & butter, 6" d., amber 2.50
Plate, bread & butter, 6" d., blue ... 6.00
Plate, bread & butter, 6" d., clear or green 4.00
Plate, bread & butter, 6" d., pink ... 3.00
Plate, salad, 7½" d., amber or green 7.50
Plate, salad, 7½" d., blue 16.00
Plate, salad, 7½" d., clear 5.00
Plate, luncheon, 9" d., amber or clear 5.00
Plate, luncheon, 9" d., blue 15.00
Plate, luncheon, 9" d., green 8.00
Plate, dinner, 10½" d., amber...... 22.00
Plate, dinner, 10½" d., blue 53.00
Plate, dinner, 10½" d., clear 25.00
Plate, dinner, 10½" d., green 29.50
Plate, dinner, 10½" d., pink 21.00
Plate, grill, 10½" d., amber or clear 7.00
Plate, grill, 10½" d., carnival 6.00
Plate, grill, 10½" d., green 12.00
Plate, grill, 10½" d., pink.......... 8.00
Platter, 11½" oval, amber or pink .. 10.50
Platter, 11½" oval, blue 26.00
Platter, 11½" oval, clear........... 7.00
Platter, 11½" oval, green 13.00
Relish, amber, 10½" d. 9.00
Relish, clear, 10½" d. 8.00
Relish, pink, 10½" d. 10.00
Salt & pepper shakers, amber, 3½" h., pr. 35.50

Salt & pepper shakers, blue, 3½" h., pr. . . . 120.00
Salt & pepper shakers, clear or pink, 3½" h., pr. . . . 40.00
Salt & pepper shakers, green, 3½" h., pr. . . . 60.00
Salt & pepper shakers, footed, amber, 3½" h., pr. . . . 52.50
Salt & pepper shakers, footed, blue, 3½" h., pr. . . . 115.00
Salt & pepper shakers, footed, clear, 3½" h., pr. . . . 36.00
Salt & pepper shakers, footed, green, 3½" h., pr. . . . 74.00
Saucer, amber . . . 2.00
Saucer, blue . . . 5.00
Sherbet, amber . . . 5.00
Sherbet, blue . . . 10.00
Sherbet, clear . . . 4.00
Sherbet, green . . . 6.00
Sherbet, pink . . . 7.00
Sugar bowl, cov., amber . . . 28.50
Sugar bowl, cov., blue . . . 125.00
Sugar bowl, cov., clear . . . 29.50
Sugar bowl, cov., green . . . 42.50
Sugar bowl, cov., pink . . . 5.50
Sugar bowl, open, amber . . . 5.00
Sugar bowl, open, blue . . . 14.00
Sugar bowl, open, clear . . . 3.00
Sugar bowl, open, green . . . 7.00
Sugar bowl, open, pink . . . 6.00
Tumbler, juice, amber, 3 7/8" h., 5 oz. . . . 11.00
Tumbler, juice, blue, 3 7/8" h., 5 oz. . . . 20.00
Tumbler, juice, green, 3 7/8" h., 5 oz. . . . 47.00
Tumbler, footed, amber, 4" h., 5 oz. . . . 13.00
Tumbler, footed, green, 4" h., 5 oz. . . . 44.00
Tumbler, amber, clear or pink, 4½" h., 9 oz. . . . 10.00
Tumbler, blue, 4½" h., 9 oz. . . . 22.00
Tumbler, green, 4½" h., 9 oz. . . . 18.00
Tumbler, footed, amber, 5¼" h., 10 oz. . . . 18.50
Tumbler, footed, blue, 5¼" h., 10 oz. . . . 21.00
Tumbler, footed, green, 5¼" h., 10 oz. . . . 24.50
Tumbler, amber, 5½" h., 12 oz. . . . 16.00
Tumbler, blue, 5½" h., 12 oz. . . . 35.50
Tumbler, green, 5½" h., 12 oz. . . . 26.00
Water set: pitcher & 6 tumblers; amber, 7 pcs. . . . 135.00

MANHATTAN or Ribbed Horizontal (Press-mold)

Ashtray, clear . . . 7.50
Bowl, dessert, 4½" d., clear . . . 4.50
Bowl, fruit, 5 3/8" d., handled, clear . . . 9.50
Bowl, fruit, 5 3/8" d., handled, pink . . . 8.50
Bowl, 7½" d., clear . . . 8.00
Bowl, 7½" d., pink . . . 5.50
Bowl, 8" d., 2-handled, clear . . . 11.00
Bowl, 9" d., clear . . . 17.00
Bowl, 9" d., pink . . . 13.00
Bowl, fruit, 9½" d., clear . . . 19.50
Bowl, fruit, 9½" d., pink . . . 25.00
Candleholder, square, clear, pr. . . . 8.00
Candlesticks, double, square, clear, 4¼" h., pr. . . . 9.00
Candy dish, cov., clear . . . 19.00
Candy dish, cov., pink . . . 6.00
Candy dish, open, 3-legged, clear . . . 9.00
Candy dish, open, 3-legged, pink . . . 5.50
Coaster, clear, 3½" d. . . . 8.00
Coaster, pink, 3½" d. . . . 5.50
Compote, 5¾" d., clear . . . 16.50
Compote, 5¾" d., pink . . . 17.00
Creamer & open sugar bowl, clear, pr. . . . 11.00
Creamer & open sugar bowl, pink, pr. . . . 10.50
Cup & saucer, clear . . . 14.50
Pitcher, juice, 42 oz., clear . . . 14.00
Pitcher, juice, 42 oz., pink . . . 28.50
Pitcher, juice, 42 oz., ruby . . . 750.00
Pitcher w/ice lip, 80 oz., ball tilt type, clear . . . 24.50
Pitcher w/ice lip, 80 oz., ball tilt type, pink . . . 35.50
Plate, sherbet, 6" d., clear . . . 3.50
Plate, salad, 8½" d., clear . . . 7.50
Plate, dinner, 10½" d., clear . . . 10.50
Plate, 14" d., clear . . . 11.00

Manhattan Relish Tray

Relish, 4-part, clear, 14" (ILLUS.) . . . 14.00
Relish, 4-part, pink, 14" . . . 37.50
Relish, 5-part, clear, 14" . . . 16.00
Relish, 5-part, clear w/pink inserts, 14" . . . 36.00
Relish, 5-part, clear w/ruby inserts, 14" . . . 31.50
Relish tray insert, clear . . . 3.00
Relish tray insert, green . . . 7.50
Relish tray insert, pink . . . 5.00
Relish tray insert, ruby . . . 3.50
Salt & pepper shakers, clear, 2" h., pr. . . . 13.50
Salt & pepper shakers, pink, 2" h., pr. . . . 31.00

Sherbet, clear or pink 5.50
Tumbler, footed, clear, 10 oz. 9.00
Tumbler, footed, green or pink, 10 oz. 10.00
Vase, 8" h., clear 9.50
Vase, 8" h., pink 15.00
Water bottle, cov., clear 13.50
Water set: pitcher & 6 tumblers; pink, 7 pcs. 79.00
Wine, clear, 3½" 4.50

MAYFAIR or Open Rose (Process-etched)

Mayfair Sherbet & Plate

Bowl, cream soup, 5" d., blue 43.00
Bowl, cream soup, 5" d., pink 33.00
Bowl, cream soup, 5" d., pink frosted 22.00
Bowl, fruit, 5½" d., blue 35.00
Bowl, fruit, 5½" d., pink 14.50
Bowl, fruit, 5½" d., pink frosted 9.00
Bowl, nappy, 7" d., blue 33.50
Bowl, nappy, 7" d., pink 15.00
Bowl, 9½" oval vegetable, blue 38.00
Bowl, 9½" oval vegetable, pink 17.00
Bowl, cov. vegetable, 10" d., blue .. 78.50
Bowl, cov. vegetable, 10" d., pink .. 63.00
Bowl, 10" d., blue 33.00
Bowl, 10" d., pink 15.00
Bowl, 10" d., handled, blue 35.00
Bowl, 10" d., handled, pink 16.00
Bowl, 10" d., handled, pink frosted 12.00
Bowl, 11¾" d., blue 44.50
Bowl, 11¾" d., green 19.00
Bowl, 11¾" d., pink 36.00
Bowl, fruit, 12" d., flared, blue 46.00
Bowl, fruit, 12" d., flared, green 23.00
Bowl, fruit, 12" d., flared, pink 36.00
Butter dish, cov., blue 206.00
Butter dish, cov., pink 41.00
Cake plate, footed, blue, 10" d. 40.00
Cake plate, footed, green, 10" d. 18.00
Cake plate, footed, pink, 10" d. 19.00
Cake plate, handled, blue, 12" d. ... 43.00
Cake plate, handled, green or pink, 12" d. 30.00
Cake plate, handled, pink frosted, 12" d. 23.00
Candy jar, cov., blue 140.00
Candy jar, cov., pink 34.00
Candy jar, cov., pink frosted 31.00
Celery dish, blue, 10" d. 25.00
Celery dish, pink, 10" d. 23.00
Celery dish, 2-part, blue, 10" d. 33.00
Celery dish, 2-part, pink, 10" d. 111.00
Cookie jar, cov., blue 166.00
Cookie jar, cov., green 587.50
Cookie jar, cov., pink 27.50
Cookie jar, cov., pink frosted 26.50
Creamer, blue 43.50
Creamer, green 135.00
Creamer, pink 14.50
Creamer, pink frosted 10.00
Cup, pink 12.00
Cup & saucer, demitasse, yellow ... 20.00
Cup & saucer, blue 42.50
Decanter w/stopper, pink, 10" h. ... 105.00
Decanter, no stopper, pink 54.50
Goblet, pink, 4" h., 2½" oz. 62.00
Goblet, wine, green, 4½" h., 3 oz. 300.00
Goblet, wine, pink, 4½" h., 3 oz.... 54.50
Goblet, cocktail, pink, 4" h., 3½ oz. 53.00
Goblet, champagne, blue, 5¼" h., 4½ oz. 65.00
Goblet, champagne, pink, 5¼" h., 4½ oz. 74.00
Goblet, water, pink, 5¾" h., 9 oz. 43.50
Goblet, water, thin, blue, 7¼" h., 9 oz. 96.50
Goblet, water, thin, pink, 7¼" h., 9 oz. 112.50
Juice set: pitcher & 6 tumblers; pink, 7 pcs. 200.00
Pitcher, juice, 6" h., 37 oz., blue.... 92.00
Pitcher, juice, 6" h., 37 oz., clear ... 10.00
Pitcher, juice, 6" h., 37 oz., pink.... 32.00
Pitcher, 8" h., 60 oz., jug-type, blue 107.50
Pitcher, 8" h., 60 oz., jug-type, pink 31.50
Pitcher, 8½" h., 80 oz., jug-type, blue 124.00
Pitcher, 8½" h., 80 oz., jug-type, pink 55.50
Plate, bread & butter, 6" w., blue .. 12.50
Plate, bread & butter, 6" w., pink ... 7.50
Plate, bread & butter, 6" w., yellow 2.00
Plate, sherbet, 6½" d., blue 9.50
Plate, sherbet, 6½" d., green 40.00
Plate, sherbet, 6½" d., pink (ILLUS.) 8.00
Plate, sherbet, 6½" d., off-center indentation, blue 17.50
Plate, sherbet, 6½" d., off-center indentation, pink 19.50
Plate, luncheon, 8½" d., blue 24.50
Plate, luncheon, 8½" d., pink 15.50
Plate, luncheon, 8½" d., yellow 72.50
Plate, dinner, 9½" d., blue 42.00

Plate, dinner, 9½" d., pink 36.50
Plate, dinner, 9½" d., yellow 11.00
Plate, grill, 9½" d., blue 25.00
Plate, grill, 9½" d., pink 23.50
Plate, grill, 11½" d., yellow 87.50
Plate, 12" d., 2-handled, blue 36.00
Plate, 12" d., 2-handled, pink 26.50
Plate, 12" d., 2-handled, pink frosted 20.00
Platter, 12" oval, pierced handles, blue 34.50
Platter, 12" oval, pierced handles, clear 15.50
Platter, 12" oval, pierced handles, pink 17.50
Relish, 2-part, blue 29.50
Relish, 2-part, clear 11.00
Relish, 4-part, blue 32.50
Relish, 4-part, pink 23.00
Relish, 4-part, pink frosted 13.50
Salt & pepper shakers, blue, pr. 185.00
Salt & pepper shakers, pink, pr. 41.50
Salt & pepper shakers, pink frosted, pr. 29.00
Salt & pepper shakers, footed, blue, pr. 155.00
Sandwich server w/center handle, blue, 12" 44.00
Sandwich server w/center handle, green, 12" 18.00
Sandwich server w/center handle, pink, 12" 26.00
Sandwich server w/center handle, pink frosted, 12" 22.00
Saucer w/cup ring, pink 22.00
Sherbet, blue, 2¼" h. 64.00
Sherbet, pink, 2¼" h. 107.50
Sherbet, footed, pink, 3" h. (ILLUS.) 11.50
Sherbet, footed, blue, 4¾" h. 58.50
Sherbet, footed, pink, 4¾" h. 43.00
Sherbet w/underplate, blue, 2¼" h. sherbet 73.00
Sugar bowl, cov., blue (rare) 1,250.00
Sugar bowl, open, blue 42.50
Sugar bowl, open, green 98.00
Sugar bowl, open, pink 17.00
Sugar bowl, open, pink frosted 11.00
Tumbler, whiskey, green, 2¼" h., 1½ oz. 40.00
Tumbler, whiskey, pink, 2¼" h., 1½ oz. 50.00
Tumbler, cocktail, pink, 2 oz. 62.50
Tumbler, juice, footed, pink, 3¼" h., 3 oz. 48.50
Tumbler, juice, blue, 3½" h., 5 oz. 76.00
Tumbler, juice, pink, 3½" h., 5 oz. 33.00
Tumbler, water, blue, 4¼" h., 9 oz. 76.50
Tumbler, water, pink, 4¼" h., 9 oz. 21.50
Tumbler, footed, blue, 5¼" h., 10 oz. 103.00
Tumbler, footed, pink, 5¼" h., 10 oz. 25.50
Tumbler, blue, 4¾" h., 11 oz. 90.00
Tumbler, pink, 4¾" h., 11 oz. 105.00
Tumbler, water, footed, pink, 4¾" h., 11 oz. 87.00
Tumbler, iced tea, blue, 5¼" h., 13½ oz. 106.00
Tumbler, iced tea, pink, 5¼" h., 13½ oz. 31.50
Tumbler, iced tea, footed, blue, 6½" h., 15 oz. 102.50
Tumbler, iced tea, footed, pink, 6½" h., 15 oz. 27.00
Vase, 5½ x 8½", sweetpea, hat-shaped, blue 66.50
Vase, 5½ x 8½", sweetpea, hat-shaped, pink 105.00
Water set: pitcher & 6 tumblers; blue, 7 pcs. 695.00
Water set: pitcher & 6 tumblers; pink, 7 pcs. 150.00

MISS AMERICA (Press-mold)

Miss America Candy Jar

Bowl, nappy, 4½" d., clear 5.00
Bowl, nappy, 4½" d., green 8.00
Bowl, nappy, 4½" d., pink 12.50
Bowl, cereal, 6¼" d., clear 5.50
Bowl, cereal, 6¼" d., green 8.50
Bowl, cereal, 6¼" d., pink 11.50
Bowl, fruit, 8" d., curved top, clear 26.00
Bowl, fruit, 8" d., curved top, pink .. 44.50
Bowl, fruit, 8" d., curved top, ruby .. 125.00
Bowl, fruit, 8¾" d., deep, clear 23.00
Bowl, fruit, 8¾" d., deep, pink 39.00
Bowl, 10" oval vegetable, clear 9.00
Bowl, 10" oval vegetable, pink 14.50
Butter dish, cov., clear 150.00
Butter dish, cov., pink 347.50
Cake plate, footed, clear, 12" d. 15.00
Cake plate, footed, pink, 12" d. 28.00
Candy dish w/metal lid, clear, 6¼" d. 20.00

Candy jar, cov., clear 45.00
Candy jar, cov., pink (ILLUS.) 95.00
Celery tray, clear, 10½" oblong 7.50
Celery tray, pink, 10½" oblong 14.00
Coaster, clear, 5¾" d. 11.00
Coaster, green, 5¾" d. 6.00
Coaster, pink, 5¾" d. 17.50
Compote, 5" d., clear 9.00
Compote, 5" d., pink 13.00
Creamer, clear 6.00
Creamer, pink 11.50
Cup, clear 6.50
Cup, green 7.00
Cup, pink 14.00
Goblet, wine, clear, 3¾" h., 3 oz. . . 13.00
Goblet, wine, pink, 3¾" h., 3 oz. . . . 45.00
Goblet, wine, ruby, 3¾" h., 3 oz. . . 175.00
Goblet, juice, clear, 4¾" h., 5 oz. . . 15.50
Goblet, juice, pink, 4¾" h., 5 oz. . . . 52.50
Goblet, water, clear, 5½" h., 10 oz. 16.00
Goblet, water, pink, 5½" h., 10 oz. 34.50
Goblet, water, ruby, 5½" h., 10 oz. 150.00
Pitcher, 8½" h., 65 oz., clear 45.50
Pitcher, 8½" h., 65 oz., pink 72.00
Pitcher w/ice lip, 8½" h., 65 oz., clear 47.00
Pitcher w/ice lip, 8½" h., 65 oz., pink 92.50
Plate, sherbet, 5¾" d., clear 3.00
Plate, sherbet, 5¾" d., pink 5.00
Plate, bread & butter, 6¾" d., clear 2.00
Plate, bread & butter, 6¾" d., green 5.00
Plate, bread & butter, 6¾" d., pink 6.00
Plate, salad, 8½" d., clear 4.50
Plate, salad, 8½" d., pink 12.50
Plate, dinner, 10¼" d., clear 8.50
Plate, dinner, 10¼" d., pink 16.50
Plate, grill, 10¼" d., clear 6.50
Plate, grill, 10¼" d., pink 12.50
Platter, 12" oval, clear 10.50
Platter, 12" oval, pink 15.50
Relish, 4-part, clear, 8½" d. 6.50
Relish, 4-part, pink, 8½" d. 12.50
Relish, divided, clear, 12" d. 13.50
Relish, divided, pink, 12" d. 13.00
Salt & pepper shakers, clear, pr. . . . 19.50
Salt & pepper shakers, green, pr. . . . 170.00
Salt & pepper shakers, pink, pr. 39.00
Saucer, clear 3.00
Saucer, pink 3.50
Sherbet, clear 6.00
Sherbet, pink 10.00
Sugar bowl, open, clear 5.50
Sugar bowl, open, green 6.00
Sugar bowl, open, pink 12.00
Tidbit server, 2-tier, clear 15.00
Tumbler, clear, 4" h., 5 oz. 10.00
Tumbler, green, 4" h., 5 oz. 15.00
Tumbler, pink, 4" h., 5 oz. 32.50
Tumbler, clear, 4½" h., 10 oz. 12.50
Tumbler, green, 4½" h., 10 oz. 12.00
Tumbler, pink, 4½" h., 10 oz. 24.00
Tumbler, clear, 6¾" h., 14 oz. 19.50
Tumbler, pink, 6¾" h., 14 oz. 46.00
Tumbler, ruby, 6¾" h., 14 oz. 41.00

MODERNTONE (Press-mold)

Moderntone Pattern

Ashtray, blue, 5½" d. 31.00
Ashtray w/match holder, blue, 7¾" d. 145.00
Bowl, cream soup, 4¾" d., amethyst 9.00
Bowl, cream soup, 4¾" d., blue 11.50
Bowl, berry, 5" d., blue 13.00
Bowl, cream soup w/ruffled rim, 5" d., amethyst 9.00
Bowl, cream soup w/ruffled rim, 5" d., blue 17.00
Bowl, cereal, 6½" d., blue 39.50
Bowl, soup, 7½" d., blue 75.00
Bowl, 8¾" d., amethyst 13.00
Bowl, 8¾" d., blue 25.00
Butter dish w/metal lid, blue 65.00
Creamer & open sugar bowl, amethyst, pr. 11.50
Creamer & open sugar bowl, blue, pr. (ILLUS.) 13.50
Creamer & sugar bowl w/metal lid, blue, pr. 31.00
Cup, amethyst 6.00
Cup, blue 7.00
Custard cup, amethyst or blue 9.50
Plate, sherbet, 5¾" d., amethyst or blue 3.00
Plate, salad, 6¾" d., amethyst 4.50
Plate, salad, 6¾" d., blue 6.00
Plate, luncheon, 7¾" d., amethyst . . 5.00
Plate, luncheon, 7¾" d., blue 5.50
Plate, dinner, 8 7/8" d., amethyst . . 7.00
Plate, dinner, 8 7/8" d., blue 9.00
Plate, 10½" d., amethyst or blue . . . 19.50
Platter, 11" oval, amethyst 17.50
Platter, 11" oval, blue 24.00
Platter, 12" oval, amethyst 19.00
Platter, 12" oval, blue 24.00
Punch bowl w/metal holder, blue . . . 35.00
Punch set: punch bowl in metal holder, 8 cups & ladle w/blue knob; blue, 11 pcs. 130.00
Salt & pepper shakers, amethyst, pr. 28.50

Salt & pepper shakers, blue, pr. (ILLUS.) 24.50
Saucer, amethyst or blue 2.00
Sherbet, amethyst 6.00
Sherbet, blue 7.50
Tea set, "Little Hostess," 16 pcs. 70.00
Tumbler, whiskey, blue, 1½ oz. 16.00
Tumbler, amethyst, 5 oz. 28.00
Tumbler, blue, 5 oz. 20.50
Tumbler, amethyst, 4" h., 9 oz. 16.50
Tumbler, blue, 4" h., 9 oz. 17.50
Tumbler, amethyst, 12 oz. 43.00
Tumbler, blue, 12 oz. 31.00

MOONSTONE (Press-mold)

(All items clear to opalescent only. Also see Hobnail.)

Moonstone Candleholders

Berry set, master bowl & 6 sauce dishes, 7 pcs. 38.00
Bonbon, heart-shaped, 6½" w. 7.00
Bowl, dessert, 5½" d., crimped 6.00
Bowl, 5½" d., straight 10.00
Bowl, cov., 6" d. 11.00
Bowl, 6½" d., handled, crimped 7.00
Bowl, 7¾" d. 7.50
Bowl, 9½" d., crimped 12.50
Candleholders, pr. (ILLUS.) 13.00
Candy jar, cov. 15.00
Cigarette box, cov. 13.50
Creamer 5.00
Cruet w/stopper 16.25
Cup 5.50
Cup & saucer 8.50
Dish, cloverleaf-shaped, 6" w. 7.00
Goblet, 10 oz. 13.00
Perfume bottle w/stopper, 5¼" h. 8.50
Plate, sherbet, 6¼" d. 3.00
Plate, luncheon, 8" d. 8.00
Plate, 10" d., crimped 16.50
Plate, 11" d. 15.00
Puff box, cov. 13.50
Relish, divided 6.50
Salt & pepper shakers, pr. 39.00
Sherbet 5.50
Sugar bowl 5.00

Tumbler, 3½" h., 4 oz. 11.00
Tumbler, footed, 5½" h. 13.00
Vase, 3½" h. 11.00
Vase, 5" h. 8.50
Vase, 10" h. 50.00

MOROCCAN AMETHYST (Early 1960's - not true Depression)

Moroccan Amethyst Cup & Saucer

Ashtray, 6 7/8" triangle 8.00
Basket 28.00
Bowl, fruit, 4¾" d. 3.50
Bowl, cereal, 5¾" d. 5.00
Candy jar, cov. 18.00
Cocktail shaker w/chrome lid 14.00
Creamer 8.00
Cup & saucer (ILLUS.) 5.00
Plate, 6" w. 3.50
Plate, salad, 7¼" w. 4.00
Plate, dinner, 9 3/8" w. 5.00
Punch cup 4.00
Relish, 8" 6.50
Tidbit server, 2-tier 16.50
Tidbit server, 3-tier 17.50
Tumbler, juice, 2½" h., 4 oz. 4.50
Tumbler, old fashion, 3¼" h., 8 oz. 6.00
Tumbler, water, 4½" h., 11 oz. 4.50
Tumbler, iced tea, 16 oz. 8.50

NORMANDIE or Bouquet and Lattice (Process-etched)

Normandie Cup & Saucer

Bowl, berry, 5" d., amber or carnival 3.50
Bowl, berry, 5" d., pink 5.00
Bowl, 6½" d., amber 7.00
Bowl, 6½" d., carnival 5.50
Bowl, 6½" d., pink 16.50
Bowl, nappy, 8½" d., amber or carnival 10.00
Bowl, nappy, 8½" d., pink 13.50
Bowl, 9½" oval vegetable, amber 11.50
Bowl, 9½" oval vegetable, carnival 12.50
Bowl, 9½" oval vegetable, pink 21.00
Creamer, amber or carnival 5.50
Creamer, pink 7.00
Cup & saucer, amber 6.00
Cup & saucer, carnival (ILLUS.) 5.50
Cup & saucer, pink 6.50
Pitcher, 8" h., 80 oz., amber 44.00
Pitcher, 8" h., 80 oz., clear 50.00
Pitcher, 8" h., 80 oz., pink 72.00
Plate, bread & butter, 6" d., amber 2.50
Plate, bread & butter, 6" d., carnival 1.50
Plate, bread & butter, 6" d., pink 4.00
Plate, salad, 8" d., amber or carnival 5.50
Plate, salad, 8" d., pink 7.00
Plate, luncheon, 9¼" d., amber 5.50
Plate, luncheon, 9¼" d., carnival 9.00
Plate, luncheon, 9¼" d., pink 8.00
Plate, dinner, 10½" d., amber 17.00
Plate, dinner, 10½" d., carnival 10.50
Plate, dinner, 10½" d., pink 41.00
Plate, grill, 10½" d., amber 8.00
Plate, grill, 10½" d., carnival 6.00
Plate, grill, 10½" d., pink 16.00
Platter, 12" oval, amber or carnival 10.50
Platter, 12" oval, pink 13.00
Salt & pepper shakers, amber, pr. 33.00
Salt & pepper shakers, carnival, pr. 28.00
Salt & pepper shakers, pink, pr. 53.00
Sherbet, amber or pink 5.50
Sherbet, carnival 4.00
Sherbet, clear 3.00
Sugar bowl, cov., amber 57.50
Sugar bowl, cov., pink 70.00
Sugar bowl, open, amber or carnival 5.00
Tumbler, amber, 4" h., 5 oz. 11.00
Tumbler, pink, 4" h., 5 oz. 28.50
Tumbler, amber, 4½" h., 9 oz. 11.00
Tumbler, pink, 4½" h., 9 oz. 24.50
Tumbler, amber, 5" h., 12 oz. 16.50
Tumbler, pink, 5" h., 12 oz. 40.00

NUMBER 612 or Horseshoe (Process-etched)

Bowl, berry, 4½" d., green 17.50
Bowl, berry, 4½" d., yellow 16.00
Bowl, cereal, 6½" d., green or yellow 16.00
Bowl, salad, 7½" d., green 14.00
Bowl, salad, 7½" d., yellow 17.50
Bowl, berry, 9" d., green 22.00
Bowl, berry, 9" d., yellow 24.00
Bowl, 10½" oval vegetable, green 18.00
Bowl, 10½" oval vegetable, yellow 23.50
Butter dish, cov., green 625.00
Candy in metal holder, motif on lid, pink 89.00
Creamer, footed, green 10.50
Creamer, footed, yellow 12.00
Pitcher, 8½" h., 64 oz., green 165.00
Pitcher, 8½" h., 64 oz., yellow 240.00
Plate, sherbet, 6" d., green 2.50
Plate, sherbet, 6" d., yellow 4.00
Plate, salad, 8 3/8" d., green or yellow 5.50
Plate, luncheon, 9 3/8" d., green 10.00
Plate, luncheon, 9 3/8" d., yellow 7.50
Plate, dinner, 10 3/8" d., green 11.50
Plate, dinner, 10 3/8" d., yellow 10.50
Plate, grill, 10 3/8" d., green 26.50
Plate, 11¼" d., green 10.50
Plate, 11¼" d., yellow 11.50
Platter, 10¾" oval, green or yellow 14.50
Relish, 3-part, footed, green 15.50
Relish, 3-part, footed, yellow 27.00
Saucer, green 3.00
Saucer, yellow 3.50
Sherbet, green 9.50

Number 612 Sherbet

Sherbet, yellow (ILLUS.) 12.00
Sugar bowl, open, footed, green or yellow 9.00
Tumbler, green, 4¼" h., 9 oz. 45.00
Tumbler, footed, green, 9 oz. 15.00
Tumbler, footed, yellow, 9 oz. 14.00
Tumbler, footed, green, 12 oz. 75.00
Tumbler, footed, yellow, 12 oz. 105.00

OLD CAFE (Press-mold)

Bowl, berry, 3¾" d., clear 2.50
Bowl, berry, 3¾" d., pink 4.50
Bowl, berry, 3¾" d., ruby 3.50
Bowl, nappy, 5" d., handled, clear 4.00
Bowl, nappy, 5" d., handled, pink 5.00
Bowl, cereal, 5½" d., pink 7.50
Bowl, cereal, 5½" d., ruby 8.50

Bowl, 9" d., handled, clear or pink 7.50
Bowl, 9" d., handled, ruby 8.50

Old Cafe Candy Dishes

Candy dish, clear, 8" d. (ILLUS. right) 4.00
Candy dish, pink, 8" d. 5.00
Candy dish, ruby, 8" d. (ILLUS. left) 8.00
Cookie jar, cov., pink 32.50
Cup & saucer, pink 10.50
Cup & saucer, ruby cup, clear saucer 6.50
Olive dish, clear or pink, 6" oblong 4.00
Pitcher, 8" h., 80 oz., pink 83.00
Plate, sherbet, 6" d., clear 2.50
Plate, sherbet, 6" d., pink 5.50
Plate, dinner, 10" d., pink 15.50
Sherbet, clear 3.00
Sherbet, pink 6.00
Tumbler, juice, clear, 3" h. 4.00
Tumbler, juice, pink, 3" h. 5.50
Tumbler, clear, 4" h. 4.00
Tumbler, pink, 4" h. 8.00
Tumbler, ruby, 4" h. 10.00
Vase, 7¼" h., clear 6.50

OYSTER & PEARL (Press-mold)

Bowl, 5¼" heart-shaped, handled, clear, white w/green or white w/pink 5.00
Bowl, 5¼" heart-shaped, handled, pink 6.50
Bowl, 5½" d., handled, clear 4.00
Bowl, 5½" d., handled, pink 4.50
Bowl, 5½" d., handled, ruby 7.50
Bowl, 6½" d., handled, clear 4.00
Bowl, 6½" d., handled, pink 6.50
Bowl, 6½" d., handled, ruby 14.00
Bowl, fruit, clear, 10½" d. 14.50
Bowl, fruit, pink, 10½" d. 15.50
Bowl, fruit, ruby, 10½" d. 29.50
Bowl, fruit, white or white w/green, 10½" d. 10.50
Bowl, fruit, white w/pink, 10½" d. 11.50
Candleholders, clear or pink, 3½" h., pr. 14.50
Candleholders, green, 3½" h., pr. 8.00
Candleholders, ruby, 3½" h., pr. 29.00
Candleholders, white, 3½" h., pr. 10.00
Candleholders, white w/green, 3½" h., pr. 11.50
Candleholders, white w/pink, 3½" h., pr. 13.50
Plate, 13½" d., clear 9.50
Plate, 13½" d., pink 14.00
Plate, 13½" d., ruby 20.00
Relish, divided, clear or pink, 10¼" oval 6.00

PARROT or Sylvan (Process-etched)

Parrot Sherbet

Bowl, berry, 5" sq., amber 10.50
Bowl, berry, 5" sq., green 16.00
Bowl, soup, 7" sq., amber or green 25.00
Bowl, berry, 8" sq., green 48.00
Bowl, 10" oval vegetable, green 34.00
Butter dish, cov., green 292.50
Creamer & cov. sugar bowl, green, pr. 102.00
Creamer & open sugar bowl, amber, pr. 46.00
Creamer & open sugar bowl, green, pr. 36.00
Cup & saucer, amber 33.50
Cup & saucer, green 31.00
Plate, sherbet, 5¾" sq., amber 8.00
Plate, sherbet, 5¾" sq., green 11.50
Plate, salad, 7½" sq., amber 22.50
Plate, salad, 7½" sq., green 13.50
Plate, dinner, 9" sq., amber 25.00
Plate, dinner, 9" sq., green 28.50
Plate, grill, 10½" sq., amber 16.00
Plate, grill, 10½" d., amber 15.50
Plate, grill, 10½" d., green 19.50
Platter, 11¼" oblong, amber 34.50
Platter, 11¼" oblong, green 25.50
Salt & pepper shakers, green, pr. 177.00
Sherbet, cone-shaped, amber 14.00
Sherbet, cone-shaped, green (ILLUS.) 16.50
Sherbet, amber, 4¼" h. 13.00
Sherbet, green, 4¼" h. 15.00
Tumbler, green, 4¼" h., 10 oz. 91.00
Tumbler, amber or green, 5½" h., 12 oz. 110.00
Tumbler, footed, cone-shaped, amber, 5¾" h. 89.00
Tumbler, footed, cone-shaped, green, 5¾" h. 97.00

PATRICIAN or Spoke (Process-etched)

Bowl, cream soup, 4¾" d., amber .. 9.00
Bowl, cream soup, 4¾" d., clear ... 5.50
Bowl, cream soup, 4¾" d., green or pink ... 14.50
Bowl, berry, 5" d., amber or green ... 7.00
Bowl, berry, 5" d., clear ... 5.00
Bowl, berry, 5" d., pink ... 8.50
Bowl, cereal, 6" d., amber ... 14.00
Bowl, cereal, 6" d., clear ... 11.00
Bowl, cereal, 6" d., green ... 17.00
Bowl, cereal, 6" d., pink ... 16.00
Bowl, nappy, 8½" d., amber ... 26.50
Bowl, nappy, 8½" d., clear or pink ... 16.50
Bowl, nappy, 8½" d., green ... 18.50
Bowl, 10" oval vegetable, amber ... 18.00
Bowl, 10" oval vegetable, clear ... 13.00
Bowl, 10" oval vegetable, green ... 17.00
Bowl, 10" oval vegetable, pink ... 14.00
Butter dish, cov., amber or clear ... 63.00
Butter dish, cov., green ... 79.00
Butter dish, cov., pink ... 188.00
Cookie jar, cov., amber or clear ... 56.00
Cookie jar, cov., green ... 242.50
Creamer, clear ... 5.50
Creamer & cov. sugar bowl, amber, pr. ... 46.50
Creamer & cov. sugar bowl, green, pr. ... 55.00
Creamer & cov. sugar bowl, pink, pr. ... 60.00
Creamer & open sugar bowl, amber, pr. ... 11.50
Creamer & open sugar bowl, clear, pr. ... 10.00
Creamer & open sugar bowl, green or pink, pr. ... 15.50

Patrician Cup & Saucer

Cup & saucer, amber (ILLUS.) ... 11.00
Cup & saucer, clear ... 8.00
Cup & saucer, green or pink ... 12.50
Jam dish, amber, 6" ... 19.00
Jam dish, green, 6" ... 21.00
Jam dish, pink, 6" ... 17.00
Pitcher, 8" h., 75 oz., amber ... 78.00
Pitcher, 8" h., 75 oz., clear ... 68.00
Pitcher, 8" h., 75 oz., green ... 73.50
Pitcher, 8" h., 75 oz., pink ... 112.50
Pitcher, 8¼" h., 75 oz., applied handle, amber ... 77.50
Pitcher, 8¼" h., 75 oz., applied handle, clear ... 71.00
Pitcher, 8¼" h., 75 oz., applied handle, green ... 80.00
Pitcher, 8¼" h., 75 oz., applied handle, pink ... 65.00
Plate, sherbet, 6" d., amber ... 6.00
Plate, sherbet, 6" d., clear, green or pink ... 4.00
Plate, salad, 7½" d., amber or green ... 9.00
Plate, salad, 7½" d., clear ... 6.50
Plate, salad, 7½" d., pink ... 10.50
Plate, luncheon, 9" d., amber or clear ... 6.00
Plate, luncheon, 9" d., green or pink ... 7.00
Plate, dinner, 10½" d., amber or clear ... 4.50
Plate, dinner, 10½" d., green ... 32.50
Plate, dinner, 10½" d., pink ... 21.00
Plate, grill, 10½" d., amber or clear ... 6.50
Plate, grill, 10½" d., green or pink ... 10.00
Platter, 11½" oval, amber ... 16.50
Platter, 11½" oval, clear ... 12.00
Platter, 11½" oval, green ... 9.50
Platter, 11½" oval, pink ... 12.50
Salt & pepper shakers, amber or clear, pr. ... 39.00
Salt & pepper shakers, green, pr. ... 43.50
Salt & pepper shakers, pink, pr. ... 61.50
Sherbet, amber ... 6.50
Sherbet, clear ... 5.50
Sherbet, green or pink ... 8.00
Sugar bowl, cov., clear ... 55.50
Tumbler, amber, 4" h., 5 oz. ... 20.50
Tumbler, green, 4" h., 5 oz. ... 22.00
Tumbler, footed, amber, 5¼" h., 8 oz. ... 28.00
Tumbler, footed, clear, 5¼" h., 8 oz. ... 32.50
Tumbler, footed, green, 5¼" h., 8 oz. ... 40.00
Tumbler, amber, clear or pink, 4½" h., 9 oz. ... 17.50
Tumbler, green, 4½" h., 9 oz. ... 19.00
Tumbler, iced tea, amber, 5½" h., 14 oz. ... 26.00
Tumbler, iced tea, clear, 5½" h., 14 oz. ... 21.50
Tumbler, iced tea, green, 5½" h., 14 oz. ... 29.50
Tumbler, iced tea, pink, 5½" h., 14 oz. ... 32.50
Water set: pitcher & five 4½" h. tumblers; amber, 6 pcs. ... 145.00

PETALWARE (Press-mold)

Bowl, cream soup, 4½" d., clear ... 5.00

Bowl, cream soup, 4½" d., Cremax or Monax 7.00
Bowl, cream soup, 4½" d., pink 6.00
Bowl, cereal, 5¾" d., clear 3.50
Bowl, cereal, 5¾" d., Cremax or Monax 5.00
Bowl, cereal, 5¾" d., pink 4.00
Bowl, 9" d., clear 6.50
Bowl, 9" d., Cremax 12.50
Bowl, 9" d., Monax 11.50
Bowl, 9" d., pink 9.00
Creamer, clear 2.50
Creamer, Cremax or Monax 4.00
Creamer, pink 5.00
Cup & saucer, clear 3.00
Cup & saucer, Cremax 5.00
Cup & saucer, Monax or pink 6.00
Lamp shade, Monax, 6" h. 7.50
Lamp shade, pink, 10" h. 8.00
Lamp shade, Monax, 11" h. 13.50
Mustard jar w/metal cover, cobalt blue 7.50
Plate, sherbet, 6" d., clear or Monax 1.50
Plate, sherbet, 6" d., Cremax or pink 2.00
Plate, salad, 8" d., clear 2.50
Plate, salad, 8" d., Cremax 3.50
Plate, salad, 8" d., Monax 4.50
Plate, salad, 8" d., pink 3.00
Plate, dinner, 9" d., clear, Cremax or Monax 4.00
Plate, dinner, 9" d., pink 5.00
Plate, salver, 11" d., clear 4.00
Plate, salver, 11" d., Cremax 5.00
Plate, salver, 11" d., Monax 6.50
Plate, salver, 11" d., pink 8.00
Plate, salver, 12" d., Cremax 6.00
Plate, salver, 12" d., Monax 7.50
Plate, salver, 12" d., pink 3.00
Platter, 13" oval, clear 7.50
Platter, 13" oval, Cremax 8.50
Platter, 13" oval, Monax 10.50
Platter, 13" oval, pink 9.50
Sherbet, Cremax or Monax 6.00
Sherbet, pink 7.50
Sugar bowl, open, footed, Cremax or Monax 4.00
Sugar bowl, open, footed, pink 3.50
Tidbit server, Monax 18.00

PINEAPPLE & FLORAL or Number 618 or Wildflower (Press-mold)

Ashtray, clear, 4½" 12.00
Bowl, berry, 4¾" d., amber 14.50
Bowl, berry, 4¾" d., clear 31.00
Bowl, cream soup, 4 5/8" d., amber 15.50
Bowl, cream soup, 4 5/8" d., clear 17.00
Bowl, cereal, 6" d., clear 18.00
Bowl, salad, 7" d., clear 4.00
Bowl, 10" oval vegetable, amber 13.00
Bowl, 10" oval vegetable, clear 19.50
Compote, diamond-shaped, amber 7.00
Compote, diamond-shaped, clear 2.50
Creamer, diamond-shaped, amber 6.50
Creamer, diamond-shaped, clear 5.50
Creamer & open sugar bowl, diamond-shaped, amber, pr. 14.50
Creamer & open sugar bowl, diamond-shaped, clear, pr. 12.00
Cup & saucer, amber or clear 9.00

Pineapple & Floral Sherbet Plate

Plate, sherbet, 6" d., amber (ILLUS.) 4.00
Plate, sherbet, 6" d., clear 3.00
Plate, salad, 8 3/8" d., amber or clear 5.50
Plate, dinner, 9 3/8" d., amber 11.50
Plate, dinner, 9 3/8" d., clear 9.00
Plate, 11½" d., amber 10.50
Plate, 11½" d., clear 11.50
Plate, 11½" d., w/indentation, clear 15.00
Platter, 11", closed handles, amber 11.50
Platter, 11", closed handles, clear 9.00
Relish, divided, clear, 11½" 11.50
Sherbet, footed, amber 9.00
Sherbet, footed, clear 12.50
Sugar bowl, open, diamond-shaped, amber 6.50
Sugar bowl, open, diamond-shaped, clear 5.50
Tumbler, clear, 4¼" h., 8 oz. 21.00
Tumbler, iced tea, clear, 5" h., 12 oz. 40.50
Vase, 12½" h., cone-shaped, clear 23.00

PRINCESS (Process-etched)

Ashtray, green, 4" 48.00
Bowl, berry, 4½" d., green 18.00
Bowl, berry, 4½" d., pink 11.50
Bowl, berry, 4½" d., yellow 35.00
Bowl, 5" d., amber or green 18.50
Bowl, 5" d., pink 15.00
Bowl, 5" d., pink frosted 7.00
Bowl, 5" d., yellow 21.00
Bowl, salad, 9" octagon, green or pink 24.00
Bowl, salad, 9" octagon, yellow 71.50

Bowl, 9½" hat shape, green 24.00
Bowl, 9½" hat shape, green frosted 10.00
Bowl, 9½" hat shape, pink 23.00
Bowl, 9½" hat shape, pink frosted . . 12.50
Bowl, 10" oval vegetable, green 17.50
Bowl, 10" oval vegetable, pink 14.50
Bowl, 10" oval vegetable, yellow 42.50
Butter dish, cov., green or pink 64.00
Cake stand, footed, green, 10" d. . . . 14.50
Cake stand, footed, pink, 10" d. 10.50
Candy jar, cov., green 32.00
Candy jar, cov., pink 36.00
Coaster, green or pink, 4" 21.00
Cookie jar, cov., green 33.00
Cookie jar, cov., green frosted 21.00
Cookie jar, cov., pink 36.00
Creamer, oval, amber or yellow 9.00
Creamer, oval, green 10.50
Creamer, oval, pink 8.00
Cup & saucer, amber, pink or yellow 9.00
Cup & saucer, green 11.00
Pitcher, 6" h., 37 oz., jug-type, green 33.00
Pitcher, 6" h., 37 oz., jug-type, pink 34.50
Pitcher, 8" h., 60 oz., jug-type, amber 49.00
Pitcher, 8" h., 60 oz., jug-type, green 32.50
Pitcher, 8" h., 60 oz., jug-type, pink 31.50
Pitcher, 8" h., 60 oz., jug-type, yellow 56.50
Plate, sherbet, 5½" d., amber or green 5.00
Plate, sherbet, 5½" d., pink 2.50
Plate, sherbet, 5½" d., yellow 3.00
Plate, salad, 8" d., amber 6.00
Plate, salad, 8" d., green 8.00
Plate, salad, 8" d., pink or yellow . . 7.00
Plate, dinner, 9" d., amber 8.00
Plate, dinner, 9" d., green 18.00
Plate, dinner, 9" d., pink or yellow 11.00
Plate, grill, 9" d., amber or yellow 6.50
Plate, grill, 9" d., green or pink 8.00
Plate, grill, 10½" d., handled, amber, pink or yellow 6.00
Plate, grill, 10½" d., handled, green 10.00
Plate, 11½" d., handled, green 12.50
Plate, 11½" d., handled, pink 11.00
Platter, 12" oval, green 15.00
Platter, 12" oval, pink 13.00
Platter, 12" oval, yellow 48.00
Relish, plain, green, 7½" 60.00
Relish, divided, green, 7½" 17.00
Relish, divided, pink, 7½" 13.00
Salt & pepper shakers, green, 4½" h., pr. 40.00
Salt & pepper shakers, pink, 4½" h., pr. 33.50
Salt & pepper shakers, yellow, 4½" h., pr. 51.00
Salt & pepper (or spice) shakers, green, 5½" h., pr. 33.00
Sherbet, green 12.00
Sherbet, pink 10.00
Sherbet, yellow 23.00
Sugar bowl, cov., amber or yellow . . 22.00

Princess Sugar Bowl

Sugar bowl, cov., green (ILLUS.) . . . 21.00
Sugar bowl, cov., pink 18.50
Sugar bowl, open, amber 5.50
Sugar bowl, open, green or yellow 8.50
Sugar bowl, open, pink 7.00
Sugar bowl, open, pink frosted 4.50
Tumbler, green, 3" h., 5 oz. 20.50
Tumbler, pink, 3" h., 5 oz. 16.00
Tumbler, yellow, 3" h., 5 oz. 18.00
Tumbler, green, 4" h., 9 oz. 17.00
Tumbler, pink, 4" h., 9 oz. 13.50
Tumbler, yellow, 4" h., 9 oz. 14.50
Tumbler, footed, green, 5¼" h., 10 oz. 21.50
Tumbler, footed, pink or yellow, 5¼" h., 10 oz. 16.00
Tumbler, footed, green, 6½" h., 12 oz. 59.50
Tumbler, footed, pink, 6½" h., 12 oz. 30.00
Tumbler, footed, yellow, 6½" h., 12 oz. 19.50
Tumbler, green, 5¼" h., 13 oz. 25.50
Tumbler, pink, 5¼" h., 13 oz. 14.00
Tumbler, yellow, 5¼" h., 13 oz. 17.00
Vase, 8" h., green 20.00
Vase, 8" h., pink 18.00
Vase, 8" h., pink frosted 12.00

QUEEN MARY or Vertical Ribbed (Press-mold)

Ashtray, clear, 2 x 3¾" oval 2.50
Ashtray, clear, 3½" d. 4.00
Bowl, nappy, 4" d., clear or pink . . . 3.00
Bowl, nappy, 4" d., handled, clear . . 2.50
Bowl, nappy, 4" d., handled, pink . . 3.50
Bowl, berry, 5" d., clear or pink 3.00
Bowl, 5½" d., 2-handled, clear 2.50
Bowl, 5½" d., 2-handled, pink 3.50
Bowl, cereal, 6" d., clear 4.00

Bowl, cereal, 6" d., pink ... 6.50
Bowl, nappy, 7" d., clear or pink ... 5.50
Bowl, 8¾" d., clear ... 7.50
Bowl, 8¾" d., pink ... 14.00
Butter (or jam) dish, cov., clear ... 18.00
Butter (or jam) dish, cov., pink ... 78.00
Candlesticks, 2-light, clear, 4½" h., pr. ... 11.00
Candy jar, cov., clear ... 11.50
Candy jar, cov., pink ... 24.50
Celery (or pickle) dish, clear, 5 x 10" oval ... 6.50
Celery (or pickle) dish, pink, 5 x 10" oval ... 16.00
Cigarette jar, clear, 2 x 3" oval ... 3.50
Coaster, clear or pink, 3½" d. ... 2.00
Coaster-ashtray, clear, 4¼" sq. ... 2.50
Coaster-ashtray, pink, 4¼" sq. ... 9.00
Coaster-ashtray, ruby, 4¼" sq. ... 4.00
Compote, 5¾" d., clear ... 5.00
Creamer, oval, clear ... 3.50
Creamer, oval, pink ... 4.50
Cup & saucer, clear ... 4.50

Queen Mary Cup & Saucer

Cup & saucer, pink (ILLUS.) ... 6.50
Plate, sherbet, 6" d., clear or pink ... 2.00
Plate, 6¾" d., clear ... 2.00
Plate, 6¾" d., pink ... 3.50
Plate, salad, 8½" d., clear ... 3.50
Plate, salad, 8½" d., pink ... 4.50
Plate, dinner, 9¾" d., clear ... 17.50
Plate, dinner, 9¾" d., pink ... 22.50
Plate, 12" d., clear ... 6.00
Plate, 12" d., pink ... 13.50
Plate, 14" d., pink ... 15.00
Relish, 3-part, clear or pink, 12" d. ... 6.00
Relish, 4-part, clear, 14" d. ... 8.00
Relish, 4-part, pink, 14" d. ... 14.00
Salt & pepper shakers, clear, pr. ... 14.50
Sherbet, clear ... 3.00
Sherbet, pink ... 4.50
Sugar bowl, open, oval, clear ... 3.50
Sugar bowl, open, oval, pink ... 4.50
Tumbler, juice, pink, 3½" h., 5 oz. ... 6.00
Tumbler, water, clear, 4" h., 9 oz. ... 4.50
Tumbler, water, pink, 4" h., 9 oz. ... 5.50
Tumbler, footed, clear, 5" h., 10 oz. ... 12.00
Tumbler, footed, pink, 5" h., 10 oz. ... 23.50

RAINDROPS or Optic Design (Press-mold)

(All items listed are green.)

Bowl, fruit, 4½" d. ... 4.00
Bowl, cereal, 6" d. ... 5.50
Creamer ... 6.00
Cup & saucer ... 5.00
Plate, sherbet, 6" d. ... 2.00
Plate, luncheon, 8" d. ... 3.00
Sherbet ... 4.50
Sugar bowl, cov. ... 15.00
Tumbler, whiskey, 1 7/8" h., 1 oz. ... 3.00
Tumbler, 3" h., 4 oz. ... 3.50
Tumbler, 3 7/8" h., 5 oz. ... 4.50
Tumbler, 4 1/8" h., 9½ oz. ... 5.50
Tumbler, 5" h., 10 oz. ... 8.50

RIBBON (Press-mold)

(While pattern was also made in black, all items listed are green.)

Bowl, 4" d. ... 10.00
Bowl, 8" d. ... 15.50
Candy dish, cov. ... 22.50
Creamer & open sugar bowl, footed, pr. ... 11.50
Cup & saucer ... 6.00
Plate, sherbet, 6¼" d. ... 1.50
Plate, luncheon, 8" d. ... 3.00
Salt & pepper shakers, pr. ... 13.50
Sherbet, footed ... 4.00
Tumbler 6" h., 10 oz. ... 14.50

RING or Banded Rings (Press-mold)

Bowl, berry, 5" d., clear ... 3.00
Bowl, berry, 5" d., green ... 4.50
Bowl, 8" d., green ... 8.00
Butter tub or ice bucket, clear ... 9.50
Butter tub or ice bucket, green ... 17.00
Cocktail shaker, clear ... 9.50
Cocktail shaker, green ... 12.00
Creamer & open sugar bowl, footed, clear, pr. ... 6.50
Creamer & open sugar bowl, footed, green, pr. ... 9.50
Cup & saucer, clear or green ... 4.50
Decanter w/stopper, clear ... 14.50
Decanter w/stopper, green ... 18.50
Goblet, clear, 7" h., 9 oz. ... 5.00
Goblet, green, 7" h., 9 oz. ... 8.00
Pitcher, 8" h., 60 oz., clear or green ... 10.00
Pitcher, 8½" h., 80 oz., clear ... 11.00
Pitcher, 8½" h., 80 oz., green ... 20.00
Plate, sherbet, 6¼" d., clear ... 1.00
Plate, sherbet, 6¼" d., green ... 2.00
Plate, 6½" d., off-center ring, clear ... 1.50
Plate, 6½" d., off-center ring, green ... 3.50
Plate, luncheon, 8" d., clear ... 4.50
Plate, luncheon, 8" d., green ... 3.50
Salt & pepper shakers, clear, 3" h., pr. ... 19.00

Sandwich server w/center handle, clear ... 9.50
Sandwich server w/center handle, green ... 16.50
Sherbet, low, clear ... 3.50
Sherbet, low, green ... 7.50
Sherbet, footed, clear, 4¾" ... 3.50
Sherbet, footed, green, 4¾" ... 5.00
Tumbler, whiskey, clear, 2" h., 1½ oz. ... 3.50
Tumbler, clear, 3½" h., 5 oz. ... 2.00
Tumbler, green, 3½" h., 5 oz. ... 3.50
Tumbler, clear, 4¼" h., 9 oz. ... 3.00
Tumbler, green, 4¼" h., 9 oz. ... 6.00
Tumbler, clear, 5 1/8" h., 12 oz. ... 3.50
Tumbler, green, 5 1/8" h., 12 oz. ... 5.50
Tumbler, cocktail, footed, clear, 3½" h. ... 3.00
Tumbler, water, footed, clear, 5½" h. ... 3.00
Tumbler, water, footed, green, 5½" h. ... 7.50
Tumbler, iced tea, footed, clear or green, 6½" h. ... 4.50

ROULETTE or Many Windows (Press-mold)

Bowl, fruit, 9" d., green ... 10.00
Cup & saucer, green ... 5.00
Pitcher, 8" h., 64 oz., green ... 26.50
Pitcher, 8" h., 64 oz., pink ... 23.00
Plate, sherbet, 6" d., green ... 2.50
Plate, luncheon, 8½" d., clear ... 3.00
Plate, luncheon, 8½" d., green ... 4.00
Plate, 12" d., green ... 8.00
Sherbet, green ... 3.50
Sherbet, pink ... 2.50
Tumbler, whiskey, green or pink, 2½" h., 1½ oz. ... 6.50
Tumbler, juice, green, 3¼" h., 5 oz. ... 12.00
Tumbler, juice, pink, 3¼" h., 5 oz. ... 5.00
Tumbler, old fashioned, green, 3¼" h., 8 oz. ... 3.00
Tumbler, water, green, 4 1/8" h., 9 oz. ... 12.00
Tumbler, water, pink, 4 1/8" h., 9 oz. ... 10.50
Tumbler, footed, green, 5½" h., 10 oz. ... 15.00
Tumbler, iced tea, green, 5 1/8" h., 12 oz. ... 16.00
Tumbler, iced tea, pink, 5 1/8" h., 12 oz. ... 8.50

ROYAL LACE (Process-etched)

Bowl, cream soup, 4¾" d., blue ... 23.00
Bowl, cream soup, 4¾" d., clear ... 8.00
Bowl, cream soup, 4¾" d., green ... 21.50
Bowl, cream soup, 4¾" d., pink ... 12.50
Bowl, berry, 5" d., blue ... 28.00
Bowl, berry, 5" d., clear ... 9.50
Bowl, berry, 5" d., green ... 18.00
Bowl, berry, 5" d., pink ... 13.50
Bowl, nappy, 10" d., blue ... 36.00
Bowl, nappy, 10" d., clear ... 11.50
Bowl, nappy, 10" d., green ... 19.00
Bowl, nappy, 10" d., pink ... 17.00
Bowl, 10" d., 3-footed, rolled edge, blue ... 225.00
Bowl, 10" d., 3-footed, rolled edge, pink ... 33.50
Bowl, 10" d., 3-footed, ruffled edge, blue ... 185.00
Bowl, 10" d., 3-footed, ruffled edge, clear ... 15.50
Bowl, 10" d., 3-footed, ruffled edge, green ... 32.00
Bowl, 10" d., 3-footed, ruffled edge, pink ... 36.50
Bowl, 10" d., 3-footed, straight edge, blue ... 45.50
Bowl, 10" d., 3-footed, straight edge, clear ... 12.00
Bowl, 10" d., 3-footed, straight edge, pink ... 22.50
Bowl, 11" oval vegetable, blue ... 38.00
Bowl, 11" oval vegetable, clear ... 14.00
Bowl, 11" oval vegetable, green ... 20.00
Bowl, 11" oval vegetable, pink ... 18.50
Butter dish, cov., blue ... 375.00

Royal Lace Butter Dish

Butter dish, cov., clear (ILLUS.) ... 52.00
Butter dish, cov., green ... 219.00
Butter dish, cov., pink ... 112.00
Candlesticks, rolled edge, blue, pr. ... 95.00
Candlesticks, rolled edge, clear, pr. ... 31.00
Candlesticks, rolled edge, green, pr. ... 56.00
Candlesticks, rolled edge, pink, pr. ... 39.00
Candlesticks, ruffled edge, blue, pr. ... 97.50
Candlesticks, ruffled edge, clear, pr. ... 28.50
Candlesticks, ruffled edge, green, pr. ... 42.50
Candlesticks, ruffled edge, pink, pr. ... 38.00
Candlesticks, straight edge, blue, pr. ... 90.00
Candlesticks, straight edge, clear, pr. ... 25.00

Candlesticks, straight edge, green, pr. 56.00
Candlesticks, straight edge, pink, pr. 31.00
Cookie jar, cov., blue 215.00
Cookie jar, cov., clear 26.00
Cookie jar, cov., green 54.00
Cookie jar, cov., pink 37.00
Creamer & cov. sugar bowl, blue, pr. 145.00
Creamer & cov. sugar bowl, clear, pr. 28.00
Creamer & cov. sugar bowl, green, pr. 60.00
Creamer & cov. sugar bowl, pink, pr. 39.50
Creamer & open sugar bowl, blue, pr. 48.50
Creamer & open sugar bowl, clear, pr. 14.00
Creamer & open sugar bowl, green, pr. 31.00
Creamer & open sugar bowl, pink, pr. 18.50
Cup & saucer, blue 29.50
Cup & saucer, clear 8.50
Cup & saucer, green 16.50
Cup & saucer, pink 13.50
Pitcher, 48 oz., straight sides, blue 85.00
Pitcher, 48 oz., straight sides, clear 34.00
Pitcher, 48 oz., straight sides, green 75.00
Pitcher, 48 oz., straight sides, pink 56.00
Pitcher, 8" h., 68 oz., blue 119.00
Pitcher, 8" h., 68 oz., clear 36.50
Pitcher, 8" h., 68 oz., green 73.50
Pitcher, 8" h., 68 oz., pink 55.50
Pitcher, 8" h., 86 oz., blue 102.50
Pitcher, 8" h., 86 oz., clear 35.50
Pitcher, 8" h., 86 oz., green 76.00
Pitcher, 8" h., 86 oz., pink 52.50
Pitcher, 8½" h., 96 oz., blue 162.00
Pitcher, 8½" h., 96 oz., clear 43.00
Pitcher, 8½" h., 96 oz., green 107.50
Pitcher, 8½" h., 96 oz., pink 64.00
Plate, sherbet, 6" d., blue 7.50
Plate, sherbet, 6" d., clear 3.00
Plate, sherbet, 6" d., green 6.00
Plate, sherbet, 6" d., pink 4.00
Plate, luncheon, 8½" d., blue 23.50
Plate, luncheon, 8½" d., clear 4.50
Plate, luncheon, 8½" d., green or pink 13.50
Plate, dinner, 10" d., blue 28.00
Plate, dinner, 10" d., clear 8.00
Plate, dinner, 10" d., green 18.50
Plate, dinner, 10" d., pink 12.00
Plate, grill, 10" d., blue 22.50
Plate, grill, 10" d., clear or green 10.50
Plate, grill, 10" d., pink 9.00
Platter, 13" oval, blue 37.00
Platter, 13" oval, clear 12.00
Platter, 13" oval, green 26.00
Platter, 13" oval, pink 15.00
Salt & pepper shakers, blue, pr. 204.00
Salt & pepper shakers, clear, pr. 35.00
Salt & pepper shakers, green, pr. 95.00
Salt & pepper shakers, pink, pr. 42.50
Sherbet, footed, blue 24.50
Sherbet, footed, clear 7.50
Sherbet, footed, green 15.00
Sherbet, footed, pink 10.00
Sherbet in metal holder, blue 17.00
Sherbet in metal holder, clear 11.50
Toddy set: cookie jar w/metal lid & 5 roly-poly tumblers; amethyst, 6 pcs. 90.00
Toddy set: cookie jar w/metal lid, 8 roly-poly tumblers, metal tray & ladle; blue, 11 pcs. 140.00
Tumbler, blue, 3½" h., 5 oz. 27.00
Tumbler, clear, 3½" h., 5 oz. 9.50
Tumbler, green, 3½" h., 5 oz. 20.00
Tumbler, pink, 3½" h., 5 oz. 14.00
Tumbler, blue, 4" h., 9 oz. 25.50
Tumbler, clear, 4" h., 9 oz. 8.00
Tumbler, green, 4" h., 9 oz. 18.50
Tumbler, pink, 4" h., 9 oz. 10.50
Tumbler, blue, 4¾" h., 10 oz. 46.50
Tumbler, clear, 4¾" h., 10 oz. 12.00
Tumbler, green, 4¾" h., 10 oz. 40.00
Tumbler, pink, 4¾" h., 10 oz. 20.00
Tumbler, blue, 5 3/8" h., 12 oz. 47.00
Tumbler, clear, 5 3/8" h., 12 oz. 21.50
Tumbler, green, 5 3/8" h., 12 oz. 39.00
Tumbler, pink, 5 3/8" h., 12 oz. 41.00

ROYAL RUBY (Press-mold)

(All items in ruby red.)

Ashtray, 4½" sq. 3.50
Bowl, berry, 4¼" d. 4.00
Bowl, 5¼" d. 6.00
Bowl, soup, 7½" d. 8.50
Bowl, 8" oval vegetable 19.00
Bowl, berry, 8½" d. 14.00
Bowl, salad, 11½" d. 22.00
Creamer, flat 5.00
Creamer, footed 6.00
Cup & saucer 5.00
Goblet, ball stem 7.50
Lamp 23.50
Pitcher, 22 oz., tilted or upright 21.50
Pitcher, 3 qt., tilted or upright 28.00
Plate, sherbet, 6½" d. 3.50
Plate, salad, 7" d. 4.00
Plate, luncheon, 7¾" d. 4.50
Plate, dinner, 9" d. 7.00
Plate, 13¾" d. 25.00
Playing card box, divided clear base 30.00
Punch bowl 27.00
Punch bowl & base 36.50
Punch cup 2.00
Punch set, punch bowl, base, 11 cups & ladle, 14 pcs. 99.50

Sherbet, footed 5.50
Sugar bowl, flat 5.00
Sugar bowl, footed 5.50
Sugar bowl w/slotted lid, footed 14.00
Tumbler, cocktail, 3½ oz. 4.00
Tumbler, juice, 5 oz. 4.00
Tumbler, water, 9 oz. 4.00
Tumbler, water, 10 oz. 5.50
Tumbler, iced tea, 13 oz. 7.00
Vase, 4" h., ball-shaped 4.00
Vase, bud, 5½" h., ruffled top 5.50
Vase, 6½" h., bulbous 6.00
Wine, 2½ oz. 7.50

SANDWICH (Press-mold)

Sandwich Cup & Saucer

Berry set: master bowl & 8 sauce dishes; clear, 9 pcs. 30.00
Bowl, berry, 4 7/8" d., amber or clear 3.00
Bowl, berry, 4 7/8" d., green 2.00
Bowl, berry, 4 7/8" d., pink 4.00
Bowl, 5¼" d., ruby 14.00
Bowl, cereal, 6½" d., amber 7.50
Bowl, cereal, 6½" d., clear 10.00
Bowl, 6½" d., smooth or scalloped, amber 7.00
Bowl, 6½" d., smooth or scalloped, clear 5.00
Bowl, 6½" d., smooth or scalloped, green 26.50
Bowl, 6½" d., smooth or scalloped, ruby 23.00
Bowl, salad, 7" d., clear 6.50
Bowl, salad, 7" d., green 37.00
Bowl, 8" d., smooth or scalloped, clear 6.00
Bowl, 8" d., smooth or scalloped, green 44.00
Bowl, 8" d., smooth or scalloped, pink 7.50
Bowl, 8" d., smooth or scalloped, ruby 24.50
Bowl, 8½" oval vegetable, clear 5.00
Bowl, salad, 9" d., clear 17.50
Butter dish, cov., clear 28.50
Cookie jar, cov., amber 25.50
Cookie jar, cov., clear 27.00
Cookie jar, cov., green 17.50
Creamer, clear 3.50
Creamer, green 13.00
Cup & saucer, amber (ILLUS.) 5.50
Cup & saucer, clear 3.00
Cup & saucer, green 17.50
Custard cup, clear 4.50
Custard cup, green 2.00
Pitcher, juice, 6" h., 36 oz., clear 49.50
Pitcher, juice, 6" h., 36 oz., green 84.50
Pitcher w/ice lip, 2 qt., clear 46.00
Pitcher w/ice lip, 2 qt., green 134.00
Plate, 4½" d., clear 6.00
Plate, 4½" d., green 1.50
Plate, dessert, 7" d., amber 4.50
Plate, dessert, 7" d., clear 6.50
Plate, 8" d., clear 3.50
Plate, dinner, 9" d., amber 5.00
Plate, dinner, 9" d., clear 9.50
Plate, dinner, 9" d., green 44.50
Plate, snack, 9" d., clear 4.50
Plate, sandwich, 12" d., amber 8.00
Plate, sandwich, 12" d., clear 13.50
Punch bowl, clear (no base) 13.50
Punch bowl & base, clear 27.00
Punch bowl & base, white 15.00
Punch cup, clear or white 1.50
Punch set: punch bowl & 7 cups; clear, 8 pcs. 37.00
Punch set: punch bowl, base & 8 cups; white, 10 pcs. 25.00
Sherbet, footed, clear 4.00
Sugar bowl, cov., clear 11.00
Sugar bowl, cov., green 16.50
Sugar bowl, open, clear 3.50
Sugar bowl, open, green 13.00
Tumbler, clear, 5 oz. 4.50
Tumbler, green, 5 oz. 3.00
Tumbler, water, clear, 9 oz. 7.00
Tumbler, water, green, 9 oz. 3.00
Tumbler, footed, clear, 9 oz. 14.50
Water set: 36 oz. pitcher & 6 tumblers; green, 7 pcs. 97.00

SHARON or Cabbage Rose (Chip-mold)

Bowl, cream soup, 5" d., amber 16.50
Bowl, cream soup, 5" d., green 27.50
Bowl, cream soup, 5" d., pink 25.50
Bowl, berry, 5" d., amber 5.50
Bowl, berry, 5" d., green 8.50
Bowl, berry, 5" d., pink 6.00
Bowl, cereal, 6" d., amber 10.50
Bowl, cereal, 6" d., green 16.50
Bowl, cereal, 6" d., pink 13.50
Bowl, soup, 7½" d., amber or pink 24.50
Bowl, berry, 8½" d., amber 4.00
Bowl, berry, 8½" d., green 21.00
Bowl, berry, 8½" d., pink 15.00
Bowl, 9½" oval vegetable, amber 9.50
Bowl, 9½" oval vegetable, green 16.00
Bowl, 9½" oval vegetable, pink 13.50
Bowl, fruit, 10½" d., amber 13.00
Bowl, fruit, 10½" d., green 21.00

Bowl, fruit, 10½" d., pink 20.00
Butter dish, cov., amber or pink 34.50
Butter dish, cov., green 61.50
Cake plate, footed, amber, 11½" d. 16.00
Cake plate, footed, clear, 11½" d... 6.00
Cake plate, footed, green, 11½" d. 45.00
Cake plate, footed, pink, 11½" d. .. 22.50
Candy jar, cov., amber 34.50
Candy jar, cov., green 113.00
Candy jar, cov., pink 32.50
Cheese dish, cov., amber 140.00
Cheese dish, cov., pink 590.00
Creamer, amber 8.50
Creamer, green 11.50
Creamer, pink 9.50
Cup & saucer, amber 10.50
Cup & saucer, green 16.00
Cup & saucer, pink 12.50
Jam dish, amber, 7½" d. 24.00
Jam dish, green, 7½" d. 25.50
Jam dish, pink, 7½" d. 90.00
Pitcher, 9" h., 80 oz., amber 86.50
Pitcher, 9" h., 80 oz., green 500.00
Pitcher, 9" h., 80 oz., pink 97.50
Pitcher w/ice lip, 9" h., 80 oz., amber 92.00
Pitcher, w/ice lip, 9" h., 80 oz., green 325.00
Pitcher w/ice lip, 9" h., 80 oz., pink 98.00
Plate, bread & butter, 6" d., amber or pink 2.50
Plate, bread & butter, 6" d., green.. 4.50
Plate, salad, 7½" d., amber 10.50
Plate, salad, 7½" d., green 13.50
Plate, salad, 7½" d., pink 19.00
Plate, dinner, 9¼" d., amber or pink 9.00
Plate, dinner, 9¼" d., green 12.00
Platter, 12¼" oval, amber 10.50
Platter, 12¼" oval, green 15.00
Platter, 12¼" oval, pink 12.50
Salt & pepper shakers, amber, pr. .. 30.00
Salt & pepper shakers, green, pr.... 53.00
Salt & pepper shakers, pink, pr. 31.50
Sherbet, amber or pink 8.50
Sherbet, green 21.50
Sugar bowl, cov., amber 22.00
Sugar bowl, cov., green 34.50
Sugar bowl, cov., pink 25.50
Sugar bowl, open, amber 6.50
Sugar bowl, open, green 9.00
Sugar bowl, open, pink 7.50
Tumbler, amber or pink, 4" h., 9 oz. 19.50
Tumbler, green, 4" h., 9 oz. 52.00
Tumbler, amber, 5¼" h., 12 oz. 27.50
Tumbler, green, 5¼" h., 12 oz. 66.00
Tumbler, pink, 5¼" h., 12 oz. 33.00
Tumbler, footed, amber, 6½" h., 15 oz. 56.00
Tumbler, footed, clear, 6½" h., 15 oz. 17.50
Tumbler, footed, pink, 6½" h., 15 oz. 32.50
Water set: ice lip pitcher & 8 tumblers; amber, 9 pcs. 245.00

SIERRA or Pinwheel (Press-mold)

Bowl, cereal, 5½" d., green or pink 7.00
Bowl, berry, 8½" d., green 15.50
Bowl, berry, 8½" d., pink 12.50
Bowl, 9½" oval vegetable, green ... 47.00
Bowl, 9½" oval vegetable, pink 22.50
Butter dish, cov., green 47.00
Butter dish, cov., pink 42.00
Creamer, green 12.00
Creamer, pink 9.00
Cup & saucer, green 11.50
Cup & saucer, pink 10.00
Pitcher, 6½" h., 32 oz., green 64.50
Pitcher, 6½" h., 32 oz., pink 46.00
Plate, dinner, 9" d., green 12.00
Plate, dinner, 9" d., pink 9.50
Platter, 11" oval, green 27.50
Platter, 11" oval, pink 20.00
Salt & pepper shakers, green, pr. ... 34.50
Salt & pepper shakers, pink, pr. 26.50
Serving tray, 2-handled, green or pink, 10¼" oval 11.00
Sugar bowl, cov., green 19.00
Sugar bowl, cov., pink 23.00
Tumbler, footed, green, 4½" h., 9 oz. 47.50
Tumbler, footed, pink, 4½" h., 9 oz. 25.50

SPIRAL (Press-mold)

(All items in green only.)

Bowl, berry, 4" d. 7.00
Bowl, salad, 6½" d., deep 16.50
Bowl, berry, 7½" d. 14.50
Creamer, footed 7.00
Cup & saucer 6.00
Pitcher, 7 5/8" h., 58 oz. 23.50
Plate, sherbet, 6" d. 2.00
Plate, salad, 7½" d. 2.50
Sandwich server w/center handle .. 18.50
Sherbet 3.00
Sugar bowl, flat 8.50
Sugar bowl, footed 6.00
Tumbler, water, 5" h., 9 oz. 8.50

SWIRL or Petal Swirl (Press-mold)

Ashtray, ultramarine, 5 3/8" 10.00
Berry set: master bowl & 6 sauce dishes; Delfite, 7 pcs. 35.00
Bowl, cereal, 5¼" d., Delfite or ultramarine 7.00
Bowl, cereal, 5¼" d., pink 5.00
Bowl, salad, 9" d., Delfite 13.50
Bowl, salad, 9" d., pink 12.50
Bowl, salad, 9" d., ultramarine 15.00

Bowl, fruit, 10" d., closed handles, footed, ultramarine 19.00
Butter dish, cov., pink 110.00
Butter dish, cov., ultramarine 172.50
Candlesticks, double, pink, pr. 23.50
Candlesticks, double, ultramarine, pr. 29.00
Candy dish, cov., pink 50.00
Candy dish, cov., ultramarine 63.00
Candy dish, open, 3-footed, pink, 5½" d. 5.50
Candy dish, open, 3-footed, ultramarine, 5½" d. 9.00
Coaster, pink, 3¼" d., 1" h. 5.50
Coaster, ultramarine, 3¼" d., 1" h. 8.00
Console bowl, footed, ultramarine, 10½" d. 18.50
Creamer, Delfite 6.00
Creamer, pink 7.00
Creamer, ultramarine 8.50
Cup & saucer, Delfite or ultramarine 10.50
Cup & saucer, pink 6.50
Plate, sherbet, 6½" d., Delfite 3.50
Plate, sherbet, 6½" d., pink 2.00
Plate, sherbet, 6½" d., ultramarine 4.50
Plate, 7¼" d., ultramarine 7.50
Plate, salad, 8" d., pink 5.50
Plate, salad, 8" d., ultramarine 8.50
Plate, dinner, 9½" d., Delfite 8.00
Plate, dinner, 9½" d., pink 7.00
Plate, dinner, 9½" d., ultramarine .. 9.50
Plate, sandwich, 12½" d., pink 8.00
Plate, sandwich, 12½" d., ultramarine 12.50
Platter, 12" oval, Delfite 17.00
Salt & pepper shakers, ultramarine, pr. 28.50
Sherbet, pink 7.50
Sherbet, ultramarine 10.50
Soup bowl w/lug handles, pink 9.50
Soup bowl w/lug handles, ultramarine 15.50
Sugar bowl, open, Delfite 7.00
Sugar bowl, open, pink 4.00
Sugar bowl, open, ultramarine 8.50

Swirl Vase

Tumbler, pink, 4" h., 9 oz. 9.50
Tumbler, ultramarine, 4" h., 9 oz. 13.50
Tumbler, footed, pink, 9 oz. 10.00
Tumbler, footed, ultramarine, 9 oz. 19.50
Tumbler, pink, 4¾" h., 12 oz. 13.50
Tumbler, ultramarine, 4¾" h., 12 oz. 24.00
Vase, 6½" h., pink 8.00
Vase, 6½" h., ultramarine 14.50
Vase, 8½" h., ultramarine (ILLUS.) .. 14.00

TEA ROOM (Press-mold)

Tea Room Tumbler

Banana split dish, clear, 7½" 31.00
Banana split dish, green, 7½" 71.00
Banana split dish, pink, 7½" 102.50
Bowl, salad, 8¾" d., green 65.00
Bowl, salad, 8¾" d., pink 48.00
Bowl, 9½" oval vegetable, green ... 49.00
Bowl, 9½" oval vegetable, pink 38.50
Candlesticks, green, pr. 38.50
Candlesticks, pink, pr. 37.00
Celery or pickle dish, green, 8½" .. 22.00
Creamer, clear, 4" h. 8.50
Creamer, green, 4" h. 11.50
Creamer, pink, 4" h. 13.00
Creamer & open sugar bowl on center handled tray, green 50.50
Creamer & open sugar bowl on center handled tray, pink 53.00
Cup & saucer, green 32.50
Cup & saucer, pink 36.50
Finger bowl, pink 40.00
Goblet, green, 9 oz. 64.00
Goblet, pink, 9 oz. 52.00
Ice bucket, green 51.00
Ice bucket, pink 47.50
Lamp, electric, green, 9" 46.00
Lamp, electric, pink, 9" 57.50
Marmalade, w/notched lid, clear ... 110.00
Mustard, cov., clear 55.00
Mustard, cov., green 125.00
Mustard, cov., pink 120.00
Parfait, green 52.00
Parfait, pink 29.00
Pitcher, 64 oz., green 98.00

Pitcher, 64 oz., pink 94.50
Plate, sherbet, 6½" d., green or pink 16.50
Plate, luncheon, 8¼" d., green 35.00
Plate, luncheon, 8¼" d., pink 31.00
Plate, 10½" d., 2-handled, green 45.00
Plate, 10½" d., 2-handled, pink 60.00
Plate, sandwich, w/center handle, green 137.00
Plate, sandwich, w/center handle, pink 115.00
Relish, divided, green or pink 15.00
Salt & pepper shakers, green, pr. 44.00
Salt & pepper shakers, pink, pr. 36.50
Sherbet, low footed, green 27.00
Sherbet, low footed, pink 22.00
Sherbet, low, flared edge, clear or pink 17.50
Sherbet, low, flared edge, green 15.50
Sherbet, tall footed, clear 25.50
Sherbet, tall footed, green 35.00
Sherbet, tall footed, pink 28.00
Sugar bowl, green, 4" h. 10.50
Sugar bowl, pink, 4" h. 8.00
Sugar bowl, open, footed, amber, 4½" h. 47.50
Sugar bowl, open, footed, clear, 4½" h. 9.00
Sugar bowl, open, footed, green, 4½" h. 18.50
Sugar bowl, open, footed, pink, 4½" h. 10.00
Sugar bowl, open, rectangular, green 12.50
Sugar bowl, open, rectangular, pink 11.00
Tray w/center handle, for creamer & sugar bowl, pink 46.00
Tumbler, footed, clear, 6 oz. 28.00
Tumbler, footed, green, 6 oz. 25.50
Tumbler, footed, pink, 6 oz. 23.00
Tumbler, green or pink, 8½ oz. 17.50
Tumbler, footed, green, 9 oz. 24.00
Tumbler, footed, pink, 9 oz. 22.00
Tumbler, footed, green, 11 oz. 28.50
Tumbler, footed, pink, 11 oz. (ILLUS.) 25.00
Tumbler, footed, clear, 12 oz. 14.50
Tumbler, footed, green or pink, 12 oz. 35.50
Vase, 6" h., ruffled rim, green 69.00
Vase, 6" h., ruffled rim, pink 61.50
Vase, 9" h., ruffled rim, clear 18.00
Vase, 9" h., ruffled rim, green 73.50
Vase, 11" h., ruffled rim, green 92.50
Vase, 11" h., ruffled rim, pink 105.00
Vase, 11" h., straight, green 65.00
Vase, 11" h., straight, pink 60.00
Water set: pitcher & 4 tumblers; green, 5 pcs. 225.00

TWISTED OPTIC (Press-mold)

Bowl, cream soup, 4¾" d., green or pink 7.00
Bowl, cereal, 5" d., green or pink 7.50
Candlesticks, amber or clear, 3", pr. 9.50
Candlesticks, green, 3", pr. 12.50
Candlesticks, pink, 3", pr. 11.00
Candlesticks, yellow, 3", pr. 22.50
Candy jar, cov., green 15.50
Candy jar, cov., pink 28.00
Creamer, amber or yellow 8.50
Creamer, green 6.00
Creamer, pink 4.50
Cup & saucer, amber or pink 5.00
Cup & saucer, green 11.00
Cup & saucer, yellow 9.00
Plate, sherbet, 6" d., amber or green 1.50
Plate, sherbet, 6" d., pink 3.00
Plate, sherbet, 6" d., yellow 4.00
Plate, salad, 7" d., green 3.00
Plate, 9 x 7½" oval, w/indentation, yellow 6.50
Plate, luncheon, 8" d., amber, clear or green 3.00
Plate, luncheon, 8" d., pink 3.50
Plate, luncheon, 8" d., yellow 4.50
Preserve jar w/slotted lid, amber or pink 12.00
Preserve jar w/slotted lid, green 16.50
Sandwich server w/center handle, amber or green 14.00
Sandwich server w/center handle, yellow 27.50
Sandwich server, 2-handled, amber 13.00
Sandwich server, 2-handled, yellow 20.00
Sherbet, amber, green or pink 4.00
Sherbet, yellow 5.50
Sugar bowl, open, amber, green or pink 4.50
Tumbler, pink, 4½" h., 9 oz. 7.00
Tumbler, green, 5¼" h., 12 oz. 4.00
Tumbler, pink, 5¼" h., 12 oz. 8.00

WATERFORD or Waffle (Press-mold)

Waterford Pattern

Ashtray, clear, 4" 4.00
Bowl, berry, 4¾" d., clear 3.50
Bowl, berry, 4¾" d., pink 6.50

Bowl, cereal, 5½" d., clear 9.50
Bowl, cereal, 5½" d., pink 18.50
Bowl, berry, 8¼" d., clear 6.00
Bowl, berry, 8¼" d., pink 11.00
Butter dish, cov., clear 18.00
Butter dish, cov., pink 152.50
Cake plate, handled, clear, 10¼" d. 4.50
Cake plate, handled, pink, 10¼" d. 8.50
Coaster, clear, 4" d. 1.50
Coaster, pink, 4" d. 2.50
Creamer, oval, clear 2.50
Creamer, oval, pink 8.00
Cup & saucer, clear (ILLUS. right) . . . 5.50
Cup & saucer, pink 12.50
Dinner service for eight: dinner plates, cups & saucers & 10 oz. tumblers; clear, 32 pcs. 144.00
Goblet, clear, 5¼" h. 11.50
Goblet, clear, 5½" h. 14.50
Goblet, pink, 5½" h. 40.00
Lamp, clear, 4" h. 29.00
Pitcher, juice, 42 oz., tilt-type, clear 16.00
Pitcher w/ice lip, 80 oz., clear 21.50
Pitcher w/ice lip, 80 oz., pink 100.00
Plate, sherbet, 6" d., clear 1.50
Plate, sherbet, 6" d., pink 5.00
Plate, salad, 7½" d., clear 2.50
Plate, salad, 7½" d., pink 6.00
Plate, dinner, 9 5/8" d., clear 5.00
Plate, dinner, 9 5/8" d., pink 10.50
Plate, sandwich, 13¾" d., clear 6.50
Plate, sandwich, 13¾" d., pink 17.00
Relish, 5-section, clear, 13¾" d. 13.50
Relish, 5-section, clear w/ruby inserts, 13¾" d. 23.50
Relish, 5-section, green w/ivory inserts, 13¾" d. 34.50
Salt & pepper shakers, clear, short, pr. 5.50
Salt & pepper shakers, clear, tall, pr. 7.00
Sherbet, footed, clear 2.50
Sherbet, footed, pink 7.00
Sugar bowl, cov., oval, clear 6.00
Sugar bowl, open, footed, clear 2.00
Tumbler, footed, pink, 3½" h., 5 oz. 12.00
Tumbler, footed, clear, 5" h., 10 oz. (ILLUS. left) 8.00
Tumbler, footed, pink, 5" h., 10 oz. 9.50

WINDSOR DIAMOND or Windsor (Press-mold)

Ashtray, Delfite, 5¾" d. 37.00
Ashtray, green, 5¾" d. 45.00
Ashtray, pink, 5¾" d. 28.50
Bowl, berry, 4¾" d., clear 3.50
Bowl, berry, 4¾" d., green 6.00
Bowl, berry, 4¾" d., pink 5.50
Bowl, cream soup, 5" d., green or pink 14.50
Bowl, cereal, 5 1/8" or 5 3/8" d., green 14.50
Bowl, cereal, 5 1/8" or 5 3/8" d., pink 10.50
Bowl, 7 1/8" d., 3-footed, clear 6.00
Bowl, 7 1/8" d., 3-footed, pink 17.00
Bowl, 8" d., pointed edge, pink 23.00
Bowl, 8" d., 2-handled, clear 6.00
Bowl, 8" d., 2-handled, green 14.50
Bowl, 8" d., 2-handled, pink 11.50
Bowl, berry, 8½" d., clear 10.50
Bowl, berry, 8½" d., green 11.50
Bowl, berry, 8½" d., pink 9.50
Bowl, 9½" oval vegetable, clear 9.50
Bowl, 9½" oval vegetable, green 14.00
Bowl, 9½" oval vegetable, pink 12.50
Bowl, 10½" d., pointed edge, pink 105.00
Bowl, salad, 10½" d., clear 18.50
Bowl, 11¾ x 7" boat shape, clear 16.00
Bowl, 11¾ x 7" boat shape, green 21.50
Bowl, 11¾ x 7" boat shape, pink 19.00
Bowl, fruit, 12½" d., pink 72.00
Butter dish, cov., clear 18.00
Butter dish, cov., green 63.50
Butter dish, cov., pink 35.50
Cake plate, footed, clear, 10¾" d. . . . 4.50
Cake plate, footed, green, 10¾" d. 13.00
Cake plate, footed, pink, 10¾" d. . . . 10.00
Cake plate, green, 13½" d. 15.50
Cake plate, pink, 13½" d. 13.00
Candlesticks, clear, 3" h., pr. 12.50
Candlesticks, pink, 3" h., pr. 67.00
Candy jar, cov., clear 9.00
Coaster, clear, 3¼" d. 4.50
Coaster, green, 3¼" d. 12.00
Coaster, pink, 3¼" d. 9.50
Creamer, flat, clear 3.00
Creamer, flat, green 7.50
Creamer, flat, pink 6.50
Creamer, footed, clear 3.50
Cup & saucer, clear 4.00
Cup & saucer, green 10.00
Cup & saucer, pink 8.50
Pitcher, 4½" h., 16 oz., clear 12.50
Pitcher, 4½" h., 16 oz., pink 107.00
Pitcher, 5" h., 20 oz., clear 5.50
Pitcher, 5" h., 20 oz., pink 18.50
Pitcher, 6¾" h., 52 oz., clear 11.50
Pitcher, 6¾" h., 52 oz., green 35.00
Pitcher, 6¾" h., 52 oz., pink 19.50
Plate, sherbet, 6" d., clear 1.50
Plate, sherbet, 6" d., green 3.50
Plate, sherbet, 6" d., pink 2.50
Plate, salad, 7" d., clear 3.50
Plate, salad, 7" d., green 11.00
Plate, salad, 7" d., pink 9.50
Plate, dinner, 9" d., clear 4.00
Plate, dinner, 9" d., green 10.00
Plate, dinner, 9" d., pink 9.00
Plate, sandwich, 10¼" d., handled, clear 3.50

Windsor Diamond Sandwich Plate

Plate, sandwich, 10¼" d., handled, pink (ILLUS.) 9.00
Plate, sandwich, 10¼" d., handled, green 12.00
Plate, chop, 13 5/8" d., clear 6.50
Plate, chop, 13 5/8" d., green 19.00
Plate, chop, 13 5/8" d., pink 18.00
Platter, 11½" oval, clear 5.00
Platter, 11½" oval, green 15.00
Platter, 11½" oval, pink 11.00
Relish, divided, clear, 11½" 5.50
Salt & pepper shakers, clear, pr. 11.00
Salt & pepper shakers, green, pr. 35.50
Salt & pepper shakers, pink, pr. 26.00
Sherbet, footed, clear 3.00
Sherbet, footed, green 8.50
Sherbet, footed, pink 6.00
Sugar bowl, cov., flat, clear 7.50
Sugar bowl, cov., flat, green 17.00
Sugar bowl, cov., flat, pink 14.00
Sugar bowl, cov., footed, clear 4.00
Sugar bowl, open, clear 2.00
Sugar bowl, open, green or pink 6.50
Tray, clear, 4" sq. 2.00
Tray, green, 4" sq. 9.00
Tray, pink, 4" sq. 24.50
Tray, clear, 9 x 4 1/8" 3.50
Tray, green, 9 x 4 1/8" 15.50
Tray, pink, 9 x 4 1/8" 25.00
Tray, pink, 9¾ x 8½" 34.50
Tray, handled, clear, 9¾ x 8½" 5.00
Tray, handled, green, 9¾ x 8½" 19.50
Tray, handled, pink, 9¾ x 8½" 28.00
Tumbler, clear, 3¼" h., 5 oz. 4.50
Tumbler, green, 3¼" h., 5 oz. 24.50
Tumbler, pink, 3¼" h., 5 oz. 10.00
Tumbler, clear, 4" h., 9 oz. 4.00
Tumbler, green, 4" h., 9 oz. 15.00
Tumbler, pink, 4" h., 9 oz. 9.50
Tumbler, footed, clear, 4" h., 9 oz. 5.50
Tumbler, clear, 5" h., 12 oz. 6.50
Tumbler, green, 5" h., 12 oz. 26.00
Tumbler, pink, 5" h., 12 oz. 17.00
Tumbler, footed, clear, 7¼" h. 8.00

(End of Depression Glass Section)

DE VEZ & DEGUE

Large De Vez Cameo Vase

Cameo glass with the name De Vez was made in Pantin, France, by Saint-Hilaire, Touvier De Varreaux and Company. Some pieces made by this firm were signed "Degue," after one of the firm's glassmakers. The official company name was "Cristallerie de Pantin."

Cameo vase, 3½" h., carved dark blue florals against frosted ground, signed Degue $295.00
Cameo vase, 5¼" h., 2¼" d., carved navy blue to creamy yellow tree landscape along a river w/mountainous background against soft pink translucent frosted ground, signed DeVez 495.00
Cameo vase, 5½" h., carved blue, orange & yellow scene w/trees, mountains & buildings, signed DeVez 740.00
Cameo vase, 6" h., 2¾" d., carved navy blue to creamy yellow scene w/trees on foreground shore, water, islands & mountainous background & tree branches framing top of scene against soft shell pink frosted ground, signed DeVez 550.00
Cameo vase, 7½" h., 3" d., carved navy to rose scene of water w/boat & village against yellow satin translucent ground w/leafy branches w/florals framing top of scene, signed DeVez 495.00
Cameo vase, 8 1/8" h., 3" d., carved navy blue to yellow scene w/sailboat on water, house on island, mountains in background & tree branches framing top of scene against soft pink translucent satin ground, signed DeVez 695.00
Cameo vase, 8¼" h., carved shaded

orange marsh, winding stream, trees, florals & grass against yellow ground, signed DeVez 995.00

Cameo vase, 8¾" h., 3 3/8" d., carved navy blue to soft yellow landscape w/island in water, trees & mountainous background against shell pink frosted translucent ground, signed DeVez....... 595.00

Cameo vase, 9 5/8" h., 3 3/8" d., carved maroon to rose scene w/ten sailboats, clouds & background shore w/tree branches framing scene against soft translucent green satin ground, signed DeVez 775.00

Cameo vase, 13¼" h., three carved swirling branches of leaves & drooping flowers, maroon over silvery inner layer w/internal twist in the opposite direction, signed Pantin 1,400.00

Cameo vase, 14 3/8" h., carved deep blue to pink florals against pale pink ground, signed Degue .. 395.00

Cameo vase, 19" h., ovoid, dusty rose glass overlaid in navy blue & lemon yellow & carved on the obverse w/a woman dressed in flowing scarves & fringed dress within a floral surround, ca. 1920, signed DeVez (ILLUS.) 3,025.00

DUNCAN & MILLER

Teardrop Pattern Champagne

Duncan & Miller Glass Company, a successor firm to George A. Duncan & Sons Company, was operated by George A. Duncan & Edwin C. Miller in Washington, Pa., from the late 19th century and produced many types of pressed wares and novelty pieces, many of which are now eagerly sought by collectors. George A. Duncan was a pioneer glass manufacturer, associated earlier with several firms.

Ashtray, Pall Mall patt. (No. 30), model of a duck, clear, 7" l. $22.00

Basket, loop handle, Early American Sandwich patt. (No. 41), clear, 11½" h. 105.00

Bowl, 14" d., Sanibel patt. (No. 130), blue opalescent or yellow opalescent, each 75.00

Butter pat, Pall Mall patt., clear 15.00

Cake stand, Early American Sandwich patt., clear, 13" d. 60.00

Champagne, Hobnail patt. (No. 118), pink 20.00

Champagne, Teardrop patt. (No. 301), clear (ILLUS.) 7.00

Cigarette box, cov., Pall Mall patt., model of a duck, clear........... 40.00

Cocktail, Chanticleer patt., blue frosted 75.00

Cracker jar, cov., Mardi Gras patt. (No. 42), clear 110.00

Creamer, Bag Ware, amber 45.00

Creamer & open sugar bowl, Festive patt. (No. 155), aqua or honey, each pr. 50.00

Cruet w/original stopper, blown, Hobnail patt., amber 50.00

Cup & saucer, etched First Love patt., clear 32.00

Pitcher w/ice lip, applied ruby handle, Caribbean patt. (No. 112), clear 80.00

Plate, 7½" d., Teardrop patt., clear 5.00

Plate, 8½" d., Hobnail patt., pink .. 30.00

Punch set: bowl, 12 cups & ladle; Caribbean patt., clear w/ruby handles, 14 pcs. ....135.00 to 175.00

Swan, Pall Mall patt., clear, 5" 45.00

Swan, blue opalescent, 7" 70.00

Swan, sapphire blue w/clear neck, 10½" 95.00

Table set: cov. sugar bowl, creamer & spooner; Ellrose Ware (Amberette), clear, 3 pcs. 150.00

Tumbler, footed, Terrace patt. (No. 111), cobalt blue, 4½" 30.00

Wine, Plaza patt. (No. 21), cobalt blue 25.00

DURAND

Fine decorative glass similar to that made by Tiffany and other outstanding glasshouses of its day was made by the Vineland Flint Glass Works Co. in Vineland, N.J., first headed by Victor Durand, Sr., and subsequently by his son Victor Durand, Jr., in the 1920's.

Boudoir lamp, blue pulled feather design & threading, marble base, overall 12" h. $850.00

Rose bowl, egg-shaped, bright yellow Cluthra-type w/vivid orange splotches 450.00

Tumbler, juice, lily pad design, signed 250.00

Vase, 4" h., bulbous w/flared mouth, vines & leaves decoration, blue, signed 350.00

Vase, 7½" h., urn-shaped, turned out collar, applied raised opal feather-shaped outlines from bottom to top, unsigned 450.00

Vase, 8" h., baluster-form, overall orange iridescence, signed & numbered 462.00

Durand Iridescent Vase

Vase, 10¼" h., inverted pyriform w/flaring lip, deep amber iridescence, inscribed "Durand - 20139 - 10" (ILLUS.) 715.00

Vase, 12" h., bulbous bottle-shape, ribbed, iridescent blue 600.00

Vase, 12¼" h., 6" d., white pulled feather design in clear w/green upper body, signed 375.00

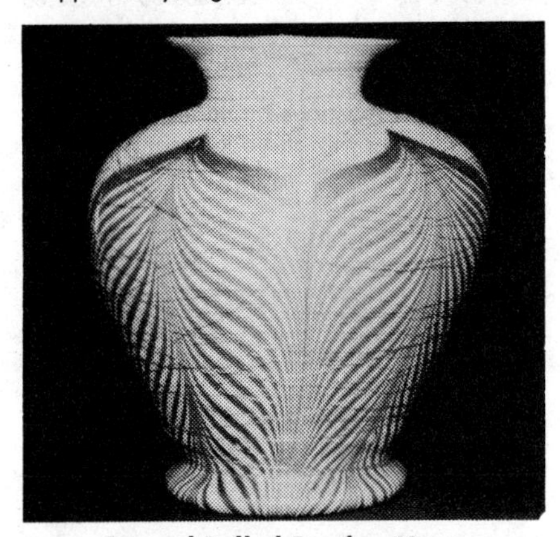

Durand Pulled Feather Vase

Vase, bulbous ovoid body w/low flared neck, wide green pulled feather design on creamy white ground, overall fine gold threading, gold iridescent lining (ILLUS.) 1,300.00

FENTON

Cranberry Opalescent Hobnail Bowl

Fenton Art Glass Company began producing glass at Williamstown, West Virginia, in January 1907. Organized by Frank L. and John W. Fenton, the company began operations in a newly built glass factory with an experienced master glass craftsman, Jacob Rosenthal, as their factory manager. Fenton has produced a wide variety of collectible glassware through the years, including Carnival (which see). Still in production today, their current productions may be found at finer gift shops across the country.

Basket, Hobnail patt., blue opalescent, ca. 1948-54, 4½" d. $25.00

Basket, low, ruffled, Silver Crest, 8" d. 18.00

Basket, hat-shape, Big Cookies patt., Mandarin Red (red slag), ca. 1933, 10½ x 5" 95.00

Bonbon, Hobnail patt., cranberry opalescent, 6" d. 15.00

Bonbon, Strawberry patt., Amberina 250.00

Bonbon, cov., footed, stretch glass, paneled pattern (No. 643), Celeste blue 24.00

Bowl, 5½" d., 4½" h., ruffled rim, Hobnail patt., cranberry opalescent, ca. 1941-77 (ILLUS.) 30.00

Bowl, 6½" d., Blackberry Spray patt., Custard w/red staining 48.00

Bowl, 7" d., Hobnail patt., Topaz opalescent 22.00

Bowl, 7" d., ruffled rim, Walking Lion patt., Custard 65.00

Bowl, 9" d., Open Edge Basketweave patt., Mandarin Red 75.00

Bowl, 12" d., 6" h., footed, Crystal Crest, w/paper label 50.00

Cake salver, pedestal base, Emerald Crest 65.00

Candlestick, simple baluster form w/round base, Flame (yellow-orange), ca. 1924-26, 8" h. 66.00

Candlesticks, Mandarin Red, 8" h., pr. 113.00

Candy dish, footed, Dolphin

handles, Diamond Optic patt., green, 4" 55.00
Candy jar, cov., Lamb's Tongue patt., turquoise, ca. 1955-56, 5½" h. 35.00
Chamberstick, Hobnail patt., cranberry opalescent 35.00
Cologne bottle, Moonstone w/ebony stopper 22.00
Creamer, Dot Optic patt., cranberry opalescent...................... 25.00
Cruet w/original stopper, Hobnail patt., cranberry opalescent....... 64.00
Epergne, Diamond Lace patt., blue opalescent, 10" 115.00
Ginger jar, cov., Mandarin Red w/black cover & base, ca. 1934... 220.00
Ivy balls, Polka Dot patt., cranberry opalescent w/clear pedestal base, ca. 1955-56, 9" h., pr. 150.00
Mayonnaise dish, heart-shaped w/one spoon, emerald green Snow Crest, 2 pcs. 65.00
Pitcher, 6½" h., Coin Dot patt., cranberry opalescent 77.00
Plate, 7½" d., Horse Medallion patt., pink satin................. 120.00
Tumbler, Coin Dot patt., Honeysuckle opalescent 28.00
Vases, 4½" h., ruffled, Hobnail patt., blue opalescent, pr. 45.00

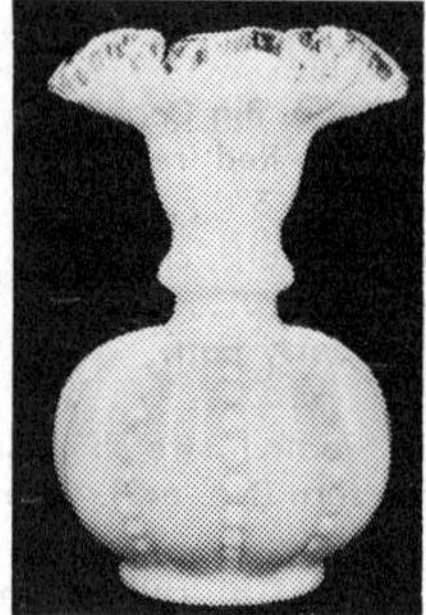

Beaded Melon Vase

Vase, 6¼" h., Beaded Melon patt., Peach Crest (ILLUS.) 40.00
Vase, 10" h., Spiral Optic patt., cranberry opalescent 75.00
Whimsey, hat w/ruffled brim, Ivory Crest, 3½" base 55.00

FINDLAY ONYX & FLORADINE

These wares were introduced by Dalzell, Gilmore & Leighton Co. of Findlay, Ohio, in January 1889. Onyx ware is a white-lined glass and was produced primarily in onyx (creamy yellowish-white) but also bronze and ruby, which are sometimes described as cinnamon, rose or raspberry. The raised flowers and leaves are silver colored or, less often, bronze. The Floradine line was made in ruby and autumn leaf (gold) with opalescent flowers and leaves and is not lined.

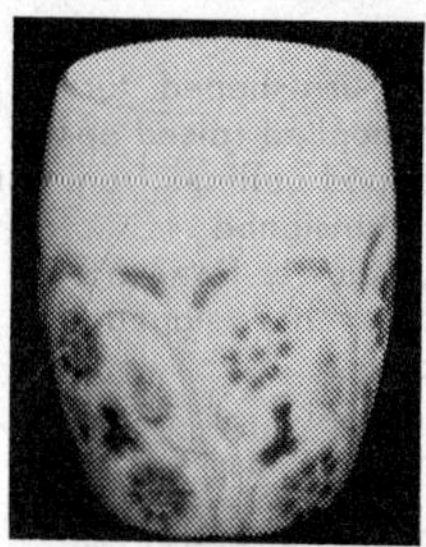

Findlay Oynx Tumbler

Celery vase, creamy white w/silver flowers & leaves, 6½" h. (rim roughness) $220.00
Creamer, unlined ruby w/white opalescent flowers & leaves, clear applied handle................. 945.00
Creamer, creamy white w/silver flowers & leaves, 4" w., 4¾" h. .. 395.00
Mustard pot, cov., creamy white w/silver flowers & leaves 395.00
Mustard pot, cov., unlined ruby w/white opalescent flowers & leaves 850.00
Pitcher, 8" h., creamy white w/silver flowers & leaves, applied opalescent handle, rare size 750.00
Sugar bowl, open, unlined ruby w/white opalescent flowers & leaves 570.00
Sugar shaker w/original top, creamy white w/silver flowers & leaves ....300.00 to 350.00
Tumbler, barrel-shaped, creamy white w/silver flowers & leaves (ILLUS.)......................... 165.00
Tumbler, barrel-shaped, unlined frosted ruby w/white opalescent flowers & leaves 785.00

FOSTORIA

Fostoria Glass Company, founded in 1887, is still in operation today in Moundsville, West Va. It has produced numerous types of fine wares through the years, many of which are now being collected. Also see ANIMALS under Glass.

Appetizer set: oblong tray fitted w/six tab-handled inserts; American patt., clear, 10½ x 8¾", 1¾" h., 7 pcs. $250.00
Ashtray, June patt., yellow 30.00
Bowl, 10½" d., Morning Glory patt., clear 50.00

Breakfast set: individual size creamer & sugar bowl on tray; Chintz patt., clear, 3 pcs. 45.00
Candelabrum, 2-light, Flame patt., clear, 10¼" w., 6¾" h. 95.00
Centerpiece bowl, footed, Versailles patt., topaz, 12" d. 50.00
Champagne, Fairfax patt., Azure blue 18.00
Cocktail, Versailles patt., Azure blue 40.00
Cordial, Versailles patt., topaz 75.00
Creamer & sugar bowl, Fairfax patt., Dawn rose, pr. 80.00
Cruet w/original stopper, Baroque patt., topaz 250.00
Cup & saucer, demitasse, June patt., topaz 39.50
Goblet, June patt., Dawn rose 26.00
Hurricane lamps, American patt., clear, 12" h., pr. 250.00
Ice bucket, Willowmere patt., clear 60.00
Ice tub w/tab handles & underplate, American patt., clear, 6½" top d., 4½" h., 2 pcs. 125.00
Oil bottle w/replaced stopper, footed, Trojan patt., topaz 220.00
Pitcher (or water jug), footed, Hermitage patt., topaz, 3 pt. 95.00
Plate, 10" d., Fairfax patt., Dawn rose 12.00
Punch set: 13¼" top d. bowl & ten 6 oz. cups; Baroque patt., clear, 11 pcs. 250.00
Relish, divided, June patt., topaz, 8½" l. 22.00
Salt & pepper shakers w/original tops, Beverly patt., green, pr. 69.00
Sandwich server, handled, June patt., Azure blue 40.00
Sherbet, June patt., Azure blue 25.00
Syrup pitcher w/original top, Priscilla patt., emerald green 195.00
Toothpick holder, Brazilian patt., clear 25.00

Lido Pattern Tumbler

Tumbler, footed, Lido patt., clear, 6" h. (ILLUS.) 17.00

Vase, 8" h., June patt., topaz 125.00
Vase, 10" h., cupped, American patt., clear 175.00
Water set: pitcher & 6 tumblers; Rosby patt., clear, 7 pcs. 150.00
Wine, Beacon patt., clear 25.00

FRANCES WARE

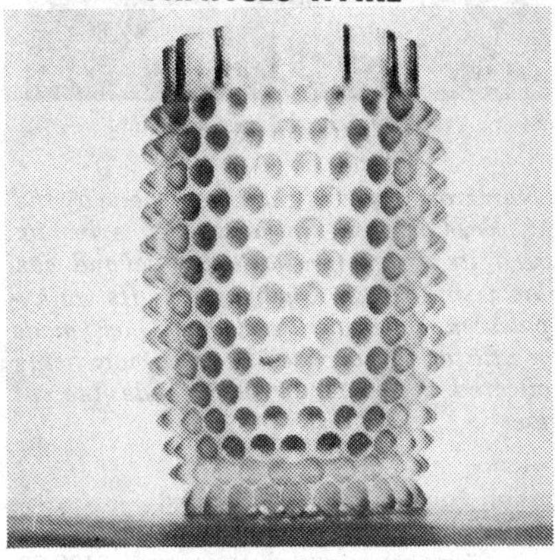

Frances Ware Celery Vase

This was made by Hobbs, Brockunier & Co., Wheeling, West Va., in the 1880's. It is frosted or clear glass with stained amber tops or rims and was both mold-blown and pressed. It usually has a pattern of hobnails or swirled ribs.

Celery vase, frosted hobnail w/amber rim (ILLUS.) $112.00
Cruet w/original stopper, frosted swirl w/amber rim 325.00
Pitcher, water, 8¼" h., bulbous, clear hobnail w/amber rim....... 165.00
Pitcher, frosted swirl w/amber rim 85.00
Salt & pepper shakers w/original tops, frosted swirl w/amber rim, pr. 115.00
Sauce dish, frosted hobnail w/amber rim 28.00
Spooner, frosted hobnail w/amber rim 65.00
Sugar shaker w/original top, frosted swirl w/amber rim 145.00
Table set: cov. butter dish, cov. sugar bowl, creamer & spooner; frosted hobnail w/amber rim, 4 pcs. 330.00
Toothpick holder, frosted hobnail w/amber rim 67.50
Tumbler, frosted swirl w/amber rim 35.00
Water set: pitcher & four tumblers; clear hobnail w/amber rim, 5 pcs. ....250.00 to 300.00

FRY

Fry Foval Tea Set

Numerous types of glass were made by the H.C. Fry Company, Rochester, Pennsylvania. One of its art lines was called Foval and was blown in 1926-27. Cheaper was its milky-opalescent ovenware (Pearl Oven Glass) made for utilitarian purposes but also now being collected. The company also made fine cut glass.

Basket, Foval, opaline w/applied Delft blue trim & handle, 7 5/8" h. $135.00

Bowl, 9½" d., 4½" h., flaring rolled rim, applied foot & stem, Foval, opaline w/applied Delft blue trim 105.00

Bowl, 11 7/8" d., 5 3/8" h ., Foval, opaline w/flaring Delft blue foot 115.00

Candlesticks, Foval, opaline w/Delft blue spiral threading & blue wafers, 10¾" h., pr. 250.00

Centerpiece bowl, pedestal base, Foval, opaline w/applied Delft blue trim, 12" d. 325.00

Creamer & sugar bowl, Foval, opaline w/applied Delft blue handles, 3 3/8" h., pr. 200.00

Cup & saucer, Foval, opaline w/applied Jade green handle ... 50.00 to 65.00

Custard cup, Pearl Oven Ware 8.00

Juice reamer, Pearl Oven Ware 26.00

Pitcher, 8 1/8" h., Foval, opaline w/applied Delft blue handle 145.00

Tea set: cov. teapot & six cups & saucers; Foval, opaline w/applied Jade green handles, spout & knob finial, 13 pcs. (ILLUS.) ... 500.00 to 550.00

Vase, 10" h., footed, Foval, opaline w/cobalt blue base & trim 185.00

GALLE'

Galle' glass was made in Nancy, France, by Emile Galle', a founder of the Nancy School and a leader in the Art Nouveau movement in France. Much of his glass, both enameled and cameo, is decorated with naturalistic motifs. The finest pieces were made in the last two decades of the 19th century and the opening years of the present one. Pieces marked with a star preceding the name were made between Gulle's death in 1904 and 1914.

Galle' Cameo Lamp

Cameo lamp, floriform shade w/carved white, rose & dark amber overlapping veined petals against grey ground, bronze leafy socket continuing to an elongated C-scroll arm ending in a shield-form base, ca. 1900, signed, 16¼" h. (ILLUS.) $14,850.00

Galle' Cameo Miniature Lamp

Cameo miniature lamp, conical shade & bulbous base in grey glass carved w/pendent cherry blossoms & leafage, overlaid & cameo-carved in maroon & deep cherry red, gilt-bronze scrolling mounts, signed, minor restoration to top of base, 8" h. (ILLUS.) 9,350.00

Cameo powder box, carved green leaves against lemon yellow ground, signed & w/original sticker, 7" d., 2¾" h. 950.00

Cameo rose bowl, spherical w/undulating rim, grey shaded w/pale aqua blue & overlaid w/caramel & mustard & cut w/a circular building w/thatched roof surrounded by leafy trees in foreground & a cluster of rooftops in background, ca. 1920, signed, 8" d. . . 2,640.00

Cameo vase, 4½" h., carved orange-red florals & leaves against frosted ground, signed w/star (1904-14) 365.00

Cameo vase, 4 5/8" h., slightly sloping sides, waisted foot, carved & intaglio deep chocolate brown fruiting chestnut branches & leafage against grey & turquoise ground, w/silver foil & oxblood red inclusions revealed through intaglio-carved leafage, whole against *martele'* ground, dated 1894, signed 10,175.00

Cameo vase, 5¾" h., 3" d., carved blue florals w/green leaves against lime to frosted to green ground, signed 995.00

Cameo vase, 5¾" h., 3½" d., carved brown to green scene of water lily buds & pads w/leafy green trees on distant shore against frosted shell pink & white ground, signed 595.00

Cameo vase, 6½" h., ovoid, mold-blown & cameo-carved white & cranberry clematis blossoms & vines against dusty rose ground, ca. 1925, signed 2,750.00

Cameo vase, 7¼" h., footed softened square form w/everted neck, carved sapphire blue & purple leafy blossoms against mottled yellow & frosted ground, signed 1,980.00

Cameo vase, 8" h., stick-type, carved light blue, violet, dark blue & lavender violets, florals & leaves against pale yellow ground 675.00

Cameo vase, 8½" h., teardrop-shaped, mold-blown & cameo-carved lavender & green budding & flowering croci against yellow ground, ca. 1920, signed 3,850.00

Cameo vase, 9 3/8" h., 10¼" w., flattened globular form w/cut away rim, carved olive green to lime green scenic landscape w/fisherman in foreground & trees along a river shore against frosted ground, ca. 1900, signed 1,980.00

Cameo vase, 9 3/8" h., globular body of oval section, carved cream mountain poppy blossoms & leafage one side, reverse w/snow-covered mountains against lime green ground mottled & splashed w/turquoise, apricot & navy *martele'* ground, ca. 1900, signed 31,900.00

Cameo vase, 10¾" h., pilgrim flask form, mold-blown & cameo carved mauve & mahogany pendent leafy fruiting grape vines against lemon yellow ground, ca. 1920, signed . . 7,975.00

Cameo vase, 11½" h., elongated ovoid w/short straight neck, mold-blown & cameo-carved lime green & medium brown pendent fruiting leafy branches against yellow-green ground, ca. 1925, signed 6,600.00

Cameo vase, 11¾" h., 4" widest d., carved brown, yellow & frosted pine cones, signed w/star 900.00

Pitcher, 9" h., flattened bulbous form w/pulled spout, applied C-scroll handle, green-tinted clear sides engraved w/spirals partially *martele'*, sides further decorated w/tendrils about the body, ca. 1894, signed 5,500.00

Galle' Etched & Enameled Vase

Vase, 6¾" h., ovoid, green-streaked translucent ground etched enameled & gilded on the obverse w/a medallion enclosing a seated male playing a lyre & "Echoes of Hellas," flanked by two ornate cartouches enclosing an applied & carved scarab, the reverse etched w/an angled column enclosing animals, signed (ILLUS.) 9,900.00

Vase, 7¾" h., broad ovoid, four angled handles, enameled white & silver-grey arabesque design of foliate tendrils delineated in gilt on amber ground w/gold inclusions, signed 1,870.00

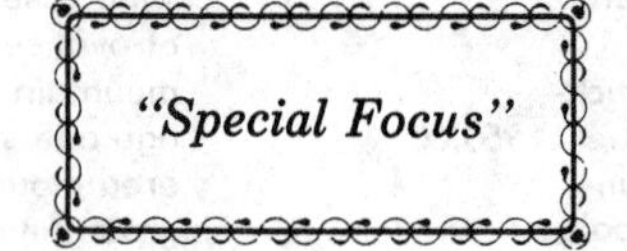

Greentown Glass

by James Measell

Over a decade ago, this Price Guide featured a special focus on Greentown glass. Since that publication appeared in the fall of 1977, Greentown glass collectors and researchers have been busy! The Greentown Glass Museum in Greentown, Indiana, has attracted thousands, particularly during the annual Greentown Glass Festival which is held the second full weekend in June. The National Greentown Glass Association was formed in 1974, and this active group of 250 collectors issues a quarterly newsletter and holds an annual meeting and dinner at the Greentown Glass Festival.

The Grand Rapids (Michigan) Public Museum has, on permanent display, a representative selection from the Greentown glass collection assembled by the late Dr. Ruth Herrick. In 1979 this museum published *Greentown Glass: The Indiana Tumbler and Goblet Company.* The book is the definitive study of this interesting tableware factory which operated in Greentown from 1894 to 1903 when it was destroyed by fire.

The old Indiana Tumbler and Goblet Company was founded in 1894 by D.C. Jenkins, Jr., an experienced glassman who had been involved with the Columbia Glass Company at Findlay, Ohio (1886-92) and the U.S. Glass Company's plant at Gas City, Indiana (1892-94). Jenkins left the Greentown works in 1901 to start his own plant at nearby Kokomo, and the D.C. Jenkins Glass Company operated there for over 25 years and also established a branch plant at Arcadia.

In its early years, the Greentown firm made rather ordinary clear pressed glass — jelly tumblers, bar goods, goblets, etc. The first pattern line, introduced in 1895, was called simply *No. 11* and it bore an unfortunate resemblance to McKee's *Champion* pattern, which probably far outdistanced it in the marketplace. Over the next few years, more patterns were added: *Shuttle; Beehive; Overall Lattice; Flatiron; Diamond Prisms; Scalloped Flange* and *Early Diamond.*

The *Austrian* and *Pleat Band* patterns were introduced in 1897-98, and several other major lines soon followed: *Dewey; Herringbone Buttress* and *Teardrop and Tassel.* Transparent colored glass in amber, several shades of blue, canary, and emerald green was added to the plant's capabilities in the late 1890's, but the various colors were not always used for each pattern. *Austrian,* for instance, is well-known in canary but scarce in emerald green. *Herringbone Buttress* occurs mainly in emerald green, but *Teardrop and Tassel* is best known in cobalt blue. All three patterns are hard to find in amber, but *Dewey* is often found in amber as well as canary and emerald green. One must study the patterns and colors for a considerable time before becoming able to recognize Greentown patterns and estimate relative rarity.

The continued success of the Greentown firm was assured by glassmaker Jacob Rosenthal when he came to Greentown in 1900. By November, he had perfected his secret formula and techniques for Chocolate glass, a unique opaque glassware. Two new patterns, *Leaf Bracket* and *Cactus,* were quickly put into production, and both were exhibited at the Pan-American Exposition in Buffalo, New York, in 1901. The *Cactus* line was extensive, embracing about three dozen different articles.

Some moulds from earlier pattern lines were soon put back into production to meet the public demand for the new color, so one finds various Chocolate glass items in *Shuttle, Austrian, Dewey,* and *Teardrop and Tassel* from time to time.

Sometime in 1902, Rosenthal reached an agreement with the National Glass Company for the sale of his Chocolate glass secrets. At this time, the National controlled nineteen glass tableware factories, including the Greentown plant. Many Chocolate glass patterns were made at other National plants, especially the large McKee and Brothers firm in Jeannette, Pennsylvania. Among the best-known of these are some sizeable lines: *Chrysanthemum Leaf; Geneva; Melrose* and *Wild Rose with Bowknot.* Others, which are generally hard to find and occur only in a few articles, are *Aldine, File, Honeycomb, Rose Garland, Shield with Daisy and Button, Touching Squares,* and *Venetian.*

Rosenthal joined the Fenton Art Glass Company in 1906, and this plant made some Chocolate glass, too, mostly in a *Water Lily and Cattails* line introduced in 1907. The *Vintage* bowl is a Fenton product, as are the *Orange Tree* hatpin holder and covered powder jar.

In letters written during the 1930's, Rosenthal also described his creation of an opaque green glass at Greentown. This color is called Nile Green by today's collectors. The *Dewey* and *Teardrop and Tassel* moulds were utilized for production, although articles are generally hard to find.

Chocolate glass occupied center stage at Greentown during the first two years of the twentieth century, but the firm added several clear glass pattern lines *(Beaded Panel* and *Invincible).* Colored glass production continued, too, in lines such as blue *Brazen Shield* which the factory may have rescued from the National's defunct plant at nearby Summitville.

The best-known Greentown glass is Holly Amber. Originally called "Golden Agate," this semi-opaque glassware was yet another Rosenthal creation. A new pattern, featuring a Holly motif, was developed for the formula, and an extensive array of tableware (more than 40 different items) was made in Golden Agate. Advertising began in January, 1903, and the new product was soon quite a success. Unfortunately, the devastating fire of June 13, 1903, brought all of this to a tragic end.

In addition to the pattern glass lines made at Greentown, the factory also produced a large number of "novelty" items. Some of these, such as the standard covered animal dishes (*Hen* and *Rabbit*), were the stock in trade of many similar glass plants, but many of Greentown's novelties were unique. Designer and mouldmaker Charles E. Beam was probably responsible for these: *Bird with Berry; Fighting Cocks* and two styles of *Cat on Hamper.* Beam's greatest success, by today's standards, is the *Dolphin* covered dish, the single article most strongly associated with Greentown glass.

Other novelties included three animal water pitchers — *Squirrel, Racing Deer,* and *Heron* - as well as various toothpick holders *(Sheaf of Wheat, Picture Frame, Dog Head,* and *Witch Head).* Mugs and steins were popular, also, and the *Indoor* and *Outdoor Drinking Scene* mugs are found in several sizes and with pouring lips.

Among the most sought-after Greentown novelties are the *Buffalo paperweight,* the *Cuff Set,* and the *Indian Head.* One sees the *Dewey Bust* relatively frequently, and the *Wheelbarrow* and *Dustpan* turn up from time to time. Four other novelties occur in clear, Chocolate glass and Nile Green: *Scotch Thistle; Hairbrush; Mitted Hand* and *Connecticut Skillet.*

Because the National Glass Company had Rosenthal's Chocolate glass secrets, they were able to make novelty items, too. Like the Chocolate glass patterns produced by the National, these are not, strictly speaking, "Greentown glass," but they are scarce, desirable, and expensive! The animal dishes are a veritable barnyard: *Cow, Duck; Hen with Peeps; Lamb; Turkey* and *Two-Headed Chick.* Most of these were made at McKee, as were the *Serenade* mugs and plates, the *Wild Rose with Festoon* lamps, and the popular *Wild Rose with Scrolling* children's set.

Studying Greentown glass can be a bewildering experience for the novice. Some pattern lines contain only a few articles, but others are extensive. Not every pattern occurs in every color, and not all Chocolate glass is Greentown-made, of course. No original catalogs from the plant are known, but the wholesale and mail-order catalogs of the times (Butler Brothers, Montgomery Ward, etc.) have been very helpful to researchers. The quarterly NGGA newsletter keeps members up-to-date on newly-discovered items in Greentown glass.

Some Greentown articles have been reproduced since World War II by such firms as the Kemple Glass Company, the Crystal Art Glass Company (Degenhart), and the St. Clair Glass Company. Kemple made both the *Dolphin* and the *Rabbit* covered dishes, but both Degenhart and St. Clair concentrated on attempts to duplicate Greentown's Chocolate glass. Many of the items made bear no resemblance to actual Greentown pieces, nor do the recent issues from the Boyd and Mosser firms in Cambridge, Ohio.

Fenton made a *Cactus* line in both milk glass and vaseline opalescent (called Topaz) in the 1950's, and this same firm made a special series in Chocolate glass in 1976. Some large covered animal dishes were made in Chocolate glass by Westmoreland, and the Summit Art Glass Company has issued a few brightly-colored reproductions.

The coming years will likely see even more activity in the ranks of Greentown glass collectors. The centennial of the Indiana Tumbler and Goblet Company's inception is less than a decade away. Both the Greentown Glass Museum and the Grand Rapids Public Museum will continue to display noteworthy examples of Greentown and Greentown-related glass. Further research and documentation work will occupy the National Greentown Glass Association, and all pattern glass enthusiasts will benefit.

About the Author

James Measell, who has prepared this overview on Greentown glass, is well-known to readers of The Antique Trader Weekly *and other publications in the antiques and collectibles fields. He has authored several publications on Greentown glass as well as a recent book on glass made at Findlay, Ohio. Request information on these publications from him at Box 1052, Berkley, Michigan 48072.*

The National Greentown Glass Association produces a regular newsletter for its members which deals with Greentown glass and related topics. For more details readers can contact the NGGA Treasurer, Charles Sterba, at Box 508037, Cicero, Illinois 60650.

The following listings are organized according to general categories with pattern and individual pieces listed alphabetically. Space precludes our listing every variation and color for all Greentown patterns, but we feel the following offers a good cross-section of current price ranges.

TABLEWARE PATTERNS

Austrian

Bowl, 7 1/8 x 4 5/8" rectangle, clear $45.00
Butter dish, cov., clear 90.00

Austrian Child's Set in Chocolate

Child's set: cov. butter, creamer, cov. sugar bowl & spooner; Chocolate glass, original box, 4 pcs. (ILLUS.) 2,000.00
Compote, open, 5" h., clear (ILLUS.) 75.00
Cordial, canary 125.00
Cordial, clear 50.00

Austrian Compote

Austrian Cordials

Cordial, emerald green (ILLUS. of two) 200.00
Creamer, Chocolate glass 150.00

Austrian Creamer, Small Pedestal Base

Creamer, small pedestal base, clear (ILLUS.) 52.00
Nappy, cov., clear 55.00
Punch cup, clear 10.00
Punch cup, clear w/gold 20.00
Spooner, clear 35.00
Spooner, child's size, clear 20.00

Sugar bowl, cov., clear, large 52.00
Tumbler, clear 22.50

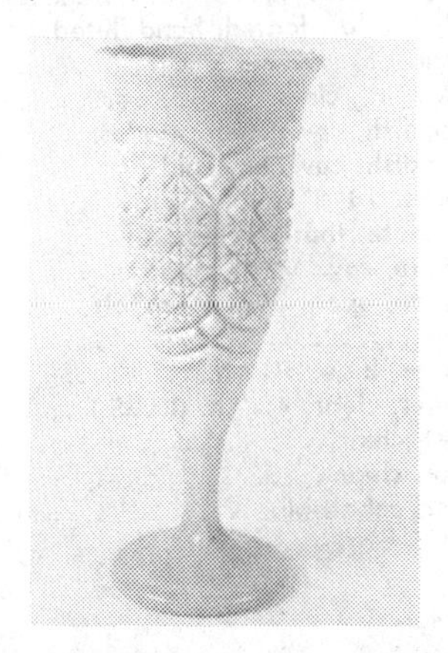

Nile Green Austrian Vase

Vase, 6" h., Nile Green (ILLUS.) 325.00
Vase, 8¼" h., clear 45.00
Wine, canary 110.00

Beaded Panel

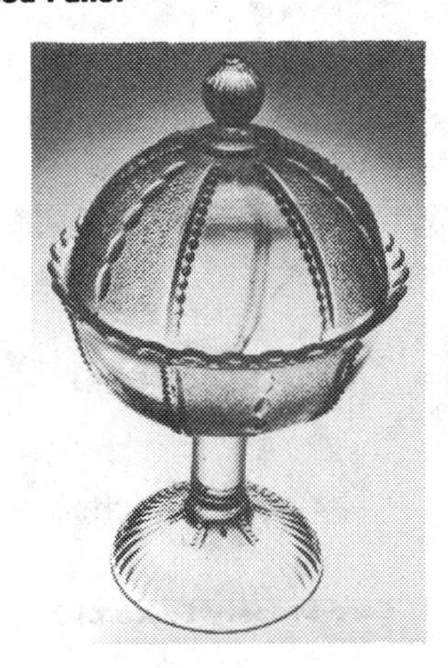

Beaded Panel Compote

Bowl, 6¼" d., clear 60.00
Celery vase, clear, 6" h. 90.00
Compote, cov., 5½" d., clear (ILLUS.) 145.00
Creamer, clear (ILLUS.) 65.00
Cruet w/stopper, clear 175.00
Pitcher, clear (two sizes) 150.00
Plate, 7¼" d., clear 75.00
Salt shaker, clear 75.00
Spooner, clear 55.00
Sugar bowl, cov., clear 90.00
Tumbler, clear 100.00

Beaded Panel Creamer

Beehive

Goblet, clear 80.00
Tumbler, Chocolate glass 350.00
Tumbler, clear 75.00
Vase, bud, clear 85.00
Wine, clear 60.00

Brazen Shield

Butter dish, cov., blue 175.00
Cake stand, clear, 9 3/8" d. 75.00
Goblet, clear 50.00
Spooner, clear 25.00
Sugar bowl, cov., clear 50.00
Tumbler, blue 47.50
Water set: pitcher & 6 tumblers; blue, 7 pcs. 450.00

Cactus

Berry set: footed master bowl & 6 sauce dishes; Chocolate glass, 7 pcs. 295.00
Bowl, 6¼" d., clear 50.00
Bowl, 7¼" d., Chocolate glass 125.00
Bowl, 7¼" d., clear 55.00
Bowl, 8¼" d., Chocolate glass 135.00
Butter dish, cov., Chocolate glass ... 175.00
Butter dish, cov., clear 150.00
Celery vase, clear, 7½" h. 75.00
Compote, jelly, 5¼" d., 5" h., Chocolate glass 150.00
Compote, open, 6¼" d., Chocolate glass 175.00
Compote, 8¼" d., Chocolate glass .. 200.00
Compote, open, 9¼" d., Chocolate glass 250.00
Compote, open, 9¼" d., clear 150.00
Cracker jar, Chocolate glass 260.00
Creamer w/Dewey lid, Chocolate glass 100.00
Creamer w/Dewey lid, clear, 2¼" d. 90.00
Cruet w/original stopper, Chocolate glass 190.00
Iced tea tumbler, Chocolate glass, 5" 68.00

Mug, Chocolate glass 70.00
Pitcher, Chocolate glass 400.00

Cactus Pitcher

Pitcher, clear (ILLUS.) 200.00
Plate, 7½" d., Chocolate glass 95.00
Salt shaker w/original top, Chocolate glass (single) 65.00
Sauce dish, flat, clear 60.00
Sauce dish, footed, Chocolate glass 45.00
Sauce dish, footed, clear 35.00
Sugar bowl, cov., Chocolate glass .. 175.00
Sugar bowl, cov., clear 85.00
Syrup jug w/original metal lid, Chocolate glass 175.00
Syrup jug w/metal lid, clear 85.00
Table set: cov. butter dish, cov. sugar bowl, creamer & spooner; Chocolate glass, 4 pcs. 600.00
Toothpick holder, Chocolate glass .. 80.00
Tumbler, Chocolate glass 55.00
Water set: pitcher & 6 tumblers; Chocolate glass, 7 pcs. 750.00

Cord Drapery

Cord Drapery Creamer

Bowl, 6¼" d., footed, hand-fluted, amber 175.00
Bowl, 6¼" d., footed, hand-fluted, clear 75.00
Bowl, 7" d., clear 25.00
Butter dish, cov., clear, 4¾" d. 85.00
Butter dish, cov., emerald green, 5 1/8" d. 175.00
Cake plate, footed, clear 40.00
Compote, cov., 9" d., clear 70.00
Compote, open, 8½" d., cobalt blue 180.00
Creamer, blue, 4¼" h. 125.00
Creamer, clear, 4¼" h. (ILLUS.) 45.00
Goblet, clear 100.00
Pitcher, clear 60.00
Pitcher, cobalt blue 225.00

Cord Drapery Punch Cup

Punch cup, clear (ILLUS.) 15.00
Salt & pepper shakers, clear, pr. ... 110.00

Cord Drapery Sauce Dish

Sauce dish, flat, clear (ILLUS.) 10.00
Sugar bowl, cov., clear 60.00
Sugar bowl, cov., emerald green ... 165.00
Syrup jug w/original metal top, Chocolate glass, 6 5/8" h. 175.00
Toothpick holder, clear 95.00
Tumbler, Chocolate glass 215.00
Wine, amber 225.00
Wine, clear 90.00

Cupid

Four piece table set only.

Butter dish, cov., Chocolate glass (ILLUS.) 550.00

Cupid Butter Dish

Butter dish, cov., clear 90.00
Creamer, clear 85.00

Cupid Nile Green Creamer

Creamer, Nile Green (ILLUS.) 400.00
Creamer, opaque white 75.00
Spooner, Chocolate glass 275.00
Spooner, clear 75.00
Sugar bowl, cov., clear 85.00
Sugar bowl, cov., opaque white 95.00

Daisy

Made in only four pieces.

Butter dish, cov., Chocolate glass ... 245.00
Butter dish, cov., clear 55.00
Butter dish, cov., frosted emerald green 100.00
Creamer, cov., Chocolate glass, w/lid - 175.00 (ILLUS. without lid) 100.00
Creamer, cov., clear 45.00
Mustard pot, cov., clear 45.00
Mustard pot, cov., frosted clear 40.00

Daisy Creamer

Sugar bowl, cov., clear 45.00
Sugar bowl, cov., frosted emerald green 75.00

Dewey

Dewey Nile Green Creamer

Bowl, 8" d., Chocolate glass 225.00
Butter dish, cov., Chocolate glass, 4" d. 145.00
Butter dish, cov., emerald green, 4" d. 70.00
Butter dish, cov., canary, 5" d. 100.00
Creamer, clear, 4" h. 30.00
Creamer, Nile Green, 5" h. (ILLUS.) 225.00
Cruet w/original stopper, amber (ILLUS.) 145.00
Cruet w/original stopper, emerald green 150.00
Mug, Chocolate glass 380.00
Mug, emerald green 65.00
Pitcher, canary 145.00
Pitcher, clear 85.00
Salt shaker, clear 50.00
Salt shaker, Nile Green 250.00

Dewey Cruet

Sauce dish, canary 45.00
Spooner, amber 60.00
Spooner, clear, 5" h. 45.00
Sugar bowl, cov., clear, 2¼" d. 35.00
Sugar bowl, cov., cobalt blue, 2½" d. 125.00
Tray, serpentine, Nile Green, small 250.00
Tumbler, canary 60.00

Herringbone Buttress

Bowl, 6¼" d., clear 65.00
Bowl, 8¼" d., emerald green 200.00
Butter dish, cov., clear 125.00
Butter dish on pedestal, emerald green 400.00
Cake stand, clear 175.00
Cordial, clear, 3" h. 100.00
Creamer, clear 100.00
Goblet, clear 110.00
Pitcher, clear 225.00
Pitcher, emerald green 375.00
Salt shaker, clear 135.00
Spooner, clear 85.00
Sugar bowl, cov., clear 100.00
Sugar bowl, cov., emerald green . . . 225.00
Syrup jug w/metal lid, clear 125.00
Tumbler, type 1, clear 100.00
Tumbler, type 2, clear 75.00
Vase, 8" h., clear 100.00
Vase, 10" h., emerald green 275.00
Wine, clear, 4" h. 90.00

Holly (Clear)

Bowl, 7½" d. 85.00
Bowl, 10¾ x 4¾" rectangle 200.00
Bowl, oval, on pedestal 175.00
Butter dish, cov. 250.00
Compote, cov., jelly, 4½" d. 250.00
Compote, cov., 6½" d. 275.00
Compote, cov., 8¼" d. 350.00

Holly Creamer

Creamer (ILLUS.) 145.00
Mug, 4" h. 90.00

Holly Pickle Dish

Pickle dish, oval, handled (ILLUS.) . . 60.00
Sauce dish, 3½" d. 50.00
Spooner 125.00

Holly Sugar Bowl

Sugar bowl, cov. (ILLUS.) 200.00
Toothpick holder 75.00
Tumbler with beaded rim, Chocolate glass, only one known (ILLUS.) . . . 4,000.00
Tumbler, clear 175.00
Vase, 6" h. 175.00
Vase on pedestal, 8" h. 275.00

Only Known Chocolate Holly Tumbler

Leaf Bracket

Leaf Bracket Cruet

Item	Price
Berry set: master bowl & 6 sauce dishes; Chocolate glass, 7 pcs.	300.00
Bowl, 8" d., clear	30.00
Butter dish, cov., Chocolate glass	150.00
Butter dish, cov., clear	100.00
Creamer, Chocolate glass	90.00
Creamer, clear	55.00
Cruet w/original stopper, Chocolate glass (ILLUS.)	200.00
Cruet w/original stopper, clear	160.00
Nappy, triangular, Chocolate glass	65.00
Nappy, clear	55.00
Pitcher, Chocolate glass	400.00
Pitcher, clear	165.00
Relish, clear, 8 x 5"	45.00
Salt shaker, clear	85.00
Sauce dish, Chocolate glass, 4¾" d.	40.00
Spooner, clear	50.00
Sugar bowl, cov., Chocolate glass	145.00
Sugar bowl, cov., clear	80.00
Toothpick holder, clear	90.00
Tumbler, clear	50.00

Overall Lattice

Overall Lattice Mug

Item	Price
Bowl, berry, clear	30.00
Creamer, clear	30.00
Goblet, clear	35.00
Mug, clear (ILLUS.)	40.00
Pitcher, clear	60.00
Sauce dish, flat, clear	15.00
Spooner, clear	25.00
Sugar bowl, cov., clear	45.00
Tumbler, clear	35.00
Wine, clear	25.00

Pattern No. 11

Item	Price
Bowl, 8 x 6½" rectangle, clear	25.00
Goblet, clear	25.00
Plate, 8" square, clear	30.00
Plate, 8" square, emerald green	55.00
Relish tray, clear, 6" l.	20.00
Toothpick holder, clear	35.00
Tumbler, iced tea, clear	10.00
Vase, 6" h., clear	20.00
Vase, 6" h., emerald green	50.00
Vase, 8" h., clear	20.00

Pleat Band

Item	Price
Bowl, 6¼" d., clear	20.00
Butter dish, cov., clear	60.00
Cake stand, clear (two sizes)	60.00
Compote, cov., 4¼" d., clear	35.00
Compote, cov., 7¼" d., clear	35.00
Compote, cov., 10¼" d., clear	50.00
Compote, open, 4¼" d., clear	25.00
Compote, open, 7¼" d., clear	30.00
Compote, open, 9¼" d., clear	35.00
Creamer, clear	35.00
Goblet, clear	30.00
Pitcher, clear	90.00
Salt shaker, amber	55.00
Salt shaker, canary or teal blue	45.00
Salt shaker, clear	15.00
Spooner, clear	25.00
Sugar bowl, cov., clear	35.00
Tumbler, clear	30.00
Wine, canary	100.00
Wine, clear	25.00

Shuttle

Shuttle Tankard Creamer

Butter dish, cov., Chocolate glass ... 850.00
Butter dish, cov., clear 110.00
Cake stand, clear 125.00
Champagne, clear 40.00
Cordial, clear 35.00
Creamer, Chocolate glass 500.00
Creamer, tankard, Chocolate glass 75.00
Creamer, tankard, clear (ILLUS.) 35.00
Goblet, Chocolate glass 650.00
Goblet, clear 60.00
Mug, amber 300.00
Mug, Chocolate glass 75.00

Shuttle Mug

Mug, clear (ILLUS.) 25.00
Mug, cobalt blue 275.00
Pitcher, Chocolate glass 3,000.00
Pitcher, clear 140.00
Punch cup, clear 10.00
Salt shaker, clear 60.00
Spooner, Chocolate glass 350.00
Spooner, clear 50.00
Sugar bowl, cov., Chocolate glass .. 600.00
Sugar bowl, cov., clear 80.00
Tumbler, Chocolate glass 85.00
Tumbler, clear 50.00
Wine, clear 10.00

Teardrop & Tassel

Teardrop & Tassel Spooner

Bowl, 7¼" d., clear 35.00
Butter dish, cov., clear 60.00
Butter dish, cov., cobalt blue 185.00
Compote, cov., 4 5/8" d., clear 65.00
Compote, cov., 6½" d., Nile Green 375.00
Creamer, amber 175.00
Creamer, clear 35.00
Goblet, clear 150.00
Goblet, emerald green 225.00
Pickle dish, emerald green 90.00
Pitcher, clear 65.00
Pitcher, cobalt blue 175.00
Salt shaker, clear 125.00
Sauce dish, clear, 4" d. 10.00
Spooner, clear 40.00
Spooner, emerald green (ILLUS.) 85.00
Sugar bowl, cov., Chocolate glass .. 475.00
Sugar bowl, cov., clear 60.00

Teardrop & Tassel Sugar Bowl

Sugar bowl, cov., cobalt blue (ILLUS.) 135.00
Tumbler, type 2, amber 225.00
Tumbler, type 1, clear 35.00
Water set: pitcher & 6 tumblers; cobalt blue, 7 pcs. 550.00

HOLLY AMBER (GOLDEN AGATE)

Holly Amber Butter Dish

Bowl, 7½" d. 550.00
Bowl, 10 x 4" rectangle 1,000.00
Bowl, oval 400.00
Butter dish, cov. (ILLUS.) 1,600.00
Cake stand 2,300.00

Holly Amber Compote

Compote, cov., 6½" d. (ILLUS.) 1,450.00
Compote, cov., 8¼" d. 2,200.00
Creamer 600.00
Cruet w/original stopper 1,850.00
Mug, 4½" h. 450.00
Pitcher 2,400.00
Plate, 7½" d. 700.00
Salt shaker 325.00

Holly Amber Sauce Dish

Sauce dish, 4½" d. (ILLUS.) 275.00
Spooner 650.00
Sugar bowl, cov. 850.00
Sugar bowl, cov., on pedestal 2,500.00

Holly Amber Syrup Jug

Syrup jug w/metal lid (ILLUS. without lid) 900.00

Holly Amber Toothpick Holder

Toothpick holder (ILLUS.) 400.00
Tray, 9¼" d. 1,150.00

Holly Amber Tumbler with Beaded Rim

Tumbler with beaded rim (ILLUS.) ... 650.00

NOVELTY & MISCELLANEOUS ITEMS

Admiral Dewey covered dish, full figure bust of Admiral Dewey as finial on cover, ribbed base, amber 250.00
Buffalo paperweight, dated 1901, opaque white 325.00

Nile Green Buffalo Paperweight

Buffalo paperweight, no date, Nile Green (ILLUS.) 600.00

Connecticut Skillet

Connecticut Skillet dish, clear (ILLUS.) 35.00

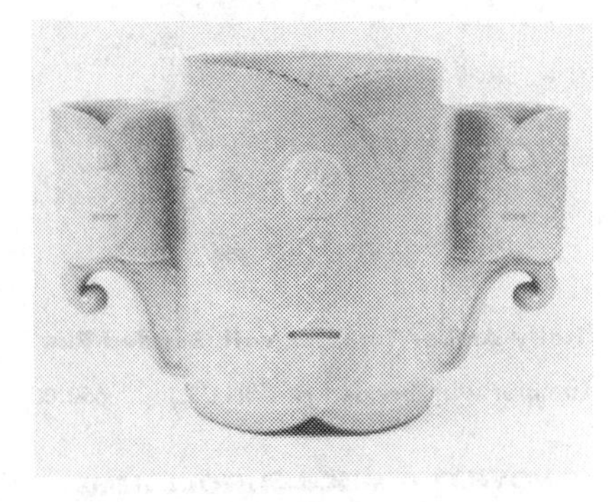

Cuff Set Novelty

Cuff Set novelty, Nile Green (ILLUS.) 450.00

Dog's Head toothpick holder, frosted clear 125.00

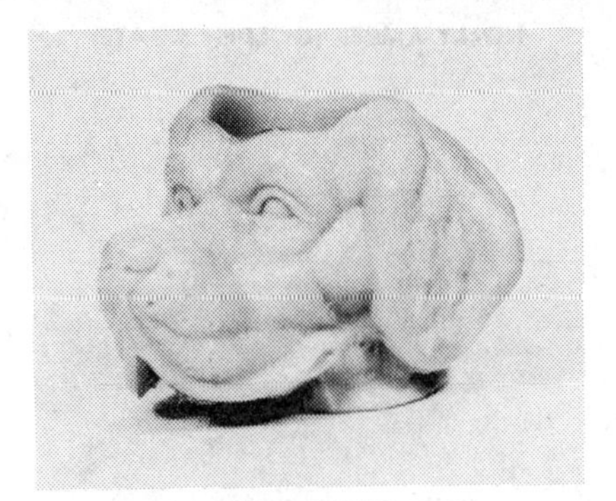

Dog's Head Toothpick Holder

Dog's Head toothpick holder, Nile Green (ILLUS.) 150.00

Dolphin Covered Dish

Dolphin covered dish, beaded edge, clear (ILLUS.) 225.00

Dustpan novelty, teal blue 75.00

Hen covered dish, amber 135.00

Hen Covered Dish

Hen covered dish, Nile Green (ILLUS.) 1,100.00

Indian Head creamer, Nile Green (ILLUS.)........................ 650.00

Indian Head creamer, opaque white 450.00

Indoor Drinking Scene mug, Chocolate glass, 5" h.................. 175.00

Indoor Drinking Scene mug, Nile Green, 5" h...................... 110.00

Indian Head Creamer

Mitted Hand novelty, clear 40.00

Outdoor Drinking Scene mug, Chocolate glass 145.00

Sheaf of Wheat & Picture Frame Toothpicks

Picture Frame toothpick holder, Nile Green (ILLUS. right) 375.00

Rabbit covered dish, amber 135.00

Racing Deer and Doe water pitcher, Chocolate glass 475.00

Racing Deer & Doe Water Pitcher

Racing Deer & Doe water pitcher, clear (ILLUS.) 150.00

Ruffled Eye Water Pitcher

Ruffled Eye water pitcher, amber (ILLUS.) 135.00

Ruffled Eye water pitcher, Chocolate glass 495.00

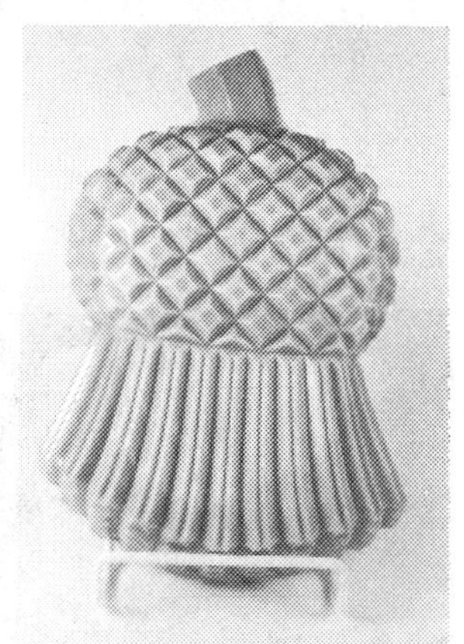

Scotch Thistle Novelty

Scotch Thistle novelty, Nile Green (ILLUS.) 475.00

Sheaf of Wheat toothpick holder, Nile Green (ILLUS. left) 310.00

Squirrel water pitcher, Chocolate glass 475.00

Squirrel water pitcher, clear 175.00

Wheelbarrow Novelty in Chocolate Glass

Wheelbarrow novelty, Chocolate glass (ILLUS.) 800.00
Wheelbarrow novelty, teal blue 150.00

NON-GREENTOWN PIECES

Listed here are a number of pieces, many of them in Chocolate glass, which are confused with Greentown products. Current research indicates that most, if not all, were actually produced by McKee and Brothers.

File Pattern Creamer

File patt. creamer, Chocolate glass (ILLUS.) 450.00

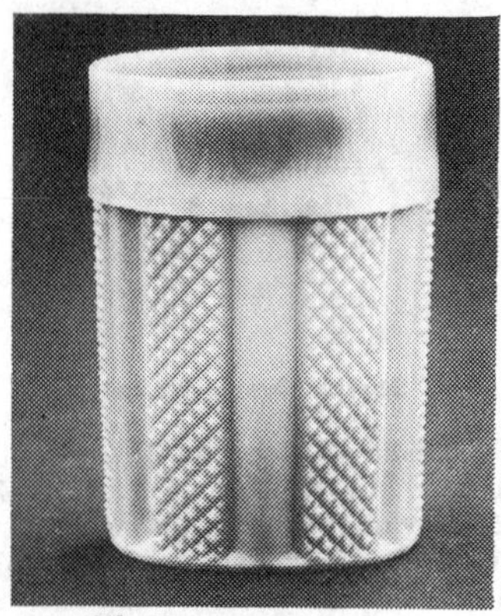

File Pattern Tumbler

File patt. tumbler, Chocolate glass (ILLUS.) 425.00
Shield with Daisy and Button patt. sauce dish, Chocolate glass (ILLUS. of bottom) 375.00
Troubadour or Serenade mug, amber, 4¾" h. 90.00
Troubadour or Serenade mug, clear, 4¾" h. 50.00
Troubadour or Serenade mug, cobalt blue, 4¾" h. 325.00
Troubadour or Serenade mug, opaque green, 5" h. 50.00

Shield with Daisy & Button Sauce

Troubadour or Serenade mug, opaque white 40.00

Troubadour or Serenade Plate

Troubadour or Serenade plate, 6" d., opaque white (ILLUS.)...... 50.00

Two-Headed Chick Covered Dish

Two-Headed Chick covered dish, Chocolate glass, 4¾" l. (ILLUS.) . . 2,600.00
Wild Rose with Bowknot water pitcher, Chocolate glass 480.00
Wild Rose with Bowknot patt. sauce dish, Chocolate glass 85.00

(End of Special Focus)

HEISEY

Heisey Trident Candelbrum

Numerous types of fine glass were made by the A.H. Heisey Glass Co., Newark, Ohio, from 1895. The company's trade-mark — an H enclosed within a diamond — has become known to most glass collectors. The company's name and molds were acquired by Imperial Glass Co., Bellaire, Ohio, in 1958, and some pieces have been reissued. The glass listed below consists of miscellaneous pieces and types. Also see ANIMALS under Glass and PATTERN GLASS.

Banana split dish, footed, Yeoman patt., Moongleam (green) $35.00
Basket, Crystolite patt., clear, 6" h. 165.00
Basket, notched handle & rim, etched flowers, clear, 14" h. 195.00
Berry set: master bowl & 6 sauce dishes; Empress patt., Flamingo (pink), 7 pcs. 120.00
Bonbon, Lariat patt., clear 23.50
Bowl, 8" d., footed, Beaded Panel & Sunburst patt., clear 65.00
Bowl, 10" d., dolphin-footed, Empress patt., Stiegel (cobalt blue) .. 350.00
Butter dish, cov., Waverly patt., Orchid etching, clear 165.00
Candelabra, 2-light, Thumbprint & Panel patt., Stiegel, pr. 275.00
Candelabrum, 2-light, Trident patt., Sahara (yellow), 5" h. (ILLUS.) 90.00
Candy dish, cov., Flat Panel patt., clear, 5" 149.00
Celery tray, Twist patt., Moongleam 32.00
Cocktail, Carcassone patt., Sahara, 3 oz. 25.00
Cocktail, Waldorf patt., Tally Ho etching, clear, 3 oz. 47.50
Cocktail shaker w/rooster stopper, Tally Ho etching, clear 165.00
Compote, 6¼" d., low stand, Waverly patt., Orchid etching, clear 52.00
Compote, cov., 7", Pleat & Panel patt., Flamingo w/gold trim 60.00
Cordial, Jamestown patt., Rosalie etching, clear 75.00
Cornucopia-vases, Warwick patt., clear, 9½", pr. 75.00
Creamer & sugar bowl, Empress patt., Sahara, pr. 60.00
Creamer & sugar bowl on tray, individual size, Crystolite patt., clear, 3 pcs. 30.00
Cruet w/original stopper, 8-sided, Colonial patt., Flamingo 590.00
Cruet w/original stopper, Ipswich patt., clear 60.00
Cup & saucer, Empress patt., Sahara 40.00
Decanter w/stopper, Carcassonne patt., clear, pt. 189.00
Goblet, Duquesne patt., clear, 9 oz. 9.50
Goblet, Trojan patt., Flamingo, 8 oz. 19.50
Ice tub, Twist patt., Moongleam 75.00
Ladle, Moongleam (green), signed .. 25.00
Lemon dish, cov., Pleat & Panel patt., Flamingo (pink), signed, 5" 42.50
Marmalade jar, Plantation patt., clear 75.00
Marmalade jar, footed, Pleat & Panel patt., clear 18.50
Mayonnaise, underplate & ladle, Orchid etching, clear, 3 pcs. 145.00
Mustard jar, cov., Double Rib & Panel patt., Moongleam 50.00
Nappy, crimped, Old Queen Anne patt., clear, 9" 60.00
Nut dish, individual, Octagon patt., Flamingo 11.00
Nut dish, individual, Twist patt., Moongleam 25.00
Oil bottle w/loop stopper & handle, Lariat patt., clear, original label, 4 oz. 65.00
Oyster cocktail, Wabash patt., Frontenac etching, clear 12.00
Pickle dish, Coarse Rib patt., Sahara (yellow), w/handled pewter holder, 6" 18.00
Pitcher, jug-type, footed, Carcassone patt., Sahara, 3 pt. 130.00
Pitcher, jug-type, Greek Key patt., clear, 3 pt. 200.00
Pitcher, tankard, Pied Piper patt., clear 130.00
Pitcher, cov., Rib & Panel patt., clear, qt. 125.00
Plate, 6" d., Acorn patt., Hawthorne etching, clear 12.50
Plate, 7½" d., Empress patt., Alexandrite (orchid) 39.00
Plate, 8" d., Waverly patt., Narcissus etching, clear 17.50

Plate, 9" d., Twist patt., Marigold (yellow) 20.00
Plate, 12" d., Wampum patt., clear 35.00
Punch bowl & base, Colonial patt., clear, 13" d. 155.00
Punch cup, Greek Key patt., clear .. 15.00
Punch set: bowl, base & 12 cups; Prince of Wales - Plumes patt., clear, 14 pcs. 235.00
Relish, three-section, Orchid etching, clear, 11" 45.00
Salt & pepper shakers w/original tops, Empress patt., Sahara, pr. .. 70.00
Salt & pepper shakers w/original tops, Plantation patt., clear, pr. .. 48.00
Sherbet, Ipswich patt., Sahara 30.00
Sherbet, Jamestown patt., Barcelona etching, clear 15.00
Sugar bowl, individual size, Cut Block patt., Custard w/enameling 55.00
Sugar bowl, open, footed, Classic patt., clear 135.00
Syrup pitcher w/original top, Plantation patt., clear 70.00
Table set: cov. butter dish, sugar bowl, creamer & spooner; Plain Band patt., clear, 4 pcs. 97.50
Toothpick holder, Pineapple & Fan patt., green w/gold 195.00
Tumbler, juice, Victorian patt., clear, 5 oz. 6.00
Tumbler, Pineapple & Fan patt., clear w/gold 35.00
Vase, 8" h., Ridgeleigh patt., Sahara 110.00

Heisey Warwick Cornucopia Vase

Vase, 9" h., cornucopia shape, Warwick patt., cobalt blue (ILLUS.) ... 165.00
Wine, Apollo patt., etched, clear ... 9.00
Wines, Old Dominion patt., Sahara, signed, set of 7 .... 150.00

HISTORICAL & COMMEMORATIVE

Reference numbers are to Bessie M. Lindsey's book, "American Historical Glass." Also see MILK WHITE GLASS.

Absecon Lighthouse Plate

Absecon Lighthouse plate, clear, 7½" d., No. 25 (ILLUS.) $65.00
Admiral Dewey tumbler, clear w/transfer commemorating Manila Bay Battle, 3 5/8" h., No. 397 .... 30.00
Admiral Dewey tumbler, portrait of Dewey within laurel wreath topped by spread-winged eagle, flagship "Olympia," ammunition, mounted cannon, etc., stippled & clear, 4" h., No. 398 .... 56.00
Battleship Oregon covered dish, milk white, 6 7/8" l., 3 5/8" w., 4" h., No. 469 ....30.00 to 40.00
Bible bread tray, open Bible center, clear, 10½ x 7", No. 200......... 55.00
Bishop's bread plate, open Bible handles, w/"Daily Bread" motto on one, clear, No. 201 .... 140.00
California Bear plate, "California Mid-Winter Fair," milk white, No. 104 .... 135.00
Cannon covered dish, milk white, 4¼" d., No. 147 .... 55.00
Charley Ross cologne bottle, kidnapping victim, bust of child w/name above, placed within a medallion, clear, 6 5/8" h., No. 460 .... 35.00
Civil War liquor glass, shield, flag w/thirty-five stars, inscribed "A Bumper to the Flag," 3¼" h., No. 480 .... 115.00
Columbia bread tray, shield-shaped, Columbia superimposed against 13 vertical bars, yellow, 11½ x 9½", No. 54 (ILLUS. next page) ... 140.00
Constitution platter, eagle & banner center, clear, 12½" l., No. 43 .... 55.00
Currier & Ives "Balky Mule" tray, clear, 9½" d., No. 135.....60.00 to 75.00
Faith, Hope & Charity plate,

maidens posed as Three Graces center, w/1875 patent date, clear w/milk white center, 10" d., No. 230 .... 165.00

Columbia Bread Tray

Folding Fan dish, w/Daisy & Button patt., clear, 10¾" spread, No. 172 .... 10.50

Garfield Drape patt. plate,, "We Mourn, etc.," clear, 10" d., No. 303 .... 55.00

Garfield Memorial mug, handled, embossed bust of Garfield, date of birth & death, clear, 2 5/8" h., No. 294 .... 55.00

Grand Army of the Republic goblet, inscribed "21 Encampment, September 27, 28, St. Louis, Mo.," clear, ca. 1887, 6¾" h., No. 596 .. 56.00

Grant Peace plate, bust portrait of Grant center, maple leaf border, blue, 10½" d., No. 289 .... 75.00

Lantern, clear, 3" w., 5¾" h., No. 156 .... 30.00

Liberty Bell patt. plate, closed handles, scalloped rim w/thirteen original states & "100 Years Ago," clear, 10¼" d., No. 37 ...95.00 to 110.00

Log watering trough, blue opalescent, No. 151 .... 25.00

McCormick reaper platter, clear, 13 x 8", No. 119 ....75.00 to 85.00

McKinley (William B.) covered cup, bust portrait opposite handle, "Protection & Prosperity," clear, overall 5" h., No. 335 .....55.00 to 70.00

McKinley-Hobart tumbler, "Protection & Prosperity," bust portrait medallions w/names inscribed, clear, 2½" h., No. 338 .... 48.50

McKinley-Roosevelt tumbler, etched oval portrait medallions of candidates, clear, 3¾" h., No. 353 .... 62.50

Mitchell (John) bread tray, gilded portrait of Mitchell center, "Leader, Counsellor, Friend, President United Mine Workers of America," clear, 10¾ x 6¾", No. 448 .... 195.00

Moses in the Bulrushes tray, milk white, 8¾ x 6 5/8", No. 213 ....55.00 to 70.00

Motto tumbler, inscribed "Make Haste to Live and Consider Each Day a New Life," clear, No. 228 .. 7.00

Motto tumbler, inscribed "Rock of Ages," clear, No. 224 .... 7.00

Nellie Bly platter, full figure of Nellie Bly (Elizabeth Cochrane) center, inscribed "Around the World in 72 D's, etc.," clear, 12¾ x 6¾", No. 136 .... 200.00

Niagara Falls tray, frosted scene of Niagara Falls from American side center, clear, 11½ x 16", No. 489 ....110.00 to 125.00

Old Abe (eagle) covered sugar bowl, frosted eagle, etched, clear 225.00

Old Glory plate, Betsy Ross making first flag pictured in center, clear, 5½" d., No. 52 .... 32.00

Old Statehouse Philadelphia tray, clear, round, No. 32 .... 65.00

Owens statuette, bust of Owens inscribed "1859 M.J. Owens, 1923," frosted, 5" h., No. 450 .... 75.00

Paperweight, round slab type w/frosted bust portrait of George Washington & beveled rim, clear, 3 1/8" d., 1" h., No. 257 .... 100.00

Pershing paperweight, bust portrait center, inscribed "General John J. Pershing, 1917," clear flat disc, 4" d., No. 404 ....25.00 to 35.00

Plymouth Rock paperweight, "A rock in the wilderness, etc." & "Providence Inkstand Co., 1876," clear, 3¾" l., No. 18 .... 80.00

Plymouth Rock paperweight, "Mary Chilton was, etc." & "Inkstand Co., Prov., R.I.," clear, No. 19.... 100.00

Pope Leo XIII plate, portrait center, alternate church symbols & hobnail border, clear, 10" d., No. 240 .... 32.00

Railroad train platter, Union Pacific Engine No. 350, clear, 12 x 9", No. 134 ....95.00 to 125.00

Rock of Ages bread tray, clear, No. 236 (ILLUS. next page) 60.00

Roosevelt (Theodore) platter, frosted portrait center, teddy bears, etc., border, clear, 10¼ x 7¾", No. 357 .... 105.00

Ruth statuette, frosted, marked "Gillinder & Sons Centennial Exposition" on base, 4½" h., No. 216 ... 135.00

Three Presidents goblet, frosted, bust portraits of Washington, Lincoln & Garfield framed in medallion settings, clear, 3" d., 6¼" h., No. 250 ....300.00 to 325.00

Rock of Ages Bread Tray

Three Presidents platter, bust portraits of Garfield, Washington & Lincoln, inscribed "In Remembrance," clear, 12½ x 10", No. 249 .... 65.00

Washington Centennial patt. platter w/bear paw handles, frosted center, "First in War," etc., clear, 12 x 8½", No. 27 ....75.00 to 95.00

Washington Monument paperweight, deep blue, 2¾" sq. base, 5½" h., No. 255 .... 165.00

IMPERIAL

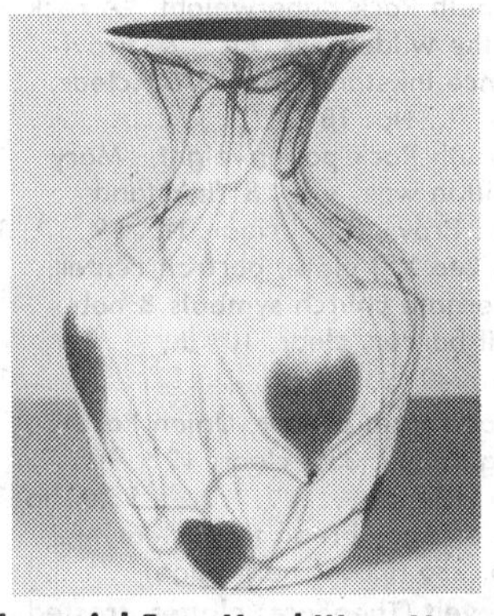

Imperial Free Hand Ware Vase

Imperial Glass Company, Bellaire, Ohio, was organized in 1901 and was in continuous production, except for very brief periods, until its closing in June, 1984. It had been a major producer of Carnival Glass (which see) earlier in this century and also produced other types of glass, including an Art Glass line called "Free Hand Ware" during the 1920's and its "Jewels" about 1916. The company acquired a number of molds of other earlier factories, including the Cambridge and A.H. Heisey companies, and had reissued numerous items through the years.

Bowl, fruit, 5" d., Candlewick patt., clear $11.50

Bowl, fruit, 6" d., Cape Cod patt., clear 6.00

Bowl, 9" w., heart-shaped w/handle, Candlewick patt., clear 80.00

Butter dish, cov., Candlewick patt., clear, ¼ lb. 22.00

Cake stand, Candlewick patt., clear, 11" h. 52.00

Candlesticks, Candlewick patt., clear, 3½" h., pr. 18.00

Champagne, Candlewick patt., clear 17.00

Cocktail pitcher, Candlewick patt., clear, 40 oz. 145.00

Creamer & sugar bowl, footed, Cape Cod patt., clear, pr. 18.00

Free Hand Ware pitcher, 10" h., applied clear handle, pale yellow lustre w/white drag loops 225.00

Free Hand Ware vase, 6" h., oyster white w/imbedded green hearts & vines, deep orange lustre lining (ILLUS.) 250.00

Free Hand Ware vase, 10¼" h., dark blue w/light blue drag loops 225.00

Free Hand Ware vase, 11¾" h., baluster-shaped, triangular pull-ups at mouth, opalescent opaque white w/imbedded iridescent blue trailing vines, original paper label 325.00

Ice bucket, 2-handled, Candlewick patt., clear, 7" h. 90.00

Mayonnaise bowl, underplate & ladle, Candlewick patt., clear, 3 pcs. 65.00

Pitcher, Candlewick patt., clear, 80 oz. 185.00

Plate, 7" d., Candlewick patt., clear 8.00

Plate, 8" d., Cape Cod patt., clear 6.00

Plate, dinner, 10" d., Candlewick patt., clear 20.00

Plate, dinner, 10" d., Cape Cod patt., clear 12.00

Punch set: 6 qt. bowl, 17" d. plate & 12 cups; Candlewick patt., clear, 14 pcs. 175.00

Tumbler, juice, beaded foot, Candlewick patt., clear, 5 oz. 10.00

Vase, 8" h., base handles, Candlewick patt., clear 80.00

Wine, Candlewick patt., clear, 4 oz. 12.00

IOWA CITY GLASS

This ware, made by the Iowa City Glass Manufacturing Co., Iowa City, Iowa, from 1880 to about 1883, was produced in many shapes and patterns.

Bread plate, round, "Elaine," 1-0-1 border, 9" d. $90.00
Bread plate, round, "Elaine," frosted center, leaf spray handles, 9" d... 95.00
Plate, child's, "Be True," dog center.......................... 90.00
Platter, oval, "Be Industrious," beehive center scene, 1-0-1 border ... 100.00
Platter, oval, "Be Industrious," frosted beehive center, laurel leaf handles 95.00
Platter, oval, Frosted Stork patt., flower pot handles, deer & doe edge scenes 75.00
Platter, oval, Frosted Stork patt., 1-0-1 border 65.00
Spooner, Stork patt. 50.00

JACK-IN-PULPIT VASES

Jack-in-Pulpit Vase

Glass vases in varying sizes and resembling in appearance the flower of this name have been popular with collectors since the 19th century. They were produced in various solid colors and in shaded wares.

Apple green opaque w/ruffled maroon edging, hobnail edge, 7½" h. (ILLUS.) $110.00
Cased, white exterior, soft green interior, applied clear feet, 5¾" widest d., 6¼" h. 95.00
Cased, white exterior, shaded green hobnail ruffled interior, 6¾" widest d., 7¼" h. 100.00
Chartreuse green opalescent, coil stem, vaseline five-petal foot, 5¼" widest d., 8½" h. 88.00
Cranberry, Diamond Quilted patt., applied clear wishbone feet & ruffled leaf, 4¼" widest d., 6 3/8" h. 125.00
Cranberry, applied clear spirals & pedestal foot, 4¼" widest d., 9½" h. 118.00
Creamy opalescent, brown leaf overlay, gold leaf & flower decoration, gold trim, England, 12½" h. 160.00
Green opalescent stripes, applied green leaf & pink flower, 9" h. ... 125.00
Opaline w/ruby red ruffles, 9" h. 95.00
Pastel yellow, pink & blue stripes, clear base, 10" h. 215.00
Spangled, white exterior w/mica flecks, pink interior w/clear edging, 5½" widest d., 5¾" h. 110.00
White opaque w/cranberry edging, 6" widest d., 7½" h. 98.00
Yellow, small gold leaf design, 7½" h., pr. 125.00

KELVA

Kelva Jewelry Box

Kelva was made early in this century by the C.F. Monroe Co., Meriden, Conn., and was a type of decorated opal glass very like the same company's Wave Crest and Nakara wares. This type of glass was produced until about the time of the first World War. Also see NAKARA and WAVE CREST.

Box w/hinged lid, mottled moss green w/h.p. variegated orange & white poppy & trailing stems w/bluish tinged buds, original lining, signed, 4½" d., 2¾" h.......$315.00
Box w/hinged lid, octagonal, mottled sage green w/h.p. orange & white florals, ormolu fittings, original lime green lining, signed, 4" w., 3" h......................... 335.00
Jewelry box w/hinged lid, mottled green w/large h.p. pink & white

florals w/green leaves, signed, 8" d., 3¾" h. (ILLUS.) 650.00
Powder jar, cov., blown-mold rose in full relief on lid, signed, 3 x 3" 300.00
Vase, 13" h., mottled green w/h.p. pink florals, signed 600.00
Vase, 18" h. to top of ornate silver plate handles, mottled green w/h.p. full-blown pink & white roses, silver plate footed base ... 1,600.00

KEW BLAS

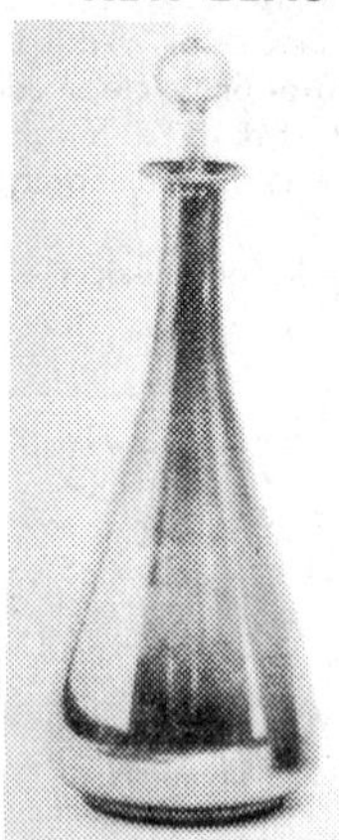

Kew Blas Decanter

Glass of this name was made by the Union Glass Works, Somerville, Mass. These iridescent wares were similar to those produced by other art glass firms during the same period in the late 19th and early 20th centuries.

Decanter w/spherical long-stemmed stopper, club-shaped body, green-gold iridescence, early 20th c., signed, 13 9/16" h. (ILLUS.) $275.00
Plate, 6" d., iridescent gold, signed 145.00
Vase, 4¾" h., baluster form, opal w/gold pulled feathering & green threads, signed 650.00
Vase, 6" h., pulled feather design, apricot, signed 850.00
Vase, 6 1/8" h., swelled cylinder w/ring neck, gold lustre pulled feathering on tan, early 20th c., signed 412.50
Vase, 6½" h., dark blue w/light blue draped swirls 775.00
Vase, 7½" h., bell-form w/ruffled everted rim, pulled feather design, iridescent gold, early 20th c. 385.00

LALIQUE

Lalique Hood Ornaments

Fine glass, including numerous extraordinary molded articles, has been made by the glasshouse established by Rene' Lalique early in this century in France. The firm was carried on by his son, Marc, until his death in 1977 and is now headed by Marc's daughter, Marie-Claude. All Lalique glass is marked, usually on or near the bottom, with either an engraved or molded signature. Unless otherwise noted we list only those pieces marked "R. Lalique" produced before the death of Rene' Lalique in 1945.

Ashtray, "Louise," black enamel center, 3" d. $135.00
Bowl, 8" d., "Gui," mistletoe design, green wash 325.00
Bowl, 14 3/8" d., "Assiette Calypso," molded mermaids (5), clear & opalescent 3,080.00
Box, cov., "Messanges," cover molded w/six sparrows, amber, 6 5/8" d. 715.00
Brooch, molded grasshoppers amongst blades of grass, frosted & clear blue, gilt-metal backing, ca. 1910, 3½" oval (pin missing) .. 990.00
Carafe w/sharply tapered ribbed stopper, "Sirenes," expanding neck of square section above gourd form body molded w/four frogs issuing streams of water forming panels alternating w/groups of sinuous water maidens molded in low relief, whole washed in a charcoal grey stain, ca. 1910, 15½" h. 1,650.00
Charger, slender, swirling opalescent fish, w/small bubbles in center, 11¼" d. 495.00
Clock, "Le Jour et La Nuit," charcoal circular face molded in positive & negative relief w/nude male & female figures arched above circular frosted dial w/white enamel chapter ring, on bronze truncated pyramidal base, ca. 1932, 14¾" h. 12,650.00

Dresser set: powder box, medium cologne bottle & large scent bottle; "Epines," molded entwined brambles, brown-stained, w/silver bands, 3 pcs. 1,850.00

Figure of "Joueuse de Flute," oviform molded w/border of roses enclosing draped maiden holding double flute to her mouth & standing on mound of overlapping petals, clear & frosted, 14½" h. 1,950.00

Figure of "Suzanne," nude but for drapery descending from her outstretched arms, milky opalescent, ca. 1932, 9" h. 4,675.00

Figure of "Thais," nude but for drapery suspended from her outstretched arms, opalescent, ca. 1932, 8¾" h. 9,900.00

Hood ornament, "Archer," molded nude male archer, clear & frosted, 5" h. (ILLUS. right) 1,650.00

Hood ornament, "Cinq Chevaux," molded 5 rearing horses in profile, clear, ca. 1925, chrome metal mount 6,325.00

Hood ornament, "Faucon," model of a falcon, clear & frosted, 6 1/8" h. (ILLUS. left) . . . . 1,430.00 to 1,760.00

Pendant, "Floret," nudes w/flowers, brown wash, round 495.00

Perfume bottle w/stopper, "Camille," flattened bulbous form, molded in medium relief w/protruding ruffled fan devices, bright grass green, ca. 1925, 2 5/8" h. . . 1,870.00

Perfume bottle w/stopper, "Epines," shouldered cylindrical vessel & flattened domical stopper each molded in relief w/entwined scrolling vines w/thorns, the recesses tinted w/grey-blue enamel, ca. 1925, engraved in script "R. Lalique France," 4¼" h. 467.50

Perfume bottle, "Amphytrite," body molded as a shell, stopper as a kneeling nude figure, frosted, 3½" h. 770.00

Plaque, "Deux Figurines et Fleurs," footed medallion molded w/two female nudes bearing urns beneath a flowering bower, 2 1/8" d. 352.00

Powder box, cov., "Emiliane," lid w/florals & some light brown tinting, "D'Orsay," 4" d. 150.00

Punch cup, "Butterfly" handle 75.00

Vase, 4¾" h., "Grenade," spherical, molded rows of serrated arches, clear & frosted amber 1,650.00

Vase, 6" h., "Lievres," globular body & tapering cylindrical neck molded w/swirling leafy branches, a band

Lalique "Lievres" Vase

on the upper half w/running rabbits, turquoise blue, ca. 1930, molded "R. Lalique" (ILLUS.) 3,850.00

Vase, 6 1/8" h., "Pierrefonds," scrolled thorny strap handles, etched, frosted & clear amber . . . 5,885.00

Vase, 6 1/8" h., "Renoncules," truncated trumpet form, bulbous lower section molded in medium relief w/stylized peonies & leafage, frosted & tinged w/pearly iridescence, ca. 1930 . . . . 990.00

Vase, 6½" h., "Formose," bulbous, molded swimming goldfish, frosted highlighted w/dusty blue, ca. 1925 . . . . 605.00

Vase, 6½" h., "Ormeaux," bulbous shape, overlapping wide leaves molded in medium relief, opalescent, ca. 1925 . . . . 605.00

Vase, 7" h., "Soucis," spherical w/conical neck, molded marigolds, frosted blue 1,980.00

Vase, 7¼" h., "Chevaux," cylindrical w/flaring rim, molded in medium relief w/frieze of wild horses against tall grasses, deep grey, ca. 1925 . . . . 2,090.00

Vase, 8 5/8" h., "Actina," flared cylinder, molded columns of serrated curves, frosted opalescent 880.00

Lalique Vase

Vase, 9 5/8" h., "Poissons," spher-

ical molded large fish, frosted red 5,500.00
Vase, 10" h., "Perruches," ovoid, molded parakeets amongst flowering branches, frosted green (ILLUS. previous page) 6,600.00
Vase, 11½" h., "Gros Scarabees," spherical, molded beetles, clear & frosted amber, ca. 1920 . . . . 9,900.00
Vase, 16¼" h., "Palastre," oviform, molded standing nude men in various poses, frosted, ca. 1922 . . . . 20,900.00

LEAF MOLD

Though the maker of this attractive glass pattern remains elusive, the Leaf Mold pattern becomes more popular with collectors each year. Thought to have been made in the 1890's, there are several colors and color combinations available and it was made in both satin and shiny finish as well as in a cased version.

Rose bowl, vaseline w/cranberry spatter $95.00
Salt shaker, cranberry spatter 65.00
Salt & pepper shakers w/original tops, cased cranberry w/mica flecks, 2½" h., pr. 125.00
Salt & pepper shakers w/original tops, vaseline w/cranberry spatter, pr. . . . . 150.00 to 200.00
Sauce dish, cranberry spatter 30.00
Spooner, vaseline w/cranberry spatter 125.00
Sugar shaker w/original top, pink & white spatter 195.00
Syrup jug w/original top, vaseline w/cranberry spatter, shiny finish 395.00
Water set: pitcher & six tumblers; vaseline w/cranberry spatter, 7 pcs. . . . . 525.00 to 575.00

LEAF UMBRELLA

This attractive pattern is attributed to the Northwood Company and dates from 1889. A complete table service was made in cranberry glass and cased glass in shades of blue, pink, mauve and yellow. Some cased cranberry and white spatter glass is also found and sometimes the wares were given a satin finish. A somewhat brittle glassware that readily flakes, items offered for sale have sometimes had the rims polished or smoothed.

Butter dish, cov., cranberry $595.00
Cologne bottle w/original stopper, cased mauve 225.00
Creamer, breakfast size, cranberry 200.00
Finger bowl, cased blue 85.00
Pitcher, bulbous, cranberry 220.00
Pitcher, cased vaseline 295.00
Pitcher, water, cased mauve 295.00
Salt shaker, cranberry 50.00
Salt & pepper shakers w/original pewter tops, cased mauve, pr. . . . 110.00
Syrup pitcher w/original top, cranberry spatter 200.00

LE GRAS

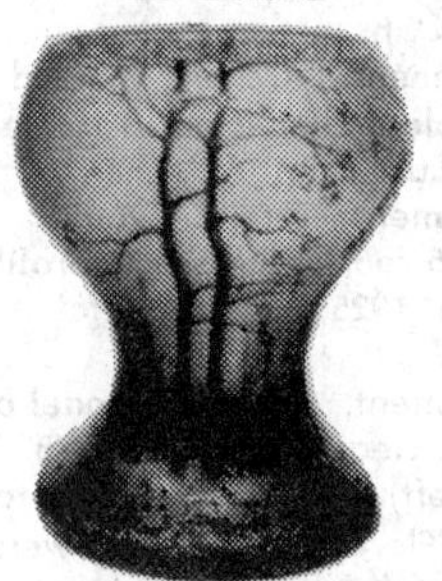

Le Gras Cameo Vase

Cameo and enameled glass somewhat similar to that made by Galle', Daum Nancy and other factories of the period was made at the Le Gras works in Saint Denis, France, late last century and until the outbreak of World War I.

Cameo bowl, 12" d., 3½" h., carved winter scene w/snow, trees & birds, signed $750.00
Cameo table lamp, domical shade, baluster form base, top & base acid-cut & enameled in The Winter Scene snowy landscape against mottled pink shaded to brown frosted ground, signed, 19½" h. 2,475.00
Cameo vase, 4½" h., 3½" d., oval top, carved & enameled barren trees w/last few leaves against mottled blue to chartreuse to green frosted ground, signed (ILLUS.) 600.00
Cameo vase, 9" h., carved magenta maple leaves against frosted ground, signed 535.00
Cameo vase, 13" h., cylindrical, carved maroon grapes & leafy branches against grey ground, signed 425.00
Cameo vase, 23" h., elongated tear-

drop form, waxy pale salmon & peach sides overlaid in rust & olive green & cut w/sea grasses, weeds & seashells, ca. 1910, signed 1,650.00

Cameo vases, 26½" h., bulbous w/tapering cylindrical neck, carved purple grape leaves & vines against clear ground, pr. 2,090.00

Vase, 8" h., cylindrical w/flaring base, enameled mountainous lake scene on sunset pink ground, frosted finish, signed 275.00

Vases, 12" h., tapered cylinder, enameled brown & green decoration, silver mounts, signed, pr. 715.00

Vase, 15¾" h., flaring four-sided form, enameled snowy landscape w/tall snow-covered trees, early 20th c., signed 357.50

LIBBEY

In 1878, William L. Libbey obtained a lease on the New England Glass Company of Cambridge, Massachusetts, changing the name to the New England Glass Works, W.L. Libbey and Son, Proprietors. After his death in 1883, his son, Edward D. Libbey, continued to operate the company at Cambridge until 1888 when the factory was closed. Edward Libbey moved to Toledo, Ohio, and set up the company subsequently known as Libbey Glass Co. During the 1880's, the firm's master technician, Joseph Locke, developed the now much desired colored art glass lines of Agata, Amberina, Peach Blow and Pomona. Renowned for its Cut Glass of the Brilliant Period, the company continues in operation today as Libbey Glassware, a division of Owens-Illinois, Inc.

Bowl, 7" d., 1¾" h., ruffled turned out rim, Amberina, signed $350.00

Cocktail, clear bowl, black silhouette of kangaroo in stem 135.00

Compote, twisted stem, engraved florals on bowl, clear, signed 250.00

Cordial, Concord patt., clear, signed 45.00

Cordial, Embassy patt., clear, signed, 6¾" h. 75.00

Goblet, clear bowl, opalescent silhouette of cat in stem, signed, 7" h. 125.00

Maize bowl, master berry 100.00

Maize butter dish, cov., pale green gold-trimmed husks, 7¼" d., 6" h. 485.00

Maize pitcher, water, barrel-shaped, 8¾" h., 5½" d., applied strap handle, creamy opaque w/green husks 550.00

Maize salt shaker w/original top, creamy opaque w/yellow husks . . 85.00

Maize spooner, creamy opaque w/gold-trimmed blue husks 165.00

Maize sugar shaker w/original top, creamy opaque w/gold-trimmed blue husks 205.00

Maize toothpick holder, creamy opaque w/blue husks 295.00

Sherry, clear bowl, black silhouette of monkey in stem, 5" h. 85.00

Sugar bowl, cov., optic ribbed, pale blue opalescent, satin finish, enameled "World's Fair 1893" in gold, 2¾" h. 150.00

Wine, clear bowl, black silhouette of bear in stem, 7" h. 165.00

Wine, clear bowl, opalescent silhouette of cat in stem, signed, 7" h. 110.00

LOETZ

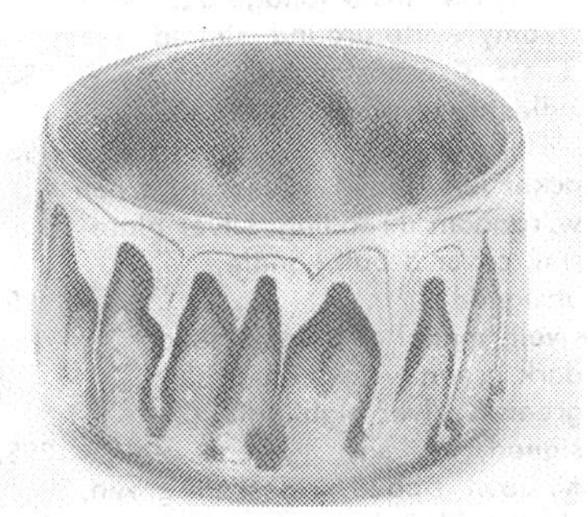

Loetz Bowl

Iridescent glass, some of it somewhat resembling that of Tiffany and other contemporary glasshouses, was produced by the Bohemian firm of J. Loetz Witwe of Klostermule and is referred to as Loetz. Some cameo pieces were also made. Not all pieces are marked.

Bowl, 4 1/8" d., squat cylinder, yellow-cased clear ground w/columns of iridescent gold dots & an irregular wide iridescent caramel, dark green & gold band, unsigned (ILLUS.) $1,980.00

Bowl, 9" d., scalloped rim, ribbed, iridescent pink, signed 210.00

Bowl, 9" d., 6-sided, iridescent gold, signed 155.00

Bowl, 9½" d., footed, iridescent pink w/silver & copper highlights 125.00

Cameo bowl, 6½ x 3¾", 2½" h.,

ovoid w/flaring rim, carved lavender field flowers, grasses & pods against white ground, signed "La Loetz, Made in Cechoslovakia" (sic) 330.00

Loetz Cameo Jar

Cameo jar, cov., cylindrical, carved black overall leaf design w/latticework border at base & on cover against opaque white ground, designed by Hans Block, overall 7" h. (ILLUS.) 4,675.00

Cameo vase, 12" h., flared rim, reverse baluster form, carved light & dark brown tulips & iris blossoms w/stems & foliage against creamy white ground, signed "Loetz, Czechoslovakia" 880.00

Candlesticks, iridescent green, 6½" h., pr. 195.00

Cracker jar, ribbed, iridescent green w/random threading, silver plate rim, cover & bail handle, unsigned 95.00

Inkwell, model of a lion's head, dark green w/iridescent blue-green & silver highlights, unsigned, 4½" sq. 395.00

Rose bowl, ribbed, iridescent green, signed, 5½" d. 175.00

Rose bowl, 2 applied handles, iridescent green, signed, 8½" . . . 225.00

Vase, 4" h., deeply scalloped rim, creamy blue exterior w/purple threading, deep iridescent purple interior, signed 250.00

Vase, 4½" h., squared dimpled sides, amber w/striated silvery blue feathering, ca. 1900, unsigned 550.00

Vase, 5" h., circular w/pinched in sides, mottled iridescent amber & peach w/pale silvery blue undulating bands, ca. 1900, signed . . 935.00

Vase, 5¼" h., iridescent blue & purple w/silver overlay floral spray center 350.00

Vase, 6¼" h., ovoid w/waisted neck & everted rim, iridescent amber w/irregular bands of silver-blue & striated iridescent amber loops & trails, ca. 1900, signed 880.00

Vase, 6 7/8" h., broad body, dimpled below flaring neck, iridescent pearly salmon pink w/applied iridescent blue trailings, shoulder applied w/iridescent caramel lily pads trailed in silver, the stems descending to base, signed 2,420.00

Vase, 8¼" h., baluster form w/inverted bulbous rim, tortoise shell (amber w/darker amber splotches) w/overall opalescent trailing, early 20th c., signed 412.50

Vase, 8¼" h., pale salmon bulbous mouth, iridescent midnight blue baluster form body & waisted circular foot w/overall silvery green oil splotches, overlaid w/pierced silver mounts in the form of blossoms & undulating leaves, ca. 1900, unsigned 2,090.00

Loetz Vase

Vase, 8 5/8" h., twisted rectangle w/scalloped rim, transparent ruby w/iridescent purple, blue & yellow-tan waves, unsigned (ILLUS.) 825.00

Vase, 8¾" h., paperweight-type, tapered cylinder, clear cased in brilliant tangerine w/striated silvery blue & burgundy lappets against silvery blue ground, ca. 1900, unsigned 1,210.00

Vase, 10½" h., iridescent gold w/applied green rigaree, signed 185.00

Vase, 11" h., 4" widest d., ruffled lip, iridescent blue-green over cranberry w/raised irregular stripes, unsigned 385.00

Vase, 11 7/8" h., cylindrical w/flaring mouth, cushion foot, deep red w/iridescent blue horizontal wave designs, unsigned 935.00

Vase, 12" h., baluster-shaped, iridescent cobalt blue w/angled pulled feathering, unsigned, in brass framework of undulating leaves signed "Van Hauten" 365.00

Vase, 13" h., jack-in-pulpit type,

green w/peacock eye design throughout the bottom 1,150.00

Vase, 14¾" h., cylindrical w/outward flaring base, deep green w/iridescent blue, purple & gold mottling, applied snake-like matching threading forming multiple coils around upper portion, signed "Loetz, Austria" 880.00

LUSTRES

Cut Glass Lustres

Lustres are glass vase-like decorative vessels with prisms designed to hold candles and intended as mantel and tabletop decorative adjuncts.

Bohemian, ruby red w/etched design, hollow flat base, open conical stem, notched petal-form rim, single row of clear spear-point prisms, 18" h., pr. $270.00

Bristol, creamy opaque w/enameled florals & foliage, single row of clear prisms, pr. 235.00

Clear, Regency, cut in a spiraling motif, ray-cut bobeche & spiral-cut saucer (chips), single row of clear prisms, gilt-bronze fittings, ca. 1820, 10¼" h., pr. (ILLUS.) 825.00

Clear, enameled white & pink flowers w/gold trim within sanded bands, domed base, scalloped rim, single row of clear prisms, 14¼" h., pr. 350.00

Green, circular base, fluted standard, crenelated rim, upper section heightened w/gilt scrolling foliage, single row of clear prisms, probably Bohemian, last half 19th c., 14" h., pr. 825.00

Ruby, enameled white & gold scrolling leafy decoration, stepped base, knopped stem, arch-cut rim, single row of clear prisms, 19th c., 13" h., pr. 247.50

MARY GREGORY

Glass enameled in white with silhouette-type figures, primarily children, is now termed "Mary Gregory" and was attributed to the Boston and Sandwich Glass Company. However, recent research has proven conclusively that this ware was not decorated by Mary Gregory nor was it made at the Sandwich factory. Miss Gregory was employed by the Boston and Sandwich Glass Company as a decorator; however, records show her assignment was the painting of naturalistic landscape scenes on larger items such as lamps and shades but never the charming children for which her name has become synonymous. Further, in the inspection of fragments from the factory site, no paintings of children were found. It is now believed that the original "Mary Gregory" glass came from England, Germany and Bohemia by way of an English import wholesale house. For further information see The Glass Industry in Sandwich, Volume 4, *by Raymond E. Barlow and Joan E. Kaiser.*

Barber bottle w/stopper, cobalt blue, white enameled figure, 10" h. $195.00

Barber bottle w/original stopper, cranberry, white enameled girl ... 325.00

Bottle, internal ribbing, green, white enameled boy & flowers, 3¾" d., 7¼" h. 135.00

Box w/lift-off lid, cranberry, white enameled boy w/hat & girl by fence on lid, leaf sprays around sides, 2 1/8" d., 1½" h. 175.00

Box w/hinged lid, emerald green, white enameled girl holding flowers, 4½" d. 400.00

Box, cov., royal blue, white enameled boy feeding two ducks on a pond on lid, 5½" d., 4¾" h. 630.00

Card tray, cobalt blue, white enameled girl w/butterfly net chasing a butterfly, mounted in brass stand w/three ring handles, 6½" d., 4" h. 135.00

Cruet w/clear facet-cut stopper, applied clear reeded handle, amethyst, white enameled boy sitting on fence w/two birds, 3" d., 8½" h. 375.00

Decanter w/original green blown ball stopper, applied green handle trimmed in gold, emerald green, white enameled boy in pink suit &

lilies of the valley, 4¼" d., 11½" h. 150.00
Dresser tray, ruby, white enameled girl watching seated boy blowing bubbles, 9½ x 6½" 330.00
Dresser tray, cobalt blue, white enameled boy pulling tree branch w/another boy w/hat riding it, 7 x 10" rectangle 255.00
Ewer, 6¾" h., 2 5/8" d., applied clear handle, lime green, white enameled boy w/hat 100.00
Goblet, cranberry w/clear foot, white enameled girl w/hat, 2¾" d., 5" h. 100.00
Jewelry box w/hinged lid, ormolu feet, cobalt blue, white enameled girl w/hat on lid & floral garlands around sides, w/original key, 3 x 4 5/8" rectangle, 4 5/8" h. 475.00

Mary Gregory Mug

Mug, applied clear handle, cranberry, white enameled girl, 2 1/8" d., 2¾" h. (ILLUS.) 69.00
Mug, applied clear handle, amber, white enameled girl holding flag 60.00
Patch box w/hinged lid, cobalt blue, white enameled young girl w/hat, 1 7/8" d., 1¼" h. 175.00
Perfume atomizer, bulbous, Optic Panel patt., cranberry, white enameled girl holding blossoms & standing in foliage, 5½" h. 275.00
Pin tray, oval, cranberry, white enameled young girl holding flower amid foliage, 2 x 4½" 95.00
Pitcher, jug-type, 1¾" h., cranberry, white enameled boy, gold on handle & rim 225.00
Pitcher, 6" h., sapphire blue, white enameled boy w/sailboat 210.00
Pitcher, 6¾" h., 4" d., fluted top, applied clear handle, cranberry, white enameled boy w/hat, gold trim 180.00
Pitcher, 7" h., 3½" d., applied clear handle, ruffled top, slight ribbing, cranberry, white enameled boy w/horn around neck & holding a staff, gold trim on suit & horn 195.00
Pitcher, tankard, 7 1/8" h., 4½" d., applied clear handle, lime green, white enameled girl holding basket of flowers & bird in hand 265.00
Pitcher, water, 8½" h., 5 1/8" d., squared bulbous shape, applied sapphire blue handle, amber, white enameled girl 275.00
Pitcher, 9½" h., applied clear handle, crimped rim, clear, white enameled girl chasing butterfly 120.00
Pitcher, water, tankard, 9 7/8" h., 4 5/8" d., applied sapphire blue handle, amber, white enameled man w/cane & hat 230.00
Pitcher, water, 10¾" h., 4½" d., applied clear reeded handle, light sapphire blue, white enameled girl w/gold dress amid foliage 275.00
Rose bowl, 7-crimp top, cranberry, white enameled boy, 3¼" d., 3¼" h. 225.00
Rose bowl, 6-crimp top, amethyst, white enameled boy, gold trim, 4 3/8" d., 4" h. 265.00
Salt dip, cranberry, white enameled boy & foliage, 2¼" d. 135.00
Stein w/hinged pewter-fitted glass lid, applied clear handle, cranberry, white enameled girl watching butterfly, 2 5/8" base d., 3¾" h. 235.00
Sugar shaker w/original brass top, Optic Panel patt., cranberry, white enameled boy holding flower & standing amid foliage, 5" h. 395.00
Tumbler, cranberry, white enameled boy holding hand out for butterfly 65.00
Tumble-up set, blue, white enameled boy on tumbler & girl on carafe, 2 pcs. 395.00
Tumble-up set, clear, white enameled girl holding flower, 7" h., 2 pcs. 115.00
Vase, 3" h., cranberry, white enameled girl in garden 230.00
Vase, bud, 6¾" h., 1¼" d., cranberry, white enameled boy, three brass feet, brass filigree top & bottom mounts 300.00
Vase, 7 3/8" h., 4" d., cut scalloped top, applied ribbed "snail" handles, golden amber, white enameled boy 145.00
Vase, 8½" h., applied clear rigaree down sides, green, white enameled girl & butterfly net 195.00
Vases, 10" h., 6 1/8" d., applied reeded scroll handles w/gold

trim, scalloped top, golden honey amber, white enameled boy on one & girl on other, pr. 485.00

Vases, 10½" h., Amberina, white enameled boy on one, girl on the other, pr. 550.00

Mary Gregory Vases

Vases, 10¾" h., 4 7/8" d., black amethyst, white enameled boy on one & girl on the other, facing pr. (ILLUS.) 450.00

Vases, 10 7/8" h., 5¼" d., black amethyst, white enameled children sitting in branch of tree watching dragonfly, facing pr. 495.00

Vases, 12 3/8" h., 4½" d., cut scalloped top, pedestal foot, electric blue, white enameled girl w/hat & butterfly net, pr. 575.00

Wine decanter w/original bubble stopper, applied green handle w/gold trim, emerald green, white enameled boy in pink suit & lilies of the valley, 4¼" d., 11½" h. 165.00

MC KEE

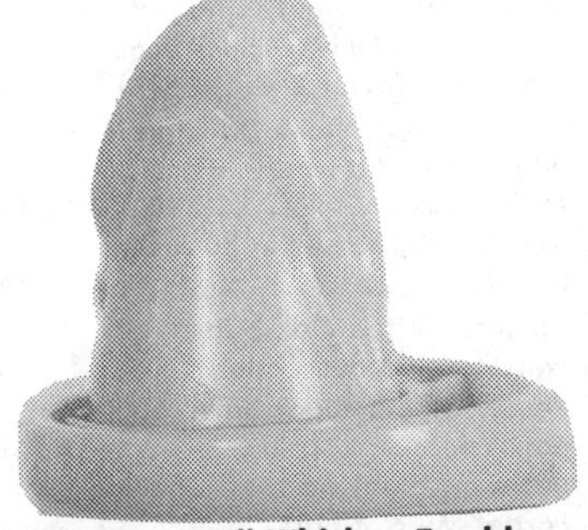

"Bottoms Up" Whiskey Tumbler

The McKee name has been associated with glass production since 1834, first producing window glass and later bottles. In the 1850's a new factory was established in Pittsburgh, Pennsylvania for production of flint and pressed glass. The plant was relocated in Jeannette, Pennsylvania in 1888 and operated there as an independent company almost continuously until 1951 when it sold out to Thatcher Glass Manufacturing Company. Many types of collectible glass were produced by McKee through the years including Depression, Pattern, Milk White and a variety of utility kitchen wares.

Bowl, 5" d., Rock Crystal patt., ruby $22.00

Candlestick, baluster-form stem, Rock Crystal patt., ruby, 8½" h. (single) 65.00

Candlestick, hexagonal base, crucifix w/figure of Christ & "INRI," clear, 10" h. (single) 110.00

Canister, "Coffee," Skokie green ... 25.00

Canister, "Sugar," French ivory 16.00

Celery, Rock Crystal patt., clear, 12" oblong 18.00

Creamer, Comet patt., clear 39.00

Creamer & sugar bowl, footed, Rock Crystal patt., clear, pr. 35.00

Cruet w/original stopper, Rock Crystal patt., amber 185.00

Juice reamer, Chalaine blue 300.00

Juice reamer, French ivory 37.50

Juice reamer, Seville yellow 150.00

Pitcher, 5" h., Aztec patt., clear 15.00

Plate, 6 3/8" d., Serenade (Troubador) patt., opaque white .. 55.00

Refrigerator water dispenser, Jade green, 11 x 5", 4" h. 85.00

Tom & Jerry set: bowl & 12 cups; White Opal w/red lettering, 13 pcs. 85.00

Toothpick holder, Rock Crystal patt., clear 35.00

Vase, 8½" h., open foot, triangular, relief-molded nude woman against latticework ground, Skokie green 129.00

Whiskey tumbler w/coaster base, "Bottoms Up," French ivory 110.00

Whiskey tumbler w/coaster base, "Bottoms Up," Skokie green, set of 4 (ILLUS. of one) ......250.00 to 300.00

MERCURY

This glass has a silvery appearance due to a coating of silver nitrate in double-walled objects. A gold effect was obtained by placing the silver nitrate in amber glass. The hole through which the solution was injected was subsequently sealed. It was made in this country and England from the middle of the 19th century.

Mercury Glass Master Salt Dips

Candleholders, low, pr. $45.00
Candlestick, enameled pastel florals, 7" h. 40.00
Candlestick, 9" h. 30.00
Candlestick, amber socket for gold-washed effect, 10" h. 30.00
Candlestick, overall enameled foliage, 10" h. 30.00
Candlesticks, cylindrical, 11" h., pr. 56.00
Curtain tiebacks w/original pewter shanks, etched vintage design, 2½" d., pr. 20.00
Rose bowl, enameled florals, 5" h. 60.00
Salt dips, master size, pedestal base, etched design, signed "N.E.G." (New England Glass Co.), 3½" d., 3" h., pr. (ILLUS.) . . . 325.00
Vase, 4" h., amber interior for gold-washed effect, enameled blue & pink florals 40.00

MILK WHITE

Robin on Nest Covered Dish

This is opaque white glass that resembles the color of and was used as a substitute for white porcelain. Opacity was obtained by adding oxide of tin to a batch of clear glass. It has been made in numerous forms and shapes in this country and abroad from about the first quarter of last century. It is still being produced, and there are many reproductions of earlier pieces. Also see HISTORICAL and PATTERN GLASS.

Animal covered dish, "American Hen," w/eggs inscribed "Porto Rico," "Cuba" & "Philippines," 6" l., 4" h. $65.00
Animal covered dish, Boar's Head w/glass eyes 800.00
Animal covered dish, Duck w/amethyst head, Atterbury, 11" l., 5" h. . . . . .175.00 to 235.00
Animal covered dish, Fox on ribbed top & ribbed base, Atterbury . . . . .125.00 to 155.00
Animal covered dish, Frog sitting, mouth slightly open 125.00
Animal covered dish, Hen w/amethyst head, lacy base, Atterbury . . 200.00
Animal covered dish, Hen on Sleigh 45.00
Animal covered dish, Quail on scroll-embossed oval base w/scalloped top, 6½" l., 4½" h. 105.00
Animal covered dish, Rabbit, original red glass eyes, patent date stamped on bottom, Atterbury . . . 145.00
Animal covered dish, Robin on Nest, 6¼" d. (ILLUS.) 145.00
Animal covered dish, Swan w/raised wings & glass eyes on lacy-edge base 135.00
Bowl, 8" d., 3" h., Open Lattice Edge, apple blossom decor center, Atterbury 45.00
Bowl, 9" d., 4½" h., Waffle patt. . . . . .45.00 to 55.00
Butter dish, cov., Strawberry patt. . . 50.00
Candlesticks, Cruciform, hexagonal base, 10" h., pr. 110.00
Compote, open, 8¼" d., 8¼" h., Atlas stem, scalloped rim, Atterbury . . . . .100.00 to 125.00
Compote, open, Jenny Lind patt. . . . 110.00
Covered dish, Fish w/glass eyes, Challinor, Taylor & Co., 8¾" l. . . . 185.00
Covered dish, Hand & Dove on lacy-edge base, Atterbury, 8¾" l., 4¾" h. . . . . .100.00 to 125.00
Covered dish, Moses in Bulrushes, 5½" l. 135.00
Creamer, Netted Oak patt., w/enameled decoration 45.00
Creamer & cov. sugar bowl, Swan patt., pr. 75.00
Cruet w/original stopper, Challinor's Forget-Me-Not patt. 45.00
Dresser bottles w/stoppers, Leaf patt., green & gold decoration, 10" h., pr. 40.00

Dresser tray, Chrysanthemum patt., 10 x 7½" 33.00
Goblet, Princess Feather patt. 40.00
Humidor w/screw top dated 1886, figural pouch tied w/bow 65.00
Jar, cov., model of the American Eagle 100.00
Jar, cov., embossed British royal arms on sides, figural portrait bust of Queen Victoria on cover .. 95.00
Match holder, Indian Head 50.00
Novelty, Sprinkler, covered jar in shape of sprinkling can, 3½" h. .. 35.00
Pickle dish, boat-shaped, "Pickle" embossed at front end & "Patented Feb. 17, 1874" on bottom, 9½" l. 28.00
Pickle dish, figural fish w/glass eyes, waffle-type body, Challinor, Taylor & Company, 9 x 4¼" 70.00
Pitcher, milk, 7" h., Block Daisy patt. 55.00
Pitcher, 7½" h., Owl w/glass eyes 150.00
Pitcher, tankard, Opaque Scroll patt. 75.00
Plate, 6¼" d., Mother Goose w/bunnies in relief 60.00
Plate, 7" d., Anchor & Belaying Pin 27.50
Plate, 7" w., diamond-shaped, Easter Chicks (2), openwork scroll & leaf border 40.00
Plate, 7" d., diamond-shaped, Niagara Falls center, openwork scroll & leaf border 28.00
Plate, 7" d., Peg Border 18.00

Three Bears Plate

Plate, 7" d., Three Bears, w/traces of original brown, green & gilt (ILLUS.) 35.00
Plate, 7¼" d., Cupid & Psyche w/leaf & lace border 22.00
Plate, 7¼" d., Little Red Hen, openwork lacy border 45.00
Plate, 7¼" d., "No Easter Without Us," rooster & hens (ILLUS.) 38.00
Plate, 7¼" d., Spring Meets Winter, openwork border 50.00

"No Easter Without Us" Plate

Plate, 7¼" d., Sunken Rabbit 35.00
Plate, 7¼" d., Yacht & Anchor 24.00
Plate, 7½" d., "Easter Opening," two chicks emerging from eggs & lily-of-the-valley 67.50
Plate, 7½" d., Hare & Cloverleaf center, scalloped & beaded border 36.00
Plate, 7½" d., Indian Head center, Beaded Loop border 38.00
Plate, 8" d., Hearts & Anchor border 26.00
Plate, 9" d., Angel Head, openwork border 18.00
Plate, 9½" d., Columbus bust center, Club & Shell border 36.00
Plate, 10" d., Scroll & Eye openwork border 18.00
Plate, 10½" d., Trumpet Vine, enameled flowers in center, Lattice Edge border 48.00
Plate, Niagara Falls, plain center, wide border w/embossed spread-winged American eagle, American flag, British merchant flag & scenes of Niagara Falls, probably from 1901 Pan-American Exhibition in Buffalo, New York 60.00
Platter, 13¼ x 9¾", Retriever, lily pad border 84.00
Salt dip, scoop-like w/handle & four feet 15.00
Salt shaker, egg-shaped, two embossed rabbits on one side & one on the other, rabbits covered w/gold, 2¼" d., 3½" h. 35.00
Smoke bell w/ruffled edge applied w/cobalt blue edging, 7½" h. 46.00
Sugar bowl, cov., Blackberry patt. 55.00
Sugar shaker w/original top, Challinor's Forget-Me-Not patt. 65.00
Syrup pitcher w/original top, Coreopsis patt. w/enameled decoration 145.00
Syrup pitcher w/original top, Challinor's Forget-Me-Not patt. 75.00

Syrup pitcher w/original pewter top, applied strap handle, Hobnail patt. 135.00
Toothpick holder, Acorn patt., enameled flower decoration 35.00
Tray, Lady & Fan patt., 7 x 5¼" 40.00
Tumbler, Netted Oak patt. 39.00
Whimsey, canoe, enameled flowers, "Souvenir of Toledo, Ohio," 6" ... 16.00

MONOT & STUMPF

A glassworks was established by E.S. Monot at La Villette, near Paris, in 1850. This operation was moved to Pantin in 1858 and became Monot & Stumpf as Mr. F. Stumpf joined the firm in 1868. Monot's son also entered the firm and, in 1873, it became Monot, Pere et Fils, et Stumpf. According to an article by Albert Christian Revi, recognized authority on glasswares and paperweights, their iridescent wares were called "Chine Metallique," a patented process they used beginning in 1878. The firm continued business in Pantin into the early 1890's but by the beginning of the 20th century the company had become Cristallerie de Pantin and was operated by Saint-Hilaire, Touvier, de Varreux & Company.

Bowl, ruffled rim, "Chine Metallique," soft opalescent pink-striped effect exterior, lustred gold interior, ormolu holder, overall 10¾" d., 6¼" h. $225.00
Salt dip, four-petal top, "Chine Metallique," opalescent brown w/applied tan edging, lustred gold interior, 1 7/8" d., 1½" h.... 65.00
Salt dip, ruffled top, "Chine Metallique," deep rose pink opalescent exterior, lustred gold interior, 2" d., 1¼" h. 65.00
Salt dip, square top, "Chine Metallique," opalescent rose pink striped effect exterior, lustred gold interior, 2" sq., 1½" h. 75.00
Salt dip, light cranberry w/gold striping 68.00
Sauce dish, "Chine Metallique," 4" sq. 145.00
Vase, 4½" h., swirled, cranberry, iridescent lining 195.00
Vase, 8" h., 7¾" d., fan-shaped, ruffled top, deep rose pink opalescent 225.00

MONT JOYE

Cameo and enameled glass bearing this mark was made in Pantin, France, by the same works that produced pieces signed De Vez.

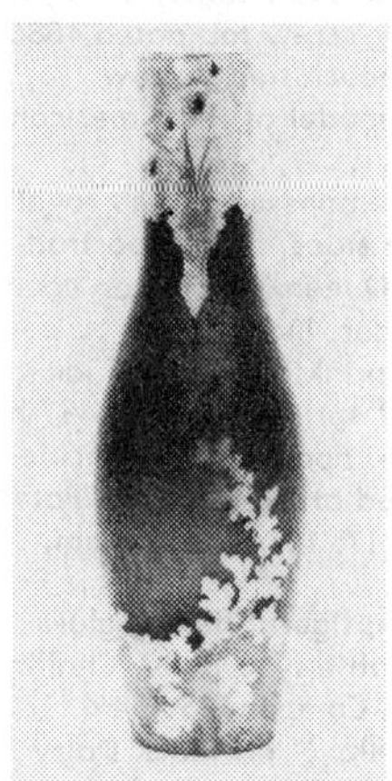

Mont Joye Cameo Vase

Cameo planter, carved green leaves against frosted amethyst ground, signed, 7½ x 2½ x 4" $245.00
Cameo vase, 8½" h., carved & enameled deep red poppies & green leaves against "chipped ice" ground, signed 410.00
Cameo vase, 11 1/8" h., flared body tapering toward base, long cylindrical neck, carved & enameled poppies against frosted ground, early 20th c. 467.50
Cameo vase, 12" h., carved & enameled gold florals & green leaves against frosted rose ground, unsigned 300.00
Cameo vase, 25¼" h., elongated baluster form, gold decorated oak leaves w/silvered acorns on an emerald acid-etched ground, rim slightly worn & base drilled, early 20th c. (ILLUS.) 990.00
Vase, 9¾" h., 3 1/8" d., cylindrical, enameled green & bronze Art Nouveau style poppy w/gilt highlights, early 20th c., signed 357.50

MOSER

High-quality Art Nouveau glass was produced from around the turn of the century by Moser, Ludwig & Sohne in Carlsbad and Mierhofen. Much of the base glass was amethyst in color, but this expert craftsman turned out various types of glass, some with exquisite enameling.

Box w/lift-off lid, slightly flared

Moser Covered Box

cylindrical form, transparent green, paneled body, lid & finial, designed by Josef Hoffmann, executed by Moser for the Wiener Werkstatte, signed, 6" d. (ILLUS.) $1,430.00

Cameo vase, 8" h., carved pink florals & leaves against mottled clear ground, signed 425.00

Cameo vase, 11½" h., carved & enameled African landscape w/family of elephants browsing on jungle foliage against transparent golden amber ground, signed 1,450.00

Cologne bottle w/clear ball stopper, cranberry w/enameled white, blue & yellow florals & green leaves outlined in gold, 3 1/8" d., 7½" h. 195.00

Cup & saucer, clear w/raised ruby panels surrounded by gold embellishments & enhanced by burnished gold borders, unsigned 185.00

Decanter w/stopper, clear cut to emerald green at the top, cut poppy design on sides, 10½" h. .. 695.00

Finger bowl, tricornered, Inverted Thumbprint patt., Amberina w/enameled multicolored grape leaves, lacy gold foliage & applied red, blue & green grape clusters, signed & w/original paper label, 4½" w., 2 5/8" h. 495.00

Goblet, golden amber w/enameled green oak leaves outlined in gold, two white & pink insects & ten applied acorns, 5 3/8" h. 375.00

Jardiniere, pink w/wide band of gold scrollwork alternating w/green & clear jeweling at top & base, signed, 9" d., 7¼" h. 950.00

Mug, applied green handle, lime green w/enameled multicolored oak leaves, lacy gold foliage & insect, applied gold lustred acorns, gold trim, unsigned, 2 5/8" d., 3¼" h. 295.00

Pitcher, 7½" h., ruby red w/enameled scene of knight on horseback surrounded by multicolored florals & gold foliage, signed 230.00

Pitcher, 12" h., enameled white lilies of the valley w/gold foliage 600.00

Powder box, cov., green w/enameled florals & gold trim, signed 210.00

Rose bowl, cranberry w/enameled florals & gold rope ribbing, signed, 9" d. 265.00

Tumbler, juice, cranberry shading to clear w/enameled multicolored oak leaves & lacy gold foliage & four applied lustred acorns, unsigned, 2¼" d., 3 7/8" h. 195.00

Vase, 4¼" h., 2¼" d., sapphire blue w/enameled multicolored grape leaves, lacy gold tendrils & a bee, applied grape clusters, unsigned 365.00

Vase, cov., 26½" h., 5¾" d., transparent green w/enameled multicolored oak leaves w/gold branches & foliage, applied lustred acorns, applied gold berry prunts around stem, unsigned 6,000.00

Wine, turquoise shaded to clear, bowl w/overall enameled & gold leaf fern motif & enameled white dots, open stem embellished w/gold-encrusted berry prunts, fluting at base decorated w/gold leaf 370.00

MOUNT WASHINGTON

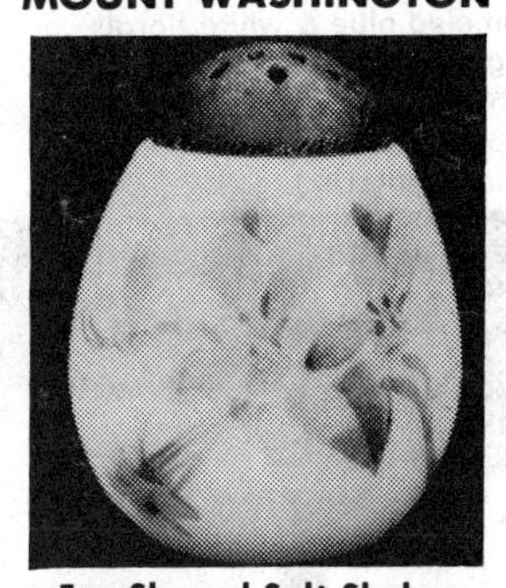

Egg-Shaped Salt Shaker

A wide diversity of glass was made by the Mt. Washington Glass Company, of New Bedford, Massachusetts, between 1869 and 1900. It was succeeded in 1900 by the Pairpoint Corporation. Miscellaneous types are listed below, but also see CROWN MILANO, PEACH BLOW and SMITH BROTHERS.

Bowl, 8¾" d., 2 5/8" h., "Peppermint Stick," clear acid finish w/"rosaria" overlay at lip cut in picket fence design, 24-point star-cut base $125.00
Cameo bowl, 9" d., carved winged griffins & shields, pink & white ... 795.00
Card tray, ribbed foot, camphor rim, sky blue satin finish, enameled florals, ca. 1890, 9½ x 8" 195.00
Compote, 6¼" d., 10" h., scalloped rim, "Napoli," clear w/pastel green chrysanthemum leaves on wafer base, continuing up encircling stem & bursting into four golden yellow chrysanthemum blossoms on underside of bowl, gold outlining interior, unsigned .. 585.00
Cracker jar, melon ribbed, shaded blue ground, h.p. gold daisies, silver plated lid, handle & rim, 6½" d., 9¼" h. 1,190.00
Cracker jar, soft green w/pale pink highlights on relief-molded florals, h.p. scene of tranquil lake shore w/home, trees, mountains & sailing ship, silver plate rim & lid, signed & numbered 575.00
Creamer, tomato-shaped, overall multicolored leaves, silver plate collar, 4" w., 3½" h. 225.00
Mustard pot, ribbed, satin finish, enameled purple violets, silver plate spoon w/bird, butterfly & foliage engraved on handle, marked H. B. & Haydens, 2¾" h., 2 pcs. .. 275.00
Rose bowl, miniature, scalloped rim, lustreless white h.p. w/Shasta daisy decoration, 3" h. 75.00
Salt shaker w/original top, egg-shaped, blended deep yellow, enameled blue & white florals (single) 48.00
Salt shaker w/original top, egg-shaped, lustreless white h.p. w/florals (ILLUS.) 80.00

Mt. Washington Fig Mold Shakers

Salt shaker w/original top, fig mold, white w/creases tinted pale yellow, enameled blue & yellow florals (ILLUS. left) 135.00
Salt shaker, model of a chick w/silver plate head, enameled white five-petal blossoms, green leaves & tracery on mauve-pink stippled ground 275.00
Salt & pepper shakers, shell-shaped, enameled pink, white & yellow blossoms w/blue highlights, original shell-form metal insert lids, pr. 412.50
Sugar shaker w/original top, egg-shaped, shaded pink to creamy yellow satin finish, enameled white daisies w/yellow centers & green leaves, embossed "Pat ppd." on base, 4¼" h. 155.00
Sugar shaker w/original top, fig mold, white w/creases tinted pale yellow, enameled blue & yellow florals (ILLUS. right) 450.00
Sugar shaker, egg-shaped, clear frosted glass w/Royal Flemish-type h.p. pansy decoration 495.00
Syrup jug, cov., miniature, raised curved gold traced panels divide the body into six blown-out sections, floral decoration shaded from pink to rose on lustreless white ground, original cover w/metal handle, 4" h. 395.00

Mt. Washington Toothpick Holder

Toothpick holder, narrow ribbed, lustreless white, enameled prunus blossoms & blue beading (ILLUS.) 135.00
Tumbler, "Verona," h.p. exterior irises w/flowing green leaves & heavy gold trim, 3½" h. 75.00
Vase, 3¾" h., "Lava," classic shape, two curled handles, shiny jet black body inlaid w/bold chips of blue, green & pink w/gold trim 1,750.00
Vase, 8" h., 3" w., peach, enameled florals, 1885-90 .... 145.00

MULLER FRERES

The Muller Brothers made acid-etched cameo and other fine glass at Luneville, France, starting in 1910 and until the outbreak of World War II in Europe.

Muller Freres Cameo Lamp & Vase

Cameo lamp, one-piece molded cylinder w/squared raised dome, carved orange, tan & brown peony blossoms, buds & leaves against frosted ground w/carved & etched enhancements, signed, in electrified metal base, 9½" h. (ILLUS. left) $1,760.00

Cameo vase, 6¼" h., ovoid, carved yellow, light mahogany & sienna zinnia blossoms & leafage against opalescent ground changing to salmon in transmitted light, mottled mauve & green at base, ca. 1920, signed 3,025.00

Cameo vase, 7½" h., baluster form w/flared rim, acid-cut & enameled maroon vines, leaves & berries against frosted & yellow mottled ground, signed (ILLUS. right) 330.00

Cameo vase, 10" h., spherical w/bulbous neck, carved shaded brown exotic forest landscape w/monkeys perched on branches or walking among the grasses against pale yellow ground streaked w/grey, ca. 1925, signed 2,750.00

Cameo vase, 13" h., ovoid, carved shaded forest green mountain landscape w/stately firs & old stone bridge crossing a winding river against grey ground mottled w/pale apricot & mint green, ca. 1920, signed 6,050.00

Cameo vase, 15½" h., baluster form w/spreading circular foot, carved orange & deep plum mountainous landscape w/an eagle perched on a thick branch in the foreground against mottled lemon yellow ground, ca. 1920, signed 5,575.00

Vase, 3 5/8" h., tapering bulbous form w/everted circular rim, enameled green & black continuous shore scene w/trees in foreground & sailboats on the lake against variegated yellow ground, signed 357.50

Vase, 11¼" h., oviform body tapering inward to short waisted neck & everted flattened rim, internally decorated, pink w/white, purple & brown mottled swirled design w/occasional silver flecks, ca. 1900, signed 192.50

NAILSEA

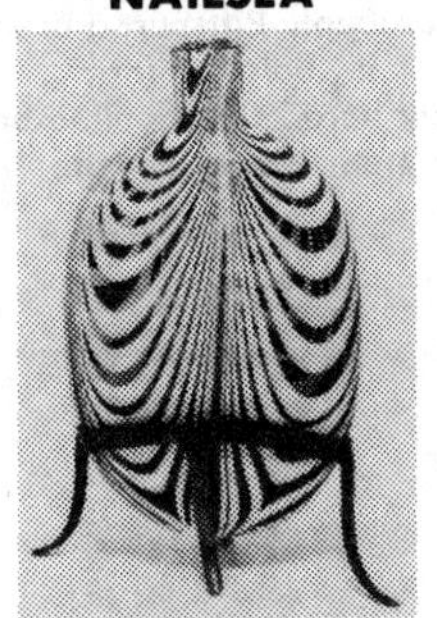

Nailsea Flask

Glass was made at Nailsea, near Bristol, England, from 1788 to 1873. Although the bulk of the products were similar to Bristol wares, collectors today visualize Nailsea primarily as a glass characterized by swirls and loopings, usually white, on a colored ground. Much glass attributed to Nailsea was made in glasshouses elsewhere.

Bowl, 7 5/8" d., 6¼" h., applied clear feet & handles, applied clear trim pulled to points around top, sapphire blue w/opaque white loopings $175.00

Candlestick, clear w/white loopings, hollow blown socket drawn out to a double knop then further drawn out to an inverted cone-shaped base, folded rim on socket, plain, sheared base, rare form, first half 19th c., England or America, 10" h. 325.00

Flask, white w/pink loopings, 6½" l. 160.00

Flask, clear w/white loopings, slightly flared, tooled mouth, 8" l. (ILLUS.) 85.00

Pitcher, 6¾" h., aqua w/opalescent loopings, applied strap handle & crimped foot, 19th c. 325.00

Pitcher & bowl, clear w/opalescent loopings, pitcher w/applied strap handle & foot, bowl w/folded rim & applied foot, 19th c., 8½" d., 7 3/8" h., the set (heat check in pitcher handle) 1,200.00

Rolling pin, free-blown, two handled, aquamarine w/white loopings, New Jersey, 9¼" l. 260.00

Rolling pin, cylindrical w/knopped ends, clear w/pink & white loopings, America, late 19th c., 17" l. 154.00

Rose bowl, egg-shaped, 8-crimp top, frosted heavenly blue w/white opaque loopings, 4" d., 5" h. 175.00

Vase, 8" h., 5" d., cylindrical w/flaring mouth & base, clear w/white loopings, plain sheared rim & pontil, probably Pittsburgh area . . 140.00

Vase, 13½" h., baluster form w/widely flared rim, applied base w/knob stem, clear w/white loopings 325.00

NAKARA

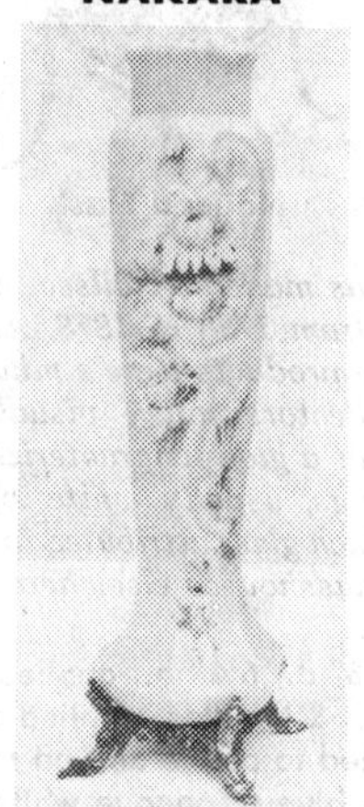

Nakara Vase

Like Kelva (which see), Nakara ware was made early in this century by C.F. Monroe Company. For details see WAVE CREST.

Bonbon tray w/ormolu collar & bail handle, octagonal, pastel florals & foliage on soft pink ground, signed $325.00

Box w/hinged lid, pink & white apple blossoms on shaded pink to blue ground, original lining, signed, 3¾" d., 2¾" h. 235.00

Box w/hinged lid, octagonal, pastel florals on apricot ground enhanced w/enameled white beading, signed, 4½" w. 425.00

Box w/hinged lid, enameled yellow flowers w/pink centers on pale peach ground w/light brown highlights, original lining, 6¼" d., 4½" h. 950.00

Box w/hinged lid, Bishop's hat shape, portrait of beautiful lady center, signed, 7" d. 625.00

Box w/hinged lid, Crown mold, enameled pink roses on green ground, signed, 9" d. 895.00

Dresser box w/hinged lid & interior mirror, scene of 2 ladies in a landscape setting within framework of enameled white beading on lid, base w/pink roses on soft green ground w/pink highlights, signed, 8" d., 3¾" h. 1,200.00

Hair receiver, cov., Bishop's hat shape, pastel florals on pink ground, signed 345.00

Vase, 8¾" h., scrollwork & white flowers outlined w/enameled white beading on pink to steel blue ground, footed ormolu base 405.00

Vase, 13½" h., pink florals on soft green ground highlighted w/enameled scrollwork & beading, footed ormolu base (ILLUS.) . . 650.00

NASH

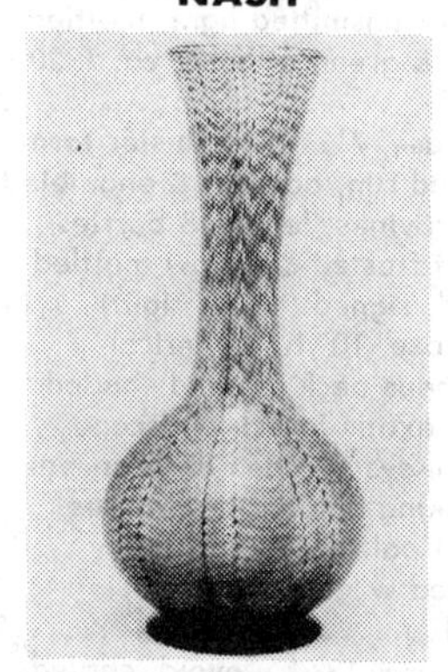

Nash Chintz Pattern Vase

This glass was made by A. Douglas Nash Corp., which purchased the Corona Works from L.C. Tiffany in December 1928. Nash, who formerly worked for Tiffany, produced outstanding glass for a brief period of time since the manufacture ceased prior to March of 1931, when A. Douglas Nash became associated with Libbey Glass in Toledo, Ohio. This fine quality ware is scarce.

Candlesticks, Chintz patt., blood red w/silver, 5" h., pr. $750.00

Cordial, Chintz patt., blue & green, 4" h. ... 55.00
Goblet, Chintz patt., blue & green, 6½" h. ... 60.00
Vase, 4½" h., scalloped rim, molded pattern on lower half of body, iridescent gold, signed ... 225.00
Vase, 6½" h., bulbous, feathery blue strokes & bubbly lime green streaks, signed ... 395.00
Vase, 17 5/8" h., baluster form, Chintz patt., blue & green draped stripes, signed (ILLUS.) ... 412.50
Wine, Chintz patt., blue & green, 3¾" h. ... 55.00

OPALESCENT

Presently, this is one of the most popular areas of glass collecting. The opalescent effect was attained by adding bone ash chemicals to areas of an item while still hot and refiring the object at tremendous heat. Both pressed and mold-blown patterns are available to collectors and we distinguish the types in our listing below. Opalescent Glass From A to Z *by William Heacock is the definitive reference book for collectors. Also see PATTERN GLASS.*

MOLD-BLOWN OPALESCENT PATTERNS

CHRYSANTHEMUM BASE SWIRL

Butter dish, cov., cranberry, satin finish ... $225.00 to 250.00
Cruet w/original stopper, cranberry ... 395.00
Toothpick holder, cranberry ... 150.00
Tumbler, cranberry ... 65.00

COIN SPOT

Coin Spot Tumbler

Creamer, blue, 4" h. ... 32.50
Pitcher, milk, blue ... 135.00
Pitcher, water, cranberry ... 295.00
Syrup pitcher w/original top, squatty, white ... 65.00
Tumbler, blue ... 30.00
Tumbler, cranberry (ILLUS.) ... 45.00
Tumblers, green, set of 6 ... 250.00
Tumbler, white ... 32.00
Tumble-up (water carafe w/tumbler lid), cranberry ... 295.00
Vase, 4" h., ruffled rim, cranberry ... 40.00
Vase, 5" h., 5½" d., bulbous, ruffled rim, white ... 45.00
Vase, 9" h., ruffled rim, cranberry ... 80.00

DAISY & FERN

Daisy & Fern Pitcher

Bowl, berry, ruffled rim, blue ... 75.00
Cruet w/original stopper, blue ... 97.50
Cruet w/original stopper, white ... 55.00
Pitcher, 5" h., applied clear reeded handle, ruffled rim, cranberry ... 75.00
Pitcher, water, blue ... 265.00
Pitcher, water, ruffled rim, cranberry (ILLUS.) ... 250.00
Pitcher, water, white ... 105.00
Sugar shaker w/original top, cranberry ... 110.00
Syrup pitcher w/original top, cranberry ... 125.00
Tumbler, blue ... 40.00
Tumbler, cranberry ... 40.00

HOBNAIL, HOBBS

Barber bottle, blue ... 110.00
Barber bottle, cranberry ... 135.00 to 165.00
Bowl, 8" d., 3" h., vaseline ... 65.00
Bowl, 10" d., fluted, cranberry ... 55.00
Butter dish, cov., blue ... 165.00
Cruet w/original stopper, cranberry ... 250.00
Finger bowl w/underplate, ruffled rim, cranberry, 2 pcs. ... 62.50
Pitcher, 5½" h., 5½" w., ruffled rim, applied clear handle, cranberry ... 230.00

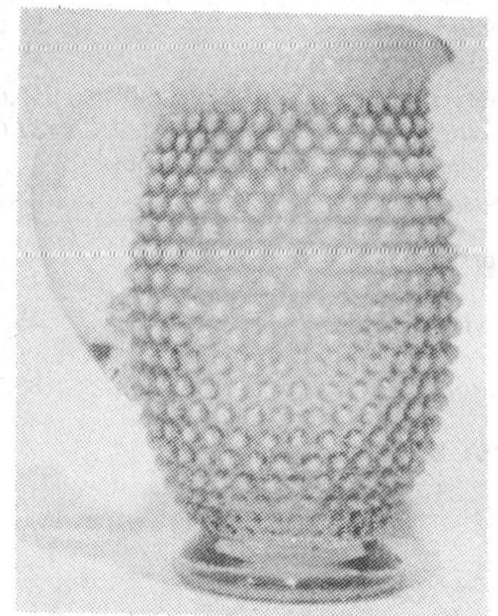

Hobnail Pitcher

Pitcher, milk, cranberry (ILLUS.) 265.00
Pitcher, milk, vaseline 175.00
Pitcher, water, square mouth, white 250.00
Table set: cov. butter dish, cov. sugar bowl, creamer & spooner; vaseline, 4 pcs. 370.00
Tumbler, cranberry 50.00

PANELED SPRIG

Cruet w/original stopper, white 90.00
Salt & pepper shakers w/original tops, white, pr. 75.00
Toothpick holder, white 47.00

POINSETTIA

Pitcher, 9¾" h., applied blue handle, fluted top, blue 135.00
Pitcher, water, tankard, 13" h., blue 195.00
Tumbler, blue 37.00

POLKA DOT

Barber bottle, blue 110.00
Cruet w/original stopper, cranberry 295.00
Water set: pitcher & 6 tumblers; cranberry, 7 pcs. 390.00

REVERSE SWIRL

Reverse Swirl Syrup Pitcher

Celery vase, canary yellow 35.00
Creamer, blue 125.00
Finger bowl, blue 28.00
Mustard jar, cranberry 55.00
Pitcher, water, white 110.00
Salt & pepper shakers w/original tops, canary yellow, pr. 70.00
Salt shaker w/original top, cranberry 45.00
Spooner, blue 68.00
Syrup pitcher w/original top, cranberry (ILLUS.) 225.00
Tumbler, blue 48.00
Tumbler, cranberry 95.00

RIBBED OPAL LATTICE

Ribbed Opal Lattice Syrup Pitcher

Cruet w/original stopper, cranberry 245.00
Salt shaker w/original top, cranberry 95.00
Sugar shaker w/original top, white 75.00
Syrup pitcher w/original top, blue (ILLUS.) 185.00
Syrup pitcher w/original top, cranberry 215.00
Toothpick holder, blue 95.00
Toothpick holder, cranberry 65.00

RING-NECK COINSPOT

Cruet w/original stopper, cranberry 275.00
Sugar shaker w/original top, cranberry 120.00
Syrup pitcher w/original top, blue 78.00

SEAWEED

Barber bottle, cranberry 165.00
Cruet w/original stopper, blue 125.00
Finger bowl, blue 45.00
Pitcher, water, blue 160.00
Pitcher, water, cranberry 275.00
Salt & pepper shakers w/original tops, cranberry, pr. 55.00
Sugar bowl, cov., cranberry .... 195.00 to 225.00
Water set: pitcher & 6 tumblers; blue, 7 pcs. 450.00

SPANISH LACE

Spanish Lace Bowl

Bowl, 7" d., ruffled rim, blue (ILLUS.) 85.00
Celery vase, blue 95.00
Celery vase, canary yellow 48.50
Cruet w/original stopper, canary yellow 160.00
Pitcher, water, white 125.00
Salt shaker w/original top, blue 75.00
Salt shaker w/original top, canary yellow 85.00
Sugar shaker w/original top, blue ....130.00 to 150.00
Water set: tankard pitcher & 6 tumblers; green, 7 pcs. .....490.00 to 525.00

STARS & STRIPES

Stars & Stripes Tumbler

Barber bottle, blue 150.00
Barber bottle, cranberry ...195.00 to 250.00
Barber bottle, white 150.00
Tumbler, cranberry (ILLUS.) 65.00

STRIPE

Barber bottle, cranberry 200.00
Celery vase, blue 85.00
Cruet w/original stopper, blue 125.00
Cruet w/original stopper, white 95.00

SWIRL

Celery vase, blue 75.00
Celery vase, cranberry 85.00
Pitcher, water, blue 95.00
Pitcher, water, square ruffled top, applied clear handle, white ....100.00 to 125.00
Rose bowl, blue 60.00
Rose bowl, canary yellow 42.00
Salt & pepper shakers w/original tops, cranberry, pr. 125.00
Sugar shaker w/original top, cranberry 150.00
Toothpick holder, cranberry 87.50
Water set: pitcher w/square ruffled top & 4 tumblers; cranberry, 5 pcs. 350.00

PRESSED OPALESCENT PATTERNS

ARGONAUT SHELL

Argonaut Shell Water Pitcher

Banana dish, canary yellow, 8½ x 6¼ x 3½" 58.00
Berry set: master bowl & 6 sauce dishes; blue, 7 pcs. 395.00
Berry set: master bowl & 6 sauce dishes; white, 7 pcs. 375.00
Compote, jelly, canary yellow 45.00
Creamer, blue 120.00
Creamer, canary yellow 175.00
Cruet w/original stopper, blue 275.00
Pitcher, water, white (ILLUS.) 135.00

BEADED FAN

Bowl, blue 45.00
Bowl, green 25.00
Compote, blue 31.50
Rose bowl, blue 65.00
Rose bowl, footed, blue 38.00
Rose bowl, white 45.00

BEATTY HONEYCOMB

Spooner, blue 45.00
Sugar bowl, cov., blue 85.00
Toothpick holder, blue 46.00

BEATTY RIB

Berry set: master bowl & 7 sauce dishes; white, 8 pcs. (ILLUS. of master bowl) 65.00
Relish dish, blue 25.00
Sugar bowl, cov., blue 125.00
Table set: cov. butter dish, cov.

sugar bowl, creamer & spooner; blue, 4 pcs. 265.00

Beatty Rib Berry Bowl

Toothpick holder, blue 35.00
Toothpick holder, white 30.00

BEATTY SWIRL

Beatty Swirl Water Pitcher

Butter dish, cov., blue 100.00
Celery vase, blue 75.00
Pitcher, water, blue (ILLUS.) 165.00
Spooner, white 35.00
Tumbler, blue 55.00
Water tray, blue 55.00
Water tray, canary yellow 60.00

CIRCLED SCROLL

Bowl, master berry, blue 75.00
Creamer, blue 45.00
Creamer, green 49.00
Spooner, green 45.00
Sugar bowl, cov., green 80.00

DIAMOND SPEARHEAD

Diamond Spearhead Butter Dish

Berry set: master bowl & 6 sauce dishes; vaseline, 7 pcs. 250.00
Butter dish, cov., vaseline (ILLUS.) . . 195.00
Creamer, vaseline, miniature 45.00
Spooner, vaseline 105.00
Sugar bowl, cov., vaseline 115.00
Toothpick holder, green 85.00
Toothpick holder, vaseline 65.00

DRAPERY

Drapery Water Pitcher

Creamer, white 35.00
Pitcher, water, blue (ILLUS.) 165.00
Pitcher, water, white 70.00
Sauce dish, blue 22.00
Sauce dish, white 10.00
Tumbler, blue 45.00
Water set: pitcher & 5 tumblers; white, 6 pcs. 225.00
Water set: pitcher & 6 tumblers; blue, 7 pcs. 375.00

EVERGLADES

Everglades Sugar Bowl

Berry set: master bowl & 6 sauce dishes; canary yellow, 7 pcs. 375.00
Compote, jelly, blue w/gold 160.00
Compote, jelly, canary yellow 112.00
Compote, jelly, white 45.00
Creamer, canary yellow w/gold 60.00
Creamer, white 40.00

Cruet, canary yellow 415.00
Pitcher, water, canary yellow 375.00
Sauce dish, canary yellow.......... 30.00
Sauce dish, white 15.00
Spooner, canary yellow 75.00
Spooner, white w/gold 45.00
Sugar bowl, cov., blue (ILLUS.) 115.00
Sugar bowl, cov., canary yellow 122.00
Sugar bowl, cov., white w/gold 65.00
Table set, canary yellow, 4 pcs. 425.00
Tumbler, white w/gold 67.50

FLORA

Bowl, master berry, canary yellow .. 80.00
Butter dish, cov., blue 225.00
Butter dish, cov., canary yellow w/gold 195.00
Spooner, canary yellow 70.00
Sugar bowl, cov., canary yellow 110.00
Toothpick holder, white w/gold 140.00

FLUTED SCROLLS

Fluted Scrolls Pieces

Bowl, 7" d., three-footed, white 25.00
Bowl, 7" d., three-footed, vaseline .. 26.00
Bowl, 7" d., three-footed, blue 25.00
Butter dish, cov. (ILLUS. front) 150.00
Creamer, blue (ILLUS. right) 40.00
Creamer, blue w/enameled florals .. 65.00
Cruet w/original stopper, blue (ILLUS. back) ....150.00 to 200.00
Cruet w/original stopper, vaseline .. 175.00
Pitcher, water, blue 160.00
Powder jar, cov., vaseline 65.00
Sauce dish, vaseline, enameled florals........................ 35.00
Spooner, white.................... 35.00
Table set, vaseline, 4 pcs. 350.00

HOBNAIL & PANELED THUMBPRINT

Hobnail & Paneled Thumbprint Table Set

Butter dish, cov., blue 110.00
Sauce dish, blue 22.00
Spooner, blue..................... 52.00
Spooner, canary yellow 45.00
Sugar bowl, cov., canary yellow 75.00
Table set: cov. butter dish, cov. sugar bowl, creamer & spooner; canary yellow, 4 pcs. (ILLUS.) ....285.00 to 335.00

HONEYCOMB & CLOVER

Bowl, master berry, blue 20.00
Bowl, master berry, white 18.00
Pitcher, water, green 175.00

INTAGLIO

Compote, jelly, blue 50.00
Compote, jelly, canary yellow 40.00
Creamer, blue 70.00
Creamer, white 47.50
Cruet w/original stopper, blue 195.00
Cruet w/original stopper, canary yellow 425.00
Cruet w/original stopper, white 60.00
Sauce dish, blue 20.00
Sauce dish, canary yellow.......... 19.00
Sauce dish, white 35.00
Spooner, blue..................... 55.00
Spooner, white.................... 35.00
Sugar bowl, cov., blue............. 85.00
Tumbler, white.................... 36.00
Water set: pitcher & 5 tumblers; white, 6 pcs..................... 225.00

INVERTED FAN & FEATHER

Bowl, 6½" d., flared, blue 39.00
Rose bowl, canary yellow 40.00
Sauce dish, blue 27.50
Spooner, blue..................... 45.00

IRIS WITH MEANDER

Berry set: master bowl & 5 sauce dishes; canary yellow, 6 pcs...... 220.00
Bowl, master berry, blue 90.00
Bowl, master berry, green 85.00
Butter dish, cov., canary yellow 175.00
Compote, jelly, blue 50.00
Pitcher, water, canary yellow 285.00
Spooner, canary yellow 85.00
Toothpick holder, blue 80.00
Toothpick holder, canary yellow 100.00
Toothpick holder, green 65.00
Tumbler, blue..................... 15.00

JACKSON

Butter dish, cov., canary yellow 185.00
Candy dish, canary yellow 30.00
Creamer, blue 50.00
Creamer, canary yellow 110.00
Powder jar, cov., blue 55.00

JEWEL & FLOWER

Creamer, canary yellow (ILLUS.) 70.00
Pitcher, water, white 115.00

Jewel & Flower Creamer

Salt shaker w/original top, blue 50.00
Spooner, white 35.00
Table set, white, 4 pcs. 245.00

JEWELED HEART

Jeweled Heart Berry Set

Berry set: master bowl & 3 sauce dishes; white, 4 pcs. (ILLUS. of part) 110.00
Berry set: master bowl & 4 sauce dishes; blue, 5 pcs. 125.00
Bowl, master berry, 10" d., ruffled rim, blue 48.00
Creamer, green 95.00
Sauce dish, white, 5½" d. 22.00
Spooner, green 40.00
Tumbler, blue 40.00
Tumbler, green 55.00
Water set: pitcher & 2 tumblers; green, 3 pcs. 345.00
Water set: pitcher & 4 tumblers; white, 5 pcs. 185.00

PALM BEACH

Sauce dish, blue 22.50
Table set, blue, 4 pcs. 550.00
Tumbler, canary yellow 50.00

PANELED HOLLY

Berry set: master bowl & 5 sauce dishes; blue, 6 pcs. 350.00
Spooner, blue (ILLUS.) 150.00
Sugar bowl, cov., blue 225.00
Table set, white, 4 pcs. (smoothed chip on sugar bowl base) 245.00
Water set: pitcher & 3 tumblers; blue, 4 pcs. 350.00

Paneled Holly Spooner

REGAL

Butter dish, cov., green 150.00
Sauce dish, blue 29.00
Spooner, blue 95.00
Sugar bowl, cov., green 85.00
Tumbler, blue 45.00

RIBBED SPIRAL

Ribbed Spiral Jelly Compote

Bowl, 8" d., canary yellow 40.00
Compote, jelly, blue (ILLUS.) 50.00
Toothpick holder, canary yellow 85.00
Tumbler, canary yellow 55.00

SHELL

Berry set: master bowl & 6 sauce dishes; blue, 7 pcs. 300.00
Bowl, master berry, blue 125.00
Creamer, blue 36.00

SWAG WITH BRACKETS

Compote, jelly, canary yellow 55.00
Compote, jelly, green 20.00
Cruet w/original stopper, canary yellow 195.00
Sugar bowl, cov., canary yellow 125.00
Water set: pitcher & 3 tumblers; green, 4 pcs. 200.00

TOKYO

Bowl, master berry, green 60.00
Compote, jelly, green 27.00

Creamer, green 46.00
Cruet w/original stopper, blue 200.00
Cruet w/clear stopper, blue 150.00
Pitcher, water, green 125.00
Sauce dish, green, 6" d. 58.00
Spooner, blue 76.00
Toothpick holder, green 110.00

WATERLILY WITH CATTAILS

Bonbon, tri-cornered, green 32.50
Bowl, 6 3/8" d., two-handled, green 29.00
Bowl, 9" d., blue 50.00
Plate 11" d., white 15.00
Spooner, blue 70.00
Tumbler, blue 30.00

Waterlily with Cattails Tumbler

Tumbler, white (ILLUS.) 24.00

WILD BOUQUET

Wild Bouquet Tumbler

Butter dish, cov., blue 350.00
Creamer, blue 48.00
Cruet w/original clear stopper, blue ....245.00 to 265.00
Pitcher, water, blue 150.00
Sauce dish, blue 20.00
Sugar bowl, cov., white 45.00
Tumbler, blue (ILLUS.) 70.00

WREATH & SHELL

Berry set: master bowl & 2 sauce dishes; canary yellow, 3 pcs. 185.00
Berry set: master bowl & 6 sauce dishes; blue or vaseline, 7 pcs., each set 265.00
Berry set: master bowl & 6 sauce dishes; white, 7 pcs. 185.00
Berry set: master bowl & 8 sauce dishes; vaseline, 9 pcs. 190.00
Butter dish, cov., blue 225.00
Butter dish, cov., vaseline w/enameled decor 200.00
Butter dish, cov., white 110.00
Creamer, blue 110.00
Cuspidor, lady's, vaseline 110.00
Rose bowl, blue 75.00
Salt dip, blue 105.00

Wreath & Shell Spooner

Spooner, blue (ILLUS.) 55.00
Spooner, canary yellow 85.00
Spooner, vaseline ....55.00 to 75.00
Sugar bowl, cov., vaseline 140.00
Table set, vaseline, 4 pcs. 475.00
Table set, white w/enameled florals, 4 pcs. 425.00
Toothpick holder, vaseline ..85.00 to 100.00
Toothpick holder, vaseline, enameled decoration 195.00
Tumbler, blue 60.00

(End of Opalescent Glass Section)

ORREFORS

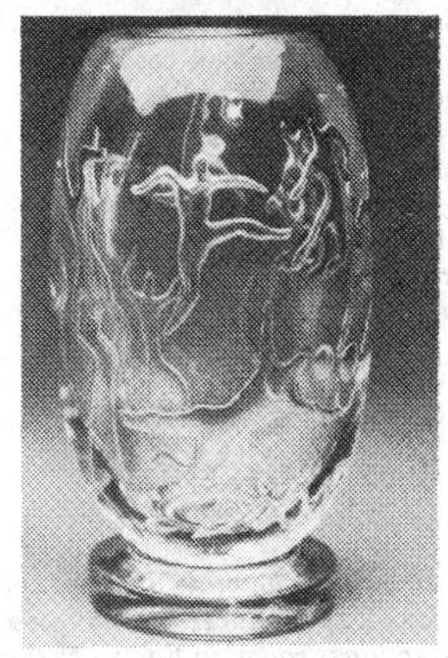

Orrefors Vase by Edwin Ohrstrom

This Swedish glasshouse, founded in 1898 for production of tablewares, has made decorative wares as well since 1915. By 1925, Orrefors had achieved an international reputation for its Graal glass, an engraved art glass developed by master glass blower Knut

Bergqvist and artist-designers, Simon Gate and Edward Hald. Ariel glass, recognized by a design of controlled air traps, and the heavy Ravenna glass, usually tinted, were both developed in the 1930's. While all Orrefors glass is collectible, pieces signed by early designers and artists are now bringing high prices.

Candleholders, ball-shaped, clear, pr. $75.00

Perfume bottle w/ball stopper, bulbous w/flat front & back, clear, engrave swan w/wings up on front, 2" w., 3¾" h. ....70.00 to 85.00

Vase, 3½" h., clear w/engraved girl & duck, signed "Simon Gate" 150.00

Vase, 4" h., teardrop-shaped, paperweight-type, ruby cased in clear 85.00

Vase, 4½" h., Graal, paperweight-type, internally decorated w/ten green fish in an underwater scene 565.00

Vase, 5" h., clear w/engraved bird in flight, artist-signed 85.00

Vase, 5" h., clear w/engraved scene of kneeling girl & birds, artist-signed 210.00

Vase, 6½" h., 4 x 2½" rectangle, pale blue, engraved w/pair of tropical fish swimming past a branch 85.00

Vase, 6½" h., 4¾ x 3¼" oblong, clear, engraved w/two nude children carrying basket of flowers, by Sven Palmquist ......300.00 to 385.00

Vase, 7½" h., paperweight-type, teardrop-shaped, ruby shaded to clear, artist-signed 140.00

Vase, bud, 8" h., smoke cased in clear 95.00

Vase, 8¾" h., Graal, clear, internally decorated w/amorphic figures engaged in games, designed by Edwin Ohrstrom, inscribed "Orrefors 1938 Graal nr 781 E. Ohrstrom" (ILLUS.) ...6,000.00 to 6,600.00

OVERSHOT

Popular since the mid-19th century, Overshot glass was produced by having a gather of molten glass rolled in finely crushed glass to produce a rough exterior finish. The piece was then blown to the desired size and shape. The finished piece has a frosted or iced finish and is sometimes referred to as "ice glass." Early producers referred to this glass as "Craquelle" and, although Overshot is sometimes lumped together with the glass collectors now call "Crackle," that type was produced using a totally different technique.

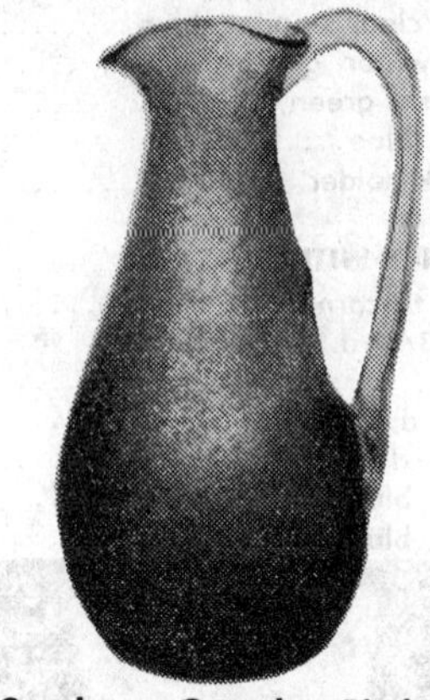

Cranberry Overshot Pitcher

Pitcher, tankard, 7¼" h., 3¾" d., cranberry, applied clear reeded handle $135.00

Pitcher w/ice bladder, 11¼" h., 5½" d., bulbous w/three-petal top, cranberry w/applied clear handle (ILLUS.) 550.00

Pitcher, 12¾" h., clear w/applied twisted-rope handle 235.00

Pitcher, water, light blue w/applied amber handle, ground pontil 165.00

PAIRPOINT

Compote with "Controlled Bubble" Stem

Originally organized in New Bedford, Massachusetts, in 1880, as the Pairpoint Manufacturing Company, on land adjacent to the famed Mount Washington Glass Works, this company first manufactured silver and plated wares. In 1894, the two famous factories merged as the Pairpoint Corporation and enjoyed renowned success for more than forty years. The company was sold in 1939 to a group of local businessmen and eventually bought out by one of the group who turned the management over to Robert M. Gunderson. Subsequently, it operated as the Gunderson Glass Works until 1952 when, after Gunderson's death, the name was changed to Gunderson-Pairpoint. This factory closed in 1956. Subsequently, Robert Bryden took charge of this glassworks, at first producing glass for Pairpoint abroad and eventually, in 1970, beginning glass production in Sagamore, Massachusetts. Bryden's Pairpoint company continues in operation today manufacturing fine quality blown and pressed glass.

Box w/hinged lid, opal w/raised gold florals, signed $375.00

Candlesticks, clear w/engraved designs, large removable candle sockets, pr. 89.00

Candlesticks, engraved Hampton patt., Auroria (reddish amber), Shape 1600, 12" h., pr. 295.00

Card holder, cranberry Diamond Quilted patt. holder w/clear "controlled bubble" stem & cranberry base 125.00

Compote, 5¾" d., overall engraved florals, bows & leaves, clear 70.00

Compote, 6", engraved Vintage patt., amber 42.00

Compote, 6½" d., 6" h., engraved Buckingham patt., cut stem, clear 80.00

Compote, 6¾" d., 8" h., engraved Chelsea patt., clear 97.50

Compote, 7" d., 5" h., ruby w/clear "controlled bubble" paperweight base, Gunderson-Pairpoint 80.00

Compote, 8" d., 5" h., amber w/clear "controlled bubble" ball connector (ILLUS.) 95.00

Compote, 8" d., 7" h., green w/clear "controlled bubble" ball connector 135.00

Console bowl, light green w/clear "controlled bubble" connector, 12" d. 145.00

Cornucopia-vase, Marina Blue w/clear "controlled bubble" paperweight base, Gunderson-Pairpoint, 11" h. 135.00

Ferner, six-sided, h.p. lilies on peach ground, silver plate rim, signed, 6" w., 4½" h. 275.00

Perfume bottle w/stopper, clear w/"controlled bubble" base & stopper, 5½" h. 75.00

Rose bowl, clear w/waterbird engraving, made for Alcoa Aluminum, 1940's, Gunderson Glass Works 97.50

Vase, 8" h., 8" widest d., trumpet-shaped, amber w/clear "controlled bubble" ball connector 65.00

Vase, 9" h., trumpet-shaped, ruby w/clear "controlled bubble" ball connector 135.00

Vase, 10½" h., bulbous bottom w/slender neck, florals on white opaque ground, signed 100.00

Vase, 11" h., engraved Vintage patt., green w/clear "controlled bubble" ball connector, ten prisms 135.00

Vase, 12" h., trumpet-shaped, engraved Colias patt., green w/clear "controlled bubble" ball connector 95.00

Vase, 13" h., ruby w/clear "controlled bubble" ball connector 145.00

Vase, trumpet-shaped, lightly ribbed, green w/clear "controlled bubble" ball connector 80.00

Vase, turquoise w/mottled pinks, Bryden Pairpoint 48.00

Wine, Flambeau (ruby) bowl w/black stem, early 1920's 65.00

PATE DE VERRE

Pate de Verre Covered Bowl

Pate de Verre, or "paste of glass," was molded by very few glass artisans. In the pate de verre technique, powdered glass is mixed with a liquid to make a paste which is then placed in a mold and baked at a high temperature. These articles have a finely-pitted or matte finish and are easily distinguished from blown glass. Duplicate pieces are possible with this technique.

Ashtray, circular w/stepped lug handles, translucent emerald green heightened w/purple speckling, signed Decorchemont, 4¾" d. $660.00

Bowl, 5¼" d., interior molded in low relief w/pale yellow-orange honeysuckle blossoms & green leaves against a pale yellow ground, faceted exterior continuing to a streaked umber & ochre conical foot molded w/dots within arches, ca. 1920, signed A. Walter, Nancy & h Berge.......................2,200.00

Bowl, cov., 6 7/8" l. across handles, mustard & ochre molded berried branches on sides, cover molded in full relief w/a green snail w/mustard shell slithering over a brown branch w/green leaves & berries, restored & chipped, ca. 1920, signed AW/N & hB/sc. (ILLUS.)...1,760.00

Box, cov., rectangular, base molded w/yellow-centered white flowers among green leaves on blue ground w/brown-spotted black lizard at each corner, cover w/molded ochre-centered yellow flowers, signed A. Walter, Nancy & Berge, Sc., 3½" l.......................2,860.00

Clock, upright rectangular form w/triangular top, molded small garland of yellow & red-tinged blossoms w/green leaves & a red & black dragonfly w/aqua wings hovering above an oval concave section against a green ground, circular metal dial, ca. 1920, signed A. Walter, Nancy & h Berge, Sc., 5¾" h. 3,575.00

Dish, oval, shaded aquamarine to sea green w/navy blue, emerald green & blue-green chameleon perched on greenish brown branch on end, ca. 1920, signed A. Walter, Nancy & h Berge, Sc., 5¾" l. 4,950.00

Dish, shallow shaped triangle, pale turquoise shading to cream splashed w/sky blue, modeled in high relief one side w/sand crab in chocolate brown, brown-black, lemon yellow & deep turquoise, ca. 1920, signed A. Walter, Nancy and h Berge, Sc., 7¾" l. 5,775.00

Figure of a nude woman kneeling w/her face uplifted, her right leg outstretched & her extended arms draped w/a robe, yellow, on rectangular green base, signed A. Walter, Nancy, 11¼" l. 6,600.00

Jar, cov., waisted globular form, molded in high relief w/green spotted deep aquamarine lizard coiling around sides, against deep raspberry & yellow berries amid spring green leaves, cover molded w/berries, ca. 1900, signed A. Walter, Nancy, h Berge, Sc., 3½" h. 7,425.00

Lamp base, flecked pale ground w/aubergine & spinach green band molded w/brick red masks, first quarter 20th c., signed G. Argy-Rousseau, 9¾" h. (2 hairlines occuring during mold removal)...1,100.00

Model of a frog, yellow-streaked green & navy frog on rounded blue base molded w/green leaves & an ochre snail, signed Daum Nancy, 4 1/8" l. 2,640.00

Night lamp, tapering cylinder, cream mottled w/lavender, orange & emerald green, molded in medium relief w/pendant rose branches w/emerald green & brown leafage & Chinese red blossoms, base further molded in low relief w/band of rose petals, in a wrought-iron circular base raised on three ball feet, cap pierced & applied w/berried leafy knopped finial, ca. 1920, signed G. Argy-Rousseau, 8" h. 4,400.00

Paperweight, model of a plump mint green bird floating contentedly on darker green waves, ca. 1900, signed A. Walter, Nancy, 3 3/8" l. 770.00

Paperweight, rust & black crustacean bracing itself against churning deep olive & mustard sea, ca. 1920, signed A. Walter, Nancy & ...rge, Sc., 4¾" l. 3,850.00

Pendant, red berries on lavender ground, original silk cord & finial 1,250.00

Tray, trapezoidal, ends w/brown & yellow moths, matte yellow ground molded in low relief w/trailing green & yellow flower sprays, signed Berge, Sc. & A. Walter, Nancy, 13½" l. 4,400.00

Vase, 3½" h., flared cylinder, molded clusters of cobalt blue berries among red & brown leaves on purple-streaked ground, signed G. Argy-Rousseau, France 2,860.00

Vase, 6½" h., trumpet-shaped, molded lower band of yellow-centered flowers & upper band of brick red & purple raspberries among green leaves on transparent blue & navy ground, signed A. Walter, Nancy 2,860.00

Vase, 9½" h., ovoid, "The Apple Pickers," cream lightly splashed w/ochre, upper section molded in medium relief w/three maidens in tiered Grecian costumes picking ripe golden apples from spreading branches, lower section incised in low relief w/continuous band of angular coils, all in shades of charcoal, tangerine & lemon yellow, ca. 1920, signed G. Argy-Rousseau 13,200.00

PATTERN GLASS

Though it has never been ascertained whether glass was first pressed in the United States or abroad, the development of the glass pressing machine revolutionized the glass industry in the United States and this country receives the credit for improving the method to make this process feasible. The first wares pressed were probably small flat plates of the type now referred to as "lacy" Sandwich, the intricacy of the design concealing flaws.

In 1827, both the New England Glass Co., Cambridge, Massachusetts and Bakewell & Co., Pittsburgh, took out patents for pressing glass furniture knobs and soon other pieces followed. This early pressed glass contained red lead which made it clear and resonant when tapped (flint). Made primarily in clear, it is rarer in blue, amethyst, olive green and yellow.

By the 1840's, early simple patterns such as Ashburton, Argus and Excelsior appeared. Ribbed Bellflower seems to have been one of the earliest patterns to have had complete sets. By the 1860's, a wide range of patterns were available.

In 1864, William Leighton of Hobbs, Brockunier & Co., Wheeling, West Virginia, developed a formula for "soda lime" glass which did not require the expensive red lead for clarity. Although "soda lime" glass did not have the brilliance of the earlier flint glass, the formula came into widespread use because glass could be produced cheaply.

By 1900, patterns had become ornate in imitation of the expensive brilliant cut glass.

ACTRESS

Actress Covered Compote

Bowl, 6" d., footed $40.00
Bowl, 8" d., Adelaide Neilson 85.00
Bread tray, Miss Neilson, 12½" l.... 72.00
Butter dish, cov., Fanny Davenport & Miss Neilson 82.00
Cake stand, Maude Granger & Annie Pixley, 10" d., 7" h. 140.00
Celery vase, Pinafore scene 158.00
Cheese dish, cov., "Lone Fisherman" on cover, "The Two Dromios" on underplate 230.00
Cologne bottle w/original stopper, 11" h. 47.00
Compote, cov., 6" d., 10" h. 100.00
Compote, cov., 8" d., 12" h. 147.00
Compote, cov., 10" d., 14½" h., Fanny Davenport & Maggie Mitchell (ILLUS.) 150.00
Compote, open, 6" d., 11" h. 130.00
Compote, open, 7" d., 7" h., Miss Neilson 145.00
Compote, open, 10" d., 9" h. 100.00
Creamer, Miss Neilson & Fanny Davenport 80.00
Goblet, Lotta Crabtree & Kate Claxton 62.00
Marmalade jar, cov., Maude Granger & Annie Pixley 107.00
Mug, Pinafore scene 47.50
Pickle dish, Kate Claxton, "Love's Request is Pickles," 9¼ x 5¼" ... 46.00
Pitcher, water, 9" h., Miss Neilson & Maggie Mitchell 250.00
Platter, 11½ x 7", Pinafore scene ... 81.00
Relish, Miss Neilson, 8 x 5" 32.50
Relish, Maude Granger, 9 x 5" 67.00
Salt dip, master size 68.00
Salt shaker w/original pewter top (single) 45.00
Sauce dish, Maggie Mitchell & Fanny Davenport, 4½" d., 2½" h. 19.00
Spooner, Mary Anderson & Maude Granger 73.00
Sugar bowl, cov., Lotta Crabtree & Kate Claxton 135.00
Sugar bowl, open 42.50

ADONIS (Pleat & Tuck or Washboard)

Bowl, master berry, canary yellow .. 12.00
Creamer, blue 35.00
Creamer, clear 15.00
Sauce dish, canary yellow 12.00

ALABAMA (Beaded Bull's Eye with Drape)

Butter dish, cov., ruby-stained 80.00
Butter dish, cov. 55.00
Castor set, 4-bottle, original silver plate stand 135.00
Compote, cov., 5" d. 65.00
Creamer 37.00
Creamer, individual size 13.00
Cruet w/original stopper 55.00
Mustard pot & cover w/slot for spoon 55.00
Pitcher, water 75.00

Relish, 8 1/8 x 5" 29.00
Sauce dish 17.00
Spooner 35.00
Sugar bowl, cov. 45.00
Syrup pitcher w/original top 94.00
Table set, creamer, cov. sugar bowl, spooner & cov. butter dish, 4 pcs. 250.00
Toothpick holder 50.00
Tray, water, 10½" 42.50

ALASKA (Lion's Leg)

Alaska Water Set

Banana boat, blue opalescent 215.00
Banana boat, emerald green 85.00
Berry set: master bowl & 6 sauce dishes; blue opalescent, 7 pcs. 325.00
Berry set: master bowl & 6 sauce dishes; vaseline opalescent, 7 pcs. .... 250.00 to 275.00
Bowl, 8" sq., blue opalescent 95.00
Bowl, 8" sq., clear w/enameled florals 65.00
Bowl, 8" sq., green w/enameled florals 65.00
Butter dish, cov., blue opalescent 225.00
Butter dish, cov., green w/enameled florals 155.00
Butter dish, cov., vaseline opalescent 250.00
Butter dish, cov., white w/enameled florals 85.00
Card tray, blue opalescent 28.50
Card tray, vaseline opalescent 30.00
Celery (or jewel) tray, blue opalescent 130.00
Celery tray, blue opalescent w/enameled florals 200.00
Celery tray, vaseline opalescent 140.00
Celery tray, vaseline opalescent w/enameled florals 175.00
Creamer, blue opalescent 72.00
Creamer, clear to opalescent 45.00
Creamer, green 38.00
Creamer, green w/enameled florals 70.00
Creamer, vaseline opalescent 57.00
Cruet w/original stopper, blue opalescent 263.00
Cruet w/original stopper, green w/enameled florals 175.00
Cruet w/original stopper, vaseline opalescent 240.00
Cruet w/original stopper, vaseline opalescent w/enameled florals 255.00
Pitcher, water, blue opalescent 308.00
Pitcher, water, clear to opalescent 125.00
Pitcher, water, green 88.00
Pitcher, water, vaseline opalescent .... 325.00 to 385.00
Salt shaker w/original top, blue opalescent (single) 40.00
Salt shaker w/original top, clear to opalescent (single) 25.00
Salt & pepper shakers w/original tops, blue opalescent, pr. 125.00
Salt & pepper shakers w/original tops, vaseline opalescent, pr. 105.00
Sauce dish, blue opalescent 50.00
Sauce dish, clear to opalescent 25.00
Sauce dish, green w/enameled florals & leaves 38.00
Sauce dish, vaseline opalescent 42.50
Spooner, blue opalescent 54.00
Spooner, clear to opalescent 30.00
Spooner, green 36.50
Spooner, green w/enameled florals 65.00
Spooner, vaseline opalescent 54.00
Sugar bowl, cov., blue opalescent 143.00
Sugar bowl, cov., blue opalescent w/enameled florals 135.00
Sugar bowl, cov., green w/enameled florals 95.00
Sugar bowl, cov., vaseline opalescent .... 125.00 to 150.00
Sugar bowl, cov., vaseline opalescent w/enameled florals 135.00
Sugar bowl, cov., white w/enameled florals 65.00
Table set, blue opalescent, 4 pcs. .... 625.00 to 750.00
Table set, vaseline opalescent, 4 pcs. 615.00
Tumbler, green 45.00
Tumbler, vaseline opalescent 63.00
Tumbler, vaseline opalescent w/enameled florals 50.00
Water set: pitcher & 4 tumblers; blue opalescent, 5 pcs. 485.00
Water set: pitcher & 6 tumblers; vaseline opalescent, 7 pcs. (ILLUS.) 725.00

ALEXIS - See Priscilla Pattern

ALMOND THUMBPRINT (Pointed Thumbprint)

Bowl, 4½" d., 4 7/8" h., footed, non-flint 20.00
Butter dish, cov., ruby-stained, non-flint 105.00
Champagne, flint 67.50
Compote, cov., 6½" d., 8" h., flint (ILLUS.) .... 75.00 to 85.00

Almond Thumbprint Compote

Egg cup, flint 25.00
Salt dip, master size, flint 20.00
Spooner, fluted, non-flint 20.00
Sugar bowl, cov., non-flint 35.00
Wine, flint 24.00

AMAZON (Sawtooth Band)

Amazon Child's Creamer

Banana stand 65.00
Bowl, 6" d. 22.00
Bowl, 9" d. 20.00
Butter dish, cov. 50.00
Cake stand, 8" to 9½" d. ....37.50 to 47.50
Celery vase 33.00
Champagne 32.00
Claret 37.50
Compote, open, jelly, 4½" d. 22.50
Compote, open, 6" d., high stand ... 28.00
Cordial 32.50
Creamer 32.00
Creamer, child's miniature (ILLUS.) .. 27.50
Creamer & cov. sugar bowl, pr. 65.00
Cruet w/bar in hand stopper, amethyst 250.00
Cruet w/bar in hand stopper 55.00
Egg cup 14.00
Goblet 23.00
Pitcher, water 53.00
Salt dip, master size..........12.50 to 18.00
Sauce dish, flat or footed .....4.00 to 11.50
Spooner 20.00
Sugar bowl, cov. 40.00
Syrup pitcher w/original top 42.50
Table set, child's miniature, 4 pcs. 150.00
Tumbler 23.00
Wine 21.00

AMBERETTE (English Hobnail Cross or Klondike)

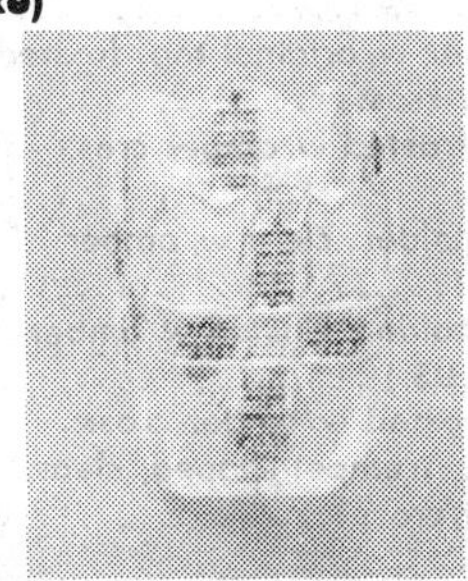

Amberette Toothpick Holder

Berry set: master bowl & 4 sauce dishes; frosted w/amber cross, 5 pcs. 385.00
Bowl, master berry or fruit, 8" sq., clear w/amber cross 75.00
Bowl, master berry or fruit, 8" sq., frosted w/amber cross 250.00
Bowl, 11" sq., flared, clear w/amber cross 130.00
Butter dish, cov., clear w/amber cross 250.00
Butter dish, cov., frosted w/amber cross 373.00
Celery tray, frosted w/amber cross, 10 7/8 x 4½", 2 7/8" h. 185.00
Celery vase, clear w/amber cross .. 142.50
Celery vase, frosted w/amber cross 200.00
Creamer, clear w/amber cross 75.00
Creamer, frosted w/amber cross ... 160.00
Goblet, frosted w/amber cross 250.00
Pitcher, water, clear w/amber cross 285.00
Pitcher, water, frosted w/amber cross...................600.00 to 900.00
Punch cup, clear w/amber cross 60.00
Punch cup, frosted w/amber cross .. 110.00
Relish, clear w/amber cross, boat-shaped, 9 x 4" 114.00
Relish, frosted w/amber cross, 9 x 4" w/silver plate holder, overall 6" h. 145.00
Salt shaker w/original top, clear w/amber cross (single) 69.00
Salt shaker w/original top, frosted w/amber cross (single) 100.00
Salt & pepper shakers w/original tops, frosted w/amber cross, pr. 192.00

Sauce dish, flat or footed, clear w/amber cross 20.00
Sauce dish, flat or footed, frosted w/amber cross 97.00
Spooner, clear w/amber cross 50.00
Spooner, frosted w/amber cross 200.00
Sugar bowl, cov., clear w/amber cross, 6¾" h. 185.00
Sugar bowl, cov., frosted w/amber cross, 4" d., 6¾" h. 250.00
Sugar bowl, open, frosted w/amber cross 175.00
Syrup pitcher w/original top, frosted w/amber cross 766.00
Table set, frosted w/amber cross, 4 pcs. 825.00
Toothpick holder, clear w/amber cross 205.00
Toothpick holder, frosted w/amber cross (ILLUS.) 415.00
Tumbler, frosted w/amber cross 138.00
Vase, 8" h., trumpet-shaped, clear w/amber cross 130.00

APOLLO

(Items may be plain or with etched designs)

Bowl, 8" d. 22.50
Bread tray, square 27.50
Butter dish, cov. 50.00
Cake stand, 9" to 10½" d. 53.00
Celery tray 22.50
Celery vase................37.50 to 45.00
Compote, cov., 6" d. 55.00
Compote, open, 5" d. 36.00
Compote, open, 7" d., low stand ... 25.00
Creamer ....30.00 to 40.00
Cruet w/original stopper 45.00
Goblet 27.50
Lamp, kerosene-type, canary yellow, 9" h. 165.00
Lamp, kerosene-type, clear, 10" h... 48.00
Lamp, kerosene-type, canary yellow w/frosted font & stem w/enameling, 12" h. 260.00
Pitcher, water, bulbous 65.00
Plate, 9½" sq. 26.50
Sauce dish, flat or footed .....6.00 to 10.50
Spooner 32.50
Sugar bowl, cov. 45.00
Sugar shaker w/original top 45.00
Syrup pitcher w/original top 110.00
Tumbler 21.00
Water set, pitcher & 6 tumblers, 7 pcs. 200.00

ARGUS (McKee & Brother, Pittsburgh)

Ale glass, footed, flint, 5½" h. 70.00
Butter dish, footed, flint, 8" d. 85.00
Celery vase, flint 50.00
Champagne, flint 50.00
Champagne (Hotel Argus), non-flint 18.50
Compote, open, 6" d., 4½" h., flint 55.00
Creamer, applied handle, flint 110.00
Egg cup, flint 24.00
Egg cup, handled, flint 70.00
Goblet, flint 42.00
Goblet (Barrel Argus), flint 42.00
Goblet (Hotel Argus), non-flint...................25.00 to 30.00
Goblet, master size, flint 37.50
Honey dish, flint 20.00
Mug, applied handle, flint 60.00
Pitcher, water, 8¼" h., applied handle, flint 200.00
Punch bowl, pedestal base, scalloped rim, 11½" d., 9½" h. 160.00
Salt dip, master size, flint 27.50

Argus Spillholder

Spillholder, flint (ILLUS.) 45.00
Spooner, flint 43.00
Sugar bowl, cov., flint 65.00
Tumbler (Barrel Argus), flint 60.00
Tumbler, bar-type, flint 60.00
Tumbler, footed, flint, 4" h. 40.00
Tumbler, footed, flint, 5" h. 60.00
Tumbler, whiskey, handled 57.50
Wine, flint, 4" h. 45.00
Wine (Hotel Argus), non-flint 20.00

ART (Job's Tears)

Art Open Compote

Banana stand 99.00
Bowl, 8½" d. 38.00
Bowl, 9¾" d. 37.00
Butter dish, cov. 52.50
Butter dish, cov., ruby-stained 65.00
Cake stand, 9" to 10½" d. 56.00
Celery vase 32.50
Compote, open, 8" d., high stand . . . 35.00
Compote, open, 9" d., 7¼" h. 45.00
Compote, open, 10" d., 9" h. (ILLUS.) 55.00
Creamer 43.00
Cruet w/original stopper 88.00
Goblet 28.00
Pitcher, milk, ruby-stained . . 95.00 to 150.00
Pitcher, water, bulbous 85.00
Plate, 10" d. 55.00
Relish, 7¾ x 4¼" 18.50
Relish, ruby-stained 65.00
Sauce dish, flat or footed 18.00
Spooner 27.00
Sugar bowl, cov. 42.00
Tumbler 20.00

ASHBURTON

Ashburton Covered Sugar

Ale glass, flint, 5" h. 87.50
Ale glass, flint, 6½" h. 65.00
Bowl, 6½" d., low, footed, flint 72.50
Celery vase, scalloped rim, canary yellow, flint 400.00
Celery vase, plain rim, flint 64.00
Celery vase, scalloped rim, flint 115.00
Champagne, flint 55.00
Champagne, creased ovals, flint 60.00
Champagne, cut ovals, flint 75.00
Claret, flint, 5¼" h. 50.00
Cordial, flint, 4¼" h. 70.00
Cordial, non-flint 42.50
Creamer, applied handle, flint 180.00
Decanter w/original stopper, canary yellow, flint . . . . . 850.00 to 1,000.00
Decanter, bar lip, canary yellow, flint 550.00
Decanter w/original stopper, flint, qt. 62.00
Decanter, bar lip & facet-cut neck, qt. 50.00
Egg cup, clambroth, flint 125.00
Egg cup, flint 27.00
Egg cup, non-flint 15.00
Egg cup, double, flint 95.00
Flip glass, handled, flint, 7" h. 212.00
Goblet, barrel-shaped, flint 38.00
Goblet, flared, flint 52.50
Goblet, non-flint 25.00
Goblet, disconnected ovals 35.00
Goblet, "giant," straight stem, flint 55.00
Honey dish, 3½" d. 8.50
Mug, applied handle, 4¾" h. 110.00
Pitcher, water, applied hollow handle, flint 450.00
Plate, 6 5/8" d., flint 60.00
Sauce dish, flint 7.50
Sugar bowl, cov., flint (ILLUS.) 140.00
Sugar bowl, open, non-flint 32.50
Tumbler, bar, flint 60.00
Tumbler, water, flint 55.00
Tumbler, water, footed 67.50
Tumbler, whiskey, applied handle, flint 125.00
Vase, 10½" h., flint 80.00
Wine, barrel-shaped, flint 41.50
Wine, flint 35.00
Wine, non-flint 20.00
Wine, emerald green, flint 425.00
Wine, peacock green, flint 525.00

ATLANTA - See Lion Pattern

ATLAS (Crystal Ball or Cannon Ball)

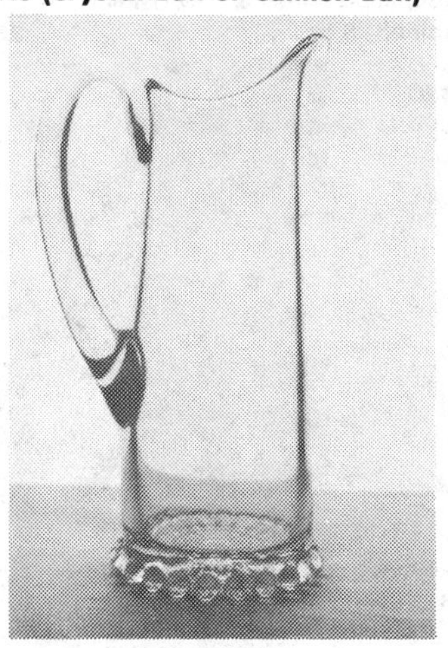

Atlas Pitcher

Bowl, cov., large, flat 35.00
Bowl, open, 9" d. 20.00
Butter dish, cov. 45.00
Cake stand, 8" to 10" d. 32.00
Cake stand, ruby-stained, 8" to 10" d. 95.00
Celery vase 25.00

Champagne, 5½" h. 22.50
Compote, cov., 8" d., 8" h. 55.00
Cordial 35.00
Creamer, flat or pedestal base 22.50
Goblet 30.00
Pitcher, milk, tankard, applied handle 38.00
Pitcher, water, tankard, applied handle (ILLUS.) 55.00
Salt dip, individual size 8.00
Salt dip, master size 18.00
Sauce dish, flat or footed . . . . 7.50 to 12.50
Spooner 26.00
Toothpick holder 20.00
Tumbler 27.50
Wine 21.00

AURORA (Diamond Horseshoe)

(Items may be plain or with etched designs)

Celery vase 32.50
Creamer, applied handle 38.00
Decanter w/original stopper 30.00
Decanter w/original stopper, ruby-stained 135.00
Goblet 27.50
Pitcher, water, tankard, 9½" h. 40.00
Pitcher, water, tankard, 12" h. 45.00
Salt & pepper shakers w/original tops, pr. 75.00
Tray, wine, 10" d. 24.00
Tray, wine, ruby-stained, 10" d. 45.00
Wine 37.00
Wine, ruby-stained 40.00
Wine set: decanter w/original ruby stopper, 6 wines & tray; ruby-stained, 8 pcs. 375.00

AZTEC

Aztec Creamer

Bowl, cov., 8½" d. 75.00
Butter dish, cov. 40.00
Carafe, water 37.50
Champagne 15.00
Cordial 17.00
Creamer (ILLUS.) 26.50
Creamer, individual size 16.00
Cruet w/original stopper 48.00
Dresser bottle w/original stopper . . . 37.50
Goblet 30.00
Pitcher, water 60.00
Punch cup 5.00
Salt shaker w/original top (single) . . 14.50
Sugar bowl, cov. 35.00
Sugar bowl, open 25.00
Tumbler 20.00
Wine 16.00

BABY FACE

Baby Face Compote

Butter dish, cov., 5¼" d. 150.00
Compote, cov., 5¼" d., 6½" h. 140.00
Compote, open, 8" d., 4¾" h. 85.00
Compote, open, 8" d., 8" h. (ILLUS.) 95.00
Creamer 110.00
Goblet . . . . 85.00 to 150.00
Pitcher, water 175.00
Spooner 80.00

BABY THUMBPRINT - See Dakota Pattern

BALDER (Kamoni or Pennsylvania - Late)

Bowl, berry or fruit, 8½" d., clear w/gold trim 24.00
Butter dish, cov., clear 49.00
Carafe, clear 45.00
Celery tray, clear, 11 x 4½" 28.00
Cheese dish, cov., clear 62.50

Balder Individual Creamer With Gold Trim

Creamer, clear w/gold trim, small, 3" h. (ILLUS.) 18.00
Creamer, green w/gold trim, small, 3" h. 50.00

Creamer, clear, large, 4" h. 32.50
Creamer & open sugar bowl, clear w/gold trim, pr. 35.00
Creamer & open sugar bowl, individual size, clear w/gold trim, pr. 40.00
Cruet w/original stopper, clear 47.50
Decanter w/original stopper, clear, 10¾" h. 65.00
Goblet, clear 22.00
Pitcher, water, clear 45.00
Plate, 8" d., clear 29.50
Punch cup, clear 12.50
Relish, clear 10.00
Salt shaker w/original top, clear (single) 35.00
Sauce dish, boat-shaped, clear 22.00
Sauce dish, round or square, clear . . . . 8.00 to 15.00
Spooner, clear 22.00
Sugar bowl, cov., child's, green w/gold trim 135.00
Sugar bowl, cov., clear 45.00
Sugar bowl, open, clear 25.00
Syrup pitcher w/original top, clear . . 37.50
Table set, clear, 3 pcs. 125.00
Toothpick holder, clear 28.00
Tumbler, juice, clear 10.50
Tumbler, water, blue, souvenir 42.00
Tumbler, water, clear 23.00
Tumbler, water, clear w/gold trim 25.00
Tumbler, water, ruby-stained 49.00
Tumbler, whiskey, clear 13.00
Vase, 5¾" h., clear w/gold trim 17.50
Wine, clear 16.50
Wine, green w/gold trim 40.00

BALTIMORE PEAR

Baltimore Pear Creamer

Bowl, 6" d. 29.00
Bowl, berry or fruit, 9" d., footed . . . 40.00
Bread plate, 12½" l. 50.00
Butter dish, cov. 50.00
Cake stand, high pedestal 55.00
Celery vase 50.00
Compote, cov., 7" d., high stand . . . 75.00
Creamer (ILLUS.) 30.00
Creamer & open sugar bowl, pr. 50.00
Goblet 31.00
Pitcher, water . . . . 75.00 to 95.00
Plate, 9" d. 35.00
Relish, 8¼" l. 25.00
Sauce dish, flat or footed . . . . 15.00 to 23.00
Spooner 32.50
Sugar bowl, cov. 43.00
Sugar bowl, open 30.00

BAMBOO - See Broken Column Pattern

BANDED BEADED GRAPE MEDALLION

Creamer 41.00
Goblet 30.00
Spooner 29.00
Sugar bowl, open 25.00
Tumbler, footed 35.00

BANDED BUCKLE

Spooner 26.50
Tumbler, bar 55.00

BANDED PORTLAND (Portland w/Diamond Point Band)

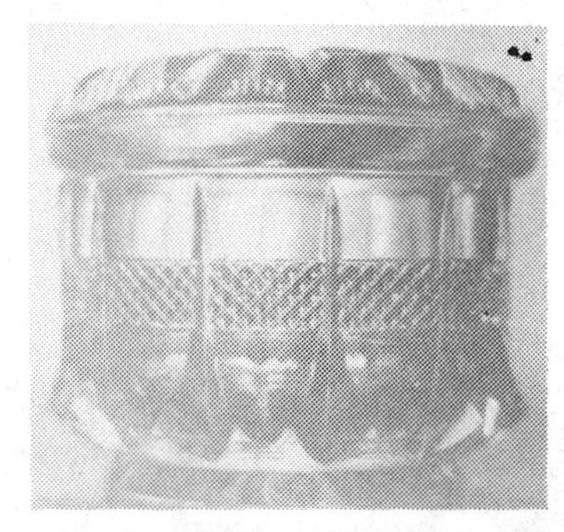

Banded Portland Dresser Jar

Butter pat 18.00
Candlesticks, pr. 75.00
Carafe, water 82.50
Celery tray, gold-stained, 12 x 5" . . . 25.00
Cologne bottle w/original stopper . . 48.00
Compote, cov., jelly 35.00
Compote, open, 10" d., high stand . . 50.00
Creamer 35.00
Creamer, individual size 29.00
Dresser jar, cov., 3½" d. (ILLUS.) . . . 33.50
Dresser set: large tray, pin tray, pr. cov. pomade jars, pr. cologne bottles w/original stoppers & ring tree; gold trim, 7 pcs. 195.00
Goblet 34.00
Pickle dish, 6 x 4" 15.00
Pitcher, water 65.00
Punch cup, gold trim 18.00
Relish, 8½ x 4" oval 10.00
Ring tree, gold-stained 40.00
Salt shaker w/original top (single) . . 25.00

Salt & pepper shakers w/original tops, pr. 50.00
Sauce dish 11.50
Spooner 35.00
Sugar bowl, cov., gold-stained 36.00
Sugar bowl, individual size 22.50
Sugar bowl, individual size, green-stained 25.00
Sugar shaker w/original top 39.00
Syrup jug w/original top 75.00
Toothpick holder 32.00
Tumbler 27.00
Vase, 6" h., flared 16.50
Vase, 9" h. 18.50
Vase, gold-stained 15.00
Wine 26.00
Wine, blue-stained 28.00
Wine, gold-stained 35.00
Wine set, tray & 6 wines, 7 pcs. 145.00

BANDED PORTLAND W/COLOR - See Portland Maiden Blush Pattern

BAR & DIAMOND - See Kokomo Pattern

BARBERRY

Barberry Water Pitcher

Bowl, 8" oval 20.00
Bread plate 23.00
Butter dish, cov., shell finial 60.00
Cake stand, 9½" d. 35.00
Celery vase 35.00
Compote, cov., 6" d., high stand, shell finial 45.00
Compote, cov., 8" d., low stand, shell finial 72.00
Compote, open, 8½" d., 7" h. 25.00
Creamer 32.50
Egg cup 20.00
Goblet 25.00
Pitcher, water, 9½" h., applied handle (ILLUS.) 85.00
Plate, 6" d. 18.00
Salt dip, master size 18.00
Sauce dish, flat or footed .....8.00 to 18.00
Spooner, footed 36.00
Sugar bowl, cov., shell finial 42.00
Sugar bowl, open 27.50
Syrup jug w/original top ....85.00 to 110.00
Tumbler, footed 23.00
Wine 26.00

BARLEY

Barley Open Compote

Bowl, 10" oval 18.50
Bread platter, plain rim, 11½ x 9½" 22.00
Bread platter, scalloped rim, 11½ x 9½" 32.50
Butter dish, cov. 29.00
Cake stand, 8" to 10½" d. 37.50
Celery vase 32.50
Compote, cov., 7" d., high stand 60.00
Compote, open, 6" d., high stand 30.00
Compote, open, 8½" d., 8" h. 35.00
Compote, open, 8¾" d., 6½" h., scalloped rim (ILLUS.) 32.00
Creamer 23.00
Egg cup 17.50
Goblet 25.00
Pickle castor w/frame & tongs 82.50
Pitcher, milk 30.00
Pitcher, water 47.00
Plate, 6" d. 25.00
Relish, 8 x 6" 15.00
Relish, handled, 9½ x 5¼" 18.00
Sauce dish, flat or footed 8.00
Spooner 21.50
Sugar bowl, cov. 27.00
Table set, creamer, open sugar bowl & cov. butter dish, 3 pcs. 110.00
Wheelbarrow sugar cube dish w/metal wheels 65.00
Wine, 3¾" h. 30.00

BARRED HOBSTAR - See Checkerboard Pattern

BARRED STAR - See Spartan Pattern

BASKETWEAVE

Bread plate, amber 35.00
Bread plate, blue 35.00

Goblet, amber 22.50
Goblet, blue 35.00
Goblet, clear 20.00
Mug, clear, 3" h. 12.00
Pitcher, water, amber 42.50
Plate, 8¾" d., handled, blue 19.50
Plate, 8¾" d., handled, clear 11.00
Tray, water, scenic center, vaseline, 12" 47.50
Vase, 8½" h., clear 12.50

BEADED BAND

Butter dish, cov. 40.00
Cake stand, 9" 27.00
Creamer 18.00
Goblet 26.50
Relish, 8½ x 5¼" 9.50
Sauce dish, flat, 4¼" d. 5.00
Sugar bowl, cov. 40.00

BEADED BULL'S EYE WITH DRAPE - See Alabama Pattern

BEADED DEWDROP - See Wisconsin Pattern

BEADED GRAPE (California)

Beaded Grape Plate

Bowl, 5½" sq., clear 16.50
Bowl, 5½" sq., green 19.50
Bowl, 6½" sq., green 35.00
Bowl, 8" sq., clear (ILLUS.) 27.00
Bowl, 8" sq., green 35.00
Bowl, 8½ x 6¼" rectangle, green 30.00
Bread tray, clear, 10 x 7" 25.00
Bread tray, green, 10 x 7" 40.00
Butter dish, cov., sq., clear 58.00
Butter dish, cov., sq., green 82.00
Cake stand, clear, 9" sq., 6" h. 55.00
Cake stand, green, 9" sq., 6" h. 85.00
Celery tray, clear 33.00
Celery tray, green 42.00
Celery vase, clear 32.00
Compote, cov., 6½" sq., high stand, clear 75.00
Compote, open, 7" sq., high stand, clear 38.00
Compote, open, 8½" sq., high stand, clear 72.50
Compote, open, 8½" sq., high stand, green 75.00
Creamer, clear 35.00
Creamer, green 45.00
Cruet w/original stopper, clear 65.00
Cruet, w/original stopper, green 125.00
Dish, clear, 8¼" sq. 30.00
Egg cup, clear 16.00
Goblet, clear 25.00
Goblet, green 45.00
Pitcher, water, round, green 82.00
Pitcher, water, square, green 100.00
Pitcher, water, tankard, clear 78.00
Plate, 8" sq., clear 25.00
Plate, 8" sq.,, green 40.00
Relish, clear, 7 x 4" 20.00
Salt shaker w/original top, clear (single) 22.50
Salt shaker w/original top, green (single) 25.00
Salt & pepper shakers w/original tops, clear, pr. 42.50
Sauce dish, clear 12.00
Sauce dish, green 15.00
Sauce dish, handled, green 30.00
Spooner, clear 35.00
Spooner, green 40.00
Sugar bowl, cov., clear 47.50
Sugar bowl, cov., green 60.00
Sugar bowl, open, clear 19.00
Sugar bowl, open, green 28.00
Table set, green, 4 pcs. 300.00
Toothpick holder, clear 27.50
Toothpick holder, green 55.00
Tumbler, clear 27.50
Tumbler, green 40.00
Vase, 7" h., green 32.50
Water set: pitcher & 6 tumblers; green, 7 pcs. 255.00
Wine, clear 35.00
Wine, green 65.00

BEADED GRAPE MEDALLION

Butter dish, cov. 38.00
Celery vase 55.00
Compote, cov., 8¼" d., low stand 75.00
Creamer, applied handle 58.00
Egg cup 29.00
Goblet 28.00
Goblet, buttermilk 40.00
Goblet, lady's 29.00
Honey dish, 3½" d. 8.00
Pitcher, water, applied handle 80.00
Salt dip, master size, footed, oval 40.00
Salt dip, flat 15.00
Sauce dish 8.00
Spooner 28.00
Sugar bowl, cov. 45.00
Sugar bowl, open 27.50
Wine 50.00

BEADED LOOP (Oregon)

Beaded Loop Goblet

Berry set, master bowl & 5 sauce dishes, 6 pcs. 50.00
Bread platter 26.50
Butter dish, cov. 50.00
Cake stand, 9" to 10½" d. ...28.00 to 45.00
Celery vase, 7" h. 27.00
Compote, open, jelly 37.50
Compote, open, 7½" d., low stand 20.00
Compote, open, 9" d., 7¼" h. 50.00
Creamer 21.50
Cruet w/faceted stopper 49.00
Cruet, no stopper 41.00
Goblet (ILLUS.) 30.00
Mug, footed 38.00
Mug, ruby-stained 25.00
Pickle dish, boat-shaped, 9" l. 15.00
Pitcher, milk, 8½" h. 38.00
Pitcher, water, tankard 51.00
Relish 12.00
Relish, w/advertising in base for "Denver Furniture & Carpet Company" 45.00
Salt shaker w/original top (single) .. 15.00
Salt & pepper shakers w/original tops, pr. 32.50
Sauce dish, flat or footed .....8.00 to 13.00
Spooner, ruby-stained 55.00
Sugar bowl, cov., ruby-stained 42.50
Sugar bowl, open 18.00
Syrup pitcher w/original top 65.00
Table set, 4 pcs. 200.00
Tumbler, ruby-stained 35.00
Vase, small 20.00
Wine 65.00

BEADED MIRROR

Butter dish, cov. 40.00
Castor bottle (mustard) 15.00
Castor bottle w/original stopper, "Oil" 25.00
Celery vase 36.50
Egg cup 18.50
Goblet 25.00
Salt dip 18.00
Sauce dish, flat 8.00
Spooner 22.50
Sugar bowl, cov. 45.00
Sugar bowl, open 23.50

BEADED TULIP

Bowl, 9½ x 6 5/8" oval 20.00
Creamer 85.00
Goblet 38.00
Pitcher, water 67.50
Wine 29.00

BEARDED HEAD - **See Viking Pattern**

BEARDED MAN (Old Man of the Woods or Neptune)

Bearded Man Covered Compote

Butter dish, cov. 52.50
Celery vase 35.00
Compote, cov., 9" h. (ILLUS.) 60.00
Creamer 40.00
Pitcher, water, 2-qt. 58.00
Spooner 40.00
Sugar bowl, open 50.00
Table set, 4 pcs. 250.00

BELLFLOWER

Bowl, 8" d., 4½" h., scalloped rim .. 70.00
Bowl, 9 x 6" oval, rayed base 125.00
Butter dish, cov. 80.00
Castor bottle w/original stopper 28.00
Celery vase, fine rib, single vine ... 80.00
Celery vase, w/cut bellflowers 175.00
Champagne, barrel-shaped, fine rib, knob stem, plain base 95.00
Champagne, barrel-shaped, fine rib, single vine, knob stem, rayed base 95.00
Compote, open, 4½" d., low stand, scalloped rim 100.00
Compote, open, 7" d., low stand, scalloped rim 35.00

Compote, open, 8" d., 5" h., scalloped rim, single vine 67.50
Compote, open, 8" d., 8" h., single vine 245.00
Compote, open, 8¼" d., 7" h., scalloped base, w/cut bellflowers 130.00
Compote, open, 9½" d., 8½" h., scalloped rim, single vine 100.00
Cordial, fine rib, single vine........ 165.00
Creamer, fine rib, double vine, applied handle 187.00
Creamer, fine rib, single vine 135.00
Decanter w/bar lip, double vine, pt. 225.00
Decanter w/bar lip, patent stopper, double vine, qt. 250.00
Egg cup, coarse rib 20.00
Egg cup, fine rib, single vine 38.00

Bellflower Knob-Stem Goblet

Goblet, barrel-shaped, fine rib, single vine, knob stem (ILLUS.)...... 50.00
Goblet, barrel-shaped, fine rib, single vine, plain stem 46.00
Goblet, coarse rib 30.00
Goblet, double vine 65.00
Goblet, single vine, rayed base 42.50
Goblet, fine rib, double vine, w/cut bellflowers 300.00
Goblet, buttermilk 55.00
Lamp, kerosene-type, 7½" h. 275.00
Lamp, kerosene-type, clear font, milk white base, flint, 9½" h. 165.00
Lamp, whale oil, brass stem, marble base ....95.00 to 125.00
Pitcher, water, 8¾" h., coarse rib, double vine 325.00
Pitcher, water, single vine 295.00
Plate, 6" d., fine rib, single vine.... 90.00
Salt dip, cov., master size, footed, beaded rim, fine rib, single vine.. 75.00
Salt dip, open, master size, footed, scalloped rim, single vine 32.00
Sauce dish, single vine 18.00
Spillholder 42.00
Spooner, low foot, double vine 47.00
Spooner, scalloped rim, single vine . 35.00

Sugar bowl, open, double vine 40.00
Syrup pitcher w/original top, applied handle, fine rib, single vine, clear 750.00
Syrup pitcher w/original top, applied handle, fine rib, single vine, fiery opalescent 1,100.00
Table set: cov. butter dish, creamer, open sugar bowl & spooner; fine rib, single vine, 4 pcs. 325.00
Tumbler, bar 78.00
Tumbler, coarse rib, double vine ... 95.00
Tumbler, fine rib, single vine, w/cut bellflowers 65.00
Wine, barrel-shaped, knob stem, fine rib, single vine, rayed base .. 75.00
Wine, straight sides, plain stem, rayed base 60.00

BIGLER

Bowl, 9 1/8" d., 2 5/8" h. 50.00
Celery vase 75.00
Champagne 95.00
Decanter w/bar lip, pt. 50.00
Goblet, 6" h. 40.00
Honey dish, canary yellow, 4 1/8" d. 110.00
Lamp, whale oil, 7" h. 125.00
Plate, toddy, 4" d. 11.00
Plate, 6" d., amethyst 193.00
Plate, 6" d., canary yellow 135.00
Plate, 6" d., clear 30.00
Sauce dish, canary yellow 95.00
Vase, tulip form, amethyst 935.00
Whiskey, handled, electric blue 95.00
Wine 70.00

BIRD & FERN - **See Hummingbird Pattern**

BIRD & STRAWBERRY (Bluebird)

Berry set, master bowl & 4 sauce dishes, 5 pcs. 150.00
Bowl, 5½" d. 27.00
Bowl, 7½" d., footed 65.00
Bowl, 7½" d., footed, w/color...... 72.50
Bowl, 9½ x 6" oval, footed 48.00
Bowl, 10" d., flat 45.00
Bowl, 10" d., flat, w/color & gold trim 92.00
Butter dish, cov. ....85.00 to 110.00
Butter dish, cov., w/color 205.00
Cake stand, 9" to 9½" d. 53.00
Celery tray, 10" l. 35.00
Compote, cov., 6½" d., 9½" h. 85.00
Compote, cov., 7" d., high stand ... 125.00
Compote, cov., 8" d., low stand 65.00
Compote, open, 4½" d., 5" h. 55.00
Compote, open, 6" d., ruffled rim .. 18.00
Compote, open, 8" d., 6" h. 80.00
Compote, open, 8" d., 6" h., scalloped & ruffled rim, w/color 110.00
Creamer 50.00
Creamer, w/color 118.00
Dish, heart-shaped 50.00

Pitcher, water 238.00
Pitcher, water, w/color 265.00
Punch cup 22.00

Bird & Strawberry Sauce Dish

Sauce dish, flat or footed (ILLUS.) . . . 23.00
Spooner 42.00
Sugar bowl, cov. 55.00
Sugar bowl, open 27.00
Table set, creamer, cov. butter dish & spooner, 3 pcs. 350.00
Table set, w/color, 4 pcs. 450.00
Tumbler 47.00
Tumbler, w/color 57.00
Wine 45.00

BIRD IN RING (Butterfly & Fan)

Bread tray 39.00
Spooner 28.50

BLEEDING HEART

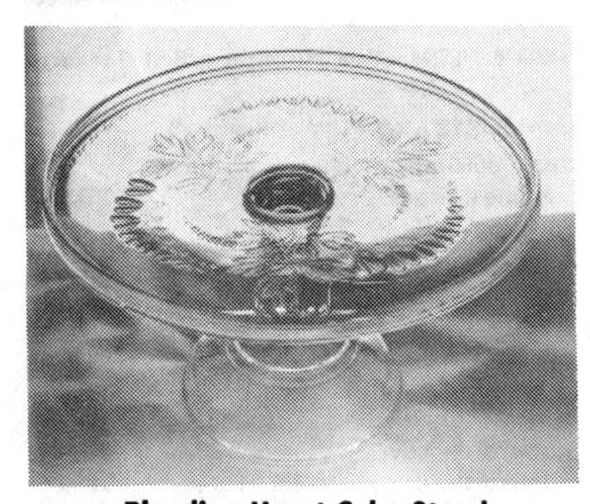

Bleeding Heart Cake Stand

Bowl, cov., 9½" d. 55.00
Bowl, 7¼" oval 27.50
Bowl, 8" 35.00
Bowl, 9¼" oval 30.00
Butter dish, cov. 46.50
Cake stand, 9½" to 11" d. (ILLUS.) . . 60.00
Compote, cov., 7" d., w/Bleeding Heart finial 65.00
Compote, cov., 9" d., 12" h., w/Bleeding Heart finial 115.00
Compote, open, 7" d., 6" h. 25.00
Creamer 40.00
Egg cup 42.00
Goblet, buttermilk 25.00
Goblet, knob stem 32.00
Mug, 3" h. 60.00
Pitcher, water 100.00
Relish, 5 1/8 x 3 5/8" oval 27.00
Salt dip, master size, footed 42.50
Sauce dish, flat 10.00
Spooner 32.00
Sugar bowl, cov. 52.50
Sugar bowl, open 25.00
Table set, 4 pcs. 325.00
Tumbler, flat 75.00
Wine, plain stem 42.50
Wine, knob stem 175.00

BLOCK

(Also see Red Block)

Celery 15.00
Creamer, large 15.00
Pitcher, water 65.00
Punch cup, applied handle 8.00
Spooner 15.00
Sugar bowl, cov. 15.00
Tumbler 32.00
Wine 14.50

BLOCK & FAN

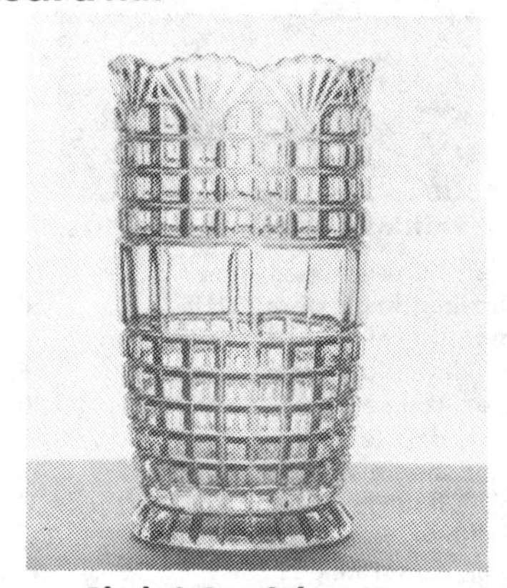

Block & Fan Celery Vase

Bowl, berry, 8" d., footed 22.50
Bowl, 9¾" d. 32.50
Bowl, 10 x 6" rectangle 50.00
Cake stand, 9" to 10" d. 30.00
Carafe, water 47.50
Celery tray 30.00
Celery vase (ILLUS.) 30.00
Compote, open, 8" d., high stand . . . 50.00
Cookie jar, cov. 65.00
Creamer 38.00
Creamer, individual size, ruby-stained 32.50
Cruet w/original stopper, small, 6" h. 22.00
Cruet w/original stopper, medium . . 35.00
Finger bowl 29.50

Goblet 57.50
Goblet, ruby-stained 95.00
Ice bucket 42.50
Pitcher, milk 35.00
Pitcher, water 45.00
Plate, 6" d. 21.50
Plate, 10" d. 19.50
Rose bowl 25.00
Salt shaker w/original top (single) 14.50
Sauce dish, flat or footed 9.25
Sauce flat or footed, ruby-stained 25.00
Spooner, ruby-stained 30.00
Sugar bowl, open 18.00
Sugar shaker w/original top 35.00
Syrup pitcher w/original top, 7" h. 75.00
Tumbler 30.00
Wine 45.00

BLOCK & STAR - See Valencia Waffle Pattern

BLUEBIRD - See Bird & Strawberry Pattern

BOW TIE

Bowl, berry, 8" d. 27.50
Bowl, 10" d., 5" h. 60.00
Butter dish, cov. 80.00
Cake stand, 9" d. 55.00
Compote, open, 5½" d., 10½" h. 60.00
Compote, open, 8" d., low stand 40.00
Compote, open, 9¼" d., high stand 65.00
Compote, open, 10½" d., 10½" h. 70.00
Creamer 43.00
Goblet 43.00
Marmalade jar w/cover 60.00
Marmalade jar (no cover) 32.50
Pitcher, water 70.00
Relish, rectangular 25.00
Salt dip, master size 40.00
Salt shaker w/original top (single) 35.00
Spooner 35.00

BRAZILIAN

Celery vase 30.00
Olive dish, ring handle 15.00
Spooner, emerald green 40.00
Sugar bowl, cov. 35.00

BROKEN COLUMN (Irish Column, Notched Rib or Bamboo)

Banana stand 100.00
Bowl, 7¼" d. 40.00
Bowl, 9" d. 32.00
Butter dish, cov. 60.00
Cake stand, 9" to 10" d. 70.00
Carafe, water 72.50
Celery vase 46.00
Celery vase, w/red notches 155.00
Champagne 65.00
Compote, cov., 5¼" d., 10½" h. 60.00
Compote, cov., 5¼" d., 10½" h., w/red notches 225.00
Compote, cov., 7" d., 12" h. 125.00
Compote, open, jelly, w/red notches 195.00
Compote, open, 5" d., 6" h. 35.00
Compote, open, 6" d., low stand, flared rim 50.00
Compote, open, 7" d., low stand 56.00
Compote, open, 8" d., 8¾" h., w/red notches 186.00
Compote, open, 10" d., low stand 110.00
Cookie jar, cov. 72.00
Creamer 37.50
Creamer, w/red notches 108.00
Cruet w/original stopper 57.00
Decanter w/original stopper, 10½" h. 85.00

Broken Column Goblet

Goblet (ILLUS.) 65.00
Pitcher, water 90.00
Pitcher, water, w/red notches 250.00
Plate, 7" d. 32.50
Plate, 8" d. 35.00
Powder jar, cov. 25.00
Punch cup, blue 75.00
Punch cup 15.00
Relish, 9 x 5" 30.00
Relish, w/red notches, 9 x 5" 110.00
Salt shaker w/original top (single) 30.00
Sauce dish 10.00
Sauce dish, w/red notches 37.50
Spooner 27.00
Spooner, w/red notches 100.00
Sugar bowl, cov. 55.00
Sugar bowl, cov., w/red notches 112.00
Syrup pitcher w/metal top 135.00
Tumbler 39.00
Tumbler, w/red notches 52.00

BRYCE - See Ribbon Candy Pattern

BUCKLE

Bowl, 10" d., rolled edge 75.00
Butter dish, cov. 52.00
Champagne, flint 60.00
Compote, cov., 6" d., 8½" h. 80.00

Compote, open, 8" d., low stand, flint 35.00
Creamer, applied handle, flint 110.00
Creamer, small size, non-flint 25.00
Egg cup, flint 38.00
Egg cup, non-flint 25.00
Goblet, flint 34.00

Buckle Goblet

Goblet, non-flint (ILLUS.) 20.00
Goblet, buttermilk, non-flint 24.00
Lamp, kerosene-type, brass & iron base 165.00
Lamp, kerosene-type, clear font, clambroth base 125.00
Pitcher, water, bulbous, applied handle, non-flint 85.00
Salt dip, master size, footed, flint .. 35.00
Sauce dish, flint ....10.00 to 15.00
Sauce dish, non-flint 7.00
Spooner, flint 37.50
Spooner, non-flint 23.00
Sugar bowl, cov., w/acorn finial, flint 65.00
Sugar bowl, cov., w/acorn finial, non-flint 43.00
Sugar bowl, open, non-flint 20.00
Tumbler, non-flint 29.00
Wine, flint 77.50
Wine, non-flint 27.50

BUCKLE WITH STAR

Bowl, 8" oval 15.00
Butter dish, cov. 35.00
Cake stand, 9" d. 35.00
Celery vase 32.00
Compote, cov., 7" d. (ILLUS.) 60.00
Compote, open, 7" d., 5½" h. 19.50
Compote, open, 10" d., 7" h. 30.00
Creamer 35.00
Goblet 25.00
Salt dip 25.00
Sauce dish, flat or footed .....5.00 to 12.00
Spillholder 50.00
Spooner 20.00
Sugar bowl, cov. 42.50

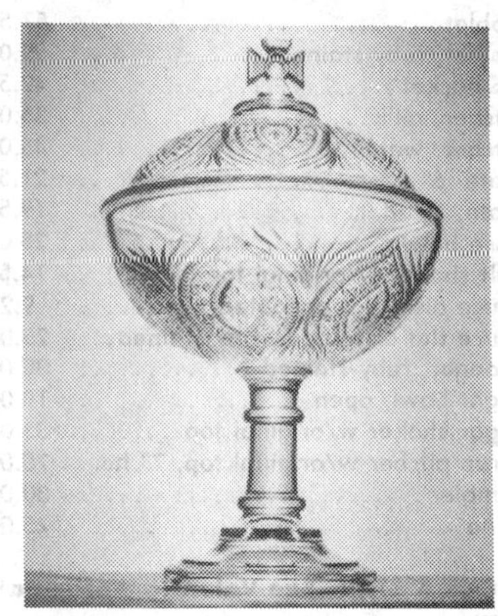

Buckle with Star Compote

Sugar bowl, open 25.00
Tumbler, bar 65.00
Wine 26.00

BULL'S EYE

Celery vase, flint 85.00
Cordial, flint 45.00
Creamer, applied handle, flint 110.00
Decanter w/bar lip, flint, qt. 120.00
Egg cup, flint 47.00
Egg cup, opaque blue 575.00
Goblet, flint 72.00
Salt dip, individual size, rectangular 32.50
Salt dip, master size, footed, flint .. 32.50
Spillholder, flint 32.50
Spooner, flint 95.00
Sugar bowl, cov., flint 135.00
Tumbler, flat, flint 75.00
Wine, knob stem, flint 47.00

BULL'S EYE VARIANT - See Texas Bull's Eye Pattern

BULL'S EYE WITH DIAMOND POINT

Bull's Eye with Diamond Point Goblet

Celery vase 147.00
Cologne bottle 85.00
Creamer, applied handle 175.00
Goblet (ILLUS.) 120.00
Honey dish 30.00
Salt dip, master size 45.00
Salt dip, basket-shaped 85.00
Sauce dish 25.00
Spillholder 75.00
Spooner 135.00
Tumbler, bar 138.00
Wine 120.00

BULL'S EYE WITH FLEUR DE LIS

Bull's Eye with Fleur de Lis Goblet

Bowl, 7½" d. 75.00
Butter dish, cov. 95.00
Creamer 65.00
Goblet (ILLUS.) 75.00
Lamp, kerosene-type, pear-shaped font w/brass standard on marble base 150.00
Salt dip, master size 52.50
Sugar bowl, cov. 135.00
Sugar bowl, open 55.00

BUTTERFLY & FAN - **See Bird in Ring Pattern**

BUTTON ARCHES

Button Arches Tumbler with Engraving

Basket, ruby-stained handle 25.00
Berry set: 8" d. master bowl & 6 sauce dishes; ruby-stained, 7 pcs. 58.00
Bowl, 8" d., ruby-stained, souvenir 45.00
Butter dish, cov., clear 48.00
Butter dish, cov., ruby-stained, souvenir 65.00
Compote, open, jelly, 4½" h., ruby-stained 45.00
Creamer, clear 18.50
Creamer, ruby-stained 42.50
Creamer, ruby-stained, souvenir, 4½" h. 45.00
Creamer, individual size, ruby-stained . . . . 18.50 to 25.00
Cruet w/original stopper, ruby-stained 175.00
Goblet, clambroth 28.50
Goblet, clear 24.00
Goblet, ruby-stained 37.50
Mug, ruby-stained 25.00
Mug, ruby-stained, souvenir, 3½" h. 30.00
Pitcher, 7" h., ruby-stained, souvenir 60.00
Pitcher, tankard, 8¾" h., clear 100.00
Pitcher, water, tankard, 12" h., ruby-stained 115.00
Punch cup, clear 10.00
Punch cup, ruby-stained 17.50
Salt shaker w/original top, ruby-stained (single) 26.00
Sauce dish, ruby-stained 35.00
Spooner, clear 27.50
Spooner, ruby-stained & etched 42.50
Sugar bowl, cov., clear 30.00
Sugar bowl, cov., ruby-stained 65.00
Sugar bowl, cov., ruby-stained & etched . . . . 65.00 to 80.00
Syrup pitcher w/original top, clear . . 40.00
Syrup pitcher w/original top, ruby-stained 125.00
Table set, ruby-stained, 4 pcs. 235.00
Toothpick holder, clear 14.50
Toothpick holder, ruby-stained 30.00
Tumbler, clear 17.50
Tumbler, ruby-stained 34.00
Tumbler, ruby-stained, souvenir (ILLUS.) 29.00
Water set: pitcher & 5 tumblers; clear w/frosted band & gold, 6 pcs. 225.00
Water set: pitcher & 6 tumblers; ruby-stained, 7 pcs. 256.00
Whiskey shot glass, ruby-stained . . . 14.50
Wine, clambroth 25.00
Wine, clear 15.00
Wine, ruby-stained, souvenir 32.50

CABBAGE LEAF

Butter dish, cov., frosted 500.00
Celery vase, clear & frosted 85.00

Custard cup, frosted, marked Libbey Glass Co., "Columbian Expo" on base 80.00
Pitcher, water, frosted 135.00
Rose bowl, amber 175.00
Sauce dish, frosted, w/rabbit center 45.00

CABBAGE ROSE

Cabbage Rose Tumbler

Bitters bottle, 6½" h. 100.00
Bowl, master berry, 9" oval 40.00
Butter dish, cov. 62.50
Cake stand, 9½" to 12½" d. 54.00
Celery vase 50.00
Champagne 42.50
Compote, cov., 6" d., low stand 95.00
Compote, cov., 7½" d., high stand 110.00
Compote, cov., 8½" d., 7" h. 120.00
Compote, open, 7½" d., high stand 70.00
Compote, open, 9½" d., low stand 90.00
Compote, open, 9½" d., high stand 100.00
Cordial 50.00
Creamer, applied handle 56.00
Dish, 7" d. .... 25.00 to 32.50
Egg cup 33.00
Goblet 36.00
Goblet, buttermilk 46.00
Mug, child's 65.00
Pickle or relish, 7½" to 8½" l. 27.50
Pitcher, water, qt. 125.00
Pitcher, 3-pint 165.00
Salt dip, master size 20.00
Sauce dish 20.00
Spooner 28.00
Sugar bowl, cov. 55.00
Sugar bowl, open 40.00
Tumbler (ILLUS.) 40.00
Wine 42.50

CABLE

Bowl, 8" d. 45.00
Bowl, 9" d. 70.00
Butter dish, cov. 88.00
Celery vase 68.00
Compote, open, 7" d., 5" h. 55.00
Compote, open, 8" d., 4¾" h. 65.00
Compote, open, 9" d., 4½" h. 55.00
Creamer .... 365.00 to 500.00
Decanter w/bar lip, qt. .... 95.00 to 125.00
Decanter w/stopper, qt. 295.00
Egg cup, cov., blue opaque, 5¼" h. 2,200.00
Egg cup, clambroth, flint 550.00
Egg cup, clear 40.00
Goblet 60.00
Honey dish, 3½" d., 1" h. 12.00
Lamp, whale oil, 11" h. 122.50
Plate, 6" d. 85.00
Salt dip, master size 35.00
Sauce dish 25.00
Spooner, clambroth 185.00
Spooner, clear 35.00
Spooner, starch blue w/original gilt decor of grape leaves 1,500.00
Sugar bowl, cov. 95.00
Wine 77.50

CABLE WITH RING

Lamp, kerosene-type, w/ring handle, flint 175.00
Lamp, whale oil, clambroth font, flint, reeded brass stem, marble base 325.00
Sugar bowl, cov., flint 78.00

CALIFORNIA - See Beaded Grape Pattern

CAMEO - See Classic Medallion Pattern

CANADIAN

Canadian Wine

Bowl, berry, 7" d., 4½" h., footed 75.00
Bread plate, handled, 10" d. 50.00
Butter dish, cov. 85.00
Cake stand, 9¾" d., 5" h. .... 32.50 to 50.00
Celery vase 55.00
Compote, cov., 6" d., 9" h. 124.00

Compote, cov., 7" d., 11" h. 85.00
Compote, open, 6" d., footed 40.00
Compote, open, 8" d., 5" h. 45.00
Creamer 48.00
Goblet 55.00
Pitcher, milk, 8" h. 140.00
Pitcher, water 92.50
Plate, 8" d., handled 30.00
Sauce dish, flat or footed .... 12.50 to 28.00
Spooner 45.00
Sugar bowl, cov. 75.00
Wine (ILLUS.) 40.00

CANE

Cane Water Pitcher

Bread platter, amber 125.00
Candlestick, clear (single) 15.00
Creamer, amber 30.00
Creamer, clear 25.00
Goblet, amber 25.00
Goblet, apple green 35.00
Goblet, blue 35.00
Goblet, clear 16.00
Goblet, vaseline 39.00
Match holder, model of a cauldron, amber 18.00
Match holder, model of a cauldron, blue 16.00
Pickle castor w/tongs, amber 150.00
Pitcher, water, amber 57.00
Pitcher, water, apple green 47.00
Pitcher, water, blue 61.50
Pitcher, water, clear (ILLUS.) 40.00
Plate, 6" d., amber 12.00
Relish, blue 50.00
Relish, clear, 8 x 5¼" oval 12.50
Sauce dish, footed, clear 10.50
Spooner, amber 42.00
Spooner, apple green 35.00
Sugar bowl, cov., amber 55.00
Toddy plate, amber, 4½" d. 12.00
Toddy plate, apple green, 4½" d. .. 12.00
Toddy plate, blue, 4½" d. 16.50
Toddy plate, clear, 4½" d. 14.00
Tray, water, blue 60.00
Tumbler, blue 25.00

Waste bowl, amber or apple green, each 30.00

CANNON BALL - See Atlas Pattern

CAPE COD

Cape Cod Spooner

Bowl, 6" d., handled 20.00
Bowl, 8" d. 32.00
Bread platter 55.00
Compote, cov., 8" d., 12" h. 130.00
Compote, open, 7" d., 6" h. 37.00
Compote, open, 8" d., 5½" h. 37.50
Cruet w/original stopper 25.00
Goblet 42.00
Pitcher, water 95.00
Plate, 10" d., open handles 30.00
Sauce dish, flat or footed .... 14.00 to 18.50
Spooner (ILLUS.) 35.00

CARDINAL BIRD

Cardinal Bird Footed Sauce Dish

Butter dish, cov. 65.00
Butter dish, cov., 3 unidentified birds 100.00
Creamer 35.00
Goblet 32.00
Honey dish, open 18.50
Sauce dish, flat or footed (ILLUS.) ... 16.00
Spooner 35.50
Sugar bowl, cov. 60.00

CATHEDRAL

Bowl, 6" d., clear 20.00

Cathedral Compote

Bowl, 6" d., crimped rim, vaseline .. 35.00
Bowl, berry, 8" d., amber 48.00
Bowl, berry, 8" d., amethyst 60.00
Butter dish, cov., clear 42.50
Cake stand, blue, 10" d., 4½" h. 45.00
Cake stand, vaseline 65.00
Compote, cov., 7¼" d., 10½" h., clear 75.00
Compote, open, 7" d., fluted rim, amber 30.00
Compote, open, 7½" d., high stand, fluted rim, amethyst 145.00
Compote, open, 9" d., 5½" h., amber 50.00
Compote, open, 9" d., 5½" h., blue 65.00
Compote, open, 9" d., 7" h., amethyst 75.00
Compote, open, 9" d., 7" h., clear .. 55.00
Compote, open, 10" d., 6" h., amethyst 58.00
Compote, open, 10½" d., 8" h., shaped rim, clear (ILLUS.) 55.00
Creamer, clear 22.50
Creamer, ruby-stained 50.00
Cruet w/original stopper, amber 58.00
Goblet, amber 40.00
Goblet, amethyst 70.00
Goblet, clear 27.50
Goblet, vaseline 60.00
Pitcher, water, ruby-stained 145.00
Relish, fish-shaped, amber 35.00
Relish, fish-shaped, blue 38.00
Salt dip, master size, amber 25.00
Sauce dish, flat or footed, amethyst 35.00
Sauce dish, flat or footed, blue 22.00
Sauce dish, flat or footed, clear 10.00
Sauce dish, flat or footed, ruby-stained ....15.00 to 22.00
Sauce dish, flat or footed, vaseline ....12.00 to 24.00
Spooner, amber 42.50
Spooner, clear 27.50
Spooner, vaseline 42.50
Sugar bowl, cov., clear 40.00
Sugar bowl, cov., ruby-stained 70.00
Sugar bowl, open, clear 22.50
Table set: creamer, sugar bowl & spooner; vaseline, 3 pcs. 75.00
Tumbler, clear 25.00
Tumbler, ruby-stained 42.50
Wine, amber 38.00
Wine, blue 49.00
Wine, clear 27.00
Wine, ruby-stained 45.00
Wine, vaseline 37.50

CERES (Goddess of Liberty)

Compote, open, 6" d., low stand, clear 25.00
Creamer, clear 22.50
Mug, blue 22.50
Mug, clear 17.50
Mug, purple-black 53.00
Spooner, milk white 22.00
Sugar bowl, open, clear 20.00

CHAIN

Chain Sauce Dish

Bread plate 27.00
Butter dish, cov. 35.00
Compote, cov., 7½" d., 12" h........ 45.00
Creamer 18.50
Creamer & cov. sugar bowl, pr. 35.00
Goblet 18.00
Plate, 7" d. 14.50
Relish, 8" oval 11.00
Sauce dish, flat or footed (ILLUS.) 8.50
Spooner 22.00
Sugar bowl, cov. 35.00
Wine 17.00

CHAIN & SHIELD

Creamer 25.00
Goblet 24.00
Pitcher, water 50.00
Platter, oval 25.00

CHAIN WITH STAR

Bread plate, handled 33.00
Butter dish, cov. 32.50
Cake stand, 8¾" to 10" d. ....30.00 to 42.50
Compote, jelly 17.00
Compote, open, 8" d., 4" h. 18.50
Compote, open, 8" d., 6½" h. 20.00
Compote, open, 9½" d. 29.00
Creamer 25.00

Goblet 20.00
Pickle dish, oval 12.50
Pitcher, water 55.00

Chain With Star Plate

Plate, 7" d. (ILLUS.) 16.50
Relish 15.00
Sauce dish 12.50
Spooner 22.50
Sugar bowl, cov. 37.50
Syrup pitcher (no lid) 45.00
Wine 27.50

CHANDELIER (Crown Jewel)

Bowl, 8" d., 3¼" h. 25.00
Butter dish, cov. 60.00
Cake stand, 10" d. 67.50

Chandelier Celery Vase

Celery vase (ILLUS.) 32.50
Compote, open, 8" d., high stand, etched 95.00
Creamer 45.00
Goblet 52.00
Inkwell 70.00
Salt dip, footed 36.00
Sauce dish, amber 35.00
Sauce dish, flat, clear 12.00
Spooner 26.50

Sugar bowl, cov. 37.50
Sugar shaker w/original top 60.00
Tumbler 35.00
Wine 32.00

CHECKERBOARD (Barred Hobstar)

Bowl, 9" d., flat 20.00
Butter dish, cov. 42.50
Celery tray 30.00
Compote, jelly 25.00
Creamer .... 12.00 to 20.00
Cruet w/blown stopper 40.00
Goblet 20.00
Honey dish, cov., 5" w. 35.00
Pitcher, milk 35.00
Pitcher, water 30.00
Punch cup 4.50
Sauce dish, flat 14.50
Sauce dish, flat, ruby-stained, gilt trim, 4½" d. 14.50
Spooner 22.50
Sugar bowl, cov. 30.00
Tumbler 15.00
Wine 17.50

CHERRY THUMBPRINT - See Paneled Cherry With Thumbprints Pattern

CLASSIC

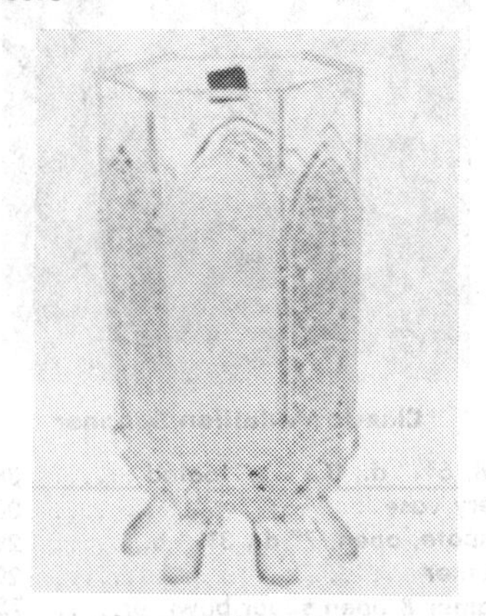

Classic Celery Vase

Berry set, master bowl & 4 sauce dishes, 5 pcs. 275.00
Bowl, cov., 7" hexagon, open log feet 145.00
Bowl, open, 8" hexagon, open log feet 98.00
Butter dish, cov., open log feet 175.00
Celery vase, collared base 142.00
Celery vase, open log feet (ILLUS.) 170.00
Compote, cov., 6½" d., collared base 150.00
Compote, cov., 7½" d., 8" h., open log feet 200.00
Compote, cov., 10" d., open log feet 295.00

Compote, open, 7¾" d., open log feet 160.00
Creamer, collared base 105.00
Creamer, open log feet 150.00
Goblet .... 195.00 to 225.00
Pitcher, milk, 8½" h., open log feet .... 450.00 to 600.00
Pitcher, water, collared base 280.00
Pitcher, water, 9½" h., open log feet 325.00
Plate, 10" d., "Blaine" or "Hendricks," signed Jacobus, each 185.00
Plate, 10" d., "Warrior" 134.00
Plate, 10" d., "Warrior," signed Jacobus 160.00
Sauce dish, collared base 30.00
Sauce dish, open log feet 28.00
Spooner, collared base 90.00
Spooner, open log feet 105.00
Sugar bowl, open, collared base 115.00
Sugar bowl, open, log feet 150.00

CLASSIC MEDALLION (Cameo)

Classic Medallion Spooner

Bowl, 6¾" d., 3½" h., footed 38.00
Celery vase 30.00
Compote, open, 7" d., 3¾" h. 29.00
Creamer 29.00
Creamer & open sugar bowl, pr. 75.00
Pitcher, water 52.50
Sauce dish, footed 9.00
Spooner (ILLUS.) 25.50

COLLINS - See Crystal Wedding Pattern

COLONIAL (Empire Colonial)

Celery vase, flint 75.00
Claret, 5½" h. (ILLUS.) 47.50
Goblet, flint 55.00
Plate, 6¼" d., canary yellow 225.00
Salt dip, master size 17.50
Spooner 40.00
Sugar bowl, cov. 95.00
Tumbler, footed, flint 34.00
Wine, flint 75.00

Colonial Claret

COLORADO

Berry set: master bowl & 6 sauce dishes; green w/gold, 7 pcs. 137.50
Bowl, 5" d., ruffled rim, blue 35.00
Bowl, 5" d., flared edge, clear 20.00
Bowl, 5" d., green w/gold 45.00
Bowl, 7" d., footed, scalloped rim, blue 25.00
Bowl, 7" d., footed, clear 20.00
Bowl, 7½" d., footed, turned-up sides, blue w/gold 55.00
Bowl, 7½" d., footed, turned-up sides, green 30.00
Bowl, 8½" d., footed, crimped edge, green 35.00
Bowl, 9" d., footed, 3 turned-up sides, clear 29.00
Bowl, 9" d., green w/gold 36.50
Bowl, 10" d., footed, fluted, green 39.00
Butter dish, cov., clear 65.00
Butter dish, cov., green 115.00
Cake stand, clear 50.00
Card tray, blue 40.00
Card tray, clear 20.00
Card tray, green 32.50
Celery vase, green 48.00
Compote, open, 6" d., 4" h., crimped rim, clear 25.00
Compote, open, 8" d., 7" h., beaded rim, green 77.50
Compote, open, 9½" d., blue 95.00
Compote, open, 10½" d., high stand, blue 215.00
Creamer, blue 85.00
Creamer, clear 32.00
Creamer, clear, individual size 34.00
Creamer, green w/gold, individual size 32.50
Creamer, green w/gold, large 57.00
Creamer, green w/gold, souvenir 35.00
Cup, clear 11.00
Cup, green 30.00
Cup, green, souvenir 25.00

Custard cup, green, large 28.00
Dish, clear, 6" sq. 15.00
Mug, clear, souvenir 18.50
Mug, green, souvenir 34.00
Nappy, tricornered, blue w/gold 38.00
Nappy, tricornered, clear 20.00
Nappy, tricornered, green w/gold .. 32.50
Pitcher, 6" h., green w/gold 42.00
Pitcher, water, green w/gold 176.00
Plate, 7" d., footed, clear 17.50
Punch cup, clear 13.50
Punch cup, green 25.00
Punch cup, green w/gold, souvenir..................20.00 to 30.00
Salt dip, master size, footed, clear 30.00
Salt & pepper shakers w/original tops, green, pr. 95.00
Sauce dish, blue w/gold 27.00
Sauce dish, clear 12.00
Sauce dish, green w/gold 27.00
Sauce dish, green, souvenir 35.00
Spooner, clear 25.00
Spooner, green w/gold 55.00
Sugar bowl, cov., large, clear 30.00
Sugar bowl, cov., individual size, green 35.00
Sugar bowl, cov., large, green 85.00
Sugar bowl, open, large, clear 25.00
Sugar bowl, open, large, green..... 32.50
Sugar bowl, open, individual size, blue or green, each 27.50
Table set: creamer, cov. sugar bowl & cov. butter dish; blue w/gold, 3 pcs. 395.00
Table set, green w/gold, 4 pcs. 350.00
Toothpick holder, blue w/gold...... 41.00
Toothpick holder, clear w/gold 23.00

Colorado Toothpick Holder

Toothpick holder, green w/gold (ILLUS.)......................... 30.00
Toothpick holder, green w/gold, souvenir........................ 27.00
Tumbler, green w/gold 31.00
Vase, 10½" h., blue 80.00
Vase, 12" h., trumpet-shaped, blue w/gold 100.00
Vase, 12" h., trumpet-shaped, green 55.00
Vase, 14½" h., green w/gold 60.00
Violet vase, blue 28.00
Wine, clear 20.00
Wine, green w/gold 28.00

Wine, green, souvenir 35.00
Wine, ruby-stained w/gold 40.00

COLUMBIAN COIN

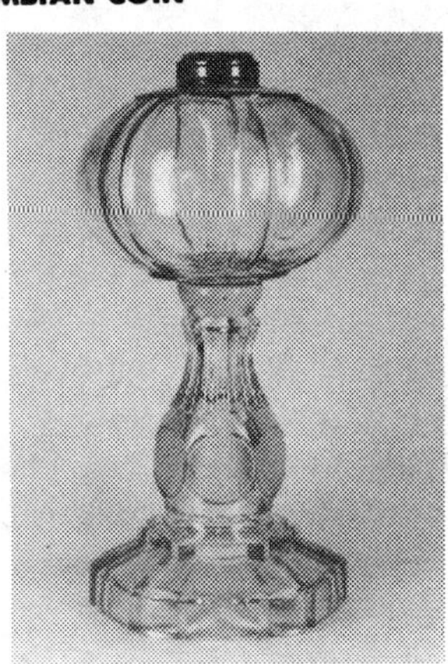

Columbian Coin Lamp

Butter dish, cov., frosted coins..................125.00 to 175.00
Butter dish, cov., gilded coins 175.00
Celery vase, frosted coins.......... 85.00
Celery vase, gilded coins 90.00
Claret, gilded coins................ 75.00
Compote, open, 8" d., clear coins .. 68.00
Creamer, gilded coins 150.00
Goblet, gilded coins 67.50
Lamp, kerosene-type, 9½" h. 165.00
Lamp, kerosene-type, frosted coins, 12" h. (ILLUS.) 180.00
Pitcher, milk, gilded coins 165.00
Pitcher, water, 10" h., gilded coins..................125.00 to 145.00
Salt & pepper shakers w/original tops, frosted coins, pr. 100.00
Sauce dish, flat or footed, gilded coins 32.50
Spooner, frosted coins 42.50
Spooner, gilded coins.............. 47.50
Syrup pitcher w/original top, clear coins 125.00
Syrup pitcher w/original top, frosted coins 180.00
Toothpick holder, frosted coins 95.00
Toothpick holder, gilded coins 135.00
Toothpick holder, red coins 195.00
Tumbler, gilded coins.............. 55.00
Wine, frosted coins..........55.00 to 80.00

COMET (Early Comet)

Goblet 80.00
Spooner 95.00
Sugar bowl, cov. 175.00
Tumbler, bar...................... 95.00
Tumbler, water 110.00
Tumbler, whiskey, handled......... 250.00

COMPACT - See Snail Pattern

CORD & TASSEL

Cord & Tassel Creamer

Bowl, oval 20.00
Butter dish, cov. 48.00
Cake stand, 9½" d. 44.00
Castor bottle 32.00
Compote, open, 8" d., low stand 26.50
Creamer (ILLUS.) 32.00
Goblet 34.00
Lamp, kerosene-type, applied handle 85.00
Pitcher, water 95.00
Salt & pepper shakers w/original tops, pr. 55.00
Sauce dish, flat 7.50
Spooner 23.00
Sugar bowl, open 26.00
Syrup pitcher w/original top, applied handle 110.00
Table set, creamer, open sugar bowl & spooner, 3 pcs. 68.00
Wine 35.00

CORD DRAPERY - *See Greentown "Special Focus"*

CORDOVA

Banana stand 90.00
Butter dish, cov. 50.00
Celery vase 45.00
Cologne bottle, 5" h. 20.00
Creamer 22.50
Creamer, individual size 35.00
Creamer & cov. sugar bowl, pr. 65.00
Mug 16.50
Pitcher, milk 30.00
Pitcher, water 52.50
Punch cup 7.50
Spooner 27.50
Sugar bowl, cov. .... 35.00 to 40.00
Sugar bowl, cov., individual size 40.00
Syrup pitcher w/pewter top .... 85.00 to 125.00
Toothpick holder 22.50
Tumbler 15.00
Vase, bud 15.00

Water set, pitcher & 5 tumblers, 6 pcs. 95.00

CORD ROSETTE

Goblet .... 30.00 to 40.00
Lamp, kerosene, pedestal base, original burner 70.00

COTTAGE (Dinner Bell or Finecut Band)

Cottage Goblet

Bowl, berry, 9¼ x 6½" oval, clear .. 16.00
Butter dish, cov., clear 42.00
Butter dish, cov., green 78.00
Cake stand, amber 50.00
Cake stand, clear 41.00
Celery vase, clear 29.00
Champagne, clear 52.50
Compote, cov., 7" d., high stand, clear 30.00
Compote, open, jelly, 4½" d., 4" h., blue 28.50
Compote, open, jelly, 4½" d., 4" h., clear 27.00
Compote, open, jelly, 4½" d., 4" h., green 39.00
Creamer, amber 76.50
Creamer, clear 22.00
Cruet w/original stopper, clear 37.50
Cup & saucer, clear 35.00
Finger bowl, clear 15.00
Goblet, amber 45.00
Goblet, clear (ILLUS.) 24.00
Pitcher, milk, amber 60.00
Pitcher, milk, clear 35.00
Pitcher, water, clear, 2-qt. 40.00
Plate, 5" d., clear 11.50
Plate, 6" d., clear 12.00
Plate, 7" d., clear 18.00
Plate, 9" d., clear 35.00
Plate, 10" d., clear 45.00
Salt shaker w/original top, clear (single) 25.00
Sauce dish, clear 7.50
Saucer, clear, 6" d. 10.00
Saucer, green, 6" d. 20.00

Spooner, clear 20.00
Sugar bowl, cov., clear 47.00
Sugar bowl, open, clear 14.00
Syrup pitcher w/original top, clear .. 57.50
Tray, water, clear 27.50
Tumbler, clear 20.00
Waste bowl, clear 38.00
Wine, blue 45.00
Wine, clear 21.00

CROESUS

Croesus Covered Sugar

Berry set: master bowl & 6 sauce dishes; green, 7 pcs. 325.00
Berry set: master bowl & 6 sauce dishes; purple, 7 pcs. 425.00
Bowl, 6¾" d., 4" h., footed, green w/gold 65.00
Bowl, 6¾" d., 4" h., footed, purple w/gold 185.00
Bowl, 8" d., green 100.00
Bowl, 8" d., purple 175.00
Bowl, berry or fruit, 9" d., green .... 100.00 to 125.00
Bowl, berry or fruit, 9" d., purple ... 155.00
Butter dish, cov., clear 75.00
Butter dish, cov., green 132.00
Butter dish, cov., purple 204.00
Celery vase, green w/gold 135.00
Compote, open, jelly, purple 255.00
Condiment set: cruet, salt & pepper shakers & tray; green w/gold, 4 pcs. 365.00
Condiment set: cruet, salt & pepper shakers & tray; purple w/gold, 4 pcs. 375.00
Condiment tray, clear 27.00
Condiment tray, green 60.00
Creamer, green 70.00
Creamer, purple 145.00
Creamer, individual size, green, 3" h. 193.00
Creamer, individual size, purple, 3" h. 165.00
Creamer & cov. sugar bowl, green, pr. 225.00
Cruet w/original stopper, green 184.00
Cruet w/original stopper, purple ... 350.00
Cruet w/original stopper, miniature, green w/gold, 4" h. 85.00
Cruet w/original stopper, miniature, purple, 4" h. 189.00
Pickle, purple 78.00
Pitcher, water, green 225.00
Pitcher, water, purple 550.00
Plate, 8" d., scalloped rim, green w/gold 110.00
Salt & pepper shakers w/original tops, green, pr. .... 120.00 to 135.00
Salt & pepper shakers w/original tops, purple, pr. 143.00
Sauce dish, clear 13.50
Sauce dish, green w/gold 34.00
Sauce dish, purple w/gold 45.00
Spooner, green 65.00
Spooner, purple 114.00
Sugar bowl, cov., green 110.00
Sugar bowl, cov., purple (ILLUS.) ... 174.00
Sugar bowl, open, green 85.00
Table set: creamer, cov. sugar bowl, cov. butter dish & spooner; green, 4 pcs. 398.00
Table set, purple, 4 pcs. 603.00
Toothpick holder, clear 25.00
Toothpick holder, green 81.00
Toothpick holder, purple 95.00
Tumbler, green 39.00
Tumbler, purple 57.00
Water set: pitcher & 6 tumblers; green, 7 pcs. 695.00
Water set: pitcher & 6 tumblers; purple, 7 pcs. 850.00

CROWFOOT (Turkey Track)

Butter dish, cov. 55.00
Cake stand, 9" d. 48.00
Goblet 32.50
Sauce dish, flat 12.00
Spooner 24.50

CROWN JEWEL - See Chandelier Pattern

CRYSTAL WEDDING (Collins)

(Items may be plain or with etched designs)

Banana stand, 10"h 87.00
Berry set, 8" sq. bowl & 6 sauce dishes, 7 pcs. 125.00
Bowl, cov., 7" sq. 75.00
Butter dish, cov. 65.00
Butter dish, cov., ruby-stained 75.00
Cake stand, 9" sq., 8" h. 57.50
Cake stand, 10" sq. 75.00
Celery vase 45.00
Compote, cov., 4" sq., 6½" h. 35.00
Compote, cov., 6" sq., 9½" h. 52.50
Compote, cov., 7" sq. 85.00
Compote, cov., 11" 60.00
Compote, open, 4" sq., 6" h. 22.50

Compote, open, 5" sq. 42.50
Compote, open, 6¼" sq., 8" h., scalloped rim 45.00
Compote, open, 7" sq., 8¾" h. 75.00
Compote, open, 8" sq., low stand .. 36.00
Creamer 45.00
Creamer, ruby-stained 52.50
Creamer & cov. sugar bowl, amber-stained, pr. ....180.00 to 195.00
Cruet w/original stopper, amber-stained 175.00
Goblet 40.00
Goblet, ruby-stained 64.00
Lamp, base, kerosene-type, square font, 10" h. 375.00
Pitcher, water 125.00
Salt dip 35.00
Salt shaker w/original top, ruby-stained (single) 68.00
Sauce dish 12.00
Spooner, amber-stained 45.00
Spooner 35.00
Spooner, ruby-stained 55.00
Sugar bowl, cov. 48.00

Crystal Wedding Sugar Bowl

Sugar bowl, cov., ruby-stained (ILLUS.) 100.00
Sugar bowl, open, scalloped rim 30.00
Syrup pitcher w/original top, ruby-stained 210.00
Table set: cov. butter dish, cov. sugar bowl, creamer & spooner; ruby-stained, 4 pcs. 400.00
Tumbler 38.50
Wine 68.00

CUPID & VENUS (Guardian Angel)

Bowl, cov., 8" d., footed 125.00
Bowl, 6½" d. 20.00
Bowl, 9" d., scalloped rim, footed .. 37.50
Bread plate, amber, 10½" d. 115.00
Bread plate, 10½" d. 35.00
Butter dish, cov. 55.00
Cake plate 40.00
Celery vase 45.00
Champagne 62.50
Compote, cov., 7" d., high stand ... 110.00
Compote, cov., 9½" d., low stand .. 95.00
Compote, open, 6" d., low stand 35.00
Compote, open, 8½" d., low stand, scalloped rim 40.00
Cordial 85.00
Creamer 36.50
Goblet 65.00
Goblet, buttermilk 50.00
Honey dish, 3½" d. 7.50
Marmalade jar, cov. 85.00
Mug, 2½" h. 30.00
Mug, 3½" h. 34.00
Pickle castor w/resilvered frame, cover & tongs 80.00
Pitcher, milk, amber 190.00
Pitcher, milk 55.00
Pitcher, water 50.00
Sauce dish, footed, 3½" to 4½" d. 10.00
Spooner 38.00
Sugar bowl, cov. 65.00
Wine 103.00

CURRANT

Butter dish, cov. 75.00
Cake stand, 9¼" d., 4¼" h. 75.00
Cake stand, 11" d. 65.00
Celery vase 40.00
Compote, cov., 8" d., high stand ... 195.00
Compote, open, 10½" d. 50.00
Creamer 38.00
Egg cup 20.00
Goblet 30.00
Goblet, buttermilk 40.00
Honey dish, 3½" d. 16.00
Pitcher, water 70.00
Relish, 8 x 5" 12.00
Spooner 26.00
Wine 37.50

CURRIER & IVES

Currier & Ives Lamp

Bitters bottle 38.00
Bowl, master berry or fruit, 10" oval, flat w/collared base 33.00

Bread plate, Balky Mule on Railroad Tracks, blue 85.00
Bread plate, Balky Mule on Railroad Tracks 50.00
Bread plate, children sawing felled log, frosted center 75.00
Compote, cov., 7½" d., high stand 95.00
Compote, open, 7½" d., 9" h., scalloped rim........................ 45.00
Creamer 30.00
Cup 15.00
Cup & saucer, blue 85.00
Decanter w/original stopper 55.00
Goblet 20.00
Lamp, kerosene-type, 11" h. (ILLUS.)........................ 70.00
Pitcher, milk 46.00
Pitcher, water, amber 110.00
Pitcher, water 53.00
Relish, 10" oval ....16.00 to 20.00
Salt shaker w/original top, amber (single)........................ 45.00
Salt shaker w/original top, blue (single)........................ 55.00
Salt shaker w/original top (single) .. 19.00
Salt shaker w/original top, vaseline (single)........................ 52.50
Salt & pepper shakers w/original tops, blue, pr. 90.00
Salt & pepper shakers w/original tops, pr........................ 58.00
Sauce dish, flat or footed, amber ... 20.00
Sauce dish, flat or footed, blue 25.00
Sauce dish, flat or footed 10.00
Spooner 23.00
Sugar bowl, cov. ....35.00 to 45.00
Syrup jug w/original top, blue...... 202.00
Syrup jug w/original top 82.50
Tray, wine, 9½" d. 48.00
Tray, water, Balky Mule on Railroad Tracks, blue, 12" d. 110.00
Tray, water, Balky Mule on Railroad Tracks, 12" d.................. 64.00
Tray, water, Balky Mule on Railroad Tracks, vaseline, 12" d...100.00 to 125.00
Waste bowl........................ 43.00
Wine 16.00
Wine set, decanter w/original stopper & 6 wines, 7 pcs. 180.00

CURTAIN

Bowl, 7½" d., ... 25.00
Butter dish, cov. 50.00
Cake stand, 9½" d. 36.00
Celery boat 48.50
Celery vase 30.00
Compote, open, 10" d., 8" h. 35.00
Condiment set, pr. salt & pepper shakers & mustard jar, 3 pcs. 65.00
Creamer ....25.00 to 35.00
Goblet 35.00
Mug, amber 65.00

Curtain Salt Shaker

Salt shaker w/original top (ILLUS.) .. 15.00
Salt & pepper shakers (no tops), pr........................ 24.00
Sauce dish, flat or footed, 4¾" d. ... 8.00
Spooner 25.00
Sugar bowl, cov. 40.00
Tumbler 20.00

CURTAIN TIEBACK

Curtain Tieback Celery

Bowl, 7½" sq., flat 18.00
Bread tray 37.00
Butter dish, cov. 38.00
Cake stand, 9" d., 6½" h. 25.00
Celery vase (ILLUS.) 30.00
Compote, cov., 7½" d., low stand .. 28.00
Creamer 35.00
Goblet 25.00
Pitcher, water 55.00
Relish 10.00
Sauce dish, flat or footed ....10.00 to 15.00
Spooner 28.00
Sugar bowl, cov. 30.00

CUT LOG

Bowl, cov., 3" d. 16.00
Bowl, 8½" d., scalloped rim........ 27.50

Bowl, master berry or fruit, 10½" d., footed . . . 40.00
Butter dish, cov. . . . 65.00 to 70.00
Cake stand, 9" d., 6" h. . . . 55.00
Cake stand, 10" d. . . . 68.00
Celery tray . . . 15.00
Celery vase . . . 32.00
Compote, cov., 5½" d., 7½" h. . . . 47.50
Compote, cov., 7" d., 10" h. . . . 60.00
Compote, cov., 8" d., 12½" h. . . . 75.00
Compote, open, 5" d. . . . 21.00
Compote, open, 6" d., 4¾" h. . . . 38.00
Compote, open, 8" d., 6½" h. . . . 28.00
Compote, open, 9" d., 6¼" h. . . . 35.00
Compote, open, 10" d., 8½" h., scalloped rim . . . 75.00 to 85.00
Creamer . . . 38.50
Creamer, individual size . . . 13.00
Cruet w/original stopper, small . . . 38.00
Cruet w/original stopper, large . . . 50.00
Goblet . . . 44.00
Jelly, cov. . . . 55.00
Mug . . . 15.00
Mug, large . . . 65.00
Nappy, handled, 5" d. . . . 18.50
Olive dish . . . 20.00
Pitcher, water, tankard . . . 66.00

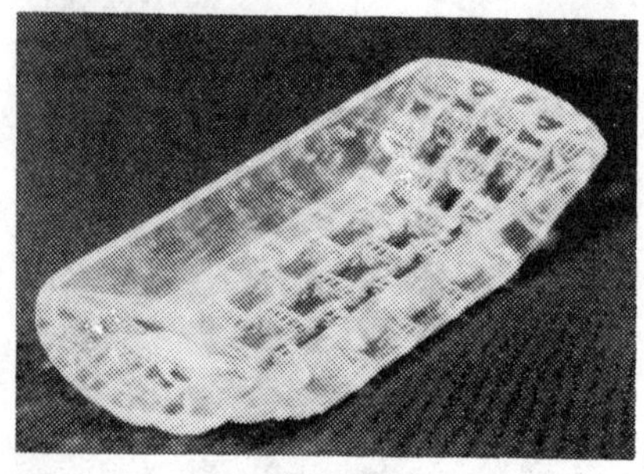

Cut Log Relish

Relish, boat-shaped, 9¼" l. (ILLUS.) . . . 30.00
Salt shaker w/original tin top (single) . . . 37.50
Sauce dish, flat or footed . . . 25.00 to 30.00
Spooner . . . 27.50
Sugar bowl, cov. . . . 52.50
Sugar bowl, cov., individual size . . . 32.50
Sugar bowl, open, individual size . . . 20.00
Tumbler . . . 45.00
Tumbler, juice . . . 22.50
Vase, 16" h. . . . 35.00
Wine . . . 22.00

DAHLIA

Bowl, 9 x 6" oval . . . 16.50
Bread platter, 12 x 8" . . . 36.00
Butter dish, cov. . . . 55.00
Cake stand, amber, 9" d. . . . 50.00
Cake stand, clear, 9" d. . . . 22.50
Champagne . . . 55.00
Compote, cov., 7" d., high stand . . . 50.00
Creamer . . . 15.00
Goblet . . . 32.50
Mug, amber . . . 42.50
Mug, clear . . . 32.00
Mug, vaseline . . . 38.00
Mug, yellow . . . 45.00
Mug, child's, blue . . . 40.00
Mug, child's, clear . . . 20.00
Pitcher, milk, applied handle, clear . . . 36.00
Pitcher, milk, yellow . . . 58.00
Pitcher, water, amber . . . 67.50

Dahlia Water Pitcher

Pitcher, water, blue (ILLUS.) . . . 95.00
Pitcher, water, clear . . . 51.00
Pitcher, water, vaseline . . . 77.00
Plate, 7" d. . . . 20.00
Plate, 9" d., w/handles, amber . . . 25.00
Plate, 9" d., w/handles, clear . . . 17.50
Plate, 9" d., w/handles, vaseline . . . 38.50
Relish, 9½ x 5" . . . 13.00
Sauce dish, flat, amber . . . 9.00
Sauce dish, flat, blue . . . 15.00
Sauce dish, flat, clear . . . 8.50
Spooner, amber . . . 45.00
Spooner, clear . . . 25.00
Sugar bowl, cov. . . . 28.00
Sugar bowl, open . . . 16.00
Wine . . . 34.00

DAISY & BUTTON

Basket, nickel silver handle, 6" h. . . . 125.00
Berry set: master bowl & 6 sauce dishes; blue, 7 pcs. . . . 85.00
Berry set: octagonal master bowl & 10 sauce dishes; amber, 11 pcs. . . . 140.00
Berry set: master bowl & 12 sauce dishes; vaseline, 13 pcs. . . . 225.00
Boot, high top, ruby-stained buttons . . . 125.00
Bowl, 8" w., tricornered, vaseline . . . 37.50
Bowl, berry or fruit, 8½" d. . . . 40.00
Bowl, 9" sq., Amberina . . . 200.00
Bowl, 9¼" oblong, amber . . . 32.00
Bowl, 11 x 8" oval, 3" h., amber . . . 65.00

Bowl, 11 x 10" oval, 7¾" h., flared, vaseline 95.00
Bowl, 11" d., amber 38.00
Bowl, fruit, rectangular, ornate silver plate frame 250.00
Bread tray, amber 25.00
Butter chip, fan-shaped 9.50
Butter chip, round, amber 9.00
Butter chip, round, clear 6.00
Butter chip, square, amber 15.00
Butter chip, square, blue 17.50
Butter chip, square, clear 7.50
Butter chip, cov., scalloped base, blue 65.00
Butter dish, cov., square 45.00
Butter dish, cov., model of Victorian stove, blue 52.50
Butter tub, cov., 2-handled, vaseline 55.00
Canoe, amber, 8" l. 35.00
Canoe, Amberina, 8" l. 495.00
Canoe, apple green, 8" l. 32.50
Canoe, vaseline, 8" l. 90.00
Canoe, amber, 11" l 85.00
Castor set, 3-bottle, in glass frame w/toothpick holder at top 50.00
Castor set, 5-bottle, blue, in original frame 225.00
Castor shaker bottle w/original top, amber 16.50
Celery vase, triangular, amber 43.00
Celery vase, triangular, green 35.00
Cheese dish, cov. 65.00
Cologne bottle w/original stopper 22.50
Compote, cov., 8" d., 12" h. 55.00
Compote, cov., 8½" d., 4½" h., amber 60.00
Creamer, amber 32.50
Creamer, clear 29.00
Creamer, ruby-stained buttons 45.00
Cruet w/original stopper, amber 100.00
Dish, amber, deep, 5" sq. 85.00
Dish, fan-shaped, 10" w. 11.50
Goblet, amber 26.00
Goblet, clear 22.50
Hat shape, canary yellow, 1¾" h. 22.50
Hat shape, amber, 2½" h. 30.00
Hat shape, blue, 2½" h. 35.00
Hat shape, clear, 2½" h. 20.00
Hat shape, vaseline, 2½" h. 37.50
Hat shape, clear, from tumbler mold, 4½" widest d. 55.00
Hat shape, blue, from tumbler mold, 4¾" widest d. 47.50
Hat shape, canary yellow, from tumbler mold, 5" widest d., 3¾" h. 48.00
Humidor, cov., amber 185.00
Ice cream dish, scalloped corners, Amberina, 5¾" d. .... 95.00 to 125.00
Ice cream dish, cut corners, 6" sq. 9.00
Inkwell, amber 145.00
Inkwell w/original insert, cat seated on cover 245.00

Match holder, cauldron w/original bail handle, amber 29.50
Match holder, wall-hanging scuff, amber, 4½" l 30.00
Match holder, wall-hanging scuff, blue .... 60.00 to 75.00
Pickle castor, amber insert, w/silver plate frame & tongs 120.00
Pickle castor, sapphire blue insert, w/silver plate frame & tongs 250.00
Pitcher, 5 1/8" h., applied handle, amber 55.00
Pitcher, water, bulbous, applied handle 55.00

Water Pitcher with Ruby Buttons

Pitcher, water, bulbous, applied handle, ruby-stained buttons (ILLUS.) 325.00
Pitcher, water, square 58.00
Plate, 5½" sq., Amberina 85.00
Plate, 7" sq., amber 18.00
Plate, 7" sq., blue 20.00
Plate, 7" sq., clear 15.00
Plate, 10" d., scalloped rim, amber 28.00
Plate, 10" d., blue 35.00
Platter, 13 x 9" oval, open handles, amber 35.00
Platter, 13 x 9" oval, open handles, blue 40.00
Platter, 13 x 9" oval, open handles, yellow 40.00
Powder jar, cov., amber, 3¾" d., 2" h. 30.00
Relish, model of "Sitz" bathtub 65.00
Salt dip, canoe-shaped, amber, 4 x 2" 19.50
Salt dip, canoe-shaped, clear, 4 x 2" 14.50
Salt dip, master size, blue, 3½" d. 12.50
Salt shaker w/original top, corset-shaped, blue (single) 25.00
Salt & pepper shakers w/original tops, clear, pr. 20.00
Salt & pepper shakers w/original tops, vaseline, pr. 30.00
Sauce dish, amber, 4" to 5" sq. 17.00
Sauce dish, Amberina, 4" to 5" sq. .... 85.00 to 100.00

Sauce dish, blue, 4" to 5" sq. 16.00
Sauce dish, clear, 4" to 5" sq. . . . . 6.00 to 12.00
Sauce dish, cloverleaf-shaped, amber 14.50
Sauce dish, tricornered, clear 16.00
Sauce dish, tricornered, vaseline . . . 15.00
Sauce dish, tricornered, yellow . . . . 9.00 to 15.00
Slipper, "1886 patent," blue 40.00
Slipper, "1887 patent" 52.50
Slipper, ruby-stained buttons 80.00
Smoke bell, amber 65.00
Spooner, amber 37.50
Spooner, blue 40.00
Spooner, clear 35.00
Spooner, hat-shaped, amber 32.00
Sugar bowl, cov., amber . . . . . 35.00 to 45.00
Sugar bowl, cov., barrel-shaped, blue 50.00
Sugar bowl, cov., clear 30.00
Sugar bowl, open, purple 55.00
Syrup pitcher w/original pewter top, blue 175.00
Table set: creamer, open sugar bowl & spooner; vaseline, 3 pcs. 65.00
Toothpick holder (or salt dip), "Bandmaster's cap," blue 35.00
Toothpick holder, 3-footed, amber . . 30.00
Toothpick holder, 3-footed, Amberina . . . . 145.00 to 185.00
Toothpick holder, 3-footed, vaseline 39.50
Toothpick holder, urn-shaped 28.00
Toothpick holder, amber, w/brass rim & base 22.00
Tray, ice cream, handled, 16½ x 9¼", blue 30.00
Tray, water, triangular, green 45.00
Tumbler, water, amber 17.00
Tumbler, water, blue 28.00
Tumbler, water, clear 13.00
Tumbler, water, vaseline 21.00
Vase, 6" h., hand holding cornucopia, blue 50.00
Vase, 6" h., hand holding cornucopia, ruby-stained buttons 58.50
Waste bowl, blue 28.00
Whimsey, sleigh, amber, 7¾ x 4½" 115.00
Whimsey, "whisk broom" dish, amber 28.00

DAISY & BUTTON WITH CROSSBARS (Mikado)

Berry set: master bowl & 4 sauce dishes; blue, 5 pcs. 85.00
Bowl, 9 x 6", canary yellow 30.00
Bread tray, apple green 32.50
Bread tray, blue 42.00
Bread tray, clear 25.00
Bread tray, vaseline 55.00
Butter dish, cov. 45.00
Cake stand, blue 85.00
Cake stand, clear 55.00
Celery vase, amber 39.00
Celery vase, blue 40.00
Celery vase, clear 27.00
Celery vase, vaseline 50.00
Compote, open, 6" h., canary yellow 38.00
Compote, open, 7" d., 4" h., amber 26.50
Compote, open, 8½" d., 7½" h., amber 45.00
Compote, open, 8½" d., 7½" h., blue 45.00
Compote, open, 8½" d., 7½" h., clear 32.50
Compote, open, 9½" d., clear 35.00
Compote, open, 10" d., amber 60.00
Creamer, amber . . . . 30.00 to 40.00
Creamer, blue 45.00
Creamer, clear 30.00
Creamer, individual size, blue 30.00
Creamer, individual size, clear 15.00
Creamer & open sugar bowl, amber, pr. 70.00
Cruet w/original stopper, amber . . . 117.00
Cruet w/original stopper, clear 55.00
Cruet w/original stopper, vaseline . . 125.00
Cruet w/replaced stopper, blue 70.00
Goblet, amber 35.00
Goblet, blue 38.00

Daisy & Button with Crossbars Goblet

Goblet, clear (ILLUS.) 22.50
Goblet, vaseline 40.00
Mug, amber, 3" h. 18.00
Mug, canary yellow, 3" h. 22.50
Mug, clear, 3" h. 12.00
Pitcher, milk, amber 45.00
Pitcher, milk, blue 55.00
Pitcher, milk, clear 42.50
Pitcher, water, amber 83.00
Pitcher, water, blue 90.00
Pitcher, water, clear 52.50
Pitcher, water, vaseline 60.00
Sauce dish, flat or footed, amber . . . . 12.50 to 15.00

Sauce dish, flat or footed, canary yellow 16.50
Spooner, amber 50.00
Spooner, clear 23.50
Spooner, vaseline 30.00
Sugar bowl, cov., blue 55.00
Sugar bowl, cov., clear 25.00
Toothpick holder 28.00
Tumbler, amber 22.00
Tumbler, blue 30.00
Tumbler, clear 15.00
Tumbler, vaseline 25.00
Vase, vaseline 45.00
Waste bowl, canary yellow 22.50
Water set: pitcher & 8 tumblers; amber, 9 pcs. 185.00
Wine 27.00

DAISY & BUTTON WITH NARCISSUS

Daisy & Button with Narcissus Pitcher

Bowl, 9½ x 6" oval, footed 45.00
Butter dish, cov. 50.00
Creamer 45.00
Decanter w/original stopper 65.00
Goblet .... 18.00 to 22.50
Nappy, leaf-shaped 65.00
Pitcher, water (ILLUS.) 70.00
Sauce dish, flat or 3-footed ... 8.00 to 15.00
Spooner 30.00
Sugar bowl, cov. 42.50
Tray, 10½" d. 30.00
Tumbler 16.50
Wine 15.50
Wine set, decanter w/original stopper & 4 wines, 5 pcs. 75.00

DAISY & BUTTON WITH THUMBPRINT PANELS

Bowl, berry, cov., 8" d., 8" h., amber panels 130.00
Bowl, 8" sq. 25.00
Bowl, 9" oval, amber panels 50.00
Bowl, 11" d., collared base, amber panels 52.00
Bride's basket, w/silver plate holder, amber panels 125.00
Butter dish, cov. 78.00
Cake basket, amber panels, 11 x 7", 5½" h. 125.00
Cake stand, 9½" d. 48.00
Cake stand, canary yellow, 10½" d., 7¼" h. 55.00
Celery vase 30.00

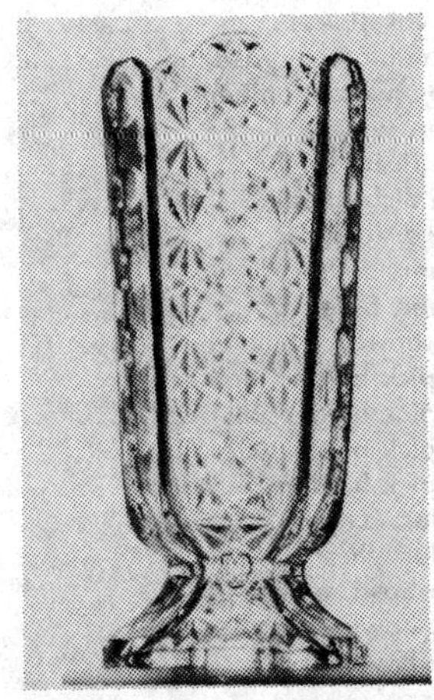

Daisy & Button with Thumbprint Panels

Celery vase, amber panels (ILLUS.) 85.00
Champagne, amber panels 25.00
Compote, cov., 6¾" d., 10½" h. 62.50
Creamer, applied handle, amber panels 59.00
Dish, triangular, 5" w., 2" h. 20.00
Finger bowl 22.50
Goblet 27.50
Goblet, amber panels 45.00
Goblet, blue panels 42.50
Pitcher, water, applied handle, amber panels 135.00
Pitcher, water, applied handle, blue panels 85.00
Sauce dish, flat or footed, 5" sq. .... 9.00 to 12.50
Sauce dish, flat or footed, amber panels, 5" sq. .... 15.00 to 30.00
Sugar bowl, open, amber panels ... 32.50
Syrup jug w/original top, amber panels 125.00
Tumbler, amber 22.50
Tumbler, blue 25.00
Tumbler, clear 20.00
Water set: pitcher & 5 tumblers; vaseline, 6 pcs. 295.00
Wine 15.00
Wine, amber panels 35.00
Wine, blue panels 40.00

DAISY & BUTTON WITH "V" ORNAMENT

Bowl, 9" d., vaseline 50.00
Butter dish, cov., canary yellow 68.00
Butter dish, cov., clear 45.00
Celery vase, amber 40.00
Celery vase, canary yellow 65.00

Celery vase, clear 25.00
Creamer, amber 27.50
Creamer, clear 30.00
Finger bowl, blue 45.00
Mug, blue 22.50
Mug, clear 17.50
Mug, vaseline 25.00
Mug, miniature, vaseline 26.00
Pitcher, water, amber 90.00
Pitcher, water, clear 48.00
Sauce dish, amber 15.00
Sauce dish, blue 15.00
Sauce dish, clear 10.00
Spooner, amber 37.50
Spooner, blue 20.00
Sugar bowl, cov., blue 49.00
Toothpick holder, amber 30.00
Toothpick holder, blue 32.00
Toothpick holder, clear 24.00
Toothpick holder, vaseline 35.00
Tumbler, amber 22.00
Tumbler, clear 15.00
Waste bowl, amber 29.00
Waste bowl, clear 22.50
Waste bowl, vaseline 28.00

DAISY IN PANEL - See Two Panel Pattern

DAKOTA (Baby Thumbprint)

(Items may be plain or with etched designs)

Dakota Covered Sugar with Etching

Butter dish, cov. 54.00
Cake stand, 8" d. 51.00
Cake stand, 9¼" d. 65.00
Cake stand, 10¼" d. 45.00
Celery vase, flat base 32.50
Celery vase, flat base, etched 45.00
Celery vase, pedestal base 41.00
Compote, cov., jelly, 5" d., 5" h. 46.50
Compote, cov., 6" d., high stand 65.00
Compote, open, jelly, 5" d., 5" h. 30.00
Compote, open, 6" d. 27.50
Compote, open, 7" d. 41.00
Compote, open, 8" d., low stand 32.50
Compote, open, 8" d., 9" h. 60.00
Compote, open, 10" d. 55.00
Creamer 45.00
Finger bowl 45.00
Goblet 26.00
Goblet, ruby-stained 40.00
Lamp, kerosene-type . . . . . . 110.00 to 135.00
Mug, ruby-stained, 3½" h. 35.00
Pitcher, milk 80.00
Pitcher, water, 10" to 12" h. 78.00
Pitcher, water, 10" to 12" h., ruby-stained 125.00
Plate, 10" d. 63.00
Salt shaker w/original top (single) . . . 42.50
Salt & pepper shakers w/original tops, pr. 90.00
Sauce dish, flat or footed 13.00
Sauce dish, flat or footed, etched . . . 24.50
Shaker bottle w/original top, 5" h. 35.00
Shaker bottle w/original top, hotel size, 6½" h. 58.00
Spooner 32.00
Sugar bowl, cov. 50.00
Sugar bowl, cov., etched (ILLUS.) . . . 58.00
Sugar bowl, open, breakfast size . . . 21.00
Table set, 4 pcs. 275.00
Tray, water, piecrust rim, 13" d. 93.00
Tray, wine 77.50
Tumbler 29.00
Tumbler, ruby-stained 32.00
Waste bowl 60.00
Water set, pitcher & 1 tumbler, 2 pcs. 75.00
Wine 22.00
Wine, ruby-stained 46.00

DARBY - See Pleat & Panel Pattern

DART

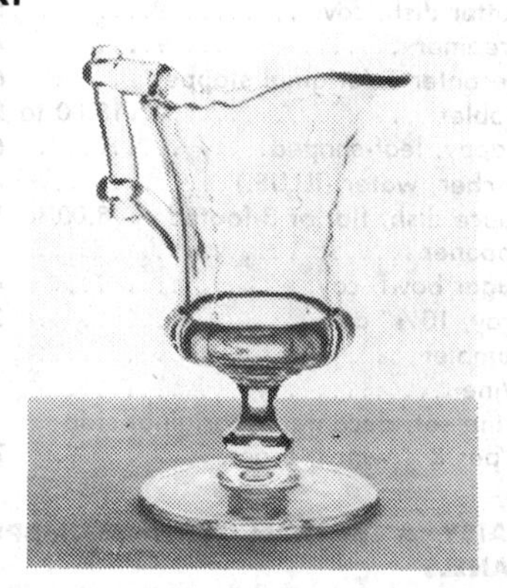

Dart Creamer

Butter dish, cov. 28.00
Compote, cov., 8½" d., high stand 35.00
Compote, open, jelly 17.00
Creamer (ILLUS.) 31.00
Goblet 25.00
Lamp, kerosene 45.00
Sauce dish, footed 10.00

Spooner 30.00
Sugar bowl, cov. 32.50
Table set, creamer, spooner & cov. sugar bowl, 3 pcs. 85.00

DEER & DOG

(Each piece etched w/scene of deer, dog & hunter)

Deer & Dog Pitcher

Butter dish, cov., pedestal base & frosted dog finial.................. 130.00
Celery vase, scalloped rim, signed "Gillinder"...................... 95.00
Compote, cov., 8" oval, 8¾" h., frosted dog finial................ 155.00
Compote, cov., 8" d., 13" h., frosted dog finial..................... 250.00
Compote, open, 8" d.............. 175.00
Cordial 95.00
Creamer 75.00
Goblet, straight sides.............. 53.00
Goblet, U-shaped 75.00
Goblet, V-shaped 50.00
Marmalade jar, cov................ 78.00
Pitcher, milk, 9" h. 165.00
Pitcher, water, applied reeded handle (ILLUS.) ....180.00 to 195.00
Sauce dish, footed 18.00
Spooner 52.00
Sugar bowl, cov., frosted dog finial.............................110.00
Wine.......................60.00 to 85.00

DEER & PINE TREE

Bowl, 8 x 5"...................... 22.00
Bread tray, amber, 13 x 8"......... 50.00
Bread tray, apple green, 13 x 8".... 78.00
Bread tray, blue, 13 x 8"........... 75.00
Bread tray, clear, 13 x 8" (ILLUS.)........................ 40.00
Bread tray, vaseline, 13 x 8" 80.00
Butter dish, cov. 88.00
Cake stand 100.00
Celery vase....................... 70.00
Compote, cov., 8" sq., 6" h......... 68.00

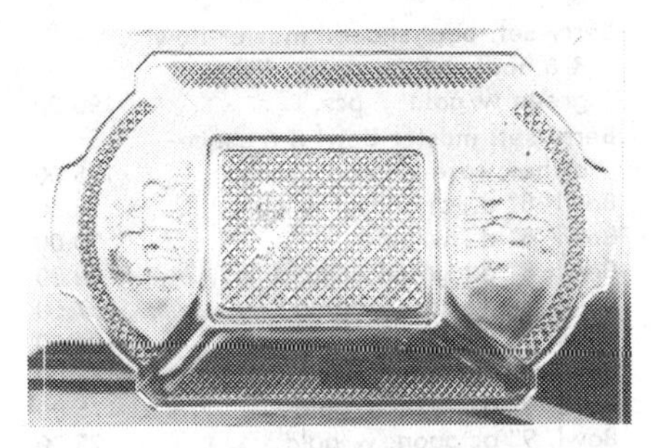

Deer & Pine Tree Bread Tray

Compote, cov., 8" sq., 12" h........ 160.00
Compote, open, 8" sq., high stand .. 48.00
Creamer 62.50
Finger bowl....................... 57.50
Goblet 43.00
Mug, child's, amber 45.00
Mug, child's, apple green 45.00
Mug, child's, vaseline.............. 55.00
Mug, large, apple green 65.00
Mug, large, blue 48.00
Mug, large, clear 40.00
Pickle dish........................ 18.00
Pitcher, milk 70.00
Pitcher, water ....85.00 to 95.00
Sauce dish, flat or footed ....12.00 to 22.00
Spooner 35.00
Sugar bowl, cov. 62.50
Tray, water, handled, amber, 15 x 9" 54.00
Tray, water, handled, clear, 15 x 9" 55.00
Vegetable dish, 9 x 5¾" 50.00

DELAWARE (Four Petal Flower)

Delaware Water Set

Banana boat, amethyst w/gold, 11¾" l. 125.00
Banana boat, w/gold, 11¾" l. 50.00
Banana boat, green w/gold, 11¾" l. 50.00
Banana boat, rose w/gold, 11¾" l. 58.00
Berry set: boat-shaped master bowl & 4 boat-shaped sauce dishes; w/rose flowers & gold, 5 pcs. 145.00
Berry set: master bowl & 4 sauce dishes; green w/gold, 5 pcs. 125.00
Berry set: master bowl & 4 sauce dishes; rose w/gold, 5 pcs. 155.00

Berry set: boat-shaped master bowl & 6 boat-shaped sauce dishes; green w/gold, 7 pcs. 190.00
Berry set: master bowl & 6 sauce dishes; rose w/gold, 7 pcs. 195.00
Bowl, 8" d., amethyst w/gold 75.00
Bowl, 8" d., w/gold 30.00
Bowl, 8" d., green w/gold 50.00
Bowl, 8" d., rose w/gold........... 57.50
Bowl, 9" d., w/gold 24.50
Bowl, 9" d., green w/gold 48.00
Bowl, 9" d., rose w/gold........... 75.00
Bowl, 9" octagon, w/gold 25.00
Bowl, 10" octagon, green w/gold ... 50.00
Bride's basket, boat-shaped open bowl, green w/gold, w/silver plate frame, 11½" oval 160.00
Bride's basket, boat-shaped open bowl, green w/gold, miniature ... 175.00
Butter dish, cov. 90.00
Butter dish, cov., green w/gold..... 105.00
Butter dish, cov., rose w/gold...... 145.00
Celery vase, green w/gold 65.00
Celery vase, rose w/gold 72.50
Claret jug, green w/gold 175.00
Creamer, w/gold.................... 43.00
Creamer, green w/gold.............. 50.00
Creamer, rose w/gold 68.00
Creamer, individual size, w/gold ... 25.00
Creamer & open sugar bowl in silver plate holder, individual size, green w/gold, pr. 75.00
Creamer & open sugar bowl, rose w/gold, pr. 95.00
Creamer & sugar bowl, breakfast size, rose w/gold, pr. 125.00
Cruet w/original stopper........... 100.00
Cruet w/original stopper, green w/gold 150.00
Dresser tray 30.00
Dresser tray, green w/gold 60.00
Dresser tray, rose w/gold.......... 65.00
Finger bowl, w/gold................ 22.00
Marmalade dish w/silver plate holder, amethyst w/gold.......... 45.00
Marmalade dish w/silver plate holder, green w/gold............ 45.00
Marmalade dish w/silver plate holder, rose w/gold 95.00
Pin tray, 7 x 3½" 14.50
Pin tray, 9 x 4¾" 17.50
Pitcher, milk, green w/gold . . 60.00 to 85.00
Pitcher, tankard, w/cranberry & green florals & gold trim......... 125.00
Pitcher, tankard, green w/gold 80.00
Pitcher, tankard, rose w/gold 148.00
Pitcher, water, bulbous, rose w/gold 125.00
Pomade jar w/jeweled cover, green w/gold 195.00
Pomade jar w/jeweled cover, rose w/gold 215.00
Powder jar, cov., green w/gold 135.00
Powder jar, cov., rose w/gold...... 145.00
Punch cup 15.00
Punch cup, green, souvenir 15.00
Punch cup, green w/gold 35.00
Punch cup, rose w/gold........... 38.00
Salt shaker w/original top, rose w/gold (single) 45.00
Sauce dish, boat-shaped 30.00
Sauce dish, boat-shaped, green w/gold 30.00
Sauce dish, boat-shaped, rose w/gold 40.00
Sauce dish, round, green w/gold ... 21.50
Sauce dish, round, rose w/gold..... 22.50
Shade, rose w/gold 105.00
Spooner, w/gold 35.00
Spooner, green w/gold 45.00
Spooner, rose w/gold 55.00
Sugar bowl, cov. 65.00
Sugar bowl, cov., green w/gold 120.00
Sugar bowl, cov., rose w/gold...... 100.00
Sugar bowl, individual size, green .. 55.00
Table set, green w/gold, 4 pcs. 400.00
Table set, rose w/gold, 4 pcs....... 450.00
Toothpick holder 30.00
Toothpick holder, w/rose-stained florals & gold 65.00
Toothpick holder, green w/gold 70.00
Toothpick holder, rose w/gold...... 115.00
Tumbler.......................... 12.00
Tumbler, w/rose-stained florals 26.50
Tumbler, custard w/stained florals . . 65.00
Tumbler, green w/gold 39.00
Tumbler, rose w/gold 33.00
Vase, 6" h., green w/gold 40.00
Vase, 8" h., green w/gold 115.00
Vase, 9½" h., green w/gold 84.00
Vase, 9½" h., rose w/gold......... 126.00
Water set: pitcher & 6 tumblers; green w/gold, 7 pcs. (ILLUS.) ....400.00 to 500.00
Water set: pitcher & 6 tumblers; rose w/gold, 7 pcs. 325.00

DEW & RAINDROP

Dew & Raindrop Punch Cup

Bowl, 6½" d. 28.00
Bowl, berry, 8" d. 38.00
Butter dish, cov. 50.00
Compote, cov., jelly 50.00
Compote, open, jelly 35.00
Cordial 18.00
Creamer 28.50

Goblet 30.00
Pitcher, water 48.00
Punch cup (ILLUS.) 7.50
Salt & pepper shakers w/original tops, pr. 40.00
Sauce dish, flat or footed . . . . 10.00 to 12.00
Spooner 35.00
Sugar bowl, cov. 50.00
Tumbler 16.50
Vase, bud, 6" h. 27.50
Wine 20.00

DEWDROP

Bread tray 25.00
Butter dish, cov. 30.00
Cake stand, 8½" d. 20.00
Cordial 40.00
Creamer 25.00
Egg cup, double 20.00
Goblet, amber 25.00
Goblet, blue 25.00
Goblet, clear 20.00
Mug, applied handle 24.00
Pitcher, water, collared base 50.00
Relish 15.00
Salt shaker w/original top, footed (single) 22.00
Sauce dish 8.00
Spooner 25.00
Sugar bowl, open 40.00
Tumbler, blue 27.50
Tumbler, clear 15.00

DEWDROP WITH STAR

Dewdrop with Star Sauce Dish

Bowl, 7" d. 14.00
Butter dish, cov. 45.00
Cake stand, 9" d. 42.50
Celery vase 40.00
Cheese dish, cov. 95.00
Compote, cov., 5" d. 60.00
Compote, open, 9" d., 9" h. 45.00
Creamer, applied handle 25.00
Pitcher, water, 8" h. 95.00
Plate, 5" d. 12.00
Plate 9" d. 13.50
Plate, 11" d. 15.00
Relish, 9" l. 15.00
Sauce dish, flat (ILLUS.) . . . . 8.00 to 10.00
Sugar bowl, cov. 50.00

DEWEY (Flower Flange)

Dewey Cruet

Bowl, 8" d., amber 30.00
Bowl, 8" d., yellow 45.00
Butter dish, cov., amber 65.00
Butter dish, cov., clear 55.00
Butter dish, cov., green 82.00
Butter dish, cov., yellow 95.00
Creamer, amber 42.00
Creamer, clear 30.00
Creamer, green 42.50
Creamer, yellow 32.00
Creamer & cov. sugar bowl, breakfast size, vaseline, pr. 95.00
Cruet w/original stopper, amber . . . 145.00
Cruet w/original stopper, clear (ILLUS.) 95.00
Cruet w/original stopper, green 150.00
Cruet w/original stopper, Nile green 750.00
Cruet w/original stopper, yellow . . . 134.00
Mug, amber 65.00
Mug, clear 35.00
Mug, green 65.00
Mug, Nile green 275.00
Parfait, green 35.00
Pitcher, water, amber 95.00
Pitcher, water, clear 85.00
Plate, footed, amber 42.00
Plate, footed, clear 15.00
Plate, footed, green 45.00
Plate, footed, yellow 55.00
Relish, serpentine shape, amber, small 35.00
Relish, serpentine shape, clear, small 20.00
Relish, serpentine shape, green, small 38.50
Relish, serpentine shape, Nile green, small 225.00

Relish, serpentine shape, yellow, small 42.50
Relish, serpentine shape, amber, large 62.50
Relish, serpentine shape, Nile green, large 265.00
Salt shaker w/original top, amber or green (single) 55.00
Salt shaker w/original top, yellow (single) 45.00
Sauce dish, amber 40.00
Sauce dish, green 40.00
Sauce dish, yellow 45.00
Spooner, amber 60.00
Spooner, green 60.00
Spooner, yellow 60.00
Sugar bowl, cov., green 75.00
Sugar bowl, open, amber 32.50
Tumbler, amber 50.00
Tumbler, clear 45.00
Tumbler, green 45.00
Tumbler, yellow 60.00
Water set: pitcher & 6 tumblers; clear, 7 pcs. 250.00
Water set: pitcher & 6 tumblers; yellow, 7 pcs. ....225.00 to 300.00

DIAGONAL BAND

Diagonal Band Goblet

Butter dish, cov. 35.00
Cake stand 30.00
Celery vase 30.00
Compote, cov., 7½" d., 9¼" h. 45.00
Compote, open, 7½" d., high stand 18.00
Creamer 30.00
Creamer & open sugar bowl, pr. 50.00
Goblet (ILLUS.) 24.00
Marmalade jar w/original lid 22.00
Pitcher, milk 32.00
Pitcher, water 39.00
Plate, 8" d. 10.50
Relish, 6 7/8" oval 7.50
Salt dip, footed 25.00
Salt & pepper shakers w/original tops, pr. 30.00
Sauce dish, flat or footed ....7.00 to 10.00
Spooner 22.50
Sugar bowl, open 15.00
Wine 24.00

DIAGONAL BAND & FAN

Diagonal Band & Fan Relish

Butter dish, cov. 40.00
Champagne 30.00
Compote, open 25.00
Creamer 35.00
Goblet 19.00
Pitcher, milk 38.00
Plate, 6" d. 11.50
Plate, 8" d. 12.50
Relish, 8" oval (ILLUS.) 15.00
Sauce dish, footed 13.50
Spooner 22.50
Wine 21.00

DIAMOND & BULL'S EYE BAND - **See Reverse Torpedo Pattern**

DIAMOND & SUNBURST

Diamond & Sunburst Goblet

Bowl, cov., 8" d. 35.00
Cake stand, 8" d. 28.00
Celery vase 35.00
Compote, cov., 7" d., high stand 48.00
Compote, open, jelly 15.00

Goblet (ILLUS.) 20.00
Pitcher w/applied handle, milk 40.00
Spooner 15.00
Sugar bowl, open 25.00
Sugar shaker 22.00
Syrup jug w/original top, applied handle 45.00
Toothpick holder 18.50
Tumbler 25.00
Wine 20.00

DIAMOND BAR - See Lattice Pattern

DIAMOND HORSESHOE - See Aurora Pattern

DIAMOND MEDALLION (Finecut & Diamond or Grand)

Diamond Medallion Creamer

Bowl, 9 x 6¼" oval 12.50
Bread plate, 10" d. 21.50
Butter dish, cov. 35.00
Cake stand, 8" d. 20.00
Cake stand, 10" d. 30.00
Celery vase 25.00
Compote, cov., 7" d., high stand 36.00
Compote, open, 7" d., high stand 22.50
Compote, open, 8" d., 6" h. 19.50
Compote, open, 9" d., high stand 17.50
Creamer, footed (ILLUS.) 24.00
Goblet 22.50
Pitcher, water 45.00
Relish, 7½" oval 12.00
Salt & pepper shakers w/original tops, pr. 35.00
Sauce dish, flat or footed .....6.50 to 9.00
Spooner 20.00
Sugar bowl, cov. 35.00
Sugar bowl, open 15.00
Wine 35.00

DIAMOND POINT

Bar bottle, flint 55.00
Bowl, 8½" d., flint 95.00
Bread plate 28.00
Butter dish, cov., flint 85.00
Castor set, 4-bottle, flint, w/silver plate frame 600.00
Celery vase, pedestal base w/knob stem, flint 65.00
Champagne, flint 75.00
Claret, flint 130.00
Compote, open, 6" d., high stand, flint ....65.00 to 100.00
Compote, open, 7½" d., low stand, non-flint 25.00
Compote, open, 10½" d., 8½" h., flared rim, flint 98.00
Creamer, applied handle, flint ....100.00 to 130.00
Decanter w/original stopper, qt. 70.00
Decanter w/bar lip, qt. ......69.00 to 85.00
Egg cup, cov., clambroth, flint 550.00

Diamond Point Covered Egg Cup

Egg cup, cov., powder blue opaque, flint (ILLUS.) 750.00
Egg cup, canary yellow, flint ....200.00 to 350.00
Egg cup, chartreuse opaque, flint ... 425.00
Egg cup, clambroth, flint 115.00
Egg cup, flint, clear 37.50
Goblet, flint 50.00
Goblet, non-flint 20.00
Honey dish, flint 15.00
Honey dish, coarse points, non-flint 7.00
Pitcher, tankard, applied handle, flint, qt. 170.00
Pitcher, water, bulbous, flint 160.00
Plate, 6" d., non-flint 13.50
Salt dip, cov., master size 27.50
Sauce dish, non-flint, 3½" to 5½" d. ....6.00 to 12.50
Spillholder, flint 52.00
Spooner, flint 40.00
Spooner, non-flint 22.00
Sugar bowl, cov., flint 95.00
Sugar bowl, cov., non-flint 40.00
Tumbler, flint 47.50
Tumbler, bar, flint 65.00

Wine, flint 47.50
Wine, non-flint 10.00

DIAMOND POINT WITH PANELS - See Hinoto Pattern

DIAMOND QUILTED

Diamond Quilted Open Compote

Bowl, 6" d., clear 12.50
Bowl, 6" d., turquoise blue 12.50
Bowl, 7" d., amber 17.50
Bowl, 7" d., vaseline 22.00
Bowl, 8" d., amber 38.00
Bowl, 8" d., vaseline 30.00
Bowl, 9" d., amber 50.00
Butter dish, cov., amber . . . . .42.00 to 50.00
Butter dish, cov., vaseline 75.00
Celery vase, amber 35.00
Celery vase, vaseline 40.00
Champagne, clear 21.50
Champagne, turquoise blue 30.00
Compote, cov., 8" d., 13" h., amber 95.00
Compote, cov., 8" d., 13" h., clear . . 75.00
Compote, open, 6" d., 6" h., amber (ILLUS.) 25.00
Compote, open, 7" d., low stand, amber 17.50
Compote, open, 7" d., high stand, amber 30.00
Compote, open, 7" d., high stand, vaseline 38.00
Compote, open, 8" d., low stand, amber 19.50
Compote, open, 9" d., low stand, amber 22.00
Creamer, amber 37.50
Creamer & sugar bowl, amber, pr. . . 85.00
Goblet, amber 50.00
Goblet, amethyst 35.00
Goblet, blue 36.00
Goblet, vaseline 36.00
Mug, amber 20.00
Mug, clear 15.00
Pitcher, water, amber 57.50
Pitcher, water, vaseline 75.00
Relish, amber, 7½ x 4½" 10.00
Relish, leaf-shaped, amber, 9 x 5½" 13.50
Relish. leaf-shaped, turquoise blue, 9 x 5½" 22.00
Relish, leaf-shaped, vaseline, 9 x 5½" 22.00
Relish, leaf-shaped, vaseline, 12 x 10" 28.00
Salt dip, vaseline 16.00
Sauce dish, flat or footed, amber 9.00
Sauce dish, flat or footed, amethyst . . . . .12.00 to 18.00
Sauce dish, flat or footed, turquoise blue 13.00
Sauce dish, flat or footed, vaseline 15.00
Spooner, amber 30.00
Spooner, turquoise blue 40.00
Spooner, vaseline 40.00
Sugar bowl, cov., blue 43.50
Sugar bowl, cov., vaseline 60.00
Sugar bowl, open, turquoise blue . . . 30.00
Sugar bowl, open, vaseline 30.00
Tray, water, cloverleaf-shaped, amber, 12 x 10" . . . . .22.00 to 30.00
Tray, water, cloverleaf-shaped, vaseline, 12 x 10" 28.00
Tumbler, juice, amber 20.00
Tumbler, vaseline 25.00
Wine, amber 22.50
Wine, clear 12.50
Wine, vaseline 26.00

DIAMOND THUMBPRINT

Diamond Thumbprint Pitcher

Butter dish, cov. . . . . .140.00 to 200.00
Cake stand, 12" d. 195.00
Celery vase 150.00
Champagne 350.00
Compote, open, 7" d., 4½" h., extended scalloped rim 68.00
Compote, open, 8" d., 3¼" h. 45.00
Compote, open, 8" d., 6" h. 75.00
Compote, open, 10½" d., 7½" h. . . . 285.00
Compote, open, 11½" d., 8" h. 375.00
Creamer, applied handle 200.00
Cup plate 50.00

Decanter w/original stopper, qt. 195.00
Goblet 325.00
Lamp, whale oil, original burner, brass stem, marble base 265.00
Pitcher, water (ILLUS.) 575.00
Punch bowl, scalloped rim, pedestal base, 11½" d., 9 1/8" h. 425.00
Salt dip, master size 45.00
Sauce dish, flat . . . . .11.00 to 20.00
Sauce dish, footed 45.00
Spillholder, clear 45.00
Spillholder, vaseline 875.00
Spooner 88.00
Sugar bowl, cov. 165.00
Tumbler 92.00
Tumbler, bar, 3¾" h. 135.00
Tumbler, whiskey, handled 300.00
Wine 245.00

DINNER BELL - See Cottage Pattern

DORIC - See Feather Pattern

DOUBLE LEAF & DART - See Leaf & Dart Pattern

DOUBLE LOOP - See Ribbon Candy Pattern

DOUBLE WEDDING RING (Wedding Ring)

Double Wedding Ring Footed Tumbler

Champagne 90.00
Goblet 65.00
Lamp, kerosene, hand-type w/flat base, applied handle 97.00
Sauce dish 25.00
Tumbler, bar 90.00
Tumbler, footed (ILLUS.) 80.00
Wine 75.00

DRAPERY

Butter dish, cov. 40.00
Cake plate, square, footed . . .40.00 to 45.00
Creamer, applied handle 29.00
Egg cup 21.00
Goblet 26.00

Drapery Buttermilk Goblet

Goblet, buttermilk (ILLUS.) 30.00
Pitcher, water, applied handle 75.00
Plate, 6" d. 24.50
Sauce dish, flat 10.00
Spooner 27.00
Sugar bowl, cov. 40.00
Sugar bowl, open 25.00
Tumbler 27.00
Water set, pitcher & 6 tumblers, 7 pcs. . . . . .275.00 to 325.00

EGG IN SAND

Egg in Sand Goblet

Bread tray, handled 32.50
Butter dish, cov. 48.00
Creamer 25.00
Goblet, blue 40.00
Goblet, clear (ILLUS.) 24.00
Pitcher, milk 45.00
Pitcher, water, amber 70.00
Pitcher, water, clear 40.00
Relish, 9 x 5½" 18.50
Sauce dish 12.00
Spooner, amber 47.50
Spooner, clear 25.00

Sugar bowl, cov. 37.50
Tray, water, 12½" oblong 38.50
Tumbler 36.00

EGYPTIAN

Egyptian Footed Sauce Dish

Berry set, master bowl & 5 sauce dishes, 6 pcs. 150.00
Bowl, 8½" d. 48.00
Bread platter, Cleopatra center, 12 x 9" 45.00
Bread platter, Salt Lake Temple center 248.00
Butter dish, cov. 67.50
Celery vase 95.00
Compote, cov., 7" d., 12" h., sphinx base 168.00
Compote, cov., 8" d., high stand, sphinx base 200.00
Compote, open, 6" d., low stand 50.00
Compote, open, 7½" d., sphinx base 65.00
Creamer 36.00
Goblet 40.00
Pickle dish 20.00
Pitcher, water .... 145.00 to 175.00
Plate, 10" d. 40.00
Plate, 12" d. 85.00
Relish, 8½ x 5½" 20.00
Sauce dish, flat or footed (ILLUS.) 19.00
Spooner 35.00
Sugar bowl, cov. 67.50
Sugar bowl, open 35.00
Table set, cov. butter dish, spooner & creamer, 3 pcs. 145.00

EMERALD GREEN HERRINGBONE - See Paneled Herringbone Pattern

EMPIRE COLONIAL - See Colonial Pattern

ENGLISH HOBNAIL CROSS - See Amberette Pattern

ESTHER

(Items may be plain or with etched designs)

Esther Sauce Dish

Berry set: master bowl & 6 sauce dishes; green, 7 pcs. 290.00
Butter dish, cov., amber-stained 110.00
Butter dish, cov., clear 70.00
Butter dish, cov., green 123.00
Celery vase, clear 70.00
Celery vase, green 135.00
Compote, cov., high stand 110.00
Compote, open, 5" d., 6½" h., green 57.00
Cookie jar, cov., amber-stained 225.00
Creamer, clear 70.00
Creamer, green 135.00
Creamer & cov. sugar bowl, individual size, pr. 95.00
Cruet w/ball-shaped stopper, clear 40.00
Cruet w/ball-shaped stopper, green .... 200.00 to 250.00
Cruet w/original stopper, clear, miniature 28.00
Cruet w/original stopper, green, miniature 95.00
Goblet, clear 52.00
Goblet, green 90.00
Goblet, ruby-stained, souvenir 55.00
Pitcher, water, green 150.00
Plate, 10¼" d. 27.50
Relish, clear, 8 x 4½" 22.50
Relish, green, 8½ x 4½" 24.00
Relish, green, 11 x 5½" 45.00
Salt & pepper shakers w/original tops, pr. 95.00
Sauce dish (ILLUS.) 17.00
Spooner, clear 38.00
Spooner, green 65.00
Sugar bowl, cov., clear 40.00
Sugar bowl, cov., green 87.50
Table set, green, 4 pcs. 475.00
Toothpick holder, amber-stained 100.00
Toothpick holder, clear 40.00
Toothpick holder, green 76.00
Tray, ice cream, green 145.00
Tumbler, clear 32.00
Tumbler, green 47.00
Water set: pitcher & 5 tumblers; green, 6 pcs. 310.00
Wine 32.50

EUREKA

Bowl, 9" oval 30.00
Bread tray 29.00
Butter dish 80.00
Compote, open, jelly 55.00
Compote, open, jelly, ruby-stained . . 75.00
Creamer 45.00
Creamer, ruby-stained 65.00
Egg cup 15.00
Goblet 25.00
Salt dip, master size 25.00
Salt & pepper shakers w/original tops, ruby-stained, pr. 48.00
Spooner 40.00
Sugar bowl, cov. 55.00
Sugar bowl, open 25.00
Toothpick holder 25.00
Toothpick holder, ruby-stained 85.00
Tumbler, footed 25.00
Wine 30.00

EXCELSIOR

Excelsior Flip

Bar bottle, pt. . . . . 35.00 to 50.00
Bar bottle, flint, qt. 70.00
Cake stand, flint, 9¼" h. 150.00
Candlestick, flint (single) 96.00
Castor set, 4-bottle, non-flint, w/pewter frame 65.00
Celery vase, flint 78.00
Claret, non-flint 16.00
Cordial 35.00
Creamer 55.00
Egg cup 28.00
Egg cup, double 35.00
Egg cup, double, fiery opalescent, flint 225.00
Flip glass, 8" h. (ILLUS.) 200.00
Goblet, "barrel" 38.00
Goblet, flint 50.00
Mug 25.00
Pitcher, water, flint 325.00
Platter, 9¼" l. 22.00
Salt dip, master size 18.50
Spillholder, flint 76.00
Sugar bowl, cov. 90.00
Syrup pitcher, applied handle 110.00
Syrup pitcher w/original top, green 750.00
Tumbler, bar, flint, 3½" h. 55.00
Tumbler, footed, flint 47.50
Wine, flint 65.00

EYEWINKER

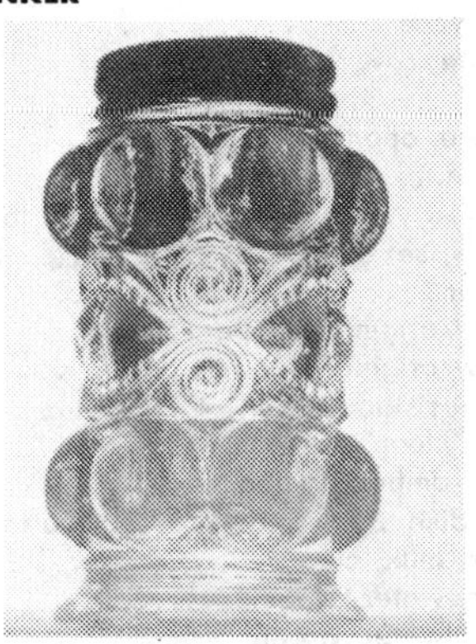

Eyewinker Salt Shaker

Banana boat, flat, 8½" 85.00
Bowl, master berry or fruit, 9" sq., 4½" h. . . . . 65.00 to 75.00
Butter dish, cov. 65.00
Cake stand, 8½" to 9½" d. 75.00
Celery vase, 6½" h. 55.00
Compote, cov., 6½" d., 11" h. 49.00
Compote, open, 4" d., 5" h., scalloped rim 31.50
Compote, open, 6½" sq., 8½" h. 70.00
Compote, open, 7½" sq., 4½" h. 37.50
Compote, open, 9½" d., 6½" h. 90.00
Cookie jar, cov. 125.00
Creamer 45.00
Creamer, miniature 50.00
Creamer & cov. sugar bowl, pr. 100.00
Lamp, kerosene-type, w/original burner, 9½" h. 125.00
Pitcher, water 85.00
Plate, 9" sq., 2" h., turned-up sides 32.50
Salt shaker w/original top, single (ILLUS.) 32.50
Sauce dish, round 35.00
Sauce dish, square 12.00
Spooner 45.00
Sugar bowl, cov. 55.00
Syrup pitcher w/silver plate top 112.00
Tumbler 24.00

FEATHER (Doric, Indiana Swirl or Finecut & Feather)

Banana boat, footed 75.00
Berry set, master bowl & 6 sauce dishes, 7 pcs. 120.00
Bowl, 6½" d. 12.00
Bowl, 7" oval 18.00
Bowl, 7½" d. 20.00

Bowl, 8½" oval, flat 25.00
Butter dish, cov., clear 50.00
Butter dish, cov., green 175.00
Cake stand, clear, 8½" d. 25.00
Cake stand, clear, 9½" d. . . . 35.00 to 45.00
Cake stand, green, 9½" d. . . . . 150.00 to 175.00
Cake stand, clear, 11" d. 72.00
Celery vase 34.00
Compote, cov., 8½" d., high stand 125.00
Compote, open, jelly, 5" d., 4¾" h. 22.00
Cordial . . . . 45.00 to 55.00
Cordials, set of 6 . . . . 300.00
Creamer 32.00
Cruet w/original stopper, clear 48.00
Cruet w/original stopper, green 185.00
Doughnut stand, 8" w., 4½" h. 36.00
Goblet, clear 57.00
Goblet, amber-stained 150.00
Honey dish, 3½" d. . . . . 9.00 to 15.00
Pitcher, milk, clear 48.00
Pitcher, water, clear 52.00
Pitcher, water, green 200.00
Plate, 10" d. 40.00
Relish, clear, 8¼" oval 15.00
Relish, amber-stained, 8¼" oval 45.00
Salt shaker w/original top (single) . . 25.00
Sauce dish, flat or footed 12.00
Spooner 25.00

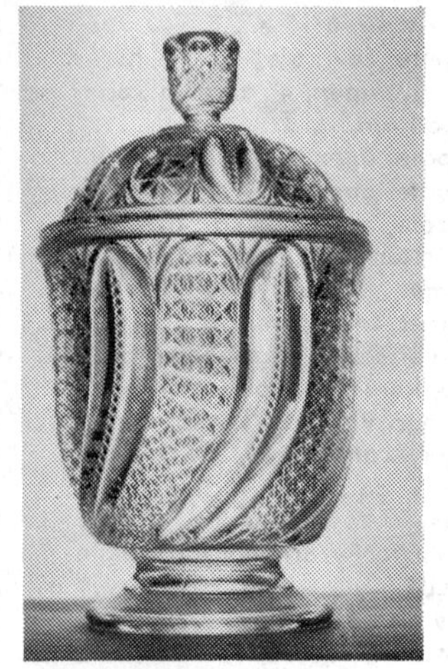

Feather Sugar Bowl

Sugar bowl, cov. (ILLUS.) 42.00
Sugar bowl, open, large 22.00
Syrup pitcher w/original top, clear . . 100.00
Syrup pitcher w/original top, green 315.00
Table set, cov. butter dish, cov. sugar bowl, creamer & spooner, 4 pcs. 125.00
Toothpick holder, clear 50.00
Toothpick holder, green 185.00
Tumbler 50.00
Wine 33.00

FESTOON

Festoon Cake Stand

Berry set, 9¼" d. master bowl & 6 sauce dishes, 7 pcs. 70.00
Bowl, 7 x 4½" rectangle 22.50
Bowl, berry, 8" rectangle 25.00
Bowl, berry, 9 x 5½" rectangle 31.50
Butter dish, cov. 45.00
Cake stand, high pedestal, 9" d. (ILLUS.) 42.00
Cake stand, high pedestal, 10" d. . . . 46.00
Compote, open, 9" d., high stand . . . 58.00
Creamer 22.00
Finger bowl, 4½" d., 2" h. 30.00
Marmalade jar, cov. 37.50
Pickle castor, silver plate frame & cover w/bird finial 85.00
Pitcher, water 59.00
Plate, 7" d. 35.00
Plate, 8" d. 35.00
Plate, 9" d. 29.00
Relish, 7 x 4" 15.00
Sauce dish 8.00
Spooner 30.00
Sugar bowl, cov. 50.00
Table set, 4 pcs. 185.00
Tray, water, 10" d. 32.50
Tumbler 25.00
Waste bowl 40.00
Water set, pitcher, tray & 4 tumblers, 6 pcs. . . . . 195.00 to 250.00

FINECUT

Bread tray, amber 40.00
Butter dish, cov. 45.00
Cake stand 30.00
Celery vase, vaseline, ornate square silver plate holder 115.00
Compote, cov., 9¼" d., 7" h., amber 135.00
Creamer, blue 37.50
Creamer, clear 35.00
Cruet w/matching stopper, amber . . 165.00
Goblet, amber 45.00
Goblet, clear 17.50
Goblet, vaseline 40.00
Pickle dish, 9 x 6" 12.00
Pitcher, water, amber 75.00

Pitcher, water, clear ... 40.00
Plate, 6" d., blue ... 20.00
Plate, 6" d., clear ... 10.00
Plate, 6" d., vaseline ... 22.50
Plate, 7" d., amber ... 20.00
Plate, 7" d., clear ... 20.00
Plate, 7" d., vaseline ... 20.00
Plate, 10" d., amber ... 20.00
Plate, 10" d., clear ... 18.00
Salt & pepper shakers w/original tops, pr. ... 25.00
Salt & pepper shakers w/original tops, vaseline, pr. ... 40.00
Sauce dish, vaseline ... 18.00
Spooner, amber ... 35.00
Spooner, clear ... 17.00
Spooner, vaseline ... 38.00
Sugar bowl, cov. ... 35.00
Table set, amber, 4 pcs. ... 300.00
Toothpick holder, hat shape on plate, amber ... 21.00
Toothpick holder, hat shape on plate, blue ... 28.50
Toothpick holder, hat shape on plate, clear ... 26.00
Toothpick holder, hat shape on plate, vaseline ... 30.00
Tray, ice cream, lion's head handles, amber ... 40.00
Tray, water, amber ... 45.00
Tray, water, clear ... 45.00
Tray, water, vaseline, 9¼" d. ... 48.00
Tumbler, clear ... 15.00
Tumbler, vaseline ... 28.00
Waste bowl, vaseline ... 32.50
Whimsey, shoe on skate, amber ... 30.00
Whimsey, slipper, blue, 4" l. ... 35.00
Wine ... 14.00

FINECUT & BLOCK

Finecut & Block Pitcher

Butter dish, cov., 2-handled ... 75.00
Butter pat, clear w/blue blocks ... 18.00
Cake stand ... 35.00
Celery tray, blue, 11" l. ... 65.00
Celery tray, clear, 11" l. ... 27.50
Celery tray, clear w/blue blocks, 11" l. ... 60.00
Celery tray, clear w/yellow blocks ... 65.00
Champagne, clear w/blue blocks ... 85.00
Compote, open, jelly, blue ... 50.00
Compote, open, jelly, clear ... 18.00
Compote, open, jelly, clear w/blue blocks ... 50.00
Compote, open, 8" d., 6½" h., clear ... 32.50
Compote, open, 8" d., clear w/blue blocks ... 65.00
Compote, open, 8" d., 4¼" h., clear w/yellow blocks ... 45.00
Cordial ... 85.00
Creamer, clear ... 30.00
Creamer, clear w/amber blocks ... 67.00
Creamer, clear w/blue blocks ... 70.00
Creamer, clear w/pink blocks ... 75.00
Creamer, clear w/yellow blocks ... 76.50
Egg cup, single ... 27.50
Egg cup, double ... 29.00
Goblet, amber ... 50.00
Goblet, clear ... 30.00
Goblet, clear w/blue blocks ... 65.00
Goblet, clear w/pink blocks ... 50.00
Goblet, clear w/yellow blocks ... 50.00
Goblet, buttermilk, clear ... 25.00
Goblet, buttermilk, clear w/blue blocks ... 50.00
Goblet, buttermilk, clear w/pink blocks ... 80.00
Ice cream tray, clear w/amber blocks ... 85.00
Pitcher, water, amber (ILLUS.) ... 85.00
Pitcher, water, clear ... 42.50
Pitcher, water, clear w/amber blocks ... 85.00
Pitcher, water, clear w/blue blocks ... 90.00
Pitcher, water, clear w/pink blocks ... 125.00
Pitcher, water, clear w/yellow blocks ... 85.00
Plate, 5¾" d. ... 23.50
Relish, handled, clear w/yellow blocks, 7½" ... 140.00
Salt dip, clear w/blue blocks ... 20.00
Salt dip, clear w/pink blocks ... 20.00
Sauce dish, blue ... 14.50
Sauce dish, clear ... 8.50
Sauce dish, clear w/amber blocks ... 20.00
Spooner, clear ... 45.00
Spooner, clear w/amber blocks ... 45.00
Spooner, clear w/blue blocks ... 55.00
Sugar bowl, open, clear w/blue blocks ... 35.00
Table set, clear w/yellow blocks, 4 pcs. ... 265.00
Tray, corset-shaped, clear w/blue blocks, 14½ x 12½" ... 75.00
Tumbler, amber ... 22.50
Tumbler, blue ... 30.00
Tumbler, clear ... 17.50

Tumbler, clear w/blue blocks 40.00
Tumbler, clear w/pink blocks 40.00
Waste bowl, amber 45.00
Waste bowl, clear w/yellow blocks 95.00
Wine, clear 25.00
Wine, clear w/blue blocks 55.00

FINECUT & DIAMOND - **See Diamond Medallion Pattern**

FINECUT & FEATHER - **See Feather Pattern**

FINECUT & PANEL (Paneled Finecut)

Finecut & Panel Plate

Bowl, 8" oval, amber 18.50
Bowl, 8" oval, clear 18.00
Bread tray, amber, 13 x 9" ... 35.00 to 50.00
Bread tray, blue, 13 x 9" 45.00
Bread tray, clear, 13 x 9" 28.00
Butter dish, cov., amber 65.00
Cake stand, sq., blue 75.00
Cake stand, vaseline 50.00
Celery vase 35.00
Compote, open, high stand, amber 47.50
Compote, open, high stand, blue ... 50.00
Compote, open, high stand, clear ... 32.00
Creamer, amber 35.00
Goblet, amber 40.00
Goblet, clear 18.00
Goblet, clear w/amber bars 35.00
Goblet, vaseline 28.00
Pitcher, water, amber 80.00
Pitcher, water, blue 55.00
Plate, 6" d., amber 25.00
Plate, 6" d., blue 30.00
Plate, 6" d., clear 14.00
Plate, 6" d., vaseline (ILLUS.) 25.00
Plate, 7" d. 11.00
Relish, 7 x 3½" 22.50
Salt shaker w/original top (single) .. 10.00
Sauce dish, amber 12.00
Sauce dish, clear 8.00
Sauce dish, vaseline 13.50
Spooner, vaseline 30.00
Sugar bowl, cov., canary yellow 60.00
Tray, water, canary yellow, 12" w. 40.00
Tumbler, clear 18.00
Tumbler, vaseline 38.00
Wine, amber 30.00
Wine, blue 35.00
Wine, canary yellow 35.00
Wine, clear 14.00
Wine, vaseline 30.00
Wine set: decanter & 4 wines; vaseline, 5 pcs. 185.00

FINECUT BAND - **See Cottage Pattern**

FINE RIB

Butter dish, cov. 75.00
Castor set, complete w/frame 190.00
Celery vase 42.00
Champagne 75.00
Champagne, cut ovals 85.00
Compote, open, 10¼" d., 8¼" h., scalloped foot 185.00
Cordial 130.00
Creamer, 6" h. 325.00
Decanter w/bar lip, qt. 95.00
Egg cup, single 42.00
Egg cup, double 35.00
Goblet 75.00
Goblet, non-flint 35.00
Honey dish, 3½" d. 14.00
Pitcher, water, bulbous, applied handle 425.00
Salt dip, individual size 14.00
Salt dip, master size, footed, scalloped rim 30.00
Sauce dish, non-flint 7.50
Spoonholder 52.50
Sugar bowl, cov. 135.00
Tumbler 75.00
Tumbler, whiskey, handled, 3" h. 85.00
Tumbler, whiskey, blue 125.00
Tumbler, whiskey, non-flint 35.00
Wine 45.00

FISHSCALE

Fishscale Open Compote

Berry set, 8½" d. master bowl & 8 sauce dishes, 9 pcs. 85.00
Bowl, cov., 7" d. 55.00
Bowl, cov., 8½" d. 35.00
Bowl, cov., 9½" d. 40.00
Bowl, 8" d. 18.00
Bowl, 9½" d. 22.00
Bread platter 26.00
Butter dish, cov. 45.00
Cake stand, 8" d. 33.00
Cake stand, 10" d. 35.00
Celery vase 27.50
Compote, cov., 7½" d. 45.00
Compote, open, jelly 16.00
Compote, open, 6" d. 25.00
Compote, open, 7" d., high stand (ILLUS.) 32.50
Compote, open, 8" d., high stand . . . 25.00
Compote, open, 9" d., high stand . . . 45.00
Condiment tray, rectangular 35.00
Creamer 26.50
Goblet 26.00
Lamp, kerosene, hand-type w/finger grip 65.00
Pickle dish 18.50
Pitcher, milk 33.00
Pitcher, water 42.50
Plate, 7" d. 15.00
Plate, 8" d. 22.00
Plate, 9" sq. 26.00
Relish, 8½ x 5" 17.00
Salt shaker w/original top (single) . . 27.50
Sauce dish, flat or footed 9.00
Spooner 22.50
Sugar bowl, cov. 36.50
Tray, water, round 35.00
Tumbler 45.00

FLORIDA - See Paneled Herringbone Pattern

FLORIDA PALM

Florida Palm Goblet

Cake stand, 9½" d. 25.00
Celery vase 18.00
Compote, cov., 7" d., high stand . . . 50.00
Compote, open, 9" d. 35.00
Creamer 18.50
Goblet (ILLUS.) 22.50
Plate, 9" d. 15.00
Spooner 20.00
Sugar bowl, cov. 35.00
Tumbler, footed 28.00
Wine 23.50

FLOWER FLANGE - See Dewey Pattern

FLOWER POT (Potted Plant)

Flower Pot Creamer

Bread tray 45.00
Butter dish, cov. 40.00
Compote, open, 7¼" h. 18.00
Creamer, clear (ILLUS.) 30.00
Creamer, vaseline 45.00
Goblet 40.00
Pitcher, milk 40.00
Pitcher, water 58.00
Salt shaker w/original top (single) . . 20.00
Sauce dish 9.00
Spooner, clear 22.00
Spooner, vaseline 45.00
Sugar bowl, cov. 37.50

FLUTE

Flute Claret

Ale glass 50.00
Bar bottle, qt. 72.00
Bar bottle, blue, flint, qt. 250.00

Celery vase 80.00
Claret (ILLUS.) 25.00
Compote, open, 8¼" d., 3" h. 35.00
Egg cup, single 20.00
Egg cup, single, handled 60.00
Egg cup, double 24.00
Goblet, Bessimer Flute 20.00
Goblet, Brooklyn Flute 35.00
Goblet, Connecticut or New England Flute 17.50
Goblet 21.00
Tumbler, 6 panels, deep purple 120.00
Tumbler, jelly glass shape, 3½" h. . . 16.00
Tumbler, whiskey, handled 27.50
Whiskey shot glass, footed 25.00
Wine, New England Flute 20.00
Wine, Pittsburgh Flute 45.00
Wine, knob stem 15.00

FLYING ROBIN - See Hummingbird Pattern

FOUR PETAL

Four Petal Sugar Bowl

Creamer, applied handle 125.00
Sugar bowl, cov., rounded lid (ILLUS.) 75.00
Sugar bowl, open 45.00

FOUR PETAL FLOWER - See Delaware Pattern

FROSTED CIRCLE

Frosted Circle Sauce Dish

Bowl, 6" d. 28.00
Bowl, 8" d., 3¼" h. 25.00
Butter dish, cov. 45.00
Cake stand, 9½" d. 37.50
Celery tray 20.00
Champagne 55.00
Claret 45.00
Compote, cov., 5" d., 9" h. 43.50
Compote, open, 7" d., 6" h. 25.00
Compote, open, 9" d., 6" h. 32.50
Compote, open, 9" d., 8½" h. 50.00
Compote, open, 10" d., high stand, scalloped rim 57.50
Creamer 35.00
Cruet w/original stopper 42.50
Goblet 32.50
Pitcher, water, tankard 80.00
Plate, 9" d. 65.00
Punch cup 15.00
Relish, 8 x 4½" 20.00
Salt shaker w/original top (single) . . 35.00
Sauce dish (ILLUS.) 10.00
Spooner 32.00
Sugar bowl, cov. 49.00
Sugar shaker w/original top 48.00
Syrup pitcher w/original top 110.00
Table set, 4 pcs. 145.00
Tumbler 30.00
Wine 32.50

FROSTED LEAF

Celery vase 140.00
Creamer 395.00
Egg cup 90.00
Goblet 82.00
Salt dip 50.00
Sauce dish 22.50
Spooner 65.00
Tumbler, footed 95.00
Wine 110.00

FROSTED LION (Rampant Lion)

(Items may be plain or with etched designs)

Frosted Lion Covered Compote

Bowl, cov., 6 7/8 x 3 7/8" oblong, collared base 110.00

Bowl, cov., 8 7/8 x 5½" oblong, collared base 125.00
Bowl, open, oval 73.00
Bread plate, rope edge, closed handles, 10½" d. 89.00
Butter dish, cov., rampant lion finial 102.00
Celery vase 70.00
Compote, cov., 5" d., 8½" h. 155.00
Compote, cov., 6¾" oval, 7" h., collared base, rampant lion finial .... 165.00 to 245.00
Compote, cov., 7" d., 11" h., lion head finial (ILLUS.) 165.00
Compote, cov., 7¾" oval, low collared base, rampant lion finial .... 100.00 to 125.00
Compote, cov., 8" d., 13" h., rampant lion finial .... 145.00 to 195.00
Compote, cov., 8½ x 7¾" oval, low collared base, rampant lion finial .... 85.00 to 120.00
Compote, cov., 8¾ x 5½" oval, 8¼" h., rampant lion finial 110.00
Compote, cov., 10" d., collared base, rampant lion finial 88.00
Compote, open, 7" d., 6¼" h. 70.00
Compote, open, 7¾" d., high stand 60.00
Compote, open, 8" oblong, low stand 80.00
Creamer 62.00
Creamer & cov. sugar bowl, child's, pr. 175.00
Egg cup 72.00
Goblet 58.00
Marmalade jar, cov., rampant lion finial 88.00
Paperweight, embossed "Gillinder & Sons, Centennial" 110.00
Pickle dish 60.00
Pitcher, water .... 250.00 to 275.00
Platter, 10½ x 9" oval, lion handles 80.00
Relish 38.00
Salt dip, cov., master size, collared base, rectangular 290.00
Sauce dish, 4" to 5" d. 20.00
Spooner 56.00
Sugar bowl, cov., rampant lion finial 80.00
Syrup pitcher w/original top 300.00
Wine, 4 1/8" h. .... 125.00 to 150.00

FROSTED RIBBON

Bowl, low 22.00
Bread platter 32.50
Butter dish, cov. 45.00
Celery vase 39.00
Champagne 100.00
Cologne bottle w/stopper 45.00
Compote, cov., 6½" d. 55.00
Compote, cov., 8" d., 11" h. 85.00
Compote, open, 10" d., high stand 40.00
Creamer 50.00
Goblet 30.00
Pitcher, water 65.00
Salt dip, individual size 5.00
Salt dip, master size 8.50
Sauce dish 12.00
Spooner 28.00
Sugar bowl, cov. 54.00
Tray, water 95.00

FROSTED ROMAN KEY (Roman Key With Flutes or Ribs)

Frosted Roman Key Creamer

Bowl, 9¾" d., 3½" h. 42.50
Butter dish, cov. 55.00
Celery vase 75.00
Champagne 77.50
Compote, cov., 7" d. 75.00
Compote, open, 6½" d. 78.00
Cordial 45.00
Creamer, applied handle (ILLUS.) 56.00
Decanter w/stopper, qt. 85.00
Egg cup 44.00
Goblet 46.00
Goblet, buttermilk 42.50
Sauce dish 13.00
Spooner 32.00
Sugar bowl, cov. 82.50
Tumbler, bar 98.00
Tumbler, footed 63.00
Wine 58.00

FROSTED STORK

Bowl, 9" oval, 101 border 45.00
Bread plate, round 58.00
Butter dish, cov. 70.00
Creamer 54.00
Finger bowl 90.00
Goblet 70.00
Pickle castor w/original frame 195.00
Platter, 11½ x 8" oval, 101 border 70.00
Platter, 12 x 8" oval 49.00
Platter, deer & doe border 82.00
Relish, 101 border 58.00
Sauce dish 32.00

Spooner 50.00
Sugar bowl, cov., stork finial 95.00
Tray, water, 15½ x 11" 115.00
Waste bowl 40.00

FROSTED WAFFLE - See Hidalgo Pattern

GALLOWAY (Mirror or Virginia)

Basket, twisted handle, 8½ x 5 x 10" 75.00
Berry set: master bowl & 3 sauce dishes; ruby-stained, 4 pcs. 95.00
Berry set: master bowl & 4 sauce dishes; clear, 5 pcs. 48.50
Berry set: master bowl & 6 sauce dishes; ruby-stained, 7 pcs. 135.00
Bowl, 5¼ x 3½" rectangle 10.00
Bowl, 5½" d. 10.00
Bowl, 6½" d. 17.50
Bowl, 7¼" d., 3½" h. 19.50
Bowl, 8½" oval, flared rim 14.00
Bowl, 9¾" d., flat 35.00
Bowl, ice cream, 11" d., 3½" h. 45.00
Butter dish, cov., clear 55.00
Butter dish, cov., ruby-stained 110.00
Cake stand, 9¼" d., 6" h. 65.00
Carafe 75.00
Celery vase, clear 30.00
Celery vase, ruby-stained 75.00
Compote, open, 4¼" d., 6" h. 30.00
Compote, open, 8½" d., 7" h. 58.00
Creamer 23.00
Creamer, individual size 15.00
Creamer & cov. sugar bowl, etched, pr. 95.00
Cruet w/stopper 38.00
Cruet, no stopper 24.00
Finger bowl, 6" d. 22.00
Goblet 72.00
Mug, 4½" d. 40.00
Olive dish, 6 x 4" ....16.50 to 25.00
Pickle castor w/silver plate lid & frame 125.00
Pitcher, child's 22.50
Pitcher, lemonade, applied handle .. 70.00
Pitcher, milk 72.00
Pitcher, water, 9" h. 55.00
Plate, 6½" d. 20.00
Plate, 8" d. 20.00
Punch bowl, 14" d. 145.00
Punch cup ....6.50 to 10.00
Relish, clear, 8¼" l. 14.00
Relish, ruby-stained 30.00
Salt shaker w/original top (single) .. 14.50
Salt & pepper shakers w/original tops, gold trim, 3" h., pr. 35.00
Sauce dish, flat or footed 12.00
Spooner, amber-stained 35.00
Spooner, clear 25.00
Sugar bowl, cov. 42.50
Sugar bowl, open, individual size ... 12.00
Sugar shaker w/original top 37.50
Syrup pitcher w/metal spring top ... 57.50
Syrup pitcher w/metal spring top, ruby-stained 135.00
Toothpick holder, clear 27.00
Toothpick holder, green 52.00
Tumbler 30.00
Vase, 8" h. 25.00
Vase, 9½" h. 30.00
Vase, 11" h. 35.00
Vase, 14" h. 20.00
Waste bowl 25.00
Water set, pitcher & 6 tumblers, 7 pcs. ....165.00 to 225.00
Water set, child's, pitcher & 4 tumblers, 5 pcs. 50.00
Wine 36.00

GARFIELD DRAPE

Garfield Drape Bread Plate

Bread plate, "We Mourn Our Nation's Loss," 11½" d. (ILLUS.) 50.00
Butter dish, cov. 59.00
Cake stand, 9½" d. 47.50
Celery vase, pedestal base 42.00
Compote, cov., 6" d., low stand 50.00
Compote, cov., 8" d., 12½" h. 135.00
Creamer 34.00
Goblet 35.00
Lamp, kerosene-type, cobalt blue, 9" h. 150.00
Pickle dish, 7¼" oval 20.00
Pitcher, milk 62.00
Pitcher, water 78.00
Plate, 10" d., star center 60.00
Sauce dish, flat or footed 9.00
Spooner 26.00
Sugar bowl, cov. 60.00
Tumbler 30.00

GEORGIA - See Peacock Feather Pattern

GODDESS OF LIBERTY - See Ceres Pattern

GOOD LUCK - See Horseshoe Pattern

GOOSEBERRY

Butter dish, cov. 50.00

Gooseberry Compote

Compote, cov., 7" d. (ILLUS.) 70.00
Creamer 28.00
Goblet 28.00
Mug 26.00
Sauce dish 8.00
Spooner 18.00
Sugar bowl, open 40.00
Tumbler, bar 30.00
Tumbler, water .... 22.00 to 30.00

GOTHIC

Gothic Egg Cup

Bowl, master berry or fruit, flat 70.00
Butter dish, cov. 85.00
Castor bottle 18.00
Castor set, 5-bottle, w/pewter
frame 125.00
Celery vase 90.00
Champagne 165.00
Compote, open, 8" d., 4" h. 65.00
Creamer, applied handle 90.00
Egg cup (ILLUS.) 42.00
Goblet 58.00
Relish 65.00
Sauce dish 14.00

Spooner 40.00
Sugar bowl, cov. 80.00
Tumbler 95.00
Wine, 3¾" h. .... 100.00 to 130.00

GRAND - See Diamond Medallion Pattern

GRAPE & FESTOON

Grape & Festoon Spooner

Butter dish, cov., stippled leaf 50.00
Celery vase, stippled leaf .... 30.00 to 45.00
Compote, cov., 8" d., high stand,
acorn finial, stippled leaf 115.00
Compote, open, 8" d., low stand ... 75.00
Creamer, stippled leaf 56.00
Egg cup, stippled leaf 30.00
Goblet, stippled leaf 25.00
Goblet, buttermilk, stippled leaf 29.00
Goblet, veined leaf 25.00
Pitcher, water, stippled leaf 97.50
Plate, 6" d., stippled leaf 17.50
Relish, stippled leaf 6.00
Salt dip, footed, stippled leaf 24.00
Sauce dish, flat, stippled leaf,
4" d. 8.50
Sauce dish, flat, veined leaf 13.00
Spooner, stippled leaf (ILLUS.) 22.00
Spooner, veined leaf 22.50
Sugar bowl, cov., stippled leaf 50.00
Sugar bowl, open, stippled leaf 25.00

GRAPE & FESTOON WITH SHIELD

Compote, cov., 8" d., low stand 39.00
Creamer, applied handle 35.00
Goblet, w/American shield 47.50
Goblet, w/shield & grapes 22.50
Mug, 1 7/8" h. 16.50
Mug, cobalt blue, 2½" h. 27.50
Mug, 3¼" h. 18.50
Pitcher, water, applied
handle .... 65.00 to 70.00
Relish, 7 x 4¼" 16.50
Sauce dish, flat or footed ..... 6.00 to 12.00
Spooner 26.50

GRASSHOPPER (Locust)

(Items may be plain or with etched designs)

Berry set, footed master bowl & 11 sauce dishes, 12 pcs. 127.00
Bowl, cov., 7" d. 27.50
Bowl, open, 7" d., footed 20.00
Butter dish, cov. 50.00
Butter dish, cov., w/insect 55.00
Celery vase, w/insect 62.50
Compote, cov., 8¼" d. 52.00
Creamer 34.00
Goblet, w/insect, amber 85.00
Goblet, w/insect, clear 27.00
Pitcher, water 72.50
Plate, 8½" d., footed 20.00
Sauce dish, footed 7.00
Spooner 35.00
Spooner, w/insect 44.00
Sugar bowl, cov. 40.00
Sugar bowl, cov., w/insect 55.00

GREEK KEY (Heisey's Greek Key)

Butter dish, cov. 125.00
Celery tray, 9" l. 38.00
Compote, open, jelly, 5" d., low stand 28.00
Creamer & open sugar bowl, pr. 56.00
Goblet .... 70.00 to 90.00
Humidor, cov. 285.00
Ice tub, small 95.00
Lamp, kerosene-type, miniature 75.00
Lamp, kerosene-type, large 95.00
Nut dish, individual size 22.00
Pitcher, pt. 125.00
Pitcher, tankard, 1½ qt. 225.00
Punch bowl & pedestal base, 2 pcs. 250.00
Punch cup 15.00
Punch set, bowl, base & 12 cups, 14 pcs. 425.00
Salt dip, master size 20.00
Sauce dish 20.00
Sherbet 22.50
Soda fountain (straw-holder) jar 128.00
Spooner 25.00
Tumbler 75.00

GUARDIAN ANGEL - See Cupid & Venus Pattern

HAIRPIN (Sandwich Loop)

Bowl, 5½" hexagon 100.00
Bowl, 6¼" d. 100.00
Bowl, 8¼" d., 1½" h. 300.00
Celery vase 38.00
Champagne 85.00
Compote, open, 8" d., 4¼" h. 85.00
Compote, open, 9½" d., 9" h., milk white 225.00
Decanter w/stopper, qt. 90.00
Egg cup 17.50
Egg cup, fiery opalescent 75.00
Goblet 38.00
Pitcher, 8" h. 175.00
Plate, 6¼" d. 100.00
Plate, 7" d. 120.00
Salt dip, cov. 85.00
Salt dip, master size 20.00
Sauce dish, 4" d. 11.00
Spooner 36.00
Sugar bowl, cov. 95.00
Tumbler 45.00
Tumbler, whiskey, handled 45.00
Wine 55.00

HALLEY'S COMET

Halley's Comet Wine

Celery vase 30.00
Goblet 35.00
Jar, cov., 3-footed 49.00
Pitcher, water 98.00
Relish, 7 x 4½" 15.00
Salt dip 20.00
Spooner .... 40.00 to 55.00
Tumbler 26.00
Wine (ILLUS.) 25.00

HAMILTON

Hamilton Compote

Bar bottle, qt. 135.00
Butter dish, cov. 80.00
Cake stand 175.00
Compote, open, 7" d., low stand 44.00
Compote, open, 8" d., 5½" h. (ILLUS.) 45.00

Compote, open, 8" d., 8" h. 70.00
Creamer 65.00
Egg cup 32.50
Goblet 40.00
Pitcher, water . . . . .255.00 to 335.00
Salt dip, footed 30.00
Sauce dish 12.00
Spooner 32.00
Sugar bowl, cov. 125.00
Tumbler, bar 65.00
Tumbler, water 80.00
Tumbler, whiskey, applied handle . . 90.00
Wine 90.00

HAMILTON WITH LEAF

Butter dish, cov., frosted leaf 80.00
Compote, open, 6" d., 4½" h. 78.00
Creamer, frosted leaf 55.00
Egg cup, clear leaf 55.00
Goblet, clear leaf 50.00
Goblet, frosted leaf 55.00
Lamp base, kerosene-type, scalloped foot, clear leaf 80.00
Spooner, clear leaf 30.00
Sugar bowl, cov., clear leaf 90.00
Sweetmeat dish, cov., clear leaf 90.00
Tumbler, clear leaf 55.00
Tumbler, frosted leaf 125.00
Tumbler, bar, frosted leaf 125.00
Tumbler, whiskey, handled, clear leaf 100.00
Wine 70.00

HAND (Pennsylvania, Early)

Bowl, 9" d. 37.00
Bread plate, 10½ x 8" oval 28.00
Butter dish, cov. 85.00
Cake stand 55.00
Celery vase 42.00
Compote, cov., 8" d., high stand . . . 92.50
Compote, open, 7¾" d., 6¾" h. 42.50
Compote, open, 9" d., low stand . . . 27.50
Compote, open, electric blue 145.00
Cordial 85.00
Creamer 35.00
Creamer, child's 45.00
Goblet 42.00
Marmalade jar, cov. 49.00
Mug 45.00
Pitcher, water 70.00
Sauce dish, 4½" d. 12.00
Spooner 24.00
Sugar bowl, cov. 65.00
Tumbler, water 135.00
Wine, clear 35.00
Wine, green 38.00

HARP

Bowl, 6½"d., 1½" h., 10-sided, opaque white 375.00
Goblet, flared sides 650.00
Goblet, straight sides 250.00
Lamp, kerosene, hand-type w/applied finger grip 195.00

Harp Spillholder

Spillholder (ILLUS.) 67.50

HEARTS OF LOCH LAVEN - *See Shuttle Pattern & Greentown "Special Focus"*

HEART WITH THUMBPRINT

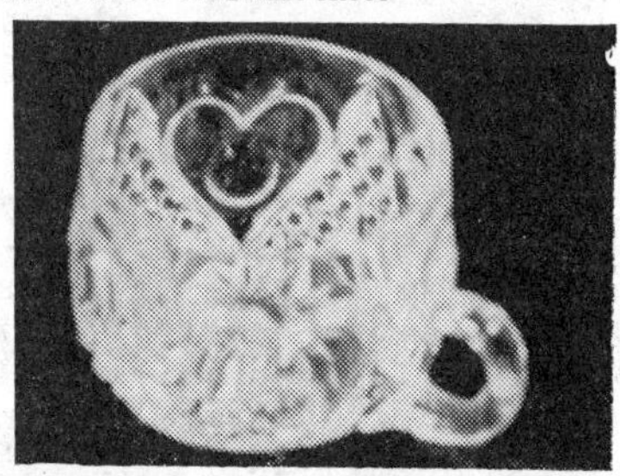

Heart with Thumbprint Punch Cup

Banana boat, 7½ x 6½" 85.00
Barber bottle w/original pewter stopper 125.00
Berry set, master bowl & 6 sauce dishes, 7 pcs. 110.00
Bowl, 7" sq., 3½" h. 37.50
Bowl, 9" d. 34.00
Bowl, 10" d., scalloped rim 36.00
Carafe 55.00
Card tray, clear 27.50
Card tray, green 45.00
Celery vase 49.00
Cordial, 3" h. 150.00
Creamer 30.00
Creamer & open sugar bowl, individual size, green w/gold, pr. . . 80.00
Cruet w/original stopper 68.00
Goblet, clear 50.00
Goblet, green w/gold 83.00
Ice bucket 58.00
Lamp, kerosene-type, green, 9" h. . . 117.00
Mustard jar w/silver plate cover 95.00
Nappy, heart-shaped 30.00
Olive dish, handled, green 42.50
Pitcher, water 50.00

Plate, 6" d. 20.00
Plate, 12" d. 47.50
Powder jar w/silver plate cover 45.00
Punch cup, clear (ILLUS.) 17.50
Punch cup, green 22.50
Relish, w/gold 17.50
Rose bowl, 5" d. 32.50
Salt shaker w/original top (single) .. 50.00
Sauce dish, clear 15.00
Sauce dish, green 32.00
Spooner 40.00
Sugar bowl, cov., large 45.00
Sugar bowl, open, individual size, clear, pewter rim 21.00
Sugar bowl, open, individual size, green w/gold, pewter rim 40.00
Syrup jug w/original pewter top .... 100.00 to 125.00
Tray, 8 1/8 x 4 1/8" 25.00
Tumbler, water, clear 42.00
Tumbler, water, ruby-stained 115.00
Vase, 6" h., trumpet-shaped 21.00
Vase, 6" h., green 42.00
Vase, 10" h., trumpet-shaped 51.00
Waste bowl 65.00
Water set, carafe & 6 tumblers, 7 pcs. 265.00
Wine 45.00

HERCULES PILLAR (Pillar Variant)

Butter dish, cov. 32.00
Celery vase 47.00
Cordial, 3¾" h. 38.00
Egg cup, double 27.50
Goblet 27.50
Syrup jug w/pewter top, amber, 8" h. 125.00
Syrup jug w/original top, blue 140.00
Tumbler 45.00
Whiskey taster 13.50
Wine 35.00

HERRINGBONE (Herringbone with Star & Shield Motif)

Berry set, master bowl & 6 sauce dishes, 7 pcs. 125.00
Celery vase 30.00
Creamer 20.00
Goblet 20.00
Salt dip, master size 14.00
Sauce dish 10.50
Spooner 20.00
Sugar bowl, cov. 24.00

HERRINGBONE BAND

Egg cup 18.50
Goblet 13.00
Sauce dish, 4" sq. 9.50
Spooner, pedestal base, scalloped rim 22.00
Sugar bowl, open 15.00
Wine 20.00

HICKMAN (Le Clede)

Hickman Creamer

Banana stand 65.00
Bowl, 5" d., green w/gold 8.00
Bowl, 7" sq. 15.00
Bowl, 7 x 6", green w/gold 25.00
Butter dish, cov. 37.50
Cake stand, 8½" to 9½" d. 30.00
Celery dish, boat-shaped, green 22.00
Champagne 21.50
Compote, cov., 5" d. 36.00
Compote, cov., 7" d., high stand ... 55.00
Compote, open, jelly, green 16.00
Compote, open, 7½" d., 5½" h. 19.50
Compote, open, 8" d., 6½" h. 32.50
Condiment set: salt & pepper shakers & cruet w/original stopper on cloverleaf-shaped tray; green, miniature, 4 pcs. 65.00
Creamer, green (ILLUS.) 22.50
Cruet w/ball-shaped stopper 45.00
Doughnut stand, scalloped rim, 8" d. 45.00
Goblet, clear 30.00
Goblet, green w/gold 35.00
Ice tub 47.50
Pickle dish, green 15.00
Pitcher, water 60.00
Punch cup, clear 8.00
Punch cup, green 15.00
Relish, clear, 4" sq. 14.00
Relish, green 15.00
Rose bowl 27.50
Salt shaker w/original top (single) .. 9.50
Sauce dish, clear 7.00
Sauce dish, green 10.00
Spooner 22.50
Sugar bowl, cov., clear 35.00
Sugar bowl, cov., green 45.00
Sugar shaker w/original top 40.00
Table set, w/gold, 4 pcs. 175.00
Toothpick holder 50.00
Tumbler 25.00
Vase, 10" h. 37.00
Vase, 10½" h., purple 45.00
Water set: pitcher & 6 tumblers; w/gold, 7 pcs. 225.00
Wine, clear 28.00
Wine, green 30.00

HIDALGO (Frosted Waffle)

(Items may be plain or with etched designs)

Hidalgo Compote

Bowl, 9" d., clear & frosted 24.00
Bowl, salad, 11" sq. 22.00
Butter dish, cov. 45.00
Celery dish, boat-shaped, 13" l. 50.00
Celery vase 30.00
Compote, open, 7" d. (ILLUS.) 20.00
Creamer 36.00
Cruet w/original stopper 60.00
Egg cup 30.00
Goblet 16.50
Pitcher, water 50.00
Relish, shell-shaped ....8.00 to 15.00
Sauce dish, handled 10.50
Spooner 40.00
Sugar bowl, cov. 35.00
Sugar shaker w/original top 45.00
Syrup pitcher w/original top 70.00
Tray, water 55.00
Tumbler 15.00
Tumbler, ruby-stained 25.00

HINOTO (Diamond Point with Panels)

Hinoto Creamer

Butter dish, cov. 90.00
Celery vase 42.50
Champagne 75.00
Creamer, applied handle (ILLUS.) ... 75.00
Egg cup, handled 23.00
Goblet 45.00
Pitcher, tankard, 9" h., applied handle 110.00
Spooner 38.00
Sugar bowl, cov. 50.00
Tumbler, footed 38.00
Tumbler, whiskey, handled, footed 45.00
Wine 57.50

HOBNAIL

Hobnail Creamer

Barber bottle, applied rigaree at neck, blue 90.00
Bowl, 7½" d., ruffled rim, blue 35.00
Butter dish, cov., amber 35.00
Cake stand, pedestal base, square .. 85.00
Cologne bottle, 6½" h. 22.00
Compote, 6" h., fluted rim, blue 55.00
Creamer, fluted top, applied handle, amber, 3 x 2" 25.00
Creamer, 3-footed, blue 35.00
Creamer, scalloped & ornamented top, 6" h. (ILLUS.) 45.00
Creamer, individual size, amber 35.00
Cruet w/original stopper, 4½" h. 45.00
Goblet, amber 27.50
Goblet, blue 26.00
Goblet, clear 15.00
Hat shape, 10" d., 6" h. 49.00
Lamp, kerosene, hand-type w/finger grip, clear 48.00
Lamp, kerosene, hand-type w/finger grip, opaque white w/amber foot & handle, 4¼" d., 6" h. 110.00
Mayonnaise dish, cov. 12.00
Mug, amber ....22.50 to 35.00
Mug, clear 15.00
Pitcher, 8" h., flat base, blue 195.00
Pitcher, 8" h., square top 60.00
Pitcher, 8" h., ruby-stained 45.00
Punch cup 22.50

Rose bowl, 6" d., 5½" h. 85.00
Salt & pepper shakers w/original tops, sapphire blue, pr. 27.50
Sauce dish, square, ruby-stained ... 45.00
Spooner, ruffled rim, amber 32.00
Spooner, clear 26.50
Sugar shaker w/original top 42.50
Syrup pitcher w/original top 72.00
Toothpick holder, amber 30.00
Toothpick holder, blue 25.00
Toothpick holder, vaseline 32.50
Tray, water, blue, 11½" d. 55.00
Tumbler, amber 30.00
Tumbler, 10-row, blue 30.00
Tumbler, 10-row, clear 25.00
Tumbler, 10-row, Rubina Frosted ... 95.00
Tumbler, ruby-stained 45.00
Tumbler, vaseline 46.50
Vase, 3¾" h., 4¼" widest d., squat, cranberry 79.00
Wine, amber 20.00
Wine, blue 25.00
Wine, clear 20.00

HOBNAIL WITH FAN

Hobnail with Fan Bowl

Bowl, 6" d. 20.00
Bowl, 7" d., blue (ILLUS.) 47.50
Celery vase 38.00
Creamer, blue 20.00
Goblet 30.00
Sauce dish 8.00
Spooner, blue 45.00

HOBNAIL WITH THUMBPRINT BASE

Hobnail with Thumbprint Pitcher

Butter dish, cov. 55.00
Butter dish, cov., child's, amber 95.00
Creamer, amber 37.50
Creamer, blue 45.00
Creamer, child's, blue 23.00
Pitcher, 7" h., ruby-stained rim 57.50
Pitcher, 8" h., amber 90.00
Pitcher, 8" h., blue (ILLUS.) 80.00
Spooner, blue 45.00
Sugar bowl, cov. 35.00
Table set, child's, 3 pcs. 50.00
Table set, vaseline, 4 pcs. 255.00
Waste bowl, amber 40.00

HONEYCOMB

Honeycomb Celery Vase

Ale glass 42.00
Barber bottle w/pewter top 45.00
Butter dish & cover w/knob finial, flint 60.00
Cake stand, 10½" d. 35.00
Candlesticks, cobalt blue, flint, 9½" h., pr. 575.00
Celery vase, flint 30.00
Celery vase, Loredo Honeycomb, flint 35.00
Celery vase, Vernon Honeycomb, flint, 9" h. (ILLUS.) 65.00
Champagne, flint 40.00
Champagne, non-flint 8.00
Compote, cov., 6½" d., 8½" h., flint 80.00
Compote, cov., 9¼" d., 11½" h., flint 90.00
Compote, open, 8¾" d., 7" h., non-flint 45.00
Compote, open, 11" d., 8" h., flint ....100.00 to 125.00
Cordial, flint, 3¼" h. 25.00
Creamer, applied handle, flint 30.00
Decanter w/bar lip, flint, 10½" h. .. 75.00
Decanter w/original stopper, flint, 13" h. 150.00
Egg cup 18.00
Goblet, flint 30.00
Goblet, non-flint 13.00
Goblet, Banded Vernon Honeycomb 18.00

Goblet, Barrel Honeycomb w/knob stem 14.50
Goblet, New York Honeycomb 17.00
Mug 30.00
Pitcher, water, 8½" h., molded handle, polished pontil, flint 160.00
Pitcher, water, 9" h., applied handle, flint 96.00
Pomade jar, cov., flint 48.00
Relish 30.00
Salt dip, pedestal base, flint 35.00
Sauce dish, flint 11.00
Spillholder, flint 22.00
Spooner, flint 33.50
Spooner, non-flint 20.00
Sugar bowl, cov., flint 75.00
Syrup pitcher w/pewter top, flint ... 128.00
Tumbler, bar 24.00
Tumbler, footed, flint 26.00
Tumbler, Vernon Honeycomb, flint .. 55.00
Tumbler, whiskey, Vernon Honeycomb, flint 125.00
Vases, 10¼" h., Vernon Honeycomb, flint, pr. 150.00
Wine, flint 25.00
Wine, non-flint 13.00

HORN OF PLENTY

Horn of Plenty Compote

Bar bottle w/pewter pour spout, 8" 135.00
Bowl, 9 x 6¼" oval 145.00
Butter dish, cov. .... 100.00 to 140.00
Butter dish & cover w/Washington's head finial 1,100.00
Celery vase 132.00
Champagne 160.00
Compote, cov., 6¼" d., 7½" h. 175.00
Compote, cov., 8¼" oval, 5¾" h. ... 350.00
Compote, open, 7" d., 3" h. 125.00
Compote, open, 8" d., low stand ... 55.00
Compote, open, 8" d., 8" h. (ILLUS.) 118.00
Compote, open, 9" d., 8½" h. 200.00
Creamer, applied handle, 5½" h. ... 235.00
Decanter w/original stopper, pt. 135.00
Decanter w/original stopper, qt. 145.00
Dish, low foot, 7¼" d. 85.00
Dish, low foot, 8" d. 95.00
Egg cup, 3¾" h. 42.00
Goblet 62.00
Honey dish 17.50
Lamp, w/whale oil burner, 11" h. ... 175.00
Peppersauce bottle w/stopper 168.00
Pitcher, water 575.00
Plate, 6" d. 65.00
Relish, 7 x 5" oval 55.00
Salt dip, master size, oval 90.00
Sauce dish, 3½" to 5" d. 90.00
Spillholder, clambroth 650.00
Spillholder 55.00
Spooner 45.00
Spooner w/yellow-stained rim 225.00
Sugar bowl, cov. 112.00
Tumbler, bar 70.00
Tumbler, water, 3 5/8" h. 95.00
Tumbler, whiskey, 3" h. 134.00
Tumbler, whiskey, handled 235.00
Wine 120.00

HORSESHOE (Good Luck or Prayer Rug)

Horseshoe Cake Stand

Bowl, cov., 8 x 5" oval, flat, triple horseshoe finial 195.00
Bowl, open, 6" d. 12.50
Bowl, open, 8 x 5" oval, footed 37.50
Bowl, open, 10 x 6½" oval 25.00
Bread tray, single horseshoe handles 32.00
Bread tray, double horseshoe handles 65.00
Butter dish, cov. 68.00
Cake stand, 9" d., 6½" h. (ILLUS.) .. 62.00
Cake stand, upright horseshoe stem, 12 x 10" 200.00
Celery vase 50.00
Cheese dish, cov., w/woman churning butter in base 225.00
Compote, cov., 8" d., 9" h. 100.00
Compote, cov., 8" d., 11" h. 125.00
Compote, open, 8" d., 7¾" h. 35.00
Creamer 36.00
Creamer, individual size 38.50
Doughnut stand 57.50

Goblet, knob stem 40.00
Goblet, plain stem 28.00
Marmalade jar, cov. 97.50
Pitcher, milk 105.00
Pitcher, water 72.00
Plate, 7" d. 28.00
Plate, 10" d. 50.00
Relish, 8 x 5" 12.50
Relish, 9 x 5½" 22.50
Salt dip, individual size 19.00
Salt dip, master size, horseshoe shape 90.00
Sauce dish, flat or footed 12.00
Spooner 24.00
Sugar bowl, cov. 50.00
Sugar shaker w/original top 29.00
Tray, double horseshoe handles, 10 x 15" 84.00
Waste bowl, 4" d., 2½" h. 55.00
Wine 135.00

HUBER

(Items may be plain or with engraved designs)

Huber Compote

Celery vase 38.50
Champagne, barrel-shaped 25.00
Champagne, straight sides 40.00
Claret 27.00
Compote, open, 7" d. 55.00
Compote, open, engraved, 8" d. (ILLUS.) 75.00
Cordial .... 25.00 to 50.00
Creamer 80.00
Egg cup, single 14.00
Egg cup, double 30.00
Goblet .... 20.00 to 30.00
Goblet, buttermilk 16.50
Salt dip, master size 17.50
Spooner 20.00
Sugar bowl, cov. 56.00
Tumbler, bar 22.50
Tumbler, water 20.00
Vase 18.50
Wine 15.00

HUMMINGBIRD (Flying Robin or Bird & Fern)

Bowl, 6" d., amber 35.00
Butter dish, cov. 49.00
Celery vase, amber 68.00
Celery vase, clear 35.00
Compote, open, 7" d. 48.00
Creamer, amber 52.50
Creamer, blue 50.00
Creamer, clear 28.00
Goblet, amber 58.00
Goblet, blue 65.00
Goblet, clear 32.50
Pitcher, milk, amber 65.00
Pitcher, milk, blue 120.00
Pitcher, milk, clear 47.50
Pitcher, water, amber 105.00
Pitcher, water, blue 122.50
Pitcher, water, clear 80.00
Sauce dish 12.00
Spooner, amber 40.00
Spooner, blue 50.00
Spooner, clear 28.00
Sugar bowl, cov. 55.00
Tray, water, amber 165.00
Tray, water, blue 125.00
Tumbler, amber 55.00
Tumbler, clear 32.50
Tumbler, bar, amber 45.00
Waste bowl 35.00
Water set: pitcher & 6 tumblers; amber, 7 pcs. 350.00

HUNDRED EYE

Compote, open, 5" d., low stand 15.00
Creamer 18.50
Goblet 14.50
Mug, blue 25.00
Wine 9.00

ILLINOIS

Basket, applied reeded handle, 11½ x 7" 140.00
Bowl, 5¼" sq. 25.00
Butter dish, cov., 7" sq. 60.00
Candlestick (single) 70.00
Celery tray 40.00
Cheese dish, cov., square 60.00
Compote, open 145.00
Creamer, large 30.00
Cruet w/original stopper 40.00
Marmalade jar in silver plate frame w/spoon, 3 pcs. 135.00
Pitcher, water, tankard .... 50.00 to 65.00
Pitcher, water, silver plate rim 85.00
Plate, 7" sq. 20.00
Relish, 8½ x 3" 11.50
Salt dip, individual size 12.50
Salt & pepper shakers w/original tops, pr. 35.00
Sauce dish 15.00
Soda fountain (straw-holder) jar, cov., clear, 12½" h. 180.00
Soda fountain (straw-holder) jar, cov., green, 12½" h. .... 250.00 to 300.00
Spooner 27.50
Sugar bowl, cov. 50.00
Sugar bowl, cov., individual size 30.00

Sugar shaker w/original pewter top 65.00
Syrup pitcher w/original pewter top 95.00
Table set, cov. butter dish, open sugar bowl, creamer & spooner, 4 pcs. 200.00
Toothpick holder 29.00
Vase, 5¾" h. 25.00
Vase, 9" h., 4" d. 40.00

INDIANA SWIRL - See Feather Pattern

INVERTED FERN

Inverted Fern Goblet

Bowl, 7" d. 45.00
Butter dish, cov. 57.50
Cake stand 475.00
Champagne 115.00
Compote, open, 8" d. 55.00
Creamer, applied handle 122.00
Egg cup 28.00
Goblet (ILLUS.) 34.00
Honey dish, 4" d. 18.00
Pitcher, water 360.00
Salt dip, master size, footed 38.00
Sauce dish, 4" d. 12.50
Spooner 42.50
Sugar bowl, cov. 78.00
Tumbler 95.00
Wine 55.00

INVERTED LOOPS & FANS - See Maryland Pattern

INVERTED THISTLE - See Paneled Thistle Pattern

IOWA (Paneled Zipper or Zippered Block)

Bowl, 9" d., 5½" h., ruby-stained . . . 135.00
Carafe, water, clear 35.00
Carafe, water, ruby-stained 60.00
Compote, 8½" d., high stand 95.00
Creamer, ruby-stained 65.00
Cruet w/original stopper 52.50
Lamp, kerosene-type . . . . . 95.00 to 125.00
Nappy, handled 10.00
Olive dish 16.00
Punch cup 14.00
Salt & pepper shakers w/original tops, ruby-stained, pr. 55.00
Sauce dish, flat 7.50
Spooner 16.50
Sugar bowl, cov., ruby-stained 75.00
Sugar bowl, cov., small 20.00
Toothpick holder, clear 20.00
Toothpick holder, ruby-stained 65.00
Tumbler, clear 20.00
Tumbler, ruby-stained 37.50
Vases, gold trim, pr. 18.00
Wine 27.00

IRISH COLUMN - See Broken Column Pattern

IVY IN SNOW

Ivy in Snow Compote

Butter dish, cov. 50.00
Cake stand, 8" to 10" d. . . . . . 30.00 to 45.00
Celery vase, 8" h. 27.50
Compote, cov., 8" d., 13" h. (ILLUS.) 60.00
Compote, open, jelly 25.00
Creamer 17.50
Creamer, ruby-stained ivy sprigs . . . 65.00
Goblet 22.50
Pitcher, water 47.50
Plate, 7" d. 17.50
Plate, 10" d. 22.50
Relish 20.00
Sauce dish, flat or footed 12.00
Spooner 30.00
Syrup jug w/original top 70.00
Syrup jug w/original top, ruby-stained ivy sprigs 295.00
Tumbler 22.50
Wine 30.00
Wine, ruby-stained, souvenir 70.00

JACOB'S LADDER (Maltese)

Bowl, 6¾" d., 4¾" h., footed 25.00

Bowl, 7¼" d., footed 30.00
Bowl, 8½ x 5½" oval, flat 21.00
Bowl, 10" d., flat 27.00
Butter dish, cov., Maltese Cross finial 60.00
Butter dish, cov., pedestal base 65.00
Cake stand, 8" to 12" d. .....30.00 to 52.50
Castor set, cruet w/original Maltese Cross stopper, salt & pepper shakers & mustard jar w/original tops & pewter frame, 5 pcs. 200.00

Jacob's Ladder Celery Vase

Celery vase (ILLUS.) 38.50
Cologne bottle w/original Maltese Cross stopper, footed 125.00
Compote, cov., 6½" d., 10¼" h..... 60.00
Compote, cov., 9½" d., high stand 165.00
Compote, open, 6" d., 7" h. 20.00
Compote, open, 7" d., high stand ... 41.00
Compote, open, 8" d., low stand ... 19.00
Compote, open, 8" d., high stand ... 33.00
Compote, open, 9½" d., high stand ....45.00 to 68.00
Compote, open, 13½" d., 9" h. 75.00
Creamer 35.00
Cruet w/original stopper, footed ....85.00 to 110.00
Dish, 7¾" oval 18.00
Goblet 55.00
Marmalade jar, cov. 85.00
Pickle castor, complete w/stand 135.00
Pickle dish, Maltese Cross handle, blue 65.00
Pickle dish, Maltese Cross handle ... 18.00
Pitcher, water, applied handle 130.00
Plate, 6" d. 22.00
Relish, Maltese Cross handles, 10 x 5½" 17.00
Salt dip, master size, footed 27.00
Sauce dish, flat or footed 9.00
Spooner 30.00
Sugar bowl, cov. 43.50
Syrup jug w/pewter top 83.00
Tumbler, bar 75.00
Wine 32.00

JEWEL & DEWDROP (Kansas)

Jewel & Dewdrop Pitcher

Banana bowl 65.00
Bowl, 8½" d. 36.00
Bread tray, "Our Daily Bread," 10½" oval 40.00
Butter dish, cov. 64.00
Cake stand, 8" to 10" d. 54.00
Cake tray, "Cake Plate," 10½" oval ....60.00 to 75.00
Celery vase 34.00
Compote, cov., 6" d., high stand ... 67.50
Compote, cov., 7" d., 12" h. 100.00
Compote, cov., 8" d., high stand ... 55.00
Compote, open, 6" d. (jelly) 45.00
Compote, open, 7" d., high stand ... 88.00
Creamer 35.00
Dish, cov., 4½" d. 40.00
Doughnut stand 35.00
Goblet 45.00
Mug, child's, 3½" h. 32.00
Mug 14.00
Pitcher, milk 70.00
Pitcher, water (ILLUS.) 48.00
Plate, 7" sq. 15.00
Relish, 8½" oval 17.50
Salt shaker w/original top (single) .. 45.00
Sauce dish, 4" d. 12.00
Sugar bowl, cov. 65.00
Syrup jug w/original top 125.00
Toothpick holder 56.00
Tumbler, water, footed 50.00
Whiskey, handled 8.00
Wine 72.00
Wine, ruby-stained w/gilt trim 98.00

JEWEL & FESTOON (Loop & Jewel)

Butter dish, cov. 35.00
Champagne 42.00
Creamer 24.00
Creamer, individual size 35.00
Dish, 5½" sq. 7.50

Goblet 16.50
Pickle dish 17.50
Punch cup 18.00
Sauce dish 12.00
Spooner 29.00
Sugar bowl, cov. 32.50

Jewel & Festoon Sugar Bowl

Sugar bowl, open, individual size (ILLUS.) 25.00
Toothpick holder 30.00
Vase, 8¾" h. 40.00
Wine 30.00

JEWEL BAND (Scalloped Tape)

Jewel Band Covered Bowl

Bowl, cov., 8" rectangle (ILLUS.) 35.00
Bread platter .... 35.00 to 45.00
Cake stand, 9½" d. 32.50
Celery vase, 8" h. 20.00
Compote, cov., 8¼" d., 12" h. 38.50
Creamer 30.00
Egg cup 20.00
Goblet 16.00
Pitcher, water, 9¼" h. 38.00
Relish, 7" l. 9.50
Sauce dish, flat or footed .... 8.00 to 10.00
Sugar bowl, cov. 35.00
Wine 18.00

JEWELED MOON & STAR (Moon & Star with Waffle)

Bowl, 6¾" d., flat 13.50
Butter dish, cov. 70.00
Cake stand, 8½" d. 29.50
Cake stand, w/amber & blue staining, 8½" d. 125.00
Carafe 42.00
Celery 35.00
Compote, open, 9" d., 8" h. 40.00
Creamer, w/amber & blue staining 47.50
Cruet 19.50
Goblet 31.00
Pitcher, water, bulbous, applied handle 153.00
Salt shaker w/original top (single) 20.00
Salt shaker w/original top, w/amber & blue staining (single) 27.00
Sauce dish 8.50
Sauce dish, w/amber & blue staining 19.50
Spooner, w/amber & blue staining 48.00
Sugar bowl, cov., w/amber & blue staining .... 78.00 to 100.00
Table set: cov. butter dish, spooner & cov. sugar bowl; w/amber & blue staining, 3 pcs. 250.00
Tumbler 22.50
Wine 23.50

JOB'S TEARS - See Art Pattern

JUMBO and JUMBO & BARNUM

Butter dish & cover w/frosted elephant finial, oblong 550.00
Butter dish & cover w/frosted elephant finial, round 450.00
Castor holder (no bottles) 100.00
Compote, cov., 12" h., frosted elephant finial .... 325.00 to 475.00
Creamer 154.00
Creamer, w/Barnum head at handle 250.00
Goblet 700.00
Match holder 40.00
Pitcher, water, w/elephant in base 695.00
Spooner 95.00
Spoon rack 800.00
Sugar bowl w/Barnum head handles & cover w/frosted elephant finial 458.00
Toothpick holder, "Baby Mine" 70.00

KAMONI - See Balder Pattern

KANSAS - See Jewel & Dewdrop Pattern

KENTUCKY

Cake stand, 9½" d. 37.50
Cruet w/original stopper 35.00
Nappy, handled 10.00
Pitcher, water 55.00
Plate, 7" sq. 17.50
Punch cup, green 16.00
Sauce dish, footed, blue w/gold 16.00
Sauce dish, footed, clear 6.50
Sauce dish, footed, green 12.50
Spooner 35.00
Sugar bowl, cov. 30.00
Toothpick holder, clear 26.50
Toothpick holder, green 100.00

Tumbler, green 21.50
Wine, clear 24.00
Wine, green 38.00

KING'S CROWN (Also see Ruby Thumbprint)

King's Crown Punch Cup

Banana stand 50.00
Bowl, 9¼" oval, scalloped rim, round base 40.00
Butter dish, cov. 37.50
Cake stand, 10" d. 45.00
Celery vase 40.00
Compote, cov., 6" d., 6" h. 85.00
Compote, open, jelly 30.00
Compote, open, 7½" d., high stand 45.00
Compote, open, 8½" d., high stand 67.50
Compote, open, 9" d., low stand ... 38.50
Cordial 48.00
Creamer, clear 40.00
Creamer, individual size, clear 18.50
Creamer, green 75.00
Creamer, individual size, green 60.00
Cup & saucer 55.00
Goblet, clear 27.00
Goblet, cobalt blue 165.00
Goblet, w/green thumbprints 21.00
Lamp, kerosene-type, stem base, 10" h. 135.00
Mustard jar, cov. 48.00
Pitcher, tankard, 8½" h. 75.00
Pitcher, tankard, 13" h. 95.00
Pitcher, bulbous 115.00
Plate, 7" d. 20.00
Punch bowl, footed 275.00
Punch cup (ILLUS.) 18.00
Salt dip, individual size 20.00
Salt dip, master size, footed 22.50
Salt & pepper shakers w/original tops, pr. 55.00
Sauce dish, boat-shaped 20.00
Sauce dish, round 7.50
Spooner 43.00
Toothpick holder 25.00
Tumbler, amber 38.00
Tumbler, blue 75.00
Tumbler, clear 25.00
Water set, bulbous pitcher & 6 goblets, 7 pcs. 225.00
Wine 20.00

KLONDIKE - See Amberette Pattern

KOKOMO (Bar & Diamond)

Bowl, 8½" d., footed 22.50
Butter dish, cov., pedestal base 30.00
Cake stand 40.00
Celery vase 35.00
Compote, cov., 7½" d., low stand .. 28.00
Compote, open, 8½" d., low stand 15.00
Creamer, applied handle 40.00
Cruet w/stopper 22.50
Decanter 65.00
Goblet 22.00
Pitcher, water, bulbous, ruby-stained 95.00
Pitcher, water, tankard 40.00
Salt & pepper shakers w/original tops, pr. 45.00
Sauce dish, footed 7.50
Spooner 22.50
Sugar bowl, cov. 45.00
Syrup pitcher w/original top 55.00
Wine 28.00

LACY MEDALLION - See Colorado Pattern

LATTICE (Diamond Bar)

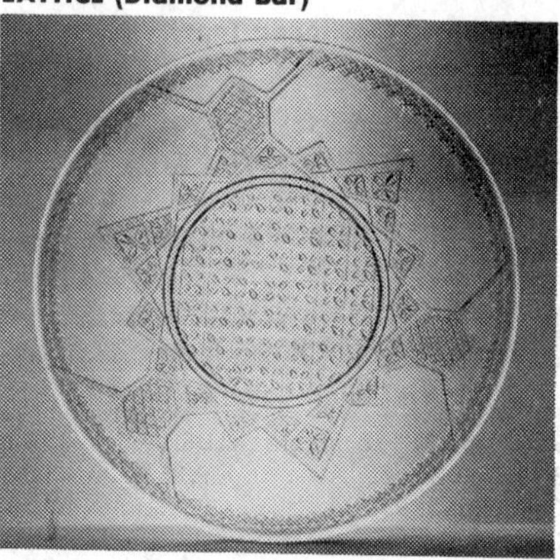

Lattice Plate

Bread plate, "Waste Not - Want Not," 10" d. 40.00
Cake stand, 8" d., 5" h. 38.00
Cake stand, 12½" d. 48.00
Cordial 23.00
Creamer 35.00
Goblet 27.50
Pitcher, water 40.00
Plate, 6" d. 12.00
Plate, 7" d. (ILLUS.) 15.00
Spooner 25.00
Sugar bowl, cov. 30.00
Syrup pitcher w/original tin top 70.00
Wine 20.00

LEAF & DART (Double Leaf & Dart)

Bowl, 8¼" d., low foot 20.00
Butter dish, cov., pedestal base 72.00

Celery vase, pedestal base 32.00
Creamer, applied handle 38.00
Cruet w/original stopper 110.00
Egg cup 22.00
Goblet 30.00
Goblet, buttermilk 35.00
Honey dish, 3½" d. 5.00
Lamp, kerosene-type, applied handle 75.00
Pitcher, milk 125.00
Pitcher, water, applied handle 95.00
Relish 18.00
Salt dip, cov., master size 68.00
Salt dip, open, master size 25.00
Sauce dish 7.50
Spooner 23.00
Sugar bowl, cov. 45.00
Sugar bowl, open 20.00

Leaf & Dart Tumbler

Tumbler, footed (ILLUS.) 25.00
Water set, pitcher & 5 footed tumblers, 6 pcs. 290.00
Wine 35.00

LE CLEDE - See Hickman Pattern

LIBERTY BELL

Liberty Bell Signer's Platter

Bread platter, "John Hancock," shell handles, 11½ x 7 1/8" 150.00
Bread platter, shell handles, without John Hancock signature, 11½ x 7 1/8" 170.00
Bread platter, "John Hancock," shell handles, milk white, 11½ x 7 1/8" 295.00
Bread platter, "John Hancock," twig handles, milk white, 13½ x 9½" 235.00
Bread platter, "Signer's," twig handles (ILLUS.) 110.00
Butter dish, cov. 130.00
Butter dish, cov., miniature 150.00
Compote, open, 6" d. 95.00
Creamer, applied handle 115.00
Goblet 45.00
Mug, miniature, 2" h. 110.00
Mug, snake handle 375.00
Pickle dish, closed handles, 1776-1876, w/thirteen original states, 9¼ x 5½" oval 50.00
Pitcher, water .... 550.00 to 850.00
Plate, 6" d., closed handles, scalloped rim, w/thirteen original states 75.00
Plate, 6" d., no states, dated 58.00
Plate, 8" d., closed handles, scalloped rim, w/thirteen original states 75.00
Plate, 10" d., closed handles, scalloped rim, w/thirteen original states 105.00
Platter, 13 x 8¼", twig handles, w/thirteen original states 90.00
Relish, shell handles, 11¼ x 7" 75.00
Salt dip 35.00
Sauce dish, flat or footed, each 29.00
Spooner 80.00
Sugar bowl, cov. 110.00
Sugar bowl, open 50.00
Table set, cov. butter dish, creamer, cov. sugar bowl & spooner, 4 pcs. 425.00

LILY-OF-THE-VALLEY

Lily-of-the-Valley Sauce Dish

Butter dish, cov. 70.00
Celery vase 50.00

Compote, cov., 8½" d., high stand 125.00
Compote, open, 8½" d., 5" h. 42.50
Creamer, 3-footed, molded handle 65.00
Creamer, plain base, applied handle 60.00
Cruet w/original stopper 80.00
Egg cup 50.00
Goblet 48.00
Honey dish 12.00
Pitcher, milk, applied handle 112.00
Pitcher, water, bulbous, applied handle ....85.00 to 125.00
Relish, 8 x 5½" 20.00
Salt dip, cov., master size, 3-footed 125.00
Salt dip, open, master size, 3-footed 27.50
Sauce dish (ILLUS.) 10.00
Spooner 35.00
Sugar bowl, cov., 3-footed 80.00
Sugar bowl, open, plain base 50.00
Tumbler, flat 9.50
Tumbler, footed 55.00
Wine 130.00

LINCOLN DRAPE & LINCOLN DRAPE WITH TASSEL

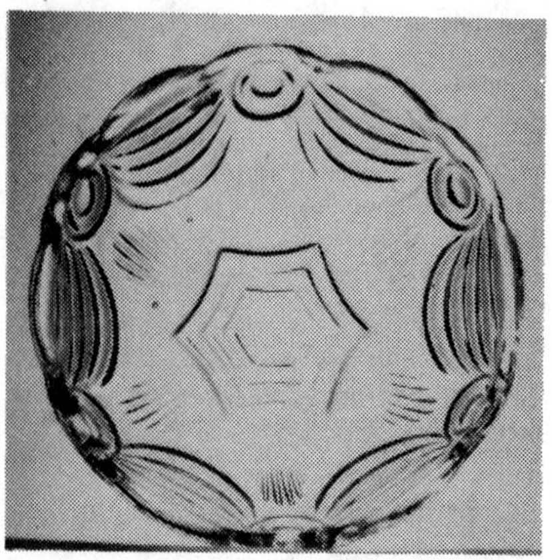

Lincoln Drape Sauce Dish

Celery vase 90.00
Compote, open, 7½" d., 3½" h. 50.00
Compote, open, 8" d., medium stand 65.00
Compote, open, 9" d. 105.00
Creamer 200.00
Egg cup 35.00
Goblet 82.00
Goblet w/tassel 128.00
Lamp, kerosene-type, miniature 125.00
Salt dip, master size 35.00
Sauce dish, 4" d. (ILLUS.) 20.00
Spillholder 52.50
Spooner 52.50
Sugar bowl, cov. 92.50
Sugar bowl, open 85.00

Syrup pitcher w/original pewter top 120.00
Syrup pitcher w/original top, opaque white 600.00
Wine 55.00

LION (Square Lion's Head or Atlanta)

Bowl, 6½ x 4¼" oblong, flat 55.00
Bowl, 8 x 5" oblong, flat 52.00
Bread plate, "Give Us....," 12" sq. ....55.00 to 75.00
Butter dish, cov. 90.00
Butter dish, cov., miniature 110.00
Cake stand 75.00
Celery vase 60.00
Cheese dish, cov. 175.00
Compote, cov., 5" sq., 6" h. 85.00
Compote, cov., 7" sq., high stand 150.00
Compote, cov., 8" sq., 9½" h. 125.00
Compote, open, 4¼" sq., 4" h. 52.00
Compote, open, 6" sq., 7½" h. 57.50
Compote, open, 8" sq., high stand 75.00
Creamer 45.00
Creamer, miniature 95.00
Cup & saucer, miniature 62.50
Dish, cov., oblong 85.00
Goblet 58.00
Pitcher, water 110.00
Platter, handled 80.00
Relish, boat-shaped 35.00
Salt shaker w/original top (single) 45.00
Sauce dish 22.00
Spooner 52.00
Spooner, miniature 28.00
Sugar bowl, cov. 95.00
Sugar bowl, cov., miniature 78.00
Sugar bowl, open, miniature 35.00
Syrup pitcher w/original top 240.00
Table set, miniature, 4 pcs. 350.00
Toothpick holder 45.00
Tumbler 45.00

LION & BABOON

Sauce dish 30.00
Spooner 85.00

LION, FROSTED - See Frosted Lion Pattern

LION'S LEG - See Alaska Pattern

LOCUST - See Grasshopper Pattern

LOG CABIN

Butter dish, cov. 250.00
Compote, cov. 330.00
Creamer, 4¼" h. 130.00
Pitcher, water 325.00
Sauce dish, flat, oblong 52.50
Spooner ....98.00 to 125.00
Sugar bowl, cov., 8" h. (ILLUS.) 250.00

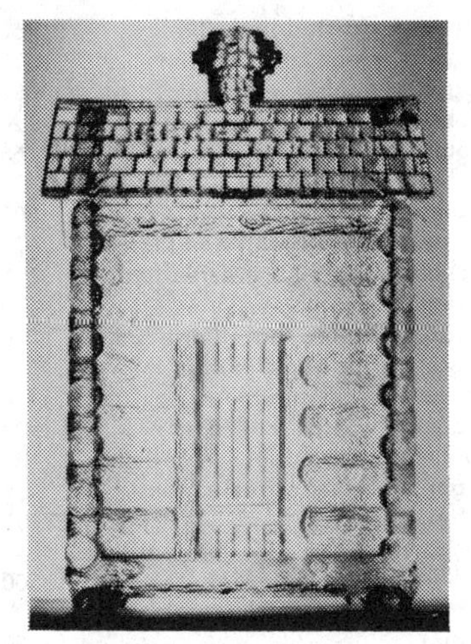

Log Cabin Sugar Bowl

Sugar bowl, cov., vaseline 675.00

LOOP (Seneca Loop)

Loop Goblet

Bowl, 9" d., flint 80.00
Butter dish, cov., flint 150.00
Celery vase, flint 57.50
Celery vase, non-flint 32.00
Champagne, non-flint 15.00
Compote, open, 8" d., 6" h., non-flint 30.00
Compote, open, 9" d., 7" h., flint ... 125.00
Compote, open, 10" d., 8" h., flint .. 85.00
Cordial, non-flint, 2¾" h. 18.50
Creamer, flint 50.00
Creamer, ruby-stained 30.00
Decanter, pt., w/original stopper, flint 130.00
Egg cup, flint 28.50
Egg cup, non-flint 12.00
Goblet, flint (ILLUS.) 25.00
Goblet, non-flint 15.00
Pitcher, water, applied handle, flint 140.00
Pitcher, water, non-flint 60.00
Salt dip, individual size, flint 18.00
Salt dip, master size, flint 22.50
Sauce dish, non-flint 6.50
Spooner, flint 34.50
Spooner, non-flint 16.00
Spooner, ruby-stained 30.00
Sugar bowl, cov., flint 115.00
Sugar bowl, cov., non-flint 29.50
Tumbler, flint 18.00
Tumbler, bar, non-flint 14.00
Wine, flint 30.00
Wine, non-flint 15.00

LOOP & DART

Loop & Dart Compote

Bowl, 9 x 6" oval, round ornaments 19.50
Butter dish, cov., diamond ornaments, non-flint ....35.00 to 45.00
Butter dish, cov., round ornaments, flint 85.00
Butter pat, round ornaments 18.00
Celery vase, round ornaments 44.00
Champagne, round ornaments, flint 65.00
Compote, cov., 6½" d., high stand, round ornaments 95.00
Compote, cov., 8" d., 10" h., round ornaments (ILLUS.) 85.00
Compote, cov., 8" d., low stand, round ornaments 75.00
Compote, open, 8" d., 4½" h., round ornaments 42.50
Cordial, 3¾" h. 22.00
Creamer, applied handle, diamond ornaments 32.50
Creamer, applied handle, round ornaments 38.00
Egg cup, diamond ornaments 18.00
Egg cup, round ornaments 23.00
Goblet, diamond ornaments 26.00
Goblet, round ornaments 29.00

Goblet, buttermilk, round ornaments 39.00
Lamp, kerosene-type, round ornaments on font, milk white base . . . 85.00
Pitcher, water, round ornaments 90.00
Plate, 6" d., round ornaments 35.00
Relish, diamond ornaments 15.00
Relish, round ornaments 25.00
Salt dip, master size, diamond ornaments 15.00
Salt dip, master size, round ornaments 28.50
Sauce dish, diamond ornaments 5.00
Sauce dish, round ornaments 6.50
Spooner, diamond ornaments 18.00
Spooner, round ornaments 28.00
Sugar bowl, cov., diamond ornaments 30.00
Sugar bowl, cov., round ornaments, flint 57.50
Sugar bowl, open, diamond ornaments 17.50
Sugar bowl, open, round ornaments 25.00
Sugar bowl, open, round ornaments, flint 35.00
Tumbler, flat or footed, diamond ornaments 25.00
Tumbler, flat or footed, round ornaments 24.00
Wine, diamond ornaments 32.50
Wine, round ornaments 32.50

LOOP & JEWEL - See Jewel & Festoon Pattern

LOOP & PILLAR - See Michigan Pattern

LOOPS & DROPS - See New Jersey Pattern

LOOPS & FANS - See Maryland Pattern

LOOP WITH DEWDROPS

Bowl, 7" to 8" d. 17.50
Butter dish, cov. 27.50
Creamer 20.00
Goblet 22.50
Pitcher, water 65.00
Sugar bowl, cov. 25.00
Tumbler 17.00
Wine 27.00

LOOP WITH STIPPLED PANELS - See Texas Pattern

MAGNET & GRAPE

Butter dish, cov., frosted leaf, flint 185.00
Celery vase, frosted leaf, flint 150.00
Compote, cov., 4½" d., 9" h., frosted leaf, flint 125.00
Compote, open, 7½" d., high stand, stippled leaf, non-flint 68.00
Cordial, frosted leaf, flint, 4" h. . . . . . 110.00 to 165.00
Creamer, frosted leaf, flint 160.00
Egg cup, clear leuf, non-flint 20.00
Egg cup, frosted leaf, flint 85.00
Goblet, clear leaf, non-flint 20.00
Goblet, frosted leaf, flint 65.00
Goblet, frosted leaf & American Shield, flint 300.00
Goblet, stippled leaf, non-flint 24.00
Goblet, buttermilk, frosted leaf, flint 45.00
Salt dip, frosted leaf, flint 50.00
Sauce dish, frosted leaf, flint 18.00
Sauce dish, stippled leaf, non-flint . . 4.50
Spooner, frosted leaf, flint 77.50
Spooner, stippled leaf, non-flint 30.00
Sugar bowl, cov., frosted leaf, flint 95.00
Sugar bowl, cov., frosted leaf & American Shield, flint 300.00
Sugar bowl, cov., stippled leaf, non-flint 50.00
Tumbler, frosted leaf, flint 85.00
Tumbler, stippled leaf, non-flint 24.00
Wine, frosted leaf, flint 135.00
Wine, stippled leaf, non-flint 40.00

MAINE (Stippled Flower Panels)

Maine Jelly Compote

Bowl, 6" d. 32.00
Bowl, master berry, 8½" d., clear 40.00
Bowl, master berry, 8½" d., green 32.50
Bread plate 26.00
Butter dish, cov. 45.00
Cake stand, green, 8½" d. 46.00
Compote, cov., small, green 65.00
Compote, open, jelly, 4¾" d. (ILLUS.) 26.00
Compote, open, 7" d. 32.00
Compote, open, 8" d., clear 38.00
Compote, open, 8" d., green 58.00
Creamer 28.50
Cruet w/original stopper 60.00
Pitcher, water 85.00
Pitcher, water, w/red & green stain 125.00

Platter, oval 38.00
Relish, 7¼" l. 14.00
Salt shaker w/original top (single) .. 20.00
Sauce dish 12.50
Spooner 30.00
Sugar bowl, cov., green 60.00
Syrup pitcher w/original top 75.00
Toothpick holder, pink-stained 95.00
Tumbler, w/red & green stain 45.00
Wine, clear 50.00
Wine, green 65.00

MALTESE - See Jacob's Ladder Pattern

MANHATTAN

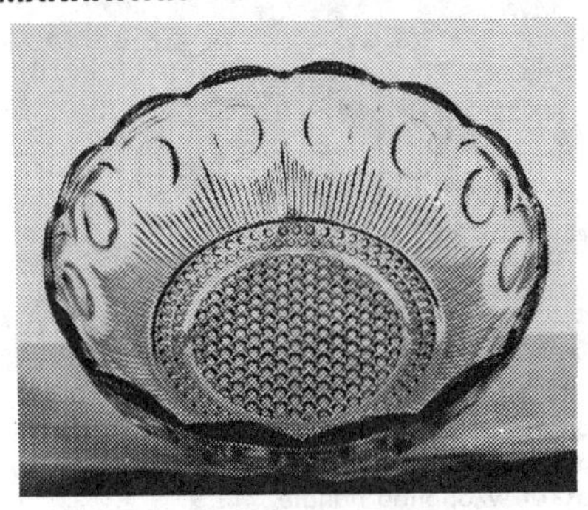

Manhattan Bowl

Basket, large 225.00
Berry set, master bowl & 3 flat sauce dishes, 4 pcs. 35.00
Bowl, 6" d. 27.00
Bowl, 8¼" d. 20.00
Bowl, 9" d. (ILLUS.) 25.00
Bowl, master berry, pink-stained 48.00
Bread plate 20.00
Butter dish, cov. 55.00
Cake stand 45.00
Carafe, water 40.00
Carafe, water, pink-stained 65.00
Cracker jar, cov. 60.00
Cracker jar, cov., pink-stained 85.00
Creamer 20.00
Creamer, individual size 22.50
Creamer & open sugar bowl, pr. 35.00
Creamer & open sugar bowl, individual size, pr. 32.50
Cruet w/original stopper 46.00
Goblet 15.00
Pickle dish, 8 x 6" oval 25.00
Pitcher, water, w/silver rim 100.00
Plate, 5" d. 10.00
Plate, 5" d., pink-stained 25.00
Plate, 8" d. 16.00
Plate, 10¾" d. 22.50
Punch bowl, 14" d., 8" h. 110.00
Punch cup 15.00
Relish, 6" l. 10.00
Salt & pepper shakers w/original tops, pr. 30.00

Sauce dish, flat, amber or pink-stained 12.00
Sauce dish, flat 9.00
Sugar bowl, open 20.00
Toothpick holder 22.00
Toothpick holder, blue-stained 55.00
Vase, 7" h. 15.00
Violet bowl 20.00
Wine 25.00

MAPLE LEAF (Leaf)

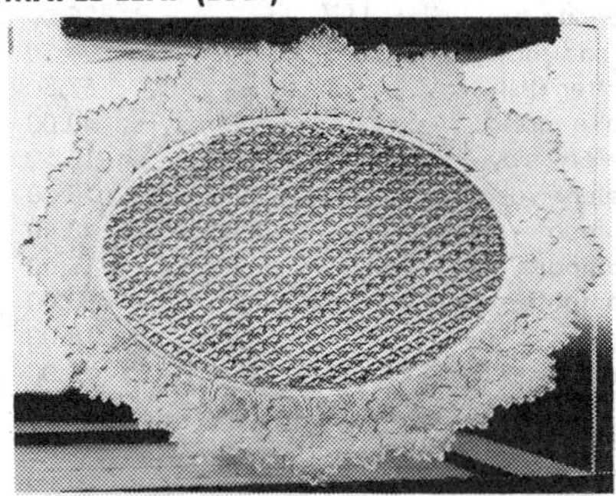

Maple Leaf Bread Tray

Berry set: oval master bowl, oval tray & 6 leaf-shaped sauce dishes; amber, 8 pcs. 95.00
Bowl, 5½" oval, clear 25.00
Bowl, 5½" oval, vaseline 45.00
Bowl, 10 x 6" oval, footed, blue 60.00
Bowl, 10 x 6" oval, footed, clear 35.00
Bowl, 10 x 6" oval, footed, green 55.00
Bowl, 10 x 6" oval, footed, vaseline 65.00
Bowl, 10" sq., crimped rim, blue 85.00
Bowl, 12 x 7½" oval, amber 70.00
Bowl, 12 x 7½" oval, blue 85.00
Bread plate, Grant, "Let Us Have Peace," amber, 9½" d. 65.00
Bread plate, Grant, "Let Us Have Peace," blue, 9½" d. 75.00
Bread plate, Grant, "Let Us Have Peace," clear, 9½" d. 75.00
Bread plate, Grant, "Let Us Have Peace," vaseline, 9½" d. 55.00
Bread tray, clear, 13¼ x 9¼" (ILLUS.) 35.00
Bread tray, vaseline, 13¼ x 9¼" 60.00
Butter dish, cov. 80.00
Celery vase 36.00
Compote, open, jelly, green 45.00
Creamer, blue 65.00
Creamer, clear 52.50
Creamer, vaseline 50.00
Goblet, amber .... 85.00 to 110.00
Goblet, frosted tree trunk stem 150.00
Goblet, vaseline .... 90.00 to 110.00
Pitcher, water 67.50
Plate, 9" d., blue 35.00
Platter, 10½" oval, blue 50.00
Platter, 10½" oval, clear 40.00
Platter, 10½" oval, vaseline 48.00

Sauce dish, leaf-shaped, 5½" l. 23.00
Spooner, blue 55.00
Spooner, clear 40.00
Spooner, green 45.00
Spooner, vaseline 65.00
Sugar bowl, cov., blue 95.00
Sugar bowl, open 40.00
Tumbler 35.00

MARYLAND (Inverted Loops & Fans or Loops & Fans)

Banana bowl, flat, 11¼ x 5" 25.00
Bread platter 28.50
Butter dish, cov. 57.50
Cake stand, 8" d. 40.00
Celery tray, 12" l. 13.50
Celery vase 25.00
Compote, cov., 7" d., high stand 48.00
Compote, open, jelly 17.50
Compote, open, medium 30.00
Creamer 16.00
Goblet 25.00
Pickle dish 16.50
Pitcher, milk 42.00
Pitcher, water 50.00
Pitcher, water, ruby-stained 105.00
Plate, 7" d. 9.00
Relish 13.50
Salt & pepper shakers w/original tops, pr. 65.00
Sauce dish 8.00
Spooner 27.50
Sugar bowl, cov. 40.00
Table set, 4 pcs. 150.00
Toothpick holder 25.00
Tumbler 24.00
Wine 36.00

MASCOTTE

Mascotte Cheese Dish

Butter dish, cov. 45.00
Butter dish, cov., etched 50.00
Butter pat 15.00
Cake basket w/handle 50.00
Cake stand 35.00
Celery vase 32.00
Cheese dish, cov. (ILLUS.) 65.00
Compote, cov., 5" d. 33.00
Compote, cov., 7" d. 45.00
Compote, cov., 9" d., high stand 175.00
Compote, open, jelly 22.00
Creamer 28.00
Goblet 24.00
Pitcher, water 60.00
Salt shaker w/original top (single) 9.00
Sauce dish, flat or footed, each 14.00
Spooner 26.00
Sugar bowl, cov. 38.00
Tray, wine 20.00
Tumbler 18.00
Wine 25.00

MASSACHUSETTS

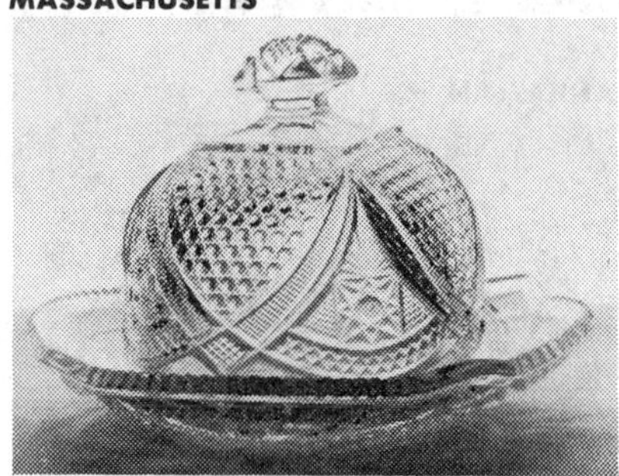

Massachusetts Butter Dish

Banana boat, 8½ x 6½" 55.00
Bar bottle, 11" h. 49.00
Basket w/applied handle, 4½ x 4½", 4¾" h. 55.00
Bowl, 6" sq. 18.00
Bowl, master berry, 8½" sq. 25.00
Butter dish, cov. (ILLUS.) 52.50
Cologne bottle w/stopper 37.50
Cordial 57.50
Creamer 24.00
Creamer, breakfast size 15.00
Cruet w/original stopper 45.00
Cruet w/original stopper, miniature 55.00
Decanter w/stopper 90.00
Goblet 45.00
Ice cream tray, 8" 16.50
Mug, 3½" h. 20.00
Olive dish, 5 x 3½" 8.50
Pitcher, water 75.00
Plate, 5" sq., serrated rim 19.00
Plate, 6" sq., w/advertising 16.50
Plate, 8" sq. 28.00
Punch cup 12.00
Relish, 8½" l. 12.50
Rum jug, 5" h. 75.00
Spooner 20.00
Sugar bowl, open, 2-handled 17.50
Sugar bowl, open, breakfast size 15.00
Table set, 4 pcs. 215.00
Toothpick holder 42.50
Tumbler, juice 16.00
Tumbler, water 35.00
Vase, 6½" h., trumpet-shaped, clear 22.50
Vase, 6½" h., trumpet-shaped, cobalt blue w/gold .... 40.00 to 60.00

Vase, 9" h., trumpet-shaped, clear . . . 35.00
Vase, 10" h., trumpet-shaped, green . . . 35.00
Whiskey set, bar bottle & 6 shot glasses, 7 pcs. . . . 125.00
Whiskey shot glass . . . 12.00
Wine, blue . . . 110.00
Wine, clear . . . 40.00

MELROSE

Butter dish, cov. . . . 45.00
Cake stand, 8" to 10" d. . . . 27.50
Celery vase . . . 27.50
Celery vase, ruby-stained . . . 65.00
Compote, open, jelly, 5½" d. . . . 14.00
Compote, open, 7" d., 7" h. . . . 25.00
Compote, open, 7½" d., 5¾" h. . . . 23.00
Compote, open, 9" d., high stand . . . 35.00
Creamer . . . 30.00
Goblet . . . 16.00
Pitcher, water . . . 32.00
Plate, 7" d. . . . 16.00
Plate, 8" d. . . . 10.00
Spooner . . . 30.00
Sugar bowl, cov. . . . 38.00
Tray, water, 11½" d. . . . 45.00
Wine . . . 20.00

MICHIGAN (Paneled Jewel or Loop & Pillar)

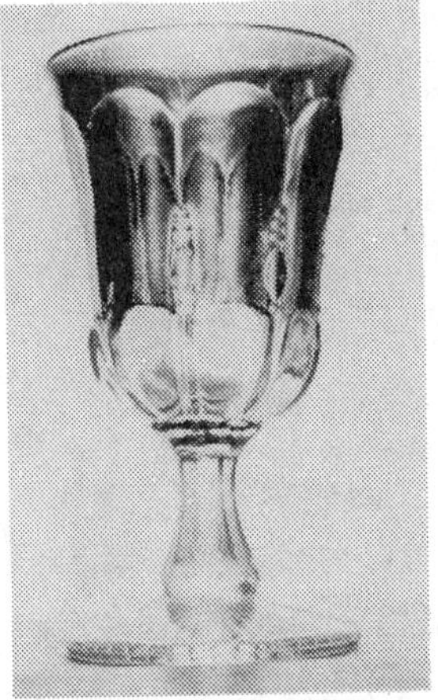

Michigan Goblet

Berry set: master bowl & 4 sauce dishes; pink-stained, 5 pcs. . . . 75.00
Bowl, cov., master berry or fruit . . . 75.00
Bowl, 8" d. . . . 28.50
Bowl, 9" d., pink-stained . . . 45.00
Bowl, 10" d. . . . 35.00
Butter dish, cov. . . . 45.00
Butter dish, cov., pink-stained . . . 125.00
Butter dish, cov., yellow-stained, enameled florals . . . 175.00
Carafe, water . . . 150.00
Celery vase . . . 36.00
Compote, open, jelly, 4½" d. . . . 23.00
Compote, open, 8½" d., high stand . . . 52.50
Compote, open, 8½" d., pink-stained . . . 40.00
Compote, open, 9¼" d. . . . 62.50
Creamer, 5" h. . . . 30.00
Creamer, individual size . . . 14.00
Creamer, individual size, yellow-stained, enameled florals . . . 22.00
Cruet w/original stopper . . . 57.00
Finger bowl . . . 14.50
Goblet (ILLUS.) . . . 32.50
Goblet, green-stained, w/enamel . . . 48.00
Honey dish, 3½" d. . . . 8.00
Mug . . . 22.50
Mug, pink-stained, gold trim . . . 38.00
Mug, yellow-stained, enameled florals . . . 33.00
Pickle dish . . . 12.00
Pitcher, water, 8" h. . . . 40.00
Pitcher, water, 12" h. . . . 68.00
Pitcher, water, 12" h., pink-stained . . . 135.00
Platters, 12½ x 8½", 10¼ x 7¼" & 9½ x 6½", nested set of 3 . . . 125.00
Punch bowl, 8" d., 4½" h. . . . 50.00
Punch cup, enameled decor . . . 13.00
Relish . . . 20.00
Salt shaker w/original top, enameled decor (single) . . . 32.00
Salt shaker w/original top, yellow-stained, enameled florals (single) . . . 45.00
Salt & pepper shakers, individual size, w/original tops, pr. . . . 75.00
Sauce dish . . . 10.50
Sauce dish, pink-stained . . . 20.00
Spooner . . . 25.00
Spooner, miniature . . . 25.00
Spooner, pink-stained . . . 72.50
Sugar bowl, cov. . . . 50.00
Sugar bowl, cov., pink-stained, gold trim . . . 130.00
Sugar bowl, individual size . . . 26.00
Syrup jug w/pewter top . . . 95.00
Table set, pink-stained, 4 pcs. . . . 375.00
Toddy mug, tall . . . 45.00
Toothpick holder, blue-stained . . . 75.00
Toothpick holder, clear . . . 38.00
Toothpick holder, enameled florals . . . 45.00
Toothpick holder, yellow-stained . . . 50.00
Toothpick holder, yellow-stained, enameled florals . . . 72.00
Tumbler . . . 30.00
Tumbler, enameled decor . . . 25.00
Tumbler, pink-stained, gold trim . . . 50.00
Vase, 6" h. . . . 10.00
Vase, 6" h., pink-stained, gold trim . . . 18.00
Vase, 8" h., green-stained, white enameled dots . . . 35.00
Water set: pitcher & 6 tumblers; pink-stained, 7 pcs. . . . 325.00

Wine 28.00

MIKADO - See Daisy & Button with Crossbars Pattern

MINERVA

Minerva "Mars" Plate

Bread tray, 13" l. 61.00
Butter dish, cov. 75.00
Cake stand, 9" d. 105.00
Cake stand, 10½" d. 92.50
Cake stand, 12½" d. 145.00
Compote, cov., 7" d., 10¾" h. 115.00
Compote, cov., 8" d., low stand 95.00
Compote, open, 8" d., 8½" h. 85.00
Creamer 50.00
Creamer & open sugar bowl, pr. 75.00
Goblet 80.00
Honey dish 17.50
Marmalade jar, cov. 150.00
Pickle dish, "Love's Request is Pickles," oval 28.00
Pitcher, milk, 7½" h. 72.50
Pitcher, water 202.00
Plate, 8" d., Bates (J.C.) portrait center, scalloped rim . . . . . 75.00 to 100.00
Plate, 9" d., handled, plain center . . 56.00
Plate, 10" d., Mars center (ILLUS.) . . 50.00
Relish, 8 x 5" oblong 23.00
Salt dip, footed, master size 25.00
Sauce dish, flat or footed, each 14.00
Spooner 37.50
Sugar bowl, cov. 65.00
Tumbler 22.50
Waste bowl, 6" d. 55.00
Wine 40.00

MINNESOTA

Banana bowl, flat 50.00
Basket w/applied reeded handle . . . 50.00
Berry set, 10" d. master bowl & 5 sauce dishes, 6 pcs. 55.00
Bowl, 8½" d. 30.00
Bowl, 8½" d., ruby-stained 100.00
Butter dish, cov. 50.00
Carafe 35.00
Celery tray, 13" l. 25.00
Compote, open, 9" sq. 55.00
Creamer, 3½" h. 22.50
Creamer, individual size 16.50
Cruet w/original stopper 32.50
Flower frog, green, 2 pcs. 45.00
Goblet 20.00
Mug 18.00
Mustard jar w/silver plate lid, handled 40.00
Nappy, 4½" d. 12.00
Olive dish, oval 12.50
Pickle dish 10.00
Pitcher, water, tankard 75.00
Plate, 7 3/8" d., turned-up rim 12.50

Minnesota Relish

Relish, 5 x 3" (ILLUS.) 9.00
Relish, 8¾ x 6½" oblong 15.00
Salt shaker w/original top, ruby-stained (single) 50.00
Sauce dish 12.00
Spooner 17.00
Sugar bowl, cov. 30.00
Table set, 4 pcs. 125.00
Toothpick holder, 3-handled 26.00
Tumbler 16.00
Water set: pitcher & 4 tumblers; gold trim, 5 pcs. 115.00
Wine 20.00

MIRROR

Mirror Pomade Jar

Bar bottle 40.00
Bowl, 7" d. 17.50
Celery vase 75.00
Compote, open, 7 1/8" d., 5 7/8" h. 40.00
Compote, open, 10" d., 7½" h. 120.00
Goblet 32.00

Goblet, bulb stem 62.50
Pomade jar w/ground stopper, 3½" h. (ILLUS.) 35.00
Spillholder 40.00
Spooner 22.00
Sugar bowl, cov. 60.00
Sugar bowl, open 18.50
Tumbler, bar 30.00
Tumbler, footed 45.00
Wine 37.50

MISSOURI (Palm & Scroll)

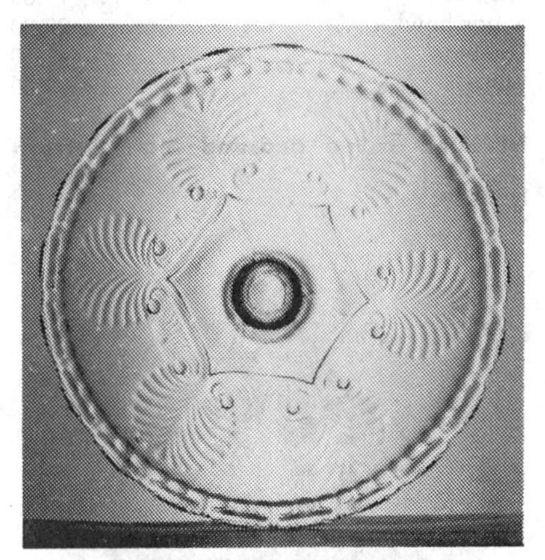

Missouri Doughnut Stand

Bowl, 8¾" d., green 38.00
Butter dish, cov., clear 55.00
Butter dish, cov., green 65.00
Cake stand, 9" d., 4¾" h. 44.00
Celery vase 28.00
Compote, open, 9" d., 7½" h., green 120.00
Compote, jelly 22.50
Creamer, clear 25.00
Creamer, green 30.00
Cruet w/original stopper, clear 45.00
Cruet w/original stopper, green 160.00
Doughnut stand, 6" d. (ILLUS.) 35.00
Goblet 45.00
Mug, green 40.00
Pitcher, milk 41.00
Pitcher, water ....40.00 to 60.00
Pitcher, water, tankard, green 75.00
Relish, clear 10.00
Relish, green 12.50
Salt & pepper shakers w/original tops, pr. 50.00
Sauce dish, clear 10.50
Sauce dish, green 12.50
Spooner, clear 24.00
Spooner, green 40.00
Sugar bowl, cov. 50.00
Syrup pitcher 68.00
Table set, green, 4 pcs. 325.00
Tumbler, green 38.00
Water set: pitcher & 6 tumblers; green, 7 pcs. 285.00

Wine, clear 36.00
Wine, green 45.00

MONKEY

Butter dish, cov. 195.00
Dish, cov., milk white 99.00
Mug ....50.00 to 90.00
Pickle jar, cov., 7 3/8" h. 100.00
Spooner 50.00

MOON & STARS

Moon & Stars Table Set

Berry set, master bowl & 6 sauce dishes, 7 pcs. 95.00
Bowl, cov., 6" d. 30.00
Bowl, cov., 7" d. 28.00
Bowl, 7" d., footed 25.00
Bowl, 8" d. 26.00
Bowl, 9" d., flat 40.00
Bowl, fruit, 9" d., footed 30.00
Bowl, 10 x 7", teardrop-shaped 42.00
Bread tray, scalloped rim, 10¾ x 6½" 24.50
Butter dish, cov. (ILLUS. left) 46.00
Cake stand, 10" d. 55.00
Celery vase 40.00
Compote, cov., 6" d., 10" h. 55.00
Compote, cov., 8" d., 12" h. 65.00
Compote, cov., 10½" d., 16¼" h. 185.00
Compote, open, 8" d., 8" h. 45.00
Compote, open, 10" d., high stand 125.00
Creamer (ILLUS. right) 50.00
Creamer & open sugar bowl, pr. 96.00
Cruet w/original stopper, applied handle 55.00
Goblet 36.00
Lamp, kerosene-type, table model, amber 190.00
Pickle dish, 8" l. 17.00
Pitcher, water, 9¼" h., applied rope handle 145.00
Relish, oblong 16.00
Salt dip, individual size, footed 15.00
Salt shaker w/original top (single) 20.00
Sauce dish, flat or footed 12.00
Spillholder 55.00
Spooner 45.00
Sugar bowl, cov. (ILLUS. center) 62.00
Toothpick holder 21.00
Tumbler, flat 45.00
Tumbler, footed, flint 67.50
Wine 35.00

MOON & STAR WITH WAFFLE - **See Jeweled Moon & Star Pattern**

MORNING GLORY

Compote, 9" d., 8" h., flint 165.00
Egg cup, flint 325.00
Honey dish, flint, 3½" 45.00
Sauce dish, flat, flint 45.00
Syrup pitcher w/original pewter top, opaque white 85.00

NAIL

(Items may be plain or with etched designs)

Bowl, 6" d., flat, ruby-stained 45.00
Butter dish, cov. 70.00
Cake stand 45.00
Celery tray, flat, 11 x 5" 22.50
Celery vase 28.00
Celery vase, ruby-stained 55.00
Compote, jelly, 5¼" 47.00
Compote, jelly, ruby-stained 85.00
Cordial 45.00
Decanter 40.00
Goblet 48.00
Goblet, ruby-stained............... 56.00
Pitcher, water 58.00
Sauce dish, flat or footed 11.00
Spooner, ruby-stained 60.00
Sugar bowl, open 17.00
Table set, 4 pcs. 175.00
Tumbler, ruby-stained 62.50
Water set: pitcher & 5 tumblers; ruby-stained, 6 pcs. 365.00
Wine 62.00

NAILHEAD

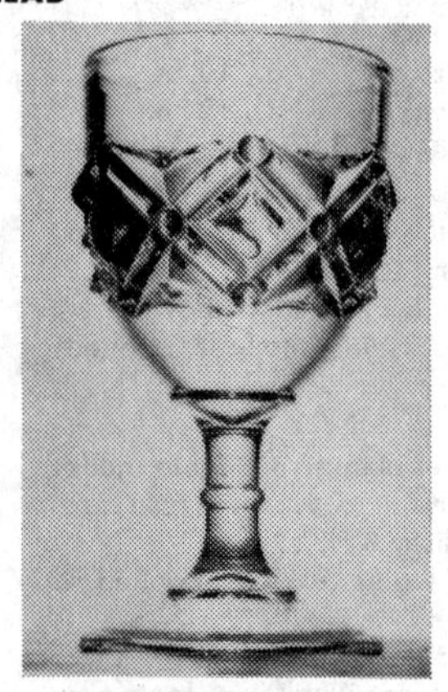

Nailhead Goblet

Bowl, 6" d. 16.00
Butter dish, cov. 46.50
Cake stand, 9" to 12" d. 26.00
Celery vase 48.00
Compote, cov., 6¼" d., 6¼" h...... 40.00
Compote, cov., 6¼" d., 9½" h...... 45.00
Compote, cov., 7" d., low stand 45.00
Compote, cov., 12" d. 65.00
Compote, open, 6½" d., 6¾" h. 25.00
Compote, open, 9" d., 6½" h. 35.00
Compote, open, 10" d., 7" h. 45.00
Creamer 20.00
Goblet (ILLUS.) 22.00
Goblet, etched 65.00
Pitcher, water 30.00
Plate, 6", 7" or 9" d. ....14.00 to 18.00
Plate, 7" sq. 15.00
Relish, 8¾ x 5¼" 10.00
Sauce dish, 4" 7.00
Spooner 19.00
Sugar bowl, cov. 28.00
Tumbler 42.50
Wine 22.00

NEPTUNE - **See Bearded Man Pattern**

NESTOR

Nestor Butter Dish

Butter dish, cov., blue w/gold trim (ILLUS.) 95.00
Butter dish, cov., gold trim 65.00
Creamer, blue 40.00
Cruet w/original stopper, blue, gold trim 100.00
Cruet w/original stopper, green 70.00
Cruet w/original stopper, purple ... 95.00
Sauce dish, purple, gold trim 25.00
Spooner, purple, gold trim 30.00
Table set, blue, 4 pcs. 525.00
Toothpick holder, blue 60.00
Tumbler, blue, gold trim 75.00
Tumbler, purple, gold trim 28.00
Water set: pitcher & 6 tumblers; green w/gold & enameled decoration, 7 pcs. 315.00

NEW ENGLAND PINEAPPLE

Bowl, 8" d., footed, scalloped rim, flint 80.00
Cake stand, flint 115.00
Champagne, flint.................. 170.00
Compote, cov., 5" d., 8½" h., flint.. 150.00
Compote, open, 7" d., 4" h., flint ... 65.00
Compote, open, 8" d., 5" h., flint ... 75.00
Cordial, flint, 4" h. 95.00

Creamer, applied handle, flint 160.00
Decanter w/bar lip, flint, qt. 175.00
Decanter w/original stopper, flint, qt. 200.00

New England Pineapple Egg Cup

Egg cup, flint (ILLUS.) 26.00
Goblet, flint 60.00
Honey dish, flint 17.00
Plate, 6" d., flint 85.00
Salt dip, individual size, flint 25.00
Salt dip, master size, flint 40.00
Sauce dish, flint 10.00
Spillholder, flint 58.00
Spooner, flint 46.00
Sugar bowl, cov., flint 95.00
Sugar bowl, open, flint 60.00
Tumbler, bar, flint 115.00
Tumbler, water, flint 85.00
Wine, flint 135.00

NEW JERSEY (Loops & Drops)

Bowl, flat 20.00
Bread plate 30.00
Butter dish, cov., w/gold trim 68.00
Compote, open, jelly 20.00
Compote, open, 7" d., 3½" h. 12.50
Creamer 35.00
Cruet w/original stopper 45.00
Goblet 34.00
Olive dish 18.00
Pitcher, water 48.00
Plate, 8" d. 12.00
Plate, 8¾" d. 13.00
Plate, 11" d. 23.00
Relish 15.00
Salt shaker (single) 35.00
Sauce dish, flat 10.00
Sugar bowl, cov. 40.00
Toothpick holder 40.00
Tumbler 25.00
Tumbler, ruby-stained 50.00
Water set, pitcher & 6 tumblers, 7 pcs. 165.00
Wine 32.00

NORTHWOOD DRAPERY - See Opalescent Glass

NOTCHED RIB - See Broken Column Pattern

OAKEN BUCKET (Wooden Pail)

Oaken Bucket Water Pitcher

Butter dish, cov., blue 85.00
Butter dish, cov., clear 65.00
Creamer, amber 40.00
Creamer, amethyst 85.00
Creamer, clear 36.50
Creamer, vaseline 40.00
Match holder w/original wire handle, amber, 2 5/8" d., 2 5/8" h. . . 20.00
Pitcher, water, amber 78.00
Pitcher, water, amethyst (ILLUS.) . . . . .80.00 to 120.00
Pitcher, water, blue 90.00
Pitcher, water, clear 52.00
Spooner, amber 40.00
Spooner, blue 45.00
Spooner, clear 17.50
Spooner, vaseline 48.00
Sugar bowl, cov., blue 48.00
Sugar bowl, cov., clear 35.00
Sugar bowl, cov., vaseline 55.00
Sugar bowl, open, blue 20.00
Sugar bowl, open, miniature, amethyst 22.50
Toothpick holder, blue 22.50
Toothpick holder, vaseline 27.50
Tumbler 15.00
Tumbler, bar, amethyst 35.00

OAK LEAF BAND

Bowl, 8 x 5½" oval 9.50
Butter dish, cov. 45.00
Goblet 32.50
Mug, applied handle, 3½" h. 37.50
Pitcher, 6" h. 36.00
Relish 10.00

OLD MAN OF THE MOUNTAIN - See Viking Pattern

OLD MAN OF THE WOODS - See Bearded Man Pattern

ONE-HUNDRED-ONE

Bread plate, 10" d. 44.00
Creamer, 4¾" h. 35.00
Goblet 32.00
Pitcher, water 125.00

Plate, 8" d.	30.00
Sauce dish	15.00
Sugar bowl, cov.	45.00

OPEN ROSE

Open Rose Goblet

Compote, open, 7½" d.	32.50
Creamer	36.00
Egg cup	22.00
Goblet (ILLUS.)	26.00
Goblet, buttermilk	22.00
Goblet, lady's	28.00
Pitcher, water, applied handle	170.00
Relish, 8 x 5½"	13.50
Salt dip, master size	22.00
Sauce dish	10.00
Spooner	26.00
Sugar bowl, cov.	52.50
Sugar bowl, open	25.00
Tumbler	40.00
Tumbler, applied handle	65.00
Water set, pitcher & 6 goblets, 7 pcs.	325.00

OREGON No. 1 - See Beaded Loop Pattern

OREGON No. 2 (Skilton)

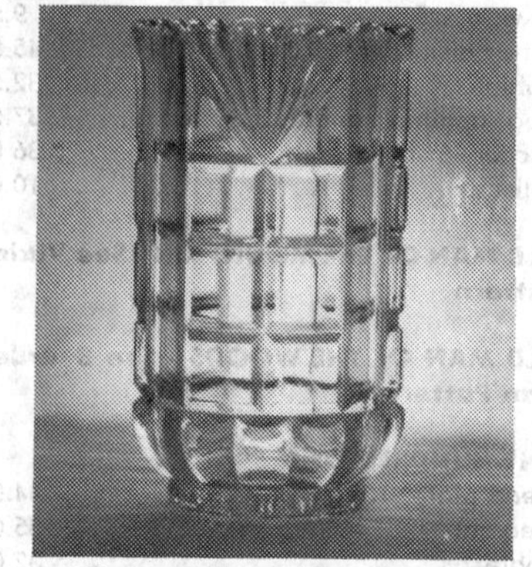

Oregon No. 2 Celery Vase

Bowl, 7¾" d., 2½" h.	12.50
Bowl, 8" d., 2½" h., ruby-stained	30.00
Butter dish, cov.	40.00
Cake stand, 9" d.	43.00
Celery vase (ILLUS.)	27.50
Compote, open, 5½" d., 4½" h.	22.50
Compote, open, 8½" d., low stand	28.00
Compote, open, 8½" d., low stand, ruby-stained	50.00
Creamer, ruby-stained	40.00
Decanter, whiskey	29.00
Goblet	28.00
Pitcher, milk	25.00
Pitcher, water, tankard	40.00
Relish	15.00
Sauce dish	11.00
Spooner, ruby-stained	38.00
Syrup pitcher w/original top	65.00
Tumbler, ruby-stained	40.00
Wine	32.50

OWL IN FAN - See Parrot Pattern

PALM & SCROLL - See Missouri Pattern

PALMETTE

Palmette Goblet

Bowl, 8" d., flat	25.00
Bread tray, handled, 9"	30.00
Butter dish, cov.	49.00
Butter pat	45.00
Cake stand	45.00
Castor set, 3-bottle, complete	75.00
Castor set, 5-bottle, complete	125.00
Celery vase	31.50
Champagne	68.00
Compote, cov., 8" d., high stand	85.00
Compote, open, 7" d., low stand	30.00
Compote, open, 8" d., low stand	27.50
Creamer, applied handle	50.00
Cup plate	45.00
Egg cup	22.00
Goblet (ILLUS.)	32.00

Lamp, kerosene-type, table model w/stem ... 75.00
Lamp, kerosene-type, table model w/stem, milk white ... 135.00
Pickle dish, scoop-shaped ... 13.50
Pitcher, water, applied handle ... 125.00
Relish ... 17.00
Salt dip, master size, footed ... 20.00
Salt & pepper shakers w/original tops, 5½" h., pr. ... 55.00
Sauce dish ... 12.00
Spooner ... 30.00
Sugar bowl, cov. ... 42.50
Sugar bowl, open ... 22.50
Syrup pitcher w/original top, applied handle ... 110.00
Tumbler, water, footed ... 47.50

PANELED CANE

Creamer & cov. sugar bowl, pr. ... 32.00
Goblet, amber ... 25.00
Goblet, blue ... 30.00
Goblet, clear ... 18.00
Mug, 2¼" h. ... 9.50
Tray, water ... 12.00

PANELED CHERRY WITH THUMBPRINTS (Cherry Thumbprints, Paneled Cherry)

(All pieces in clear glass w/red-stained cherries & gilt cable trim.)

Paneled Cherry Creamer & Sugar Bowl

Berry set, master bowl & 6 sauce dishes, 7 pcs. ... 135.00
Butter dish, cov. ... 85.00 to 100.00
Celery dish ... 45.00
Creamer (ILLUS. right) ... 45.00
Pitcher, water ... 110.00 to 125.00
Punch cup, footed ... 26.00
Sauce dish ... 12.50
Spooner ... 42.00
Sugar bowl, cov. (ILLUS. left) ... 75.00
Table set, 4 pcs. ... 250.00
Tumbler ... 22.50
Water set, pitcher & 6 tumblers, 7 pcs. ... 225.00

PANELED DAISY

Berry set, master bowl & 6 sauce dishes, 7 pcs. ... 75.00
Bowl, 7 x 5" oval ... 12.50
Bowl, berry, 8¼ x 5¾" oval ... 20.00
Butter dish, cov. ... 40.00
Cake stand, high stand, 8" to 11" d. ... 45.00
Cake stand, 11½" d. ... 45.00
Celery vase ... 29.00
Compote, cov., 5" d., high stand ... 50.00
Compote, cov., 6" d., low stand ... 35.00
Compote, cov., large ... 47.50
Creamer ... 35.00
Goblet ... 25.00
Mug ... 30.00

Paneled Daisy Pickle Dish

Pickle dish, handled, 8½" l. (ILLUS.) ... 15.00
Pitcher, water ... 45.00
Plate, 9" sq. ... 22.50
Relish, 7 x 5" oval ... 12.00
Sauce dish, flat or footed, each ... 11.00
Spooner ... 22.50
Sugar shaker w/original top ... 35.00
Toothpick holder, footed, amber ... 25.00
Tray, water ... 32.00

PANELED DEWDROP

Bowl, 8½" oval ... 24.00
Bread platter, 12½ x 9½" ... 52.50
Butter dish, cov. ... 65.00
Celery vase ... 38.00
Cordial, 3¼" h. ... 28.50
Creamer ... 22.50
Creamer, individual size ... 20.00
Goblet ... 22.00
Marmalade jar, cov. ... 42.50
Mug, applied handle ... 35.00
Pitcher, milk ... 42.50
Plate, 7" to 10" d. ... 15.00 to 30.00
Sauce dish, flat or footed ... 5.00 to 10.00
Spooner ... 35.00
Sugar bowl, cov. ... 38.00
Wine ... 20.00

PANELED FINECUT - See Finecut & Panel Pattern

PANELED FORGET-ME-NOT

Bread platter, 11 x 7" oval ... 30.00
Butter dish, cov. ... 45.00
Cake stand ... 38.50
Celery vase ... 33.00
Compote, cov., 6" d., 9½" h. ... 45.00
Compote, cov., 7" d., 10" h. ... 67.50
Compote, cov., 8" d., high stand (ILLUS.) ... 59.00

Paneled Forget-Me-Not Covered Compote

Compote, open, 7¼" d., 7" h. 30.00
Compote, open, 8½" d., 6½" h. 30.00
Compote, open, 8½" d., 12" h. 40.00
Creamer 32.00
Goblet 30.00
Marmalade jar, cov. 54.00
Pitcher, milk 47.50
Pitcher, water 65.00
Relish, handled, 7¾ x 4½" 15.00
Relish, scoop-shaped, 9" l. 19.50
Salt & pepper shakers w/original tops, pr. 65.00
Sauce dish, flat or footed, each 13.00
Spooner 32.00
Sugar bowl, cov. 35.00
Wine 38.50

PANELED GRAPE

Butter dish, cov. 68.00
Compote, open, 6½" h. 65.00
Creamer 25.00
Pitcher, water, 8¾" h. 65.00
Sauce dish 10.00
Sugar bowl, cov., small 25.00
Sugar bowl, open 25.00
Tumbler 18.00
Wine 15.00

PANELED HEATHER

Paneled Heather Jelly Compote

Bowl, 7" d. 12.50
Bowl, 8¼" d., 3¾" h. 27.50
Butter dish, cov., ruby-stained 40.00
Cake stand 30.00
Compote, cov. 40.00
Compote, open, jelly (ILLUS.) 20.00
Compote, open, 8" d. 27.50
Creamer 18.00
Cruet w/original stopper 30.00
Goblet 24.00
Pitcher, water 38.00
Plate, 12" d. 15.00
Sauce dish, flat or footed 7.50
Spooner 18.00
Sugar bowl, cov. 32.50
Tumbler 25.00
Vase, 6½" h. 17.50
Water set, pitcher & 5 tumblers, 6 pcs. 150.00
Wine 18.50

PANELED HERRINGBONE (Emerald Green Herringbone or Florida)

Paneled Herringbone Goblet

Berry set: 9" d. master bowl & 6 sauce dishes; green, 7 pcs. 105.00
Bowl, master berry, 9" sq., green . . 38.00
Bowl, oval vegetable, green, medium 17.50
Butter dish, cov., green 60.00
Cake stand, clear 25.00
Cake stand, green 75.00
Celery vase, green 55.00
Creamer, clear 20.00
Creamer, green 30.00
Cruet w/original stopper, green 105.00
Goblet, clear 14.50
Goblet, green (ILLUS.) 35.00
Mustard pot, cov. 22.50
Nappy, green 19.00
Pickle dish, green 22.50
Pitcher, milk, green 75.00
Pitcher, water, clear 42.00
Pitcher, water, green 58.00
Plate, 5" to 7" d., green 22.00

Plate, 9" sq., clear 28.00
Plate, 9" d., green 37.50
Relish, green, 6" sq. 15.00
Relish, green, 8 x 4½" oval . . 13.50 to 20.00
Sauce dish, green 12.00
Spooner, green 24.00
Sugar bowl, cov., green 50.00
Syrup pitcher w/original top, clear . . 175.00
Syrup pitcher w/original top, green 225.00
Table set, green, 4 pcs. 175.00
Tumbler, green 22.50
Water set: pitcher & 6 goblets; green, 7 pcs. 250.00
Water set: pitcher & 6 tumblers; green, 7 pcs. 195.00
Wine, clear 22.50
Wine, green 48.00

PANELED HOBNAIL

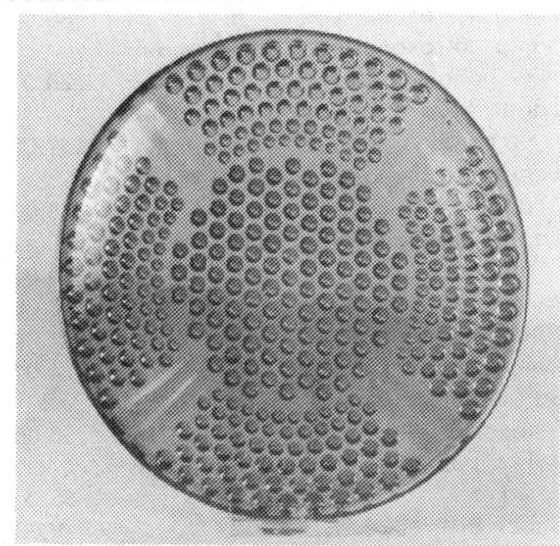

Paneled Hobnail Plate

Creamer, blue 65.00
Plate, 7" d., sapphire blue (ILLUS.) . . 25.00
Spooner, blue opaque 27.50
Toddy plate, 4½" d., blue 15.00

PANELED JEWEL - See Michigan Pattern

PANELED STAR & BUTTON - See Sedan Pattern

PANELED THISTLE (Inverted Thistle)

Basket w/applied handle, 7 x 4¾", 2½" h. 35.00
Bowl, cov., 5½" d., 4" h., w/bee in base 48.00
Bowl, 6" d., 2½" h., footed 12.50
Bowl, 7" oval, 1¾" h. 15.00
Bowl, 9" d., deep, w/bee 29.00
Bowl, 10" d., flattened rim 27.50
Bread plate 40.00
Butter dish, cov., w/bee 58.00
Cake stand 40.00
Cake stand, w/bee 65.00
Candy dish, cov., footed, 5" sq., 6¼" h. 30.00
Celery tray 13.50
Celery vase 30.00
Champagne, flared, w/bee 37.00
Compote, open, 5" d., low stand 15.00
Compote, open, 5" d., high stand 25.00
Compote, open, 7½" d., 7" h. 35.00
Compote, open, 9" d., 6½" h. 35.00

Paneled Thistle Creamer

Creamer (ILLUS.) 30.00
Cruet w/stopper 40.00
Goblet 36.00
Honey dish, cov., square 50.00
Pitcher, water, w/bee 68.00
Plate, 7" sq., w/bee 20.00
Plate, 9½" d. 36.00
Punch cup 16.00
Relish, 8½ x 4" 16.50
Relish, w/bee, 9½ x 4" 24.00
Rose bowl, 5" d., 2¾" h. 20.00
Rose bowl, extra large 50.00
Salt dip, master size 12.50
Sauce dish, flat or footed, each 16.00
Spooner, handled 18.50
Sugar bowl, cov. 30.00
Toothpick holder 29.00
Tumbler, ruby-stained 45.00
Vase, 8" h., trumpet-shaped 35.00
Vase, 9¼" h., fan-shaped 25.00
Wine 26.50

PANELED ZIPPER - See Iowa Pattern

PARROT (Owl in Fan)

Goblet 32.50
Pitcher, water 75.00
Spooner 25.00
Wine 50.00

PAVONIA (Pineapple Stem)

(Items may be plain or with etched designs)

Butter dish, cov. 78.00
Butter dish, cov., ruby-stained 110.00
Cake stand, 10" d. 44.00
Celery vase 40.00
Compote, cov., 6" d., high stand 60.00
Compote, open, jelly 38.00
Compote, open, 7" d. 50.00

Creamer 42.50
Creamer, ruby-stained 62.50
Creamer & cov. sugar bowl, ruby-stained, pr. 125.00
Cup plate 28.00
Finger bowl, 7" d. 36.00
Goblet 27.50
Mug, applied handle 15.00
Mug, ruby-stained, souvenir 28.00
Pitcher, water, tall tankard 59.00
Pitcher, water, tall tankard, ruby-stained 95.00
Salt dip, master size 19.00
Sauce dish, flat or footed, each 10.00
Spooner 35.00
Spooner, ruby-stained 45.00
Sugar bowl, cov. 55.00
Sugar bowl, cov., ruby-stained 75.00
Table set, ruby-stained, 4 pcs. ..... 250.00 to 300.00
Tray, water 60.00

Pavonia Tumbler

Tumbler (ILLUS.) 32.50
Tumbler, ruby-stained 40.00
Water set, tankard pitcher & 4 tumblers, 5 pcs. 120.00
Water set: pitcher & 6 tumblers; ruby-stained, 7 pcs. 350.00
Wine 26.00
Wine, ruby-stained 29.00

PEACOCK FEATHER (Georgia)

Bonbon dish, footed 25.00
Bowl, 8" d. 24.00
Butter dish, cov. 45.00
Cake stand, 8½" d., 5" h. 31.00
Cake stand, 10" d. 50.00
Celery tray, 11¾" l. 35.00
Compote, open, 6½" d., high stand 23.00
Compote, open, 8" d., high stand (ILLUS.) 42.50
Compote, open, 10" d., low stand 27.00
Creamer 29.00
Cruet w/original stopper 46.00

Peacock Feather Compote

Cup plate 25.00
Decanter w/original stopper 70.00
Dish, tricornered 24.00
Lamp, kerosene-type, low hand-type w/handle, blue, 5¼" h. 135.00
Lamp, kerosene-type, low hand-type w/handle, 5½" h. 55.00
Lamp, kerosene-type, 7" h. 80.00
Lamp, kerosene-type, table model w/handle, blue, 9" h. 220.00
Lamp, kerosene-type, table model w/handle, clear, 9" h. 62.00
Lamp, kerosene-type, table model, amber, 10" h. 275.00
Lamp, kerosene-type, table model, amber, 12" h. 325.00
Mug 20.00
Pitcher, water 54.00
Relish, 8" oval 14.00
Salt & pepper shakers w/original tops, pr. 50.00
Salt & pepper shakers w/glass tray, set 65.00
Sauce dish 9.00
Spooner 38.00
Sugar bowl, cov. 47.00
Table set, creamer, cov. sugar bowl & cov. butter dish, 3 pcs. 125.00
Tumbler 32.00

PENNSYLVANIA, EARLY - See Hand Pattern

PENNSYLVANIA, LATE - See Balder Pattern

PICKET

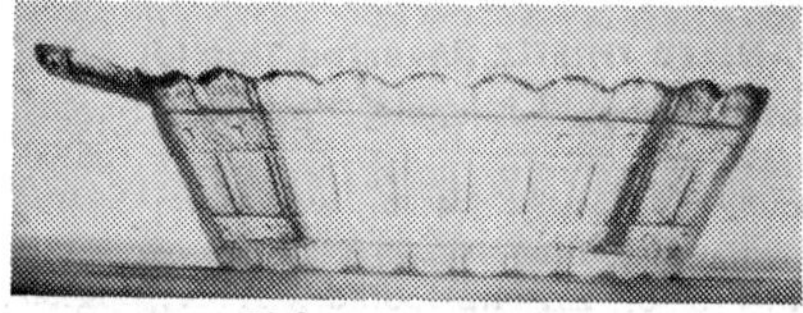

Picket Sauce Dish

Bread tray, 13 x 8" 67.50
Butter dish, cov. 50.00
Celery vase 55.00
Compote, cov., 8" d., low stand 125.00
Compote, open, 7" sq., 7" h. 30.00
Compote, open, 8" sq., 8" h. 40.00
Creamer 42.50
Goblet 45.00

Lamp, kerosene-type, amber-stained ... 195.00
Pitcher, water ... 75.00
Salt dip, master size ... 32.50
Sauce dish (ILLUS.) ... 8.00 to 12.50
Spooner ... 30.00
Sugar bowl, cov. ... 45.00
Toothpick holder ... 30.00
Wine ... 50.00

PILLAR

Ale glass, 6½" h. ... 42.50
Claret ... 55.00
Compote, open, 8" d. ... 55.00
Creamer ... 70.00
Decanter w/bar lip, pt. ... 52.50
Goblet ... 40.00 to 50.00
Wine ... 45.00

PILLAR & BULL'S EYE

Pillar & Bull's Eye Decanter

Decanter w/bar lip, 10" h. (ILLUS.) ... 80.00
Goblet ... 45.00 to 70.00
Pitcher, water, applied handle ... 325.00
Tumbler ... 65.00
Wine ... 50.00 to 65.00

PILLAR VARIANT - See Hercules Pillar Pattern

PILLOW & SUNBURST

Creamer ... 20.00
Creamer & sugar bowl, pr. ... 32.50
Plate, 10¼" d. ... 30.00
Spooner ... 30.00

PILLOW ENCIRCLED

(Called Ruby Rosette when ruby-stained)

Berry set: master bowl & 3 sauce dishes; Ruby Rosette, 4 pcs. ... 125.00
Bowl, 7" d., 3" h., Ruby Rosette ... 27.00
Bowl, 8" d., clear ... 28.00
Bowl, 8" d., Ruby Rosette ... 51.00
Butter dish, cov., clear ... 65.00
Butter dish, cov., Ruby Rosette ... 65.00
Celery vase, clear ... 35.00
Celery vase, Ruby Rosette ... 50.00
Condiment set: 9½ x 5½" tray, cruet w/original stopper, salt & pepper shakers w/original tops; Ruby Rosette, 4 pcs. ... 210.00
Creamer, clear ... 30.00
Creamer, Ruby Rosette ... 37.50
Creamer & cov. sugar bowl, clear, pr. ... 75.00
Cruet w/original stopper, enameled floral decoration ... 25.00
Cruet w/original stopper, Ruby Rosette ... 135.00
Honey dish, cov., 2-handled, oval, clear ... 10.00
Lamp, kerosene, w/stem, clear, 10¼" h. ... 36.50
Lamp, kerosene, finger-type, sapphire blue ... 195.00
Pitcher, milk, Ruby Rosette ... 85.00
Pitcher, water, tankard, clear ... 42.00
Pitcher, water, tankard, Ruby Rosette ... 108.00
Salt & pepper shakers w/original tops, clear, pr. ... 65.00
Sauce dish, footed, clear ... 13.50
Sauce dish, footed, Ruby Rosette ... 20.00
Spooner, clear ... 25.00 to 30.00
Spooner, Ruby Rosette ... 62.00
Sugar bowl, cov., clear ... 32.50
Sugar bowl, cov., Ruby Rosette ... 41.00
Table set: cov. butter dish, sugar bowl & spooner; Ruby Rosette, 3 pcs. ... 285.00
Tumbler, clear ... 16.00
Tumbler, Ruby Rosette ... 25.00
Water set: pitcher & 5 tumblers; clear, 6 pcs. ... 120.00
Water set: tankard pitcher & 6 tumblers; Ruby Rosette, 7 pcs. ... 215.00

PINEAPPLE & FAN

Butter dish, cov. ... 35.00
Celery tray ... 38.00
Creamer ... 30.00
Pickle castor in silver plate holder, w/tongs ... 65.00
Spooner ... 15.00
Sugar shaker ... 27.50
Tumbler, green w/gold ... 25.00

PINEAPPLE STEM - See Pavonia Pattern

PLEAT & PANEL (Darby)

Bowl, 6" sq., flat ... 13.50
Bowl, 7" d., 4½" h., footed ... 22.50
Box, cov., 8 x 5" ... 42.50
Bread tray, closed handles, 13 x 8½" ... 28.00
Bread tray, pierced handles ... 32.50
Butter dish, cov., footed ... 55.00
Cake stand, 8" sq. ... 31.00
Cake stand, 9" to 10" sq. ... 38.00

Celery vase, footed 35.00
Compote, cov., 7" sq., 10½" h...... 46.00
Compote, cov., 8" d., 12" h......... 43.00
Compote, open, 7" d., high stand... 27.50
Creamer 26.00
Finger bowl....................... 37.50

Pleat & Panel Goblet

Goblet (ILLUS.)................... 27.00
Lamp, kerosene, stem 85.00
Marmalade jar, cov. & underplate .. 135.00
Pickle dish........................ 20.00
Pitcher, milk...................... 40.00
Pitcher, water 75.00
Plate, 5" sq. 24.00
Plate, 6" sq. 20.00
Plate, 7" sq., amber 32.50
Plate, 7" sq., amethyst 95.00
Plate, 7" sq., canary yellow 25.00
Plate, 7" sq., clear 18.00
Plate, 8" sq., clear 22.50
Platter w/open handles 40.00
Relish, 7 x 4½" 12.00
Relish, 9½" l....................... 25.00
Salt dip, master size............... 18.00
Salt & pepper shakers w/original tops, pr.......................... 65.00
Sauce dish, flat, handled........... 10.50
Sauce dish, footed 14.50
Spooner 28.00
Sugar bowl, cov. 43.50
Tray, water 52.00
Waste bowl 25.00
Wine 75.00

PLEAT & TUCK - See Adonis Pattern

PLUME

Berry set, 8½" sq. master bowl & five 4½" sq. sauce dishes, 6 pcs. 95.00
Bowl, 6" d. 22.50
Bowl, 8" d., shallow 28.00
Bowl, 8½" sq. master berry 35.00
Bowl, 9¼" d. 20.00
Butter dish, cov., clear 45.00
Butter dish, cov., ruby-stained 135.00
Cake stand, 9" d., 5¾" h. 47.50
Cake stand, 10¼" d. 55.00
Celery vase, clear 23.50
Celery vase, ruby-stained & etched 85.00
Compote, cov., 6½" d., 12" h....... 95.00
Compote, open, 7" d., 6¾" h. 28.00
Compote, open, 8" d., 8" h. 42.00

Plume Open Compote

Compote, open, 9" d., 6½" h. (ILLUS.)......................... 48.00
Cracker jar w/original metal cover 75.00
Creamer, applied handle, clear..... 30.00
Creamer, ruby-stained 60.00
Goblet, clear 26.00
Goblet, ruby-stained & etched 55.00
Lamp, kerosene 60.00
Pitcher, water, clear............... 82.50
Pitcher, water, ruby-stained 140.00
Relish 25.00
Sauce dish, flat or footed, clear 12.00
Sauce dish, ruby-stained 20.00
Spooner, clear 26.50
Spooner, ruby-stained 55.00
Sugar bowl, cov., clear 30.00
Sugar bowl, cov., ruby-stained 90.00
Sugar bowl, open, clear 20.00
Sugar bowl, open, ruby-stained..... 37.50
Syrup pitcher w/original top, applied handle 50.00
Tumbler 35.00
Waste bowl 45.00
Water set, pitcher & 6 tumblers, 7 pcs. 165.00

POINTED THUMBPRINT - See Almond Thumbprint Pattern

POLAR BEAR

Bread tray, frosted 175.00
Claret 120.00
Goblet 110.00
Goblet, clear & frosted 102.00
Pitcher, water, frosted ....250.00 to 350.00
Tray, water, 16" l. 95.00
Tray, water, frosted, 16" l. 178.00
Tumbler 95.00

Waste bowl 87.50

Polar Bear Waste Bowl

Waste bowl, frosted (ILLUS.) 110.00

POPCORN

Popcorn Cake Stand

Butter dish, cov. 49.00
Cake stand, 11" d. (ILLUS.) 78.00
Celery tray 17.50
Celery vase, 6½" h. 40.00
Cheese dish, cov., 11 x 8" 185.00
Creamer w/raised ears 47.50
Creamer & cov. sugar bowl, pr. 110.00
Goblet w/raised ears 42.50
Goblet 30.00
Pickle dish, oval 12.50
Pitcher, milk 75.00
Pitcher, water 80.00
Spooner w/raised ears 40.00
Spooner 35.00
Sugar bowl, cov. 47.50
Wine w/raised ears 58.00
Wine 31.00

PORTLAND

Basket w/high handle 125.00
Bowl, 4½" d., 3" h. 20.00
Bowl, 9" d. 25.00
Butter dish, cov. 49.00
Cake stand, 10½" 45.00
Candlestick (single) 50.00
Carafe 30.00
Celery tray 18.00
Celery vase 35.00
Compote, cov., 6½" d., high stand 115.00
Compote, open, 7½" d., 5½" h. 48.00
Cordial 30.00

Portland Creamer

Creamer (ILLUS.) 20.00
Creamer, individual size 14.00
Cruet w/original stopper 40.00
Dresser jar, cov., 5" d. 22.50
Goblet 28.00
Lamp, kerosene, 9" h. 65.00
Pitcher, water 55.00
Pitcher, water, miniature 20.00
Punch bowl, 5" d., 8½" h. 150.00
Punch cup 12.00
Relish, boat-shaped, 9" l. 12.50
Relish, boat-shaped, 12" l. 18.50
Salt shaker w/original top (single) 16.00
Sauce dish, 4½" d. 7.50
Spooner 32.50
Sugar bowl, cov. 35.00
Syrup pitcher w/original top 125.00
Toothpick holder 23.00
Tumbler 15.00
Vase, 6" h., scalloped rim 17.00
Vase, 9" h. 30.00
Water set, pitcher & 4 tumblers, 5 pcs. 100.00
Wine 23.50

PORTLAND MAIDEN BLUSH (Banded Portland with Color)

Portland Maiden Blush Sauce Dish

Bowl, 5½ x 3½" oval 35.00
Butter dish, cov. 165.00
Celery tray, 10" oval 65.00
Celery vase 67.50
Creamer 75.00
Creamer, breakfast size 26.00
Finger bowl, 4½" d., 2" h. 28.00
Goblet 56.00
Marmalade jar w/silver plate cover, frame & spoon, 3 pcs. 95.00
Olive dish 28.00
Perfume bottle w/original stopper 85.00
Pin tray, souvenir 12.50

Pitcher, tankard, 11" h. 167.50
Pitcher, water, child's 32.50
Powder jar, cov. 85.00
Punch cup 18.00 to 25.00
Relish, 6½ x 4" 25.00
Relish, boat-shaped, 8¾ x 4¼" 36.00
Salt shaker w/original top (single) 39.00
Sauce dish, boat-shaped, 4¾" l. 25.00
Sauce dish, 4½" d. (ILLUS.) 30.00
Sugar bowl, cov., large 115.00
Sugar shaker w/original top 120.00
Table set, cov. butter dish, creamer, cov. sugar bowl & spooner, 4 pcs. 285.00
Toothpick holder 50.00
Tumbler 27.00
Vase, 4" h. 25.00
Vase, 6" h. 27.50
Wine 55.00

PORTLAND WITH DIAMOND POINT BAND - See Banded Portland Pattern

POST (Square Panes)

Bowl, cov., 6¾" d., footed 45.00
Bowl, 8" sq. 25.00
Butter dish, cov. 42.50
Cake stand, 9½" d. 60.00
Celery vase 42.50
Compote, cov., 5" sq., 10" h. 45.00
Compote, cov., 6" d., high stand 57.00
Creamer 35.00
Goblet 41.00
Lamp, kerosene, 7½" h. 120.00
Lamp, kerosene, 8½" h. 80.00
Lamp, kerosene, 11" h. 75.00
Pitcher, water 75.00
Relish, 7¼ x 4¾" 8.00
Salt dip, master size 7.00
Spooner 26.00
Sugar bowl, cov. 42.00
Table set, cov. sugar bowl, creamer & spooner, 3 pcs. 125.00

POTTED PLANT - See Flower Pot Pattern

POWDER & SHOT

Butter dish, cov. 80.00
Compote, open, 7 7/8" d., low stand 55.00
Creamer, applied handle, flint 95.00
Egg cup, flint 46.00
Goblet, flint 59.00
Goblet, buttermilk 37.50
Salt dip, master size 44.00
Sauce dish 20.00
Spooner 45.00
Sugar bowl, cov. 85.00
Table set, 4 pcs. 350.00

PRAYER RUG - See Horseshoe Pattern

PRESSED LEAF

Bowl, 7" oval 40.00
Butter dish, cov. 50.00
Champagne 21.50
Compote, cov., acorn finial, low stand 47.50
Compote, cov., acorn finial, high stand 65.00
Cordial 20.00
Creamer, applied handle 35.00
Goblet 20.00
Goblet, buttermilk 25.00
Pitcher, water, applied handle 84.50
Relish, 7 x 5" 12.50
Salt dip, master size 15.00
Sauce dish 9.00

Pressed Leaf Spooner

Spooner (ILLUS.) 22.00
Sugar bowl, cov. 40.00
Wine 33.00

PRIMROSE

Primrose Sauce Dish

Bowl, 8" d., flat 25.00
Bread plate 30.00
Butter dish, cov. 40.00
Cake plate, 2-handled, amber, 9" d. 27.00
Cake plate, 2-handled, clear, 9" d. 15.00
Cake stand, clear, 9" d. 29.00
Cake stand, blue, 10" d. 47.00
Card tray, amber w/wire frame, 4½" d. 32.00
Celery vase 18.50

Compote, cov., 5" d., milk white . . . 28.00
Compote, open, low stand, large . . . 25.00
Creamer . . . 30.00
Goblet . . . 40.00
Lamp, kerosene, clear to opalescent, complete, 8" h. . . . 195.00
Pickle dish, amber . . . 17.50
Pickle dish, clear . . . 13.00
Pitcher, milk, amber . . . 65.00
Pitcher, milk, clear . . . 26.00
Pitcher, water, amber . . . 55.00
Pitcher, water, clear . . . 42.50
Plate, 4½" d., amber or blue . . . 11.00
Plate, 4½" d., clear . . . 8.50
Plate, 6" d., amber . . . 16.50
Plate, 6" d., clear . . . 13.00
Plate, 7" d., amber . . . 16.00
Platter, 12 x 8", amber . . . 22.50
Relish, amber, 9¼ x 5" . . . 18.00
Relish, blue . . . 22.00
Relish, clear . . . 12.50
Sauce dish, flat, blue . . . 9.00
Sauce dish, flat or footed, clear (ILLUS.) . . . 10.00
Spooner . . . 21.00
Sugar bowl, cov. . . . 42.50
Tray, water, blue, 11" d. . . . 58.00
Tray, water, clear, 11" d. . . . 25.00
Wine, amber . . . 37.00
Wine, clear . . . 20.00
Wine, opaque turquoise . . . 60.00

PRINCESS FEATHER (Rochelle)

Princess Feather Goblet

Bowl, cov., 7½" d. . . . 35.00
Bowl, 7¼ x 5" oval . . . 25.00
Bowl, 9 x 6" oval . . . 30.00
Butter dish, cov. . . . 50.00
Celery vase . . . 41.00
Compote, cov., 8" d., low stand . . . 130.00
Creamer . . . 45.00
Egg cup, clear . . . 28.50
Egg cup, opalescent, 3¾" h. . . . 180.00
Goblet (ILLUS.) . . . 34.00
Goblet, buttermilk . . . 25.00
Honey dish . . . 12.50
Lamp, kerosene, clear, 12" h. . . . 75.00
Lamp, kerosene, green, 9½" h. . . . 175.00
Pitcher, water, bulbous, applied handle, flint . . . 112.00
Plate, 6" d., clear, non-flint . . . 36.00
Plate, 7" d., amber, flint . . . 165.00
Plate, 7" d., clear, non-flint . . . 28.00
Plate, 8" d., clear, non-flint . . . 29.50
Relish, 7 x 5" oval . . . 17.50
Salt dip, master size . . . 29.00
Sauce dish, blue, flint . . . 145.00
Sauce dish, clear, non-flint . . . 10.00
Spooner, clear, non-flint . . . 28.00
Spooner, fiery opalescent milk white, flint, 5 1/8" h. . . . 120.00
Sugar bowl, cov., clear, non-flint . . . 55.00
Sugar bowl, cov., milk white, flint . . 140.00

PRISCILLA (Alexis)

Priscilla Tumbler

Banana stand . . . 75.00
Basket . . . 85.00
Bowl, 7" d., flat . . . 28.00
Bowl, 8" d., 3½" h., straight sides, flat . . . 38.00
Bowl, 8" d., 3½" h., w/pattern on base . . . 48.00
Bowl, 8¾" d., 3 3/8" h., flared sides . . . 55.00
Bowl, 9" d., shallow . . . 38.00
Bowl, 9¼" d., 5" h. . . . 37.50
Bowl, 9 7/8" d., 2" h. . . . 35.00
Bowl, 10¾" d., shallow . . . 31.00
Butter dish, cov. . . . 127.00
Cake stand, 9" to 10" d., high stand . . . 60.00
Compote, cov., jelly . . . 50.00
Compote, cov., 6" d., 10" h. . . 55.00 to 65.00
Compote, cov., 8" d. . . . 110.00
Compote, cov., 12" d. . . . 145.00
Compote, open, 4¾" d., 4 7/8" h., flared sides . . . 35.00
Compote, open, 6 7/8" d., 7" h. . . . 45.00
Compote, open, 8" d., 8" h. . . . 55.00
Compote, open, 8¾" d., 9¾" h., flared rim . . . 55.00
Compote, open, 9" d., 7" h. . . . 33.00
Compote, open, 9½" d., 9" h. . . . 55.00
Cracker jar, cov. . . . 175.00
Creamer . . . 38.00
Creamer, individual size . . . 29.00

Cruet w/original stopper 61.00
Doughnut stand, 5¾ x 4¼" 47.50
Egg cup 17.00
Goblet 42.00
Mug 15.00
Mustard jar, open 25.00
Nappy, handled 28.00
Pitcher, water ....85.00 to 115.00
Plate, 10½" d., turned-up rim 26.00
Punch cup 15.00
Relish ....20.00 to 28.00
Rose bowl, 3¾" h. 35.00
Salt shaker w/original top (single) .. 35.00
Sauce dish, flat, 4½" to 5" d. 12.50
Spooner 28.00
Sugar bowl, cov. 31.00
Sugar bowl, cov., individual size 32.50
Syrup pitcher w/original pewter top 135.00
Table set, 4 pcs. 235.00
Toothpick holder 44.50
Tumbler (ILLUS.) 25.00
Wine 28.00

PRISM

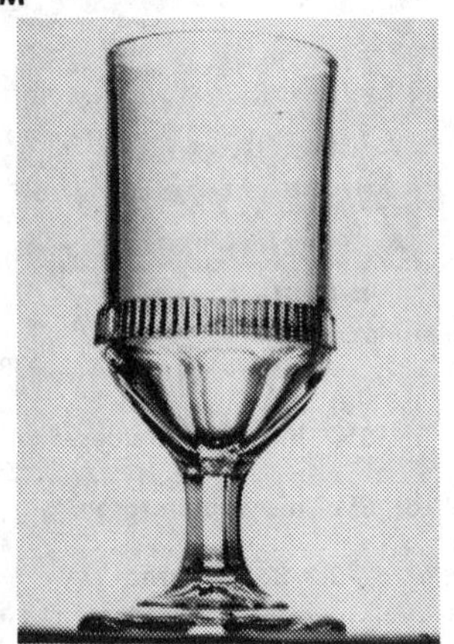

Prism Claret

Bowl, 7" d., flat 8.00
Celery vase 30.00
Champagne 45.00
Claret, 6" h. (ILLUS.) 22.00
Compote, open, 7" d., 5" h. 65.00
Compote, 7½" triangle, 4½" h. 45.00
Creamer 55.00
Decanter, bar lip, qt. 125.00
Egg cup 25.00
Egg cup, double 27.00
Goblet 35.00
Honey dish 9.50
Pickle dish 15.00
Pitcher, water 100.00
Plate, 7½" d. 25.00
Sauce dish 16.00
Spooner 35.00
Sugar bowl, open 18.00
Tumbler, buttermilk 35.00
Wine 38.00

PRISM WITH DIAMOND POINT

Goblet 45.00
Salt dip, master size 17.50
Tumbler, bar 65.00

PSYCHE & CUPID

Bread tray 35.00
Butter dish, cov. 65.00
Celery vase 32.00
Compote, open, 5" d., 6¾" h. 45.00
Creamer 53.00
Goblet 36.00
Pitcher, water 78.00
Plate, 7" d., milk white 18.00
Relish, 9½ x 6½" 32.50
Sauce dish, footed 11.50
Spooner 38.00
Sugar bowl, cov. 42.50
Table set, 4 pcs. 210.00

PYGMY - **See Torpedo Pattern**

RED BLOCK

Red Block Spooner

Bowl, berry or fruit, 8" d. 65.00
Butter dish, cov. 72.00
Celery vase, 6½" h. 84.00
Creamer, large 58.00
Creamer, small, applied handle 35.00
Creamer & open sugar bowl, pr. 65.00
Creamer & cov. sugar bowl, individual size, pr. 135.00
Cruet w/original stopper 135.00
Decanter, whiskey, w/original stopper, 12" h. 164.00
Goblet 41.00
Mug 27.00
Mug, souvenir, 3" h. 43.00
Pansy bowl, 2¾" h. 65.00
Pitcher, 8" h., bulbous 120.00
Pitcher, tankard, 9 5/8" h. 120.00
Rose bowl 55.00
Salt dip, individual size, 2-handled .. 48.00
Salt shaker w/original top (single) .. 49.00
Sauce dish, 4½" 24.00
Spooner (ILLUS.) 40.00
Sugar bowl, cov. 55.00
Sugar shaker w/original top 75.00

Table set, creamer, sugar bowl & spooner, 3 pcs. 150.00
Table set, 4 pcs. 210.00
Tumbler 28.00
Water set, pitcher & 6 tumblers, 7 pcs. 225.00
Wine 35.00

REVERSE TORPEDO (Diamond & Bull's Eye Band)

Reverse Torpedo Covered Bowl

Banana stand 115.00
Basket 65.00
Bowl, cov., 9" d. (ILLUS.) 75.00
Bowl, 5¾" d., piecrust rim 35.00
Bowl, 6¾" d. 35.00
Bowl, 7½" d., piecrust rim 70.00
Bowl, 9" d., piecrust rim 65.00
Bowl, 10¼" d., piecrust rim 70.00
Bowl, 11¼" d., 7" h., footed 85.00
Butter dish, cov. 80.00
Cake stand 75.00
Celery vase 70.00
Compote, cov., jelly 39.00
Compote, cov., 6" d., high stand 95.00
Compote, cov., 7" d., low stand 98.00
Compote, open, 5" d., flared rim 50.00
Compote, open, 7" d., 8" h. 55.00
Compote, open, 8" d., piecrust rim 62.50
Compote, open, 9" d., 7" h., turned-over piecrust rim 82.00
Compote, open, 10" d., 6½" h. 70.00
Compote, open, 10 x 8½" oval, 9¼" h., ruffled rim 122.00
Creamer 66.00
Dish, ruffled, 11¼" d., 2¾" h. 85.00
Goblet 85.00
Honey dish, cov., square 145.00
Pitcher, water 165.00
Salt shaker w/original top (single) 45.00
Sauce dish 25.00
Spooner 55.00
Sugar bowl, cov. 75.00
Syrup pitcher w/original top 165.00
Tumbler 75.00

RIBBED GRAPE

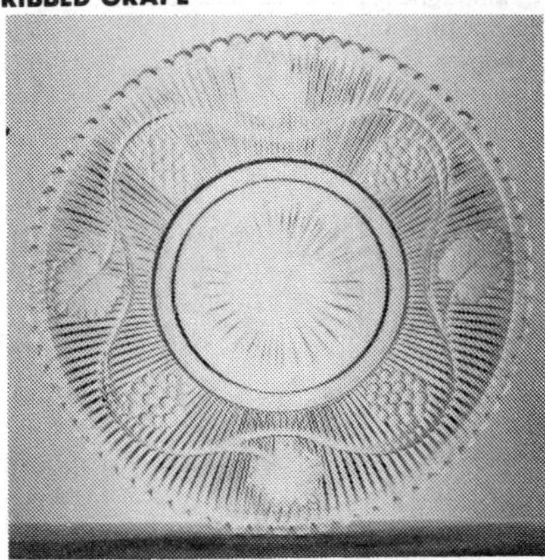

Ribbed Grape Plate

Compote, open, 7½" d. 42.00
Creamer, applied handle 130.00
Goblet 38.00
Goblet, buttermilk 50.00
Plate, 6" d. (ILLUS.) 34.00
Sauce dish, 4" d. 20.00
Spooner 37.00
Sugar bowl, cov. 95.00

RIBBED IVY

Berry set, master bowl & 4 sauce dishes, 5 pcs. 105.00
Bitters bottle w/original tulip-shaped stopper 175.00
Bowl, 8" d., 2" h. 67.50
Butter dish, cov. 95.00
Celery 225.00
Champagne 145.00
Compote, cov., 6" d., high stand 250.00
Compote, open, 7½" d., high stand, rope edge rim 100.00
Compote, open, 8" d., 5" h. 62.50
Creamer, applied handle 110.00
Decanter w/original tulip-shaped stopper, ½ pt. 120.00
Egg cup 34.00
Goblet 35.00
Honey dish 15.00
Salt dip, cov., master size 115.00
Salt dip, open, master size, beaded rim 40.00
Sauce dish 12.00
Spooner 40.00
Sugar bowl, cov. 87.50
Sweetmeat, cov. 325.00
Tumbler, bar .... 105.00 to 125.00
Tumbler, water 80.00
Tumbler, whiskey 82.00
Tumbler, whiskey, handled 150.00
Wine 97.00

RIBBED PALM

Bowl, 8" d., footed 65.00
Butter dish, cov. 88.00
Celery vase 85.00

Champagne 113.00
Compote, open, 8" d. 85.00
Creamer 145.00
Egg cup 29.00

Ribbed Palm Goblet

Goblet (ILLUS.) 31.00
Goblet, buttermilk 37.50
Honey dish 12.50
Pitcher, water, 9" h., applied handle 255.00
Plate, 6" d. 60.00
Relish, 8 x 5" 40.00
Salt dip, master size, footed 50.00
Sauce dish 14.00
Spillholder 45.00
Spooner 42.00
Sugar bowl, cov. 68.00
Tumbler, bar 110.00
Wine 49.00

RIBBON (Early Ribbon)

Ribbon Spooner

Bowl, 3½" d., flat 8.50
Bowl, 8" d. 15.00
Bowl, 9 x 5" 20.00
Bread tray 40.00
Butter dish, cov. 69.00
Cake stand, 8½" d. 50.00
Cake stand, 9¼" d. 27.50
Cake stand, 10" d., high stand 35.00
Celery vase 42.00
Cheese dish, cov. 145.00
Compote, cov., 6" d. 32.00
Compote, cov., 8" d. 88.00
Compote, open, 7" d., low stand ... 30.00
Compote, open, 8" d., 8" h., frosted dolphin stem on dome base 250.00
Compote, open, 8 x 5½" rectangular bowl, 7" h., frosted dolphin stem on dome base 160.00
Compote, open, 8½" d., 4½" h. 50.00
Creamer 34.00
Creamer & cov. sugar bowl, pr. 110.00
Goblet 33.00
Marmalade jar, cov. 45.00
Pitcher, water 90.00
Plate, 7" d. 35.00
Platter, 13 x 9" 62.50
Pomade jar, cov., squat 35.00
Sauce dish, flat or footed 12.50
Spooner (ILLUS.) 24.00
Sugar bowl, cov., 4¼" d., 7¾" h. .. 72.00
Sugar bowl, open 40.00
Table set, 4 pcs. 225.00
Tray, water, 15" 115.00
Wine 110.00

RIBBON CANDY (Bryce or Double Loop)

Ribbon Candy Plate

Bowl, cov., 6¼" d., footed 35.00
Bowl, 8" d., flat 20.00
Butter dish, cov. 45.00
Cake stand, child's, 6½" d., 3" h. ... 35.50
Cake stand, 8" to 10½" d. 28.00
Celery vase 28.00
Compote, cov., 5" d., 8½" h. 47.50
Compote, cov., 6¼" d., 7½" h. 35.00
Compote, open, jelly 22.50
Compote, open, 5¾" d., 4½" h. 16.50
Compote, open, 8" d. 30.00
Compote, open, w/dolphin stem 110.00

Creamer 20.00
Doughnut stand 35.00
Goblet 30.00
Mug 22.50
Pitcher, milk 47.50
Pitcher, water 70.00
Plate, 8½" d. 14.00
Plate, 9½" d. 17.00
Plate, 10½" d. 32.00
Plate, 12" d. (ILLUS.) 45.00
Relish, 8½" l. 11.00
Salt shaker w/original top (single) .. 25.00
Spooner 18.00
Sugar bowl, cov. 35.00
Syrup pitcher w/original top 85.00
Wine 27.50

RISING SUN

Rising Sun Toothpick Holder

Berry set: master bowl & 6 sauce dishes; clear, 7 pcs. 120.00
Bowl, 4½" d., handled, purple suns 9.00
Bowl, 6½" d., pink suns 8.00
Bowl, master berry, pink suns 30.00
Butter dish, cov., clear 68.00
Butter dish, cov., green suns 40.00
Celery vase, gold suns 18.00
Celery vase, pink suns 32.50
Compote, open, jelly, purple suns .. 22.00
Compote, open, 7" d., 6" h. 18.50
Creamer 22.00
Cruet w/stopper 28.00
Goblet, clear 24.00
Goblet, gold suns 17.50
Goblet, green suns 25.00
Goblet, pink suns 20.00
Goblet, purple suns 22.50
Pitcher, water, clear 65.00
Pitcher, water, gold suns 35.00
Punch cup, green suns 20.00
Sauce dish, red suns 8.00
Spooner 40.00
Sugar bowl, open, scalloped rim, green suns 22.00
Table set, 4 pcs. 110.00
Toothpick holder, 3-handled, clear .. 18.00
Toothpick holder, 3-handled, gold suns (ILLUS.) 25.00
Toothpick holder, 3-handled, green suns 32.50
Toothpick holder, 3-handled, purple suns 25.00
Toothpick holder, 3-handled, red suns 14.00
Tumbler, clear 15.00
Tumbler, gold suns 13.50
Tumbler, green suns 25.00
Tumbler, pink suns 22.00
Tumbler, whiskey 8.50
Vase, 6½" h., 4½" d., gold suns ... 25.00
Vase, 6½" h., 4½" d., red suns .. 18.00
Water set: pitcher & 4 tumblers; clear, 5 pcs. 120.00
Water set: pitcher & 4 tumblers; green suns, 5 pcs. ......140.00 to 195.00
Water set: pitcher & 6 tumblers; gold suns, 7 pcs. 90.00
Water set: pitcher & 6 tumblers; green suns, 7 pcs. 80.00
Wine, clear 16.00
Wine, green suns 30.00
Wine, pink suns 30.00
Wine, purple suns 20.00

ROCHELLE - See Princess Feather Pattern

ROMAN KEY - See Frosted Roman Key Pattern

ROMAN ROSETTE

Roman Rosette Creamer

Berry set, 8" d. master bowl & six 5" d. sauce dishes, 7 pcs. 90.00
Bowl, 6" d. 16.00
Bowl, 7" d. 22.50
Bowl, 8" d. 24.00
Bowl, 9½ x 6¼" oval 22.00
Bread platter, 11 x 9" 27.00
Butter dish, cov., clear 47.00
Butter dish, cov., ruby-stained 105.00
Cake stand, 9" to 10" d. .....45.00 to 55.00
Castor set, salt & pepper shakers & cov. condiment jar, set 36.50

Celery vase, clear 20.00
Celery vase, ruby-stained 95.00
Compote, cov., 5″ d. 58.00
Compote, cov., 6″ d., 10″ h. 62.50
Compote, open, jelly, 5″ d. 26.50
Cordial 44.00
Creamer, clear (ILLUS.) 27.00
Creamer, ruby-stained 46.00
Goblet 36.00
Honey dish, cov. 42.50 to 60.00
Marmalade dish, footed, clear 38.00
Marmalade dish, footed, ruby-stained 45.00
Mug, 3″ h. 14.00
Pickle dish, oval 19.50
Pitcher, milk 40.00
Pitcher, water 70.00
Plate, 6″ d., fiery opalescent, flint 140.00
Plate, 7″ d. 18.00
Plate, 8″ d., flint 45.00
Relish, 8½ x 3½″ 10.00
Relish, 9 x 6″ 20.00
Salt & pepper shakers w/original tops, clear, pr. 32.00
Salt & pepper shakers w/original tops, ruby-stained, pr. 90.00
Salt & pepper shakers w/original tops on original glass stand w/handle, set 42.00
Sauce dish 10.00
Spooner, clear 21.00
Spooner, ruby-stained 50.00
Sugar bowl, cov. 32.50
Toddy plate, clear, 5½″ d. 35.00
Toddy plate, purple, flint, 5½″ d. 325.00
Tumbler, clear 30.00
Tumbler, ruby-stained 38.50
Tumbler, lemonade 16.00
Water set, pitcher & 6 tumblers, 7 pcs. 195.00
Wine 35.00

ROSE IN SNOW

Rose in Snow Creamer

Berry set, 8¼″ sq. footed bowl & 4 footed sauce dishes, 5 pcs. 75.00
Bitters bottle w/original stopper 55.00
Bowl, 7″ d., footed 32.00
Bowl, 10 x 7¼″ oval 47.00
Butter dish, cov., round 46.00
Cake plate, handled, amber, 10″ d. 42.00
Cake plate, handled, clear, 10″ d. 25.00
Cake stand, clear, 9″ d. 73.00
Cologne bottle w/original stopper 90.00
Compote, cov., 6″ d., 8″ h. 70.00
Compote, cov., 7″ d., 8″ h. 85.00
Compote, cov., 8″ d., 10″ h., clear 80.00
Compote, cov., 8″ d., 10″ h., vaseline 110.00
Compote, open, 5″ d., 5½″ h. 55.00
Compote, open, 5½″ d., high stand 36.00
Compote, open, 5¾″ d., vaseline 55.00
Compote, open, 6″ d., 5″ h., blue 70.00
Compote, open, 6″ d., low stand 24.00
Compote, open, 7″ d., low stand 40.00
Compote, open, 7″ d., 7″ h. 45.00
Creamer, round, amber 45.00
Creamer, round, blue 55.00
Creamer, round, clear 23.00
Creamer, square, clear (ILLUS.) 34.00
Creamer, square, vaseline 60.00
Creamer & open sugar bowl, round, pr. 90.00
Creamer & sugar bowl, square, pr. 95.00
Goblet, amber 41.50
Goblet, blue 34.00
Goblet, clear 30.00
Mug, clear, 3½″ h. 45.00
Mug, applied handle, "In Fond Remembrance," clear 29.00
Mug, applied handle, "In Fond Remembrance," yellow 45.00
Pitcher, water, applied handle, amber 112.50
Pitcher, water, applied handle, blue 225.00
Pitcher, water, applied handle, clear 80.00
Plate, 5″ d. 30.00
Plate, 7″ d. 20.00
Powder jar, cov. 21.00
Relish, 8 x 5½″ oval 15.00
Relish, 9¼ x 6¼″ 19.00
Relish, double 88.00
Sauce dish, flat or footed 12.00
Spooner, round 25.00
Spooner, square 35.00
Sugar bowl, cov., round 37.50
Sugar bowl, cov., square 45.00
Table set, square, 4 pcs. 170.00
Tumbler 38.00
Wine 20.00

ROSE SPRIG

Bowl, 8 x 7½″, footed, clear 32.00
Bowl, 9″ d., footed, clear 23.00
Bowl, 9 x 6″ rectangle, vaseline 27.50
Bowl, 9 x 8¼″ oval, footed, clear 32.00

Bread tray, 2-handled, blue 35.00
Bread tray, 2-handled, yellow 40.00
Cake stand, amber, 9" octagon, 6½" h. 60.00
Cake stand, blue, 9" octagon, 6½" h. 65.00
Cake stand, clear, 9" octagon, 6½" h. 62.00
Cake stand, yellow, 9" octagon, 6½" h. 85.00
Celery vase, amber 45.00
Celery vase, clear 32.00
Celery vase, yellow 36.00
Compote, cov., high stand, large, clear 75.00
Compote, open, 7" oval, amber 36.00
Compote, open, 7" d., 5" h., yellow 37.00
Compote, open, 9" d., low stand, clear 19.00
Compote, open, 9" d., high stand, amber 37.50
Creamer, amber 40.00
Creamer, yellow 40.00
Goblet, amber 30.00
Goblet, blue 48.00
Goblet, clear 32.00
Goblet, yellow 32.00
Honey dish, cov., amber, square 23.00
Nappy, handled, clear, 6" sq. 18.00
Pitcher, milk, amber 55.00
Pitcher, milk, clear 45.00
Pitcher, water, amber 65.00
Pitcher, water, clear 48.00
Pitcher, water, yellow 70.00
Plate, 6" sq., amber 26.50
Plate, 6" sq., blue 30.00
Plate, 6" sq., clear 20.00
Relish, handled, blue, 6 x 4" 32.50
Relish, handled, clear, 6 x 4" 7.50
Relish, handled, yellow, 6 x 4" 20.00
Relish, boat-shaped, amber, 8" l. 30.00
Relish, boat-shaped, blue, 8" l. 36.00
Relish, boat-shaped, clear, 8" l. 20.00
Relish, boat-shaped, yellow, 8" l. 32.00
Sauce dish, flat, amber 15.00
Sauce dish, flat, clear 12.50
Sauce dish, footed, blue 17.50

Rose Sprig Handled Tumbler

Sauce dish, footed, clear 8.00
Spooner, clear 15.00
Tumbler, amber 30.00
Tumbler, clear 40.00
Tumbler w/applied handle, clear (ILLUS.) 45.00
Wine, blue 50.00
Wine, clear 28.00
Whimsey, sleigh (salt dip), amber, 4 x 6 x 4" 47.00

ROSETTE

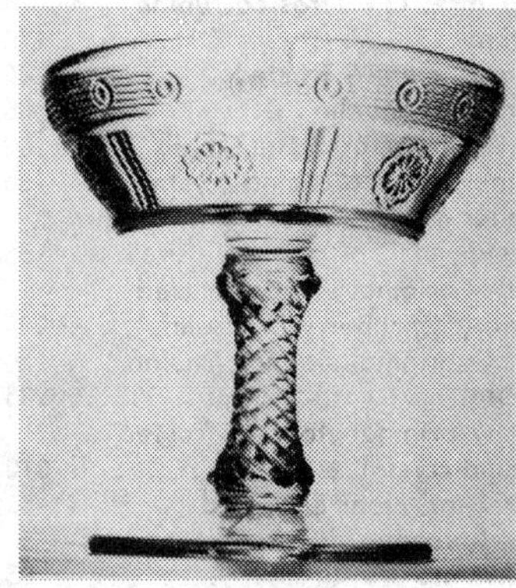

Rosette Jelly Compote

Bowl, cov., 7¼" d., flat 30.00
Bowl, 7½" d. 16.00
Bread plate, handled, 11" d. 25.00
Butter dish, cov. 40.00
Cake stand, 8½" to 11" d. 27.00
Celery vase 21.00
Compote, cov., 6" d., 9" h. 70.00
Compote, cov., 11½" h. 50.00
Compote, open, jelly, 4½" d., 5" h. (ILLUS.) 16.00
Compote, open, 7¼" d., 6" h. 30.00
Compote, open, 9" d., low stand 14.00
Creamer 25.00
Goblet 20.00
Pitcher, milk 42.00
Pitcher, water, tankard 45.00
Plate, 7" d. 22.50
Plate, 9" d., 2-handled 21.00
Relish, fish-shaped 12.00
Salt shaker w/replaced top (single) 23.00
Sauce dish 8.00
Spooner 32.00
Sugar bowl, cov. 33.00
Tumbler, clear 16.00
Tumbler, ruby-stained 29.00
Wine 25.00

ROYAL IVY

Berry set: master bowl & 5 sauce dishes; frosted rubina crystal, 6 pcs. 295.00
Berry set: master bowl & 8 sauce dishes; clear & frosted, 9 pcs. 250.00
Bowl, 8" d., rubina crystal 95.00

Bowl, 8" d., frosted rubina crystal 120.00
Bowl, fruit, 9" d., craquelle (cranberry & vaseline spatter) 125.00
Bowl, fruit, 9" d., frosted craquelle 150.00
Bowl, fruit, 9" d., frosted rubina crystal 100.00
Butter dish, cov., clear & frosted . . . 175.00
Butter dish, cov., frosted craquelle . . 137.50
Butter dish, cov., rubina crystal 162.00
Butter dish, cov., frosted rubina crystal 175.00
Creamer, clear & frosted 45.00
Creamer, craquelle 85.00
Creamer, rubina crystal 100.00
Creamer, frosted rubina crystal 165.00
Creamer & open sugar bowl, rubina crystal, pr. 155.00
Cruet w/original stopper, cased spatter (cranberry & vaseline) 395.00
Cruet w/original stopper, rubina crystal 285.00
Cruet w/original stopper, frosted rubina crystal 310.00
Dresser jar, clear & frosted 85.00
Lamp, kerosene, frosted rubina crystal, miniature 85.00
Marmalade jar, cov., rubina crystal 100.00
Pickle castor, clear & frosted insert, complete w/silver plate frame . . . 140.00
Pickle castor, rubina crystal insert, complete w/silver plate frame . . . 260.00
Pickle castor, frosted rubina crystal insert, complete w/silver plate frame 395.00
Pickle castor, cased spatter insert, complete w/silver plate frame & tongs 350.00
Pitcher, water, cased spatter 285.00
Pitcher, water, clear & frosted 102.00
Pitcher, water, craquelle 450.00
Pitcher, water, frosted craquelle 400.00
Pitcher, water, rubina crystal . . . . 165.00 to 225.00
Pitcher, water, frosted rubina crystal 275.00
Rose bowl, cased spatter 295.00
Rose bowl, clear & frosted 85.00
Rose bowl, rubina crystal 92.00
Rose bowl, frosted rubina crystal . . . 80.00
Salt shaker w/original top, rubina crystal (single) 46.00
Salt & pepper shakers w/original tops, clear & frosted, pr. 69.00
Salt & pepper shakers w/original tops, rubina crystal, pr. 78.00
Salt & pepper shakers w/original tops, frosted rubina crystal, pr. . . . 78.00
Sauce dish, clear & frosted 37.50
Sauce dish, frosted rubina crystal . . . 32.00
Spooner, clear & frosted 38.00
Spooner, rubina crystal 79.00
Spooner, frosted rubina crystal 75.00
Sugar bowl, cov., clear & frosted . . . 45.00
Sugar bowl, cov., rubina crystal 128.00
Sugar bowl, cov., frosted rubina crystal 130.00
Sugar shaker w/original top, cased spatter 175.00
Sugar shaker w/original top, clear & frosted . . . . 58.00 to 75.00
Sugar shaker w/original top, frosted craquelle 200.00
Sugar shaker w/original top, rubina crystal 110.00
Sugar shaker w/original top, frosted rubina crystal 135.00
Sweetmeat jar w/silver plate top, cased spatter, 4½" d., 3½" h. . . . 195.00
Syrup pitcher w/original top, cased spatter 490.00
Syrup pitcher w/original top, clear & frosted 155.00
Syrup pitcher w/original top, rubina crystal 250.00
Syrup pitcher w/original top, frosted rubina crystal 450.00
Table set, cased spatter, 4 pcs. 875.00
Table set, clear & frosted, 4 pcs. . . . 265.00
Table set, craquelle, 4 pcs. 850.00
Table set, frosted rubina crystal, 4 pcs. 624.00
Toothpick holder, clear & frosted . . . 30.00
Toothpick holder, craquelle 182.00
Toothpick holder, rubina crystal 85.00
Toothpick holder, frosted rubina crystal 125.00
Tumbler, whiskey, handled, flint 95.00
Tumbler, cased spatter 85.00
Tumbler, clear & frosted 25.00
Tumbler, craquelle 76.00
Tumbler, frosted craquelle 125.00
Tumbler, rubina crystal 42.50
Tumbler, frosted rubina crystal 65.00
Water set: pitcher & 4 tumblers; frosted rubina crystal, 5 pcs. 650.00
Water set: pitcher & 5 tumblers; cased spatter, 6 pcs. 850.00
Water set: pitcher & 6 tumblers; rubina crystal, 7 pcs. . . . 400.00 to 500.00

ROYAL OAK

Berry set: master bowl & 4 sauce dishes; rubina crystal, 5 pcs. 225.00
Bowl, berry, 7½" d., frosted crystal 65.00
Butter dish, cov., frosted crystal 55.00
Butter dish, cov., rubina crystal 135.00
Butter dish, cov., frosted rubina crystal 180.00
Creamer, frosted crystal 82.00
Creamer, rubina crystal 85.00
Creamer, frosted rubina crystal 245.00
Cruet w/original stopper, frosted crystal 95.00

Cruet w/original stopper, rubina crystal 425.00
Cruet w/original stopper, frosted rubina crystal 310.00

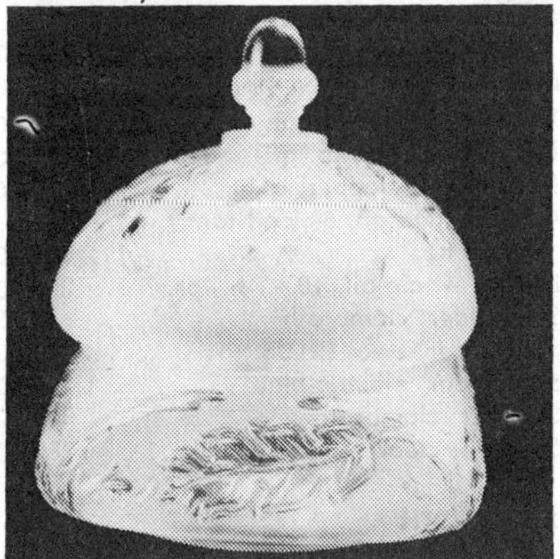

Royal Oak Dresser Jar

Dresser jar, cov., frosted crystal, 5" w., 5½" h. (ILLUS.) 150.00
Nappy, frosted crystal 30.00
Pickle castor, frosted rubina crystal insert, w/silver plate frame & cover 225.00
Pitcher, 8½" h., frosted crystal 100.00
Pitcher, water, rubina crystal 260.00
Pitcher, water, frosted rubina crystal 312.00
Salt shaker w/original top, frosted crystal (single) 60.00
Salt shaker w/original top, rubina crystal (single) 54.00
Salt shaker w/original top, frosted rubina crystal (single) 65.00
Salt & pepper shakers w/original tops, frosted crystal, pr. 135.00
Salt & pepper shakers w/original tops, frosted rubina crystal, pr. 150.00
Sauce dish, frosted crystal 12.50
Sauce dish, rubina crystal 40.00
Spooner, frosted crystal 58.00
Spooner, rubina crystal 60.00
Spooner, frosted rubina crystal 100.00
Sugar bowl, cov., frosted crystal 55.00
Sugar bowl, cov., rubina crystal 140.00
Sugar bowl, cov., frosted rubina crystal 130.00
Sugar bowl, open, frosted rubina crystal 60.00
Sugar shaker w/original top, frosted crystal 65.00
Sugar shaker w/original top, rubina crystal 125.00
Sugar shaker w/original top, frosted rubina crystal 165.00
Syrup pitcher w/original (repaired) top, rubina crystal 275.00
Table set, frosted rubina crystal, 4 pcs. 600.00
Toothpick holder, frosted crystal 52.00
Toothpick holder, rubina crystal 89.00
Toothpick holder, frosted rubina crystal 125.00
Tumbler, frosted crystal 75.00
Tumbler, frosted rubina crystal 80.00
Water set: pitcher & 5 tumblers; frosted crystal, 6 pcs. 425.00

RUBY ROSETTE - See Pillow Encircled Pattern

RUBY THUMBPRINT

Ruby Thumbprint Tankard Pitcher

(Items may be plain or with engraved designs)

Berry set, boat-shaped master bowl & 5 boat-shaped sauce dishes, 6 pcs. 195.00
Berry set: master bowl & 8 sauce dishes; round, 9 pcs. 250.00
Bowl, 6½" d. 33.50
Bowl, 7½" d. 52.00
Bowl, 8½" d. 45.00
Bowl, master berry or fruit, 10" l., boat-shaped 125.00
Butter dish, cov. 105.00
Cake stand, 10" d. 125.00
Castor set, 4-bottle, w/frame ....325.00 to 425.00
Celery vase 50.00
Champagne 35.00
Cheese dish, cov., 7" d. 55.00
Claret 46.50
Compote, open, jelly, 5¼" h. 58.00
Compote, open, 7" d. 90.00
Compote, open, 8½" d., 7½" h., scalloped rim 230.00
Cordial 28.00
Creamer 58.00
Creamer, souvenir, "Dear Mother" & date 63.00
Creamer, individual size 30.00
Creamer & sugar bowl, individual size, pr. 85.00
Cup & saucer 53.00

Dish, cov., 8" d., 7" h. 68.00
Goblet 36.00
Mustard jar, cov. 58.00
Mustard jar, cov., etched "World's Fair, 1893" 127.50
Olive dish 125.00
Pitcher, milk, 7½" h., bulbous 120.00
Pitcher, milk, tankard, 8 3/8" h. 82.00
Pitcher, water, bulbous, large 250.00
Pitcher, water, tankard, 11" h. 132.00
Pitcher, water, tankard, 11" h., w/engraved leaf band (ILLUS.) ... 170.00
Plate, 5" d. 22.00
Plate, 7½" d. 22.00
Punch cup 18.00
Relish, 8" oblong 35.00
Salt dip, individual size 145.00
Salt shaker w/original top (single) .. 28.00
Salt & pepper shakers w/original tops, pr. 70.00
Salt & pepper shakers w/original tops, individual size, pr. 95.00
Sauce dish, boat-shaped 28.00
Sauce dish, round 20.00
Spooner 52.50
Sugar bowl, cov. 77.50
Sugar bowl, open 32.50
Sugar bowl, open, individual size, 2¼" h. 26.00
Table set, 4 pcs. ....250.00 to 350.00
Toothpick holder 27.00
Tumbler 38.00
Water set, bulbous pitcher & 5 tumblers, 6 pcs. 315.00
Water set, tankard pitcher & 5 tumblers, 6 pcs. 295.00
Water set, tankard pitcher & 7 tumblers, 8 pcs. 395.00
Wine 33.00

SANDWICH LOOP - **See Hairpin Pattern**

SANDWICH STAR

Sandwich Star Spillholder

Butter dish, cov. 195.00
Compote, open, 8½" d., low stand 60.00
Compote, open, 12" d., 9½" h., scalloped rim, three-dolphins base, canary, flint, unique example (running crack) 3,600.00
Compote, open, 12" d., 9½" h., clear 265.00
Decanter w/patented stopper, pt. .. 135.00
Decanter w/bar lip, pt. 70.00
Decanter w/bar lip, qt. 85.00
Decanter w/stopper, qt. 110.00
Lamp, whale oil, 6-sided font, 10½" h. 125.00
Lamps, whale oil, 10½" h., pr. 300.00
Spillholder, clambroth 440.00
Spillholder, clear (ILLUS.) 50.00
Spillholder, electric blue 1,200.00
Spooner, clambroth 400.00
Spooner, clear 85.00

SAWTOOTH

Sawtooth Compote

Ale glass 35.00
Banana boat, non-flint 57.50
Bitters bottle w/stopper, flint 47.50
Butter dish, cov., flint, clear 80.00
Butter dish, cov., non-flint, clear 35.00
Butter dish, cov., non-flint, sapphire blue 230.00
Cake stand, non-flint, 7½" d., 6" h. 35.00
Cake stand, non-flint, 9½" d., 4½" h. 75.00
Carafe 45.00
Celery vases, knob stem, flint, pr. .. 105.00
Celery vase, knob stem, non-flint ... 38.00
Champagne, knob stem, flint 55.00
Champagne, non-flint 32.50
Compote, cov., 6½" d., 9" h., milk white, flint 105.00
Compote, cov., 7½" d., 8¼" h., flint 65.00
Compote, cov., 7½" d., 11½" h., flint 85.00
Compote, cov., 8" d., low stand, flint 125.00
Compote, cov., 8" d., high stand, flint 82.00

Compote, cov., 9¼" d., 4" h., non-flint 48.00
Compote, cov., 9½" d., 14" h., flint 200.00
Compote, cov., 9½" d., 14" h., non-flint 72.50
Compote, open, 7½" d., 5½" h., flint 40.00
Compote, open, 7½" d., 7½" h., flint (ILLUS.) 55.00
Compote, open, 7¾" d., 6¼" h., flint 72.00
Compote, open, 8" d., 6" h., non-flint 36.00
Compote, open, 10" d., 9" h., flint 60.00
Cordial, non-flint, clear 20.00
Cordial, ruby-stained 40.00
Creamer, applied handle, clear, flint 75.00
Creamer, applied handle, cobalt blue, flint 230.00
Creamer, applied handle, non-flint .. 30.00
Creamer, miniature 14.00
Cruet w/original stopper, applied handle, flint 85.00
Cruet w/original stopper, non-flint .. 22.50
Decanter w/acorn stopper, flint, ½ pt. 105.00
Egg cup, cov., flint 65.00
Egg cup, flint 43.00
Goblet, flattened sawtooth 47.00
Goblet, knob stem, flint 34.00
Goblet, knob stem, non-flint 20.00
Goblet, plain stem, non-flint 19.00
Honey dish, 3½" d. 28.00
Pickle jar w/original cover 65.00
Pitcher, milk, non-flint 25.00
Pitcher, water, applied handle, clear, flint 115.00
Pitcher, water, applied handle, milk white, flint 345.00
Plate, 6" d., rayed center 17.00
Salt dip, cov., individual size, footed, flint 35.00
Salt dip, individual size, footed, flint 18.00
Salt dip, cov., master size, footed, flint 58.00
Salt dip, master size, clear, flint 34.00
Salt dip, master size, clear, non-flint 15.00
Salt dip, master size, fiery opalescent, flint 150.00
Salt dip, master size, milk white, non-flint 19.50
Salt shaker w/original top, milk white, non-flint (single) 19.50
Salt shaker w/original top, bulbous, sapphire blue (single) 22.00
Spillholder, flint 53.00
Spillholder, non-flint 22.50
Spooner, clear, flint 45.00
Spooner, clear, non-flint 22.00
Spooner, cobalt blue, non-flint 85.00
Spooner, milk white 48.00
Spooner, sapphire blue, jagged sawtooth rim, 5½" h., flint 700.00
Spooner, child's 30.00
Sugar bowl, cov., flint 75.00
Sugar bowl, cov., non-flint 28.50
Sugar bowl, cov., miniature 45.00
Sugar bowl, open, flint 48.00
Table set, clear, 4 pcs. 125.00
Table set, milk white, 4 pcs. 310.00
Tumbler, bar, flint, 4½" h. 58.00
Tumbler, bar, non-flint 35.00
Tumbler, flat, flint 36.00
Tumbler, footed, flint 65.00
Tumble-up (carafe w/tumbler lid) ... 175.00
Vase, 9 7/8" h. 25.00
Wine, flint 35.00
Wine, non-flint 25.00

SAWTOOTH BAND - See Amazon Pattern

SCALLOPED TAPE - See Jewel Band Pattern

SEDAN (Paneled Star & Button)

Sedan Sauce Dish

Butter dish, cov. 38.00
Compote, cov., 8" d., high stand ... 26.00
Compote, open, high stand 20.00
Creamer 25.00
Goblet 22.00
Mug, miniature 12.50
Pitcher, water 45.00
Relish, 10" l. 10.00
Salt dip, master size 12.50
Sauce dish, flat, 4½" d. (ILLUS.) 6.00
Spooner 25.00
Sugar bowl, cov. 45.00
Sugar bowl, open 36.00
Wine 15.00

SENECA LOOP - See Loop Pattern

SHELL & JEWEL (Victor)

Berry set, 8" d. bowl & 8 sauce dishes, 9 pcs. 55.00
Bowl, 8" d., clear 30.00

Bowl, 10" d., clear 25.00
Butter dish, cov. 60.00
Cake stand, 10" d., 5" h. 40.00
Compote, cov., 8½" d., high stand 75.00
Compote, open, 7" d., 7½" h. 40.00
Creamer 35.00
Pitcher, milk, blue 75.00
Pitcher, milk, clear 35.00
Pitcher, water, amber 100.00
Pitcher, water, blue or green 80.00

Shell & Jewel Pitcher

Pitcher, water, clear (ILLUS.) 39.50
Relish, oblong 18.00
Sauce dish, amber 15.00
Sauce dish, clear 8.00
Spooner 22.00
Sugar bowl, cov. 42.50
Tumbler, amber 32.00
Tumbler, blue 36.00
Tumbler, clear 16.00
Tumbler, green 36.00
Water set: pitcher & 6 tumblers; amber, 7 pcs. 260.00
Water set: pitcher & 6 tumblers; blue, 7 pcs. 245.00
Water set: pitcher & 6 tumblers; clear, 7 pcs. 150.00
Water set: pitcher & 6 tumblers; green, 7 pcs. 225.00

SHELL & TASSEL

Berry set, 10" oval master bowl & 6 square footed sauce dishes, 7 pcs. 190.00
Bowl, 8 x 5" rectangle, clear 24.00
Bowl, 9" oval, amber 50.00
Bowl, 9" oval, clear 40.00
Bowl, 9" oval, vaseline 57.50
Bowl, 11½ x 6½" oval, amber 90.00
Bowl, 11½ x 6½" oval, blue 95.00
Bowl, 11½ x 6½" oval, clear 49.00
Bowl, 12" oval, clear 75.00
Bowl, rectangular, amber 75.00
Bread tray, 13 x 9" 52.00
Bride's basket, 8" oval bowl in silver plate frame 125.00
Bride's basket, 10 x 5" oval amber bowl in silver plate frame 275.00
Butter dish, cov., round, dog finial .. 120.00
Cake stand, shell corners, 8" sq. 42.50
Cake stand, shell corners, 9" sq. 50.00
Cake stand, shell corners, 10" sq. .. 65.00
Cake stand, shell corners, 12" sq. .. 82.00
Celery vase, round, handled 51.00
Celery vase, square 48.00
Compote, cov., 4¼" sq., 8" h. 47.50
Compote, cov., 5¼" sq. 65.00
Compote, cov., 7" d., dog finial 155.00
Compote, cov., 7½" d., 8" h. 75.00
Compote, open, jelly 50.00
Compote, open, 4½" sq., high stand 35.00
Compote, open, 5½" sq., 6" h. 29.50
Compote, open, 6½" sq., 6½" h. 32.50
Compote, open, 7½" sq., 7½" h. 45.00
Compote, open, 7½" sq., 9" h. 44.00

Shell & Tassel Compote

Compote, open, 8½" sq., 8" h. (ILLUS.) 60.00
Compote, open, 9½" d., 9" h. 82.00
Compote, open, 10" sq., 8" h. ....60.00 to 75.00
Creamer, round 32.00
Creamer, square 45.00
Creamer & cov. sugar bowl, square, pr. 120.00
Dish, 10 x 7" 25.00
Doughnut stand, 8" sq. 55.00
Goblet, round, knob stem 40.00
Goblet, square, knob stem 24.50
Mug, miniature, blue 35.00
Oyster plate, 9½" d. 210.00
Pickle dish 22.00
Pitcher, water, round 60.00
Pitcher, water, square 68.00
Plate, shell-shaped w/three shell-shaped feet, large 67.50
Platter, 11 x 8" oblong 50.00
Platter, 13 x 9" oval 50.00
Relish, blue, 8 x 5" 85.00

Relish, clear, 8 x 5" 40.00
Salt dip, shell-shaped 20.00
Salt & pepper shakers w/original tops, pr. 125.00
Sauce dish, flat or footed, 4" to 5" d. 10.00
Sauce dish, footed, w/shell handle 13.50
Spooner, round 37.00
Spooner, square 29.00
Sugar bowl, cov., round, dog finial 90.00
Sugar bowl, cov., square, shell finial 75.00
Sugar bowl, open, round 52.00
Sugar bowl, open, square 25.00
Table set, 4 pcs. 295.00
Tray, ice cream 44.00
Tumbler 15.50
Vase 110.00

SHERATON

Sheraton Compote

Bowl, 6 5/8 x 4 7/8", amber 23.00
Bowl, 10 x 8", 8-sided, clear 18.50
Bread platter, amber, 10 x 8" 42.50
Bread platter, blue, 10 x 8" 33.00
Bread platter, clear, 10 x 8" 20.00
Butter dish, cov., blue 50.00
Butter dish, cov., clear 40.00
Cake stand, amber, 10¼" d. 45.00
Cake stand, clear, 10½" d. 32.00
Celery vase 24.00
Compote, cov., 8" d., clear 35.00
Compote, open, 7" d., 5" h., amber 28.00
Compote, open, 7" d., 5" h., clear 21.00
Compote, open, 8" d., 7¾" h. (ILLUS.) 28.00
Compote, open, 8" d., low stand 24.00
Compote, open, 10" d. 45.00
Creamer, amber 27.00
Creamer, blue 37.00
Creamer, clear 23.00
Goblet, blue 43.00
Goblet, clear 22.00
Pickle dish, amber 16.00
Pickle dish, clear 7.00
Pitcher, milk, amber 40.00
Pitcher, milk, clear 24.00
Pitcher, water, amber 55.00
Pitcher, water, blue 85.00
Pitcher, water, clear 45.00
Plate, 7" sq., amber 20.00
Plate, 8½" sq., clear 8.50
Relish, handled, amber 16.50
Relish, handled, blue 31.00
Relish, handled, clear 14.50
Sauce dish, blue, 4" d. 12.00
Sauce dish, clear, 4" d. 9.00
Spooner, amber 30.00
Spooner, blue 32.50
Spooner, clear 22.00
Sugar bowl, cov., amber 44.00
Sugar bowl, cov., clear 25.00
Tumbler 22.00
Wine 21.00

SHOSHONE

Bowl, 7", flat 11.00
Cake stand, clear 23.50
Cake stand, green 55.00
Compote, jelly 17.50
Creamer, amber-stained 47.50
Creamer, green 37.50
Cruet w/original stopper, clear 55.00
Cruet w/original stopper, green 95.00
Plate, 11" d., reticulated rim, milk white 35.00
Relish, 7½" l. 11.00
Sauce dish, w/gold, 5" sq. 12.50
Spooner 35.00
Toothpick holder, clear w/gold 30.00

SHOVEL

Shovel Goblet

Compote, open, jelly 18.00
Goblet (ILLUS.) 19.00
Syrup pitcher w/glass top 19.00
Tumbler 16.00
Wine 18.00

SHRINE

Bowl, 6½" d., scalloped rim 20.00
Bowl, 8¼" d. 31.50
Butter dish, cov. 45.00
Champagne 58.50
Compote, cov., high stand 75.00
Compote, open, jelly 22.50
Creamer 32.50
Goblet 37.50
Lamp, kerosene, w/fingergrip, pedestal base, 10" h. 145.00
Mug 32.00
Pickle dish 16.00
Pitcher, cider, ½ gal 125.00
Pitcher, water 45.00
Plate, 6" d., scalloped rim 46.00
Salt shaker w/original top (single) .. 28.50
Salt & pepper shakers w/replaced tops, pr. 45.00
Sauce dish 13.00
Spooner 26.50
Sugar bowl, cov. 47.50
Toothpick holder 85.00
Tumbler, 4" h. 37.50
Wine 45.00

SHUTTLE (Hearts of Loch Laven)

Shuttle Mug

Bowl, berry, large 30.00
Butter dish, cov. 110.00
Cake stand 125.00
Celery vase 48.00
Champagne 36.00
Cordial, small 32.00
Creamer, tall tankard 35.00
Goblet 60.00
Mug, amber 300.00
Mug, clear (ILLUS.) 28.00
Pitcher, water 140.00
Punch cup 12.00
Salt shaker w/original top (single) .. 60.00
Spooner, scalloped rim 50.00
Tumbler 50.00
Wine 12.50

SKILTON - See Oregon Pattern

SMOCKING

Bowl, 7" d., footed 38.50
Butter dish, cov. 90.00
Cake stand, purple, 8½" d. 750.00
Champagne, knob stem 85.00
Compote, 6" d., 4" h. 50.00
Compote, 7¾" d., low stand 52.00

Smocking Creamer & Sugar Bowl

Creamer, applied handle (ILLUS. left) 150.00
Creamer, individual size 125.00
Goblet 45.00
Spillholder 39.50
Spooner 37.50
Sugar bowl, cov. (ILLUS. right) 150.00
Wine 65.00

SNAIL (Compact)

Snail Banana Stand

Banana stand, 10" d., 7" h. (ILLUS.) 190.00
Bowl, 7" d., low 34.00
Bowl, berry, 8" d., 4" h. 32.50
Bowl, 9" d., 2" h. 30.00
Butter dish, cov. 80.00
Cake stand, 10" d. 87.50
Celery vase 52.00
Cheese dish, cov. 80.00
Compote, cov., 7" d., 11½" h. 130.00
Compote, open, 8" d., 9" h. 65.00
Cracker jar, cov., 8" d., 9" h. 125.00
Creamer, clear 50.00
Creamer, ruby-stained 75.00
Cruet w/original stopper, clear 93.00
Cruet w/original stopper, ruby-stained 225.00
Goblet 90.00
Honey dish, cov. 95.00
Pickle dish, 8 x 5½" 28.00
Pitcher, cider, bulbous 150.00

Pitcher, milk, bulbous, applied handle, large 120.00
Pitcher, water, tankard 89.00
Pitcher, wine, tankard 155.00
Plate, 7" d. 27.50
Plate, 9" d. 34.00
Punch cup 27.00
Relish, 7" oval 22.50
Rose bowl, double, miniature 35.00
Rose bowl, large 85.00
Salt dip, individual size 20.00
Salt dip, master size, 3" d. 50.00
Salt shaker w/original top, clear (single) 23.00
Salt shaker w/original top, ruby-stained (single) 50.00
Salt & pepper shakers w/original tops, clear, pr. 55.00
Salt & pepper shakers w/original tops, ruby-stained, pr. 95.00
Sauce dish ...... 9.00 to 15.00
Spooner, clear 33.00
Spooner, ruby-stained 85.00
Sugar bowl, cov. 60.00
Sugar bowl, cov., engraved leaf band 85.00
Sugar shaker w/original top, clear 100.00
Sugar shaker w/original top, ruby-stained 193.00
Syrup jug w/original brass top 75.00
Tumbler, clear 48.00
Tumbler, ruby-stained 54.00
Vase, 12½" h., scalloped rim 55.00
Vase, 17" h. 65.00

SNAKESKIN & DOT

Bread tray 140.00
Celery vase 35.00
Compote, cov. 60.00
Creamer 30.00
Goblet 30.00
Plate, 4½" d., amber 9.00
Plate, 7" d., milk white 15.00
Plate, 9" d., clear 25.00
Sugar bowl, cov. 45.00

SPARTAN (Barred Star)

Cordial 15.00
Goblet 22.50
Sauce dish, flat 10.00
Sugar bowl, cov. 60.00
Tumbler 17.50

SPIREA BAND

Bowl, 8" oval, flat, blue 39.00
Butter dish, cov., amber 50.00
Butter dish, cov., blue 57.50
Butter dish, cov., clear 40.00
Cake stand, amber, 8½" d. 45.00
Celery vase, blue 35.00
Compote, cov., 7" d., high stand, blue 65.00
Compote, cov., 7" d., low stand, amber 55.00
Compote, open, 7" d., low stand, amber 26.00
Compote, open, 8" d. 25.00
Creamer, amber 36.50
Creamer, blue 32.50
Creamer, clear 20.00
Goblet, amber 24.50
Goblet, blue 36.00
Goblet, clear 22.00
Pickle castor, amber insert, w/silver plate frame, lid & tongs 100.00
Pickle dish 7.00
Pitcher, water, amber 42.50
Pitcher, water, blue 90.00
Pitcher, water, clear 45.00
Platter, 10½ x 8½", amber 25.00
Platter, 10½ x 8½", blue 32.00
Platter, 10½ x 8½", clear 20.00
Platter, 10½ x 8½", vaseline 28.00
Relish, amber, 7 x 4½" 10.00
Relish, amber, 9 x 5½" 18.50
Salt shaker w/original top, blue (single) 37.50
Salt & pepper shakers w/original tops, amber, pr. 30.00
Sauce dish, flat or footed, amber ...... 6.00 to 12.00
Sauce dish, flat or footed, blue 12.00
Spooner, amber 26.00
Spooner, blue 33.00
Spooner, clear 18.00
Spooner, vaseline 26.00
Sugar bowl, cov., blue 55.00
Sugar bowl, cov., clear 32.50
Sugar bowl, open, amber 22.00
Tumbler, blue 50.00
Wine, amber 24.00
Wine, blue 28.00
Wine, clear 18.50

SPRIG

Sprig Relish

Berry set, 8½" d. master bowl & 6 sauce dishes, 7 pcs. 80.00
Bowl, 8" oval, footed 42.00
Bowl, 9" oval 40.00
Bread platter, 11" oval 32.00
Butter dish, cov. 47.50
Cake stand 44.00
Celery vase 36.50
Compote, cov., 6" d., high stand 50.00
Compote, cov., 8" d., low stand 45.00
Compote, open, 6" d. 32.50
Compote, open, 6¾" d., 5½" h. 17.50
Compote, open, 7" d., low stand 24.00
Compote, open, 8" d., high stand 24.00
Compote, open, 10" d., high stand 42.50

Creamer 30.00
Goblet 31.00
Pickle castor, resilvered frame & tongs 85.00
Pitcher, water 50.00
Relish, 6¾" oval 11.00
Relish, 8¾" oval (ILLUS.) 22.00
Salt dip, master size 45.00
Sauce dish, flat or footed 10.50
Spooner 23.50
Sugar bowl, cov. 48.00
Sugar bowl, open 20.00
Wine 38.00

SQUARE LION'S HEAD - See Lion Pattern

SQUARE PANES - See Post Pattern

STAR ROSETTED

Bowl, 7¼ x 5" oval 6.50
Butter dish, cov. 40.00
Cake (or bread) plate, "A Good Mother Makes A Happy Home" 55.00
Creamer 30.00
Goblet 28.00
Relish, 3-handled, 9¾ x 5" 6.50
Sauce dish, flat or footed 4.50
Spooner 25.00
Sugar bowl, cov. 40.00

STATES (THE)

Bowl, 7" d., 3-handled 55.00
Bowl, 7½" d. 25.00
Bowl, 9" d. 60.00
Butter dish, cov. 58.00
Card tray, 7 3/8 x 5" 15.00
Celery 30.00
Cocktail, flared 22.00
Compote, open, 5½ x 5" 27.00
Compote, open, 9¼" d., 9" h. 80.00
Creamer 30.00
Creamer, individual size 30.00
Creamer & sugar bowl, individual size, pr. 42.50
Goblet 32.00
Nappy, 2-handled 22.50
Olive dish 17.50
Pitcher, water 65.00
Punch bowl, 13" d., 5½" h. 70.00
Punch cup 12.50
Salt shaker w/original top (single) . . 16.50
Salt & pepper shakers w/original tops, pr. 54.00
Sauce dish 12.00
Spooner 26.50
Sugar bowl, cov. 48.00
Sugar bowl, open, individual size . 17.50
Syrup jug 95.00
Toothpick holder 32.00
Tumbler 18.50
Water set, pitcher & 6 tumblers, 7 pcs. 125.00
Wine 27.00

STEDMAN

Champagne 35.00
Compote, open, 7½" d., 7" h. 45.00
Creamer 40.00
Egg cup 20.00
Goblet 27.50
Sauce dish, flat 14.00
Spooner 40.00
Syrup pitcher, applied handle, 4¼" d., 8¼" h. 100.00
Wine 45.00

STIPPLED CHAIN

Creamer 30.00
Goblet 20.00
Relish, 8¼ x 6 1/8" 10.00
Salt dip, master size 19.50
Sauce dish 4.50
Spooner 20.00
Sugar bowl, cov. 29.50
Tumbler 20.00

STIPPLED CHERRY

Bowl, master berry, 8" d. 28.00
Bread platter 26.00
Butter dish, cov. 42.00
Celery 35.00
Creamer 22.50
Pitcher, water 52.00
Plate, 6" d. 20.00
Sauce dish, flat 6.50
Spooner 25.00
Tumbler 22.00

STIPPLED DOUBLE LOOP

Butter dish, cov. 40.00
Creamer 30.00
Goblet 28.00
Spooner 20.00
Sugar bowl, cov. 35.00
Tumbler 15.00

STIPPLED FLOWER PANELS - See Maine Pattern

STIPPLED FORGET-ME-NOT

Stippled Forget-Me-Not Compote

Bread platter 37.00

Butter dish, cov. 48.00
Cake stand, 8" to 9" d. 42.50
Celery vase 31.00
Compote, cov., 8" d., high stand ... 55.00
Compote, open, 6" d., 6½" h. (ILLUS.) 32.50
Compote, open, 8" d. 45.00
Creamer 24.00
Cup & saucer 35.00
Goblet 35.00
Mug 20.00
Pitcher, milk 37.00
Pitcher, water 52.00
Plate, 7" d., w/kitten center 45.00
Plate, 9" d., w/kitten center, handles 27.50
Salt dip, master size, oval 35.00
Salt shaker w/original top (single) .. 25.00
Syrup pitcher w/original top 80.00
Tray, water 75.00
Tumbler 30.00
Wine 42.50

STIPPLED GRAPE & FESTOON

Celery vase 28.00
Compote, 8" d., low stand 38.50
Creamer, w/clear leaf 38.50
Egg cup 25.00
Goblet 30.00
Pitcher, water 98.00
Spooner, w/clear leaf 25.00
Sugar bowl, open 21.00

STIPPLED IVY

Butter dish, cov. 45.00
Creamer, applied handle 35.00
Egg cup 28.00
Goblet 24.00
Salt dip, master size 23.00
Sauce dish, flat 8.00
Spooner 27.50
Sugar bowl, cov. 35.00
Sugar bowl, open 27.50

STIPPLED ROMAN KEY

Goblet 36.50
Tumbler 18.00

SUNK HONEYCOMB (Corona)

Cracker jar, cov., ruby-stained 485.00
Creamer, ruby-stained, 4½" h. 30.00
Cruet w/original stopper, ruby-stained, enameled floral decoration 135.00
Cup & saucer, ruby-stained 35.00
Mug, ruby-stained, 3" h. 16.00
Pitcher, 6½" h., ruby-stained, souvenir 20.00
Punch cup 6.50
Salt dip, master size, ruby-stained .. 65.00
Salt shaker w/original top (single) .. 6.50
Salt shaker w/original top, ruby-stained (single) 19.50
Syrup pitcher w/original top, ruby-stained 120.00

Toothpick holder, ruby-stained, souvenir 52.00
Tumbler, ruby-stained 32.00
Wine, etched 15.00
Wine, ruby-stained 32.50
Wine, ruby-stained, etched 40.00

SWAN

Butter dish, cov., swan finial 90.00
Celery vase 60.00
Compote, cov., w/swan finial, 8" d. 185.00
Compote, open, 8½" h. 53.00
Creamer 47.00
Goblet, canary yellow 70.00
Goblet, clear 50.00
Marmalade jar, cov. 57.50
Mug, footed, clear 27.50
Mug, footed, ring handle, opaque blue 68.00
Mug, footed, ring handle, opaque purple 68.00
Mustard jar, cov., amber 75.00
Pitcher, water 140.00
Sauce dish, flat or footed 12.00
Spooner 55.00
Sugar bowl, cov. 185.00
Sugar bowl, open 40.00

TEARDROP & TASSEL

Teardrop & Tassel Butter Dish

Bowl, 7½" d., clear 40.00
Bowl, 7½" d., Nile green 35.00
Bowl, master berry or fruit, cobalt blue 45.00
Butter dish, cov., clear (ILLUS.) 60.00
Butter dish, cov., cobalt blue 185.00
Butter dish, cov., emerald green 200.00
Compote, cov., 5" d., 7½" h. 65.00
Compote, cov., 7" d., 11½" h. 85.00
Compote, cov., 9½" d. 95.00
Compote, open, 8½" d. 45.00
Compote, open, Nile green 250.00
Creamer, amber 175.00
Creamer, clear 35.00
Creamer, cobalt blue 125.00
Creamer, Nile green 200.00
Creamer, white opaque 75.00
Creamer & cov. sugar bowl, emerald green, pr. 325.00

Creamer & cov. sugar bowl, white opaque, pr. 150.00
Goblet, clear 150.00
Goblet, emerald green 225.00
Pitcher, water, clear 65.00
Pitcher, water, cobalt blue 175.00
Pitcher, water emerald green 200.00
Relish, clear 35.00
Relish, emerald green 100.00
Relish, Nile green 175.00
Relish, teal blue 175.00
Salt shaker w/original top, clear (single) 125.00
Salt & pepper shakers w/original tops, Nile green, pr. 350.00
Sauce dish, cobalt blue 45.00
Sauce dish, emerald green 75.00
Spooner, clear 40.00
Spooner, cobalt blue 90.00
Spooner, Nile green 175.00
Spooner, white opaque 65.00
Sugar bowl, cov., clear 60.00
Sugar bowl, cov., Nile green 300.00
Tumbler, clear 35.00
Tumbler, cobalt blue 55.00
Tumbler, emerald green 165.00

TEASEL

Celery 20.00
Goblet 25.00
Plate, 7" to 9" d. .... 12.00 to 20.00
Sauce dish 5.50
Sugar bowl, open 30.00
Tumbler 10.00
Wine 12.00

TEXAS (Loop with Stippled Panels)

Texas Toothpick Holder

Bowl, 8" oval 30.00
Butter dish, cov. 112.50
Cake stand, 9½" to 10¾" d. 65.00
Compote, cov., 6" d., 11" h. 90.00
Creamer 15.50
Creamer, individual size 16.00
Creamer & sugar bowl, individual size, pr. 29.00
Cruet w/original stopper 70.00
Cruet w/original stopper, ruby-stained 165.00
Goblet 45.00
Goblet, ruby-stained 95.00
Pitcher, water, 8½" h. 120.00
Plate, 8¾" d. 62.50
Relish, handled, 8½" l. 25.50
Salt dip, master size, footed, 3" d., 2¾" h. 22.00
Sauce dish, flat or footed 13.50
Spooner 52.50
Sugar bowl, cov. 60.00
Sugar bowl, open, individual size 16.00
Toothpick holder (ILLUS.) 26.00
Vase, bud, 8" h. 24.00
Vase, 9" h. 36.00
Vase, 10" h. 27.50
Wine 78.00
Wine, ruby-stained 95.00

TEXAS BULL'S EYE (Bull's Eye Variant)

Celery vase 32.00
Egg cup 15.00
Goblet 22.50
Lamp, kerosene-type, footed, hand-type w/finger grip 37.50
Sugar bowl, open 30.00
Tumbler 22.50
Wine 21.00

THISTLE - See Paneled Thistle Pattern

THOUSAND EYE

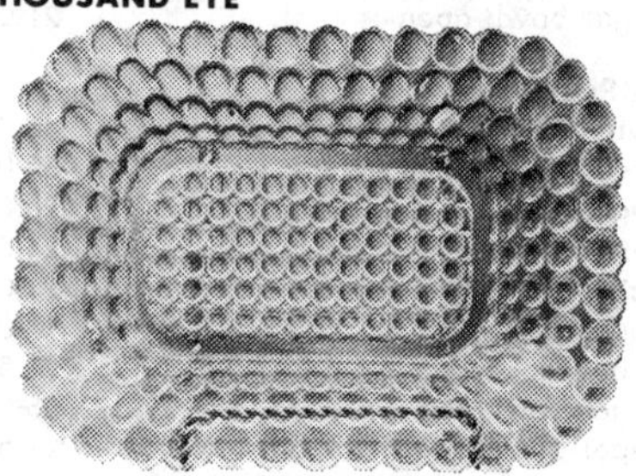

Thousand Eye Dish

Bowl, 8" d., 4½" h., footed, blue opaque 55.00
Bowl, 11" rectangle, shallow, amber 32.00
Bread tray, blue 43.00
Butter dish, cov., amber 70.00
Butter dish, cov., apple green 80.00
Butter dish, cov., clear 44.00
Cake stand, apple green, 8½" to 10" d. 67.50
Cake stand, clear, 8½" to 10" d. 28.00
Celery vase, 3-knob stem, amber 48.00
Celery vase, 3-knob stem, apple green 60.00
Celery vase, 3-knob stem, clear 33.00
Celery vase, plain stem, amber 46.00
Celery vase, plain stem, clear 35.00
Compote, cov., 12" h., clear 115.00
Compote, open, 6" d., low stand, amber 22.00

Compote, open, 6" d., low stand, apple green 31.00
Compote, open, 6" d., low stand, blue 34.00
Compote, open, 6½" d., 3-knob stem, blue 30.00
Compote, open, 7½" d., 3-knob stem, amber 47.50
Compote, open, 7½" d., 3-knob stem, blue 55.00
Compote, open, 8" d., 3¾" h., apple green 37.50
Compote, open, 8" d., 6" h., 3-knob stem, amber 32.50
Compote, open, 8" d., 6" h., 3-knob stem, apple green 40.00
Compote, open, 8" d., 6" h., 3-knob stem, blue 38.00
Compote, open, 10" d., 6½" h., apple green 45.00
Compote, open, 10" d., 6½" h., 3-knob stem, blue 75.00
Creamer, clear 21.00
Creamer, vaseline 47.50
Creamer & cov. sugar bowl, amber, pr. 100.00
Cruet w/original 3-knob stopper, amber 72.00
Cruet w/original 3-knob stopper, apple green 135.00
Cruet w/original 3-knob stopper, blue 75.00
Cruet w/original 3-knob stopper, vaseline 95.00
Cruet stand w/pr. cruets w/original stoppers, knob stem, amber, set 210.00
Dish, apple green, 7 x 5" (ILLUS.) . . . 25.00
Egg cup, blue 75.00
Goblet, amber 30.00
Goblet, apple green 33.50
Goblet, blue 46.00
Goblet, clear 27.50
Goblet, vaseline 34.00
Honey dish, cov., apple green 125.00
Honey dish, cover w/knob finial, rectangular, vaseline 135.00
Inkwell, cov., 2" sq. 30.00
Lamp, kerosene-type, pedestal base, blue, 12" h. 165.00
Lamp, kerosene-type, flat base, ring handle, clear . . . . . . 105.00 to 120.00
Lemonade set: tankard pitcher, lemon dish, 12" tray & 3 goblets; apple green, 6 pcs. 165.00
Mug, amber, 3½" h. 21.00
Mug, blue, 3½" h. 30.00
Mug, clear, 3½" h. 12.50
Mug, vaseline, 3½" h. 27.50
Mug, miniature, amber 19.00
Mug, miniature, apple green 17.50
Mug, miniature, vaseline 25.00
Pitcher, milk, 3-knob stem, clear . . . 35.00
Pitcher, water, clear 57.50
Pitcher, water, vaseline 60.00
Plate, 6" d., amber 30.00
Plate, 6" d., apple green 18.00
Plate, 6" d., clear 12.00
Plate, 8" d., amber 22.00
Plate, 8" d., apple green 25.00
Plate, 8" d., blue 30.00
Plate, 8" d., clear 18.00
Plate, 8" d., vaseline 26.00
Plate, 10" sq., w/folded corners, apple green 120.00
Plate, 10" sq., w/folded corners, clear 27.00
Plate, 10" sq., w/folded corners, vaseline 35.00
Platter, 11 x 8", blue 42.50
Platter, 11 x 8", clear 30.00
Salt dip, master size 20.00
Salt shaker w/original top, amber (single) 21.00
Salt shaker w/original top, blue (single) 40.00
Salt shaker w/original top, clear (single) 18.50
Salt & pepper shakers w/original tops, amber, pr. 45.00
Salt & pepper shakers w/original tops, blue, pr. 88.00
Sauce dish, flat or footed, amber . . . 10.00
Sauce dish, flat or footed, blue . . . . . . 12.00 to 25.00
Sauce dish, flat or footed, vaseline . . . . . . 15.00 to 27.00
Spooner, 3-knob stem, amber 29.50
Spooner, 3-knob stem, apple green 35.00
Spooner, 3-knob stem, blue 38.00
Spooner, 3-knob stem, clear 18.00
Sugar bowl, cov., 3-knob stem, apple green 45.00
Sugar bowl, cov., clear 37.50
Syrup pitcher w/original pewter top, footed, apple green 113.00
Toothpick holder, amber 32.50
Toothpick holder, blue 32.50
Toothpick holder, clear 30.00
Toothpick holder, vaseline 39.00
Tray, water, clear, 12½" d. 38.00
Tray, clear, 14" oval 50.00
Tumbler, amber 24.00
Tumbler, blue 35.00
Tumbler, clear 18.00
Water set: oval tray, pitcher & 5 tumblers; apple green, 7 pcs. 240.00
Whimsey, model of a 4-wheeled cart, amber 115.00
Wine, blue 40.00
Wine, vaseline 42.50

THREE FACE

Bread plate 78.00
Butter dish, cov. 112.00
Cake stand, 8" to 10½" d. 145.00
Celery vase 100.00
Champagne 175.00
Claret (ILLUS.) 132.00

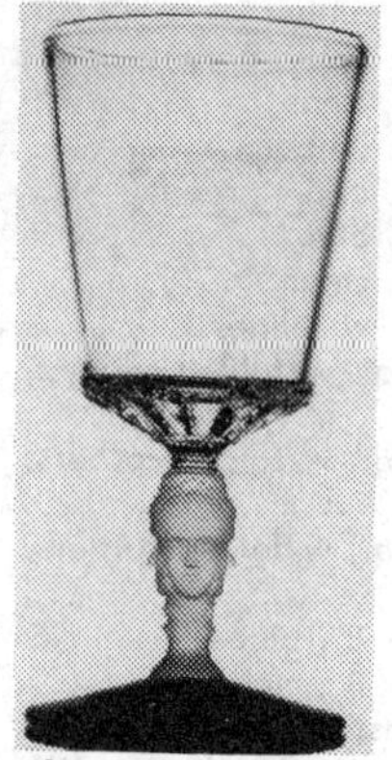

Three Face Claret

Compote, cov., 4½" d., 6½" h. 75.00
Compote, cov., 6" d. 135.00
Compote, cov., 8" d., 13" h. 195.00
Compote, cov., 10" d. 145.00
Compote, open, 6" d., 7½" h. 70.00
Compote, open, 8½" d., 8½" h. 107.00
Compote, open, 9½"d., 9½" h. 160.00
Cracker jar, cov. 1,250.00
Creamer 85.00
Creamer w/mask spout 135.00
Creamer w/mask spout & cov. sugar bowl, pr. 265.00
Goblet 80.00
Lamp, kerosene-type, pedestal base, 8" h. 148.00
Pitcher, water 285.00
Salt dip 50.00
Salt & pepper shakers w/original tops, pr. 110.00
Sauce dish 18.50
Spooner 85.00
Sugar bowl, cov. 115.00
Sugar bowl, open 75.00
Table set, creamer, cov. sugar bowl & spooner, 3 pcs. 285.00
Toothpick holder 50.00
Wine 98.00

THREE PANEL

Three Panel Compote

Berry set: 7" d. footed bowl & 4 footed sauce dishes; blue, 5 pcs. 75.00
Berry set: master bowl & 8 sauce dishes; amber, 9 pcs. 150.00
Bowl, 7" d., footed, amber 25.00
Bowl, 7" d., footed, blue 30.00
Bowl, 9" d., footed, blue 25.00
Bowl, 10" d., amber 49.00
Bowl, 10" d., blue 47.00
Bowl, 10" d., clear 20.00
Bowl, 10" d., vaseline 45.00
Butter dish, cov., amber 55.00
Butter dish, cov., clear 55.00
Celery vase, amber 40.00
Celery vase, blue 37.50
Celery vase, clear 35.00
Compote, open, 5½" d., 4" h., amber 28.00
Compote, open, 7" d., low stand, blue 32.50
Compote, open, 7" d., low stand, clear 20.00
Compote, open, 8½" d., low stand, blue 43.00
Compote, open, 8½" d., low stand, vaseline (ILLUS.) 32.50
Creamer, amber 36.00
Creamer, blue 46.00
Creamer, clear 22.00
Creamer, vaseline 50.00
Goblet, amber 27.00
Goblet, blue 39.00
Goblet, clear 24.50
Goblet, vaseline 38.00
Lamp, kerosene-type, amber 145.00
Mug, amber 32.00
Mug, vaseline 35.00
Pitcher, milk, 7" h., clear 44.50
Pitcher, water, amber 85.00
Pitcher, water, vaseline 110.00
Sauce dish, footed, amber 17.50
Sauce dish, footed, blue 13.00
Sauce dish, footed, clear 8.00
Spooner, blue 40.00
Spooner, clear 18.00
Spooner, vaseline 30.00
Sugar bowl, cov., amber 55.00
Sugar bowl, cov., blue 65.00
Sugar bowl, cov., clear 45.00
Sugar bowl, cov., vaseline 65.00
Sugar bowl, open, clear 25.00
Table set, blue, 4 pcs. 235.00
Tumbler, amber 35.00
Tumbler, clear 12.00

THUMBPRINT, EARLY

Ale glass, footed, 5" h. 31.00
Bowl, 5" d., 5" h., footed 32.00
Bowl, 8" d., flat 85.00
Butter dish, cov. 115.00
Cake stand, 8" to 9½" d. 85.00
Celery vase, plain base 90.00
Celery vase, scalloped rim, pattern in base (ILLUS. next page) 135.00
Compote, cov., 6" d., 7½" h. 225.00
Compote, cov., 7½" d., 11½" h. 85.00

Early Thumbprint Celery Vase

Compote, open, 5" d., 5½" h., scalloped rim 65.00
Compote, open, 8" d., low stand .. 36.00
Compote, open, 8½" d., high stand, scalloped rim 155.00
Compote, open, 12½" d., 11¼" h. .. 400.00
Creamer 70.00
Decanter, 11" h. 110.00
Egg cup 40.00
Goblet, baluster stem 55.00
Honey dish 16.00
Paperweight, panel-cut top 350.00
Pickle dish 40.00
Pitcher, milk 95.00
Pitcher, water, 8¼" h. 275.00
Salt dip, individual size 15.00
Salt dip, master size, footed 27.50
Sauce dish 9.00
Spillholder 45.00
Spooner 48.50
Sugar bowl, cov. 55.00
Tumbler, bar 30.00
Tumbler, footed 48.50
Tumbler, whiskey, footed 32.50
Tumbler, whiskey, handled, footed 150.00
Wine, baluster stem 44.00

TONG

Celery vase 60.00
Spillholder 30.00
Sugar bowl, cov. 50.00

TORPEDO (Pygmy)

Banana stand 55.00
Bowl, cov., master berry 80.00
Bowl, 7" d., flat, clear (ILLUS.) 16.00
Bowl, 7" d., flat, ruby-stained 40.00
Bowl, 8" d., clear 17.50
Bowl, 8" d., ruby-stained 35.00
Bowl, 9" d., clear 31.00
Bowl, 9½" d., clear 32.00
Butter dish, cov. 75.00
Cake stand, 9" to 11" d. .....55.00 to 82.50
Celery vase 42.00

Torpedo Bowl

Compote, cov., jelly 43.00
Compote, cov., 6" d. 78.00
Compote, cov., 7" d., 7¼" h. 65.00
Compote, cov., 8" d., 14" h. 135.00
Compote, open, jelly, 5" d., 5" h. 45.00
Compote, open, 7" d., high stand ... 52.00
Compote, open, 8" d., high stand, flared rim 50.00
Compote, open, 9" d., low stand ... 55.00
Creamer 42.00
Cruet w/original faceted stopper ... 49.00
Cup 25.00
Cup & saucer 60.00
Decanter w/original stopper 123.00
Goblet, clear 50.00
Goblet, ruby-stained 85.00
Honey dish, cov. 20.00
Lamp, kerosene, hand-type w/finger grip, w/burner & chimney 75.00
Lamp, kerosene-type, pedestal base, 8½" h. 110.00
Marmalade jar, cov. 55.00
Pickle castor insert 28.00
Pitcher, milk, 7" h. 50.00
Pitcher, milk, 8½" h., clear 62.00
Pitcher, milk, 8½" h., ruby-stained 90.00
Pitcher, water, 10" h., clear 84.00
Pitcher, water, 10" h., ruby-stained 90.00
Pitcher, water, tankard, 12" h., clear 70.00
Salt dip, individual size, 1½" d. 32.50
Salt dip, master size 60.00
Salt shaker w/original top (single) .. 25.00
Sauce dish 16.00
Spooner 32.00
Sugar bowl, cov. 68.00
Sugar bowl, open 25.00
Syrup jug w/original top, clear 74.00
Syrup jug w/original top, ruby-stained 186.00
Tray, 9¾" d. 70.00
Tumbler, clear 32.00
Tumbler, ruby-stained 52.00
Waste bowl 60.00
Wine, clear 67.00
Wine, ruby-stained, souvenir 45.00

TREE OF LIFE - PITTSBURGH (Tree of Life with Hand)

Butter dish, cov. 55.00
Cake stand, 8¾" d. 75.00
Compote, cov., 6" d., 8" h., frosted hand & ball stem 65.00
Compote, open, 5½" d., 5½" h., clear hand & ball stem 36.00
Compote, open, 5½" d., 5½" h., frosted hand & ball stem 47.50
Compote, open, 8" d., clear hand & ball stem 60.00
Compote, open, 8" d., 8½" h., frosted hand & ball stem 57.50
Compote, open, 9" d., frosted hand & ball stem 85.00
Compote, open, 10" d., 10" h., frosted hand & ball stem 95.00
Creamer, w/hand & ball handle 48.00
Creamer & sugar bowl, pr. 110.00
Pitcher, water, 9" h. 60.00
Relish, oval 29.00
Sauce dish, flat or footed . . . . 12.00 to 20.00
Spooner 45.00
Sugar bowl, cov. 52.50
Sugar bowl, open 19.00
Tumbler 23.00
Waste bowl 22.00
Waste bowl w/underplate 60.00
Wine 28.00

TREE OF LIFE - PORTLAND

Portland Tree of Life Waste Bowl

Berry set: master bowl & 4 sauce dishes; blue, 5 pcs. 325.00
Bowl, 5½" d., flat 12.00
Bowl, signed "Davis," green, in silver plate holder marked "Meriden Britannia Co." 235.00
Bread tray 40.00
Butter dish, cov. 55.00
Butter pat, vaseline 25.00
Cake stand, signed "Davis," 9" to 11½" d. . . . . 45.00 to 60.00
Celery vase, in metal holder 75.00
Cologne bottle w/faceted stopper . . 48.00
Compote, open, 6" d., 6" h. 35.00
Compote, open, 7¾" d., signed "P.G. Co." 75.00
Compote, open, 7¾" d., 11" h., Infant Samuel stand, signed "Davis" 150.00
Compote, open, 8½" d., 5" h., signed "Davis" 60.00
Compote, open, 10" d., 6" h., signed "Davis" 125.00
Creamer, signed "Davis" 65.00
Creamer, cranberry in silver plate holder 85.00
Cruet w/original stopper, blue 90.00
Dish, leaf handle, blue 40.00
Epergne, single lily, red snake around stem, 18" h. 450.00
Goblet 43.00
Goblet, signed "Davis" . . . . . . 50.00 to 65.00
Ice cream set, tray & 5 leaf-shaped desserts, 6 pcs. 70.00
Ice cream set, tray & 6 leaf-shaped desserts, 7 pcs. 105.00
Pitcher, water, applied handle, signed "Davis," amber . . . 225.00 to 250.00
Plate, 6½" d. 18.00
Plate, 7¼" d. 50.00
Plate, 10" l., 3-footed, shell-shaped 85.00
Powder jar, cov., red coiled snake finial on cover 350.00
Salt dip, flat, clear, 3" d. 10.00
Salt dip, footed, "Salt" embossed in bowl, clear 135.00
Salt dip, footed, opaque green 95.00
Salt shaker w/original top (single) . . 25.00
Sauce dish, leaf-shaped, clear 15.00
Spooner, handled silver plate holder w/two Griffin heads 57.50
Sugar bowl, cov. 55.00
Sugar bowl, silver plate holder 70.00
Table set: cov. sugar bowl, creamer & spooner; ornate silver plate holder, 4 pcs. 175.00
Toothpick holder, blue 75.00
Tray, ice cream, 14" rectangle 28.00
Tumbler, 4½" h. 22.50
Tumbler, footed, 6" h. 40.00
Waste bowl w/ornate silver plate holder, blue 175.00
Waste bowl, clear 14.00
Waste bowl, cranberry, flint (ILLUS.) 145.00
Wine 45.00

TULIP WITH SAWTOOTH

Celery vase, flint 65.00
Celery vase, non-flint 34.00
Champagne, non-flint 40.00
Compote, cov., 6" d., high stand, flint 120.00
Compote, open, 7" d., low stand, non-flint 69.00
Creamer, applied handle, flint 75.00
Cruet w/original stopper, non-flint . . 205.00
Decanter w/tulip-form stopper, flint, 12" h., pt. 150.00
Decanter w/bar lip, flint, pt. 68.00

Goblet, flint 45.00
Goblet, non-flint 20.00
Pitcher, water, flint 175.00
Salt dip, master size, scalloped rim, flint 27.00
Salt dip, open, non-flint 15.00
Sauce dish, flat, non-flint, 3 7/8" d. 8.00
Spooner, flint 45.00
Spooner, non-flint 28.00
Sugar bowl, open, non-flint 32.50
Tumbler, bar, flint 85.00
Tumbler, bar, non-flint 27.50
Tumbler, flint 30.00
Tumbler, footed, flint 55.00
Wine, flint 60.00
Wine, non-flint 22.50

TWO PANEL (Daisy in Panel)

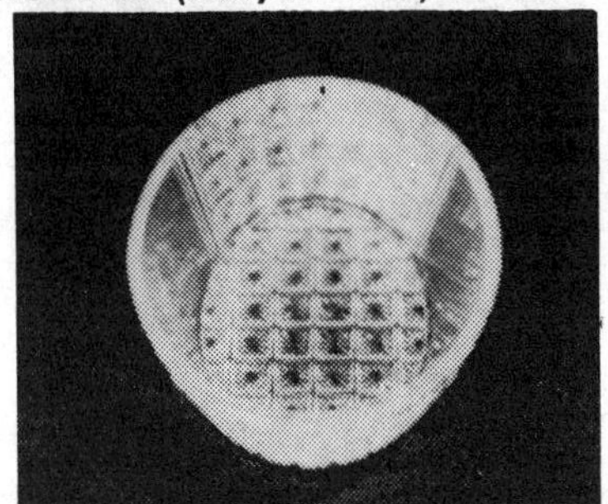

Two Panel Sauce Dish

Bowl, cov., 7" oval, vaseline 55.00
Bowl, 7 x 5½" oval, amber 25.00
Bowl, 9 x 7½" oval, amber 35.00
Bowl, 9 x 7½" oval, apple green . . . 37.50
Bowl, 9 x 7½" oval, clear 15.00
Bowl, 10 x 8" oval, blue 65.00
Bowl, 10 x 8" oval, vaseline 50.00
Bread tray, apple green 39.00
Bread tray, blue 45.00
Bread tray, clear 27.00
Butter dish, cov., amber 50.00
Butter dish, cov., blue 90.00
Butter dish, cov., vaseline 55.00
Celery vase, amber 30.00
Celery vase, blue 50.00
Celery vase, clear 25.00
Compote, cov., 8 x 6½", 11" h., vaseline 85.00
Compote, cov., high stand, apple green 130.00
Compote, open, 9" oval, amber 37.00
Compote, open, 9" oval, blue 40.00
Creamer, amber 60.00
Creamer, apple green 40.00
Creamer, blue 35.00
Creamer, clear 22.50
Creamer, vaseline 35.00
Goblet, amber 32.50
Goblet, apple green 31.00
Goblet, blue 40.00
Goblet, clear 22.50
Goblet, vaseline 33.00
Lamp, kerosene-type, pedestal base, apple green, 9½" h. 90.00
Marmalade jar, cov., clear 36.50
Marmalade jar, cov., vaseline 65.00
Pitcher, water, amber 50.00
Pitcher, water, apple green 55.00
Pitcher, water, blue 95.00
Pitcher, water, clear 36.00
Pitcher, water, vaseline 65.00
Relish, amber 16.00
Relish, blue 22.50
Relish, vaseline 22.50
Salt dip, master size, amber 20.00
Salt dip, master size, apple green . . 18.50
Salt dip, master size, vaseline 22.00
Salt dip, individual size, apple green 14.00
Salt dip, individual size, blue 12.00
Sauce dish, flat or footed, amber . . . 11.00
Sauce dish, flat or footed, apple green . . . . . 13.50 to 22.00
Sauce dish, flat or footed, blue . . . . . 14.00 to 18.00
Sauce dish, flat or footed, clear . . . . . 7.50 to 15.00
Sauce dish, flat or footed, vaseline (ILLUS.) . . . . . 15.00 to 19.00
Spooner, amber 35.00
Spooner, blue 35.00
Spooner, clear 25.00
Spooner, vaseline 32.50
Sugar bowl, cov., amber 50.00
Sugar bowl, cov., clear 30.00
Tray, water, cloverleaf shape, vaseline, 10½ x 8¾" 55.00
Tray, water, amber, 15 x 10" oval . . 47.50
Tumbler, amber 25.00
Tumbler, vaseline 32.50
Waste bowl, blue 30.00
Water set: pitcher & 6 tumblers; blue, 7 pcs. 300.00
Wine, amber 35.00
Wine, apple green 35.00
Wine, blue 35.00
Wine, clear 19.50
Wine, vaseline 35.00

U.S. COIN

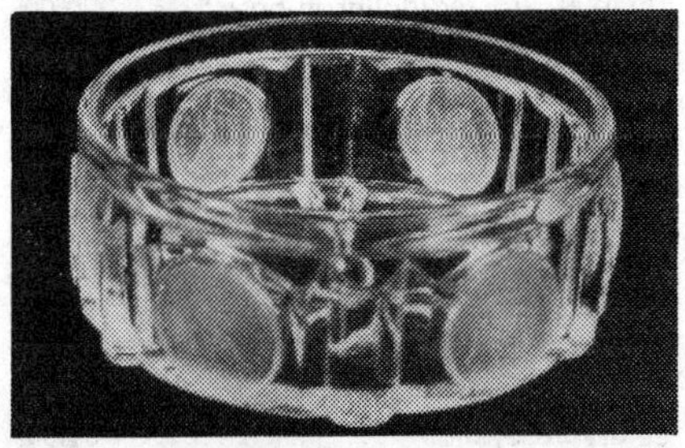

U.S. Coin Sauce Dish

Bowl, 8" oval, frosted coins 308.00
Bread tray, dollars & half dollars . . . 390.00

Butter dish, cov., dollars & half dollars 525.00
Cake plate, frosted coins, 7" d. 485.00
Cake stand, clear dollars, 10" d. 265.00
Cake stand, frosted dollars, 10" d. .. 450.00
Candy dish, cov., 6" d. 275.00
Celery vase, clear quarters 245.00
Celery vase, frosted quarters 350.00
Champagne, frosted dimes 325.00
Compote, cov., 6 7/8" d., high stand, frosted coins 485.00
Compote, cov., 8" d., 11½" h., frosted coins 535.00
Compote, cov., 9" d., frosted coins 500.00
Compote, open, 6½" d., 8" h., frosted dimes & quarters 215.00
Compote, open, 7" d., 5¾" h., frosted dimes & quarters 400.00
Compote, open, 8" d., 6½" h., frosted coins 475.00
Compote, open, 8½" d., 6½" h., frosted quarters on bowl, dimes on stem 242.00
Compote, open, 9¼" d., 7" h., frosted half dollars on bowl, quarters on stem 375.00
Epergne, frosted dollars 1,100.00
Goblet, frosted dimes 325.00
Goblet, flared, half dollars 395.00
Lamp, kerosene-type, round font, frosted dollars in base 850.00
Lamp, kerosene-type, round font, handled, clear quarters in base ... 500.00
Mug, frosted coins 345.00
Pickle dish, clear coins, 7½ x 3¾" .. 220.00
Pickle dish, frosted coins 180.00
Pitcher, water, frosted dollars 495.00
Relish, frosted coins 185.00
Salt shaker w/original top (single) .. 125.00
Sauce dish, frosted quarters, 4" d. (ILLUS.) 120.00
Spooner, clear quarters 225.00
Spooner, frosted quarters 375.00
Sugar bowl, cov., frosted coins 425.00
Syrup jug w/original dated pewter top, frosted coins 500.00
Toothpick holder, frosted coins 190.00
Tumbler, frosted dollar in base 220.00
Wine, frosted half dimes 450.00

VALENCIA WAFFLE (Block & Star)

Bread platter 25.00
Butter dish, cov., amber 70.00
Butter dish, cov., apple green 60.00
Butter dish, cov., clear 42.50
Butter dish, cov., ruby-stained 110.00
Cake stand, amber 70.00
Cake stand, 10" d., clear 70.00
Celery vase, blue 39.00
Celery vase, clear 32.00
Celery vase, yellow 35.00
Compote, cov., 6" d., 10" h., clear .. 75.00
Compote, cov., 7" sq., low stand, amber 64.00
Compote, cov., 7" sq., low stand, apple green 75.00
Compote, cov., 7" sq., low stand, blue 76.00
Compote, cov., 7" sq., low stand, clear 50.00
Compote, cov., 8" d., clear 45.00
Compote, open, 6" d., low stand, apple green 35.00

Valencia Waffle Open Compote

Compote, open, 6" sq., low stand, blue (ILLUS.) 30.00
Compote, open, 8" d., low stand, blue 29.50
Goblet, amber 38.00
Goblet, clear 24.00
Pitcher, water, 7½" h., amber 65.00
Pitcher, water, apple green 95.00
Pitcher, water, clear 40.00
Relish, amber, 10¾ x 7½" 30.00
Relish, clear, 7½ x 10¾ 10.00
Salt dip, master size, amber 22.50
Salt dip, master size, clear 15.00
Salt dip, master size, yellow 26.00
Salt shaker w/original top (single) .. 20.00
Salt & pepper shakers w/original tops, apple green, pr. 50.00
Sauce dish, footed, amber 13.50
Sauce dish, footed, blue 14.00
Sauce dish, footed, clear 12.50
Spooner, amber 40.00
Spooner, clear 18.00
Syrup jug w/original top, amber 100.00
Syrup jug w/original top, blue 75.00
Tray, water, amber, 13¼ x 9½", amber ....37.50 to 45.00
Tray, water, clear 26.00
Tumbler, ruby-stained 30.00

VICTOR - See Shell & Jewel Pattern

VICTORIA

Compote, cov., 8" d., low foot 150.00
Compote, cov., 8" d., high stand ... 200.00
Compote, cov., 10½" d., 15¼" h.... 215.00

VIKING (Bearded Head or Old Man of the Mountain)

Viking Butter Dish

Apothecary jar w/original stopper . . 95.00
Bowl, cov., 8" oval 65.00
Bowl, 7" d., 4" h. 25.00
Bread tray, cupid hunt scene center 68.00
Butter dish, cov. (ILLUS.) 58.00
Cake stand, 10" d. 67.50
Celery vase 52.00
Compote, cov., 7" d., low stand 75.00
Compote, cov., 8" d., low stand 70.00
Compote, cov., 9" d., low stand 89.00
Compote, open, 8" d., high stand . . . 62.50
Creamer 50.00
Creamer & cov. sugar bowl, pr. 79.00
Egg cup 35.00
Goblet 95.00
Marmalade jar, footed, etched (no cover) 27.50
Mug, applied handle 62.50
Pickle jar w/cover 95.00
Pitcher, water, 8¾" h. 82.00
Salt dip, master size 43.50
Sauce dish, footed 13.50
Shaving mug, milk white 62.50
Spooner 34.00
Sugar bowl, cov. 57.00

VIRGINIA - See Galloway Pattern

WAFFLE

Celery vase, flint 56.00
Champagne 135.00
Compote, open, 7" d., 5¼" h. 32.50
Compote, open, 9½" d., 8" h. 75.00
Creamer, applied handle 125.00
Creamer, footed 45.00
Cruet 27.50
Egg cup 35.00
Goblet 58.00
Salt dip, master size 27.50
Sugar bowl, cov. 55.00
Syrup pitcher, applied handle 85.00
Tumbler, footed 18.00
Tumbler, bar 75.00
Waste bowl, ruffled top 75.00

WAFFLE AND THUMBPRINT

Bowl, 7¼" d., flint 35.00
Celery vase, flint . . . . .85.00 to 100.00
Compote, open, 8" d., high stand, flint 80.00
Cordial, flint 85.00
Creamer, applied handle, flint 250.00
Egg cup, flint 31.00
Goblet, flint 60.00
Lamp, w/original 2-tube burner, hand-type w/applied handle, flint, 3" h. 135.00
Lamp, w/original whale oil burner, flint, 11" h. 153.00
Pitcher, water, flint 300.00
Salt dip, master size, flint 27.00
Spillholder, flint 115.00
Sugar bowl, cov., flint 175.00
Tumbler, bar, flint 79.00
Tumbler, footed, flint 110.00
Tumbler, whiskey, flint 79.00
Wine, flint 50.00

WASHBOARD - See Adonis Pattern

WASHINGTON (Early)

Early Washington Celery Vase

Celery vase (ILLUS.) 95.00
Claret, flint 135.00
Decanter w/original stopper, qt. 225.00
Egg cup, flint 55.00
Goblet, flint . . . . .60.00 to 80.00
Lamp, kerosene-type, cast iron base 125.00
Pitcher, water, flint 225.00
Salt dip, individual size 29.00
Salt dip, master size, flat, round 27.50

WASHINGTON CENTENNIAL

Bowl, 8½" oval 22.50
Bread platter, Carpenter's Hall 100.00
Bread platter, Carpenter's Hall, frosted 125.00
Bread platter, George Washington center 84.00

Bread platter, George Washington center, frosted 101.00
Bread platter, Independence Hall center 85.00
Butter dish, cov., footed 87.50
Cake stand, 8½" to 11½" d. 46.00
Celery vase 39.50
Champagne 42.50
Compote, cov., 8½" d., 12" h. 105.00
Compote, open, 7" d., low stand 45.00
Compote, open, 8" d., 6½" h. 37.50
Compote, open, 10½" d., high stand 70.00
Creamer, applied handle 80.00
Egg cup 39.00
Goblet 37.00
Pickle dish 34.00
Pitcher, milk 104.00
Pitcher, water 95.00
Relish, bear paw handles, dated 1876 .... 56.00
Salt dip, master size 25.00
Sauce dish, flat or footed 11.00
Spooner 42.00
Sugar bowl, cov. 75.00
Sugar bowl, open 20.00
Syrup pitcher w/original metal top, applied handle, milk white 140.00
Toothpick holder 60.00
Tumbler, bar 65.00
Wine 40.00

WEDDING BELLS

Bowl, 8" d., flat, ruby-stained 32.50
Bowl, master berry, gold trim 28.00
Butter dish, cov. 38.00
Celery tray, pink-stained 27.50
Celery vase, clear 27.50
Creamer, 4-footed 48.00
Goblet 50.00
Pitcher, water, clear 48.00
Pitcher, water, alternate ruby-stained panels 85.00
Punch cup 15.00
Salt shaker w/original top (single) 20.00
Spooner 40.00
Sugar bowl, cov. 55.00
Toothpick holder, gold trim 55.00
Toothpick holder, pink-stained 80.00
Tumbler 18.00
Water set, pitcher & 4 tumblers, 5 pcs. 135.00
Wine 22.00
Wine, pink-stained 40.00

WEDDING RING - See Double Wedding Ring Pattern

WESTWARD HO

Bread platter 112.00
Butter dish, cov. 150.00
Celery vase 125.00
Compote, cov., 5" d., 9" h. 92.00
Compote, cov., 6" d., low stand 120.00
Compote, cov., 6" d., 12" h. 183.00
Compote, cov., 6¾ x 4" oval 136.00
Compote, cov., 7¾ x 5" oval, 10" h. 160.00
Compote, cov., 8" d., low stand 244.00
Compote, cov., 8" d., 11½" h. 250.00
Compote, cov., 8 x 5½" oval, 12" h. 290.00
Compote, cov., 8" d., 14" h. 290.00
Compote, cov., 10 x 6½" oval, low stand 292.00
Compote, open, 6" d., low stand 60.00
Compote, open, 6" d., high stand 127.00
Compote, open, 8 1/16" d., 8" h. 65.00
Creamer 120.00
Creamer & cov. sugar bowl, pr. 275.00
Creamer & open sugar bowl, pr. 175.00
Goblet 73.00
Marmalade jar, cov. 157.00
Mug, child's, 2½" h. 225.00
Pickle dish, oval 55.00
Pitcher, milk, 8" h. 250.00
Pitcher, water 240.00
Platter, 13 x 9" 170.00
Relish, deer handles 115.00
Sauce dish, footed 40.00

Westward Ho Spooner

Spooner (ILLUS.) 82.50
Sugar bowl, cov. 156.00
Sugar bowl, open 35.00
Water set, pitcher & 6 goblets, 7 pcs. 595.00

WHEAT & BARLEY

Bowl, cov., 8" d., flat 38.00
Bread plate, amber 25.00
Butter dish, cov., blue 75.00
Butter dish, cov., clear 35.00
Cake stand, amber, 8" to 10" d. 35.00
Cake stand, clear, 8" to 10" d. 36.00
Compote, cov., 8½" h., high stand 55.00
Compote, open, jelly, blue 35.00
Compote, open, jelly, clear 18.50
Compote, open, 8¼" d., amber 75.00
Compote, open, 8¾" d., 6¾" h., clear 37.00

Creamer, amber ... 33.00
Creamer, blue ... 45.00
Creamer, clear ... 20.00
Doughnut stand, blue ... 58.00
Goblet, amber ... 38.00
Goblet, blue ... 31.00
Goblet, clear ... 25.00
Mug, amber ... 32.50
Mug, clear ... 20.00
Pitcher, milk, blue ... 65.00
Pitcher, milk, clear ... 37.50
Pitcher, water, amber ... 85.00
Pitcher, water, blue ... 72.50
Pitcher, water, clear ... 53.00
Plate, 7" d., blue ... 30.00
Plate, 7" d., clear ... 18.00
Plate, 9" d., closed handles, amber ... 35.00
Plate, 9" d., closed handles, blue ... 27.50
Plate, 9" d., closed handles, clear ... 19.00
Plate, 9" d., closed handles, vaseline ... 35.00
Salt shaker w/original top, blue (single) ... 44.00
Salt shaker w/original top, clear (single) ... 14.50
Salt & pepper shakers w/original tops, clear, pr. ... 30.00
Sauce dish, flat, handled, amber ... 13.00
Sauce dish, flat, handled, clear ... 10.00
Sauce dish, footed, amber ... 14.50
Spooner, amber ... 32.50
Spooner, blue ... 30.00
Spooner, clear ... 19.50
Sugar bowl, cov., clear ... 30.00
Tumbler, amber ... 32.50
Tumbler, blue ... 30.00
Tumbler, clear ... 20.00
Wine, amber ... 20.00

WILDFLOWER

Wildflower Sauce Dish

Bowl, 5¾" sq., clear ... 15.00
Bowl, 6½" sq., blue ... 22.50
Bowl, 7" sq., footed, amber ... 29.00
Bowl, 7" sq., clear ... 14.50
Bowl, 8" sq., 5" h., footed, apple green ... 35.00
Bowl, 8" sq., 5" h., footed, blue ... 50.00
Butter dish, cov., amber ... 75.00
Butter dish, cov., clear ... 35.00
Butter dish, cov., collared base, vaseline ... 60.00
Cake stand, amber, 9½" to 11" ... 48.50 to 65.00
Cake stand, apple green, 9½" to 11" ... 60.00 to 95.00
Cake stand, blue, 9½" to 11" ... 50.00 to 85.00
Cake stand, clear, 9½" to 11" ... 50.00 to 65.00
Cake stand, vaseline, 9½" to 11" ... 82.00
Celery vase, amber ... 57.50
Celery vase, blue ... 62.50
Celery vase, clear ... 28.00
Champagne, amber ... 50.00
Champagne, blue ... 50.00
Champagne, clear ... 30.00
Compote, cov., 6" d., blue ... 70.00
Compote, cov., 6" d., clear ... 42.00
Compote, cov., 7" d., amber ... 50.00
Compote, cov., 8" d., amber ... 90.00
Compote, cov., 8" d., clear ... 29.00
Compote, cov., 10" d., clear ... 55.00
Compote, open, jelly ... 30.00
Compote, open, 7" d., low stand, apple green ... 23.50
Compote, open, 7" d., low stand, blue ... 38.00
Compote, open, 9½" d., amber ... 45.00
Compote, open, 10½" d., 8¼" h., amber ... 78.00
Creamer, amber ... 36.00
Creamer, apple green ... 40.00
Creamer, blue ... 42.00
Creamer, clear ... 29.00
Creamer, vaseline ... 40.00
Creamer & sugar bowl, clear, pr. ... 65.00
Goblet, amber ... 36.00
Goblet, apple green ... 35.00
Goblet, blue ... 35.00
Goblet, clear ... 26.00
Goblet, vaseline ... 41.00
Pitcher, water, amber ... 52.50
Pitcher, water, apple green ... 75.00
Pitcher, water, blue ... 75.00
Pitcher, water, clear ... 42.00
Pitcher, water, vaseline ... 62.00
Plate, 7" sq., apple green ... 24.50
Plate, 7" sq., blue ... 45.00
Plate, 10" sq., amber ... 35.00
Plate, 10" sq., apple green ... 32.50
Plate, 10" sq., blue ... 35.00
Plate, 10" sq., clear ... 25.00
Platter, 11 x 8", apple green ... 45.00 to 69.00
Platter, 11 x 8", clear ... 35.00
Relish, amber ... 17.50
Relish, apple green ... 19.50
Relish, clear ... 22.50
Salt dip, turtle-shaped, amber ... 45.00
Salt shaker w/original top, amber (single) ... 26.00
Salt shaker w/original top, apple green (single) ... 30.00

Salt shaker w/original top, vaseline (single) 45.00
Salt & pepper shakers w/original tops, blue, pr. 70.00
Salt & pepper shakers w/original tops, clear, pr. 45.00
Sauce dish, flat or footed, amber 12.00
Sauce dish, flat or footed, apple green 13.50
Sauce dish, flat or footed, blue 18.00
Sauce dish, flat or footed, clear (ILLUS.) 10.00
Sauce dish, flat or footed, vaseline 15.00
Spooner, amber 32.50
Spooner, apple green 35.00
Spooner, clear 31.00
Spooner, vaseline 34.00
Sugar bowl, cov., blue 54.00
Sugar bowl, cov., clear 33.00
Sugar bowl, open, amber 20.00
Sugar bowl, open, apple green 35.00
Sugar bowl, open, blue 30.00
Sugar bowl, open, clear 19.00
Syrup pitcher w/original top, amber 160.00
Syrup pitcher w/original top, blue 130.00
Syrup pitcher w/original top, clear 115.00
Tray, dresser, amber, 9 x 4" 30.00
Tray, dresser, blue, 9 x 4" 45.00
Tray, water, amber, 13 x 11" 44.00
Tray, water, apple green, 13 x 11" 55.00
Tray, water, clear, 13 x 11" 39.00
Tray, water, vaseline, 13 x 11" 50.00
Tumbler, amber 33.00
Tumbler, apple green 28.00
Tumbler, blue 27.50
Tumbler, clear 22.00
Tumbler, vaseline 30.00
Tumbler, yellow 27.50
Vase, 10½" h. 58.00
Water set: pitcher, tray & 6 tumblers; apple green, 8 pcs. 325.00

WILLOW OAK

Willow Oak Water Pitcher

Bowl, cov., 7" d., flat 39.00
Bowl, 7" d., amber 20.00
Bowl, 7" d., blue 30.00
Bowl, 7" d., clear 14.50
Bowl, 8" d., 2½" h. 19.50
Bread plate, clear, 9" d. 35.00
Bread plate, amber, 11" d. 42.00
Butter dish, cov., amber 65.00
Butter dish, cov., clear 52.50
Cake stand, amber, 8" to 10" d. 55.00
Cake stand, blue, 8" to 10" d. 58.00
Cake stand, clear, 8" to 10" d. 38.00
Celery vase, amber 49.00
Celery vase, clear 39.00
Compote, cov., 6½" d., 9" h. 47.50
Compote, open, 6" d., scalloped top 39.00
Compote, open, 7" d., high stand, amber 40.00
Compote, open, 7" d., high stand, blue 60.00
Compote, open, 7" d., high stand, clear 32.00
Creamer, amber 35.00
Creamer, blue 42.50
Creamer, clear 32.00
Goblet, amber 40.00
Goblet, blue 37.00
Goblet, clear 32.00
Mug, amber 35.00
Mug, blue 42.50
Mug, clear 27.00
Pitcher, milk, amber 55.00
Pitcher, milk, clear 40.00
Pitcher, water, amber (ILLUS.) 85.00
Pitcher, water, clear 46.00
Plate, 7" d., amber 35.00
Plate, 7" d., clear 23.00
Plate, 9" d., handled, amber 30.00
Plate, 9" d., handled, blue 45.00
Plate, 9" d., handled, clear 25.00
Salt shaker w/original top, blue (single) 68.00
Salt shaker w/original top, clear (single) 25.00
Sauce dish, flat or footed 12.50
Spooner, amber 40.00
Spooner, blue 38.00
Spooner, clear 22.00
Sugar bowl, cov., amber 62.50
Sugar bowl, cov., clear 39.00
Sugar bowl, open 20.00
Tray, water, blue, 10½" d. 58.00
Tray, water, clear, 10½" d. 32.00
Tumbler, amber 35.00
Tumbler, blue 37.50
Tumbler, clear 32.50
Waste bowl, amber 48.00
Waste bowl, clear 29.00
Water set: pitcher, tray & 2 tumblers; clear, 4 pcs. 170.00
Water set: pitcher & 8 goblets; amber, 9 pcs. 325.00

WINDFLOWER

Bowl, 7 x 5" oval 27.50

- Butter dish, cov. 55.00
- Celery vase 40.00
- Compote, cov., 8½" d., low stand .. 45.00
- Compote, open, 8" d. 16.50
- Creamer 34.00
- Egg cup 20.00
- Goblet 39.00
- Pitcher, water 65.00
- Sauce dish 10.00
- Spooner 28.00
- Sugar bowl, cov. 29.00
- Sugar bowl, open 18.00
- Tumbler, bar 35.00
- Tumbler, water 40.00
- Wine 29.00

WISCONSIN (Beaded Dewdrop)

- Banana stand, turned-up sides, 7½" w., 4" h. 75.00
- Bonbon, handled, 4" 27.50
- Bowl, 6½" d. 37.00
- Bowl, 8" d. 24.00
- Bread tray 45.00
- Butter dish, cov. 92.00
- Cake stand, 8¼" d., 4¾" h. 30.00
- Cake stand, 9¾" d. 40.00
- Celery tray, flat, 10 x 5" 42.50
- Celery vase 45.00
- Compote, cov., 10½" d. 65.00
- Compote, open, 6½" d., 6½" h. ... 26.00
- Compote, open, 7½" d., 5½" h. ... 39.00
- Creamer, individual size 49.00
- Cup & saucer 45.00
- Dish, cov., oval 26.50
- Goblet 49.00
- Mug, 3½" h. 37.00
- Nappy, handled, 4" d. 22.00
- Olive dish, 2-handled 35.00
- Pickle dish 24.00
- Pitcher, milk 48.00
- Pitcher, water, 8" h. 46.00
- Plate, 5" sq. 15.00
- Plate, 6½" sq. 27.50
- Punch cup 15.00
- Relish, 8½ x 4" 22.50
- Salt & pepper shakers w/original tops, pr. 45.00
- Sauce dish 12.50
- Spooner 30.00
- Sugar bowl, cov., 5" h. 37.50
- Sugar shaker w/original top 58.00
- Syrup pitcher w/original top, 6½" h. 82.00
- Toothpick holder 41.00
- Tumbler 38.00
- Wine 55.00

WOODEN PAIL - See Oaken Bucket Pattern

ZIPPER

- Bowl, 8" oval 18.00
- Butter dish, cov. 39.00
- Celery vase 21.00
- Cheese dish, cov. 50.00
- Compote, cov., low stand 40.00
- Creamer 20.00
- Cruet w/original stopper, clear 38.00
- Cruet w/original stopper, ruby-stained 145.00
- Goblet 20.00
- Humidor, cov. 45.00
- Marmalade jar, cov. 35.00
- Pitcher, water 35.00
- Relish 15.00
- Sauce dish, flat or footed ..... 6.00 to 8.00
- Spooner 20.00
- Sugar bowl, cov. 25.00
- Sugar shaker w/silver plate top 28.00
- Toothpick holder, clear 15.00
- Toothpick holder, ruby-stained 25.00
- Wine 18.00

ZIPPERED BLOCK See Iowa Pattern

(End of Pattern Glass Section)

PEACH BLOW

Several types of glass lumped together by collectors as Peach Blow were produced by half a dozen glasshouses. Hobbs, Brockunier & Co., Wheeling, West Virginia made Peach Blow as a plated ware that shaded from red at the top to yellow at the bottom and is referred to as Wheeling Peach Blow. Mt. Washington Glass Works produced an homogeneous Peach Blow shading from a rose color at the top to pale blue in the lower portion. The New England Glass Works' Peach Blow, called Wild Rose, shaded from rose at the top to white. Gunderson—Pairpoint Co. also reproduced some of the Mt. Washington Peach Blow in the early 1950's and some glass of a somewhat similar type was made by Steuben Glass Works, the Boston & Sandwich Factory and by Thomas Webb & Sons and Stevens & Williams of England. Sandwich Peach Blow is one-layered glass and the English is two-layered. A relative newcomer to the fold is called New Martinsville "Peach Blow." It is a single-layered glass.

GUNDERSON - PAIRPOINT

- Decanter w/original stopper, applied shell handle, glossy finish, 12" h. $750.00
- Vase, 9¼" h., trefoil form 225.00

MT. WASHINGTON

- Creamer, applied handle, ribbed, 3" h. 350.00
- Pitcher, 6 7/8" h., bulbous, square handle 4,300.00
- Sugar bowl, cov., original paper label 1,750.00

Tumbler 1,450.00
Vase, 3¼" h., 2 7/8" d., flower petal top, acid finish 850.00
Vase, 7" h., rose bowl shape w/short feet, wishbone-shaped turned down points around top, berry pontil 2,500.00
Vase, 8¼" h., lily form 2,450.00

NEW ENGLAND

New England Peach Blow Pear

Celery vase 870.00
Creamer, satin finish, marked "World's Fair 1893" (Chicago's Columbian Exposition) 295.00
Creamer & sugar bowl, white handles, pr. 750.00
Creamer & sugar bowl, white handles, ribbed, pr. 1,100.00
Darner, glossy finish, 6 x 2½" .... 150.00 to 175.00
Finger bowl, 5¼" w., 2½" h. 335.00
Pear w/stem, glossy finish (ILLUS.) .. 155.00
Pitcher, milk, 6¼" h., applied handle, ten-crimp top with tenth elongated to form the spout, satin finish 1,285.00
Punch cup, applied opaque white handle, gold rim, marked "World's Fair 1893" 400.00
Rose bowl, seven-crimp top, acid finish, 3¾" d., 3½" h. ... 350.00 to 450.00
Spooner, 4 5/8" h. 385.00
Syrup pitcher, tapering to top, applied handle, original tin lid dated "1884" 765.00
Tumbler, 3¾" h., glossy finish (ILLUS. right) .... 275.00 to 295.00
Tumbler, satin finish, 3¾" h. (ILLUS. left) .... 350.00 to 450.00
Vase, 6 1/8" h., lily form, deep rose to creamy white 425.00
Vase, 6¼" h., ball-shaped base w/slender long neck, glossy finish 565.00
Vase, 8¼" h., lily form, glossy finish (ILLUS.) 650.00

New England Peach Blow Tumblers & Vase

Vase, 10" h., lily form, acid finish 1,250.00

NEW MARTINSVILLE

Bowl, 7½" d., 3½" h., ribbed sides, crimped & ruffled top, wafer base 345.00
Cheese dish, cov., satin finish 195.00

WEBB

Webb Peach Blow Decorated Vase

Bottle vases, bulbous base, ribbed narrow neck, pr. 285.00
Bowl, 4 5/8" d., 5" h., three clear feet, clear rigaree around top edge, applied clear branches, leaves & flowers, clear flower prunt on pontil, glossy finish, creamy white lining 395.00
Butter dish, cov. 390.00
Finger bowl, six-crimp top, applied clear rigaree, glossy finish, creamy white lining, 5" d., 2¼" h. 175.00

Ginger jar, cov., enameled blue & white blossoms & white & brown leaves, signed 395.00

Ivy bowl, enameled florals & coralene trim 135.00

Pitcher, 3½" h., 2½" d., bulbous w/round mouth, applied clear handle, glossy finish............. 225.00

Scent bottle w/hallmarked silver screw-on dome top, enameled blue, white & yellow forget-me-nots w/green leaves decoration, acid finish, creamy white lining, 2¾" d., 3¾" h. 650.00

Scent bottle w/hallmarked silver screw-on top, lay-down type, acid finish, gold prunus blossoms decoration, 1½" d., 3¾" l. 365.00

Vases, 5" h., 3 5/8" d., branches, gold prunus blossoms & dragonfly decoration, glossy finish, creamy white lining, pr. 495.00

Vase, 7½" h., 4¾" w., gold encrusted florals, leaves, butterflies & insects decoration, acid finish, creamy white lining (ILLUS.) 850.00

Vase, 9 3/8" h., 5 1/8" flattened oval shape, gold & silver flowers, leaves & birds decoration, glossy finish, creamy white lining 675.00

Vase, 15" h., 6¾" d., two gold-encrusted slightly protruding birds, gold branches & leaves w/silver floral decoration, glossy finish 1,150.00

WHEELING

Wheeling Peach Blow Cruet

Creamer, bulbous, four-cornered top, glossy finish, 4" h. 435.00

Cruet w/original diamond-cut amber stopper, trefoil top, applied amber handle, glossy finish, white lining, 6½" h. (ILLUS.) 1,285.00

Cruet w/original teardrop-shaped stopper, applied amber reeded handle, glossy finish 1,185.00

Decanter, "pilgrim flask" shaped, cut amber stopper, applied amber rope handle 1,500.00

Morgan vase replica in original amber glass base, overall 10" h., satin finish 3,100.00

Mustard, metal lid & handle 750.00

Wheeling Drape Pattern Pitcher

Pitcher, 5¼" h., squat bulbous form w/pinched square neck, applied clear ribbed handle, Drape patt., ca. 1886 (ILLUS.) 1,200.00

Vase, 7" h., cylindrical, flared & gently ruffled top w/narrow amber border, Drape patt. 650.00

PEKING

Peking Overlay Vase

This is Chinese glass, some of which has overlay in one to five colors, that has attracted collector interest.

Bowls, 4¼" d., bell-shaped w/sloping sides & lip, overlay blossoming prunus & lily against white ground, pr. $220.00

Bowls, 4 3/8" d., flared rim, ring foot, purple, pr. 220.00
Bowl, 7" d., 3" h., overlay blue florals, butterfly & leaves against white ground, on teakwood stand 250.00
Vases, 8 7/8" h., baluster form, overlay royal blue peony & cicada design against white ground, 20th c., pr. 440.00
Vase, 9½" h., overlay red stork in flight against white ground (ILLUS.) 224.00
Vase, 10" h., baluster form, overlay yellow monkey on pine tree against white ground, early 20th c., pr. 300.00
Vase, 12" h., overlay yellow fish against white ground 375.00
Vase, 12" h., baluster form, overlay green crane perched on limb of a pine tree against white ground 425.00

PELOTON

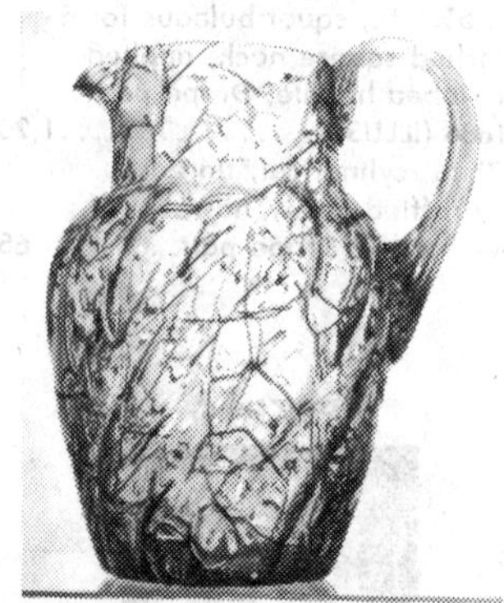

Peloton Water Pitcher

Made in Bohemia, Germany and England in the late 19th century, this glassware is characterized by threads or filaments of glass rolled into the glass body of the objects in random patterns. Some of these wares were decorated.

Cracker jar, melon-ribbed, opaque white w/pink, blue, yellow & white "coconut" threading, silver plate rim, cover & bail handle, 5¾" d., 5½" h. $595.00
Cracker jar, melon-ribbed, light blue w/multicolored "coconut" threading, satin finish, white lining, silver plate rim, cover & bail handle, 4½" d., 6¾" h. 600.00
Pitcher, 7" h., amber w/multicolored "coconut" threading 295.00
Pitcher, water, 11" h., applied clear handle, amber w/multicolored "coconut" threading (ILLUS.) 545.00
Plate, dessert, 6¼" d., ruffled, clear w/pink, blue, yellow & white "coconut" threading 100.00
Sweetmeat jar, robin's egg blue w/pink, yellow, white & blue "coconut" threading, cased in clear, white lining, silver plate rim, lid & bail handle, 5¼" d., 2¾" h. plus handle 585.00
Vase, 5" h., 4 3/8" d., ruffled fan top, orchid pink w/pink, blue, yellow & white "coconut" threading 295.00
Vase, 6¼" h., 4" d., clear wafer foot, round mouth, orchid pink w/pink, blue, yellow & white "coconut" threading 275.00

PHOENIX

Phoenix Vase

This ware was made by the Phoenix Glass Co. of Beaver County, Pennsylvania, which produced various types of glass from the 1880's. One special type that attracts collectors now is a molded ware with a vague resemblance to cameo in its "sculptured" decoration.

Box, cov., scalloped, sculptured fruits & leaves on white ground, 7¼ x 4¾" oval $75.00
Cigarette box, cov., sculptured white florals on blue ground, 4½ x 3½" 60.00
Vase, 5" h., sculptured white pinecones on green ground, paper label 55.00
Vase, 7" h., sculptured white fern fronds on brown or powder blue ground, original paper label, each 80.00 to 100.00
Vase, 8½" h., sculptured white dancing nudes on light green ground 129.00
Vase, 9" h., pillow-shaped, sculp-

tured deep blue fish on white ground 195.00
Vase, 9¼" h., pillow-shaped, iridescent flying geese on brownish red ground, original paper label 215.00
Vase, 10" h., four sculptured opalescent cameos, each w/three zodiac signs on slate grey ground 700.00
Vase, 10¼" h., sculptured white Madonna bust front & back on blue ground 250.00
Vase, 10½" h., 9" d., sculptured white daisies on light brown ground, original sticker (ILLUS.) .. 130.00
Vase, 11½" h., sculptured white philodendron leaves on blue ground 89.00
Vase, 12" h., sculptured gold flying geese on white ground 100.00

PIGEON BLOOD

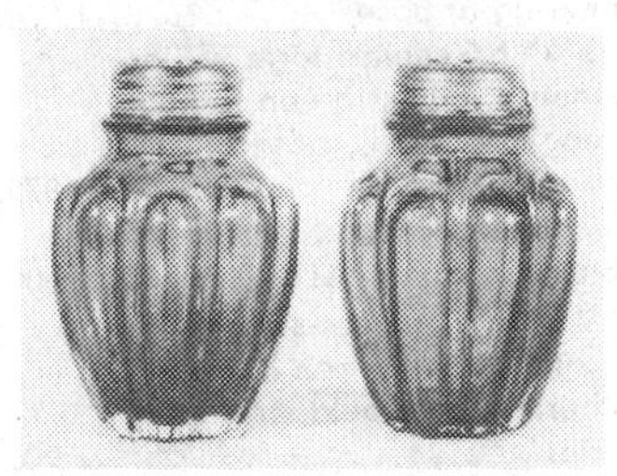

Bulging Loops Pattern Shakers

This name refers to the color of the glass, which was blood-red, and many wares have been lumped into this category.

Cracker jar, Beaded Drapery patt., ornate silver plate rim, cover & handle $185.00
Creamer, Torquay patt., silver plate rim & handle 115.00
Cruet w/original stopper, Inverted Thumbprint patt. 225.00
Lamp, hanging hall fixture, paneled, original brass frame 250.00
Pitcher, water, Torquay patt. 315.00
Salt & pepper shakers w/original tops, Bulging Loops patt., pr. (ILLUS.) ....95.00 to 120.00
Salt & pepper shakers w/original tops, Globule patt., pr. 135.00
Salt & pepper shakers w/original tops, squatty, raised fleur-de-lis & white enameled floral decor, pr. 150.00
Salt dip, scalloped rim 25.00
Syrup pitcher w/original top, applied frosted handle, Scroll & Net patt., satin finish 575.00

Table set: cov. butter dish, cov. sugar bowl, creamer & spooner; Torquay patt., w/original silver plate rims & lids, 4 pcs. 575.00

POMONA

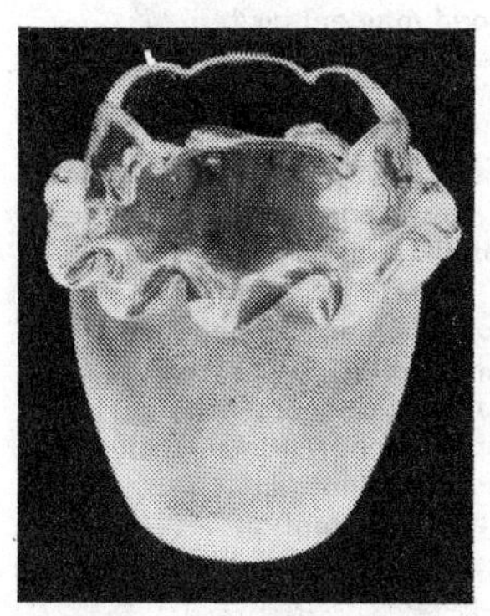

Pomona Toothpick Holder

First produced by the New England Glass Company under a patent received by Joseph Locke in 1885, Pomona has a frosted ground on clear glass decorated with mineral stains, most frequently amber-yellow, sometimes pale blue. Some pieces bore smooth etched floral decorations highlighted with staining. Two types of Pomona were made. The first Locke patent covered a technique whereby the piece was first covered with an acid-resistant coating which was then needle-carved with thousands of minute criss-crossing lines. The piece was then dipped into acid which cut into the etched lines, giving the finished piece a notable "brilliance." A cheaper method, covered by a second Locke patent on June 15, 1886, was accomplished by rolling the glass piece in particles of acid-resistant material which were picked up by it. The glass was then etched by acid which attacked areas not protected by the resistant particles. A favorite design on Pomona was the cornflower.

Cruet w/original stopper, leafy stem w/amber- and blue-stained pansy at front & amber- and blue-stained butterfly reverse, 2nd patent, 7¼" h. $465.00
Ice cream tray, blue-stained cornflowers, 2nd patent, 12½ x 7½" .. 395.00
Lemonade tumbler, clear handle & rim, Diamond Quilted patt., 1st patent, 5¾" h. 165.00
Lemonade tumbler, applied handle, Inverted Thumbprint patt., amber-

stained top, blue-stained cornflowers, 2nd patent, 5¾" h. 175.00
Pitcher, milk, 4½" h., square top, Inverted Thumbprint patt., 1st patent 350.00
Pitcher, water, 6½" h., clear handle, amber-stained square top, 1st patent 185.00
Pitcher, 7" h., red- and jade green-stained maidenhair fern, 1st patent 385.00
Pitcher, 8" h., bulbous, Diamond Quilted patt., amber-stained band at neck, 2nd patent 225.00
Punch cup, clear handle, blue-stained cornflowers, 1st patent, 2¾" d., 2½" h. 295.00
Toothpick holder, applied clear rigaree collar, 1st patent 265.00
Toothpick holder, applied clear rigaree, amber-stained scalloped rim, 2nd patent (ILLUS.) 245.00
Tumbler, 1st patent 90.00
Tumbler, blue-stained blueberries, 2nd patent 165.00
Vase, 2½" h., 4" w., fan-shaped, pie crust crimped amber-stained rim, 1st patent 185.00
Vase, 6¼" h., ovoid w/wafer base & amber-stained flared rim, 1st patent 285.00
Water set: pitcher & eight tumblers; amber-stained rim & blue-stained cornflowers, 1st patent, 9 pcs..... 950.00
Wine, applied clear stem & foot, Diamond Quilted patt., 2nd patent, 4 5/8" h. 88.00

QUEZAL

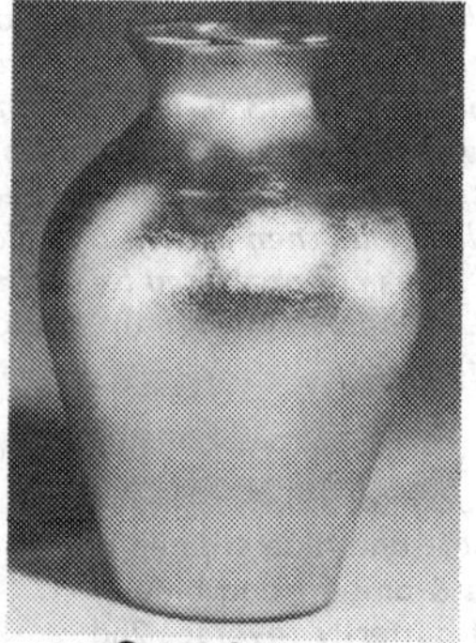

Quezal Vase

These wares resemble those of Tiffany and other glasshouses which produced lustred glass pieces in the late 19th and early 20th centuries. They were made by the Quezal Art Glass and Decorating Co. of Brooklyn, New York, early in this century and until its closing in the mid-1920's.

Candy dish, ribbed w/ruffled squared top, iridescent gold, signed, 4½" d., 2½" h. $175.00
Chandelier, 7-light, brass vasiform standard cast w/foliage & strapwork & supporting six brass candelarms, each supporting an iridescent amber floriform shade, brass drop finial w/additional iridescent amber floriform shade, early 20th c., 17" h. 1,100.00
Compote, 3¾" widest d., 2¾" h., ribbed, flared, scalloped edge, iridescent gold, signed 395.00
Cup & saucer, S-shaped handle, iridescent gold, signed 475.00
Salt dip, raised ribbed body, iridescent gold, signed 110.00
Vase, 4½" h., bulbous base, graceful gold neck continuing to opalescent body decorated w/a green, gold & opal fan-like diamond pattern over gold pulled feathering at base 1,200.00
Vase, 5¼" h., chalice-form w/flaring mouth, pulled green feathering edged in gold, iridescent gold interior, signed 875.00
Vase, 7¼" h., iridescent gold w/blue highlights (ILLUS.) 600.00
Vase, 7½" h., trumpet-shaped, ruffled rim, pulled green & gold feathering, pale gold striated interior 1,200.00
Vase, 8" h., baluster form w/flared rim, pulled & coiled swirls of iridescent ambergris, gold, green & blue on opalescent ground, gold interior, signed 550.00
Vase, 8½" h., ruffled top, iridescent gold w/rainbow highlights, signed 375.00
Vase, 9¾" h., bulbous, slender standard, outward flaring neck, pulled green feathering edged in iridescent amber on an opalescent ground, 1904-20, signed.......... 770.00
Vase, 10" h., bulbous w/flared top, iridescent gold w/pink highlights 525.00
Vase, 11½" h., baluster form, spreading circular foot, iridescent amber neck, shoulder w/scrolling opalescent lappets edged in olive green & amber iridescence continuing in the lower body to striated amber iridescent & opalescent feathering, 1905-25, signed 1,100.00
Vase, 13" h., jack-in-pulpit type, large iridescent gold face, body w/green & gold pulled feathering, signed 3,250.00
Vases, 15 1/8" & 16" h., slender

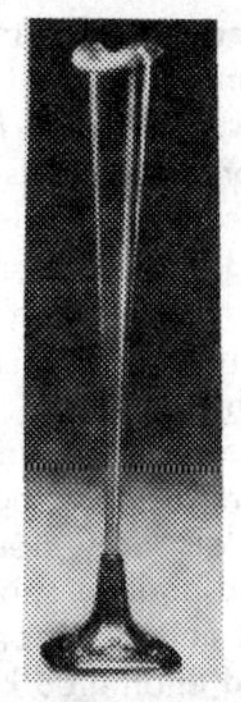

Quezal Vase

elongated trumpet form w/curling lip, iridescent amber, each signed, in flaring, faceted square metal base cast w/swans & lotus blossoms, 1905-20, pr. (ILLUS. of one) 605.00

RICHARD

Richard Cameo Vase

This is cameo glass made in France.

Cameo jar, cov., carved deep blue scene of castle reflected in lake w/forest & mountains in the distance against white ground, signed, 6" h. $475.00

Cameo vase, 4" h., carved deep blue floral spray against citron shaded to deep blue at foot, signed (ILLUS.) 325.00

Cameo vase, 4 3/8" h., carved black holly leaves & berries against tomato red ground 275.00

Cameo vase, 5" h., carved chocolate brown trailing leaves & florals against lemon yellow ground, signed (ILLUS.) 395.00

Cameo vase, 8" h., 5 1/8" d., 4 applied blue fin feet, carved navy blue scene of house by arched bridge, river & trees against orange opaque satin ground, signed 550.00

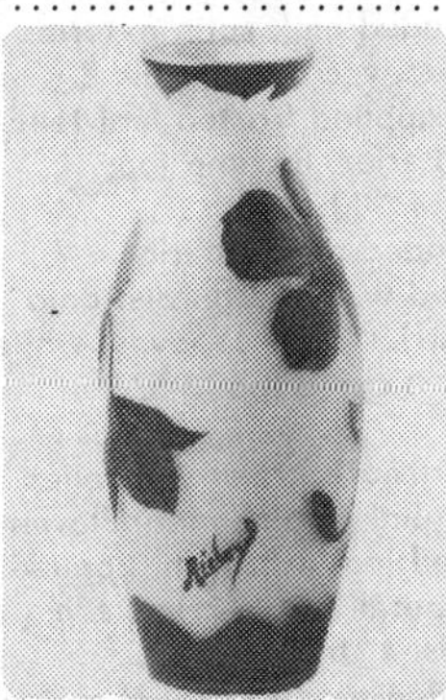

Richard Cameo Vase

Cameo vase, 9 7/8" h., 2¾" d., carved green to rosy peach scene of lady in headdress & flowing scarves dancing amidst a profusion of roses & foliage against soft blue frosted ground, signed .. 995.00

Cameo vase, 14½" h., baluster form, carved brown village scene w/mountains in background & leafy trees in foreground against pumpkin orange ground, ca. 1920, signed 935.00

ROSE BOWLS

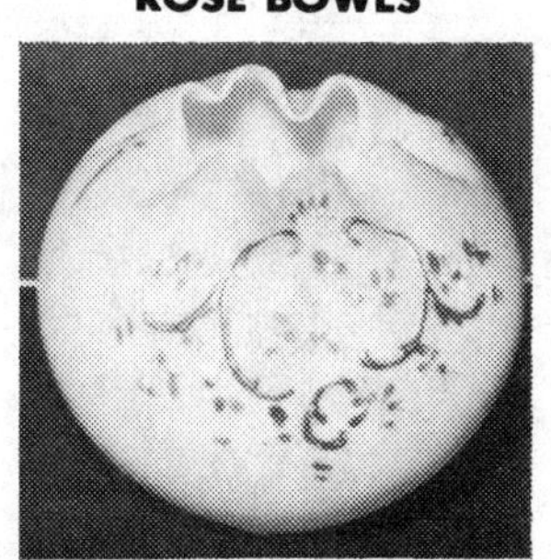

Pink Satin Decorated Rose Bowl

Cameo, carved white to blue leaves & berries against chartreuse green satin ground, white interior, English, 2 5/8" d., 2" h. $875.00

Cased, shaded heavenly blue satin exterior enameled w/Monarch butterfly in flight, cream florals & green leaves, lacy crystalline trim & applied frosted petal feet, white interior, 4-crimp top, 4 3/8" d., 5 3/8" h. 135.00

Cased, egg-shaped, pink satin exterior enameled w/three blue birds on branch & cream & blue florals, applied frosted handles, white interior, 8-crimp top, 6" d., 6½" h. 150.00

Cased, shaded pink satin exterior enameled w/cream florals & leaves, applied frosted leaf feet, white interior, 8-crimp top, 4¼" d., 4¾" h. 135.00

Cased, shaded pink exterior enameled w/white florals, gold strawberries & gold leaves, white interior, 8-crimp top, 3 5/8" d., 3" h. 75.00

Satin, chartreuse green w/applied white & pink satin spatter flower w/frosted leaf & branch, applied frosted petal feet, 8-crimp top, 3 5/8" d., 4" h. 95.00

Satin, shaded green w/relief-molded five-petal flower & leaves, 4½" d. 275.00

Satin, pink w/white enameled florals w/lavender centers & branches, 8-crimp top, 5½" d., 4¾" h. (ILLUS.) 150.00

Satin, yellow w/enameled floral decoration, 4¼" h. 35.00

Verre Moire, egg-shaped, frosted blue w/opaque white loopings, 8-crimp top, 3 5/8" d., 4¾" h. 175.00

ROYAL FLEMISH

Royal Flemish Vase

This ware, made by Mt. Washington Glass Co., is characterized by very heavy enameled gold lines dividing the surface into separate areas or sections. The body, with a matte finish, is variously decorated.

Bowl, 9" d., h.p. w/seven flying ducks against frosted white ground divided by gold-outlined geometric panels, signed $575.00

Cracker jar, cov., four gold Roman coin medallions interspersed against multicolored stained panels w/raised gold enameled tracery, silver plate rim, cover marked "MW" & bail handle, ca. 1893, overall 7½" h. 1,430.00

Cracker jar, decorated overall w/two clusters of pink-tinged roses, leaves & thorny stems super-imposed against subtle scroll-painted panels separated by raised gold enameled border-lines, silver plate rim, lid marked "MW" & bail handle, overall 7¾" h. 1,210.00

Vase, 11" h., bulbous base w/long neck, base shades of stained tan & brown w/gold-outlined scrolls on neck & geometric panels on body outlined w/heavy gold & enamel w/scattered round dragon head medallions (ILLUS.) 1,700.00

Vase, 13½" h., deeply ruffled trefoil rim, baluster form body, decorated overall w/ornate enameled leafy scrolls & arabesques centering a horned & winged dragon against a stained background of pastel green, lavender, blue & pink panels separated by raised gold enameled webbing interconnected by deeper blue & maroon devices 2,090.00

Vase, bulbous modified square shape w/short neck & two loop handles at neck, five Roman medallions raised on light brown & pastel green panels separated by raised gold borders 1,985.00

RUBINA CRYSTAL

This glass, sometimes spelled "Rubena," is a flashed ware, shading from ruby to clear. Some pieces are decorated, others are plain.

Basket, applied clear twisted handle, threaded decoration, 3½" d., 5½" h. $118.00

Compote, open, 8¼" d., low stand, Honeycomb patt. 60.00

Cruet w/original cut stopper, applied clear reeded handle, Inverted Thumbprint patt., Hobbs, Brockunier & Co. (ILLUS.) 385.00

Mug, applied clear handle, marked "Brother" 55.00

Perfume bottle w/clear cut faceted

stopper, cut panels, 1¾" d., 5 5/8" h. 80.00

Rubina Cruet

Pitcher, 7" h., 4½" d., applied clear handle, cut-diamond patt., star-cut base 125.00
Pitcher, 8½" h., Inverted Thumbprint patt. 245.00
Pitcher, water, 10" h., 5¼" d., applied clear reeded handle, "overshot" decoration 185.00
Pitcher, water, applied vaseline handle, square top, Reverse Thumbprint patt., Hobbs, Brockunier & Co. 250.00
Tumblers, Inverted Thumbprint patt., pr. 80.00
Water set: tankard pitcher w/applied clear handle & six tumblers; embossed floral design outlined w/gold, lower part w/satin finish separated from top by white enamel scrollwork, 7 pcs. 880.00

RUBINA VERDE

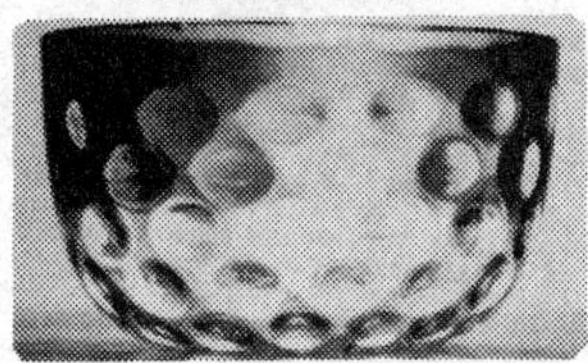

Rubina Verde Finger Bowl

This glass shades from ruby or deep cranberry to green.

Bowl, 5½" d., seven shell feet, opalescent crimped top, rigaree trim $95.00
Butter dish, cov. 395.00
Epergnes, single lily, applied rigaree, 16" h., pr. 495.00
Finger bowl, Inverted Thumbprint patt. (ILLUS.) 39.00
Pitcher, Bull's Eye patt. 395.00

Rubina Verde Pitcher

Pitcher, 6½" h., squared rim, Inverted Thumbprint patt. (ILLUS.) 260.00
Salt shaker w/pewter top, enameled floral decoration, 4¼" h. 185.00
Syrup pitcher w/pewter lid marked "Pat. Mar 29, '83," applied handle, Inverted Thumbprint patt. 335.00
Tumbler 70.00
Vase, 6" h., ruffled rim, melon-ribbed w/beading between ribs, enameled floral decoration 310.00
Vase, 7¼" h., jack-in-the-pulpit form 135.00
Vase, 10" h., enameled florals w/gold trim ....150.00 to 200.00

RUBY

Diamond Peg Pattern Napkin Ring

This name derives from the color of the glass — a deep red. Most ruby glass was stained and was produced as souvenir items late last century and in the present one. Also see PATTERN GLASS.

Berry set: master bowl & 6 sauce dishes; Carnation patt., 7 pcs. ....$155.00 to 175.00

Berry set: master bowl & 6 sauce dishes; Hexagon Block patt., etched, 7 pcs. 160.00
Butter dish, cov., Block & Lattice patt. 75.00
Butter dish, cov., O'Hara Diamond patt., w/vintage etching 110.00
Butter dish, cov., Pioneer's Victoria patt. . . . . .85.00 to 100.00
Butter dish, cov., Scroll with Cane Band patt. 95.00
Celery vase, Bar & Flute patt., 6" h. 40.00
Celery vase, Nail patt. 42.00
Compote, jelly, Diamond Spearpoint patt. 60.00
Compote, 5¾" d., 5¾" h., Column Block patt. 110.00
Creamer, individual size, Cut Block patt. 40.00
Creamer, O'Hara Diamond patt., w/vintage etching 65.00
Creamer, Spearpoint Band patt., frosted band 38.00
Cruet w/original stopper, Button Arches patt., w/frosted band 175.00
Cruet w/original stopper, Button Panel patt. 135.00
Cruet w/original stopper, O'Hara Diamond patt. 130.00
Goblet, Lace Band patt., souvenir . . . 21.00
Goblet, Toltec patt. 40.00
Goblet, Triple Triangle patt. 38.00
Goblet, Truncated Cube patt. 40.00
Mug, Arched Fleur de Lis patt. 40.00
Mug, Nail patt. 35.00
Mug, Triple Triangle patt. 25.00
Napkin ring, Diamond Peg patt., etched "Happy Halloween" (ILLUS.) 75.00
Pitcher, milk, Sheaf & Block patt. 80.00
Pitcher, water, bulbous, Loop & Block patt. 75.00
Pitcher, water, Swirl with Diamond patt. 225.00
Relish dish, Greensburg's Florida patt. 40.00
Rose bowl, Late Block patt. 60.00
Salt & pepper shakers w/original tops, Heart Band patt., pr. 55.00
Sauce dish, Flower & Pleat patt. 25.00
Spooner, Barred Oval patt. 65.00
Spooner, Diamonds with Double Fans patt. 45.00
Spooner, Millard patt. 30.00
Sugar bowl, cov., Beaded Swag patt. 65.00
Sugar bowl, cov., Triple Triangle patt. . . . . .65.00 to 80.00
Syrup pitcher w/original top, Prize patt. . . . . .235.00 to 295.00
Syrup pitcher w/original top, Truncated Cube patt. 155.00
Table set: cov. butter dish, cov. sugar bowl, creamer & spooner; Pearl patt., 4 pcs. 425.00
Table set, Prize patt., 4 pcs. 550.00
Toothpick holder, Britannic patt. 55.00

Naomi Pattern Toothpick Holder

Toothpick holder, Naomi (Rib & Bead) patt., souvenir (ILLUS.) 60.00
Toothpick holder, Riverside's Victoria patt. 275.00
Toothpick holder, Tacoma patt. 165.00
Tumbler, Big Button patt. 49.00
Tumbler, Heart Band patt., souvenir 30.00
Tumbler, Spearpoint Band patt. 45.00
Tumbler, York Herringbone patt., souvenir 45.00
Water set: pitcher & 5 tumblers; Triple Triangle patt., 6 pcs. 285.00
Wine, Arched Ovals patt. 28.00
Wine, Triple Triangle patt. 35.00
Wine set: decanter w/original stopper, tray & 5 wines; Aurora patt., 7 pcs. 350.00

SANDWICH

Sandwich Columnar Candlesticks

Numerous types of glass were produced at The Boston & Sandwich Glass Works in Sandwich, Massachusetts, on Cape Cod, from

1826 to 1888. Those listed here represent a sampling. Also see PATTERN GLASS.

Bitters bottle, Loop patt., flint, clear ... $85.00

Bowl, 6 x 8½" oval, 2" h., lacy, clear w/Crossed Peacock Feathers patt. ... 135.00

Candlesticks, columnar standard & petal socket, stepped square base, clambroth, 9¼" h., pr. (ILLUS.) ... 575.00

Candlesticks, dolphin stem w/petal socket, two-step base, clear, pr. ... 650.00

Cologne bottle, square base, herringbone corners, sapphire blue, 11" h. ... 2,300.00

Custard cup, applied clear handle, cranberry "overshot" ... 35.00

Custard cup, applied clear handle, pink "overshot" ... 50.00

Finger bowl, ruby cut to clear, 4½" d. ... 95.00

Finger bowl & underplate, wild rose decoration, 2 pcs. ... 95.00

Mucilage pot, lady's, octagonal ending in eight base scallops, canary yellow, original brush in stopper dated 1840, 1 5/8" w. base, 2¼" h. ... 295.00

Pepper shaker, "Christmas" type, dated top w/fixed finial, deep teal green, 2½" h. (single) ... 55.00

Pitcher, 10" h., applied reeded handle, clear "overshot" ... 125.00

Plate, 6" d., lacy, Hairpin patt., clear ... 85.00

Plate, 8" d., lacy, Peacock Eye & Thistle patt., clear ... 145.00

Pomade jar w/original pewter lid, octagonal, Diamond, Punty & Plume patt., opalescent, ca. 1840, 2½" w. ... 195.00

Relish, lacy, gothic arches, leaves & thistles, clear, 7½" oblong ... 135.00

Salt dip, lacy, model of wheeled wagon w/paneled sides w/lacy diamond in center panel, 1830's, clear (some damage) ... 110.00

Salt dip, rectangular, lacy, Strawberry Diamond patt., clear ... 36.00

Salt shaker, "Christmas" salt w/agitator & dated top, amber ... 100.00

Salt shaker, "Christmas" salt w/agitator & dated top, cobalt blue ... 110.00

Salt shaker, "Christmas" salt w/agitator & dated top, cranberry ... 75.00

Salt shaker, "Christmas" salt w/agitator & dated top, green ... 65.00

String holder, Bull's-eye patt., cased ruby on clear ... 195.00

Tray, scalloped, lacy, Scrolled Leaf & Fleur de Lis patt., clear, 5 x 6½" rectangle ... 65.00

SATIN & MOTHER-OF-PEARL

Satin Glass Ewer

Satin and Mother-of-Pearl wares were made by numerous glasshouses over a large part of the world. They continue in production today.

Basket, fan-shaped, applied frosted twisted thorn handle & tightly crimped edge, pinkish salmon mother-of-pearl Herringbone patt., 8½" w., 9½" h. ... $635.00

Bowl, 5" w., 4¼" h., tricornered, applied clear ruffle & three wishbone feet, heavenly blue mother-of-pearl Diamond Quilted patt., glossy cream lining, marked "Patent" ... 595.00

Bowl, 7½" w., 8¾" h., deeply ruffled w/applied clear trim at edge, shaded blue mother-of-pearl Diamond Quilted patt. w/enameled blue, green & white bird & florals, on ornate brass-finish metal base ... 1,070.00

Bowl, 13 3/8" d., 6 3/8" h., ruffled, heavenly blue w/enameled white florals w/gold & green branches interior, white exterior ... 295.00

Box, cov., h.p. roses on light blue, 5¾" d., 3¾" h. ... 240.00

Cracker jar, blue Swirl patt., silver plate rim, lid & bail handle ... 245.00

Ewer, ruffled rim, applied frosted handle, shaded soft peach mother-of-pearl Herringbone patt., white lining, 3½" d., 8½" h. (ILLUS.) ... 200.00

Finger bowl, 9-crimp top, shaded rose mother-of-pearl Diamond Quilted patt., cream lining, Webb, 4½" d., 2" h. ... 350.00

Finger bowl & underplate, Amberina mother-of-pearl Diamond Quilted patt., cream lining ... 900.00

Paperweight, shaded rose mother-of-pearl Diamond Quilted patt. 150.00
Perfume bottle w/silver screw-on top, lay-down type, shaded pink mother-of-pearl Swirl patt., 5½" l. 445.00
Pitcher, 3 7/8" h., applied ribbed handle, shaded pink mother-of-pearl Drapery patt. 105.00
Pitcher, water, 9" h., applied frosted reeded handle, shaded blue mother-of-pearl Raindrop patt. ... 350.00
Rose bowl, 3-crimp top, frosted wafer foot, rose mother-of-pearl Ribbon patt. w/gold prunus decoration, white lining, 2¾" d., 3" h. 335.00
Rose bowl, 4-crimp top, frosted wafer foot, peach mother-of-pearl Ribbon patt., white lining, 3½" d., 3½" h. 195.00
Rose bowl, 9-crimp top, blue mother-of-pearl Ribbon patt., white lining, 3¾" d., 2½" h. 225.00
Rose bowl, 13-crimp top, "petit point" enamel on rose, overall lavender, blue, yellow, green & white dots w/gold trim, white lining, 5 3/8" d., 4" h. 325.00
Salt shaker w/pewter top, rosy pink mother-of-pearl Herringbone patt. 235.00
Sweetmeat jar, American Beauty Rose mother-of-pearl Diamond Quilted patt., white lining, silver plate rim, cover & handle, 4¾" d., 3 1/8" h. 365.00
Tumbler, blue shaded to white mother-of-pearl Raindrops patt. .. 75.00
Tumbler, deep blue to pearly white mother-of-pearl Diamond Quilted patt., w/enameled pink blossoms & colorful foliage.............. 285.00

Satin Glass Tumbler

Tumbler, shaded pink mother-of-pearl Herringbone patt., 3¾" h. (ILLUS.)............................ 100.00
Tumbler, yellow shaded to white mother-of-pearl Diamond Quilted patt. 80.00
Vase, 3 5/8" h., 2¾" d., frosted wafer foot, American Beauty Rose mother-of-pearl Ribbon patt. w/gold prunus decoration, white lining 350.00
Vase, 6¼" h., 3 5/8" d., frosted binding around ruffled rim, shaded apricot mother-of-pearl Herringbone patt. w/enameled light gold florals & butterfly, white lining 245.00
Vase, 10½" h., 6 3/8" d., deep brown mother-of-pearl Federziechnung patt. w/gold decor, cream lining.........................1,650.00
Vases, 11 1/8" h., 6 1/8" d., ruffled, shaded green mother-of-pearl Coin Spot patt., one w/gold leaves & pink florals, other w/gold leaves & lavender florals, pr. 1,895.00
Vase, 13" h., 5 5/8" d., ewer-shaped, applied frosted thorn handle, shaded heavenly blue w/enameled creamy white flowers w/gold trim, white lining 225.00
Water set: pitcher & five tumblers; blue mother-of-pearl Herringbone patt., 6 pcs. 460.00

SCHNEIDER

This ware is made in France at Cristallerie Schneider, established in 1913 near Paris by Ernest and Charles Schneider. Some pieces of cameo were marked "Le Verre Francais" and others were signed "Charder."

Bowl, 9¼" d., flattened globular form, clear mottled w/cream shading to magenta & splashed w/orange & deep purple, ca. 1925 ....$165.00
Candlestick, paperweight-type, coral & pink double clematis, 5½" h.... 165.00
Compote, 6¼" d., 7½" h., pale peach bowl w/applied band of blue at rim, amethyst base & stem 380.00
Compote, 12" w., 4" h., mottled amethyst bowl, black base & stem... 400.00
Console bowl, mottled red & yellow bowl, wrought-iron vining floral base, signed, 10" d. 295.00
Vase, 7½" h., stylized lavender florals against mottled milky white and orange streaked ground, signed Charder 375.00
Vase, 9" h., 9" d., blood red w/drip effect at shoulders.............1,150.00

Vase, 12" h., puffy ribbed body, mottled royal blue against orange ground, heavy royal blue base . . . 275.00
Vase, 17¼" h., teardrop form w/wide flaring lip, mottled periwinkle blue on cherry red ground, ca. 1925, signed 935.00
Vase, 21½" h., urn-form, shoulder w/two angular applied handles, mottled lemon yellow & purple on orange ground, ca. 1920, signed . . 715.00

SILVER OVERLAY-SILVER DEPOSIT

Silver Overlay Miniature Vases

Silver Deposit and Silver Overlay have been made commercially since the last quarter of the 19th century. Silver is deposited on the glass by various means, the most widely adapted utilizing an electric current. The glass was very popular during the first three decades of this century, and some pieces are still being produced. During the late 1970's, silver commanded exceptionally high prices and this was reflected in a surge of interest in silver overlay glass, especially in pieces marked "sterling" or "925" on the heavy silver overlay.

Card tray, footed, ruffled upturned edge, black w/silver overlay, 9½" d. $40.00
Console set: large footed bowl & pair of candlesticks; black w/silver overlay, 3 pcs. 225.00
Cracker jar, cov., black w/silver deposit florals, 6½" d. 65.00
Decanter w/hollow stopper, emerald green w/silver deposit, 9" h. 55.00
Flask w/hinged sterling silver top, lady's, clear w/silver overlay scrolls, 2¼" w., 4¼" h. 140.00
Perfume bottle w/original stopper, cranberry w/silver overlay, 3½" h. 210.00
Perfume bottle w/original stopper, ball-shaped, cranberry w/sterling silver overlay florals & scrolls, 4" h. 300.00
Perfume bottle w/original stopper, bulbous, green w/silver overlay, 5" h. 375.00
Serving plate, 10-sided, pierced handles, black amethyst w/silver deposit Art Nouveau lilies, 12½" d. 55.00
Vase, 2 5/8" h., bulbous w/flared polished rim, amber w/iridescent gold, pink & blue-green highlights w/silver overlay intricately cut w/foliate & scrolled designs & marked "Sterling" near base (ILLUS.) 495.00
Vase, 3½" h., dimpled bulbous body w/ruffled trefoil rim, clear & amber body w/gold iridescence w/blue & pink highlights, silver overlay cut w/scrolled floral design marked "Sterling" at side (ILLUS. right) 715.00
Vase, 6" h., 2¾" widest d., flat bulbous base, trumpet-shaped top, cranberry w/sterling silver overlay florals & scrolls 475.00
Whiskey bottle w/sterling silver corked stopper, clear w/silver overlay leaves & thistles, glass signed "Hawkes," 11¾" h. 275.00
Whiskey decanter w/original stopper, pinched shape, white w/silver overlay, 10" h. 75.00
Wine set: decanter & four wines; green w/silver deposit, 5 pcs. 75.00

SLAG

Purple Slag Plate

Marble and Agate glass are other names applied to this variegated glass ware made from the middle until the close of the last century and now being reproduced. It is characterized by variegated streaks of color. Pink slag was made only in the Inverted Fan & Feather Pattern and is rare.

Basket, tall loop handle, crimped ruffled rim, cherry & leaf in relief, blue, 8 x 9½" $65.00
Butter dish & cover w/cow finial, purple 30.00
Cake stand, plain, purple 120.00
Celery vase, fluted, purple 80.00
Compote, 5" d., 4½" h., Beaded Hearts patt., purple 68.00
Compote, 5" h., Scroll with Acanthus patt., purple 40.00
Compote, Spool patt., purple 45.00
Compote, jelly, threaded, purple 55.00
Cruet w/(replaced) clear stopper, Inverted Fan & Feather patt., pink .. 995.00
Cup, square foot, purple, 1877 English Registry mark, 4" h. (tiny base chip) 20.00
Plate, 10" d., lattice edge, purple (ILLUS.) ....75.00 to 90.00
Salt dip, two-handled, oval, embossed florals, purple 32.00
Spooner, Scroll with Acanthus patt., purple 60.00
Toothpick holder, Inverted Fan & Feather patt., pink 625.00
Toothpick holder, Scroll with Acanthus patt., purple 115.00
Tumbler, souvenir, "A Present From the Bristol Expo 1893," purple 45.00

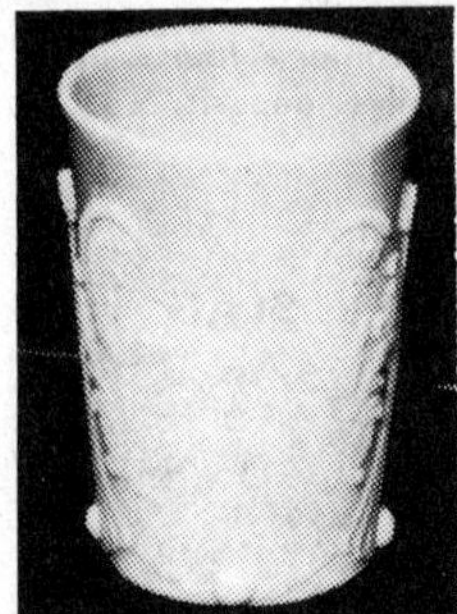

Pink Slag Tumbler

Tumbler, Inverted Fan & Feather patt., pink, 3 7/8" h. (ILLUS.) 350.00
Tumbler, whiskey, model of a thimble, purple, 2½" h. 32.00
Vase, 6" h., jack-in-pulpit type, purple 25.00

SMITH BROTHERS

This company first operated as a decorating department of the Mt. Washington Glass Works in the 1870's and later on as an independent business in New Bedford, Massachusetts. The firm was noted for its outstanding decorating work on glass and also carried on a glass cutting trade.

"Santa Maria" Plate

Bowl, 5½" d., 3" h., melon-ribbed, beaded rim, pale blue & violet pansies on biscuit colored ground, signed $275.00
Bowl, 9" d., melon-ribbed, satin finish, decorated 100.00
Cracker jar, cov., melon-ribbed, barrel shape, enameled blue open-faced pansies & buds on cream ground, 6½" d., 7¼" h. 585.00
Perfume bottle w/embossed flower cap, enameled decoration, signed, 5" h. 340.00
Plate, 7½" d., h.p. "Santa Maria" ship, blue & sepia, dated "1893," made for Chicago's "Columbian Exposition" (ILLUS.) 295.00
Powder box, cov., melon-ribbed, decorated w/pansies, 5" d. 395.00
Powder box, cov., roses outlined in pencil gold, 5" 450.00

Smith Brothers Vase

Rose bowl, ribbed, blue & orange floral decoration, signed 249.00
Toothpick holder, ribbed, opaque white w/blue dot rim & pastel floral decoration 135.00
Vase, 6" h., cylindrical, scene of heron in rushes, butterscotch ground, unsigned (ILLUS.) 100.00
Vase, 7¼" h., 8 x 2", double pilgrim flask shape, lavender wisteria traced in gold, gold beading on top, unsigned 1,215.00
Vase, 8¾" h., pillow-shaped, front w/leafy vine w/one pink & one blue clematis blossom w/raised gold borders, reverse w/one blue blossom, unsigned 385.00

SPANGLED

Spangled Glass Rose Bowl

Spangled glass incorporated particles of mica or metallic flakes and variegated colored glass particles imbedded in the transparent glass. Usually made of two layers, it might have either an opaque or transparent casing. The Vasa Murrhina Glass Company of Sandwich, Massachusetts, first patented the process for producing Spangled glass in 1884 and this factory is known to have produced great quantities of this ware. It was, however, also produced by numerous other American and English glasshouses. This type, along with Spatter, which see below, is often erroneously called "End of Day."

A related decorative glass, Aventurine, features a fine speckled pattern resembling gold dust on solid color ground.

Basket, applied clear handle, white exterior, clear edging, rich blue w/mica flecks, 4 7/8 x 5¾", 4¾" h. $125.00
Basket, applied clear handle, white exterior, shaded pink interior w/mica flecks, 4 x 6", 5½" h. 114.00
Basket, melon-ribbed, crimped ruffled top w/clear edging, pointed clear twist handle, white exterior, deep rose to pink w/silver mica flecks, 5¾ x 8½", 6½" h. 245.00
Basket, melon-ribbed, clear fishscale handle, clear edging around closely crimped flared top, white exterior, caramel interior w/gold mica flecks, 8¾ x 10", 8½" h. 295.00
Cologne bottle w/stopper, ruby & cream w/gold mica flecks, clear overlay, 5½" h. 80.00
Cruet w/clear faceted stopper, bulbous, clear applied handle, clear w/hint of blue at base, silver mica flecks, profuse random white mottling, Hobbs, Brockunier & Company 435.00
Ewer, applied clear thorn handle, apricot w/mica flecks, white lining, 3½" d., 8 3/8" h. 125.00
Pitcher, water, cranberry spatter w/gold mica flecks 265.00
Plate, 6 5/8" d., shallow w/swirled design of gold Aventurine threads emanating from center, pontil on base 25.00
Rose bowl, 8-crimp top, deep rose w/mica flecks in coralene-like pattern, white lining, 3½" d., 3 5/8" h. (ILLUS.) 110.00
Tumbler, molded Honeycomb patt., white, red, cranberry & amber spatter w/silver mica flecks, white lining, 3¾" h. 45.00
Vase, 5¾" h., 5½" d., jack-in-pulpit shape, ruffled rim, white exterior, pink interior w/clear edging & mica flecks 118.00
Vase, 6 1/8" h., applied striped side handles, bulbous w/tapering neck & flared rim, green, red, chartreuse, blue, yellow, white spatter w/mica flecks.................... 55.00
Vase, 8½" h., flattened oval, applied cranberry rigaree, scroll handles & ribs, copper colored Aventurine flecks, ca. 1880 ...... 302.50
Vase, 9¾" h., 4 1/8" d., applied vaseline loop handles & shell trim, pink w/mica flecks, white lining 95.00

SPATTER

This variegated-color ware is similar to Spangled glass but does not contain metallic flakes. The various colors are applied on a clear, opaque white or colored body. Much of it was made in Europe and England. It is sometimes called "End of Day."

Basket, applied clear thorn handle,

closely ruffled top, pink, white & tan spatter, white lining, 5" d., 5 5/8" h. $145.00

Basket, applied clear thorn handle, ruffled top, embossed swirled ribs, shaded aqua and brown spatter in white cased in clear, 5" w., 6½" h. 240.00

Basket, applied clear thorn handle, ruffled oval top, embossed swirls, peach & white spatter, 6 x 5¼", 6½" h. 165.00

Basket, applied blue twisted thorn handle, square ruffled top, embossed swirled ribs, blue w/light opaque blue spatter, 4½" d., 8" h. 175.00

Candlestick, domed ribbed base, twisted ribbed hourglass-form stem & flared socket w/ribbed base, yellow, red & white spatter in clear, 7½" h. (single) 35.00

Cruet w/clear stopper, applied clear handle, footed, red & white spatter 85.00

Spatter Glass Covered Jar

Jar & cover w/clear ball finial, base w/applied clear ruffled rim, white, pink, maroon & green spatter, white lining, 5" d., 4" h. (ILLUS.) 55.00

Pitcher, water, 6½" h., 6" d., bulbous w/round mouth, applied clear reeded handle, dark red spatter on opaque yellow, yellow lining 195.00

Pitcher, 9" h., swirl ribbed body, applied clear handle, brown, blue & white spatter 85.00

Pitcher, 9" h., pink & green spatter, white lining..................... 150.00

Pitcher, 10" h., fluted rim, applied clear handle, ruby spatter, yellow lining 365.00

Salt dip, applied clear shell trim around top, maroon, white & yellow spatter, white lining, 3¾ x 3", 1½" h. 50.00

Sugar shaker w/brass top, bulbous, ribbed, cranberry & white spatter, 5" h. 95.00

Tumbler, yellow & brown spatter ... 27.00

Vase, 7¼" h., 4 1/8" widest d., jack-in-pulpit type, green, peach, yellow & white spatter top, green Diamond Quilted patt. body 55.00

Water set: 9" h. bulbous pitcher & two tumblers; embossed Swirl patt., pink & yellow spatter, 3 pcs. 125.00

Water set: 7 7/8" h., 6" d. bulbous pitcher w/square mouth & dimpled sides, applied clear reeded handle & four 3¾" h. tumblers; embossed Swirl patt., pink, white, maroon, green & yellow spatter, white lining, 5 pcs. (hairline at top of one tumbler) 325.00

STEUBEN

The Steuben glass listed below was made at the Steuben Glass Works, now a division of Corning Glass, between 1903, when the factory was organized by T.G. Hawkes, Sr., the late Frederick Carder, and others, until about 1933. Mr. Carder developed many types of glass and revived many old techniques.

ALABASTER

Lamp, cylindrical Alabaster column w/etched decor, applied leaves & loop handles at base, fitted in metal holder above bulbous column set on heavy metal base, overall 10" h. $1,500.00

Vase, 5¾" h., double gourd shape, raised ribs, signed 225.00

ANIMALS

Duck, stylized vertical version, signed, 8½" h. ....275.00 to 300.00

Gazelles, leaping, base of molded, scrolled grass design, signed, 5½" l., 6¾" h., pr. 550.00

Pigeons, cut feathers on wings & tails, signed, 6" h., pr. 1,100.00

Robin, beak open, ca. 1950, signed, 5" l. 185.00

AURENE

Basket, cylindrical w/pinched flared rim, upright handle, blue Aurene, early 20th c., signed, 11¼" h. 825.00

Bowl, 10" d., 6" h., blue Aurene, signed (ILLUS.) 950.00

Bowl, 12" d., 3" h., folded-in top, 3-footed, blue Aurene, signed & numbered 725.00

Candlesticks, twisted stem, blue Aurene, signed & numbered, 8" h., pr. . . . 825.00

Blue Aurene Bowl

Centerpiece bowl, gold Aurene & Calcite, signed, 14¼" d. . . . 435.00
Compote, 6¼", gold Aurene, signed & numbered . . . 420.00
Cordial, twisted stem, gold Aurene, signed, shape No. 2361 3½" h. . . . 275.00
Perfume atomizer, deep violet blue Aurene, 8" h. . . . 475.00
Perfume bottle w/original ball stopper, gold Aurene w/blue, pink & green highlights, signed & numbered, 3 1/8" d., 3¼" h. . . . 545.00
Sherbet & underplate, Aurene & Calcite, 2 pcs. . . . 135.00
Vase, 4¾" h., blue Aurene, shape No. 2633 . . . 595.00

Gold Aurene Vase

Vase, 10" h., bulbous ovoid w/waisted neck & everted rim, gold Aurene w/mottled amber iridescence, shaded to silver at rim, 1st quarter 20th c., signed (ILLUS.) . . . 935.00
Vase, 12" h., blue Aurene, signed & w/paper label . . . 950.00

BRISTOL YELLOW

Bowl & underplate, lotus leaf form, signed, 2 pcs. . . . 125.00
Candlestick, twisted stem, clear & Bristol yellow, 10" h. (single) . . . 115.00
Centerpiece bowl, diagonally ribbed, turned over rim, signed, 12" d., 4½" h. . . . 110.00
Compote, 6" h., clear stem . . . 65.00
Goblet, signed, 6" h. . . . 55.00

CALCITE

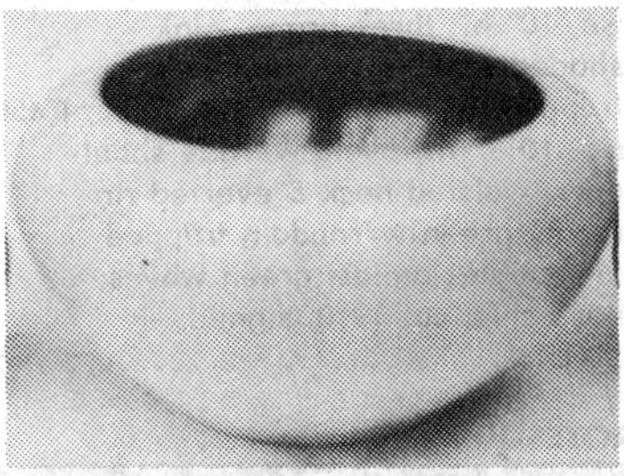

Calcite & Blue Aurene Bowl

Bowl, 5¾" d., 3" h., Calcite exterior, blue Aurene lining (ILLUS.) . . . 350.00
Compote, 8" d., Calcite exterior, gold Aurene lining . . . 375.00
Finger bowl & underplate, Calcite & gold Aurene, 2 pcs. . . . 375.00
Rose bowl, Calcite exterior, gold Aurene interior, shape No. 2687, 6½" w., 4" h. . . . 350.00
Salt dip, pedestal base, Calcite & gold Aurene, 1½" h. . . . 195.00
Vase, 3" h., 6" top d., futuristic shape w/turned down rim, Calcite & gold Aurene, signed . . . 250.00

CLUTHRA

Cluthra Vase

Chalice, green shaded to white w/random trapped air bubbles . . . 125.00
Vase, 6½" h., 6¼" d., rose quartz shaded to white w/random trapped air bubbles . . . 400.00
Vase, 8" h., white w/random trapped air bubbles, shape No. 2683 . . . 895.00 to 975.00
Vase, 8" h., 11½" widest d., flaring rim, alternating white & clear

w/random trapped air bubbles, shape No. 7564 .... 525.00

Vase, 8¼" h., Pomona green w/random trapped air bubbles ... 650.00

Vase, 10" h., 9½" d., bulbous, blue w/random trapped air bubbles, signed 700.00

Vase, 10" h., three-prong, pink shaded to white w/random trapped air bubbles, signed 1,450.00

Vase, 10½" h., ovoid w/wide shoulders, waisted neck & everted rim, foamy green w/random trapped air bubbles amidst green waves, base chip, ca. 1910, signed (ILLUS.)........................ 715.00

GROTESQUE

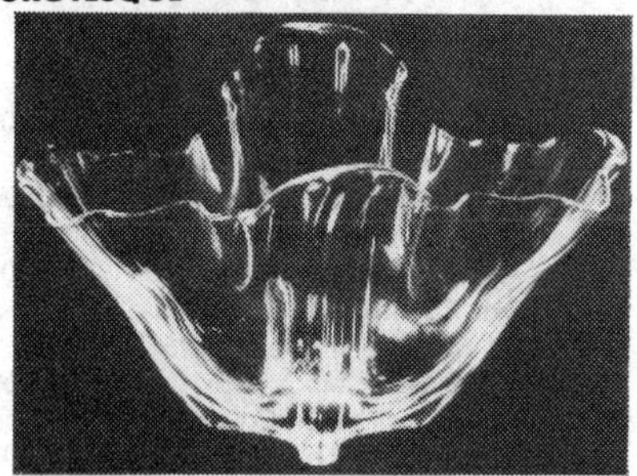

Grotesque Bowl

Bowl, 8" d., cobalt blue shaded to clear, signed ....160.00 to 185.00

Bowl, 5½ x 9", 5" h., fluted, clear, signed (ILLUS.) 175.00

Bowl, 12" w., 6½" h., green, unsigned ....90.00 to 120.00

Vase, 7" h., 12" w., clear 125.00

Vase, 11" h., red shaded to clear ... 295.00

JADE

Jade Sherbet & Underplate

Bowl, 10¾" d., 5" h., light blue Jade 495.00

Candleholder, green Jade & Alabaster, unsigned, 11¾" h. 210.00

Centerpiece, fan-shaped green Jade bowl on ribbed, domed Alabaster foot, shape No. 7307, 12" w. across top, 8" h. 295.00

Goblet, green Jade w/twisted Alabaster stem, signed, 8" h. 115.00

Plate, 8½" d., green Jade, signed .. 50.00

Sherbet, scalloped, green Jade 50.00

Sherbet & underplate, green Jade w/Alabaster stem & foot, pr. (ILLUS.)......................... 190.00

Vase, 4" h., dark blue Jade 1,150.00

Vase, 7" h., slightly ovoid, green Jade, signed, shape No. 6031 .... 125.00

Vase, 9½" h., 6" w. rectangle, diagonally ribbed, green Jade, signed, shape No. 6199 .... 125.00

Vase, 10" h., hexagonal, low foot w/knopped stem, green Jade & Alabaster, unsigned, shape No. 7188 .... 195.00

ROSALINE

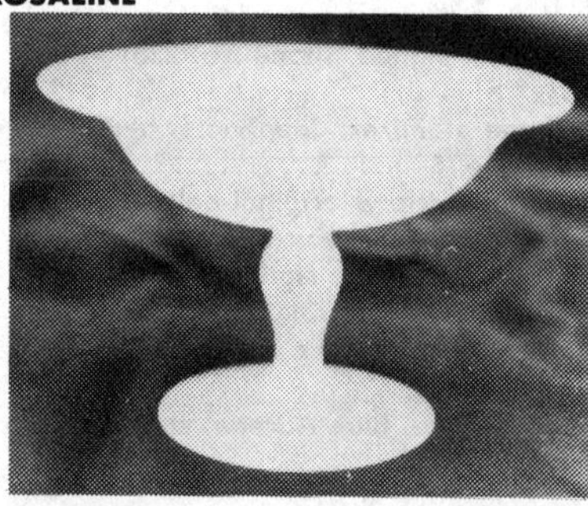

Rosaline & Alabaster Compote

Bowl & underplate, Alabaster foot, signed, pr. 125.00

Compote, 6" d., 2¾" h., Alabaster foot & stem..................... 165.00

Compote, 6¼" d., 4" h., Alabaster foot & stem (ILLUS.) 185.00

Compote, 8" w., 2" h., Alabaster foot.......................... 235.00

Cup & saucer, Alabaster handle, unsigned 150.00

Dish, apple-shaped, applied Alabaster leaves & stem, 4¾" 135.00

Goblet, cone-shaped w/flaring rim, twisted Alabaster stem & foot, signed, shape No. 5154, 7 1/8" h. 165.00

Plate, 8½" d., unsigned 25.00

Vase, 6" h., Alabaster pedestal foot.......................... 150.00

Vase, bud, 8" h., Alabaster foot, signed 200.00

Wine, Alabaster stem & foot, 7½" h.......................... 90.00

SELENIUM RUBY

Luncheon service for six: 8¼" d. plates, footed bowls w/underliners & goblets w/applied prunts & twisted stems; signed, 24 pcs... 660.00

Vase, 5" h., 4" top d., signed, shape No. 2013 .... 165.00

THREADED

Bowl, 12" d., clear w/blue threading, signed 265.00
Compote, clear w/Bristol yellow threading, controlled bubble stem w/teardrop 85.00
Dresser jars, square, clear w/Gold Ruby threading, Gold Ruby flower-form stoppers, etched fleur-de-lis mark, graduated sizes from 3½" to 4¾" h., set of 3 .... 467.50
Goblet, clear w/green threading, controlled bubble stem 55.00
Goblet, clear w/pink threading, signed 90.00
Liqueur, clear w/green threading, controlled bubble stem 55.00
Sherbet & underplate, clear w/blue threading, signed 95.00
Wine, clear w/green threading, controlled bubble stem 55.00

VERRE DE SOIE

Bowl, 8" d., 3" h., signed 90.00
Compote, 6" d., white, unsigned.... 90.00
Compote, 8" d., green trim 175.00
Nappy, unsigned, 6¼" d. 40.00
Perfume bottle w/Nile green steeple stopper, shape No. 1988, 10" h. .. 395.00
Perfume bottle w/pastel blue stopper, 10¾" h. 365.00
Sherbets & underplates, unsigned, set of 4 .... 800.00
Vase, 3" h. 150.00

(End of Steuben Glass Section)

STEVENS & WILLIAMS

Rose Bowl with Applied Decoration

This long-established English glasshouse has turned out a wide variety of artistic glasswares through the years. Fine satin glass pieces and items with applied decoration (sometimes referred to as "Matsu-No-Ke") are especially sought-after today. The following represents a cross-section of its wares.

Basket, applied amber feet & handle, creamy opaque w/applied green & amber ruffled leaves, rose pink lining w/amber edging, 5" d., 9" h. $350.00
Bonbons, flared, threaded rose & clear, ca. 1890, unsigned, 5½" d., 2¾" h., pr. 90.00
Bowl, 6¾" d., 3¼" h., box pleated top, pink mother-of-pearl satin Swirl patt., cream lining 495.00
Cameo bowl, 5 5/8" d., 3½" h., 8-crimp rose bowl style top, applied clear feet w/flower prunt, carved cream bamboo leaves & florals against deep pink ground, yellow lining, unsigned 595.00
Cruet w/original flattened amber stopper, amber pedestal foot, applied amber handle, amber w/opaque white "Arboresque," 3½" d., 9½" h. 145.00
Decanter w/clear cut steeple stopper, intaglio cut green to clear cherries & leaves, 3 7/8" d., 16½" h. 325.00
Pitcher, 10½" h., applied amber feet & rim, green handle continuing to form green leaves & yellow flower, cranberry overlay, blue interior 595.00
Plate, 4¾" d., ruffled shell shape, shaded pink to green mother-of-pearl satin Swirl patt., cream underside 175.00
Rose bowl, 8-crimp top, creamy opaque w/applied pink, amber & gold leaves & florals, signed, 6" d. (ILLUS.) 165.00
Vase, 5" h., pink mother-of-pearl satin Swirl patt. 85.00
Vase, 6¼" h., fluted, white to pink w/applied gold & green florals & leaves, signed 210.00
Vase, 8¼" h., 5 1/8" d., applied amber loop feet, shaded pink w/applied amber & green leaf & branches w/applied soft blue & cream florals w/amber centers, white lining..................... 295.00
Vase, 11½" h., gourd-shaped, footed, pink mother-of-pearl satin, applied Matsu-No-Ke trim 650.00

TIFFANY

This glassware, covering a wide diversity of types, was produced in glasshouses operated by Louis Comfort Tiffany, America's outstanding glass designer of the Art Nouveau period, from the last quarter of the 19th century until the early 1930's. Tiffany revived early techniques and devised many new ones.

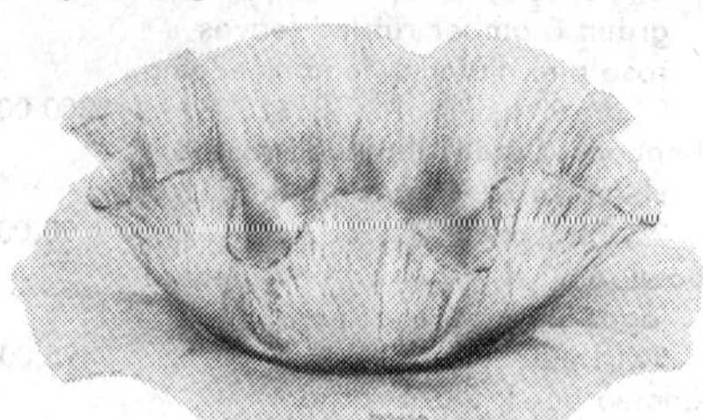

Tiffany Finger Bowl & Underplate

Bowl, 5" d., turned-in & ruffled rim, ribbed body, clear w/lavender internal decor, signed & numbered $325.00

Bowl, 7" d., 3" h., ruffled rim, gold, signed "L.C.T. - Favrile" & numbered 590.00

Bowl, 8 3/8" d., hemispherical, scalloped rim, ribbed body, deep blue w/pale amber iridescence, ca. 1893, signed "L.C. Tiffany-Favrile" 412.50

Bowl, 9" d., ruffled rim, gold w/purple iridescence, signed 460.00

Bowl, 12" d., 3½" h., stretched edge, iridescent gold w/bronze, blue & lavender iridescence, intaglio-cut butterfly, signed "L.C. Tiffany-Favrile" & w/original foil label, w/teakwood stand 1,100.00

Butter pat, scalloped edge, iridescent gold, signed "L.C.T.-Favrile" & w/original label, 3¼" w. 195.00

Cameo vase, 15 1/8" h., baluster-shaped, carved central dogwood spray & applied & carved flowers among carved metallic gold leaves against iridescent silvery blue ground shading to peacock blue below, signed "Louis C. Tiffany Furnaces, Inc.-Favrile" 3,630.00

Centerpiece bowl, footed, iridescent blue, signed "L.C. Tiffany, Inc.-Favrile," 11" d. 770.00

Centerpiece bowl w/attached flower frog at center, blue w/gold lily pads & gold trailings, signed, 11" d. 1,400.00

Compote, 6" d., 4½" h., Laurel patt. in white on pastel purple, clear base & pedestal, signed "L.C. Tiffany-Favrile" 895.00

Compote, 8½" d., 4" h., iridescent gold, signed "L.C.T.-Favrile" 600.00

Compote, 9¾" w., 5¼" h., iridescent gold, signed & w/paper label 925.00

Creamer, pastel pink & white, signed, 3¼" h. 425.00

Finger bowls & underplates, iridescent amber flaring floriform bowl w/crimped rim w/blue, pink, rust, aqua & violet iridescence, iridescent amber underplate w/petal-form rim w/yellow-green, deep aqua, berry red, pink & blue iridescence, ca. 1910, signed "L.C.T.," set of 6 (ILLUS. of one set) 1,650.00

Goblet, iridescent gold, applied lily pad decoration, original label, 5¼" h. 650.00

Goblet, circular base, iridescent gold, signed, 5½" h. 300.00

Liqueur, clear iridized stem & foot, iridized opalescent green exterior, green interior, signed "L.C.T.-Favrile," 4¾" h. 275.00

Nut cup, iridescent amber, signed "L.C. Tiffany-Favrile," 2 7/8" d. 182.00

Panel, mosaic, two opposing parrots against ground of exotic leafage, brilliant iridescent colors, 1899-1920, unsigned, 16½ x 14 1/8" rectangle 6,325.00

Parfait, opalescent & iridescent aqua, signed "L.C.T.-Favrile" 255.00

Perfume bottle w/stopper, iridescent blue, paper label, 4¼" h. 575.00

Plate, 6¼" d., shallow cavetto, five evenly spaced peacock "eyes" within undulating feathering, iridescent amber, blue-green & brown w/pale green sides, signed "L.C.T. Favrile," ca. 1896 .... 1,540.00

Plate, 8½" d., footed, gold w/silver & lavender highlights, signed & numbered 295.00

Punch cup, applied handle, green lily pad decoration on iridescent gold ground, signed 185.00

Rose bowl, light diamond quilted effect, gold w/iridescent rainbow highlights, signed & numbered, 5½" widest d., 5" h. 1,400.00

Salt dip, four pulled feet, iridescent gold w/pigtail prunts, signed "L.C.T.," 2" d. 145.00

Tile, highly iridescent pale green, signed "L.C. Tiffany" & dated, 3½" sq. 230.00

Toothpick holder, dimpled sides, iridescent gold, signed "L.C.T.," 1½" d., 1 7/8" h. 225.00

Tumbler, Vintage patt., iridescent gold, intaglio-cut clusters of grapes w/vines, signed, 3" h. 185.00

Vase, 2½" h., sharply waisted neck decorated about the angled shoulder w/iridescent amber striated lappets on tomato red ground, ca. 1906, signed "L.C.T." & w/partial paper label 3,025.00

Vase, 4" h., paperweight-type, bulbous w/short neck, iridescent grey w/white blossoming daffodils w/orange-red centers on green stalks, ca. 1913, signed "L.C. Tiffany Favrile" 1,540.00

Vase, 4¼" h., baluster-shaped, three pulled openwork handles, translucent red shading to amber, original paper label 825.00

Vase, 4¾" h., "millefiore," rolled collar, green leaves, florettes & reddish brown vines on an iridescent gold ground w/rainbow highlights, signed "L. C. Tiffany, Inc. Favrile"........................1,800.00

Vase, 5½" h., "Cypriote," shouldered ovoid, green scrolling vines & leafage against silvery amber lightly pitted ground, ca. 1915, signed "L.C. Tiffany Favrile"............2,750.00

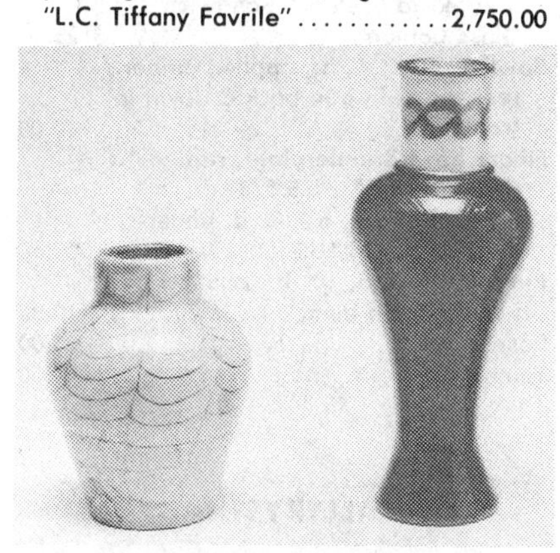

Tiffany Favrile Vases

Vase, 5¾" h., ovoid, transparent amber cased w/beige-streaked sky blue divided by vertical lines & bands of horizontal waves, signed "L.C.T. Favrile" (ILLUS. left)........................... 935.00

Vase, 8" h., baluster form, iridescent emerald green, opalescent interior tinged w/amber, ca. 1916, signed "L.C. Tiffany Favrile"............1,045.00

Vase, 9" h., jack-in-pulpit type, iridescent amber, ca. 1905, signed "L.C.T." 990.00

Vase, 9½" h., wide raised cuffed rim, baluster-form body, cobalt blue lustred brilliant turquoise blue, black rim decorated w/lighter turquoise blue chain border w/silver iridescent centers in the Egyptian patt., opalescent interior, signed "L.C. Tiffany-Favrile, 3433E" 3,740.00

Vase, 9 5/8" h., baluster form, opalescent-cased red w/white neck bordered by applied red bands, w/gold iridescence & chain of red links enclosing iridescent gold lines connected by purple bars, signed "L.C. Tiffany-Favrile" (ILLUS. right)..........................17,600.00

Vase, 10¼" h., trumpet-shaped, ribbed domed foot, ball stem, iridescent gold w/pink highlights, signed 675.00

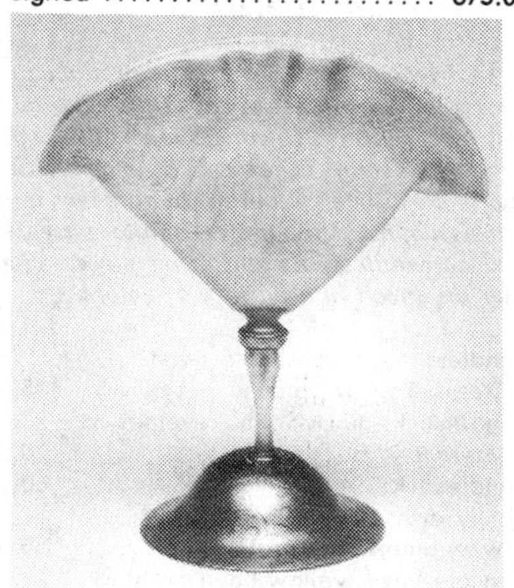

Tiffany Fan-shaped Vase

Vase, 11½" h., fan-shaped, transparent amber ruffled bowl w/textured design of swirls & a heavy gold & violet iridescence supported by a short spiralled stem raised on a domed base w/a design matching the bowl, signed "Louis C. Tiffany, o3423" (ILLUS.) 13,200.00

Vase, 12¼" h., slender baluster form w/knopped stem above circular spreading foot, iridescent brilliant deep blue trailed w/apple green lily pad leaves about the shoulder, signed "L.C. Tiffany-Favrile" 1,870.00

Vase, 13¾" h., floriform, pale iridescent amber ovoid bowl w/elongated ruffled rim w/amber-green striated feather devices edged in iridescent amber-blue, pale green slender knopped standard continuing to an iridescent amber domed circular foot w/green feathering, ca. 1900, signed "L.C.T." 3,025.00

Vase, 16" h., jack-in-pulpit type, iridescent amber tinged w/pink, obverse w/amber & opalescent graduated bands of interlaced scrolling waves continuing into slender stem & domed circular base, ca. 1905, signed "L.C.T." 9,900.00

Whiskey shot glass, pinched, iridescent rust brown, signed......... 110.00

Wine, iridescent pastel blue w/blue opalescent shaded to vaseline stem & foot, signed "L.C.T. Favrile," 5½" h. 275.00

Wines, iridescent opalescent aqua-green, knopped stem, opalescent-edged pedestal, signed "L.C.T.-Favrile," 4" h., set of 6 .... 935.00

TIFFIN

A variety of glasswares were produced by the Tiffin Glass Company of Tiffin, Ohio earlier in this century. One type especially popular with collectors is now called "Black Satin" and is most often found in round vases with a design of molded poppies. Similar vases, as well as candlesticks and other pieces, were also produced in a variety of colors.

Candlesticks, Black Satin, twist-stems, 7½" h., pr. $35.00
Candlestick, Black Satin, reverses to vase, 8½" h. (single) 20.00
Candlesticks, yellow, tall, pr. 60.00
Candy dish, cov., Black Satin w/enameled decoration.......... 55.00
Console bowl, yellow bowl on black base, 2 pcs. 50.00
Console set: 10½" d. footed bowl & pair reversible 8½" h., candlesticks; Black Satin, 3 pcs. 145.00
Console set: 11" d. footed orange bowl on separate black base & pair 9" h. twist-stem candlesticks; Peach Blow, 4 pcs. 215.00
Vase, 5" h., round bulbous shape, black w/shiny finish, molded poppies design 27.50
Vase, 8½" h., round bulbous shape, blue w/satin finish, molded poppies design 48.00
Vase, 6½" h., Black Satin w/h.p. iris & coralene beading 95.00
Vase, 8" h., Black Satin w/silver overlay trim 95.00
Vase, 8" h., round bulbous shape, Black Satin w/h.p. daffodils & coralene beading................ 79.00
Vase, round bulbous shape, Black Satin, molded poppies design w/red coralene trim 50.00
Vase, round bulbous shape, vaseline, molded poppies design, large........................... 85.00

TORTOISE SHELL

Tortoise Shell glass is primarily amber with splotches of darker amber or brown and resembles actual tortoise shell, hence the name. Some of this ware is attributed to Sandwich, but it was also made in numerous European glasshouses. Readily identified by its peculiar coloring, it is admired by many collectors.

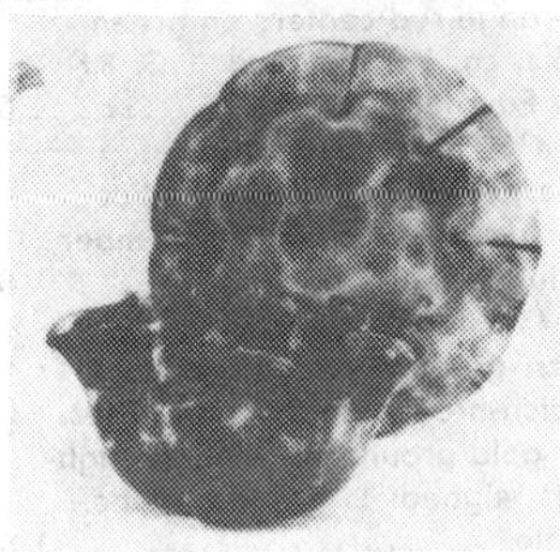

Tortoise Shell Finger Bowl

Bowl, 4½" d., round w/two sides turned-in, applied clear feet, attributed to Boston & Sandwich Glass Company $125.00
Bowl, 7¾" d., 4" h., applied amber feet, turned up in back & down in front 110.00
Finger bowl & underplate, ruffled rims, late 19th c., 5 5/8" d., 2 7/8" h. bowl, 6 1/8" d. underplate, 2 pcs. (ILLUS.)............ 302.50
Pitcher, tankard, 10" h., applied handle & rim band 110.00
Rose bowl 55.00
Tumbler 40.00

VALLERYSTHAL

Glass was made in Vallerysthal, France, for several centuries until 1939 when the factory there was demolished during the war. Most of its glass available to the collector today is of fairly recent vintage.

Animal covered dish, dog on rug, milk white, signed $90.00
Animal covered dish, fish 85.00
Animal covered dish, rabbit crouching...................... 85.00
Butter dish, figural radish, signed... 75.00
Candy jar, cov., blue w/gold trim, signed 90.00
Covered dish, figural lemon, yellow 50.00
Vase, stick-type, green intaglio-cut dragonfly & bullrushes........... 750.00

VAL ST. LAMBERT

This Belgian glassworks was founded in 1790. Items listed here represent a sampling of its numerous types of productions.

Cameo vase, 6½" h., pyriform, frosted grey shaded to iridescent grass green, maroon & amber at neck & foot, overlaid in similar colors & cut w/berry-laden leafy branches, ca. 1900, signed $550.00

Val St. Lambert Cameo Vase

Cameo vase, 7¼" h., ovoid w/pinched sides & trefoil lip, clear opalescent sides overlaid in oxblood & impressionistically carved w/leafy trees, the obverse further carved w/two peacocks, signed (ILLUS.) 605.00

Cameo vase, 9½" h., carved deep purple tulips against frosted ground, purple collar, signed 775.00

Cordial decanter w/original stopper, cranberry cut to clear, signed & w/paper label, 12½" h. 165.00

Powder jar, cov., clear w/amber stain, signed, 2½" 45.00

Ring tree, acid cut-back royal blue to clear orchid-like flowers, acid etched background, cut center column, signed, 4¼" d., 3½" h. . . 175.00

Toothbrush holder, clear w/amber stain, signed 50.00

Wines, heavily intaglio cut, ribbons & bows, cranberry cameos, gold trimmed stems, set of 12 .... 480.00

VASELINE

This glass takes its name from its color, which is akin to that of petroleum jelly used for medicinal purposes. Pieces below are miscellaneous. Also see PATTERN GLASS.

Butter dish, cov., Daisy & Button patt., faceted knob finial, 6½ x 5" $125.00

Celery vase, Leaf & Panel patt. 35.00

Cruet w/original stopper, Beaumont's Columbia patt., gold trim . . 99.00

Cruet w/original stopper, Riverside's Ranson patt. 145.00

Pitcher, 3½" h., 2 3/8" d., embossed ovals & quilting, opalescent rim, English 40.00

Salt dip, applied vaseline shell trim, opalescent rim, in silver plate stand, 2¾" d., 2¼" h. 85.00

Salt dip, open, six panels each w/impressed star, starred base . . 7.00

Salt dip, open, tulip-shaped 42.50

Salt shaker w/original top, Riverside's Ranson patt. 28.00

Vaseline Inverted Thumbprint Syrup

Syrup jug w/original pewter lid marked "OK Pat. Jan. 29 '84," Inverted Thumbprint patt., 6½" h. (ILLUS.) 80.00

Syrup pitcher, Rope & Thumbprint patt. 125.00

Toothpick holder, Ribbed Spiral patt. 60.00

Tumbler, Cane patt. 35.00

Tumbler, Diamond Quilted patt. 25.00

Wine, Paneled Jewel patt. 35.00

Wines, hourglass shape, set of 8 ... 200.00

VERLYS

Verlys Frosted Tassel Bowl

This glass is a relative newcomer for collectors and is not old enough to be antique, having been made for less than half a century in France and the United States, but fine pieces are collected. Blown and molded pieces have been produced.

Bowl, 6" d., Cupid & Hearts patt., clear $45.00
Bowl, 6" d., Pinecone patt., clear ... 49.00
Bowl, 6" d., Thistle patt., cobalt blue 65.00
Bowl, 8", Thistle patt., clear 40.00
Bowl, 10" d., Chrysanthemum patt., clear & frosted 125.00
Bowl, 11½" d., 2¾" h., Frosted Tassel patt., clear, signed (ILLUS.) ... 110.00
Bowl, 12" d., birds & bees design, clear 210.00
Console bowl, 14", Butterfly patt., clear 125.00
Console bowl, Goldfish patt., clear, signed 100.00
Vase, 10" h., Thistle patt., clear & frosted, signed 239.00
Vase, Alpine Thistle patt., dusty rose, signed 325.00
Vase, fan-shaped, sculptured lovebirds, clear & frosted 95.00

WAVE CREST

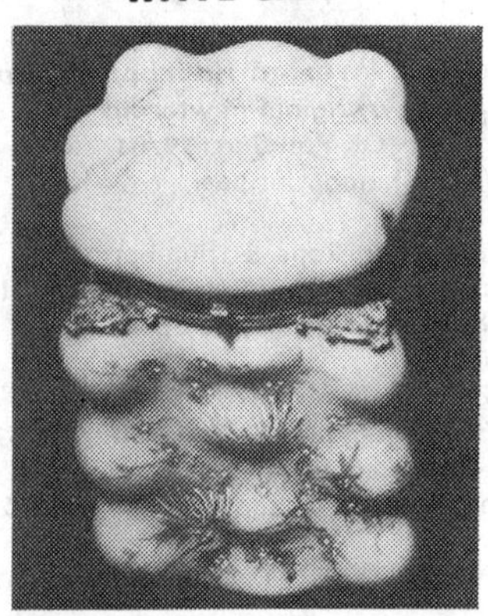

Wave Crest Collars & Cuffs Box

Now much sought after, Wave Crest was produced by the C.F. Monroe Co., Meriden, Conn., in the late 19th and early 20th centuries from opaque white glass blown into molds. It was then hand-decorated in enamels and metal trims were often added. Boudoir accessories such as jewel boxes, hair receivers, etc., were predominant. Also see KELVA and NAKARA.

Bowl, 5½" d., footed, Embossed Rococo mold, h.p. cherubs & enameled florals, ormolu rim & foot, signed $310.00
Box w/hinged lid, h.p. scene of house, pond & trees on pale pink ground, original lining, unsigned, 3¾" d., 3" h. 145.00
Box w/hinged lid, Embossed Rococo mold, cupids & florals on pale yellow ground, 5¼" d., 3" h. 500.00
Box w/hinged lid, Egg Crate mold, enameled florals on creamy white ground, ormolu feet, w/lining, signed, 6½" sq., 6½" h. 650.00
Box w/hinged lid, Helmschmied Swirl mold, enameled florals on pale pink ground, w/lining, signed, 7¼" d. 450.00
Cameo box, cov., 8-sided, carved brown, blue & green woodland scene on lid, 9" w., 5¼" h. 1,500.00
Cigarette container, Embossed Rococo mold, enameled florals on creamy white ground, ornate ormolu footed base & rim w/tab handles, 4" h. 325.00
Collars & cuffs box w/hinged lid, Egg Crate mold, "Collars and Cuffs" & h.p. pastel florals on heavenly blue ground, signed, 7" sq. (ILLUS.) 725.00
Cracker jar, 4-sided w/vertical ribbing, Embossed Rococo mold, pink florals on creamy white ground, silver plate rim, cover & bail handle, unsigned, 8¾" h. 250.00
Cracker jar, Egg Crate mold, pink & yellow roses decor, silver plate rim, cover & bail handle 240.00
Dresser box w/hinged lid, Baroque Shell mold, large enameled white daisies & pink & blue florals on sky blue ground, scrolled ormolu feet, beaded collar, original lining, signed, 9½ x 6¼", 5½" h. 1,200.00
Ferner, Egg Crate mold, enameled French blue florals on pale blue ground, ornate ormolu feet & rim, 7" sq. 310.00
Glove box w/hinged lid, Embossed Rococo mold, florals on robin's egg blue ground, ormolu feet, signed, 9½ x 4½", 6" h. 1,150.00
Humidor w/hinged lid, Baroque Shell mold, pink lustre "Cigars" & pink roses outlined in white enameled dots on robin's egg blue ground, signed, 6" h. 495.00
Jardiniere, Embossed Rococo mold, enameled spider chrysanthemums front & Shasta daisies reverse on robin's egg blue ground, beaded ormolu rim, 9" d., 7¼" h. 595.00
Jewelry box w/hinged lid, Helmschmied Swirl mold, enameled florals & beading on soft pink ground, original lining, 6" d. 420.00
Match holder, enameled florals on creamy white ground, ornate ormolu feet, 2" h. 125.00
Memo spindle, enameled violets &

green foliage on domed creamy white base, ormolu trim, unsigned 350.00

Paperweight, domed, pastel florals on white ground, ornate ormolu knob, 3¼" d. 450.00

Wave Crest Photo Receiver

Photo receiver, Egg Crate mold, enameled florals on creamy white ground, beaded ormolu rim, unsigned, 5¾" l., 4¼" h. (ILLUS.) . . . 350.00

Pin tray, Helmschmied Swirl mold, enameled pastel florals, ormolu rim w/handles, signed, 3" d. 125.00

Plaque, h.p. sailboat scene, cobalt blue border, ornate ormolu frame, 11½" 1,400.00

Ring box, cov., h.p. scene w/lake, trees & house, 3" d. 195.00

Salt & pepper shakers w/original pewter tops, "Daisy," squatty enameled lilies of the valley on pastel blue ground, signed & marked "Patented June 2nd, 1891," pr. 285.00

Salt & pepper shakers w/original spiked pewter tops, enameled blue blossoms & green foliage on white shading to blush pink at base, pr. 335.00

Table set: creamer, sugar bowl & spooner; Helmschmied Swirl mold, enameled apple blossoms, 3 pcs. 650.00

Toothpick holder, enameled pansy decoration, ormolu feet & rim, signed 145.00

Vase, 6½" h., overall enameled pink apple blossoms w/purple highlights centering transfer scene of Niagara Falls, ormolu base 425.00

Vase, 8" h., 9" w. across ormolu handles, enameled large petaled flowers, buds & trailing stems on pale lemon yellow shading to pink ground, signed 285.00

Vase, 10¼" h., Embossed Rococo mold, h.p. burgundy & pink florals on shaded yellow ground, ormolu foot, signed 400.00

Vase, 13½" h., Embossed Rococo Spindrift mold, h.p. roses on creamy white ground, ornate ormolu base w/dolphin feet 890.00

WEBB

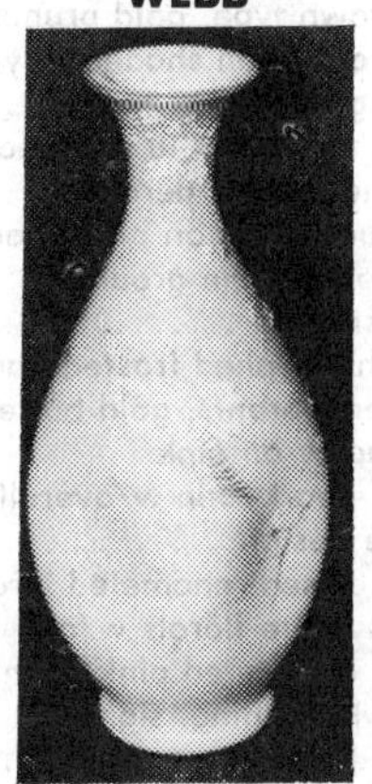

Webb Vase

This glass is made by Thomas Webb & Sons, of Stourbridge, one of England's most prolific glasshouses. Numerous types of glass, including cameo, have been produced by this firm through the years. The company also produced various types of novelty and "art" glass during the late Victorian period.

Bowl-vase, cased, gold prunus blossoms & butterfly on yellow satin ground, gold trim, cream lining, 4¼" d., 3½" h. $295.00

Cameo cologne bottle w/silver top & closure, carved white florals against amber ground 1,250.00

Cameo perfume bottle w/silver screw-on cap, fat round shape, carved white blossoms against blue satin ground, 3½" h. 875.00

Cameo vase, 4½" h., 2¾" d., carved opaque white florals & leaves against rose shaded to amber ground, white top & bottom bands, creamy opaque lining, unsigned 1,575.00

Cameo vase, 6" h., globular, carved coral morning glories against yellow satin ground, white lining . . . 2,150.00

Cameo vase, 8" h., 4" widest d., carved white grape clusters clinging to leafy tendrils & tiny 13-petaled daisies against ruby red ground, signed 3,450.00

Cameo vase, 12" h., carved white florals, bee & butterfly against blue ground 3,200.00

Centerpiece bowl, cased, fluted, folded top, opaque white exterior, blush pink lining, signed, 12" d. . . 225.00

Pitcher, 5½" h., applied frosted handle, scalloped top, gold shaded to white, signed 145.00

Scent bottle w/hallmarked silver screw-on domed monogrammed cap, lay-down type, gold prunus blossoms on green shaded to yellow satin ground, 1¼ x 4¼" 395.00

Vase, 3 3/8" h., 3 1/8" d., ruffled top, enameled bird perched amidst blue florals on pink shaded to vaseline satin ground w/white striping 195.00

Vase, 6¼" h., applied frosted handles w/berry prunts, gold butterflies & tracery on pink mother-of-pearl satin w/overall snowflake design 595.00

Vase, 7" h., cased, enameled birds in flight & white florals w/gilt highlights on shaded pink satin ground, white lining, signed (ILLUS.) 265.00

Vase, 13" h., 7" w. at shoulders, cased, pleated top, four gnarled feet, white enameled butterflies hovering over a branch laden w/leaves & berries on dark mahogany ground, gold & silver highlights, robin's egg blue lining 1,350.00

(End of Glass Section)

GLOBE MAPS

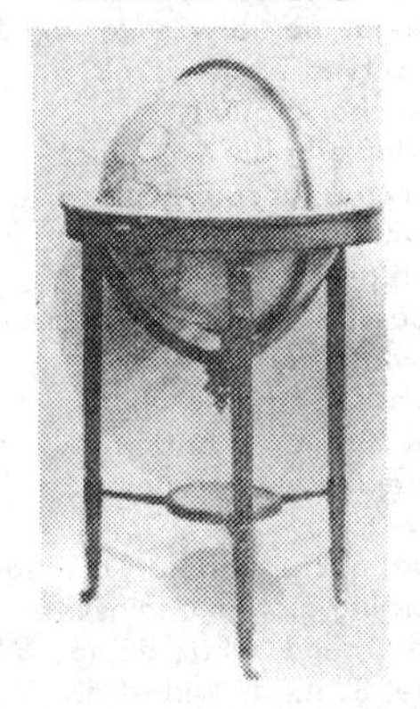

19th Century Terrestrial Globe Map

Celestial globe, floor-standing model, issued by Nevil Maskelyne, early 19th c., on mahogany stand w/reeded legs joined by compass-centered stretcher, 44" h. $6,600.00

Terrestrial globes, engraved ivory, 1¾" d., pr. 770.00

Terrestrial globe, table model, issued by Weber Costello Co., Chicago, on wooden frame w/three short turned legs set on round wooden base, 8¼" h. 105.00

Terrestrial globe, table model, "Newton's New & Improved Terrestrial Globe, London 1836," w/engraved brass circumference ring & raised on wooden stand w/turned legs joined by X-stretcher, 18½" h. 525.00

Terrestrial globe, floor-standing model, issued by Cary of London, 1815, on Regency-style mahogany stand w/three turned, tapered & reeded legs joined by compass-centered stretcher, 28" d. globe, 48" h. (ILLUS.) 5,100.00

GRANITEWARE

Blue & White Graniteware Coffeepot

This is a name given to metal (customarily iron) kitchenwares covered with an enamel coating. Featured at the 1876 Philadelphia Centennial Exposition, it became quite popular for it was lightweight, attractive, and easy to clean. Although it was made in huge quantities and is still produced, it has caught the attention of a young generation of collectors and prices have steadily risen over the past five years. There continues to be a consistent demand for the wide variety of these utilitarian articles turned out earlier in this century and rare forms now command high prices.

Baby bottle warmer, electric-type, grey & white speckled $55.00

Basin, blue & white speckled 10.00
Beer bucket, cov., grey 49.00
Berry bucket w/lid & bail handle, blue & white marbleized, 7½" 72.00
Berry bucket w/lid & bail handle, brown & white marbleized 135.00
Cake pan, Chrysolite (dark green w/white swirls) 38.00
Cake pan, tube-type, octagonal, grey mottled, "L & G" label, Lalance and Grosjean Mfg. Co., Woodhaven, New York 28.00
Candleholder, blue & white marbleized 115.00
Canister, cov., "Tea," blue, 5¾" d., 5½" h. 52.00
Casserole dish, cov., cobalt blue & white marbleized................ 45.00
Chamber pot, cov., blue & white marbleized 72.00
Coffee boiler, cov., blue & white marbleized 70.00
Coffee boiler, cov., turquoise & white marbleized................ 42.50
Coffee cup, blue & white marbleized 26.00
Coffeepot, cov., gooseneck spout, blue & white marbleized, 9" h. (ILLUS.) 55.00
Coffeepot, cov., gooseneck spout, brown & white marbleized 90.00
Coffeepot, cov., white w/colorful mill scene on two sides, pewter trim 195.00
Coffee set: 10¼" h. cov. coffeepot, 6½" h. creamer & 8¼" h. cov. sugar bowl; spray of oak leaves, acorns, maple leaf & fern decor on white ground, silver plate spout, lids & handles w/copper bandings & base rim, ca. 1880, 3 pcs. 225.00
Colander, blue & white marbleized, large 175.00
Colander, footed, handled, orange mottled w/blue trim 45.00
Cream can, blue & white marbleized 90.00
Cream can w/tin lid, grey mottled .. 50.00
Creamer, bulbous, grey mottled, 3½" h. 53.00
Cup, green & white marbleized 20.00
Cuspidor, grey mottled, marked "Agate Ware" 22.00
Dipper w/long handle, grey mottled 12.00
Double boiler, angled sides, Chrysolite 92.50
Fish boiler, grey mottled 55.00
Flask, grey mottled................ 70.00
Food mold, Turk's turban, grey mottled, marked "L & G" 45.00
Frying pan, cobalt blue & white marbleized, small 90.00
Funnel, blue & white mottled, 7" d. 35.00
Grater, grey mottled, miniature 125.00
Ham boiler, w/drain insert, grey mottled, large 118.00

Graniteware Kettle

Kettle, cov., w/wire bail handle, dark brown & white marbleized, 8½" d., 7" h. (ILLUS.) 65.00
Kettle, cov., 2-handled, green speckled, 6 qt. 18.00
Liquid measure, grey mottled, 1 gal. 45.00
Lunch box, turquoise & white marbleized, oval 190.00
Milk can w/lid & bail, grey mottled, 1 gal. 45.00
Milk cooling basin, Chrysolite (dark green w/white swirls), 12" d. 15.00
Muffin pan, 8-cup, iris blue & white mottled 75.00
Muffin pan, fluted, 12-cup, grey mottled 45.00
Mug, cobalt blue & white marbleized, miniature, 1" d., 1" h. ... 140.00
Mug, turquoise & white marbleized 12.00
Mustard pot, cov., w/ladle, white, ladle 4½" l., pot 3½" h., the set 78.00
Pie pan, blue & white marbleized ... 20.00
Pie pan, Chrysolite, 8¾" d. (tiny chip) 25.00
Pitcher, water, grey mottled, 10½" h. 36.00
Pitcher, robin's egg blue, 16" h. 85.00
Pitcher, child's, blue mottled 22.00
Roaster, blue & white marbleized, large......................... 40.00
Salt box, hanging-type, brown...... 45.00
Salt box w/hinged wooden lid, hanging-type, white, early 1900's 75.00
Sauce pan, green speckled, 9" d. ... 20.00
Sauce pan, turquoise & white marbleized, 1 qt. 30.00
Soap dish, hanging-type, blue & white marbleized................ 45.00

Soap dish, w/drain insert, high back, ornate, sky blue, 10" h. 50.00
Spatula, pierced, blue & white speckled 58.00
Tea kettle, blue swirl over heavy cast iron, pit bottom, swing lid marked "Wrought Iron Range Co., St. Louis, Mo.," premium given for purchase of kitchen stove 80.00
Tea kettle, turquoise & white marbleized 185.00
Teapot, cov., blue w/pewter trim, marked "Manning-Bowman" 45.00
Teapot, cov., gooseneck spout, buff w/green trim, small 18.00
Teapot, cov., florals on beige, embossed pewter handle, spout & lid w/finial, English 225.00
Tea strainer, turquoise & white marbleized 175.00
Wash basin, two-handled, brown & white marbleized 55.00
Wash basin, grey mottled 20.00
Washboard, wooden frame w/cobalt blue corrugated scrubbing surface, marked "Imperial" 75.00
Water cooler w/lid & brass spigot, grey mottled, 5 gal. 225.00
Whiskey flask, grey mottled 85.00

GREENAWAY (Kate) ITEMS

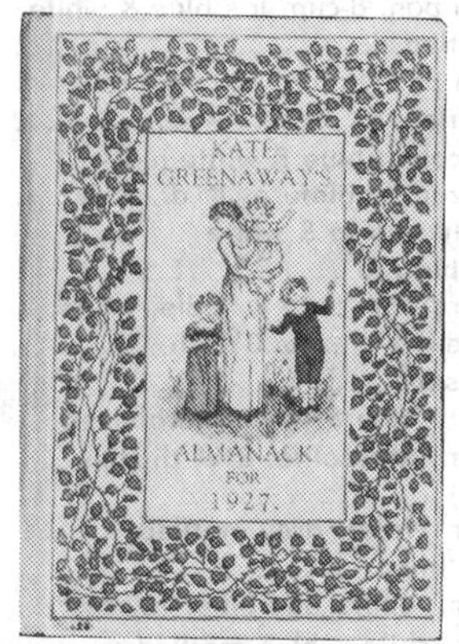

Almanac for 1927

Numerous objects in pottery, porcelain, glass and other materials were made in or with the likenesses of the appealing children created by the famous 19th century English artist, Kate Greenaway. These are now eagerly sought along with the original Greenaway books.

Almanac for 1927 (ILLUS.) $40.00
Book, "Babies' Book," linen cover, published by Saalfield, illustrated by Kate Greenaway 45.00
Book, "Chatterbox Hall," illustrated by Kate Greenaway, 1884 (few loose pages) 35.00
Book, "Kate Greenaway's Birthday Book for Children," verses by Mrs. Sale Barker, illustrated by Kate Greenaway, 1880, 4 x 4" 95.00
Book, "Marigold Gardens," engraved by Edmond Evans, published by Frederick Warne & Co., London, illustrated by Kate Greenaway, 1880's 125.00
Tea set: cov. teapot, cov. sugar bowl, creamer, four cups & six tea plates; blue & white Kate Greenaway scenes, Staffordshire, 13 pcs. (no saucers) 245.00
Toothpick holder, clear glass, two little girls sitting beside basket for toothpicks 95.00

GUTMANN ARTWORK

"Good Morning"

This American artist, Bessie Pease Gutmann (1876-1960), is noted for her illustrations in baby's and children's books and for her published art prints which won acclaim not only in the United States, but in Canada, Europe, Japan and Australia as well. Often her subjects were her own children, nieces or nephews. The most famous of these prints, "A Little Bit of Heaven" and "Awakening" (depicting infants asleep and awake), were published in 1916 and 1918, respectively. Prints entitled "In Disgrace" and "The Reward" (depicting a child and puppy standing in the corner and a child sharing an ice cream cone with her puppy) became record sellers as a pair of matched prints during 1935-36.

Print, "Awakening," 1918, 14 x 21", framed $55.00
Print, "Bedtime Story" (The), 1923, 14 x 21" 75.00
Print, "Bride" (The), 1913, 10½ x 15½", original Art Nouveau frame 40.00
Print, "Butterfly" (The), 1912, 15 x 19", original frame 65.00
Print, "Contentment," 1929, 8 x 10", framed & matted 45.00
Print, "Friendly Enemies," 1937, 11 x 14", framed & matted .....55.00 to 68.00
Print, "Good Morning," 1940, 11 x 14," framed & matted (ILLUS.) 68.00
Print, "His Majesty," 1913, 15 x 19" 37.00
Print, "In Disgrace," 1935, 14 x 18" 32.00
Print, "Little Bit of Heaven" (A), 1916, 14 x 21", original frame ....50.00 to 65.00
Print, "Lullaby" (The), 1949, 14 x 21" 45.00
Print, "Message of the Roses" (The), 1915, 14 x 21" 135.00
Print, "Mischief," 1907, 9 x 12", framed 85.00
Print, "My Baby," 1952, 11 x 14", framed & matted 68.00
Print, "Nitey-Nite," 1952, 13 x 17" .. 30.00
Print, "On Dreamland's Border," 1921, 14 x 17½", original frame ....45.00 to 55.00
Print, "On the Up & Up," toddler followed up stairway by pup, 1938, 14 x 21" 65.00
Print, "Reward" (The), 1936, 14 x 21" 45.00
Print, "Rosebud," 1926, 14 x 21", framed 65.00
Print, "Symphony," 1921, 14 x 21" .. 165.00
Print, "Television," 1949, 11 x 14", framed & matted 68.00
Print, "To Love and to Cherish," 1911, 15 x 13" ....125.00 to 175.00

HATPIN HOLDERS

Austrian china, h.p. roses w/gold top $55.00
Belleek china, gold paste decoration, Willets 55.00
Belleek china, h.p. "E" & floral decoration, Willets 65.00
Bisque, Art Nouveau style ladies' faces, lavender 175.00
China, figural bust, king's face on one side, queen's face on other .. 300.00
China, h.p. rose on black ground, unsigned 40.00
China, tiny pink florals on tan ground, unsigned 50.00
Geisha Girl china, decorated w/figure of a Geisha Girl 45.00
Limoges china, cream ground, gold embossed border 65.00
Nippon china, h.p. pink roses w/gold trim, 4" h. 45.00
Nippon china, h.p. Washington, D.C. Capitol Building, ornate beading top & base, 5" h. 35.00
Pickard china, h.p. violets 125.00
Royal Bayreuth china, Rose Tapestry patt., pale green ground w/pink roses decoration, w/gold 395.00
Royal Doulton china, figural Dickensware "Sam Weller," typical earth tone colors, 2" diameter flaring to 4" base, 6" h. 250.00

R.S. Germany Hatpin Holder

R.S. Germany china, waisted cylinder w/concave pierced top, single flower decoration, 4½" h. (ILLUS.) 50.00
R.S. Germany china, blue forget-me-not decoration 85.00
R.S. Prussia china, roses, lustre finish, scalloped base, 4¾" h. 235.00
R.S. Prussia china, portrait of standing young girl in yellow dress & hat w/pink roses, small pink roses all around, embossed mold & scalloped top & bottom, 5" h. .. 450.00
R.S. Prussia china, six-sided, bluebirds scene 275.00
Schafer & Vater china, pink bisque lady w/fan 185.00
Torquay pottery, footed, h.p. rooster decoration w/"Keep Me on the Dressing Table," 5" h. 85.00

HATPINS

Advertising, "The Malleable Steel Range Mfg. Co., South Bend, Ind." $25.00
Aquamarine glass 24.00
Brass, openwork, concave oval at top w/engraving around, 1 x ¾" top, 9" l. 14.00
Brass, lacy openwork, large rhinestones on domed 1¼" top, 10½" l. 30.00
Brass, figural owl 37.50
Brass, Oriental design 12.50
Carnival glass, figural flying bat, black w/silver lustre 32.00
China, relief-molded pink flowers 35.00
Gold, 18k, hand-made wire flowers, 1852, 4½" l. 335.00
Gold-filled, green stone 15.00
Gold-filled w/gilt crown & monogram, fob style, 7½" l. 35.00
Jet, large 16.00
Mother-of-pearl, 2" d. top 16.75
Rhinestones & pink stones in swirled design, 2" d. top 12.00
Rhinestones in triangular frame w/filigree border, Austria, 12¼" l. 135.00
Sterling silver, figural bear standing by tree 125.00
Sterling silver, figural cherub, ¾" d. top 49.00
Sterling silver, figural owl, ¾" d. top 89.00

HEINTZ ART WARES

Beginning in 1915 the Heintz Art Metal shop of Buffalo, New York began producing an interesting line of jewelry and decorative items, especially vases and desk accessories, in brass, bronze, copper and silver. Their distinctive brass and bronze wares overlayed with sterling silver Art Nouveau and Art Deco designs are much sought after today. Collectors eagerly search for pieces bearing their stamped mark consisting of a diamond surrounding the initials "HAMS." Around 1935 the firm became Heintz Brothers, Manufacturers.

Ashtray, copper w/sterling overlay in Art Deco style $46.00
Book ends, bronze w/sterling overlay, monogram "U," pr. 42.00
Bowl, bronze w/sterling overlay, 9" d. 130.00
Box w/hinged lid, bronze w/sterling overlay of two Art Deco style birds on lid, green patina, cedar lining, signed, 3¼ x 4" 95.00
Calendar-letter rack combination, bronze w/sterling overlay 55.00
Candlesticks, bronze w/sterling overlay, 12" h., pr. 140.00
Desk set: letter caddy, calendar & inkwell; bronze w/sterling overlay of pussy willows, 3 pcs. 125.00
Inkwell, cov., oval, bronze w/sterling overlay, glass insert, marked & numbered "1165," 4" w., 2½" h. 95.00
Smoker set, bronze w/sterling overlay, 4 pcs. 140.00
Vase, bronze w/sterling overlay of swirling iris, 4½" h. 68.00
Vase, bronze w/sterling overlay of large rose w/stem & leaves, 5" h. 95.00
Vase, bronze w/sterling overlay, marked & numbered "3763," 6¾" h. 60.00
Vase, bronze w/sterling overlay in Art Deco designs, 8" h. 145.00
Vase, bronze w/sterling overlay of grape leaves, 10" h. 75.00
Vase, 2-handled, bronze w/sterling overlay of golfer 245.00

HOOKED & NEEDLEWORK RUGS

Cheetah Hooked Rug

A true form of American folk art, hooked rugs have caught the attention of numerous collectors. It is believed this rug-making technique (pulling yarn or fabric strips through a woven fabric background) originated in America. Jute burlap (gunny-sacking) provides the ideal background material and after this fabric was brought out around the 1850's, rug hooking became quite a vogue. It provided the opportunity to thriftily use up leftover burlap sacks and the remains of discarded clothing to produce attractive floor coverings. Geometric and floral design rugs are the most common while animals, houses, figures, landscapes and ships are scarcer. Bold colorful, original designs are most appealing to collectors, but those hooked on stamped burlap patterns, even during the 20th century, are also avidly sought.

American Eagle in flight holding arrows w/feet, stars in background, 23 x 35" $385.00
Basket of colored flowers in center on dark grey-green ground, pink & yellow florals at each end, early 20th c., 27 x 41" 295.00
Cat reclining on an ottoman, black & orange calico animal on beige ground w/foliate scrolls in shades of salmon pink, maroon & olive green, 28 x 44½" (wear & repair) 225.00
Checkerboard pattern w/floral design in each square, rich colors, 35 x 87" 325.00
Cheetah, crouching figure of cat against dark ground, border pattern of leafy scrolls, good overall condition (ILLUS.) 797.50
Chickens (2 large & 2 small) in faded colors on black ground, 27 x 40" (edges frayed) 160.00
Deer leaping, brown animal against salmon, grey, green, black, blue & beige abstract ground, yarn stitched binding, 24 x 38" 85.00
Deer recumbent, antlered stag at center framed by pointed trees (2 large, 2 small), two stars & round moon, good colors, 25 x 40" (minor fading) 700.00

Hooked Rug with Flowers & Vines

Flowers & vines, group of three rose sprigs across the center framed by undulating flowering vines, shades of red, yellow, blue & pink on pale blue ground, 19th c., 26 x 62½" (ILLUS.) 3,300.00
Heart, stars & leaf scrolls, red, pink, white & olive gold on grey ground, 31½ x 43" (wear & repair) 95.00
Horse running, red animal w/saddle & reins on black ground w/grey, orange, blue, brown & purple flowers & foliage w/a butterfly in each upper corner, within narrow border of multicolored blocks, 30 x 53" 600.00
Lion, tan w/blue eye, outlined in black, on a neutral ground, early 20th c., 24 x 40" 247.50

HORSE & BUGGY COLLECTIBLES

Iron Dog Hitching Post

Blacksmith's carry-all, wooden, scalloped sides, divided interior, turned handles, old red paint, 8 x 28¾" $95.00
Bridle, Indian-type, leather & horsehair (two breaks) 75.00
Bridle, military-type, blinders w/brass "U.S." 75.00
Bridle, rolled leather w/glass rosettes, Victorian 25.00
Bridle rosette, brass w/iron star in center, "Texas Rangers" 150.00
Buggy steps, cast iron, pr. 15.00
Driving lamp, one red & one clear lens, kerosene burner, wire bail, Rayo, 10½" h. 65.00
Hitching post, cast iron, jockey w/removable top hat, traces of old polychrome paint, 26" h. (ring missing) 125.00
Hitching post, cast iron, model of a Mastiff dog's head, mounted on squared stepped wooden platform painted grey, 19th c., overall 11" h. 302.50
Hitching post, cast iron, model of seated dog w/molded fur, rectangular base, ca. 1850, overall 35½" h. (ILLUS.) 4,950.00
Hoof trimmer, cast iron, w/handles, 12" 5.00
Horse bit, cast iron, England 20.00
Horse bit, medicine-type 135.00

Horse brass, round scalloped shape w/pierce-cut rayed heart in center, England, 3½" d. 95.00
Horse brasses, hearts, shield & crescent moon on original shaped leather strap, ca. 1840, 11" l. 85.00
Horse brush, soft leather, monogrammed 15.00
Horse collar, leather 15.00
Horse comb, marked "Oliver Slant Tooth" 6.00
Horse sling, canvas, complete 115.00
Horsetail fly whisk, bay color, hewn wood handle 45.00
Horse tooth rasp 15.00
Lap robe, horse hide w/mohair backing 80.00
Lap robe, wool, lady in red on white horse (moth holes) 55.00
Pony bridle blinders, studded, pr.... 85.00
Saddle, cowboy-type, tooled leather, w/name, 1860 to 1870 .... 275.00
Saddle, plantation-type, "Clark" 225.00
Saddle, woman's, side-saddle type, hand-tooled leather w/worn carpet seat, small, 11" l. 165.00
Saddle, woman's, side-saddle type, hand-tooled leather 249.00
Saddle, wooden horn & seat, Mexican 150.00
Shoulder drops, leather & brass, 4' l., 6" w. 300.00
Spurs, brass & leather strap, Maltese Cross on sides w/sprig of leaves growing down & up from it, pointed, 1½" across, pr. 75.00
Stirrup, hand-forged iron, pony saddle size, one-piece w/ring for strap at top & open figural heart foot rest 45.00
Vehicle, buckboard, child-size, two spring seats, doubletree, tongue, neck yoke, painted red, white & blue 800.00

Early Express Wagon

Vehicle, express coach, leather roof & roll-down sides, marked "U.S. Mail - Washington & Maybert - Express," built by Abbott & Downing (ILLUS.) 12,000.00
Vehicle, hunting trap, four-wheel carriage w/rear wheels larger than front wheels, open seats on high body, two-tongue (one w/lead bars), black w/burgundy trim 8,500.00
Vehicle, jaunting cart, open one-horse style, carries seven passengers, Irish 2,500.00
Vehicle, mail wagon, government issue, windows, lights, doubletree, tongue, neck yoke & wheels 1,500.00
Vehicle, spring wagon, doubletree, tongue, neck yoke, wheels, leather seats, Velie Carriage Co., Moline, Ill., 1906 .... 2,700.00
Vehicle, surrey, doubletree, tongue, neck yoke, lights, leather seats .. 3,000.00
Wagon jack, wood & iron, worn red paint on base, stamped name & engraved date, "P. Shaeffer, 1794," 20" h. (crank old replacement) 150.00
Whip rack, marked "Reed's," pat. 1883 .... 35.00

HOUSEHOLD APPLIANCES

Labor saving devices for the housewife as well as appliances to improve the quality of life of the American family began to proliferate in the 19th century. The introduction of electricity helped expand the field even more and today early appliances, especially electric models, are increasingly collectible. Many serious collectors search for early fans and toasters in particular, but old coffee makers, steam irons and vacuum cleaners also have dedicated enthusiasts.

Electric fan, Emerson, ceiling-type, w/original blades, 1920's $200.00
Electric fan, General Electric "Whiz" model, brass blades, 10" d. 27.00
Electric fan, General Electric, oscillating-type w/brass blades, 13" d. 35.00
Electric fan, A.C. Gilbert "Polar Cub" model, 6" 60.00
Electric fan, "Manhattan No. 3," battery-operated 300.00
Electric fan, Singer "Ribbonaire" model 125.00
Electric fan, "Super Blueline," brass blades, 8" 30.00
Electric fan, Western Electric "Hawthorn Victor Vane" flag fan, 16" brass blades 350.00

Electric fan, Westinghouse, iron base, w/blade guard, 6 x 15" 12.00
Electric toaster, Cookenette 17.50
Electric toaster, Hotpoint, Art Deco style 28.00
Electric toaster, "Super Electric," Art Deco style 18.00
Electric toaster, "Toastmaker," Art Deco style w/chrome finish 25.00
Vacuum cleaner, hand-pump type, Regina Model A, 1903 .... 150.00

ICART PRINTS

Elephants

The works of Louis Icart, the successful French artist whose working years spanned the Art Nouveau and Art Deco movements, first became popular in the United States shortly after World War I. His limited edition etchings were much in vogue during those years that the fashion trends were established in Paris. These prints were later relegated to closet shelves and basements but they have now re-entered the art market and are avidly sought by collectors. Listed by their American titles, those appearing below have been sold within the past eighteen months.

Alms, 1926, 17½ x 13" $880.00
Angry Steed, 1917, 16¼ x 10¼" ...1,650.00
Autumn Leaves, 1926, 21 x 16¾" ...1,430.00
Backstage, 11½ x 8¼" 990.00
Black Fan, 1931, 21 x 16" oval (repair) 990.00
Casanova, 1928, 14 x 21" 1,100.00
Cat and Mouse, 1920, 8¾ x 11" 1,100.00
Chestnut Vendor, 1928, 14 x 19" ...1,210.00
Choice Morsel, 1927, 18¼ x 13¾" .. 935.00
Cinderella, 1927, 14½ x 18¼" oval 1,100.00
Conchita, 1929, 14 x 21" ....1,300.00 to 1,700.00
Confidence (The), 1926, 20½ x 16" 1,210.00
Coursing III, 1930, 26 x 16" 5,225.00
Cuddling, 1926, 11½ x 16¾" 990.00
Dalila, 1929, 13½ x 20½" 880.00
Don Juan, 1928, 14 x 21" 1,100.00
Elephants, 1925, 11½ x 16½" (ILLUS.) 1,650.00
Embrace (The), 14 x 17" oval 990.00
Eve, 1928, 19½ x 14" oval ....1,000.00 to 1,800.00
Fair Dancer, 1939, 22 x 19" 1,210.00
Fair Model, 1937, 11 x 18½" 2,800.00
Faust, 1928, 13 x 21" 1,540.00
Flower Seller, 1928, 14 x 19" 1,340.00
Fluttering Butterfly, 1936, 7 x 9" ...6,050.00
Forsythia, 1926, 19¼ x 15½" 1,870.00
Four Dears, Tamed Hind, 1929, 15 x 21" ....1,300.00 to 1,500.00
French Quadrille, 1935, 16½ x 25" 6,050.00
Gay Senorita, 1939, 21½ x 18¼" ...1,320.00
Gossip, 1926, 13 x 16½" oval 900.00
Hiding Place (The), 1927, 14½ x 18" ....700.00 to 1,000.00
Intimacy, The Green Screen, 1928, 18 x 16" 1,650.00
Joy of Life, 1929, 15 x 23½" 3,025.00
Lady of the Camelias, 1927, 24¼ x 16½" oval ....550.00 to 750.00
Letter (The), original print, ca. 1928 .... 250.00
Little Book (The), 1925, 13¼ x 17½" 1,045.00
Lovers (The), 1930, 14 x 21" 1,210.00
Madame Butterfly, 1927, 21 x 14" ..1,320.00
Manon, 1927, 13 x 20" 1,100.00
Mardi Gras, 1936, 18½ x 18½" 4,675.00
Martini, 1932, 13¼ x 17¼" 4,400.00
Mimi, 1927, 13 x 20" 990.00
Mimi Pinson, 1927, 20½ x 13½" ...5,060.00
Morning Cup, 1940, 17½ x 19½" ...2,475.00
Musetta, 1927, 13 x 20" 750.00
Open Cage (The), 1926, 13 x 17" oval 1,210.00
Orange Seller, 1929, 14 x 19" oval .. 990.00
Orchids, 1937, 19½ x 28" 3,520.00
Peacock (The), 1925, 15 x 18½" (ILLUS. top next page) 1,980.00
Peonies, 1935, 11 x 8½" 1,210.00
Poem (The), 1928, 22 x 18" 5,500.00
Recollections, 1928, 17 x 12" 1,760.00
Red Cage (The), 1928, 11¾ x 9¼" .. 770.00
Sleeping Beauty, 1927, 19½ x 15½" oval 1,485.00
Smoke, 1926, 20 x 15" 1,760.00
Speed, 1933, 25 x 15½" 2,750.00
Swallows, 1926, 19¼ x 11½" 1,540.00

The Peacock

Unmasked, 1933, 8½ x 13" 1,210.00
White Underwear, 1925, 19 x 15" . . 1,100.00
Wisteria, 1940, 21 x 17½" 2,420.00
Woman in the Wings, 1936,
9 x 7" 6,600.00
Wounded Dove, 1929, 21 x 16¾"
oval . . . . 1,000.00 to 1,760.00

ICE CREAM SCOOPS & SERVERS

During the past decade, the ice cream scoop and ice cream server have become very popular with a growing number of collectors and prices have soared. While the nickel-plated brass scoop with a lever-operated blade that eases the ball-shaped scoop of ice cream from the server seems to be the most popular, there is also interest in the earlier cone-shaped tin scoops and in pewter or aluminum servers. Collectors can select a scoop that served up a small penny-size ice cream cone, a larger nickel-size cone, or a square slice for an ice cream sandwich.

"Benedict Indestructo No. 4," nickel-plated brass, wooden handle, 1920's, 10" l. $42.00
"Benedict Indestructo No. 20," Bakelite handle 30.00
"Cake Cone Co. - Rainbow Ice Cream Dispenser, St. Louis, Mo.," ice cream slice for ice cream sandwiches, brass, 9" l. 225.00
"V. Clad Co. - Philadelphia, Pa.," conical bowl, steel w/tubular steel handle, 1876 patent, 8½" l. 30.00
"Dover Mfg. Co.," No. 20, right-left handed, nickel-plated brass, 1920's . . . . 75.00 to 100.00
"Fisher - Made in Canada, Orillia, On.," nickel-plated brass, wooden handle, 10¼" l. 22.00
"Gilchrist No. 30," size 12, nickel-plated brass, metal squeeze handle, 10½" l. 48.00
"Gilchrist No. 30," size 20, nickel-plated brass, metal squeeze handle, 10½" l. 32.00
"Gilchrist No. 31," size 6, nickel-plated brass, wooden handle, 11" l. 50.00
"Gilchrist No. 31," size 10, nickel-plated brass, wooden handle, 11" l. 35.00
"Gilchrist No. 31," size 16 or 24, nickel-plated brass, wooden handle, 11" l., each 25.00
"Hamilton Beach Disher No. 40," size 16, chromium-plated brass, wooden handles, 1930's, 10" l. . . . 22.00
"ICYPI - Automatic Cone Co., Cambridge, Mass.," nickel-plated brass, wooden handle, ca. 1924-30, 10" l. 125.00
"New Gem, Newark, N.J., Made in U.S.A.," nickel-plated brass, wooden handle, ca. 1932-40, 10½" l. 20.00
"Perfection Equipment Co., Kansas City, Mo.," cylinder-type, nickel-plated brass, ca. 1933, 8½" l. 400.00
"The 'Polar Pak' Disher - Made by Phila. Ice Cream Cone Machinery Co., Phila., Pa.," ice cream slice for ice cream sandwiches, nickel-plated brass, wooden handle, ca. 1932, 10½" l. 250.00

ICONS

Icon is the Latin word meaning likeness or image and is applied to small pictures meant to be hung on the iconostasis, a screen dividing the sanctuary from the main body of Eastern Orthodox Churches. Examples may be found all over Europe. The Greek, Russian and other Orthodox churches developed their own styles, but the Russian contribution to this form of art is considered outstanding.

Christ Pantocrater, the Savior holding open Book of Gospels in His left hand & w/His right hand raised in blessing, silver & enamel okhlad, Ovchinnikov, Russia, 1893, 10½ x 12½" $2,750.00

The Holy Visage, silver-gilt & shaded enamel okhlad, Cyrillic maker's mark "N.G.," Moscow, Russia, ca. 1910, 10½ x 12¼" 3,025.00

Iverskaya Mother of God, silver-gilt okhlad, crown set w/"jewels" & w/seed pearl robes set w/simulated diamonds, Khlebnikov, Moscow, Russia, 1877, 11½ x 18¼" . .4,400.00

Kazan Mother of God, rectangular wood panel painted in tones of red, brown, black & gilt, border w/two saints, Russian, 19th c., 12 x 14" (panel cradled) 660.00

Tichvin Mother of God

Tichvin Mother of God, finely chased silver-gilt okhlad, the border repousse & chased w/fruiting vine, St. Petersburg, Russia, 1814, 10½ x 12½" (ILLUS.) 2,640.00

Triptych, central panel painted w/a male saint, the wings w/Ss. Nicholas & Barbara, silver borders chased w/scrolling foliage, the doors also chased w/foliage & a cross, Ivan Khlebnikov, Moscow, Russia, ca. 1910, 7 1/8" h. 3,520.00

The Virgin, holding a scroll in both hands, painted in tones of red, gilt, green, white & umber, silver plate okhlad, Russian, 19th c., 10½ x 12 7/8" 495.00

INDIAN ARTIFACTS & JEWELRY

Agency voucher, from Oregon, signed by Indian Chief Horolish Wampo with an "X," 1870. . . . .$165.00

Amulet, Central Plains, umbilical cord, lozenge-shaped, beaded in blue, green & red on white, sinew-sewn, ca. 1870, 5" l. 205.00

Axe, trade-type, iron, touchmarked on both sides w/three circles w/raised cross, 17th c., 7½" l. . . . 150.00

Bag, Nez Perce, cornhusk, woven w/polychrome aniline dye design of trees & flowers one side & geometric motif reverse, 17½ x 13¼" (minor wear in bottom corners). . . 175.00

Ball-head club, Eastern Plains, wooden, incised animals & teepees on shaft 4,950.00

Basket, Pomo, boat-shaped one rod coil treasure-type, stepped triangular design in redbud, excellent condition, 4½ x 7½", 2" h. 375.00

Basket, White Mountain Apache, large round shape w/dark radiating design on natural, ca. 1885, 14" d., 4" h. (minor wear) 750.00

Basket, Yokuts, bottleneck form w/flared sides to flat shoulder, design of alternating men & women around middle, shoulder trimmed w/yarn fringe & remnants of quail topknots, 7" d., 4½" h. (minor wear to yarn). 2,650.00

Blanket, Cayuse, car lap robe w/cloth label reading "Pendleton Woolen Mills," late 1920's, 60 x 66" 95.00

Blanket, child's, Navajo, woven in handspun wool, red, indigo & ivory stripes & zigzags 9,350.00

Bottle, Tlinglit, basketry-covered, elongated gourd shape, finely woven w/sea wolf design & flowers, faded aniline colors, mid-19th c., 10½" h. 625.00

Bowl, Yokuts, basketry, large flaring shape w/classic rattlesnake design in redbud & martynia, excellent condition, 15" d., 6" h. 1,150.00

Bowl, Hopi, pottery, umber & red ochre geometric design on smoky buff slip, ca. 1920, 7¾" d., 3½" h. 150.00

Bowl, Northwest Coast, wooden, carved w/facing eagles at each end, wing details on sides, mellow patina, 15¾" l., 4" h. 425.00

Brooches, Iroquois, German silver, set of four in the Masonic (Council fire) design, stamping & rouletting, 1 7/8 to 2" l., the set 325.00

Bucket, Upper Missouri River area, rawhide leather, stretched & laced over top & bottom bentwood rim, 18" d., 12½" h. 155.00

Club-whip, Blackfoot, dog soldier style, club stained black w/brass tack decoration, one side incised w/carved figures of a man, stained red ochre, & a light brown horse w/brass tack eye, other side carved w/incised figure of a horse, stained red ochre, fine old patina, 21½" l. (one tab reattached) 2,500.00

Concho belt, Navajo, silver, link construction, alternating oval & butterfly-shaped conchos w/stamped design, 32½" l. 230.00

Cradleboard, Eastern Woodland, rounded backboard tapering to squared base, crocheted ribbon wrapping, footrest & perimeter w/brass tack decoration, painted face of Indian baby added to upper backboard, ca. 1870, 26" l. (age cracks) 325.00

Sioux Beaded Cradle Cover

Cradle cover, Sioux, beaded hide w/diamond patterns on dark ground (ILLUS.) 3,190.00

Doll, Sioux, leather head & body, dressed in long dress w/nice fringe detailing w/beaded yoke & bands in light & dark blue, red, green & white beads, 20" h. (hair missing, hole worn in leather at side of head) 950.00

Dress, girl's, Osage, deerskin w/intricate designs worked in beading & sequins, ca. 1870, size 2. . . . . . .1,500.00

Dress, Plains, white smoked elkhide w/large red & blue beads around neck & down shoulder seam, bands of blue & black cut glass tube beads alternating w/elk teeth across bodice & back, beaded fringe & blue & red felt ornaments on skirt, 50" l. 725.00

Drum, Plains, double-faced style w/fine painted geometric designs on each side in red, yellow, green & purple, brass bells & feather attachments, 12" d. (small stain & split in leather at rim) 225.00

Gorget, trade silver, round concave disk w/engraved central star & border, stamped "NV" for silversmith, American or Canadian, late 18th or early 19th century, 4 1/16" d. (one button suspension missing, cracked through center, edge chip) 800.00

Jacket, Plains, beaded hide, beaded elk on front in gold & blue beads w/white beaded antlers, warriors beaded in light & dark blue, white & red white-heart beads, pockets quilled in red & orange, back beading in red white-heart, light & dark blue, green, yellow & white w/a few metallic beads dating around 1890, beaded band around edges in green, yellow, blue & red white-heart bands, fringed at all seams, 34" l. (few loose beads, 1" back split) 2,600.00

Jar, Acoma, pottery, flattened ovoid form w/red-orange & umber design on white slip over dark red bottle bottom, ca. 1930, 6" d., 4" h. 85.00

Jar, Zuni, redware, umber curvilinear design w/deer in medallions around top & medallions of arrow designs around body, red ochre accents, ca. 1910, 8½" d., 9½" h. (worn slip & minor repairs) 500.00

Knife sheath, Northern Plains (Crow), beaded leather, sinew sewn w/dark blue, greens & red beading on sky blue ground, tin dangles, w/bone handled steel knife, 10" l. sheath plus 9" l. beaded dangle, 12½" l. knife, two pcs. 550.00

Mask, Iroquois (Seneca), carved wood, false face type w/classic curing ritual smiling face in dark red w/tin eye plates, five hole attachments, fine old patina, four tiny cloth pouches containing sacred Indian tobacco, 10¼" l., 6¼" w., plus horsehair hair 2,900.00

Moccasins, Sioux, burial-type, fully beaded, including soles, red, white, blue, gold & yellow beadwork in beautiful design, pr. 995.00

Moccasins w/attached leggings, Sioux, woman's, beaded hide, finely beaded in blue, dark blue, red & green on white, sinew sewn, leather colored w/yellow-ochre, 10" l., 18" h., pr. 1,050.00

Mukluks, Eskimo, seal fur decorated w/red trade cloth & beads, red &

indigo yarn & wild mink fur, sea grass insulation, wolverine fur insole, w/tassels & binding, 11" l. sole, 16" h., pr. 500.00

Necklace, Southwest, shell, three strands of rolled beads w/pieces of turquoise & shell interspersed w/incised silver crosses, 27" l. 225.00

Peace medal of President Andrew Johnson, silver, 62mm diameter 7,480.00

Pipe bag, Sioux, beaded leather, sinew sewn, dark & light blue, yellow, red & green geometric beaded design on white ground, red, yellow & faded blue quilled slat band w/red & gold Germantown yarn tin cone tassels, 19th c., excellent condition, 26" l. 900.00

Pipe bowl & stem, Eastern Woodlands (Ojibwa), Catlinite stone, twisted stem w/one side stained green, Catlinite bowl inlaid w/pewter, finely patinated stem signed "Bear Heart/Medicine Priest-Cannonball Sun Dance - July 3-4, 1937 - He Topa" & number "H 321," 23½" l. stem, 6¾" l., 4" h. bowl 875.00

Rug, Navajo, transitional twill weave w/cochineal red, analine red, recarded mix red & orange stripe w/black & light grey design elements, Germantown yarn fringe at corners, string warp, ca. 1885, 33 x 53" (selvage breaks, three holes) 350.00

Rug, Navajo, Klagetoh area, Good Spirit or Weaver's Pathway, dark red center & corner stars w/further designs in light & dark browns, tan on natural ground, ca. 1925, 43 x 59" (small break in selvage thread) 1,050.00

Navajo Yei-bei-chai Rug

Rug, Navajo, Yei-bei-chai, finely detailed dancing figures w/Rainbow God border, multicolor on dark red background, excellent condition, 51 x 76" (ILLUS.) 1,100.00

Saddle, Crow, woman's, wooden w/sinew stitched rawhide covering, red, white & blue beaded fringe & brass tack trim, complete w/stirrups & cinch, 33" l., 19" h. . . 100.00

Shirt, Eastern Plains, man's, quilled & fringed hide, decorated w/two quilled & plaited roundels front & three on back, fringe trim along inner sleeve seams 10,175.00

Totem pole, Northwest Coast, carved wood, stylized figure of an eagle, spirit w/otter, face, snake & raven, reticulated crest & edge, painted blue, black, gold & dark ochre, ca. 1900, 36½" h. 1,050.00

Trade beads, clear red & blue 3 3/8" d. glass beads interspersed w/round shell disks, paper tag "Columbia River, The Dalles, 1921," 29" l. 35.00

Vest, Sioux, child's, beaded leather, sinew sewn beading of red, white & blue flags (crow stitch) on white ground on front, fine geometric design in red, yellow, blue & green on white ground on back, red beads have white hearts, 11 x 13" (minute bead damage) 1,000.00

Water jar, Northern Paiute, basketry, ovoid form w/narrow neck & two horsehair handles at neck, pitched w/banded rattlesnake design around middle, 6" d., 8" h. 450.00

IVORY

Ornately Carved Ivory Stein

Brush holder, curved cylinder, carved diagonal spiral pattern stopping short of the slanted scalloped edge collar at the rim, fitted into wooden base, Chinese, 9 7/8" h. $880.00

Brushpot, continuous scene of a herdboy resting on a water buffalo w/a young water buffalo trailing behind in a bamboo forest, decoration picked out in black, carved wood stand base, Chinese, 18th 19th c., 6" 825.00

Candlesticks, tapered cylindrical shaft supporting a bulbous socket above a spindle-form base, whole raised on a square silver-rimmed carved ivory foot, 19th c., 5½" h., pr. 990.00

Chess set, hand-carved, in original wood box, Japan 800.00

Cue balls (for pool), three in original wooden box (one has chip) ... 145.00

Figure of "Christo Morto," mounted on an ebonized wood cross, Germany, 17th-18th c., 11¼" h. figure 770.00

Figure of a smiling farmer, holds woven bag over his shoulder, hoe near his feet, Japanese, 19th c., 7 1/8" h. 225.00

Jagging wheel, in the form of a sea horse, center band of ebony, horns continuous w/head, two-pronged pickle fork flanked by triangularly shaped ears, eyes inlaid w/tiny pieces of ebony, forelegs grasping a crenelated wheel held in place w/tiny silver pins, hub of the wheel a thick, five-pointed star, ca. 1870, 7¾" l. (repair to one leg) 5,500.00

Models of foo lions, fierce expressions, on carved oval bases, Chinese, 19th c., 5¼" h., pr. (age cracks) 357.50

Plaque, relief-molded depicting Venus & a goat attended by a putto & two satyrs, on a lapis lazuli ground, 19th c., framed, 4¼ x 6" 550.00

Puzzle ball, outer sphere w/entwined dragons & clouds motif, 13 inner spheres w/reticulated stars & trefoils, on wooden stand, Chinese, 3" d. 412.50

Rule, folding-type, nickel-plated fittings, engraved "T. M. Nelson, 3 Charles St., St. James Sq." (London), 24" l. 175.00

Stein, carved Renaissance style w/standing Roman finial over carved lid & cylindrical body carved w/continuous scene of warriors in battle, handle carved w/satyr mask & dragon w/intertwined warriors, the base carved w/satyr marks, Germany, 19th c., age cracks, repairs, 5½" d., 19" h. (ILLUS.) 4,510.00

JADE

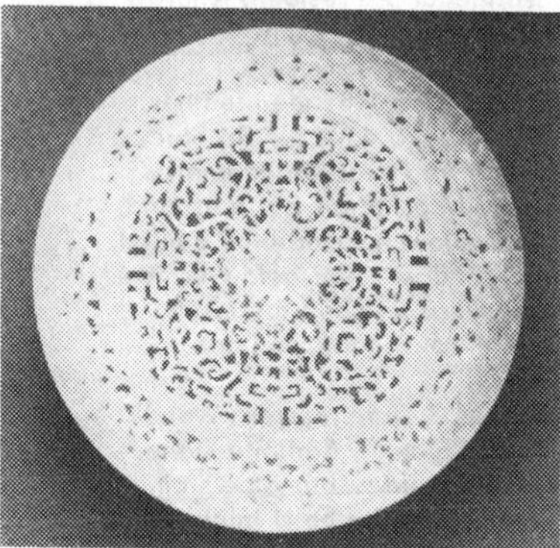

Carved Jade Box

Bowl, carved paper-thin in the Mogul style w/radiating concentric circles of fluted chrysanthemum petals simulating an open flower, low foot carved in the same manner, spinach green w/dark green flecks, 19th c., 4½" d. $3,575.00

Box, reticulated cover finely carved in openwork w/a circular floral medallion surrounded by foliage, enclosed in a rim of scrollwork containing the eight precious Buddhist objects (*ba jixiang*), pale celadon green, 18th c., 6 1/8" d. (ILLUS.) 4,950.00

Censer, cov., ribbed ovoid form, overall relief scrolling decoration, lion head loop handle suspending loose rings & decorative flower ring around base, chrysanthemum & ring finial on domed cover, spinach green, China, 5 1/8" l., 3 3/8" h. 495.00

Cup, slightly flared rim, raised on splayed foot, white, Qianlong seal mark & period (1736-96), 3¼" d. 1,320.00

Figure of Guanyin seated & holding a scroll w/one elbow on an armrest carved w/a mask & claw support, translucent suffused w/emerald green on the face & gathered folds of her gown, 19th c., 8½" h. ...12,100.00

Hat stand, domed circular top carved w/a central medallion containing a four-character seal mark, *Qianlong yu yong*, surrounded by two ferocious five-claw dragons amid cloud scrolls, the dragon & scroll motif repeated on the small central knop & heavy circular base, the two wood standards incised w/lengthy inscriptions copying Qianlong's calligraphy, filled w/gilding & w/small seals dated *Dingwei yu ti*, corresponding to 1787, wooden tab in bottom of knop fitting into a square aperture in the bottom standard, Qianlong mark & period, 11 5/8" h. 8,800.00

Model of two cats, bushy-tailed feline poised on the underside of the other, even-toned pale white stone carved to leave orange skin along the back of one animal, 17th c., 2½" l. 990.00

Pomander, purse form, two sides pierced & w/panels of lotus blossoms among scrolling leaves, top carved w/flowers on a lobed ground w/two holes to admit a handle carved in the form of a two-headed dragon, surmounted by a pierced & carved ball w/*shou* medallions, moss green, 18th c., 3¼" h. 2,750.00

Urn, cov., flattened ovoid, carved w/*taotie* masks below narrow neck w/flanking handles suspending carved chains attached to domed lid & connected to a yoke-shaped hanger, spinach green, 8" h. 715.00

Vase, slender baluster form, body encircled by *ruyi* & leaf lappet bands, waisted neck flanked by *chilong* handles, pale greenish white, Qianlong, 5¼" h. 3,850.00

JEWELRY

ANTIQUE

Victorian Gold Bangle Bracelet

Bar pin, brass w/garnets, 2½" l. $45.00

Bar pin, 10k gold, two rubies & one diamond 125.00

Bracelet, bangle-type, gold, overall finely engraved ground w/black enamel highlights, 19th c. (ILLUS.)......................... 495.00

Bracelet, 14k gold, round, stippled gold discs joined by links, w/larger center disc set w/small diamond 325.00

Brooch, 15k gold, engraved ribbon highlighted by turquoise & two gold tassels....................... 400.00

Brooch & pendant, cameo profile of maiden w/pearls in hair, calla lilies at shoulder, 14k white gold rectangular filigree framing, engraved bows at corners, 1½ x 1 1/8" 135.00

Cameo, Victorian lady on pink ground, 10k gold frame w/fifty seed pearls 250.00

Chain & pendant, seed pearls spaced by platinum wires supporting a platinum topped gold, seed pearl & diamond circle pendant, Edwardian 650.00

Chatelaine, silver gilt mesh purse, match safe, letter opener, mirror, knife & telescoping pencil designed as a bullet, 18k gold chain, "Tiffany & Co." 700.00

Earrings, 14k gold, loops w/deep red coral teardrops, gypsy-type, pr. 65.00

Locket brass, embossed Art Nouveau maiden's head w/flowers & scrolls, on woven chain, overall 19" l. 58.00

Locket-pendant, 14k gold rectangular plaque on onyx, w/cultured pearls in the form of a fan 350.00

Mourning brooch, black drawing on ivory of woman at a tomb w/willow tree, almond-shaped gold case engraved on back, "A.P. 1796. F.S.J. May 9, 1844," 1 1/8 x 1¾" (lens worn & cracked) 250.00

Necklace, Art Nouveau style, turquoise & freshwater pearls in an 18k gold mounting 950.00

Pendant, oval pink tourmaline suspended within a pear-shaped foliate mounting, set w/tiny diamonds, Edwardian 2,100.00

Pin, Art Nouveau style, 14k gold scrolled mounting w/green enamel & pearl highlights set w/square-cut peridot & an oval peridot drop 325.00

Pin, heart-shaped, 14k gold set w/fifteen demantoid garnets alternating w/fifteen diamonds, Edwardian 1,100.00

Ring, lady's, 14k gold, polished onyx carbuncle, gold leaves & petals motif, ca. 1870................. 110.00

Ring, lady's, opal stone in sterling filigree mount, ca. 1870.......... 225.00

Watch chain, woven hair, two-

pattern, slide w/two garnets & one seed pearl, 6" l. 95.00
Watch chain w/slide, 14k gold, sliding "T" bar, 13" l. 295.00

RHINESTONE & COSTUME

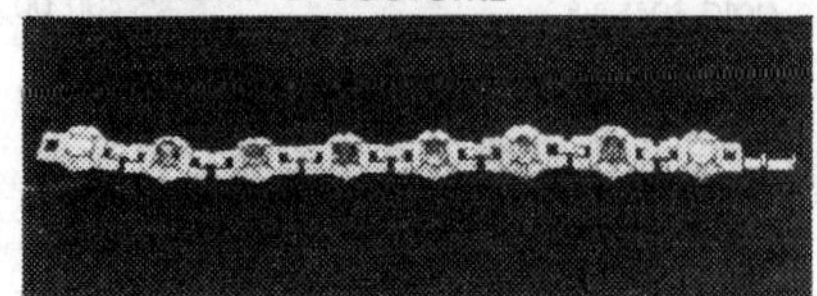

Link-type Bracelet

Bar pin, silver filigree set w/rhinestones, 2" l. 25.00
Bar pin, sterling silver set w/rhinestones, large 40.00
Belt, lady's, Art Deco style, overall rhinestones on fabric backing, diamond-shaped buckle, 1½" w., 30" l. 150.00
Bracelet, gold-plated metal set w/amber stones, "Lisner" 28.00
Bracelet, blue stones w/drop, narrow, "Weiss" 15.00
Bracelet, link-type, multicolored stones surrounded by rhinestones, 7¾" l. (ILLUS.) 35.00
Bracelet, 150 rhinestones set between two rows of large rhinestone baguettes, w/guard chain, 1¼" w. 45.00
Bracelet, four-row, set w/round & emerald-cut rhinestones, Germany 80.00
Bracelet, rhinestones & grey stones, ornate, "Weiss" 18.00
Clip, large turquoise blue stones, "Eisenberg" 65.00
Earrings, amber stones, marked "Eisenberg Ice," pr. 24.00
Earrings, drop-style, 196 amber stones, 1½" w., 3" l., pr. 35.00
Earrings, clip-type, 27 hand-set blue stones, pr. 15.00
Earrings, gunmetal filigree set w/green stones, marked "Dior by Kramer," pr. 15.00
Earrings, pink stones, marked "Eisenberg Ice," pr. 35.00
Earrings, clip-type, gold flower set w/large pink stone, pr. 40.00
Earrings, clip-type, 40 rhinestones, marked "Trifari," pr. 12.00
Earrings, drop-style, set overall w/rhinestones, "Eisenberg," 1" l., pr. 45.00
Earrings, screw-type, rhinestone teardrop within circle, pr. 20.00
Earrings, screw-type, set w/round faceted rhinestones, marked "Austria," pr. (ILLUS.) 20.00

Rhinestone Earrings

Hair clip, heart-shaped, set w/rhinestones 6.00
Hair comb, set w/45 rhinestones 25.00
Hair combs, hand-set rhinestones, set of 3 .... 18.00
Necklace, black stones w/random rhinestones, "Weiss" 25.00
Necklace, gold-plated metal set w/dark blue stones, "Lisner" 35.00
Necklace, silver links set w/blue & pink stones forming floral clusters, firey opal center, "Coro" 35.00
Necklace, floral spray, large round & oval rhinestones on blossoms w/smaller rhinestones on leaves, in original grey box, marked "Eisenberg Ice" 120.00
Necklace, pave-set w/rhinestones, multiple rhinestone drops, 250 stones, "Weiss" 50.00
Necklace, ornate rhodium mounting set w/rhinestones, "Eisenberg" 85.00
Necklace, sterling silver set w/155 rhinestones, 15½" l. 65.00
Necklace, single strand w/pave-set rhinestones, "Eisenberg" 75.00
Necklace, single strand of rhinestones, "Weiss," 16" l. 45.00
Pin, sterling silver set w/amethyst stones, "Eisenberg" 125.00
Pin, floral spray set w/blue stones, "Hobe" 18.00
Pin, sunburst design, pale blue stones, "Regency," 2" d. 18.00
Pin, pinwheel form, set w/alternating bands of blue & green stones, marked "Weiss," 2½" d. 17.00
Pin, butterfly, body & wings set w/blue & pink stones, "Regency," 2½" w. 26.00
Pin, floral spray set w/pink stones, marked "Czechoslovakia" 35.00
Pin, ornate cluster set w/pink & lavender stones, "Eisenberg" 60.00
Pin, bow-shaped, sterling silver set w/pink stones & rhinestones, "Eisenberg" 75.00
Pin, American flag, gold-plated metal set w/red & blue stones & rhinestones, prong-set, 2" w. 20.00
Pin, airplane, set w/rhinestones, inscribed "Spirit of St. Louis," 1¾" l. 55.00
Pin, rhinestone-studded bird on gold-plated half moon, "Jomaz" 20.00

Pin, butterfly, sterling silver, wings set w/large faceted rhinestones, "Eisenberg" 200.00
Pin, cluster of three flowers w/foliage set w/large & small rhinestones, marked "Eisenberg Ice," 2" w. 55.00
Pin, comet w/three tails, set w/rhinestones, "Kramer" 20.00
Pin, four-leaf clover, set w/rhinestones, 1 x 1½" 11.00
Pin, golf bag, set w/round rhinestones surrounding central row of oblong rhinestones, gold-tone club heads at top of bag, ½" w., 2" h. 20.00
Pin, ladybug set w/rhinestones, "Kenneth Jay Lane" 25.00
Pin, set w/two large pear-shaped rhinestones & seven marquise rhinestones, "Eisenberg" 55.00
Pin, set w/28 oval, round & marquise rhinestones, "Eisenberg," 1½ x 1¾" 90.00
Shoe clips, designed by "Musi," 3 x 1¾", pr. 65.00
Sweater guard, blue stones, ca. 1950 . . . . . 15.00
Tiara, set w/rhinestones 35.00

SETS

Bracelet & earrings, large pink stones, "Schaiparelli" 35.00
Bracelet & earrings, floral design set w/rhinestones 45.00
Bracelet & long drop earrings, Art Deco style, rhinestones & smokey grey stones, "Weiss" 95.00
Necklace & earrings, necklace set w/100 stones in shades of amber, matching earrings, "Lisner" 30.00
Necklace & earrings, blue stones set in swag design 45.00
Pin & earrings, 1½ x 2¾" pin, marked "Eisenberg Ice" 65.00
Pin & earrings, star-shaped, w/rows of rhinestones & green center stone, "Hattie Carnegie" 95.00
Pin & earrings, rhinestones & green stones, "Lisner" 35.00
Pin & earrings, rhinestones, multicolored stones & pearls, marked "B. David" 75.00

JUKE BOXES

AMI (Automatic Musical Instrument Co.) Model D-40 . . . . . $600.00
Gabel's Jr., 1930's, twelve plays 750.00
Mills "Panorama Video," 1940 . . . . . 2,500.00

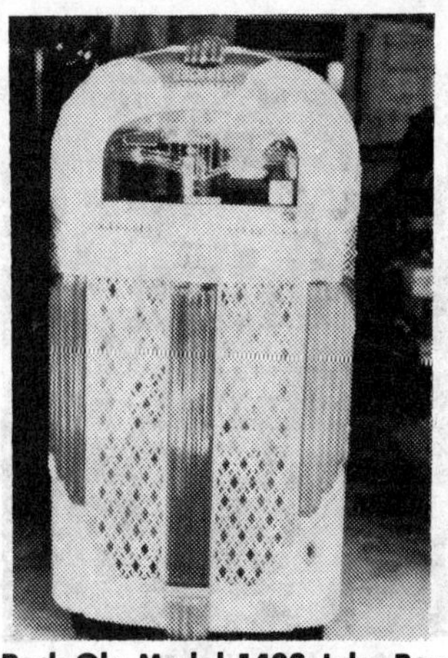

Rock-Ola Model 1428 Juke Box

Rock-Ola Model 1428, 1948 (ILLUS.) 3,250.00
Rock-Ola Fireball, Model 1436, 1952 . . . . . 490.00
Rock-Ola Master Rocolite (Luxury light-up), 1940 . . . . . 1,500.00
Rock-Ola Multi Selector Model "B" . . 550.00
Seeburg Audiophone, disc-type, eight-selection, 1920's 2,800.00
Seeburg Model P147 (Trashcan), 1947, restored 1,200.00
Seeburg Model HF100R, 1950's 450.00
Wurlitzer Model 71, table-type, walnut case w/yellow & red plastic panels, plays twelve 78 rpm records, 1940-41 . . . . . 3,500.00
Wurlitzer Wireless Remote Wallbox Model 125 . . . . . 150.00
Wurlitzer Model 600, 1938-39 . . . . . 1,600.00
Wurlitzer Model 600A, 1939 . . . . . 1,500.00
Wurlitzer Model 616, 1938 . . . . . 900.00
Wurlitzer Model 800, glazed front revealing 24 selections, bubble tubes centering front decorative panel, flanked by illuminated full-length plastic cylinders, 1940 . . . . . 3,800.00
Wurlitzer Model 950, 1942 . . . . . 6,800.00
Wurlitzer Model 1050, 1973 . . . . . 3,800.00 to 4,500.00
Wurlitzer Colonial Model 1080, 1947-48 . . . . . 4,200.00 to 5,200.00
Wurlitzer Model 1100, veneered case w/window at front revealing 24 selection mechanism above chrome-trimmed selector buttons & revolving colored lights either side, 1948-49, 60" h. (restored) 2,700.00
Wurlitzer Model 1400, 1951 . . . . . 500.00 to 1,000.00
Wurlitzer Model 1650 . . . . . 895.00
Wurlitzer Model 2100, w/200 selections, 1956 . . . . . 350.00

KEWPIE COLLECTIBLES

Kewpie Indian Figure

Rose O'Neill's Kewpies were so popular in their heyday that numerous objects depicting them were produced and are now collectible. The following represents a sampling.

Advertisement, lithographed paper, "Hendler's Golden French - A Special Ice Cream," Kewpie standing & eating ice cream at one end, open carton & dish of ice cream at other end w/wording between, red & blue lettering on gold ground $67.00

Booklet, "Jell-O & The Kewpies," 1915 . . . . . 15.00 to 30.00

Cake decoration, celluloid, Kewpie bride & groom wearing paper clothing, paper bell, paper platform, overall 4¾" h. 48.00

Charm, carved bone, model of a Kewpie 45.00

Clock, jasperware, dome-shaped, three relief-molded white action Kewpies on green ground, German works, 5" h. 375.00

Figure, bisque, Kewpie w/hands on stomach, original Rose O'Neill label, "Germany" & "Pat. 1913," 2½" h. 80.00

Figure, bisque, Kewpie w/hands upraised, original Rose O'Neill label, "Germany" & "Pat. 1913," 2½" h. 80.00

Figure, bisque, Kewpie Civil War soldier, red cap, rifle in one hand, sabre in other, signed "O'Neill," 3½" h. 300.00

Figure, chalkware, standing Kewpie Indian holding tomahawk, polychrome paint in excellent condition, 7" h. (ILLUS.) 900.00

Figure, bisque, Kewpie "Governor," Kewpie seated in wicker chair, arms folded, feet crossed, Germany 425.00

Handkerchief, action Kewpies decoration, "Blowing Bubbles," signed "Rose O'Neill," registered & dated 1915 (unused) 65.00

Magazine cover, *Ladies' Home Journal*, Christmas 1927, action Kewpies on pink ribbons surrounding Santa Claus, signed "O'Neill," framed 110.00

Magazine page, *Woman's Home Companion*, November 1910, full-page color Kewpie w/verse & picture 15.00

Place card holder, bisque, figural Kewpie lying on back, legs in air, attached to rectangular base of white bisque, copyright mark, Germany 110.00

Plaque, pierced to hang, jasperware, triangular, three relief-molded white Kewpies sitting on a bench surrounded by flowers & butterflies on blue ground, signed "Rose O'Neill," 4½" each side 265.00

Postcard, girl & two Kewpies by Christmas tree, 1918, signed "R. O'Neill" 20.00

Posy pot, jasperware, footed, w/original liner, relief-molded white Kewpies (6) & floral decoration on green ground, signed "Rose O'Neill," 3 5/8" d., 2¼" h. . . 395.00

Vase, jasperware, relief-molded white Kewpies on blue ground, relief-molded white floral trim, signed "Rose O'Neill," 3½" w., 1½" deep, 4" h. 295.00

Whistle, brass, figural Kewpie 25.00

KITCHENWARES

Also see ADVERTISING ITEMS, BOTTLE OPENERS, CERAMICS, CHARACTER COLLECTIBLES, CLOCKS, COCA-COLA ITEMS, COFFEE GRINDERS, COOKBOOKS, COOKIE CUTTERS, FOOD, CANDY & MISCELLANEOUS MOLDS, GLASS, METALS, OCCUPIED JAPAN and WOODENWARES.

Apple corer, tin & wood, "Boye," 1916 . . . . . $12.00

Apple parer, cast iron, eight-gear, "Sinclair, Scott Co., Baltimore" . . . 45.00

Batter pitcher, utilitarian crockery, brown glaze, 2 qt. 68.00

Bean pot, stoneware, dark brown

glaze & grey, w/South Dakota advertising 35.00
Beater jar, grey stoneware w/blue banding ....30.00 to 40.00
Berry basket, woven tin strips, old red paint, ca. 1880, 4½" sq., 3½" h., qt. 110.00
Biscuit pricker, cherrywood, round, mushroom knob handle, metal teeth, "patent applied for," 3½ x 4" 220.00
Boiler, tin, two-handled, marked "Toledo Cooker Co. pat. 1900," 16½" h. 39.00
Bread board, poplar, applied edges & table edge lips on two sides, single board w/old patina, 20 x 31½" 47.50
Bread dough knife, hand-carved maple, ca. 1830, 12" l. 26.00
Bread (or meat) slicer, "Gem Slicing Machine," slicing carriage moves to meet slanted fixed blade, cherry & hardwood w/iron & steel hardware, dated 1903, 7½ x 8½ x 20" 150.00
Butter churn, "Elgin," glass jar, 2 qt. 85.00
Butter churn, tin, mustard yellow paint, w/original wooden lid & dasher, 13" top d., 23" h. 260.00

"The Dazey Churn"

Butter churn, "The Dazey Churn No. 300," blue galvanized tin, wooden lid & two-wheel paddle, 1917 patent, 3 gal., 25" h. (ILLUS.) 110.00
Butter dish, cov., utilitarian crockery, Daisy patt., green & yellow .. 100.00
Cabbage cutting board, bird's-eye maple, carved offset pistol grip handle at top, pierced to hang, 5 x 15" 50.00
Cake pan, bundt-type, tin, 9½" d. .. 10.00
Canister, pressed emerald green glass, embossed "Cereal" or "Flour," 7¼" h., each 20.00
Can opener, cast iron w/wooden handle, "Boye Needle Co.," ca. 1913 .... 7.50
Carpet beater, Shaker-style, bentwood 67.50
Carpet beater, wicker, orange & green basketweave splint handle 27.50
Charcoal iron, cast iron w/rooster finial 47.50
Cheese ladder, hickory, hand-hewn, mortised & wedged, 11 x 25" 95.00
Cherry pitter, cast iron, "Enterprise No. 2" 32.50
Cherry pitter, cast iron, "Enterprise No. 18," 1903, 2" 24.00

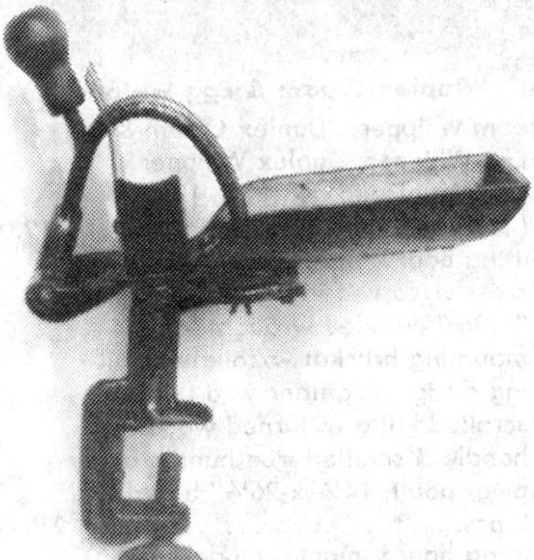

Cherry Pitter

Cherry pitter, cast iron, double, "Goodell Co., Antrim, New Hampshire," clamp-type (ILLUS.) 55.00
Chopping bowl, turned wood, cylindrical, worn blue painted exterior, early 19th c., 17½" d. 150.00
Colander, tin, pierced w/six-pointed star in bottom & w/half-circles & arches in sides 65.00
Cookie board, carved granite, bird on branch one side, initials & flowers reverse, early 1800's, 4 x 6" 120.00
Cookie board, carved wood, double-faced, full-length man & dog one side & woman w/bird on shoulder reverse, 8¾ x 21½" 275.00
Cookie peel, wrought iron, open ring handle, 18th c., 24" l. overall 130.00
Cookie stamp, cast iron, butterfly design, "Albany Foundry," early 1800's, 5½" oval 175.00
Cornstick pan, cast iron, "Griswold No. 6," in original wrapper 60.00
Cornstick pan, cast iron, "Griswold No. 28" 45.00

Cottage cheese sieve, tin, heart-shaped w/ring feet & side handles, 4½" h. 200.00
Cranberry scoop, wood w/tin & canvas, dark finish, 19" w. (old splits & repairs) 125.00
Cream skimmer, pierced brass bowl, wrought-iron open ring handle, ca. 1800, 4" d., 11" l. 120.00

"Duplex Cream & Egg Whipper"

Cream whipper, "Duplex Cream & Egg Whipper, Duplex Whipper Corp., Chicago, Nov. 25, 1919" (ILLUS.) 12.00
Cutting board, hardwood, scalloped crest w/carved initials & dated "1736," detailed wrought-iron mounting bracket w/foliate scrolling design, together w/a flat scrolled knife w/turned wood handle & scrolled iron handle at pivot point, 14¼ x 26½" board, 2 pcs. 275.00
Cutting board, maple, model of a pig w/carved open curly tail, 11½ x 33" (tip of one foot missing) 140.00
Dish cover, blown clear glass, ball knob finial, folded rim, square shoulder, 6" d. 150.00
Dish cover (fly screen), domed wire mesh, ring handle, 10 x 14", 7" h. 85.00
Dish covers (fly screens), domed wire mesh, round, nested set of 5 .... 195.00
Drying rack, hanging-type, "Empire Clothes Dryer Made by American Wringer Co., New York" 70.00
Drying rack, mahogany, three horizontal bars, well-shaped dainty shoe feet, 25¾" w., 42½" h. 225.00
Dutch oven, cov., cast iron, "D.R. Sperry Co. No. 3, 1896," 11½" d. 95.00
Dutch oven, cov., "Griswold Tite Top," emblem on lid & base 38.00
Dye tub, wooden, stave construction w/three loop handles, old red paint w/indigo blue stained interior, 18th c., 13" d., 12" h. 175.00
Egg basket, wire, folding-type .... 16.00 to 24.00
Egg beater, cast iron, "Cyclone," dated 1901 .... 30.00
Egg beater, cast iron, "Dover Pattern Improved," Taplin 22.00
Egg beater, tin, turbine-type, "Cassady-Fairbanks" 25.00
Egg crock, utilitarian crockery, white w/blue banding 95.00
Egg rack, birch, 12-hole w/salt dip pockets each corner, splayed arched feet, early 1800's 220.00
Flour measure & scoop, wooden, turned side handle, "Wilton, New Hampshire" 130.00
Fluting iron, cast iron, "American," 1880 patent date, 2 pcs. 60.00
Fluting iron, cast iron, "Indicator - Illion, New York, Pat'd. 1878," 2 pcs. 75.00
Food chopper, small wooden bar handle, wrought-iron blade, 18th c., 4 x 4½" 40.00

Early 19th Century Food Chopper

Food chopper, cast iron & oak, boat-shaped container raised on spatula feet, chopping disk fitted on oak handle, 16" l. (ILLUS.) 605.00
Food grinder, cast iron w/tinned finish, "Griswold No. 2" 20.00
Fork, wrought iron, two-tine w/flattened handle ending in flattened knob, good detail, 17" l. 85.00
Fruit & lard press, "Griswold No. 2," 4 qt. 65.00
Frying pan, cast iron, "Griswold," 20" d. 150.00
Funnel, salt-glazed stoneware, grey, 5" h. 40.00
Grater, table clamp-on type, cast iron, "Regina" 40.00
Grater, table clamp-on type, cast iron & graniteware, "Julius" 35.00
Griddle, cast iron, "Griswold No. 107" 35.00
Grid iron (for broiling meat on range over coals), cast iron, side handles, parallel grids w/drip trays on four sides, ca. 1860, 9½ x 19½" 48.00
Herb grinder, burl, turned mortar & close fitting pestle, top of pestle w/carved date "1805," base w/carved date "1825," 7¼" h. (wear & worm holes) 675.00

Ice cream freezer, wooden stave construction, "White Mountain, Jr." 250.00

Ice cream measure, tin, cup-type, 1 pint 40.00

Knife Tray

Knife tray, grain-painted finish (ILLUS.) 145.00

Ladle, copper bowl w/wrought-iron rat-tail handle w/hanging hook, ca. 1800, 6" d. bowl, overall 22" l. 150.00

Lemon squeezer, cast iron w/glass inserts, "Kings," 1882 .... 22.00

Lemon squeezer, wooden, hinged, 1880's 42.00

Measuring cup, clear glass, three-spout 3.00

Meat fork w/ring handle, wrought iron, ca. 1810, 18" l. 47.00

Meat tenderizer, grey stoneware head w/cobalt blue trim, square wooden handle 450.00

Muffin pan, cast iron, 12 round fluted cups in handled frame, 10 x 14" 95.00

Nutmeg grater, tin, w/flip top compartment for storing nutmeg 17.00

Oven peel, wrought iron, open ring handle, 18th c., 24" l. 130.00

Parer, "Reading Hdw. Co.," table model 49.00

Pastry peel, wrought iron, ram's head handle, 19" l. 80.00

Pastry wheel, wooden, well-carved wheel, handle w/relief-carved florals, serrated stamp at end, 6 3/8" l. 175.00

Pie lifter, tin & wire, dated 1898 .... 48.00

Pillow (or drapery) beater, bent iron wire loop w/two intertwined hearts center, wooden handle 45.00

Pitcher, utilitarian crockery, Cow patt., green & tan w/brown shading, 8" h. 185.00

Pitcher, utilitarian crockery, Love Bird patt., brown 75.00

Pitcher, utilitarian crockery, Swan patt., brown 70.00

Plate drying rack, wooden, dowel rod shelves, on wheels, 42½" w., 55½" h. 75.00

Popover pan, cast iron, "Griswold No. 10," finger grips, ca. 1890 .... 45.00

Poppy seed grinder, cast iron & brass 50.00

Potato boiling basket, wire, folding-type, two-handled, large 25.00

Pumpkin chopper, hand-crank, dated 1869 .... 350.00

Raisin seeder, cast iron, clamp-on type, lever operated w/waffled head press & thin wires over oval tin tray, late 1800's 260.00

Rolling pin, blown amethyst glass, 15" l. .... 75.00 to 85.00

Rolling pin, milk white glass, worn decals each of a sailing ship & a verse ending "Success to the Baltic Fleet," dated 1856 .... 110.00

Sausage stuffer, "Enterprise," 4 qt. 45.00

Shrimp boiling basket, wire, arched handle, seven-sided, ca. 1870 .... 75.00

Skillet, brass & iron, deep brass pan mounted in a wrought-iron frame w/long shaped iron handle w/ram's horn end, mid-handle leg, England, early 18th c., 5¾" d., 18½" l. 165.00

Skillet, cast iron, "Griswold No. 0" 30.00

Skillet, cast iron, "Griswold No. 1" 120.00

Skillet, cast iron, "Griswold No. 8" 12.00

Skillet w/lid, cast iron, "Griswold No. 10" 35.00

Skimmer, tin, round strap handle at edge, 8" d. 45.00

Skimmer, brass & cast iron, pierced, open ring handle, 18th c., 23" l. 150.00

Soap shaver, tin, "Sunny Monday Soap Shaver" 17.50

Spatula, brass blade & wrought-iron handle marked "F.B.S. Canton O. Pat Jan 26, '86," 14¼" l. 125.00

Spice mill, wall-type, cast iron w/original stenciling, "Enterprise" 75.00

Steamer kettle, cov., tin, handled, perforated holes 12.00

Painted Tin Strainer

Strainer, painted tin, 6½" l. (ILLUS. previous page) 20.00
String bean slicer, cast iron 60.00
Sugar nippers, steel, spring keeper & rest, 18th c., marked "steel," 8½" l. 165.00
Syllabub churn (or cream whipper), tin, four looped feet, side crank handle moves beater in rectangular container, ca. 1880, 5½ x 8½ x 9½" 85.00
"Taster" spoon, brass bowl w/tooled wrought iron handle, 6 5/8" l. 250.00
Tea kettle, copper w/brass trim, dovetail construction, overhead handle w/milk white glass handgrip, oval, 8¼" h. (polished) 105.00
Tea strainer, tin, ornate leaf design, 1800's 10.00
Tub, fiber w/embossed label "United Indurated Fibre Co.," wire & wood rim handles, 21¾" d., 12¾" h. (minor edge damage) ... 45.00
Utensil rack, wrought iron, flat bar w/five hooks, rounded crest w/applied curliques, late 19th c., 18" w., 18" h. 225.00
Waffle iron, cast iron, "Griswold No. 7," bail handle, dated 1908 .... 75.00
Waffle iron, cast iron, "Griswold No. 9" 45.00
Waffle iron, cast iron, "Keen Kutter" 175.00
Waffle iron w/bail handle, cast iron, "Wagner," Feb. 2, 1910 patent, 2-pc. 35.00

KNIFE RESTS

Cut glass, notched prism cutting overall, dumbbell shape, 4¼" l. $35.00
Pottery, h.p. peasant decoration, marked "H.B. Quimper" 45.00
Pressed glass, clear w/blue candy cane swirls, 3½" l. 45.00
Silver plate, figural Dachshund at each end 37.00
Silver plate, figural lion at each end 45.00
Silver plate, figural seated squirrel at each end, large 36.00
Silver plate, semi-circular bar raised on twin arched ribbed feet, impressed "Christofle," original fitted case, 3¼" l., set of 12 ..... 825.00
Sterling silver, leaf-form ends 45.00

KNIVES

Remington Pocket Knife

Advertising, "Firestone," pocket knife, bone handle w/silver inlay $38.00
Advertising, "Russel Road Grader Co.," pocket knife, chrome-plated brass, early machine pictured 65.00
Bowie knife, English Sheffield spearpoint, brass & wood grip w/inlaid British lion, leather scabbard, 6" blade, 10" overall 145.00
Case Tested two-blade pocket knife, genuine stag handles, pre-1940, No. 5264, 3 1/8" l. closed 100.00
Farriers knife, bone handle, Sheffield 25.00
Ka-Bar U.S.N. belt knife, 1943, original sheath 20.00
Marbles Arms & Manufacturing Company, Gladstone, Michigan, one-blade folding safety hunting knife 595.00
Remington two-blade pocket knife, pyremite handle, No. 2105, 3 1/8" l. closed 25.00
Remington three-blade pocket knife, green marbleized Pyremite handle w/emblem shield, No. R3555, 4" l. closed (ILLUS.) 90.00
Remington two-blade w/punch blade & hook "Bullet" camp knife, bone handle, No. 4243, 4¾" l. closed ....385.00 to 450.00
Robeson one-blade pocket knife, genuine stag handle, brass lining, No. 512224, 5" l. closed 110.00
Silver one-blade pocket knife, florals & foliage in relief, marked "Luzern" & "800" 28.00
Sterling silver one-blade pocket knife, tapestry-type engraving w/scrolled medallion enclosing name, 3¼" l. closed 32.00
Winchester one-blade "Pruner" knife, cocobola handle, steel bolster, steel lining, No. H1610P, 4" l. closed 75.00
Winchester three-blade "Cattle" knife, brown bone handle, No. 3952, 3¾" l. closed 275.00

Wostenholm (George) & Son Cutlery Company, (I*XL), Sheffield, England, three pence facsimiles on each side of handle, etched "1943" on can opener blade 40.00

LACQUER

Cinnabar Squash-Form Box

Most desirable of the lacquer articles available for collectors are those of Japanese and Chinese origin, and the finest of these were produced during the Ming and Ching dynasties, although the Chinese knew the art of fashioning articles of lacquer centuries before. Cinnabar is carved red lacquer.

Box w/slightly domed cover, polygonal, four giltwood claw feet, gilt chinoiserie figures & foliate borders, China, late 18th/early 19th c., 6" w. $660.00

Box, cov., multicolored w/fairy tale decor of numerous people & a village, Russia, 9½ x 4¼" 625.00

Cinnabar bowl, carved reserve panels of fruit & florals on overall floral-carved ground, 8" d., w/wooden stand 495.00

Cinnabar box, cov., squash-form two-part box well-carved & undercut w/overall design of insects & butterflies hovering over fruiting & flowering vines w/leafy tendrils, black ground (chips), 18th-19th c., 4 5/8" l., w/carved wood base (ILLUS.) 605.00

Cinnabar tray, carved scene of a pagoda, house, bridge & two people, 14 x 12" 125.00

Plaque, multicolored troika scene w/inset iridescent silver & gold foil, artist-signed "Fedoskino," Russia, large 820.00

Table, dark lacquer over cinnabar lacquer, carved scene of trees & people, China, 12½ x 12½", 5" h. 490.00

Writing box, rectangular, fitted at each end w/cut glass inkwell w/faceted stopper & two graduated racks for storage, gold chinoiserie decor on black ground, 13" l., 10" h. 440.00

LAW ENFORCEMENT ITEMS

All types of objects relating to law enforcement activities of earlier days are now being collected, just as are fire-fighting mementoes. The range extends from badges and insignia to leg irons and weapons. The following compilation represents a cross-section.

Badge, "Arizona State Prison," spread-winged eagle above embossed shield w/lettering around color-enameled Arizona State Seal center, gold-plated metal, 2 x 3" $37.00

Badge, "Chicago Police Dept.," pie plate shape, ca. 1910 .... 95.00

Badge, "Deputy Sheriff, Westchester County, New York," 14k gold..... 175.00

Belt buckle w/insignia 75.00

Billy club, leather 20.00

Billy club, oak 15.00

Billy club, w/whistle in handle, 1880's, 14" l. 60.00

Finger printing set, 1918, original metal box 32.00

Handcuffs, w/iron claw "come-along," dated 1869, pr. 45.00

Handcuffs, nickel-plated, w/"come-along" chain, ca. 1870, pr. 45.00

Handcuffs, "H & R Arms," pr. 85.00

Helmet, Keystone Cop type, w/badge "No. 85" (outside band missing) 75.00

Lantern, brass w/kerosene burner, brass top & wire cage connecting to domed brass foot, clear blown globe engraved w/five-pointed star & "Thos. Barrett, First Precinct, Serge. of Police, Chicago, Ill.," 10½" h. 350.00

Leg irons, shackle-type, "Hartford Lock Co.," w/key, pr. 55.00

Night stick, oak, "Helms, Boston, No. 18" 12.00

Suspenders, embossed night stick & "Police" on adjusting catches 25.00

Wanted brochure, "15,900.00 Reward in Gold - Train Hold-Up and Murder..." w/information on three brothers wanted for robbery & murder, 1920's, 9 pp. 25.00

LIGHTING DEVICES

CHANDELIERS

Neoclassical Style Candle Chandelier

Candle chandelier, ormolu & cut glass, 8-light, pendant hung corona suspending acanthus scroll candle arms w/ram heads divided by plume-form decoration w/cut glass flowerheads, Neoclassical style, Continental, 37½" d., 38" h. (ILLUS.) $8,800.00

Chandelier, brass frame w/four matching Quezal shades in waisted bell-form w/ruffled bases, shades w/Feather pattern in gold threading, gold iridescent interiors, each shade signed 800.00

Chandelier, Lalique signed, domical clear glass bowl molded in medium relief w/radiating meandering vines covered w/plump leaves washed in brown, suspended from four rectangular glass supports, molded w/conforming decoration, continuing to twisted silk cords, ca. 1925 (minor chips to supports), 27" h. (ILLUS.) 4,400.00

Chandelier, Mission-style (Arts & Crafts movement), four rectangular metal-framed shades w/slag glass panels suspended from rectangular center post w/four cast monks' heads, frame of heavy copper-washed iron w/hammered surface, 20" w. 425.00

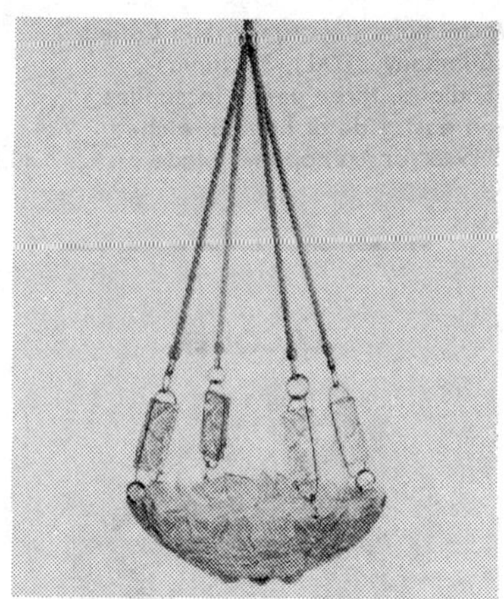

Signed Lalique Chandelier

Chandelier, Mission-style (Arts & Crafts movement), 3-light, three copper lanterns (one w/original frosted amber glass) on wrought-iron chains w/copper canopies pendent from a chambered oak board, w/original bolts for attachment, Gustav Stickley lantern Model No. 205, ca. 1904, 36" w., 28½" h. 4,400.00

Chandelier shade, Tiffany signed, deep domical shade composed of bands of brilliant red turtleback tiles surrounded by ochre & pale green continuous borders against red ground, tiles washed in iridescent amber, suspended from a gilt cap, 1899-1920, 18¼" d. 24,200.00

FAIRY LAMPS

These are candle burning night lights of the Victorian era. Best known are the Clarke Fairy Lamps made in England, but they were also made by other firms. They were produced in two sizes, each with a base and a shade. The Fairy Pyramid Lamps listed below all have a clear glass base and are approximately 2 7/8" d. and 3¼" h. The Fairy Lamps are usually at least 4" d. and 5" h. when assembled and these may or may not have an additional saucer or bottom holder to match the shade in addition to the clear base.

Fairy Pyramid Lamps

Amber w/white opal swirl glass shade, marked "Clarke" clear glass base, 3" d., 3 5/8" h. 95.00

Apple green satin glass shade w/embossed ribs, marked "Clarke" clear glass base, 2 7/8" d., 3½" h. 110.00

Blue diamond-quilted mother-of-pearl satin glass shade w/white lining on marked "Clarke" clear glass base, 2 7/8" d., 3½" h. 140.00

Burmese glass shade, salmon pink shaded to yellow, acid finish, marked "Clarke" clear glass base, 2 7/8" d., 3 7/8" h. 171.00

Green overshot glass shade w/overall round bumps, marked "Clarke" clear glass base, 3" d., 3¾" h. . . . 110.00

Rose mother-of-pearl satin glass shade w/white lining, Diamond Quilted patt., marked "Clarke" clear glass base, 2 7/8" d., 3½" h. 145.00

Ruby Diamond Quilted patt. shade, marked "Clarke" clear glass base, 2 7/8" d., 3½" h. 79.00

Fairy Lamps

Baccarat Fairy Lamp

Blue mother-of-pearl satin glass shade w/stippled & beaded pattern w/matching blue pedestal base, 2¾" d., 5¾" h. 115.00

Blue shaded frosted glass ruffled shade w/molded pattern of cords, medallions & petals, matching saucer base, 6¼" h. 450.00

Burmese glass shades, salmon pink shaded to yellow, two domed shades on marked "Clarke" clear glass bases in oval silver plate holder, 7 x 10½", 7" h. 850.00

Cranberry "overshot" crown-shaped glass shade (made for Victoria's 1887 Jubilee), marked "Clarke" clear glass base, 3" d., 4½" h. 200.00

Green overlay glass shade w/white lining, marked "Clarke" clear glass base, 4" d., 4¼" h. 115.00

Green shaded frosted glass shade w/scalloped base & frosted garlands & bows, marked "Clarke" clear glass base, 3¼" d., 5¾" h. 180.00

Heavenly blue mother-of-pearl satin glass shade w/white lining, Diamond Quilted patt., on opaque white satin glass base, marked "Clarke" clear glass candle cup, 3 5/8" d., 5¼" h. 335.00

Rose Tiente Sunburst patt. Baccarat shade w/matching saucer base, 5¼" d., 4" h. (ILLUS.) 235.00

Royal blue "overshot" crown-shaped glass shade (made for Victoria's 1887 Jubilee), marked "Clarke" clear glass base, 3" d., 4½" h. . . . 185.00

Spatter glass shade, Swirl patt., gold, white & pink spatter, white lining, marked "Clarke" clear glass peg base, in brass candlestick, 4" d., 14" h. 235.00

Verre Moire (Nailsea) glass shade & matching ruffled base, frosted blue w/opaque white loopings, marked "Clarke" clear glass candle cup, 5½" d., 5½" h. 425.00

Figural Fairy Lamps

Bisque, kitten's head, grey w/blue collar & green eyes 485.00

Bisque, monkey's head, natural coloring w/amber eyes, 3½" h. . . 365.00

Bisque, model of an owl, base on three sides, amber w/black glass eyes, marked "KPM," 4 x 4" 345.00

Bisque, Pekingese pup's head, amber eyes, black nose, tiny protruding tongue, blue collar 485.00

Glass, model of an owl, frosted cranberry body, marked "Clarke" clear glass base, 3½" d., 4¾" h. 195.00

LAMPS, MISCELLANEOUS

French "Bouillotte" Lamp

Aladdin, Diamond Quilted Model No. B91 . . . . 95.00

Aladdin, Lincoln Drape Model No. B75, ivory Alacite glass, 12-sided foot, w/burner (no filler cap) 225.00

Aladdin, Model No. 12, w/original No. 601 shade 150.00

Banquet lamp, black pottery base, brass stem, shaded peach glass embossed font, matching peach frosted glass shade, 23" h. 695.00

Betty lamp, copper, shaped lamp

w/hinged lid, hanging from a chain w/an iron spike, 3½" h. . . 198.00

Bouillotte lamps, Directoire, ormolu, 3-light, adjustable candle branches above circular stem & dished base chiselled w/basketweave, palmettes & leaf tips, adjustable green tole shade, late 18th c., France, 24¼" h., pr. (ILLUS. of one) 8,800.00

Daum Nancy signed table lamp, cameo glass & wrought iron, bulbous shade carved w/pale aubergine view of a tranquil lake w/sailing boats, trees in foreground & mountains in distance against mottled orange, rose & lemon yellow ground, raised on three-arm support, baluster form standard w/carved tall leafy trees & sailboats on a lake, ca. 1910, 19¾" h. (shade aperture reduced) 9,350.00

Desk lamp, "Emeralite," double knuckler, extension arm, clamp, No. 8734TW 345.00

Flint glass, deep amethyst, hexagonal form w/high domed top on font above waisted font w/a loop in each panel, octagonal columnar base w/stepped foot, ca. 1860, 8½" h. 1,400.00

Fluid lamps, pewter, dished circular base, baluster stem w/strap handle, cylindrical font, w/brass double wick holder w/pewter snuffers, unmarked American, 1825-50, 8¼" h., pr. 462.00

Gone-with-the-Wind Lamps

Gone-with-the-Wind lamp, ball-shaped shade decorated w/lion & lioness on shaded ground, inverted pear-shaped font w/matching lion decoration, ornate brass fittings & four-footed base (ILLUS. left) 1,500.00

Gone-with-the-Wind lamp, ball-shaped shade decorated w/Hansel & Gretel & the witch on a shaded ground, ovoid font decorated w/Little Red Riding Hood & the wolf, ornate brass fittings & four-footed base (ILLUS. right) 1,650.00

Gone-with-the-Wind lamp, red satin glass Quilted Diamond Drape patt., ornate footed brass base, 27½" h. 650.00

Kerosene hand lamp w/finger grip, blown Bristol glass, turquoise blue, applied blue handle, enameled rose & blue florals & green leaves, 4 3/8" d., 5 5/8" h. 110.00

Kerosene hand lamp w/finger grip, pressed glass, Coolidge Drape patt., clear 75.00

Kerosene hand lamp, pressed glass, Double Rib & Oval patt., clear 55.00

Kerosene hand lamp w/finger grip, footed, pressed glass, Filley patt., opaline font on blue opaline foot, Atterbury, 5¼" h. 1,375.00

Kerosene hand lamp, pressed glass, Fishscale patt., purple, original chimney & reflector 285.00

Kerosene lamp, hanging-type, signed "Angle Lamp Co., N.Y.," four-arm fixture, antiqued brass & copper finish, original shades 725.00

Kerosene lamp, hanging-type, white opalescent font & matching shade, ruffled rim w/pattern resembling Double Greek Key, shade 8" deep, 10" across bottom & 7" across ruffled top (electrified) 395.00

Kerosene table lamp, brass, font marked "Perkins & House Safety Lamp Clev'd Non-explosive Lamp Co., Cleveland & New York," w/last patent date of 1871, 8¾" h. 200.00

Kerosene table lamp, pressed glass, Aquarius patt., amber, round base w/original burner 165.00

Kerosene table lamp, pressed glass, Canadian Heart patt., green 150.00

Kerosene table lamp, Coin Spot patt., cranberry opalescent. 595.00

Kerosene table lamp, pressed glass, Peacock Feather patt., amber (base only) 175.00

Kerosene table lamp, pressed glass, Peanut patt., 9", clear 55.00

Kerosene table lamp, pressed glass, Six Panel patt., clear (replaced collar) 45.00

Lacemaker's lamp, cranberry glass Diamond Quilted patt. shade, brass base w/handles, w/chimney, 11½" d., 16½" h. 425.00

Leaded Glass Table Lamp

Leaded glass table lamp, 22" d. domical leaded glass shade composed of opaque yellow scale-shaped tiles w/a colorful border of water lilies in white & amber w/green leafage on a blue ground, raised on a brown tree-trunk form column w/roots spreading to a circular base, early 20th c., 25½" h. (ILLUS.) 1,045.00

Miner's lamp, iron, hanging-type, squat ovoid font w/figural chicken finial in top, arched swing handle w/twisted hanger, 7" h. plus hanger 75.00

Moe Bridges signed table lamp, 18" d. reverse-painted glass shade w/flowers of various sizes and shapes in purple, pink, white & orange w/green leaves & black border, above border are four sections of open field gold outlined w/black lines, black urn-shaped base 2,250.00

Muller Freres signed table lamp, cameo glass & wrought iron, helmet form shade, bulbous base, carved deep red & crimson blossoming rose bushes against pale yellow ground randomly splashed w/lemon yellow, emerald green & lavender, wrought-iron foliate mounts, ca. 1920, 12 5/8" d. shade, 12 3/8" h......................14,300.00

Pairpoint signed boudoir lamp, "puffy," 9¾" d. shade w/pink & yellow flowerheads on blue & white gingham ground, bronzed metal base of inverted trumpet form, early 20th c., 14½" h......1,100.00

Pairpoint signed table lamp, 15" d. reverse-painted domical shade decorated w/three masted ships under sail & small boat of sailors in foreground, seagulls in flight, pinkish sunset sky over greenish blue water, brass-colored metal base 2,050.00

Pairpoint signed table lamp, reverse-painted domical shade in Bird of Paradise patt., signed bronze-finish base, 17½" h. 3,500.00

Peg lamp, acid cut-back red florals on green, Val St. Lambert, original burner, set in Rogers silver plate candlestick, 2 pcs. 125.00

Peg lamp, lemon yellow overlay Satin glass, melon sectioned shade & font embossed w/scrolls w/matching mushroom shade in brass candlestick base, ruffled top on shade, white lining, 5½" d., 18 7/8" h., 3 pcs. 505.00

Peg lamp, shaded pink mother-of-pearl Satin glass Swirl patt. font & shade, brass base, clear chimney, 3½" d., 12" h., 4 pcs. 550.00

Brass Lamp with Quezal Shades

Quezal floriform pulled feather shades issuing from three shaped arms, supported on a baluster standard, round domed foot, 18½" h. (ILLUS.) 385.00

Rush light holder, wrought iron, spiral-forged candle arm & standard culminating in a clamp, raised on a spiral wrought-iron base, America, 19th c., 12½" h. . . 302.50

Sinumbra brass lamp, four column stem on baluster pedestal & square base, clear shade w/frosted interior, Perry & Co., New Bond Street, London, ca. 1845, 23¾" h. (electrified)............ 880.00

Student lamp, single, bronze w/ball counterweight, leaded glass shade in lavender & yellow drape design by Lundberg Studio, 15" h.......................... 275.00

Student lamp, double, brass reservoir & lamp adjustable on rod standard & domed base, clear shades w/white enameling & clear glass chimneys, signed "The Solar, E.N. & Co.," 21½" h. (electrified) 550.00

Table lamp, blown glass, onion-form blown font in amethyst w/white Nailsea-type loopings on blown clear glass hourglass form stem w/round applied clear foot, brass collar, 10½" h. 675.00

Fulper Pottery Lamp

Table lamp, Fulper pottery, mushroom-shaped shade of mirrored black glaze over green flambe inset w/leaded glass of alternating coloration, the base *en suite* w/black glaze dripping over green, base & shade marked, 13 7/8" d., 15½" h. (ILLUS.) 14,300.00

Whale oil lamp, pewter & tin, disc-shaped base, ring-turned stem, original burner, R. Gleason, Dorchester, Massachusetts, 7" h. 260.00

Whale oil lamp, pressed flint glass, Heart patt., 8¾" h. 125.00

Whale oil lamp, tole, saucer base, tubular stem & cone-shaped oil font, removable shade, worn original dark green paint w/yellow striping, original burner & filler cap, 11½" h. 250.00

HANDEL LAMPS (All Signed)

Desk lamp, Aladdin lamp-shaped font w/bird head loop handle raised on bulbous knob column on square domed base w/embossed designs, lamp supports domed leaded glass shade composed of rectangular tiles & four flower & leaf sprigs (ILLUS.) 2,100.00

Table lamp, 14" d. reverse-painted "chipped ice" domical shade decorated w/pink to white wild roses w/yellow center petals, dark blue flowers w/yellow centers, intertwined green leafage & vine obversely outlined in dark green, light blue-grey to light grey-green ground from top to bottom, bronzed metal signed base w/circular foot having low relief leaves at bottom of simple baluster stem 2,200.00

Handel Desk Lamp

Table lamp, three-light, 15" d. reverse-painted "chipped ice" domical shade w/Dutch village windmill scene reflected in foreground canal in monochromatic green, yellow interior, No. 5465, classically-molded standard w/circular base, 23½" h. 1,760.00

Table lamp, 18" d., reverse-painted "chipped ice" domical shade, design of a frosted autumn scene all around, 23" h. 2,640.00

Handel Table Lamp

Table lamp, reverse-painted "chipped ice" domical shade w/a continuous landscape scene of small trees & bushes on islet surrounded by marshy landscape, patinated metal standard w/domed ribbed round base (ILLUS.) 3,080.00

TIFFANY LAMPS (All Signed)

Tiffany Floor Lamp

Bridge lamp/ash receiver, twelve-sided shade set w/linenfold panels between linenfold panel borders, pivoting between a bronze harp-shaped support & an ash receiver w/iridescent amber bowl, a circular wooden shelf & a U-form magazine holder, bronze flattened circular base cast w/gadrooning & raised on four animal-paw feet, shade marked "Tiffany Studios 1938," base marked "Tiffany Studios New York," 1899-1920, 56" h. 4,400.00

Desk lamp, 7" d., 4" h. ribbed opalescent & green Favrile shade w/iridescent pulled decoration, bell-form patinated holder w/footed base, shade marked "L.C. Tiffany-Favrile," overall 13" h. 2,640.00

Desk lamp, 12½" d. conical shade composed of radiating amber linenfold panels, gilt-bronze American Indian base cast w/Indian motifs, w/finial, shade impressed "Tiffany Studios New York," 1899-1920, 17½" h. 4,950.00

Floor lamp, "Ivy," 12" d. domical shade w/radiating bands of striated opalescent green tiles w/band of green ivy leaves, pivoting on slender gilt-bronze standard w/undulating contour cast at top, midpoint w/rococo scrolls & leaves & continuing to four elongated legs wrought w/scrolls on upturned feet, on ribbed domed foot cast w/scrollwork about the edge, finial, shade impressed "Tiffany Studios," base impressed "Tiffany Studios New York," 1899-1920, 55" h. 5,500.00

Floor lamp, "Peony Border," 24" d. leaded glass domical shade w/broad band of white-streaked red & crimson peonies among violet & blue-streaked green leaves on a mottled green ground, bronze base w/ribbed column & platform cast w/stylized flowers, raised on four carved feet, cap lacking tip of pig-tail, 76" h. (ILLUS.) 35,200.00

Tiffany Student Lamp

Student lamp, double, two pale green Favrile glass shades w/gold pulled feather design fitted on two adjustable arms centering patinated bronze cylindrical font w/rope & beaded detail in Moorish influence, round stepped base w/coiled rope medallions, 27½" w., 29½"h. (ILLUS.) 4,675.00

Table lamp, "Apple Blossom," 25" d. leaded glass shouldered shade w/irregular lower rim w/profusion of yellow-centered pink, burgundy & white blossoms & green leaves on brown stems beneath pierced network of branches at the top on pale green ground, bronze tree-form base, 29½" h. 28,600.00

Table lamp, "Bamboo," 21¾" d. leaded glass domical shade w/overall striated emerald green, lime green, avocado & deep ochre bamboo leafage & stalks against opalescent ground, bronze adjustable base in the form of a bamboo stalk splitting at the base to form eight spreading roots & raised on circular foot, 1899-1920, 30½" h. (replaced finial) 37,400.00

Table lamp, "Crocus," 16¼" d. leaded glass domical shade w/overall pendant mottled lemon yellow

Tiffany "Crocus" Lamp

crocus blossoms & mottled grass green & lemon yellow stalks reserved against mottled grass green shading to opalescent ground, bronze urn-form base raised on four slightly scrolling legs ending in spatulate feet on a shaped square stepped base, 1899-1920, 21" h. (ILLUS.) 8,250.00

Table lamp, "Daffodil," 16" d. leaded glass hemispherical shade w/orange-centered yellow blossoms among tall green leaves on an emerald green shaded to milky white ground, bronze base, 21¼" h. 10,450.00

Table lamp, "Dragonfly," 20¼" d. leaded glass sharply conical shade w/lower border w/lavender, purple, royal blue & grey rippled dragonflies w/overlapping wings & red eyes against striated shaded royal blue to emerald green & deep ochre & amber ground, further set w/amber & ochre "jewels," bronze baluster standard w/applied spiralling stringing, dished circular base cast w/tiers of overlapping lappets, w/finial, 1899-1920, 25¾" h. 44,000.00

Table lamp, "Gentian," 17½" d. leaded glass domical shade w/lappets of aquamarine & powder blue gentian blossoms within striated olive & spring green leafy borders against mottled white ground, above a border of emerald green glass "jewels," bronze standard pierced w/gentian blossoms continuing to a circular foot cast w/rows of lappets, beading & further gentian blossoms, 23½" h. (replaced finial) 24,200.00

Table lamp, mushroom-form, the shaped mushroom-form shade in opalescent glass decorated w/pink-amber oil spottings, fitting onto a cylindrical amber iridescent standard ending in a domed circular base decorated w/amber & caramel interlocking coils, raised on five ball feet, 1892-1902, 8" h. (ILLUS.) 3,850.00

Tiffany Mushroom-Form Lamp

Table lamp, "Oak Leaf," 18" d. leaded glass domed shade w/central band of deeply mottled green & amber scrolling leaves & deep orange acorns on mottled sage green ground, bronze base w/greenish brown patina, 25¼" h. 6,600.00

Table lamp, "Poppy," 20" d. leaded glass conical shade w/crimson, purple, orange & burgundy blossoms & buds against streaked blue-green sky above band of bright green filigreed leaves, bronze base w/adjustable stem separating below into four feet each applied w/four gold Favrile glass balls, circular base, 24¾" h. 44,000.00

Table lamp, "Rosebush," 26" d. leaded glass domed shade w/profusion of bright pink & fuchsia-colored roses among mottled green leaves against a streaked turquoise blue sky, adjustable gilt-bronze base, 30" h. unextended 52,800.00

Table lamp, "Zodiac," 22" d. leaded glass domed shade w/lower band of panels centering circular iridescent green turtle-back tiles within scrolling green & brown borders on a midnight blue ground alternating w/smaller panels centering bronze filigrees depicting the signs of the Zodiac, upper band of panels similarly decorated, bronze Louis XIV base, 33¼" h. 18,700.00

MINIATURE LAMPS

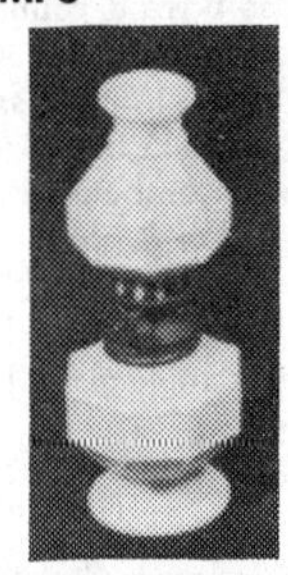

Block Pattern Miniature Lamp

Our listings are arranged numerically according to the numbers assigned to the various miniature lamps pictured in Frank R. & Ruth E. Smith's book, "Miniature Lamps," now referred to as Smith's Book I, and Ruth Smith's sequel, "Miniature Lamps II."

Milk white glass pedestal base, pressed clear glass font, Olmsted burner, milk white glass chimney-shade, 6½" h., No. 11 .... 280.00

"Improved Banner" & three stars embossed on clear glass pedestal base, Olmsted burner, white Bristol glass shade, 3" h., No. 20 .... 80.00

"Little Duchess" & three stars embossed on milk white glass font in brass saucer base w/brass spring-type clamp, Acorn burner, clear glass chimney, 3" h., No. 32 ..... 110.00

"Little Buttercup" embossed on clear glass font w/handle, Nutmeg burner, clear glass chimney, 2¾" h. base, No. 36 .... 46.00

Clear glass, "Fire-Fly" embossed on font, collar marked "pat'd. 4/13/75" and "3/21/76," string-type wick, unmarked burner, 2" h., No. 55 (Book II) 120.00

Brass "Beauty Night Lamp" embossed wall lamp, w/filling spout on wall reservoir & lion's mouth supporting tubing to burner, milk white glass beehive chimney-shade, No. 77 .... 72.00

Finger lamp, light amber base, applied handle, embossed large bull's eye foot & shoulder, Acorn burner, 3 11/16" h., No. 96 (Book II) 75.00

Clear glass stem lamp w/square base, Acorn burner, clear glass chimney, advertised in Butler Brothers "Our Drummer" 1912 catalog, 4" h., No. 103 .... 45.00

Green glass Bull's Eye patt. stem lamp, Nutmeg burner, clear glass chimney, advertised as "Daisy" in Butler Brothers "Our Drummer" 1912 catalog, 5" h., No. 112 ...... 84.00

Clear glass stem lamp w/embossed medallions, Acorn burner, clear glass chimney, 5½" h., No. 113 .. 77.00

Clear glass Waffle patt. font on embossed brass pedestal base, Acorn burner, clear glass chimney, 4½" h., No. 117 .... 100.00

Clear & frosted glass Octagon-type patt. globular base & overlapping leaf patt. umbrella-type shade, Nutmeg burner, clear glass chimney, 6¾" h., No. 148 .... 140.00

Milk white glass w/ovoid footed base & matching ovoid chimney, each w/embossed flowers & scrolls painted in pink, brown & gold, Acorn burner, called "Jupiter" & pictured in Butler Brothers April 1912 catalog, 8" h., No. 156 .... 99.00

Milk white glass footed base & matching globe-chimney w/embossed design highlighted in gilt, Acorn burner, 7¾" h., No. 173 ... 117.00

Custard glass Leon's Ribbed patt. base & globe-chimney shade, Acorn burner, 6" h., No. 177 ..... 270.00

Milk white glass footed Block patt. base & globe-chimney w/h.p. blue & green florals, Acorn burner, advertised as "Mission" design in Butler Brothers "Our Drummer" 1912 catalog, 6½" h., No. 192 (ILLUS.) 100.00

Milk white glass w/embossed rims around top of base & top & bottom of shade which are painted green, painted red, pink & green flowers, Nutmeg burner, 6½" h., No. 196 .... 163.00

Milk white glass Plume patt. base & umbrella shade w/gilt highlights, Nutmeg burner, clear glass chimney, 7½" h., No. 203 .... 184.00

Milk white glass Chrysanthemum & Swirl patt. base & globe-chimney w/painted pink & yellow florals, Hornet burner, 9" h., No. 213 .... 312.00

Milk white glass base & globe-chimney w/embossed Maltese Cross & other designs highlighted in gilt, Hornet burner, 9½" h., No. 214 .... 170.00

Milk white glass base & ball-shaped shade embossed w/fleur-de-lis & other designs, Acorn burner, clear glass chimney, 7" h., No. 228 .... 235.00

Milk white glass Acanthus Swirl patt. base & ball-shaped shade w/green-painted trim, Nutmeg burner, clear glass chimney, No. 230 .... 226.00

Milk white glass 8-sided base & ball shade w/embossed scrolls & florals highlighted w/pink, blue, yellow & green enameling, sometimes called "Paneled Cosmos," Nutmeg burner, 8½" h., No. 241 . . . . 270.00

White opaque glass, Delft blue windmills on base & shade, marked "Delft" on bottom, Mt. Washington Glass Co., Acorn burner, 8½" h., No. 267 variant (Book II) 585.00

Milk white glass Eagle patt. base & ball-shaped shade w/American Eagle in relief in diamond form w/beaded & leaf-molded framework, Nutmeg burner, clear glass chimney, 7½" h., No. 275 . . . . 360.00

Red Satin glass embossed base & petal-molded globe-chimney shade, Nutmeg burner, clear glass chimney, 9" h., No. 284 . . . . 207.00

Milk white glass Cosmos patt. base & umbrella shade w/pink-stained band & colored florals, Nutmeg burner, 7½" h., No. 286 . . . . 287.00

Milk white glass painted yellow around top of shade & base, transfer-printed flower bouquets in shades of brown & green, Nutmeg burner, 8¾" h., No. 308 . . . . 315.00

Milk white glass painted blue around top of shade & base, blue & green h.p. floral decorations, Nutmeg burner, 8¼" h., No. 315 . . . . 265.00

Milk white glass base w/painted blue ship scene & blue-stained embossed corners, foreign burner, white Bristol glass chimney-shade, 6" h., No. 338 . . . . 135.00

Cranberry beaded ribbed "End-of-Day" (spatter) base & chimney, Hornet burner, 9" h., No. 367 . . . . 375.00

Embossed beaded swirl, iridescent cranberry glass w/greyish overshot, Hornet burner, 8¾" h., No. 370 . . . . 295.00

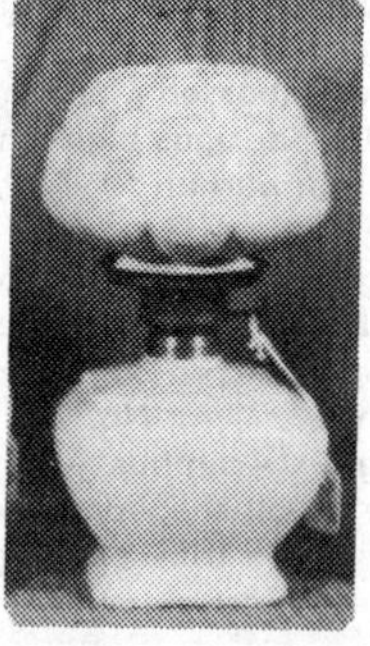

Pink Satin Miniature Lamp

Pink Satin glass base & rounded petal-molded ball-shaped shade, Nutmeg burner, clear glass chimney, 7" h., No. 385 (ILLUS.) 390.00

"Twinkle" & stars embossed on amethyst glass base & globe-chimney, Nutmeg burner, 7" h., No. 432 . . . . 290.00

Swan lamp, pink milk glass base, Nutmeg burner, 7½" h., No. 499 . . . . 300.00

LANTERNS

Primitive Hand Lantern

Barn lantern, tin, kerosene-type, "Dietz Farm," red globe, 6½" 35.00

Barn lantern, tin, kerosene-type, cobalt blue globe, marked "Norleigh Diamond," "Shapleigh Hardware Co.," St. Louis, 15" 30.00

Bicycle lantern, brass, kerosene-type, two red, one green gem-like lens, cracked clear front lens, top cap marked "The Neverout Insulated Kerosene Safety Lamp," 6½" h. 40.00

Candle lantern, hanging-type, blown glass, tapering cylinder, clear w/etched design, prunted knop, circular low-domed smoke cover, fitted for suspension, Anglo-Indian, early 19th c., 7 5/8" d. cover, lantern 8¾" h. 1,320.00

Candle lantern, tin, half-round, glass front, hinged back door w/hasp, cone-shaped top w/crimped wafer & ring, ca. 1810, 18" h. overall 220.00

Candle lantern, tin, conical smoke chamber w/punched decoration, three sides w/double bull's-eye inserts encircled w/punched decoration, hinged door w/single bull's-eye insert & punched decoration, ring handle, America, ca. 1800, 12" h. (some damage to bull's-eyes) 715.00

Coach lanterns, black-painted sheet metal w/copper & brass trim, curved & beveled glass engraved "W," w/kerosene burners, labeled "The James Cunningham Son & Co., Rochester, N.Y.," w/mounting brackets, 24¾" h., pr. 410.00
Folding lantern, tin, rectangular sides w/mica panels, brass hook fasteners, w/tin storage case, 7" h. 60.00
Hand lantern, painted pine & glass, rectangular lantern of pine w/hinged door fitted w/glass panels & a bail handle, painted dark green, America, early 19th c., 15" h. (ILLUS.) 605.00
Hanging lantern, bell-shaped frosted glass shade etched w/grape & vintage decoration, w/pierced & molded metal fittings, 19th c., 14" h. shade (electrified) 660.00
Miner's lantern, brass, carbide-type, w/7½" reflector, "Justrite" 32.00
Skater's lantern, tin, pear-shaped blue glass globe marked "Jewel," bail handle, 7" h. 150.00
Skater's lantern, tin, pear-shaped clear glass globe, marked "Jewel," bail handle, 7" h. 55.00

SHADES

Acid cut-back, elongated bell-form, green, pink & orange, unsigned, pr. 250.00
Art Deco style, hall-type, amber glass ball w/Handel-type crackled exterior, each side internally painted w/a parrot on a tree branch, molded brass tassel at base, 10" d. (minor rim roughness) 412.50
Clear frosted shading to cranberry, frosted leaves & flowers around middle, ruffled rim, 7" d. 55.00
Hobnail patt., ruffled rim, blue, 6" h. 135.00
Lustre Art, opal feathering on gold w/overall gold threading, scalloped edge, 5¼" h., pr. 300.00
Quezal, blue feathering in opposed hooks design 225.00
Quezal, fiery opalescent, floriform body w/delicate ribbing & shallow flared outer rim, 4½" h., set of 4 .... 165.00
Quezal, gold iridescent, bell-form w/flared flange at base opening, signed on lip, 4 1/8" d., 6½" h., pr. 200.00
Quezal, gold King Tut patt. & gold zipper on opal, squatty, 3½" h., pr. 325.00
Quezal, gold pulled feathers on Calcite, gold interior, 6 x 4½", pr. 260.00
Quezal, lily form, five green & white feathers on pearly opalescent w/iridescent gold borders, iridescent stretch gold interior, 5" h. 285.00
Quezal, gold zipper design, set of 6 .... 900.00
Quezal, opal w/fishnet design, gold interior, ruffled edge, 7" 685.00
Quezal, raised dark blue latticework on opal & gold, gold interior, 4" d. 950.00
Rubina crystal, etched frosted & clear small florals & leaves, 7 5/8" h. 175.00
Rubina Verde, Seashell patt. 395.00
Shaded yellow mother-of-pearl satin glass Diamond Quilted patt., melon ribbed, ruffled, white lining, 9" d., 6¼" h. 165.00
Steuben, blue drape w/gold hooked feather border on Calcite, ruffled rim, unsigned 265.00
Steuben, Calcite exterior w/gold & green pulled feathering, gold Aurene interior, bell-shaped, etched fleur-de-lis mark, 4½" h., set of 3 .... 302.50
Steuben, gold Aurene w/pink & blue iridescence, ribbed body w/flared rim, etched fleur-de-lis mark, 5" h., pr. 165.00
Tiffany, iridescent blue w/yellow pulled-up feather design, scalloped rim, 3" h. 245.00
Verlys, soft lavender, raised birds & fish design, 5¾" h. 275.00

(End of Lighting Devices Section)

MAGAZINES

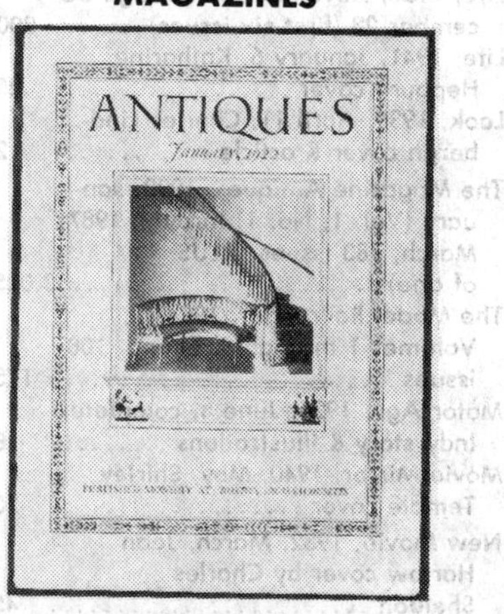

The Magazine Antiques

Advertising Arts, 1934, November, posters, layouts & design $20.00
The American Inventor, 1903, February 15 .... 7.50
Arizona Highways, 1952, February, Nicolai Fechin prints 20.00
Cartoons Magazine, 1917, May, color cover by Raphael Kirchner, black & white illustrations & one Icart illustration 65.00
Cosmopolitan, 1930, January, Harrison Fisher cover 10.00
Country Gentleman, 1922, March, Norman Rockwell cover 25.00
Country Life in America, 1901, November, Vol. 1, No. 1 .... 17.50
Electric Railway Journal, 1915, September or November, 98 pp., 9 x 12", each 15.00
Fortune, 1930, February or March, each 30.00
Godey's Lady's Book, 1862, full year bound 100.00
Harper's Bazaar, 1934, June or August, Erte' cover, each 60.00
Harper's Weekly, 1864, December 31, Christmas issue, double-page woodcut by Nast, Civil War scenes 25.00
Hearst's International, 1921, December, Alphonse Mucha cover 50.00
Ladies' Home Journal, 1914, June, Maxfield Parrish cover, color fashions feature 28.00
La Mode Illustree, 1882 or 1886, full year bound, folio size weekly, France, each 95.00
Landscape Architecture, 1912, October, article, illustrations & map of Boston Zoological Park 13.50
Life, 1921, December, Maxfield Parrish cover 38.50
Life, 1936, November 23 through December 28 (first six issues) 300.00
Life, 1941, January 6, Katharine Hepburn cover 25.00
Look, 1939, April 11, Charles Lindbergh cover & article 12.50
The Magazine Antiques, 1922, January (Vol. 1, No. 1) through 1987, March, 783 issues (ILLUS. of one) 3,025.00
The Model Railroader, 1934-42, Volumes 1 through 9, bound, 108 issues 175.00
Motor Age, 1925, June 4, complete Indy story & illustrations 8.50
Movie Mirror, 1940, May, Shirley Temple cover 20.00
New Movie, 1932, March, Jean Harlow cover by Charles Sheldon 45.00
Oui, 1972, October, Vol. 1, No. 1 ... 25.00
Photoplay, 1940, April, Tyrone Power cover 45.00
Pictorial Review, 1913, July, Harrison Fisher cover 15.00
Picture Play, 1916, April, Mary Pickford cover 20.00
Playboy, 1953, December, Vol. 1, No. 1 ....600.00 to 750.00
Radio Guide, 1937, October 9, Jeanette MacDonald cover 25.00
Red Cross, 1918, November, four Norman Rockwell color Boy Scout illustrations 10.00
Saturday Evening Post, 1904, full year bound 150.00

Saturday Evening Post

Saturday Evening Post, 1908, June 20, President Cleveland cover by Edward Penfield (ILLUS.) 10.00
Scribner's, 1899, April, Maxfield Parrish cover 55.00
Show Business Illustrated, 1961, September 5, Vol. 1, No. 1 .... 400.00
Sports Illustrated, 1954, August 16, Vol. 1, No. 1 .... 125.00
Vogue, 1939, February 1, World Fair features 13.00
Woman's Home Companion, 1914, February, Kewpie valentines, Kewpies & Little Peggy, Jack & Betty 32.00

MAGIC LANTERNS

These devices were used to project slide pictures on a screen and were popular from the late 19th to the early 20th century. Prices range from $60.00 to $250.00, or more.

Magic lantern, electric, "Lilley Electric," w/key, wood case & instructions, 12 x 20" $295.00

Magic lantern, electric, wooden case w/key, instructions, adjusting accessories, 33 7 x 4" slides (blank), France 425.00
Magic lantern, "German Pat. 1866," tin, w/glass slides & box, complete 185.00
Magic lantern, "The London," brass & black painted metal, 21" l. 245.00
Magic lantern slide, Civil War, Northern & Southern soldiers clasping hands, an angel w/outspread wings above them, man lying on a bier draped w/American flag, above angel, "Let us have peace," below two wreaths, "North" & "South" 125.00
Magic lantern slides, Black Americana, series of six different progressively tell funny story, great comic pictures, the set 75.00

MARBLES

Bennington-type Clay Marbles

Bennington-type, mottled blue, 3¼" d. $8.00
Bennington-type, mottled brown, 4¼" d. 10.00
Glass, Akro Agate, Cardinal, red box w/marbles 90.00
Glass, "onionskin," Lutz-type, swirls of red, green, white & orange, 3/8" d. 50.00
Glass, "onionskin," overall swirled white & yellow w/mica, ¾" d. ... 25.00
Glass, "onionskin," red, green & yellow swirls, 1 1/8" d. 60.00
Glass, sulphide, w/baboon sitting, 1 3/8" d. 155.00
Glass, sulphide, w/bear sitting, 1¾" d. 125.00
Glass, sulphide, w/billy goat, 1¾" d. 100.00
Glass, sulphide, w/boy on stump, 1 21/32" d. 550.00
Glass, sulphide, w/bull, 2 1/8" d. 225.00
Glass, sulphide, child w/ball & mallet, 1¾" d. 1,050.00
Glass, sulphide, w/cow, 1½" d. 80.00
Glass, sulphide, w/dog w/collar, 1 5/8" d. 150.00
Glass, sulphide, w/donkey, 1 5/8" d. 125.00
Glass, sulphide, w/dove on post, 1 1/8" d. 185.00
Glass, sulphide, w/spread-winged eagle, 1 3/8" d. 120.00
Glass, sulphide, w/fox running, 1 7/16" d. 165.00
Glass, sulphide, w/frog, 1 3/8" d. 110.00
Glass, sulphide, w/hawk, 1 7/16" d. 175.00
Glass, sulphide, w/horse grazing, 1 3/8" d. 150.00
Glass, sulphide, w/lion, 1 3/8" d. 75.00
Glass, sulphide, w/llama, 1 5/8" d. 90.00
Glass, sulphide, w/monkey sitting, 1 3/8" d. 135.00
Glass, sulphide, w/parrot, 2 3/8" d. 275.00
Glass, sulphide, w/pigeon, 1 3/8" d. 125.00
Glass, sulphide, w/rooster, 1½" d. 100.00
Glass, sulphide, w/sheep, 1 3/32" d. 90.00
Glass, sulphide, w/turtle, 1¼" d. 125.00
Glass, sulphide, w/"2" inside, wear & small flakes, 1 5/8" d. 130.00
Glass, swirl, w/white center & multicolored outer swirls, polished, 1½" d. 38.00
Glass, swirl, w/silvery tiny beads core "caged" by a yellow swirl striped interior & red & blue striped exterior, 2½" d. 195.00

MATCH SAFES & CONTAINERS

Cast Iron Match Container

Advertising container, wall-type, tin, "Clover Brand Shoes" $30.00
Advertising container, wall-type, tin, "Kelly's Famous Flour" 35.00

Advertising container, wall-type, cardboard, "Occident Flour" 90.00
Advertising container, wall-type, diecut tin, "Vulcan Farm Machinery," man pictured 295.00
Advertising safe, pocket-type, gutta percha, "Arm & Hammer Baking Soda" 65.00
Advertising safe, pocket-type, brass, "Griesedick Bros." 38.00
Advertising safe, pocket-type, celluloid, "Mollassine" horse & cattle food 55.00
Bisque container, table model, model of a pink pig holding orange pot embossed "Boston Baked Beans," Germany 48.00
Brass container, table model, figural spread-winged eagle above rectangular container w/ribbed sides, scroll-decorated column, rectangular plinth base on four small feet, 7¼" h. 165.00
Brass safe, pocket-type, figural man's head w/moustache & beard, 1½ x 2" 114.00
Cast iron container, table model, rectangular pedestal base, full-bodied rooster on lid 130.00
Cast iron container, wall-type, openwork scrolling vines, 2¾" l., 3½" h. (ILLUS.) 37.50
Cast iron container, wall-type, full figural head of Mephistopheles, circle of grape leaves above head, 7" l. 85.00
Ivory safe, pocket-type, cylindrical w/cross-hatched striking surface on base, screw-on lid, 2¾" h. 120.00
Leather safe, pocket-type, w/silver plate bust of Dewey on front, cigar cutter in base, tiny ball on base pulls out cigar cutter 110.00
Pewter safe, pocket-type, model of a mouse, 2" 145.00
Silver plate safe, pocket-type, figural "Punch," opens at base, w/striker, 1¼" d., 2 3/8" h. 139.00
Sterling silver safe, Art Nouveau dancing lady decor 65.00
Stoneware container, table model, model of owl, cobalt blue on grey, hollow stump, striker base, 6" 450.00
Tin container, wall-type, embossed light house & ships, open pocket, painted, 3½ x 8" overall 65.00
Wooden container, wall-type, carved walnut, leaf sprig at top w/game suspended at each side above hunting pouch holder at base, 11¾" l. (minor damage) 105.00

MEDICAL COLLECTIBLES

Amputation bow saw, ebony handle $120.00
Bleeder w/bone handle, three blades 95.00
Bleeder, solid brass, 12 blades, spring loaded, original case 200.00
Bodyscope, heavy cardboard, color fold-out in sleeve, moving wheels explaining & illustrating parts of male & female bodies, 16 x 20" ... 20.00
Book, "Depolaray, College of Electronic Medicine, San Francisco," w/case 38.00
Book, "A Textbook of Practical Gynecology," by Gilliam, 1913 ...... 15.00
Book, "Genito-Urinary & Venereal Diseases," 1897, 1,060 pp. 29.00
Breast shield, blown glass 50.00
Chiropractic treatment table, portable, oak & leather, folds up into carrying case, 22½ x 12½" 50.00
Dental instruments, ebony handles, ca. 1860, set of 6 .... 160.00
Lamp, "Vapo-Cresolene," for catarrh, whooping cough, asthma & spasmodic croup, w/bottle of Cresolene, in original box 52.00
Machine, hand-held shock treatment, "Branston Standard Electrode," original box 185.00
Machine, Cardiograph, electric, portable, 1930's 95.00
Machine, "Electric Nerve Stimulator," by E.J. Colby 175.00
Machine, "Master Violet Ray No. 11" 39.00
Machine, "Relaxacizor," size 5, 1955 .... 17.00
Machine, "Renulife" (violet ray), hand-blown glass attachments & instruction booklet in case 125.00
Retinoscope, ebony & brass handle 75.00
Tooth display, 834 teeth mounted in carrying case, made by Trubyte Dentist Supply Co. of New York, the set 125.00
Tooth display, "New Century," wood box containing 150 steel tooth forms, made by Cetral Tool Co., Auburn, Rhode Island, for the SS White Dental Manufacturing Co., dated September 27, 1910, the set 200.00
Tooth extractor 85.00
Urologist's "Kystoskop," ca. 1910, original box 75.00
Vials, glass, w/catgut sutures, six vials in box 30.00
Vibrator, "Cesco" label, w/glass attachment, original box 15.00

METALS

ALUMINUM

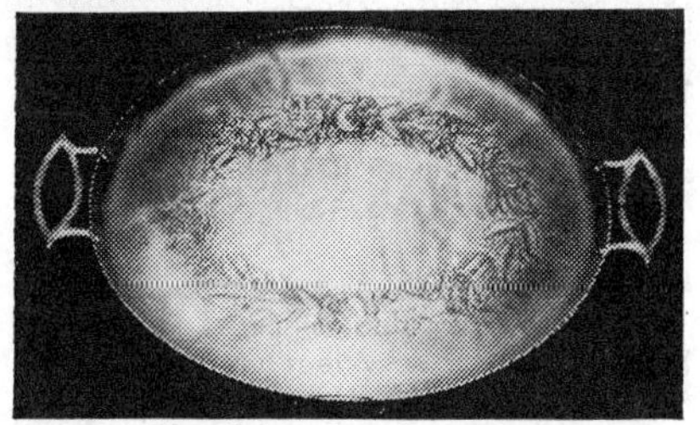

Aluminum Serving Tray

Bowl, Chrysanthemum patt. w/applied leaves, marked "Continental Silverlook No. 715," ca. 1950, 11¼" $14.00
Bowl, grapes on hammered ground, West Bend, 1950, 14" d. 15.00
Crumber, hammered shiny finish, Farberware, 1950 .... 6.00
Dish, handled, Wild Rose patt. on hammered ground, Continental No. 1088, ca. 1950, 7¾" d. 10.00
Tray, two-handled, flowers & foliage in relief on lightly hammered ground, 20½" l. across handles (ILLUS.) 28.00
Tumblers, colored, 1940's, set of 6 .. 15.00

BRASS

Brass Jardinieres

Alms dish, flat bottom repousse w/scene of the Crucifixion, w/Christ flanked by two standing figures & two partial figures hovering above, slightly flaring sides w/flat narrow border stamped w/a repeating foliate motif, ca. 1550, 9 9/10" d. ..3,850.00
Ashtray & matchbox holder combination, Gustav Stickley logo "Als ik Kan" stamped on sides of holder attached to oval dish-shaped tray, ca. 1912, 4" l., 3½" h. 110.00
Barber's basin, footed, cut to fit around neck, rolled edges, ring for hanging, 18th c., 6" d. 175.00
Bill clip, hanging-type, cast, bust of an Indian w/full headdress, 4½" h. 45.00
Bill clip, hanging-type, cast, model of a Turkish Sultan reading book, 4" h. 38.00
Box, cov., hanging-type, embossed scene of two men netting birds, 6¾" l. 130.00
Document carrier for saddle bag, cylindrical, 1" d., 8" l. 49.00
Dog collar, plain w/raised borders, adjustable to two sizes, w/padlock, engraved "Mr. James Barker, Olridge Taunton," ca. 1850, 6" widest d. 715.00
Footrests from shoe shine stand, 16" h., pr. 75.00
Grain scale bucket, "Howe," large .. 85.00
Jardinieres, neoclassical style globular body incised around rim w/thin band of vitruvian scrolls & rosettes supported by three acanthus leaves raised on a tripartite base, 10½" h., pr. (ILLUS.) 880.00
Jardiniere, three paw feet, lion's mask drop ring handles at sides, 13¾" h. 275.00
Letter rack, stag, hunting dogs & fence scene, Bradley & Hubbard .. 60.00
Mold for fishing sinkers, fish-shaped, two-part 140.00
Potter's coggle wheel for incising & decorating stoneware pottery, 2" d., 7" l. 85.00

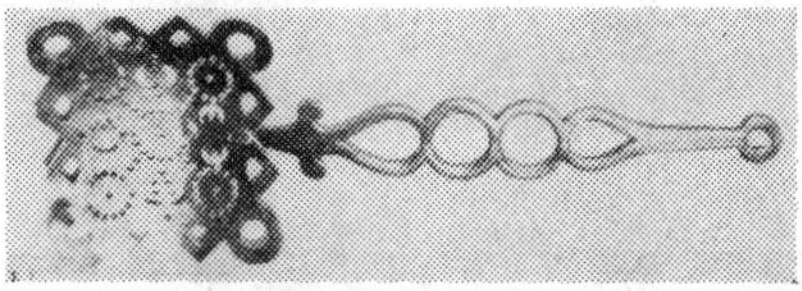

Brass Skimmer

Skimmer, overall 22½" l. (ILLUS.) ... 115.00
Stencil for apple crate, ornate lettering, "Russet" or "Wealthy," 2½ x 7", each 10.00
Stencils for flour barrel, ornate lettering, "Silver Lake Mills, St. Louis, Mo.," 16" d. 175.00
Tobacco box w/hinged lid, embossed floral design, 4¼ x 5 1/8" oval 75.00
Tobacco box w/hinged lid, man, woman & farm scene, 18th c., Dutch, oval 350.00
Whisk broom holder, hanging-type, ornate, Victorian 65.00

BRONZE

Blotter, rocker-type, caramel slag glass inserts, signed "Tiffany Studios, No. 995" 150.00
Blotter corners, pierced floral & leaf design, signed "Tiffany Studios, No. 997," set of 4 .... 150.00
Blotter ends, Chinese patt., signed "Tiffany Studios," pr. 150.00

Bowl, pine cone & pine needles in high relief, signed "Slot, Paris, 121, C. Delaherche," 3" w., 9" l., 2" h. 275.00
Box w/hinged lid, footed, Pine Needle patt. w/caramel slag glass inserts, signed "Tiffany Studios," 3½ x 4½" 200.00
Calendar frame, easel-type, Venetian patt., "dore" finish, signed "Tiffany Studios" & numbered, 6 x 6½" 225.00
Desk set: ink stand w/original milk white glass insert & pen rest, rocker blotter, long stamp box & letter rack; ornate ovals framing Art Nouveau type woman w/flowing gown & long hair, Jennings Bros., 4 pcs. 115.00
Desk set: pair blotter ends, inkwell, pen tray, perpetual calendar, rocker blotter, letter rack & stamp box; Adams patt., enameled gilt-bronze, signed "Tiffany Studios, New York," 8 pcs. 1,320.00

Bronze Ewers

Ewers, cast w/continuous panel of putti in various pursuits, strap handle w/a satyr mask applied at the base & a trailing vine issuing to a mounted putto amidst grape clusters, 23" h., pr. (ILLUS.) 990.00
Letter clip, Adam patt., signed "Tiffany Studios" 170.00
Letter clip, Grapevine patt., signed "Tiffany Studios" 160.00
Letter rack, black marble base, Liberty & Co., 1900's 75.00
Letter rack, Zodiac patt., "dore" finish, signed "Tiffany Studios" & numbered (ILLUS. right) . . 175.00 to 225.00
Memo pad holder, caramel slag glass inserts, signed "Tiffany Studios, No. 1022" 200.00
Mirror, easel-type, circular bevelled glass within a border cast w/band of linked peacock "eyes," mount cast w/matching peacock plumage set w/iridescent blue "eyes," reverse w/incised peacock feathers, signed "Tiffany Studios," 12¾" h. 5,500.00
Models of cat musicians, 1½" h. animals each w/different musical instrument, signed "Bergman," Vienna, Austria, ca. 1890, set of 10 .... 1,000.00
Paperweight, model of a spaniel, signed "Tiffany Studios" 295.00
Planter, shallow w/wide mouth, molded in low relief w/undulating flowers & leafage, gilt-bronze, signed "Tiffany Studios, New York," 10¾" d. 2,970.00
Plate, mosaic design, Tiffany, 1902, 12" d. 900.00

Tiffany Zodiac Pattern

Postal scale, Zodiac patt., "dore" finish, signed "Tiffany Studios" & numbered (ILLUS. left) 275.00
Pot, cast, three-footed, handle stamped "Robt. Street & Co.," polished, 5¾" d., 8" l. handle 310.00
Stamp box, three-section insert, Zodiac patt., "dore" finish, signed "Tiffany Studios" .... 125.00 to 150.00
Urns, shouldered ovoid, cast in relief w/classical sacrificial scenes within lobed borders, cast either side w/grotesque animal masks w/intertwined horn form handles, raised on waisted circular base w/laurel wreath border, inscribed "F. Barbedienne," late 19th c., 13¾" h., pr. 1,650.00

COPPER

Ale pitcher, dovetail construction, 18th c. (dents) 225.00
Apple butter kettle, dovetail construction, wrought-iron bail handle, w/cast-iron stand, J.P. Schaum, Lancaster, Pennsylvania, 22" d. 350.00
Bucket, w/bail handle & pouring lip, marked "5 gal. liquid, N.Y. City" 185.00
Cauldron, oval, lipped rim, wrought-iron handle, 18th c., 18" w., 14" h. 1,210.00
Cauldron, cov., swelled oval base w/wrought-iron handles, stepped

oval lid w/strap handle, late 18th-early 19th c., 19" l., 15" h. 286.00

Copper Chocolate Pot

Chocolate pot & cover w/brass flame finial, tapering cylinder, strap handle, brass button at center of side, France, ca. 1900, 8¼" h. (ILLUS.) 200.00

Coffeepot & domed lid w/brass finial, dovetail construction, tapering cylinder w/flared base, gooseneck spout, turned wood side handle in ferrule w/heart-shaped attachment, 11½" h. (slightly battered & seam separation at base) 95.00

Fish kettle, oval w/tubular handles, removable pierced liner w/strap handles, 21" l. 264.00

Funnel, 10" l. 25.00

Hot water bottle, brass stopper & bail handle, marked "Norman-Warmflasche, AEMA, Garantiert Reines Kupper" 75.00

Kettle, dovetail construction, wrought-iron handle, 30½" d., 20" h. 220.00

Measuring pitcher, haystack form, arched block center swing handle, handle at base, ca. 1860, 1 gal. .. 85.00

Mug, cylindrical, curving handle, spreading foot, hammer-faceted body & handle glazed in deep pink enamel, rim w/patinated silver die-rolled leaf border, one side applied w/patinated silver branch of cherry blossoms, other w/a silver butterfly, interior gilt, bottom w/inscription "Won by Dottie at New York Horse Show 1888," Gorham Manufacturing Company, Providence, 1881, 6½" h. 1,650.00

Pail, dovetail construction, iron bail handle, 12¾" d., 9" h. 105.00

Platter cover, tinned interior, brass Queen Anne style twisted open oval ring handle, 7¼ x 10½" oval 75.00

Sauce pan, dovetail construction, wrought copper handle, 9" d., 9½" l. handle 45.00

Tea kettle, cov., dovetail construction, gooseneck spout, fixed overhead brass handle stamped "J.M. Schwarz, Julje 1856," 8½" h. plus handle 130.00

Early 19th Century Tea Kettle

Tea kettle, cov., dovetail construction, gooseneck spout, arched swing handle, signed "W. Wolf," probably Pennsylvania, early 19th c., 11" h. (ILLUS.) 550.00

Teapot, embossed florals, copper & brass handle, impressed "London" 135.00

Vase, patinated, Dirk Van Erp, 8½" h. 85.00

IRON

18th Century Stove Plate

Ashtray, cast, model of cupped hands w/leaves & gilt grapes at wrist, painted black, ca. 1860 .... 50.00

Blacksmith's buttress, hand-wrought, offset handle w/shoulder rest 75.00

Bundt pan, cast, scalloped rim, solid center post, 18th c., 10½" d. 120.00

Cookie board, cast, spread-winged American eagle above shield w/"E Pluribus Unum" & 16 stars, 5 3/8" d. 85.00

Curling iron, hand-wrought, scissors-type, ball ends atop handles, 18th c., 10" l. 65.00

Fireback, cast, dolphin crest w/cherub, scene of nursing mother & two children, 24" w., 36" h. 285.00

Fork, hand-wrought, two-tine, delicate tines & slender handle w/hanging ring at end, 16 5/8" l. 45.00

Gas fixture, wall-type, cast, winged cherub blowing horn, hinged hardware, original paint 135.00

Hooks, hand-wrought, spike ends & decorative bird silhouettes w/brass eyes, 4½" l., pr. (lightly pitted) 230.00

Model of a frog, cast, old green & yellow paint, 5" h. 60.00

Oven peel, hand-wrought, ram's horn handle ends, 43½" l. 115.00

Pipe tongs, hand-wrought, well-detailed, 21" l. 550.00

Porringer, cast, lacy tab handle marked "Bellevue," bottom marked "E & T Clark, 1 pint," 5¼" d. (pitted) 75.00

Rendering kettle on furnace base, cast, removable jacket around kettle cast w/ears of corn & double steer's head medallions in relief, marked "Warranted 45 gal." on rim, furnace base w/cast paw feet & ears of corn, impressed "Kenwood Neward Stove Wks, Chicago," 37¾" d. kettle, overall 36" h. 350.00

Roasting skewer, hand-wrought, twisted handle, 29" l. 30.00

Rope maker, cast, "New Era Rope Machine," manufactured by A.D. Long, Fairfield, Iowa, 1911 patent date 32.50

Snowbirds, cast, model of an eagle, pr. 110.00

Spatula, hand-wrought, broom-shaped blade, well-shaped handle w/doughnut terminal, 16¾" l. 45.00

Stove plate, cast & painted, two canopies supported by three twisted columns, tulips, stars, an aureole on sheep legs, flower pots w/tulips & "1769" beneath inscription "DIE ERDE IST HERREN" & a medallion w/inscription "WILEHELM BENET, HA LEM FUR," flanked by tulips below, Hellam Furnace, York County, Pennsylvania, 27" w., 24½" h. 1,540.00

Stove plate, cast, depicting a woman in a canopied bed grasping the cloaks of a gentleman standing beside a column & tasseled curtain, above inscription "DAS WEIB DES SUCHT JOSEPH ZV ENTZVNDE IM. I. B. MOSE. 13 C. 1749," Pennsylvania, 18th c., 25" w., 26½" h. (ILLUS.) 1,320.00

Sugar nippers, hand-wrought w/wooden handle, shaped cutting device w/baluster-turned handle above a square base w/applied molding & short drawer, on molded base, 19th c., 12" h. 528.00

"Taster" spoon, hand-wrought, shaped shaft w/rat-tail end, 1835, 15" l. 150.00

Cast-Iron Footed Tea Kettle

Tea kettle, cov., cast, round body, gooseneck spout, swing handle, peg feet, 1770-1800, 9" h. (ILLUS.) 660.00

Tea kettle, cov., cast, graceful swan's neck spout, brass lid, wrought-iron handle, worn black paint 120.00

Teapot, cov., cast, gooseneck spout, marked "No. 1 J & J Siddons, West Bromwich," 4 pt. 69.00

Utensil rack, hand-wrought, D-shaped w/four hooks each w/bird-form scroll finial, 23" l. 550.00

Wafer iron, cast grid w/double eagle, 16 stars, shield & other devices, wrought-iron handles, 21½" l. 500.00

PEWTER

Pewter Chalice

Basin, molded brim, Thomas Boardman, Hartford, Connecticut, 1810-30, 6½" d. 418.00

Basin, Parks Boyd, Philadelphia, Pennsylvania, early 19th c., 12" d. 3,300.00

Basin, plain narrow brim, touchmarks for Townsend & Compton, London, 13¼" d., 3½" h. 425.00

Basket, floral & leaf design inside bowl, floral bud at top of handle, Kayserzinn, Germany, early 20th c., 10" d. 215.00

Beaker, flaring cylinder, double incised midband lines, molded base, Boardman & Hart, New York, New York, 1828-53, 5¼" h. 685.00

Bowl, footed, Leonard, Reed & Barton, Taunton, Massachusetts, 6¼" h. 175.00

Bowl & cover w/knob finial, two-handled, footed, rim engraved "B.G.Z., 1857," unmarked, 9¾" h. 325.00

Canisters, cov., graduated sizes, possibly American, 18th c., 13" h. largest, set of 6 ....1,760.00

Chalice, Reed & Barton, 1850-60, 7¼" h. (ILLUS.) 145.00

Charger, single reed brim, Thomas Badger, Boston, Massachusetts, 1787-1815, 15" d. 550.00

Coffeepot, cov., pear-shaped, S-scroll spout, spurred C-scroll handle, high domed lid, Sellew & Co., Cincinnati, Ohio, 2nd quarter 19th c., 10 3/8" h. 225.00

Coffeepot, cov., baluster form, octagonal base, scrolled spout, wooden handle, Britannia, Leonard, Reed & Barton, 1st half 19th c., 12½" h. 330.00

Communion chalices, high foot, unmarked, American, 7 1/8" h., set of 6 ....1,080.00

Dish, deep, Peter Young, New York City and Albany, New York, ca. 1785, 13½" d. 770.00

Flagon, flared cylinder, domed lid w/three-tiered finial, scrolled thumbpiece, curved spout, double scrolled handle w/bud terminal, body w/molded midband, flaring molded base, Boardman & Co., New York, 1825-30, 12 1/8" h. 1,760.00

Funnel, dome-shaped, w/cylindrical nozzle & suspension loop, probably European, late 18th-early 19th c., 8" h. 88.00

Ladle, Thomas & Sherman Boardman, Hartford, Connecticut, ca. 1820, 13" l. 247.50

Mug, tapering cylinder w/midband, flaring foot rim, double scroll handle, Samuel Hamlin, Providence, Rhode Island, 1771-1801, 4½" h. ... 990.00

Mug, tapering cylinder, S-scroll han-

Pewter Mug

dle w/bud terminal, midband & banded foot rim, Thomas D. & Sherman Boardman, Hartford, Connecticut, 1810-30, qt., 5¾" h. (ILLUS.) 715.00

Pitcher, tapering cylinder w/curving spout, handle w/bud terminal, William Savage, Middletown, Connecticut, ca. 1838, 4½" h. 275.00

Pitcher, baluster form, Rufus Dunham, Westbrook, Maine, 1st half 19th c., 6¼" h. 330.00

Pitcher, bust of Mephistopheles, signed "Kayserzinn" & numbered, Germany, early 20th c. 210.00

Plate, single reed brim, George Lightner, Baltimore, Maryland, 1806-15, 7¾" d. 385.00

Plate, "Love" touchmarks, Pennsylvania, 1750-93, 8½" d. 350.00

Plate, beaded rim, bottom incised w/initials "MVSV," Peter Young, New York City & Albany, New York, 1775-95, 8¾" d. (pitting, bruising) 660.00

Plate, single reed brim, Timothy Boardman & Co., New York, 1820-30, 9¼" d. 176.00

Plate, Thomas D. Boardman, Hartford, Connecticut, 1804-60 & later, eagle touchmark, 10¾" d. 400.00

Porringer, pierced crescent handle, everted brim, curved sides, Richard Lee, Vermont, 1795-1816, 4" d. 352.00

Porringer, old English handle, everted brim, Samuel Hamlin, Providence, Rhode Island, 1771-1801, 4 1/8" d. 495.00

Porringer, old English handle, everted brim, Samuel Danforth, Hartford, Connecticut, 1795-1816, 5" d. 1,210.00

Porringer, cast scroll handle, Thomas D. Sherman Boardman, Hartford, Connecticut, 1810-30, 5" d. 475.00

Porringer, plain tab handle pierced w/single hole for hanging, attributed to Elisha Kirk, York, Pennsylvania, 5¼" d. (small break in rim at handle) 660.00

Soup plate, Boardman & Hart, New York, New York, 1828-53, 11" d. .. 300.00

Sugar bowl & domed lid w/ball finial, globular, open handles, circular foot, George Richardson, Cranston, Rhode Island, 1830-45, 6½" d., 5" h. 2,200.00

Sugar bowl, open, dragon ship form, Kayserzinn, No. 4502, Germany, early 20th c., 8" l. 150.00

Tablespoons, leaf design on handle, marked "L.B." (Luther Boardman), 8¼" l., set of 6 .... 240.00

Scottish "Tappit Hen" Measure

"Tappit hen" (measure), Scotland, late 18th c. (ILLUS.).............. 895.00

Teapot, cov., pear-shaped body, footed, swan's neck spout, wooden C-scroll handle, domed lid w/wooden finial, Townsend touchmark for 1748, 6¾" h. 2,400.00

Teapot, cov., bulbous body, flaring foot, ornate C-scroll handle, William McQuilkin, Philadelphia, Pennsylvania, 2nd quarter 19th c., 7½" h. 250.00

Teapot, cov., stepped conical body, footed, gooseneck spout, ornate C-scroll handle, Roswell Gleason, Dorchester, Massachusetts, 8½" h. 200.00

Tray, leaf-shaped, w/handle, signed "Kayserzinn," Germany, early 20th c., 11½" l. 75.00

Vase, hammered body set w/three green stones, marked "Liberty of London," England, early 20th c., 7½" h. 150.00

SHEFFIELD PLATE

Candlesticks, shaped hexagonal base, knopped & tapered fluted stem, campana-shaped sconce w/detachable nozzle, borders of beading, acanthus, flowers & anthemia, Matthew Boulton & Co., ca. 1830, 11 5/8" h., set of four 1,650.00

Candlesticks, square base decorated on three sides w/urns & on other w/vacant oval cartouche all flanked by scrolled foliage, twisted bamboo column stem headed by overlapping leaf-tips, detachable

Sheffield Plate Gilt Candlesticks

nozzle, gilding of later date, ca. 1780, 12½" h., pr. (ILLUS.)....... 1,210.00

Card tray, flat chased center w/vintage border, raised on three vintage supports, 7" l., 7/8" h. 45.00

Chamberstick, octafoil base w/flying scroll handle fitted w/conical extinguisher, Matthew Boulton, early 19th c., 5¾" d. (lacking scissors snuffer) 165.00

Soup tureen & cover, fluted oval bombe form, foliate scroll, floral & shellwork rim & handles, leaf-capped scrolled panel feet headed by a flowerhead, domed cover w/oak branch finial, ca. 1820, 15 5/8" l. 1,980.00

Tea & coffee service: hot water kettle & lamp stand, cov. teapot, cov. coffeepot, waste bowl, creamer & cov. sugar bowl; in the George III style, hallmarked E.V., 6 pcs. 2,585.00

Tray, shaped rectangle, face flat chased w/scrolls & flower bands centered by a crest, applied molded rim of scrolls & shells, bracket handles, early 19th c., 24½" l. plus handles 357.50

Wine coolers, George III, cylindrical, molded rim, two pendant ring handles, detachable cover w/galleried rim, engraved crests, w/interior cylinder, felt-covered wood base, ca. 1800, 5¾" h., pr. 1,210.00

Sheffield Wine Coolers

Wine coolers, fluted & lobed campana form, pedestal base, gadroon borders w/foliate shells at intervals, reeded handles rising from lion's masks, detachable rim & liner, 10 5/8" h., pr. (ILLUS.) 2,970.00

SILVER, AMERICAN (Hollowware)

Tiffany Silver Centerpiece Bowl

Beakers, plain barrel form w/reeded foot rim, contemporary monogram, Churchill & Treadwell, Boston, 1814, 3¼" h., pr. 660.00

Bread tray, shaped rectangle, border repousse & chased in Kirk style w/flowers & foliage on matte ground, Baltimore Silver Co., ca. 1904, 14 1/8" l. 770.00

Cake basket, molded incised loop handle, circular pierced basket w/scalloped edge on circular footed base, reticulated, Tiffany & Co., New York, early 20th c., 12½" d. 825.00

Cann, baluster form, molded rim, spreading base, scroll handle engraved w/initials "T W," side later engraved w/"N.H." in script within wreath, "E.C." in shaped Roman letters, Jacob Hurd, Boston, ca. 1750, 5" h. 1,210.00

Centerpiece bowl, shaped oval, Chrysanthemum patt., border applied w/chrysanthemum blossoms & scrolling leaves, raised on four matching feet, Tiffany & Co., New York, 1880-91, 19" l. (ILLUS.) 5,610.00

Compotes, shaped edge, repousse & chased w/garden flowers on rim, stem & base, Tiffany & Co., New York, 1875-91, 8 9/16" d., 5" h., pr. 825.00

Creamer & sugar bowl, rectangular baluster form on pedestal base, gadroon rim, angled scroll handles, w/monogram "J.E.L.," Samuel Williamson, Philadelphia, ca. 1810, pr. 440.00

Cups & saucers, demitasse, Lily patt., Black, Starr & Frost, New York, set of 6 ....1,200.00

Cuspidor, Martele, paneled bag form w/gilt interior, wide slightly waved flat rim chased w/flower border & a cipher, Gorham Mfg. Co., Providence, 12½" d., 4" h. 5,225.00

Entree dish, cov., oval, engraved w/presentation on interior of bowl & dated 1910, base raised on four foliate headed supports w/shell pads, floral chased bracket handles, domed lid w/detachable handle, floral & landscape decor, S. Kirk & Son Co., Baltimore, 1896-1925, 10½" l. plus handles 2,475.00

Flask, overall embossed basketweave design, hinged lid, Gorham Mfg. Co., Providence, 7" l. 250.00

Julep cup, faceted cylinder, circular molded rim, molded octagonal foot rim, engraved "MM," J. Coning, Mobile, Alabama, ca. 1845, 3 5/8" h. 1,045.00

Mug, barrel-shaped, S-scroll strap handle, reeded rim & foot rim, engraved in script "SCJ," Thaddeus Keller, New York, 1805-13 (minor repairs) 440.00

18th Century Silver Pitcher

Pitcher, barrel form applied w/hoops, scroll strap handle, short angled spout, front engraved w/contemporary monogram, Thomas Shields, Philadelphia, ca. 1785, 6" h. (ILLUS.) 9,625.00

Pitcher, bombe form, lower body chased w/vertical lobes, entwined twig handle continuing below the rim into chased foliage & berries, molded rim, Lincoln & Foss, Boston, ca. 1850, 10" h. 1,100.00

Platter, border repousse & chased w/florals & leaves on matte ground, foliate rim, base engraved "Julia J. Ramsey, 1919," S. Kirk & Son Co., Baltimore, 17" oval 660.00

Porringer, pierced keyhole handle engraved in script "W & CDW," marked "Davis," possibly Issac Davis of Boston, early 19th c., 5½" d. 1,540.00

Salt dip, corn-shaped w/tassels at

ends, vermeil interior, Wood & Hughes, New York 200.00

Salver, square, hammered finish, curved rim applied in three corners w/lady bug, pinwheel & quince floral branches, fourth corner w/scarab beetle, Bigelow, Kennard & Co., Boston, 8" sq. 880.00

Sauceboat, oval bombe form w/shaped rim, leaf-capped double scroll handle, three hoof feet headed by shells, base engraved w/contemporary initials "IMI," Simeon Soumaine, New York, ca. 1740, 7¾" l. 8,250.00

Sugar bowl, cov., plain pear shape w/molded borders, slip-on cover w/molded ring finial for use as a foot when cover everted, base & cover engraved "LKC," base w/scratch weight, Myer Myers, New York, 1760-70, 4¾" h. 14,300.00

Tablespoon, spatulate-end mid-rib handle w/rat-tail on bowl, W. Simpkins, Boston, 1704-80, 8" l. . . . 330.00

Tea & coffee service: cov. teapot, cov. coffeepot, cov. sugar bowl, creamer & waste bowl; circular bombe form, pedestal bases, chased w/scrolling foliage & florals, straight gadroon borders, compressed bud finials, w/monogram, Gorham Mfg. Co., Providence, 1891-92, 5 pcs. 1,760.00

Teapot, cov., inverted pear shape, shell-decorated swan's neck spout capped by a leaf, matching upper handle terminal, shoulders flat-chased w/shaped border of shell & scrollwork, (repaired) pedestal foot, engraved "S. Gibbs," silver & wood urn finial, Samuel Casey, Exeter and South Kingston, Rhode Island, ca. 1760, 4¾" h. 9,625.00

Vases, faceted trumpet-shaped basket-form on conforming circular base, fixed arched handle, Tiffany & Co., New York, 1907-38, 11½" h., pr. 357.50

SILVER, COIN

Asparagus tongs, Bailey & Co., Philadelphia, ca. 1850 . . . . 475.00

Butter dish w/domed cover & liner, circular base w/beaded edge raised by three griffin form supports, cover w/three arched reserves engraved w/romantic landscapes alternating w/engine-turned panels, knob finial, w/star pattern pierced liner, Gorham, Providence, ca. 1860, retailed by Geo. C. Shreve & Co., 6½" d. 605.00

Canister, D. Tyler, Boston, ca. 1800, 7½" h. 1,200.00

Cheese scoop, large ball finial, Wood & Hughes, New York City, ca. 1860 . . . . 185.00

Coffee spoon, E. Lang, Salem, ca. 1770 . . . . 75.00

Condiment ladle, Fiddle Tip patt., Palmer & Batchelder, Boston, ca. 1850, 5 1/8" l. 30.00

Creamer & sugar bowl, Basket of Flowers patt., J. Crawford, New York City, ca. 1825, pr. 850.00

Dessert spoon, Olive patt., O. Reed, Philadelphia, ca. 1850 . . . . 29.00

Dinner fork, Josephine patt., Haas & Trau, probably Philadelphia, ca. 1860 . . . . 45.00

Coin Silver Ewer

Ewer, Hyde & Goodrich, New Orleans, ca. 1850, 15½" h. (ILLUS.) 5,750.00

Fruit knife, Grape patt., A. Coles, New York City, ca. 1860 . . . . 45.00

Ladle, bright-cut, H. Robinson, Wilmington, Delaware, ca. 1860, 9 1/8" l 375.00

Marrow scoop, Hayden & Whilden, Charleston, South Carolina, ca. 1850 . . . . 950.00

Mint julep cup, engraved presentation inscription, John Kitts, Louisville, Kentucky, ca. 1838, 3¾" h. (dents) 400.00

Mustard pot, N. Harding, Boston, ca. 1850 . . . . 195.00

Pastry server, Oval Thread patt., openwork & bright-cut blade, Tiffany & Co., New York City, ca. 1850 . . . . 195.00

Pitcher, milk, repousse florals & Dover, New Hampshire, textile industry inscription, N. Harding & Co., Boston, ca. 1850 . . . . 525.00

Punch ladle, bright-cut, H. Robinson, Wilimington, Delaware, ca. 1860 . . 375.00

Salt dip, boat-shaped, stag head at

ends, John Westervelt, Newburgh, New York, 1826-50 .... 500.00

Salt dips, twig feet, repousse grapes & leaves, P. Krider, Philadelphia, ca. 1865, pr. 450.00

Salt spoon, J. Basset, Philadelphia, ca. 1815 .... 21.00

Sauce ladle, T.K. Emery, Boston, ca. 1810 .... 75.00

Serving spoon, Farrington & Hunnewell, Boston, 1835-50 .... 35.00

Soup ladle, Olive patt., A.F. Burbank, Worcester, ca. 1850 .... 180.00

Stuffing spoon, P. Krider, Philadelphia, ca. 1860, 13½" l. 350.00

Sugar shell, twisted handle, bright-cut bowl, S. & T. Child, Philadelphia, ca. 1860.................. 48.00

Sugar sifter, Honeysuckle patt., John Polhemus, New York City, ca. 1862 .... 145.00

Sugar tongs, Sheaf of Wheat patt., Benjamin Benjamin, New Haven, ca. 1825 .... 175.00

Tablespoon, bright-cut, Ephraim Brasher, New York City, ca. 1790 .... 300.00

Tablespoon, E. Chittenden, New Haven, ca. 1750 .... 425.00

Teapot, cov., pear-shaped body, chased w/oak leaf & acorn designs, pedestal base, high domed cover w/acorn finial, marked "Bailey, Kettle & Chapman, Boston, Pure Coin," 10" h. 440.00

Teapot, cov., Basket of Flowers patt., Frederick Marquand, Savannah, ca. 1825..................2,400.00

Teaspoon, N. Coleman, Burlington, New Jersey, ca. 1790 .... 95.00

Teaspoon, shell-back, J. Richardson, Jr., Philadelphia, ca. 1770........ 195.00

Waste bowl, Basket of Flowers patt., J. Crawford, New York City, ca. 1825 .... 325.00

SILVER, ENGLISH & OTHERS

Apostle spoon, gold-washed bowl, Charles Stuart Harris, England, ca. 1885, 7" l. 125.00

Beaker, tapered cylindrical form w/molded rim above broad matted band, engraved w/later monogram, gilt interior, George Lotter I, Augsburg, Germany, 1652, 3¼" h. 1,540.00

Bowl, cov., Art Nouveau style, conical bowl w/flared rim held within slender leaves rising from low domed foot, domed cover w/curled leaf finial, Georg Jensen, Denmark, 5 5/8" h. 315.00

Cake basket, George III, oval w/gadroon rim, lower part of body chased w/vertical lobes, spreading foot rim, reeded swing handle rising from acanthus terminals, Paul Storr, London, 1799, 14 7/8" l. 5,500.00

Hot water pitcher, cylindrical, body embossed & chased w/detailed scene of a river procession arriving at the steps of a nobleman's house, winged dragon spout, foliage scroll handle, spray of pea pods finial, Chinese Export, Luen. Wo., Shanghai, late 19th c., 9" h. 990.00

Russian Silver Ice Bucket

Ice bucket, banded body repousse & chased w/continuous view of the Moscow Kremlin, strap swing handle, Andrei Alexandrov, Moscow, Russia, 1885, 11¼" h. (ILLUS.) ...3,740.00

Monteith, scalloped rim w/ring handles, simple horizontal line design, Charles Aldridge & Henry Green, 1784, w/retailer's stamp "Lambert Coventry St. London"............2,200.00

Salver, George II, molded shell & scroll rim, center engraved w/contemporary armorials within band of contemporary chased rococo decor, raised on three hoof feet, Robert Abercromby, London, 1742, 10" d. 715.00

Samovar, inverted pear shape, domed base raised on four ball feet, C-scroll handles, ivory fittings, maker's mark, "V.K.," St. Petersburg, Russia, ca. 1910, 14½" h. ..3,300.00

Tazza, Augsburg style w/applied shaped molded rim, flat-chased w/narrow border of strapwork on diaper, scalework & matted grounds, matching shaped domed foot, maker's mark "I.P.," Vienna, Austria, 1741, 8¾" d. 4,125.00

Tea caddy spoon, George III, long narrow fluted bowl w/serpentine sides, shaped Fiddle handle,

Richard Sawyer, Jr., Dublin, Ireland, 1812 .... 275.00

Tea set: tray, cov. teapot, creamer & sugar bowl; overall embossed hunting scenes, ca. 1880, India, marked 750 silver, 4 pcs. 550.00

Wine coasters, George III, gallery sides w/bright-cut floral swags interrupted by openwork paterae & bordered by two pierced bands of conjoined scrolls, beaded rims, turned wood bases, Hester Bateman, London, 1786, 4¾" d., set of 4 ....5,225.00

SILVER PLATE (Hollowware)

Silver Plate Cake Basket

Bath tub, typical form w/rolled top, engraved inside w/wide band of vitruvian scrollwork sprouting floral sprays & later applied (ca. 1890) w/copper shield engraved w/monogram "P de D," on black iron base, probably French, ca. 1870, 64½" l., 37¼" h..........22,000.00

Butter dish, cov., circular, w/pierced liner & bell-form cover, Gothic arch handle, domed base raised on four palmette decorated supports, multiple die-rolled borders, Meriden Silver Plate Co., Meriden, Connecticut, 14½" h. 165.00

Cake basket, ornate pierced feet, repousse florals & foliage, pierced movable handle, Simpson, Hall, Miller & Co., Wallingford, Connecticut (ILLUS.) 125.00

Cake holder, round dish-shaped top on pedestal base w/"Japanesque" border on rim, neck & foot, Hartford Silver Plate Co., Hartford, Connecticut, ca. 1890, 7" h. 165.00

Candelabrum, seven-light, naturalistic form, rocky base rising to entwined grapevine stems & branches hung w/bunches of grapes, Elkington & Co., Birmingham, England, ca. 1870, 24" h., pr. 2,475.00

Card tray, coral branch on pedestal base raised on three turtle feet, nautilus shell-form dish, Meriden Silver Plate Co., Meriden, Connecticut, 6" h. 85.00

Coffeepot, cov., etched ivy design, polar bear finial on handle, porcelain liner, w/inscription dated "1872," marked "Jas. Stimpson Pat. 1854," Baltimore, 2½ qt., 7" d., 13" h. 245.00

Egg caddy: footed tray w/center handle, four egg cups & four spoons; Florida patt., Wm. Rogers Mfg. Co., Hartford, 5 pcs......... 60.00

Flask, round w/puffy fluted edge, screw-on cap, comic engraving of standing golfer wearing knickers, resting stick on shoulder & holding flask in hand, 4¼ x 4¾" 145.00

Goblets, gilt lined, inverted bell-form cup on stepped pedestal base, 8½" h., pr. 44.00

Mirror, hand-type, beveled edge, back embossed w/cherubs, fish & waves 65.00

Model of a poodle standing beside enameled blue bud vase, ornate base, James W. Tufts, Boston 275.00

Mug, bright-cut design, James W. Tufts, Boston, 4" h. 18.00

Nut bowl, leaf-shaped w/squirrel on rim, cabbage feet, Pairpoint Mfg. Co., New Bedford, Massachusetts 110.00

Plateau mirror, double beveled mirror plate within chased scrolls & strawberries framework, 12" d. .. 80.00

Punch bowl, hemispherical bowl on domed pedestal base, top & base rims w/die-rolled band depicting sporting motifs, James W. Tufts, Boston, 19½" d. 1,210.00

Punch ladle, Pearl patt., semi-nude woman w/flowing hair holding dish, bird overhead, Reed & Barton, Taunton, Massachusetts 110.00

Sugar bowl-spoonholder combination, 12 spoon slots, domed lid, handled, sapphire blue glass Inverted Thumbprint patt. insert, Heron inset each leg, Rogers Brothers, Hartford 105.00

Syrup pitcher, hinged lid w/full figure of nude child standing on molded floral mound blowing a horn, mask spout & handle, Viking heads either side, engraved body, pedestal foot, 8" h. 65.00

Tray, two-handled, Art Nouveau style border, quadruple plate, Meriden Silver Plate Co., Meriden, Connecticut, overall 17½ x 30½" 350.00

Water tippling stand w/drip tray & tumbler, lined, quadruple plate, No. 163, Middletown Plate Co., Middletown, Connecticut 350.00

SILVER PLATE (Flatware)

HANOVER (Wm. A. Rogers)

Bouillon spoon 7.50
Butter spreader 7.00
Dinner knife, hollow handle 13.50
Pickle fork, long handle 27.00
Salad fork 12.00
Sauce ladle 18.00
Sugar tongs 27.00
Tomato server 55.00

IRIS (E. H. H. Smith Silver Co.)

Cold meat fork, large 15.00
Demitasse spoon 5.00
Luncheon knife, hollow handle 6.00
Olive fork, 6" l. 6.00
Pickle fork, 5 5/8" l. 5.00
Sugar tongs 12.00
Tomato server 16.00

LA VIGNE (Wm. A. Rogers)

Berry spoon 38.50
Butter serving knife, twist handle 11.00
Cold meat fork 17.50
Cream ladle 25.00
Demitasse spoon 15.00
Dinner knife, hollow handle 45.00
Ice cream fork 45.00
Salad fork 25.00
Sauce ladle 25.00
Soup ladle, 10½" l. .... 95.00 to 110.00

MOSELLE (American Silver Co.)

Berry spoon 76.00
Bouillon spoon 40.00
Cake server, hollow handle 125.00
Dinner fork 40.00
Dinner knife 40.00
Fruit knife, hollow handle 50.00
Gravy ladle 75.00
Luncheon fork 17.00
Luncheon knife 22.50
Pickle fork 62.50
Salad serving fork 175.00
Sardine fork 95.00

MYSTIC (Rogers & Bro.)

Cold meat fork 24.00
Dessert server 15.00
Dinner fork 4.00
Gravy ladle, gold-washed bowl 16.50
Ice cream spoon 14.00
Olive spoon, long handle 25.00
Oyster ladle, 10¾" l. 40.00

ORANGE BLOSSOM (Wm. Rogers & Son)

Butter spreader 5.00
Citrus spoon 7.50
Dinner knife, hollow handle 15.00
Iced tea spoon 16.00
Luncheon knife, hollow handle 15.00
Pie server, decorated blade 21.00
Sauce ladle 12.00
Sugar spoon 9.00
Tablespoon 9.00
Tomato server 22.00

VINTAGE (1847 Rogers Bros.)

Baby spoon w/curved handle & food pusher, original box, the set 75.00
Butter pick 49.00
Cake lifter 89.00
Cocktail fork 18.00
Cold meat fork 22.00
Demitasse spoon 15.00
Ice cream fork 69.00
Iced tea spoon 55.00
Lettuce fork, hollow handle 250.00
Olive spoon, long handle 75.00
Punch ladle, hollow handle 445.00
Salad fork 32.00
Soup ladle 68.00
Tongs, 4½" l. 35.00

STERLING SILVER (Flatware)

ACORN (Georg Jensen)

Bouillon spoon 40.00
Cheese scoop 100.00
Cold meat fork 135.00
Fruit knife 45.00
Gravy ladle 190.00
Salad fork 67.00
Serving spoon 175.00
Teaspoon 41.00

ANTIQUE LILY ENGRAVED (Whiting Mfg. Co.)

Berry spoon 165.00
Butter serving knife 58.00
Demitasse spoon 18.50
Iced tea spoon 59.00
Nut pick 30.00
Soup ladle 220.00
Tablespoon 62.00
Youth set: knife, fork & spoon, 3 pcs. 115.00

BEEKMAN (Tiffany & Co.)

Asparagus tongs, 10" l. 650.00
Bouillon ladle, 10½" l. 320.00
Fish slice & fork, vine engraving, 2 pcs. 495.00
Ice cream spoon 65.00
Oyster ladle 395.00
Stuffing spoon 225.00
Tablespoon, pierced, 8½" l. 95.00
Tomato server 230.00

CHARLES II (Dominick & Haff)

Berry fork 15.00
Claret ladle 120.00

Cream soup spoon 21.00
Jelly trowel 145.00
Olive fork 37.50
Pie server, silver blade 175.00
Sugar sifter 70.00
Teaspoon 20.00
Vegetable spoon, large 175.00

ENGLISH KING (Tiffany & Co.)

Tiffany's English King Pattern

Bonbon spoon, heart-shaped bowl .. 165.00
Pickle fork 62.00
Sugar shell, gold-washed bowl 75.00
Table service for twelve: dinner forks, dinner knives, luncheon forks, luncheon knives, salad forks, teaspoons, soup spoons, tablespoons, seafood forks & demitasse spoons plus 10 large tablespoons, 8 iced tea spoons, 11 butter spreaders, 3 serving forks, 3 serving spoons & large carving fork & knife, 157 pcs. (ILLUS. of part) 10,450.00

HERALDIC (Whiting Mfg. Co.)

Berry spoon 125.00
Butter serving knife 34.00
Dinner fork 32.00
Luncheon fork 23.00
Macaroni server 315.00
Mustard ladle 32.50
Pancake server 195.00
Salt spoon, master size 39.00
Sardine fork 69.00

MAZARIN (Dominick & Haff)

Asparagus server 190.00
Cold meat fork, gold-washed tines .. 95.00
Cream soup spoon 35.00
Dinner fork 30.00
Ice cream slice 205.00
Strawberry fork 40.00

Tablespoon 35.00
Teaspoon 14.00

PERSIAN (Tiffany & Co.)

Tiffany's Persian Pattern

Crumb knife 285.00
Cheese scoop 295.00
Dinner fork 65.00
Gravy ladle, gold-washed bowl 150.00
Ice cream serving spoon 295.00
Luncheon fork 47.50
Sugar sifter 220.00
Tablespoon 70.00
Vegetable fork, large 295.00

POPPY (Gorham Mfg. Co.)

Berry fork 30.00
Chocolate spoon 25.00
Cold meat fork 85.00
Fish server 135.00
Grapefruit spoon 30.00
Ice tongs 195.00
Preserve spoon 46.00
Teaspoon 15.00

RENAISSANCE (Dominick & Haff)

Renaissance Pattern

Asparagus server 325.00
Butter pick 75.00
Fish serving fork 130.00
Jelly spoon, large 110.00
Luncheon fork 32.50
Salad serving set 290.00
Sauce ladle 70.00
Teaspoon 17.50

VERSAILLES (Gorham Mfg. Co.)

Beef fork 95.00
Bonbon spoon, pierced bowl 95.00
Butter serving knife 73.00
Carving set, large, 3 pcs. 285.00
Gravy ladle 125.00
Ice cream slice, large 340.00
Lettuce fork, bright-cut design on tines 235.00
Pastry fork, gold-washed tines 67.00
Preserve spoon 82.50
Sardine fork 120.00

TIN & TOLE

Pennsylvania Punched Tin Coffeepot

Basket, woven tin, picnic hamper type w/two-section hinged lid, 6¾" h. plus handle 185.00

Beaker, tole, polkadot daubing, red & yellow rim design & yellow striping on original dark brown japanned ground, 3¾" h. 105.00

Bread tray, tole, oblong w/canted sides & rounded ends, free-hand yellow, red, green & black florals on sides, original dark brown japanned ground w/crystalized center, signed "Jacob Small" on back, 7½ x 12½" 300.00

Butler's tray on a stand, tole, painted w/pastoral scene of a man & woman w/farm animals in a country landscape w/buildings in the distance, within gilt & black painted borders, 19th c., stand of later date, 19 x 24", 19" h. 1,760.00

Candle mold, tin, 6-tube, large strap handle, 11¼" h. 80.00

Candle mold, tin, 12-tube, circular w/conical top & ring handle, 14½" h. plus handle 475.00

Candle mold, tin, 55-tube, 5 rows of 11 in footed pine frame, 35½" l. (4 tubes missing & 1 mismatched) 675.00

Candle sconces, wall-type, tin, oval curved reflector backs, crimped saucer pan w/cylindrical candle nozzle, 12" h., pr. 1,050.00

Candle snuffer, tin, w/wire handle, hook end, ca. 1830, 12" l. 25.00

Canisters, tole, molded circular body, slightly domed lid, front w/coat of arms painted in tones of red, green, blue & yellow on yellow ochre ground, w/gilt trim, 17½" h., pr. 990.00

Coffeepot w/hinged lid, tin, punched design of urn w/flowers & tulips each side, strap handle impressed "M. Uebele," Pennsylvania, early 19th c., 10½" h. (ILLUS.) 2,750.00

Creamer, tole, tapering cylinder, free-hand crystallized silver & red decor on dark brown japanned ground, 5½" h. 175.00

Document box w/domed lid, tole, free-hand red & amber swags on original dark brown japanned ground, 6 3/8" l. 120.00

Ice cream pail, tin, side blocked arched handle & inset lid, ca. 1840, 1 qt. 60.00

Jardinieres, tole, flaring square on lion's paw feet over a square base, painted landscape scene each side, 12¼" h., pr. 1,430.00

Tole Oil Lamp

Lamp, tole, dished base w/polychrome floral & leaf motifs on dark ground, American, early 19th c., 7¼" h. (ILLUS.) 770.00

Liquid measure, tin, 2 qt. 9.00

Maple syrup pitcher w/hinged lid, tole, haystack form, stenciled gilt flowers on black japanned ground, shell finial, ca. 1830 .... 130.00

Tole Measure

Measure, tole, conical w/strap handle, polychrome fruit & floral motifs on lacquered ground, inscribed on sides w/level indicators, American, early 19th c., 7" h. (ILLUS.) 5,775.00

Model of a star, tin, nine-pointed, three-dimensional, worn old bronze paint, w/hanging ring, 6" h. 315.00

Mug, tole, straight sides, strap handle, free-hand yellow, red & dark green design on green ground, 2" h. 185.00

Tin Oil Can

Oil can, tin, cylindrical w/strap handle at base & wire bail handle at shoulder, 10¾" h. (ILLUS.) 72.50

Sugar bowl, cov., tole, free-hand red, yellow & green florals on dark brown japanned ground, 3½" h. 110.00

Teapot, cov., tin, simple punched design, C-scroll handle, 5½" h. 195.00

Tray, tole, dished rectangular top w/scene of pagodas, Chinese figures, foliage & birds in shaded gilding on black ground, Victorian, 19th c., on later stand, 30½" l. .. 2,310.00

Whale oil lamp filler, tin, cone-shaped, crooked spout, strap handle, brass screw-on lid, 1830, 6 x 7½ x 9" 75.00

(End of Metals Section)

MILITARY COLLECTIBLES

Civil War bowie knife, hand-forged blade, brass guard, overall 18" l. $400.00

Civil War cavalry saber, ca. 1860 ... 200.00

Civil War field cage for carrier pigeons, wicker & leather 24.00

Civil War musket, Springfield (restored) 295.00

Civil War pike, Confederate cavalry, crude iron blade on original wooden staff, 6' l. 450.00

Nazi ammunition box, Luftwaffe, pine 75.00

Nazi belt buckle, Army officer's 25.00

Nazi cap, Luftwaffe officer's, w/visor 75.00

Nazi dagger, 1st pattern Luftwaffe officer's, plain blade, aluminum hilt mounts, swastikas to pommel & crossguard w/gilt, wire bound blue leather grip, by Eickhorn, Solingen, blue leather covered scabbard w/aluminum mounts & chain hanger, w/dress knot, 1935-41 .... 395.00

Nazi sun helmet 85.00

Nazi sword, Luftwaffe officer's, silver plate hilt mounts, pommel w/engraved oak leaves around outer circumference, swastikas to pommel & crosspiece, wire bound blue leather covered grips, by E. & F. Horster, Solingen, in blue leather covered steel scabbard w/silver plate mounts, w/hanging frog 720.00

Revolutionary War sword, American officer's 145.00

Spanish American War helmet, khaki 50.00

Spanish American War summer helmet, white, w/infantry helmet plate 90.00

World War I book, "Non-Commissioned Officers Manual," by Col. James A. Moss, 1917 ..... 5.00

World War I compass, "Waltham" ... 20.00

World War I forge, U.S. Army, field-type, sheet metal box on four wrought-iron legs 185.00

World War I freight wagon, U.S. Army, canvas-covered, wooden bed, (rebuilt) spoke wheels 2,500.00

World War I machine gun & ammunition cart, U.S. Army, dated 1917 .... 850.00

World War I propeller, U.S. Army Air Forces, w/plates & original shipping tag, 56" l. 350.00

World War I trumpet, brass, "U.S. Regulation" 78.00

World War I water bucket, canvas, collapsible 28.00

World War II book, "30 Seconds Over Tokyo," by T. Lawson, actual photographs, hardbound, 1943 .... 9.00

World War II field telephone, w/case 24.00

World War II flight jacket, U.S. Army Air Forces, original 8th Air Force patch, leather name tag, size 44 .... 150.00

World War II flight pants, U.S. Navy

pilot's, leather & fleece, w/suspenders 200.00

World War II mess kit, U.S. Army field officer's, 30 pieces of grey graniteware cooking & eating utensils in compartmented trunk, 14 x 14 x 18" 150.00

World War II sextant, U.S. Army Air Forces, model A-10A, mint in box w/instructions 100.00

World War II sword, U.S. Navy officer's, dress-type, w/scabbard & leather belt w/bronze dore buckle 1,500.00

MINIATURES (Paintings)

Miniature Painting of a Gentleman

Bust portraits of a lady & a gentleman on ivory, she w/an ornate upswept hair style, white collar & gold jewelry, he w/high collar, black tie & coat, each in oval gilt case w/window reverse enclosing black cloth & lock of hair, 2 x 2 3/8", pr. (woman's dress repainted) $650.00

Bust portrait of a plump young man on ivory, curly hair, wearing black coat w/high rolled collar & brass buttons over a white shirt & stock, gilt oval frame w/braided lock of hair in back of case, late 1820's, 2½ x 3" 357.50

Bust portraits of a gentleman & lady, water-color & pencil on paper, he in topcoat shown in profile facing right, she in Empire-style gown & bonnet facing left, original h.p. black eglomise mats, early gilt frames, from Conway, New Hampshire, early 19th c., 6½ x 7½", pr. (ILLUS. of one) 1,050.00

Half-figure of a child on ivory, wearing red calico dress w/lace trim, executed in water-color, unsigned, ca. 1830, in red morocco leather case w/brass mat, 1¾ x 2¼" 522.50

Full-length figure of a mature woman seen quarter right on ivory, wearing white cap w/blue ribbon, high white ruff collar over black dress w/high collar, paper label reverse "Hannah C. (?) Born at Portsmouth, N.H. (?) November, 1755 Died at Nantucket, Mass. (?) 1829 A.E. (?) June (?) Boston," original square wooden frame w/brass liner, 2¼ x 2¾" 302.50

Waist length portrait of Henry Floyd Jones facing right on ivory, brown curly hair, deep blue coat, white waistcoat, seated in red chair w/sky blue background, attributed to Joseph Wood, ca. 1816, 3" l. rectangle 2,090.00

Young girl on ivory, dark hair parted in the middle & falling to shoulders, low-cut pink dress w/white lace trim, doll duplicate of little girl dressed in blue is held on left arm, touches of green in back & base, unsigned, w/braided lock of hair in back of case, early 19th c., 2¾ x 2¼" 2,860.00

MINIATURES (Replicas)

Miniature Federal Wall Mirror

Basket, field or gathering type, bentwood staves w/wood & metal banding, wooden bottom & bentwood handles, old white paint over earlier red, 5½" d., 3" h. ...$325.00

Blanket chest, Federal, inlaid & painted cherry, rectangular hinged top lifting to deep well, line-inlaid base, high French feet, painted oval on the front decorated w/floral vines & centering the name "Maria Seigrift," 11" l., 7¾" h. 2,090.00

Book jacket, sterling silver, embossed each side w/scene of nude child on floral chariot drawn by large bumble bee within scrollwork, French hallmarks, 18th c., 2" w., 2¼" h. 120.00

Candlesticks, flint glass, hexagonal, deep purple-blue, 1 9/16" h., pr. (minor flake) 2,100.00

Chest, rectangular w/leather-hinged lid opening to deep well, top & sides painted w/circle & dot decoration in dark green & red on a mustard yellow ground, raised on turned feet, Shenandoah County, Virginia, ca. 1850, 8¾ x 5", 6" h. 9,075.00

Chest of drawers, Chippendale, walnut, rectangular molded top above four graduated drawers w/original brass bat's wing handles, bracket feet, Pennsylvania, ca. 1780, 12¾" w., 10" deep, 19¾" h. 15,400.00

Chest of drawers, Federal, inlaid cherry, rectangular top w/bowed line-inlaid front above a conforming case w/two graduated line inlaid drawers flanked by trailing vine & urn decorations over a shaped skirt, French feet, probably Kentucky, 1820-30, 11½ x 7½", 12 7/8" h. 2,420.00

Chest of drawers, Empire-transitional, cherry, oblong top over deep overhanging long drawer over three graduated long drawers flanked by spiral-turned columns, wood knobs, turned feet, 9¾ x 14¾", 18½" h. 1,450.00

Cupboard, step-back type, pine, two-part construction: upper part w/molded projecting cornice above single open shelf; lower section w/single paneled cupboard door, cut-out skirt at either end, old red paint, America, early 19th c., 10¼" w., 17¾" h. 1,320.00

Footstool, painted & decorated pine, stenciled fruit & foliage in shades of green & black w/bronze highlights on light green painted ground, 8½ x 4½" 200.00

Furniture knobs, flint glass, clear, mushroom-shaped w/rosette design, pr. (shank chip on one) 95.00

Ice cream freezer, tin drum, cast iron top marked "Made in U.S.A.," scale model in working condition, 7" h. 65.00

Mirror, Federal, wall-type, mahogany, carved molded cornice above picture panel enclosing a colored print & rectangular mirror flanked by reeded half-columns, molded base, America, 19th c., 9½" h. (ILLUS.) 1,210.00

Piano, grand, w/bench, sterling silver filigree, Germany 145.00

Salute cannon, brass & steel-mounted mahogany & oak, w/caisson & fitments, a front carriage supporting an adjustable brass cannon w/rifled aperture flanked by pole supports for carrying a munitions box & pair hinged powder boxes, caisson w/removable munitions box before two planks for a driver, w/a removable carriage, English, 19th c., 4' 4" l. 9,900.00

Settee, painted & decorated, plain crestrail above 9-spindle back, shaped arms on turned support, plank seat, splayed turned legs w/stretchers, crestrail w/stenciled stylized leaf & stellate devices in yellow on red & black grain-painted ground, Pennsylvania, ca. 1840, 15¼" l. 2,970.00

Tea table, Federal, tilt-top, mahogany, octagonal tilting top above baluster-turned standard, three arched legs w/pad feet, America, early 19th c., 9" h. 990.00

Trunk, flat-top, red leather w/black trim & brass studding, iron lock w/brass trim, brass bail handle, original marbleized paper lining w/paper label "Robert Burr...Boston," 8" l. 215.00

Miniature Freight Wagon

Wagon, freight-type, carved wood & metal, rectangular wagon bed w/sliding boards, metal fittings, wheels & brakes, Pennsylvania, 19th c., 16½" l., 12½" h. (ILLUS.) 4,675.00

MUCHA (Alphonse) ARTWORK

A leader in the Art Nouveau movement,

Alphonse Maria Mucha was born in Moravia (now part of Czechoslovakia) in 1860. Displaying considerable artistic talent as a child, he began formal studies locally, later continuing his work in Munich and then Paris, where it became necessary for him to undertake commercial artwork. In 1894, the renowned actress Sarah Bernhardt commissioned Mucha to create a poster for her play "Gismonda" and this opportunity proved to be the turning point in his career. While continuing his association with Bernhardt, he began creating numerous advertising posters, packaging designs, book and magazine illustrations and "panneaux decoratifs" (decorative pictures).

"Iris" by Mucha

Poster, "Biscuits Le Fevre Utile," 1897, 23 x 30" $3,000.00

Poster, "Casan Fils," 32 x 70" 4,500.00

Poster, "Job," cigarette paper advertisement, 1896, printed by F. Champenois, Paris, framed, 20¼ x 15 3/8" 8,250.00

Poster, "Job," cigarette paper advertisement, 24 x 29" 9,500.00

Poster, "Job," cigarette paper advertisement, 1898, 38 x 58" 8,000.00

Poster, "Leon Maillard Menus & Programmes Illustres," 21 x 29" . . 950.00

Poster, "Printemps," 1900, framed, 11 3/8 x 27 1/8" 4,400.00

Print, "Iris," printed in colors, 1898, trimmed to the subject, framed, image 15¾ x 39¼" (ILLUS.) 2,420.00

MUSIC BOXES

Baker-Troll & Co. (Swiss) interchangeable cylinder music box,

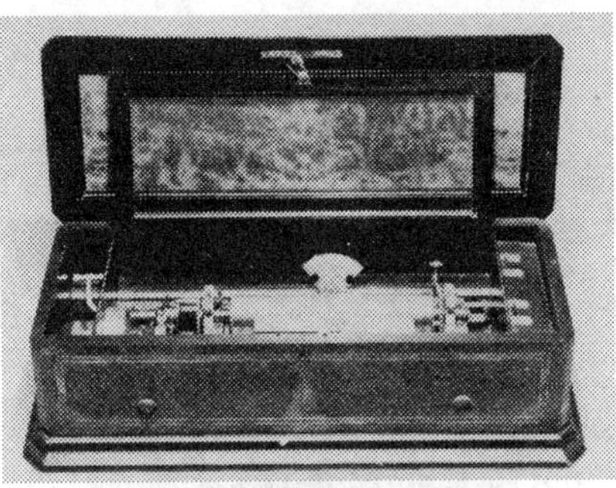

Baker-Troll Cylinder Music Box

6-tune, w/tune indicator, start-stop levers, w/zither attachment, needs damper repair, walnut case w/fruitwood banding, late 19th c., 21" l. (ILLUS.) $880.00

Bremond (Swiss) cylinder music box, 12-tune, rosewood box w/fruitwood stringing & an inlaid central floral motif, late 19th c., 15" cylinder, 24" w. 605.00

Conchon, Francois Michel (Swiss) cylinder music box, 12-tune, lever wind, w/original tune sheet, rosewood & mahogany case w/inlaid floral designs & boxwood stringing, ca. 1870, 9 x 21", 6" h. (professionally restored, glass damage) 1,650.00

Heller, J.H. (Swiss) cylinder music box, 8-tune, inlaid rosewood case, late 19th c., 13" cylinder 1,900.00

Mermod Freres (Swiss) interchangeable cylinder music box, 6-tune, wooden case w/floral inlay on lid, late 19th c., 9" cylinder, 24" l. . . . 1,320.00

Paillard (Swiss) cylinder music box, 10-tune, rosewood case w/floral inlay on lid, 11½" cylinder, 24" l. (needs damper repair) 715.00

Regina (American subsidiary of Polyphon Musikwerks, Rahway, New Jersey) disc music box, Style 17a, double comb, oak upright case, w/seventeen 12¼" discs 2,800.00

Regina disc music box w/automatic changer, w/thirty-six 20¾" discs 12,000.00

Polyphon (Polyphon Musikwerke, Leipzig, Germany) disc music box w/bells, double comb w/twelve bells, crank handle wound, professionally restored, walnut case w/inlaid lid, bracket feet, sepia lithograph set inside lid, ca. 1900, w/twelve 14½" discs, 25" w., 12" h. (ILLUS.) 5,170.00

Stella (Swiss) disc music box, table model, mahogany case w/drawer, 17¼" disc 4,200.00

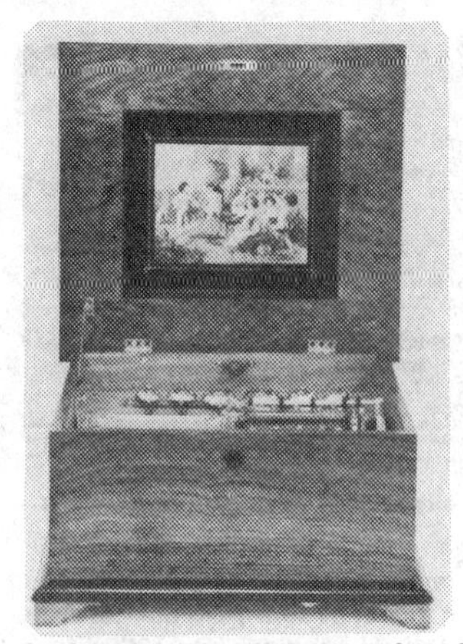

Polyphon Disc Music Box with Bells

Symphonion (German) disc music box, Style 30A Deluxe, double comb, walnut case w/inlaid lid, brass end handles, 13 5/8" disc (restored) 3,250.00

MUSICAL INSTRUMENTS

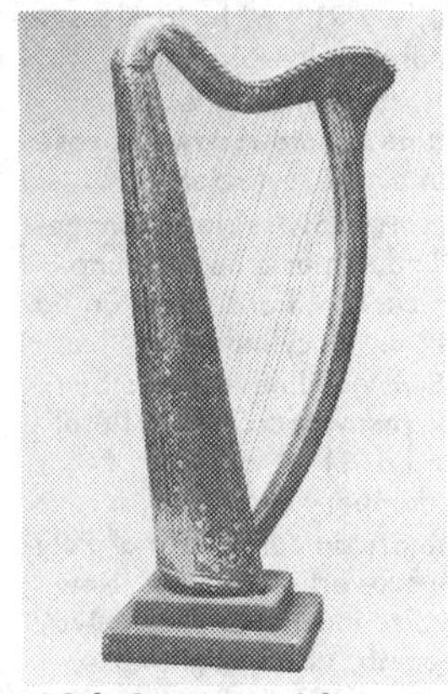

18th Century Irish Harp

Accordion, "Crucianelli," Bakelite case, 1937 .... $60.00

Autoharp, "The Zimmerman Autoharph Co., Dolgeville, New York, USA," original black painted finish w/gold embossed advertising & design in 2-tone brown of a winged lion, 21 x 10" 55.00

Banjo, "Orpheum No. 2," 5-string, neck carved w/flower & scroll at either end of base, fingerboard w/mother-of-pearl inlays, imitation ivory tuners, Serial No. 724833, w/green velvet lined hardshell case 507.00

Bugle, brass, "J.W. York & Sons, Grand Rapids, Mich., Phila. Depot Spec. 1152 cont. 7-10-17," 9" l. . . . 75.00

Cello bow, "Colin - Mezin," silver & ebony mounted w/pearl inlaid frog, silver wrapped, 28" l. 650.00

Clarinet, "Klemm & Bro., Phia.," B-flat, boxwood, 6 brass keys, block mounted w/five ivory rings, ca. 1845, 26" l.................... 175.00

Cornet, "Aschbach, Allentown, Pa.," B-flat, brass, ca. 1890, leather satchel case 125.00

Drum, worn original paint w/American eagle w/shields, flags & "E Pluribus Unum" in oval, 22½" d., 25" h. 500.00

Flute, "Haynes," sterling silver, dated August, 1909, w/case 2,200.00

Guitar, "C.F. Martin," ivory & abalone trim, pre-1930 ....1,500.00

Guitar, "National Resophonic Dobro," 4-string, nickel-plated mother-of-pearl dots inlaid on ebony fingerboard, Serial No. 616, ca. 1926, original leatherette hard case lined in purple velvet, 36" l. 275.00

Harmonica, "Hohner - Chromonica 10," double hole model, ca. 1937 .... 25.00

Harp, Irish, green-painted w/parcel-gilt foliate scrolls & flowering vine borders, third quarter 18th c., 36" h. (ILLUS.) 990.00

Mandolin, "Gibson Style A" 325.00

Metronome, "Seth Thomas," wooden case 38.00

Ocarina, "Ewa" 40.00

Organ, "Clough & Warren," pump model, solid walnut tall-back case w/burl trim, patented 1884 (tuned & reconditioned) 1,600.00

Organ, "Gulbransen," traveling model, 4-octave keyboard, case 30½ x 16½ x 11½" closed, 72" h. open 165.00

Piano, grand, "Bluthner, No. 57202," rosewood case, 89" l. 4,950.00

Piano, grand, "Niendorf," Louis XVI-style, shaped rectangular case painted w/floral swags & medallions centering putti on light green ground, hinged top painted in 18th century style w/figures in landscape scenes, raised on fluted circular legs, ca. 1915, w/piano stool, 5' 11" l., 2 pcs. 7,700.00

Piano, square grand, "Hallet Davis," rosewood case, ca. 1850 ....1,000.00

Piano, square grand, "Kimball," walnut case, 1892 (refinished & restrung), w/stool, 2 pcs. 2,000.00

Trumpet, "C.G. Conn, Ltd.," B-flat,

silver plate "peashooter" style, ca. 1925, original green velvet lined hardshell case, 22" l. 90.00

Tuba, E-flat, three Berliner valves, brass w/nickel silver trim, ca. 1870 .... 138.00

Ukelele, concert model, "Gretsch," mahogany, h.p. tuning plate, triplex ring around tone hole, straight neck w/small circular pearl inlays on fingerboard, ca. 1920 .... 75.00

Violin, "Amati" style, w/two bows, deluxe case, 1894 (restored) 775.00

Violin, "Copie De Antonius Stradivarius Cremonenfis, Faciebat Anno 1726," 2-piece grained back, light brown, contemporary wooden chin rest replacement, lined hardshell case 210.00

Zither, "Class Instrument," original black paint finish w/gold embossed decor, patented 1894, original label, w/tuner & music sheets, 19½ x 11" 45.00

MUSICAL INSTRUMENTS, MECHANICAL

Band organ, "Wurlitzer 146B," double track w/bells, converted to blower operation, 1940's, rebuilt 1966 ....$16,500.00

Barrel organ, "Gavioli Harmoniflute & Trombone" (needs restoration)...........................3,250.00

Caliola (calliope), "Wurlitzer," antique white finish w/varied color trim 15,500.00

Coin-operated piano, "Coinola Cupid," w/mandolin attachment..4,250.00

Coin-operated piano, "Cremona Style G," Marquette Piano Company (restored)................11,500.00

Coin-operated piano, "Seeburg Style E," w/xylophone, 1910-15, unrestored 4,000.00

Orchestrion, "Berry-Wood Style A.O.H.R.," w/rewind rolls (restored) 21,000.00

Orchestrion, "Coinola Midget X," w/xylophone (restored) 16,000.00

Orchestrion, "Philipps Violin Orchestra" (restored & refinished) 44,000.00

Orchestrion, "Seeburg Style E Special," quarter-sawn oak case (restored)....................14,995.00

Organ, "Mortier Concert," 67 keys, 350 wooden pipes, 12' w. front 16,000.00

Player piano, baby grand, "Chickering," mahogany, w/Stoddard Ampico player, 1912, 5' 8" (restored, refinished & restrung)...........7,850.00

Player piano, upright, "Alexander Debain Antiphonel," plays movement from rectangular "planchettes" studded w/pins, walnut case w/operating handle at front flanked by pair of brass candleholders above carved baluster supports, ornate cast brass carrying handles at sides, France, mid-19th c., 51" w. 5,500.00

Player piano, upright, "Decker," black walnut, ornate scrolled music board, carved legs, 1888 (unrestored)...................1,950.00

Player piano, baby grand, "George Steck Duo-Art," 1923, w/rolls 2,500.00

Player reed organ, "Wilcox & White Symphony," 58-note, ornately carved mahogany cabinet w/large griffins supporting keyboard, w/rolls 4,250.00

Reproducing piano, "Marshall & Wendell Ampico Model A," walnut, Louis XV style, highly carved, 5' 8" (unrestored)...................7,900.00

Reproducing pipe organ, "Seeburg Style M.O." 3,900.00

Violano (violin player), "Mills Deluxe," double violins, restored 23,100.00

MUSTACHE CUPS & SAUCERS

China Mustache Cup

China, Coalport, dark blue birds & bamboo decor on white ground, wide geometric border, 1880's....$110.00

China, inscribed "Forget Me Not" ... 17.00

China, Paragon, rust & green decor on white ground, ca. 1904 .... 68.00

China, pink & white floral decor, gold trim, Germany (ILLUS.) 40.00

China, fluted rim, pink flowers on white ground 35.00

China, roses decor on green ground, marked Germany 27.00

China, scenic medallion on purple ground, unmarked 45.00

China, h.p. violets decor, Bavaria . . . 37.50
Silver plate, engraved "Charlie - December 25, 1892," Pairpoint Corp. (cup only) 75.00
Silver plate, engraved florals, inscription & "1869-1887," James W. Tufts (cup only) 85.00

NAPKIN RINGS

Silver Plate Napkin Ring

All napkin rings listed are silver plate unless otherwise noted.

Art Nouveau style water lilies decor, sterling silver $50.00
Barefoot girl seated to one side of ring w/book on lap on oblong base, Simpson, Hall, Miller & Co. 110.00
Baseball player in uniform & holding bat, bell in front, 1870's 235.00
Bulldog w/glass eyes beside ring, Derby Silver Co. 150.00
Butterflies (2) on flat fan base & supporting ring between wings, Meriden Britannia Co. 90.00
Cherub pulling wheeled wagon w/ring, salt & pepper shakers & butter pat, Simpson, Hall, Miller & Co. 450.00
Chick & wishbone beside ring inscribed "Best Wishes," Derby Silver Co. 90.00
Cockatoo on branch beside ring, No. 228, Meriden Britannia Co. . . . 140.00
Dogs (2) barking at bird on ring, tree trunk base, Meriden Britannia Co. 155.00
Eagles (2) w/spread wings on either side of floral engraved ring, Meriden Britannia Co. 80.00
Frog marching & playing drum forming ring, Reed & Barton 150.00
Gargoyle heads either side of ring, coin silver 400.00
Goat pulling ring on wheels, Meriden Britannia Co. 275.00
Greenaway boy w/baseball bat in elbow crook, ball front of foot . . . 250.00
Greenaway boy offering cookie to dog beside ring, flat rectangular base 185.00
Holly engraving overall, sterling silver 30.00
Husky-type dog pulling ring cart w/movable wheels 260.00
Jester standing in front of ring, pointing & holding torch, Meriden Britannia Co. 295.00
Jockey cap atop horseshoe w/initials "GPM" on side, clover reverse, Derby Silver Co. 195.00
Kitten pulling ring cart w/movable wheels 295.00
Leaves & branches supporting barrel form ring (ILLUS.) 65.00
Man w/top hat, holding long staff & standing before pedestaled ring, octagonal base 155.00
Peacock on ring, No. 234, Meriden Britannia Co. 110.00
Stag supporting ring on back, No. 204, Meriden Britannia Co. . . . 225.00

NAUTICAL ITEMS

Brass Diver's Helmet

The romantic lure of the sea, and of ships in general, has opened up a new area of collector interest. Nautical gear, especially items made of brass or with brass trim, is sought out for its decorative appeal. Virtually all items that can be associated with ships, along with items used or made by sailors, are now considered collectible for technological advances have rendered them obsolete. Listed below are but a few of the numerous nautical items sold in recent months.

Anchor lamp, schooner-type, 1880's, 24" h. $80.00

Binnacle, brass casing, door w/kerosene light, underplate showing ships, w/information on sister ships, "H. Edinburgh Castle" & "Pretoria Castle" 200.00
Boatswain's pipe, silver w/macrame cord 24.00
Book, "Keel to Truck," by Capt. H. Paasch, 1885, dictionary of naval terms in English, French & German, 1st edition 310.00
Cannon, black powder-type, line shooter (used to shoot line from one ship to another), 1880's 225.00
Compass, in liquid, enclosed in covered copper box, John E. Hands & Sons Co., Phila., USA, U.S. Coast Guard, 6" sq., 8" h. 185.00
Diver's helmet, brass, A.J. Morse & Sons, Inc., Boston, Massachusetts, 22½" h. (ILLUS.) 825.00
Fid (tapering needle), carved whalebone 375.00
Mast top, carved wooden crown, decorated, 7¾" h. 600.00
Medal, bronze, commemorative, "Nautilus - 1st Atomic Submarine - Launched Nov. 1954" 18.00
Net maker's needle holder, wooden, bottle-shaped w/hewn stopper, w/24 netting needles, early 1800's, 2" d., 12½" l. 65.00
Quadrant, brass, w/extra lens in a fitted walnut case, marked "England No. 9052," also "Kelvin & Wilfred O. White Co., Boston, U.S.A.," late 19th c., 9½ x 10¾", 5" h. case 250.00
Sailor's valentine, double-hinged octagon filled with tiny shells in various colors arranged around central reserve w/"Forget Me Not," 9½" w. 900.00
Seaman's chest, painted finish, six-board construction w/canted front, grommet handles at sides, original green paint, 10 x 23¾", 9½" h. 325.00
Ship's lamp, hanging-type, pewter, acorn font w/two covered wick holders suspended over a stepped circular base w/ring handle, Yale & Curtis, New York, 1858-67, 7 7/8" h. 550.00
Ship's masthead & starboard lanterns, copper, quarter-round w/oil burner, w/molded copper tag, G.B. Seahorse, 26" h., 2 pcs.. ..... 264.00
Ship's wheel, mahogany, complete w/stand, 28" d. 800.00
Telescope, captain's, leather-covered white metal, tapering cylinder w/retractable sections, Ross, London, late 19th c., 41" l. extended 462.00

NEEDLEWORK PICTURES

19th Century Needlework Picture

Berlin wool work is embroidery with wool on a canvas pattern, sometimes erroneously referred to as tapestry, which was a popular pastime of ladies of the 19th century. Wool embroidery with glass beads worked in the design became fashionable about 1850 and this type is known as "German Embroidery." Stool and book covers, panels for fire screens and pictures are among the items available to collectors today. Fine early pictures were often embroidered on silk.

Needlework embroidered on wool flannel, scene of beautiful woman in garden setting, paper face w/pen & ink & water-color detail, oval gold mat & giltwood frame, 11¼ x 13 3/8" $175.00
Needlework embroidered & painted on silk, depicting Marie of Sterne's *Sentimental Journey*, executed in gold, green, beige, pale yellow & rose silk threads w/sky, mountains, face & limbs rendered in water-color, black glass eglomise mat inscribed "Wrought by Ann Faulkner, A.D. 1814," New England, in original giltwood & gesso frame, 13½ x 17¼" (ILLUS.) 5,225.00
Needlework embroidered on wool, scene of three children on a park

bench above date "1857," hourglass in each corner, worked in needle point & petit point on black, beveled wood frame, 14 x 18½" 90.00

Needlework embroidered on silk, Biblical scene in New England setting w/figures of a king in rich robes proffering a feather to the queen richly dressed & attended by a hand-maiden, painted townscape in distance, executed in moss green, gold, vermillion, beige & brown silk w/costumes trimmed in gilt metal threads & gold sequins, anonymous, Miss Patten's School, Hartford, Connecticut, early 19th c., giltwood frame, 17 x 20½" 660.00

Needlework embroidered full figure of a crouching tiger in a landscape setting, worked w/wool yarns in long stitch & French knots in shades of brown, blue, green & gold, probably English, ca. 1840, framed, 17 x 22¼" 330.00

Needlework embroidered on linen canvas, hunting scene w/five men on horseback chasing a pack of dogs against a bucolic landscape w/farm houses, grazing cattle, roaming horses & trees w/hills & a townscape on the horizon, polychrome silk threads, signed "Mary Flower 1768" on lower border, mounted on cedar panel w/ink inscription "Mary Flower her Work in the Year 1768," now in shadowbox frame, 23" w., 18½" h. ...187,000.00

Needlework embroidered on silk, map of the United States, depicting the country as it appeared in 1809, the state lines, rivers, lakes & mountain ranges rendered in fine black silk stitches on a white ground, the state borders executed in red, yellow & black chenille, along with the longitude & latitudes, inscribed within banner, stitched in the lower right corner "United States, Ann E. Colson, 1809," the banner flanked by sprays of rose blossoms & buds, probably Pennsylvania, framed, 25¼ x 27" (minor stains) 4,400.00

NETSUKE

These decorative toggles were used by the Japanese to secure a purse or other small personal article by means of a cord slipped through a Kimono sash. They are carved of ivory and other materials. There are many reproductions.

Fox Priest Netsuke

Figure of European man carrying a rabbit over his back, ivory, 19th c., 2½" h. $110.00

Figure of Hannya, ivory, 19th c., 2½" h. 220.00

Figure of a man sitting & holding a large fish, boxwood, 19th c., 1½" h. 165.00

Figure of Shishi w/his head resting on a reticulated ball, fruitwood, 19th c., 1 5/8" h. 175.00

Figure of a woman, ivory, crouching figure pats hair & gazes into mirror, faint image reflected in glass, 19th c., 1¾" h. 125.00

Figure of a woman diver, ivory, standing woman wearing grass skirt, holds basket over her back, late 19th c., 2 3/16" h. 150.00

Figure group, mountain witch, Yama Abu, suckles her son, Kintoki, ivory, rabbit w/coral eyes stands by, 20th c., 2" h. 175.00

Model of a fox priest, ivory, standing robed figure scatters beans during Setsubun, 19th c., 1 11/16" h. (ILLUS.) 200.00

Model of a human skull without lower jaw, hardwood, 19th c., 1¾" l. 70.00

Model of a recumbent ram, boxwood, inlaid brass eyes, signed Minko, 18th c., 1 5/8" l. 175.00

Model of rats (2) on a bale of rice, hardwood, 19th c., 2" l. 200.00

NUTTING (Wallace) COLLECTIBLES

In 1898, Wallace Nutting published his first hand-tinted pictures and these were popular for more than 20 years. An "assembly line" subsequently colored and placed a signature and (sometimes) a title on the mat of these copyrighted photographs. Interior scenes featuring Early American furniture are considered the most desirable of these photographs.

Nutting's photographically illustrated travel books and early editions of his antiques reference books are also highly collectible.

A Sip of Tea

BOOKS

"The Clock Book," 1924 .... $35.00
"England Beautiful" 17.50
"Ireland Beautiful," 1925, first edition 27.00
"Pennsylvania Beautiful," 1924, Old America Co., first edition 25.00
"Vermont Beautiful," 1922, first edition 25.00

PRINTS

Afternoon Tea, interior scene, ladies in parlor w/scenic wall covering, framed, 10 x 8¾" 65.00
Among the Beeches, exterior scene, winding road between beech trees, framed, 18 x 16" 40.00
An Eventful Journey, exterior scene, carved brown frame, copyright 1909, 12 x 14" (several tiny white spots on left edge) 140.00
Bit of Sewing (A), interior scene, woman sewing in room w/rocking chair, mirrors, rugs & fireplace, framed, 14¾ x 11¾" 80.00
Book Settle (The), interior scene, lady sewing, seated on high backed bench w/two shelves of books, framed, 11 x 15¾" 90.00
Careful Mother (The), interior scene, mother watches cradle in lovely furnished bedroom, copyright 1911, framed, 12¾" 125.00
Gathering a Bouquet, exterior scene, lady at back door of Nantucket-type house w/basket of flowers, framed, 15½ x 9½" 110.00
Hawthorn Dell (The), exterior scene, framed, 11¼ x 14¼" 37.00
Home Lane, exterior scene, dirt lane, fence, flowering tree in a rolling countryside setting, framed, 18 x 12" 35.00
Irish Hawthorn, exterior scene, red flowering trees & blue sky, framed, 17 x 13" 55.00
Leaf Strewn Brook (A), exterior scene, trees w/brilliant autumn foliage beside small brook, framed, 18½ x 14¼" 65.00
Maple Sugar Cupboard (The), interior scene, lady opening door above fireplace mantel, framed, 13 x 10½" 125.00
October Glories, exterior scene, colorful autumnal trees, framed, 21 x 18" 55.00
Pergola, Amalfi (The), exterior scene, foreground w/columns, arbors & flowers overlooking the Amalfi & Italian villas w/ocean in distance, framed, 18½ x 15½" ... 65.00
Ripening Year (The), exterior scene, tranquil bend in river w/autumn foliage either side, framed, 18 x 12" 28.00
Sip of Tea (A), interior scene, copyright 1907, framed, 14½ x 17" (ILLUS.) 125.00
Swimming Pool (The), exterior scene, water w/reflecting foliage, framed, 17 x 13" 68.00
Warm Spring Day (A), exterior scene, sheep grazing near water & trees against blue sky, framed, 14 x 17" 130.00

OCCUPIED JAPAN

Moriage-decorated Cup & Saucer

American troops occupied the country of Japan from September 2, 1945, until April 28, 1952, following World War II. All wares made for export during this period were required to be marked "Made in Occupied Japan." Now these items, mostly small ceramic and metal trifles of varying quality, are sought out by a growing number of collectors.

Binoculars, w/case, 7 x 50, Meibo mark $30.00

Bowl, china, lattice sides, h.p. fruit w/gold trim decor, marked, 6" d. 18.00
Bowls w/underplates, lacquer ware, red w/birds & branches, set of 4 . . . . . 65.00
Candlestick, bisque, figural shepherdess, 9½" h. 125.00
Cigarette lighter, silver plate, w/separate underplate ashtray, Aladdin lamp-shaped 20.00
Creamer, sugar bowl & tray, china, tomato-shaped, 3 pcs. 25.00
Cup & saucer, porcelain, moriage dragon decor, saucer 5" d., cup 2" h. (ILLUS.) 35.00
Dinner service for 8, plus serving pieces, marked "Ivory China Meito," 63 pcs. 300.00
Doll, celluloid w/movable arms, painted eyes, 6½" h. 10.00
Dresser lamps, china, figural Colonial man & Colonial woman, pr. 50.00
Figure of a baby in cradle, bisque, marked, 2 pcs. 35.00
Figures, Bride & Groom, bisque, 4" h., pr. 20.00
Figure of Santa Claus, composition, red plush coat & pipe cleaner trim, 4" h. 40.00
Figure of football player, celluloid, red & black decor, 4½" h. 15.00
Figure of little boy w/Scottie dog pulling on shirt, 8" h. 25.00
Figure group, musicians, china, five black figures, each playing different instrument, 5" h. 150.00
Gravy boat w/underplate, china, Blue Willow patt. w/gold trim 32.00
Liquor bottle, porcelain, model of a parrot, 5" h. 25.00
Luncheon set, china, Ivy patt., Ardalt mark, 20 pcs. 68.00
Model of dog, Scottie, china, 8" l., 6" h. 35.00
Plates, china, lattice border, floral decor, 8¼" d., pr. 25.00
Salt & pepper shakers, china, Hummel-like boy & girl figures, pr. 24.00
Tea set: cov. teapot, creamer, cov. sugar bowl & six cups & saucers; china, floral decor, 15 pcs. 88.00
Toby mug, china, full figure bartender, 6" h. 55.00
Toy, jointed celluloid dog, 5" l. 15.00
Toy, windup, celluloid, "Arty the Trapeze Artist," boxed 140.00
Toy, windup, "Sweet Melodeon Monkey," boxed 70.00
Vase, bisque, figural girl seated near tree stump, 6" h. 25.00
Vase, children in relief decoration, 7¼" h. 38.00

OLYMPIC GAMES MEMORABILIA

First begun in Ancient Greece as a Pan-Hellenic festival of athletic games, as well as choral poetry and dance contests, the Games were held every four years until the 4th century A.D. Not until 1896 were the Olympics revived under the leadership of Baron deCoubertin of France. The first modern Games were held in Athens, Greece and have continued throughout this century with lapses during the two World Wars. It was in 1924 that the first Winter Olympics were initiated so the numbering for the Summer and Winter Olympics does not coincide. Posters, pins and other items from past Olympiads are today highly collectible.

Book, hardbound, "III Olympic Games Lake Placid 1932," issued by the Olympic Committee, IIIrd Winter Olympiad, Lake Placid, New York, 1932, illustrated, 291 pp. $52.00
Books, "Die Olympischen Spiele," XIth Olympiad, Berlin, Germany, 1936, 300 photographs, 2 vols. 95.00
Books, one hardbound w/original dust jacket containing photographs of contestants for the Winter & Summer Olympics; second w/soft cover containing color photographs of the Summer Olympics, XIth Olympiad, Berlin, Germany, 1936, 2 pcs. 375.00
Brochure, "Olympic Winter Games 1948," Vth Winter Olympiad, St. Moritz, Switzerland, 1948 . . . . . 5.00
Cigar case, leather & Bakelite, XIth Olympiad, Berlin, Germany, 1936 . . . . . 45.00
Magazine, "Pennant," Xth Olympiad, Los Angeles, California, 1932 . . . . . 13.00
Model of Olympic grounds & stadium, plastic, original box w/legend, XIth Olympiad, Berlin, Germany, 1936, 11½" 75.00
Photograph, panorama of Los Angeles Coliseum Opening Ceremonies, Xth Olympiad, Los Angeles, California, 1932, 9 x 36" 185.00
Pin, enameled, German eagle w/swastika on chest over rings, "XI Olympaide Berlin" underneath, 1936 . . . . . 45.00
Program, "Official Souvenir Pro-

gram," Xth Olympiad, Los Angeles, California, 1932 . . . . 38.00
Tickets (3), plus postcard of Los Angeles Coliseum at night, Xth Olympiad, Los Angeles, California, 1932, 4 pcs. 25.00

OPERA GLASSES, LORGNETTES & EYEGLASSES

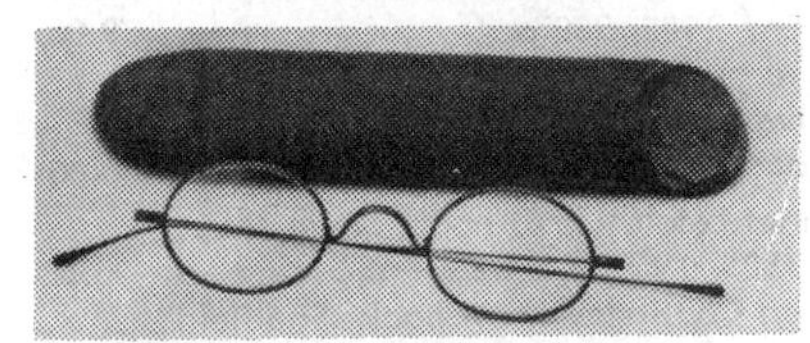

Late 19th Century Eyeglasses

Eyeglasses, coin silver frames, J. Owen, Philadelphia, Pennsylvania, ca. 1830 . . . .$195.00
Eyeglasses, silver frames w/sliding ear pieces, folding double lenses, marked "Bolles & Day, Hartford" 100.00
Eyeglasses, stamped "Adolphus Goldstein, Louisville, Ky.," late 1800's, w/leather case (ILLUS.) . . . 20.00
Lorgnette, 14k gold, frame heavily chased w/Art Nouveau style florals 550.00
Lorgnette, folding-type, tortoise shell frame 52.50
Opera glasses, enamel & mother-of-pearl, each eyepiece enameled w/bust portrait of a maiden wearing a classical gown, w/flower & jewels in her hair, a continuous landscape w/trees in the distance, handle similarly decorated w/three-quarter length portrait, all on a shaded lavender guilloche patterned ground, France, late 19th c. 550.00
Opera glasses, mother-of-pearl, marked "LeMaire, Paris" 30.00
Opera glasses, lorgnette-style w/telescoping handle, nickel-plated frame w/blue enameled decoration & polychrome painted scenes, mother-of-pearl eyepieces marked "Le Fils, Paris," France, ca. 1900 . . . . 145.00
Opera glasses w/long handle, polished brass w/cobalt blue star design, Paris, 1920's 75.00

PAPER COLLECTIBLES

Buffalo Bill's Wild West Show Program

Also see FISHER GIRLS, MAGAZINES, MUCHA ARTWORK, PAPER DOLLS, ROYCROFT ITEMS, SIGNS & SIGNBOARDS, STEAMSHIP COLLECTIBLES and WORLD'S FAIR COLLECTIBLES.

Admission ticket, "Official Reception to Capt. Charles Lindbergh-June 13, 1927" $20.00
Book, "Souvenir of Chicago in Color," 100 pages showing Chicago in 1910, soft cover, 6 x 8" 40.00
Broadside, printed paper, "A Proclamation for a Thanksgiving," printed in Boston by Richard Draper in 1703, large lion & unicorn crest at top of page, framed, 15½ x 18½" (stains & fold lines) 775.00
Calendar, 1929, "Horse Review Calendar of Champions," each month w/picture of a Trotter, 12 pgs. 36.00
Calligraphic specimen, pen & ink drawing of a rabbit, birds, scrolls & flags above inscription in Spencerian script "Miss Marie, 1895, from a friend....," contemporary grain-painted frame, 10 x 12¼" . . 105.00
City directory, New York City, 1853, fold-out map w/advertising, hardbound 45.00
Map, Nebraska, mounted on linen, 1920, 30 x 42" 40.00
Menu, "Hotel New Yorker," 1941, exceptional steel engraving of a New York view, in original envelope 15.00
Newspaper, "Pittsburgh Sun," April 19, 1912, the sinking of the Titanic, complete 60.00
Program, "Buffalo Bill's Wild West -- Historical Sketches & Programme," chromolithograph covers, 64 pp. (ILLUS.) 75.00
Scherenschnitt (cut work), delicate

white paper scene of various birds, wild flowers & foliage, blue paper backing, Victorian, mounted in reeded criss-cross frame w/porcelain corner buttons, 8¼ x 8½" 625.00
Scherenschnitt (cut work), ornate lacy square signed "Henry Snyder, 24 December 1849," mounted on blue paper, flame-grained beveled wood frame, 15 7/8" sq. 445.00
Telephone directory, Greater Houston area, 1943 ..... 15.00
Tour book, "Europe," by Cook, 1923 ..... 6.00

PAPER DOLLS

Roy Rogers & Dale Evans Paper Dolls

Advertising, "Clark's Spool Cotton," assorted lot of 9 ..... $80.00
Advertising, "Duplex Corset," uncut sheet 75.00
Advertising, "Lion Coffee," Nursery Rhyme series, assorted set of 6 ..... 55.00
Advertising, "McLaughlin Coffee," Teddy Bears (2), each w/set of clothes, 6" h. 35.00
Advertising, "None Such Mince Meat," 5 dolls, 10 outfits 75.00
Ava Gardner, uncut book, Whitman No. 965, 1949 ..... 25.00
Barbie & Ken Suitcase (box), Whitman No. 4797, 1962 ..... 22.00
Betty Grable, three dolls, uncut book, Merrill No. 1558, 1951 ..... 60.00
Blondie, uncut book, Whitman No. 987, 1945 ..... 135.00
Carol Lynley, uncut book, Whitman No. 2089, 1960 ..... 15.00
Carolyn Lee by Queen Holden, uncut book, Whitman No. 997, 1943 ..... 15.00
Campus Queen, uncut book, Abbott Co., Kenosha, Wisconsin, 1940's 25.00
Dionne Quintuplets, uncut book, Merrill No. 3488, 1935 ..... 85.00
Dionne Quintuplets by Avis Mac, uncut books, Whitman No. 1055, 1936, set of 5 ..... 400.00
Dolly Dingle, Bridesmaid, uncut sheet, Pictorial Review, October 1929 ..... 20.00
Elizabeth Taylor, uncut book, Whitman No. 1951, 1955 ..... 30.00
"Family Affair," w/Buffy, uncut book, Whitman No. 1985, 1968 ..... 10.00 to 15.00
George Montgomery & Dinah Shore, uncut book, Whitman No. 1970, 1959 ..... 40.00
Indian & Cowboy Cut-Outs, uncut book, Platt & Munk No. 260, 1934 ..... 34.00
Introducing Lettie Lane, Geo. Jacobs Co., 1908, 288 pcs. 79.00
Jane and Jill's New Frocks & Frills, two dolls, six dresses, original package, copyright 1925 ..... 60.00
Janet Leigh, uncut book, Lowe No. 1805, 1958 ..... 26.50
Joan Caulfield, uncut book, Saalfield No. 1578, 1953 ..... 85.00
Judy Garland, by Queen Holden, uncut book, Whitman No. 999, 1940 ..... 185.00
Lennon Sisters, uncut book, Whitman No. 1979, 1957 ..... 12.50
Linda Darnell, uncut book, Saalfield No. 1584, 1953 ..... 65.00
"The Loves of Carmen," w/Rita Hayworth, Saalfield No. 1529, 1948 ..... 45.00
Moving Picture Dolls (with color movable tabs that change clothes), black dolls, pat. Jan. 15, 1907 ..... 65.00
Natalie Wood, uncut book, Whitman No. 2086, 1958 ..... 30.00
Polly's Paper Playmates (Folk Dances of the Nations), uncut sheet, Boston Globe, April 16, 1911 ..... 40.00
Roy Rogers & Dale Evans, uncut book, Whitman No. 1950, 1956 (ILLUS.) 30.00
Snow White & the Seven Dwarfs, uncut book, Tomart No. D7807 ..... 125.00
Tricia Nixon, uncut book, Saalfield No. 1248, 1970 ..... 17.50
Trixie (from Hi & Lois Comic Strip), uncut book, Lowe No. 3920, 1961 ..... 32.00
Tuck (Raphael), Courtley Beatrice, Prince & Princess series, w/four outfits & a hat 65.00
Tuck (Raphael), Washing Day, No. 215A; At the Spinning Wheel, No. 215D; A Young Gardener, No. 2151A; A Young Carpenter, No. 215J; set of 4 ..... 125.00
The Waltons, uncut book, Whitman No. 1995, 1975 ..... 10.00

PAPERWEIGHTS

Baccarat Garlanded Butterfly Weight

Advertising, rectangular glass over fancy black lettering & picture of a trestle, "Groton Bridge and Mfg. Co.," patented 1882, 3½" l., 2" w. $23.00

Baccarat, "Convolvulus" weight, clear encasing on enameled metal enclosure of a vermillion shaded convolvulus growing from a curved green stalk w/a bud & two green leaves near the base, star-cut base, 2 7/16" d. 6,050.00

Baccarat, "Garlanded Butterfly" weight, clear glass set w/an insect composed of a deep purple body w/turquoise eyes, dark grey antennae & w/yellow, red, green, purple & cobalt blue marbled wings, set at the periphery w/a garland of alternating green, red, white & cobalt blue canes, star-cut base, 2 13/16" d. (ILLUS.) 2,200.00

Baccarat, sulphide of Joan of Arc w/sprays of foliage on either side of the standing figure, on red translucent ground, sides cut w/geometric facets, 3 3/8" d. 2,420.00

Clichy, scattered millefiori weight, clear w/brightly colored assorted millefiori canes including two green & pink roses, 2 5/8" d. 385.00

Clichy, faceted mushroom weight, tuft of four concentric rows of brightly colored assorted millefiori canes including seven white & green roses about a central pink & green rose, w/outer row of elongated opaque turquoise blue & white alternating staves, cut w/top & six side printies, star-cut base, 2 13/16" d. 2,640.00

Malachite & ormolu, formed as an exotic bird, on rectangular malachite base, Russian, late 19th c., 5" h. 1,980.00

Millville, "Rose" weight on pedestal base, spherical, enclosing a yellow flower composed of numerous petals set on three dark green leaves extended above the flower, set on a circular base, 2 5/8" base d., 4" h. 1,045.00

New England, "Upright Bouquet" weight, large central white flower w/ochre cane center surrounded by cobalt blue bud & red bud & three millefiori canes in shades of cobalt blue, red & white, resting on six dark green leaf tips & set in a basket of swirling white latticinio, 2 9/16" d. 495.00

St. Clair, "Apple" weight, cobalt blue Carnival glass 70.00

St. Louis, "Fruit" weight, clear w/cluster of three red cherries, one russet colored apple, one ripened pear & one unripened apple, set among numerous green leaves on a swirling white latticinio ground, 2½" d. 715.00

St. Louis, "Pompon" weight, numerous rows of white recessed petals w/pale yellow stamen centers growing from a short green stalk w/four green leaves & white bud about the flower, set on swirling pink latticinio ground, 2 1/8" d. ..2,200.00

Sandwich, "Poinsettia" on blue ground, attributed to Nicholas Lutz 650.00

Snow-type weight, Empire State Building, New York.............. 22.50

Souvenir, glass dome over color lithograph of castle-type building, "The World's Only Corn Palace, Mitchell, S. Dakota," 3" d., 2" h. 12.00

U.S. Glass Co., Pittsburgh, Pennsylvania, clear, oval glass w/bust of woman cut on the underside, ca. 1910 .... 65.00

PAPIER-MACHE

Various objects including decorative adjuncts were made of papier-mache, which is a substance made of pulped paper mixed with glue and other materials or layers of paper glued and pressed and then molded.

Box, cov., gilt birds & flowers within an inlaid mother-of-pearl border on black ground, circular bun feet, 19th c., 13½" w. $412.50

Bread tray, cartouche-shaped, blood

red surface floral spray & a butterfly, cavetto & shaped border w/gilt floral & leaf sprigs highlighted w/colors, gilt edge, black undersurface, England, ca. 1820, 14¼" l. 495.00

Candy containers, figural Hansel, Gretel & Witch, Germany, 3 pcs. 250.00

Candy container, model of a duck w/googly-eyes, 9¼" h. 45.00

Candy container, model of a rabbit dressed in tuxedo 120.00

Figure of a winged cherub, gilt paint, ca. 1900, 12" h. 95.00

Victorian Tilt-Top Table

Table, shaped oval tilt-top centrally painted w/a stag, inlaid mother-of-pearl & gilt floral borders, ring- & baluster-turned standard, footed circular molded base w/further gilt trim, mid-19th c., 29" w. (ILLUS.) 1,870.00

Tray, scalloped oval, inlaid w/mother-of-pearl floral vine border & foliate edge, Victorian, 25½" l. (on faux bamboo stand of later date) 550.00

PARRISH (Maxfield) ARTWORK

During the 1920's and 1930's, Maxfield Parrish (1870-1966) was considered the most popular artist-illustrator in the United States. His illustrations graced the covers of the most noted magazines of the day- Scribner's, Century, Life, Harper's, Ladies' Home Journal *and others. High quality art prints, copies of his original paintings usually in a range of sizes, graced the walls of homes and offices across the country. Today all Maxfield Parrish artwork, including magazine covers, advertisements and calendar art, is considered collectible but it is the fine art prints that command the most attention.*

Advertisement for Djer-Kiss cosmetics, girl & gnomes, ca. 1918, framed $87.50

Book, "A Wonderbook of Tanglewood Tales," by Nathaniel Hawthorne, illustrated by Maxfield Parrish, 1928 ....55.00 to 70.00

Book, "Dream Days," by Kenneth Grahame, illustrated by Maxfield Parrish, 1902 .... 75.00

Book, "The Knave of Hearts," by Louise Sanders, illustrated by Maxfield Parrish, spiral-bound ....325.00 to 400.00

Calendar, 1927, for Edison-Mazda, entitled "Reveries," small 175.00

Calendar, 1941, for Brown & Bigelow Publishing Co., entitled "Village Brook," overall 16 x 22½" 100.00

Calendar, 1948, for Brown & Bigelow Publishing Co., entitled "The Mill Pond," overall 16 x 22" 145.00

Calendar, 1956, for Brown & Bigelow Publishing Co., entitled "Misty Morn" 240.00

Magazine ad, for Jell-O, "Polly Put the Kettle On," ca. 1920, matted, small 25.00

Menu, for St. Regis Hotel, entitled "Old King Cole," 1920's, 3¼ x 9" 40.00

Playing cards, for Edison-Mazda, full deck 125.00

Print, "Daybreak," original frame, 6 x 10" 45.00

Print, "Daybreak," original blue frame & braided blue silk hanging cord, 12 x 24" 65.00

Print, "The Dinkey Bird," framed, 14½ x 18½"..........135.00 to 150.00

Print, "Enchantment," framed, small 95.00

Print, "Evening," framed, 6 x 10" ... 70.00

Print, "Garden of Allah," framed, 15 x 30" 165.00

Print, "Golden Hours," framed, small 145.00

Print, "Lute Players," House of Arts, ca. 1924, original frame, medium 125.00

Print, "Night is Fled," framed, large (trimmed margins) 485.00

Print, "Old Glen Mill," 13¼ x 16¾" 150.00

Print, "The Prince," original frame, 1928, 10 x 12" 75.00

Print, "Romance," original frame, large 200.00

Print, "Rubaiyat," framed, large 385.00

Print, "Spirit of Transportation," framed 485.00

Print, "Stars," framed, medium 375.00
Print, "Twilight," ca. 1935, framed, 18 x 24" 95.00
Print, "Wynken, Blynken & Nod," signed on the mat "To Walter A Fuller, Maxfield Parrish, July 31st, 1912," original frame 375.00
Tobacco tin, "Old King Cole" 800.00

PERFUME, SCENT & COLOGNE BOTTLES

Decorative accessories from milady's boudoir have always been highly collectible and in recent years there has been an especially strong surge of interest in perfume bottles. Our listings also include related containers such as pocket bottles and vials, tabletop containers and atomizers. Most readily available are examples from the 19th through the mid-20th century, but earlier examples do surface occasionally. The myriad varieties have now been documented in several recent reference books which should further popularize this collecting specialty.

ATOMIZERS

Blue opalescent Coin Spot patt., DeVilbiss $55.00
Crystal green glass w/pebbled effect, molded crown shape, heavy gold trim, paper label reading "Imperial Art Glass" 100.00
French enameled art glass, frosted blue body w/panel cutting & enameled thistle & vine decoration, 4" h. 125.00
Gold crackle glass, beaded flower on top, DeVilbiss, 4¾" h. 48.00
Layered mottled glass, yellow & black w/orange highlights, DeVilbiss 40.00
Light blue glass w/gold panels, all original, DeVilbiss, 5½" h. 70.00

BOTTLES & FLASKS

Amber glass, square, w/original amber cut faceted stopper, engraved roses & leaves cut through amber to crystal, 2" d., 5" h. 95.00
Amethyst glass, cut sides, rectangular pedestal base, original cut flat steeple stopper, 3" h. 195.00
Baccarat glass, Guerlain "Vague" bottle, signed, mint in box 145.00
Cameo & enameled glass, bell form, green w/enameled neck & applied scenic cameo bosses & trailing vine, signed "Daum Nancy," 8" h. 880.00
Canary yellow flint glass, hexagonal Star & Punty patt., faceted stopper, 7½" h. 275.00
Clear glass, paperweight base, lovely intaglio cutting of crosshatching, flowers, etc., pear-shaped oval stopper, 6½" h. 300.00
Cranberry glass, w/enameled blue, white & yellow flowers & green leaves outlined in gold, original clear ball stopper, 2" d., 4 5/8" h. 118.00
Cranberry glass, finger ring w/attached chains, engraved & openwork ormolu-encased bottle, hinged star engraved top, original stopper, ¾" oval bottle, 4 7/8" l. including chains & ring 225.00
Cut glass, clear, floral design, pedestal base, signed "Hawkes" & numbered, 8½" h. dauber, 9½" h. bottle 240.00
English cameo glass, bulbous, carved white flowers & leafage against lemon yellow ground, neck carved w/X's between line borders, neck w/silver conical cover, signed "Thomas Webb & Sons," 1889, 5½" h. 1,320.00
Fiery opalescent glass, four nudes design, signed in script, "Sabino, Paris" 160.00
Figural black cat & moon, blown glass, Germany 15.00
Figural dog, porcelain, Germany, 2¾" h. 30.00
Free-blown glass, "seahorse" form, 24 swirled ribs, 2¾" h. (shallow chip on one side of neck) 80.00

Enameled Scent Flask

Gold-mounted enameled scent flask, waisted cylinder painted w/putti & neo-classical scenes of couples in a garden, gold mounts engraved w/leaftips, fitted case, Continental, ca. 1900, 3½" h. (ILLUS.) 1,540.00

Lalique glass, heart-shaped, "Farouche," made for Nina Ricci, signed, w/red plush box, 4" h. . . . 295.00

Mold-blown aqua glass, scrolls & stars design, rolled lip, pontil, from two-part mold, early 19th c., 3" h. . . . 25.00

Mold-blown bright sapphire blue glass, twisted-rib patt., original tam stopper (damaged), early 19th c., GI-3, type 2 . . . 475.00

Moser glass, cylindrical, cobalt blue, enameled multicolor leaves w/lacy gold foliage & small gold berries, matching cobalt blue stopper w/gold trim, 5½" h., 2" d. . . . 135.00

Overlay glass, three layers, clear cut to white then cut to blue, overall cuttings w/tiny clear ovals outlined w/white on a blue ground, each tiny oval has a gold decoration in center, 2½" l. . . . 210.00

Pressed glass, clear, Queens Necklace patt., bulbous, triple ring stopper, 4" h. . . . 75.00

Sapphire blue glass, enameled white flowers, green leaves & small peach flowers, original blue ball stopper w/gold trim, 2" d., 4¾" h. . . . 100.00

Silver-cased glass, chatelaine form, Continental style cylindrical faceted bottle mounted at the tip, neck & shoulder, the body w/an openwork embossed design of 18th c. figures seated at tables outdoors, the ball-shaped hinged lid opening to reveal a cork stopper, the rope twisted silver cord now mostly removed, unmarked, late 19th c., 10¾" l. . . . 247.50

Spatter glass, yellow & white spatter w/enameled pink flowers, green leaves & gold foliage & scrolls cased in clear, original ball stopper, 2½" d., 5½" h. . . . 95.00

Vaseline cut glass, overall Diamond patt., matching stopper, 2 1/8" d., 5½" h. . . . 98.00

PHONOGRAPHS

Brunswick Parisiane, w/collapsible cardboard horn . . . $395.00

Carron Model 1000, child's, dated 1953, plays 78's . . . 45.00

Columbia "Grafonola Baby Regent" . . . 400.00

Columbia Model BII "Improved Sterling," oak cabinet, oak morning glory horn (ILLUS.) . . . 2,750.00

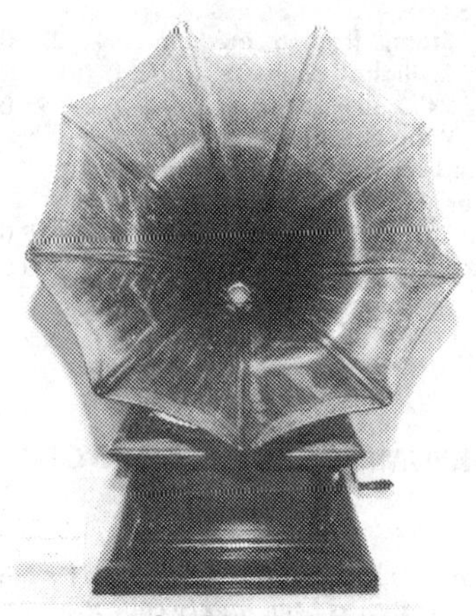

Columbia Model BII

Edison Amberola Model A, type Sm. 100, floor model, drawers full of cylinder records . . . 995.00

Edison Amberola X, w/recorder attachment, 1913-1914, original box . . . 525.00

Edison "Chippendale" Diamond Disc Model C250, floor model, mahogany cabinet . . . 250.00

Edison Diamond Disc Model No. S19 . . . 150.00

Edison Home Model A, "suitcase" style oak carrying case, 1 & 2 speed, pat. 1905 . . . 395.00

Garrand, hand-crafted snakeskin horn, 1920 . . . 1,250.00

Victor II, w/morning glory horn . . . 575.00

Victor Model XVI, Electrola . . . 350.00

Victor Model 1050 w/record changer . . . 450.00

Victor Model R, oak case, brass horn on oak arm, w/six "Little Wonder" records . . . 445.00

Victrola Model No. 300 "Humpback" . . . 175.00

Zonophone Grand Concert, front mount, original condition . . . 1,650.00

PHOTOGRAPHIC ITEMS

Ambrotype, sixth plate (2¾ x 3¼"), Civil War soldier, w/case . . . $27.00

Book, "How To Make Good Pictures," Kodak, 1921 . . . 7.00

Cabinet photograph, barber shop interior, early 1900's . . . 15.00

Cabinet photograph, cowboy wearing fringed buckskin outfit w/two Colt revolvers & Marlin rifle . . . 150.00

Camera, Ansco No. 4, Model D, wooden case 65.00
Camera, Eastman Kodak No. 2, factory loaded w/sixty exposures, 1890 . . . . 225.00
Camera, Jumbo Century Studio Camera No. 4A, all-wooden w/lens & hand-held rubber squeeze bulb, original label, brass hardware, made by Folmer Graphflex Corp., Rochester, New York, 12½ x 25", 16½" h. 100.00
Camera, Zeiss Contaflex, 1:28 lens, wide angle & telephoto lens, Walz filter kit & close-up lens, instruction booklet & case 250.00
Carte de visite, Alexander Dumas, w/autograph 42.00
Carte de visite, General Ulysses S. Grant & Schuyler Colfax, 1868 presidential campaign 15.00
Carte de visite, Mr. & Mrs. Tom Thumb, autographed & dated 100.00
Catalog, Kodak, 1910, 64 pp., 5½ x 8" 30.00
Daguerreotype, ninth plate, Mexican War soldier by White 27.50
Daguerreotype, sixth plate, Indian in Eastern dress 150.00
Daguerreotype, sixth plate, occupational, butcher holding a cleaver-type knife standing by a large piece of meat on a butcher block, oval mat in partial soft case 440.00
Daguerreotype, half plate, John Greenleaf Whittier 16,000.00
Daguerreotype case, thermoplastic, "The Fireman" 85.00
Daguerreotype case, thermoplastic, fortune teller scene, 4 x 5" 125.00
Darkroom lantern, tin, original black paint w/white striping & label "Carbutt's Dry Plate Lantern, Pat. April 25th 1882," w/tin kerosene font & burner, copy of patent drawing attached, 17" h. 55.00
Darkroom timer, cast iron, "Kodak" 35.00
Glass negatives, "Decatur, Illinois," scenes of homes, people & cars, set of 64 . . . . 80.00
Photograph, John Wilkes Booth, 1865 . . . . 30.00
Photograph, President Lincoln on Battlefield of Antietam, October 1862 . . . . 3,500.00
Photograph, San Francisco, Clay Street Cable Car, by Watkins, 1870's 75.00
Photographer's bench, carved oak, child's seat in the form of an eagle, 34" w., 22½" h. 385.00
Scales, avoirdupois, Eastman Kodak 45.00
Tintype, ninth plate, Annie Oakley, ca. 1883 . . . . 115.00
Tintype, sixth plate, woman playing guitar 35.00

Civil War Tintype

Tintype, quarter plate, Civil War Union soldier (ILLUS.) 95.00
Tintype, whole plate, black man in Civil War uniform 250.00

PINCUSHION DOLLS

Assortment of Pincushion Dolls

These china half figures were never intended to use as dolls, but rather to serve as ornamental tops to their functional pincushion bases which were discreetly covered with silk and lace skirts. They were produced in a wide variety of forms and quality, all of which are now deemed collectible, and were especially popular during the first quarter of this century.

Bisque half figure of a Dutch girl, w/original clothing, marked "Heubach," 7" h. $65.00
Bisque half figure of a lady w/arms away from body, blonde attached wig, original dress of purple & black tiers w/pink velvet flowers, flower in hair, 3" d., 5½" h., overall 13" h. 232.00
China half figure of a "flapper" w/hands to chest, red curls, black hat, impressed "Germany, 6349," 3½" h. 50.00
China half figure of a lady w/hands on hips, painted beaded filet en-

circles her brown hair w/blue flower centered above her brow, yellow bodice, impressed "Germany, 6099," 3" h. 32.00

China half figure of a lady w/yellow band & flowers in her grey hair, arms away from body & holding closed yellow fan in one hand, impressed "Germany, 2735," 4" h. 27.00

China half figure of a lady w/her grey hair in an ornate 18th century coiffure topped w/lavender & cream plumes, arms away from body, impressed "21275," 2 7/8" d., 4 3/8" h. 79.00

China half figure of a lady w/ornate coiffure, arms free & away from body, impressed "13273," 3½" d., 6" h. 156.00

China half figure of a lady w/deeply molded hair, one hand raised to place a rose in her hair, the other held in front, h.p. features, original clothing, 7" h. 65.00

China half figure of a lady w/hands slightly away from body, purple band in her ornately styled grey hair, pale blue dress w/overall white roses design, china legs, 3¾" d., 7½" h. 175.00

China half figure of a lady w/applied pink roses in her grey hair, hands outstretched & holding a pink rose, marked "Dressel & Kister" 200.00

China half figure of a lady w/dark brown hair wearing red cloche hat w/feather, holding fan in right hand, left hand on bosom ... 37.00

China half figure of a Spanish dancer w/right hand at waist & left hand at neck, black hair w/blue comb, impressed "Germany, 8033," 3¾" h. 35.00

China half figure of top-hatted man, 1½" h. 25.00

Wax half figure of a lady w/bisque arms, lovely face w/shaded eyes, red lips & beauty mark, blonde attached hair, original black & pink silk dress w/black feather, 2" d., 4½" h., overall 12" h. 180.00

Whisk broom doll, china half figure of a lady w/blonde hair wearing blue shawl, 7½" h. 35.00

PIPES

Amber etched & carved bowl w/winged bare-breasted angel w/wings wrapped around bowl itself, ivory stem, 12" l. $150.00

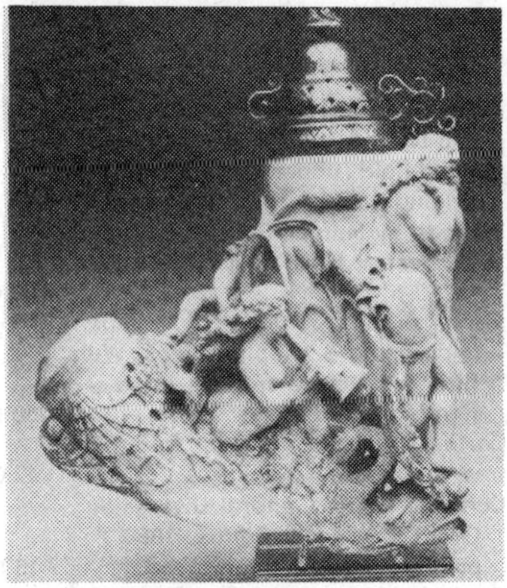

Elaborate Meerschaum Pipe Bowl

Meerschaum bowl, curved cylindrical vessel carved in high relief w/a central figure of Poseidon & Aphrodite embracing before a large shell, flanked by naiads, tritons & dolphins rising from the waves, the naiads blowing pipes, gilt-metal pierced cap, w/fitted leather case, late 19th c., chips, losses, some discoloration, 7" w., 9" h. (ILLUS.) 2,200.00

Meerschaum, carved figure of an elf on bowl, amber stem, w/case 95.00

Meerschaum, carved figure of a nude woman w/flowing hair, amber stem, original case, 7" l. 125.00

Meerschaum, carved head of Bacchus, w/carved wooden case 245.00

Meerschaum, carved model of a horse's hoof w/carving of terrier w/paws resting on saddle, amber stem, w/original fitted case, 4" l. (flake on dog's ear) 75.00

Meerschaum, carved reindeer behind bowl, two bands of carved flowers, yellow-amber stem, original case, 19" l. 350.00

Meerschaum, miniature, carved full-figure dog standing on stem, original case 65.00

Opium, bamboo stem w/brass tips .. 225.00

PITCHER & BOWL SETS

Basket & Vase patt., medium blue transfer, early Staffordshire ware, Clews mark, the set $550.00

Blue & white pottery, Fishscale & Wild Rose patt., the set 275.00
Cairo patt., Art Deco design, blue, black & white, S. Hancock & Sons Coronaware, Stoke on Trent, England, the set 250.00
Flow Blue, overall h.p. dark blue floral & leaf bands on ironstone body, 12-sided geometric bowl & matching pitcher, ca. 1850, 11 7/8" h. pitcher, 14¼" d. bowl (some wear, hairline in base of bowl), the set 425.00
Flow Blue, Saskia patt., Ridgway mark, the set 500.00
"Gaudy" Ironstone, orange & cobalt blue w/gold decoration, scalloped 13½" d. bowl & 12" h. pitcher w/applied handle which ends in five spread fingers w/fingernails, marked "Stone China" on base, the set 495.00
Ironstone, colorful florals & birds decoration on white, Mason's Pottery, Staffordshire, England, 8" d. cov. soap dish, 12½" h. pitcher & 15½" d. basin, 3 pcs. 130.00
Mulberry Ware, Jeddo patt., Adams mark, the set 495.00

Early Pearlware Pitcher & Bowl Set

Pearlware, pitcher & interior of the basin painted w/garland of ochre & underglaze-blue tulips amid green leaves, the basin w/a central large blue flowerhead surrounded by tulip buds & blossoms & green leaves, exterior of basin w/three ochre & green floral sprays, the rims edged in underglaze-blue, Staffordshire, 1830-40, 12 1/8" d. bowl, 8" h. pitcher, the set (ILLUS.) 880.00

POLITICAL, CAMPAIGN & PRESIDENTIAL ITEMS

CAMPAIGN ITEMS

Bandanna, 1904 campaign, Parker (Alton B.) & Davis (Henry G.), American flags & single star above oval bust portraits of Parker & Davis over banner inscribed "Good Government for the People," faded red, blue & brown on white cotton, 25 x 22½" $127.50
Book, 1936 campaign, Landon (Alfred), "Deeds Not Deficits" 10.00
Compact, 1940 campaign, Willkie (Wendell), red, white & blue cover & "Elect Willkie President," 3" d. 75.00
Earrings, 1952 campaign, Eisenhower (Dwight D.), rhinestone, "Ike," pr. 13.50
Knife, pocket-type, 1916 campaign, Wilson (Woodrow), bust portrait obverse, Uncle Sam reverse 45.00
Lapel pin, 1928 campaign, Hoover (Herbert), model of an elephant, embossed "Hoover" 14.00
License plate attachment, 1942 campaign, Roosevelt (Franklin D.), die-cut tin, red, white & blue, "America Needs Roosevelt" 30.00
Match safe, 1888 campaign, Cleveland (Grover), brass, figural bust, 2½" h. 225.00
Mirror, pocket-type, 1932 campaign, Roosevelt (Franklin D.) 20.00
Paperweight, 1896 campaign, McKinley (William), sepia-tone photograph under glass dome 14.00
Paperweight, 1904 campaign, Parker (Alton B.) & Davis (Henry G.), rectangular glass block over bust portraits w/spread-winged eagle, wreaths & flags in color, 2½ x 4" 95.00
Poster, 1948 campaign, Truman (Harry S), paper, red, white & blue background w/"Vote Democratic November 2, 1948" & photographs of Truman, Barkley, Smith, Blair, Toberman, Holmes, Morris & Taylor, 14 x 22" (unused) 35.00
Poster, 1968 campaign, McCarthy (Eugene), "Peace," signed Ben Shahan 90.00
Quilt, 1844 campaign, Clay (Henry), eight-pointed stars in triangular & square blue & white patches on blue background framed by white bands, middle star centering a political bandanna w/a printed likeness of Henry Clay within a wreath of oak leaves, framed by 26 five-pointed stars, 15¼" sq. bandanna, overall 88" sq. (ILLUS. top of next page) 1,320.00
Ribbon, 1844 campaign, Clay (Henry), Frelinghuysen (Theodore) &

Gubernatorial candidate Markle (Joseph), silk 200.00

Patchwork Campaign Quilt

Toothpick holder, 1904 campaign, Roosevelt (Theodore) & Fairbanks (Charles), custard glass, jugate photograph transfer 155.00

Tray, 1904 campaign, Roosevelt (Theodore), tin, Roosevelt in military uniform w/sword raised, astride horse, red, white & blue border w/stars & draped flags, 16½" oval 250.00

Tumbler, 1904 campaign, Parker (Alton) & Davis (Henry), clear glass, etched "Parker For President" & "Davis For Vice President" w/shield & eagle & portraits of candidates........................ 85.00

Watch fob, 1900 campaign, Bryan (William J.), celluloid & leather ... 225.00

NON-CAMPAIGN ITEMS

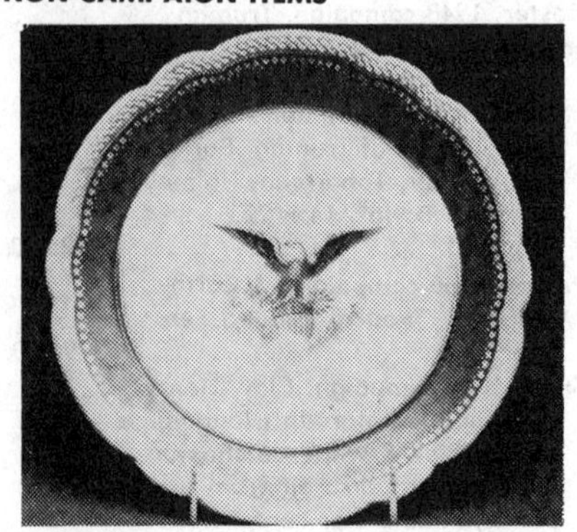

Abraham Lincoln's Presidential China

Banner, printed on fabric, oval cartouche w/star border centering figure of George Washington standing beside his horse, holding a paper, American shield above & below, alternating red & white striped background, America, 19th c., framed, 19 x 23½" (fading & staining) 247.50

Inaugural medal, 1917, Wilson (Woodrow), bronze, 3" d. 45.00

Inaugural plate, 1973, Nixon (Richard M.) & Agnew (Spiro T.), sterling silver, Franklin Mint, 8" d. 137.50

Membership card of the National Democratic Club, 14k gold, given to John F. Kennedy in 1961, rectangular form engraved w/dates "1834" & "1961" flanking the club's monogram above the name of the President & the words "Honorary Life Member" w/names of club president & secretary, w/velvet envelope, 4" l. 1,870.00

Music box, John F. Kennedy seated in a rocking chair, mint in box ... 150.00

Photographs, President John F. Kennedy & family, captions reverse, postcard-size, set of 42 .... 75.00

Plate, gold floral border, center portrait of John F. Kennedy, "In Memoriam, 1917-63"............ 30.00

Playing cards, John F. Kennedy & family pictured 22.00

Presidential china, Grant (Ulysses S.), plates, each centrally painted in various colors w/different floral sprig or spray, gilt-edged scalloped rim w/buff-colored border edged in black & gilt lines interrupted at the top w/the Great Seal in gilt, Haviland & Cie, Limoges, France, 1870-73, 9 3/8" d., set of 8 ......1,760.00

Presidential china, Hayes (Rutherford B.), fish plates, each formed on lower half as a gilt-edged scallop shell & on upper half as a ruffled shell printed in sepia & naturalistically painted w/a fish or other water creature in its habitat, Haviland & Co., Limoges, France, ca. 1880, 8¼" to 8 3/8" d., set of 12 (chips & hairline crack) 2,750.00

Presidential china, Lincoln (Abraham), dinner plate, center printed & painted w/a brown eagle clasping a red-berried green laurel branch & a cluster of black arrows in his talons, standing on a red, white & blue shield above a pink banderole inscribed "E PLURIBUS UNUM" amidst clouds shading from grey to pink & yellow, puce rim edged w/a border of gilt dots & "Alhambra" tracery, Haviland, Limoges, France, ca. 1861, 9½" d. (ILLUS.) 9,350.00

Spoons, silver plate, Presidents Washington to Hoover, each w/relief of President on handle &

scene from presidency in bowl, boxed w/brochures, William Rogers Manufacturing Co., Hartford, Connecticut, 1930's, set of 30 .... 38.50

POSTCARDS

Sleepy Eye Flour Postcard

Advertising, "Bell Telephone," "The Social Call by Bell Telephone," R-6 .... $22.00
Advertising, "Bromo-Seltzer," horse drawn wagon w/logo 10.00
Advertising, "Bull Durham" tobacco 8.00
Advertising, "Cracker Jacks," Roosevelt Bears on card, No. 15 .. 12.50
Advertising, "Elgin," raggedly clothed boy w/watch 9.00
Advertising, "Round Oak Stoves," Hunting Moon decoration 12.00
Advertising, "Sleepy Eye Flour," Indian looking down at factory (ILLUS.) 42.00
Advertising, "Swift & Co.," 1909, lot of 4 .... 24.95
Atlantic City, N.J., views, 1909 ..... 5.00
Bird series, Church & Dwight, Series No. 5, 1904-24, set of 150 .... 225.00
Black Americana, black man w/feather portruding from overcoat telling black mammy "No ma'am I ain't seen no stray rooster over heah!," 1900 .... 100.00
Boy & dog, "In His Element" 3.00
Christmas Greetings, Ellen H. Clapsaddle, Santa Claus, telephones, girl & toys 5.00
Christmas Greetings, Pioneer type, primitive looking Santa Claus full length carrying wicker basket packed full of toys at door 25.00
Easter Greetings, "Easter Happiness," bulldog scene 4.00
Easter Greetings, embossed bunnies, chicks, etc., pre-1915, set of 10 .... 15.00
Halloween Greetings, embossed owls, pumpkins & lady, John Winsch, 1911 .... 50.00
Hold-to-light, Brooklyn Bridge 25.00
Hold-to-light, St. Louis, Mississippi River steamer 25.00
Indians, various Reinhart photographs including Sitting Bull, 1904-1906, set of 11 .... 29.00
Jack Dempsey & Jess Willard, J.M. Flagg 15.00
Kentucky, mounted in album, set of 85 .... 26.00
Leather, "Teddy Roosevelt," w/stamp 10.00
Leather, shoe-shaped, w/original stamp, early 1900's, coin purse ... 15.00
Moose Jaw, Saskatchewan, Canada, 1908, C.P. Ry., depot w/train pictured 5.00
New York City, streets, buildings, etc., pre-1920, set of 105 .... 69.00
Roosevelt bears, "Fleet Around the World" 18.00
San Francisco earthquake scene, "San Francisco Disaster By Quake & Fire," copyright 1906, postmarked Ohio, June 18, 1907 ...... 15.00
Tacoma, Washington, street scene, 1940 .... 2.00
Tournament of Roses Parade, Pasadena, California, 1911 .... 20.00
Tuck (Raphael), Doll Baby Series, "Your Dolly" 40.00
West Virginia scenes, set of 13 ..... 8.00
World War II, colored, Eagles, airplanes, V-signs, etc., set of 10 ... 28.00

POSTERS

Art Salon Poster

Art salon, "Salon des Artistes Decorateurs," lithograph in colors on

paper, signed & dated, Jean Dupas, 1924, 15¼ x 23" (ILLUS.) $1,650.00
Boxing, "World's Champions and Past Greats of the Prize Ring," 35 fighters listed and photographed in black & white, the last listed in 1947, also printed information on each fighter's record, 22½ x 28" .. 60.00
Buffalo Bill's Wild West Shows, "A Group of Wild West Girls & Cowboys - The Virginia Reel on Horseback," 10 ft. l. 3,300.00
Cigarette papers, "Le Nil Cigarette Papers," French lithograph, scene of trumpeting elephant, linen backing, 47 x 58" 195.00
Skin cream, "Satin Skin Cream," lovely young Japanese lady holding fan in background behind containers of skin cream, yellow background, black lettering, green border, 28" w., 41" h. (small edge tears) 50.00
World War I, "Buy Bonds," scene of General Pershing & two children, 20 x 36" 250.00
World War I, "Navy-Gee! I Wish I Were a Man," Howard Chandler Christy, 1918 .... 350.00
World War I, "Ring It Again...3rd Liberty Loan," 20 x 30" 28.00
World War I, "They Said We Couldn't Fight," 30 x 41" 65.00
World War I, "Together We Win," James Montgomery Flagg 100.00
World War I, "The Triumph of Justice," 1918, James Lee, framed, 18 x 21½" 45.00
World War II, "Award for Careless Talk," hand comes out to award viewer iron cross, 20 x 30" 75.00
World War II, "Careless Talk Got There First," dead soldier falling to ground, 20 x 30" 65.00
World War II, "Don't Let That Shadow Touch Them," children playing w/shadow of swastika over them, 14 x 20" 48.00
World War II, "Freedom of Worship," Norman Rockwell, 28 x 40" 250.00
World War II, "Join the Cadet Nurse Corps," young woman in uniform, 20 x 30" 35.00
World War II, "Less Dangerous Than Careless Talk," pictures bloody rattlesnake, 20 x 30" 55.00
World War II, "Let's Give Him Enough & On Time," Army soldier firing machine gun, Norman Rockwell, 27 x 41" 400.00
World War II, "Use It Up—Wear It Out—Make It Do!," woman sewing patch on seat of pants of man bending over, 1943, 22 x 28" 20.00

PYROGRAPHY

Pyrography is the process of producing designs on wood, leather or other materials by using heated tools or a fine flame. Commonly referred to as "burnt-wood" wares, creating these articles became a popular home craft earlier in this century after the invention of the platinum-pointed needle which could be safely heated. Prior to this a hot poker was used to scorch a design in the wood. But because of the accuracy the needle allowed, burning a design into wood became a hobby with many and companies issued kits with all the tools necessary to create the design on a pre-stamped soft wood box or article. A wide variety of designs was available including flowers, animals and scrolls. Women were popular subjects and the rights to Charles Dana Gibson's famous "Gibson Girl" were obtained by Thayer and Chandler Co. of Chicago who also sold items pre-stamped with the Sunbonnet Babies. Modest prices are still associated with burnt-wood wares unless the overall workmanship or design is exceptional.

Box, cov., burnt period scene & "Velma Chocolates, Roddewig-Schmidt Candy Co., Davenport, Iowa" $24.00
Checkerboard, hinged, burnt & plain squares 38.50
Frame, burnt holly leaves decor & inscription "Merry Christmas 1904" 19.00
Glove box w/hinged lid, burnt portrait of 1920's lady on cover 15.00
Glove box w/hinged lid, burnt roses decor 10.00
Model of puppy w/wide leather collar, burnt details, 14" h. 27.00
Plaque, burnt grape clusters & acorn decor, 30 x 16" ....60.00 to 70.00
Tie rack, burnt likeness of Will Rogers 28.00

RADIOS & ACCESSORIES

Early model radios, transmitting equipment and components are now being sought by a special group of collectors.

Books, "Perpetual Trouble Shooter's

Manuals," by John F. Rider, Volumes 1 through 20 .... $550.00
Brochure, Atwater Kent Radio Cabinet models, fold-out, 1927 .... 6.00
Catalog, "Lafayette Radio Co.," 1940, 120 pp. 25.00
Manual, Atwater Kent Instruction Manual, for Models 55 & 60, 1929 .... 7.50
Radio, Admiral "Super Airoscope," table model, standard broadcast .. 65.00
Radio, Atwater Kent Model 12, w/six brass base tubes, breadboard case 835.00
Radio, Atwater Kent Model 20, 1924 .... 70.00
Radio, Atwater Kent "Cathedral" Model 84, 1931 .... 150.00
Radio, Buckingham Model 30, w/inside speaker 115.00

Crosley "Showbox" Radio & Speaker

Radio, Crosley Model 706 "Showbox," 8-tube, w/speaker, 120-volt, 1928 (ILLUS.) 80.00
Radio, Emerson Model 157, black plastic case, 1937 .... 55.00
Radio, Federal, crystal set, patented 1917, Buffalo, New York 200.00
Radio, General Model BC14A, crystal set, dated 1918 .... 450.00
Radio, Grebe Model CR-9, 1921 ..... 525.00
Radio, Grebe "Synchophase" Model MU-1, 1925 .... 150.00
Radio, Majestic "Cathedral" Model 151 .... 100.00
Radio, Metro "Super 7," gold silk screen, good tubes, 1926 .... 125.00
Radio, Murdock "Neutrodyne" battery-operated, 1924 .... 120.00
Radio, Philco "Baby Grand" Model 37-84B, 1937 .... 125.00
Radio, RCA "Radiola IIIA," 1924 ..... 125.00
Radio, RCA "Radiola 60," 9-tube, w/No. 103 speaker, 1928 .... 495.00
Radio, Setchell Carlson Model 427, table model, brown Bakelite case, 1940's 46.00
Radio, Silvertone "Cathedral" Model 1291, battery-operated pat. No. 1-537-708 .... 110.00
Radio, Spartan, glass, nickel-plated metal & wood, circular dial surrounded by a speaker, peach mirrored-glass body intersected by three nickel-plated bands, raised on a black-painted wood base, face printed "Spartan Jackson, Michigan Made in U.S.A.," 15" h. 1,210.00
Radio, Truetone, red Bakelite case, 1930's 40.00
Radio, Tuska Model 224, 1922 ...... 175.00
Radio, Volta, crystal set 185.00
Radio, Walter Electrical Mfg., crystal set 240.00
Radio, Zenith "Trans-Oceanic" Model 8G005, portable, 1946-50 .. 80.00
Radio-phonograph combination, Majestic Model M-100-B 125.00
Radio-phonograph combination, Westinghouse Model H-171, chairside model, brown plastic case, 1946 .... 30.00
Radio speaker, Atwater Kent, gooseneck, 1926 .... 70.00
Radio speaker, Operadio, 1925 ..... 75.00
Radio tubes, WD-11, pr. 100.00

RAILROADIANA

Early Locomotive Lantern

Almanac, "Milwaukee R.R.," 1941 ... $5.00
Badge, metal, "N.P.R.R." (Northern Pacific Railroad) 25.00
Bell, "Santa Fe," steam engine-type, solid bronze 300.00
Blanket, "C.N." (Canadian National), maple leaf logo 60.00
Bond, "Plymouth, Kankakee & Pacific Railroad Co.," dated 1871, framed 229.00
Book, "Chicago, Compliments Chicago & NW Railway," Art Deco cover by Welch, 1929 .... 100.00
Book, "General Motors Locomotives

Operating Manual," Kansas City Southern Railway, 1946 .... 16.95
Bowl, "Soo Line," china, Only At Grandpa's patt., 5½" d. 140.00
Bowl, "Missouri Pacific Lines," china, Eagle patt., Syracuse (O.P. & Co.), 8" d. 38.00
Brochure, "Illinois Central," Mardi Gras Tour, 1934 .... 20.00
Butter pat, "Canadian National Railways," china 12.50
Cabinet photograph, uniformed conductor, 1890's 5.00
Caboose lamp, brass, Aladdin, w/unique leveling holder, w/original tag 125.00
Calendar, 1947, "Pennsylvania R.R.," full pad, full color, in original mailing tube, 28½" square 75.00
Chromolithograph, side view of steam locomotive, "The Hinkley Locomotive Works, Boston," printed by C.H. Crosby & Co., ca. 1860, 15 3/8 x 25 3/8" image size, 19 7/8 x 30" overall 1,100.00
Coal shovel, "MO. PAC. R.R." (Missouri Pacific Railroad), back of shank marked "ABW CO - CAR HT - 3-36" 55.00
Coffeepot, cov., "Great Northern," silver plate, ca. 1910 .... 75.00
Conductor's uniform, "C&NW" (Chicago & Northwestern), 4 pcs. including hat 85.00
Creamer w/hinged lid, "Northern Pacific," silver plate 65.00
Cuspidor, "Union Pacific," brass & copper, large 90.00
Fire extinguisher, "Louisville & Nashville Railroad," copper 50.00
Gravy ladle, "New Haven R.R.," silver plate 40.00
Handsaw, "Frisco Lines," logo on saw 40.00
Insulator, "Union Pacific R.R.," glass, threadless pilgrim's hat style 75.00
Lantern, locomotive, tin, original nickel-plated kerosene burner & reflector, old worn black paint on exterior, marked "Star Head-Light Co., Rochester, N.Y., U.S.A.," w/newspaper article about manufacturer, 27½" h. (ILLUS.) 210.00
Lantern, "C St P M & O Ry." (Chicago, St. Paul, Minneapolis & Omaha), Adlake Reliable, tin frame, clear cast logo globe marked "The Northwestern Line," 5 3/8" globe 225.00
Match safe, "Monon Route," alligator-shaped, promotional piece 275.00
Mustard pot, cov., "New York Central System," china 18.00
Padlock, "Missouri R.R. Co.," brass 95.00
Padlock, "Oregon-California R.R.," brass 100.00
Plate, "Northern Pacific," china, Monad patt., 7" d. 60.00
Plate, dinner, "Denver & Rio Grande," china, Adam Blue patt., 9" d. 32.00
Plate, "Missouri Pacific Lines," china, State Flowers patt. w/"The Sunshine Special" center, Syracuse China, 10 5/8" d. 184.00
Playing cards, Denver & Rio Grande Railroad, different scene on each card, w/wood box w/slide drawer, complete deck 26.00
Poster, "Great Northern Railway," canvas, scene of Many Glacier Hotel, in original advertising frame, ca. 1910, 18 x 48" 400.00
Switch key, "Oregon Short Line Railroad," brass 30.00
Tablespoon, "Rock Island Railroad," silver plate, 1912 .... 25.00
Timetable, "Baltimore & Ohio," April 28, 1929 .... 12.00
Wrench, "C.R.I. & P.R.R. No. 2" (Chicago, Rock Island & Pacific), bulldog design 25.00

ROGERS (JOHN) GROUPS

"Checkers Up At The Farm"

Cast plaster and terra cotta figure groups made by John Rogers in New York City in the mid to late 19th century were highly popular in their day, originally selling for $10 to $25. Many offer charming vignettes of Victorian domestic life or events of historic or *literary importance and those in good condition are prized today.*

"Checker Players" $1,500.00
"Checkers Up At the Farm" (ILLUS.) 835.00
"Coming to the Parson" 600.00
"Favored Scholar" 385.00
"Fighting Bob" 1,500.00
"The Foundling" 625.00
"George Washington" 1,300.00
"One More Shot" 550.00
"Peddler at the Fair" 300.00
"Photographer" 1,000.00
"Playing Doctor" 550.00
"Rip Van Winkle Returned" 475.00
"School Examination" 500.00
"Speak For Yourself, John" 525.00
"Uncle Ned's School" 1,500.00
"The Watch On The Santa Maria" ... 475.00

ROYALTY COMMEMORATIVES

Queen Victoria Jubilee Plate

QUEEN VICTORIA (1837-1901)

Book, "Diamond Jubilee," by Raphael Tuck, 12 colored embossed scenes of Victoria's reign $125.00

Bread tray, glass, portrait of Victoria, 1897 Jubilee 125.00

Figurine, parian, Queen Victoria seated on ornate chair w/British Royal Crest embossed on back, ca. 1850, 7½" h. 325.00

Handkerchief, portrait of Queen Victoria, 1897 Jubilee 75.00

Match safe, sterling silver, w/enameled "VR" & British flag, 1897 Jubilee 95.00

Pinback button, celluloid, 1897 Jubilee, six different, the set 75.00

Pitcher, china, cobalt blue w/silver rim, 1897 Jubilee, Doulton, 10" h. 525.00

Pitcher, porcelain, round medallion center, black transfer w/gold trim, 1887 Jubilee, 5" w., 5" h. ... 85.00

Pitcher, jug-type, stoneware, portrait of Queen Victoria seated on throne surrounded w/embossed emblems of Commonwealth nations, tan & cream ground, Doulton Lambeth, 1887 Jubilee, 6" h... 225.00

Plate, china, royal blue w/"Dominion of Canada" & seven Provincial crests centered around likeness of Queen Victoria, 19th century, 8" d. 65.00

Plate, china, transfer print of Queen's wedding, ca. 1840 .... 185.00

Plate, pressed glass, clear w/gold, 1887 Jubilee, 9¾" d. (ILLUS.) 50.00

Spoon, sterling silver, Queen Victoria head handle w/blue enameling & dated "1837/1897," picture of crown, two men & bird from Halifax, Nova Scotia in bowl, 1897 Jubilee 45.00

EDWARD VII (1901-1910)

Woven Silk Portrait of Edward VII

Book, "London at the Coronation of King Edward VII," 1902 .... 50.00

Medallion, metal, 1908 .... 12.00

Mug, stoneware, cobalt blue, Royal Doulton 145.00

Plate, pressed glass, handled, clear, 25th Wedding Anniversary of Prince of Wales, Edward, & Princess of Wales, marked "March 10, 1863-1888," Prince of Wales plumes in center 85.00

Woven silk portrait of Edward VII, in cardboard mount, by W.H. Grant (ILLUS.) .... 150.00 to 200.00

ROYCROFT ITEMS

Roycroft Floor Ashtray

Elbert Hubbard, eccentric entrepreneur of the late 19th century, founded Roycroft Shops and established a craft community in East Aurora, New York in 1895. Individuals were trained in the trades of bookbinding, leather tooling and printing. Craft-style furniture in the manner of Gustav Stickley and known as "Aurora Colonial" furniture was produced. A copper workshop, begun in 1908, turned out numerous items. All of these, along with the Buffalo Pottery china which was produced exclusively for use at the Roycroft Inn and carries the Roycroft symbol, constitute a special category associated with the Arts and Crafts movement.

Ashtray, floor-type, hand-hammered copper & oak, strap handle on match box holder at top above shallow round bowl fitted on tapering oak pedestal & round base, marked, ca. 1915, 29" h. (ILLUS.) $175.00

Book, "The Five Human Types - How To Analyze People On Sight," Elsie Lincoln Benedict, 1921, seven pamphlets & chart 15.00

Book, "Patrick Henry," by Elbert Hubbard, 1903 .... 6.00

Book, "The Roycrofters - The Date Book of Elbert Hubbard," 1927, leather bound, 208 pp. 20.00

Book ends, hand-hammered copper, embossed poppies, brass wash, die-stamped mark, 5 x 5½", pr. .. 275.00

Bookstand, oak, tall w/tapering sides, overhanging top & five open shelves, four keyed through-tenons on either side, marked on each side w/carved orb & fleur de lis, 20 x 17½", 63" h. (partially refinished) 5,775.00

Box, mahogany, iron fittings at each lower corner, iron handles either side, hinged iron clasp at front, die-stamped mark, 9¼ x 25½ x 12" 412.50

Roycroft Buffet-Serving Table

Buffet - serving table, oak, plate rail at top above rectangular top above one long drawer w/metal bail pulls & metal keyhole escutcheon above pair of leaded glass cabinet doors w/"Butterfly" metal hinges, w/metal presentation tag, ca. 1906, 20 1/8" w., 42" h. (ILLUS.) 4,620.00

Candleholders, hand-hammered copper, circular base, cylindrical shaft, flaring bobeche, original dark brown patina, die-stamped mark, 4" d., 9½" h., pr. 605.00

Candlesticks, hand-hammered copper, flattened rim & socket on cylindrical stem & wide floriform base, early 20th c., 8" h., pr...... 150.00

Child's chair, mahogany, four vertical slats at back, rounded tops on back posts, front legs end in tenons through the seat, uneven stretchers on the sides, front & back, Macmurdo feet, burned-in orb across front seat rail, original finish & leather seat, 29" h. 715.00

Conference table, oak, rectangular top on four heavy square legs w/low, uneven stretchers on all four sides, burned-in orb mark one leg, fully pinned, new dark brown finish, 74 x 37½", 30" h. 1,760.00

Desk lamp, wide domed shade w/four straps & band of mica, on flaring cylindrical shaft & broad circular base, original brass wash patina, fully riveted, die-stamped mark, 14½ x 10" 2,860.00

Desk set: document box w/hinged lid & hand-hammered surface, pair of book ends w/stylized embossed leaves, pair of blotter ends w/stylized embossed flowers in middle; copper, box 9½ x 6¼ x 2¾", 5 pcs. 450.00

Dining table, oak, round w/rolled-edge apron & four legs ending on "V" platforms, buttressed w/small, thick arched corbels, new dark brown finish, unmarked, 48" w., 28½" h. 1,760.00

Lantern, wall-type, hand-hammered copper & hammered amber glass, rectangular, hanging from L-shaped bracket, die-stamped joiner's compass mark, 13 x 8½" 2,860.00

Morris chair, oak, five vertical slats at back, flat "paddle" arms w/four slats under each, fully pinned, burned-in orb mark on front seat rail, No. 45, new red-brown finish, cushions covered in Liberty's "Hera" pattern cloth, 41½" h. . . .2,310.00

Motto on paper, calligraphy within a floral border, "Do unto others as though you were the others," wide margins, framed & matted . . 130.00

Side chair, oak, one broad & one narrow slat flanked by tall, square stiles, square upholstered seat above wide apron, heavy tapered legs, uneven stretchers at front, back & sides, burned-in orb mark on front apron, medium brown finish, 37½" h. (new leather seat) 412.50

Table, oak, four-sided taboret w/overhanging top & "key-hole" cut-outs on each flaring side, burned-in mark, new finish, 15½" w., 20¾" h. 3,520.00

Vase, hand-hammered copper, "American Beauty" design w/squatty bulbous footed base w/wide shoulder tapering to tall, narrow neck w/flared rim, red-light brown patina, die-stamped mark, 7¼" w., 22" h. 475.00

Wall sconces, hand-hammered copper, arrowhead backs incorporating candle sockets, early 20th c., 8" h., pr. (brass wash removed) . . 220.00

Writing desk, drop-front, woman's, quarter-sawn oak, rectangular overhanging top above slanting fall-front w/two long copper straps ending in curved "handles," above one long drawer w/hammered copper pulls, square tapering legs w/Macmurdo feet, burned-in orb mark on front, new finish, 38½" w., 44" h. 2,750.00

SALESMAN'S SAMPLES

Uncle Sam Jr. Cooking Range

The traveling salesman or "drummer" has all but disappeared from the American scene. In the latter part of the 19th century and up to the late 1930's, they traveled the country calling on potential customers to show them small replicas of their products. Today these small versions of kitchenwares, farm equipment, and even bath tubs, are of interest to collectors and are available in a wide price range.

Air compressor, cast iron, "Lipman," South Beloit, Illinois, 3" w., 4" h. $75.00

Axle grease bucket, tin, "Mica" 65.00

Barn stanchion, wood & iron, 13 x 21" 275.00

Bed, iron, embossed "Art Bed Co." & "Chicago," 28 x 17 x 18" 175.00

Bed, Murphy-type, folds into walnut cabinet w/maple trim, 14½" h. . . . 225.00

Blackboard, "Sterling Lifelong Blackboard," w/advertising logo on back, original mailing envelope w/company stamp, 3½ x 5" 32.50

Boots, rubber, knee-high, Goodyear Rubber Co., 2½" h., pr. 22.50

Butcher knives, "Foster Bros.," manufactured by John Chatillon & Sons, w/catalogue No. 28, dated 1940, 24 pcs. in original suitcase . . 225.00

Clothes wringer, American Wringer Co. No. 2, Gem Horseshoe Brand 75.00

Coffin, child's, wooden, w/two metal inscriptions for the lid 75.00

Cooking range, cast iron, "Favorite, Piqua, Ohio," 42 lbs. 1,500.00

Cooking range, gas, cast iron, "Superior," two-door model 175.00

Cooking range, cast iron, "Uncle Sam Jr.," complete w/three pots, pans & coal hod, ca. 1876 (ILLUS.) 900.00

Cultivator, horse-drawn, triangular wooden frame & six steel shaped

blades, turned tiger maple post, 8¾" l., 4¾" h. 295.00
Fire extinguisher, "Presto," 1940's, 6", w/box 14.00
Nozzle, brass, "Self-Propelling Nozzle Co.," pat. 1922, 7½" 42.00
Organ stool, wooden, 7½" h. 175.00
Railroad lantern, "Baltimore & Ohio," clear globe, Deltz No. 39 .. 55.00
Sewing machine w/attachments, electric w/foot pedal, Wilcox & Gibbs, walnut carrying case 495.00
Sideboard w/mirror, oak, w/manufacturer's label dated 1905, 13" w., 17" h. 195.00
Washboard, "Little Darling" 65.00
Washing machine, hand-seamed galvanized steel, cast-iron hand-cranked fly wheel, sink agitator, 12" 110.00

SCALES

Postal Scale

Apothecary scale, balance-type, oak case w/drawer, disassembles & parts fit in drawer, 10¾" l. $40.00
Baby weighing scale, cast iron, "Dayton," blue paint............ 37.50
Bathroom scale, cast iron, Art Deco style, measures to 300 lbs........ 65.00
Butter scale, ash & pine, square post supports balancing arm w/suspended wooden trays, square wood base w/chamfered sides, nut brown finish, 21" h. (repair in top of post) 115.00
Candy scale, "Anderson Computing Scale Co.," 2 lb. 250.00
Candy scale, cast iron w/brass pan, all weights, "Detecto Gram," 1930's, 3 lb. 135.00
Candy scale, lollypop-type, "O.D. Jennings," white porcelain 1,200.00
Candy scale, "National Specialty Co.," 1910, 2 lb. (restored) 225.00
Coin-operated sidewalk scale, advertising "Grapette Soda," 1-cent 2,200.00
Coin-operated sidewalk scale, "National Weigher," gilded metal, ornate claw feet, blue & white porcelain face registers up to 300 lbs., National Novelty Co., 1910 .. 850.00
Countertop scale, balance-type, walnut & brass, brass pans & crosspiece, carved hand-form support on column w/pedestal, Antico Verde marble base, Italy, 18th c., 25½" h. 330.00
Egg grading scale, copper, "Champion," ca. 1925 .... 75.00
Kitchen scale, hanging-type, brass, "Chatillons Family" 25.00
Pharmacy scale, oak case w/beveled glass & marble top, 1800's ... 295.00
Postal scale, platform-type, "Hanson Bros. Scale Co.," ca. 1925 (ILLUS.)........................... 35.00
Postal scale, "I.D.L.," 3¢............ 20.00
Spring scale, hanging-type, "Chatillons Spring Balance," brass face, measures to 144 lbs., 17 x 4½"... 60.00
Spring scale, hanging-type, brass face, "Chatillon's No. 2," dated 1892 .... 20.00
Spring scale, hanging-type, "Hanson Scale Co. Chicago, Cap. 160 Lbs." 10.00
Steelyard scale, wrought iron w/brass inlay, brass fig-shaped weight, 32" l. (pitted & old repair) 25.00

SCIENTIFIC INSTRUMENTS

Bausch & Lomb Microscope

Barometer, stick-type, mahogany veneer, broken pediment crest w/brass urn finial, long throat w/"dry and damp" indicator, a thermometer, large dial for weather conditions, ivory button & a level w/maker's name, "D. Rivolta," Edinburgh, Scotland, 19th c., 38½" h. $220.00

Barometer, stick-type, pine, w/thermometer, signed "C. Wilder, Peterboro, New Hampshire, Woodruffs pat. June 5, 1860," 38¼" h. 1,000.00

Barometer, wheel-type, gilt bronze, circular face surmounted by an urn *en flambeau* & flanked by rams' heads suspending garlands, base cast w/plumes & tassels, signed "Couilleau Paris," Louis XV style, 11½" w., 27" h. 660.00

Bipolar dynamo, Edison-type, 1870's, possibly experimental, 14" h. 800.00

Compass, turned wood case, convex glass lens, hand-colored engraved paper face, 2" d. (age cracks in lid) 150.00

Kaleidoscope, "Bush," ca. 1875, on walnut stand (restored) 1,000.00

Micrometer, "Starrett," 3", w/original case 45.00

Microscope, "Bausch & Lomb," in fitted wooden case (ILLUS.) 330.00

Microscope, brass, w/accessories, in fitted wooden case, "Universal Household Microscope," Newton Co. 95.00

Planisphere, "Hammett's" 175.00

Slide rule, wood & celluloid, "Keuffel & Esser," dated 1900, w/case 35.00

Slide rule, ivory & brass, pat. 1908, w/leather case 28.00

Telescope, brass w/leather grip, 4-section, original pigskin case, 22½" l. 85.00

Telescope, brass, on oak tripod base w/turned legs, signed "M. Jaggli, Zurich," 39" l., 65" h. (dented cylinder) 200.00

Transit, brass, demilune form, compass in oblong form, marked "Fecit Thomas Greenough, Boston," 18th c., 4¾" d. dial, 12¾" l. 4,070.00

SCOUTING ITEMS

Scout rules and regulations, handbooks and accouterments have changed with the times. Early items associated with the Scouting movements are now being collected. A sampling follows.

World War I Poster

BOY SCOUT

Axe, hand-type, "The Collins Co. Famous Conn. Axe Makers" $45.00

Beadcraft kit, "Official Boy Scout Indian Beadcraft Kit," 1940's, original box 28.00

Book, "Boy Scouts on Bob's Hill," Chas. Pierce Burton, 1912, forward by James West 20.00

Book, "The Boy Scouts Camp Book," 1914, illustrated by Norman Rockwell 30.00

Book, "Explorer Scout Manual," 1946 .... 12.00

Calendar, 1934, Norman Rockwell illustration 75.00

Calendar, 1963, Norman Rockwell illustration 25.00

Camera, Scout 120, box-type 12.50

Figure of Boy Scout, white metal, motto & "In Appreciation, 1938 Campaign" 68.00

First Aid Kit, w/book & holder, 1926 .... 23.00

Handbook, 1914, hardbound 35.00

Handbook, 1934 .... 12.00

Handbook, 1940, Norman Rockwell cover 8.00

"Handbook for Scout Masters," 1913, first edition 25.00

Knife, pocket-type, bone handle, "Ulster USA," pre-1941 .... 75.00

Knife, sheath-type, 1929, original box 25.00

Magazine, "Scouting," 1931, September 6.00

Membership cards, 1916, flag & Scouts on cover, set of 4 .... 16.00

Mess kit: aluminum cup & canteen, metal fork, spoon & knife; original canvas holders, ca. 1945 ..... 18.00

Neckerchief, National Jamboree, 1953 .... 25.00
Pin, Jubilee, 1930, New York, shows Statue of Liberty 20.00
Poster, World War I, "USA Bonds - Third Liberty Loan Campaign - Boy Scouts of America - Weapons For Liberty," kneeling Scout holding sword for Columbia, drawn by J.C. Leyendecker, 20 x 30" (ILLUS.) ....100.00 to 150.00
Program, "42nd Anniversary, 1952," U.S. Naval Air Station, Pensacola, Florida 6.00
Sign, "Boy Scout Cartridges," tin over cardboard, Boy Scout holding two flags, U.S. Cartridge Co., Lowell, Mass., Beach Co., Coshocton, Ohio, 13 x 19" 450.00
Uniform shirt, 1945, w/badges 18.00

GIRL SCOUT

Book, "Girl Scout Game Book," 1929 .... 6.00
Book, "Manual of Cooking," bear on cover 12.50
First Aid Kit, tin 25.00
Handbook, 1917, blue covers 25.00
Handbook, 1943 .... 7.50
Trivet, "50th Anniversary," 1962 .... 15.00
Uniform: jacket, hat & belt; regulation-type, 1920's 40.00

SEWING ADJUNCTS

Maple Darner

Book, "Complete Book of Sewing," by Constance Talbot, 1943, 750 explanatory pictures $12.00
Book, "How To Make Draperies," by Singer Sewing Machine Co., 1920 .... 7.00
Crochet hook, ivory, double ended, 7" 45.00
Darner, blown deep pink opaline glass 215.00
Darner, blown iridescent blue glass, ball w/handle 55.00
Darner, ebony, egg shape, sterling silver repoussé hollow handle, 4½" l. 35.00
Darner, maple, slipper-shaped, 5½" l. (ILLUS.) 18.00
Darner, sterling silver, egg shape, heavily engraved, w/thimble 140.00
Embroidery stamp, hewn pine handle & tin scroll, 18th c., 4" l. 39.00
Eyelet punch, sterling silver, w/gauge, relief engraved floral handle 30.00
Needle case, ivory, model of a fish, body has embedded silvery dots, one iridescent pink eye & one blue eye, 3¼" l. 68.00

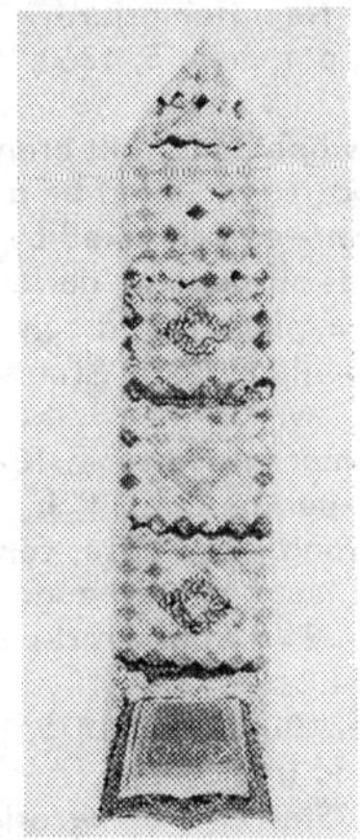

Pieced Needle Case

Needle case, pieced cotton & wool felt, elongated folding case composed entirely of small diamond patches divided into a series of three deep pockets lined w/blue fabric, the last section w/three multicolored embroidered wool needle holders, New England, dated 1781, 28½" l. (ILLUS.) 1,100.00
Pin casket, brass, figural leaf slide lid, embossed butterfly, vertical ribbed body & beading, signed "Pratt & Farmer Licenses," England, ca. 1822, 2¾" l., 1" h. 125.00
Pincushion, model of a lady's slipper, spelter, red velvet cushion, 1 x 2¼ x 3½" 25.00
Pincushion, pillow-shaped, paper covered base, velvet top theorem-painted w/red & green roses, 2¾" l. 95.00
Scissors, buttonhole-type, "Keen Kutter" 30.00
Sewing basket, woven splint w/cheese weave, octagonal base, 4" deep, 12" d. 110.00
Sewing bird, brass, flowers & leaves in relief, double silk cushions 165.00
Sewing box, heart-shaped, velvet side panels w/applied wooden hearts & inlay, heart-shaped pincushion on top, end drawer, 12" l.

(minor repairs & one foot replaced) 80.00

Sewing box, rosewood w/brass inlay, tapering rectangular form, lid w/raised center & sloping sides enclosing a series of lidded compartments, rosewood ring handles on sides, raised on gadrooned bun feet, overall brass-inlaid floral decoration & beaded edges, William IV period, ca. 1835, 7¼" h. 825.00

Sewing kit: thimble, scissors, needle case, thread puller & knife; sterling silver, fitted wooden case has silver medallions on lid of crowned male & female rulers, tattered inside lining has scrap of newspaper written in German - dated 1857, 5 pcs. w/case (scissors has been repaired) 135.00

Spool stand, wooden, circular step-down disc base, four iron spool rods, turned center post w/ring & suppressed ball finial, great patina & surface, 3½ x 5" 85.00

Tape measure, advertising, "Lewis Lye Penna., Salt Mfg. Co.," celluloid 15.00

Tape measure, celluloid, figural Indian 18.00

Tape measure, celluloid, model of an alligator 55.00

Tape measure, celluoid, model of a four-masted schooner, "Estes Park, Colorado" 45.00

Tape measure, china, figural Pierrot playing mandolin, 2¾" 45.00

Thimble, brass, marked "Her Majesty Thimble," England 20.00

Thimble, 10k gold, Simons, size 12 .... 70.00

Thimble, 14k gold, narrow engraved edge "Esther," size 8 .... 95.00

Thimble, plastic, marked "Promote Charles Scott for Chancery Clerk" 10.00

Thimble, sterling silver, engraved barnyard scene, bridge & buildings, size 7 .... 38.00

Thimble, sterling silver w/engraved wide gold band, "Ketchum & McDougal," size 8 .... 55.00

Thimble case, celluloid, figural cowboy on horse 55.00

Thimble holder, blue glass, model of Victorian shoes 88.00

SHAKER COLLECTIBLES

The Shakers, a religious sect founded by Ann Lee, first settled in this country at Watervliet, N.Y., near Albany, in 1774 and by 1880 there were nine settlements in America. Workmanship in Shaker crafts is an extension of their religious beliefs and features plain and simple designs reflecting a chaste elegance that is now much in demand though relatively few early items are available.

Shaker Basket

Almanac, 1884, thirty-two page booklet describing various medical & expression formulation advice, promoting "The Never Failing Shaker Extract of Roots, or Mother Seigel's Curative Syrup," 6 x 7 7/8" (minor losses & tears, foxing) $77.00

Basket, woven splint, finely woven w/split ash rim & carrying handle, square base, 19th c., some minor breaks, 5½" h. (ILLUS.) 660.00

Blanket chest, hinged rectangular top w/molded edge, opening to a till & storage area, the paneled front & sides raised on tapering cylindrical legs, painted red overall, Midwest, 19th c., 37½" l., 24¾" h. (till lacks cover) 990.00

Box, cov., bentwood oval, Harvard-style double tapering lappets, umber graining on yellow ochre ground, fitted cover w/yellow free-hand painted scalloped border & decorative initials "P.R.," 19th c., 4 3/8 x 5 7/8", 2" h. 3,630.00

Bucket, cov., wooden, tapering cylinder, two finger lappets at top & one at base, top w/painted floral decoration, wooden strap handle, miniature, 2 3/8" h. 550.00

Cloak, red on scarlet French wool broadcloth, label "Shaker Cloak, L.M. Noyes Agent, Sabbathday Lake Me.," late 19th-early 20th c. 500.00

Counter chair, painted & decorated wood, low back w/single arched slat above high rush seat on turned legs joined by turned stretchers, painted & decorated overall w/tones of ochre, Freegift Wells, Watervliet, New York, ca. 1845 . . 8,800.00

Cupboard, painted pine & poplar, flat molded cornice above rectangular recessed molded panel door opening to shelved interior w/six tombstone compartments & recessed drawer above shorter door flanked by rounded corners, flat base, old ivory green paint over old red stain, possibly Watervliet, New York, ca. 1830, 28" w., 86¾" h. . . 3,850.00

Dining table, trestle-type, tiger stripe maple & cherry, four-board rectangular top on chamfered tapering braces & shaped supports, joined by horizontal rail w/exposed tenon construction, arched legs, (probably) original finish, Canterbury, New Hampshire, first half 19th c., 34½ x 71¼", 27½" h. 94,600.00

Dress, homespun linen, simple pale brown dress w/double collar, w/twelve later buttons, late 19th-early 20th c. 192.50

Pantry box, cov., bentwood oval, three finger lappet construction on base w/single finger lappet on lid, worn old bluish green paint, 10¼" l. (bottom board loose & has age cracks) 250.00

Peg rack, eight turned pegs, salmon paint 302.50

Shaker No. 6 Rocking Chair

Rocking chair w/arms, four-slat back w/acorn finials on turned stiles, woven tape seat, original alligatored dark finish, stenciled "Mt. Lebanon, New York," No. 6 size (ILLUS.) 975.00

Sewing box, cov., semicircular, marbleized oilcloth on cardboard w/blue velvet interior & blue ribbon trim, stamped label "Sabbathday Lake Shakers, Maine," 6 x 9" (bottom edge & hinge retaped, front edge worn) 105.00

Work table, painted birch & pine, rectangular top w/rectangular splashboard above a single molded drawer on circular tapering legs, original red paint, New Lebanon Community, first half 19th c., 37½" l., 25½" h. 8,800.00

SHEET MUSIC

"The Alcoholic Blues," 1919, Prohibition theme, owl on moon cover . . $10.00

"Amelia Earhart's Last Flight," 1939 . . . . 20.00

"Ballad of Davy Crockett," Fess Parker on cover 6.00

"Belle of Cuba Quickstep," 1895 . . . . 15.00

"Brazil," Donald Duck & Joe Carioca on cover 12.00

"Bunch of Blackberries," vignette of black boys, 1899 . . . . 20.00

"By Radio Phone," 1922, girl operator on cover 15.00

"Casey Jones," train on cover 6.00

"Caesar & Cleopatra" theme, 1963, Elizabeth Taylor, Richard Burton & Rex Harrison on colorful cover . . . 10.00

"Darktown Is Out Tonight," couple doing Cake Walk & streetcar pictured, framed 30.00

"Don't Cry Dolly Grey," World War I uniformed soldiers w/rifles on cover, Jerome H. Remick & Co. 25.00

"Did I Remember?" Jean Harlow on cover 10.00

"Eagle of U.S.A.," Lindbergh on cover 12.00

"Fancy Free," Mickey Mouse & Donald Duck on cover 12.00

"For Me & My Gal," Judy Garland on cover 12.00

"Frankie & Johnny," Mae West on cover 15.00

"Gold Mine in the Sky," 1937, Kate Smith on cover 8.00

"Help," Beatles on cover 18.00

"I'll Have You All Over Again," 1920, cover by T. Earl Christy 15.00

"I'm A Lonely Little Petunia," Lawrence Welk on cover 4.00

"Just You & Me," 1917, Raphael Kirchner cover 45.00

"Katrina," from Disney's "The Adventures of Ichabod & Mr. Toad," Bing Crosby on cover 13.00

"Laugh Clown Laugh," 1928, Lon Chaney, Sr. on cover 5.00

"Mammy Jinny's Jubilee," 1913, blacks on cover 20.00

"The Midnight Fire Alarm," old-fashioned fire wagon on cover by E.T. Paull 20.00
"My Doughnut Girl," 1919, Salvation Army 10.00
"Oh Dem Golden Slippers," 1935, Gene Autry on cover 15.00
"Over the Rainbow," from The Wizard of Oz, whole cast on cover ... 20.00
"She'll Always Remember," Kate Smith on cover 5.00
"Stormy Weather," Lena Horne on cover surrounded by numerous black caricatures 15.00
"Teddy Bears' Picnic," 1947 .... 20.00
"We," Charles Lindbergh on cover .. 25.00
"When Our Firemen Face Their Foe," 1907, steamer racing to fire on cover 15.00
"Who's Afraid of the Big Bad Wolf," 1933, Disney cover 14.50
"You Belong To My Heart," 1943, from Walt Disney's "Three Caballeros," Donald Duck & Joe Carioca on cover 12.00

SIGNS & SIGNBOARDS

Butcher Shop Trade Sign

Ammunition, "Laflin & Rand," paperboard, four soldiers from different branches of the military, 1900, framed, 24 x 43" $290.00
Amusement park, "Pontchartrain Beach," tin, large clown mask roller coaster, 27 x 21" 95.00
Automobile parts, "Houk Hubcaps," lithographed canvas, soldiers in gun battle around 1915 automobile, framed, 23 x 33" 650.00
Automobiles, "Jaguar Sales & Service," porcelain, shows head of jaguar at top, maroon & cream, no brackets, 40 x 38" 275.00
Baking powder, "White Loaf," embossed tin, can, loaf & "Wise Women Use White Loaf," ca. 1900 .... 375.00
Barber, wooden, straight razor w/movable parts, shaped blade fits into case, copper rivets, 2' x 12" 195.00
Beer, "Champagne Velvet Beer," tin, sporting scene, 20 x 14" 75.00
Blacksmith, "Horseshoeing and Repairing," painted wood, black lettering on white, black frame, back w/traces of blue paint, 13" x 5' 9" 247.50
Blacksmith & livery, "Buck's Livery," sheet zinc anvil, silver repaint w/black lettering, mounted on wrought-iron scroll bracket, 91½" l., 29" h. 795.00
Bread, "Butter-Nut Bread," decal on canvas, Butter-Nut Bread Boy, 19 x 40" 75.00
Buggies, "Ahlbrand Carriage Co.," lithographed paper, 12 styles of buggies shown 135.00
Butcher shop, cast iron, meat saw, cleaver & knife w/bull finial, old worn gold & aluminum paint, 24½" l. (repaired break in cleaver handle) 250.00
Butcher shop, copper, full-bodied standing pig on molded copper base, 19th c., 29½" l., 19½" h. (ILLUS.) 5,225.00
Candy, "Health Chocolates," die-cut tin, baker in white outfit, Victorian woman holding candy w/tennis racket at her feet & "A Wholesome Temptation," 1890's 475.00
"Cattle Crossing," sheet iron, black & silver painted bull, 18 x 23" rectangle 160.00
Cereal, "Kellogg's Toasted Corn Flakes," double-sided, die-cut lithographed tin, child in wicker hooded seat looking at product .. 1,650.00
Champagne, "Great Western," tin, early bottle, glass & grapes, 22 x 16" 550.00
Chocolate chips, "Trowbridges'," window decal, three-color, woman eating candy, ca. 1900 .... 75.00
Cigarettes, "Egyptienne Straight," paper under glass, artist-signed, beautiful girl, ca. 1910, original frame, 25 x 36" 250.00
Cigarettes, "Mecca," paper under glass, Christy-type girl shown, ca. 1912, original frame, 11 x 19" 170.00
Cigars, "The Barrister Cigar," cardboard w/original embossed wooden frame, man smoking in den w/fireplace, 27 x 37" 550.00
Cigars, "Red Circle," reverse painting on glass, wording on either side of center circle w/Indian Chief profile & "Smooth - Soothing

"Red Circle" Cigars Sign

- Satisfying," original wide oak frame, early 20th c. (ILLUS.) 798.00

Circus banner, "Canada's Conklin Shows Main Entrance," canvas, 8 x 20 feet 500.00

Cleanser, "Borax Mule Team," self-framed tin, colorful mule team pictured, 32 x 21" 70.00

Clothing, "Munsingwear," die-cut tin, two men looking at picture of man in long johns at easel 2,200.00

Coffee, "K & B Coffee," lithographed tin, man sipping coffee & coffee tin pictured, large 750.00

Coffee, "Maxwell House," easel-type w/hanger, celluloid & metal over cardboard, red, blue & white, "Maxwell House Coffee - Good To the Last Drop," 6 x 12" .. 55.00

Fabric, "Skinner's Satin," lithographed tin, Indian chief in full headdress & adorned w/colorful beads, oval (minor scuffs & dents) 2,640.00

Firearms, "Remington Firearms," cardboard, colorful man & lady holding boxes of shells w/ducks in foreground, ca. 1930 .... 375.00

"Fire Escape," tin, pointing finger, bright red w/relief lettering 35.00

Fish monger, copper, full-bodied fish w/embossed details & soldered fins, old patina, 30" l. 700.00

Flour, "Lysle Milling Co., Leavenworth, Kansas," self-framed lithographed tin, factory scene & "Where America's Best Flour Originates," 24 x 13" 125.00

Flour, "Saxton & Thompson," Lockport, N.Y., lithographed paper, mill, city, canal & elevated railroad, 25 x 19" 925.00

Food product, "Durr's Quality Foods," lithographed tin, Indian maiden serving food to chief, 1920's, wooden frame, 27 x 20" .. 175.00

Food product, "Squire's Hams," self-framed tin, comical portrait of pig w/human facial features, 1906, 19 x 14" oval....................1,250.00

Furniture, "Daven-o-Sofa Bed Combination," wooden, sofa closed & open, 1910 .... 120.00

Gasoline, "Marine," tin, speedboat w/two pilots, 4 x 2½' 375.00

Gloves, "Adler's," paper, "Adler's Two Butt'n Kids," child & goat butting heads, wood frame 200.00

Gum, "Kis-Me," die-cut metal, lady w/flowers & gold coins, 19 x 13" 400.00

Ice cream, "Borden's," tin, embossed w/Elsie the Cow & lettering, 44 x 24" 200.00

Insurance Company Sign

Insurance, "Providence Washington Insurance Co. - Providence, R.I. - Incorporated 1799," porcelain, gold lettering, old gilt plaster frame (ILLUS.) 65.00

Lanterns, "Air-O-Lite Kerosene Lantern," embossed tin, man adjusting flame in lantern w/glass shade, ca. 1910 .... 95.00

Medical supplies, "Johnson & Johnson," cardboard, blacks picking cotton, 1894, 2' x 3' 600.00

Motor oil, "Gulf Oil," metal, w/30¢ qt. oil pictured, 1950's, 8 x 12" ... 45.00

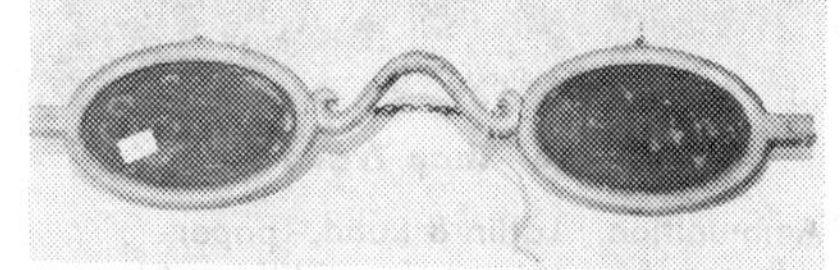

Optician's Trade Sign

Optician, wood, painted frames, w/doctor's name painted in left & "Optician" painted in right lens (ILLUS.) ....800.00 to 1,000.00

Osteopath, "Dr. Gahring Osteopathic Physician," tin, black sanded paint w/silver trim & lettering, wooden frame, 15¾ x 57" 55.00

Paint, "Sherwin Williams Paint," die-cut tin, "Covers the Earth," large............................ 160.00

Patent medicine, "Hostetter's Stomach Bitters," tin, nude man on horseback spearing dragon, 1905, 14 x 20" 1,350.00

Pharmacy, "C. H. Case Drugs and Stationery," carved & painted wood, mortar & pestle shape, old worn black repaint w/gilt lettering, 21½" w., 40½" h. plus iron brackets........................ 125.00

Pub sign, "Wheat Sheaf," painted wood, double-sided w/landscape w/windmill centering a large gilt sheaf of wheat, iron framework, England, ca. 1900, 26½ x 39" (wear, cracks) 990.00

Razor blades, "Twenty Grand Razor Blades," die-cut tin, razor blade shaped 122.50

School zone, "7-UP," tin, colorful standing policeman, double-sided, 5' h. 300.00

Shirts, "Jack Holt Shirts," canvas, color picture of famous movie star modeling a blue shirt w/yellow tie & black sports coat, framed under glass, 26 x 30" 75.00

Shoes, "Poll Parrot Shoes," glass, full-color parrot, original frame, 1920, 12 x 24" 325.00

Soap, "Milady Toilet Soap," tin, Victorian woman standing over wash bowl holding soap & "Keeps Skin Soft & Smooth 5¢" 575.00

Soft drink, "Hires," paper, copyright 1914, framed, 11 x 6½" (some corner pieces missing) 75.00

Soft drink, "Pepsi Cola," cardboard, "Say Pepsi Please," 1960's, tin frame 25.00

Soft drink, "RC Cola," cardboard, Santa decoration, 1940's, 40 x 20" 125.00

Stoves, "Majestic Ranges," colorful & graphic scene of woman cooking on Majestic stove, large 700.00

Tea, "Brooke Bond Tea," enameled sheet iron, black & white checkered border, orange ground, 20 x 30" 85.00

Tires, "Armstrong," tin, embossed "Unconditionally Guaranteed Armstrong Tires," burgundy w/yellow lettering, 1930's, 24 x 34" 68.00

Tobacco, "Honeymoon," embossed tin, man & woman sitting in moon 365.00

Tobacco, "Red Jacket," heavy cardboard, very colorful baseball scene, 22 x 28" 125.00

Tools, "True-Temper," die-cut cardboard, "Kelly Axe & Garden Tools," 1938, 18 x 24", set of 4 ... 40.00

Veterinary medicine, "Rawson's Standard Horse & Cattle Medicines," pictures horse & doctor, 10 x 15" 45.00

Watchmaker, wooden pocket watch w/iron stem & ring, worn old gold & yellow paint w/black & white face marked "G.T. Johnston," 16½ x 21½" (minor weathering w/some age cracks & wear)...... 875.00

Whiskey, "Fern Glen Rye, East St. Louis," tin, Negro crossing road w/a chicken under one arm & watermelon under other, on the road is a bottle of rye, captioned, "I'se in a perdickermunt"........3,700.00

Whiskey, "Old Barbee," self-framed tin, old man w/two farm girls by distillery, 1905, 38 x 26" 575.00

SNUFF BOTTLES & BOXES

The habit of taking snuff (powdered tobacco meant for inhaling) began in 17th century France and reached its peak during the 18th century, spreading to England, elsewhere on the Continent, and even to China, probably introduced there by Spanish or Portuguese traders. In Europe, tightly hinged porcelain or metal boxes were considered desirable containers to house the aromatic snuff. Orientals favored bottles of porcelain or glass, or carved of agate, ivory or jade, often modeled in the form of a human figure or fruit. By mid-19th century the popularity of snuff declined and consequently production of these exquisite containers diminished.

BOTTLES

Agate, carved in relief w/cat watching butterfly, 2¼" h. $85.00

Jadeite, carved in high relief w/naturalistic leaves, pale green tone w/slight russet mottling, bright green stem-form stopper .. 247.50

Mother-of-pearl, carved dragons, 2¼" h. 95.00

Peking glass, cameo-carved red to snowflake white swimming fish amidst waterweeds in red, green, yellow, blue & pink 440.00

Porcelain, multicolor enamel & gilt "Hundred Children" motif, one side w/dragon-boat festival scene, the other w/children encircling a Fu lion 247.50

BOXES

Brass, hinged lid engraved w/crowned wheel flanked by two rampant lions, monogram & "1765," 3 1/8" l. 125.00

Enamel, retangular w/gilt-metal mounts, decorated in celebration of the Prussian victory over the French & Austrians in the Seven Years War (1756-63), cover painted w/horsemen both inside & outside on a white ground, base, front & back w/German inscriptions, Germany, ca. 1757, 3 3/8" l. 1,760.00

Gold & enamel, oval, gilt stars on translucent enamel ground, borders w/white dots between green enamel leaves, hinged cover mounted w/an oval enamel miniature depicting a lady reading w/cupid at her side, Ambroise-Gregoire Retore, Paris, France, 1784, 2½" l. 8,800.00

Horn, oval, hinged cover engraved w/scene of Alpine couple, house, flowers & German inscription, 3 1/8" l. (hinge damage)......... 65.00

Ivory, circular lid inset w/a painted ivory miniature depicting figures in a landscape w/buildings, the sides inlaid w/gold-painted geometric borders, Continental, late 18th-early 19th c., 2 3/8" d. (minor losses) 137.50

Papier-mache, round w/painting on lid of young girl w/dark hair holding mirror, 2¾" d. (worn & edge damage) 150.00

Victorian Snuff Box

Silver & mother-of-pearl, rectangular w/projecting chased foliate borders & engine-turned sides, cover mounted w/mother-of-pearl panel carved w/armorials w/Masonic charges flanked by figures of Faith, Hope & Charity surrounded by clouds, inscription on base, Birmingham, England, 1839, 3 1/8" l. (ILLUS.)................1,430.00

Staffordshire enamel, modeled as a head of a dog w/features picked out in black & red, cover w/a dog seated on a cushion within a scroll border, late 18th c., 2¾" l. 1,870.00

Tortoise shell, painted w/scene of a guillotine execution w/crowd of people, including a man on horseback, gathered to watch, France, unsigned, 3½" d. 1,000.00

Wooden, round, top engraved w/a four-point flowerhead within geometric borders, interior lined w/horn, painted overall in red, America, 19th c., 3¼" d., 1" h.... 99.00

SOUVENIR SPOONS

St. Augustine, Florida Spoon

Actor's Fund Fair, Gorham $420.00

Arms of New York City on handle, Tiffany 95.00

Crab handle, Norfolk, Virginia in bowl 42.00

Easter cherub figural handle, cross & crown in bowl 45.00

Eddy, Mary Baker (founder of Church of Christ, Scientist) full figure handle 175.00

Indian head handle, U.S. Indian Industrial School, Mt. Pleasant, Michigan in bowl 45.00

Indian squaw full figure handle, Gorham 195.00

Minute Man full figure handle 65.00

Oranges & foliage handle, St. Augustine, Florida in bowl (ILLUS.) .. 30.00

Roosevelt (Theodore) on horseback full figure handle, plain bowl..... 125.00

St. Paul's Church, gold-washed bowl, Tiffany 95.00

"Salem Witch" figural handle, No. 2 (demitasse) 56.00

Statue of Liberty full figure atop handle, Brooklyn Bridge, river & boats in bowl, Gorham 235.00

SPICE CABINETS & BOXES

Bentwood box, cov., lappet construction, dark green paint, cover w/worn gold-leaf band w/inner black band, block letter initials in gold-leaf, "S.J.L.," possibly Harvard, Massachusetts, mid-19th c., 4¼ x 5¾" (small crack, sliver missing) $495.00

Bentwood box, cov., round w/tin trim & word "Spices" stenciled on front, seven matching inner containers (eighth missing), impressed label, "...N. York," 9" d., 3¾" h. 135.00

Pine cabinet, nine-drawer, original gold-stenciled labels & white porcelain knobs, cast iron carrying handle, worn original dark brown finish, 10¾" l. 135.00

Pine cabinet, nine-drawer (three rows of three each), dovetailed construction, original blue paint & worn paper labels identifying spices, original brass pulls, 33½ x 13", 25½" h. 1,500.00

Pine Hanging Spice Cabinet

Pine cabinet, hanging-type, 14-drawer, three tier step-back arrangement of three rows of three drawers each over two rows of two drawers w/single drawer below, turned wooden pulls, round doughnut-shaped hangers at top, square nail construction, damage to hanger & one top corner, 13" w., 25½" h. (ILLUS.) 810.00

Poplar box, cov., rectangular dovetailed box w/chamfered sliding lid, three-part interior, old varnish finish, 10½" l. 135.00

Poplar box, hanging-type, narrow shaped tab handle w/hole comes up from back to form hanger above rectangular lift lid on dovetailed case, dovetailed projecting drawer at base divided by diagonal strips into four compartments, dark, worn finish, 9½" w., 13½" h. (some damage, cracks & discoloration) 500.00

Poplar cabinet, hanging-type, nine-drawer, wire nail construction, arched top pierced for hanging, original brown finish w/black stenciled labels on drawer fronts, 9½" w., 16¾" h. 200.00

Tin box, cov., w/six inner containers, brass handle, original paint .. 85.00

STATUARY

Equestrian Group after Hermant

Bronzes, and other statuary, are increasingly popular with today's collectors. Particularly appealing are works by "Les Animaliers," the 19th century French school of sculptors who turned to animals for their subject-matter. These, together with figures in the Art Deco and Art Nouveau taste, are available in a wide price range.

BRONZES

Akeley, Carl E., model of an elephant w/snake twining around its right front leg, molded elliptical base, green patina, inscribed "Stung" & "1914"(?), 9½" l., 9" h. $4,675.00

Barye, Antoine-Louis, model of the stallion Cheval Turc, standing w/neck arched & one foreleg raised, on rocky ground, black-red patina, ca. 1900, 11 3/8" l. 1,980.00

Baur, Theodore, equestrian group depicting an Indian on rearing horse aiming his spear at mountain lion, on grassy & rocky base; quadrangular base w/incurved sides mounted w/two cast panels of an Indian buffalo hunt & the presentation of a killed stag in an Indian camp, pierced & gilt foliate borders, silvered bronze, attributed to Meriden Britannia Co., ca. 1880, overall 37¾" h. 36,300.00

Bonheur, Isidore, group of a lioness & two cubs, recumbent lioness suckling one cub while grooming the other between her front paws, naturalistic rectangular mound base, late 19th c., 27" l. 4,400.00

Chiparus, Demetre, figure of a woman dancer w/right leg upraised & arms lifted above her head, dressed in "beaded" costume w/bolero & cloche hat, polychromed bronze w/ivory head & hands, on stepped onyx base, ca. 1930, overall 21½" h. 8,800.00

Drouot, Edouard, figure of Joan of Arc, medium brown patina, late 19th-early 20th c., 28½" h. 825.00

Dubucand, Alfred, group of a Moroccan boy & a donkey, young boy w/gilt cap & parcel gilt garment standing in front of his donkey, holding the rein, brown patina, on naturalistic ground, ca. 1870, 13¾" h. 2,750.00

Fremiet, Emmanuel, figure of a Spanish guitar player seated side-saddle on donkey, molded rectangular base, dark brown patina, late 19th c., 11" l., 13" h. 1,100.00

Hermant, Leon, equestrian group of Lady Godiva as the rider of a horse w/elaborate trappings, her hair trailing about her, brown patina, inscribed "Cast by Am. Art Bronze Fdy/Chicago 1931," further inscribed "Leon Hermant" and "(to) Melvin L. Emerich (from) S.D. Zuckerman," 16" h. (ILLUS.). 1,980.00

Figure of an Athlete

Le Faguays, Pierre, figure of an athlete, the young man w/intense expression, right arm uplifted & left arm extended, on a rocky ground, green patina, inscribed "P. Le Faguays," ca. 1930, 27 7/8" h. (ILLUS.) 1,760.00

STATUE OF LIBERTY COLLECTIBLES

With the 1986 centennial celebration of Bartholdi's famous monument to Liberty the market was flooded with souvenir items representing "Lady Liberty." Interest in earlier souvenir items probably also peaked during the celebration but better quality pieces should continue to appreciate over the years.

Statue of Liberty Stein

Bank, cast iron, model of the Statue of Liberty, aluminum paint, 9 5/8" h. $155.00

Biscuit tin, "Sunshine," eight-sided, handled, Statue of Liberty decoration 25.00

Fruit crate label, "Bartlett Pears," Statue of Liberty illustrated 10.00

Lamp, spelter, light in torch, bronze finish, ca. 1930, 12½" h. 55.00

Stein, grey stoneware, model of head from the Statue of Liberty, marked on base "Stein Collectors International Convention, Limited Edition, July 1974 - Made in Brazil" (ILLUS.) 100.00

Watch fob, metal, embossed design of the Statue of Liberty 30.00

STEAMSHIP MEMORABILIA

The dawning of the age of world-wide airline travel brought about the decline of the luxury steamship liner for long-distance travel. Few large liners are still operating, but mementoes and souvenirs from their glamorous heyday are much sought-after today.

Admission ticket, launching of the liner "Titanic," May 31, 1911 . . . .$1,940.00

Ashtray, liner "R.M.S. Mauretania," china 25.00

Book, "The Only Way To Cross," 1972, w/dust jacket 5.00

Bottle opener, advertising, "Surinam Line," brass. 16.00

Brochure, "White Star Mediterranean," 1907 .... 6.00
Butter pat, "White Star Line," dated 1912, china 65.00
Candy box, liner "Queen Mary," tin 10.00
Creamer, "New England Steamship Co.," china 35.00
Cup & saucer, "Cunard," florals, china 34.00
Dish, liner "Italia," china, 8 x 5" 15.00
Lithograph, "Hartford and New York Steamboat Company, the Steamer, City of Hartford," broadside view at sea w/building specifications listed in margins, color, published by Endicott & Co., New York, ca. 1900, 21 x 35" (water stains & overall discoloration) 1,100.00
Menu, liner "S.S. Normandie," French & English, pictorial cover, 1936 .... 12.00
Model of liner "Italia Genoa," wood & metal, two stacks, 14 lifeboats, early 20th c., in 50" long case, 46½" long model 192.50
Nameplate, "S.S. Titanic," from lifeboat No. 12, brass 9,860.00
Napkin ring, "Cunard Lines," china 25.00
Passenger list, "Red Star Line," liner "Zeeland," 1907 .... 20.00
Plate, dinner, "New England Steamship Co.," china 45.00
Playing cards, "White Star Line" burgee shown, from the liner "S.S. Titanic," w/original box 700.00
Pocket mirror, "Scandinavian American Lines - Copenhagen" 50.00
Postcard, liner "Titanic," mailed from the last port of call, Queenstown, Ireland, April 11, 1912 .... 3,520.00
Poster, "Hamburg-American Line," full color scene of the ship, 1926, 37½ x 27½" 90.00

Currier & Ives Steamship Print

Print, "The Sinking of the Steamship Ville Du Havre," Currier & Ives, 1873, small folio (ILLUS.) 250.00
Sign, "Scandinavian American Line," Rudolph Valentino pictured, tin, 8"d. 45.00
Spoon, demitasse, liner "Bremen" 5.00
Timetable, "Ward Line," to Cuba, 1907 .... 12.00

STEIFF TOYS & DOLLS

From a felt pincushion in the shape of an elephant, a world-famous toy company emerged. Margarete Steiff (1847-1909), a polio victim as a child and confined to a wheelchair, planned a career as a seamstress and opened a shop in the family home. However, her plans were dramatically changed when she made her first stuffed elephant in 1880. By 1886 she was producing stuffed felt monkeys, donkeys, horses and other animal forms. In 1893 an agent sold her toys at the Leipzig Fair. This venture was so successful that a catalog was printed and a salesman hired. Margarete's nephews and nieces became involved in the business, assisting in its management and the design of new items. Through the years, the Steiff Company has produced a varied line including felt or plush animals. Descendents of the original family members continue to be active in the management of the company still adhering to Margarete's motto "For our children, the best is just good enough."

Baboon, sitting, mohair, w/button, 1950's, 12" $65.00
Bat, "Eric," grey mohair body, felt ears, plastic wings, chrome button, 1950's, mint w/all tags, 8" wingspan, 4½" h. .... 350.00 to 500.00
Camel, tan mohair, velvet legs & face, button in ear, 1950's, 5½" 150.00
Cat, standing, "Lizzy," white mohair w/black spots, green eyes, blue bow, w/tail in the air, 1950's, 5" l., 7" h. 72.00
Dog, Boxer, brown mohair, U.S. Zone Germany, button, signed by H. O. Steiff under leather collar, mint, 10 x 10" 120.00
Doll, General, dark blue uniform w/red trim, wearing cap & monocle, early, 17" h. 4,500.00
Doll, Polar Explorer, felt, short brown mohair wig, long mustache, black stud eyes, body joined at shoulder & hips, wearing long frosted mohair parka & booted leggings, probably representing Amundsen, the Norwegian who was first to reach the South Pole in 1911, 16½" 5,280.00

Hippopotamus, "Nosy," grey mohair, felt ears, mouth & foot pads, 1950's 82.00
Lobster, "Crabby," orange felt, glass eyes, w/tags, 7" l. 275.00
Monkey, dressed as bellhop, "Cocoli," early, mint 325.00
Monkey, felt, on wooden wheels, clown hat & ruff, 1926, similar to "Record Monkey" 475.00
Reindeer, "Renny," tan mohair, felt antlers, glass eyes, sewn nose & mouth, raised button, 1950's, 9" . . 225.00
Teddy bear, gold mohair, shoebutton eyes, button in ear, straw stuffed, ca. 1915, 18" h. 2,100.00
Teddy bear, gold mohair, large brown glass eyes, straw stuffed, button in ear, wears old glasses, German edition, early, 20" h. (replaced pads) 2,400.00
Turkey, "Tucky," long mohair body, felt wings & tail, velvet head, metal legs & feet, 1950's, 5½" . . . 140.00

STEINS

Character, "Bull," pottery, painted full color, pottery lid, marked "1453 Germany," ½ liter (minor scratches) $605.00
Character, "Cat," pottery, brown, ½ liter 231.00
Character, "Clown," pottery, red, grey & green, signed "J. Reinemann," 3/10 liter 990.00
Character, "Devil," pottery, tan & red, ½ liter 605.00
Character, "Monk," stoneware, deep blue glaze, inlaid stoneware lid, marked "MWG," ½ liter 231.00
Faience, cylindrical, h.p. in manganese, yellow, green & iron-red w/a rearing horse in an oval panel & foliage-scroll cartouche on a powder blue ground within green border w/manganese & iron-red lappets, pewter lid & foot-rim, inscribed "B.W. 1781 R.K.," Erfurt, Germany, 18th c., 10" h. 2,090.00
Glass, amber w/Munich Maid enameled on front, dressed in black & tan w/red shoes on branch of fruit, applied amber prunts around top & base, pewter lid & thumbpiece, applied amber handle, 5 1/8" d., 14½" h. 500.00
Mettlach, No. 24, relief-molded figures in four separate panels, inlaid pewter lid, 1 liter 341.00
Mettlach, No. 228, four relief-molded panels w/musical scenes, inlaid pewter lid, ½ liter 185.00
Mettlach, No. 1059 (2488), printed-under-the-glaze humorous scene of cartoon-style steins, dice & cards, pewter lid, 4.8 liter 1,100.00
Mettlach, No. 1132, etched, man fiddling & dancing crocodile in front of pyramids, inlaid lid, ½ liter . . . 357.50
Mettlach, No. 1266, three panels w/white relief scenes of men drinking on grey w/tan ground, inlaid pewter lid w/six-point star, bunch of grapes center, ½ liter . . 185.00
Mettlach, No. 1358 (3185), printed-under-the-glaze scene of men playing cards, inlaid pewter lid, ½ liter 385.00
Mettlach, No. 1454, etched white horse in medallion, inlaid pewter lid, ½ liter 370.00
Mettlach, No. 1469, etched gnomes celebrating, inlaid pewter lid, 6 liter 2,530.00
Mettlach, No. 1502 (1526), printed-under-the-glaze, military figure, inlaid pewter lid, ½ liter 350.00
Mettlach, No. 1526, printed-under-the-glaze standing Yale University student in cap & gown, ½ liter . . . 165.00
Mettlach, No. 1786, etched St. Florian putting out fire, handle is dragon, thumblift is ceramic dragon's head, pewter lid looks like tiled roof, 1 liter 935.00
Mettlach, No. 1986, incised w/two women in traditional dress, hops & a German verse, pewter-mounted lid, ½ liter 495.00
Mettlach, No. 2001I, Book stein, etched & glazed theology books, inlaid lid, ½ liter 840.00
Mettlach, No. 2049, etched, Chess stein, chessboard, inlaid lid, ½ liter 2,475.00
Mettlach, No. 2082, etched scene of William Tell shooting an apple off his son's head, inlaid pewter lid, 1 liter 925.00
Pottery, brown glaze, enameled flying eagle w/Iron Cross, pewter lid w/Iron Cross, 1914, ½ liter 440.00
Pottery, etched frog smoking, marked "MWG," pewter lid, ½ liter 242.00
Regimental, pottery, etched, "2 Batl., ER. II, 1904-1906," by Marzi & Remy, inlaid lid, ½ liter 880.00
Regimental, porcelain, "Bav. Inft. Nr. 13, Ingolstadt, 1910-1912," four side scenes, roster, lion thumblift, stacked bullet lid, ½ liter 1,292.50

"Special Focus"

ENCOUNTERS WITH THE THIRD DIMENSION - - -

COLLECTING STEREOGRAPHS & STEREOSCOPES

by Laurance Wolfe

While there are hundreds of different 3-D antiques and collectibles, the best known, and most sought-after, are the vintage "Holmes-type" hand-held stereoscope and the companion stereo views. These are artifacts of so recent an America—the mid-1800's through the 1930's—that there are still those who say "Granny had one of those and a basket of cards in the parlor."

The *stereograph,* or stereo view, that familiar card with two seemingly identical photographs adjacent to one another—photographs which, when viewed through a stereoscope, present the illusion of depth—evolved from photography's 1840's beginnings. But stereography caught on in the United States only after the 1859 invention of the Holmes *stereoscope.* The Holmes stereoscope (often mis-called "stereopticon"—let your fingers walk through the dictionary for confirmation!) was named in honor of its inventor: poet-author, philosopher, physician Oliver Wendell Holmes. He had become so interested in stereo viewing and stereo views that he and another Bostonian—one Joseph Bates—set about to devise a less cumbersome, cheaper viewer than the type imported from Europe. Holmes refused to patent the viewer because he looked upon it as a vital educational tool which should be available to all Americans. Individuals and companies copied the viewer, sometimes adding improvements, well into the 20th century.

The first stereoscope adapted to photographic use was an improvement by Sir David Brewster, in 1850, on a reflecting stereoscope of Sir Charles Wheatstone. Brewster's stereoscope, with a ground glass base and small trap doors to permit proper light on views, is a closed container approximately 7" x 7" x 2¼" with binocular lenses. Daguerreotype images were the initial stereographs viewed on this device.

Not long after Brewster's innovative viewer, J. F. Mascher of Philadelphia offered a folding daguerreotype case, part of which case was a pair of lenses which, when the case was opened, focused on two side-by-side stereoscopic images. These usually were the product of two daguerreotype cameras with distance between the two camera lenses being approximately 2½" (the distance between human eyes). Although the results, shown in vintage Maschers available today, were far from spectacular, the Mascher case is a very desirable collector's item. They may be found at auctions, particularly auctions of photographica, and also where antique photographica is offered.

Copies and versions of the Holmes stereoscope are legion. On one extreme is a sturdy walnut stereoscope which may be used in hand or on a stand which came with it. A brass tag, "Joseph Bates, Boston," is affixed to the viewer. At the other end of the stereoscope spectrum is the aluminum hooded product of Underwood & Underwood, Keystone, H. C. White, and other 20th century manufacturers. Then, of course, there are reproduction viewers being made today, viewers whose optics are often superior to those of earlier days.

In between the Bates-Holmes model and the last 20th century mass-produced aluminum viewers are stereoscopes both plain and fancy: bird's-eye maple, cherry wood, scalloped, embossed. Viewers with unusual card holders, with individually adjustable eyepieces, one with take-apart components to make them more portable and novelty viewers such as one which folds into an attractive "cigar box."

Table and floor model stereoscopes, introduced in the 1850's, proliferated in the period after 1860 and are greatly coveted by collectors. These ran the gamut from all-brass Holmes-type viewers with velvet covered hoods and a pedestal base, to S. Perry's patent of 1859 which held 52 single views or 104 in back of each other. This stereoscope is drum-like in appearance and inlaid with mother-of-pearl and had painted scenes on either side. In a sense, these were the Cadillacs of viewers, more costly and with greater embellishment. Comparatively few were made and they are scarce today.

Arcade machines came into being in the latter part of the 19th century. These were coin-operated stereoscopes with a revolving mechanism holding views and exposing them to stereo "fans" one at a time. They could still be activated with a penny, or a nickel, in various locations as late as the 1940's. (Cliff House, San Francisco, had one in 1940.) Arcade viewers provided users with a variety of stereo views from risque to Wild West and wondrous others of stereoscopy's vast repertoire.

Values of the various type viewers cover a wide range. With any type of stereoscopic viewing device, quality of optics, age and workmanship are vital criteria in determining prices. Holmes-type viewers in good condition, no parts missing, sell from $35 to as much as $90. Brewster stereoscopes range from $80 on up. Mascher cases rarely come in under $300 and are usually judged first on the basis of the stereo view that is in the case. Most Mascher daguerreotypes are portraits. Non-portrait views command higher prices.

Table model viewers are available for as low as $75 and can go into four figures for very unusual, hand-carved decorative ones. Floor model viewers are rarely seen for less than $1,000 and unique ones have commanded more than five times that figure.

One doesn't often run across cast iron or wooden arcade viewers. When located, they usually range from $400 to sky-high.

Between 5 and 10 million stereoscopic views are estimated to have been produced. Each of these was replicated anywhere from a dozen times to amounts in the thousands. Survivors of these views must certainly number in the millions—a mighty group from which a collector may choose in building his collection.

As in most collecting, the collector begins to specialize after his early practice of acquiring whatever comes along.

Categories to pick from include geographic areas, transportation, comics, sentimentals, expeditions, expositions and fairs, disasters, statuary, medical, mills and factories, religious groups, astronomy, blacks, natural wonders, personalities, Presidents, railroads, sports, wars, actresses, whaling, and so on.

New England and the White Mountains, Yosemite, Niagara Falls, and Mammoth Cave lead the way among sought after views. This is partly because so much of early stereography centered on the better known natural wonders of the United States. Most stereographers early on wet their feet in the snows of New Hampshire as they punctuated stereographic careers by producing views of Mt. Washington and others of the White Mountains.

The Civil War, with Mathew Brady and his corps of photographers (who, truth tells us, took a lion's share of views credited to Brady), straining to assemble the first pictorial record of a major conflict, has long been a collector's target. As a group, Civil War views may command the highest prices in the stereo marketplace. Some Brady views and ones by Alexander Gardner, bring $100 and more. Brady views of Abraham Lincoln are still extant. Three different Brady Lincoln views published by E. & H. T. Anthony, fetched $3,900 in an auction not too long ago. The buyer, an expert in stereo views, offered copies in numbered sets of three for $25.

Transportation views—railroads in particular—are prized. From the beginning of stereo, many American railroads had their own photographers, or a contract with one or more, to keep a photographic journal of the building and progress. Usually, stereography went hand in hand with photography with these professionals.

Keystone View produced a set on airline operations in the Thirties. For 20th century stereo, this is a hard-to-get set.

Comics and sentimentals, best described as poking fun at, satirizing, and/or portraying familiar family events such as a wedding, seem to have been turned out by the thousands in the late 1800's. The market is flooded with them and they are reasonable ($1 for most, with a premium on some such as the "French Cook," part of a series which was cloned by various stereo view operators).

Choice vintage stereoscopic views—in extremely short supply because of the small number manufactured over a brief span of years (1851-1862 in the United States) and their innate fragility—are glass stereo slides and "tissues." The glass slides pre-date the common stereo views. "Tissues" are stereo photos printed on translucent paper. Held to light, they offer magnificent views, depending upon the extent they have been creatively worked on by the "artist." Tinted, "pin-pricked" to emphasize a row of street lamps, windows, stars, or other details in a photograph, tissues earn premium prices when they can be found. Some glass views are listed as "priceless" by stereo historian W. C. Darrah, whose books on stereoscopy are close to being definitive writings. Glass stereo views by Platt Babbitt, noted Niagara Falls photographer, have recently been auctioned for $75 each.

Seekers after views look for these things, not necessarily in this order: subject, three-dimensional quality, condition, age and identity (i.e., photographer, publisher, etc., usually printed on front or back of view). Pseudoscopic views, ones which pair two identical photos and therefore are "flat" rather than 3-D, are discarded off-hand, unless they were intentionally produced that way. Some companies published such views to demonstrate the vast difference 3-D makes.

The infant years of stereoscopy—the 1840's—witnessed the production of a few stereo cameras—all hand-crafted. The long line of stereoscopic cameras which came on the market, starting in about 1854, paralleled that of non-stereo cameras. Nearly every kind of camera manufactured after the 1850's had its match in stereo. The quantity of stereo cameras was limited, though, partly because not all professional photographers "doubled" in stereo, and partly because fewer amateurs became engaged in stereo when it was first introduced.

By the mid-1850's, stereo cameras began to be on the shelves of all serious photographic establishments. All the major manufacturers of photographic apparatus would eventually offer stereo equipment. Around the turn of the century, stereo cameras appeared in the mail-order catalogs of Montgomery Ward and Sears, Roebuck. The stereo bubble burst in the 1920's, hastened by the advent of radio and motion pictures. It was the 1950's before stereo cameras were made in any quantity again. The Stereo Realist, invented by Seton Rochwite and put on the market in 1947, was the first of a number of modern 35 mm stereoscopic cameras produced in stereo's "born again" era. Stereo Kodak, Revere Stereo Camera and a dozen or more stereo cameras followed. Even the people who brought you Lionel Trains manufactured a stereo camera, the Linex. Most new stereos were sold with a 35 mm viewer.

Vintage stereo cameras are quoted at a wide range of prices, starting at about $200. The 35 mm stereo camera of recent origin commands from $100 to $300.

Old stereo viewers, views, cameras...these are the major goodies in the collector's cornucopia.

Other vintage and contemporary items looked for and cherished by the 3-D-er are:

Stereo projectors (they use transparent slides, product of the 35 mm or Viewmaster camera, and require polarized glasses for viewing); holograms (one appeared a couple of years ago on the cover of the *National Geographic*); 3-D comic magazines (bigger in Europe than here); Viewmaster viewers and reels (they're not just for kids!); a device named Tru-Vue and film strips that portray various people, events and activities in 3-D, available in toy stores from the 1930's until just a few years ago; books having to do with stereoscopy (one, by Sir David Brewster, is available in reprint); posters; and other stereo and stereo-related pieces, including difficult-to-find motion picture film from a dozen or so 3-D movies produced over the years.

The advanced collector—there are many of them thanks to the National Stereoscopic Association (Box 14801, Columbus, Ohio 43214)—seeks to discover unusual stereoscopic viewers or long forgotten views. Or he may seek to acquire 35 mm views shot by probably the most prominent stereographer of all—Dwight D. Eisenhower. The United States President of the 1950's took a number of views of family, friends and events. They are filed at the Eisenhower Library in Abilene, Kansas. The Library plans to make duplicates available, for a fee, to those who request them.

The National Stereoscopic Association, membership now approaching 2,000, has developed a stereo information exchange for its members that offers, through its magazine, STEREO WORLD, an outstanding resource.

(Editor's Note: *Laurance Wolfe, author of this "Special Focus," has more than twenty years of study of stereoscopic views, 15 years as a collector and dealer, and has written numerous articles on stereo views. For about ten years he has also been a practicing stereographer with a number of published views of subjects from Ronald Reagan to Jesse Jackson to a series of unusual grave markers in cemeteries in the United States.)*

ILLUSTRATED PRICE LISTING

**Denotes illustrated item.*

Stereo Views:

Geographic

NOTE: Illustrated at right is a full view of a stereo view. Due to space limitations, the remaining illustrated listings will show only the left half of each of the stereo views.

*ADIRONDACKS - Shanty on Irondeqoit (sic) Bay, by W. M. Tucker 5.00

ADIRONDACKS - Rapids, Ausable Chasm, by American Scenery 5.00

ALASKA - Bound for the Alaska Gold Fields..., by Keystone (No. 9191) 18.00

ALASKA - The Bay of Sitka, Alaska - Continent Stereoscopic Company 12.00

*ALASKA - Sitka, from Japanese Island - Muybridge (No. 462) 85.00

ALASKA - Our Alaskan Sisters..., (Litho. Ingersoll No. 258) 2.00

ALASKA - Newcomers selling out to go home, Cold Feet, Alaska - Kilburn (No. 13132) 28.00

ALASKA - At the Wharf, Dawson City..., Kilburn (No. 13103) 20.00

ALASKA - Miners leaving for home..., Kilburn (No. 13149) 12.00

*ALASKA - Panning out the Gold in the Klondyke (sic)..., Kilburn (No. 13123) 30.00

CALIFORNIA - View at Keene, S.P.R.R. - Watkins New Series(No. 4303) 10.00

CALIFORNIA - General view San Fernando Tunnel, from the south, S.P.R.R. - Watkins New Series (No. 4321) 10.00

*CALIFORNIA - The Lower Yosemite Fall, Watkins Pacific Coast (No. 1069) 15.00

CALIFORNIA - Butt end of original Big Tree..., by John P. Soule (No. 1091) 8.00

CALIFORNIA - The Plaza (San Francisco) - Muybridge (No. 391) 60.00

CANADA - Montreal from mountain, by J. G. Parks 3.00

CANADA - French Cathedral, Montreal, by J. G. Parks 3.00

COLORADO - Donkey Train, Silver Plume, Colorado - Kilburn Brothers (No. 3213) 15.00

COLORADO - Glen Eyrie Series, by W. G. Chamberlain, each 5.00

FLORIDA - Boxing pineapples for shipping, Fla., U.S.A., by Keystone View Company 2.00

*FLORIDA - St. Augustine, Treasury Street, Seven Feet Wide, by the Florida Club . . . 4.00

FLORIDA - St. Augustine, Old Fort San Marco (Dungeon Lock), by Florida Club 4.00

FLORIDA - St. Augustine, Old Slave Market, by Keystone View (No. 314) 3.00

HAWAII - In the heart of a banana plantation..., by Strohmeyer & Wyman 3.00

*HAWAII - Group of Natives Eating Poi..., by Underwood & Underwood 3.00
MARTHA'S VINEYARD - Broadway, Oak Bluffs, no ID 6.00
MARTHA'S VINEYARD - Ladies on piazza, and baby buggy, by S.F. Adams 4.00
MARTHA'S VINEYARD - Cottage at the Vineyard, by Woodward & Son 4.00
MASSACHUSETTS - Plymouth, First Street laid out by the Pilgrims, by C. H. Rogers 3.00
MASSACHUSETTS - Quinsigamond Regatta, 1868. No. 1, Causeway from West End, by I. H. Stockwell, Optician 4.00
MASSACHUSETTS - Quinsigamond Regatta, 1868. No. 2, Down the Lake, by I. H. Stockwell, Optician 4.00
MASSACHUSETTS - Quinsigamond Regatta, 1868. No. 5, Looking East from Hotel, by I. H. Stockwell, Optician 4.00
MASSACHUSETTS - New Barn at House of Correction, Ipswich, Mass., by George H. Jones 5.00
MASSACHUSETTS - The Rapids (Hoosac Tunnel and Vicinity), by E. D. Merriam . . 4.00
MASSACHUSETTS - Hoosac Mountain, by E. D. Merriam 4.00
NEW HAMPSHIRE - School House, Littleton, N.H., by Kilburn Brothers (No. 275) . . 6.00
NEW HAMPSHIRE - New London Institute, by W. G. C. Kimball 11.00
NEW HAMPSHIRE - Mossy Fountain, near Concord, by Clough & Kimball 5.00
NEW HAMPSHIRE - On Mt. Washington Carriage Road, near Half Way House, by John P. Soule (No. 22) 14.00
NEW HAMPSHIRE - Ice Jam on the Ammonoosuc, by Kilburn Brothers (No. 3) 18.00
NEW HAMPSHIRE - untitled fishing scene, by W.L. Wilber 3.00
NEW HAMPSHIRE - Orphan's Home, Franklin, N.H., by W. G. C. Kimball 5.00
NIAGARA FALLS - from New Suspension Bridge - Moonlight, by George E. Curtis 4.00
NIAGARA FALLS - Niagara, Winter, Am. Falls, fr. Luna Island, by Langenheim, Lloyd & Co. 20.00

*NIAGARA FALLS - Marie Spelterini Crossing Niagara Rapids (tightrope), by Charles Bierstadt 15.00
NIAGARA FALLS - Am. Falls from Canada side, by C. Bierstadt (No. 61) 3.00
NIAGARA FALLS - Niagara Falls from the Suspension Bridge, by Kilburn Brothers (No. 263) 3.00
OREGON - Grandeur of Columbia River..., by Keystone (9329T) 2.00
OREGON - Majestic Mt. Hood, by Keystone (W12635T) 2.00
PENNSYLVANIA - Carpenter's Hall, Phila., no ID 3.00
PENNSYLVANIA - Poet's Haunt - Along the Schuylkill, by E. & H. T. Anthony Company (No. 5672) 3.00
PENNSYLVANIA - Rock Cut, near Huntingdon, by Purviance 4.00
PENNSYLVANIA - Wissahicon Valley, by F. W. Woodward 4.00
RHODE ISLAND - Narragansett Pier View, by Thos. Lewis 5.00
RHODE ISLAND - Jewish Synagogue, Newport, by John P. Soule 6.00
RHODE ISLAND - Views of Newport, by Wm. A. Williams . . . . 4.00 to 8.00
SARATOGA, N.Y. - Congress Spring, by Baker & Record 3.00
SARATOGA, N.Y. - United States Hotel Dining Room, by Baker & Record 5.00
SARATOGA, N.Y. - Grand Union Dining Hall, by Charles Bierstadt 4.00
SARATOGA, N.Y. - Grand Hotel, by American Views 4.00
VERMONT - View from Ox Bow Cliff, Waterford, Vermont, F. B. Gage photo, E. Anthony 12.00
VERMONT - "Lake of the Clouds" and Chin, by A. F. Styles (No. 114) 6.00

VERMONT - Via Arietis, Highgate Springs, Vt., by A. F. Styles (No. 163) 5.00
VERMONT - Brattleboro, View from Brooks House, by Cheney & Clapp (C. L. Howe, artist) 8.00
WASHINGTON, D.C. - The Capitol, by H. C. White Company 3.00
WASHINGTON, D.C. - East Room, White House, by H. C. White 3.00
WASHINGTON, D.C. - Green Room in President's Mansion, by J. F. Jarvis.......4.00
WASHINGTON, D.C. - Chamber, House of Representatives, by J. F. Jarvis 3.00
WASHINGTON, D.C. - The State Department, by American Scenery 2.00
YELLOWSTONE NAT'L PARK - views by C. D. Kirkland (4.00 each):
No. 8 - Central Basin Mammoth Hot Springs
No. 21 - Formation in Hot Periodical Lake
No. 40 - Scene in the Yellowstone Canyon
No. 58 - Sentinel Rock
No. 74 - Giant Group of Geysers
No. 78 - Castle Geyser from the Grand Geyser
No. 81 - Crystal Spring and Castle Geyser
YOSEMITE - Above the clouds on Eagle Peak, by Strohmeyer and Wyman 2.00
YOSEMITE - Nevada Falls, by Strohmeyer and Wyman 2.00
YOSEMITE - Mirror View of the majestic Cathedral Rocks..., by Underwood and Underwood 2.00
YOSEMITE - Cap of Liberty, by Kilburn Brothers (No. 974) 4.00
YOSEMITE - Cathedral Rock, no ID 1.00

Stereo Views: General Subjects

*ANIMALS - A Bunch of Buffalo, New Educational Series 3.00
ANIMALS - Picturesque ramblings in old England, by London Stereoscopic Company (blind stamped) 12.00
ANIMALS - Ploughing on a prairie farm in Illinois, by Underwood & Underwood 2.00
ANIMALS - Cat, by J. Gurney and Son 4.00
ANIMALS - In the Great Union Stockyards, Chicago, by J. F. Jarvis 5.00

*ASTRONOMY - Full Moon, by S. Davis (No. 429) 6.00
AVIATION - Six American aviators who first encircled earth..., by Keystone (26408T) 10.00

*AVIATION - Zeppelin flying over a German Town, by Keystone (No. 18000) 6.00
AVIATION - Airplane factory, Wichita, Kansas, by Keystone (No. 32318T) 5.00
BLACKS - Field hands "We's done all dis s'mornin'," by Keystone (No. 9506) 4.00
BLACKS - "Take me back to Dixie," by B. W. Kilburn (No. 10726) 20.00
BLACKS - Who said Pie? (two black children posing), by B. W. Kilburn (No. 14314) 8.00
*BLACKS - "I isn't bin borned very long," by B. L. Singley, No. 6050 (Top of next column) 5.00

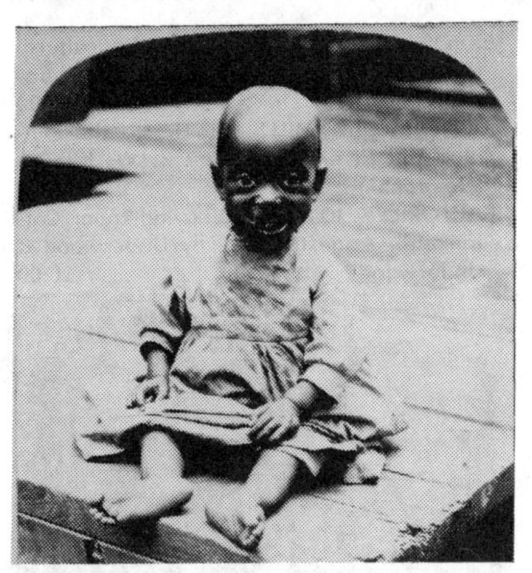

BRIDGES - Livermore Falls, Plymouth, N.H., by Kilburn Brothers (No. 503) 8.00

BRIDGES - Interior of Railway, Mt. Holyoke, no ID 6.00

*BRIDGES - Victoria Bridge, Montreal, by Alex Henderson 14.00

BRIDGES - East River Bridge, by American Views 3.00

BRIDGES - Goodrich Falls, Bartlett, N.H., by N.W. Pease 18.00

CEMETERIES - Grave of Lt. Quentin Roosevelt, by Keystone (No. V19225) 5.00

CEMETERIES - Soldiers' Cemetery, Arlington, by Kilburn Brothers (No. 322) 2.00

CEMETERIES - Tomb of Washington, by Alexander Gardner 25.00

CEMETERIES - View in Mt. Auburn, by Kilburn Brothers (No. 245) 3.00

CHILDREN - A little child shall lead them, by B. W. Kilburn (No. 6440) 5.00

CHILDREN - Weary Travelers, by Keystone (No. 3984) 2.00

*CHILDREN - A photographic feat unparalleled..., by R. B. Lewis 8.00

CIVIL WAR - Battle of Gettysburg (from L. Prang painting), by William Rau 3.00

CIVIL WAR - Ruins of Catholic Cathedral, Charleston, S.C., by E. & H. T. Anthony & Co. (No. 3075) 28.00

*CIVIL WAR - Church built by Engineers, Petersburgh, Va., by E. & H.T. Anthony & Co. (Brady Negative No. 3339) 22.50

CIVIL WAR - Court House, Yorktown, Va., by E. & H. T. Anthony & Co. (Brady Negative No. 2376) 38.00

COMICS - Bitter with the sweet, by Littleton View Co. (No. 514) 2.00

COMICS - Waiting for Pure Fresh Milk, by Underwood & Underwood (No. 1491) . . . 3.00

COMICS - "I'll not take off another stitch if I Lose My Place," by Keystone (No. 10410-b) 3.00

COMICS - Terrors of the Alligator Swamp, Florida (alligator swallowing black boy), by B. W. Kilburn (No. 472) 4.00

DISASTERS - Johnstown and Conemaugh Valley, Pa. Disaster..., by Webster & Albee 6.00

DISASTERS - The Great Johnstown Flood, by R. K. Bonine (No. 11) 4.00

DISASTERS - The Great Johnstown Flood, by R. K. Bonine (No. 21) 4.00

DISASTERS - The Great Johnstown Flood, by R. K. Bonine (No. 22) 4.00

DISASTERS - Great Disaster on Mill River, Mass., by J. A. French (No. 17) 8.00

*DOLLS AND TOYS - Tired of Play, by French & Sawyer (No. 332) 5.00

DOLLS AND TOYS - In the Hammock, Comic Series 3.00

DOLLS AND TOYS - Untitled, child, doll in doll bed, by Lewis' Galleries 4.00

DOLLS AND TOYS - Come Birdie, Come, by Kilburn Brothers (No. 187) 5.00

EXPOSITIONS & FAIRS - Interior Ag. Building, Columbian Expo., by Strohmeyer & Wyman 3.00

EXPOS & FAIRS - One of McMonnies' Horses and Liberal Arts Building, World's Fair, 1893, by Strohmeyer and Wyman 3.00

EXPOS & FAIRS - Just inside gates, Louisiana Purchase Exposition, by C. H. Graves 4.00

EXPOS & FAIRS - Philadelphia 1876 Exhibition, Group America, Art Gallery 2.00

*EXPOS & FAIRS Int. 1876 Expo. Agricultural Hall looking north, Centennial Photo. Co. (No. 746) 5.00

FACTORIES AND MILLS - The Hum of the Spindle, Fall River, Mass., by B. W. Kilburn (No. 15557) 15.00

FACTORIES AND MILLS - Weaving Room, Cotton Mill, Augusta, Ga., by Underwood & Underwood 20.00

*FACTORIES AND MILLS - Printing Room, American Print Works, by Kilburn Brothers (No. 620) 20.00

FACTORIES AND MILLS - Spinning Room, Lawrence Mill, Lowell, Mass., by B. W. Kilburn (No. 4730) 20.00

HOTELS - Fabyan House Parlor, White Mountains..., by Kilburn Brothers (No. 685) 12.00

HOTELS - Fabyan House Dining Hall, by Kilburn Brothers (No. 1789) 8.00

*HOTELS - Sinclair House, Bethlehem, N.H., by Kilburn Brothers (No. 113) 12.00

INDIANS - Piute Indian Boy, (Yosemite Valley, California) 20.00

INDIANS - Indian Wigwam, Oregon, by B. W. Kilburn (No. 10552) 25.00

*INDIANS - Indian Wigwam, Oregon, by B. W. Kilburn (No. 10552) 25.00

LADIES - Emily Rigl (ca. 1875) - stereo celebrities, by Sarony 4.00

*LADIES - Portrait, by Fritz Luckhardt . . . 5.00

LADIES - The Young Milliner, by F. G. Weller (No. 529) 5.00

*LOGGING AND LUMBERING - Poling logs in McCloud River Lumber Co., Mill Pond, by Underwood & Undersood (No. 6013) . . 4.00

LOGGING AND LUMBERING - Great Chain Log Rafts, Wash., by Keystone (No. 20031) 3.00

*PERSONALITIES - John D. Rockefeller - the Richest Man in the World, by Keystone (No. V11961) 35.00

PERSONALITIES - Gen. Pershing with Marshall Joffre, by Keystone (No. V18848) 6.00

*PRESIDENTS - President McKinley and his eight Chosen Advisors, by Underwood & Underwood 6.00

*PRESIDENTS - Mrs. McKinley in the Conservatory, by Underwood & Underwood . . . 5.00

*PRESIDENTS - Theodore Roosevelt, by Keystone (No. 11914) 10.00

PRESIDENTS - Woodrow Wilson, by Keystone (No. 11252) 8.00

*PRESIDENTS - Calvin Coolidge (while Vice President) at American Legion Convention, Kansas City, 1921, by Keystone (No. 13365) 4.00

Mrs. McKinley

Theodore Roosevelt

Calvin Coolidge

*PRISON - Chain Shop, Massachusetts State Prison, by American Views, People's series (Top of next column) 6.00

RAILROAD - Danger signal, railroad of lies, by B. W. Kilburn (No. 6810) 20.00

*RAILROAD - Mt. Washington Railway Engine, "Tip Top," by Kilburn Brothers (No. 1814) 9.00

*RAILROAD - Elevated Railway, Burling Slip, New York, by C. Bierstadt (No. 1325) 3.00

RAILROAD - Willey Brook Bridge and Mt. Webster, P. & O. R.R., by Kilburn Brothers (No. 2116) 5.00

ROGERS GROUPS - Uncle Ned's School, by Weschler Abraham & Co. 3.00

*ROGERS GROUPS - Council of War, by H. Wood, Jr. 5.00

SANTA CLAUS - Santa Claus Starting Out, by F. G. Weller (No. 6654) 5.00

SANTA CLAUS - Santa Claus at Home, by F. G. Weller (No. 653) 5.00

*SHAKER - Getting a Drink, by W. G. C. Kimball (Shaker Village, No. 22) 35.00

SHAKER - Church Family (buildings), from the south, by W. G. C. Kimball (No. 2 of Shaker Village) 35.00

SOULE (Photographer Special) - **John P. Soule was an outstanding photographer whose views of the White Mountains area are noted.** A sampling of his square-cornered yellow mounts:

No. 12 - Crystal Cascade 5.00

* No. 26 - Mt. Washington Carriage Road, at ledge, looking up 8.00

No. 37 - Summit House, Mt. Washington, 1861 . . . . 8.00

No. 47 - Snow Arch, Tuckerman's Ravine, August 28, 1861 . . . . 6.00

No. 82 - Artist's Brook, Bridge and Mill6.00

No. 108 - White Mountain Range - from Jefferson Hill 5.00

* No. 182 - The Philosopher of the Pool 10.00

*WAR - The Dog in War...World War I, by Keystone (No. V18856) 3.00

WAR - Fighting from stone wall defenses, Philippines..., by Underwood & Underwood 2.00

WAR - Fire spray captured from the Austrians... by Keystone (No. 18669) 2.00

*WAR - French Gunners in Forest of Argonne, by Keystone (No. V18908) 3.00

WAR - View in a Trench Kitchen, by Keystone (No. V18883) 2.00

Stereoscopes:

* A. Folding metal viewer made in the U.S.A. Similar to foreign-made No. 14 in cover photo. Ca. 1920's $25.00

* B. Graphoscope-style folding viewer/magnifier (American). Beautifully grained and decorated. Designed for stereo views and as magnifier for conventional photographs. Ca. 1870-1880 . . . . 225.00

* C. Becker-style Multicard Tabletop Viewer. Made in Great Britain, accommodates 50 stereo views mounted on an endless belt. Twenty-one inches high. Ca. 1870-1880 . . . . 600.00

* D. (Left) Richard Stereoscope (French), hand-held for 45 mm x 107 mm glass stereo views. Ca. 1910-1920 . . . . . 125.00

(Right) Unis-France, hand-held for 6 cm x 13 cm glass stereo views. Also shown in cover photo 55.00

* E. Richard Taxiphote Stereoscope (French). Elegant stereoscope which uses trays of 25 45 mm x 107 mm glass stereo transparencies. Crank-operated. Storage for up to 300 transparencies. Height - 20 inches. Ca. 1910-1920 ......1,100.00

* F. Telebinocular Stereoscope by Keystone, with incandescent lamp in reflector housing. Ca. 1925-1935..........110.00

* G. Zeiss Stereo Viewer. High quality optical device made by Zeiss for scientific laboratory use. Also pictured in cover photo; depending upon choice of lenses ....100.00 - 200.00

(End of Special Focus)

STOVES

The thought of a family gathered companionably around the parlor stove on a cold winter's evening, or of an apple pie baking in the wood-burning cookstove, brings to some a longing for the "good old days." On a more practical note, many people turned to wood-burning stoves during the recent energy crisis when they discovered wood was plentiful and by far cheaper than commercial fuels. Aside from the primary function, a handsome old parlor stove adds a distinctive touch with its ornate design and an old cookstove can turn a kitchen into a real family room. Whatever the reason, there has been a renewed interest in old stoves of all types.

"Glenwood" Parlor Stove

Cookstove, cast iron, w/plate warmers, "Combine," 45 x 30", 62" h. . .$575.00

Cookstove, cast iron w/salmon pink enamel finish, warming ovens w/cornucopia decor on doors, "Copper Clad" 695.00

Cookstove, blue enamel w/nickel-plated trim, w/oven thermometer & warming oven, Adam Kerr, Belleville, Illinois 2,000.00

Cookstove, blue enamel w/copper trim, w/water reservoir & warming ovens 1,800.00

Cookstove, tan enamel finish, wood-burning, w/water reservoir & two warming ovens, "West Bend"..... 300.00

Franklin stove, cast iron, "Cheerful," in the form of a house w/elaborate finial over three bays & four working doors, on lobed base, Richmond Stove Co., Richmond, Va., patented 1873, 26" w., 43" h. 330.00

Franklin stove, parlor-type, cast iron w/brass finials & inserts, w/original pair of cast iron andirons, 29 x 23 x 22" 375.00

Gas range, "Magic Chef," 4-burner, black & grey marbleized on pale yellow enamel, early 1920's 500.00

Laundry stove, cast iron, "Midget - Atlanta Stove Works," "pot-belly" type, flat top w/two lids, splayed legs, 18 x 13" top, w/two lifters .. 145.00

Parlor stove, cast iron, "Art Garland No. 46," ornate nickel trim & mica windows (restored) 2,100.00

Parlor stove, cast iron, "Favorite No. 115," base burner, eight mica doors & three windows, 5' 6" h...1,275.00

Parlor stove, cast iron, "Forest Oak," box-type, 1877 .... 265.00

Parlor stove, cast iron, wood- or coal-burning, "Glenwood No. 6" (ILLUS.).......................... 310.00

Parlor stove, cast iron, top w/two ball-turned brass finials above frieze molded w/flowerheads & leaves & "Jones and Wardell," shaped base on paw feet, Boston, ca. 1840, 20 x 18¼", 21¾" h. 275.00

Parlor stove, cast iron, "Moores Air Tight Heater No. 402B," ornate, Joliet Stove Co., Joliet, Ill., 45 x 24 x 24" 1,375.00

Parlor stove, cast iron, "Round Oak No. SB-14-T," nickel trim 400.00

Parlor stove, cast iron, "Stanley's Patent No. 2," w/cast decoration of maidens on doors & basket of fruit on double-flue to chimney pipe, cabriole legs w/scrolling toes, 26" w., 16½" deep, 35" h. .. 405.00

Parlor stove, cast iron, "Stewart Oak No. 18," ornate lacy nickel trim & mica windows 850.00

Parlor stove, cast iron, "Union Air Tight Patented 1851, Warnick & Leibrandt, Phila.," spread-wing eagle finial over pierced cover above reeded stepped top w/foliate & geometric bands above frieze of stars & frieze of American shields & wreaths over arched foliate panels flanked by fluted pilasters, side opening, stepped & molded rectangular base on molded scrolled legs, 2nd half 19th c., 20" w., 36" h.................... 770.00

STRING HOLDERS

Before the widespread use of paper bags, grocers and merchants wrapped their goods in paper, securing it with string. A string holder, usually of cast iron, was, therefore, a necessity in the store. Homemakers also found many uses for string and the ceramic or chalkware wall-type holder became a common kitchen item.

Advertising, "Jaxon Soap," cast iron $65.00

Advertising, "Post Toasties," tin 375.00

Advertising, "Postum" 145.00

Advertising, "Red Goose Shoes," tin, hanging-type, figural goose on hanger 1,200.00

Bronze, grapevine pattern over green glass, Tiffany Studios 325.00

Cast iron, ball-shaped, hanging-type, Victorian openwork style ... 55.00

Cast iron, model of beehive, dated Apr. 1865, 8" base, 6" h. 50.00

Cast iron, model of Dutch Girl, hanging-type 20.00

Cast iron, model of snail 25.00

Cast iron, model of turtle w/domed shell 25.00

Ceramic, figural rooster, Royal Bayreuth 225.00

Ceramic, heart-shaped, "String Along With Me"................ 38.00

Ceramic, pumpkin face 55.00

Chalkware, apple w/berries........ 18.00

Chalkware, Court Jester 39.00

Chalkware, figural black mammy holding flowers 85.00

Chalkware, figural chef, white & black 39.00

Chalkware, head of a black mammy & "Ty Me," 1936................. 90.00

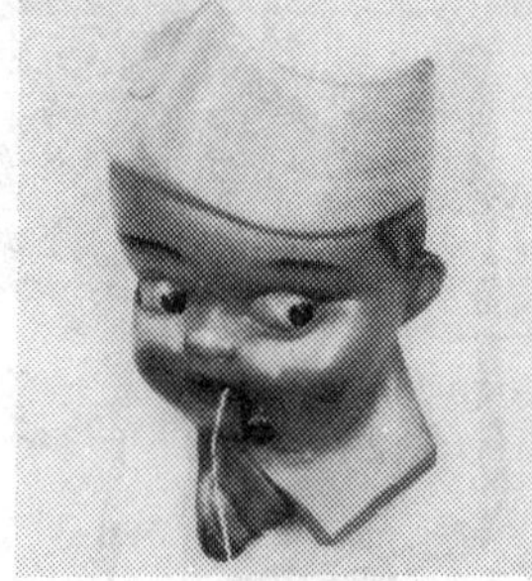

Boy with Pipe Chalkware String Holder

Chalkware, head of a boy w/pipe (ILLUS.)......................... 26.00

Redware, primitive, hanging-type, 6" d............................ 35.00

Wooden, figural black mammy, cloth clothing 95.00

Wooden, model of teapot w/chef decal 28.00

TEDDY BEAR COLLECTIBLES

Theodore (Teddy) Roosevelt had become a national hero during the Spanish-American War by leading his "Rough Riders" to victory at San Juan Hill in 1898. He became the 26th President of the United States in 1901 when President McKinley was assassinated.

The gregarious Roosevelt was fond of the outdoors and hunting. Legend has it that while on a hunting trip, soon after becoming President, he refused to shoot a bear cub because it was so small and helpless. The story was picked up by a political cartoonist who depicted President Roosevelt, attired in hunting garb, turning away and refusing to shoot a small bear cub. Shortly thereafter, toy plush bears began appearing in department stores labled "Teddy's Bears" and they became an immediate success. Books on the adventures of "The Roosevelt Bears" were written and illustrated by Paul Piper under the pseudonym of Seymour Eaton and this version of the Teddy Bear became a popular decoration on children's dishes.

Assorted Teddy Bears

Book, "More About Teddy B and Teddy G, The Roosevelt Bears," by Seymour Eaton (one plate loose, one plate chipped) $65.00
Book, "Mother Goose's Teddy Bears Book," 1907 .... 275.00
Model of a Teddy Bear, lithographed die-cut tin, pink bear wearing checked pants & red jacket, 2" h. 55.00
Playing cards, miniature, Teddy Bear wearing Fire Chief's hat, full deck 2.50
Postcards, "Days of the Week" series, signed Wm. S. Heal, 1907, set of 7 .... 140.00
Postcards, "Roosevelt Bears," set of 16 .... 320.00
Pull toy, Teddy Bear on wheels, gold mohair body, glass eyes, embroidered features, felt pads, tan ribbon & bow at neck, cast iron wheels, 12½" l. 450.00
Sand pail, lithographed tin, Teddy Bears decoration, "Chein" 26.00
Tea set, china, service for 6, Teddy Bear decoration, ca. 1910 (incomplete) 375.00
Teddy bear, white mohair body, glass eyes, Steiff, 3¾" 340.00
Teddy bear, mechanical tumbling-type, brown cotton body, black shoe button eyes, original label affixed to left arm, mechanism activated by winding arms, Germany, 7¾" 77.00
Teddy bear, light beige straw-stuffed body, fully jointed, shoe button eyes, 1910, 10½" 350.00
Teddy bear, pale gold mohair body, black shoe button eyes, blank ear button, Steiff, ca. 1905, 13" 1,210.00
Teddy bear, gold mohair straw-stuffed body w/hump, fully jointed, glass eyes, 1920's, 20" 350.00
Teddy bear, grey mohair body, jointed limbs, inset snout, w/growler, 22" 385.00
Teddy bear, beige mohair body, swivel head & jointed limbs, glass eyes, embroidered nose & mouth, felt padded feet & paws w/embroidered nails, 26" (some wear) 300.00
Teddy bear, straw-stuffed light brown mohair, glass eyes, jointed, Hermann, 1940's, 28" 695.00

TEXTILES

BEDSPREADS

Hand-crocheted white cotton, Filigree & Hobstars patt., 102 x 120" $125.00
Hand-crocheted ecru cotton, Pinwheel patt., 86 x 100" 80.00
Hand-crocheted creamy white cotton, Popcorn patt. w/hexagonal floral medallions, 90 x 90" (minor age stains) 175.00
Hand-crocheted ecru cotton, Popcorn patt., 78 x 100" 250.00
Hand-crocheted white cotton, Popcorn & Star Medallion patt., 70 x 90" 105.00
Hand-crocheted orange & white cotton, Sunflower patt., 90 x 100" (minor damage) 140.00
Hand-crocheted ecru cotton, Wheels & Six Petal patt., fringed, 86 x 108" 85.00
Linen w/lace inserts & embroidery, white, 96" sq., w/pair matching pillow shams, European style, 3 pcs. 245.00
Silk, embroidered w/blue & white doves & floral patterns on deep blue ground, braided blue & white 5" fringe on each side, 1920's, 74 x 86" 225.00

COVERLETS

Jacquard, single weave, one-piece,

floral medallion w/vintage grape vines, eagles, bird corners, tassel border & border label, red, olive green, orange & natural white, signed "Made by H. Stager, Mount Joy, Lancaster Co., Pa. Fast Color No. 1," 75 x 78" (minor wear) 500.00

Jacquard, single weave, one-piece, bold floral medallions, vining border, blue & white, 73 x 90" 300.00

One-piece Jacquard Coverlet Dated 1837

Jacquard, single weave, one-piece, floral medallions in center w/vining rose border, red, blue, green & natural, corners signed "Daniel Bordner, Millersburg, Berks County 1837," 80 x 96" (ILLUS. of one corner) 625.00

Jacquard, single weave, one-piece, rose medallions (4) center, flowers & compotes of fruit border, red, blue, green & natural white, corners signed "Made by D. Cosley, Xenia, Greene Co., Ohio, 1857," 84 x 96" (minor wear & stains) 260.00

Jacquard, double woven, two-piece, Tile patt., blue & white, bottom border w/doves in trees, eagle corners dated "1847," 81 x 82" (minor seam separation) 650.00

Jacquard, Memorial Hall in center, w/Miss Liberty, eagles & florals, "Memorial Hall" & "Centennial," red & white, 1876, 68 x 77" 375.00

Overshot, two-piece, optical design in navy blue, red, green & natural white, sewn-on fringe, 76 x 94" (minor wear) 350.00

Overshot, green, yellow, blue & red stripes in geometric floral blocks, 70 x 86" 467.50

LACES

Battenburg

Bedspread, all lace, 88 x 115" 700.00

Coat, long-sleeved bolero style w/buttoned back lapels, together w/flared skirt, ca. 1910, 2 pcs. . . . 440.00

Doilies, all lace, 10" d., pr. 20.00

Table centerpiece, all lace, 14" d. . . 30.00

Table centerpiece, drawn-work center w/initial "H," 17" sq. 42.00

Table centerpiece, 26" sq. 94.00

Tablecloth, 42" sq. 95.00

Tablecloth, 51" d. 75.00

Tablecloth, ecru, 60 x 93" 375.00

Tablecloth w/linen center, grape clusters, vines & foliage border, 70" d. 195.00

Tablecloth, linen w/Battenburg lace border, 72" d. 150.00

Tablecloth, deep Battenburg lace border & intricate center w/minimum amount of linen, 78 x 114" . . 550.00

Table runner, 4" Battenburg border, 16½ x 34" 85.00

QUILTS

Snail's Trail Crib Quilt

Crazy Quilt, ribbon-like bands of brilliant colors separated by black satin bands, 56 x 60" 245.00

Crazy Quilt, silk & various other materials, some patches w/embroidery details, wide lace edge, late 19th c., 60 x 72" 247.50

Crib-size, pieced Postage Stamp patt., pre-Depression calico patches, dark shades of blue w/red, grey & white, 825 pieces, 30 x 36" 160.00

Crib-size, pieced Snail's Trail patt., brightly colored pink & green calico patches, borders of boldly printed calico & chintz patches, reverse w/broad blue & green stripes, 19th c., 38 x 40" (ILLUS.) . . 550.00

Crib-size, pieced bluebirds carrying pink tied bow, sawtooth edge, 36 x 52" 49.00

Appliqued & pieced Carolina Lily patt. in red, goldenrod & sage green patches on white cotton field, feather wreath quilting between flower baskets, sawtooth border in matching colors, 83 x 86" 750.00

Appliqued Fleur-de-Lis patt., solid deep red pattern on white & ecru ground, red triangle border band, 76 x 78" 350.00

Appliqued & pieced Friendship patt., green, brown, red, pink & yellow cotton patches in a variety of bold floral forms, framing a rose pattern w/a bird on stem at center, names inked on white cotton, field heightened w/fan quilting, late 19th c., 68 x 78" 475.00

Rising Star Appliqued Quilt

Appliqued & pieced Rising Star of Gettysburg patt., 16 cotton blocks surrounded by double glazed blue floral chintz border, each star w/double wreath of flowers in red & green, mid-19th c., 100 x 103½" (ILLUS.) 2,420.00

Appliqued Thistle patt. variant, four boldly stylized medallions of four thistle blossoms & leaves radiating from central blossom, red, goldenrod & deep teal blue, finely quilted white ground, 82 x 82" (age stains) 600.00

Appliqued stylized meandering border & four oak leaf medallions in red & green calico on white, 92 x 94" (overall wear, stains & fading) 495.00

Pieced Anvil & Chain patt., pink & white patches, 72 x 82" 160.00

Pieced Barn Raising patt. variant, brightly colored print patches, 76 x 80" (minor wear) 425.00

Pieced Basket patt., multicolored calico baskets on white squares against bright red ground, 76 x 76" 300.00

Pieced Bear Paw patt., blue & white patches, quilted circles, never washed, pencil pattern intact, 72 x 82" 325.00

Pieced Bowtie patt., blue & white calico patches, 76 x 80" 250.00

Pieced Broken Star patt., Star Point borders, red, blue & orange patches on white, 78 x 82" 535.00

Pieced Courthouse Square patt., multicolored printed cotton patches, mainly browns, red & blues, on white ground, ca. 1880 . . . . 200.00

Pieced Double Irish Chain patt., red & white cotton patches, 71 x 80" . . 225.00

Pieced Drunkard's Path patt., red & white patches, 64 x 72" (minor stains) 200.00

Pieced Goose Tracks patt., red & muted gold patches on white, Indiana, 1900 . . . . 310.00

Pieced Log Cabin patt., red, blue & green patches, machine quilted, 70 x 70" 255.00

Pieced Monkey Wrench patt., red, blue & other colored calico patches, ca. 1910, 78 x 80" 250.00

Pieced North Star patt., indigo calico stars within white diamond-shaped blocks & set w/diagonal bands of red striped cotton, ca. 1890 . . . . 330.00

Pieced Pineapple patt., salmon patches on light green ground, diagonal line quilting, attributed to Bedford County, Pennsylvania Mennonites, 74 x 90" 350.00

Pieced Rolling Stone patt., friendship-type, white w/red & various shades of blue calico patches on blue field, each white center square w/pen & ink signature & "1858," overall diagonal line quilting within a border of spiral twist quilting, white homespun fabric backing, 76 x 89" 475.00

Pieced Single Star patt., calico & solid color red, pink, goldenrod & beige patches, sawtooth pieced border, meandering feather quilted edge, 72 x 76" (minor stains) . . 225.00

Pieced Spade & Blade patt., red, blue, brown & beige printed calico patches, elliptical quilting, diamond border, 19th c., 92 x 100" (ILLUS. top next page) 1,650.00

Pieced Sunshine & Shadow patt., blues & greens, Amish, signed & dated, queen size 500.00

Spade & Blade Pattern Quilt

Pieced Wild Goose Chase patt., pink & yellow calico patches on dark green ground, w/red, white & blue checked homespun backing, Bucks County, Pennsylvania, ca. 1900, 72 x 90" (edges rebound) . . . 175.00

SAMPLERS

Early Framed Sampler

Alphabet & inscription encircled by floral sprays stitched in blue, blue-green, apricot & ivory on natural linen, signed "Wrought by Augusta Brown, 1824," w/back label inscribed "Done in 1824 in Fitchburg, Massachusetts," 13 x 13½" 1,400.00

Alphabets & numerals above the verse "This fading Record of my hands reminds me that Another stands inscribed against my name of all this mortal part has wrought of all this thinking soul has thought for glory or for shame. Fall River, December 16 1837, Wrought by Sarah P. Carr Aged 9 yrs." above large flower basket & foliate sprigs within chain borders all within a scrolling stylized floral sprig border, square brown crash linen ground worked in black, green, beige, yellow & brown threads, framed, 17 1/8 x 19 1/8" (minor staining) 1,430.00

Alphabets in rows above name & pious verse above flowering trees, all within a chevron rimmed border & outer trellis border on linen, worked in a variety of stitches in blue, green, light yellow, signed "Charlotte Richardson 13 years," late 18th c., minor rust spots, 17 x 20" (ILLUS.) 1,650.00

Birds, figure, trees, potted flowers & butterflies on linen, inscribed within a diamond cartouche "Harriet Thorpe, Aged 12 years," framed w/narrow floral border, ca. 1830, 13 x 12" 450.00

Brick building w/black windows on scenic bottom panel, all within meandering strawberry vine border, silk stitches on linen, signed "Elizabeth Brook, aged 10, Bath 1813," 11¼ x 15" 522.50

Family record, radiating sunface peeking above an arc inscribed "Family Record" & flanked by pair of large leafy trees, above two columnar devices enclosing a listing of the members of the George & Betsy Rowe family w/their birth & death dates over a two-story yellow house w/red chimneys & roof, all within a strawberry border, executed in a variety of green, red, yellow & white silk stitches on loosely woven homespun linen fabric, by Elizabeth J. Rowe, Aged 11, probably Massachusetts, ca. 1830, 15" w., 16¾" h. 1,320.00

Landscape central scene of checkerboard house beside tall leafy tree under which is seated a young girl w/a standing dog nearby, large butterfly above house & large basket of fruit to right of tree, above scene is embroidered "Emblem of Innocence," & pious verse, all framed on three sides by running flowering vines, executed in a variety of green, blue, yellow, pale pink & gold silk stitches on loosely woven homespun linen ground, signed & dated, "Regina Rayton Made this work November 2, 1827," original frame, 16½ x 19¾" (some thread breaks & discoloration) 8,250.00

Memorial inscription above lengthy pious verse over framed short

Memorial Sampler

verse & inscription framed by large trees, floral sprigs & birds at top & surrounded by foliate scroll border on linen, signed "Emma Collins aged 11 years 1831," framed, 15 3/8 x 16¾" (ILLUS.) 550.00

Pious verse & landscape on homespun linen, vintage border framed in narrow bands surrounds center w/pious verse titled "On Youth" at top above finely stitched landscape scene of two leafy trees flanking two turbanned natives holding ropes attached to a giraffe, shades of green, brown, white, yellow, black & grey, signed "Mary Ann Goldsworthy 1837," molded wood frame w/gilt liner, 26¾ x 28½" 2,700.00

SHOW TOWELS

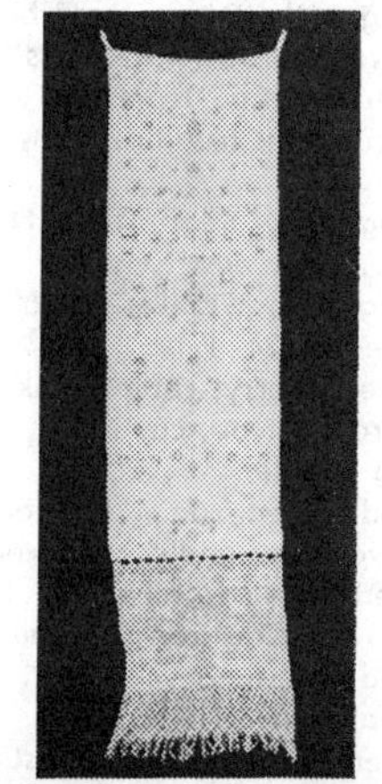

Embroidered Show Towel

Embroidered pink stars, flowerheads, birds, reindeer, dogs, potted flowering shrubs above a crocheted panel w/stars, birds & reindeer above zigzag crocheted panel w/fringe below, signed "Anna Maria Nies," dated 1816, probably Spanish, 15" w., 5' l. (ILLUS.) 330.00

Embroidered red & blue eight-point stars w/cut-work band & fringe, 12 x 14¼" plus fringe 105.00

Embroidered red designs & "C.L. 1834," woven white on white designs w/fringe, 16 x 51" (faded red, minor age stains) 95.00

Embroidered red florals & peacock on homespun linen fabric, signed "Ella Heisey, 1889," fringed end, 18 x 41" 85.00

Embroidered white bird-filled trees on homespun linen fabric, w/thread drawn-work geometric design panel at bottom, embroidered faded red initials "B.K,." two rows of fringe, 16 x 58" 145.00

TOBACCO JARS

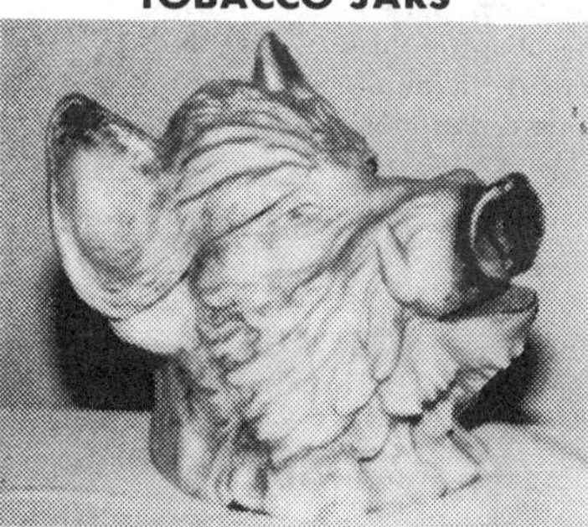

Wild Boar Tobacco Jar

Bisque, bust of Chinese man, gold skin, black hair, lavender hat, 3¼" d., 5¼" h. $100.00

Bisque, bust of Hindu man wearing white turban, dark complexion, black beard, turban forms lid, 3 5/8" d., 4 3/8" h. 115.00

Bisque, bust of Japanese lady, olive skin, black hair w/lavender combs, 3½" d., 4¾" h. 93.00

Bisque, model of a skull, cream w/black & white teeth, black eyes & nose, 4 x 5½", 5" h. 140.00

Bisque, model of a wild boar's head, light tan coloring (ILLUS.) 175.00

Ceramic, cover w/figure of man drinking from stein, banded cigar base, Bohemia 125.00

Copper, hand-hammered, threaded button finial on stepped lid, fitting onto cylindrical base w/rings of bands, Old Mission Kopper Kraft, San Francisco, California, ca. 1910, 6¼" h. 70.00

Majolica, bust of Scotsman, bearded, blue tam forms lid, 4¼" d., 6" h. 124.00

Painted treen, ovoid body w/tapered neck & outturned rim, lid w/knop finial, painted w/reserves of a ship, a bridge & pagodas, the body painted w/cream-colored cartouches depicting Chinese figures at leisure within Chinese landscapes, all within a brick-colored crosshatched background, Continental, early 18th c., 8" h. .. 880.00

Redware, three-part construction, domed lid w/ribbed spire finial & applied white clay flowers in yellow-green & clear glaze, cylindrical body w/similar flowers & glaze, round, tapering base matches other parts, 10¾" h. (edge chips) 45.00

Stoneware, round tree-trunk form grey saltglazed body highly embossed as tree bark w/leaves & knotholes highlighted in blue & olive, also applied deer, birds & cherubs, flat lid w/two seated dogs as finial, 8¼" h. (minor chips & hairlines) 375.00

TOOLS

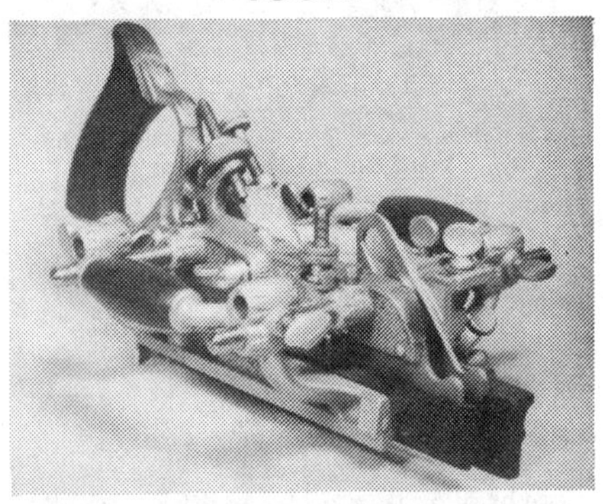

Stanley No. 55 Combination Plane

Auger, "Swan's Universal Auger," in original wooden box w/instructions $170.00

Axe, "Winchester," 7½ x 4½"...... 85.00

Bit, "Winchester," 1" 11.00

Brace, "Winchester W 210," 10"..... 50.00

Brace, hand-forged iron, "C" scroll, speckled ash burl grip, 11" l...... 95.00

Butcher's meat cleaver, stamped "New Haven Tool Edge Co."...... 30.00

Calipers, jeweler's, brass & copper rivet, inlaid brass & copper circles, 3½" l. 85.00

Chisel, "Winchester No. 4845," ¾" w/leather butt handle 25.00

Gauge, "Stanley No. 77," rosewood w/brass trim 15.00

Hand saw, "Winchester No. 10" 45.00

Leather cutter, pistol-grip worn rosewood handle w/adjustable steel & brass cutter, 6" l. 20.00

Level, "Stanley No. 36," steel 16.00

Level, rosewood trimmed in brass, marked "Stratton Brothers, Greenfield, Mass.," & patent dates 1872 & 1887, 22" l. 115.00

Mallet, burl wood, stamped "S. Coss," 11¼" l. 45.00

Mitre box, "Craftsman No. 3646" ... 20.00

Monkey wrench, "Winchester," 21" 95.00

Plane, "Bailey's Victor No. 1½," nickel-plated block-type 2,200.00

Plane, "Case & Co., Auburn, N.Y.," rosewood plow-type 210.00

Plane, "DeForest," stamped "W.W. Henderson," plow-type w/six blades 75.00

Plane, "Keen Kutter No. 10," carriagemaker's bench-type 165.00

Plane, "Sargent No. 407," smoothing-type 105.00

Plane, "Stanley 'Bailey' No. 1," smoothing-type 850.00

Plane, "Stanley 'Bailey' No. 26," jack-type 25.00

Plane, "Stanley No. 55," Universal Combination model w/three boxes of blades (ILLUS.) 350.00

Plane, "Stanley No. 100½," block-type 55.00

Rule, folding pocket-type w/combination level & protractor, brass bound, Stevens Co., Ivoryton, Connecticut, 1 ft. (repair at 1" mark) 65.00

Rule, folding-type, "Keen Kutter No. 680" 20.00

Rule, folding-type, "Stanley No. 62," w/brass edge, 24" l. 25.00

Scorp (shave), cherry, cabinetmaker's half-round type, ca. 1800, 7" curved handle 140.00

Scribe, hand-forged iron w/hooked end, 6" wooden handle w/carved full-bodied naked woman 350.00

Shipwright's hawsing iron (for caulking), hand-forged, 26" 59.00

Square, "Stanley No. 18" 12.50

"Tentlometer," brass (used to test tensile strength of wire) 225.00

Woodgraining set, Davis Co., 1904, three rollers & instruction book ... 25.00

TOOTHPICK HOLDERS

Three Dolphins Base Toothpick Holder

Reference numbers listed after the holders refer to William Heacock's book, "1000 Toothpick Holders."

Amber glass, pressed Three Dolphins Base (ILLUS.) $55.00
Amethyst glass w/enamel, Jefferson Optic patt. 45.00
Bisque, model of a cat dressed as a coachman w/barrel 55.00
Blue glass, pressed Daisy & Button patt., model of Coal Bucket, U.S. Glass, ca. 1892, No. 315 .... 30.00
Blue glass, pressed Gatling Gun, No. 741 .... 25.00
Brass, model of top hat w/umbrella 20.00
China, model of top hat, hunting dog scene on green ground & sunset on cream ground, cobalt blue bottom band 37.50
Clear glass, Pretty Maid (figure of girl standing next to basket), No. 749 .... 65.00
Majolica, model of a mouse w/ear of corn 135.00
Nippon china, gold w/floral band decoration 25.00
Purple slag glass, pressed British Boot (model of tall boot), No. 318 .... 55.00
Royal Bayreuth china, three-handled, penguins on yellow ground 85.00
R.S. Prussia china, plume mold, cobalt blue w/gold tracery, 2¼" h. 120.00
Silver plate, model of chick head emerging from egg, feet on branch, square fringed base, piercing on the egg, marked "Hartford" 70.00

TOYS

Also see CHARACTER COLLECTIBLES, CHILDREN'S DISHES and DOLLS.

Early Puzzle Blocks

Acrobats, "Crandall's Great Show, The Acrobats," lithographed paper on wood, patented Feb. 5, 1867, in original box, 7¾" h., pr. $125.00
Adding machine, tin, Wolverine Co. (Pittsburgh, Pennsylvania)........ 15.00
African Safari animal, Alligator, wooden, glass eyes, Schoenhut (Philadelphia), regular size 285.00
Airplane, "Northeast DC 9," aluminum, 27" body, 23" wing, on stand 500.00
Airplane, "Pan-Am DC 8," cast aluminum, Douglas, 36" 650.00
Airplane, rubber, Sun Rubber Company (Barberton, Ohio), 3 x 4" ... 15.00
Alphabet board, original paint, movable letters, pat. Feb. 16, 1886 ... 55.00
Armored bank truck, sheet metal, Buddy L (Moline Pressed Steel Company, East Moline, Illinois) ... 15.00
Army Supply Corps truck, pressed steel, Buddy L, 15" 60.00
Army trucks, metal, Dinky Toys (Meccano Ltd., England), set of 18 .... 265.00
Automobile, Buick Brougham, die-cast metal, Tootsietoy (Dowst Brothers, Chicago, Illinois) 48.00
Automobile, Cadillac 60 Special 4-door sedan, 1948 model, die-cast metal, yellow, Tootsietoy, 6" 18.00
Automobile, Corvette, 1953 model, cast iron, Hubley, 13" l. 375.00
Automobile, Ford Model A Tudor w/original driver, cast iron, Arcade (Freeport, Illinois), 6½" l. ... 275.00
Automobile, Ford Model T, cast iron, Arcade, 3 x 4¾" 110.00

Automobile, Futuristic sedan, die-cast metal, two-piece body, grey & black, w/six red wood wheel hubs w/removable white rubber tires, Manoil (Waverly, New York) 60.00
Automobile, Lincoln Zephyr, cast iron, Hubley, 6" 125.00
Automobile, Porsche 917, Shuco (Germany) 125.00
Balance toy, parrot, laminated wood, brightly colored bird w/weighted tail & copper tack edge, early 20th c., 12" h. 175.00
Ball, rubber, portrait of a cherub, ca. 1880 .... 55.00
Battery-operated, "Batmobile," 12" l. 85.00
Battery-operated, "Blacksmith Bear" 90.00
Battery-operated, "Buttons Puppy with a Brain," Louis Marx & Co. (New York City), 12" 85.00
Battery-operated, "Chimp Playing Cymbals," C.K. Co., 1960, 10½" .. 125.00
Battery-operated, "Cragston Crap-shooter," original box 75.00
Battery-operated, "Doxie the Dog," Line Mar (Japan) 45.00
Battery-operated, "Grandpa Rocking Bear" 180.00
Battery-operated, "Haunted House," w/original box 995.00
Battery-operated, "Miss Friday Typist" 115.00
Battery-operated, "Mr. McGregor," Japan 85.00
Battery-operated, "Phillips 66 Power Yacht," w/box 45.00
Battery-operated, "Picnic Bear" 70.00
Battery-operated, "Piggy Cook" 100.00
Battery-operated, "Popcorn Eating Panda Bear," Japan 75.00
Battery-operated, "Santa on Roof," tin, Japan, 1960 .... 95.00
Battery-operated, "Santa on Scooter," Japan 75.00
Battery-operated, "Smoking Papa Bear" 90.00
Battery-operated, "Sunnyside Service Station," Louis Marx & Co., 10 x 14" base 325.00
Battery-operated, "Telphone Bear" .. 115.00
Battery-operated, "Trumpet Monkey" 75.00
BB gun, Atlas 200.00
BB gun, HyScore Model 808 .... 45.00
Bell ringer toy, "Ding Dong Bell Pussy's Not in the Well," cast iron, Punch & Judy-type clowns rescuing cat, Gong Bell Mfg. Co. (East Hampton, Connecticut), 1890's 1,350.00
Bell ringer toy, "Rough Riders," painted cast iron & nickel-plated pressed steel, Watrous, 13" l. 375.00
Blocks, alphabet & Bible verses & stories, hand-colored printed paper-covered wood, marked "Manufactured by J.S. Wesby, Worcester, Mass.," set of 23 (one missing) in original (worn) box ... 75.00
Blocks, building-type, stone, in original box w/paper label "Richter's Anchor Blocks No. 8. Made in U.S.A.," 9¾ x 14" 115.00
Blocks, building-type, stone, in original box w/paper label "Richter's Anchor Blocks," w/U.S. patent date of 1880, large size, 14¾ x 15¾" 125.00
Blocks, building-type, "American Skyline," Elgo, 1950, large set 50.00
Blocks, puzzle-type, lithographed paper on wood, colorful scenes of children at play, set of 9, in original box (ILLUS.) 75.00
Blocks, puzzle-type, lithographed paper on wood, blocks form six different circus scenes, set of 35, in original wooden box, overall 8 x 10 7/8" 125.00

Bing Torpedo Boat

Boat, Torpedo, clockwork, painted tin, boat w/deck details including funnel, two revolving guns, ventilator, ship's wheel controlling rudder, mechanism concealed in grey painted hull, Bing (Germany), plaque on deck marked "GBN, Bravia," ca. 1910 (repainted deck, small dent on side), 15" l. (ILLUS.) 660.00
Boat, Transport, die-cast metal, Tootsietoy, 1940's 24.00
Britains (soldiers), Bahamas Police at Attention w/Sergeant & British officer, Set No. 2184, set 2,530.00
Britains (soldiers), Military Band, Set No. 2110, U.S. Army Band in yellow & black uniforms, set 4,180.00
Bus, "Fageol," die-cast metal, six windows each side, orange, Tootsietoy, 3½" 35.00
Bus, "Inter-City," die-cast metal, Buddy L, 1928, 24" l. 215.00
Bus, "Inter-State," lithographed tin, brown, Ferdinand Strauss Corp. (New York, New York), 1926, 10½" l. 450.00

Cannon, "Big Bang," cast iron, two-wheeler, 18" l. 85.00
Cannon, firecracker-type, cast iron, Kilgore Manufacturing Co. (Westerville, Ohio) 60.00
Cap pistol, "Bigger Bang," cast iron 45.00
Cap pistol, "Border Patrol," cast iron, Kilgore 17.50
Cap pistol, "Colt," cast iron, marked "Made in U.S.A., patent June 17, 1880," overall 5½ x 2¾" 40.00
Cap pistol, "Federal," cast iron, Kilgore 25.00
Cap pistol, "Jr. Ranger," cast iron, .32 cal. 40.00
Cap pistol, "Luger," lithographed tin, Louis Marx & Co. 9.00
Cap pistol, "Star," cast iron, ca. 1885 .... 110.00
Cap pistol, "Trooper," cast iron, Hubley, 6" 15.00
Cap pistol, cast iron w/white plastic handle w/applied brown bull head each side 12.00
Carpet sweeper, Bissell's "Little Helper," Mother Goose on top ... 30.00
Carpet sweeper, "Sunshine," gilt script name, varnished, early 1900's 30.00
Cash register, "Benjamin Franklin," nickel-colored metal 35.00
Cash register, "Tom Thumb," red ... 24.00
Chemistry set, Chemcraft No. 2, ca. 1927 .... 110.00
Circus animal, Buffalo, wooden, carved mane, painted eyes, Schoenhut, regular size 225.00
Circus animal, Camel (Dromedary), wooden, painted eyes, Schoenhut, regular size 160.00

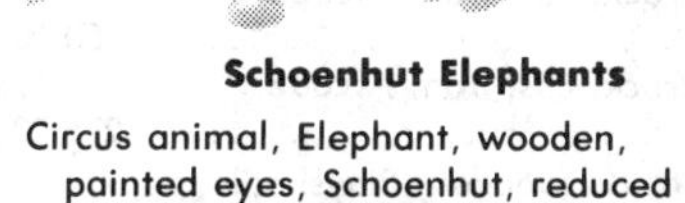

Schoenhut Elephants

Circus animal, Elephant, wooden, painted eyes, Schoenhut, reduced size, 6¼" l. (ILLUS. right) ..50.00 to 75.00
Circus animal, Elephant, wooden, glass eyes, Schoenhut, regular size (ILLUS. left) 160.00
Circus animal, Goat, wooden, painted eyes, Schoenhut, regular size 115.00
Circus animal, Hippopotamus, wooden, glass eyes, Schoenhut, regular size 255.00
Circus animal, Lion, wooden, painted eyes, Schoenhut, regular size (repainted) 200.00
Circus animal, Pig, wooden, glass eyes, leather ears & woven tail, Schoenhut, ca. 1925, 3¾" h. 275.00
Circus animal, Polar Bear, wooden, painted eyes, Schoenhut, 4¾" h. 350.00

Schoenhut Poodle

Circus animal, Poodle, wooden, cloth ruff, glass eyes, Schoenhut, regular size (ILLUS.) 190.00
Circus animal, Tiger, wooden, Schoenhut, regular size 200.00
Circus animal, Zebra, wooden, painted eyes, Schoenhut, reduced size 210.00
Circus performer, Girl Bare-Back Rider, wooden w/bisque head, Schoenhut, 8½" h. 250.00
Circus performer, "Humpty Dumpty" Clown, wooden, Schoenhut, 8½" h. 112.00
Circus performer, Lion Tamer, wooden, Schoenhut, regular size 185.00

Schoenhut Negro Dude

Circus performer, Negro Dude, wooden, Schoenhut, 8¾" h. (ILLUS.) 225.00

Circus performer, "Ringmaster," wooden w/wooden head, Schoenhut, reduced size 155.00

Circus set, "Humpty Dumpty," wooden, Schoenhut, 36 pcs. 4,620.00

Circus wagon, wooden, Fisher Price (East Aurora, New York), No. 850 .... 195.00

Clockwork mechanism, tin plate, "La Conquete du Nord," Admiral Robert Peary in sled pulled by four dogs, commemorating his 1909 journey to the North Pole F. Martin Co. (France)..........2,290.00

Bing Clockwork Limousine

Clockwork mechanism, Limousine, lithographed tin, auto w/luggage rack, pair of headlights, steering wheel, opening rear doors, hand brake, (lacking front grill), Bing (Germany), ca. 1912, 10" l. (ILLUS.) 2,970.00

Clockwork mechanism, "Peter Rabbit Chick-Mobile," composition Peter Rabbit operating a yellow hand car w/green basket at one end, w/circular track, Lionel Mfg. Corp. (New York, New York) 242.00

Clockwork Touring Car

Clockwork mechanism, Touring Car, painted tin, open-sided auto w/body painted red w/green tufted seats, celluloid windscreen & tan canvas convertible top, probably Morton E. Converse Company (Winchendon, Massachusetts), ca. 1910, 16" l. (ILLUS.) 4,400.00

Coaster wagon, "Radio Flyer," wooden, red 42.00

Coaster wagon, "Star Coaster," wooden 250.00

Coaster wagon, painted pine, rec-

Early Wooden Coaster Wagon

tangular cart w/two large wooden front wheels & two small wooden back wheels each banded in wrought iron, 19th c., 40" l., 13¾" h. (ILLUS.) 770.00

Concrete mixer truck, sheet steel, Structo Mfg. Co. (Freeport, Illinois) 45.00

Cook stove, "Crescent," cast iron, w/coal scuttle & skillet, 1935-40 .. 195.00

Cook stove, "Garland Stoves & Ranges," cast iron, w/tin chimney & hood, black paint, 12" h........ 135.00

Cook stove, "Little Fanny," cast iron, Philadelphia Stove Works, 12" l., 7¼" h. 285.00

Corn planter, cast iron, Arcade 30.00

Dairy van, die-cast metal, white body, black fenders, red wheels, replaced tires, raised black lettering "Graham," Tootsietoy, 1933-39 (restored) 75.00

Delivery truck, "Heinz Pure Food Products," pressed steel, Metalcraft, 1933, 12" l. (some wear) ... 135.00

Delivery truck, "Pepsi," metal, Buddy L, 1960's, 13" l. 48.00

Donkey cart & driver w/large nodding head, "Rubber Neck," cast iron, worn old polychrome paint, 6½" l. (repairs to donkey's neck) 215.00

Drum, lithographed tin, eagles & flag decoration, silk top & bottom, Noble & Cooley Co., 1940's, 8" h. 25.00

Dump truck, cast iron, Arcade, 4" l. 50.00

Dump truck, cast iron, Arcade, 11" 275.00

Dump truck, wooden, Playskool Mfg. Co. (Milwaukee, Wisconsin) 8.00

End loader, sheet steel, Structo, early 1950's.................... 85.00

Engine shed (railroad), orange-painted metal w/red trim, green grillwork & sliding front doors, semi-circular structure w/flat roof topped by three funnel vents, Marklin, ca. 1925, 27 x 11 x 15" .. 990.00

Erector set, A.C. Gilbert, No. 7½ . . . 40.00
Erector set, Mecanno Ltd. (England), 1914, w/instruction booklet 100.00
Farm set, Louis Marx & Co., No. 3931, w/original box 50.00
Fire chief's car, sheet steel, crank siren, Hoge Mfg. Co. (New York, New York), 1935-45 . . . . 295.00
Fire engine, cast iron, deep red w/gilt wheels, Hubley, 1920's, 6½" l. 295.00
Fire hook & ladder truck w/two firemen & three horses, cast iron & steel, rubber tires, Wilkins Toy Company (Keene, New Hampshire), 1911, 21" l. 350.00
Fire water tower truck, sheet steel, Keystone Mfg. Co. (Boston, Massachusetts), 32" l. (some wear) . . . 375.00
Friction-type, tin, 1970's Chevrolet pickup truck, Japan 15.00
Friction-type, tin, "Sea Queen" motorboat w/man at steering wheel, Japan, 10" l. 75.00
Friction-type, tin, "Tin Lizzie" sedan, Louis Marx & Co. 85.00
Friction-type, tin, street car w/cast-iron wheels, worn original paint, stamped "Pat'd Nov. 2, 1897," 14¾" l. 95.00
"Funny Andy" Street Railway Car, tin, 1920's, 14" l. 200.00
Gasoline tank truck, "Mack," cast iron, blue, 5" l. 100.00
Gasoline tank truck, "Mack," cast iron, red, Arcade, 1925, 13¼" l. . . 525.00
Gasoline tank truck, "Texaco," Buddy L, 1950's, 23" l. 35.00
Globe, tin, w/Zodiac signs & months, 1930's, 9" 45.00
Gravity-operated mechanism, two mice move up & down spiral column, tin, original paint, 15" l. 65.00
Hand-crank type, "The Little Red Hen," tin, cackles & lays eggs 50.00
Hobby horse chair rocker, wooden sides cut-out in horse form w/seat between, warm white w/stenciled red & black trim, 37" l. 145.00
Hobby horse on frame, carved wood w/black plush velvet, brown saddle, ears & bridle, swings in red painted frame, ca. 1880, 33½" l., 29½" h. 650.00
Hobby horse on frame, wooden, worn original dapple grey paint, blue oilcloth harness, upholstered seat, horsehair tail & mane, red base w/white & black decoration, 36" l. 550.00
Hobby horse on frame, wooden, original dapple grey paint, traces of old saddle & harness, red base w/yellow & black striping, 37¼" l. 550.00
Hobby horse on frame, carved & painted wood, dapple grey w/metal eyes, horsehair forelock & tail, on bentwood supports joined to wooden frame by metal brackets, New England, ca. 1880, 45" l., 38" h. 632.50

Hobby Horse on Frame

Hobby horse on frame, wooden, dappled grey & white paint, corduroy saddle seat, swings in painted frame (ILLUS.) 995.00
Hobby horse on rockers, wooden, turned & flattened legs w/one-piece body, white paint, worn oilcloth saddle & incomplete harness, red rockers w/black striping & polychrome floral decoration, 46¼" l., 22½" h. 550.00
Hobby horse on rockers, painted wood, rocking trestle base, late 19th-early 20th c., 38" h. (losses to paint) 418.00
Hobby horse on removable rocker base, wooden, worn original brown haircloth covering, very worn red striping, 50¾" l. 225.00
Hobby horse, stick-type, stuffed hound's tooth fabric horse head w/bridle, Amish, 40" l. 55.00
Horse barn, wooden, ornate cut-out trim at roof edge, lithographed paper shingle design roof, worn original polychrome paint, 23½" l., 18" h. 250.00
Horse-drawn sleigh, cast iron, painted, Dent Hardware Co. (Fullerton, Pennsylvania), 16" l. 1,200.00
Ice truck, "Ice," cast iron, red w/white rubber tires, Arcade (Freeport, Illinois), 1941, 6¾" l. . . 110.00
Ice truck, cast iron, Hubley (Lancaster, Pennsylvania), 8" l. 195.00
Ice wagon & horse, cast iron, 9" l. . . 105.00
Ice wagon w/two horses, cast iron, 12" l. 150.00

Iron, electric-type, robin's egg blue graniteware, 1920's 40.00
Ironing board, folding-type, wooden, ca. 1920, 21" l., 10" h. 18.00
Jack-in-the-box, clown, early 20th c., 4" sq. 110.00
"Jolly Jigger," Dutch boy, activated by depressing platform, Schoenhut (Philadelphia, Pennsylvania), 1910 patent . . . . 975.00 to 1,200.00
Jigsaw puzzle, circus scene, wooden, w/twelve cut-out model figures, Victory, w/box 45.00
Jigsaw puzzle, Effanbee dolls, original box 65.00
Jigsaw puzzle, girl & squirrel scene, wooden, 1900's 55.00
Jigsaw puzzle, hook & ladder fire engine, Milton Bradley (Springfield, Massachusetts), 1920, 9 x 16" 75.00
Jigsaw puzzle, soldiers one side, ABC's reverse, lithographed paper on wood, 1898 patent 250.00
Kaleidoscope, brass tube w/silver-painted metal trim, on turned wood stand, 10¾" l., 9½" h. 80.00
Kitchen, "Pretty Maid," metal, range & sink w/dish drainer & sink strainer, each 11 x 11 x 6", the set 65.00
Kitchen cabinet, lithographed tin, red & white, Wolverine Co. (Pittsburgh, Pennsylvania) 32.00
Kitchen sink, "Kohler," cast iron, Arcade, 4 5/8" h. 35.00
Lawn mower, lithographed tin, Louis Marx & Co. (New York City), 1940's 25.00
"Little Home Maker Clean-Up Set," tin, carpet sweeper, broom, dustpan & stand-up container, in unopened package, 1930's 50.00
Log truck, cast iron, w/load of logs, Hubley 98.00
Machine gun, shoots ping-pong balls, 1950's 20.00
Mail wagon, "U.S. Mail," cast iron & steel, w/driver & American flags, rubber tires, Wilkins Toy Co. (Keene, New Hampshire), 1911, 7" l. 355.00
Meccano set, No. 2A, metal, Frank Hornby (Liverpool, England), in original box 39.00
Meccano set, No. 2X, metal, w/electric engine, Frank Hornby . . 240.00
Merry-go-round, pedal-type, four wooden horses 750.00
Metallophone, Schoenhut 27.00
Microscope set, A. C. Gilbert Co. (New Haven, Connecticut), 1930's, in original box 27.00
Milk pail, lithographed tin, farm scene w/Sunbonnet girl milking cow, bail handle, Louis Marx & Co. 40.00
Milk truck, "Borden's," cast iron, Hubley, 1930, 7½" l. 600.00
Milk truck, "Cass Milk Truck," wooden, painted & stenciled, N.D. Cass (Athol, Massachusetts), 16" l. 45.00
Milk wagon, composition horse & driver, tin wagon & milk cans, Penwood Toys (Philadelphia, Pennsylvania) 135.00
Motorcycle, cast iron, Champion Hardware Co. (Geneva, Ohio), 5" l. 145.00
Motorcycle, 3-wheel, "Crash Car," cast iron, 1941 . . . . 50.00
Motorcycle w/driver, "Harley Davidson," cast iron 175.00
Motorcycle w/side car & two demountable policemen, cast iron, red, black rubber tires & spoke wheels & rachet noise attachment, Hubley, 8½" l. 485.00
Motor home, "Winnebago," Tonka . . 45.00
Movie projector, Model 535, Keystone Mfg. Co. (Boston, Massachusetts), w/catalog, film, tickets, etc. 75.00
Movie projector, "Illustravox Junior Film Strip," w/turntable record sound, ca. 1928 . . . . 97.50
Moving van, pressed steel, Keystone Mfg. Co., 26" l. 600.00

Wooden Noah's Ark

Noah's Ark, wooden, polychrome painted ark w/lift-off roof & sliding door together w/66 pairs of wooden animals, 29" l. (ILLUS.) 3,650.00
Panel truck, cast iron, blue, Champion, 7 7/8" l. (one rubber wheel replaced) 275.00
Pastry set: bowls, grater, egg beater, rolling pin, pastry board & animal-shaped cookie cutters; tin, DeLuxe Game Corp., boxed set . . 50.00
Pedal airplane, U.S. Navy Fighter . . . 950.00
Pedal car, 1935, Airflow, Steelcraft 1,750.00
Pedal car, 1953 Cadillac 600.00
Pedal car, 1916 Dodge 625.00

Pedal car, 1939 Lincoln Zephyr, Steelcraft 800.00

Pedal car, 1965 Mustang, yellow 245.00

Pedal car, Stutz Tandem, two-passenger, two-tone blue 5,000.00

Pedal tractor, D4 Caterpillar 350.00

Penny toy, sedan w/driver, Germany 75.00

Penny toy, tin, circle of jockeys on horses, operated by blowing into tin stem to make riders & horses race around 225.00

Penny toy, lithographed tin, town car w/driver & passengers, one door opens, spoke wheels 125.00

Piano, baby grand, Schoenhut, 25" w., 19" h., w/stool 350.00

Piano, grand, "Cable," cast iron, blue paint, w/stool, Arcade, 5" l. 135.00

Pickup truck, "International Harvester," plastic & metal, 1942 ...... 100.00

Playland whip & bump cars (No. 340), tin, drivers' head wobbles, J. Chein & Co. (New York City), original box 120.00

Pogo stick, wood w/cast iron foot rest, 1880's 125.00

Potbellied stove, cast iron, marked "Spark Cap & Lifter, Grey Iron Casting Co., Mt. Joy, Pa.," 13½" h. 225.00

Power plant, horizontal steam engine w/high stack mounted beside piston w/flywheel, w/operable pressure gauge, marked "Bavaria," 11 x 12½" (minor damage) 165.00

Pull toy, bear on platform w/wheels, rag-stuffed grey-tan flannel bear w/glass eyes & pink ribbon at neck, wooden base w/tin wheels, 6¾" l. 145.00

Pull toy, covered wagon & two horses, "Gypsy Wagon," metal w/cloth top, No. 57, Gibbs Mfg. Co. (Canton, Ohio), patented 1919, 19" l., 9" h. ....300.00 to 400.00

Pull toy, cow on platform w/wheels, wood & composition animal w/felt covering, white w/painted brown spots, glass eyes, moos when head is pushed, red wooden base, "Made in Germany," 12½" l. 525.00

Pull toy, dog on wheels, "Woofy Wagger," moving head w/felt ears, spring tail, Model 465, Fisher-Price, Inc. (East Aurora, New York), 1954-56, 5½" h. 48.00

Pull toy, duck on platform w/wheels, papier-mache duck & small woven basket, wooden base w/tin wheels, original polychrome paint, 6" l. 105.00

Pull toy, elephant on wheels, tan mohair w/red felt trappings, head moves from side to side when tail is turned, Schuco (Germany), 11" h. 198.00

Pull toy, grasshopper on wheels, cast-iron & aluminum grasshopper on rubber wheels, original green paint, Hubley Mfg. Co., 9" l. 225.00

Pull toy, hen on wheels, "The Cackling Hen," Model 120, Fisher-Price, Inc., 1958-67 .... 45.00

Pull toy, horse on platform w/wheels, light tan & black papier-mache body w/carved wood legs, white fleecy mane & tail, leather reins, wooden base w/cardboard wheels, ca. 1850, 7" h. plus platform 180.00

Pull toy, horse on platform w/wheels, papier-mache horse w/horsehair mane & tail, wooden base w/cast-iron wheels, overall 10½" h. 450.00

Pull toy, horse on shaped wooden platform w/turned wheels, original brown haircloth covering w/glass eyes, felt ears, black hair tail & mane, orange oil cloth harness w/yellow velvet saddle & red felt blanket, 16" l., 15¾" h. 375.00

Pull toy, horse on iron wheels, wooden horse w/dapple grey paint, red saddle, 24" h. 475.00

Pull toy, lamb on platform w/wheels, wool covering, green glass eyes, original ribbons, squeaks when head is pushed down, 12½" l., 11" h. 775.00

Pull toy, mail cart, two-wheel horse-drawn cart, "No. 27 U.S. Mail," metal, Gibbs Mfg. Co., 1922-31 ... 400.00

Pull toy, pig on wheels, "Pinky Pig," plastic umbrella, when pulled umbrella spins & hemispherical eyes roll up & down, Model 695, Fisher-Price, Inc., 1956-58, 6" l., 5½" h. 25.00

Pull toy, ram on platform w/wheels, wooden ram w/composition head & wooly coat wearing blue paperboard collar, on wooden base w/tin wheels, worn original paint, 7" h. 210.00

Pull toy, "Rich's Little Milk Man," tin milk wagon w/wooden horse on wheels, Rich & Co. (Clinton, Iowa) 265.00

Pull toy, rooster on platform w/wheels, papier-mache rooster on spring legs, wooden base w/tin wheels, bright original polychrome paint, Ultrahart, 8" h. 305.00

Puppet, painted wood, cat in Cossack outfit, w/wire & strings 125.00

Push toy, tin butterfly on cast-iron wheels, 1800's ....155.00 to 195.00

Push toy, red & green duck w/oilcloth wings & tail, 1920's......... 25.00

Push toy, tin, animated clucking hen, wooden handle, 7½" h. plus handle 30.00

Puzzle blocks, Santa Claus, child w/Teddy bear, Germany, 16 x 16", in original box.............. 585.00

Riding toy, "Rocket," Metalcraft (St. Louis, Missouri), 24" l. 150.00

Riding toy, train, "Super Yard Bird," operated by 6-volt battery, Charles William Doepke Manufacturing Co. (Rossmoyne, Ohio)...............1,100.00

"Rolly-Dolly," papier-mache w/weighted bottom, Dutch girl, patented 1908, 8" h. 138.00

Roly-poly, papier-mache clown figure w/bright original white & blue paint w/polychrome trim, green ribbon around neck, 4 1/8" h. 60.00

Painted Tin Roundhouse

Roundhouse, painted tin, two hinged doors, sides painted to simulate stone, Marklin (Germany), ca. 1910, 24" l. (ILLUS.)............. 770.00

Sad iron, "Lady Dover" 27.50

Sad iron & trivet, cast iron, swanform iron, cathedral trivet, 3" l., 2 pcs. 75.00

Sand pail, lithographed tin, girl feeding chickens, Ohio Art Co. (Bryan, Ohio) 28.00

Sand pail, lithographed tin, Peter Cottontail, Chein 18.00

Sand pail, lithographed tin, Treasure Island scene, U.S. Metal Toy Mfg. Co. 20.00

Sand pail w/matching shovel, boat-shaped, tin, animals & ark, Unique Art Mfg. Co., Inc. (New York City), 4½ x 9½" 46.00

Saxophone, "Playasax," w/twenty music rolls, Q.R.S., all in original boxes 200.00

Scale, platform-type, cast iron, w/pan & four graduated weights, 3½ x 5" 65.00

Schoolhouse set, "Pretty Village," McLoughlin Bros. (New York City), 1897 .... 95.00

Sewing machine, "American Girl," green metal w/wooden base, 4 x 7¾" 35.00

Sewing machine, "Baby Betsy Ross," electric, in carrying case 50.00

Sewing machine, "Betsy Ross," cast metal, green, in red carrying case 45.00

Sewing machine, "Little Beauty," Germany, 4½ x 4½" 26.00

Sled, original blue board w/horse-head center & daisy border, wooden runners, 10½" w., 27" l. 185.00

Sled, wooden w/metal-tipped runners & cast-iron swan finials, old worn polychrome repaint w/landscape scene, striping & "Lion," 33" l. (age cracks in top)......... 375.00

Spaceship, "Marx Mystery Spaceship," plastic, gyro powered, w/instructions, in box 75.00

Sparkler toy, tin & wood, pull string & disc spins emitting colored sparks, handle embossed "Ronson Magic Sparkler," manufactured by Art Metal Works, 1906-23 patent.. 50.00

Speed boat, "KTO Ranger," w/Hurricane outboard motor, 13" l. 90.00

Sprinkling can, tin, lithographed children in garden, Chein 30.00

Steam roller, "Old Smokey," Wilesco, w/original fuel box 175.00

Steam shovel, pressed steel, original red & black paint, "Buddy L" (Moline Pressed Steel Company, East Moline, Illinois) 100.00

Stove, "Western Electric Jr. Range," black tin plate w/nickel trim & top, has six burners & oven, 12" l., 15" h. 115.00

Taxicab, "Checker," lithographed tin, Mohawk, 6" l. 130.00

Taxicab, "Yellow Cab," cast iron, "A Century of Progress, Chicago 1933," Arcade Mfg. Co. (Freeport, Illinois), 6¾" l. 335.00

Telephone, lithographed tin, Western wall model, wooden handle, double bells, Gong Bell Co. (East Hampton, Conn.), 16" 60.00

Tool chest & tools, "The Boys Favorite Tool Chest," paper litho on inside of lid shows boy planing board, oak box, dovetailed, early 1900's 125.00

Tractor, "Ford 8600," cast iron, 12" 32.00

Tractor, "International Farmall 1466," 9½" 30.00

Tractor, "International Harvestor," cast iron, Arcade, 7" 345.00

Windup tin, automobile, "Graham-Paige Sedan," near mint in box, Kosuge, pre-war Japan, 6" 435.00

Windup black comic dancers, wood, two articulated black dancers w/wooden limbs & painted embossed brass faces & traces of original costumes stand on raised rectangular wooden box base holding clockwork mechanism, 11" h. (base top & bottom loose) 650.00

Windup tin "Bombo the Monkey," Unique Art Mfg. Co. (Newark, New Jersey) 84.00

Windup tin Harold Lloyd "Funny Face" walker, Louis Marx & Co. (New York, New York), 1929 ..... 360.00

Windup tin "Le Pochard-The Drunkard," w/part of original box w/original label attached, Martin-France 380.00

Windup tin "Nina" cat chasing a mouse, Lehmann (Germany), No. 790, original box w/chromolithographed scene of cat & mouse 1,550.00

Windup tin seal, Lehmann (Germany), early 20th c. 232.00

Windup tin "Slugger Champions," flat tin boxing figures on square boxing ring base, works, U.S. Zone, Germany, w/box (lid detached) & key, 4" sq. 85.00

Windup tin "Stubborn Donkey," Lehmann (Germany), w/clown, original box ....350.00 to 425.00

Windup tin zeppelin "Chicago," Ferdinand Strauss (Germany), ca. 1930 .... 506.00

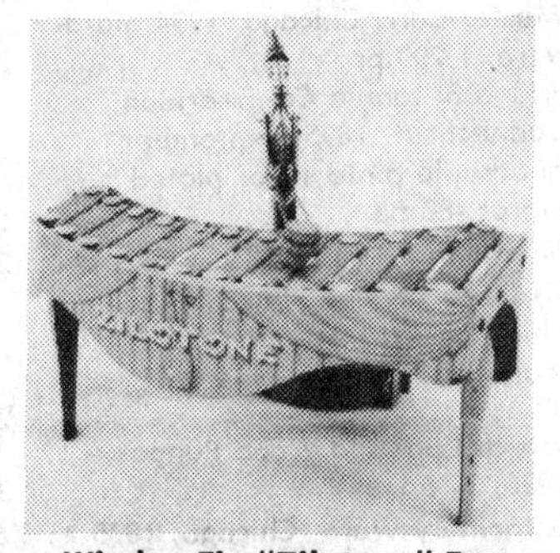

Windup Tin "Zilotone" Toy

Windup tin "Zilotone," Wolverine Supply & Manufacturing Co. (Pittsburgh, Penn.), clown figure playing xylophone, ca. 1930 (ILLUS.) .. 300.00

TRADE CATALOGS

M. W. Savage Co. Catalog

Altman (B.) & Co., New York, 1925-26, Fall & Winter, fashions for women & children, 100 pp. ... $40.00

American-LaFrance Firefighting Equipment, 1929, clothing & badges, 176 pp. 38.00

American Mechanical Toy Co., Dayton, Ohio, 1912, w/original mailing envelope.................... 37.00

Andrews School Merchandise, 1898, 197 pp. 90.00

Atlas Portland Cement Co., 1900, "Concrete Country Residences," 168 pp. 85.00

Baird (Chas.) Co., Providence, Rhode Island, 1912, jewelry, 7 x 10", 200 pp. 25.00

Barney & Berry Ice Skates, 1909, 4½ x 6½", 32 pp. 25.00

Bennett (J.M.) Wholesale Jewelers, 1928, 490 pp. 35.00

Bent (G.W.) Co., 1911, "Largest Bedding House in New England," 108 pp. 35.00

Bostwick's Gates & Gratings, 1882, 24 pp. 40.00

Bowen Wholesale Explosives, 1931, w/three inserts, original envelope, 32 pp. 45.00

Bradley (Milton), 1938-39, games, 64 pp. 40.00

Butler Bros., "Our Drummer," Minneapolis, May 1922, wholesale general merchandise 35.00

Carson Pirie Scott & Co., Chicago, 1897 .... 15.00

Clark (B.) Co., New York, 1895, jewelry, soft cover, 8 x 10½", 144 pp. 60.00

Claxton Printing Co., 1888, sample book, 86 offerings, gilt-edged 69.00
Cline (E.) & Co., Chicago, 1906, Thomas Edison motion picture projectors, magic lanterns, stereopticans & slide materials, 6 x 9", 24 pp. 95.00
Columbia Bicycles, 1881, high-wheelers 65.00
Consolidated Soda Fountain, 1929, color illustrations 50.00
Crescent Bicycles, 1898, 5 x 8", 48 pp. 20.00
Cretors, 1908, popcorn wagons, 15 x 17¼", 36 pp. 500.00
DeLaval Separators, 1918, 64 pp. ... 15.00
DeMoulin Bros. & Co., Chicago, 1905, burlesque, trickery & Lodge costumes, 6 x 9", 128 pp. 65.00
Dennison Stationers' Specialties, 1905, tags & party crafts, 149 pp. 19.00
Diamond Dyes, 1892, color illustrations 10.00
Dixon Graphite Pencils, 1879, 15 pp. 12.00
Eastman Kodak Co., 1910, 5½ x 8", 64 pp. 30.00
Evans (H.C.), 1913, trade stimulators & prizes 45.00
Fairbanks & Co., 1889, scales, 28 pp. 60.00
Falker Stern, 1899, glassware, china & fancy goods, 64 pp. 38.00
Garland Stoves, 1892, 168 pp. 120.00
Gilbert Clocks, 1918, 28 pp. 50.00
Godfrey (Chas.) Co., 1905, fishing tackle, guns & hunting knives, 5 x 7", 64 pp. 25.00
Gould (L.) Toys, 1939-40, 337 pp. 58.00
Graflex Cameras, 1915, 6½ x 10", 64 pp. 30.00
Great Western Stove Co., 1926, 215 pp. 85.00
Gregory & Sons, 1891, "Retail Catalogue of Warranted Vegetable, Flower and Grain Seeds Grown and Sold by James J. H. Gregory, Marblehead Mass.," 56 pp. 12.50
Gulbransen Player Pianos, 1920, 6¼ x 9¼", 32 pp. 17.50
Harrington, Richardson Arms Co., 1932, revolvers & shotguns, 28 pp. 30.00
Haw Hardware Co., Ottumwa, Iowa, No. 5, 612 pp. 85.00
Heinz Stove Co., 1916, stoves & ranges, 168 pp. 60.00
Hohner Piano Accordions, 1936, 23 pp. 13.00
Horder's Office Supplies, Chicago, 1922, furniture, 222 pp. 40.00
Incandescent Supply Co., 1920, lighting fixtures, lamps & shades, 9 x 12", 50 pp. 40.00
Indian Motorcycles, 1915, lithograph of Indians on cover, 24 pp. 65.00
Jewel Carriage Co., Cincinnati, 1909, "Breeze Motor Buggy," 8½ x 10", 24 pp. 65.00
Johnson (H.A.) Co., Boston, 1910, baker's & confectionary supplies, display cases, ice cream tables, refrigerators & automobile cake ornaments, 187 pp. 50.00
Keds Footwear, 1926, 48 pp. 6.00
Kenton Hardware Co., 1925, American toys 150.00
Kirk (Samuel) & Sons, Baltimore, 1933, silverware, 64 pp. 28.00
Koken, 1928, barber chairs & poles, color illustrations, 140 pp. 95.00
Larkin, 1912, Spring & Summer, 127 pp. 55.00
Lockwood Taylor Hardware Co., Cleveland, 1906, ornate lighting fixtures, lamp shades, etc., 9 x 12", 50 pp. 55.00
Mandel Bros., Chicago, 1914, ladies fashions 35.00
Marietta Chair Co., 1889, Eastlake-style furniture 95.00
Mason Machine Works, 1876, cotton machinery, 60 pp. 100.00
Maurer (W.A.), 1912, wholesale sterling silver, cut glass & dinnerware, 171 pp. 95.00
May & Malone Inc., 1927, sporting goods, 100 pages of fishing tackle, 260 pp. 35.00
McCormick-Deering Hay Machines, 1915, 31 pp. 16.00
McMaster-Carr, Chicago, 1934, hardware, 1,200 pp. 25.00
Meriden Britannia Co., Meriden, Connecticut, 1895, September, quadruple plate silver plated wares, 80 pp. 22.00
Millers Falls Tools, 1913, No. 32 .... 25.00
Mills (Thos.) & Bro., Inc., Philadelphia, ca. 1915, ice cream manufacturing equipment, 60 pp. 22.50
Monarch Coal and Wood Ranges, 1936, 34 pp. 30.00
Montgomery Ward, Chicago, 1875 .. 65.00
Montgomery Ward, 1918, October, groceries 30.00
Montgomery Ward, 1931, Spring & Summer 40.00
Montgomery Ward, 1950, Christmas 35.00
Nagel (W.G.), 1910, No. 6, lighting fixtures & chandeliers, 143 pp. ... 80.00

National Bellas Hess, 1929, Spring & Summer 26.00
National Cloak & Suit Co., 1919, Spring & Summer, color illustrations, 423 pp. 25.00
New Idea Dress Patterns, 1919, Summer, 48 pp. 16.00
Northwestern Stamp Works, 1895, police, fire & railroad badges, carriage plates, brass labels & trade checks, 34 pp. 33.00
Noyes Bros. & Cutler, 1884, "Importers & Wholesale Dealers in Drugs, Chemicals & Patent Medicines," w/advertising, hardbound, 750 pp. 200.00
Old Trusty Incubator, 1923, 65 pp. . . 16.00
Orgill Bros., 1935, plows, stoves, watches, jewelry & Remington pocket knives, hardbound 85.00
Osborne (D.M.) & Co., 1880's, farm implements, 20 pp. 15.00
Ovington's, 1923, china & crystal, 23 pp. 12.00
Peacock (C.D.), Chicago, 1921, jewelry & watches, 166 pp. 75.00
Peck & Hills Furniture Co., 1922, tapestry rugs, color illustrations, 9 x 12", 480 pp. 75.00
Pickard China, 1912, 32 pp. 44.00
Pitkin-Brooks, 1897, imported banquet, table, Gone-with-the-Wind & ceiling lamps, 25 pp. 44.00
Pressed Steel Car Co., 1922, railroad passenger cars, subway cars, mining & cattle cars, street & interurban trolleys, suede cover, 10 x 12", 289 pp. 100.00
St. Louis Jewelry, Clock & Silver Co., 1930, color illustrations, embossed brown cover, 9 x 12", 320 pp. 150.00
Savage (M.W.) Co., Minneapolis, 1923, Spring & Summer, No. 42, clothing, dry goods, jewelry, household goods & hardware, 320 pp. (ILLUS.) 22.00
Schwinn Bicycles, 1950, Black Phantom featured, 8 x 9", 12 pp. 15.00
Sears & Roebuck, 1921, Fall & Winter, 1,276 pp. 40.00
Shapleigh Hardware, 1923, 3,008 pp. 120.00
Simmons Hardware, 1880, 1,140 pp. 300.00
Stevens (Charles A.) Co., Chicago, 1904, ladies' fashions, 32 pp. 32.50
Tiffany Studios, New York, 1913, "Character & Individuality in Decorations & Furnishings" 95.00
U.S. Tent & Awning Co., Chicago, 1914, big top tents & general circus supplies 75.00
Von Lengerke & Antoine, Chicago, 1929, guns, hunting equipment, dog supplies, footballs & knives, 126 pp. 30.00
West End Pottery Co., East Liverpool, Ohio, 1920's, 9 x 12", 45 pp. 45.00
William (Charles) Stores, New York, 1928, Spring & Summer 35.00
Willowcraft Shops, 1913, wicker, 52 pp. 175.00
Wurlitzer, 1929, No. 131, musical instruments, 136 pp. plus index 95.00
Yale Locks, 1929, hard cover, leather bound, 8 x 11", 517 pp. . . . 75.00
Young (Otto) & Co., 1902, pocket watches, silver tableware items & jewelry, 576 pp. 125.00

TRAMP ART

Tramp Art Cupboard

Tramp art flourished in the United States from about 1875 into the 1930's. These chip-carved woodenwares, mostly in the form of boxes or other useful items, were made mainly from old cigar boxes although fruit and vegetable crates were also used. The wood is predominantly edge-carved and subsequently layered to create a unique effect. Completed items were given an overall stained finish which was sometimes further enhanced with painted highlights. Though there seems to be no written record of the artists, many of whom were itinerants, there is a growing interest in collecting this aptly named ware.

Box, cov., chip-carved layers on lid

& sides, gold trim, 10 x 5", 6" h. $35.00

Christmas tree holder, solid fence & arched gate enclosing stepped cylindrical holder, chip-carved pyramidal layers on sides, corner posts, worn white paint w/green trim & gold highlights, 32" sq., 8¼" h. 175.00

Cigar box, glass sides, wooden lid w/chip-carved tulip decoration ... 45.00

Cupboard, corner hanging-type, quarter-round cylinder w/leaf-carved superstructure, door applied w/a print of a lovely young woman at the helm of a boat entitled "Talk to the Man at the Wheel," surmounted by chip-carved stars & geometric motifs, opening to two shelves, heart-form handle, painted overall in black w/gilt & green highlights, America, ca. 1920, 13" w., 24½" h. (ILLUS.) 770.00

Doll dresser, shaped crest above framed mirror above rectangular top over two long drawers w/porcelain knobs above two cupboard doors w/porcelain knobs, shaped skirt, made from packing crates & boxes, chip-carved trim, old dark varnish finish, 11¾" w., 30" h. ... 65.00

Dresser, child's, original beige & green paint 125.00

Jewelry box w/hinged lid, diamond-shaped, flared rectangular base, chip-carved layers, America, ca. 1930, 9½" l., 7" h. 66.00

Jewelry box, cov., chip-carved layers forming pyramid on lid & circle designs on sides, footed, satin lined 125.00

Mirror, chip-carved frame, 5¾ x 7¾" 45.00

Picture frame, chip-carved sides w/wooden hearts at corners, 8 x 10" 24.00

Picture frame, cross-bar, intricately chip-carved, old natural finish, 16¼ x 21¼" 25.00

Rocking chair, sewing-type, slightly arched back crest w/row of low knobs above row of square chip-carved panels in crest, carved serpentine back stiles & low arms extending front of wooden seat, paneled aprons on seat, chip-carved square legs to rockers, old alligatored varnish & brown paint w/two porcelain buttons on back, found in Indiana (replaced seat) 175.00

TRAPS

Bear, "Triumph," iron, 41 x 25" $165.00

Eel, wooden, woven splint, wood top, 17½" 150.00

Fly, blown clear glass, round w/sheared mouth w/an applied ring on the neck, three applied feet w/hatch-marked decoration, 5½" h. 60.00

Fly, screen dome w/tin base, "Bug & Fly Trap, Nesko, Shur Katch" 45.00

Fly, screen w/tin top, "Sur-Katchem," 10½ x 6" 35.00

Mouse, wooden, dead-fall type, dome in frame, round dish base, 18th c., 5 x 7" 440.00

Mouse, "Victor," four-hole choker-type 14.00

TRAYS, SERVING & CHANGE

Arrow Beer Tray

Both serving & change trays once used in taverns, cafes and the like and usually bearing advertising for a beverage maker are now being widely collected. All trays listed are heavy tin serving trays, unless otherwise noted. Also see COCA-COLA ITEMS.

Akron White Rock Export, round $375.00

American Steamship Line (change) .. 60.00

American Yeoman (change) 25.00

Andrew White Cigars (change) 75.00

Anheuser-Busch Brewing Ass'n., St. Louis, Missouri, brewery & factory buildings w/trains & wagons, pre-Prohibition, 19" oval. .1,000.00 to 1,200.00

Anheuser-Busch, "Budweiser Beer," St. Louis, Missouri, fox hunters by fireplace w/shadow of fox 85.00

Anheuser-Busch Malt Nutrine, St. Louis, Missouri, Madonna Della Sedia by Raffello, Feb. 1905, 10" d. 120.00
Apollinaris Table Water (change) ... 25.00
Arrow Beer, large scene of King Gambrinus seated on throne amid wild reveling, post-Prohibition (ILLUS.) 125.00
Baker's Chocolate, "La Belle Chocolatiere," 1910, 12" d. 150.00
Baker's (Walter) Chocolate, four advertisements on oval tray 85.00
Ballentine Beer, Newark, New Jersey, three rings shown (change) .. 45.00
Bartel's Brewing Co., Syracuse, New York, "The Night Watchman," dated 1907 (change) 110.00
Bartel's $5,000 Beer, lady & bottle, pre-Prohibition 600.00
Ben Franklin Insurance (change) 15.00
Bettendorf (Iowa) Wagon Co., wagon pictured (change) 60.00
Billy Baxter Ginger Ale, bird scene 45.00
Binghamton Ice Cream (change) 125.00
Booth Shoe Co. (change) 46.00
Boston Beer Company, Boston, Massachusetts, truck pictured 475.00
Boyce Motometer, "Ford" in script (change) 50.00
Brasserie Karcher, Paris, France, girl on beer barrel (change) 65.00
Braumeister, Milwaukee's Choicest Beer, brewmaster holding bottle & glass 45.00
Buffalo Beer, New York, New York, table scene 210.00
Buffalo Brewing Co., bottle-shaped (change) 350.00
Bull Frog Ale (change) 45.00
Burkhardt's Beer, Burkhardt's Brewery, Akron, Ohio, factory scene, pre-Prohibition 450.00
Canadian Ace Beer & Ale, w/oyster shell & fish (change) 65.00
Carstairs White Seal, wood, 12" d. .. 25.00
Carta Blanca, lady & man dining 75.00
Case & Martin's Connecticut Pies (change) 22.00
Chambersburg Engineering, 50th Year, 1897-1947, brass (change) .. 12.50
Columbia Brewery, Tacoma, Washington, Liberty & eagle, pre-Prohibition, 9" d. 350.00
Congress Beer, Congress Brewing Company, Brooklyn, New York, eagle decoration in five colors, pre-1900 .... 650.00
Consumer's Brewery, New Orleans, Louisiana, factory scene, pre-Prohibition, large oval 1,100.00
Coors Beer, Adolph Coors Co., Golden, Colorado, mountain scene, pre-Prohibition 200.00
Cortez Cigars "For Men of Brains" (change) 17.00
Cudahy, boy pictured (change) 49.00
DeLaval Cream Separators, "The World's Standard," lady using separator, small child nearby (change) 95.00
Delta Air Lines To California, 20th Anniversary, 12" d. 25.00
Dick's Beer, factory scene, pre-Prohibition 259.00
Diehl (Christian) Brewing Co., Defiance, Ohio, bottle of Diehl Beer & semi-nude lady on mountain top, 1930's 250.00
Doelger (Peter) Beer, New York, factory scene (change) 95.00
Dohne's Carnation Gum, 1920's (change) 65.00
Dowagiac (Doe Wah Jack) Round Oak Stoves (change) 20.00
Dr. Pepper, girl in green dress holding two bottles of Dr. Pepper 245.00
East Side Brewing, Detroit, Michigan, Oriental boy 60.00
Eberle's Blue Star Export, Eberle Brewing Co., Jackson, Michigan, wood-grained, rectangular 45.00
Ebling Brewing Co., New York City, brewery scene, rectangular 1,150.00
El Verso Cigars, man in chair w/girl in smoke dreams (change) 40.00

Enterprise Brewing Company Tray

Enterprise Brewing Co., San Francisco, California, young lady w/horse (ILLUS.) 350.00
Enterprise Brewing Co., girl w/ribbons in hair 425.00
Falls City Brewery, Louisville, Kentucky, maid w/bottles pictured ... 450.00
Felsenbrau Beer, Cincinnati, Ohio, 18 marching waiters, post-Prohibition 85.00
Fosselmans Ice Cream, Kewpie baseball player w/bat eating ice cream, hat says "Kewpie Baseball Team," signed "O'Neill" 450.00
Fox Head 400 Beer, Waukesha, Wisconsin, fox's head pictured 52.00

Franklin Life Insurance (change) 20.00
Fuller Johnson, gas engine shown (change) 65.00
Globe Brewing, Utica, New York, old English lettering 350.00
Goebel Brewing Co., Beaver Dam, Wisconsin, Dutch girl w/baskets of beer (change) 45.00
Golden West Brewery, Oakland, California, factory scene 175.00
Grain Belt Beers, Minneapolis, Minnesota (change) 25.00
Gravel Springs Water (change) 65.00
Gretz Beer, Philadelphia, Pennsylvania, man on highwheeler bike, post-Prohibition 45.00
Hampden Brewing Co., Willimansett, Massachusetts, "Who Wants The Handsome Waiter," shows wrinkled old man as waiter, ca. 1935, 13" d. 150.00
Hanlen Bros., Harrisburg, Pennsylvania, Liquor Dealers (change) 65.00
Hanley's "Peerless Ale," Providence, Rhode Island, w/bulldog, post-Prohibition 65.00
Huebner Brewing Co., Toledo, Ohio, lady seated at table pictured, 12" d. 250.00
Hopski Soda, frog pouring drinks 50.00
Hudson County Consumers Brewing Co., Hoboken, New Jersey, brewery scene, rectangular 550.00
Iroquois Beer, bust of Indian w/full headdress (change) 110.00
Jones (Frank), "Homestead Ale," Portsmouth, New Hampshire (change) 37.50
Koppitz-Melchers Brewing Co., elves brewing beer, pre-Prohibition, oblong 225.00
Lykens Brewing Co., bust portrait of lady w/horse, 13 x 17" oval 475.00
Malto Dextrine Tonic, woman drinking, tray printed w/double image (change) 85.00
Mathie Brewing Co., Los Angeles, bear drinking beer from bottles in wooden case, ca. 1910, 13¼" sq. 400.00
Maxwell House Coffee (change) 15.00
Mitchell's Best Flour, pretty girl w/ribbon in long hair (change) 85.00
"Montgomery (Ala.) Confederate Monument & Capitol," 13 x 10½" 25.00
Monticello Whiskey, horses & dogs (change) 65.00
Montrose Dairy Parker-Brawner Co. Ice Cream, Kewpie eating from large sundae 250.00
Moroney Army & Navy Whiskey, bottle of whiskey shown (change) 65.00

National Brewing Co., St. Louis, Griesedieck Bros., Prop., bottle of beer, "G. B." & flag in circle & factory scene ....450.00 to 500.00
Neff Bros. Brewing Co., Denver, Colorado, dogs chewing cards, 1894-1916, 16 x 13" 95.00
New Home Sewing Machines, grandma sewing seat of boy's pants while he's still in them (change) .. 125.00
Oakville Co., Waterbury, Conn., hand holding safety pin, oval (change) 60.00
Old Reliable Coffee, pretty girl facing forward (change) 75.00
Oneida Brewing Co., Utica, New York, standing Indian chief in center, porcelain, 12" d. 350.00
Orange Julep, bathing beauty, ca. 1929, 10½ x 13¼" 135.00
Pacific Malt & Brewing Co., "Pacific Beer," 'Mt. Tacoma' (Mt. Rainier) scene, ca. 1912, 12" d. 125.00
Pepsi Cola, four sides marked "Enjoy Pepsi Cola," 13¼ x 13¼" 16.00
Persil Wash Compound, box pictured (change) 40.00
President Suspenders, pretty girl w/flower in her hair (change) 95.00
Priscilla, Maid of New England, Furniture & Carpet Co., Minneapolis (change) 85.00
Radnor Water, fake wood-grained background w/yellow lettering around center colored scene of monk opening bottle of water w/another bottle sitting on table next to him, Kelly green rim, 11½" d. 51.00
Rainier Beer, cowgirl on horse, ca. 1905, 13" d. 450.00
Red Cross Stoves (change) 42.50

Resinol Soap Change Tray

Resinol Soap & Ointment, bust portrait of beautiful woman, 4¼" d., change (ILLUS.) 102.00
Roi-Tan Cigar, woman lighting cigar for man (change) 100.00

Ruhstaller Beer, man wearing fez, 1910, 16 x 18" oval 450.00
Frank X. Schwab Co., Liquor Dealers, Buffalo, little boy carrying wooden keg, 10½ x 13¼" 245.00
Universal Stove & Ranges, world pictured (change) 60.00
Welsbach Lighting, woman & child in living room (change) 95.00
White Rock Table Water, semi-nude lady on rock looking into water, black border, 4½ x 6¼" (change) 100.00
William Tell Flour, pretty girl (change) 100.00

TRIVETS

George Washington Trivet

When numbers are noted following trivets listed below they refer to numbers in the long out-of-print books, "Trivets," Book I and "Trivets, Old and Re-Pro," Book II, both by Dick Hankenson. All are cast iron except where otherwise noted.

Arched brass w/openwork design top on three tall wrought-iron legs w/penny feet & cross braces, turned wood handle, 15" l., 12" h. (age crack in handle) $130.00
"Colt" in cut-out letters, Book I, No. 130 .... 12.00
Double broom & heart (brass) 75.00
Eagle & Heart center, scrolled wreath border, 9" d. 65.00
Enterprise "E," Book I, No. 114 ..... 17.00
Folded oak leaf design, footed, 19th c. 47.50
George Washington bust in center, scroll designs at end of flat handle, 9" l., brass (ILLUS.) 38.00
Harp-form brass top engraved w/foliate sprigs, on wrought-iron penny feet, black-painted turned wood handle, 11½" l. 55.00
Horse in center, footed, 6" d., 3½" h. (brass) 68.00
Horseshoe & Good Luck center, two horses at top, 8½ x 4½" 20.00
Odd Fellows, w/heart in hand, Book I, No. 12 .... 26.00
Rectangular rack w/five crossbands on short legs w/long handle w/loop at end, hand-wrought, 7¾" l. 135.00
Rectangular rack w/five crossbars on short corner legs, long handle w/heart-shaped end formed by curled tips, hand-wrought, 11" l... 225.00
Rectangular, top pierced w/design of birds, paw feet, 6 x 10½", 3¾" h. (brass) 60.00
Rope twist quatrefoil w/matching legs on shoe feet, hand-wrought, 4½ x 4½" 80.00
Round brass top w/florette pattern in center, wrought-iron legs, black painted turned wood handle, overall 12½" l. 55.00
Starflower in center & six interlocking openwork circles, round, 5¾" 45.00
Tulip, bold stylized flower w/good detail in round border, 5¼" d. ... 50.00
U-shaped pierced brass top w/wooden handle, thin flat iron legs w/medial iron support, 19th c., 11¼" 385.00

TRUNKS

Painted Immigrant Trunk

These box-like portable containers are used for transporting or storing personal possessions. There are many styles to choose from since they have been made from the 16th century onward. Thousands arrived in this country with the immigrants and more were turned out to accommodate the westward movement of the population. The popular dome-top trunk was designed to prevent water from accumulating on the top. Hinges, locks and construction, along with condition and age, greatly determine the values of older trunks.

Dome-top, miniature, painted & decorated pine, rectangular w/red-painted wire bail handle on lid opening to a paper-lined interior, the top & sides painted w/feathers, flowers, scallops & swags in red, yellow & white on a black-painted ground, Southbridge, Massachusetts area, first half 19th c., 11¾" l., 5" h. $1,375.00

Dome-top, pine, mitered corners, top & front panel w/red, yellow & white swags & arcs on black ground, iron carrying handles, central Massachusetts, ca. 1825, 28 x 14", 11¼" h. (hinge repairs) 550.00

Dome-top, painted pine, decorated overall w/boldly painted scallops in red & yellow vinegar graining, original iron hinges, end handles & lock, probably New England, ca. 1830, 26" l., 14" deep, 11½" h. . . 1,760.00

Dome-top, wooden, dovetail construction, wrought-iron hinges, lock & hasp, original brass bail side handles, original red graining w/yellow striping & green oval on lid w/initials "E.D.," 29½" l. 200.00

Dome-top, baroque studded leather, hinged top opening to a lined interior above rectangular sides w/wrought-iron hasps & carrying handles, top & three sides embellished w/nailhead decoration, Dutch, late 17th c., 33" l., 18" h. 1,870.00

Flat-top, green & tan leather w/brass stud trim, original oval brass handle, embossed brass escutcheon, 15½" l. 350.00

Immigrant-type, red-stained pine, hand-wrought iron trim & nails, carved initials on side, interior w/till, 48 x 25", 24" h. 275.00

Immigrant-type, dome-top, painted pine, three-board top opening to plain interior w/interior wrought-iron strapwork, front colorfully painted in yellow, green, blue, black & white w/floral medallions & sprigs enclosing the inscription "aurel 1850," w/further inscription above, sides w/wrought-iron loop handles, Norway, early 19th c., 46 1/5" l., 29" h. (ILLUS.) 550.00

UNGER BROTHERS

Herman and Eugene Unger worked as jewelers and silversmiths in Newark, New Jersey, from 1881. Their early productions were designed with elaborate rococo scrolls but after a visit to Paris, in 1901, their work began to reflect the Art Nouveau movement. They became masters of this style, characterized by limply swaying, curving lines enhanced with flowers and tendrils and by the appearance of figures, predominantly female, that seemed to melt away with the lines of the objects they adorned. Sterling silver dresser and desk sets, along with ashtrays, cigarette and match cases, sewing accessories and pocket flasks reflect an exquisite development of the Art Nouveau taste, so popular in the first decade of this century and collectors vie to acquire items bearing the interlaced U and B trademark of the Unger Brothers. The company's Art Nouveau productions ceased about 1910, but they continued to produce a simpler line of silver until 1914 when the firm switched their production to airplane parts.

Box, cov., sterling silver, pale enameled amethyst top, 3" d. $175.00

Brooch, sterling silver, model of a lion's head w/green stone eyes, gold-washed 235.00

Button hook, sterling silver hollow handle, cupid riding dolphin, two seahorses, etc. decoration on front & reverse, 7¾" l. 75.00

Cigarette case, hinged, curved, design of nude maiden sitting on rock w/waves & gulls, 2" w., 3" h. 140.00

Flask, sterling silver repousse floral scrolls on bottom half, diamond-cut cut glass top half, detachable cap, inscribed "3.24.'98," late 19th c., 5¼" l. 220.00

Nail buffer, Beaded patt. 25.00

Nut dishes, scalloped edges, orchids & swirled stems in relief, 3½" d., set of 6 . . . . 160.00

Pencil case, "Four Vices," embossed high relief race horse & jockey heading for homestretch, a bottle of bubbly, a charming dancing girl

& a winning poker hand w/four aces 110.00
Watch fob, four roses design, catalog No. 8085 . . . . 235.00

STERLING SILVER FLATWARE PATTERNS

DUVAINE

Almond scoop 95.00
Coffee spoon, w/monogram 29.00
Cream ladle 70.00
Demitasse spoon 18.00
Dessert spoon 45.00
Fruit spoon 39.00
Gravy ladle 115.00
Luncheon fork 42.00
Meat fork 125.00
Olive fork 65.00
Olive spoon 70.00
Pickle fork 75.00
Sardine fork 75.00
Sauce ladle 75.00
Serving spoon 55.00
Sugar shell 46.00
Sugar tongs 60.00
Tablespoon 80.00
Teaspoon 32.00

NARCISSUS

Berry spoon 85.00
Butter pick 58.00
Butter serving knife 45.00
Claret ladle 225.00
Dinner knife 30.00
Food pusher 88.00
Grapefruit spoon 38.00
Luncheon fork 35.00
Mustard spreader 45.00
Nut scoop, fluted 95.00
Olive spoon, pierced 58.00
Pickle fork 30.00
Salad serving fork, gold-washed 115.00
Serving spoon 75.00
Sugar spoon 45.00
Sugar tongs 56.00
Teaspoon 19.00
Tomato server 98.00

PASSAIC

Asparagus server, hooded 495.00
Bonbon shovel, gold-washed bowl . . 25.00
Cheese scoop, enameled 95.00
Claret ladle 160.00
Cocktail fork 25.00
Demitasse spoon, gold-washed bowl 20.00
Dinner fork 48.00
Dinner knife 49.00
Gravy ladle 90.00
Lettuce fork 88.00
Luncheon fork 38.00
Mustard ladle 69.00
Olive spoon, pierced 66.00
Sardine fork 95.00
Tablespoon 59.00
Teaspoon 25.00
Tomato server 110.00

VALENTINES

Fold-out type, lacy background w/romantic scene, Germany, ca. 1890, 6½ x 11" $25.00
Fold-out type, die-cut lady, lacy border, ca. 1890, 13 x 10" 25.00
Fraktur valentine, folding-type, pen, ink & colorful watercolor hearts & circles, verses revealed as paper is unfolded, framed under glass, 17 x 17" (minor fold damage) 385.00
Mechanical-type, bear w/movable arms 18.00
Mechanical-type, black boy & girl, chicken & duck w/Valentine cards in beaks pop out of watermelons 25.00
Raphael Tuck publisher, "Love's Greeting," five double heart-shaped cards attached by pink ribbon, little girls pictured on each card, original box 45.00
Scherenschnitte (paper cutwork) & watercolor, simple cut-out design & single verse, dated 1863 . . . . . . 85.00

VENDING/GAMBLING MACHINES

Watling's "Treasury" Slot Machine

Arcade, "Auto Stereoscope," Mills, ca. 1905, table model w/stand . . . $650.00
Arcade, "Chinese Crystal Gazer," fortune teller 495.00

Arcade, "Electricity is Life," Mills Novelty Co., 1904 .... 4,500.00
Arcade, "Grip Tester," Gatter Novelty, ca. 1925 .... 1,500.00
Arcade, "Lighthouse," strength tester, Globe Mfg., ca. 1924 ..... 1,100.00
Arcade, "Love Tester," thermometer type, Exhibit Supply, ca. 1925 .... 650.00
Arcade, "Red Top Lift," strength tester, Caille Bros., 1904 .... 1,900.00
Arcade, "Whom Shall You Marry," fortune teller, Exhibit Supply, ca. 1925 .... 1,500.00
Candy vendor, "Old Mill," International Mutoscope Co., ca. 1928 ... 2,800.00
Gambling, Bally's "Double Bell" counter-top slot machine, 5-cent & 25-cent play 2,700.00
Gambling, Bally's "Draw Bell" console slot machine, 5-cent play 570.00
Gambling, Bally's "Reliance" dice counter-top slot machine, 25-cent play 3,200.00
Gambling, Bally's "Spark Plug" horse race, 5-cent play, 1934 .... 1,600.00
Gambling, Caille's "Double Centaur" upright slot machine, 25-cent & 50-cent play, ca. 1905 .... 20,500.00
Gambling, Caille's "Liberty Bell" cast-iron counter-top slot machine, ca. 1909 .... 7,250.00
Gambling, Caille's "Lone Star" upright slot machine, 5-cent play, ca. 1902 .... 18,000.00
Gambling, Caille's "New Century" floor model slot machine, 5-cent play, 1901 .... 9,250.00
Gambling, Fey's "The Thirty-six Midget" dice game, Art Deco design, 6½ x 7½ x 9½", 1920's-1930's 595.00
Gambling, Field's "Five Jacks" counter-top slot machine, 5-cent play 900.00
Gambling, Jennings' "Club Chief" slot machine, 5-cent play, ca. 1940's 700.00
Gambling, Jennings' "Silver Moon Chief" counter-top slot machine, 5-cent play, ca. 1941 .... 1,250.00
Gambling, Keeney's "Super Bell" console slot machine, 5-cent play, 1941-51 (unrestored) 395.00
Gambling, Mills' "Cricket" upright floor model slot machine, ca. 1904 .... 11,000.00
Gambling, Mills' "Dewey" upright slot machine, 5-cent play 8,000.00
Gambling, Mills' "Dewey" upright slot machine, 25-cent play 10,500.00
Gambling, Mills' "Golden Falls" counter-top slot machine, 1-cent play 1,150.00
Gambling, Mills' "Owl" counter-top slot machine, 25-cent play, ca. 1924 .... 4,500.00
Gambling, Pace's "All-Star Comet" counter-top slot machine, 5-cent play, 1936 .... 1,200.00
Gambling, Pace's "Rocket" counter-top slot machine, 5-cent play, 1939 .... 1,100.00
Gambling, Victor's "Little Six America" counter-top slot machine, 5-cent play, ca. 1907 .... 15,000.00
Gambling, Watling's "Cherry Front - Rol-A-Top" counter-top slot machine, 5-cent play, ca. 1935 ..... 3,000.00
Gambling, Watling's "Treasury" counter-top slot machine, 1-cent play, ca. 1936 (ILLUS.) 2,900.00
Gum vendor, "Ben Franklin," 1-cent play, Mills 2,500.00
Hand lotion vendor, "Jergens Lotion," 1-cent play 175.00
Peanut vendor, "Asco Hot Nut" vendor, eight-sided globe w/light on top, 1940's, scarce 175.00
Peanut vendor, "Challenger Triple Hot" 250.00
Pinball machine, "Avalon," Exhibit Supply Co., 5-cent play, ca. 1936 (restored) 575.00
Pinball machine, "Fifty Grand," ornate legs, Automatic Games Co., Inglewood, California, ca. 1920's .. 400.00
Trade stimulator, "Ace," five card draw model, Daval, 5-cent play, ca. 1940-51 .... 150.00
Trade stimulator, "Banker," 5-reel poker type, Caille 2,100.00
Trade stimulator, "Check Boy," Mills, ca. 1907 .... 3,750.00
Trade stimulator, "High-Low," Mills, 1-cent or 5-cent play, w/marquee 6,200.00
Trade stimulator, "The Kelley," 5-reel model, Kelley Co., 1903-12 .... 2,300.00
Trade stimulator, "Penny Draw," Stevens, 1936-39 .... 250.00
Trade stimulator, "Wasp," Caille, on swivel base, ca. 1905 .... 3,800.00

VICTORIAN WHIMSEYS

Hats, boots and slippers are just a few of the knickknacks turned out in the Victorian era, in both glass and ceramics. Dishes were made in the shape of stoves; bowls were shaped as wide-brimmed hats; toothpick holders as coal scuttles. We list only a few of the wide assortment of Victorian whimseys that abounded in the late 19th century.

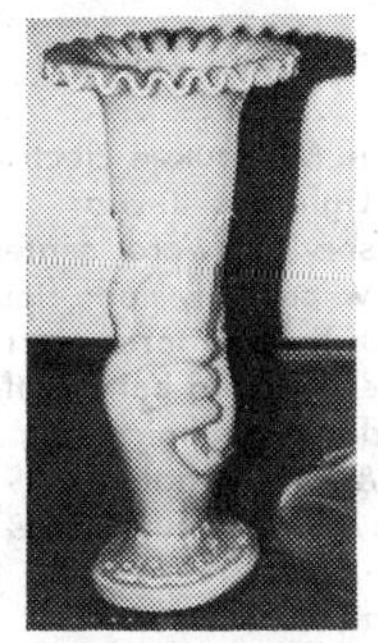

Victorian Hand Vase

GLASS

Bottle, hand-shaped, clear, "The Glad Hand," 6" h. $30.00
Boot, man's, w/spur, black amethyst 45.00
Boot, blown, rubina, applied clear rigaree on rim & leaf on boot 165.00
Cake stand, milk white, ribbed base, hand w/bracelet stem, Atterbury, 11½" d., 6½" h. 125.00
Chain, blown, links of amber, clear & aqua, 15" l. 120.00
Coal hod, pressed, amber, w/original wire bail 45.00
Figure of Buddha, seated, amber, signed "Gillinder," 6" h. 165.00
Hat, blown, aqua, derby w/double rim, 3 x 5" 125.00
Hat, blown, aqua, low crown w/wide rolled rim, sheared rim & pontil, 5 5/8" d., 1½" h. 65.00
Hat, blown, cranberry, Diamond Quilted patt., 3" h. 50.00
Hat, pressed, amber, Daisy & Button patt., 5 x 3¾" 26.00
Hat, pressed, clear, Petticoat patt., 3 1/8" across brim, 2 1/8" h. 35.00
Lady's leg bottle, pressed, frosted & clear, leg w/molded high-button shoe resting on hassock 110.00
Shoe, lady's high heeled-style, blown, clear w/applied decoration on instep 225.00
Shoe, lady's, blown, pink spatter cased w/clear, applied clear leaf rigaree 110.00
Shoe, lady's, pressed, vaseline, Daisy & Button patt., 11½" l. 165.00
Shoe, lady's, pressed, clear, Daisy & Button patt. on Fishscale patt. tray, made by Bryce Bros., Pittsburgh, dated 1886 . . . . 110.00
Shoe, lady's, pressed, olive green, puss-in-boot style w/overall Hobnail patt., 6" l. 34.00
Shoe, lady's, pressed, blue, Horizontal Ribbed patt. 95.00
Vase, pressed, frosted, hand holding torch, marked "Centennial 1876," 7" h. 40.00
Vase, green opaque, hand holding cornucopia w/beading & fluted rim, 8¾" h. (ILLUS.) 50.00

VIENNA ART TIN PLATES

Jamestown Exposition Tin Plate

Beautiful young woman w/long dark hair in low-cut gown in center, advertising on back for Anheuser-Busch's Malt Nutrine (slight paint loss) $41.00
Bust portrait of "Madonna Della Sedia," signed "Anheuser Busch, St. Louis Malt Nutrine" on back, ca. 1905, 10" d. 90.00
Bust portrait of Queen Louise, navy w/gold, 1905, 10" d. 50.00
Bust portrait of lovely woman w/brown hair, royal blue ground w/much gold, ca. 1905 . . . . 55.00
Cupid in mythological scene center 48.00
Girl in pink dress w/doll center, Christmas advertising promotion for C.D. Kenney Co. 65.00
Jamestown Exposition souvenir, center scene of Indian attack, portraits of John Smith & Pocahontas at side borders & dates 1607 & 1907 on pages of open book at bottom border, patd. 1905, 9" d. (ILLUS.) 85.00
Roses center, advertising Dr. Pepper, "King of Beverages" 295.00

WATCH FOBS

Advertising, "Avery Tractor," Bulldog, metal w/celluloid insert $60.00

"Henry Bosch Company" Watch Fob

Advertising, "Henry Bosch Company," white metal, embossed name, wall paper roll & tools, 1 1/8 x 1½" oval (ILLUS.) 40.00
Advertising, "Buffalo Brand Rubber Boots" 35.00
Advertising, "Buffalo Steam Roller Co." 135.00
Advertising, "Cherry Smash" 35.00
Advertising, "DeLaval Cream Separators" 65.00
Advertising, "Elastica Flour Finish" 30.00
Advertising, "Euclid Earth Moving Equipment" 23.00
Advertising, "Garland Stoves" 20.00
Advertising, "Hamilton-Brown Shoes" 45.00
Advertising, "Harley Davidson Cycles" 30.00
Advertising, "Heinz 57 Varieties" 28.00
Advertising, "Henderson Motorcycles" 100.00
Advertising, "Ingersoll-Rand," pewter, hard-hat construction worker w/jackhammer, w/leather strap 29.00
Advertising, "John Deere," brass deer & plow on mother-of-pearl insert 95.00
Advertising, "Keystone Watch Co.," 1893 .... 25.00
Advertising, "Mack Trucks" 45.00
Advertising, "Marion Power Shovel Co." 40.00
Advertising, "McCormick Thresher" 40.00
Advertising, "National Accident Insurance, Lincoln, Nebraska," enameled 14.00
Advertising, "NCR" (National Cash Register) 125.00
Advertising, "Oakland," oval, blue & white porcelain 150.00
Advertising, "Polarine Motor Oil," embossed bear 50.00
Advertising, "Poll Parrot Shoes" 65.00
Advertising, "Shell Oil" 120.00
Advertising, "Sherburne R.R. Supplies" 50.00
Advertising, "Western Ammunition" 200.00
Gold, 18k, The Milwaukee Electric Railway & Light Co. 40-year employee service award, center embossed w/partially nude figure of a woman holding torch aloft in one hand & lightning bolts in the other, border set w/thirty-four diamonds & a ruby, dated 1899 .. 1,800.00
Goldstone, oval, wide silveroid & brass strap, 1920 .... 22.00
Seal, Blackamoor, carved Labradorite face highlighted by diamond-set eyes, w/18k rose gold & silver vest, completed by an agate & carnelian seal 700.00
Souvenir, "National Sportsman," original strap 39.00
Souvenir, "Veterans of Foreign Wars, 21st Encampment," Rochester, New Hampshire, 1941 .... 20.00
Sterling silver, Victorian 39.00

WATCHES

Lady's American Waltham Watch

Hunting case, lady's, American Waltham Watch Co., 15-jewel nickel movement, multicolored gold case w/bird & floral motifs, ca. 1884 (ILLUS.) $412.50
Hunting case, lady's, Elgin Watch Co., Elgin, Illinois, 17-jewel movement, 0 size (1 5/30"), yellow gold-filled case chased w/bird in flight & foliage 135.00
Hunting case lapel watch w/brooch, lady's, Patek Philippe & Co., Geneva, Switzerland, gilt lever movement, gold bi-metallic compensation balance, white enamel

dial w/Arabic numerals & gold scroll hands, 18k gold case chased w/undulating floral design, w/similarly decorated Art Nouveau brooch, 1 1/8" d. case, ca. 1900 . . . . 1,870.00

Hunting case, man's, Elgin National Watch Co., 17-jewel movement, 16 size (1 21/30"), black Roman numerals w/small red numerals above, 14k yellow gold-filled case w/shield center engraved "1906" 250.00

Hunting case, man's, E. Howard & Co., Boston, Massachusetts, 23-jewel movement, 16 size, 14k gold case 800.00

Open face, man's, Arnold Adams, London, England, key wind, elaborate engraved gold dial, 18k yellow gold case 350.00

Open face, man's, Elgin Watch Co., 15-jewel movement, 14 size (1 19/30"), yellow gold-filled case w/engraved presentation inscription 125.00

Open face, man's, Hamilton Watch Co., Lancaster, Pennsylvania, Model 992, 21-jewel movement, 16 size, lever set, ca, 1933 . . . . 125.00

Open face, man's, E. Howard Watch Co., Waltham, Massachusetts, 17-jewel movement, 16 size, yellow gold-filled 20-year case, ca. 1909 . . . . 125.00

Open face, man's, Samson, London, England, key wind, white enamel dial w/scene of shepherd, engraved & signed brass works, silver inner case w/London hallmarks for 1788-9, gold outer case chased w/scene of two women & a soldier, w/key, 2" d. (old repairs to hinge & stem) 500.00

Open face, man's, South Bend Watch Co., South Bend, Indiana, Model No. 429, 19-jewel movement, 12 size (1 17/30"), double roller, yellow gold-filled case 75.00

Railroad, American Waltham Watch Co., 17-jewel nickel movement, 16 size, 10k yellow gold-filled case . . 165.00

Railroad, American Waltham Watch Co., Model 645, 21-jewel movement, 16 size, 14k gold case w/presentation inscription 500.00

Railroad, American Waltham Watch Co., Vanguard model, 23-jewel movement, 18 size (1 23/30"), up & down indicator, gold-filled case 390.00

WEATHERVANES

Angel Gabriel, molded copper, flying figure wearing robes & blowing his trumpet, American, 19th c., 24" l., 18" h. $37,400.00

Apple trees w/leaves & fruit, man on ladder w/basket picking apples & large basket of fruit on the ground at foot of ladder, sheet iron, supported by wrought iron straps & mounted on an arrow, small cutout directionals, probably early 20th c., 30" h. tree 5,600.00

Bull standing, copper, full-bodied well-muscled animal, on rod standard in black metal base, New England, 19th c., 25" l., 18" h. . . . 3,520.00

Car, copper, silhouetted car w/driver, molded rooster in front, Prides Crossing, Massachusetts, ca. 1914, 3' 8" l. 6,250.00

Cow, copper, flattened full-bodied animal w/sheet copper ears & zinc horns, on rod standard & black stepped wooden base, 19th c., 29½" l., 29½" h. 2,750.00

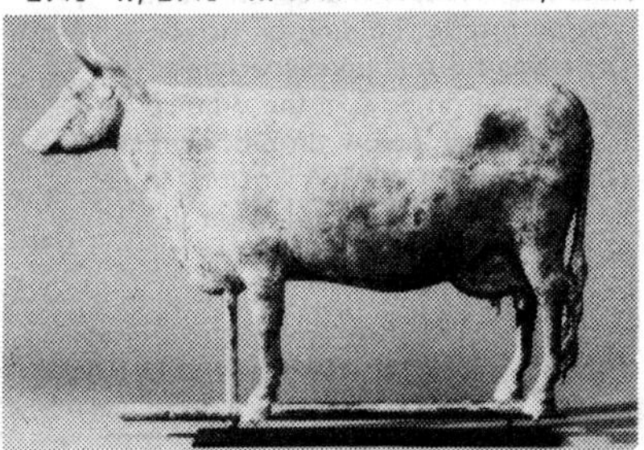

Cow Weathervane

Cow, molded copper & zinc, full-bodied animal w/cast zinc horns, mounted on a rod in a black metal base, J. Harris & Co., third quarter 19th c., restorations to gilding, 28" l., overall 24" h. (ILLUS.) 7,425.00

Eagle, molded copper & zinc, bird w/upraised wings, cast zinc head, perched on an orb, on black metal stand, A.L. Jewell & Co., Waltham, Massachusetts, third quarter 19th c., 20½" w. wingspan, 21¼" h. 3,410.00

Horse, molded copper & zinc, full-bodied horse w/left foreleg raised, forequarters & head in molded zinc w/repousse cut sheet copper mane, legs & hind quarters in molded copper w/repousse cut sheet copper tail, on rod w/arrowhead finials, in a lucite base, J. Howard & Co., West Bridgewater, Mass., third quarter 19th c., 17½" l., 16" h. 19,800.00

Horse & jockey, copper, flattened full-bodied running horse w/cast zinc head, the jockey seated on a sheet copper saddle w/stirrups & holding wire reins, original gilding, 19th c., 30½" l., 20" h. 3,025.00

Horse prancing, sheet metal, stylized figure w/pierced eyes & nostrils, raised on a wrought-iron support, painted black overall, 20th c., 17½" l., 18" h. (flaking to paint) 220.00

Horse running, copper, full-bodied, solid zinc head, flying tail, old dark patina w/traces of gilt, 29½" l. (battered, loose seams, hole in neck, front portion of mounting rod missing) 375.00

Horse & sulky w/driver, copper, full-bodied figure of a driver seated in cart w/pneumatic tires, drawn by molded trotting horse, probably J. W. Fiske, New York, third quarter 19th c., mounted on rectangular wooden base, 34½" l., 19" h. (several bulletholes, refinished) . .3,960.00

Indian, full-bodied Massasoit standing in profile, holding an arrow in one hand & a copper-sheathed wrought-iron bow in the other, posed on an arrow, in black metal base, J. Harris & Co., Boston, third quarter 19th c., 29" w., overall 37½" h. (restorations to gilding) 49,500.00

Fine Ram Weathervane

Ram, molded copper, flattened full-bodied animal w/deep repousse detail & applied repousse sheet copper horns, signed "Harris and Son, Boston," late 19th c., 28" l., 20½" h. (ILLUS.) 7,700.00

Rooster, cast iron, full-bodied bird w/well-defined feathers & sheet iron tail, later yellow paint, 19th c., 36" w., 35" h. plus rod standard 3,080.00

Rooster, copper, small cock w/molded body & pressed sheet metal tail, solid cast white metal legs, impressed maker's mark on tail, "A.B. Jewel, Waltham, Mass.," late 19th c., w/set of cast-iron directionals w/letters in brass, 23" h. 1,650.00

Sheep, sheet metal, primitive flat silhouette, traces of paint one side, worn blue & white repaint other side, iron-braced repair, wooden ball on mounting rod, modern wood base, 24½" w., 29½" h. 260.00

Stag leaping, copper, full-bodied animal w/cast zinc head & antlers, original gilding, mounted on display stand, New England, second half 19th c., 30" l. 4,510.00

Swan, wooden, flattened silhouetted form w/arched neck, incised bill painted black, tack eyes, original white paint, on black metal stand, Eastern Shore, Maryland, ca. 1920, 27½" l., 22½" h. 3,850.00

Train, copper, fashioned in the round, long engine w/straight-sided smoke stack & cow catcher, open cab & long coal car, initials "B.A." on side of coal car (Boston & Albany), early 20th c., 60" l., 12½" h. (minor damage) 12,100.00

WHISTLES

There are many types of whistles–devices used to produce whistling sounds by means of breath, air or steam forced through them. We distinguish between working steam whistles such as those used on boats, trains or in early factories as a warning, summons or command, and the small whistles used by individuals, some of which were meant to be a whimsey or toy.

Small Whistles

Earthenware pottery, model of a bird, American, mid-19th c., 2 3/8" h. $400.00

Metal, "American Song," in original box 15.00

Pewter, ca. 1880 . . . . 18.00

Steam Whistles

Brass, marked "Fulton Co.," car exhaust chime whistle 65.00

Brass, marked "Lunkenheimer," 3" d. 130.00

Brass, marked "Powell," 2" d. 75.00

WITCH BALLS

Witch Ball with Red & White Loops

Several theories exist as to the origin of these hollow balls of glass. Some believe they were originally designed to hold the then precious commodity of salt in the chimney where it would be kept dry. Eventually these blown glass spheres became associated with warding off the "evil eye" and it is known they were hung in the windows of homes of many 18th century English glassblowers. The tradition was carried to America where the balls were made from the 19th century on. They are scarce.

Amber, dark ball & matching vase w/folded rim, overall 11¾" h., 2 pcs. $440.00

Amethyst ball w/white loopings & matching tall vase w/knob stem & flared foot, vase 9¾" h., 2 pcs. ... 1,400.00

Clear ball w/white loopings & matching vase w/scalloped & folded rim, overall 10¼" h., 2 pcs. 225.00

Clear ball w/red, white & blue loopings, Pittsburgh, Pennsylvania, open pontil w/hanger set in black composition trimmed w/metallic paper, 5½" d. 475.00

Clear ball w/white loopings,& matching vase, overall 14¾" h., 2 pcs. 325.00

Cobalt blue ball, 5" d. 130.00

Opaque white ball w/red loopings, attributed to the Pittsburgh, Pennsylvania area, 5¼" d. (ILLUS.) 210.00

WOODENWARES

The patina and mellow coloring, along with the lightness and smoothness that come only with age and wear, attract collectors to old woodenwares. The earliest forms were the simplest and the shapes of items whittled out in the late 19th century varied little in form from those turned out in the American colonies two centuries earlier. Burl is a growth, or wart, on some trees in which the grain of the wood is twisted and turned in a manner which strengthens the fibers and causes a beautiful pattern to be formed. Treenware is simply a term for utilitarian items made from "treen," another word for wood. While maple was the primary wood used for these items, they are also abundant in pine, ash, oak, walnut, and other woods. "Lignum Vitae is a species of wood from the West Indies that can always be identified by the contrasting colors of the dark heartwood and light sapwood and by its heavy weight, which causes it to sink in water.

Large Burl Bowl

Apple sauce bucket, grain-painted w/wire bail & wood handle, red iron bands around sides, ca. 1840, 9½" d., 7" h. $220.00

Ballot box, two cast-ballot holders on front, 11 x 18 x 7" 55.00

Barrel w/lid, tapering cylinder, stave construction w/metal bandings, worn old blue paint, 22½" h. 295.00

Bee box, American Indian birch bark, two compartments, barrel shape, glass lid, slide partition w/tab handle, dark patina, Brantford Reservation origin, 3 x 4" ... 295.00

Biscuit prick, used for making holes in crackers or biscuits 37.50

Bowl, cov., burl, square rim, lid & base, Friesian carving, 3¾" sq., 2½" h. (age crack & small edge chips) 125.00

Bowl, burl, good figuring throughout, thin flared sides, 17 x 21" irregular oblong, 7½" h. (some wear & small holes at knots or age cracks) 700.00

Bowl, burl, molded rim, mid-19th c., 24" d. (ILLUS.) 1,980.00

Bowl, rolled rim, incised lines on exterior, footed base, deep green paint (worn), late 18th c., 6" d., 3¾" h. 425.00

Bowl, maple, factory-made, signed "Munising," 12" d. 18.00

Bowl, oblong, worn reddish stain, tool marks on exterior, 10½ x 18", 3¾" h. 75.00

Bowl, rectangular w/steeply dished sides, slightly dished out handholds on underside of rim, worn scrubbed interior, traces of old red paint exterior, 16¾ x 25½" (age cracks) 250.00

Box w/hinged lid, pine, colorful h.p. scenes of a house on original white ground, hand-wrought hinges & hasp, 4 1/8" l. 275.00

Box w/domed lid, pine, polychrome floral decor & yellow striping on original light blue ground, 4 7/8" l. (split in tin hasp) 300.00

Bucket & cover, stave construction w/metal bandings, lid w/inset wooden handle that latches into upright staves on each end, worn red paint, 7¾" d., 7¾" h. 160.00

Bucket & cover, stave construction w/metal bandings, sloping sides, wire bail handle w/wooden grip, dark red alligatored finish, 10" h. 35.00

Bucket, stave construction w/metal banding, wire bail handle w/wooden grip, worn original yellow graining, 11½" d., 9¼" h. ... 105.00

Butter carrier w/finger lappet lid, flat wooden bail handle, 9" d., 6½" h. 20.00

Butter churn, dasher-type, yellow wooden band at top, four original metal bands, knob handle on original lid, wooden dasher, 9½" d., 19½" h. 260.00

Butter churn, dasher-type, turned wood, funnel-shaped cap, worn patina, overall 21¼" h. 225.00

Butter churn, dasher-type, stave construction w/bentwood banding, tapering cylinder, 25" h. (no dasher) 145.00

Butter paddle, burl, worn surface w/age cracks, 9" l. 95.00

Butter paddle, burl w/wide blade, highly figured maple w/both burl & curl, warm brown color, 9½" l. 350.00

Ornately Carved Cake Board

Cake board, mahogany, rectangular board carved w/the figure of a soldier on horseback carrying a spear flanked by a banner inscribed "New York Lancer," two large cornucopias overflowing w/fruits & flowers at bottom, attributed to J. Conger, New York, early 19th c., 10¼ x 14" (ILLUS.) .. 990.00

Candle box, wall-type, painted pine, oblong open box w/canted backplate & round crest pierced w/hole to hang, original blue paint w/simple red geometric design on front, 11" l. 250.00

Candle box, wall-type, primitive pine, square nail construction, scalloped front & back edges, traces of old brownish red paint, 13½" l. (very worn w/minor edge damage) 130.00

Carrier, cov., bentwood round, wire bail handle w/wooden grip, worn old green paint over grey, lid branded "O. Hailey, Jr.," 11½" d., 6¼" h. 95.00

Charger, turned, wide rim, shallow center, back w/molded rim & incised line decoration, crude tin strap handle attached to back, probably England, 18th c., 16 x 17" warped d. 375.00

Cheese ring, staved open end, two wide buttonhole hoops, 18th c., 10½" d., 5½" h. 125.00

Cookie board, deeply carved one-horse sleigh w/driver, good color, 5¾ x 12" 275.00

Cookie board, carved maple (some curl), four bunches of grapes in a row, 3½" w., 13¼" l. (minor edge damage) 230.00

Cutlery tray, birds'-eye maple w/pine bottom, square nail construction, shaped center divider pierced w/hand grip, old varnished finish, 7¼ x 11¼" 115.00

Document box w/hinged flat lid, walnut, inlaid light & dark woods w/star & fan design on lid, original brass oval keyhole escutcheons, early 19th c., 7 x 12", 6" h. 275.00

Document box w/domed top, painted & decorated, hinged lid painted w/trees, peacock, fence & hex sign lifting to well w/drawer below inscribed w/initials, in shades of yellow-ochre & black on red ground w/black border & yellow pinstriping, Pennsylvania, early 19th c., 12 x 13", 11¼" h. 467.50

Dough trough, cov., painted wood, canted sides, one-board lid, old red paint, 13¼ x 25½", 9½" h. (some wear & edge damage) 225.00

Dough trough, cov., extended curved handles at each end, breadboard ends on inset lid, original dry red paint, 18th c., 15 x 44", 12" h. 375.00

Dough trough on stand, cov., pine & poplar: trough w/canted sides & breadboard lid; stand w/plain apron & turned legs; worn original yellow graining w/black striping, 23½ x 41½", 29¼" h. 325.00

Early Pine Dough Trough on Stand

Dough trough on stand, cov., pine, Chippendale style, rectangular top sliding above canted rectangular dovetailed case on block & baluster-turned legs joined by block & baluster-turned stretchers w/ball feet, 25" w., 49" l., 29" h. (ILLUS.) 1,045.00

Drying rack, folding accordion-type, ten-bar, old dark brown patina, 42 x 50" 90.00

Drying rack, folding accordion-type, floor model, 12-bar, old blue paint, 48 x 57" 300.00

Egg carrier, dovetailed box w/interior dividers & lid, marked "Star, Mfg. by John G. Elbs, Rochester, N.Y., Pat. 1903-06," 1 doz., 6½ x 8½", 2¾" h. 40.00

Egg crate, "Golden Rule Hatchery," mustard paint, 12 x 14", 14" h. . . . 55.00

Feather bed smoothing board, tapered w/chamfered top, open arched handle, nut brown patina, 2½" w. narrow end, 5" w., 37" l. 85.00

Firkin, stave construction, pegged wooden flat bail, ca. 1880, 9½ x 9½" 65.00

Firkin, cov., tapered sides w/rosehead nails holding the hoops, bail handle w/wooden button swivels, old blue paint, branded on bottom in clover leaf "Hingham," early 19th c., 14¼" h. (minor cracks on corner) 400.00

Flax break, chestnut, 4' l. 450.00

Flax hatchel, pine w/wrought-iron spikes & pierced tin trim, w/cover, 16¼" l. 75.00

Jar & cover, turned poplar w/worn red sponging, 4 3/8" h. 150.00

Jar & cover, turned poplar, original red sponged bird & other designs on yellow ground, 5¾" h. (age crack in lid & chipped finial) 1,000.00

Kraut cutter, cherry, rectangular w/heart cut-out in rounded crest, chip carving on bottom edge, old worn finish, 7¼ x 19" (age cracks) 165.00

Lemon squeezer, two-part, hinged, maple, ca. 1840 . . . . 44.00

Mangling (or smoothing) board, beech wood, carved stylized horse handle, original red paint w/polychrome vase & vining flowers & birds, 22" l. (some worm holes) . . 295.00

Walnut Mortar & Pestle

Mortar & pestle, walnut, hand-turned w/incised line bands, 1850-90, 5" w., 6½" h. (ILLUS.) . . . . .125.00 to 150.00

Mortar & pestle, ash burl mortar, round, speckled, w/short pedestal base, American, 18th c., 6 x 7" . . . 175.00

Pantry box, cov., bentwood oval, laced seams, yellow, blue & green floral decor on faded original salmon pink ground, 8¼" l. 200.00

Pepper pot, turned tall bulbous shape, pedestal base, 18th c., 6" h. 260.00

Pipe box, hanging-type, truncated body w/raised circular crest, square nail construction, traces of light blue paint over old green w/red beneath, 5½" w., 12½" h. 205.00

Porringer, child's, hand-hewn, tab handle, ca. 1800, 3 x 4½" 110.00

Potato masher, curly maple, 11" h. 25.00

Rolling pin, tiger stripe maple, knob handles, one-piece, 16" l. 85.00

Salt box w/drawer, hanging-type, poplar, rounded crest w/relief-carved details, chip-carved & stamped designs on front & sides, refinished, 8½" w., 5½" deep, 15¾" h. 220.00

Sap bucket, wooden pegged (placed at foot of tree), one-piece construction, birch bark, American Indian origin, ca. 1800, 5½ x 8 x 13½" 220.00

Sap yoke, shoulder-type, hand-hewn, painted blue, early 1800's.. 40.00

Spoon rack, hanging-type, chip-carved hex signs, pinwheels, geometric sunburst crest & date "1795," three cleats w/chip-carved edging & slots for spoons, nut brown patina, 8¾" w., 20¼" h...1,400.00

Sugar box, cov., tiger maple, hinged rectangular top above a conforming base w/one long drawer, interior fitted in a sugar cutter mounted on a pierced board (pierced board of later date), probably New England, early 19th c., 9½ x 14½", 7" h.......... 308.00

Sugar firkin (bucket of stave construction) w/lid, bentwood banding secured w/copper tacks, bentwood swing handle, 9¾" h. (glued repair to lid) 87.50

Tape loom board, pine, lollipop-form, 18th c., 7 x 22½".......... 220.00

Tool carrier, pine, dovetail construction, center handle, old blue paint, 12 x 20" 160.00

Trencher plate, birch, hand-hewn, 18th c., 10½ x 19" 150.00

Wall pocket, pine, early cut nail construction, triangular back w/big lollipop top, rectangular pocket, painted apple green, 10" w., 12½" h.................. 295.00

WOOD SCULPTURES

American folk sculpture is an important part of the American art scene today. Skilled wood carvers turned out ship's figureheads, cigar store figures, plaques and carousel animals of stylized beauty and great appeal. The wooden shipbuilding industry, which had originally nourished this folk art, declined after the Civil War and the talented carvers then turned to producing figures for tobacconist's shops, carousel animals and show figures for the circuses. These figures and other early ornamental carvings that have survived the elements and years are eagerly sought. Carousel animals are listed separately.

Washerwoman Whirligig

Cigar store figure of an Indian brave, modeled half-length, holding a bunch of cigars in one hand, probably late 19th c., on a later wooden pedestal base (repaired), overall 74" h. $1,980.00

Model of an American eagle, bird & base carved from a single block of pine, outstretched wings doweled into the body, body, legs & feet w/characteristic roughly cross-hatched carving, painted brown w/yellow markings, base painted green, w/pen inscription "For Peggs Brock, Mary H. Gibson," Wilhelm Schimmel, Cumberland County, Pennsylvania, 1860-90, 13" wingspan, 9¼" h..........10,450.00

Model of an American eagle, for ship's pilot house, carved w/outstretched wings, well-defined plumage, glass eyes, painted grey, 29" wingspan, 10½" h...... 850.00

Model of a rooster, bird & base carved from a single block of pine, rotund, pear-shaped body painted cream-yellow w/black spots, bushy upright tail similarly painted, red wattles & comb, green base, Wilhelm Schimmel, Cumberland County, Pennsylvania, 1860-90, 3½" l., 5¼" h. 2,750.00

Plaque, pine, carved spread-winged American eagle grasping banderole inscribed "While we live let us live," eagle above foreshortened shield, painted red, white & blue, attributed to John H. Bellamy, Portsmouth, New Hampshire or Kittery, Maine, late 19th c., 25" l., 9" h. (portion of flag pole finial missing) 4,950.00

Plaque, walnut, figure of an Indian carved in relief, Peter Toth....... 45.00

Whirligig, figure of a sailor in blue & white uniform, arm baffles painted red, late 19th-early

20th c., 8¼" h. figure, mounted on low stand 375.00

Whirligig, painted pine & metal, figure of a washerwoman wearing painted tin dress & sunbonnet standing over a washtub, painted blue & white, mechanism attached to wind propeller painted blue & white, figure scrubs when wind activated, mounted on brass rod in wooden base, American, ca. 1930, 29" l., overall 20½" h. (ILLUS.) 6,325.00

Whirligig, four-arm, pine, stylized birds w/paddle wings on spokes around central core, weathered grey finish, 28" d. 115.00

Whirligig, figure of black mammy hitting Uncle Tom over head w/rolling pin 160.00

Whirligig, figure of an old man chasing a mule, arm baffles w/paddles 250.00

WORLD'S FAIR COLLECTIBLES

There has been great interest in collecting items produced for the great fairs and expositions held through the years. During the 1970's, there was particular interest in items produced for the 1876 Centennial Exhibition and now interest is focusing on those items associated with the 1893 Columbian Exposition. Listed below is a random sampling of prices asked for items produced for the various fairs.

1876 PHILADELPHIA CENTENNIAL

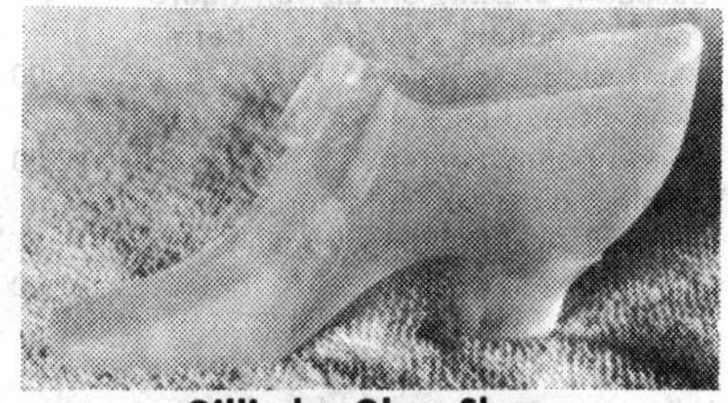

Gillinder Glass Shoe

Beer mug, clear glass, paneled body w/protruding star, "1776" & "1876" each side $47.50

Book, "Frank Leslie's Illustrated Historical Register of the Centennial Exposition 1876," large folio size w/leather bindings 125.00

Cologne bottle w/fluted stopper, camphor glass, marked "Centennial 1876" in black & gold, w/paper label 25.00

Mug, china, bust of George Washington, flags & eagle decoration & "George Washington 1776" front, "A Memorial of the Centennial 1876" reverse, Copeland, England 135.00

Picture, woven silk, Memorial Hall International Exhibition Building, 3½ x 6" 65.00

Plate, china, pink transfer of The Liberty Bell w/crossed flags & 1776-1876, "Our Union Forever - Centennial" in raised letters on border, 8½" d. 125.00

Salt shaker, clear pressed glass, in form of Liberty Bell w/pewter screw cap, marked "Liberty 1776-1876," 3" h. 42.50

Shoe, lady's, frosted glass, Gillinder & Sons, 5" l. (ILLUS.) 52.00

Trinket box, glass w/ormolu trim, reverse painting of fair scene on glass cover 60.00

1893 COLUMBIAN EXPOSITION

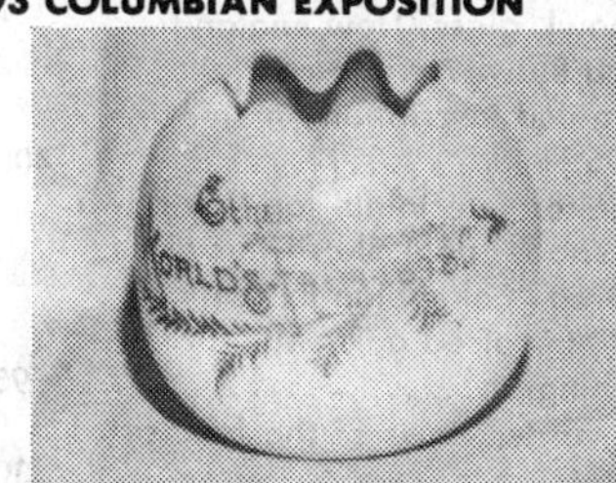

New England Peach Blow Rose Bowl

Advertising card, "The Ferris Wheel," 3½ x 5½" (slight bend mark) 40.00

Advertising card, "Sulky Cultivator," Machinery Hall at World's Fair w/water & boats, reverse picture of cultivator, 4 x 6" 15.00

Bone dish, china, transfer scene of fair buildings viewed from lagoon, marked "On Lagoon" 18.00

Book, "Bird's Eye View of Columbian Exposition," soft cover, 7 x 10" ... 12.00

Book, "The Dream City," photographic portfolio, 11 x 13½" 42.50

Booklet, "Fair Companion," Marshall Field 6.00

Coin purse, mother-of-pearl, Fine Arts Building shown 30.00

Handkerchief, panorama of fairground in center, 17 x 19" 25.00

Hatchet, clear glass, George Washington on blade, signed "Libbey Glass" 55.00

Inkwell, traveling-type, metal, shape of stack of gold coins, top coin reads "Christopher Columbus, 1492-1892, Chicago," w/bust of Columbus, 1½" 65.00

Mug, amber glass, Landing of Columbus on one side & the Flagship Santa Maria on other, base reads "World's Fair 1893" 95.00

Paperweight, "Administration Building," black & white scene under rectangular clear glass dome 42.50

Photographs, interior of Electrical Building, 7 x 9" mounted, set of 8 .... 120.00

Picture, woven silk, "Manufacturing Building," 20" 22.00

Pin, brass, model of "Santa Maria" ship w/half-round world globe reading "Columbian Exposition 1893" suspended from red, white & blue ribbons 30.00

Plate, vaseline glass, center reads "World's Columbian Exposition 1893," rim reads "Libbey Glass Co., Toledo, Ohio," 4" d. 110.00

Ribbon, woven silk, phoenix bird decoration on original card that shows Machinery Hall, 10½" 150.00

Rose bowl, glass, New England Peach Blow, 7-crimp rim, enameled inscription on side (ILLUS.) 400.00

Salt shaker w/original top, lay-down egg shape, pale bluish tint glass lettered "Columbian Exhibition 1893" in raised gold, Mt. Washington 95.00

Stereo cards, views of the fair, set of 10 .... 30.00

Stevengraph, woven silk, "Columbus Leaving Spain," replaced appropriate mat, narrow frame, overall 9½ x 12" 150.00

Teaspoons, demitasse, silver, bust of Columbus on handle, different Fair building in each bowl, marked "Standard," set of 6, original box 135.00

Teaspoon, sterling silver, little girl handle, "Chicago Children's Home Goin' to the Fair" in bowl 39.00

Thimble holder, mother-of-pearl, model of ship under sail w/banner at top of mast, h.p. lettering on sail 40.00

1901 PAN-AMERICAN EXPOSITION

Demitasse set: cov. coffeepot, creamer & cov. sugar bowl; silver, baluster-shaped, enameled lavender & pale green decor & inset w/semi-precious stones, sides, covers & handles w/cast applied stylized foliate ornament, foot rims w/guilloche border enameled in dark green, coffeepot w/ivory insulating rings, Tiffany & Co., New York, special exhibition set, 3 pcs. 24,200.00

Inkwell, pot metal, model of a crab 40.00

Buffalo Opaque White Paperweight

Paperweight, milk white glass, model of a buffalo on an octagonal base dated "1901" (ILLUS.) 325.00

Plate, china, Temple of Music scene center, lacy edge, 7" d. 20.00

Pan-American Exposition Playing Cards

Playing cards w/box, complete deck (ILLUS.) 30.00

Teaspoon, sterling silver, full figure buffalo handle, "Mfgr's & Liberal Arts Bldg." in bowl 45.00

Token, "Good Luck," w/1901 Indian Head penny center 19.00

Tumbler, glass, Manufacturing & Liberal Arts Building transfer, 3½" h. 25.00

1904 ST. LOUIS WORLD'S FAIR

Ashtray, metal, model of a skillet, "Home Comfort Range," 2½" 20.00

Badge, brass, souvenir of dedication ceremony, 1903 .... 48.50

Book, "St. Louis Universal Expo," soft cover, 9 x 12", 80 pp. 45.00

Creamer, glass, ruby-stained top, clear bottom, Star of David patt., etched "World's Fair St. Louis, 1904" 125.00

Cup, graniteware, overall color decoration w/portraits of Jeffer-

son & Napoleon 18.00
Fan, advertising, "Keen Kutter Kutlery," 35.00
Plate, china, "Festival Hall Cascade Gardens" center scene, openwork lattice edge.................... 45.00
Plate, china, "Palace of Machinery" blue transfer center scene, floral border 95.00
Plate, metal, "Hall of Festivals & Central Cascades," 4" d. 45.00
Plate, pressed glass, "Festival Hall" scene in center, openwork lattice edge 25.00
Teaspoon, sterling silver, Palace of Electricity shown 55.00
Tip tray, tin, black edge border w/yellow, orange & green leaf scrolls, center scene of dome-roofed fair building in color against a light blue background, red lettering reading "Louisiana Purchase Exposition 1904 - Souvenir made at American Can Co. Exhibit," 4" d. 125.00

1915 PANAMA-PACIFIC INTERNATIONAL EXPOSITION

Books, "Story of Panama Pacific International Exposition," by Todd, 5 vols. 300.00
Bowl, wood, redwood burl w/gold seal, 2 x 3"................... 12.00
Catalog, "California Perfume Co.," w/color plates 150.00
Postcards, picturing exhibits at Exposition, jumbo size, 5½ x 7", set of 6........................ 24.00
Postcard, advertising, "Keen Kutter," Keen Kutter exhibition pictured, jumbo size, 7 x 10" 40.00
Teaspoon, sterling silver, "Tower of Jewels" on handle 38.00

1933-34 CHICAGO WORLD'S FAIR

Ashtray, copper, "Chrysler Motor Exhibit," original box 10.00
Bank, lithographed tin, American Can Co. 23.00
Book, "1934 Chicago Expo Souvenir & Guide," by Burroughs, Wellcome & Co...................... 19.95
Booklet, Swedish exhibit of arts & crafts, 92 illustrated pp. 5.00
Bookmark-letter opener combination, Illinois Host Building pictured, mint on card 16.00
Cane, wooden, Travel & Transport Building shown, 34" l. 20.00
Compact, metal, by Girey, Hall of Science pictured................ 14.00
Creamer & sugar bowl, china, Art Institute & Chicago Court House shown, 4½" creamer, pr. 150.00

Keychain, brass, Skyride shown 8.00
Photograph, black & white, bird's-eye view of fair w/zeppelins, lake front, etc., matted 45.00
Plate, china, Science Hall scene on blue ground, Pickard 10.00
Postcards, set of 134 assorted views 75.00
Teaspoon, silver plate, Hall of Science on handle, Travel & Transportation Building in bowl........ 7.50
Toy, bus, cast iron, "Greyhound - Century of Progress," Arcade, 1934 .... 150.00
Toy, bus trailer, cast iron, "Greyhound - Century of Progress," Arcade, 10" l...................... 136.00
Walking stick, milk white glass w/brown swirls, paperweight handle 95.00

1939 NEW YORK WORLD'S FAIR

Book, "New York World's Fair Illustrated by Camera," 66 pp. 16.00
Book, "Official Souvenir Guide & Picture Book Masterpieces of Art" 33.00
Booklet, "Ballantine Inn Ballad," beer mug shaped 50.00
Booklet, "Futurama" exhibit 35.00
Booklet, "Rip Discovers Radio," illustrates Rip van Winkle, published by RCA......................... 10.00
Cane, wooden, "Kan-O-Seat," cane opens to form spectator chair, pictures Trylon & Perisphere on seat, Greyhound bus label on back 55.00
Map of fairground, foldout-type, large......................... 24.00
Model of train, balsa wood, "Railroads on Parade," original box ... 125.00
Napkin ring, Bakelite, blue, model of Trylon & Perisphere.......... 42.00
Plate, china, George Washington overlooking the Trylon & Perisphere, Lamberton China, 11" d. 65.00
Plate, china, New York City view, blue & white, Mason China....... 35.00
Program, "Billy Rose's Aquacade," featuring Johnny Weismuller, 32 pp.......................... 16.00
Program, "Cotton Club Fair," signed on cover by Cab Calloway & Bill Robinson 200.00
Teaspoon, silver plate, Food Exhibition Building in bowl 18.50
Tickets, assorted set of 9 .... 8.00

1964-65 NEW YORK WORLD'S FAIR

Coloring book.................... 12.50
Medallion, bronze, "Commemorative," mint in box 18.00
Tray, copper, 5".................. 5.00

Tumbler, glass, w/Kodak advertising 7.50

WRITING ACCESSORIES

Early writing accessories are popular collectibles and offer a wide variety to select from. A collection may be formed around any one segment–pens, letter openers, lap desks or inkwells–or the collection may revolve around choice specimens of all types. Material, design and age ususally determine the value. Pen collectors like the large fountain pens developed in the 1920's but also look for pens and mechanical pencils that are solid gold or gold-plated.

INKWELLS & STANDS

Bisque well, ornate model of an owl's head w/glass eyes, colorful $195.00

Brass well, model of a fox head, clear glass insert w/stopper, ornate, ca. 1880, 6" sq. 110.00

Tiffany Studios Inkwell

Bronze well, Spanish patt. w/original glass insert, "dore" finish, signed "Tiffany Studios 1883," 4¼" h. (ILLUS.) 550.00

Cameo glass well, carved opaque white florals & leaves on frosted citron ground, clear glass insert, sterling silver dome-shaped hinged lid, England, 3" d., 4½" h. 1,350.00

Cast iron well, modeled as a cauldron suspended over fire, hinged lid, on marble base, 3¾" 50.00

Cut glass stand, paperweight-type, diamond-cut hinged lid, Cane patt. sides w/pen rests on each side, brass fittings, 4" sq. base, 3" h. 195.00

Glass well, blown-three-mold, olive amber, GII-18, 2 5/8" d., 2" h. 125.00

Glass well, blue, pressed Double Cube patt. 160.00

Glass well, cranberry, hinged pewter lid in the form of a daisy, 4" d. 225.00

Glass well, millefiori, beehive form, concentric design, w/matching stopper, Whitefriars, England, overall 5" h. 395.00

Majolica stand, model of a lady's hand resting on two books, w/well & sander 95.00

Ormolu & malachite stand, formed as a seated soldier w/standard by his feet, pouring himself a drink into a cup engraved w/inscription & date "1812," flanked by two barrel-shaped inkpots, Russian, 19th c., 6½" l. 4,180.00

Pewter well, w/frog finial, 12" l., Kayserzinn 200.00

Silver & cut glass stand, circular dished base w/engraved inscription, beaded border, ribbed spherical glass well surmounted by an allegorical figure holding Masonic devices, all raised on black wooden base w/four bun feet, Dutch, 1885, 11½" h. 770.00

Staffordshire pottery stand, lift-off lid w/three figural girls, one seated in a chair & one standing at each side, polychrome enameling w/gilt trim, interior w/original liner & pounce sander, 5 1/8" h. 285.00

Staffordshire pottery stand, nodder-type, jolly old man seated on wine barrel & holding bottle on knee w/one hand, the other aloft w/tumbler, white jacket, knee breeches & ruffled shirt w/gold trim, flesh tones on hands, face & bald head w/fringe of grey hair, toothy grin, 3¼ x 4" well resting on molded gold & white rectangular base between his legs, pen holder at side, 6½" h. 350.00

Stoneware well, two quill holes, olive mustard glaze, 3½" d. 130.00

Wedgwood basalt well, vertical engraving around sides, center opening surrounded by three small openings, letter "B" impressed on base, 18th c., 2¼" d., 1¾" h. 135.00

Wooden stand, carved owl w/glass eyes, hinged head, carved pen rest at front, 6" l. base, 4½" h. . . . 45.00

LAP DESKS & WRITING BOXES

Mahogany, curved tambour top above fitted interior w/one of three original clear cut glass inkwells w/brass lid, narrow dovetailed drawer across base w/original brass knob, brass bail handles at ends, ivory knob on lid, 9 x 12" (some edge wear) 155.00

Mahogany, rectangular top w/brass corners opening to interior fitted w/several compartments, brass carrying handles at ends, brass plate on top engraved "S. Hornbrook," paper label "Wm. Dobson, Strand, London," England, early 19th c., 10½ x 20", 6½" h. 330.00

Painted wood, rectangular case w/hinged slant top opening to well fitted w/leather straps, grain-painted in watermelon striping, American, 19th c., 15½ x 20", 13" h. (wear & chips) 412.50

Rosewood w/brass binding, rectangular top opening to interior fitted w/a green baize hinged writing surface & compartments, w/pen & key, Regency period, England, ca. 1820, 11¾ x 20", 8¾" h. 467.50

LETTER OPENERS

Advertising, "Fuller Brush," plastic, figural salesman handle 10.00

Advertising, "Uneeda Biscuit," die-cut tin, boy in raincoat 75.00

Advertising, "Welsbach Mantel Lights," lithographed tin 30.00

Brass, figural rearing horse handle, pierced floral blade, 7¼" l. 16.00

Celluloid, carved monkey 38.00

Gold and Ivory Letter Opener

Gold & ivory, dagger-form, ivory blade, 22k gold handle surmounted w/a lion's head, its mouth open supporting the dagger mounted w/a panel of three scenes depicting the labors of Hercules, Italy, 13" l. (ILLUS.) 1,210.00

Sterling silver handle, plain, Gorham Mfg. Co., 8" l. 14.00

Sterling silver handle, Chantilly patt., Gorham Mfg. Co. 25.00

PAPER CLIPS

Brass Paper Clip

Brass, lady's hand extending from cuffed sleeve, Victorian, 6½" l. (ILLUS.) 90.00

Bronze-finish brass, model of an owl, 4" l. 75.00

Sterling silver, repousse scrolls & roses centering baby w/outstretched arms amid the flowers, Gorham Mfg. Co., 1 7/8 x 3" 150.00

Sterling silver, heavy repousse top, ornate pierced design on under piece, marked 140.00

PENS & PENCILS

Parker and Shaeffer Fountain Pens

Ballpoint pen, sterling silver, souvenir of Israel Independence Day (needs filler) 25.00

Dip pen, mother-of-pearl handle, plain, gold nib 30.00

Dip pen, mother-of-pearl spiral carved handle w/gold ferrule, velvet case 25.00

Conklin fountain pen, dark green marbleized, transparent ink chamber, 14k gold-plated Signature nib, ca. 1930 .... 25.00

Eversharp "Skyline" fountain pen, green striped, 1940's 15.00

Eversharp "Skyline Command Performance" fountain pen & repeater pencil, solid 14k gold cap, barrel & trim, pr. 525.00

Holland fountain pen & mechanical pencil, green marbleized plastic, gold-filled tip, w/box 35.00

Parker "Royal Challenger" fountain pen, silver pearl & black, chromium trim, button filler, 1934 (ILLUS. top) 32.00

Parker "Duofold" fountain pen & mechanical pencil, "Big Red," Chinese red, pr., original box 150.00

Shaeffer "No. 74C Lifetime" fountain pen, jade green, gold-filled trim, lever fill, ribbon ring, 1927 (ILLUS. bottom) 35.00

Shaeffer "Snorkle" fountain pen, blue, 1950's 60.00

Wahl-Eversharp "Equipoised" fountain pen, Rosewood finish, gold trim 58.00

Wahl-Oxford line fountain pen, bronze & brown, transparent barrel, pinch filler 32.00

Waterman "Patrician" fountain pen, gold & mother-of-pearl, 1929-34, w/case 125.00

Waterman "Patrician" fountain pen, onyx, 1930's (some discoloration in cap) 200.00

Waterman "42½" fountain pen, safety-type, gold-filled w/floral design 350.00

WAX LETTER SEALS

Faberge Seal

Glass, handle molded in the form of a female bust, gilt-bronze base w/monogram, signed "R. Papa" & dated "1923," w/silk-lined case ... 375.00

Ivory & brass, fluted knob handle & bulbous turned stem, brass base w/script initials "J H," 2 5/8" h. ... 200.00

Moss Agate w/gold & silver, 19th c. 120.00

Mother-of-pearl handle, square sterling silver base w/simple scrolled design 24.00

Porcelain, phrenology head marked w/regions of the brain & their functions, brass base, 3¼" h. 55.00

Silver & nephrite, bulbous w/plain unengraved base, signed "Faberge," workmaster August Hollming, St. Petersburg, ca. 1900, 2" h. (ILLUS.) 1,045.00

YARD LONG PICTURES

These out of proportion colorful prints were fashionable wall decorations in the waning years of the 19th century and early in the 20th century. They are all 36" wide and between 8" and 10" high. A wide variety of subjects, ranging from florals and fruits to chicks and puppies, is available to collectors. Prices for these yard-long prints have shown a dramatic increase within the past years. All included in this list are framed unless otherwise noted. Also see CAT COLLECTIBLES.

Battle of the Chicks, signed Ben Austrian, 1902 .... $135.00

Bridal Favors, violets, signed Mary E. Hart .... 48.00 to 55.00

Carnations, signed Grace Barton Allen 50.00

Chickens, signed Van Vredenburgh 130.00

Dogs, signed Guy Bedford 125.00

Fruit arrangement 80.00

Puppies 115.00

Roses in shades of red, yellow, pink & white, 1891 .... 65.00

Shaggy Dogs, signed Van Vredenburgh 135.00

Show Dogs, signed Ben Austrian 145.00

ZEPPELIN COLLECTIBLES

Not all airships are zeppelins. Only those lighter-than-air crafts that resemble the huge cigar-shaped type designed by Count Ferdinand von Zeppelin of Germany are referred to as zeppelins. The famed "Graf Zeppelin" was the only airship to fly around the world, making this trip in twenty-one days, eight hours, in 1929. Used for commercial flights from 1933 until 1937, its success led to the building of the "Hindenburg," the largest airship ever built. The tragic crash of the "Hindenburg" on May 6, 1937, ended regular airship service.

Baggage label, paper, "Luftschiffbau Zeppelin" $75.00

Book, "The Story of the Airships" ... 65.00

Ice shaver, cast aluminum, replica of "Graf Zeppelin," made in Osaka, Japan by Tomita Foundry, exceptional casting & paint, 12" w., 36" h. 600.00

Model of "Hindenburg," AMT Co., original box 18.00

Pencil sharpener, metal, model of a zeppelin, Germany 100.00

Pocket watch, commemorating round the world flight of Graf Zeppelin, heavily embossed case, colorful dial, ca. 1930 .... 150.00

Toy balloon, "The Great American Toy Dirigible Balloon -- Inflates and Performs Like the Big Ones," in mint envelope, complete 77.00

Toy, pull-type, sheet metal, Steel Craft Co., Murray, Ohio, 32" l. ... 300.00

Toy, pull-type, tin replica of airship "Akron," 25½" 185.00

Toy, tin, replica of "Sky Ranger" zeppelin, Unique Art, 9" l. 25.00

INDEX

*Denotes "Special Focus" section

THE ANTIQUE TRADER WEEKLY

The leading publication of the antiques hobby for over thirty-one years. This tabloid sized newspaper has approximately 100 pages each week and is filled with advertisements for antiques and collectibles both for sale and wanted from around the nation. It also lists auction and show information plus news, feature stories and informative question and answer columns for the antiques collector.

$24.00 per year (52 issues)
Sample copy $1.00

Your money back if not satisfied!

Send to:
THE ANTIQUE TRADER WEEKLY
P.O. Box 1050
Dubuque, Iowa 52001

Name ______________________

Address ______________________

City ______________________

State ____________ Zip ____________

Enclosed is $24.00. Please enter my subscription to **THE ANTIQUE TRADER WEEKLY** for one year.

Or charge my ( ) MasterCard, or ( ) Visa Card.

Card No. ______________________

Expiration Date ______________________

You can enter your order **FREE** by phone and charge one of the above credit cards. Have card handy.

Call **TOLL FREE 1-800-334-7165** except in Iowa, Alaska or Hawaii 1 (319) 588-2073.